FROM
SCARFACE
TO
SCARLETT

Also by Roger Dooley

LESS THAN THE ANGELS
DAYS BEYOND RECALL
THE HOUSE OF SHANAHAN
GONE TOMORROW
FLASHBACK

FROM SCARFACE TO SCARLETT

AMERICAN FILMS IN THE 1930s

ROGER DOOLEY

Harcourt Brace Jovanovich, Publishers
New York and London

Requests for permission to make copies of any part of the work should be mailed to: Permissions, Harcourt Brace Jovanovich, Inc., 757 Third Avenue, New York, N.Y. 10017.

The author is grateful to Pauline Kael for permission to quote from her writings.

Quotations from the following songs are used by permission: "Top Hat, White Tie and Tails" by Irving Berlin, © copyright 1935 Irving Berlin, © copyright renewed 1962 Irving Berlin, reprinted by permission of Irving Berlin Music Corporation, rights for the United Kingdom and Israel controlled by Chappell Music. "Poor Little Rich Girl" by Noel Coward, © 1925 Aschberg, Hopwood & Crew Ltd., copyright renewed, all rights reserved, used by permission of Warner Bros. Music. "Twentieth Century Blues" by Noel Coward, copyright © 1931 by Chappell & Co., Ltd., copyright renewed, international copyright secured, all rights reserved. "Forty-Second Street" by Harry Warren and Al Dubin, © 1932 by Warner Bros. Inc., copyright renewed, all rights reserved, used by permission of Warner Bros. Music. "Hooray for Hollywood" by Harry Warren and Al Dubin, © 1937 by Warner Bros. Inc., copyright renewed, all rights reserved, used by permission of Warner Bros. Music. "We're Working Our Way Through College" by Johnny Mercer and Richard Whiting, © 1937 by Warner Bros. Inc., copyright renewed, all rights reserved, used by permission of Warner Bros. Music. "Cocktails for Two" by Arthur Johnston and Sam Coslow, copyright © 1934 by Famous Music Corporation, copyright © renewed 1961 by Famous Music Corporation.

End-paper photograph is used by courtesy of United Press International.

Library of Congress Cataloging in Publication Data

Dooley, Roger Burke.
From Scarface to Scarlett.
Includes index.
1. Moving-pictures—United States—History.
I. Title.
PN1993.5.U6D57   791.43'75   80-8745
ISBN 0-15-133789-6

Printed in the United States of America

First edition

B C D E

To my mother,
May Riordan Dooley,
who first took me to the movies,
and to
Cathleen Nesbitt,
a great actress and a great lady

Motion pictures are very important as ART . . . the motion pictures, which are the most popular of modern arts for the masses, have their moral quality from the intentions of the minds which produce them and from their effects on the moral lives and reactions of their audiences. This gives them a most important morality.

1. *They reproduce the morality of the men who use the pictures as a medium for the expression of their ideas and ideals.*

2. *They affect the moral standards of those who, through the screen, take in these ideas and ideals.*

In the case of the motion pictures, this effect may be particularly emphasized because no art has so quick and so widespread an appeal to the masses. It has become in an incredibly short period the art of the multitudes.

—The Motion Picture Production Code
March 1930

For those who did not live through the period, the Thirties seem as well represented by breadlines as by lines at the box-office. . . . Throughout most of the Depression, Americans went assiduously, devotedly, almost compulsively, to the movies. Radio, the only rival to the motion picture on a national scale, kept families home together, clustered around the voices of Eddie Cantor and The Shadow, but the movies offered a chance to escape the cold, the heat, and loneliness; they brought strangers together, rubbing elbows in the dark of movie palaces and flea-pits, sharing in the one social event available to everyone. It is safe to assume that less people saw The Public Enemy *in its time than they did, say,* The Godfather *in the Seventies. But in a time less surfeited by the media, the impact was undoubtedly stronger and the resonances seem to last longer.*

—Carlos Clarens
From The Crash to The Fair
The Public Theatre, 1979

ACKNOWLEDGMENTS

In expressing gratitude to some of those who helped make this work possible, I must begin with my agent, Warren Bayless, whose faith in the project over a long haul kept me at it, and to Marcia Magill, the kind of editor we had always hoped to find. Paul Myers and his staff at the Theatre Collection at the New York Public Library at Lincoln Center were invaluable with prompt and courteous service in tracking down the most obscure material.

William K. Everson deserves special thanks not only for allowing me to quote from his program notes, mostly from his three annual series at the New School for Social Research, but for those series themselves, which have enabled me to see literally hundreds of '30s films available nowhere else. This is also true of the Museum of Modern Art, especially its retrospective series on the major Hollywood studios, and of those revival theaters that offer New Yorkers dozens of vintage films every week: the Carnegie Hall Cinema, the Regency, the Thalia and especially the Theatre 80 St. Mark's.

Ron Bowers, editor of *Films in Review*, was also most helpful in recommending sources for illustrative stills. For those used, I drew upon the collections of Hollywood dealers Eddie Brandt and the Collectors' Bookstore, and in New York those of Gene Andrewski, Saul Goodman, Jerry Ohlinger and Stephen Sally, and the shops known as Cinemabilia, Ron's Now & Then, Movie Star News, Photo Archives and the Silver Screen. And, of course, one must ultimately thank the studios who originally made the stills: Columbia, MGM, Paramount, RKO, 20th Century-Fox, United Artists, Universal and Warner Brothers.

CONTENTS

FROM SCARFACE TO SCARLETT

WHY THE '30s?
Or, No, No Nostalgia

"Some people think the movies should be more like life," said Myrna Loy in *To Mary— With Love* (1936). "I don't. I think life should be more like the movies." In the 1930s only critics held the first attitude; the public clearly favored the second. But in this last quarter of the twentieth century surely it is no longer necessary to defend or justify the application of the methods of scholarly research to the history of the once despised popular film, the performing art that has come closer than any other in history to achieving true universality—the only one whose masterpieces, even the earliest, can still be freshly enjoyed by each succeeding generation around the world, not merely reconstructed from fading memories or yellowed clippings, but with the original players in every glance and gesture caught forever exactly as they looked and moved at the time.

Yet, interesting as the pioneer period is, silent films were an altogether different art, dead for more than half a century, and now largely a historical curiosity. In the dazzlingly swift rise, decline and fall of Hollywood (roughly 1910–60)—that is, of the studio and star system—it now seems clear not merely in fond retrospect but in actual fact that by far the richest, liveliest, most productive decade of that all too brief golden age was the middle one, the 1930s.

As social historian Frederick Lewis Allen was among the first to observe, seldom has a decade been so clearly marked off at both ends. For his terminal dates he pinpointed September 3, 1929, the high-water mark of the bull market, and September 3, 1939, the beginning of World War II. For a film historian it will be enough merely to note that after the transitional year of 1929, 1930 brought total acceptance of talkies. Even the smallest theater in the remotest town could no longer afford not to install sound equipment, and not even the biggest stars (Chaplin always excepted) could ignore the revolution. They had either to talk or get off the screen. At the other end of the decade, the opening of *Gone With the Wind* in December 1939 marks even more precisely the climax and culmination of all that Hollywood in the '30s stood for, aspired to and achieved.

In between came those ten phenomenal years that seem ever more incredible as they recede in time. Granted that movies were then a giant industry, whose aim was to make the biggest profit by pleasing the widest public, the wonder is how many really fine pictures were produced within, or in spite of, the system. Even the most routine "B" films still show an un-self-conscious verve, pace and vitality, a crisp professionalism all too seldom seen today; dialogue is fast but clearly spoken, scenes make their point and end. The very speed of the shooting schedules left little time for self-indulgent writers, directors or stars.

Indeed, never in theatrical history was such an abundance and variety of acting, writing, directing and designing skills concentrated in one place. Hollywood at its zenith could afford the world's best talent, and that is precisely what it demanded and got. The relationship between art and commerce, after all, need not be a hostile one. However mercenary their motives, the movie moguls played Medicis to many of the finest artists of their time.

But it was the stars whom the public—at the peak in eighty million paid admissions a week —flocked to see, mobbed at personal appearances, deluged with letters, celebrated in worldwide fan clubs, read about (especially their private lives) in scores of movie magazines and syndicated gossip columns, and passionately idolized on a global scale never experienced by any royalty in history, still less by any previous generation of entertainers, nor by any since except for certain rock stars.

This flood of talent converged on early talkies from several different sources. Contrary to popular belief—fixed forever in the public mind, in tragic form by *Sunset Boulevard* (1950) and in comic form by *Singin' in the Rain* (1952) —not all silent stars were finished overnight by talkies. In fact, immediate casualties would include only Corinne Griffith, Norma Talmadge, Virginia Valli, to a lesser extent Clara Bow, May McAvoy, Mae Murray and, among the European contingent, Renee Adoree, Vilma Banky, Emil Jannings, Pola Negri and Conrad Veidt. Practically all American actors survived except John Gilbert, and that was not primarily because of his voice.

A number of silent stars retired or faded out during the '30s, for reasons of age, changing public tastes, unwillingness to accept less than top billing or play character roles. A few went to England (Esther Ralston, Bebe Daniels) ; others descended to "B" films made by obscure independents (Lila Lee, Betty Compson, Marie Prevost, William Haines, Conrad Nagel, Rod La Rocque) .

Compared to these few, the vast majority,

well over sixty others, made the transition successfully—perhaps not so surprising, after all, considering how many of the best had started on stage as children. Indeed, in 1930 it would have been impossible for any lifelong player over twenty-five *not* to have begun his or her career on the stage.

Three of the greatest silent stars not only survived the talkies but remained familiar, respected names through the 1970s: Chaplin, Gloria Swanson and Lillian Gish. Those stage actors who had made silents (e.g., George Arliss, Eddie Cantor, W. C. Fields and Will Rogers) had no problem. But the freshest faces in early talkies were not so often Broadway stars (unless comedians) as talented young players who had been promising ingenues or juveniles in stock or road companies. From this group came most of the important new stars of the '30s, including many Oscar winners.

However continually disproved in fact, a favorite Broadway myth of the '30s (dramatized in the play *Stage Door*) was that this generation of movie stars were unripened talents plucked untimely from the stage, seduced into selling their histrionic souls for a mess of Hollywood pottage. What gave this legend credence was that, with the exception of Helen Hayes, who starred in nine films between 1931 and 1935, the most celebrated and distinguished Broadway stars of the decade, most by their own choice, made few pictures, if any at all. Even their greatest hits were filmed by others.

Whatever the explanation, the result was an almost complete dichotomy between stage and screen careers, unlike the situation in England, where both theaters and film studios are centered around London, so that the same actors can and do play simultaneously in both (as did some American stars in the early '30s, when Paramount maintained its Astoria, N.Y., studio) . Over here, it was then impossible to commute back and forth between coasts; thus a Hollywood contract meant an irrevocable choice, which few were given a chance to reconsider. The consequence of this geographical barrier was that most of the '30s' greatest stage names, now either retired or dead, left little or no cinematic record of their unique talents at their peak.

Yet their contemporaries, who had been equally successful on the stage in the '20s or even earlier, some of whom had made silents, did find lucrative new film careers in middle-aged character roles. Somewhere between youth and middle age were two stage actresses whose dignity, poise and perfect diction made them among the most sought-after early talkie stars, though their success did not last through the decade: Ruth Chatterton and Ann Harding. Unique also were two stage actors, neither juveniles nor aged character men, whose fame lasted throughout their lives: Paul Muni and Edward G. Robinson.

At the same time, a still older generation, who had been Broadway stars or leading ladies or men in the 1900s, moved into those elderly character roles not already pre-empted by their British contemporaries. One reason why in '30s talkies the grandparents, spinster aunts, dowagers, lawyers, judges, elder statesmen and their wives so often steal the scenes from the stars is the authority gained in decades of stage experience.

With such a wealth of American talent available, it might have been expected that the European stars so popular in silents would fade out, but with the few exceptions noted, this did not happen. Greta Garbo was bigger than ever, and Marlene Dietrich's American career began with talkies, as did those of Maurice Chevalier, Charles Boyer, Mady Christians, Francis Lederer, Peter Lorre, Hedy Lemarr and (in 1939) Ingrid Bergman. Less lastingly successful, but not because of voice or accent, were other imports like Anna Sten, Lilian Harvey, Dorothea Wieck, Luise Rainer, Simone Simon, Danielle Darrieux, Henri Garat and Fernand Gravet.

More stable was Hollywood's large British colony. Even in silents, when diction had not mattered, some English actors had prospered, but naturally with talkies their well-bred voices were much in demand. Each year brought new arrivals, either by way of the London or New York stage or British films—literally scores of popular leading ladies and men. They were often supported by their compatriots, that host of sterling middle-aged character players who brought so much to '30s films, and by an even older generation already in their sixties or seventies.

Clearly, youth and good looks were not everything. Indeed, one of the '30s' more endearing tastes was their fondness for grandparental figures, veterans who looked and played their age: Marie Dressler, George Arliss, Will Rogers, Lionel Barrymore. Even some usually seen in supporting roles (May Robson, Edna May Oliver, Alison Skipworth, Charles Winninger, Fred Stone, Charles Grapewin, Guy Kibbee) were occasionally starred in "B" films. A less appealing phenomenon to later generations was the extraordinary popularity of child stars, led by the unique Shirley Temple.

Most fortunate of all the new talkie stars were those "discoveries" who without any significant stage or screen experience just happened to look—and sound—good to someone at the right time and caught the public fancy —e.g., Frances Dee, Jean Harlow, Maureen O'Sullivan, Lana Turner, Joel McCrea, Randolph Scott, Robert Taylor, John Wayne. A few others were signed because they were already famous in other fields: radio (usually preceded by vaudeville and/or musical comedy), notably Jack Benny, Bing Crosby and Burns and Allen, or sports (Johnny Weissmuller, Buster Crabbe, Max Baer, Sonja Henie).

Dazzled by all the new personalities on screen, however, the average movie fan cared as little about their earlier careers as about the contributions of the many craftsmen behind the camera. Women might know the names of the designers who dressed their glamorous favorites, especially Adrian at MGM, Travis Banton and later Edith Head at Paramount and Orry-Kelly at Warners, but only because their creations were regularly publicized in fan magazines and Hollywood columns. Writers were, of course, totally unknown to anyone, sometimes even to the studio heads who hired them. Few film-goers read such credits then, any more than now.

Though executives and producers were the ones who could and did make all the important decisions behind the scenes, their names were hardly known to the general public. A regular reader of reviews and credits might come to recognize those of Samuel Goldwyn, Irving Thalberg and David O. Selznick as guaranteeing a certain quality of film, and more might have heard of the Warner Brothers' frequent battles with their stars, but such powers behind all thrones as Louis B. Mayer at MGM, Harry Cohn at Columbia, Carl Laemmle at Universal, Darryl Zanuck at 20th Century-Fox, B. P. Schulberg and Adolph Zukor at Paramount seldom made the news.

As for directors, the fact is that the public—or, for that matter, most reviewers—knew very few by name or style: Frank Capra, Cecil B. De Mille, Ernst Lubitsch, Josef von Sternberg, perhaps Alfred Hitchcock, because their films were relatively few, distinctively individual and publicized as such. There was no reason for anyone to hear of the many others, some since reverently interviewed and studied by generations of film students, simply because these supremely competent craftsmen did equally well with whatever kind of film was handed to them, normally several a year.

The *auteur* theory had not yet been formulated, and in any case could hardly apply to the studio system. Even the best Hollywood directors of the 1930s did not work as independent creative artists but as top technicians. Not unreasonably, even the most enlightened producers regarded them as highly paid employees, and unless they became producers themselves, few directors were allowed choice of scripts, still less the right of final cut on their own work. Only when they had repeatedly proved themselves at the box office were they occasionally permitted to make a film of their own choice, and then, if the commercial results were not satisfactory (e.g., King Vidor's *Our Daily Bread*), the executives felt their worst fears justified.

Even if unaware of such off-screen relationships, the frequent movie-goer soon learned, if only subliminally, to distinguish the identities, qualities and stars of the eight major studios, seven of them still hanging on through the 1970s, five even using adaptations of the same logos as then. Whenever Leo, the MGM lion, roared, the audience could count on an opulently mounted production, occasionally a lavish original (*San Francisco, The Great Ziegfeld*), but, more often, adaptations of established material, carefully chosen to suit a huge stable of talent ("More stars than there are in heaven") : plays like *Grand Hotel, Dinner at Eight* and *The Women,* operettas (all the MacDonald-Eddy vehicles), novels, either classic (*David Copperfield, Anna Karenina*) or current best sellers (*The Good Earth, Goodbye, Mr. Chips*).

Paramount (now owned by Gulf + Western but still symbolized by a mountain ringed with stars) meant, at least in the early '30s, a kind of freewheeling, iconoclastic comedy not found elsewhere: the unique capers of the Marx Brothers and W. C. Fields, the sly boudoir romps of Lubitsch, the earthier ones of Mae West, and, every few years, a De Mille costume spectacle (*The Sign of the Cross, Cleopatra, The Crusades*).

When a shield-shaped emblem formed by the letters "WB" appeared, sometimes zooming out of the sky, the viewer knew even more precisely what, and whom, to expect. Warner Brothers quickly established themselves as prime purveyors of crackling timely melodramas, not only about gangsters, including the classic *Little Caesar* and *The Public Enemy,* but on other social issues, wisecracking, gold-digging comedies, backstage musicals varied only by the Busby Berkeley production numbers, and, surprisingly, a sideline in costume drama: biographies first with Arliss, then Muni, and, from 1935 on, the Errol Flynn swashbucklers.

20th Century-Fox, formed halfway through the decade when Zanuck merged his highly successful 20th Century with the old Fox studio, is still heralded, to a blare of trumpets, by monumental block letters in which the word "20th" seems to have flattened "Century" and "Fox" beneath it. Its successes were mainly in genres not likely to win critical acclaim: Shirley Temple vehicles at the rate of four a year, Alice Faye-Don Ameche musicals, Tyrone Power-Loretta Young romantic comedies—all types done more skillfully, and earlier, by other studios. Yet it also produced a number of John Ford's classics such as *Young Mr. Lincoln* and *The Grapes of Wrath.*

Universal, whose logo was a small open plane flying eastward around the world, tried classics and every other genre, but became known mainly for its horror films, starting with the original *Dracula* and *Frankenstein,* but soon degenerating into formula. At the opposite extreme, it also made the refreshing musicals of Deanna Durbin.

At first too small to be counted among the major studios, Columbia, whose symbolic goddess still carries her torch, made a double breakthrough in the mid-'30s, with the operatic musicals of Grace Moore, and, more substantially, with the warmhearted comedies of Frank Capra, guaranteed annual hits for the rest of the decade.

An Eiffel-like tower, from which chain lightning flashed amid urgent beeping sounds, on top of a revolving globe, once announced the films of RKO-Radio, which produced creditable examples of all the leading genres, especially the delightful Astaire-Rogers musicals and all Katharine Hepburn's better '30s vehicles, as well as an occasional remarkable sleeper like Ford's *The Informer.* (RKO was the only one of the eight major studios to go out of business after the first onslaught of TV in the 1950s.[1])

Finally, then as now, United Artists was not really a studio but an organization for the release and distribution of pictures by independent producers, especially the distinguished films of Samuel Goldwyn (*Dodsworth, Wuthering Heights*). The rise and fall of the independent studios, of which Monogram and Republic were the biggest, has been chronicled in Don Miller's *B Movies.*

Until compelled by law to end the practice, the major studios of the '30s controlled not only production but distribution, by blockbooking their own nationwide chains of theaters. Every sizable city offered several levels of such movie houses, starting with those vast "cathedrals of the cinema," baroque or rococo, Moorish or Egyptian, in the one vital "downtown" section (in many cities now dead after office hours), the first-run showcases for the most important productions, flagships for the chains.

Here, for less than a dollar, in addition to the standard newsreel (Paramount, Pathé or Fox Movietone), a cartoon (most frequently Disney) and short subjects (two-reel comedies, Pete Smith satires, Fitzpatrick Traveltalks, John Nesbitt's Passing Parade), fans could enjoy instead of a second feature an orchestral or organ interlude (or both), plus an elaborate stage production: a whole vaudeville program, an original revue, a "tabloid" version of a Broadway musical or a big-band show. This may be contrasted with first-run film theaters of the present, where for four or five dollars the customer sees one single film, plus perhaps an advertising trailer; between showings nothing but long, blank intermissions, with the house lights on and insipid music playing, no doubt to the great profit of the refreshment stands.

The most spectacular movie palace is, of course, Radio City Music Hall (in 1979 apparently given a new lease on life, without films), "the show place of the nation," which, though built as the premier outlet for RKO pictures, soon became known as the most prestigious possible showcase for the major productions of any studio.

Others in midtown Manhattan, around or just off Times Square, once included the Paramount, the Roxy for Fox, later 20th Century-Fox films, the Capitol and Loew's State (now divided into two smaller houses) for MGM,

[1] It seems almost too patly symbolic that the property was bought for Desilu Studios by Lucille Ball, once an RKO player.

the Hollywood and the Strand for Warners—all gone or transformed beyond recognition.

Other than the Victoria, isolated in a particularly squalid block of Broadway that it once proudly shared with the Astor, the sole survivor, still operating on something close to its original level, is one of the oldest and largest, the Rivoli, once the launching pad for the most important United Artists films, such as Samuel Goldwyn's. In other cities most such theaters have long since been torn down, converted to other uses or else stand dark and empty, forlorn monuments to the movies' golden age.

A step below these were the second-run houses (like the Loew's and RKO chains in New York), built on a scale only slightly less grandiose, where after four or five weeks those in outlying neighborhoods could see the same films, usually two at a time and changed two or three times a week. On the next level down, every few blocks along every main business artery in every American city stood the modest little third-, fourth- and even fifth-run houses—the first to close in the 1950s—the once beloved "nabes" (neighborhood theaters), where in the depths of the Depression midweek "bank nights," dish nights, even amateur nights and endless variations on Bingo lured families away from their radios, and where at "kiddie matinees" on Saturdays and Sundays millions first became addicted to movies.

Here, if one waited long enough, the same pictures that had cost fifty or seventy-five cents downtown and a quarter at the second runs could be enjoyed for ten or fifteen cents—or re-enjoyed by true fans, who often followed favorites through the whole cycle, since in the '30s the life expectancy of a film was only as long as it took to play through the circuit, three or four months at most.

Though for purposes of analysis it has been possible to unravel some fifty separate strands from the multicolored tapestry of '30s screen fare, what must be kept in mind above all is not only the endless variety and multiplicity but the simultaneity. Unlike the TV fan, limited to much the same standard brand product in prime time on the commercial channels, the urban movie-goer of the '30s had a staggering choice.

In the '30s any American city on any night of the week offered from scores to hundreds of varied films, most of them two for the price of one as double features became prevalent. Supposedly, one film was always a "big" one, the other a "B," which often proved the better of the two, but a comparison shopper who did not mind crossing town could occasionally find two "A" pictures paired.

Yet, though those films still show us the familiar faces and still speak to us in voices known the world over, a number of internal differences distinguish them as of their own time, and this is not merely a matter of fashions, slang and the absence of four-letter words. Color was perfected midway through the decade, but the process was still so expensive that by the end of 1939 barely twenty feature-length color films had been made. Except on the covers of fan magazines, most '30s stars were seen, and are remembered, only in black and white—a fact that worked to the advantage of some genres such as horror films. With such vivid personalities, lack of color is even now far easier to take for granted than lack of voices would be.

Another fact of cinematic life taken for granted at the time was that almost *all* American films, wherever set, were made in Hollywood. When an occasional company went on location, usually in California itself, this was publicized as an unusual event. Otherwise, research, careful art direction and the adroit use of process shots and back projections created as convincing an illusion of Paris, Dublin or Shanghai as if the film was actually photographed in those cities.

Audiences soon learned the standard establishing shots for each important city: for London, bicyclists and pedestrians crossing Westminster Bridge, with Parliament and Big Ben visible, or else Piccadilly Circus, looking toward Shaftesbury Avenue, with a large ad for Bovril on one building and double-decked buses; for Paris (accompanied by zippy cancan music), either the Eiffel Tower, the Place de la Concorde or the Place de l'Opéra, with a glimpse of the Café de la Paix. New York had at least three introductory images: the Manhattan skyline (often accompanied by "Manhattan Serenade" or Alfred Newman's *Street Scene* music); to suggest night life, Times Square looking north, with many lighted movie marquees along both sides, and atop a building at Forty-seventh Street huge ads in moving lights for Four Roses, Chevrolets, Planters Peanuts and Coca-Cola; for the Lower East Side (while the sound track played "The Sidewalks of New York"), a teeming street of tenements, pushcarts and children playing in the spray from a fire hydrant. All the authentic locales common since the 1950s, plus wide screens, CinemaScope and other technical advances, have failed to make films any more real.

Still another factor in Hollywood's exuberant self-confidence in the '30s was the almost complete absence of any foreign competition. After the great success of *The Private Life of Henry VIII*, British films gained a certain popularity, as well as prestige that ensured the best ones distribution, at least in the larger cities, but these were relatively few each year, presumably the cream of the crop.

In fact, German and Austrian films outnumbered them in New York—not the great ones of the silent UFA days but countless forgotten farces, Viennese operettas or heavy historical epics about Frederick the Great and other eighteenth-century royalty. (Very few shown here conveyed overt Nazi propaganda.) The far fewer Italian films shown in New York in the '30s bore all too noticeably the heavy thumbprint of Mussolini's propaganda machine, and were not widely distributed in this country.

Outside of New York, only the most prestigious and highly acclaimed French and Russian films ever found an outlet, and then only for a week or two in specialized "art" theaters (a new idea at the time), usually near universities, of which most cities could support only one, if any. Despite their earlier in-

fluence, the impact of Scandinavian films in the '30s was negligible, and, of course, Japanese and Indian films were unknown outside the countries of origin. In short, the general American public had not yet discovered the excitement of foreign films.

Thus the balance of trade was so entirely in favor of the American studios that Hollywood, flooding world markets with several hundred films a year, had no serious competition. If British or European stars or directors won international acclaim, the immediate response was simply to buy them up, make them an offer they could not refuse (as was done with almost the whole cast of *Henry VIII*), sometimes with unhappy results (as in the case of Anna Sten), sometimes with permanent American success (Alfred Hitchcock).

Even Hollywood's severest restriction on artistic maturity, the elaborately detailed Production Code, self-imposed in 1934, though rightly denounced then and ever since, at least had the side effect of forcing stars, writers and directors to hint by subtle innuendo what they could no longer say or show on screen, with results that were often far wittier than latter-day sexual explicitness.

It must be kept in mind, however, that critical appreciation of Hollywood's achievements in the '30s has grown largely by hindsight. During the decade itself most intellectuals took movies even less seriously than their successors have taken TV. Cultural mandarins like Dwight Macdonald in the liberal weeklies scorned by reflex anything that came out of Hollywood, berating a public unaware of their existence for preferring escapist entertainment to political propaganda and scolding directors like Capra for not being Eisenstein. As good Marxists they feared that not religion but movies had become the opiate of the people—yet, even if so, was ever a drug (addictive, mildly aphrodisiac, occasionally sedative as it may have been) cheaper, more readily available and less harmful in its effects?

The respectable critical attitude of the day was that the drama and the novel were the only fictional genres worthy of a true artist;

movies were by definition of, by and for morons, the sitting duck even for radio comedians, much less cynical Broadway wits. Writers who had literally never had it so good, supporting their failed poetry or novels or plays by turning out highly paid screenplays, never tired of gnawing at the hand that fed them, like the self-pitying hero of Hemingway's *The Snows of Kilimanjaro*, blaming his rich wife for having destroyed his supposed talent.

Yet on the whole the average successful movie of the '30s holds up at least as well today as the average best seller or Broadway hit of those years. As has often been noted, the most ambitious, highly praised work in any period may well look to later generations merely pretentious, while craftsmanlike productions turned out with unassuming expertise may prove the genuine works of art—especially once that expertise is lost.

Small wonder, then, that to many who lived through the '30s movies were not merely their best and cheapest escape from the Depression but remain among their brightest memories of that otherwise grim decade. No one then living could ever have imagined that the day would come when those clinging, calf-length gowns, marcelled, platinum-blond bobs, Art Deco bridge lamps and "modernistic" radios would be re-created on screen and even collected off screen as priceless examples of kitsch, pop culture or "camp."

That the '30s could ever become the subject of faithful cinematic recapture, much less nostalgia, would have seemed a bitter joke, the more so in that what seemed most fascinating to '70s film-makers were just those sordid aspects of the times that '30s people went to the movies to forget, as proved by most '30s-set films.

In *They Shoot Horses, Don't They?* it was marathon dance contests; in *The Way We Were*, radical campus protests; in *Hard Times*, the brutal lives of illegal prize fighters; in *The Sting* and *Chinatown*, the machinations of urban murderers and con men; in *Bonnie and Clyde, The Whiskey War, Fools' Parade, Paper Moon, Dillinger* and *Thieves*

Like Us, rural, especially Southern and Midwestern, petty criminals.

Even in the more sophisticated European milieux of *Julia, The Damned, Cabaret, England Made Me, Stavisky, The Conformist, The Garden of the Finzi-Continis* and other political films, emphasis has been on the sick and the decadent—almost as if the '70s were so distasteful that audiences enjoyed looking back on even the worst phases of the '30s.

Only the non-political *Murder on the Orient Express* and, to a lesser extent, Bogdanovich's witless, heavy-footed attempt at a '30s musical, *At Long Last Love*, reflected any of the carefree luxury and elegance that were so very much a part of the charm of '30s films themselves.

The most perverse twist of all is Hollywood's ugly desecration of its own golden age, which smacks less of nostalgia than of self-cannibalization. MGM's two *That's Entertainment* films, though a tacit confession of present creative impoverishment, at least lived up to their titles by giving the public its fond memories untarnished, but what is to be made of *Inserts, Hearts of the West, Won Ton Ton* and especially the incredibly pretentious *The Day of the Locust* and the utterly pallid, lifeless *The Last Tycoon?* In the last two named, the "exposure" of Hollywood corruption circa 1938 took as much courage as a 1976 declaration of war against the Nazis. Only a modest thriller, *What's the Matter with Helen?* (1971), set on the amateur fringes of Hollywood in 1934, simply re-created the time and place, with neither sentimentality nor attempted satire.

More deplorable still is the ghoulish trend of trying to cash in on the off-screen lives of once-beloved stars, either in transparent disguise, as in *The Wild Party*, or using actual names, as in *Gable and Lombard* and *W. C. Fields and Me*, which can only prove anew the unique irreplaceability of the originals. More such rip-offs of the defenseless dead have been announced, along with, even more incredibly, a "sequel" to *Gone With the Wind!* At best (if "best" is not a contradiction in terms here) any such misguided venture will probably bear the same illegitimate relation to *GWTW* as *The Black Bird* did to *The Maltese Falcon.*

Yet considering this apparent fascination with '30s films, their familiarity from TV and revivals and the general recognition of their unique qualities, they have received relatively little serious critical attention. To be sure, a few books appeared during the 1970s, but by their very nature and limited scope none attempted to take into account the Hollywood output of the '30s in its *entirety.*

The present work is the first based on research on *all* the nearly 5,000 American feature films reviewed between January 1, 1930, and December 31, 1939, the majority by the *New York Times* but more than 1,500 others covered only by *Film Daily,* omitting, along with foreign pictures, only those "B" Westerns that never played first-run theaters.

Not all are worth discussing or even mentioning, nor could even the basic facts about all be recorded in a volume of less than encyclopedic scope, yet detailed knowledge of the sheer number and nature of those forgotten films surely gives a historian an entirely different perspective from one who, on whatever basis, merely plucks out selected threads from the vast tapestry, with no attention to, or even awareness of, the rest.

Instead of a chronological survey, the chapters are organized into fifty distinct genres (some constituting trends and cycles), when necessary beginning with their roots in the '20s (especially 1928–29) or earlier and indicating survival or revival in later decades. After an introduction suggesting historical, sociological or psychological reasons for the waxing and waning of a particular type (including contemporary parallels in other media such as the stage, radio, popular songs and even comic strips), each genre is traced through the decade, with discussions of the more significant examples and variations.

Any such minute classification of such a heterogeneous medium must necessarily seem arbitrary, but in addition to the few familiar types obvious even at the time, the others have been arrived at by trial and error, with a new category opened only when as many as ten or twelve films clearly followed the same pattern.

By way of balancing contemporary judgments with those of posterity, many later sources have been used, as cited in the footnotes and bibliography. Except when directly relevant to the casting, production or reception of a film, off-screen anecdotes have been avoided, in favor of concentration on the films themselves. Likewise, except when a star made a number of films of the same type (as did most comedians and some musical performers), no player's career has been traced through the decade; the same performers recur in as many chapters as they made kinds of films.

In comparing movies of the '30s with mass entertainment of earlier eras (though none ever rivaled them in numbers of people reached), a closer analogy than the nineteenth-century novel, which presumed a literate public, reading quietly at home, would be the Elizabethan theater. There too, the groundlings were entertained by boldly drawn characters, strong speeches, violence (swordplay as well as horseplay), startling visual effects, rich costumes and the illusion of an inside glimpse into the private lives of the high and mighty—yet in these same plays the gorgeous language, sublime poetry and powerful rhetoric, the flashing wit and graceful songs, the subtle characterizations, psychological nuances and profound insights into human nature were all there, too, for those who could understand them.

Just as some paranoids really do have enemies and even hypochondriacs are sometimes sick, not all appreciation of the past can be dismissed with the catchall term "nostalgia," if that implies a sentimental retrospective softening or distortion of the truth. Thus middle-aged Londoners of the 1620s and 1630s were not merely waxing nostalgic for their lost youth when they asked each other why no one was writing any more great plays such as they remembered seeing in the 1590s and 1600s.

No one was. In fact, they *had* lived from the high noon through the sunset of a glorious age, whose towering masterpieces seem even more extraordinary with the passage of time.

This is precisely how the best American films of the 1930s now look from the vantage point of the 1980s—with the unique difference that even those not born at the time can still enjoy the original casts and performances.

Just as it is useful for scholars of the Elizabethan period to study the admittedly minor works of the contemporaries of Shakespeare, Marlowe and Jonson, the literary compost from which the rare blooms grew, so may this history of the total Hollywood product of the 1930s provide the same kind of background, against which the greatest achievements will stand out all the more clearly.

"JUST PICTURE A PENTHOUSE..."
Love Among the Millionaires

1

O MISTRESS MINE
Ladies with a Past

The presentation of evil is often essential for art or fiction or drama. This in itself is not wrong provided that evil is not presented alluringly. Even if later in the film the evil is condemned or punished, it must not be allowed to appear so attractive that the audience's emotions are drawn to desire or approve so strongly that later condemnation is forgotten and only the apparent joy of the sin remembered.
—The Motion Picture Production Code

"I'm steppin' out, my dear, to breathe an atmosphere that simply reeks with class," sang Fred Astaire in *Top Hat* (1935) —a boast that could have been echoed by the hero or heroine of almost any '30s film set in modern times. As David Shipman observes in *The Great Movie Stars,* "No matter where the characters came from in reel one, they would certainly be in evening dress by the end." This high social gloss, so utterly alien to films of the present, was a fact of cinematic life that cut across all the most popular genres.

Indeed, perhaps the most striking visual quality of Hollywood films of that decade is those production values, the taken-for-granted opulence of the settings. In clinging evening gowns or perfectly fitted tail coats, heiresses and underworld czars, chorus girls and playboys ride in chauffeured limousines from duplex penthouses (usually all white, with a curved staircase, single or double, winding down from a gallery) to choice boxes at the theater or the opera or to ringside tables in palatial Art Deco night clubs, preferably rooftop, where the dance floors are always crowded with other formally clad couples.

Or, if urban pleasures pall, they can always retreat to the race track or to the tennis courts, golf links or dining rooms of elegant country clubs, or to restored Early American country houses, usually in Connecticut, with grounds suitable for garden parties, or to hunting lodges, all knotty pine paneling, chintz-covered furniture and freshly laid fires.

Further afield, they may encounter each other in the club cars or diners of crack transcontinental express trains, the promenade decks, ship's cafes or spacious staterooms of luxury liners (after midnight sailings celebrated with lavish bon voyage parties), en route to cozy Swiss chalets, de luxe hotels on the Riviera or flower-filled suites in the Paris Ritz, with obsequious managers bowing attendance while servants unpack steamer trunks plastered with exotic luggage labels—all this at a time when most Americans had never seen Europe—typical '30s amenities which fans no doubt appreciated the more because they could glimpse them only on screen.

Such preoccupation with the trappings of wealth while millions were struggling for the bare essentials need not necessarily be taken as evidence of callous snobbery on Hollywood's part. During the first four decades of this century, much of middle-class America, especially its women, took genuine vicarious pleasure in following the well-publicized lives of the very rich.

In the worst years of the Depression, not only did *Vogue* and *Harper's Bazaar* continue to flourish at thirty-five cents a copy, when most magazines cost a nickel, chronicling on page after glossy page, with photos by Beaton or Steichen, the doings of what was then called "the international set," but every newspaper of any size devoted an inordinate number of daily pages to "society," supplemented on Sunday by rotogravure pictorial sections featuring the latest American heiresses to marry titles or to be presented at the Court of St. James, plus local and syndicated columns glittering with such once potent words and phrases as "socialite," "scion," "elite," "dowager," "subdeb," "smart set," "the best people" and "our finest families."

Even more frequently than movie stars (who, after all, had other means of getting publicity), Vanderbilts and Whitneys, Cabots and Astors, even Bourbons and Romanovs, posed for ads endorsing cigarettes, beauty products and other luxury items, with presumably the desired effect on sales. In a decade that began with front-page stories about Barbara Hutton's $100,000 debut and ended with Brenda Frazier enshrined on the cover of *Life* as America's Number One Deb, when "cafe society" became a way of life, and Elsa Maxwell and Cholly Knickerbocker were names to be reckoned with, when many looked on Edward VIII and Mrs. Simpson as the great lovers of the century and regarded being seen and photographed at the right table in El Morocco or the Stork Club as the ultimate in human achievement, how could Hollywood have ignored such a popular spectator sport?

Thus if the leading characters in '30s films had not been born in the lap of luxury, then he, or, more commonly, *she* had to attain it. His way was often to become either a ruthless tycoon or a criminal, but before the Pro-

duction Code in 1934 imposed such drastic restraints on a heroine's freedom, hers was most frequently the one known, after Eugene Walter's play, as "the easiest way"—which some suave, wealthy older man was only too eager to provide. As plot obstacles, such men were as familiar in early '30s films as testy millionaire fathers and stuffy fiancés became later in the decade.

In Victorian novels (with the exception of Becky Sharp in *Vanity Fair*), if such characters appear at all, they are permanently "ruined" maidens like Little Emily in *David Copperfield* or "unfortunates" like Nancy in *Oliver Twist*, who must either pine away or be murdered. In American nineteenth-century fiction, Hester Prynne in *The Scarlet Letter* stands alone as a convicted adulteress who not only lives down her public shame but scores a moral victory over Puritanism. She remained alone for many decades; one has but to recall the outraged protests at Crane's *Maggie, A Girl of the Streets* (1892) and the long suppression of Dreiser's *Sister Carrie* (1900) to realize the moral climate of prewar America. *The Easiest Way* caused as great a sensation in the New York of 1908 (fifty-six years after *Camille*) as Pinero's *The Second Mrs. Tanqueray* had done in the London of 1893—each the first native attempt at a sympathetic portrayal on stage of a "fallen woman."

Naturally, the earliest American films reflected not the standards of the most advanced literature but of the popular melodramas and novelettes of the day. In Griffith's films a woman is either a frail, angelic heroine (most perfectly embodied by Lillian Gish) or else a heartless adventuress, dissolute consort of the villain (Constance Collier in *Intolerance*, 1916), not far above the level of Theda Bara's wicked vamps.

But even Hollywood could not remain totally oblivious to the social revolutions of the '20s. As the importation of sophisticated European directors and stars led to pictures more subtle, adult and less simplistic in their morality, Griffith's child-heroines began to be edged out not only by peppy (though technically innocent) flappers but by experienced women of the world, occasionally played by Gloria Swanson, Norma Talmadge or Florence Vidor, but most strikingly portrayed by pseudoexotic types like Nita Naldi or genuine Continental *femmes fatales* like Pola Negri, Jetta Goudal, Olga Baclanova and Greta Garbo. (One of Negri's silents was actually called *A Woman of the World*.) [1]

1929, for instance, saw such significantly titled films (most still silent) as *The Shopworn Angel* (Nancy Carroll as a kept show girl), *A Dangerous Woman* (originally titled *The Woman Who Needed Killing*), in which Baclanova, though married to Clive Brook, drove several other men wild in East Africa, and *Shanghai Lady,* with Mary Nolan as a variation on Sadie Thompson. (Possibly in consequence of the lurid reputation of the play *The Shanghai Gesture,* the very name of the city, like those of Singapore and Panama, had become a code word for vice. A character who called herself Shanghai Mabel, Panama Flo or Singapore Sal announced her profession with her name.)

Even in pictures where the heroine was actually pure, such titles (all between 1929 and 1932) as *Street Girl, Lady of the Pavements, Lady with a Past, Ladies They Talk About, Anybody's Woman, Bought, Tarnished Lady* and *Expensive Women* were obviously meant to suggest otherwise. On the other hand, prostitute heroines often lurked behind such innocuous titles as *Inspiration* (1931), *Virtue* (1932) and *Baby Face* (1933).

During the '20s the long-despised fallen woman had gradually picked herself up from the sackcloth and ashes and risen to the role of accepted heroine. In endless variations on *Camille,* she always faced the same old question: could there be a future for a woman with a past? Indeed, a sizable bordello could have been staffed by all the shady ladies played by almost every leading actress between 1930 and 1933.

This account does not include *all* heroines who trod the primrose path. Nor does it take in countless secondary characters: the occasional clearly labeled madam (e.g., Estelle Taylor in *Cimarron,* 1931), the gangsters' brassy molls played by such as Mae Clarke, Noel Francis and the early Harlow, nor yet the sleek, svelte, slightly older blondes (Lilyan Tashman, Natalie Moorhead, Verree Teasdale, Genevieve Tobin), who, however well kept by someone else, usually the villain, were not above making a play for the hero.

In *We're in the Money, Depression America and Its Films* (1971) Andrew Bergman makes the point that only Mae West and Ernst Lubitsch's heroines broke with the prevailing code by accepting sex as a normal human activity to be enjoyed and slyly joked about—but both West's and Lubitsch's films were witty comedies, the very antitheses of the soul-searing illicit romances that were the vehicles of most actresses of the early '30s.

Bergman also asserts that in all other films involving sex, the loss of virginity was a tragedy that had to be atoned for by endless suffering according to the most rigid Mosaic code. He cites four examples: Garbo in *Susan Lenox* (1931), Dorothy Mackaill in *Safe in Hell* (1931), Tallulah Bankhead in *Faithless* (1932) and Dietrich in *Blonde Venus* (1932), which might indeed seem to support his thesis—but this ignores literally scores of other films in which such heroines are not punished at all.

Rather than proving the brutal exploitation of women in the Depression years, far more films (especially the many based on '20s plays and novels) seem rather to express the new freedom of the postwar woman, the dawning of something approaching a single standard. If their wealthy protectors could leave them at any time, such ladies of leisure had themselves the same freedom to walk out, and usually did. They used their sex appeal to attain a standard of living unattain-

[1] *The American Film Institute Catalog . . . 1921– 1930* lists thirty films about prostitutes, forty-two about mistresses.

able by most girls in any other way—for that matter, unattainable by most men of the '30s in *any* way. They seem content enough in their gilded cages until they meet their true loves and must choose between a bed of long-stemmed roses and love in a cottage. They always end up with one or the other, with luck sometimes both.

Scrimping housewives and jobless working girls struggling through the Depression could hardly have shed too many tears for poor Constance Bennett, suffering in sable while making up her mind between rich, distinguished John Halliday and handsome, promising Joel McCrea. No doubt the real demimonde of those years, as of any other, included far more sisters under the skin of such heroines, or of the gold diggers, than of those selfless wives selling their all for the sake of an ailing husband (like Bankhead in *Faithless* and Dietrich in *Blonde Venus*)—an extremely bizarre situation perhaps more traceable to Edith Wharton's novelette *New Year's Day* (1924) than to observation from life.

Among top American stars of the early '30s, undoubtedly the one kept most often, on the grandest scale, was chic, blond Constance Bennett, who drew more than her share of such roles, alternating them with drawing-room comedies, mother-love dramas and even spy pictures. Some of her most provocative titles, however, were among the most misleading. In *Bought* (1931), though illegitimate, she could not, after all, be "bought" by all the upper-class temptations of Newport, not even after a one-night fling with Ray Milland, but returned to a poor writer (Ben Lyon) and her humble home near the el. In *Lady with a Past* (1932) she was a virtuous but unpopular girl who had to go to Paris, hire a gigolo and pretend a lurid past to attract men. This was certainly not a problem for most Bennett heroines.

In *The Easiest Way* (1931), which was very loosely adapted from the 1908 shocker, Bennett was a shopgirl, then a model, not an actress as in the original play, whose taste for luxuries provided by Adolphe Menjou almost

John Halliday and Constance Bennett in Bed of Roses

costs her the love of Robert Montgomery.

In *The Common Law* (1931) it was Joel McCrea and Lew Cody who provided the other two sides of the triangle, McCrea as an artist in Paris disillusioned in Bennett, his model, when he learns of her relationship with the older man—but he takes her back to Westchester and finally marries her. In *Bed of Roses* (1933) Bennett played a thief and adventuress who achieves her bed of roses through New Orleans publisher John Halliday, but for love of a Mississippi barge skipper (McCrea again) leaves her protector and even goes so far as to work in a department store to prove her reformation.

As if in tender adieu to all her tarnished lady roles, in the musical *Moulin Rouge* (1934) the most elaborate production number is a stylized scene of Montmartre, in which Bennett as a demimondaine sits in a cafe singing wistfully about the Boulevard of Broken Dreams.

Not yet as glittering a star as Bennett, Barbara Stanwyck earned her share of the wages of sin in considerably less glamorous surroundings. Starting down the road to ruin early in 1930 in the forgotten *Mexicali Rose,* as the trampish wife of a gambler, Stanwyck came into her own in *Ladies of Leisure* (also 1930), from a play more frankly titled *Ladies of the Evening.* Though euphemistically termed a "party girl," she has acquired a sufficiently lurid reputation to give up her young lover (Ralph Graves) on the plea of his mother (Nance O'Neil). Of course he later realizes her true worth.[2]

In *Shopworn* (1932) Stanwyck played a waitress railroaded to a ninety-day jail sentence on a morals charge by the mother of a rich boy who wanted to marry her. Coming out convinced that she may as well have the game as the name, she uses a series of men to become a Broadway star—a status acceptable even to her future mother-in-law. In *The Purchase Price* (1932) she was again an entertainer, the torch-singing mistress of her married boss, bootlegger Lyle Talbot. Tired of the bright lights, she flees to Montreal, and by buying a hotel maid's credentials from a matrimonial bureau, becomes the mail-order bride of North Dakota wheat farmer George Brent. Though her former lover turns up long enough to advance $800 to save the farm, unknown to her husband, she also gets other offers, but by surmounting hazards undreamed of by the second Mrs. Tanqueray, including a blizzard, a neighbor's difficult childbirth and a fire started by a vengeful admirer, she finally manages to atone for her wicked past. (The title of *Ladies They Talk About,* 1933, was obviously meant to suggest the same sort of character, but in it Stanwyck was no worse than a bank robber—an offense

more readily forgivable by the reforming D.A., Preston Foster, who falls for her.)

The climax of her Bad, Bad Barbara phase was *Baby Face* (1933), a film that (according to the *New York Times* review) not only brought down the wrath of the Hays Office and forced the resignation of Darryl Zanuck from Warners, but no doubt helped add fuel to the purifying fires of the Legion of Decency and hasten the imposition of the Production Code. In this one Stanwyck is a speakeasy owner's blond daughter who comes to New York knowing only too well how to succeed in business without really trying, as she moves up the ladder in a bank from one executive to the next, driving infatuated Donald Cook to murder his father-in-law and rival (Henry Kolker), then kill himself.

By threatening to sell her story to the newspapers, Baby Face stays on the payroll but is sent to the Paris branch of the bank, where the new president (George Brent) meets and marries her. Later, about to desert him, taking all her jewels and cash, she does her one good deed by leaving enough to save him from imprisonment. Though Stanwyck went on to play many another hard-boiled, crooked or adulterous heroine, no other was quite so coldly amoral as Baby Face until *Double Indemnity* (1944).

In those pre-Code years Joan Crawford's career in many respects paralleled Stanwyck's, ranging from headstrong heiresses to wronged working girls. Throughout her flaming flapper phase, however "madcap," she had remained 100% pure, but *Possessed* (1931), the first of two Crawford films by that name, found her as a small-town girl in New York who becomes the mistress of a divorced lawyer (Clark Gable), but in a "stirring climax" renounces him for the sake of his political future.

In 1932 she played two more girls no better than they ought to be. In *Grand Hotel,* though the Crawford character, Flaemmchen, nominally works as a public stenographer (perhaps the better to meet lucrative contacts), she makes no bones about letting the

[2] *Ladies of Leisure* was remade as *Women of Glamour* (1937), with Virginia Bruce.

***Clark Gable and Joan Crawford in* Possessed**

nessmen. Indeed, she is all set to accompany him to Manchester (though she will still not call him by his first name), until his brutal murder of Baron von Geigern (John Barrymore) drives her into the arms of the doomed Kringelein (Lionel Barrymore). Except for her love for the Baron, her motives throughout are frankly mercenary; even Kringelein promises to leave her his money.

From there it was only a slight step downward for Crawford (in a tight, checked dress, white fox fur and feathered cloche) to play one of the most famous of all fictional prostitutes, Sadie Thompson in *Rain,* the only one of the three film versions to be called by that name. (Her Sadie was not as much admired as Gloria Swanson's 1928 silent characterization.)

It is significant that in *Chained* (1934), made after the Production Code, though Crawford readily offers to become the mistress of her employer (Otto Kruger) when his wife will not give him a divorce, she first goes on a cruise to South America to think it over. Needless to say, on board she meets the man of her dreams (Clark Gable), and is about to break off with Kruger, only to learn that his wife has at last consented to a very expensive divorce. What can the poor girl do but marry him? After a few years of luxurious and entirely chaste yearning for her lost love, she is given her freedom by her remarkably understanding husband.

After several years of glamorous, Adrian-gowned society roles, Crawford returned to earthier material as Melvyn Douglas' wife in *The Shining Hour* (1939) as "a glorified gal of the streets—an erstwhile Tenth Avenue chippy turned ballroom dancing queen" (according to the *Times*), a film that did nothing for anyone.

Later 1939, however, saw one of the best portrayals in Crawford's career (and one of the best film characterizations ever of a girl who quite coolly uses sex appeal for upward social mobility)—Crystal Allen in *The Women.* Unlike those mentioned above, however, Crystal is not the heroine but the

industrialist Herr Preysing (Wallace Beery) know that she poses nude for magazines and has taken trips with other appreciative busi-

menace, the hard-as-nails perfume salesgirl who steals infatuated Stephen Haines from the noble Mary (Norma Shearer), with more than a little help from Mary's supposed friends. As in the original play, she is doubly punished; in the end she not only loses Stephen but finds that Buck Winston, the cowboy singing star with whom she was having an affair, is penniless. With a shrug she says, "It's back to the perfume counter." Her exit line, which does not appear in the printed version of the screenplay, is: "There's a word for you ladies—but in polite society it's only used around kennels."

No discussion of hard-boiled heroines of the '30s could be complete without Jean Harlow, whose whole screen image: the plucked eyebrows and platinum-blond bob, the slinky gowns and strident voice, made it almost impossible for her to play anything else. In *Hell's Angels* (1930), though her role was small, she managed to take on both heroes and also have an affair with another man. In *The Secret Six* (1931), *The Public Enemy* (1931) and *Beast of the City* (1931), she was a typical gangster's moll of the period, in *Iron Man* (1931) the loose-living chorus girl wife of boxer Lew Ayres and in *Goldie* (1931), though nominally a high diver in a carnival, she was frankly described as "a tramp."

The major difference between Harlow and all the other cinematically fallen women (except Mae West) was that, once she hit her stride in *Red Headed Woman* (1932), she played hers most successfully for laughs. In this Anita Loos screenplay (both more dramatic and far wittier than the Katherine Brush best seller on which it was based), she played a character somewhat parallel to Stanwyck's in *Baby Face* and even closer to Crawford's in *The Women,* a scheming stenographer from the wrong side of the tracks who traps her married boss (Chester Morris) into divorce and remarriage to her. Still snubbed by the local gentry, she sets her cap for a New York tycoon (Henry Stephenson), is caught in an affair with his chauffeur (Charles

Boyer) and thus drives her husband back to his first wife (Leila Hyams). Two years later, in Paris, she has found a wealthy old French protector, but still has the chauffeur on the side—an ending that outraged the Hays Office.

In *Red Dust* (1932) Harlow's comedy potential was even more fully realized, as one of those wisecracking dames of dubious past so often found in tropical melodramas, like a less troubled kid sister of Sadie Thompson.[3] It is her common-sense lie at the end that saves ladylike Mary Astor from the consequences of her own folly in falling for Gable. So successful was Harlow in this role that it virtually set the pattern for that kind of heroine from then on (e.g., Ann Sothern in the Maisie series).

In *Hold Your Man* (1933) Harlow played another tough girl, whose source of income was described by the *Times* reviewer as "conjectural," one who aids Gable in setting up a badger game to trap unwary men—but she is redeemed by love, prison and approaching motherhood—a transformation that no one believed even in 1933.

Far more in the true Harlow vein was her unforgettably hilarious performance in *Dinner at Eight* (1933) as a petulant, *nouveau riche* wife (of obviously questionable past) who out of sheer boredom indulges in an affair with her doctor (Edmund Lowe), meanwhile managing to outargue and outshout her crude tycoon husband (Wallace Beery). As the guests wait to go in to dinner, Harlow, trying to make conversation with Marie Dressler as a retired actress, remarks that she has read a book that states that machinery is going to replace people "in every profession." Looking her up and down, Dressler replies, "Oh, my dear, that's something *you'll* never have to worry about."

In *Bombshell* (also known as *The Blonde Bombshell*, 1933), Harlow was a dumb but basically sweet sexpot movie star, and in *The*

---

[3] Incredibly, MGM in 1930 had planned to star Garbo in *Red Dust.*

Girl from Missouri (1934), no worse than a would-be gold digger.

But in *China Seas* (1935) she was back plying her old trade, this time as another tropical trollop known as China Doll. In *Wife vs Secretary* (1936) she loves her boss (Gable), but hands him back untouched to his wife (Myrna Loy). More successfully, in *Libeled Lady* (1936), extending the dumb but lovable characterization used in *Bombshell,* she played a goodhearted broad named Gladys who clearly foreshadows both Billie Dawn in *Born Yesterday* and Miss Adelaide in *Guys and Dolls*—one of those long-suffering "fiancées" who never get any closer to the altar.

Although Myrna Loy appeared as Harlow's respectable foil in the last two films mentioned, as the wife in *Wife vs Secretary* and as an heiress in *Libeled Lady,* she had done her own long apprenticeship on the other side of the street. Along with her Oriental and half-caste siren roles, she also played the thoroughly amoral Becky Sharp in a forgotten modern-dress version of *Vanity Fair* (1932).

More memorably, in *Topaze* (1933) Loy was the kindhearted mistress of industrialist Reginald Mason, actually the heroine, who gladly switches to timid schoolmaster John Barrymore. Likewise, in *Penthouse* (1933), though she starts as the moll of gangster C. Henry Gordon, she ends with lawyer Warner Baxter, in *The Prizefighter and the Lady* (1933) she leaves night club owner Otto Kruger for boxer Max Baer, and in *Manhattan Melodrama* (1934), even under the Production Code, she is openly living with Gable before marrying William Powell (and settling down with him as America's favorite wife). Only in *The Rains Came* (1939) did she return to her wicked ways, as the reportedly wanton Lady Edwina Hesketh, punished for her past, like so many post-Code sinners, by untimely death.

Among other name actresses of the early '30s, Tallulah Bankhead in her brief career (1931–32) was almost entirely limited to this kind of role, or at least to films with titles

that suggested it. In *Tarnished Lady* (1931) after marrying broker Clive Brook for his money she promptly deserts him when he loses it, but after a period of painting the town without quite committing herself to any other man, she is supposedly brought to her senses by the birth of a child.

In *My Sin* (1931) she has already sunk to the depths as a cabaret entertainer (in Panama, where else?) who shoots her blackmailing husband, but because of her unsavory reputation can find no lawyer to defend her except alcoholic derelict Fredric March. Acquitted through his efforts, she starts life afresh in New York, only to have her past catch up with her just as she is about to marry into money—so, of course, she ends up with the now regenerated lawyer.

Tallulah Bankhead in **My Sin**

In her last vehicle of this period, *Faithless* (1932), Bankhead actually takes to the streets —but only to keep her injured husband (Robert Montgomery) in food and medicine (exactly the same situation as Dietrich's in *Blonde Venus,* released by the same studio only two months before). Nobly, her husband forgives her—but Bankhead did not forgive Hollywood, refused an MGM contract and returned to the stage.

Ironically, the two actresses who from 1930 to 1933 devoted themselves most exclusively to playing courtesans are the two who are still closest to having become legends in their own time, Dietrich and Garbo. Arriving in Hollywood fresh from her triumph as the lusty Lola Lola in UFA's *The Blue Angel* (1930), Dietrich started her American career

in *Morocco* (1930), cast, naturally enough, as Amy Jolly, cafe entertainer with a past that has driven her to Morocco, where she falls in love with callow young Legionnaire Gary Cooper so deeply that at the end she is about to walk into the desert, high heels and all, as a camp follower.

In *Dishonored* (1931), anticipating Garbo's *Mata Hari* by a year, Dietrich was a patriotic streetwalker turned Austrian spy who (wearing 1931 clothes, though the year is 1915) chooses love over duty and ends before a firing squad. However, it was *Shanghai Express* (1932) that permanently established the Dietrich image of feathers, sequins and elegant sexiness.

"It took more than one man to change my name to Shanghai Lily," she murmurs to dis-

Marlene Dietrich in **Blonde Venus**

Anna Sten in **Nana**

illusioned ex-fiancé Clive Brook, explaining how she became a "China coaster." The story line owes much to *Rain*—like Sadie Thompson, Lily likes to play the phonograph and must contend with a missionary (Lawrence Grant) as ruthlessly intolerant as Reverend Davidson—but it involves enough dramatic twists and atmosphere of war-torn China to deserve its semiclassic status.

In *Blonde Venus* (1932), though happily married to Herbert Marshall and the mother of Dickie Moore, Dietrich learns that her husband is suffering from radium poisoning. She not only goes to work as an entertainer in the night club of Cary Grant but accepts his financial help, so must suffer through several reels before the beneficiary (as in *Faithless*) finally forgives her.

In *Song of Songs* (1933), the third version of the old Hermann Sudermann play, Dietrich was another of those innocent but frail country girls who poses nude for a sculptor she loves (Brian Aherne), but must marry an evil old baron (Lionel Atwill). After leaving him, she becomes a demimondaine (giving her a chance to sing her sexy song "Jonny") before returning to smash the statue and regain her true love.

Though Catherine the Great might surely be regarded as the ultimate in frank promiscuity, in Dietrich's *The Scarlet Empress* (1934), her reputation as "the Messalina of the North" was curiously underplayed in favor of the girlish naïveté, shock and disillusion that made her what she was; the film ends with her proclamation as empress.

The Devil Is a Woman (1935), her last film with von Sternberg, is usually dismissed as a static photographic tribute to Dietrich's exotic beauty, but John Dos Passos' adaptation of a Pierre Louÿs story, with Rimsky-Korsakov's *Capriccio Espagnol* woven into the background music, was praised by the *Times* as "one of the most sophisticated films ever produced in America."

Set in a turn-of-the-century Spanish town during carnival week and told largely in flashbacks, the story is remarkably parallel to *Carmen*. Concha Perez works in a cigarette factory and ruins the career of a military man (Lionel Atwill), then runs off with a bullfighter (Don Alvarado), yet she suffers no punishment. When in a duel over her Atwill spares the life of her young revolutionary lover (Cesar Romero) and is wounded himself, she sees Romero safely across the border to France, but returns to Atwill—the heavy hand of the Production Code or a classic instance of the unpredictable, not entirely bad *femme fatale*?

In *The Garden of Allah* (1936) and *Angel* (1937), however her behavior may appear, her motives are always beyond reproach—and often beyond comprehension as well. When she returned to the more lurid vein in *Destry Rides Again* (1939), it was on an altogether different level of rowdy comedy, as a dance hall girl who belts out numbers like "See What the Boys in the Back Room Will Have" and proves her heart of gold by stopping a bullet meant for Jimmy Stewart. It should be noted that, even under the Production Code, Westerns, always set in the past, seemed to enjoy more relaxed standards. Perhaps because of the shortage of women or the drabness of the "good" ones in frontier towns, what were euphemistically known as "dance hall girls" were accepted as a welcome touch of local color.[4]

Although to those more familiar with the regal Garbo of her later, better-known films it may seem incredible, she had, after all, in the early days, made her name as a "temptress," a smoldering sexpot capable of ruining any number of men, in several American silent films.

While O'Neill's *Anna Christie* (1930)—an ideal choice for her first talkie in that the title role called for a Scandinavian accent—was a departure to the extent that Garbo wore only the drabbest of clothes amid the most sordid surroundings, in another sense it

---

[4] Other beneficiaries of this dispensation include Miriam Hopkins in *Barbary Coast* (1935) and Lily Damita in *Frisco Kid* (1935), both as gamblers' mistresses.

continued her established pattern. Her anguished problem is to convince the outraged Matt Burke (Charles Bickford) that her past as a prostitute was involuntary and certainly not enjoyable.

In *Romance* (1930), another time-tested stage hit that served as Garbo's second talkie, her situation was somewhat more complex. The glamorous Italian diva Rita Cavallini, though as a girl sold by her first lover, has enjoyed not only an internationally successful operatic career but prolonged luxurious dalliance with wealthy admirers like Cornelius Van Tuyl (Lewis Stone)—hardly the woman to make a suitable wife for a young Episcopalian minister (Gavin Gordon) in New York of the 1860s.

After a tormented, *Thaïs*-like affair in which Gordon is almost driven to throw away his clerical career, Garbo (foreshadowing her renunciation of Armand in *Camille* seven years later) gives him up for his own good and sails out of his life forever. The framework prologue and epilogue fifty years later, in which as an old man, now Bishop of New York, the hero tells his story as a cautionary tale to his grandson, was a favorite device of the period.

Inspiration (1931), one of Garbo's weakest films, based on Daudet's *Sapho,* was even closer to *Camille* in its depiction of a Parisian demimonde in which a frankly promiscuous model is transformed by the passionate, jealous love of an idealistic young man (Robert Montgomery), whom she eventually frees to go on with his diplomatic career, while she marries a former lover.

In *Susan Lenox, Her Fall and Rise* (1931), adapted from a once controversial novel of an earlier generation, a country girl is seduced by an evil circus owner (John Miljan) and later becomes the mistress of an Irish politician (Hale Hamilton), complete with the inevitable penthouse, but she gives it all up and even sinks to dancing in a low dive in South America in order to redeem herself in the eyes of her one true love (Clark Gable), an engineer who, out of sheer disillusion with

her, has been going to pieces in the tropics.

Willingness to say "yes" in the line of duty might surely be considered one of the minimal professional requirements of any efficient female spy, so in that sense perhaps *Mata Hari* (1932) represented a step upward for the Garbo screen image. In any case no doubt was left that Mata Hari was ready to romance as many men as necessary in the German cause, despite her supposed love for a young Russian officer (Ramon Novarro).

In *Grand Hotel* (1932), though presumably the world-weary ballerina Grusinskaya enjoys one night of love with the Baron von Geigern (John Barrymore) and speaks wistfully of a late Grand Duke as if they had been lovers, her past for once is no problem, since the Baron is not, nor does he pretend to be, a naïve, strait-laced young man of the kind she had loved in all her previous talkies.

In Pirandello's *As You Desire Me* (1932) the emphasis has shifted from the heroine's morality to her identity. If as the Budapest cafe entertainer Zara she is obviously the mistress of Erich von Stroheim (and others before him—"Men! Men!" she groans, trying to recall her past), this may be blamed on her unhappy amnesiac state, and if her true personality was an Italian countess (the question is never conclusively settled) she was once, and may be again, the virtuous wife of Melvyn Douglas.

From then on, though Garbo on screen might indulge in premarital sex (as in *Queen Christina,* 1933, and *Ninotchka,* 1939) or adultery (*The Painted Veil,* 1934, *Anna Karenina,* 1935, *Conquest,* 1937), she never again played a kept woman except in the incomparable *Camille* (1937), regarded by most critics as her greatest performance. As Dumas' 1852 play was the ancestor and remains the archetype of all such dramas, in which an experienced woman of the world is redeemed, too late, by the love of an innocent youth, so Garbo's *Camille* remains by far the finest film ever done on this theme, as touching and haunting today as when it was made.

"1847 . . . In the gay half-world of Paris,

the gentlemen of the day met the girls of the moment at certain theaters, balls and gambling clubs, where the code was discretion, but the game was romance," the opening subtitle announces, as the lilting strains of von Weber's *Invitation to the Dance* give way to a lively cancan. "This is the story of one of those pretty creatures, living on the shifting sands of popularity—Marguerite Gautier, who brightened her wit with champagne, and sometimes her eyes with tears."

This sets the bittersweet mood for the whole exquisite film. Though perhaps all viewers may not have caught the implications of "half-world," the literal translation of "demimonde," the screenplay by Zoe Akins, Frances Marion and James Hilton delicately but unmistakably conveys Marguerite's profession as, without even trying, she attracts the Baron de Varville (Henry Daniell) from the theater box of her rival, the vulgar Olympe (Lenore Ulric), into her own, then leaves with him without a thought of Armand (Robert Taylor), the young man she has sent to buy her *marrons glacés*.

Later, at her dinner party, when an off-color joke (unheard by the audience) makes the rounds of the table and shocks Armand, she tells him, "These are the only friends I have, and I am no better than they are," but neither he nor we believe her. The film abounds in poignant touches, such as the scene in which Armand shows her a picture of his long-married parents and she murmurs: "Thirty years! You'll never love me thirty years. No one will." Though she has been only superficially corrupted by the luxuries of Paris, it is just enough to blight any other future, as we see from her face at the country wedding she has arranged for her innocent young friend Nichette (Elizabeth Allan).

On its New York opening Frank Nugent of the *Times* hailed it as Garbo's finest work, "eloquent, tragic, yet restrained . . . simply, delicately and movingly played," while Howard Barnes in the *Herald Tribune* called her characterization "breath-takingly beautiful and superbly modulated." Although *Camille*

had been filmed three times in the silents, in the more than forty years since Garbo's version no other film actress has dared risk the comparison; it seems unlikely that any will.

If even the most illustrious stars chose to play so many ladies of questionable or nonexistent virtue, it was inevitable in those pre-Code years that many less distinguished actresses would do the same. These included fading silent stars (Corinne Griffith in *Back Pay* and *Lilies of the Field,* Evelyn Brent in *Madonna of the Streets* and *Pagan Lady,* Bebe Daniels in *My Past* and *Honor of the Family,* Dorothy Mackaill in *The Love Racket, Once a Sinner* and *Safe in Hell*) and promising newcomers (Mae Clarke in *Waterloo Bridge* and *The Front Page,* Genevieve Tobin in *Up for Murder* and *Success at Any Price,* Verree Teasdale in *Skyscraper Souls* and *Payment Deferred,* Helen Twelvetrees in *Millie, Panama Flo* and *State's Attorney,* Claudette Colbert in *His Woman,* Carole Lombard in *Virtue,* Elissa Landi in *Devil's Lottery,* Wynne Gibson in *If I Had a Million*). Even wide-eyed ingenues now and then kicked over the virginal traces (Helen Chandler in *Daybreak,* Janet Gaynor in *The Man Who Came Back,* Joan Bennett in *Hush Money,* Nancy Carroll in *Hot Saturday,* Loretta Young in *Midnight Mary* and *Born to Be Bad*). It should be recalled, too, that these were the permissive years that saw Mae West at her rather brief peak (1933–35) as the screen's frankest embodiment of uninhibited sex.

When the long-threatened storm of moral outrage finally broke in 1934 with the formation of the Catholic Legion of Decency and the enforcement of the Production Code (sixteen closely printed pages written by Rev. Daniel Lord, S.J., and Martin Quigley, publisher of movie trade journals) irked producers often charged that the same professional reformers who had foisted Prohibition on the nation, now embittered by its repeal,

Lenore Ulric, Greta Garbo, Laura Hope Crews in Camille

were poking their blue noses into an artistic medium where they had no competence.[5] This may well have been true, but it must also be kept in mind that in 1934 America was much more of a "God-fearing" country than now, at least in the sense of Bible-reading, churchgoing and keeping tabs on private morality. Thus the sheer number of tarnished screen heroines was enough to make one understand, if not share, the concern of worried parents. How were they to keep their teen-aged children, especially their daughters, on the straight and narrow path they heard preached in Sunday sermons, when the rest of the week at the neighborhood theater they could see for themselves over and over again that the wages of sin was not death but a Park Avenue penthouse?

Aside from the blight of censorship that nipped Mae West's screen success in the blossom (she was through as a major star by 1938), perhaps the most unfortunate casualty of the new morality was Samuel Goldwyn's highly publicized Russian importation, Anna Sten, whom he obviously intended to be a serious rival to Garbo and Dietrich. A few years earlier she might have become just that, but despite an elaborate production, a good cast and even an insinuating Rodgers and Hart song, "That's Love" (delivered by Sten in sultry Dietrich style), *Nana* (1934), meant to launch her American career, was softened and sentimentalized beyond the recognition of Zola or anyone else.

Though briefly seen in a gaudy outfit that suggests a streetwalker, she is never shown plying her trade. Laudably ambitious to succeed as a singer, she resents the producer Greiner (Richard Bennett) for expecting too much in return, for she loves Georges Muffat, a young army lieutenant (Phillips Holmes). The machinations of his jealous

older brother, the haughty Colonel Muffat (Lionel Atwill), send the boy to Algeria, whence his love letters are intercepted by three women friends who live with, and off, Nana. Only when she believes him lost forever does she surrender to the elder Muffat. When Georges returns and the two brothers confront each other in her luxurious apartment, Nana solves everything by shooting herself.

From 1934 on, with few exceptions, mistresses, kept women or courtesans as heroines (usually punished by death) added all together scarcely number as many as in any one year between 1930 and 1933. Undoubtedly the most spectacular example was Bette Davis' antiheroine, Mildred, in *Of Human Bondage* (1934), a totally tawdry creature, whose degeneration from heartless tease to raging fury to diseased prostitute stunned critics and audiences alike. Never for an instant does Davis play for sympathy, and her death is certainly the grimmest possible wages of sin, yet in the crusading hysteria of 1934 to "clean up the movies," when countless self-appointed bands of moral vigilantes were issuing long lists of films their followers should not see, *Of Human Bondage* was one of those most widely attacked.

It is significant of the times that though Davis went on to play many a vixen, alcoholic, adulteress and murderess, she never again played a prostitute except in *Marked Woman* (1937), an exposé of the seamier, criminal side of the life, though even then the Code made it necessary to euphemize the girls as "hostesses" in a clip joint. Soon afterward Davis played the likable girl friend, presumably mistress, of Edward G. Robinson in *Kid Galahad* (1937), so had to lose Wayne Morris, whom she loved, to virtuous Jane Bryan.

Yet if the Production Code made it impossible for even the biggest star either to enjoy or to capitalize on sex and go unpunished, sex itself could hardly be altogether banished from adult films, and members of the scarlet sisterhood continued to turn up as second-

[5] According to Jack Vizzard in *See No Evil* (Simon & Schuster, 1970) the famous regulation requiring married couples to sleep in beds separated by at least eighteen inches was never in the Production Code, but was insisted upon by the British Board of Film Censors.

Reginald Sheffield, Reginald Denny, Bette Davis, Ethel Griffies in Of Human Bondage

ary characters. Thus Katie Madden, Margot Grahame's character in *The Informer* (1935), though clearly labeled from the moment she is first glimpsed leaning against a lamppost, was presumably allowable as a repentant magdalen.

"I'm not the kind of girl you are," she says humbly to virginal Heather Angel in pleading for the life of Gypo Nolan (Victor McLaglen), "but there was a time when I was." By the end she has certainly suffered enough to satisfy even Irish morality. Likewise, in cross-sectional or *Grand Hotel* films, no standard assortment of characters was considered complete without a "street girl," either redeemed (Isabel Jewell in *Lost Horizon,* 1937) or doomed to some tragic fate (Helen Mack in *The Last Train from Madrid,* also 1937).

Then too, as noted in connection with *Des-* *try Rides Again,* a period setting, especially the 1890s or 1900s, seemed to encourage greater freedom in depicting ladies of the evening—perhaps on the hopeful assumption that prostitution was, after all, an evil now as safely in the past as slavery or child labor.[6] Thus even in such a family-oriented film as *Ah, Wilderness!* (1935) Helen Flint's greedy five-dollar tart is portrayed frankly enough, and despite Mae West's own fall from favor, in *San Francisco* (1936) Margaret Irving plays a decidedly Mae Westish madam.

By the same token, the ambiguous goodbad girls who occasionally figured in nineteenth-century fiction—the villain's mistress

[6] This attitude would also account for the relatively sympathetic treatment of historic mistresses like Cleopatra, Mmes. Pompadour and Du Barry, Marie Walewska and Katie O'Shea.

who may, if cast off, switch to the right side, or the wild, lovable *gamine* who has never known any life but the streets—were also still permissible when such works were filmed— e.g., Mary Astor as Antoinette de Mauban, the mistress of Black Michael in *The Prisoner of Zenda* (1937) and Ellen Drew as Huguette in *If I Were King* (1938), the same character Lillian Roth had played in the 1930 operetta *The Vagabond King*.

But even after most heroines could no longer have love affairs, much less sell, or rent, their favors to the highest bidder, they could be, and often were, suspected of doing just that. Ingenious writers and directors outdid each other in devising new stratagems to hint at and play around with situations that could no longer simply be taken for granted. Never did the word "suggestive" narrow to a more precise meaning.

In a more serious vein, in *Dead End* (1937) two secondary characters are introduced as variations on the relentlessly hammered theme of the destructive effects of the economic system: Kay (Wendy Barrie), a luxuriously kept woman who longs for a fling with Dave (Joel McCrea), and Francie (Claire Trevor), a diseased prostitute who had been the childhood sweetheart of Baby Face Martin (Humphrey Bogart)—both punished by losing the men they love. (Earlier that year Trevor had played Akim Tamiroff's reluctant but well-kept mistress in *King of Gamblers*.) Similarly, in *Algiers* (1938) Hedy Lamarr plays an elegant Parisienne kept by Robert Greig, but loved by Pepe Le Moko (Charles Boyer), whose death she inadvertently causes, thus getting her comeuppance.

Trevor's success in *Dead End* was so striking that she continued to play that kind of role for most of her long career, three more in the '30s alone: *The Amazing Dr. Clitterhouse* (1938), *Valley of the Giants* (1938) and *Stagecoach* (1939), the latter two Westerns. Under that benign dispensation already noted, which took a more tolerant view of such women if they lived in the nineteenth century, especially in the old West, she was

allowed to reform in both. Indeed, Dallas in *Stagecoach,* first seen being run out of town by the respectable citizens, is one of the very few post-Code heroines with such a past to be allowed a happy future: a new life with the Ringo Kid (John Wayne).

Another major exception, set in the First World War era—the twentieth century, to be sure, but still in the past—was *The Shopworn Angel* (1938), a remake of a Nancy Carroll-Gary Cooper silent. Perhaps musical comedy star Daisy Heath (Margaret Sullavan) could not be promoted from mistress of the producer (Walter Pidgeon) to wife because that would have made the plot impossible. Just when he is finally willing to marry her, instead she weds out of impulsive pity a naïve young soldier (James Stewart) about to be sent overseas, presumably on the understanding that he will have the good taste not to come back. Obligingly, he doesn't.

Except for the show girl accused of murdering her protector in *The Trial of Mary Dugan* (1929), Norma Shearer's talkie heroines were usually too wealthy and independent to be kept by anyone, yet she played (and very well) the last mistress heroine of the decade, Irene in *Idiot's Delight* (1939), the exotic, Russian-accented traveling companion of munitions tycoon Achille Weber (Edward Arnold).

As it did with so many other movie trends and tastes of the '30s, *Gone With the Wind,* set nearly eighty years in the past, wrapped up at least one phase of the "scarlet woman" image—not in Scarlett O'Hara, who remains technically pure after her offer to Rhett Butler in the Atlanta jail is rejected, but in the important secondary character of Belle Watling (Ona Munson), who plays much the same role in Rhett's life as Dixie Lee did in Yancey Cravatt's in *Cimarron* (1931). Though she is warmly thanked by the good Melanie for saving Ashley's life, Scarlett continues to scorn her. Belle is the classic madam with a heart of gold, by implication more decent than many a so-called good woman, especially Scarlett herself.

2

PUTTIN' ON THE RITZ
The Gold Diggers of 1930-39

Of the stock company of stereotypes that continually recurred in 1930s films, some survived through the '40s or even later (the private eye, the brash reporter, the ruthless spy), but others for a variety of reasons perished with the decade or even before it (the runaway heiress, the playboy, the Bengal Lancer). One of the most conspicuous of these was the gold digger, who in the early '30s was almost as familiar a heroine as the wrongly imprisoned working girl, the long-suffering mother or the well-kept courtesan. Like the last-named, she was among the casualties of the Production Code.

Though it was never quite clear just how deep she had to dig before striking pay dirt, her main difference from the elegant lilies of the field played by Garbo, Dietrich, Bennett, Crawford et al. was that the true gold digger, as gaily amoral as Robin Hood, kept a wisecracking tongue planted firmly in her well-rouged cheek. Since her willing victims were usually potbellied stage-door Johnnies played by actors like Guy Kibbee, Eugene Pallette and George Barbier, who could quarrel with such an equitable redistribution of wealth?

This was one field—perhaps the only one—in which female characters enjoyed far wider latitude than male. The gigolo (another vanished '30s type) was, after all, the male counterpart of the gold digger. Both used their charms to exploit rich, gullible older members of the opposite sex, but whereas the gigolo was invariably depicted as a hand-kissing foreigner (Ivan Lebedeff, Alexander D'Arcy, Gilbert Roland), often with a phony title, or at best a harmless clown (Erik Rhodes, Mischa Auer), the gold digger, always American, was shrewd, knowing, tart-tongued, the kind of personality later associated with Eve Arden—on the assumption, no doubt valid at the time, that, with so many other options open, it was always despicable for a man to live off wealthy women, but quite understandable, even laudable, if a girl was smart enough to beat a system in which all the important cards were stacked against her. Even if she worked, how much did a chorus girl earn? (The first kept hero, John O'Hara's Pal Joey, came as a shock even to Broadway in 1941 and did not make it to the screen until 1957, ⟨...⟩ laundered and still not quite sym⟨...⟩

Presented seri⟨...⟩ easily turn int⟨...⟩ snatcher, like St⟨...⟩ in *Red Headed⟨...⟩ Women*. On tl⟨...⟩ timentality, s⟨...⟩ the poor but⟨...⟩ elderly milli⟨...⟩ some son as⟨...⟩ reward. (A⟨...⟩ marry for⟨...⟩

The earliest use of the word "gold digger" (like "flapper" and "gangster") could perhaps be traced back before World War I, but what gave it general currency in the language was Ina Claire's great Broadway success in Avery Hopwood's 1919 comedy *The Gold Diggers,* which Warners first filmed in 1923, starring, aptly enough, Hope Hampton, with Louise Fazenda as her comic sidekick. *The American Film Institute Catalog . . . 1921– 1930* lists literally one hundred other films between 1920 and 1930 dealing with chorus girls, most of the titles now forgotten, except perhaps for *Sally, Irene and Mary* (1925).

It seems probable that both the term and the idea of "gold digging" reached even wider circulation through their archetypal embodiment in Lorelei Lee, heroine of Anita Loos's 1925 novel, 1926 play and 1928 film *Gentlemen Prefer Blondes.* Whatever its origins, "gold digger" is indeed as much a part of '20s night life as "love nest," "sugar daddy," "tired businessman," "butter-and-egg man," "baldheaded row" and other slang evocative of those years when lavish Broadway musicals provided the recognized showcase where rich middle age could seek out youthful beauty, then wait in Rolls-Royces and Cadillacs to shower orchids, ermine and jewels on chorines whose on-stage talents would scarcely have kept them in silk stockings.

Even when ardor cooled, the right lawyer could always extract "heart balm" in the form of payment for indiscreet letters, breach of promise settlements or juicy alimony. In the kind of cultural lag often seen in '30s films, this was also the glittering, pre-Depression Broadway that screenwriters, eating their hearts out in exile by the waters of Hollywood Babylon, continued to evoke as a dazzling myth long after the actuality had disappeared, along with Texas Guinan, Legs Diamond and "angels" with unlimited bankrolls.

Late in 1929 Warners remade its 1923 silent *Gold Diggers* as one of its earliest musical talkies, in Technicolor, as *The Gold Diggers of Broadway,* featuring Nancy Welford, Conway Tearle and Winnie Lightner, with a score

that included "Tiptoe Through the Tulips" and "Painting the Clouds with Sunshine." After such a success, it is surprising that no other studio picked up the theme, but most 1930s backstage musicals were more concerned with male song writers or entertainers who let success go to their heads.

In *New Movietone Follies of 1930,* Noel Francis, who had been a famous Ziegfeld beauty, played a likable show girl who takes family pressure off the playboy hero (William Collier, Jr.) by revealing at the right moment that her hitherto secret protector, "Dodo," is actually the boy's stuffy old uncle, but this is not the main plot.[1]

Since writing effective comedy is never as easy as turning out melodrama, it is not surprising that many early '30s films in which the modish term "gold digger" was tossed about were no more than soap operas, in which the fortune-hunting heroine either was exposed or repented or both. Yet since such characters were not really courtesans or even promiscuous, merely designing, they seem to belong here as gold diggers who took themselves seriously. A prime example was *The Devil's Holiday* (1930), in which Nancy Carroll as a scheming manicurist marries a scion of wealth (Phillips Holmes) and leaves him for the price offered by his family, but when he loses his mind returns to him.

Perhaps because 1929 and 1930 saw so many backstage films, musical or otherwise, that reviewers were begging for mercy, 1931 and 1932 saw none at all. Thus during those years gold diggers' connection with the theater, if any, was tenuous at best; even if they had once been in show business, they were in no hurry to get back to it. Perhaps they may be regarded as the "purest" professionals, not just chorus girls between jobs.

On a relatively sophisticated level were two witty gold-digging comedies, one based on a

[1] In *Smart Woman* (1931) Francis played a much less amiable gold digger, a beauty contest winner who tries to steal first Mary Astor's husband (Robert Ames), then her even wealthier admirer (John Halliday).

Kay Francis and Lilyan Tashman in Girls About Town

story, one on a stage hit, both by Zoe Akins. Directed by George Cukor, *Girls About Town* (1931—note the playful tone of that title compared with the guilt-laden implications of *Ladies of Leisure, The Purchase Price* and other dramas of kept heroines dealt with in the previous chapter) starred the brunette Kay Francis and the blond Lilyan Tashman as apartment mates who live quite luxuriously off the fatheads of the land as paid dinner companions of visiting Babbitts, giving as little as possible in return for their glamorous evenings on the town. Kay, however, falls for Joel McCrea, and that plot turns into a kind of happily resolved, if unconvincing, *Camille* or *The Easiest Way*. A high point, anticipating the catty wit of Cukor's

The Women, is the scene in which the girls attempt to raise cash by auctioning off their gowns and jewels. Most amusing is Tashman's involvement with Eugene Pallette as a penny-pinching copper king whose wife, Lucille Gleason, frankly envious of the gold digger's life, wonders if it is too late for her to try.

"Since the world began, half of the female population has always been working women. The other half has been working men," announced the opening subtitle of *The Greeks Had a Word for Them* (1932), the definitive gold-digging comedy, which on Broadway had been called *The Greeks Had a Word for It.* Ever suspicious of an unidentified "it," United Artists (or was it Samuel Goldwyn himself?) only made it sound more incriminating, because what word for "them" would occur to most people? Probably not the Greek word Akins may have had in mind: "hetairai" (those cultivated Athenian courtesans of whom Pericles' mistress, Aspasia, was the most notable example).

Ex-*Follies* girls Jean (Ina Claire) and her oddly named friends Polaire (Madge Evans) and Schatze (Joan Blondell) are in every sense of the word past mistresses of the art of gold digging. At one point, they discover that all three have had affairs with the same, now deceased, admirer. Polaire surrenders to love in the person of wealthy David Manners, but the other two, even when Jean is offered marriage by Manners' father, sail off to Europe to continue on their merrily unregenerated way, as all three did in the play.

Blondie of the Follies (1932), written by Anita Loos, starred Marion Davies and Billie Dove, who had actually been Ziegfeld girls, as a rival pair who had grown up together in the slums. The continual contrast between their tenement background and the luxury of Park Avenue penthouses suggests a basic sociological explanation for gold digging usually not touched on in this kind of film. Dove's character, Lurleen Cavanaugh (born Lottie Callahan), takes the primrose path and becomes the mistress of playboy Robert Montgomery, but it is true-blue, straight-as-a-die Blondie who (after being seriously injured in a stage accident caused by the other girl) wins him in the end—an ironic twist, considering Davies' well-known off-screen status.

After two years in which backstage musicals had been pronounced officially dead, Warners were taking a decided risk in trying to revive them with *42nd Street* (1933), but, as any film buff knows, the gamble more than paid

Madge Evans, Ina Claire, Joan Blondell in **The Greeks Had a Word for Them**

off. Though the main plot has nothing to do with gold digging, Ann Lowell, a minor character played by Ginger Rogers, is a prime practitioner. When she turns up at the first chorus call in a smartly tailored suit, sporting a monocle, carrying a Pekingese and in a phony British accent dropping references to a summer at Deauville, the first muttered comment from one of the other girls is "Lamp Minnie the Mountaineer!"

"That's Any Time Annie," another explains. "She only said no once, and then she didn't hear the question." A third adds, "I bet *her* homework's tough!" Until Ginger and Una Merkel go into their cynical added chorus of "Shuffle Off to Buffalo," little further is made of this character, but she surely revived the comic possibilities of the chorus girl who moonlights as mistress.

Even before the release of *42nd Street,* Warners were planning a follow-up musical, to be called *High Life,* but the January 13, 1933, issue of *Film Daily* announced that the title had been changed to *The Gold Diggers of 1933.* One may infer that when even the advance response to *42nd Street* exceeded their fondest hopes, the producers, eager to get a successor into the theaters as soon as possible, decided instead of trying to devise an original screenplay to remake a proven hit. Since the production numbers would have nothing whatever to do with the story line, they could be spliced into any plot. This seems the only logical explanation of the fact, unique in film history, that a successful musical in Technicolor was remade, less than four years after its release, in black and white, with a different score.

All that remained was Hopwood's by now creaking 1919 plot, with a few Depression touches added. Once more a proper Bostonian (Warren William) accompanied by his lawyer (Guy Kibbee) comes to New York to rescue his younger brother (Dick Powell) from the toils of a supposed adventuress (Ruby Keeler). Mistaking her room-mate (Joan Blondell) for her, he is maneuvered into writing a check for $10,000 to buy her off—not, of

Una Merkel, Ginger Rogers, Ruby Keeler
in 42nd Street

course, that she wants the money but only to teach him a lesson.

By this time they are in love, he approves his brother's choice and the girls' most expertly mercenary room-mate (Aline MacMahon in the Fazenda-Lightner role) gets the lawyer. True gold diggers, of course, were more interested in money than marriage, and not interested in working at all, so the ironic fact is that in no version of this story were the heroines ever really full-time gold diggers—only hard-working chorus girls trying to raise money for a show.

Joan Blondell in The Gold Diggers of 1933

Though, presumably as a marquee attraction, the words "Gold Diggers" persisted through three more Warners musicals (*. . . of 1935, of 1937* and *in Paris*), they became as meaningless as Paramount's *Big Broadcasts* and MGM's *Broadway Melodies*—merely an easily identifiable label for an annual musical. As with most such series, the law of diminishing returns very soon set in.

Meanwhile the initial success of *The Gold Diggers of 1933* led Warners to launch concurrently another, non-musical series that teamed two of the most proficient gold diggers in the trade, Joan Blondell and Glenda Farrell, whose peppery, hard-boiled personalities probably epitomize the type better than those of any other actresses. In *Havana Widows* (1933) they try to work an extortion racket on pseudo-pious parson Guy Kibbee, until Blondell falls for his son (Lyle Talbot). *Convention City* (1933) is a variation, with many of the same supporting players, this time in the guise of a broad satire on the antics of American businessmen at an annual sales convention in Atlantic City. But when *Kansas City Princess* opened in November 1934, the *Times* called it "shopworn," noting that "the cynical gold digger has gone out of fashion lately."

It is surely no coincidence that the heyday of the gold digger was during the years of Mae West's all too brief reign. Her films are not usually considered in this connection, but her standard character of the wisecracking blond entertainer with a broad and profitable experience of men seems like an 1890s forerunner of the gold digger of the '20s and '30s, just as her famous line about her jewelry, "Goodness had nothing to do with it!" echoes Lorelei Lee's "Diamonds are a girl's best friend."

The huge success of *She Done Him Wrong* (1933) reinforced the popularity of quick-tongued, adventurous blondes whom nobody could possibly mistake for the girl next door. Thus in *Her Bodyguard* (1933) Wynne Gibson played a gold digger named Margot Brienne (nee Maggie O'Brien), whose patron (Edward Arnold) hires a detective (Edmund Lowe) to guard both her and her jewels, which she never takes off. The bodyguard does such a thorough job that he eliminates all other suitors, including his employer.

After the advent of the Production Code, only Carole Lombard was allowed to give the gold digger's tattered banner a few last flings in *The Gay Bride* (1934) as a chorine involved with gangsters and in *Hands Across the Table* (1935) as a manicurist determined to marry for money who falls for Fred Mac-Murray mistakenly thinking he's rich but eventually accepting him, anyway.

Just as surely as the seriously presented kept woman, the once lighthearted gold digger was technologically unemployed by the Production Code. Though both Ted Sennett in *Lunatics and Lovers* and Pauline Kael in her *New Yorker* profile of Cary Grant quote a line spoken by Glenda Farrell in *The Gold Diggers of 1937* as typical: "It's so hard to be good under the capitalistic system," this is just the kind of self-conscious observation a true gold digger would never have made. In this particular film, called by the *Times* "a disappointing Christmas package," the plot—a ghoulish one for a musical—centered on the efforts of Victor Moore's business partners to murder him for his insurance.

By the later '30s, a heroine could only be suspected or accused of gold digging (Simone Simon in *Josette,* Danielle Darrieux in *The Rage of Paris,* to cite but two from 1938). If indeed she ever did harbor any such base mercenary motives, she renounced them before the end in favor of the right (poor) young man. As the opposite side of this counterfeit coin, the true gold digger was accordingly reduced to the role of menace, comic (Binnie Barnes in *Three Smart Girls,* 1937) or otherwise (Virginia Bruce in *The Great Ziegfeld,* 1936, as the dissolute *Follies* beauty who comes between Flo and his first wife, Anna Held). Sometimes even the designing ex-wife or catty fiancée, determined to wrest the hero from the heroine, the kind of character played by Astrid Allwyn, Leona Maricle and Helen Vinson, might be loosely described as a gold digger, but obviously she was not the real pre-1934 stock.

In *Meet the Girls* (1937) Lynn Bari and June Lang were cast as two chorines in a projected Big Town Girls series, apparently a belated attempt to revive the breezy Blondell-Farrell tradition, but even after a better second film, *Pardon Our Nerve* (1938), the series did not catch on. By this time Blondell and Farrell, however unflappably brassy and sassy, were playing reporters, process servers, waitresses or Girls Friday, all lawfully employed.

Far commoner was the sentimental softening of the gold-digger pattern into the Cinderella tale, as in *Three Blind Mice* (1938), in which Loretta Young, Pauline Moore and Marjorie Weaver played three sisters who use their small inheritance to put up a front by which at least one of them will trap a rich husband. Young pretends to be an heiress, Moore her secretary and Weaver her maid, and, of course, all three end up with suitable mates, one actually rich.

The three small-town sisters were not designing women of the world but as 100% pure as Doris Day at her most virginal; their maneuvers to help each other to advantageous matches make them more akin to the Bennets in *Pride and Prejudice* than to Zoe Akin's coolly calculating, antiromantic ladies. It is significant that the settings for their girlish stratagems in the three versions of this story were respectively Santa Barbara (*Three Blind Mice*), Miami (*Moon over Miami*) and the Atlantic City of 1902 (*Three Little Girls in Blue*), playgrounds all of the presumably more gullible newly rich. Such Little Red Ridinghoods would have been quickly gobbled up by the more experienced wolves of Manhattan.

It is an ironic commentary that the last would-be gold digger of the 1930s, suitably chastened and reformed, was played by Joan Blondell herself—she who had merrily fleeced Guy Kibbee from Atlantic City to Havana—in *Good Girls Go to Paris* (1939), a lame title, from which a significant final *Too* had been deleted. A campus waitress in a college town, she confides to a professor (Melvyn Douglas) her girlish dream of going to Paris on money made from a breach of promise suit against a rich student (Alan Curtis), but then cannot go through with it. She even turns down a proposal from another scion of wealth (Stanley Brown) to settle for, need it be added, the professor.

By the end of the decade all that remained of the once vivid figure who had been as much a part of '30s film folklore as the mistress or the heiress was an occasional faint reminder, when in a backstage musical a chorus girl too minor to figure in the plot could be heard squealing as she opened a jewel box proffered by an elderly admirer, "Ooh, Mr. Oglethorpe, how can I *ever* thank you?"

3

HAPPILY EVER AFTER
Cinderella Romances

As temporary obstacles to true love, disparities in rank and fortune are at least as old as the myths in which gods and goddesses fell in love with attractive mortals, and the fairy tales in which the peasant lad wins the faraway princess, or, even more commonly, the beggar maid or Cinderella figure marries the King or his son. In modern dress, with the heroine as a working girl and the King replaced by the boss or owner of the firm (or his son), this was the basis for countless silent comedies made by flapper stars like Colleen Moore, Clara Bow and Alice White, and occasionally even by Mary Pickford (*My Best Girl*).

It was inevitable, then, that during the Depression years the appeal of this perennial pattern grew stronger than ever, subconsciously reassuring jobless or underpaid stenographers and salesgirls that if only they played their cards wisely and hung on to their "reputation," they, too, might one day meet Mr. Right in the person of a handsome, but honorable, young millionaire. So popular was this theme that frequently it proliferated into sets of three or more heroines, and the audience got several Cinderellas for the price of one.

In a sense more prudent than either courtesans or gold diggers, in that *their* upward mobility involved no guilty past, these girls, like Pamela (heroine of the first English novel in 1740, who by clinging tenaciously to her "virtue" eventually forces her amorous employer to capitulate and marry her), always knew when pursued by playboys or roués just how long to hold out for a wedding ring. Occasionally such a girl would find that this could be provided only by the poor but honest boy friend she had once spurned. Often this formula was used in backstage musicals, with the Cinderella figure the chorus girl who becomes a star overnight. Occasionally the rags-to-riches routine turned up in the joyous comedies of Carole Lombard, Claudette Colbert and Jean Arthur, but the more typical Cinderellas of the early '30s took themselves and their romances very seriously.

Few of these films will bear, or deserve, extended analysis. If they provided dreams of wish fulfillment and a few hours' escape from the grim realities outside, they served their purpose. Since so many of the top women stars of the early '30s were busy playing courtesans or gold diggers, Cinderella roles were usually left to the relative few who could still project girlish innocence, especially Janet Gaynor, Joan Bennett, Nancy Carroll and Mary Brian. (Oddly enough, Loretta Young, the youngest and most girlish-looking of all, was seldom cast as a pure Cinderella.)

Surprisingly, MGM's favorite working-girl Cinderella of the '30s was Joan Crawford. Often as she may have taken the primrose path as prostitute or mistress, at least as often she made it to the altar with a rich husband. In *Sadie McKee* (1934) she loves a weakling entertainer (Gene Raymond), who dies, but she marries and rehabilitates an alcoholic millionaire (Edward Arnold) before ending up with almost equally rich Franchot Tone. As noted in Chapter 1, in *Chained* (1934), her millionaire husband (Otto Kruger) gives her up to Gable—again almost as rich.

In *The Bride Wore Red* (1937) she was a cabaret girl given "two glorious weeks with high society in the Tyrol," but when her midnight strikes, she settles for the village postmaster (Tone again). In *Mannequin* (1938, as in *Sadie McKee,* she falls for the wrong man (Alan Curtis), who later tries to blackmail her, but ends up with self-made millionaire Spencer Tracy.

Even some stars not normally associated with Cinderella roles played at least one during the decade. Thus Claudette Colbert in *Secrets of a Secretary* (1931), left penniless, works as social secretary to Mary Boland, whose wild daughter (Betty Lawford) —another of those decadent heiresses—gets involved with Claudette's ex-husband (Georges Metaxa), now turned blackmailing gigolo, thus leading the girl's titled fiancé (Herbert Marshall) to turn to the secretary.

In her screen debut, *Bad Sister* (1931), Bette Davis played a "sad-faced Cinderella" (said the *Times*), constantly victimized by

her "bad sister" (Sidney Fox), who, however, makes the mistake of eloping with smooth-talking con man Humphrey Bogart and is left stranded, while Davis gets one of her rejects (Conrad Nagel), a doctor whom she has always loved.

Even after proving her dramatic worth in *Of Human Bondage* and *Bordertown,* Davis was handed another Cinderella role in *The Girl from Tenth Avenue* (1935), as a tenement girl married in drunken spite by the usual kind of playboy (Ian Hunter), whom she, of course, straightens out and wins away from the socialite (Katherine Alexander) who had jilted him.

Clara Bow, whose career declined rapidly after 1930, may have hastened the process by making three inept Cinderella romances. In *Love Among the Millionaires* (1930) she was a waitress who attracts the son (Stanley Smith) of a railroad president, but is persuaded by the father, à la *Camille,* to indulge in crude behavior to disillusion the boy—only temporarily, of course. In *No Limit* (1931) she was an usherette who marries a millionaire (Norman Foster) who is actually a thief. She's willing to take the rap for him, but he goes to jail himself. In *Call Her Savage* (1932) she was a fiery-tempered Western girl scorned by the aristocratic family of the Eastern playboy she marries (Anthony Jowitt).

Nancy Carroll soon succeeded Bow as Paramount's favorite Cinderella. In the title role of *Personal Maid* (1931) she played a New York Irish girl who straightens out and ultimately marries the wild playboy son (Gene Raymond) of her employer (Mary Boland) —an obvious link in the chain that leads from *Pamela* to *Upstairs, Downstairs.* (In fact, this sounds like a backstairs version of *Secrets of a Secretary,* released the week before by the same studio, with Mary Boland in approximately the same role.)

Wayward (1932) saw Carroll as a chorus girl married to a scion of wealth (Richard Arlen), but so relentlessly persecuted by his mother (Pauline Frederick) that she almost runs off with his brother-in-law. (The plot is almost identical with that of *The Social Register,* 1934, in which Colleen Moore was the chorus girl-wife, Alexander Kirkland the husband and Pauline Frederick again the ruthless mother-in-law.)

In *Hot Saturday* (1932), praised for its authentic small-town atmosphere, Carroll was a girl who, when wrongfully suspected of having spent a night with millionaire Cary Grant, loses her bank job and is so bitterly denounced by her parents and her long-time beau (Randolph Scott) that she decides she may as well have the game as the name, and

Cary Grant and Nancy Carroll in Hot Saturday

runs off with Grant (who only in the last scene mutters something vague about marriage). In *Child of Manhattan* (1933) Carroll was a pregnant taxi dancer who marries a millionaire (John Boles), but must lose her baby and get a Mexican divorce before convincing him that she's *not* a gold digger.

Another disenchanted taxi dancer was played by Barbara Stanwyck in *Ten Cents a Dance* (1931), in which her weakling husband (Monroe Owsley) accuses her of infidelity with wealthy Ricardo Cortez, and also robs him, before she leaves him for Cortez. Still another dancer was chorus girl Mary Brian in *The Runaround* (a.k.a. *Lovable and Sweet,* 1931), who proves she is a Cinderella, not a gold digger, by tricking playboy Geoffrey Kerr into a church wedding.

Another entertainer who ends up married to a millionaire, though only after much harsher vicissitudes, was Janet Gaynor in *The Man Who Came Back* (1931), based on a melodrama of 1916. In what must have seemed a shocking change of pace for Gaynor and Charles Farrell, "America's favorite lovebirds," she was a San Francisco cafe singer turned drug addict, he an alcoholic playboy who writes rubber checks. When both have hit rock bottom, they find each other again in an opium den in Shanghai, and, of course, redeem themselves, not without occasional threats of relapse, until they ultimately regain the respect (and inheritance) of his father.[1]

Not all early talkie Cinderellas held such relatively desirable jobs as singing or dancing. Many were described as "slaveys"—a favorite word, at least in reviews, applied alike to Winifred Westover in *Lummox,* Rose

[1] Considering all the fuss in 1955 when *The Man with the Golden Arm* broke the Production Code ban on drug addiction, it seems ironic that this 1931 film showed and discussed it quite openly, as also did *The Mad Genius* (1931), *Three on a Match* (1932) and *The Mystery of the Wax Museum* (1933), not to mention *The Masquerader* (1931) and *Heroes for Sale* (1934).

Hobart in *Liliom* and *Compromised* and especially to Gaynor, whose wistful charm made her a natural to play such downtrodden victims. In *Merely Mary Ann* (1931) she was the drudge in a London household until she inherited a fortune and married a young composer (Farrell). In *Delicious* (1931), a musical, she was a poor Scotch immigrant hounded by a customs inspector until she eventually lands a millionaire (as usual, Farrell).

Closely akin to the slavey was the ugly duckling, the drab, overlooked wallflower readily convertible into a raving beauty. A typical example was *Beauty and the Boss* (1931) (from a play called *The Church Mouse*), in which Warren William, distracted by a series of seductive secretaries, hires an apparently plain, mousy type (Marian Marsh), who, of course, at the right moment blossoms out. In *Devotion* (1931), set in London, Ann Harding for love of barrister Leslie Howard disguises herself as a dowdy, middle-aged governess to care for his child, and eventually wins him from an already estranged wife.

Marion Davies underwent similar metamorphoses in two of her last films, both so poorly received that they may well have hastened her retirement. In *Page Miss Glory* (1935) a chambermaid in a hotel turns out to resemble a composite photograph that won a contest and uses her momentary fame to win the aviator of her dreams (Dick Powell). In *Ever Since Eve* (1937) she disguises herself as a frump to become the secretary of writer Robert Montgomery, then must pretend to be her own room-mate, with predictable results.

Another hoary cliché, revived by both Gaynor and Davies, was one already so obsolete on stage that it was satirically spoofed in Ferber and Kaufman's *The Royal Family* (1927), in the no-talent Cavendish in-laws' account of their projected radio series, to be called *The Bachelor's Baby*. This is the figure of the spunky, lovable, preferably orphaned girl-child (like a lighter version of

Griffith's usually tragic nymphet), quaintly dressed in a child's short skirts, clumsy shoes and either a baggy tam-o'-shanter or one of those straw hats associated with English schoolgirls, with the brim upcurled like an angel food cake tin, and usually accompanied by her mischievous mongrel pet. In the end it is she who wins the heart of the crusty bachelor father figure (sometimes one of a trio) and becomes his wife. If this typically Victorian dream achieved its most sophisticated expression in *Gigi*, at the other end of the scale it reached its ultimate *reductio ad absurdum* in comic strip figures like Little Orphan Annie and Little Annie Rooney.

The Beloved Bachelor (1932) is a perfect example. A sculptor (Paul Lukas) and his two bachelor friends are left with the care of an orphan girl (Dorothy Jordan) who after much misunderstanding grows up to marry him. One of the most durable examples is *Daddy Long Legs* (refilmed as late as 1955), from a 1914 play based on a 1912 novel, and filmed as a silent in 1921 by Pickford, which in 1931 made a perfect vehicle for Gaynor and Warner Baxter. This is the one about the orphan girl who has seen only the elongated shadow on a wall of the deliberately mysterious benefactor who puts her through college. Never does she dream of associating him with the kindly bachelor confidant who is always urging her to go out with boys her own age.

The heroine of *Paddy the Next Best Thing* (1933) is not an orphan, but, as indicated by the coy title, is another Little Miss Slyboots (Janet Gaynor), a roguish colleen who, knowing that her sister (Margaret Lindsay) does not love the rich man (Warner Baxter) she is slated to marry, does everyone a favor by nabbing him for herself. Perhaps the most blatant example of this sort of pre-World War I sentimentality was *Peg o' My Heart*, the 1912 play of which Laurette Taylor virtually made a way of life. Two decades later, in 1933, Marion Davies filmed it, complete with a rich brogue, an added song, "Sweetheart Darlin'," and Onslow

Stevens as her cousin's wealthy suitor, whom Peg wins.

Not all girls who married money were so fortunate, and a number of films warned against the perils of becoming a bird in a gilded cage. In the much-admired *Laughter* (1930) Nancy Carroll was an ex-*Follies* girl married to a millionaire (Frank Morgan) but unhappy until she regains her true love, a lighthearted composer (Fredric March). Far more extreme was the case of Joan Bennett as a beauty contest winner in *She Wanted a Millionaire* (1932). What she gets is a sadist (James Kirkwood), who keeps her terrified with Great Danes until eventually he kills himself, leaving her only too glad to settle for faithful railroad engineer Spencer Tracy.

Carole Lombard almost made the same mistake in *Sinners in the Sun* (1932), as a high-fashion model who rejects auto mechanic Chester Morris to dally with a married tycoon (Walter Byron), without actually becoming his mistress. As a chauffeur, Morris soon attracts and marries his employer (Adrienne Ames), another of those heiresses then so prevalent on screen, but in the end both lovers give up wealth in favor of each other.

In *Walls of Gold* (1933) Sally Eilers' fiancé (Norman Foster) while drunk marries her sister (Mary Mason), so, to spite him, she marries his rich, elderly uncle (Ralph Morgan). But as fate and author Kathleen Norris would have it, the wife dies in childbirth and the old husband has a fatal heart attack, leaving his widow with the best of both worlds.

In *Splendor* (1935) Miriam Hopkins undergoes suffering of a more complex nature as a poor girl who marries Joel McCrea, son of an impoverished but ultra-aristocratic family. In a variation on de Maupassant's *Boule de Suif,* her haughty in-laws urge her to encourage the attentions of a broker (Paul Cavanagh) who can help her husband's career, but when a scandal breaks out, they turn against her. She leaves and goes to work until her husband comes to his senses.

One might note that even Hepburn's *Alice Adams* (1935), marvelously poignant though it is, was turned into a Cinderella tale by its ending, when, instead of losing the rich young man and starting business school, as in the Tarkington novel, she finds that, after all, he loves her for her real self.

A delightful exception to the run-of-the-mill Cinderella films was Margaret Sullavan's hilarious *The Good Fairy* (1935), based on a Molnár play, with the Budapest setting intact. Fresh from a girls' orphanage, she finds herself fending off amorous millionaire Frank Morgan by pretending to have a husband. Forced to produce him, she picks the name of a lawyer (Herbert Marshall) from the phone book. Expecting to be repaid by the favors of the supposed wife, Morgan offers him a contract that will make his career, then, even when the truth comes out, lets it stand, so the lawyer can marry the girl.

Individual Cinderellas continued to recur for the rest of the decade, though more and more frequently in comedies in which sentimentality was kept at a minimum. For really heavy, tear-choked problem dramas of the awful dilemmas of love vs. money, Hollywood seemed convinced that the best things in life were three.

In European fairy tales the rule of three usually took the form of three sisters (or brothers), of whom only the youngest, the one scorned by the parents and the older two, proves able to pass some crucial test. That is the basic pattern of *King Lear,* as well as *Cinderella.* Even Chekhov was not above naming a play *The Three Sisters.* The *Film Daily Yearbook* lists well over a hundred titles beginning with *Three* or *The Three,* not including all the films centered on that number of heroes or heroines.

Undoubtedly the most prominent silent film to utilize this pattern was *Sally, Irene and Mary* (1925), with Joan Crawford, Constance Bennett and Sally O'Neil in the title roles as three chorus girls; perhaps this was what established what came to be an unwritten law in this kind of film—that one of the three girls, the one who falls for the wrong man, the married tycoon or the weakling playboy, must die, either as a suicide or a murder or accident victim. Crawford went on to the definitive jazz age film, *Our Dancing Daughters* (1928), in which Anita Page and Dorothy Sebastian were the other two, and Page died in a drunken fall downstairs. In *Our Modern Maidens* (1929) Crawford again shared honors with Page, with Josephine Dunn as the not very important third girl. (No one died.)

The very first 1930 talkie to use the pattern was a minor Fox musical, *The Big Party*, in which Dixie Lee, Sue Carol and Dorothy Brown played (according to the review in *Screen Play Secrets*) "Three virtuous working girls who pass up millionaires to marry the boys of their choice." A more notable example, released in the summer of 1930, was *Our Blushing Brides*, which reunited the original trio of girls from *Our Dancing Daughters*. (There was no plot connection among the three *Our . . .* films, only the alliterative titles, which led one reviewer to conjecture that the next one would be *Our Dizzy Divorcees*.)

Instead of keeping the pace that kills as

Dorothy Sebastian, Anita Page, Joan Crawford in **Our Blushing Brides**

jazz-mad society girls, this time the three friends work in a New York department store, Crawford as a mannequin, the other two as clerks. After trying every other approach, the owner's older son (Robert Montgomery) eventually marries Crawford, but not until after his younger brother (Raymond Hackett) has set up the pathetically vulnerable Page in a love nest, then dropped her to marry on his own social level, driving her to suicide. Sebastian finds that the glib, apparently wealthy man she married (John Miljan) is a thief. Though critics at the time, especially Lucius Beebe in the *Herald Tribune,* scorned *Our Blushing Brides, The New Yorker's* anonymous note on a 1975 revival seems closer to the mark: "A lavish, lively popular film of the period."

Its success seemed to give new life to the three-girls formula, and many variations followed. In later versions, the third girl, besides the levelheaded heroine and her doomed friend, was usually comic relief. As Judith Crist noted in her review of *The Group,* in this kind of film, while the star always got Mr. Right and the second girl became fatally involved with Mr. Wrong, the comedienne settled for Mr. Mediocre.

In *Three Girls Lost* (1931) it was small-town girls Loretta Young, Joyce Compton and Joan Marsh who share an apartment in Chicago, with Marsh succumbing to roué Lew Cody, whose murder leads to further complications. (This must be the only picture in which John Wayne ever got Loretta Young.)

In *Three Wise Girls* (1931) Jean Harlow played a small-town soda jerk who comes to New York, inspired by the success of her well-kept mannequin friend (Mae Clarke), whose protector (Jameson Thomas), however, later goes back to his wife, driving Mae to suicide. Disillusioned, Harlow goes home, but *her* millionaire (Walter Byron) really does get a divorce and seeks her out. Her wisecracking roommate (Marie Prevost) settles for Byron's chauffeur (Andy Devine)—perhaps the first use of the third girl as comic relief.

By far the best of such triple threats was *Three on a Match* (1932). Even though another Warners picture later that year, *The Match King,* explained away the familiar superstition as a scheme by Ivar Kreuger to sell more matches, it is taken half seriously here as three girls who graduated from grammar school together in 1919 meet for a reunion lunch after more than ten years.

It is a neat, fast-moving, fairly realistic story of the three: the tough one (Joan Blondell), now a show girl, the hard-working secretary (Bette Davis) and the spoiled beauty (Ann Dvorak), who from sheer perversity deserts her wealthy husband (Warren William) for an underworld figure (Lyle Talbot)—a sordid affair that leads to drug addiction and the kidnaping of her little son (timely in 1932, with the Lindbergh case still unsolved) and to her own sacrifice of her life to let the police know the boy's whereabouts. Blondell has meanwhile married the ex-husband, while Davis has become the child's governess.

But what makes *Three on a Match* unique is that it was the first '30s film to reflect, if not nostalgia, at least a specific recall of the '20s as a distinct period, beginning in 1919 with a montage of sheet music, headlines, newsreel clips and the same fashion plate used as the frontispiece of Frederick Lewis Allen's best-selling social history, *Only Yesterday* (1931). The '20s flash by, year by year, with equally vivid accuracy, and even 1930, before the main story gets under way in 1931.

In *Beauty for Sale* (1933) Madge Evans, Florine McKinney and Una Merkel work together in a luxurious beauty salon, and though Evans is in love with wealthy Otto Kruger, married to Alice Brady, she is allowed a happy ending while McKinney suffers. (A year earlier, Chesterfield had beaten MGM to this particular background with a "B" called *Beauty Parlor,* in which Barbara Kent, Joyce Compton and Dorothy Revier were the standard trio.)

Every Night at Eight (1935) featured Alice Faye, Frances Langford and Patsy Kelly as three office girls in a "mint julep factory" trying to make it as a singing trio, but since it

Bette Davis, Joan Blondell, Ann Dvorak in **Three on a Match**

was a musical, no one had to die. In *Ladies in Love* (1936), though the setting was Budapest, the only difference was that this time not three but four heroines, all stars, shared the billing: Janet Gaynor, Loretta Young, Constance Bennett and Simone Simon. Only Gaynor and Simon got their men; Young, who was to get Tyrone Power in several later pictures, lost him in this, their first encounter, as Bennett lost Paul Lukas to Simon (though without being driven to suicide).

Besides all the chorines, beauticians and shopgirls with nothing more on their minds than getting a husband, others could occasionally be glimpsed actually training for a profession—though only those traditionally open to women. Thus *The White Parade* (1934) and *Four Girls in White* (1939) followed a number of nursing students through to their capping ceremony—*two* such pictures in a decade that saw literally scores of films about doctors.

Since in those years airline stewardesses had to be R.N.'s, *Flying Hostess* (1936) merely gave wings to the familiar story about the three friends, with a few added aeronautical twists.

Without even counting *Three Blind Mice*, already covered as a gold-digging comedy, 1938 saw several conventional examples. *Sally, Irene and Mary,* which used only the title of the 1925 silent, cast Alice Faye, Marjorie Weaver and Joan Davis as three stage-struck manicurists trying to raise money, by marrying it, if necessary, to put on a show.

On the theory so often practiced by 20th Century-Fox, that if one of a thing was good, two would be more than twice as good, *Walking Down Broadway* tossed no less than *six* chorus girls into the hopper: Claire Trevor, Phyllis Brooks, Leah Ray, Dixie Dunbar, Lynn Bari and Jayne Regan. By the end two are dead and one in jail, while, hopefully, the other three are safely married—a fair operation of the law of averages.

Ever quick to cannibalize its own work, Warners by mid-decade was already remaking films of only a few years before, with the title and the characters' names changed and no acknowledgment of the source, apparently hoping no one would notice. Unfortunately, one of those to be subjected to this treatment, which invariably cheapened the original, was *Three on a Match*, which became *Broadway Musketeers* (1938), with Ann Sheridan, Margaret Lindsay and Marie Wilson in the Blondell, Dvorak and Davis roles, but with none of the verve, pace or period atmosphere of the 1932 version.

Still another variation on the "just among us girls" theme was *Hotel for Women* (1939), with Elsa Maxwell playing herself, as Louella Parsons had done in *Hollywood Hotel* (1938), and Ann Sothern, Linda Darnell and Jean Rogers among the residents. Sothern played an innocent from Syracuse who becomes a top model but almost loses her true love (James Ellison).

1939 also saw two films in which the same threadbare formula of three heroines was applied to female pilots or "aviatrixes," as they were called at the time. In *Tail Spin*, Alice Faye, Nancy Kelly and Constance Bennett represented three social levels, reading from bottom to top. Inevitably, when Kelly's husband (Edward Norris), also a pilot, is killed, she joins him in death, to the strains of "their" song, "Beautiful Ohio."

Released too soon afterward, *Women in the Wind* starred Kay Francis as a pilot who must win the "Powder Puff Derby" to pay for her brother's operation, backed by such stalwart aviation pioneers as Eve Arden and Sheila Bromley. One can see by hindsight how easily these films about supposedly heroic women led into such wartime epics of selfless WACs, WAVEs or nurses as *So Proudly We Hail*, *Keep Your Powder Dry* and *Flare Path*.

Although the title of *Midnight* (1939) is taken from Claudette Colbert's line "Every Cinderella has her midnight," she is at best only a very temporary Cinderella, who chooses a cab driver over a playboy. Rather, the '30s final salute to the durable Cinderella legend was one of the most charming and open in its parallels with the original—*First Love* (1939), which transposes the tale to modern New York. Sent to live with a family rather

like the one in *My Man Godfrey*, with Eugene Pallette again the vulgar millionaire, Leatrice Joy as his scatterbrained wife and Helen Parrish as their daughter, twice as bitchy as Cinderella's two stepsisters combined, niece Deanna Durbin is left home from an all-important ball, but manages with the equivalent of a fairy godmother to get there properly gowned, loses her slipper and pines a bit until the local Prince Charming (Robert Stack) finds her again, to seal their romance with her first on-screen kiss.

Although, strictly speaking, the term "Cinderella" should be applied only to stories of poor girls who marry wealth, it was often extended by reviewers to any film in which the characters' apparently impossible dreams suddenly and unexpectedly come true. Of this, the '30s' most extraordinary example—still unique after nearly five decades—was Paramount's *If I Had a Million* (1932).

Unlike other all-star films of the period, this was not a variation of *Grand Hotel*, with the characters' lives entwined by being thrown together for a few days. Rather, it was eight separate stories, each made by a different director, held together only by one basic link: a supposedly dying millionaire (Richard Bennett), to spite his eager heirs, picks eight names at random from the city directory and personally gives each a check for a million dollars. This was a structure not seen on the screen again until *Tales of Manhattan* (1942). Released late in 1932, at rock bottom of the worst year of the Depression, *If I Had a Million* must have been the ultimate in wish fulfillment to countless viewers who didn't know where their next meal was coming from.

Predictably, a few of the episodes are ironic—the forger (George Raft) who cannot cash his check without being arrested; the condemned criminal (Gene Raymond) for whom it comes too late; the Marine (Gary Cooper) who thinks it's a joke and uses it to pay a restaurant check—but the best-remembered sequences are those of the downtrodden little people finally free to vent their frustrations—Charlie Ruggles, who smashes all the china in the prissy shop where he works; Wynne Gibson as a prostitute whose dream is a clean bed by herself; W. C. Fields and Alison Skipworth, who avenge their wrecked car by going on a joyous spree of punishing all road hogs; Charles Laughton, who makes his way through innumerable outer offices and past countless underlings, at last to give his boss a hearty Bronx cheer. This gleeful acting out of long-suppressed whims clearly anticipates screwball comedy.

However, the longest and most touching segment is the final one, in which May Robson, a rebellious inmate in a grim home for old ladies, constantly bullied and nagged by the smug, sanctimonious matron (Blanche Frederici), uses her million to buy the home and convert it into a luxurious club, where the ladies can smoke, drink, play cards and entertain gentlemen callers, while the matron is paid to sit rocking all day, doing nothing. There is even a hint of geriatric romance between Robson and the now rejuvenated millionaire.

In Frank Capra's book *The Name Above the Title,* he writes as if *Lady for a Day*

(1933) were Robson's first film, after a long stage career, but she had already made at least eight silents and ten talkies, including some very big MGM productions. Whoever thought of her as Apple Annie may well have been influenced by her highly emotional performance in *If I Had a Million. Lady for a Day* is one of the most enjoyable wish-fulfillment fantasies of the '30s, and the *Times* was quite right in terming the elderly heroine in the heading of its review "a white-haired Cinderella."

The Damon Runyon tale concerns a drunken old Times Square derelict who has been secretly hoarding money to keep her illegitimate daughter in a private school in Spain, her despair when the girl and her titled Spanish fiancé announce a visit to New York, and the elaborate hoax by which gamblers, bookies and con men rally round to make Apple Annie's dream come true.

Though Capra had already directed several successful films, this was his real breakthrough, and he did variations on the same warmhearted theme for the rest of the decade. So, of course, did others. Scarcely a

Blanche Frederici and May Robson in **If I Had a Million**

year after *Lady for a Day, Lady by Choice* (1934), directed by David Burton, starred Robson as an alcoholic old vagrant adopted as a Mother's Day publicity stunt by a fan dancer (Carole Lombard), with happy results for both. Another variation was *Lady Tubbs* (1935), directed by Alan Crosland, in which Alice Brady as a cook in a railroad construction camp inherits a fortune, trains herself to enter Long Island society and arranges her niece's wedding to a wealthy boy. In an almost exact reversal of *Lady for a Day, Star for a Night* (1936) told of three young Austrians (Claire Trevor, Evelyn Venable and Dean Jagger) not doing too well in New York, who keep their blind mother (Jane Darwell) happy by letters telling of their glowing success, until a visit from her brings the predictable crisis.

In 1936 Capra directed one of the most widely popular films of the decade, *Mr. Deeds Goes to Town,* in which a small-town tuba player (Gary Cooper) who inherits an unwanted fortune is labeled by a reporter (Jean Arthur), whom he innocently trusts, "the Cinderella Man." *Deeds* is the epitome of the "worm turns" type of comedy, in which the meek, long-suffering hero, male counterpart of the ugly duckling, gathers his strength and turns the tables on his persecutors, especially if official and institutional.

Not only did it give Gary Cooper one of his most beloved roles and launch Jean Arthur on her brilliant comedy career, it also made "doodle" and "pixilated" part of the American language. The two gently firm, dotty old spinsters (Margaret Seddon and Margaret McWade) who at first endanger Deeds' sanity hearing by declaring him "pixilated," but eventually admit that everyone is—except themselves—foreshadow the two lethal aunts in *Arsenic and Old Lace.*

Actual Cinderellas, individual and triple, survived well into the 1960s. Not so the variations, the kind of cheerful, folksy tale that some critics unkindly labeled "Capra-corn." So completely are they rooted in the '30s that even Capra's own remake of *Lady for a Day, A Pocketful of Miracles* (1961), with Bette Davis in the Robson role, was generally dismissed as dated, unconvincing and irrelevant to a later generation.

4

VIVACIOUS LADIES
Working Girl Comedies

Not all '30s heroines were courtesans, gold diggers or Cinderellas. Some of the most warmly remembered appeared in a genre that for want of a more precise term must be called "romantic comedy"—not, of course, in the literary sense, meaning Elizabethan as distinguished from classic or neoclassic, but in the more general usage: a lighthearted love story, usually triangular or quadrilateral, a type of film that reached its dazzling peak from the middle to the later years of the decade.

Although in addition to the gold-digger films noted, early talkies abounded in other sophisticated comedies, most were variations on modes long established on the stage: the French boudoir farce, the British comedy of manners, the Viennese operetta. Many were set in Europe, especially Paris, sometimes with scenes aboard a liner, with the trip serving as a catalyst or liberating experience for the American characters.

In such films the heroine was likely to be a jewel thief (like Norma Shearer in *The Last of Mrs. Cheyney* or Miriam Hopkins in *Trouble in Paradise*), a temperamental performer (Jeanette MacDonald in *Oh, for a Man!*, Gloria Swanson in *Tonight or Never*, Elissa Landi in *I Loved You Wednesday*), a potentially or actually straying wife (Genevieve Tobin in *Free Love* and *One Hour with You*), a princess or queen of a mythical kingdom (MacDonald in *The Love Parade* and *Love Me Tonight*, Hopkins in *The Smiling Lieutenant*, Claudette Colbert in *Tonight Is Ours*), a rich girl without the particular problems of an heiress (Joan Bennett in *Careless Lady*, Constance Bennett in *Lady with a Past*), occasionally even a freethinking artist or writer (Bebe Daniels in *The Cocktail Hour*, Ann Harding in *The Animal Kingdom*, Myrna Loy in *When Ladies Meet*, Hopkins in *Design for Living*).

The one problem such heroines never had to face was getting a job in the real America of the time. If a girl worked at all in early talkies, she was usually employed, like her predecessors in silents, in some quite menial capacity—but then, as has been seen, she was apt to be involved in a tearful Cinderella romance in which she proved far nobler than her boy friend's snobbish family.

As Molly Haskell, among others, points out, one positive side effect of the Production Code was to get heroines out of the boudoirs and into the offices. Perhaps this would have happened in any case as a belated reaction to the realities of the Depression, but

whatever the ultimate cause, by the mid-'30s even the sultriest stars had to direct at least some of their energies into other channels, often comedies.

No one has summed up the change in comedy style better than Ted Sennett in *Lunatics and Lovers:*

Certain biases persisted: to be rich and idle was to be a target for contempt. Poverty had its compensations. Love was more important than a bank account. But attitudes were changing, and the comedies began to center, not on grotesque figures in painted mustaches or rag-mop hair or bulbous noses, but on identifiable people, foolish, scatter-brained and laughably fallible, but also good-natured, honest and likable.[1]

None of this would have been possible without the amusing situations and witty lines supplied by some of the most talented writers of the day.

As Pauline Kael has observed in her *Citizen Kane Book:*

. . . the thirties have never been rivaled in wit and exuberance . . . largely because there was already in Hollywood in the late silent period a nucleus of the best American writers, and they either lured their friends West or were joined by them: . . . Mankiewicz and Hecht and Charles MacArthur, George S. Kaufman and Marc Connelly, Nathanael West and his brother-in-law S. J. Perelman, Preston Sturges, Dorothy Parker, Arthur Kober, Alice Duer Miller, John O'Hara, Donald Ogden Stewart, Samson Raphaelson . . . Gene Fowler, and Nunnally Johnson and such already famous playwrights as Philip Barry, S. N. Behrman, Maxwell Anderson, Robert E. Sherwood, and Sidney Howard . . . From time to time Ring Lardner and Moss Hart would turn up . . . As a group [they] were responsible for that sustained feat of careless magic we call "thirties comedy."[2]

Such writers took the Production Code as a challenge rather than an insuperable obstacle. If the rich man's mistress, whether treated seriously as a courtesan or lightly as a gold digger, was no longer salable, or even permissible, on screen, two new, more independent

[1] Ted Sennett, *Lunatics and Lovers* (Arlington House, 1973), p. 14.

[2] Pauline Kael, *The Citizen Kane Book* (Bantam Books, 1974), pp. 12–13.

types of heroines soon emerged: the self-sufficient working girl who scorned the idea of being kept by anybody, and the heiress, for whom the question never arose. The former often had to choose between marrying for love or money, the latter had to prove that in spite of her money she herself was worthy of love. It was in this new, post-Production Code comedy that a number of actresses, some of whom had been in pictures since silent days, came fully into their own as comediennes.

It seems significant that although most of the actors who co-starred in these comedies (Melvyn Douglas, Douglas Fairbanks, Jr., Henry Fonda, Cary Grant, Fred MacMurray, Ray Milland, David Niven, James Stewart, Robert Young) have remained in the public eye through the 1980s, it is the female stars, even those long dead or retired, who still glow brightest in public memory—that unparalleled galaxy who emerged in the mid-'30s to create a new, peculiarly American kind of comedienne, the attractive girl who could be funny without losing her feminine charm, lightly skimming along somewhere between the traditional low comedy of Marie Dressler and Fannie Brice and the high comedy of Lynn Fontanne and Ina Claire, but nearer the latter in their zest for tossing off witty lines with casual spontaneity.

Some, notably Claudette Colbert, Irene Dunne and Carole Lombard, could cavort with equal ease on either side of the social tracks; others could, or did, not. In particular, Katharine Hepburn's ineradicable air of breeding, authority and cool intelligence made it as impossible for her to play a convincing stenographer or shopgirl as it would have been for the equally charming but down-to-earth Jean Arthur or Ginger Rogers to play society girls.

But whether debutantes or secretaries, the true '30s heroines were breezy without being brassy, quick-witted but never smart-aleck, capable of meeting the hero on his own terms without putting him down. At best they conducted their sprightly romances with a sparkling composure worthy of Beatrice,

Millamant or Elizabeth Bennet. Indeed, they became the 1930s equivalent—a breed of heroine never seen before in American films and seldom enough since.

Again one must quote the indispensable Kael, this time in *The New Yorker* of July 14, 1975:

> The comedies celebrated a change in values . . . Impudence became a virtue. Earlier, the sweet, archly virginal heroine had often had a breezy, good-hearted confidante; now the roles were reversed, and the lively, resilient heroine might have an innocent kid sister or a naive little friend from her home town who needed looking after. What man in the Depression years would welcome a darling, dependent girl? Maybe the hero's shy buddy, but not the hero. He looked for the girl with verve; often she was so high and buoyant she could bounce right over trouble without noticing it . . . The stars came down to earth in the middle and late thirties—and became even bigger stars.

This progression from heavy drama to light comedy was nowhere more evident than in the career of Claudette Colbert. In the very same year (1934) as *Cleopatra* and *Imitation of Life*, she played the first, and still the best-remembered, of the runaway heiresses, in the Oscar-winning *It Happened One Night* (a role for which Frank Capra had wanted Myrna Loy).[3]

She also made the first good example of the typical '30s comedy described above, in *The Gilded Lily* (1935), as a stenographer who rejects a British lord incognito, and is consequently publicized by a ship's reporter (Fred MacMurray) into a night club celebrity known as the "NO Girl." Of course for a time she thinks she wants the peer, but returns to the reporter.

This might be considered almost an anti-Cinderella tale, since she turns down not some stuffy Ralph Bellamy type but a genuine Prince Charming, Ray Milland, soon to emerge as a romantic leading man in his own right. Given the choice, this kind of heroine

---

[3] All three films were nominated for best picture —the only time this has ever happened to an actress.

Ray Milland and Claudette Colbert in **The Gilded Lily**

often chose the poorer suitor not so much from sentiment or idealism as from boredom with the rich, or because she preferred hot dogs to caviar.

Though critics were quick to point out that it could hardly rival *It Happened One Night* (which was to remain the standard by which all other such comedies were judged for the rest of the decade), the *Times* found *The Gilded Lily* "a fresh and engaging screen comedy," which succeeded in recapturing "the warmth and humor of the average American without becoming average itself." The fact that the girl and the reporter customarily meet in front of the New York Public Library and whimsically debate the merits of peanuts versus popcorn is typical of the

"humanizing" touches that marked this kind of comedy, like the dunking and hitchhiking lessons in *It Happened One Night*.

Colbert followed this with *She Married Her Boss* (1935), of which the *Times* commented: "Now the studio takes out the venerable Office Wife theme with eagerness and faith, and erects a merry romantic comedy on the ruins," while the *Herald Tribune* found it "a thoroughly delightful and surprisingly heart-warming comedy," in which "all have maintained the happy, easy-going mood of *It Happened One Night.*"

As indicated by the title, Colbert is a secretary married by her employer, a department store head (Melvyn Douglas), more to retain her clerical services than for any more romantic reason, and saddled with his unpleasant family. As his inventively brattish daughter, Edith Fellows won the hearts of both New York morning reviewers, just then beginning to gag on the four-times-a-year dollops of cloying sweetness and light forced down their throats in Shirley Temple films.

Colbert ended 1935 with a third such comedy, *The Bride Comes Home,* which the *Times* described as "stemming from those earlier Paramount comedies, *The Gilded Lily* and *Hands Across the Table,* but with a story so thin as to be nearly non-existent." This time, a once rich girl (one of the few *ex*-heiresses in '30s films) must choose between rich Robert Young and poor Fred MacMurray, who is almost as bad-tempered as she is. About to elope with Young, she is, needless to say, saved in the nick of time by her own true, ill-natured love.

1934 and 1935 were also breakthrough years for three other actresses who had literally been around since silents. In the Grant profile, Kael links them thus: "It was Carole Lombard's good-hearted giddiness that made her lovable, Jean Arthur's flightiness, Myrna Loy's blithe imperviousness." David Shipman in *The Great Movie Stars* analyzes their appeal more specifically:

> . . . Myrna Loy, Carole Lombard and Jean Arthur . . . were not at all alike—except in skill . . . they were/are all highly individual; at the same time these three shared attributes with each other and with the other fine comediennes of the time. They were warm and loyal to their leading men but never taken in; were more at ease in restaurants and honking city streets than in night clubs or boudoirs; they moved quickly to keep up with their men, and spoke to them crisply and incisively; they were men's equals, but regarded the world with less illusion.[4]

Having worked her way up from gypsies and Oriental slave girls, and having successfully played a spy, an aviatrix, a jewel thief and many an adventuress, Myrna Loy no doubt *could* have played a working girl with equal ease, but for some reason, perhaps her de-

lightfully cool manner, whether cast as one of her numerous perfect wives or a single girl, she was always seen in affluent circumstances, even in the Thin Man series.

After years of being taken for granted as a sexy, elegant blonde, often cast as a gold digger or as decorative leading lady to stars like Crosby and Raft, Carole Lombard broke out of her conventionally glamorous mold with her hilarious performance as Lily Garland, overnight movie star, opposite John Barrymore's egomaniac producer in the classic comedy *Twentieth Century* (1934)—but even this did not lead at once to better opportunities; she had to make four more forgettable films before *Hands Across the Table* (1935), which the *Times* hailed as the most successful of "all the numerous efforts to recapture the

**Fred MacMurray and Carole Lombard
in Hands Across the Table**

mood of *It Happened One Night*"—perhaps because it was the first film supervised by Lubitsch in his new position as Paramount production head. Lombard played a cynical manicurist, a would-be gold digger, determined to marry kindly, crippled Ralph Bellamy for money, only to fall for an impoverished ex-playboy (Fred MacMurray).

Lombard and MacMurray were teamed three more times, most hilariously in *True Confession* (1937), a variation on the *Chicago/Roxie Hart* plot. As a compulsive liar (who telegraphs her fibs to the audience by literally putting her tongue in her cheek), the wife of a strait-laced, totally honest lawyer, when wrongly accused of a murder she finds it a better defense to confess that she did it to protect her honor. As a weird character who may well be the killer, John Barrymore keeps telling her gleefully, "You'll *fry* for this!" Meanwhile, *My Man Godfrey* (1936) had established Lombard once and for all as the very embodiment of what was now called "screwball comedy," a term that might have been invented for her.

Like Loy and Lombard, Jean Arthur had been wasted for years in dozens of forgotten films, mostly melodramas, until in *The Whole Town's Talking* (1935) she was at last given a chance to show her comic skills. Again parallel to Lombard, she had to make four more inconsequential films until, late in 1935, she appeared in *If You Could Only Cook*.

An auto tycoon (Herbert Marshall), sitting on a park bench, meets a girl (Arthur) who thinks he's unemployed, too, and suggests they answer an ad for a couple to work as cook and butler. Bored with his life, especially with his socialite fiancée (Frieda Inescort), he accepts, and they are hired by a genial ex-gangster (Leo Carrillo), who's also a gourmet. Though a similar upstairs-downstairs reversal had been used in the musical *Honey* (1930) and would turn up again in *Tovarich* (1937), this variation provides enough amusing twists (e.g., the gangland-style kidnapping of Marshall from his own formal wedding) to merit *The New Yorker*'s accolade, "remarkably

good-natured and fresh." Undoubtedly it helped pave the way for Arthur's real breakthrough in her next film, Capra's *Mr. Deeds Goes to Town* (1936), as a cynical but warmhearted reporter—a type she was to repeat with variations until well into the 1940s.

In 1936 this quartette of scintillating comediennes, Colbert, Loy, Lombard and Arthur, were joined by a fifth. Long and solidly established in drama and more recently in musicals, Irene Dunne delighted everyone in *Theodora Goes Wild,* a frequently uproarious farce which some reviewers considered Columbia's attempted follow-up on *Mr. Deeds,* since again a small-town hayseed gets the best of New York City slickers and even marries one. Dunne's slow, insinuating laugh reminded some reviewers of Lynn Fontanne's.

A demure spinster reared by two maiden aunts (one of them, Margaret McWade, had also been one of the "pixilated" sisters in *Mr. Deeds*), Dunne secretly writes a sexy best seller, then, when exposed, tosses discretion to the winds and succeeds in liberating the supposedly sophisticated jacket artist (Melvyn Douglas) from his impossible wife and stuffy parents. In the comic climax—a typical example of post-Production Code daring—Theodora returns to a brass-band reception in her home town carrying an unexplained infant (who actually belongs to the secretly married daughter of the town's worst gossip).

1937 was truly an *annus mirabilis* in the history of this kind of comedy, with Colbert, Lombard, Arthur and Dunne all starring in vehicles still regarded as among the best in this field. After making, with the professional versatility expected of '30s stars, two costume dramas, *Under Two Flags* (1936) and *Maid of Salem* (1937), Colbert returned to the métier in the highly successful *I Met Him in Paris,* in which as an American girl on a three-week fling she is pursued by three suitors, playboy Robert Young, playwright Melvyn Douglas and home-town boy Lee Bowman. Hailing it as "the brightest comedy of the year," the *Times* particularly praised the hilarious skiing scenes, in which Sun Valley doubled for the Alps.

Lombard made two of her funniest films, *True Confession* and *Nothing Sacred* (a phrase that might have been applied to almost any of these comedies), a satire so abrasively cynical about everything, especially newspaper ethics, that it alone would explode Andrew Bergman's theory that after 1934 the best film comedies tended to be "warm and healing."

Arthur also made one of her best-known, though in many opinions not one of her best, comedies, *Easy Living,* a rather prolonged one-joke affair concocted by Preston Sturges, about a poor stenographer who while riding on the open top deck of a Fifth Avenue bus is hit by a fur coat flung from a penthouse terrace by an irate millionaire (Edward Arnold). She is immediately assumed to be his mistress, installed in a plush suite by an ambitious hotel manager and subjected to endless misunderstandings until she finally wins Arnold's son (Ray Milland).

By far the best of these 1937 comedies, however, is *The Awful Truth,* in which Irene Dunne and Cary Grant were teamed for the first time, as a divorcing couple, with Ralph Bellamy on hand in one of his first dull suitor roles. Scene after scene can still reduce audiences to helpless laughter, such as the one in which Grant in Bellamy's presence needles Dunne about her probable future in Oklahoma City ("And, of course, if things *should* ever get a little dull, you can always go over to Tulsa. I do think a big change like that is good for anyone").

Especially effective is the parallel scene in which Dunne turns up at the Park Avenue home of Grant's wealthy fiancée (Molly Lamont), introducing herself as his sister, a Southern singer-stripper in a shady night club, running a chiffon handkerchief between her teeth, then purposely mislaying her purse and ordering, "Don't anybody leave this room!"

The next one to join the quintette of actresses already mentioned had also been on

Irene Dunne and Cary Grant
in **The Awful Truth**

the scene since talkies began, at first usually cast as a brash, wisecracking chorus girl—Ginger Rogers. Her series of elegant musicals (1933–39) opposite Fred Astaire, negligible though the plots were, trained her in more subtle comedy. Then in *Stage Door* (1937) she proved that she could hold her own trading polite insults with Hepburn herself. Possibly as a reward she was happily cast in *Vivacious Lady* (1938) as a likable night club singer married on impulse by a naïve young professor (James Stewart), who is so afraid to break the news to his parents (Charles Coburn and Beulah Bondi) that through most of the picture everyone thinks Ginger is the wife of a playboy cousin (James Ellison).

As William K. Everson puts it in his program notes for *Bluebeard's Eighth Wife,* "1938 saw the last of the gay and crazy comedies of the '30s: *The Rage of Paris* and *Bluebeard's Eighth Wife* were the tail end of a delightful genre that had flourished between 1932 and 1934, had been given a new impetus in '36 with *My Man Godfrey,* retained its drive in '37 with *Nothing Sacred* and *It's Love I'm After,* and now, in 1938, was beginning to lose steam."

Colbert's first picture for Lubitsch since *The Smiling Lieutenant* in 1931, with a screenplay by Charles Brackett and Billy Wilder, based on a 1921 stage farce first filmed with Gloria Swanson in 1923, *Bluebeard's Eighth Wife* cast Colbert as the daughter of a French Marquis (Edward Everett Horton) who becomes the eighth wife of an American millionaire (Gary Cooper), but, to teach him a lesson, puts off consummating the marriage until he is driven (temporarily) to a lunatic asylum. Everson calls it "the last of the vintage Lubitsch, of breezy sex farce in Paris and Monte Carlo . . . it's the kind of tasteful froth that seemed to belong so much to the prewar years—and that we've just never been able to recapture."

The same words might be applied to *The Rage of Paris* (1938), in which Danielle Darrieux made a far more auspicious American debut than had Simone Simon two years earlier, in a far more amusing role, as an innocent ma'amselle stranded in New York who on circumstantial evidence is mistaken by Douglas Fairbanks, Jr., for a gold digger, if not worse, from whom he must save his playboy friend Louis Hayward. Set up by a friendly waiter (Mischa Auer) in the usual plush hotel suite, with Helen Broderick as chaperone, Darrieux proceeds to complicate all their lives until the expected happy ending with Fairbanks. As Everson notes: "Charm . . . was a quality that the Code couldn't affect, and this film has it in full measure . . . Both of the leads play sophisticated innocents, and the risqué complications that develop are all, of course, misun-

derstandings, or carefully guided wrong 'interpretations' from the audience."

As is evident by hindsight, by 1939 the cycle had virtually ground to a halt, though the first half of the year produced two of the last, brightest examples, and the second half two more by Lubitsch. As noted in the last chapter, Colbert's *Midnight,* despite the title, belongs among anti-Cinderella tales. Under Mitchell Leisen's direction the Brackett-Wilder script and the superb performances keep the laughter constant throughout. "Rapturous fun!" says *The New Yorker.*

An American singer stranded in Paris with only an evening gown to her name, Colbert crashes a society musicale where she is spotted by French millionaire John Barrymore—not for himself but as a means of coming between his wife (Mary Astor) and her lover (Francis Lederer). When all gather at a château for a weekend house party, complications, unexpected but always logical, snowball with increasing merriment, until the end, when Colbert and Don Ameche (a taxi driver who befriended her), who have never been married, must go through the motions of a divorce.

Midnight's only rival as funniest romantic comedy of 1939 was Ginger Rogers' *Bachelor Mother.* A toy department clerk who innocently agrees to hold a strange baby, Ginger finds herself holding him for keeps. Within hours no one will believe it's not hers; within days everyone is convinced the father is the playboy son (David Niven) of the store owner (Charles Coburn), and so, as in *Easy Living,* her status quickly escalates among the other employees, including her insufferable boy friend (Frank Albertson). In the comic high point both young men, plus her landlady's son, are all claiming to be the infant's father. Says Everson:

The film's placid acceptance of the heroine as an apparently unwed mother (the audience knows she isn't, but people in the film don't and never do find out otherwise) is an indication of the new maturity Hollywood was reaching in 1939; such a situation would have been commonplace pre-1933, but would have been very much tidied up in the post-Production Code years.

Alas, this was a maturity never fully reached. In amusing complications, Rogers' other 1939 comedy, *Fifth Avenue Girl*, was a step backward. In still another variation on the *Easy Living* theme, this Cinderella serves as fairy godmother to an unhappy millionaire (Walter Connolly). Ignored by his impossible family, he turns to a poor girl met in the park, and finds her so sympathetic that he installs her in his household, letting his out-

raged wife and children assume the worst. In no time at all the girl has detached the wife (Verree Teasdale) from her gigolo, broken up the daughter's romance with a Communist chauffeur and won the son (Tim Holt) for herself.

But 1939 was not yet over. Lubitsch was still to contribute two of his most brilliant comedies, the highly original *Ninotchka*, which because of its then timely political satire will be discussed elsewhere, and the enchanting *The Shop Around the Corner*, released in January 1940, so obviously com-

Ginger Rogers, Charles Coburn, Elbert Coplen Jr., David Niven in **Bachelor Mother**

pleted in 1939. In adapting a play by Niko-laus Laszlo, Samson Raphaelson retained the Budapest setting, which, as was to be expected from Lubitsch, is so convincingly brought to life to the finest detail that one soon thinks of the familiar American actors only as their Hungarian characters.

Except for an occasional customer, the cast consists exclusively of the staff of a small but thriving leather-goods shop, of which Frank Morgan is the highly respected owner. Gen-tle spinster Sara Haden, elderly family man Felix Bressart and flip errand boy William Tracy act as chorus for the series of misun-derstandings that keep the lovers (Margaret Sullavan and James Stewart, in their third and best teaming) at cross-purposes. All day they bicker at each other, then go home to write through a lonely-hearts club to an ideal "dear friend," never suspecting that they are corresponding with each other. More serious complications arise when an affair between the owner's wife (never seen) and a ladies' man clerk (Joseph Schildkraut) is blamed on Stewart, and he is fired, but all the misunder-standings are cleared up in time for Christ-mas Eve.

No outline can begin to suggest the humor, warmth and charm of this film, unusual for Lubitsch in that the laughter is always ten-der rather than mocking. *The New Yorker* calls it "close to perfection—one of the most beautifully acted and paced romantic come-dies ever made in this country."

Although all but one of the five comedi-ennes emphasized in this chapter continued to prove their talents for several decades after the '30s (Colbert, Arthur and Rogers on Broadway itself), few ever again had as much opportunity to display or extend their mar-velous comic skills. True, Colbert did Pres-ton Sturges' *Palm Beach Story* (1942), but within a few years was bogged down in the wartime heroics of *So Proudly We Hail* and *Since You Went Away*. Similarly, Dunne made only one more memorable comedy, again pairing with Cary Grant, *My Favorite Wife* (early 1940), before going on to such out and out weepers as *A Guy Named Joe* and *The White Cliffs of Dover*, and spending the rest of her career in dignified, matronly roles.

Lombard's comedy career continued only in Hitchcock's uneven *Mr. and Mrs. Smith* (1941) and Lubitsch's bizarre anti-Nazi piece, set in occupied Warsaw, *To Be or Not to Be* (1942), her last film before her tragi-cally early death. Arthur fared perhaps best of all, since she starred in three fine '40s comedies, *The Devil and Miss Jones* (1941), *The Talk of the Town* (1942) and *The More the Merrier* (1943). Rogers, too, made a few more good comedies, though none exactly in the '30s vein, *The Primrose Path* (1940), *Tom, Dick and Harry* (1941), *Roxie Hart* and *The Major and the Minor* (both 1942), but even she was soon trapped in such lugu-brious contributions to the war effort as *Ten-der Comrade* (1943) and *I'll Be Seeing You* (1944).

Speaking for 1930s film-goers, Kael writes:

We in the audience didn't have to wake up *after-ward* to know how good those films of the thirties were; in common with millions of people, I en-joyed them while they were coming out . . . But I did take them for granted. There was such a steady flow of bright comedy that it appeared to be a Hollywood staple, and it didn't occur to me that those films wouldn't go on being made.[5]

[5] Kael, op. cit., pp. 34–35.

"WITH PLENTY OF MONEY AND YOU"
Heiresses, Madcap, Headstrong, Footloose and Runaway

"Who killed society?" asked Cleveland Amory in his book of that name, without ever arriving at a final answer. Certainly he could not have hung the rap on Hollywood in the '30s, which continually made the lives of the rich look even more glamorous than they were. In addition to all the upwardly mobile courtesans, gold diggers, Cinderellas and the surprising number of quick-witted working girls who married either the boss or his son, another whole set of heroines, equally numerous, faced precisely the opposite problem: too *much* money.

These were, of course, the heiresses, variously described as "spoiled," "madcap," "footloose," "headstrong" or "runaway," who in many a variation on *The Taming of the Shrew* or *The Admirable Crichton* had to be taught Life's True Values. To cite but one symbolic example of how tastes have changed, in 1935 *Five Little Heiresses* was evidently considered an attractive title for an Alice Duer Miller novel serialized in the *Ladies' Home Journal;* in 1975 an Otto Preminger picture specifically *about* "five little heiresses" was pointlessly titled *Rosebud*.

During the early '20s, with that preachy "Whither are we drifting?" tone so often assumed by the higher-minded silents, wealthy women had been tried and found wanting in many a lavish society drama, and Gloria Swanson, Norma Talmadge or Florence Vi-

dor suffered in the most elegant surroundings. By the middle of the decade came the exposés of flaming youth, all the exponents of which drove the latest rumble-seated roadsters to their wild parties, either went to college and frequented roadhouses, or, if slightly older, did their Charlestons at the best country clubs and, to forget unhappy love affairs, routinely sailed to Europe or around the world. It took a very good income to make whoopee on the scale shown, for instance, in *Our Dancing Daughters* (1928) and *Children of the Ritz* (1929).[1]

The popular attitude of scandalized fascination with the antics of the (moneyed) bright young people, somewhere between tongue-clicking and lip-smacking, was perfectly expressed in Noel Coward's 1925 song "Poor Little Rich Girl," which is full of words of warning: "By dancing much faster, you're chancing disaster, time alone will show . . . The life you lead sets all your nerves a-jangle, your love affairs are in a hopeless tangle . . . In lives of leisure, the craze for pleasure steadily grows. Cocktails and laughter, but what comes after? Nobody knows." Most people, however, could hazard a fairly shrewd guess.

The tone of stern indictment of the rich

[1] *The American Film Institute Catalog . . . 1921–1930* lists only twenty-five films about heiresses.

persisted in early talkies such as *Manslaughter* (1930), Claudette Colbert's remake of an Alice Duer Miller novel first filmed as a silent by Leatrice Joy in 1922. A particularly spoiled heiress who by her careless speeding causes the death of a motorcycle cop is, much to her chagrin, convicted and sentenced to prison, where, among others, she encounters her former maid, whom she had condemned for a trifling theft. But she learns her bitter lesson so well that eventually she proves worthy even of the D.A. (Fredric March) who put her behind bars.

A lighter variation on this theme was used in *The Silver Lining,* also known as *Thirty Days* (1932), in which Maureen O'Sullivan owns tenements so neglected that one causes serious injury to a child. Wandering in a park after being robbed of her purse, she is mistaken for a drunk and sentenced to thirty days, during which she learns from her fellow inmates how the other half really lives, and also wins the love of the lawyer (John Warburton) for the crippled child. (Meanwhile in 1930 O'Sullivan and Charles Farrell had made *The Princess and the Plumber,* perhaps the ultimate extreme in romance between a high-born heroine and low-born hero, a whimsical item in which an American engineer saves a Graustarkian princess from an evil suitor.)

The Dancers (1930), from a play by Gerald du Maurier, was made of sterner stuff. Lois Moran as a "daring" English girl named Diana Snowden has strayed so far from the pure ideals of her childhood that when the boy she loves (Phillips Holmes), returning from a long stay in Canada, proposes, she flees by plane to France, where he finds her a year later as a teacher (presumably not a dancing teacher) in a French village. In the same spirit of redemption through sacrifice, Carole Lombard in *No One Man* (1932), after marrying a faithless playboy (Ricardo Cortez) who's later found dead in another girl's boudoir, takes up nursing in order to prove worthy of the Viennese doctor (Paul Lukas) whom she has really loved all along.

Most early talkies dealing with wealthy girls reveal much the same punitive attitude. In the Depression years, career women were apparently too rare to pose a threat to male supremacy (and in any case were probably the first fired), so they seldom appeared on screen—but those who wielded the undeniable power of inherited wealth had to be put firmly in their place and forcefully convinced that they must first and foremost be "real women"—if necessary, ready to live on a poor husband's salary so that he could be the boss and not feel snubbed by her society friends.

Variations on the wearing-the-pants motif were seen in three films of 1931. In *Platinum Blonde* Jean Harlow, ludicrously miscast as a society girl, marries reporter Robert Ames, but he cannot conform to her constant demands and leaves her for sob sister Loretta Young. (Obviously the two actresses should have switched roles.) In *Kept Husbands* Dorothy Mackaill as a steel heiress marries a plant employee, Joel McCrea, who soon grows bored with his nominal executive job and busy social whirl, until she finally agrees to live on his income. A forgotten Rodgers and Hart musical, coyly titled *The Hot Heiress,* made the identical point, with wealthy Ona Munson falling for riveter Ben Lyon, who refuses to pretend to be anything but what he is.

One of the most inept of such early talkies was Joan Crawford's *Montana Moon* (1930), described by the *Times* as "an interminable, amateurish talking picture with spasmodic snatches of melody." Continuing her dancing daughter, modern maiden phase, Crawford was as willful an heiress as ever defied her husband. She marries cowboy Johnny Mack Brown, but is embarrassed by his simple Western ways, as when he makes a jealous scene over her passionate tango with Ricardo Cortez. She leaves him to return East, but, disguised as a Mexican bandit, he kidnaps her from the train, so naturally that solves everything.

A year later Paramount came up with a

more palatable treatment of an almost identical story, *I Take This Woman* (1931), based on a Mary Roberts Rinehart novel, with Carole Lombard as the willful heiress and Gary Cooper as a cowboy on her parents' ranch. After a year of married life in a one-room shack, she leaves him to return to her own world, and he joins a rodeo. When on the very night she attends the performance, he is thrown and badly hurt, true love eventually prevails. (Oddly enough, Cooper was cast in approximately the same role in one of the last heiress comedies of the decade, *The Cowboy and the Lady,* 1938.)

Crawford played one of her more interesting heiresses in *Dance, Fools, Dance* (1931), one of the first films to show any awareness of the changed times. At the opening, a set of rich young idlers aboard a yacht decide to go for a midnight swim, and though the girls strip only to discreet lingerie and the boys to BVDs or undershirts and boxer shorts, leaving all of them more fully covered than in bathing suits, for 1931 the very idea was provocative enough. Soon a montage of dancers dissolves into one of panic on Wall Street, and the heroine finds herself penniless, her father a suicide, her younger brother emotionally shattered. She gets a job on a newspaper, and the story turns to gangster melodrama. In her days of wine and roses, however, she has had an affair with intended fiancé Lester Vail, who is then reluctant to marry her. Not until the end, after she has helped trap the criminals, does he finally "forgive" her.

This brings us to another, rarer kind of heroine, whose money is no obstacle to happiness, but, rather, enables her to experiment and get away with unconventional conduct impossible for a girl without an impregnable bank account. In no sense a courtesan, not even necessarily promiscuous or a faithless wife, she is a new woman, or, in the slang of the day, a "daring young modern," who takes that one important step beyond all the wild but technically innocent flappers by boldly demanding the single standard, the same sex-

ual freedom always taken for granted by men.

Perhaps the classic case in the 1920s had been Iris March, the heroine of Michael Arlen's famous novel and play *The Green Hat,* played in London by Tallulah Bankhead, on Broadway by Katharine Cornell and on screen by Garbo. To millions at the time, Iris, who ends by crashing her Hispano-Suiza into an oak tree, must have seemed as fascinatingly *avant-garde,* doomed and gallant as Lady Brett Ashley or Lady Chatterley, whose upper-crust British background she shared. So "notorious" were the novel and the play that not only was the 1928 film rechristened *A Woman of Affairs* (hardly a more innocent title!), but all the characters' names were changed. Yet when Constance Bennett remade it in 1934 as *Outcast Lady,* with the original names restored, so far had public taste and what was permissible on screen changed that the *Times* found it hopelessly outmoded, a "tinny, over-theatrical roadshow edition."

This was the sort of ultra-emancipated heroine in whom Norma Shearer specialized in her earliest talkies. Sometimes, as in *Their Own Desire* (1930), the title promised more than the picture delivered, but in *Strangers May Kiss* (1931) she played a girl (like an unmarried version of the one she had played in *The Divorcee,* 1930) who openly travels to Mexico with a globe-trotting journalist (Neil Hamilton), only to be scorned by him later because her reputation is ruined. Bitterly, she goes to Europe and lives in a manner described by the *Times* as "unrestrained," until eventually the hypocritical hero forgives her.

Even more boldly defiant of convention was Barbara Stanwyck in *Illicit* (1931), a controversial drama that anticipated some of the issues of the sexual revolution of the 1960s. The heroine and her lover (James Rennie) live openly together because *she* does not believe in marriage. When they do marry, they play around with others, but end up together, thus in the classic Hollywood formula working both sides of the street, at once attacking and upholding conventional monogamy.[2]

In *A Free Soul* (1931) Shearer was the daughter of a brilliant, alcoholic lawyer (Lionel Barrymore) who becomes almost fatally infatuated with one of her father's gangster clients (Clark Gable). Decadent rich girls morbidly fascinated by criminals also turned up in *Secrets of a Secretary* (1931), *Blood Money* and *Officer 13* (both 1933), *All of Me* and *Fog over Frisco* (both 1934). Sheer melodrama, no doubt; still, not even the most lurid screenwriting imagination of the 1930s could have conjured up the 1970s, when the college-educated daughters of well-to-do American families not only sought out bizarre criminals but themselves became fugitives from justice as murderers, bank robbers, terrorists and "urban guerrillas."

1932 saw three wealthy heroines involved in murder cases. In *Letty Lynton,* whose plot so closely resembled that of the stage hit *Dishonored Lady* that the playwrights sued and won, Crawford, after a last passionate rendezvous with her blackmailing ex-lover (Nils Asther), accidentally poisons him when he drinks from a glass intended for herself, but she is cleared by using the alibi, backed by her mother, that she spent the night with her fiancé (Robert Montgomery).

Murder reared its ugly head again in *Unashamed,* in which heiress Helen Twelvetrees, refused permission to marry, goes off overnight with fortune hunter Monroe Owsley, who is next day shot, for reasons of family "honor," by her brother (Robert Young). At first she refuses to help his defense, but then manages to get an acquittal by making the jury dislike her so much that they cannot blame her brother. In an almost exact reversal, Constance Bennett in *Two Against the World* confesses to a murder she did not commit, to shield her brother and spare the family worse scandal. In a switch on *Manslaughter,* she is prosecuted by the

young lawyer she loves (Neil Hamilton). It need hardly be added that this type of heroine, never too popular at best since she had her cake and ate it without even losing the man she loved, was automatically banished by the Production Code.

Perhaps the most liberated of all unconventional heiresses was Ruth Chatterton in *Female* (1933), for she is not the usual nubile debutante or society girl but a mature woman who has already come into her inheritance, an auto-manufacturing company founded by her father and actively run by her as president. In the style of Catherine the Great, after a hard day at the office she "unwinds" with whatever young executive employee takes her fancy—until she meets the inevitable man (George Brent) who tames her. This is, of course, an early example of the "boss lady" pattern later associated with Rosalind Russell, reaching the same preordained conclusion.

In the more conventional spoiled heiress pattern, Marian Nixon in *Chance at Heaven* (1933) played a naïve rich girl who wins a resort-town gas station owner (Joel McCrea) away from his true-blue girl friend (Ginger Rogers), but eventually becomes bored with love in a cottage and returns to her mother in New York. It would seem that heiresses could sink no lower, but *All of Me* (1934) plumbed new depths of bathos when Miriam Hopkins as the standard rich bitch, unwilling to move West to help the career of her engineer fiancé (Fredric March), is inspired by the noble example of a crook and his pregnant girl (George Raft and Helen Mack), who jump out a window rather than be parted.

Presumably there was nowhere to go but up, and for the rest of the decade heiresses were treated more sympathetically, especially in dramas. If it seems ironic that poor or unemployed people would pay money to see films with titles like *The Social Register, Coming Out Party* or *Finishing School* (all 1934), much less empathize with the plights of their overrich heroines, perhaps the simplest explanation (aside from

---

[2] Surprisingly, *Illicit* was remade only two years later by Bette Davis as *Ex-Lady* (1933).

the obvious one of escape into a world of luxury) is that it must have been deeply consoling to feel that rich girls, after all, had their own peculiar problems, and no amount of money could buy true love—which invariably took the form of a clean-cut young American who earned his own living.

Or, as Everson suggests in program notes for a New School showing of *Coming Out Party* on October 6, 1978:

There seems to be a certain amount of very low-key New Deal propagandizing injected . . . It is the "little people," regardless of race or origin, who are the good guys here; it is the servants, or the poor struggling artist/musician hero, who display all the decency and compassion. The rich aren't exactly the villains, but they are shown as aloof and in need of the overhaul and reformation that the New Deal was all (or partially) about.

In *No More Orchids,* Carole Lombard, the first completely sympathetic film heiress, is almost forced by her grandfather (C. Aubrey Smith) to marry a prince (Jameson Thomas) to save her father (Walter Connolly) from financial ruin, if not prison, but, of course, she prefers an American boy (Lyle Talbot).

In *Coming Out Party,* debutante Frances Dee, daughter of snobbish Gilbert Emery and Marjorie Gateson, loves a poor musician (Gene Raymond), but finding herself pregnant as he is about to leave for Europe, elopes from her own debut with an alcoholic playboy (Clifford Jones)—a marriage quickly annulled. A few months later, Frances was at it again, in *Finishing School,* in which, neglected by her selfish parents (Billie Burke and John Halliday), she becomes pregnant by a young intern (Bruce Cabot), who is only too eager to marry her. In the first film, a ruthless arranger (Alison Skipworth—like Julianna Cutting?) of fashionable debuts is caustically depicted, as in the second is the ultrasnobbish headmistress (Beulah Bondi) of the exclusive school.

In *Servants' Entrance* (1934), set in Sweden, Janet Gaynor, anticipating the loss of her family's fortune, goes to work as a maid and falls for the chauffeur (Lew Ayres). Most elaborately, Joan Crawford in *I Live My Life* (1935), suffocated by wealth, loves a poor archaeologist (Brian Aherne), who wants to free her, but is tricked into marriage when she shows up at the church instead of jilting him as agreed.

And Sudden Death (1936) revived the *Manslaughter* syndrome; Frances Drake is tamed by policeman Randolph Scott, and even takes the blame for a fatal crash caused by her kid brother. In *Live, Love and Learn* (1937), Rosalind Russell leaves her wealthy family to marry Greenwich Village artist Robert Montgomery, but success, promoted by her, goes to his head, she leaves him, he learns and returns to his true métier—a familiar story line that owes much to *What Every Woman Knows.*

Wise Girl (1938) centered on another Village artist, this time Ray Milland, who has custody of his two small nieces, wanted by their wealthy maternal grandfather (Henry Stephenson). The late mother's sister (Miriam Hopkins) pretends to be poor, gains Milland's confidence and makes him an artistic success. Presumably they will share custody of their nieces.

The few seriously treated heiresses (fewer than ten after 1934) were vastly outnumbered by their comic counterparts. Earlier, from 1930 to 1933, the only pictures to take the rich at all lightly were occasional musicals like *The Hot Heiress* and *High Society Blues* (both 1930), two romantic comedies noted in the previous chapter (*Lady with a Past* and *Careless Lady,* both 1932) and a few comedies of manners from the stage.

But in the very same month as the abysmal *All of Me* (February 1934) came the picture that revolutionized '30s film comedy, won Oscars for all concerned and established the heiress, especially if "runaway," once and for all as one of the decade's favorite heroines, at least in comedies that took her down a few pegs. What really launched her on her merry way was, of course, Capra's *It Happened One Night,* which is full of scenes and touches familiar to every movie fan.

What charmed the whole country were the relaxed, good-humored camaraderie as the bus passengers join in singing "The Man on the Flying Trapeze"; the alternate put-downs of reporter (Gable) and heiress (Colbert), as he teaches her to dunk and she shows him how to hitchhike; the touch-and-go risqué situation when they must share a room divided only by the "walls of Jericho" blanket; and the trumpet at the end, which by implication goes well beyond the conventional fade-out kiss.

So universally popular was *It Happened One Night,* it was said that in consequence of the scene when Gable starts to strip by taking off his shirt to reveal a bare chest, undershirt manufacturers soon noted a drop in their sales. On screen, the echoes were innumerable, in its own decade and later, including the climactic wedding interrupted in the nick of time (also used in *If You Could Only Cook,* 1935, *Swing Time,* 1936, *On the Avenue,* 1937, *Four's a Crowd,* 1938, and *The Philadelphia Story,* 1940).

For the rest of the '30s, if half the heroines in romantic comedies were stenographers or stranded entertainers mistaken for rich men's mistresses, the other half were heiresses, pitted in a battle of the sexes that could end only one way, against a man from the workaday world. Most often he was a reporter, but sometimes a poor artist, salesman, song writer, once even a paleontologist. Sometimes she used her wealth to embarrass or annoy him, especially if she had been attacked in his newspaper; sometimes she pretended to be poor to test whether he or any man would love her without her money. Sometimes he was also incognito and turned out to be just as wealthy. From all the possible permutations of this situation came some of the '30s' funniest comedies.

A whole stock company of character players kept turning up in these films, serious and comic alike. If the millionaire father was a vulgar, good-natured slob, he would be played by Eugene Pallette or Guy Kibbee. If inclined to be testy and irascible (the better to conceal his heart of gold), he might be Walter Connolly, Edward Arnold, Charles Coburn, Charles Winninger or George Barbier. A really pompous stuffed shirt would be Henry Kolker, Henry Stephenson, Berton Churchill or occasionally John Halliday. The mother, if vague and dithery, would usually be Billie Burke or Alice Brady, sometimes Mary Boland or Spring Byington. If cold and snobbish, pushing her daughter into an unwelcome marriage, then she would be Marjorie Gateson or Hedda Hopper, or, if a bit younger, with perhaps a gigolo on the side, Verree Teasdale. Mary Forbes and Nella Walker, those glacially gracious *grandes dames,* usually played some other socialite's mother, not the heroine's.

As with gold diggers, this was an area where women were indulged more freely than men. Before the decade had ended, almost every American actress, with the exceptions noted, Jean Arthur and Ginger Rogers, had played an heiress or two, but there was no comparable field for male stars to play likable scions of inherited wealth. Those who did (at first Robert Montgomery, Charles Farrell, Monroe Owsley and Robert Ames, later Franchot Tone, Lew Ayres, Ray Milland, Louis Hayward and David Niven) were at best leading men for the working-girl heroines, at worst dismissed as playboys, either weakling younger brothers or the charming, perhaps alcoholic wastrel whose chief accomplishment is the ability to wear white tie and tails gracefully and who accepts with a wry smile and a shrug his loss to the red-blooded, gainfully employed hero.

Among the immediate follow-ups on *It Happened One Night* were numerous "B's," including *The Golden Arrow,* with Bette Davis and George Brent, but the next memorable '30s comedy, even more completely screwball and destined to spawn just as many imitators, was *My Man Godfrey* (1936), which, more than four decades later, continues to delight audiences. The opening credits, with the sound track playing "Manhattan Serenade" while the actors' names in neon

light up one by one atop the skyscrapers of a stylized Art Deco skyline, immediately set the tone and atmosphere of a New York as impossibly glamorous as only Hollywood in the '30s could picture it.

If not a serious picture of the Depression, *My Man Godfrey* at least attempted to touch sympathetically on the plight of the unemployed. Though neither the first nor the last of the mad families that romped through so many '30s comedies, the Bullocks remain the funniest: Eugene Pallette and Alice Brady as the parents, Gail Patrick as the bitchy sister and Mischa Auer as a well-meaning gigolo. Above all, Irene Bullock was one of Carole Lombard's most endearing zany characterizations—indeed the quintessential screwball heiress—perfectly balanced by William Powell's polished man of the world playing butler. Under Gregory La Cava's direction, all the elements blended to make the film a perennial joy.

Myrna Loy had already shown a deft light touch in the Chevalier-MacDonald musical *Love Me Tonight* (1932), as well as in such filmed comedies of manners as *Rebound* (1931), *The Animal Kingdom* (1932) and *When Ladies Meet* (1933), but when *The Thin Man* (1934) for the first time combined a genuine mystery plot with dry, witty badinage, it not only established Loy and William Powell as the screen's most sophisticated couple, in roles they repeated in several sequels, but led them on to *Libeled Lady* (1936), which, though it involves an heiress and a newspaperman, owes little to *It Happened One Night*.

When Spencer Tracy's paper wrongly brands heiress Loy as a husband-stealer and she sues for five million, with every prospect of collecting, what can he do but try to make the charge stick by arranging for Powell to lure her into a romantic relationship, then be caught by his nominal wife? Tracy's long-time girl friend, Jean Harlow, is persuaded

Carole Lombard, Franklin Pangborn, William Powell in My Man Godfrey

to go through with a marriage for just this purpose. Marvelous as all four stars were, what stands out in most memories is the scene in which Walter Connolly as Loy's father attempts to instruct Powell in the art of trout fishing.

In 1937 20th Century-Fox, then trying hard to build Tyrone Power and Loretta Young into a top romantic team by casting them in one such comedy after another (*Cafe Metropole, Second Honeymoon*), inevitably tossed them into the reporter-heiress cycle in *Love Is News,* a fast-moving but undistinguished farce about a rich girl so infuriated by a newspaper's jibes that, to embarrass the star reporter, she announces her engagement to him, along with a million-dollar settlement. Fox liked this plot so well that it was used again as a Betty Grable musical, *Sweet Rosie O'Grady,* in 1944, and again with Power in his original role in 1948 as *That Wonderful Urge.*

MGM's 1937 contribution was even slighter. *Double Wedding,* supposedly based on a play by Molnár, with Powell as a feckless artist living in a trailer and Loy and Florence Rice as wealthy sisters, so obviously

Clark Gable and Claudette Colbert in It Happened One Night

Spencer Tracy and Jean Harlow in Libeled Lady

echoed *My Man Godfrey* that the *Times* found it entirely too full of "screwball slapstick." The same charge was made with equal justice against *Merrily We Live* (1938).

By now this vein of freewheeling comedy had spread to several other genres, notably the cycle about batty families, fantasies and especially mysteries. Even actresses best remembered for serious dramatic roles did not hesitate to jump on the screwball band wagon —Joan Crawford as another runaway heiress in *Love on the Run* (1936) and Olivia De Havilland as daffy heiresses in *It's Love I'm After* (1937), *Hard to Get* and *Four's a Crowd* (both 1938).

It is only fair to report that by 1938 this kind of comedy, reduced to formula by countless "B" imitations of the outstanding films, had worn out its welcome. Both *It Happened One Night* and *My Man Godfrey* spawned an endless cycle of reasonably exact facsimiles starring minor couples like Gene Raymond and Ann Sothern or Wendy Barrie, or Kent Taylor and Irene Hervey, until reviewers winced at the first glimpse of any fey, whimsical or eccentric character, much less whole families of them.

As noted, Katharine Hepburn was always at her best in playing one to the manor born. Even in *Alice Adams,* her closest approach to a working-class background, her one aim in life was to pass as a young lady of wealth and assured social position, and in her post-1940 career woman comedies opposite Spencer Tracy she was always at the top of her profession, whether as a journalist, lawyer or athlete.

Thus while anyone might have predicted that if Hepburn ever turned to comedy, she would surely play an heiress, no one could have foreseen that she would take the total plunge and play the screwiest of all screwballs in *Bringing Up Baby* (1938), a film now regarded as a comic masterpiece, in which admirers of Howard Hawks as *auteur* profess to find all kinds of subtle symbolism in the progress from the "light" early scenes in New York to the "darkness" of the sequences in the country.

Yet, in one of the few cases when a memorable '30s film was not fully appreciated at the time, Frank Nugent in the *Times* gave *Bringing Up Baby* an unmitigated pan, listing every one of the gags as ancient and concluding:

After the first five minutes . . . we were content to play the game called "the cliché expert goes to the movies," and we are not at all proud to report that we scored 100% against Dudley Nichols, Hagar Wilde and Howard Hawks, who wrote and produced the quiz. Of course, if you've never been to the movies, "Bringing Up Baby" will be all new to you—a zany-ridden product of the goofy farce school. But who hasn't been to the movies?

Actually, none of the principal gags—the escaped wild leopard mistaken for the tame pet one, which can be soothed only by the singing of a particular song, the valuable dinosaur bone irretrievably buried by the mischievous dog, the wind-up with just about everyone in jail—had been used before in this kind of comedy. Seen now, independent of the cycle of which it was a peak, *Bringing Up Baby* ranks at least on a par with *It Happened One Night* and *My Man Godfrey*, without even a trace of the sentiment of the one or the redeeming social consciousness of the other. Peter Bogdanovich paid it the highest possible homage by frankly using it as the inspiration for his *What's Up, Doc?* (1972), which worked twice as hard without ever seeming half as funny. This is the film of which *The New Yorker* always comments, "It may be the American movies' closest equivalent to Restoration comedy."

Since it had come down hard on *Bringing Up Baby,* one would think the *Times* would have demolished *The Mad Miss Manton* (1938), but it was unaccountably kind to this veritable pastiche of current clichés, starting with the title. Four years after *The Thin Man,* the comedy-mystery was already overexposed, though this was the first to center around a conventionally unconventional heiress. From *Love Is News,* to name but one source, came the furious feud with the newspaper, from *Libeled Lady* the suit against the mocking editor (Henry Fonda), and the scene in which he pretends to be dying in order to get his way is right out of *Twentieth Century.* With Barbara Stanwyck and her debutante friends rushing frantically around in evening dress, with boxy silver fox jackets, and gardenias in their long bobs, *The Mad Miss Manton* now looks and sounds like a parody of the entire cycle.

By this time it was obvious to critics as well as the public—in fact, to everyone but the producers—that the heiress, headstrong, footloose or whatever, had thrown her madcap over the mill once too often, yet on she slogged through such tired items as *There Goes My Heart* (1938, Virginia Bruce and Fredric March in still another variation on *It Happened One Night*), *The Cowboy and the Lady* (1938, with Gary Cooper and Merle Oberon in the title roles of a lackluster script) *Cafe Society* (1939, with Madeleine Carroll as an heiress who marries yet another newspaperman, Fred MacMurray, on a bet) and *Lucky Night* (1939, Myrna Loy married to Robert Taylor, a jobless poet).

Some of the less pretentious "B" versions were actually funnier—e.g., Lucille Ball and James Ellison as the standard pair in *Next Time I Marry* (1938). Likewise, the heiress

Cary Grant, Katharine Hepburn, and Baby in Bringing Up Baby

sometimes came off more convincingly as a secondary character, like Madeleine Carroll in *On the Avenue* (1937) or Joan Bennett in *Vogues of 1938* (1937).

Although the fortune-hunting European nobleman had long since become a stock character even in comic strips, his reality was constantly reaffirmed in the much-publicized marriages and divorces of Barbara Hutton, Doris Duke, Pola Negri, Mae Murray, Gloria Swanson, Constance Bennett and the three Princes Mdivani, who married several of the above. Thus the movie heiress was often either married to a nobleman (Ruth Chatterton in *Unfaithful,* Gloria Stuart in *Sweepings,* Norma Shearer in *Riptide,* Ann Sothern in *My American Wife,* Constance Bennett in *Our Betters*), rejecting or seeking a titled match (Hopkins in *Fast and Loose,* Gaynor in *High Society Blues,* Patricia Ellis in *The World Changes,* Harlow in *Bombshell,* Anita Louise in *Our Betters,* Lombard in *No More Orchids,* Crawford in *Love on the Run,* Madeleine Carroll in *It's All Yours*) or else already divorced from a peer or two and ready to settle down with a nice, clean-cut American (Shirley Ross in *Paris Honeymoon,* Ann Sheridan in *Winter Carnival*).

Though World War II naturally put a damper on the frivolous escapades of the heiress, who as a comedy heroine gave way to the Washington government girl or the kind of tailored career woman played by Hepburn and Russell, she still hung on in a few more isolated films such as *Cross Country Romance* (1940, Wendy Barrie and Gene Raymond again) and *The Bride Came C.O.D.* (1941, starring, surprisingly, Davis and Cagney). According to Ted Sennett, the spoiled heiress did not breathe her last well-bred sigh until 1948, when Joan Fontaine played the long-threadbare role opposite James Stewart in *You Gotta Stay Happy.* The following year saw the release of a film actually called *The Heiress,* but this was a somber drama of a repressed spinster in nineteenth-century Washington Square—the furthest possible cry from the runaway rebels of the decade before.

6

SCENE: THE DRAWING ROOM, LATE AFTERNOON
Comedies of Manners from the Stage

Self-evidently, many of the best-remembered film comedies of the '30s have been covered in the last two chapters. But discriminating audiences could also enjoy another, more traditional kind of comedy, at best more subtly sophisticated, about the rich as they preferred to see themselves, leading lives in which wealth was quietly taken for granted and the antics of irascible tycoons, screwball heiresses and playboys incognito forever falling in love with someone unsuitable from across the tracks would have seemed grotesquely gauche and *nouveau riche*.

This genre is, of course, the comedy of manners (also known as "high," "polite" or "drawing room" comedy) —a form obviously well suited to the prosperous 1920s, but despite deepening economic and political crises throughout the '30s still flourishing on both sides of the Atlantic right up until World War II. It had first appeared in England with the Restoration (1660–c. 1700), disappeared in the rising sentimentality of the eighteenth century, until it surfaced briefly in a few comedies of the 1770s by Goldsmith and Sheridan, faded out again for more than a century and then returned in the 1890s for what seems to be the last time, in the brilliant line of succession that leads from Oscar Wilde to Somerset Maugham to Noel Coward (with lesser contributions by Frederick Lonsdale, A. A. Milne, Ivor Novello and others).

In the '20s, when all of the last-named but Wilde were at the peak of their powers, they were joined by three American practitioners of the form, Rachel Crothers, S. N. Behrman and Philip Barry, the first—and almost the last—writers to bring this kind of comedy successfully to Broadway and deal with a level of well-to-do American life otherwise reflected only in the novels of Edith Wharton and, to a lesser extent, F. Scott Fitzgerald. This was a world as immediately distinguishable from the wisecracking show-biz atmosphere of Kaufman and Ferber or Kaufman and Hart as from the middle-class banalities of George Kelly and Marc Connelly or the frantically paced melodramatic farces of Ben Hecht and Charles MacArthur.

Wilde's *Lady Windermere's Fan* (1892), with its semiserious plot, had pointed the way the best comedies of manners were to take. As if influenced by the problem plays of the day, the tone could become thoughtful, and some potentially serious questions were raised: Why should a woman not enjoy the same freedom as a man? Should a single act of adultery be enough to break up an otherwise good marriage? Can anyone learn from someone else's experience? But such issues are only suggested, never heavily debated, so that the bright, urbane surface of "civilized" badinage is not disturbed.

It was easy enough even then for critics to

poke fun at certain artificial conventions (some eliminated in film versions), such as the opening scene in which the curtain rises as a maid or butler crosses an elegant drawing room to answer the phone, conveying by his/her replies the needed exposition. Then two or three smartly dressed secondary characters would come on stage and (while latecomers in the audience got settled) proceed to chat over tea or cocktails about their expected hostess (the star), paving the way for her well-timed entrance.

Characters, too, tended to become stereotyped: the suave, middle-aged Lothario (often played on screen by Adolphe Menjou, Paul Cavanagh or Conway Tearle) with whom the ingenue is temporarily infatuated; the charming, mature woman (usually the star) who gets or regains him; the wise, knowing friend who serves as *raisonneur,* or, more often, *raisonneuse,* subtly underlining the theme; the imperturbable servants; that face that launched a thousand quips, the juvenile in white flannels who comes bounding through the French doors with his immortal cry of "Tennis, anyone?"; and the hostess to whose lavish country home everyone goes for the weekend that usually comprised Acts Two and Three. She would be either totally scatterbrained (Alice Brady in *When Ladies Meet* and *Should Ladies Behave?*) or a worldly, sharp-tongued old dowager (Marie Dressler in *Let Us Be Gay,* Jessie Ralph in *The Last of Mrs. Cheyney*).

Since so much of the effect of such plays lies in hearing neat epigrams crisply tossed off by polished actors, silent film versions, even Lubitsch's *Lady Windermere's Fan,* seemed at best as incomplete as silent versions of musicals. With talkies, the best works of all the playwrights mentioned above (plus many by the popular Hungarian writer Ferenc Molnár) could be played as intended. If some of the first made now seem static, photographed plays, this was true of most early talkies. The best of these comedies are historically interesting as authentic contemporary interpretations of a totally vanished art form. It is only re-

grettable that the actresses who created such roles on Broadway, Gertrude Lawrence, Lynn Fontanne and especially Ina Claire, so seldom got the chance to repeat them on screen.

Aside from his enormous output of novels and short stories, Somerset Maugham was from 1908 to 1933 an extremely prolific playwright, a master of artificial comedy. Critics agree on his three finest comedies: *Our Betters* (1917), *The Circle* (1921) and *The Constant Wife* (1927), all of which were made into early talkies, in reverse order from that of their stage productions.

Under the title of *Charming Sinners* ("Sinners" was an extremely popular word in titles of that period), *The Constant Wife* was the first such comedy to reach the talking screen, in 1929, less than two years after its Broadway opening, with Ruth Chatterton starred in the Ethel Barrymore role, supported by Clive Brook as her husband, Mary Nolan as his young mistress and William Powell as the wife's bachelor admirer. Though the *Times* reviewer complained of inadequate sound and also of a changed ending (the wife's would-be lover gets off the train instead of accompanying her to Italy, as in the play), on the whole Maugham seems to have been well served.

Unfortunately, what is generally regarded as the best of the three plays, *The Circle,* apparently got the worst production. Disguised by MGM under the typical catchpenny title of *Strictly Unconventional* (1930) (not to be confused with *Strictly Dishonorable, Strictly Modern, Strictly Personal,* etc.), the film featured Catherine Dale Owen, Paul Cavanagh, Lewis Stone, Ernest Torrence and Alison Skipworth—in 1930 an excellent cast, but the *Times* did not deign to review it, and even *Film Daily* rated it poor.

The plot depends on an ironic parallel between two generations. A young wife, so bored with her stuffy M.P. husband that she is considering running off with a lover, invites her husband's mother and *her* elderly lover, who had run off together in a great scandal thirty years before, to visit for a weekend. The once notorious Lady Kitty, now a vain, chattering creature with dyed hair and too much make-up, would seem sufficient warning, yet in spite of this apparently horrible example, the girl still goes off with her lover. Though Skipworth should have made an excellent Lady Kitty, in the film she and the lover, Lord Porteous, are *married*—which, of course, undercuts the whole point.

Our Betters (1933) —and RKO is to be commended for not renaming it *Strictly Sinners* or *She Wanted a Title*—the most caustic of the three plays, is a sharp satire on the American heiresses who for the past few generations had been buying their way into London society by marrying into the peerage. Constance Bennett was perfectly cast as Lady Grayston (the former Pearl Saunders of New York), who despite all the glaring examples of snobbery, infidelity and sexual decadence in her set, and indeed in her own life, is determined that her younger sister (Anita Louise), too, will taste the joys of a titled marriage.

Except for some expansion to include scenes like the one in which for her sister's presentation at St. James's she wears black instead of white, the one significant softening of the play (in which Pearl is shown as clever, ruthless and hard as nails, without mitigating explanation) is that on her wedding day Pearl overhears her husband (Alan Mowbray as a character who never appears in the play) reassuring his mistress that everything will go

Alan Mowbray and Constance Bennett in **Our Betters**

on as before, as he is only marrying Pearl for her money. This goes a long way toward explaining, if not justifying, her subsequent behavior. Otherwise the plot, with all its illicit affairs, culminating in the return of the horrified sister to America, most of the cynical witticisms and certainly Maugham's basic point, survives intact in this forgotten gem of sophisticated comedy.

Noel Coward, though perhaps best-known to the American public in the early '30s as the writer of *Bitter Sweet* and *Cavalcade,* did not fare as well as Maugham in film adaptations of his comedies: only one was good. Judging by contemporary accounts, photographs and the surviving recording, one would give anything to be able to see Coward and Gertrude Lawrence in a film of the original production of *Private Lives,* but in 1931 they were not movie names, and Robert Montgomery and Norma Shearer were.

That wishful reservation aside, it must be said in all justice that the MGM production, with Reginald Denny and Una Merkel as the secondary couple, holds up very well indeed, as if some of the gloss of the stage version, then scarcely closed, had rubbed off on all the players. Not only is the period detail effortlessly right, but Shearer is surprisingly effective as Amanda, and Montgomery, in one of the few opportunities he was ever given to play high comedy, is a truly delightful Elyot, far better cast than some stage Elyots of the 1970s.

Design for Living (1933) is in every respect different. The three people who comprise the central triangle are not members of the idle rich but practicing artists, two men, a playwright and a painter, and a woman commercial artist (a decorator in the play) who loves both and furthers their careers. Coward wrote it specifically as a vehicle for himself, Alfred Lunt and Lynn Fontanne, a trio whose combined glamour was enough to command seventy-five dollars each for black market opening night seats in 1932, the worst year of the Depression.

Paramount bought it, assigned Ben Hecht

to adapt it and Ernst Lubitsch to direct it, and cast Miriam Hopkins, Fredric March and Gary Cooper as the leads—all attractive young players, but hardly in the league with the originals. Typically, the men's names were changed from Otto and Leo to George and Tom. Fearing, perhaps wisely, that the Coward epigrams would not play in Peoria, Hecht according to his own boast retained only one line from the play. This one can believe, for although a number of the lines are funny, wisecracks and sight gags are no substitute for wit. In short, the film is not only not good Coward, it is not even good Lubitsch.

"Polyandry has nothing to do with Pollyanna," the ads announced coyly, and indeed the casual acceptance of sex is definitely pre-Production Code. Hopkins first lives with Cooper, then has a fling with March, leaves them both to marry Edward Everett Horton, but finally settles for a *ménage à trois* that will make all three happy. Molly Haskell gives this several pages of enthusiastic analysis, noting, "The number of sacred cows gaily demolished by the film—premarital virginity, fidelity, monogamy, marriage, and, finally, the one article of even bohemian faith, the exclusive one-to-one love relationship—is staggering." In the history of sexual politics or polemics it may well rank as a call to arms (though one that went unheeded for several decades), but compared to such vintage Lubitsch masterpieces as *Trouble in Paradise* and *Ninotchka,* it is very flat champagne.

Incredible as it may now seem, in the 1920s Frederick Lonsdale, Ivor Novello and even A. A. Milne were seriously regarded as rivals of Noel Coward, perhaps even his superiors. In movie sales, Lonsdale did the best of the three, with one of his comedies filmed three times within twenty-two years. This was *The Last of Mrs. Cheyney* (like *Our Betters,* an Ina Claire vehicle on stage), which in 1929 served as Norma Shearer's second talkie. Eight years later it was remade, with Joan Crawford as the socialite jewel thief, William Powell as her accomplice working as butler in the country house where she plans a major job and

Robert Montgomery as the nobleman for whose love she reforms. A strong supporting cast included Jessie Ralph, Frank Morgan, Nigel Bruce and Ralph Forbes. The *Times* reviewer, who had seen both the play and the 1929 film, was pleased with everyone but Crawford and Montgomery. MGM gave Mrs. Cheyney one more go-round in 1951, with Greer Garson, under the title of *The Law and the Lady.*

Meanwhile early in 1930 Paramount had filmed Lonsdale's *The High Road* as *The Lady of Scandal,* with Ruth Chatterton, Basil Rathbone, Ralph Forbes and Nance O'Neil, a production which the *Times* acclaimed: "it is not only acted by understanding players, who fill the various roles most intelligently, but . . . a work which should do a great deal to lift picture tales out of the ordinary rut."

A musical comedy star scheduled to be snubbed by the aristocratic set of the young man who loves her, the heroine has the same enlivening effect on this stuffy lot as Auntie Mame on Beauregard's Southern clan. Indeed, she does even better than planned by landing a duke instead of her original suitor. Set in a working-class background, this, of course, would have been a Cinderella romance.

A. A. Milne, whose claim to fame now rests exclusively on his Winnie-the-Pooh books and other works for children, was in his time a successful dramatist, but only one of his plays was given an American film production in the '30s. *The Dover Road,* characteristically retitled *Where Sinners Meet* (1934), "Sinners" being still as popular a word with American film-makers as "Road" was with British playwrights, reunited Clive Brook and Diana Wynyard, who had scored so heavily in *Cavalcade,* supported by the usual company of stage-experienced actors including Billie Burke, Reginald Owen and Alan Mowbray. Brook was the eccentric Dover Road resident whose hobby it is to arrange minor motor accidents so that impulsive extramarital couples running off to the Continent will have time to think it over as disillusion sets in.

Ivor Novello likewise scored only once in American films, with a version of his play *The Truth Game* titled *But the Flesh Is Weak* (1932). C. Aubrey Smith and Robert Montgomery were father and son, partners in gentlemanly fortune hunting. To save his father from suicide over a gambling debt he can't pay, the son is about to marry wealthy Heather Thatcher, but is saved and ends up with the widow he loves (Nora Gregor).

This kind of genteel comedy was, of course, far more a British than a Continental tradition, but a few European works followed the pattern, including some by the versatile Molnár. Both *The Good Fairy* (1935) and *The Bride Wore Red* (1937) were included among Cinderella romances, as *Double Wedding* (1937) was among films about heiresses. Likewise Molnár's haunting fantasy *Liliom* (1930) and the touching *No Greater Glory* (1934), based on his novel *The Paul Street Boys,* clearly belong elsewhere, but at least three of his lighter works rank with those under discussion.

Olympia, under the title of *His Glorious Night* (1929), fared no better than when it was exhumed as *A Breath of Scandal* (1960). Undaunted, MGM gave *The Swan* a similar title, *One Romantic Night* (1930), but it suffered the same fate as did the Grace Kelly remake under the original title in 1955. The pallid romance of a princess (Lillian Gish in her talkie debut) who falls in love with her brother's tutor (Conrad Nagel) but realizes she must marry a prince (Rod La Rocque) had been a great success with Eva Le Gallienne on Broadway, but the *Times* found the film distinctly inferior, especially Nagel and La Rocque in comparison with Basil Rathbone and Philip Merivale on stage.

MGM's version of Molnár's 1911 comedy *The Guardsman* (1931) is at least historically important because it is the only film of Alfred Lunt and Lynn Fontanne, already established as America's most distinguished acting couple. Though the setting is Vienna, where they are supposedly stars of the Burgtheater, by opening with them playing the last few minutes of *Elizabeth the Queen,* their most recent Broadway success, then taking bows with smiling hypocrisy while exchanging insults under their breath, the picture gives the illusion of being not merely with but *about* the Lunts.

Yet *The Guardsman* is almost as much a comedy of the boudoir as of the drawing room; there is no glimpse of any surrounding society, the secondary characters are negligible and the whole plot hinges on a single contrived situation. When the actor-husband disguises himself as a bearded Russian guardsman to make love to his wife, does she really know all the time who he is? If so, then he has failed as an actor. If not, then she is unfaithful to him. One recognizes the plot, of course, from innumerable other variations, of which *Fledermaus* is one of the oldest. As director, Sidney Franklin made a few attempts at opening up the stagy script, but the streets and buildings look nothing like Vienna.

Lunt is, of course, most amusing as the vain, shallow actor, pouting, preening and posturing in classic ham style, and Fontanne as his slyly teasing wife makes effective use of her Mona Lisa smile and famous insinuating chuckle (though her voice sounds strangely heavy and old as it never did on stage), but the one-dimensional roles make little demands on them. Only in that tantalizing bit from *Elizabeth the Queen* does one catch a glimpse of the powerful talents that for four decades kept the Lunts at the top of their profession.

Marcel Pagnol's *Topaze* (1933, no connection with Hitchcock's 1969 film *Topaz*), adapted by Benn Levy, though not squarely within the comedy of manners pattern, did treat an upper-class milieu with cheerfully urbane cynicism. In a lighter variation on the situation in Ibsen's *An Enemy of the People,* a naïve, bookish science teacher (John Barrymore, in an uncharacteristically restrained performance), discovers in his laboratory the healthful properties of a liquid, is hired by a tycoon (Reginald Mason) to mass-produce it as a soft drink, then finds it is actually harmful, with inevitable complications for himself. As the tycoon's kindhearted mistress, Myrna

Myrna Loy and John Barrymore in Topaze

Loy made the most of one of her first opportunities in a sympathetic role. In his program notes, William Everson calls the film "Lubitschian," "a fitting climax to just a few years of superlatively civilized and gentlemanly film-making" by director Harry D'Arrast. To modern viewers it remains an unmixed delight.

The only other lightly sophisticated film from a French source was Jacques Deval's *Tovarich* (1937), adapted by Robert E. Sherwood. Though the situation of aristocrats mistaken for or masquerading as servants is at least as old as Roman comedy and had been used in such varied works as *She Stoops to Conquer* and *Come Out of the Kitchen,* what added piquancy to *Tovarich* (the Russian word for "comrade") was that the leading couple are very high Russian ex-nobility who are struggling to make a living in Paris several years after the Revolution, and hence jump at the chance to work as butler and cook.

With Charles Boyer and Claudette Colbert, who had proved an effective team in *Private Worlds,* as the former Prince and his Grand Duchess wife, and Basil Rathbone as the

Soviet commissar who tries to outwit them, not without grudging respect for their sense of *noblesse oblige, Tovarich* both in its locale and its Red-White conflict over precious Czarist jewels clearly anticipates *Ninotchka* (1939), but the tone is lightheartedly romantic, with more good-natured fun poked at lingering imperial pretensions and bourgeois title worship than at Stalinist bureaucracy.

Six years before adapting *Tovarich,* Sherwood had done even better on his own, with Austrian royalty, in *Reunion in Vienna* (produced on stage in 1931, but set specifically in 1930). Indeed, he out-Molnáred Molnár by creating one of the best Continental comedies ever written by an American. Filmed by MGM in 1933, only two years after *The Guardsman,* with the same director, Sidney Franklin, and likewise a Lunts stage vehicle, it makes a kind of companion piece, but infinitely less dated and stage-bound, perhaps because its basic premise is firmly rooted in historic reality. *The Guardsman* might as well have been set in some mythical kingdom, but Sherwood made adroit use of two of the most important facts in Vienna's unique cultural identity: its past as capital of the Hapsburg Empire and its then present as the world capital of Freudian psychiatry.

Almost as if symbolizing the city, the heroine, Elena, has gone from mistress of a wildly uninhibited archduke to wife of a renowned psychiatrist. According to Everson's program notes, on Broadway "Lynn Fontanne played it full of bubbling energy, rather like the Jean Arthur heroine of a Capra movie," whereas "Diana Wynyard's . . . restraint and taste emphasize the bittersweet quality of the play."

Certainly this is the mood of the opening scene, in which she wistfully trails a party of tourists through the Schönbrunn, and, while the guide displays the bedroom of the once notorious Archduke Rudolph, drifts into a reverie, to the strains of *Tales from the Vienna Woods.* In flashback we glimpse an elaborate court function at which, as she makes a deep curtsy while the Austrian national anthem plays, Rudolph deliberately stands on the hem of her gown so that she cannot straighten up without ripping it. With a look of the most humble respect, she seems to kiss his hand, but instead bites it. The abrupt shift of mood sets the tone for the merry battle that follows between aristocrat and bourgeois, past and present, hectic romance and safe marriage.

Another poignant moment, of a kind not attempted by the later *Tovarich* and *Ninotchka,* occurs in the former imperial suite of the Hotel Lucher (a transparent disguise for the Sacher) when the forlorn survivors of the old regime—then only twelve years in the past—who have sneaked back into Vienna and gathered in their faded finery to celebrate Franz Josef's hundredth birthday, toast his portrait.

Most of the film, however, is dominated by John Barrymore's flamboyant performance. He and Frank Morgan (who had played Barrymore's role in *Topaze* on stage) as the enlightened Freudian husband who urges his wife to confront and dispel the ghost from the past, make perfect foils, strongly supported by May Robson as the rowdy, cigar-smoking Frau Lucher, who has arranged and financed the whole forbidden reunion, and Henry Travers, repeating his stage role as the doctor's inquisitive father.

Another intelligent comedy of manners was Mark Reed's *Yes, My Darling Daughter* (staged 1937, filmed 1939), in its way a modest American analogue of *The Circle.* Once a militantly radical feminist and advocate of free love in Greenwich Village, circa 1915, Ann Whitman Murray (Fay Bainter), more than twenty years later, though still politically active, seems a sedate enough Connecticut matron. When her daughter (Priscilla Lane), doing a college research paper on revolt in the earlier generation, stumbles on the truth about the past, including a well-documented love affair, the mother is in no position to take high moral stands when the girl announces her intention of spending a weekend with her boy friend (Jeffrey Lynn) before he goes off on a foreign job.

The mother's thrice-divorced sister (Gene-vieve Tobin), who represents the in-between generation, the flaming youth for whom the ashes are now cooling, seems to both other women a sad example of muddled jazz age romanticism. Even though in the film the daughter does not, as in the play, go off with her mother's blessing, its mere title and theme generated such violent attacks from would-be censors that its box-office success was guaranteed.

Later in 1939 MGM produced a much more famous comedy, the long-awaited screen version of one of the truly unique plays of the decade (if only because it has no male characters), Clare Boothe Luce's *The Women*. True, this might well be called a comedy of *bad* manners, but nevertheless it lies well within the classic tradition, not only set in the "best" society but ruthlessly exposing from within its every foible—a Juvenalian or Swiftian satire, despite the title not really against the whole female sex but, rather, against that element of it included in the author's originally intended titles, *The Ladies* or *Park Avenue*.

Called by George Jean Nathan after its 1936 Broadway opening the best argument he had ever seen for homosexuality, sternly condemned by Marjorie Rosen in *Popcorn Venus* as a betrayal of the sisterhood, *The Women* has survived these solemnly irrelevant strictures as one of the most gorgeously funny films ever made—exactly the kind of no-holds-barred '30s comedy for which Hollywood was soon to lose its knack. Said Nugent in the *Times*: "Every studio in Hollywood should make at least one thoroughly nasty picture a year . . . The women have gone on a glorious cat-clawing rampage and have turned in one of the merriest pictures of the season."

In a novel opening, the cast credits, a series of moving portraits framed against a moiré background, introduce the ten leading characters with a shot of an appropriate animal dissolving into one of the actress—a doe for heroine Mary Haines (Norma Shearer), a viciously snapping leopard on a chain for de-

Joan Crawford, Norma Shearer, Rosalind Russell in **The Women**

signing shopgirl Crystal Allen (Joan Crawford), a sleek black Persian cat seated on a cushion, delicately baring its teeth, for the gleefully malicious Sylvia Fowler (Rosalind Russell), a chattering monkey for the much-married Countess di Lave (Mary Boland) and so on. The camera's opening sweep through a luxurious Fifth Avenue beauty salon, picking up snatch after snatch of female talk of ineffable fatuity, hypocrisy and sheer bitchery, sets the tone for the whole film, which gets under way the instant Sylvia picks up from the manicurist's gossip that Mary's husband is keeping Crystal.

While Mary may indeed be almost too saccharine ("Noble Norma Shearer, weeping, weeping," as *The New Yorker* always says) and Peggy (Joan Fontaine) too naïve to count as sympathetic characters, it is not true that no one else in the cast is likable. Mary's wise old mother (Lucile Watson, symbolized in the credits by an owl), Miriam (Paulette Goddard, a fox), the *Vanities* girl who succeeds Sylvia as Mrs. Howard Fowler (after what must be the most famous female brawl in screen history), Lucy, the dude ranch owner (Marjorie Main) and Nancy Blake, the spinster novelist (Florence Nash), are all sensible women who serve at various times as *raisonneuses*—not to mention the constant background chorus of cooks, maids, beauticians, models, secretaries, salesgirls and exercise instructresses whose sardonic comments underline the shallowness of the pampered parasites they serve.

The play was so full of lines impossible to use on the screen in 1939 (e.g., someone remarks of the perpetually pregnant Edith, "She must be either Catholic or careless") that keeping within the Production Code presented unusual problems for scenarists Anita Loos and Jane Murfin, who even had to invent a new word, "beezle," as a euphemism for "floozie" or "tart," but on the whole any loss is more than compensated by an unexpected bonus. Thus a scene in a maternity hospital in which Edith's cigarette ashes keep dropping on her nursing infant is omitted, but in its place we get the hilarious scene at the perfume counter of "Black's Fifth Avenue," in which Sylvia and Edith try in vain to get the best of Crystal.

The opulent production values at which MGM excelled are almost overwhelming, including an overlong fashion show for which Adrian outdid himself; even after more than forty years, the cachet of chic elegance is unmistakable. Oddly enough, the play, revived on Broadway in 1973 with an all-star cast and proper '30s decor, seemed flat and dated, certainly not shocking, while the film, played to the hilt by a glittering galaxy of actresses then at the height of their powers, when '30s social attitudes could still be taken for granted, remains one of the dazzling comedies of the decade.

By any standard the *doyenne* of American women playwrights of the twentieth century was Rachel Crothers, who achieved her first Broadway production in 1903, antedating by nearly ten years that of her only rival, Clare Kummer. For the next thirty-four years Crothers wrote almost a play a season, most now forgotten but several included in Burns Mantle's annual *Ten Best Plays* volumes. She must also be considered the American pioneer in writing this kind of social comedy, since her career goes back so much further than those of Behrman, Barry and the others. From her large output, three films were made in the '30s, the very titles of which (*Let Us Be Gay*, *When Ladies Meet* and *As Husbands Go*) suggest the kind of lighthearted—but never light-minded—air that makes her work the very epitome of the drawing-room, or, more precisely, country house comedy.

Let Us Be Gay (1930) offered Shearer a decided change of pace between the heavy dramatics of *The Divorcee* (1930) and *Strangers May Kiss* (1931), as a dowdy, bespectacled wife who loses her philandering husband (Rod La Rocque), then spends three years in Paris, after which the hard-working silkworm emerges as a glittering butterfly and *femme fatale*. Invited for the inevitable weekend at the home of the standard determined dowager (Marie Dressler), she is asked to save the old lady's granddaughter from her infatuation with a middle-aged roué by vamping him herself. Though the others do not suspect, he is, of course, her ex-husband. (It is remarkable how many plays which seemed to deal lightly with divorce still had the original couple getting back together; nearly ten years later, Shearer was still following the same pattern in *The Women*.) With a cast that included Hedda Hopper, Sally Eilers and Gilbert Emery, *Let Us Be Gay* was, said the *Times*, "a mirthful affair . . . eight reels of carefree madness."

When Ladies Meet (1933) was an altogether more original play, its central situation the unhackneyed one of a betrayed wife and the other woman becoming good friends without knowing each other's identities, then, when they do find out, joining in telling off the man who has deceived them both. Once again Myrna Loy and Ann Harding were the rivals, as they had been the year before in Barry's *The Animal Kingdom,* but this time Loy (who lost in both cases) was the mistress and Harding the wife.

Loy as a young writer spurns the suit of a reporter (Robert Montgomery) because she is in love with her married publisher (Frank Morgan). As the chattering hostess at whose country house all the confrontations take place, Alice Brady made such a successful talkie debut that she was type-cast in such featherbrained roles.

As Husbands Go, a considerably slighter earlier play, was filmed in 1934. In yet another variation on Henry James' favorite theme of American naïveté versus European subtlety, two Midwestern matrons, a young wife (Helen Vinson) and a middle-aged widow (the inimitably flighty Catharine Doucet, repeating her stage role), return from Paris with foreign admirers in tow, in the wife's case an English poet (G. P. Huntley). The widow, whose intended is a French pseudo philosopher played by Warner Oland, meets strenuous objections from her daughter, while the wife is so disarmed by her

Robert Montgomery and Ann Harding in **When Ladies Meet**

husband's apparently total acceptance of the poet that she is eventually piqued enough to return to the fold. (The husband was Warner Baxter, who was to play Vinson's unappreciated husband again both in *Broadway Bill*, 1934, and *Vogues of 1938*, 1937.)

Crothers' last play, *Susan and God* (1937), a great hit on Broadway with Gertrude Lawrence, was also her most intelligent and serious. Amid the usual luxurious Long Island settings, a delicately devastating portrait emerges of a totally vain, frivolous woman, so hipped on a simplistic new religious fad, "Lady Wigstaff's Movement" (like the then controversial Oxford Group), that she meddles destructively in the lives of all her friends, meanwhile almost losing her own neglected husband and daughter. When it was filmed early in 1940 with Joan Crawford, Fredric March and an unusually strong cast, some critics felt Crawford's performance was too much like Lawrence's, yet under George Cukor's direction she was surprisingly convincing in an entirely new kind of role, as a vapid society matron.

The literary reputation of S. N. Behrman has survived more securely than Crothers' no doubt because, even after he himself was no longer writing Broadway hits, he turned with equal skill and success to adaptations of others' works (e.g., Maugham's story *Jane*), biographies, notably those of Lord Duveen and Max Beerbohm, and his own memoirs. During the '30s he also wrote or collaborated on several important MGM films, none comedies, including *Queen Christina, A Tale of Two Cities, Parnell* and *Conquest*—but he was given these assignments presumably because of his Broadway reputation as a master of polished dialogue, in a series of plays which the critics invariably—and quite rightly—characterized as "urbane."

The first of these was *The Second Man* (1927), in which the Lunts co-starred, a comedy so witty that Noel Coward, then at the first peak of his fame, did not hesitate to star in the London production. Under the inept title of *He Knew Women*, this was filmed in 1930, with Lowell Sherman and Alice Joyce not badly cast in the Lunts' roles, with Frances Dade and David Manners as the younger couple. That early in talkie development, it was apparently very much a photographed play, but enough of the epigrams survived to impress the reviewers.

An articulate but slothful writer, more or less kept by a wealthy widow, finds himself also besieged by a much younger girl, even though a scientist her own age loves her. The girl must pretend pregnancy and the boy fire at the hero and miss before the two couples are properly paired off. As in all Behrman's work, the charm was mainly in the dialogue.

Brief Moment (filmed 1933) was one of several novels, plays and movies inspired by the much-publicized romance of torch singer Libby Holman and tobacco heir Smith Reynolds, whose marriage ended in his mysterious death (other interpretations include *Sing, Sinner, Sing, Reckless* and *Written on the Wind*). Despite the already hackneyed Cinderella plot, Carole Lombard and Gene Raymond, according to the *Times,* made it seem fresh. The bride insists that her playboy groom go to work for his father, with predictable disastrous results. He plays truant, she finds out and the marriage is temporarily over, until he gets another job. However bright the dialogue may have been, this was certainly the least original, most obvious of Behrman's plays.

Not until 1935 did Hollywood get around to Behrman's 1932 hit, *Biography*, and then the title was coyly changed to *Biography of a Bachelor Girl*. Critics agreed that Ann Harding, long typed as the noble, superior woman, was all wrong for the lively bohemian artist played on stage by Ina Claire. Robert Montgomery was equally miscast as the venomous radical editor bent on using her to destroy one of her former lovers (Edward Everett Horton), a mediocre politician. In the play, after canceling her autobiography, she flees to Europe to escape her bitter young lover; in the film he is apparently going to follow her.

Ironically, or perhaps inevitably, Behrman's

greatest hit, *No Time for Comedy* (1939), which on stage starred Katharine Cornell and Laurence Olivier (soon succeeded by Francis Lederer), dramatized his own plight, that of a successful writer of comedy who (encouraged by a "Lorelei with an intellectual patter") feels guiltily obliged to write something reflective of the terrible political crises of the day, until convinced by his coolly rational actress-wife that his true talent is to amuse the world, not reform it. For once the film version was faithful and well cast, with James Stewart and Rosalind Russell as the couple and Genevieve Tobin as the other woman. Though not released until 1940, it seems in retrospect to capture the tone of Behrman's '30s comedies at their best.

Better-known to the general public during his career and perhaps better-remembered now than either Crothers or Behrman is Philip Barry. In a long article in *The New Yorker* of September 15, 1975, Brendan Gill suggests as well as any critic could the unique charm that has kept some of Barry's plays alive long after those of his contemporaries have been retired to American drama courses and film history books.

Of his twenty-one plays, the majority were unsuccessful, and of his hits only two filmed in the '30s (one twice) belong precisely in the realm of comedy of manners, yet the radiant impression lingers perhaps because these two are bracketed by two others, one filmed in 1929, one in 1940, to make four of the best high comedies the screen has ever seen.

One of the earliest such plays to be given talkie treatment, *Paris Bound* (1929), released scarcely a month before the Wall Street crash, would now be historically interesting if only as a living record of smart '20s comedy, but the reviews also praised its unusual intelligence and sophistication. Ann Harding in her screen debut played a young wife all in favor of free and easy marriage until her husband (Fredric March) is actually unfaithful, an infidelity that almost breaks up the marriage—another example of the pattern already noted of the marriage preserved. (If the title is in-comprehensible to later generations, it should be recalled that for the rich in the '20s Paris preceded Reno as the fashionable divorce mill.)

With her stage experience and classic beauty, Harding at this point had the field of sophisticated comedy almost to herself, so was inevitably cast in the first talkie version of Barry's 1928 hit, *Holiday,* which, released in July 1930—the same month as Maugham's *Strictly Unconventional (The Circle)*, Lonsdale's *The Lady of Scandal (The High Road)* and Crothers' *Let Us Be Gay*—"missed greatness by not so very much," according to the *Times*. "It is a good picture, filled with fine dialogue and acting, but by no means the best."

Harding and Mary Astor were the wealthy Seton sisters, tomboyish, would-be rebel Linda and socially correct Julia, rivals for the love of Johnny Case (Robert Ames), idealistic young financier who wants to rest on his Wall Street laurels and take his bride off for an indefinite holiday in Europe. The *Times* singled out Edward Everett Horton for special praise as Johnny's whimsical friend Nick Potter, who has many of the best lines. If this version has not altogether disappeared (like many films of that period), it has been so overshadowed by the 1938 remake that since the early 1950s, at least, it has never been shown in New York, either on TV or at any revival theater or museum series.

Before that remake, three other Barry plays were filmed, two of them not comedies of manners at all, *The Bargain* (1931), based on his 1923 play *You and I* and *Tomorrow and Tomorrow* (1933), but between them came a very successful lighter work, *The Animal Kingdom* (1932), which despite fears that it might be mistaken for a jungle picture, retained not only its title but its Broadway star, Leslie Howard, and two of its featured players, William Gargan and Ilka Chase.

As Gill puts it, "Barry argues that a man may be more truly married to his mistress than to his wife, and in this case an adulterous relationship is more honorable than monogamy"

Ann Harding and Mary Astor in Holiday (1930)

—surely a surprising thesis to be advanced by a happily married Irish Catholic in 1932. As her third Barry heroine, Ann Harding was the beloved mistress, and Myrna Loy, the wife (as noted, exactly the reverse of the roles they were to play the next year in *When Ladies Meet*) who resents the mistress less than her husband's friendship with his hard-drinking ex-pug butler (Gargan). The film was considered important enough to open the RKO Roxy, the smaller, 3,700-seat theater in Radio City.

Six years later, in 1938, came what remains for many viewers the quintessential Barry comedy of those filmed in the '30s, the ever-fresh Katharine Hepburn-Cary Grant *Holiday,* which the reviewer-in-brief for *The New Yorker* considers Hepburn's "archetypal" role. She had understudied the part on Broadway in 1928 and used it for her screen test, so was well qualified to be the definitive Linda Seton,

which at present writing she remains. Equally well cast are Grant and Lew Ayres, in a very fine performance as Ned, the Setons' gently alcoholic young brother.

"You can't ask a recession-ridden audience to weep over the unhappiness of people who are so filthy rich they live in a house like an apartment hotel and don't know what to do with their money," grumbled *Photoplay* (August 1938)—but actually the screenplay by Donald Ogden Stewart (who had been the original Nick Potter on stage) shows many signs of awareness that times had indeed changed. Unlike the original, this Linda *has* tried art, nursing and social work, and was serving at a strikers' canteen until she learned that her father was on the board of directors. As she says, "I can't decide whether to be Joan of Arc, Florence Nightingale or John L. Lewis."

References to America's Sixty Families and other bits of '30s social awareness add a suggestion of guilt to Linda's discontent with the trappings of wealth and at the same time underline Julia's crassness in her preoccupation with them. When the obnoxious cousin Seton Cram (Henry Daniell), presumably irked by New Deal reforms, wishes "we had the right kind of government," Susan Potter (Jean Dixon) pointedly asks him, "Just what countries do you have in mind?" Then too, Nick Potter (again played by Horton) is not a charming idler as before, but a professor about to take a long-awaited sabbatical in Europe.

From the opening scene, in which, after popping in on the Potters to break the news of his engagement, Johnny, awed by the façade of the Seton house, goes in the servants' entrance and spends several amusing moments of misunderstanding before he can grasp that Julia (Doris Nolan) is not "some kind of secretary" but actually lives here, until the end, in which he does cartwheels in the corridor outside a stateroom on a departing ocean liner (thus utilizing Grant's acrobatic skills), the film is smoothly cinematic, never more so than in the scene of Julia's elaborately formal engagement party, with hundreds of guests in

Katharine Hepburn, Cary Grant, Doris Nolan in **Holiday (1938)**

evening dress swirling through the opulent rooms.

Perhaps the theme, as phrased by Gill, "that wealth and convention suffocate the soul—that a man must take radical chances in order to find out what he is capable of becoming" may by 1938 have rung as hollow as *Photoplay* suggested to audiences whose main problem was not *enough* money, for the picture was not a box-office success. Yet to college students of the '60s and '70s, seeing *Holiday* on screen or stage, or discussing the play in class, the option of dropping out of a grossly materialistic society to do your own thing while you're young seemed perfectly natural, and Johnny Case, a prophet two generations ahead of his time.

Incredibly, after three such splendid (and varied) films as *Stage Door, Bringing Up Baby* and *Holiday,* Hepburn was among the stars named by exhibitors in 1938 as "box-office poison"—but when she asked Barry (who had not had a solid Broadway hit since *The Animal Kingdom* in 1932) to write a play for her, the result was a triumphant comeback for both, one of the greatest hits of 1939, *The Philadelphia Story.*

The 1940 film version, called by *The New Yorker* "one of the high points of the big studio system of movie making," remains perhaps the best example ever of this kind of screen comedy. Cary Grant gave another of his inimitably polished performances, and James Stewart won an Oscar for his. Though on one level it might be considered the ultimate confrontation between that favorite '30s pair, the heiress and the reporter, in a twist typical of Barry the arrogant Tracy Lord does not marry the newspaperman but her former husband, a leisured sportsman of her own class.

"There's no prettier sight than the privileged class enjoying its privileges," observes Macaulay Connor, the reporter—but it was a sight to be seen not much longer on stage or screen. History was catching up. When *The Women* opened in September 1939, war had already broken out in Europe, by the summer of 1940, when the films of *Susan and God* and *No Time for Comedy* were shown, Hitler had conquered most of the Continent, and by December, when *The Philadelphia Story* was released, just in time to be eligible for Oscars, though no one could have foreseen Pearl Harbor less than a year in the future, the draft was on, and the only question was how soon this country would be at war.

Along with the escapades of the heiresses and playboys, even the more serious problems of the rich seemed utterly irrelevant, and never again were they to recapture their hold on the American imagination. The teacups rattled no more on the country house terrace, the juvenile had turned in his white flannels for khaki and the ingenue was serving at a USO canteen. Writers and stars, if they were to survive at all, had to turn to other genres.

True, in England the form was still flickering feebly as late as the 1970s in the work of a few dramatists like William Douglas Home and Hugh and Margaret Williams, who continued to write just as if World War II, or, for that matter, World War I, had never happened. These pallid charades (e.g., *The Kingfisher*) only confirm that the comedy of manners is now as dead as the epic poem, the Elizabethan verse tragedy and the novel of sensibility. The last American plays at all reminiscent of it were Samuel Taylor's *Sabrina Fair* (1953) and *The Pleasure of His Company* (1959), both rather well filmed, but even these did not attain the effervescent sparkle of the best high comedies of the '30s. It is impossible to imagine anyone ever attempting or being allowed to write a comedy of manners for American television.

THE PLOT THICKENS
Intrigue, Boudoir and Otherwise

7

"GOOD HEAVENS, MY PEARLS!"
Gamblers and Jewel Thieves

Although some of the films already discussed bordered on melodrama, most dealt primarily with the romantic and/or marital affairs of the characters. Whatever complications developed usually rose from some misunderstanding, serious or humorous, rather than from the devious machinations of those living outside, or barely within, the law.

Yet in certain other kinds of film the two worlds mingled so freely that the character actors and actresses who played the parents of the playboys and heiresses seldom had to doff their fashionable wardrobes or leave their accustomed luxurious surroundings to become the victims of expert con men or jewel thieves, or to find themselves thrown together as guests (passengers, fellow travelers) on land, sea or air in the continual variations on *Grand Hotel*.

Or, with the backgrounds changed to staff headquarters, diplomatic balls and European embassies, the same suave dignity that made actors like Lewis Stone or Lionel Atwill, for instance, effective as the courtesan's wealthy protector or the young socialite's father fitted them equally well to play master spies, mostly during World War I.

Likable rogues who, though technically outside the law, are morally superior to those judging them or tracking them down have always been a staple in popular literature, especially when the rogue uses his ill-gotten gains to help the oppressed against an unjust or tyrannical establishment. To the English-speaking world the archetype is undoubtedly Robin Hood, who may be regarded as the ultimate ancestor of all those dashing, often disguised, figures who break a few man-made laws to uphold a higher code.

The tradition continued in the picaresque adventure tales of the seventeenth century, culminating in Defoe's narratives of low life such as *Moll Flanders*. Later in the eighteenth century the respectable middle class still loved to read the "true accounts" and "dying confessions" of such real gentlemen of the road as Jonathan Wild and hear ballad operas sung about such fictitious antiheroes as Macheath. By the twentieth century this had dwindled down to such secret benefactors as the Scarlet Pimpernel, Zorro and Superman, or, on a less philanthropic level, such dazzlingly professional crooks as Arsène Lupin, Jimmy Valentine, the Lone Wolf and Raffles, all of whose escapades were filmed again and again.

Why gangster films should enjoy their greatest popularity during the Depression decade will be discussed elsewhere. But not all audiences could identify with such violent, murderous protagonists. Others outside the law practiced bloodless rackets as gamblers, jewel thieves, phony stock promoters, mind readers, dealers in fake art or various kinds of con artists.

Only in the United States have certain forms of gambling (such as the once taboo off-track betting) been subject to puritanical preachments and legal bans. Even so, in nineteenth-century America surely one of the most romantic figures was the Mississippi gambler, typified by Gaylord Ravenal in *Show Boat*. And in the twentieth century in the night life of most large cities the professionals, especially those who ran casinos, were accepted and patronized for the same reason as bootleggers: they provided people with what they wanted, regardless of the law.

On screen, the gambler's image ranked somewhere between the jewel thief and the gangster, but nearer the former (and often played by the same suave actors) : capable of lethal violence, but only if driven to it; urbane, discreet, impeccably dressed (always in evening clothes for high-stake games) , usually married to a good woman who deplores his underworld connections even while enjoying the luxuries they provide.

He is strictly honest according to his own code; he never cheats at cards nor welches on a debt, nor does he, like the gun-toting mobsters never hesitate to do, force his illegal services on anyone. He also displays a marked penchant for self-sacrifice on behalf of wives and daughters, sons and even younger brothers.

If Al Capone is said to have been the inspiration for all the more violent movie gangsters, then surely gambler Arnold Rothstein (murdered in 1928) must be credited as the prototype of all the gambler heroes. A close parallel to Rothstein was the gambler played by William Powell in *Street of Chance* (1930). To cure his newly married kid brother (Regis Toomey) of gambling mania and spare his sister-in-law (Jean Arthur) the constant worry suffered by his wife (Kay Francis), he arranges a game with the slickest pros in New York, intending the boy to be taken for every cent.

Instead, by a streak of beginner's luck, he wins big, and the gamblers naturally assume they have been set up. Though the young

Kay Francis and William Powell
in Street of Chance

couple escape with the money, the hero pays for his good deed with his life. *Street of Chance* still holds up extremely well, dated only in the pleasing sense that it offers fascinating glimpses of the 1930 New York where it was filmed.[1]

Gamblers on a lower level figured in Warners' *Smart Money* (1931), the only film in which Robinson and Cagney ever appeared together. Though it was hardly an adequate follow-up to their respective triumphs a few months before in *Little Caesar* and *The Public Enemy,* as Everson noted, "as a non-formula offshoot of the gangster film, *Smart Money* is quite rewarding, relatively unmelodramatic and more relaxed and naturalistic than most of its genre." Robinson was a small-town barber whose skill at dice and cards leads him to brief success as the ace of gamblers in a big city. But he is undone by a series of designing blondes, especially Evalyn Knapp, and then, in an unexpectedly tragic

[1] *Street of Chance* was remade in 1938 under the misleading title of *Her Husband Lies,* with Ricardo Cortez and Gail Patrick; like most remakes, it was inferior to the original.

twist, a single blow from him kills his henchman (Cagney), and he must face a long term for manslaughter.

Gambling Lady (1934) saw Barbara Stanwyck as an honest pro who plays in a gambling house on commission, rejecting all offers to go crooked. Presumably the same could be said for Gable, who operates a luxurious casino in *Manhattan Melodrama* (1934). Even the beloved George M. Cohan appeared as the owner of a fashionable gambling club in his own film production of his play *Gambling* (1934), in which he tracks down the murderer of his adopted daughter.

Supposedly based on fact, *Now I'll Tell* (1934) was taken from a book by Rothstein's widow. Its protagonist, aptly rechristened Murray Golden (Spencer Tracy), is a gambler so insatiable that he even pawns the jewelry of his devoted wife (Helen Twelvetrees), who is at one point kidnapped to bring him to terms. Eventually she divorces him, leaving him to Alice Faye, who is killed while riding with him.

As the decade wore on, the gambler, like his occasional business associate, the gangster, grew either more out-and-out villainous (e.g., Akim Tamiroff in *King of Gamblers,* 1937) or more sentimental. Thus in *Black Sheep* (1935) Edmund Lowe, without ever revealing his identity, saves his son (Tom Brown) from an adventuress (Adrienne Ames). In *Forgotten Faces* (1936), the third of four film versions of the same story, Herbert Marshall played a gentleman gambler known as Heliotrope Harry, who at the cost of his own life saves his daughter (Jane Rhodes) from the blackmail threats of his vicious ex-wife (Gertrude Michael).

But superior even to the gambler among white-collar crooks, the one true artist, the aristocrat of his profession, was the jewel thief. To begin with, in a Depression-stricken nation, what form of conspicuous consumption could be more shamelessly provocative than flaunting gems worth enough to support a poor family for years? To relieve the insensitive rich of such needless status symbols, pre-

sumably insured, seemed almost a victimless crime.

Unlike the rank-and-file hood, the gentleman jewel thief used only skill, never violence, for his success depended on his ability to speak and wear clothes well enough to be accepted at the most exclusive playgrounds of the rich, especially Paris, Venice and the Riviera. He was, in consequence, played by some of the screen's most polished actors, including John Barrymore, Ronald Colman, Clive Brook, Herbert Marshall, William Powell, Paul Lukas, Robert Montgomery, Warner Baxter and Melvyn Douglas.

Then too, this was one kind of crime—perhaps the only one other than embezzlement or blackmail—at which a woman could not only hold her own but, by sheer feminine guile, even excel. Perhaps the light-fingered lady was only the ultimate extension of the gold digger, using even more direct methods of parting fools and their money.

She also operated in much less restricted circles, since she normally assumed not only the jewels but the clothes and manners (and sometimes the title) of an aristocrat, as evidenced by the quality of the stars who played such characters: Shearer, Hopkins, Loy, Dietrich, Crawford and Stanwyck (not to mention such lesser luminaries as Evelyn Brent, Bebe Daniels and Gertrude Michael). Some ultimately reformed, or tried to, until tempted to pull one last, irresistible job, but until the heavy hand of the Production Code clamped down, many went on their larcenous way unrepentant.

As noted in the previous chapter, Lonsdale's *The Last of Mrs. Cheyney* combined jewel thief plotting with a conventional British comedy of manners. The Shearer version (1929), her second talkie, also marked the debut of this kind of heroine on the talking screen. Leading off the line-up for 1930 was Evelyn Brent in *Slightly Scarlet,* as a self-styled Austrian countess on the French Riviera bent on stealing the priceless necklace of an American millionaire's wife—but only because she must obey master crook Paul Lukas. Clive

Brook was a British rival thief, but both eventually reform.

In July 1930 Ronald Colman made the first talking version of *Raffles,* adapted by Sidney Howard from stories by E. W. Hornung, Conan Doyle's brother-in-law. On the stage the adventures of the chivalrous "amateur cracksman," cricket champion by day, safe-cracker by night, had been a popular vehicle for such stars as Gerald du Maurier and Kyrle Bellew, John Barrymore had filmed it as a silent in 1917, and David Niven was to make yet another version in 1940, but the *Times* found the Colman film curiously unexciting, especially in comparison to his first talkie, *Bulldog Drummond,* the previous year. Ever the perfect British gentleman, Raffles, it will be recalled, pulls off the last big job only so that an impoverished friend may claim the reward by finding the missing jewels.

Another old Barrymore stage vehicle, *Kick In* (1931), from a 1914 play in which an ex-con struggling to go straight is used by police to recover a stolen necklace, failed to do anything for the careers of Clara Bow and Regis Toomey. As it happened, the next notable tale of a supercrook was *Arsène Lupin* (1932), based on a 1909 play, starring Barrymore himself, with his brother Lionel as the clubfooted Paris police chief with whom he matches wits in a cat-and-mouse game almost as intricately plotted as *Sleuth.*

Personally supervised by Irving Thalberg, this was the first of several films in which the two talented Barrymore brothers seemed to be jockeying for position. As Everson notes, "John, supremely confident, steals the scenes often in absolute silence, or by employing some of those purely physical tricks he had mastered."

In this instance the grand prize is not jewelry but the *Mona Lisa,* snatched from the Louvre, a caper managed in convincing and amusing detail. (A little later that year John Barrymore played a less successful thief, the unfortunate Baron von Geigern in *Grand Hotel,* whose initial purpose in entering Grusinskaya's room is to steal her necklace.)

The summer of 1932 also saw a film frankly titled *Jewel Robbery,* based on a Viennese comedy, with William Powell as a gentleman thief who "can kiss a woman's hand—while relieving it of a diamond bracelet," said the *Times.* He also loots jewelry shops "with the delicate touch of a surgeon." As a baroness "as weary of her lovers as of her husband," Kay Francis "finds her boudoir invaded, successively, by a box of flowers, her stolen jewels and the faultlessly attired bandit himself."[2]

Later the same year Francis played another charmed victim, in what remains by any standards the best jewel thief film of the decade, done as a sly boudoir comedy rather than a melodrama: *Trouble in Paradise,* Ernst Lubitsch's own favorite among his works, the one which perhaps more than any other sparkles with what was rightly known as "the Lubitsch touch."

As wittily cynical as any Restoration comedy, the script by Grover Jones and Samson Raphaelson, based on Laszlo Aladar's play *The Honest Finder,* makes no attempt whatever either to punish vice or reward virtue. *Trouble in Paradise* was pronounced by Dwight Macdonald, who despised most Hollywood products, "as close to perfection as anything I have ever seen in the movies"—a judgment later generations have confirmed.

From the opening rendezvous at a hotel in Venice, where prince of thieves Gaston Monescu (Herbert Marshall) and society pickpocket Lily (Miriam Hopkins) over a seductive dinner in his suite proceed simultaneously to unmask each other's titled pretensions, rob each other blind and fall in love, the pace never falters. Meanwhile in another suite a wealthy guest (Edward Everett Horton) reports having been tricked and robbed by a man posing as a doctor.

A switch to a Paris newscast about this robbery leads to a satirical theme song and commercial for the Colet perfume company ("It's

---

[2] An unusual touch was Powell's method of subduing victims without hurting them; he offers them cigarettes, presumably marijuana, which produce a giddy high.

Karen Morley, John Barrymore, Lionel Barrymore in Arsène Lupin

not how you look that counts, it's how you smell!") and thence to a meeting of the board of directors of that prestigious firm, presided over by lovely Mme. Marianne Colet (Kay Francis), who inherited the business from her late, elderly husband.

Despite a constant refrain of "In times like these—" always uttered by the wealthiest characters, Marianne amid an obsequious chorus of "Yes, madames!" buys a costly jeweled purse, and is next seen with it in her opera box, escorted by two jealous, middle-aged suitors (Horton and Charlie Ruggles). From the orchestra, Gaston is gazing up through his opera glasses not so much at Marianne as at her purse—which, of course, presently disappears.

Despite the advice of Lily, with whom he has been living for over a year, Gaston returns the purse and claims the reward. Describing himself as one of the "nouveau poor," he so thoroughly ingratiates himself with the charming widow that he is presently installed as her confidential secretary and business man-

ager, with Lily introduced as a mousy typist supposedly supporting her poor family. With inverted morality typical of the whole film, Lily, who respects Gaston as a thief, despises him as a gigolo.

In the climax he must choose between a long-deferred midnight tryst with Marianne and a planned getaway to Venice with Lily. Meanwhile Horton has recognized him and exposed him to Colet's respected chairman of the board, Giron (C. Aubrey Smith)—but Gaston has also been doing his homework by checking the books, which reveal that Giron is the biggest crook of all. Even knowing the truth, Marianne is unwilling to call the police. Gaston and Lily escape with her purse, her pearls and a good amount of her cash, but even as they drive off in a taxi are still gaily robbing each other. With the kind of gleeful amorality impossible under the Production Code, there is not the least hint that they will ever legalize their relationship, much less reform.

Amid the usual flow of "B" variations, 1933

Kay Francis and Herbert Marshall
in Trouble in Paradise

also saw such star-cast films as *Dangerously Yours* (Warner Baxter as another Raffles type), *Midnight Club* (Clive Brook again, as head of a gang who use doubles to establish perfect alibis) and *The Solitaire Man* (Marshall again, as a diamond specialist who practices his art aboard a London-Paris plane).

1934 brought *The Mystery of Mr. X.* (Robert Montgomery as a gentleman thief who solves a series of murders unconnected with his own career) and *The Notorious Sophie Lang,* the first of three films in which Gertrude Michael starred as a celebrated jewel thief who constantly outwits Scotland Yard. Sometimes such a plot was worked into the *Grand Hotel* formula, as in *Grand Hotel* itself, or in *I Am a Thief* (1935), in which everyone aboard the Paris-Istanbul express is after the stolen jewels.

Early 1936 saw Myrna Loy in *Whipsaw,* as still another jewel collector, pursued by a disguised G-man (Spencer Tracy) who falls for her, and *The Lone Wolf Returns,* with Melvyn Douglas in the title role, which the *Times* reviewer regarded as at least fifteen years out of date. The next memorable jewel thief film, however, was *Desire* (1936), directed by Frank Borzage but produced by Lubitsch,

with enough of the master's touch evident to make it at least a partly satisfying film.

If for no other reason, *Desire* would be notable for allowing Dietrich to score brilliantly in her first chance at sophisticated comedy, without in any way impairing her glamorous image. Indeed, the whole first half of the film, in which she gets away with a valuable necklace by separately convincing first a Parisian jeweler (Ernest Cossart) and then a psychiatrist (Alan Mowbray) that she is the wife of the other, and the stratagems by which she manages to plant the jewels on innocent American businessman Gary Cooper en route to the Spanish border are as fast-paced, bright and full of unexpected twists as the best of Lubitsch. (Incredibly, even Cooper himself had played a jewel thief as Shirley Temple's father in *Now and Forever,* 1934.)

It is only when her confederate, John Halliday (who before 1934 would surely have been her lover as well), recovers the pearls and the story turns to the Dietrich-Cooper romance that it begins to bog down, perhaps less the fault of Borzage's sentimental taste than simply the inescapable restrictions of the Production Code. Though Zeffie Tilbury sparkles as the *grande dame* of the gang, with no regrets for her long life of crime, Dietrich's attempted Camille-like renunciation and Cooper's moralizing (in a triumph of homespun Yankee virtue over decadent European vice), her reform, restitution and the careful explanation about her probation leave *Desire* a long way from the seamless satin fabric, the undimmed glitter of *Trouble in Paradise.*

This rigidly enforced morality had much the same effect on other jewel thieves for the rest of the decade. In *The Return of Sophie Lang* (1936), even Sophie, "notorious" only two years before, had reformed and was working as companion to an old lady, whose diamond disappears on shipboard, compelling Sophie to clear herself by recovering it. Nowadays a heroine could only be accused of theft (like Fay Wray in *They Met in a Taxi,* 1936) or pretend to be a thief in order to trap the real culprits (Claire Trevor in *15 Maiden Lane,*

Marlene Dietrich and Alan Mowbray in Desire

1936) or, of course, she could always reform (Crawford in the 1937 *Last of Mrs. Cheyney*).

Men fared little better. In *Beg, Borrow or Steal* (1937), Frank Morgan played an expatriate con man on the Riviera who specializes in selling fake art objects. In a switch on *Lady for a Day*, his estranged wife (Janet Beecher), their grown daughter (Florence Rice), her fiancé (Tom Rutherfurd) and his family announce an impending visit, so the father must rent a villa and assume all the virtues he lacks. This he manages so well that the daughter breaks with her stuffy fiancé to marry a young count (John Beal), a protégé of the father. In *Arsène Lupin Returns* (1938), Melvyn Douglas was the now retired thief who helps an American detective recover some famous emeralds, but reviews were not enthusiastic, nor were they for the equally reformed hero (Francis Lederer) of *The Lone*

Wolf in Paris (1938), who falls for a princess while saving her crown jewels.

Considerably further from the beaten path, praised for its freshness as well as its use of classical music, was *Stolen Heaven* (1938), in which Gene Raymond and Olympe Bradna as members of a gang of jewel thieves fleeing across Europe stumble on the secluded cottage of a once great pianist (Lewis Stone) dreaming of a comeback. Finding it a perfect hideout, they pretend to arrange for his return to the concert stage, but, unlike William Holden in *Sunset Boulevard,* must make good on their promise, meanwhile gradually shedding their own warped values. (A somewhat parallel transformation takes place in *The Young in Heart,* also 1938, in which a family of charming con artists is won over by the sweet old lady they intended to fleece.)

The last notable jewel thief hero of the decade was the title character in *The Amazing Dr. Clitterhouse* (1938), with Edward G. Robinson somewhat miscast in the role Sir Cedric Hardwicke had played on stage, as a suave society physician who first turns thief to do research on crime, then finds he enjoys pulling successful jobs, joins a gang headed by Humphrey Bogart, but learns he can't retire when he wants. Claire Trevor was the good-bad girl who saves the day by switching sides.

Just around the corner in early 1940 came *Remember the Night,* in which Barbara Stanwyck played a jewel thief released on bail for the holidays in the custody of an assistant D.A. (Fred MacMurray). She does indeed reform and refuses either to escape or to allow him to jeopardize his career by throwing the case, but the script by Preston Sturges (enacted to the recurrent strains of "Home in Indiana") is so warm and witty, the Christmas atmosphere of MacMurray's rural home, with Beulah Bondi as his mother, Elizabeth Patterson as his aunt and Sterling Holloway as their hired man, is so touchingly real that *Remember the Night* must always rank high among jewel thief films.

That the witty, elegant lawbreaker has not dropped entirely out of favor in subsequent decades is evident in such occasional films as Hitchcock's *To Catch a Thief* (1955), a TV series like *The Rogues* and the 1973 film *The Thief Who Came to Dinner.* Yet to a large extent these have been overshadowed, if not altogether replaced, by a newer genre: the perfect caper, of which one might cite countless examples, from *Rififi* through *Gambit* to *11 Harrowhouse.* Now the victim is no longer a wealthy widow but more likely to be some famous museum, bank, institution or corporation. The protagonist consequently depends less on his personal charm and psychological acumen or even skill than on his manipulation of superelaborate mechanical and scientific devices to overcome supposedly burglarproof security systems. As in so many other fields, the technician has replaced the hand craftsman.

8

IT'S A SMALL WORLD
The <u>Grand Hotel</u> Formula

Aside from all the films centered on jewel thieves themselves, such characters, though sharing the spotlight with others, often figured in the many variations on what came to be called the *Grand Hotel* formula, named after the most famous example. The appeal of a cross section of humanity temporarily thrown together by some special circumstance can be traced at least as far back as the Prologue to Chaucer's *Canterbury Tales,* the first literary work to present a microcosm of the society of its day. But, though in the linking pieces between the tales Chaucer's twenty-eight pilgrims exchange lively dialogue, nothing really happens to any of them to change their lives.

Perhaps the closest dramatic precursors of the *Grand Hotel* pattern were those once popular, vaguely inspirational semifantasies such as Charles Kennedy's *The Servant in the House* (1908), Jerome K. Jerome's *The Passing of the Third Floor Back* (1909) and Barrie's *Dear Brutus* (1918), in which a mysterious, perhaps supernatural visitor (is he a harmless madman or does he represent Some Higher Power?) straightens out the lives of a number of troubled people—but these never strayed beyond the familiar stereotypes of the genteel, well-made play.

Except for *Outward Bound* (1930), to be dealt with among fantasies, the only talkie example of the above genre was *The Way of All Men* (1930), remake of a 1921 silent,

which the *Times* called "an unbelievable tale with evangelical leanings," in which all the characters are in "some fantastic way . . . bound up in the affairs of the others. This situation, while lending imagination and interest, strains credulity to the breaking point."

In a pattern that anticipates the disaster films of the 1970s, they are trapped in an underground cafe in a Southern city when a levee breaks and the Mississippi overflows. Under this strain, all the former friends, enemies, sweethearts and business partners, confronted with their misdeeds, undergo a great "spiritual" change, only to revert to their normally nasty selves when the danger is past.

Thus, except for *Transatlantic* (1931), to be treated with other seagoing melodramas, the first talkie to present a cross section of humanity without moralistic pretensions was a remarkably faithful transcription of that masterpiece of American naturalism, Elmer Rice's Pulitzer Prize-winning hit *Street Scene* (1931). Here in addition to a constant stream of passers-by the characters are the eight Manhattan families living in a dilapidated brownstone tenement, not so much thrown together by chance as permanently bound together by economic lot.

Like the play, King Vidor's film scrupulously preserves the classical unities of time and place, with all the action unfolding in front of the grim old house, between one evening and the next afternoon, during a June heat wave. The climactic double murder takes place within the house, unseen by the audience, so, if the gossiping neighbors can be considered a kind of chorus, *Street Scene* is very close to a Greek tragedy—with the difference that instead of kings and queens the fatal triangle involves an Irish stagehand, his wife and a collector for a milk company.

Resisting the temptation to dilute the effect of the play by moving inside the house, Vidor nevertheless kept the film cinematically fluid by showing the whole block, as well as part of an adjoining avenue along which runs an elevated line. In the most vividly realized scenes, immediately after the murder of Mrs. Maurrant (Estelle Taylor) and her lover (Russell Hopton) by her drink-crazed husband (David Landau), we glimpse reactions of the whole neighborhood in Fellini-like flashes of unprettied, gaping faces. As the camera pans back, a mob soon gathers, through which the ambulance must inch its way, and Rose Maurrant (Sylvia Sidney), getting off the el, instantly guesses what has happened. The irony of urban tragedy as casual spectator sport achieves

something of the shattering impact of *Dog Day Afternoon* (1975).

Among the film's unique qualities (along with a haunting Alfred Newman score later used in many 20th Century-Fox films set in New York), not the least is the faithful reflection of lower-middle-class New York's actual ethnic mix, in what an earlier generation had overoptimistically called "the melting pot." Except for routine Irish and Jewish stereotypes in endless variations on *Abie's Irish Rose* (a cliché that was done to death in the late silents), few other films of this period, even the best, ever dealt with any Americans but WASPs. Unlike *Dead End*, with which it is sometimes compared because of the setting, *Street Scene* has no particular social axes to grind; the universal human problems would be the same under any economic system.

Rice's play, which had opened on Broadway early in 1929, was a boldly original concept, with no literary ancestors and few descendants, so its inclusion here is not intended to suggest any debt to Vicki Baum's *Grand Hotel*, which, though already popular in Europe as a novel and a play in the '20s, did not open in New

Sylvia Sidney, David Landau, and extras in Street Scene

York until November 1930. Its success helped the novel become an American best seller, widely serialized in newspapers, so that by 1931 almost any literate person must have been aware of both the title and the general pattern. Thus it was no coincidence that while MGM was preparing its superelaborate, all-star production for release in April 1932, three other variations, in addition to *Shanghai Express,* beat it to the screen earlier that year. The reviewers were quite aware of the parallels.

Opening in January, *Union Depot,* based on a play by Gene Fowler, was described as "ingenious rather than artistic," notable for an all-seeing camera eye roving over the huge terminal set, picking up a variety of vignettes amid the constant hustle and bustle. A young hobo (Douglas Fairbanks, Jr.) meets a chorus girl (Joan Blondell) who's determined to get to Salt Lake City, but they are only two out of the twenty comic and dramatic figures whose affairs, mostly extralegal, interweave.

The *Grand Hotel* influence on Paramount's *Hotel Continental* was even more obvious to the *Times* reviewer, who had already spotted the new cycle. In this case he also gave some credit to an actual event, the demolition of the old Waldorf-Astoria at Fifth Avenue and Thirty-fourth Street, since the action takes place "on the last night of a famous Gotham hostelry." Among the former guests is still another jewel thief, an ex-con (Theodore Von Eltz), returned to retrieve a fortune in jewels he had hidden in one of the rooms. Two rivals bent on the same end hire a girl (Peggy Shannon) to lure and betray him, but she relents in time. The *Times* was displeased by the trite dialogue, poor continuity and unsatisfactory performances.

The next variation was *The Devil's Lottery,* which brought together the winners of the Calcutta Sweepstakes, among them the beautiful mistress (Elissa Landi) of a card-cheating cad (Paul Cavanagh), a Cockney ex-pug (Victory McLaglen) and his mother (Beryl Mercer), who insists on carrying her winnings around with her. The peer who owns the winning horse invites all the lucky ticket holders to his estate, where it soon becomes clear that so much sudden wealth can only bring trouble to most. Indeed, it leads to two deaths, one a murder, before the heroine, freed of her obnoxious partner, can go off with a nice young American (Alexander Kirkland). This is, of course, a variation on the "fatal gift" motif so familiar in folklore (e.g., the golden apple of discord) and in such fantasy-melodramas as William Wymark Jacobs' *The Monkey's Paw.*

Thus when *Grand Hotel* itself opened at the Astor on April 12, 1932, with all possible fanfare, its thunder had not been stolen, after all. A genuinely strong script, Cedric Gibbons' sumptuous Art Deco settings, gowns by Adrian, the most illustrious cast the screen had thus far seen, giving performances that still hold up nearly five decades later, all combined to make it a "production thoroughly worthy of all the talk it has created," said Mordaunt Hall in the *Times.* Since Garbo, Crawford, the Barrymore brothers and Wallace Beery were all major stars in their own right, not accustomed to sharing top billing with more than one co-star, it was a triumph of the studio system (and of Edmund Goulding's direction) to cast them all so perfectly that the roles might have been written for them; the effect is one of polished ensemble playing, not competing ego trips.

Although Garbo was only twenty-six at the time, the role of Grusinskaya, the melancholy, aging ballerina, was a natural for her. Every gesture and inflection conveys ineffable world-weariness. John Barrymore was never more charming than as her overnight lover, the luckless Baron von Geigern, who wins all hearts but one. As Flaemmchen, the stenographer who has found that typing will get her nowhere, the youthful Crawford was at her most jauntily attractive, while the versatile Lionel Barrymore achieves both humor and genuine pathos as Kringelein, the downtrodden white-collar wage slave trying for one worldly fling in the short time he has left to live. The real surprise is Wallace Beery, who, for once not cast in his standard lovable slob role, contributes a grimly convincing portrait of Herr Preysing, the ruthless Prussian industrialist, the only totally unsympathetic character among the five, whose brutal murder of the Baron provides the climax for all the intersecting plots.

Supporting the five stars is a distinguished cast of a dozen character players, all well-known at the time, led by two whose careers spanned several decades, from silent pictures until their deaths. Lewis Stone is the cynical Dr. Otternschlag, crippled and hideously disfigured by the war, who asks every day for mail that never arrives and turns away muttering, "They come, they go, but nothing ever happens"—perhaps the most famous line in the film. Jean Hersholt is Senf, the hotel porter, whose anxiety about his wife's difficulty in bearing their first child serves as a leitmotif throughout the film; in the end his relief at the news that both are safe provides the same closing grace note as the birth of Mrs. Buchanan's baby in *Street Scene;* despite heartbreak and death, the cycle of life goes on.

Though of the cast only Garbo, Hersholt and Rafaela Ottiano were actually European, the illusion of Continental atmosphere, as in so many Hollywood films of the period, is perfectly maintained throughout, even to the military bearing of the bellboys and the right German newspapers and magazines to be found in such a Berlin hotel. To be sure, the frequent use of familiar Strauss waltzes on the sound track, as well as "Vienna, City of My Dreams" whenever Grusinskaya speaks of her plans to have the Baron join her in Vienna, may now seem heavy-handed, but at the time it was not customary to compose original scores for even the most important non-musical films.

Visually, the frequent overhead shots, with the viewer gazing downward through seven floors of circular balconies to the lobby, also circular, tiled in a concentric checkerboard pattern, certainly made the Grand Hotel look more impressive than any most Americans had seen in 1932. Likewise, the thrice-repeated

image of Garbo, in a long "polo coat," now mink, now chinchilla, with a pillbox hat on her shoulder-length bob, sweeping through the lobby like an empress, with her entourage hurrying after, oblivious to the awed stares of onlookers, still seems the very epitome of '30s elegance.

Given "road show" treatment—i.e., shown at only one theater in each city, with a limited number of performances and high-priced tickets sold in advance—*Grand Hotel* was even in the worst Depression year such a critical and financial hit that during the remainder of 1932 half a dozen variations followed, each in a different setting. As ultimate proof of its total popular acceptance, Jack Benny parodied it on his radio program as "Grind Hotel," with Mary Livingstone as a stenographer named Flim-Flam.

Universal's *Night World,* released in May 1932, which Everson calls "clearly an attempt to both jump the gun on *Grand Hotel . . .* and to repeat the success of Universal's own *Broadway,*" used as its microcosm a seedy night club. Here the several story lines include those of a drunken young playboy (Lew Ayres) befriended by a dancer (Mae Clarke) and the club owner (Boris Karloff in a sympathetic role), whose faithless wife (Dorothy Revier) arranges his murder. The Negro doorman (Clarence Muse), standing outside in the snow, is, like Senf, worried about his wife, who, however, dies. The whole sordid milieu of betrayal and corruption, symbolizing the society outside, curiously anticipates Sidney Kingsley's play *Night Life,* more than thirty years later.

In *Skyscraper Souls,* based on a Faith Baldwin novel, the unifying setting is a thirty-million-dollar office tower supposedly taller than the Empire State, built by a ruthless banker (Warren William), who manipulates a stock debacle to his own advantage, meanwhile stringing along his faithful secretary-mistress (Verree Teasdale) with the story that his wife (Hedda Hopper) will not divorce him. When the secretary discovers that he is making a play for a younger girl (Maureen O'Sullivan), she

Lionel Barrymore, Joan Crawford, John Barrymore in **Grand Hotel**

shoots him and jumps off the top of his building—which his indifferent widow promptly sells, while the girl settles for a humble bank teller (Norman Foster).

Life Begins, from a play by Mary McDougal Axelson, had an ironic sequel more than four decades later when the then elderly author was murdered in her hospital bed by the crazed daughter whose birth inspired the original play. The setting is a maternity ward where, under the benign supervision of head nurse Aline MacMahon, a full range of expectant mothers await their time, including a hard-boiled floozie (Glenda Farrell) who would sell her child if she could, one who has already had too many children, one who's not married, and especially a convicted murderess (Loretta Young) guarded by a prison matron.

Despite all the new lives begun, including that of Young's baby, she herself dies in childbirth. (*Life Begins* was remade early in 1940 under the title of *A Child Is Born.*)

The Night of June 13, from *Suburbs,* a story by Vera Caspary, offered a finely detailed picture of several families living on the same street in a suburb of New York. An extremely neurotic wife (Adrianne Allen) kills herself, leaving a letter blaming her husband's (Clive Brook) attentions to a young neighbor (Lila Lee). To spare the girl's name, he burns the note, and so is accused of the wife's murder. Various witnesses who could clear him all have their own reasons for lying about what really happened on the night of June 13, among them Mary Boland (playing Charlie Ruggles' wife for the first of many times), a young couple secretly married (Frances Dee and Gene Raymond) and a woman ashamed to admit she patronizes a bootlegger. Only the last-minute testimony of an old man (Charles Grapewin) clears the hero and exposes the weaknesses of the others. With its believable characters and recognizable milieu, this was a long way from the prevailing old-house, assorted-heirs murder mystery formula of the day.

When Strangers Meet (1934), from a story by Zona Gale, dealt with a similar community of families, facing each other across a narrow, flagged path, like a mews. Hidden hostilities erupt in a double murder, solved when a long-suffering wife pins it on her husband. Both the cast, which included Richard Cromwell, Arline Judge and Lucien Littlefield, and the story were praised by *Film Daily*, but the *Times* did not review it.

On a "B" level also too lowly for the *Times, Manhattan Tower* (1932), set in the Empire State Building, nevertheless boasted an excellent cast headed by Mary Brian, Irene Rich, James Hall and Hale Hamilton. In what sounds like a variation on *Skyscraper Souls,* a scheming financier involves a whole assortment of victims in a stock market crash. It also included two love stories, one among the bosses, one among the workers.

First National offered the last *Grand Hotel* variant of the year in *Central Park,* for which it reassembled some of the cast of *Union Depot* (Joan Blondell, Guy Kibbee) and moved the formula outdoors. With only a few establishing shots made on location, the rest, though supposedly set entirely in Central Park, was filmed in Hollywood. Blondell and Wallace Ford are two hungry young people innocently involved with gangsters, but the climax comes when a lion escaped from the zoo invades a dinner dance in the Central Park Casino.

From Hell to Heaven (1933) takes place at a resort hotel near a race track. Jack Oakie played a sports announcer eager to become a crooner, but his is only one of half a dozen stories combining the usual ingredients of

murder, theft and adultery, all hinging on the outcome of a crucial race. When at the end Oakie actually says, "People come and people go, but nothing ever happens at the Luray Spring Hotel," surely the writers must have wished to call attention to the obvious parallel.

1933 also saw two modest "B" variations, both set in New York boardinghouses. In *Hotel Variety* a night club dancer (Olive Borden) who has witnessed a gang murder, while hiding out in a refuge of hard-hit vaudevillians, falls for a hoofer (Hal Skelly), left with his little boy. When he fails to get a promised job, his ex-wife claims the child, but meanwhile another boarder sells a scenario and hires everyone else to play in the film.

In *East of Fifth Avenue* the boarders include a pregnant show girl (Mary Carlisle), her married gambler-lover (Walter Byron), his faithless wife (Dorothy Tree) and a kindly old couple (Walter Connolly was the husband), one of whom commits suicide after the death of the other, in classic *deus ex machina* style leaving enough money to solve everyone else's problems.

A genuinely distinguished film was *Zoo in Budapest* (1933), Jesse Lasky's first production for Fox. Its fairy-tale quality was emphasized in the reviews, and Rowland V. Lee's direction was even likened to F. W. Murnau's. A strange youth who virtually lives in the zoo (Gene Raymond) enjoys such uncanny rapport with the animals that (anticipating crusades of later decades) he steals women's furs and burns them. Befriending a lovely girl (Loretta Young) who is escaping from an orphanage, he takes her to hide in an unused bear cavern, where they are joined by a little runaway boy, who accidentally releases many of the animals. When they run wild and begin to fight each other, only the hero can calm them down, rescue the boy and, of course, bargain for freedom for himself and the girl.

Paramount's *International House* (1933) attempted to spoof the whole *Grand Hotel* genre. The usual all-star cast, Peggy Hopkins

Joyce (as herself), W. C. Fields, Burns and Allen, Bela Lugosi and Stuart Erwin, are all drawn to the same hotel by the announcement of an "invention which combines the best features of radio and television." Erwin comes down with measles, so all are quarantined. None of it made much sense, but it was often hilarious.

By far the most important such film of 1933, however, was that true American equivalent of *Grand Hotel,* with which it is often double-billed in classic film revivals, MGM's *Dinner at Eight,* in which George Cukor brought the Kaufman-Ferber stage hit of 1932 to unforgettably vivid life with the most glittering cast ever assembled.[1] Beery and the Barrymore brothers were reunited, but instead of Garbo and Crawford, who would not have fitted any of the women's roles, there are Marie Dressler and Jean Harlow, who most brilliantly did. Besides these five major stars, or six, if one adds Lee Tracy, eight other well-known players lent strong support: Edmund Lowe, Billie Burke, Madge Evans, Jean Hersholt, Karen Morley, Louise Closser Hale, Phillips Holmes and May Robson. From the opening credits, in which the cast is introduced visually, each famous face framed by the rim of a plate and silver service set for dinner, until Dressler's priceless closing line to Harlow, *Dinner at Eight* pulses with pace, energy and sharpness of characterization undimmed by nearly fifty years.

The continually mounting dramatic crises, the sardonic sting of the dialogue and the keen insights into such then timely phenomena as a silent star ruined by talkies and an old family firm going under in the Depression vigorously recall Broadway of the '30s, when even

[1] Although the *Bluebook of Hollywood Musicals* lists two songs written for *Dinner at Eight,* a title number and "Don't Blame Me," neither is played in the film as now shown. "I Kiss Your Little Hand, Madame" is heard with the credits, and, as the dinner guests assemble, on-screen musicians hired by Millicent play a few standards like "There's Danger in Your Eyes, Cherie," but otherwise the film uses *no* background music.

frankly commercial plays could bite sizable chunks out of the American hide. Unlike the characters in *Grand Hotel,* the only ones in the least sympathetic are the silently suffering Oliver Jordan (Lionel Barrymore), head of a declining shipping company and victim of heart disease, and Lucy Talbot (Karen Morley), the patient wife of a philandering doctor (Edmund Lowe). The others are quite ready to claw each other to bits, if necessary, in their ruthless drive toward their particular sexual, social and financial goals.

The connecting thread is the dinner of the title, to which Jordan's social butterfly wife Millicent (Billie Burke) has for various reasons invited all the others, to meet Lord and Lady Ferncliffe. Thus, unlike most films of this genre, it moves freely through several different milieux over a period of days. Revival theater audiences still savor the flair with which Dressler, cast against type, carries off the imperious theatrical *grande dame,* Carlotta Vance; they roar with laughter at the raucous cat-and-dog battles between Beery and Harlow as Dan and Kitty Packard, the vulgar tycoon who is taking over Jordan's business and his brassy, two-timing second wife, and they are moved by the quiet dignity with which alcoholic ex-film idol Larry Renault (John Barrymore, as if foreshadowing his own future), his last self-deluding vanity stripped away, arranges his suicide so that whoever finds him will first see the once-famous profile. They also burst into applause at Millicent Jordan's hysterical tirade in which she dismisses the genuinely serious problems of her husband and daughter (Madge Evans) as trifles compared to the threatened ruin of her dinner party. Just as with *The Women,* the film is totally right, definitive and part of its own time. As the *Times* comments whenever it is scheduled for TV: "Still the best meal in town."

1934 saw, if no falling off of the *Grand Hotel* cycle, a trend to move the action to ships, trains or buses, as will be detailed in the next chapter. Among the few that stayed in the same place was *Wonder Bar,* in which the

Grant Mitchell, Louise Closser Hale, Jean Harlow, Wallace Beery, Edmund Lowe, Karen Morley, Billie Burke in **Dinner at Eight**

all-star cast were all either entertainers, employees or patrons in a lavish Montmartre night club, but this is obviously a backstage musical.

At the opposite end of the social scale was *Heat Lightning* (1934), which directly anticipated both *The Petrified Forest* and *Bus Stop*. As the owner of an isolated gas station and cafe in a Western desert, Aline MacMahon finds among those passing through an evil ex-lover (Preston Foster) whom she must kill to protect her sister (Ann Dvorak). *Helldorado* (1935) used a somewhat similar setting. Motorists and hitchhikers trapped by a cloudburst take refuge in a ghost town, where a half-mad prospector actually finds gold.

Another 1935 entry, *Four Hours to Kill*, based on Norman Krasna's Broadway success *Small Miracle*, turned the familiar formula

into a tense melodrama set in the lounge of "the West 43rd Street Theatre" during the performance and between the acts of a play. Among the customary assortment are the checkroom boy (Joe Morrison), his filing clerk sweetheart (Helen Mack), the usherette (Dorothy Tree), who is trying to blackmail him for "an operation," a cheating wife (Gertrude Michael) and her lover (Ray Milland), but the drama centers on a convict (Richard Barthelmess) manacled to a detective (Charles Wilson) and on his way to be hanged—who at the crucial moment breaks loose and sets a trap for the man responsible for his death sentence.

Since by the mid-'30s the *Grand Hotel* pattern was hardly a novelty, most films that used it at all had some other, ostensibly more serious purpose in mind than mere melodrama.

Thus *The Petrified Forest* (1936), *Dead End* (1937) and *Idiot's Delight* (1939) will be discussed elsewhere.

But the *Grand Hotel* formula was not dead yet, even though a dismal 1945 remake, *Weekend at the Waldorf,* with Grusinskaya turned into a bored movie star (Ginger Rogers) and the Kringelein character transformed to a doomed war hero (Van Johnson), might have seemed enough to bury it forever. When well written, sustained by crisp dialogue and good performances, the formula continued to produce some solidly engrossing films, some even embracing whole communities (e.g., *Kings Row,* 1942, *Peyton Place,* 1957, and *Nashville,* 1976), as well as such entertaining variations as *Separate Tables* (1958), *The*

VIP's (1963) and *Hotel* (1967), whose cast in the classic tradition actually included a jewel thief.

In the 1970s the cross-section-of-humanity pattern took a decidedly macabre turn in the rash of disaster films (the four *Airport* pictures, *Earthquake, The Towering Inferno, The Poseidon Adventure, Juggernaut,* etc.), and, in a lighter vein, such all-star mysteries as *Murder on the Orient Express, Murder by Death* and *Death on the Nile.* Though set mainly in a hotel, *California Suite* (1978) does not count, since the four sets of characters never meet. Perhaps closest to the true formula is *When You Comin' Back, Red Ryder?* (1979), which is essentially a variation on *The Petrified Forest.*

9

"HURTLING THROUGH THE NIGHT"
<u>Grand Hotel</u> in Transit

To enterprising writers in search of new twists on an already familiar pattern, it presently occurred that if a hotel, park, depot or hospital could serve as an effective crucible for juxtaposing the lives of people who might otherwise never have met, even more dramatic pressure might be applied by confining them to some means of public transportation from which there was no possible escape. Granted, they might maintain a certain amount of privacy aboard an ocean liner, but how long could they avoid each other on a train, a bus or a 1930s passenger plane? Thus, along with all the stationary versions of *Grand Hotel,* the decade saw numerous oth-

ers set afloat, aloft or aboard some moving vehicle. The very first cross-sectional film of 1931, antedating even *Street Scene,* was Fox's *Transatlantic*—which, said the *Times,* had almost as many plots as the ship had officers.

In one of them, Myrna Loy, for a change, played an unhappy wife, in danger of losing her banker husband, John Halliday, to dancer Greta Nissen; in another a gambler (Edmund Lowe) shoots it out in the engine room with four desperadoes who stole some securities from the banker, but not before he has wooed the daughter (Lois Moran) of an elderly lens grinder (Jean Hersholt) making his first trip to Europe. The banker's murder adds a note of mystery, though not enough to class this as a pure mystery film. All these plot elements: marital triangles, thefts, frustrated romances, murder, recurred, as we have seen, again and again in the *Grand Hotel* variants.

The next seagoing version was *Luxury Liner* (1933), which incidentally provides further evidence of a rather surprising trend: the popularity of German subjects and characters in the few years from the late silent era (e.g., *Four Sons*) through the early '30s (*All Quiet on the Western Front, Grand Hotel, The Man I Killed*) until Hitler came to power—as it happened, later in the very month *Luxury Liner* was released.

George Brent played a doctor (German, like all the other characters) who at the last minute comes aboard a liner leaving Hamburg for New York, to overtake his wife (Vivienne Osborne) and her lover (Frank Morgan), another of those ruthless millionaires. The passenger list also includes a pert little gold digger (Alice White) and a once rich man (C. Aubrey Smith) ruined by others who saves a number of third-class passengers from buying worthless stock. When the millionaire turns his interest to an opera singer (Verree Teasdale), he is eventually murdered. Despite the period and setting, this was evidently no *Ship of Fools*.

Directly anticipating the 1970s' disaster films, especially *Juggernaut, Infernal Machine* (1933) centered on an ocean liner threatened by a bomb timed to go off at midnight. A young stowaway (Chester Morris) falsely confesses to being the terrorist, and as his price for saving the ship demands an hour alone with the girl he loves (Genevieve Tobin). Just as in de Maupassant's *Boule de Suif*, all the respectable passengers vie with each other in urging the girl to sacrifice her "honor" for their safety—though it turns out not to be necessary, after all.

Transatlantic Merry Go Round (1934) was described by Frank Nugent in the *Times* as "a blend of *Grand Hotel* and *42nd Street*, to which have been added dashes of Wheeler

and Woolsey, Philo Vance and Janet Gaynor . . . but that does not prevent it from going down with the cinema public as a smooth and zestful screen cocktail."

Less melodramatic than *Wonder Bar,* the only other musical to attempt this formula, "the story defies synopsis," Nugent admitted, but it involved ship's entertainers Jack Benny and Nancy Carroll, a handsome thief (Gene Raymond), the usual erring wife (Shirley Grey) and pursuing husband (Ralph Morgan), an escaped convict as a stowaway, a vacationing detective and two crooked gamblers with a sinister hold over Carroll's kid brother. Long before 1934, any experienced movie-goer could have taken it from there, but the musical and comedy numbers (including one in which Carroll and Benny burlesqued Garbo and Barrymore in *Grand Hotel* (as Marion Davies and Jimmy Durante had done in *Blondie of the Follies*) kept the audience amused.

That was more than could be said for *The Captain Hates the Sea* (1934), which had the misfortune to open in New York just four weeks later, with essentially the same format. As an alcoholic, John Gilbert made one of his last vain attempts at a comeback, but only Walter Connolly as the irascible captain got good notices. The by now thoroughly predictable human cargo included Fred Keating and Helen Vinson as a bond thief and his girl, Victor McLaglen as a private detective who falls for Vinson while trailing the bonds, Wynne Gibson as a woman with a past and John Wray as her husband who can't forget it. Said the *Times,* with rare understatement: "Something seems to have gone agley."

As usual, MGM topped the field, with a slam-bang melodrama, *China Seas* (1935), a kind of seagoing *Shanghai Express,* which surely must rank as the nearest nautical equivalent of *Grand Hotel* and *Dinner at Eight.* The stars were that proven sure-fire combination, Gable and Harlow (the latter, as noted in Chapter 1, in one of her best hard-boiled hussy roles), but they were strongly supported by Wallace Beery, Lewis

Stone, Rosalind Russell, Dudley Digges, C. Aubrey Smith and Robert Benchley.

Embittered by captain Gable's attentions to British aristocrat Russell, China Doll (Harlow) turns to Beery, realizing too late that he is in league with pirates bent on seizing the ship. Some of the scenes, such as coolies being crushed by a careening steam roller during a storm and Gable and Stone being tortured by the pirates, were regarded as excessively brutal.

As *Grand Hotel* pictures in general began to fade out, so did the maritime species, though *Till We Meet Again* (1938), a misguided remake of *One Way Passage,* almost expanded that simple love story into a conventional ship-wide panorama. The last such film to appear during the decade was *Pacific Liner* (1939), in which a ship was threatened

by cholera. The cast included Victor McLaglen, Chester Morris, Wendy Barrie, Alan Hale and Barry Fitzgerald, but the *Times* dismissed it as "a story calculated to make Conrad shudder in his grave, to turn O'Neill green, but not with envy, to give Masefield something more painful than *mal de mer.*"

As the great ocean-spanning *Queens* whose majestic bulk once spelled to travelers everywhere the ultimate in luxurious escape are now retired as cruise ships or museums, so the once famous crack express trains have been rendered equally obsolete, except to nostalgia buffs, by the supremacy of air travel. But in the '30s their names: the Twentieth Century, the Wolverine, the Empire State, and especially those crisscrossing Europe: the Blue Train, the Golden Arrow, the Orient Express, still cast their own

Wallace Beery and Clark Gable in China Seas

peculiar magic, as film-makers were well aware. This was the inviting ambiance so delightfully recaptured in *Murder on the Orient Express* (1974).

"Hurtling through the night . . ." the newspaper ads and "coming attraction" trailers would proclaim, "laden with romance . . . adventure . . . mystery . . . intrigue . ." Usually they were hurtling from Budapest to Bucharest by way of Belgrade, or other faraway places with strange-sounding names equally unfamiliar to most Americans. One advantage the train films had over those set on ships was that the writers (and the audience) were not necessarily limited to those passengers who came on board in the opening scenes. Every stop (and even expresses sometimes made unscheduled stops) could bring significant additions to or subtractions from the human equation that could change the whole outcome.

Oddly enough, the first such film was a Russian one, *China Express* (1930), quite evidently the inspiration for von Sternberg's much more famous *Shanghai Express* (1932). In the latter film, Dietrich's conflict with a missionary has already been discussed, but the train also carries a full complement of other, mostly expatriate, characters on its frequently interrupted journey from Peiping to Shanghai: the British army surgeon (Clive Brook) who is Shanghai Lily's one true love, a fussy old lady (Louise Closser Hale) and her dog, an American gambler (Eugene Pallette), a Chinese "girl of the town" (Anna May Wong) and a sinister Eurasian (Warner Oland) who turns out to be not only a revolutionary general, but a sadistic villain as well. The vivid local color (all painstakingly created in Hollywood), the constant movement and dramatic twists make *Shanghai Express* a deserved favorite at revival theaters—by far the best of the Dietrich-von Sternberg collaborations.

A British production, *Rome Express* (1933), was the first follow-up, in what was soon to become a flourishing cycle, but the next American entry was *The Silk Express*

(1933), which takes place aboard a train bound from Seattle to New York, carrying three million dollars' worth of silk—enough for the hero (Neil Hamilton) to break an attempted price monopoly by an evil speculator (Arthur Hohl). Just as the special train is about to pull out, a girl (Sheila Terry) and her father (Dudley Digges) beg to be taken aboard so that the old man can get prompt medical attention in New York: as the only woman in the cast, however, Terry was hardly competition for Dietrich.

India provided the colorful backdrop for *Bombay Mail* (1934), titled after a train bound from Calcutta, a thirty-six-hour run first disturbed by the murder of a high-ranking British official. A maharaja is also killed, and someone else bitten by a cobra before the inspector (Edmund Lowe) clears things up. *Orient Express* (1934)—based on one of Graham Greene's early "entertainments" —bound from Ostend to Constantinople, bore the usual motley passenger list: an ambitious dancer (Heather Angel), a youthful date merchant (Norman Foster), a vulgar Cockney couple (Herbert Mundin and Una O'Connor), a sneak thief (Roy D'Arcy) who looks like a diplomat and an anarchist (Ralph Morgan) who sounds like a family doctor. The *Times* found the script an ineffective patchwork, with too much evidence of rewriting.

Despite a good cast headed by Mary Astor and Ricardo Cortez, *I Am a Thief* (1935) inspired a rueful essay by Nugent of the *Times,* on the fatal easiness of mounting a melodrama on railroad tracks.

A shot of clicking wheels or of a train passing through a tunnel conveys a sense of action even when the story does not . . . There is more than a suspicion that its present name was selected only after the discovery that the stock of "express" titles had run out.

Movie-makers are convinced that the trains of Central Europe carry a few bona fide passengers but derive their chief revenue from the transport of international jewel thieves, their potential victims and secret police agents; that sinister men and women are always prowling through compartments and leering into the camera with-

Anna May Wong and Marlene Dietrich in **Shanghai Express**

out any one ever noticing, and that the conductors never bother about tickets, but just poke about in the corridors, looking for murdered passengers.

As a matter of fact, there were no more train pictures for the next few years, at least none of the international kind. Even *Film Daily* was not much impressed with *Streamline Express* (1935), in which a streamlined train on an inaugural cross-country run is the scene of the birth of twins, the disentangling of a triangle and, in what seems a faint echo of *Twentieth Century* (1934), the efforts of a

producer (Victor Jory) to recapture his star (Evelyn Venable). *Florida Special* (1936), from a Clarence Budington Kelland story, *Recreation Car,* was a routine mystery involving the usual jewel thieves, an elderly millionaire (Claude Gillingwater), a brash reporter (Jack Oakie) and other familiar types.

The next notable example was *Last Train from Madrid* (1937), dismissed by the *Times* as "a glib little fiction built along the lines of *Grand Hotel*," yet its attempt to deal, however inadequately, with the then raging Spanish Civil War would seem to rate it a place among those films which at least tried to use the *Grand Hotel* formula for more than pure escapist entertainment.

What gave the obviously moribund train cycle a whole new lease on life was, of course, *The Lady Vanishes* (1938), the immensely successful British classic that led to Hitchcock's American career and remains a dazzling example of the tongue-in-cheek spy thriller, rivaled only by Carol Reed's *Night Train* (1940), also British. The only remaining American example of the decade, *Exile Express* (1939), though it also involved espionage, did not fare as well, in spite of the presence of the talented Anna Sten and a cast of nearly twenty recognizable character players. The plot involved a secret poison gas formula, a spy ring, an innocent dupe and a dashing newspaperman.

Despite a number of wartime films, mostly comedies, with scenes aboard overcrowded trains in cramped or unwillingly shared accommodations, once the war was over, the train picture as such ground to a permanent halt, as did most trains, except for commuter lines, in American life. The two rival means of transport, buses and planes, that were to displace both ships and trains forever were in the '30s still in their infancy. Artistically, one remained there. The increasing availability of long-range, especially transcontinental, bus lines must indeed have been a boon to Depression-stricken travelers, a trend which was duly reflected by three films released early in 1934—but, cinematically, two of them never left the terminal.

Fugitive Lovers saw Robert Montgomery and Madge Evans in the title roles in a comedy-drama involving an escaped convict fleeing across the country by bus. In *Cross Country Cruise* Lew Ayres, a playboy, solves a disappearance among the passengers when he discover that two-timing Alan Dinehart has murdered his wife (Minna Gombell) and placed her body among the bridge-playing dummies in a department store window.

The most famous picture involving a bus,

It Happened One Night, does not belong here since it is entirely concerned with the romance of the heiress and the reporter, not with the lives of the other passengers, and most of the best scenes do not take place on the bus. In more recent decades this still flourishing means of travel has been reflected only in such occasional films as *Bus Stop* (1956), *The Wayward Bus* (1957) and *The Big Bus* (1976).

Ever since silents, aviation had been a natural subject for films, but despite many in the early '30s about World War I aces, army and navy flyers, stunt, test and mail pilots, parachute jumpers, barnstormers and other daredevil pioneer figures, commercial passenger travel was for the vast majority of Americans still such an extremely rare, expensive and daring venture that no one even thought of applying the *Grand Hotel* formula to a plane until in 1936 Paramount began to make a film originally called *Twenty Hours by Air,* about a coast-to-coast flight, which then had to be made in several jumps and stages. During production, the flying time was at least theoretically cut so that the picture was released as *Thirteen Hours by Air.*

United Airlines, which had co-operated with the studio in all technical details, may well have had second thoughts, for the particular flight dramatized included every possible crisis, even a forced landing in a blizzard (thereby scooping *Airport* by thirty-four years). A number of standard characters reappeared: a criminal trio who have just committed a huge gem theft, a mysterious count (Fred Keating) who offers the pilot (Fred MacMurray) $5,000 to land short of San Francisco, an obnoxious brat (Bennie Bartlett) who proves an unexpected help.

This was followed a few days later by MGM's *Absolute Quiet,* in which a plane full of friends and enemies tries to make a forced landing at the private air strip of a recluse financier (Lionel Atwill), but is compelled by crooks who have taken control to crack up instead. Inside the house, the passengers, too,

Joan Bennett and Fred MacMurray in **Thirteen Hours by Air**

crack up under the emotional stress of all the crisscrossed relationships revealed.

Warners' *Fugitive in the Sky* (1937) seemed to the *Times* a direct steal from *Thirteen Hours by Air,* but it had the distinction of presenting the first film hijacking, when a wanted killer takes over control of the plane until it is forced down by a dust storm. The most famous hijacking in screen history was first seen a little later in 1937: the kidnapping of the passengers hand-picked for Shangri-La in *Lost Horizon,* which clearly belongs among film fantasies.

Two other films with planes full of assorted passengers (both to be discussed elsewhere) involved crashes or forced landings in the tropics. *Sinners in Paradise* revived the timeworn *Admirable Crichton* situation, while *Five Came Back* posed the more serious question of who will be allowed to survive if not all can.

It was perhaps inevitable that all six films about passenger planes involved crashes or forced landings, and that most of the action in three of them took place on the ground. Because '30s planes could hold few people by today's standards and stay aloft for only relatively short periods of time, even the most ingenious writers could not possibly draw out the mechanical suspense as excruciatingly or with such variety of reaction as in the later

The High and the Mighty (1954), *Airport* (1970), *Airport 1975* (1974), *Airport '77* (1977) and *The Concorde—Airport '79* (1979).

Yet of all the *Grand Hotel*-in-motion films of the 1930s, the one critically most admired, the one undisputed classic, depends not on any power-driven mechanism but on a simple horse-drawn vehicle—John Ford's *Stagecoach* (1939), which not only restored the threadbare pattern to brilliant life but is regarded by many as the finest Western ever made.

10

"YOU KNOW WHAT HAPPENS TO THOSE WHO FAIL..."
Espionage, Mostly World War I

To audiences of later decades, the term "spy film" may well conjure up the lurid exploits of Agent 007, complete with supervillains bent on world domination, comic-strip death devices and an endless succession of invitingly named beauties as disposable as Kleenex. Or, at the opposite extreme, the phrase may suggest the tired, gray world of John Le Carre and Graham Greene, where there is no choice morally between the two sides of the Cold War, everyone is expendable and the most unspeakable betrayals may be committed by a man's own superiors.

In the '30s, both these milieux, one so flamboyantly overcolored, the other so relentlessly drab, would have been equally disconcerting to espionage fans. As noted, the better ocean liners and especially the best European express trains often carried, besides

their quota of jewel thieves, ladies with a past, fleeing extramarital lovers and absconding embezzlers, one or more mysterious agents of unnamed foreign powers who, without necessarily affecting the plot, deepened the general fog of mystification.

But in most '30s films espionage meant not so much a sinister fact of contemporary international politics as an exciting, often romantic battle of wits, set in the past, most often during World War I, in Paris, London or especially Vienna, amid embassy balls, high-level staff conferences, midnight suppers in elegant hotel suites and coded messages slipped to the waiter during rendezvous in quaint Old World cafes or beer gardens. Sooner or later, hero and heroine would be shocked to discover that they were, alas, spying for opposite sides, and the stage would be set for the inevitable conflict between love and duty.

To deal with the least typical examples first, Gary Cooper, whether by coincidence or choice, co-starred in two of the three '30s spy films set in the American Civil War, all in the romantic nineteenth-century tradition of *Shenandoah,* in which no issues were raised, both blue and gray were portrayed with equal gallantry and the peculiar anguish of brother-against-brother struggles was stressed.

In *Only the Brave* (1930) Cooper played a Union soldier who, finding his sweetheart in the arms of another man, volunteers for a suicidal spy mission that involves letting himself be caught behind Confederate lines with false plans to mislead the enemy. A Southern belle (Mary Brian) falls for him, but not even she can save him from the firing squad, until in the nick of time Union troops arrive —a fairly simple-minded plot even in 1930.

Between Cooper's two stints, RKO resurrected William Gillette's 1895 melodrama *Secret Service* (1931), with Richard Dix as a Union spy posing as a Confederate officer in besieged Richmond. Put in a position to telegraph false orders that will divert a Southern battalion, he is torn by his love for a local belle (Shirley Grey). The *Times* called it "good enough . . . to fill that gap between the vaudeville and the newsreels."

In *Operator 13* (1934), one of Marion Davies' better costume films, based on a Robert W. Chambers novel, and given a Grade A MGM production, Cooper returned to the fray, this time as a Confederate captain in intelligence who penetrates the successive disguises of a Northern actress spying for the Union—but she saves his life, and after the war they are "no longer enemies."

The first '30s espionage film involving World War I was Paramount's *Young Eagles* (1930), in which William A. Wellman again directed Charles "Buddy" Rogers, as he had done in *Wings,* in a bizarre tale that mixed flying with spying. Rogers and his sidekick, Stuart Erwin, are set up by their superiors in an elaborate plot in which they are apparently duped by a German spy (Paul Lukas), who escapes with his accomplice (Jean Arthur). The girl turns out to be a double agent, merely using the German to get behind enemy lines.[1] Surprisingly, her dresses and those of other women in a party scene in Paris are authentic to the war period—most unusual in 1930.

Far more typical was *Inside the Lines* (1930), from a play by Earl Derr Biggers (the author of the Charlie Chan stories), set in the novel background of Gibraltar, where an English girl (Betty Compson) encounters a German (Ralph Forbes) whom she had loved just before the war. Each suspects the other of being a German agent bent on destroying the British fleet, until it turns out that both are in His Majesty's service. Thus did the writer avoid one cliché only to fall into another.

Released a few weeks later, *This Mad World* took itself far more seriously. A French spy (Basil Rathbone) born in Alsace returns by plane to his home behind the lines, where he is recognized by a German general's wife (Kay Johnson). They fall in love, but duty wins out; she reports him as a spy, then shoots herself, while he is taken off presumably to be executed.

In a more popular vein was another 1930 film, *Three Faces East,* the first talking version of a 1918 melodrama that had been made as a silent by Jetta Goudal in 1926 and would be remade by Margaret Lindsay in 1940 as *British Intelligence.* Erich von Stroheim not only took top billing over Constance Bennett, then at her height, but drew all the good notices as the head of a German spy ring in London who just happens to be the butler for "Sir Winston Chamberlain, First Lord of the Admiralty." Bennett is a British agent, double, triple or possibly quadruple, with more layers to her identity than an onion, so that at any given moment it is impossible to

---

[1] Somewhat similar was Fox's *Body and Soul* (1931), in which Elissa Landi is suspected of being a spy who has caused aviators' deaths, but Myrna Loy is the real culprit.

be sure who is deceiving whom. One unique feature: she does not fall in love with the enemy agent.

1931 saw even higher casualty rates among cinematic spies. In *Dishonored* Dietrich was a Viennese streetwalker who as X 27 makes a most efficient spy, until she falls for a Russian agent (Victor McLaglen) and is executed for letting him escape. In *The Spy* Neil Hamilton as an exiled noble returns to Russia to visit his wife (Kay Johnson again) and child and also kill the head of the Cheka secret police, but finds his wife is involved

Marlene Dietrich and Warner Oland
in Dishonored

with a spy for the system, with tragic results for all.

More directly in the mainstream was *A Woman of Experience,* based on a play called *The Registered Woman,* set in wartime Vienna, where Helen Twelvetrees, a girl with a past like Dietrich's in *Dishonored,* seeks to redeem herself by volunteering as a spy. While trapping a treacherous officer (Lew Cody) she is wounded, after having fallen for a naval officer (William Bakewell). When he wants to marry her, his mother (Nance O'Neil) objects, but the girl's service to the crown, recognized by Franz Josef himself, plus the fact that her wound leaves her only six months to live, allows for the marriage, if not a happy ending.

Men of the Sky, originally planned as a musical by Jerome Kern and Otto Harbach, but apparently abandoned as such, dealt with a brave French girl (Irene Delroy) who plays the piano as a signal to an aviator to come and steal secret plans while she diverts a German officer. Both lovers are executed. The only lighter note of the year was sounded in *The Gay Diplomat,* written by Benn W. Levy, in which Russian captain Ivan Lebedeff meets two beautiful spies, Genevieve Tobin and Betty Compson (no doubt profiting by her experience in *Inside the Lines*), *one* of whom proves to be innocent.

The very first film to be reviewed by the *Times* in 1932 was Garbo's *Mata Hari,* co-starring Ramon Novarro, with Lionel Barrymore, Lewis Stone, Karen Morley and a strong supporting cast. Released nearly a year after *Dishonored,* this was surely meant to prove that anything Dietrich could do, Garbo (who had already played a spy in the silent *Mysterious Lady*) could do better, including facing a firing squad.

In this fanciful version of the historic spy case, the exotic Javanese-born dancer, directed by the head German spy in Paris (Stone), becomes the mistress of a Russian general (Barrymore), but falls in love with his young lieutenant (Novarro), who is blinded when shot down in a plane, so does not know when she is arrested as a spy. Rather than have him testify at her trial and learn the whole truth, she pleads guilty. Even when he is brought to visit her in prison, he thinks it is a hospital.

Despite the praise of contemporary critics, this is one Garbo film that does *not* hold up well. As in *Dishonored,* not the slightest attempt is made to suggest the actual period; Garbo wears superglamorous, strictly 1932 Adrian creations throughout. More seriously, Novarro was a weak leading man, and much of the dialogue now sounds ludicrous, as when Stone, calmly looking down at a courtyard where Karen Morley, Garbo's predecessor, is being executed, mutters, "So much for Carlotta."

But not, alas, "So much for spy pictures." On and on they went, with only an occasional attempt at something different. One such effort, in several ways unique, was Barbara Stanwyck's *Ever in My Heart* (1933), which her biographer, Ella Smith, regards as "her first chance to play tragedy—with hauntingly beautiful results." In 1909 a New England girl falls in love with a German (Otto Kruger), to the strains of "Du, du, liegst mir in Herzen," which is used for emotional effect throughout. Happily married, they are drawn even closer by the death of their only child, but with the outbreak of the war and especially the sinking of the *Lusitania* anti-German hysteria sweeps the country. The husband loses his job, their friends turn against them, even their dachshund is stoned to death. To spare his wife further suffering, he returns to fight for his own country.

A year later, working at a canteen in France, she discovers him as a spy. Though she saves him from exposure, after a last night together she quietly, without telling him, poisons their wine, so that they die together. Among other distinctions, this seems to be the only picture ever to dramatize a subject most Americans would rather forget, the extremes of anti-German fury during World War I.

Unfortunately it was to remain unique.

Ramon Novarro and Greta Garbo in **Mata Hari**

Less than a month later, Constance Bennett and Gilbert Roland in *After Tonight* were going through the same old love versus duty routine, she as a Russian spy, he as an Austrian captain in Vienna (where else?) who must trap the woman he loves—though the tone of the reviews does not suggest an unhappy ending. Likewise in *Madame Spy* (1934) Fay Wray was a Russian agent spying on her German husband (Nils Asther) in wartime Austria, but she escapes execution by crawling through no man's land to the Russian lines. Nevertheless, the *Times* praised Karl Freund's direction and the authenticity with which the espionage was managed.

1934 also saw Myrna Loy in *Stamboul Quest,* one of several films based on the career of the successful German spy known as "Fräu-

Barbara Stanwyck and Otto Kruger in **Ever in My Heart**

lein Doktor." Beginning and ending in a sanatorium where she is confined after a mental breakdown induced by the belief that she caused the death of the man she loved, the story traces her operations in Istanbul in 1915, with George Brent as an American whose country was still neutral. The *Times* praised it for "a good story and a better cast . . . the heroine is not torn between love for her country and unwillingness to betray her lover. There is conflict, of course, but happily it does not center in the traditional dilemma of the traditional cinema Mata Hari."

Also hailed as superior was *British Agent* (1934), based on R. H. Bruce Lockhart's account of his role as England's unofficial emissary to the Russian revolutionary government in 1917. Anticipating *The Spy Who Came in from the Cold,* the story has the hero (Leslie Howard) betrayed by his own government and his life jeopardized for the sake of diplomatic appearances. One critic's complaint was that a romance with a Russian spy for the Cheka (Kay Francis) distracted too much attention from the genuinely dramatic efforts to persuade the Bolsheviks not to sign a separate peace with Germany. Finally he joins the counterrevolutionaries and barely escapes with his life.

For later generations the political assumptions may seem far more dubious, as Everson noted at a 1960s screening:

It's rather difficult to have too much sympathy for the British agent—or his American cohorts—who are clearly . . . diverting another nation's affairs for reasons of their own country's politics. The underhanded tricks that Leslie Howard and Co. get up are the kind of things that we are now told only those sneaky Communists perpetrate.

The first American spy film with a sense of humor was MGM's *Rendezvous* (1935), set in Washington in 1917, with William Powell as a cryptographer and Rosalind Russell in her first leading role as a scatterbrained society girl (another variation on the madcap heiress?) whose efforts to be helpful almost lead to the triumph of the German spy ring, led by Cesar Romero and Binnie Barnes.

One might have hoped that by now the classic romance of the two lovers on opposite sides had been laid to rest, but Paramount gave it one more go-round in a rather pleasing example titled *Till We Meet Again* (1936). Herbert Marshall played a British actor and Gertrude Michael a German actress who fall in love in London in 1914, just before the war, then later find themselves playing the usual cat-and-mouse game for their respective countries until, in a fairly novel twist, they decide with the connivance of her superior (that familiar master spy, Lionel Atwill) to chuck their duties and elope to neutral Holland. One other noteworthy feature of *Till We Meet Again* was that the period atmosphere of 1914–17 was precise and accurate throughout.

The last American spy melodrama of the decade to be set in World War I, and rated one of the best, was *Lancer Spy* (1937), Gregory Ratoff's debut as a director. A British officer (George Sanders) is called upon to impersonate a German nobleman prisoner and take over his life. Despite a Keystone Kops

***Rosalind Russell and William Powell*
in** Rendezvous

chase in which he escapes over the Swiss border, the cast, including Dolores Del Rio, Sig Rumann and Joseph Schildkraut, gave top-notch performances.

More than four decades and several wars later, the '30s spy films seem not only romantic but rather charmingly innocent in ways no spy story can ever be again. Even when they ended unhappily, as a surprising number of them did, this was always the heroine's own decision in deliberately choosing love over duty (as in *Dishonored* and *Mata Hari*), or, if necessary, sacrificing both lives (as in *This Mad World* and *Ever in My Heart*).

Considering the ambiguous role of Russia in the war and the remoteness of its front and its interests from those of the other Allies, it is also surprising in how many cases (five by actual count) one of the spy-crossed lovers was Russian. But one thing these films definitely were not was political, chauvinistic or in any way slanted in favor of what had, after all, been "our" side. Indeed, the most sympathetic heroines (those played by Garbo, Dietrich, Loy, Twelvetrees and Michael) were all spying for the Germans or Austrians. In fact, these often beguiling tales of lovelorn spies in World War I were at worst better than most of those that attempted to tackle espionage in the contemporary world.

The presidential year 1932 had seen an unusual number of films, most set in Washington, sharply critical or satirical of American politics. A variation on these was a muddled melodrama of Washington, *Man About Town,* with Warner Baxter—the first spy film set in modern America.

Others followed on the same undistinguished level: *Marie Galante* (1934) was about spies in the Panama Canal Zone trying to blow up the fleet; in *Murder in the Fleet* (1935) the same sort of agents were after a new electric firing device; in *Mystery Woman* (1935) a wife clears her husband, wrongfully sent to Devil's Island for supposed espionage; *The House of 1000 Candles* (1936) centered on a crucial document that could preserve world peace if it reached Geneva in time; in *Crack Up* (1937) spies were seeking the design of a giant plane; in *Espionage* (1937), despite the title, a munitions magnate pursued across Europe by various agents proves a harmless fellow, after all; in *The Spy Ring* (1938) a blonde lures officers at a California army base to get her hands on "the plans"; by *Cipher Bureau* (1938) the spy ring of the unnamed foreign power was beginning to sound suspiciously Teutonic.

By 1939, as the world moved ever more clearly from a postwar into a prewar period, the tone of such American-set spy plots had begun to take on a heavily hortatory tone, as drama was sacrificed to a pot of message. Reviewing *They Made Her a Spy* ("her" being Sally Eilers), Nugent sardonically noted that it seemed an immediate response to Will Hays' current call to Hollywood for "more pictures emphasizing Americanism."

In this one the head of the spy ring is trapped in the top of the Washington Monument, where he must listen to an endlessly garrulous elevator operator who says things like "Every time I look out at Washington, I kinda get the feelin' that all this is permanent, that it's strong, that it's here to stay." When the spy jumps out the Monument window, it is less to avoid arrest, the reviewer suggested, than to escape the elevator man.

A month later, in April 1939, came *Confessions of a Nazi Spy,* in which Warner Brothers, anticipating the American Government by nearly three years, unilaterally declared its own war against Germany, and the question of propaganda was no longer a laughing matter. Though many viewers were impressed by the bold courage and timeliness of the film, based on records of actual trials of the previous year, Nugent "thought that school of villainy had gone out with *The Beast of Berlin* made back in '14." (A few years later such reservations might well have led him to be denounced as an appeaser, isolationist or America Firster.)

Edward G. Robinson played a G-man, Paul Lukas the Nazi propaganda chief in the United States and Francis Lederer the weak link in the spy network. Yet even aside from the diplomatic impropriety of a film studio attacking the incumbent government of a country with which we were not at war (nor was anyone else at the time), most Americans, once bitten by World War I tales of Hunnish atrocities later exposed as propaganda, were twice shy of being taken in again. Naïve as it may seem by hindsight, in 1939 many decent people simply could not believe that the rulers of a major European country long known for its cultural achievements could really be as evil as in fact history has proved them to be.

Even before *Confessions,* early 1939 had seen a rash of forgotten "B" films reflecting the mounting fear of sinister forces at work in this country. *Smashing the Spy Ring,* set in Washington, featured a head spy who ran a sanatorium; *Navy Secrets* was a variation on the old formula with both lovers turning out to be on the American side; *Trapped in the Sky* was "a timely espionage drama" about a foreign government's attempt to buy the plans for "a new electric plane"; in *Panama Patrol* the Canal was once again imperiled, this time by an interpreter working for the cipher bureau itself; in *Mystery Plane,* the first of the Tailspin Tommy series, the hero invents a bombing device which the villain wants to sell abroad.

These last five films, all released in January and February 1939, were not even reviewed by the *Times,* only by *Film Daily.* (This was also true of *Television Spy,* released in October, in which the hero perfects a TV system which will carry "further than the present fifty-mile limit," but the mistress of one of the backers duplicates the plans and the two sets cross waves, revealing each other.)

On a slightly higher level, Warners in *Espionage Agent* pressed so hard in its campaign against current spies, presumably German, and the need for countermeasures, that the *Times* feared it might inflame too many would-be spy catchers and set off a witch hunt. Less militantly, *Sabotage* dealt with dirty work in a plane factory which is cleared up by the doddering night watchman (Charles Grapewin) and his cronies. The last 1939 film released by a major studio to involve spies was *Nick Carter, Master Detective.*

But while Hollywood had continued to pluck too long on the same old romantic string, only to give it up for the even drearier clichés of the films just noted, the British had carried the spy film to new levels of cinematic achievement, first with the soberly realistic *I Was a Spy* (1934), then in the brilliant series of films that made Alfred Hitchcock an international name: *The Man Who Knew Too Much* (1934), *The 39 Steps* (1935), *Secret Agent* (1936), *The Woman Alone* (1937) and especially *The Lady Vanishes* (1938).

In all these, romance, if any, was strictly subordinate to breathless suspense, bizarre settings, truly sinister characters and startling twists, especially when some sudden, unnerving detail gives the game away. Who could ever forget the missing finger on the genial host in *The 39 Steps* or the high heels on the supposed nun in *The Lady Vanishes?* Not surprisingly, the first American film to embody these elements to the same high degree, still one of the best of all World War II spy films, was Hitchcock's own second Hollywood production, *Foreign Correspondent* (1940).

REMEMBRANCE OF THINGS PAST
Wistful Glances Back

11

DAYS BEYOND RECALL
Nostalgia for the Prewar Era

In a sense, all the genres discussed so far were forms of escape—but one other avenue grew ever more popular as the decade wore on: escape into the safe, unalterable past, especially into certain fondly remembered years. Still well within the memory of adults, World War I continued to haunt '30s film-makers not only in spy melodramas and antiwar pictures, but as the watershed event of the twentieth century thus far, the great divide, on the other side of which glowed a golden age of irrevocably lost innocence.

Nostalgia, not as the private yearning of each person and generation for some phase of the past, but as a public mood, consciously indulged, catered to and commercialized, seems a phenomenon peculiar to the twentieth century, but it was not invented by the 1970s; in fact, it was the '30s themselves that first tasted its painful joys and savored them to the last bittersweet pang, gazing back through ever rosier glasses at those years from the 1880s to the outbreak of the war in 1914, the period known in France as "La Belle Époque," in England loosely styled "Edwardian" and in America evoked by the equally elastic term "the Gay '90s."

As attested by countless plays, novels, memoirs and obvious social facts, in the brave new world of the '20s the first postwar reaction had been to spit squarely in the eyes of the older generation, they who had started the war and kept it going for four senseless years. Every popular writer told the bright young people what they wanted to hear: that the values they had been brought up to accept with blind faith, if indeed they had ever existed, had been blasted forever by the war. The ultimate damning epithet was "Victorian."

In Europe this rejection of the past could be wholly consistent; for Americans it was qualified by one inescapable fact: Prohibition. It was not so easy to scoff at the prewar years when they remembered that their parents, however inhibited they may have been in other ways, had at least been free to drink what, when and where they pleased, with no expensive, illegal encumbrance of bootleggers, speakeasies and bathtub gin.

With this irony ever more glaring, America was even in the '20s inclining toward a mellower view of what were already being called the Gay '90s. Thus in 1926, the same year as Thomas Beer's highly unflattering book *The Mauve Decade*, came *The Turn of the Century*, the first volume of Mark Sullivan's monumental *Our Times* series, a social history of America 1900–25, which looked back not in anger but in affection.

Even the younger generation was intrigued by the livelier, saloon-bar aspects of the old days, as witness the popularity of anthologies like *Ballads from the Dear Dead Days*, illustrated by John Held, Jr., in a style parodying nineteenth-century woodcuts like those in the *Police Gazette*. This was the taste boldly appealed to in Mae West's play *Diamond Lil* (1928) and more discreetly in the Kern-Hammerstein musical *Sweet Adeline* (1929).

But it was, of course, the 1929 crash, followed by the worst depression in history, that broke the dam and turned what had been a mild trickle of interest in the '90s into a raging flood of nostalgia, as if America had suddenly come face to face with the future and found it intolerable. What safer, cozier retreat from bread lines and ragged veterans peddling apples than the warmly remembered past, the good old sheltered days before the war?

It should be kept in mind that in 1930 not only the old and middle-aged but anyone over twenty could remember at least some of the prewar years, centuries away though they already seemed. Old family photograph albums and postcard collections revealed scenes and people that now looked to be from a different world—on the whole a kindlier, more leisurely world.

Wherever popular music was played—in the remaining vaudeville houses, at band concerts in parks, on middle-brow radio programs like the *Cities Service Concert* and the *Bayer Album of Familiar Music,* in the tabloid revues and orchestral interludes that were still featured at the largest "cathedrals of the cinema" and in those organ recitals where the audience was urged to sing the words flashed on the screen—few weeks passed without some variations on a Gay '90s medley. Thus in the *Ziegfeld Follies* of 1931 the biggest hit was a number titled "Rector's—Before Prohibition," in which Harry Richman and Ruth Etting sang songs of that era.

As the diluted "3.2" beer gave way to the real thing with Repeal, in cities all over the country couples who before Prohibition would never have entered a saloon were sitting in taverns or lounges, as they were now known, in hotel rathskellers or even in reopened beer gardens, wearing cardboard hats supplied by the management. As they happily pounded steins on checkered tablecloths, they sang from printed song sheets, rollicking choruses of songs like "After the Ball," "In the Good Old Summer Time" and "The Sidewalks of New York." (By now the women looked as unlike flappers as possible. Even before the influence of Mae West, the natural figure had returned, along with form-fitting, high-waisted, long-skirted dresses, often with puffed sleeves, and shallow-crowned hats tilted saucily over one eye—all styles reminiscent of the same beloved Gibson girl era.[1])

Even children who read the comics could not but be aware of all this continual gazing back at supposedly happier times. The nonnarrative, one-panel cartoons of Gluyas Williams, Clare Briggs and others, under recurrent titles like "Then and Now," "Born Thirty Years Too Soon," "Those Days Are Gone Forever" and "When Mother Was a Girl," constantly contrasted the old and the new in every phase of daily life.

In a bizarre and psychologically revealing episode that lasted several months, comic-strip heroine Ella Cinders, the freckled, lank-haired slavey whom Colleen Moore had played in a 1926 silent comedy, found herself trapped, perhaps for life, in a town called Deweyville, cut off as completely as one of Tarzan's lost civilizations from the outside world by an impenetrable mountain barrier. Here literally nothing had changed since 1898, and the strong-willed mayor was determined to keep it just that way. His sweetheart had been killed by an early horseless carriage, so, by deliberately isolating the town, he hoped to save it at all costs from any further inroads of "progress."

To adult readers, an American town forever 1898, where people thought a stock crash meant cattle falling off a cliff, must have anticipated the charm of Shangri-La or Brigadoon, all the more appealing because it was a return to their own childhood.

Thus when movies began turning back to those dear dead days before 1914, they were,

[1] The costumes worn by Ruby Keeler and the chorus girls in the title number of *42nd Street* (1933) perfectly illustrate this trend.

in fact, only catching up with a trend already apparent in every other popular medium. In *My Man* (1928) Fannie Brice sang "I Was a Florodora Baby," and both MGM's *Hollywood Revue of 1929* and Warners' *Show of Shows* (1929) featured elaborate Gay '90s numbers.

Then in May 1930 came the first talkie specifically devoted to the '90s. *The Florodora Girl* (which was to have been called *The Gay Nineties* and on screen is still subtitled *A Story of the Gay Nineties*) starred Marion Davies, who, contrary to the impression left by the second Mrs. Citizen Kane, was a most delightful comedienne.[2]

The Florodora Girl was not, as David Shipman asserts in *The Great Movie Stars*, "from the old musical," but a lively original screenplay by Gene Markey, about Daisy Dell, who

[2] *Florodora* was an extraordinarily popular British musical that ran over five hundred performances on Broadway (1900–2), in which the high point was a number in which six top-hatted, frock-coated gentlemen wooed six beruffled, parasoled young ladies, the famous sextette, with "Oh, Tell Me, Pretty Maiden."

The Florodora Sextette in The Florodora Girl; *Lawrence Gray and Marion Davies (far left), Ilka Chase (far right)*

after several seasons in *Florodora* finds herself the only survivor of the original sextette, the others all having landed wealthy husbands. In a cheerful variation on *Camille,* Daisy, in love with young socialite Jack Vibart (Lawrence Gray), is persuaded by his mother (Nance O'Neil) to give him up so that he can marry much-needed money—but the charm of the film (which still holds up) is in the variety of New York '90s atmosphere adroitly introduced.

Daisy not only rides on a bicycle built for two but escorts her father home from a typical saloon, enjoys a picnic at Coney Island, where many of the old songs are sung, a tally-ho ride through Central Park, a ball at the old Waldorf and a slumming party in a Bowery dive. Eventually learning the truth, Jack elbows one of the chorus boys aside to follow Daisy on stage during an encore of "Oh, Tell Me, Pretty Maiden" and fall on his knee at the right moment, so that the finale of *Florodora* also provides the happy ending of the film.

Yet in spite of the public's ever-growing appetite for all things connected with the '90s, for nearly three years after *The Florodora Girl,* except for incidental scenes (minimally suggested) in through-the-years chronicles like *Cimarron* (1931) and sagas of long-suffering mothers like *Frisco Jenny* (1933), no other full-length film made any use of this time period. Thus America was more than ready when Mae West burst in full-figured glory on the screen in *She Done Him Wrong* (1933)—a twist on a line from "Frankie and Johnny," a ballad not singable in respectable company before the war, so actually more suggestive than *Diamond Lil,* the title of West's 1928 play on which the film was based. As all the world knows, it was Mae who really brought the '90s back with a bang (or, rather, a pompadour).

From the introductory subtitle evoking the earthy joys of the '90s and Mae's famous opening line: "I'm the finest woman that ever walked the streets," *She Done Him Wrong,* written by Mae herself, was clearly meant to celebrate (with a gusto no doubt the more

Cary Grant and Mae West in She Done Him Wrong

joyous in anticipation of the New Deal and the certainty of Repeal) all the gaudier, lustier, tenderloin aspects of the decade. Doubtless drawing on her own Brooklyn childhood, Mae delivered to the worldwide movie public the same message that had delighted Broadway five years before—that to those who knew their way around, the supposedly prim Mauve Decade had been far more than "pink innocence trying to be purple passion"—had, in fact, been wide open in many ways forgotten by the '20s and '30s.

How Mae West revolutionized movie sex by kidding it, how she saved Paramount and almost singlehanded (though double-breasted) brought on the Legion of Decency—these are well-known facts of film history. Her fourth film, in mid-1934, heralded by the slogan "When Mae's good, she's very, very good, but when she's bad, she's better," was to have been called *It Ain't No Sin*. After all, Clara Bow had once been known as the "It Girl," and only the previous spring *It Happened One Night* had won great acclaim—perhaps because it was so clear that nothing *had* happened. But in a Mae West film no one could doubt what the "it" meant, so the ever-stronger forces of righteousness blew the whistle.

Since she was plying the Mississippi in this one, the title was first changed to *St. Louis Woman,* but this brought outraged protests from that pure city. *Belle of New Orleans* drew even louder shrieks from New Orleans, so the picture was finally released as *Belle of the Nineties.* As *Film Daily* observed, it might better have been called *Belle of the Nighties.*

In *Klondike Annie* (1936), however, Mae was kept literally and figuratively under wraps in the assumed identity of a Salvation Army lassie, and when in *Every Day's a Holiday* (1938) she once again returned to the decade she had made her own, her words and actions were completely hobbled by the Production Code. Though Sheilah Graham in *Film Daily* virtuously hailed it as "a better picture than *She Done Him Wrong*—and clean, which should make it a hit all around," *Photoplay* observed: "They'll all be holidays for Mae pretty soon, if this little number's any indication. Since film sex has gone subtle, she's left with little to do but walk, which isn't enough." Or as the *Times* reviewer put it: "Yesterday was not Mae Day." Nor did *My Little Chickadee* (1939) help bring her back.

Since comparatively few people remember her four films in modern dress, Mae's dazzling image remains fixed forever with the hour-glass curves, the plumed picture hat, feather boa and ruffled parasol of the '90s. Although film commentators and historians from Parker Tyler on down to Andrew Bergman, Marjorie Rosen and Molly Haskell have attempted to analyze her unique impact from every angle (or curve), even to suggesting that she did not look like a woman at all but like a female impersonator, no one has ever speculated on

how much she might have owed to the inbuilt nostalgia of her image. To adults of the '30s, here was a mature, almost matronly type who would once have been described as "a fine figure of a woman," like a sexier Lillian Russell, pompadoured, tightly corseted, in the street-sweeping skirts they remembered Mother wearing. How could anyone so reminiscent of those hallowed years of innocence possibly be offensive?

The most immediate follow-up to *She Done Him Wrong,* even to the same kind of prefatory subtitle full of words like "lusty," "rowdy" and "roistering," was *The Bowery* (1933), Darryl F. Zanuck's first production for his newly formed 20th Century studio. Display ads printed in circus poster type, illustrated with simulated woodcuts, hailed "The Bowery of Al Smith, Jimmy Walker and Irving Berlin! The bailiwick of Chuck Conners and Steve Brodie! East side, west side, all around the town and country, every one will be flocking to the sidewalks of New York to see *The Bowery!*"

The background was Bowery saloons, with bouncers giving drunks the bums' rush through the swinging doors, foaming shoopers of beer being slid across the bar, and suds wiped appreciatively from handle-bar mustaches. Fay Wray was even threatened with white slavery, as Rochelle Hudson had been in *She Done Him Wrong.* Cashing in on the success of *The Champ,* Zanuck teamed Wallace Beery as Chuck Conners and Jackie Cooper as Swipes the newsboy, with George Raft as Conners' arch-rival saloonkeeper, Steve Brodie.

Although the real Brodie had been a tall, slim newsboy who had supposedly made his famous jump from the Brooklyn Bridge in 1886, in the film it is followed very shortly by the Spanish-American War, which provides a pseudopatriotic and thoroughly feeble ending to an otherwise entertaining comedy. Without speaking a word, Pert Kelton provided the necessary dash of Mae Western spice as a saucy soubrette singing "Naughty '90s" numbers of the kind later recorded by Beatrice

Kay, including "Ta-ra-ra-boom-der-e" and "Strike Up the Band—Here Comes a Sailor."

1934 brought *The Old-Fashioned Way,* in which W. C. Fields played to the hilt an old-time ham actor leading a broken-down touring troupe in *The Drunkard,* with much scope for the by now familiar burlesque of melodrama. When in 1935 Warners belatedly filmed the 1929 Kern-Hammerstein musical *Sweet Adeline,* though Irene Dunne as the daughter of a Hoboken beer-garden owner sang the Helen Morgan numbers competently enough, the atmosphere seemed pallid, not to be compared with *The Florodora Girl* (1930), still less with the West vehicles.[3]

More successful, though hardly notable for authenticity, was Universal's *Diamond Jim* (1935), in which Edward Arnold played one of his more sympathetic tycoons, a completely sentimentalized Diamond Jim Brady opposite Binnie Barnes as Lillian Russell, with an absolute minimum of period atmosphere. At the end, rejected by his fictitious true love (Jean Arthur), he takes the glutton's way out by ordering a meal he knows will kill him.

As a kind of symbol of his era, Diamond Jim had also been glimpsed sitting in a theater box in *Broadway to Hollywood* (1933), and in *The Great Ziegfeld* (1936) he and Lillian Russell are briefly introduced as celebrities of the day at Anna Held's Broadway debut.[4] (And early 1940 brought a biographical film on Lillian Russell herself, starring Alice Faye, with Arnold repeating his characterization of Diamond Jim.) Indeed, to the otherwise uninformed movie-goer Diamond Jim must have seemed a far more important person than he had ever been in real life.

[3] '90s numbers introduced into modern backstage musicals included "The Girl at the Ironing Board" in *Dames* (1934), "I Was Born Too Late" in *George White's 1935 Scandals* and "The Girl on the Police Gazette" in *On the Avenue* (1937).

[4] Played by Charles Wilson and Ruth Gillette, they also appeared as important characters in *The Gentleman from Louisiana* (1936), based on the career of jockey Tod Sloan.

However, by far the most successful and full-bodied evocation of the atmosphere the public had by then come to associate with the prewar years was MGM's extraordinary blend of melodrama, historical spectacle and musical entertainment, *San Francisco* (1936). Just as in *She Done Him Wrong* and *The Bowery,* the opening subtitle used adjectives like "splendid and sensuous," "vulgar and magnificent," but added a more solemn, elegiac note, as if the earthquake had been visited as fit punishment upon a city whose flagrant wickedness put Sodom and Gomorrah to shame.

Like the other two films, *San Francisco* was set almost entirely in and around a music hall-saloon, this time in the heart of the Barbary Coast, with only occasional glimpses of Nob Hill. Besides all the featured songs sung by Jeanette MacDonald, everything from two new popular hits to hymns to opera, in all the cafe scenes the background sound track is constantly playing such atmospheric numbers as "After the Ball," "A Hot Time in the Old Town," "Hello! Ma Baby" and "Bill Bailey, Won't You Please Come Home?"

When on New Year's Eve 1905 Mary Blake (MacDonald), a small-town minister's daughter seeking a singing career in San Francisco, wanders into the Paradise, a notorious Barbary Coast joint owned by lovable rogue Blackie Norton (Clark Gable), he can scarcely believe her innocence, but respects it, especially under the wary eye of his lifelong best friend, Father Tim Mullin (Spencer Tracy), pastor of a nearby slum parish.

Mary is obviously such a gifted singer that she attracts the attention of a party of slumming socialites, particularly Jack Burley (Jack Holt), patron of the arts and political rival of Blackie in an upcoming election. He buys Mary's contract, and after introducing her to Maizie, his delightful old Irish mother (Jessie Ralph), a Nob Hill dowager who first came to town as a washwoman during the gold rush, he arranges for Mary's highly successful debut at the San Francisco Opera, in *Faust.*

When Blackie reluctantly agrees to marry

Clark Gable, Jack Holt, Spencer Tracy, Jeanette MacDonald in San Francisco

her, however, she returns to his place and is even ready to let him publicize her, cheaply posed in tights, as "The Colorado Nightingale," until the priest forcefully intervenes and Blackie strikes him—a stunning shocker in 1936. Resuming her operatic career in *La Traviata,* Mary seems set to marry Burley, until, on the night of the annual Chicken Ball, April 17, 1906, when all the Barbary Coast saloons compete in presenting musical numbers, she learns from Della (Margaret Irving), a Mae Westish madam who also loves Blackie, that his place has been raided and closed through Burley's influence, and tonight he has no one to represent him.

To the dismay of Burley and his society friends, Mary fills in with a very spirited rendition of "San Francisco," which will clearly win the prize, but Blackie, thinking she is patronizing him, publicly repudiates her help. Just as she is leaving, humiliated, with Burley, the chandelier overhead begins to sway and the ceiling cracks.

In the quake sequence, which lasts several minutes, the quick, terrifying images of destruction and human suffering speak so eloquently for themselves that no moral underlining is necessary. When Blackie and the priest meet, they are reconciled without a word; when he learns Mary is alive, his falling on his knees to thank God (which must be taken in the context of both 1906 and 1936) is also done with a minimum of maudlin verbalizing. Likewise, when he and Mary find each other, they embrace in silence—one reason why the scene still plays well.

Though Judy Garland's 1960s version of the title song, written for her night club act ("I never will forget how that brave Jeanette stood there in the ruins and sang"), may well have given *San Francisco* an undeserved reputation as typical '30s movie corn, the fact is that it combined in one well-knit structure (written by Anita Loos) several built-in popular appeals: attractive roles for three top stars, lavish evocation of the period, even a painless touch of spiritual uplift, and the most spectacular catastrophe the screen had yet seen.

In a sense, *San Francisco*, with its strong, dramatic story line and vigorous use of authentic Americana, anticipates the Rodgers-Hammerstein musical plays of the 1940s and 1950s, but, however well the music may reflect the mood of the scene, each number is introduced only at a time when MacDonald would actually be rehearsing or performing it, so in a sense *San Francisco* is also a spectacular backstage musical.

Although by the late 1930s the Chicago fire of 1871 could hardly have been a nostalgic memory for even the elderly, nevertheless Zanuck's *In Old Chicago* (1937) belongs here, because it is so clearly a spin-off from (if not a rip-off of) *San Francisco*. The parallels are too numerous and close to be coincidence. In both cases a historic American urban catastrophe serves as the climax of a story about a lovable rogue (here Tyrone Power) who owns a rowdy music hall-saloon involved in a love-hate conflict with a conventionally good, strait-laced type (here his brother, Don Ameche), a star performer (Alice Faye) who belts out the rousing title song, a political campaign to clean up the city's tenderloin (here called "the Patch"), and a heroic Irish washwoman (Alice Brady), who, just like old Maizie in *San Francisco*, wonders where all this wickedness will end. Even the name of her son who is killed in the disaster is the same: Jack.

But, though Power, Faye and Ameche were younger than Gable, MacDonald and Tracy, they were by no means as polished perform-

ers; the knockdown battles between the lovers are ludicrous. Even the Irish brogues sound as synthetic and forced as the idea of making the central family the O'Learys, owners of the famous cow.

20th Century-Fox showed better taste in its British-made vehicle for Gracie Fields' international film debut, *We're Going to Be Rich* (1938), which did for the music halls of Melbourne and Johannesburg "in the robustious Eighties" (to quote the *Times*) what so many other pictures had done for those of the Bowery and the Barbary Coast, with Gracie rendering such ballads as "Walter, Walter, Lead Me to the Altar" and "Don't 'Ang My 'Arry."

Perhaps most directly nostalgic of all to those then middle-aged, in 1939, after eight successful musicals as the ideally elegant young couple of the '30s, Fred Astaire and Ginger Rogers leaped gracefully aboard the ragtime band wagon in *The Story of Vernon and Irene Castle*, and, with dances supervised by Irene Castle herself, fox-trotted, tangoed and maxixed their way from 1911 to 1918, "an era," as the inevitable introductory subtitle put it, "still near enough to be warmly remembered."

Though generally successful, the above films may well have appealed most strongly to those who had grown up in large cities and remembered concert saloons, music halls and ballroom dance teams—but it must not be supposed that the gentler, more pastoral side of the prewar years recalled by millions of others, the even more idealized semirural America associated with Currier and Ives prints, radio's Seth Parker and the *Soconyland Sketches*, and strawberry festivals with Japanese lanterns strung between the trees, was forgotten—certainly not by 20th Century-Fox.

In five of Will Rogers' vehicles—*David Harum* (1934), in which he played a bachelor in an upstate New York town with a passion for trotting races, *Judge Priest* (1934), set in Kentucky in the 1900s, *The County Chairman* (1935), from a 1903 play laid in a Western town, *Steamboat Round the Bend*

(1935), set on the Mississippi, and his last film, *In Old Kentucky* (1935), from an 1894 play about horse racing—Rogers' sly country-codger maneuvers in uniting the juvenile and the ingenue were considerably enhanced by the homespun period atmosphere of various regions of the country. Indeed, Rogers became as perfect a symbol of the small-town virtues of prewar America as Mae West was of its big-city vices.

The same studio also starred Henry Fonda in *Way Down East* (1935), considered a chestnut even when filmed by Griffith in 1920, but redeemed for many viewers by its authentic re-creation of New England farm life in the 1880s. In the same year Paramount produced the definitive version of *Ruggles of Red Gap* (1935), set in 1908, in which, leading a brilliant cast of comedians, Charles

Laughton as a gentleman's gentleman won in a poker game by Charlie Ruggles becomes his own man in an American Western town and silences a saloon by reciting the Gettysburg Address.

Equally memorable was MGM's ideally cast version of *Ah, Wilderness!*, Eugene O'Neill's only comedy, about (it has been surmised) the kind of nice, normal family he would like to have had rather than the one he actually did have, depicted in *Long Day's Journey into Night*. With Lionel Barrymore and Spring Byington as the parents, Aline Mac-Mahon and Wallace Beery as the aunt and uncle, and Eric Linden and Cecilia Parker as the troubled young sweethearts, the film opened up the play just enough, with a 1906 high school dance, street scenes, a graduation, a Fourth of July picnic and other bits of

Wallace Beery and Aline MacMahon in Ah, Wilderness!

small-town Americana, all done with much nostalgic atmosphere. The tone of tender reminiscence, certainly unique in O'Neill's work, places *Ah, Wilderness!* as the first of that family memory cycle (*Life with Father, I Remember Mama*, etc., etc.) that became so popular in the 1940s.

When Warners, which except for *Sweet Adeline* (1935) had made no contribution to the nostalgic cycle, produced *The Sisters* (1938), from a novel by Myron Brinig, its appeal was twofold, since it was set in the two favorite milieux, a small town (Silver Bow, Montana) and a big city (San Francisco), both depicted with a wealth of authentic detail (though this was only director Anatole Litvak's second American film).

In a warmly sympathetic role, for a change, Bette Davis played Louise Elliott, oldest of the three daughters of a druggist (Henry Travers) and his wife (Beulah Bondi). Her sisters were plain Grace (Jane Bryan) and Helen, the family beauty (Anita Louise). At a ball celebrating the 1904 election of Teddy Roosevelt, the men who are to marry all three girls are present. Helen quite cold-bloodedly sets her cap for a friend's wealthy father (Alan Hale) and goes on to become an international society figure. Grace quickly catches on the rebound a dull young banker (Dick Foran) rejected by Louise, while Louise herself elopes with Frank Medlin (Errol Flynn), a dashing newspaperman who takes her to live in San Francisco.

But Frank is a restless wanderer, given to drinking and feeling trapped by domesticity. Not knowing Louise is pregnant, he goes off on a tramp steamer the night before the 1906 earthquake. She wanders dazed until rescued by a tartish neighbor (Lee Patrick), whose mother (Laura Hope Crews) runs a thinly disguised brothel in Oakland. There Louise loses her child but is nursed back to health and found by her father and her employer, William Benson (Ian Hunter), who loves her.

Both she and Helen, now widowed, are summoned back to Silver Bow by a crisis in Grace's marriage; with their help she manages to get rid of the milliner with whom her husband has been having an affair. On the night of Taft's election in 1908, just four years after the opening sequence, the family is reunited, and the unselfish Benson even brings penitent Frank from San Francisco for a happy reunion with Louise.

Just beyond the '30s but presumably planned in 1939 was the filmed *Our Town* (1940), even with a happy ending a beautiful rendition of Wilder's 1938 play, one of the most poignant of all the 1930s' lingering backward glances at America's lost innocence.

In real life nostalgia was commercialized perhaps most spectacularly by Billy Rose's Diamond Horseshoe on West Forty-sixth Street, where he regaled 1939 World's Fair visitors with a revue titled *The Turn of the Century,* featuring numbers supposedly set in Rector's, Steve Brodie's, Ziegfeld's Midnight Frolics and Delmonico's, for which Rose resurrected, like living pages from one of *Stage* magazine's annual "Fond Memories" issues, once famous stars like Fritzi Scheff, Joe Howard and Noble Sissle, while others impersonated Lillian Russell, Diamond Jim and the Florodora Sextette.

Even now anyone familiar with New York has only to contemplate the continued success of Lüchow's, Bill's Gay Nineties, Gage and Tollner's in Brooklyn and, most elegantly, the Plaza, where in 1974 public protests led the management to reconvert the super-mod Green Tulip Room back to its original 1907 look as the Edwardian Room.

Theatrically the 1930s' rediscovery of the charms of the Florodora era has left at least one permanent legacy. As a graceful setting for musicals, it has become Broadway's most durable cliché. It is impossible to imagine what contemporary dress and decor would have done to any number of hits of the past three decades, all the way from *Oklahoma!* down through *My Fair Lady, The Music Man* and *Hello, Dolly* right up to *A Little Night Music.*

In screen musicals, the prewar era soon became so taken for granted as to pass unnoticed, in countless show-biz biographies ranging from good (*Yankee Doodle Dandy*, 1942) through mediocre (*Shine On, Harvest Moon*, 1944) to awful (*The Great Victor Herbert*, 1939), not to mention the numerous undistinguished and indistinguishable vehicles for Betty Grable and Alice Faye. On the other hand, the same trend, handled with better taste at MGM, produced *Meet Me in St. Louis* (1944), *The Harvey Girls* (1945), *Easter Parade* (1948) and *Gigi* (1958). That many

of these are now doubly layered in nostalgia is evidenced by the very warm reception of MGM's two *That's Entertainment* films (1974 and 1976).

As a final footnote to the enduring charm of the Edwardian era for later generations, one has only to cite the enormous international success of the British TV series *The Forsyte Saga*, followed by *Jennie, Upstairs, Downstairs, The Duchess of Duke Street, Edward the King* and *Lillie*.

12

AS TIME GOES BY
Through-the-Years Cavalcades

It seems significant that the Pulitzer Prize for fiction in 1920 was won by *The Age of Innocence,* Edith Wharton's quietly devastating study of the crippling repressions imposed by the elaborate code of New York society in the 1870s. But by 1930, after a decade of the new freedom and a year of the Depression, the Pulitzer Prize went, perhaps for some of the psychological reasons suggested in the last chapter, to Margaret Ayer Barnes' *Years of Grace,* a charming novel of Chicago society from 1890 through the late 1920s, which delicately but unmistakably conveys that none of the postwar social changes had been for the better.

The Pulitzer Prize was but one small straw in the changing wind that had begun to sweep across America. Inevitably, as the Depression deepened, novels, plays and films began to look back more seriously, as if the time had come to question when and how everything

had gone so wrong, by retracing what had happened to the world between the confident nineteenth century and the troubled present.

Thus *Years of Grace* differed from *The Age of Innocence* not only in tone but in structure; it belonged to the genre of the *roman fleuve* or chronicle novel, pioneered by the French, occasionally written by others (e.g., Thomas Mann's *Buddenbrooks*), but at its most popular in the 1920s, with the completion of Galsworthy's *Forsyte Saga,* the beginning of Hugh Walpole's Herries series (1930) and the success of Canadian Mazo De la Roche's Jalna novels, which eventually spread over several generations.

In America in the '20s something like this pattern had already appeared in the colorful regional novels of Edna Ferber, especially *Show Boat,* which though not predominantly nostalgic, made the most of the picturesque aspects of the changing times.

This was equally true of the film *Cimarron* (1931), based on Ferber's 1929 novel, one of the first talkies other than the operetta *Viennese Nights* (1930) to follow the through-the-years pattern. While it records in vivid detail the growth of a one-street Oklahoma village of 1889 to a booming metropolis by 1929, even as the heroine (Irene Dunne) grows from Southern belle to pioneer wife to crusading editor to liberal congresswoman, the tone is less one of nostalgia than of chamber of commerce civic pride.

If the theme of *Cimarron* could be summed up in the 1970s advertising slogan "You've come a long way, baby!", then its most obvious follow-up, *The Conquerors* (1932), hailed by *Photoplay* as "a worthy successor to *Cimarron*," one that "makes you proud to be an American," might be epitomized in the phrase "Look, we've come through!" A pioneer couple, ultra-WASPishly named Roger Standish and Caroline Ogden (Richard Dix and Ann Harding), who found the first bank in a Nebraska town, are followed with excellent period atmosphere from 1873 through nearly six decades. Though they lose their only son in an accident the day the Union Pacific reaches the town and the husband (Donald Cook) of their daughter (Julie Haydon) kills himself after embezzling bank funds in

Richard Dix, unidentified player, Donald Cook in **The Conquerors**

the panic of 1893, their grandson (also played by Dix) survives World War I and brings the bank safely through the 1929 crash.

Yet in the fall of that same year (1932) even the optimistic Ferber, or perhaps her co-author, George S. Kaufman, in the play *Dinner at Eight* (in the first scene of which the society hostess is planning to attend a costume ball as a Florodora girl) allows a moment of rueful nostalgia when Carlotta Vance, a retired actress returning to New York after several decades in Europe, exclaims: "Everything's changed! I'd die here. I belong to the Delmonico period. A table by the window, facing Fifth Avenue, with the flower boxes and the pink lampshades and the string orchestra. Oh, I don't know—willow plumes and Inverness capes, dry champagne and snow on the ground—God, they don't even have snow any more!"

Meanwhile one of the first British stage works to express a growing ambivalence toward the old days (as implied in its very title) had been Noel Coward's internationally successful operetta *Bitter Sweet* (1929), first filmed by the British in 1932, a kind of parallel to *Show Boat* in its time span, enduring music and pleasingly romantic tone. Though the young lovers flee a conventionally stuffy Victorian household in 1875, the act set in 1895 (not used in either film version) first revealed that indulgent fondness for Edwardian foibles, especially theatrical foibles, that was to recur in several later Coward works.

Always sensitive to shifts in public taste and quick to reflect them, Coward crossed the border into pure nostalgia with *Cavalcade* (1931), researched while he was starring in his own *Private Lives* in New York in 1930, just as his generation was beginning to realize that the decade-long party of the '20s was over. Jane Marryot's prescient line in a 1918 scene of *Cavalcade* summed it up: "Something seems to have gone out of all of us, and I'm not sure I like what's left."

The play was transferred directly from the London stage to the Hollywood sound stages, with no Broadway production, and the

stiff-upper-lip restraint, the sharp class distinctions and the use of "Soldiers of the Queen," "Land of Hope and Glory" and, at the end, "God Save the King" for patriotic appeal might have seemed too exclusively British for the American public, but *Cavalcade* was one of the most highly praised and successful films of 1933, well worthy of its three Oscars (best production, director, Frank Lloyd, art direction, William Darling).

The story of Robert and Jane Marryot (Clive Brook and Diana Wynyard, who was also nominated for an Oscar), their former servants, Alf and Ellen Bridges (Herbert Mundin and Una O'Connor), their sons Edward (John Warburton) and Joe (Frank Lawton) and the girls they love, Edith Harris (Margaret Lindsay, the only adult American in the cast) and Fanny Bridges (Ursula Jeans), seemed to touch a universal chord.

From the opening subtitle, noting how "our London family, sheltered through two generations of Victorian prosperity, awaits the headlong cavalcade of the twentieth century," to the final scene, over thirty years later, in which the white-haired Marryots, who have lost both sons, gallantly toast the new year with the forlorn hope that their beloved country "may find dignity and greatness and peace again," the elegiac note is unmistakable, and nearly half a century later, with the knowledge of all that has happened to England since then, even more poignant now.

Though faithful to the play, the film was able to achieve effects impossible on stage, not only in massive spectacles like the troop ship leaving for the Boer War, a London theater on the night Mafeking is relieved, an Edwardian ball, a lower-class London street scene, a crowded seaside resort in 1909 and Trafalgar Square on Armistice night, but by purely cinematic devices.

The passing years throughout are indicated not by the conventional calendar pages but by a cavalcade of medieval riders, men and women on caparisoned horses, cantering forever through a darkening wood, downhill

Diana Wynyard and Clive Brook in Cavalcade

Beryl Mercer, Herbert Mundin, Tempe Pigott, Una O'Connor in Cavalcade

from 1914 on—a haunting variation on the Four Horsemen of the Apocalypse. And Coward's most celebrated *coup de théâtre* worked even better on screen—the scene of the honeymooning couple (Edward and Edith) on an ocean liner, in which only at the very end is the name on the life preserver revealed as TITANIC.

The mass tragedy of 1914–18 is brilliantly conveyed by a montage (designed by William Cameron Menzies) of three girl entertainers in a London cabaret singing recruiting songs less and less gaily, until at last tears are streaming down their faces, while simultaneously endless soldiers march across the screen through a French village, at first smiling, then ever more wearily, at last dragging themselves and each other along in unrelieved agony, as

shells gradually reduce the village to rubble, the sky darkens and even a surviving wayside shrine is destroyed. Their songs change, too, as the jaunty "It's a Long, Long Way to Tipperary" gives way to the determinedly cheerful "Pack Up Your Troubles," and that in turn to the wistful "Keep the Home Fires Burning."

The postwar montage cuts back and forth among quick shots of blinded veterans learning to weave baskets and read Braille, endless rows of white crosses in a military cemetery, disarmament conferences dragging on while governments secretly plan to buy "improved" poison gas that will guarantee "security." A Communist soapbox orator tells his listeners, "The whole world's broke! The whole thing is a heartless mockery!", a suave radio speaker denounces all religion as childish, while a clergyman preaches to a church empty except for a few old people on the theme of "What shall it profit a man?", intercut with headlines of depression and war threats. Then to a decadent night club, where older women are dancing, too close, with younger men, and one plump, effete young man puts a slave bracelet on the wrist of another.

"Twentieth Century Blues," described in the stage directions as "oddly discordant," sung by Fanny Bridges (whose lover, Joe Marryot, was killed in the war), leaning against a piano in the same night club, only underlines the implications of what we have already seen, in such despairing lines as "Why, if there's a God in the sky, why shouldn't He grin, high above this dreary twentieth-century din?"

Pacifism was certainly not new to 1933 audiences after three years of antiwar films, but seldom had the heartbreak been dramatized so movingly through the eyes of the bereft parents, nor had any previous film except *The Conquerors* offered such an atmospheric march of time through the twentieth century. No wonder the word "cavalcade" took on the extended meaning it has had ever since, in such expressions as "Cavalcade of America" and "cavalcade of sports."

The parallels between *Cavalcade* and the popular BBC TV series *Upstairs, Downstairs,* written more than forty years later, seem too numerous to be mere coincidence: the whole concept of following a comfortable London family and their servants from the turn of the century to the early '30s; the use of the name "Bridges" and a plump, sharp-tongued cook; a dim-witted kitchen maid (Annie in *Cavalcade,* Ruby in *Upstairs, Downstairs*); the rise of a "downstairs" girl to a popular stage performer (Fanny Bridges, Sarah); the death of an important character on the *Titanic* (Edward Marryot, Lady Marjorie); a fashionable widowed friend who remains constant throughout (Margaret Harris, Lady Prue); the anguished scenes of the badly wounded being brought off trains into Victoria Station; the frantic social upheavals of the '20s— but what took *Upstairs, Downstairs* at least thirty-nine episodes to cover, *Cavalcade* accomplished in less than two hours.

Though *Cavalcade* remains the finest film to look back on the prewar years with frank nostalgia, it by no means stood alone. 1933 saw at least a dozen other variations on the through-the-years pattern. While the number was small in comparison to other types of film, enough were made so that the constant moviegoer very soon learned what to expect: Gibson girls and bicycles built for two, the Spanish-American War, with "Goodbye, Dolly Gray" played in the background, references to McKinley and Teddy Roosevelt, the horseless carriage derided as a passing fad, girls denounced as hussies for showing an ankle, the Sarajevo assassination mentioned and dismissed as unimportant, scare headlines: WAR DECLARED!, predictions that it would be over in a few months, the inevitable battlefield montage, old newsreel shots of returning troopships and victorious Yanks marching up Fifth Avenue, then the postwar chaos, futility and sense of loss, a shot of panic on the floor of the Stock Exchange and tall towers of coins symbolically collapsing. And if no one had gone down on the *Titanic,* then it would surely be the *Lusitania.* By the end of 1933 even the least-informed movie-goer must have had a fairly good grasp of at least the sequence, if not the cause and effect, of the major events of the century.

It is surely no coincidence that in *Cavalcade,* the only such film about a British subject, we are never told nor do we even wonder what, if anything, Robert Marryot does for a living, while all the American counterparts put the strongest possible emphasis on the protagonists' business careers. Looking over the bumper crop of such films in the early '30s, one is struck by the recurrence of a single theme: the betrayal or corruption or destruction of the American dream of success. As the *New York Post* noted in its review of *The World Changes* (1933): "Despite the richness and variety of the source, it seems that American history in the hands of the movies is capable of only one interpretation, namely, that the pioneering spirit is subject to an inevitable decadence when traced down through the corrupting influence of the materialistic twentieth century." The typical structure was the rise and fall of a tycoon, preferably self-made, who claws his way to the top, usually in Chicago or points west, along the way ruthlessly disposing of rivals and, if necessary, friends, driving his neglected wife to insanity and/or suicide, becoming entangled with a younger woman, always with disastrous results, and, of course, finally getting his comeuppance.

Why so many of these sagas were set in Chicago rather than in New York, where the greatest fortunes were made and spent, remains an open question, but one possible reason is that the studios had friends at Chase Manhattan—i.e., they were controlled from New York by banks still owned by the descendants of the city's leading Robber Baron families, whereas their Chicago counterparts, like the Fields, Swifts, Armours and McCormicks, seemed safe targets.

Not only were the tycoon films variations on that favorite Depression film formula: "What's money? It can't buy happiness," they also stirred righteous biblical echoes of "Pride

goeth before a fall." To a public that had lived through all the bank failures and political scandals of 1930–33, had heard FDR announce in his inaugural address, "The money-changers have fled from their high places in the temple of our civilization" and had seen so many once respected figures of the '20s either leave office under a cloud (like Jimmy Walker), flee the country in disgrace (Samuel Insull) or kill themselves (Ivar Kreuger), no message could have seemed more welcome, more grimly true to life nor more in keeping with the "soak the rich" spirit of the New Deal.

Other than *The Conquerors,* the only exception to the pattern of ruthless rise was *Sweepings* (1933), in which Lionel Barrymore, made up to look like a young man in the early sequences, was almost a Chicago Lear. In the aftermath of the great fire of 1871, he opens a small dry-goods shop, which eventually grows into one of the world's great department stores, inevitably suggestive of Marshall Field. However, his three sons (William Gargan, George Meeker and Eric Linden) disappoint him by taking no interest in the business, and his daughter (Gloria Stuart) marries and divorces a worthless prince; not until the end of his life do they show any sign of remorse. Only his Jewish manager (Gregory Ratoff), whom he refused to make a partner, has seen the truth all along and quietly bought out the children's shares of the store.[1]

More typically, *Silver Dollar* (1932) traced the bizarre, almost incredibly melodramatic career of Colorado silver king H. A. W. Tabor, the same career that later inspired the libretto (by John LaTouche) of Douglas Moore's opera *The Ballad of Baby Doe.* Per-

---

[1] For this kind of film, *Sweepings,* unlike *The Conquerors,* is almost totally lacking in period sense. Not a date is mentioned throughout nor any historical event but the fire. Though the children would have been young in the 1900s at latest and middle-aged by the '30s, they wear modern clothes throughout and scarcely age at all.

haps because the real Baby Doe was still living in 1932, the film changed the names of the principals to Yates Martin and Lily Owens, but the story was unmistakably Tabor's in every detail. Hailed by the *Herald Tribune* for dealing with a type that "could be brought forth in all of his glory only by the America that died with Teddy Roosevelt and William Jennings Bryan," the film depicted its hero in all his naïve *nouveau riche* vulgarity, naming the town of Denver and building an opera house for it, buying his way into the Senate, hobnobbing with Presidents Grant and Arthur and the young Bryan.

His downfall with the decline of silver and his last half-mad days, haunted by ghosts of vanished glory, were compared by the *Times* reviewer to those of Beau Brummell (presumably the John Barrymore version). Edward G. Robinson was highly praised for his forceful portrayal of "Martin," as were Aline MacMahon as his first wife and Bebe Daniels as "Lily." (No scenarist could have imagined an ending as macabre as the death of the real Baby Doe in her eighties in 1935: she was found frozen to death in her shack at the head of the Matchless Mine, where she had lived as a recluse, waiting for silver to come back.)

Within a year Robinson was tycooning it again in *I Loved a Woman,* in which the once powerful hero dies in lonely exile in Greece, while the love of his life (Kay Francis), whose

Edward G. Robinson and Kay Francis in **I Loved a Woman**

career he sponsored at the Chicago Opera House, remains politely indifferent. The real-life parallel was unmistakable, but in 1933 Samuel Insull was in no position to sue. Instead of a utilities magnate, the protagonist starts out as the sensitive, art-loving heir to a meat-packing fortune, but soon learns to play the game, cheating the government with tainted meat both in the Spanish-American and First World wars, meanwhile embittering his society wife (Genevieve Tobin) by his prolonged dalliance with the singer. Anticipations of *Citizen Kane* are obvious.

Even more sweeping was *The World Changes* (1933), which with the aid of Dos Passos-like newsreel interludes spanned more than seventy years, from South Dakota in 1856 to New York in 1929. (It followed so close upon the heels of *I Loved a Woman* that reviewers wondered what Warner Brothers had against Chicago meat packers.) Paul Muni, the son of sturdy Swedish immigrants, by driving a herd of cattle from Abilene to Omaha makes such an impression on a packer (Guy Kibbee) that he presently leaves his prairie sweetheart (Jean Muir) to go to Chicago, become the packer's partner and marry his socially ambitious daughter (Mary Astor).

By the '90s he is the world's greatest meat packer, but his wife is so enraged at his refusal to retire from the distasteful business that she dies insane. However, she has reared their two sons to despise their father's work. One (Gordon Westcott) is a general wastrel, while the other (Donald Cook) marries a New York socialite (Margaret Lindsay) and becomes a Wall Street broker.

By 1929 *their* daughter (Patricia Ellis) is about to marry a mercenary British peer (Alan Mowbray), while the disappointed grandfather can only sit brooding in the Union Club. *His* mother (Aline MacMahon), still vigorous in her nineties, perhaps because she never left Dakota, comes to New York to attend the wedding and also to tell off her useless descendants. It is the day of the stock-market crash, and the bride loses fiancé, father and fortune, for Cook, who has learned of his

wife's infidelity as well as his own financial ruin, kills himself (just as he did in *The Conquerors*), after an embezzling son (Theodore Newton) flees to South America. Understandably, Muni collapses and dies, on the stairs of his son's mortgaged mansion—but all is not lost. A worthier grandson, his namesake (William Janney), in a variation on that favorite '30s theme "back to the land," is to return to Dakota with his great-grandmother and there, we assume, marry the granddaughter (again Jean Muir) of Muni's original love.

However, the most generally admired film of this type was *The Power and the Glory* (1933), an original by Preston Sturges which even used the same framework as *Citizen Kane*, beginning at the hero's funeral and reconstructing his life in flashbacks, not necessarily chronological—an idea considered so novel that it was called "narratage" and a bronze tablet was placed in the New York theater where the picture opened.

Spencer Tracy's performance in the central role, a trackwalker who rises to head of the Chicago and Southwestern Railroad, made him a star, according to Pauline Kael, while as the wife who made him a success (and whom he drives to suicide) Colleen Moore played one of her last important parts. Helen Vinson was the faithless second wife who à la Phaedra becomes involved with her young stepson.

But seen now the film is the very antithesis of *Kane*: thin, simplistic, unconvincing, with no sense of period or passing time. The hero's business career is simply stated rather than shown; at one point he settles a strike (the issues of which are never clear) in which over four hundred men are killed! The ironies are too pat, the climaxes too abrupt—e.g., when his first wife comes to his office to ask him to take her to Europe and instead learns he wants a divorce, she leaves, dismisses her chauffeur and walks in front of a streetcar. Later, coming home to celebrate his first wedding anniversary with the second wife, he conveniently overhears a phone conversation that instantly convinces him that the child he

Colleen Moore and Spencer Tracy in **The Power and the Glory**

thought his own is actually his grandchild (just as in *Desire Under the Elms*). Without a moment's hesitation he walks into the next room and shoots himself, with a cry of "Sally!" (the first wife's name).

Not all the through-the-years films of 1933, of course, brought in such stern indictments as those discussed above. *Broadway to Hollywood,* for instance, was pure show-biz nostalgia; *The Man Who Dared* dealt with an *admirable* mayor of Chicago; *Song of the Eagle* sympathically portrayed a German-American brewing family before and during Prohibition; *Secrets,* Mary Pickford's last film, in which she and Leslie Howard went from

youth in New England in the 1860s to happy, rich old age in California, was dismissed by the *Times* as sentimental twaddle.

More successful were two comedies with remarkably parallel structures—presumably a coincidence, as they were released within a few days of each other. In *Turn Back the Clock,* Lee Tracy was a dissatisfied cigar store owner transported under anesthetic back to his prewar youth, with full memory of all that happened in the interim (as in *A Connecticut Yankee, Berkeley Square* and other fantasies of time travel), so that he is able to make all the right decisions, avoid the draft, amass a fortune and even marry Peggy Shannon, whom in his other life he had lost to Otto Kruger—but, of course, he finds himself so unhappy that he is glad to wake up to his real life and wife (Mae Clarke). To an extraordinary degree, the plot anticipated Maxwell Anderson's play *The Star Wagon* (1937).

One Sunday Afternoon used straight flashbacks in telling a similar story, of a discontented dentist (Gary Cooper) who as he treats his erstwhile rival (Neil Hamilton) recalls the youthful triangle in which he was the loser—only to find his idealized girl (Fay Wray) now a hard, vampish type, not to be compared with his loyal wife (Frances Fuller). Both pictures depend strongly on 1900s atmosphere.

By 1934 this cycle was beginning to wear thin. *Beloved*, borrowing from *Bitter Sweet*, *Viennese Nights* and even *Broadway to Hollywood*, though not considered an operetta, traced four generations of a musical family. This time it was John Boles and Gloria Stuart who went from youth to extreme old age, but the *Times* found their lives "morose and interminable," just as it found *A Modern Hero*, though directed by G. W. Pabst from a novel by Louis Bromfield and starring Richard Barthelmess, "earnest, sketchy and spiritless." The illegitimate son of a drunken circus performer (Marjorie Rambeau) rises to wealth and power by using women but eventually outsmarts himself and admits his failure.

Apparently meant to outdo even *The World Changes*, by broadening its scope to international dimensions, with echoes both of *The Four Horsemen of the Apocalypse* and *The House of Rothschild*, Fox's *The World Moves On* (1934) proved as ponderous as its title. Despite an original script by Reginald Berkeley, who had adapted *Cavalcade* for the screen, the same pointed antiwar message, direction by John Ford, and a large, able cast headed by Franchot Tone and Madeleine Carroll, this one bit off perhaps more than any one picture could comfortably chew. Two families of cotton brokers, one New Orleans French, one Manchester English, in 1825 form a business alliance cemented by intermarriage,

and later establish branches in Germany and France, so that by World War I descendants of Forsytean complexity are fighting and being killed on both sides.

The surviving family head becomes so engrossed in the greedy speculation of the '20s that his wife considers financial ruin a blessing in disguise. At the end they are ready to start afresh in the same Louisiana house where it all began (including an earlier, frustrated romance between two ancestors also played by Tone and Carroll). The main difficulty with *The World Moves On* was that by mid-1934 its every point had been made better, by too many other films.

In 1935 the only film in any way suggestive of this pattern was Hugh Walpole's highly selective adaptation of the last of his Herries novels, *Vanessa*. The screen title, *Vanessa: Her Love Story*, was apt enough, for that was certainly all that was left of the book. Since the film stops in 1912, with a falsely happy ending and no hint of the war or its aftermath, omitting and distorting many of the characters, perhaps it does not belong to this cycle at all. In any case, it was Helen Hayes' last film for many years.

Why such a flourishing genre should have faded by mid-decade is not clear; perhaps the gradual easing of the Depression under the New Deal made people less fearful of the present and the future, so less eager to cling to the past. Typically, just as the major studios were losing interest in the through-the-years pattern, one independent example appeared, Republic's *Born to Gamble* (1935), in which H. B. Warner as a cautionary antigambling warning tells in flashback the fate of his four sons: one was killed in the war, one shot by bootleggers, one killed himself after the 1929 crash. Only Onslow Stevens. escaped the curse.[2]

[2] The only three '30s films to deal accurately with the 1920s also followed this pattern, though over shorter spans: *Three on a Match* (1932), which covered 1919–32, *To Mary with Love* (1936), 1925–35, and *The Roaring Twenties* (1939), 1918–32.

As a last feeble gasp of the through-the-years pattern, *Fifty-Second Street* (1937) traced the vicissitudes of a Manhattan brownstone from 1912 on, as it went from private home to speakeasy to night club. As one reviewer put it, it showed how "a high-hat street gone honky-tonk returned to hoity-toity by way of hi-de-ho."

The only other notable film of the decade, except for those to be covered under other categories, to revive the now moribund pattern was *Goodbye, Mr. Chips* (1939), from James Hilton's 1934 novel. Since apart from the Austrian interlude in which the hero meets his wife, the action is entirely confined to a boys' school, there was little scope to reflect the changing times except for the war.

That the chronicle film when done well could still pack a wallop was, of course, most brilliantly proved in 1941 by *Citizen Kane,* which viewed in this context, as Kael points out in her *Citizen Kane Book,* while no less an achievement, seems less a trail-blazing,

unique phenomenon than the ultimate culmination of the cycle of tycoon films.

The '40s also brought a number of lesser examples, like *My Son, My Son* (1940), *Forever and a Day* (1943), *Mr. Skeffington* (1944), *Mrs. Parkington* (1944) and *The Valley of Decision* (1945). Yet if such pictures have vanished from the theaters, family chronicles have never died out in other popular media.

Perhaps (as first proved by *Mama,* which over several seasons gradually moved from 1910 through the First World War) the ideal medium for such leisurely, ample narratives is TV. Except for *Roots,* most recent American efforts such as *Beacon Hill, The Best of Families* and *The Adams Chronicles* have ranged from inept to disastrous—but the half-dozen "Edwardian" BBC series cited at the end of the last chapter (not to mention others like *The First Churchills* and *I, Claudius*) have all followed the through-the-years patterns with exemplary success.

13

MOTHER'S DAY
Women Who Paid

One other genre remains which usually covered the same years as the cavalcades: the endless variations on the theme of *Madame X.* It is typical of the taken-for-granted sex roles of the time, both on screen and off, that although the tycoons' private lives abounded in neglected wives, designing mistresses and thankless children, the concentration was al-

ways, as noted, on the men's business careers, while in the films to be discussed here the heroines, who in reality would have been the exact contemporaries of the tycoons, led lives exclusively determined by their relationship to men.

This was one phase of the "women's films" which Molly Haskell in *From Reverence to*

Rape divides into four overlapping categories: sacrifice, affliction, choice and competition. In "mother" films it was sacrifice and affliction all the way. They were enormously popular with women themselves, perhaps because they made even the unhappiest woman in the audience feel lucky by comparison, or perhaps simply because they played so directly on the most basic emotions. Who could resist a frail, white-haired old lady in the snow of a Christmas Eve pressing her face against the gaily lighted window of a rich man's home, hoping in vain for a glimpse of the son she had given up for his own good? In the words of a 1930s music hall ballad sung by Gracie Fields, in which a working girl recounts the plots of her favorite weepy movies: "Oh, I never cried so much in all me life!"[1]

The long-suffering mother, ready to make any sacrifice even for a son or daughter torn from her in childhood, presumably dates to nineteenth-century melodrama or sentimental novels like Mrs. Henry Wood's *East Lynne* (1861), certainly not to any more respectable literary antecedent. Foolish, managing, indifferent or completely selfish mothers are so common in Jane Austen, Dickens, Thackeray, Balzac, Zola, Tolstoy and other classic novelists that it almost seems as if the only good mother was a dead mother, preferably one who had died at the heroine's birth.

Beyond that fact, with the discoveries of Freud ever more widely disseminated, one would have thought that by the '30s the time had come for America to drop the bomb on Mom—and indeed a number of realistic films did, though usually in the form of a mother-in-*law* battling her son's wife—but it is doubtful if they were ever as popular as those which tugged at the heartstrings by following the downward path of women who paid and paid.

It was perhaps to be expected that the country which had in 1914 proclaimed Mother's Day, which still choked up at songs like

"Mother Machree," "Mammy," "Meine Yiddishe Mama" and the Italian "Mam-ma," would be particularly susceptible to such appeals—yet it must be kept in mind that *Madame X,* the mother of them all, started out as a French play.

Less shrewd than the courtesans, gold diggers or Cinderella working girls, the betrayed heroine either gave up her child, if illegitimate, or, even if married, lost him to the law, heartless in-laws or wealthy foster parents ("You must think of *his* future, my dear. *We* can give him everything")—after which she could only sink to the very depths, walking the streets, ending on the wrong side of the law, usually charged with murder in the film's climax. She follows her child's life from afar, and decades later encounters the long-lost son (or, more rarely, daughter) as the judge, defense attorney, prosecutor or key witness at her trial, without his (or her) ever suspecting her identity—or at the very least she gets the chance to make some dramatic sacrifice on the child's behalf. About the only variation *not* tried was for her to have twelve illegitimate children who turn up as members of the jury.

The assumption in all such films was based on a premise—possibly valid in France in 1908 when Alexandre Bisson wrote the play *Madame X,* but certainly not in later societies—that without the "protection" of a father or husband a woman had no choice but prostitution on one level or another—the very antithesis of feminist thinking in that day or this.

After her 1929 triumph in the first talking version of *Madame X,* Ruth Chatterton was inevitably cast again and again as a bereft mother. In *Sarah and Son* (1930) her child is given away by her worthless husband, who dies muttering only the name of the foster parents. Returning from Europe as a successful opera singer, she finds and fights them, in the end winning not only her son (Philippe de Lacy) but their lawyer (Fredric March).

Her problem was nothing compared to those of Dorothy Peterson in *Mothers' Cry* (1930), who went from 1900 to 1930 as the mother of several troublesome children, in-

[1] *The American Film Institute Catalog . . . 1921–1930* lists 139 films about mothers, 15 more about mothers-in-law.

cluding a son who kills his sister while she's shielding her lover; the picture ends with his execution.

In 1931 Chatterton returned twice to the maternal fray, first in *The Right to Love,* in which she played dual roles, a mother and her illegitimate daughter, for whose sake she marries a man she does not love—but the daughter rejects her advice, favors her stepfather and achieves happiness after all. In *Once a Lady* (implication: "always a lady") Chatterton plays a pre-Revolutionary Russian married and divorced by a cold English aristocrat; after eighteen years, presumably in the demimonde, she returns, like Mrs. Erlynne in *Lady Windermere's Fan,* to save her daughter from a serious mistake and ensure her happy marriage.

Even the elegant Constance Bennett, when she was not being luxuriously kept by John Halliday or Adolphe Menjou, found time for an annual mother-love drama, though never the decade-spanning variety. In *Common Clay* (1930), from an old Jane Cowl hit, a speakeasy "hostess" tries to go straight by working as a servant, only to be seduced by the young master (Lew Ayres) and bear his child. In the climactic custody battle with his family, their lawyer (Tully Marshall) is revealed as our heroine's father, given up by her mother for the sake of his career. This solves everything.

In *Born to Love* (1931) Bennett was an American nurse in wartime London who falls in love with a U.S. flyer (Joel McCrea). After he is reported missing while she is pregnant, she marries an understanding British aristocrat (Paul Cavanagh). Later when the lover turns up, however, the husband claims custody, but eventually the heroine regains both her child and the man she loves.

Rockabye (1932) saw Bennett as a Broadway star noted for sophisticated roles. When headlines reveal that she was the mistress of an indicted politician (Walter Pidgeon), authorities take her adopted child away. Then she stars in a drama of mother love and falls in love with the playwright (McCrea again),

but on learning that his estranged wife has borne a son, she gives him up. (After all this maternal litigation, it seems only fair that more than three decades later Constance evened the score as the bitchy mother-in-law who wrecks Lana Turner's marriage in the 1966 *Madame X*—a character who does not appear in any other version.)

Far more luridly publicized than any of those was Donald Henderson Clarke's *Millie,* who was nothing if not thoroughly modern for 1931. "Drama Crying Out to All Womanhood!" screamed the ads. "Torn from her Arms . . . A Child of the Love a Woman Can Give But Once! . . . One Woman's Story for Every Woman Who Ever Loved a Home and Children!" The truth, however, was not quite that sensational. Millie's child is perfectly legitimate; a small-town girl (Helen Twelvetrees) elopes with a rich boy (James Hall) and lives with him in the family mansion, but leaves when she finds him deceiving her with a former mistress, entrusting her child for the usual noble reasons to her kindly mother-in-law.

Embittered against all men, she nevertheless gets to know quite a few, including a wealthy man about town (John Halliday). Years later, when he secretly lures her daughter (now grown into Anita Louise) to his country house for no good purpose, Millie speeds there in the nick of time and shoots him à la Mildred Pierce. At her trial her daughter's testimony clears her, and she ends up with a reporter (Robert Ames) who had been hanging around through the whole picture.[2]

Not at all incidentally, 1931 also saw two versions of *East Lynne* itself, one in modern dress under the title of *Ex-Flame,* with Ma-

---

[2] A similar situation was used in *Confession* (1937), already made under other titles by both Gloria Swanson and Pola Negri, in which Kay Francis as an ex-opera singer kills the pianist (Basil Rathbone) who ruined her marriage, to keep him from seducing the daughter (Jane Bryan) whom she lost through her brief indiscretion.

rian Nixon, one in proper 1870s decor, with Ann Harding as that Victorian equivalent of Anna Karenina, Lady Isabel Carlyle. However, even against such competition, the champion maternal tear-jerker of the year was undoubtedly *The Sin of Madelon Claudet,* for which Helen Hayes in her film debut received her first Oscar, winning over Marie Dressler and Lynn Fontanne.

A French peasant girl seduced by an American artist (Neil Hamilton) bears his child, gives it up to an orphanage, is later sentenced to ten years in prison as the unwitting accomplice of a kindly jewel thief (Lewis Stone), and comes out to sink to the conventional depths, all the while sending money to a doctor (Jean Hersholt) for her son's education. He, too, becomes a doctor (played, prophetically enough, by Robert Young), and Madelon at least has the satisfaction of visiting him in his office, after which, taking pity on her as a poor old woman, he sees that she has a home.

Among other effects, the success of *The Sin of Madelon Claudet* seemed to establish a pattern in titles for this kind of film: The Abstraction of First Name Last Name. *Madelon* was soon followed by *The Strange Case of Clara Deane* (1932), *The Past of Mary Holmes* and *The Secret of Madame Blanche* (both 1933) and *The Life of Vergie Winters* (1934), all centered on unhappy mothers.

As Clara Deane, Wynne Gibson, an innocent designer, marries a crook (Pat O'Brien), is sentenced to fifteen years as his accomplice and ends by killing him to protect their daughter (Frances Dee).[3] As Madame Blanche, Irene Dunne in a remake of a 1924 Norma Talmadge silent, based on a 1923 British play, *The Lady,* was an American show girl in Paris whose husband's aristocratic British family disowns him, driving him to suicide, then claims their child. When twenty

years later as a soldier he kills someone in her French cafe, guess who takes the blame. Yet later that year Dunne in *Ann Vickers* (1933) was an unwed mother who paid no price except losing her job—the only one in the decade to get off so easily.

1932 saw one realistic variation on the selfless mother theme, without murder or melodrama, Barbara Stanwyck as Selina Peake in Edna Ferber's *So Big,* the second of its three film versions and considered by many the best. Though it spans several decades in the hard-working life of a widowed truck farmer in a Dutch community near Chicago, unlike the tycoon films, it still reflected the basic optimism of the '20s when it was written. The heroine's disappointment that her son (Hardie Albright) grows up to be a bond salesman rather than an architect is more than balanced by her satisfaction in the successful sculpturing career of a neighbor's boy (George Brent) whom she had encouraged.

Now at Warners, Ruth Chatterton returned to the genre in *Frisco Jenny* (1933), in which the San Francisco earthquake (the first use of it in a '30s film) leaves Jenny, a Barbary Coast saloonkeeper's daughter, both orphaned and minus the lover who was about to marry her, none too soon. With only her Chinese amah to turn to, she secretly bears a child and later gives him up to the usual wealthy couple. Aided by politician Louis Calhern, she soon rises (with perfect period atmosphere all the way) to become the city's top madam, with a hand in other lucrative rackets as well—until in the early '30s her son (Donald Cook), now a crusading D.A., determines to clean up the city. The one way to stop him would be to blackmail him about his real parentage, but when Calhern threatens to do this, Jenny silences him for good, and so must face murder prosecution by her own son, without any usable defense—a twist of the knife even more excruciating than in *Madame X* (in which the son is her court-appointed defense attorney). She goes to the gallows without ever telling him the truth.

As Chatterton's career faded, it was, sur-

---

[3] *Forbidden* (1932) used a very similar plot. Barbara Stanwyck has a child by D.A. Adolph Menjou, gives it up to him and his wife, later murders her editor husband Ralph Bellamy to save Menjou's career from exposure of the truth.

Louis Calhern and Ruth Chatterton in Frisco Jenny

prisingly, the glamorous Kay Francis who took up the hopeless torch as the most put-upon mother on the screen, at least at Warner Brothers. Just as, among *Madame X* variations, 1933 had opened with *Frisco Jenny,* so it closed with *The House on 56th Street.*

Starting in a *Florodora*-like chorus line singing "Strolling Through the Park One Day" in a Broadway musical of 1905, Kay Francis as Peggy breaks with her middle-aged admirer (John Halliday in his usual role) to marry a generous young millionaire (Gene Raymond), who presents her with a house on Fifty-sixth Street which he promises will be her home forever. But when a few years later she tries to prevent Halliday's suicide, the gun goes off, and she is convicted of manslaughter. Naturally, her husband's haughty family promptly arrange a divorce and tell her little girl her mother is dead, he himself is killed in

the war, and Peggy, paid never to contact her daughter, emerges in the late '20s to make a new life as hostess and dealer in the elegant gambling casino of Ricardo Cortez in guess what house on Fifty-sixth Street.

Who should soon become an all too steady habitué but the daughter (Margaret Lindsay), now a young society matron turned feverishly compulsive gambler. When she runs up debts over her head and Cortez threatens blackmail, she impulsively shoots him. Her mother tries to take the blame, but an even bigger shot than Cortez (William "Stage" Boyd) covers for her on the condition that she will remain, presumably as his mistress, forever in the house on Fifty-sixth Street.

Francis apparently did so well in her first mother role that she played four more in the next few years: *I Found Stella Parish* (1935), *Give Me Your Heart* (1936), *Confession* (1937) and *My Bill* (1938).

Mid-1933 meanwhile had produced a creditable version of Dreiser's *Jennie Gerhardt,* praised by the *Times* for "laudable sincerity." Sylvia Sidney suffered from 1904 onward as a scrubwoman's daughter who for her family's sake becomes the mistress of a senator (Edward Arnold), only to lose him in a railroad accident before he can marry her. Driven from home, she goes to live in Cincinnati with a cousin, leaving her child with her while she goes to work as a lady's maid for a wealthy girl.

Soon the young master (Donald Cook) falls in love with her, and she lives with him in Chicago for five years before his family breaks it up. Even reunited, knowledge of her child keeps him from marrying her, though he does marry a widowed former flame (Mary Astor). When Jennie's daughter dies at seventeen after falling from the stage at her graduation, she is left with nothing but the bleak satisfaction of being summoned to Cook's deathbed to hear that she was, after all, the only one he really loved.

Judging by the press book, Paramount meant to push the period atmosphere for all

Donald Cook and Sylvia Sidney in **Jennie Gerhardt**

it was worth. The costumes, 1904–32, were "the most embracing parade of American styles ever conceived for the screen," announced designer Travis Banton. Another release hopefully proclaimed "Real beer, a Roosevelt as president, bicycles built for two, mutton-chop sleeves, double-breasted jackets —current events of 1904 . . . cold proof that a complete reversion is taking place in American life back to the 1904 morals, manners and modes!"—cold proof, rather, of the 1930s' pathetic eagerness to forget the '20s and identify with the prewar years.

Late 1933 also saw *Only Yesterday,* which, though obviously meant to cash in on the popularity of Frederick Lewis Allen's best-selling social history, contains no '20s atmosphere whatever. (An opening credit stating that it is "based on the novel by Frederick Lewis Allen" indicates that the writers were ignorant of even the nature of the book, much less its contents.) From the first scene, supposedly in 1929, through the end a few days later, with the past, 1917–28, recalled in a long flashback that makes up most of the picture, the dresses, hats, furniture and every other visible detail are relentlessly 1933—a total anachronism that even in that year must have disappointed many viewers expecting some fictional equivalent of Allen's book.

But if the writers knew nothing of the book whose title they were using, they were certainly familiar enough with Stefan Zweig's *Letter from an Unknown Woman* (beautifully filmed by Max Ophuls in 1948). Except for the ending, the screenplay of *Only Yester-*

day is a total, unacknowledged use of Zweig's exact plot, including the framework, the long flashback, even the letter itself.

On the day of the 1929 market crash, a prosperous New Yorker (John Boles), married to an indifferent, if not faithless, woman (Benita Hume), receives a long letter that reminds him how as an army officer in 1917 he casually seduced a Southern girl (Margaret Sullavan, in an auspicious screen debut). Never letting him know, she moved to New York, bore his son and with the aid of kindly relatives (Billie Burke and Reginald Denny) made a life of her own, running a dress shop.

Twice when they met, once even when they spent a night together, he failed to recognize her; now it is too late, as she is dying of heart disease. But, unlike the ending of the Zweig novel, the man does acknowledge and claim his son. Despite Sullavan's glowing performance, *Only Yesterday* remains a peculiarly unsatisfactory film.

In 1934 Ann Harding (after warming up in *Gallant Lady,* in which she became the unwed mother of Dickie Moore but was fortunately able in a few years to marry the man who adopted him) really joined the ranks of martyred motherhood in *The Life of Vergie Winters.* In '30s films a mistress' lot was at best not an easy one, but it became even harder under the Production Code. After losing the man she loves (Boles again) through her father's interference, Vergie, a small-town milliner, endures a fate "pliant with sadness and martyrdom," said the *Herald Tribune,* "another version of *Back Street* or *Jennie Gerhardt.*"

This time it is her lover who eventually becomes a senator; she even lets him and his wife (Helen Vinson) adopt her daughter. Boles seemed to specialize in such heartless heels, as casually indifferent to the sacrifices of Irene Dunne in *Back Street* as to Margaret Sullavan's in *Only Yesterday,* Lois Wilson's in *Seed* and later Barbara Stanwyck's in *Stella Dallas.* In this one, at least, he is shot by his jealous wife, but, predictably, it is noble Vergie who takes the blame and goes to prison

until cleared by her daughter (Betty Furness).

The same year, most incredibly, even Jean Arthur, then still in pre-Capra obscurity, paid her dues to the maternal cause in a forgotten item called *The Most Precious Thing in Life* (1934). A poor girl working as a waitress at a college attracts a wealthy student (the ubiquitous Donald Cook), who even marries her, but after bearing his son, she is eased out by his family, who keep the child. Twenty years later, now scrubbing floors at the same college, she befriends a certain wealthy young student involved in a parallel romance with a poor girl. Without ever revealing her identity, she not only saves the young lovers (Richard Cromwell and Anita Louise) from the machinations of the boy's father, but convinces her son that he should play football and win for his alma mater.

A far more realistic film of 1934 was Fannie Hurst's *Imitation of Life,* in which Claudette Colbert and Louise Beavers as two young widows, one white, one black, pool their resources to package a special pancake flour, Aunt Delilah, which makes them rich. (In Ross Hunter's vastly inferior version in 1959 Lana Turner in the Colbert role becomes a Broadway star overnight, with the black woman as her servant, not her business partner.) The white heroine's story involves a mother-daughter rivalry of a kind often used, as in *Desirable,* released only a few months before *Imitation of Life.*

But what made the film stand out is the subplot—except for *Show Boat* the only actual racial problem reflected in any generally released American film of the entire decade. This came through even in the 1959 version, but in 1934 it was both startling and deeply moving, thanks to the fine performances of Louise Beavers as the gentle, self-effacing black mother and Fredi Washington as her rebellious daughter, determined to pass as white even if it means denying her own mother. Her hysterical remorse at the mother's funeral pulls out all the emotional stops, yet the situation itself was close enough to a painful social fact otherwise ignored by Hollywood to

have far deeper impact than the legal difficulties of the various Mesdames X.

Motherhood clearly was a duty not even
the greatest stars could hope to avoid. Dietrich, for instance, was a mother in *Blonde
Venus* and *The Garden of Allah*. One hardly
thinks of Garbo as the maternal type, yet in
Anna Karenina (1935) some of her tenderest
scenes are with Freddie Bartholomew as her
little son, and being forbidden to see him is
one of the most painful conditions of her social ostracism. She was also the mother of a
son by Napoleon in *Conquest* (1937).

On and on they suffered through the '30s,
all those countless, dauntless movie mothers:
mothers whose scandalous ways of life when
discovered by their grown children called for
extremes of sacrifice: Clara Kimball Young in
Mother and Son, Louise Dresser in *Caught,*
Pauline Frederick in both *This Modern Age*
and *Self Defense;* a panhandling mother who
pretends to a social grandeur she does not
possess (Robson in *Lady for a Day*); younger
mothers who ran chic little dress shops (Sullavan in *Only Yesterday*) or became interior
decorators (Harding in *Gallant Lady*); a
shopkeeper who makes her son a gentleman
by convincing him he belongs to an actress
(Pauline Lord in *A Feather in Her Hat*); a
wife who kills her worthless husband in self-
defense, flees with her four children, then,
after rearing them successfully, returns to face
the charge and be acquitted (Mady Christians
in *A Wicked Woman*); a "woman of the
town" who breaks with her lurid past for the
sake of two adopted children (Gladys George
in *Valiant Is the Word for Carrie*); besides all
those already mentioned who are driven to
commit murder or at least take the blame for
the child's sake.

It will be noted that when forced to support
themselves and/or the child, those who did
not take to the oldest profession went in for
others almost equally traditional—genteel occupations that had always been considered
suitable for "the fair sex." Even Colbert's
success in *Imitation of Life* was based on pancake flour. With the exception of Chatterton

in *Female* (who had, after all, inherited a going concern), a few daring doctors, lawyers,
reporters and entertainers, employed heroines
in '30s films were working girls, not career
women.

Altogether unique, then, was Katharine
Hepburn in *A Woman Rebels* (1936), all the
more remarkable because her rebellion was
fought out amid the gentilities of Victorian
England, from 1869 to 1890. Not only does
this heroine survive her affair (with Van Heflin) and rear her daughter (Doris Dudley) as
her niece, she refuses to marry her faithful
suitor (Herbert Marshall) until she has first
proved her independence by becoming the
crusading editor of a pioneering women's
magazine.

When in 1937 *Madame X,* like Halley's
comet, made one of its periodic returns, the
fourth in twenty-one years, this time with
Gladys George in the title role and John Beal
as the son, the *Times* dismissed it as a museum
piece.

After spending all of *Internes Can't Take
Money* (early 1937) searching for the child
taken from her by her late gangster husband,
Barbara Stanwyck then rose to true maternal
heights in *Stella Dallas* (1937), called by the
Times the "most satisfactory" remake the
screen had yet attempted. Many reviewers felt
that by this time the ubiquitous influence of
movies and women's magazines had made
Stella's atrocious taste in clothes obsolete, if
not impossible—but perhaps beneath a certain social and educational level this was not
necessarily true. In a role that at one point in
her life would have been exactly right for
Shelley Winters, Stanwyck gave one of the
strongest performances in her long career,
well worthy of her Oscar nomination.

As the loving, innocently vulgar small-town
girl who through passing attraction wins a
husband far above her (John Boles, who
else?), Stanwyck outdid even Belle Bennett's
silent version. Viewers were equally enchanted by the dewy freshness of Anne Shirley
as Laurel, Stella's instinctively refined daughter whom she pushes into choosing the more

Barbara Stanwyck in Stella Dallas

novelettes, which had also been (as adapted by Zoe Akins) the 1934–35 Pulitzer Prize play. Charlotte Lovell (Davis) briefly catches on the rebound the man (George Brent) loved but rejected by her mercenary cousin Delia (Miriam Hopkins)—just long enough to bear his child, whom she later cares for under the guise of running a small orphanage. She is about to marry Delia's brother-in-law (Jerome Cowan), who may even let her keep the child, but when Delia learns the paternity she instantly interferes and breaks off the match.

Although the play, like the novelette, had been set from 1830 to 1850, the film updated it to 1861–81, making functional use of the Civil War to dispose of the lover and to account for a home for war orphans. Pictorially, it also enabled Davis to age from the light-hearted young bridesmaid in hoop skirt and poke bonnet to a prim-lipped, angular woman whose severe iron-gray pompadour,

Bette Davis in The Old Maid

elegant world of her father and his second wife (Barbara O'Neil). The fact that *Stella Dallas* went on to dubious immortality as a long-running soap opera with a gravel-voiced actress constantly muttering "Lolly, baby, I ain't good enough fer ya!" should not detract from the solid merits of the film.

As it did in so many other genres, 1939 produced perhaps the decade's finest example of the mother-love drama, a high point even in the endlessly distinguished career of Bette Davis: *The Old Maid*. It was based on one of Edith Wharton's four *Old New York*

jet brooch and earrings, knitted shawl, fussy lace jabot and cuffs, rigid posture, stiff gestures and perpetual slight frown make her the very embodiment of a Victorian maiden aunt.

The poignance of all the 1880s scenes, as "Aunt Charlotte" sternly represses her motherly feelings and assumes the chiding tone of a censorious spinster lest her daughter (Jane Bryan) be spoiled by the wealthy, widowed Delia with whom they live, her wistful longing to tell the girl the truth at last the night before her wedding (and her inability to do so), the complex nuances of the long love-hate relationship between Charlotte and Delia, the use of eloquent silence, restraint and muted pathos—all this and its superb production values make *The Old Maid* the crowning example of the 1930s mother-love film.

Except for the previously noted cycle of family reminiscence, which usually included an idealized mother or mother surrogate, later decades have been much harder on motherhood. Their film characters have tended to be social dropouts with no visible family ties, or, if mothers did appear, they were oversexed, hateful, grotesque or at least foolish, especially if Jewish, as in *Portnoy's Complaint, Goodbye Columbus* and the driving stage mamas in *I'll Cry Tomorrow, Gypsy* and *Funny Girl*. Occasionally they were downright psychopathic, as in *Die, Die, My Darling, Bloody Mama, The Anniversary, My Lover, My Son* and *The Damned*.

When—rarely—a warmhearted and loving mother was sympathetically portrayed, without Oedipal implications, like Melina Mercouri's character in *Promise at Dawn* (1971) or Shirley MacLaine's in *The Turning Point* (1977), she seemed a strange throwback to a long-vanished age—in fact, to the '30s.

◀ SECTION 4 ▶

LONG AGO AND FAR AWAY
Escapes Still Further into the Past

14

AMERICANA
Literary Classics, Biography and Historical Fiction

To later generations, even the films discussed in the last three chapters may look like costume pictures, but, as noted, for '30s audiences the prewar years held a unique, family-album familiarity, colored with fond childhood memories, even if only absorbed by hearsay, of those days not quite beyond recall. This special nostalgia is not to be confused with the romantic fascination, inherited from the nineteenth century, of times no living person could possibly remember—those "olden" days so dear to historical novelists.

From the very first, long-established classics had attracted pioneer film-makers, as attested by any number of early silents. Not only did their titles ensure a presold audience; even more temptingly, they were in public domain, with no temperamental author to claim royalties or demand script approval. Indeed, although by actual count more silent films must have been set in the contemporary world, most of the best-*remembered* silents—the ones given the most publicity at the time, those with stupendous sets and spectacular effects, "road-shown" at advanced prices, accompanied by specially composed musical scores, with souvenir booklets on sale in the lobby—were costume pieces.

This obviously popular trend reached its dazzling zenith in the superelaborate spectacles of the late '20s, as if the silent directors were determined to go out in a blaze of glory. Indeed, the ring of clashing swords in the dueling scenes of *Don Juan* (1926), among the first audible effects ever heard from the screen, were in effect sounding the temporary death knell of just this kind of swashbuckler.

Aside from a few major studio Westerns and the even fewer films that included 1890s sequences, 1930 produced a scant dozen costume films of any kind, none in the league with the great silent spectacles. One reason, not suspected by the public at the time, was economy. As Andrew Bergman verifies in *We're in the Money,* contrary to the popular impression—that thanks to the simultaneous novelty of talkies and the influx of new acting talent from the stage, movies were the one industry to escape the effects of the 1929 crash—all the major studios were operating in the red throughout 1931 and 1932, and began to recover only late in 1933.

What better way to economize than to write scripts with only the minimum number of characters, a few modern interiors—apartments, night clubs, newspaper offices—and standard city street scenes, where extras, if any, could wear their own clothes? In the opinion of Pauline Kael, Hollywood did more than make a virtue of necessity. When films about the current scene were handled by a brilliant galaxy of New York writers, the results were bracingly astringent. Says Kael:

Even those of us who were children at the time loved the fast-moving modern city stories. The commonplaceness—even the tawdriness of the imagery was such a relief from all that silent "poetry" . . . It's hard to make clear to people who didn't live through the transition how sickly and unpleasant many of those "artistic" silent pictures were—how you wanted to scrape off all that mist and sentiment.[1]

Undoubtedly the combination of impoverished Wall Street backers and clever Broadway writers had much to do with Hollywood's temporary neglect of the picturesque past, but another, even more fundamental explanation occurs. Despite Kael's strictures, the fact remains that many silents did cast a dreamlike spell over millions, never more potently than in tales of heroes in doublet and hose, long-haired, languishing maidens, ogreish villains and pathetic monsters (like Conrad Veidt in *The Man Who Laughs*, Chaney in almost anything)—perhaps playing on subliminal childhood memories of fairy-tale books illustrated by artists like Maxfield Parrish and Howard Pyle.

It was one thing for silent audiences, lulled by theme music from the orchestra, organ or piano, to read flowery subtitles, often printed in antique type, and imagine them ideally spoken; it was quite another to hear untrained, uneducated voices, perhaps with accents made harsher by the abrasive tone of early sound systems, trying to cope with lines like "Odds bodkins! Methinks yon scurvy knave doth court a broken pate."[2]

With so many factors working against them, small wonder that costume pictures almost disappeared from the screen 1930–32, and the few that were made were almost all safe, time-tested material, old stage hits or romantic operettas, mostly starring players with stage-trained diction—e.g., *Kismet, Ro-*

mance, *Sweet Kitty Bellairs, A Connecticut Yankee* and *Alexander Hamilton*.

What is more remarkable is, once the financial and vocal difficulties had been surmounted, how strongly period films came back, produced on a more elaborate scale than ever. This was in part due to a change of taste roughly coinciding with the advent of Roosevelt's New Deal, a revulsion from the sordid realities in favor of more purely escapist fare, and partly a side effect of the Production Code, self-imposed in 1934, which turned producers' interest back to the past, especially to nineteenth-century English novels, whose writers had faced similar problems with Victorian prudery, and to French and Russian classics which frankly handled adult material impossible to touch in a modern American setting.

By the mid-'30s, Hollywood was turning out at least twenty lavish costume films a year, set in almost every conceivable historical background, from ancient Rome through Renaissance Italy to nineteenth-century England—an endless fancy-dress parade guaranteed to transport any audience out of the Depression.

To that generation, "American classics" meant the New England poets they had read in school, plus a few other nineteenth-century writers—not Melville or James, of whom they would scarcely have heard, but Poe, Irving, Cooper, Hawthorne, Louisa May Alcott and Mark Twain. Several novels by writers then living, now considered classic, were filmed in the '30s, but most dealt with contemporary life, so have been or will be treated in other chapters. (Ironically, though F. Scott Fitzgerald was working in Hollywood during the decade, none of his works was filmed.)

The first undisputed American classic to be filmed in 1930, though not updated, was subjected to other "improvements" equally highhanded. This was *Moby Dick,* based less on Melville than on a 1926 silent adaptation known as *The Sea Beast*. John Barrymore starred in both versions, starting as a young,

---

[1] *The Citizen Kane Book* (Bantam Books, 1974), p. 18.

[2] This was the situation hilariously satirized in *Singin' in the Rain* (1952).

romantic Ahab in love with a beautiful girl (Dolores Costello as "Esther" in the first film, Joan Bennett as "Faith" in the second). He loses his leg through the fault of his scheming half brother Derek—another character undreamed of by Melville. This sort of adaptation, which gave rise to the definition of love as "what's left of the book in the movie version," was fortunately less typical of filmed classics of the later '30s than of the silents, when audience naïveté and ignorance were apparently assumed to be unlimited.

Far more faithful in letter and spirit to its original was *Tom Sawyer,* directed by John Cromwell, Paramount's Christmas 1930 show at its first-run theaters across the country. In the title role, Jackie Coogan, then fifteen, once the world's best-known child star, after several years as a teen-aged has-been, made a temporarily successful comeback, with precocious Mitzi Green as Becky Thatcher, Junior Durkin as Huck Finn and Jackie Searl, then the screen's favorite brat, as the odious Sid. All the familiar episodes were included: whitewashing the fence, the boys' attendance at their own funeral service and the climactic battle in the cave with Injun Joe. The *Times* reviewed it much more favorably than it did Selznick's more elaborately produced and expensively cast Technicolor *Adventures of Tom Sawyer* (1938).

So successful was Paramount's version that the studio used the same cast in the same roles (including Clara Blandick as Aunt Polly and Jane Darwell as the Widow Douglas) in the first talkie version of *Huckleberry Finn* (1931), though without quite the same fidelity to Twain. Eugene Pallette and Oscar Apfel were effective as the King and the Duke, but critics noted too much emphasis on the youthful romances of Tom and Becky, Huck and Mary Jane, and complained of the omission of the brutal Grangerford-Shepherdson feud so important in the book and the downplaying of Huck's relationship with Jim. On the other hand, the *Times* was even unhappier with the updated social attitudes of MGM's 1939 version (Mickey Rooney as

Huck, Walter Connolly and William Frawley as the King and the Duke), which turned Huck into a convinced abolitionist, who at last persuades the Widow Douglas to free Jim.

Two other Twain works successfully filmed in the '30s, *A Connecticut Yankee* (1931) and *The Prince and the Pauper* (1937), were both set in the British past, so will be discussed in Chapter 16. The most memorable '30s screen version of an American classic, one which has indeed become something of a classic itself, was undoubtedly RKO's *Little Women* (1933). According to David O. Selznick, quoted by Michael Pointer in *American Film,* RKO executives and sales heads so far misread the changing public mood that they at first wanted to subject the beloved novel to the "modernizing" treatment that had proved so disastrous whenever tried. As it is, what gives *Little Women* its enduring charm is its tender respect for both the period and the values of the novel.

Although, incredibly enough, the role of Jo had been coveted by Constance Bennett, whose brittle sophistication would have been totally wrong, Katharine Hepburn, perfectly cast as the moody, tomboyish girl whose spunky independence ranges far beyond the ladylike limitations of her time, contributed to this, her fourth film, a characterization that she has never surpassed. The prolonged illness and death of Beth, the only sentimentalized sister, is a problem in any version of *Little Women,* but Jean Parker is at least inoffensive, while, as Meg and Amy, Frances Dee and Joan Bennett fit in beautifully, with no trace of the brisk modern heroines they usually played. All the character players are equally fine: Paul Lukas as Professor Bhaer, Spring Byington as Marmee, Henry Stephenson as Mr. Lawrence and especially Edna May Oliver as the testy Aunt March.

"It is, of course, the mood which is the important part of the work," observed Richard Watts in the *Herald Tribune,* "and it is the unashamed straightforwardness of the writing, the unpatronizing shrewdness of George Cukor's direction and, above all, Miss Hep-

burn's beautiful playing which make *Little Women* an exquisite screen drama."

With *Little Women* such a resounding success, setting new box-office records at the Music Hall and being nominated for three Oscars, it was inevitable that its sequel (but not equal), *Little Men,* would be filmed, and so it was, late in 1934, by an independent studio, Mascot, with Erin O'Brien Moore and Ralph Morgan taking over from Hepburn and Lukas as Jo and Professor Bhaer, now married and running a predecessor of Boys' Town, a very special school for boys, even rebellious street urchins. The cast included just about every boy actor in Hollywood, from Frankie Darro to Dickie Moore, but the *Times* found the whole affair too deliberately tear-jerking. In all fairness to the film, it must be noted that the same charge might be made against the novel, which, unlike its predecessor, was written for the edification of children. (*Little Men* was remade in 1940 with Kay Francis and Carl Esmond, with even more deplorable results.)

As is evident, many of these homespun favorites, most centered around children or adolescents, lingered in that mythical realm that many Americans, at least those of WASP descent, had absorbed from parents and grandparents, an idyllic, Norman Rockwell America of quaint villages, little red schoolhouses, covered bridges and swimming holes, idealized in many a forgotten rustic romance once read by millions—for example, the works of Gene Stratton Porter, Mary Jane Holmes and Harold Bell Wright. With such emphasis on down-home folksiness, calico and gingham, overalls and straw hats, against a background of country kitchens and general stores, the visual appeal, if any, of films in this genre was the very opposite of that associated with costume pictures set in more picturesque periods of the European past.

In this subliterary limbo of vaguely familiar titles, surely not classics, but of some historic interest as barometers of American taste, would belong such '30s films, most of them remakes of silents, as *Tol'able David* (1930), *Lena Rivers, Rebecca of Sunnybrook Farm, Tess of the Storm Country* (all 1932), *Peck's Bad Boy, The Hoosier Schoolmaster* (both 1935) and *Mother Carey's Chickens* (1938).

A few, of course, rose above the general level of mediocrity, such as *Ruggles of Red Gap* (1935), *Mrs. Wiggs of the Cabbage Patch* (1934), *Anne of Green Gables* (1934) and *Little Lord Fauntleroy* (1936). Clearly those set in the 1880s or later blend and overlap with the nostalgia for rural Americana exemplified by *Way Down East* and several Will Rogers vehicles.

In fact, with the exception of *The Last of the Mohicans* (1936), the only American-set native classic filmed in the '30s to go further back than the nineteenth century for its background was Monogram's *The Scarlet Letter* (1934), which the *Times* did not review. Though it may not have equaled the Victor Seastrom silent (1926), which starred Lillian Gish and Lars Hanson, it was a faithful version of the novel, authentically set and costumed (to judge by surviving stills) and sensibly cast, with Colleen Moore (who, unlike Clara Bow, had developed from a flapper star into an actress) as Hester Prynne, Hardie Albright (a specialist in young weaklings) as Reverend Dimmesdale and Henry B. Walthall, as in the silent, as Roger Chillingworth.

Not all films dramatizing the American past were drawn from acknowledged classics. A far larger number were either screen originals or based on currently popular novels or plays. In time they ranged from the New England settlements of the seventeenth century down to the post-Civil War decades on the frontier and in the cities, there merging with the through-the-years chronicles and nostalgic films.

Here it must be frankly acknowledged that compared to European and British history the American past offered far less colorful possibilities. Undoubtedly decent family

Katharine Hepburn, Joan Bennett, Frances Dee, Jean Parker in Little Women

men, churchgoers, good administrators, fond of dogs and children, patiently hammering out political and diplomatic compromises for the common good, make more reliable rulers of a country than mad emperors, royal favorites or crafty powers behind the throne, but they are not the stuff of which intriguing drama is made, as proved on TV by the admirable but unexciting *Adams Chronicles.*

Other than *The Scarlet Letter,* the only '30s film to touch on the New England Puritan experience utilized, not surprisingly, the Salem witchcraft persecutions of 1692. Though it cannot compare with Arthur Miller's *The Crucible* or other more serious fictional treatments of America's most appalling recorded case of mass hysteria, *Maid of Salem* (1937), directed by Frank Lloyd, was an excellent melodrama which used many actual characters and incidents to build a fictitious story about a girl whose parents had been burned as witches in England and whose secret meetings in the forest with a rebel exile from Virginia are taken to be rendezvous with the devil.

Claudette Colbert and Fred MacMurray were rather surprising choices for the put-upon lovers, and his last-minute horseback rescue of her from the gallows strained credibility, but both stars performed well, assisted by an unusually distinguished cast of those character players who so often gave this kind of picture its strength. Bonita Granville, who had been the malicious brat in *These Three* (1936), scored again as one of the apparently possessed girls whose accusations start the trouble. Her parents were Edward Ellis and Beulah Bondi, and among the other Puritan accusers or accused were Gale Sondergaard, Harvey Stephens, E. E. Clive, Ivan Simpson and Pedro De Cordoba.

Unless one counts *Naughty Marietta* (1935), set in French colonial New Orleans, the century and a half between the Salem hangings and the French and Indian War was ignored in '30s films, as indeed it has been in historical fiction. *The Last of the Mohicans* (1936) was a competent version of Cooper's familiar old warhorse, featuring a number of attractive players of the second rank of stardom, with British and American roles appropriately distributed. Randolph Scott was Hawkeye, Robert Barrat Chingachgook and Phillip Reed Uncas, the somewhat overshadowed title character, all of whose "noble savage" simplicity is presumably meant to contrast with the British spit-and-polish attitude of Major Heyward (Henry Wilcoxon).

The two Munro sisters were oddly cast, or miscast; the usually blond, sophisticated Binnie Barnes as a brunette ingenue, Alice, the usually dark and wistful Heather Angel as a blond Cora—exactly the opposite from their descriptions in the book—almost as if someone had mistakenly reversed their roles. One critic complained bitterly of the emphasis on a romantic attachment between Hawkeye and Alice undreamed of by Cooper, but since she ends with Heyward and Hawkeye with his rifle, this hardly violates the integrity of the novel, such as it was.

Far more interesting are the other pair of lovers, Uncas and Cora. In the novel General Munro is careful to explain that the mother of his "dusky" Cora was actually a native of the West Indies, hence the attraction between her and Uncas can be understood, if not encouraged. Since in the film it is limited to chaste, yearning glances and tender gestures, this would hardly seem to matter. In the book both are murdered by Hurons; in the film Uncas is kicked off a cliff by the villainous Magua (Bruce Cabot), whereupon thoroughly Caucasian Cora leaps after him. Unless it could have been proved that Uncas was really white, some tragic outcome for any interracial romance was inevitable, or so '30s movie-goers had been conditioned to believe.

Set in the same period, a few decades before the Revolution, on the Pennsylvania frontier, where a group called the Black Boys rebelled against the disciplinary forces of the crown, *Allegheny Uprising* (1939) proved a general disappointment. Not even John Wayne and Claire Trevor, fresh from their triumph in *Stagecoach* (1939), could save

Fred MacMurray and Claudette Colbert in **Maid of Salem**

what the *Times* called "a sprawling, confused costume picture."

Despite George Washington's much-publicized bicentennial in 1932, Hollywood made no dramatic use of the best-known figures, battles or incidents of the Revolution. In fact, only three films touched on those crucial years at all, and then only as they affected rural folk far removed from the stirring events in Boston, New York and Philadelphia.

The Great Meadow (1931), a faithful transcription of Elizabeth Madox Roberts' novel, concerned those Virginians who, inspired by Daniel Boone's glowing description of the new land, pioneered the wilderness of Kentucky while the Revolution was being fought along the Eastern seaboard. The valiant mother (Lucille La Verne) of the hero (John Mack Brown) is killed protecting his young wife (Eleanor Boardman) from Indians, he himself is later reported dead, his supposed widow marries another, and a frontier Enoch Arden triangle develops. Though praised for its rugged authenticity, the film sounds like no more than a superior Eastern Western, and certainly had no direct relation to the issues of the Revolution.

Even further removed from the shot and shell was *The Pursuit of Happiness* (1934), based on a stage hit by Lawrence Langner and Armina Marshall, which, despite its

Revolutionary Connecticut setting, was a lighthearted romantic comedy. This was the one that rediscovered the old New England custom of "bundling," by which, to keep warm on cold winter evenings, courting couples were allowed to share a bed—but fully clothed and firmly separated by a center board that folded down from the head. As the daughter of Charlie Ruggles and Mary Boland, Joan Bennett falls in love with a young Hessian deserter (Francis Lederer), who takes too literally the assurances of the Declaration of Independence. (The plot obviously owes something to Shaw's *Arms and the Man,* and indeed a 1950 stage musical version was called *Arms and the Girl.*)

The only picture of the 1930s to deal seriously with any phase of the Revolution was *Drums Along the Mohawk* (1939), based on Walter D. Edmonds' best-selling novel, directed by John Ford, one of the first outdoor historical films to be made in color. Henry Fonda played a young farmer of the Mohawk Valley in upstate New York during the years when such settlers were constantly harassed not only by the British but by hostile Indians and Tories.

"A first-rate historical film, as rich atmospherically as it is in action," said the *Times.* Claudette Colbert was Fonda's wife, and the supporting cast included many familiar faces (John Carradine, Ward Bond, Jessie Ralph, Arthur Shields), but Edna May Oliver as "war-like Widow McKlennan, with a tongue sharper than a tomahawk and a soft spot in her heart for a handsome man" walked off with character player honors. Even this excellent picture did not attempt to dramatize any major event of the Revolution.

The immediate post-Revolutionary years were reflected only in *Alexander Hamilton* (1931). In an unusual opening, under the credits the three familiar figures from the painting *The Spirit of '76* march toward the camera, to the shrill accompaniment of "Yankee Doodle," setting the mood for the first scene, a well-staged re-enactment of Washington's farewell to his troops. Alan

Mowbray was highly praised as Washington, Montagu Love was Jefferson and Morgan Wallace, Monroe.

Like all George Arliss' early talkies, this was based on one of his old stage vehicles, in this case one he himself had co-authored. Even school children studying American history from illustrated texts must have noticed that Arliss, then a withered sixty-three, bore no resemblance to the handsome Hamilton in his thirties.

The plot concerned Hamilton's brief dalliance, during his wife's long stay in London, with a Mrs. Reynolds (June Collyer), whose husband (Ralf Harolde), hired by a crooked, fictitious senator (Dudley Digges), tries to blackmail Hamilton and circulates gossip to prevent the passage of his "Assumption Bill," by which the federal government was to assume the debts of the individual states. The most dramatic phase of Hamilton's life— perhaps the only one—his running feud with Aaron Burr, culminating in the fatal duel, was not used; the film ends, as did all Arliss' historical vehicles, with the hero outwitting his enemies.

The War of 1812, beginning with the burning of Washington (with Spring Byington as Dolley Madison) and ending after the Battle of New Orleans, was the background of Cecil B. De Mille's *The Buccaneer* (1938), starring Fredric March as Jean Lafitte. This is the film whose Hollywood premiere was for some unfathomable reason fictitiously used to trigger the apocalyptic riot that climaxes *The Day of the Locust* (1975). In reviewing it, Nugent of the *Times* fairly outpunned himself, referring to De Mille as "professor demeritus," for whom "the De Millennium has come," and the picture as "run of De Mille." He dismissed the star in a widely quoted phrase: "March comes in like a lion and goes out like a ham."

In the midst of all his piratical and military adventures, Lafitte must choose between a Dutch girl (Franciska Gaal) who loves him and a New Orleans belle (Margot Grahame) whom he loves. As Dominic You, erstwhile cannoneer to Napoleon, Akim Tamiroff got the best notices. Unlike the 1958 *Buccaneer* (only a partial remake, with an altered story line), in which Charlton Heston, playing Andrew Jackson for the second time, was co-starred with Yul Brynner as Lafitte, the 1938 cast lists Jackson (Hugh Sothern) twelfth, too minor to be mentioned in the reviews.

Old Hickory as President, played by Lionel Barrymore, came in for much fuller treatment in *The Gorgeous Hussy* (1936), Joan Crawford's only venture into costume drama. Supposedly based on the life of Margaret O'Neill Eaton, wife of a cabinet member whose snubbing by other Washington matrons led Jackson to form his "kitchen cabinet," the film was richly produced, with an impressive cast that included Melvyn Douglas, Franchot Tone, Robert Taylor, James Stewart, Louis Calhern, Alison Skipworth and especially Beulah Bondi (then Hollywood's favorite backwoods matron) as the pipe-smoking Rachel Jackson.

But "Pothouse Peg," as she was known because her father kept a tavern, was cleaned up and idealized beyond all recognition. An apologetic foreword to the film warned "This story of Peggy Eaton and her times is not presented as a precise account of either— rather as fiction founded upon historical fact. Except for historically important personages, the characters are fictional." Since most of the characters *were* "historically important personages," this left confusion thrice confounded. What was most puzzling to the audience was that Crawford, who had played so many hard-boiled working girls, mistresses and even prostitutes, was, according to the *Times,* "gorgeous, but not a hussy." Rather, she was "a maligned Anne of Green Gables, a persecuted Pollyanna, a dismayed Dolly Dimple."

Jackson, this time played by Edward Ellis, also figured importantly in *Man of Conquest* (1939), an ambitious, well-received Republic production, with Richard Dix as Sam Houston. The unusually strong cast included Gail Patrick, Joan Fontaine, Victor Jory,

Ralph Morgan and Robert Barrat. Considering the newly proclaimed Good Neighbor policy toward Latin America, this was "not a tactful film," said the *Times,* "but it's a remarkably good one." It covered almost all of Houston's public career, including the fall of the Alamo, his victory over Santa Ana in 1838 and at the end of the admission of Texas to the Union seen as a triumph of Jacksonian democracy over Mexican dictatorship.

Although no '30s film (nor any later, for that matter) directly dramatized the Mexican War of 1846–48, several dealt with the aftermath in California, the conflict between land-grabbing Yankees and the aristocratic *hacendados,* who held their frequently vast *ranchos* under centuries-old grants from the Spanish crown.

Most such films were variations on *The Mark of Zorro,* in which an embittered young Spanish Californian turns outlaw in disguise to right the wrongs done to his people. The first of these—the first film reviewed by the *Times* in 1931—was *The Lash* (originally titled *Adios*), set specifically in 1848, with Richard Barthelmess as the hero, who under the sobriquet of "El Puma" stirs rebellion and after shooting a crooked land agent and tax collector (Fred Kohler) must flee to Mexico. The cast included two attractive pseudo-señoritas, Mary Astor as his sweetheart, who follows him into exile, and Marian Nixon as his sister, who stays to marry the head of a vigilante committee.

The Bold Caballero (1935), a "B" variation starring Robert Livingston and Heather Angel, sounds like an actual remake of *Zorro,* except that the hero is protecting oppressed Indians under the Spanish rule.

1936 saw four films set in old California, of which by far the best reviewed was *The Robin Hood of El Dorado,* in which Warner Baxter (who had already played the Indian hero in the silent *Ramona,* the Cisco Kid and "the squaw man") was Joaquin Murrieta, a Mexican peon turned outlaw to avenge the murder of his wife (Margo) and the lynching of his brother.

The *Times* was pleasantly amazed at Hollywood's courage in making it:

It is ironic that Hollywood, unable to make films of *It Can't Happen Here*, *Paths of Glory* or *The Forty Days of Musa Dagh* through fear of treading on foreign sensibilities, is not restrained at all when it comes to pointing an accusing finger at certain unpalatable phases of our own national history. It would seem that the only toes we safely may tread upon are our own.

Released the same month, set in exactly the same period and background, *Sutter's Gold*, starring Edward Arnold as the Swiss upon whose property gold was discovered, was denounced by one reviewer as a complete falsification of Sutter's genuinely tragic story. Instead, it depicted him as just as gold-mad as the rest and involved him in a fictitious affair with a European adventuress (Binnie Barnes) suggestive of Lola Montez.

Rebellion starred Tom Keene, Duncan Renaldo and Margarita Cansino (the future Rita Hayworth). The daughter of a California Spanish ranch owner murdered in 1850, she goes to Washington to protest, and Keene is sent back with her to clean out the gang stealing the homes and lands of the rightful owners. (In the same vein, the next year Rita starred in *Old Louisiana*, in which she was the daughter of a Spanish governor before the Louisiana Purchase. Keene was among the settlers who had to fight the villain who monopolized the fur concession from the Spaniards.)

Within a few days of the release of *Rebellion* came *Ramona*, the first 20th Century-Fox production in the improved color. The 1884 Helen Hunt Jackson novel had been filmed twice in silents, in 1916 with Mary Pickford and in 1928 with Dolores Del Rio, but reviewers of 1936 were not at all impressed by Loretta Young as the beautiful half-breed, still less by Don Ameche as her Indian husband, Alessandro, murdered by whites, Kent Taylor as Felipe, the Spanish aristocrat who loves her, nor even by Pauline Frederick as his heartless mother, Señora

Moreno, who, far from the usual lovable *hacendada*, was a dyed-in-the-wool white supremacist. (It seems her sister, equally haughty, had turned down Ramona's Scotch father, thereby driving him into the arms of an Indian bride.) *Ramona* was praised, if at all, for its new achievements in outdoor color effects.

The following year the same studio, perhaps making use of some of the same sets and costumes, offered yet another *Zorro* variation, *The Californian* (1937), in which Ricardo Cortez returns from Spain to Southern California and turns outlaw to protect his people from the ruthless Americans. As noted, this seemed a very safe conflict to deal with. The much more serious 1840s–50s problem involved in the continual westward expansion, the increasingly bitter national division over the extension of slavery into the new territories, was never touched. Most films about the advancing frontier were simple Westerns which ignored any such social implications.

Possibly inspired by the success of *Mutiny on the Bounty* (1935) or by the African sequences in *Anthony Adverse* (1936), two seagoing melodramas of 1937 purported to deal with the iniquities of the slave trade. In the more dubious of the two, *Slave Ship*, Warner Baxter was the captain of a jinxed slaver called the *Albatross*, prospering at his trade in the late 1850s, until love for a Virginia belle (Elizabeth Allan) makes him see the error of his profitable ways. Ordering his first mate (Wallace Beery) to pay off his hard-bitten crew and hire honest replacements, he takes his bride aboard for what he plans as a honeymoon to Jamaica, where they will settle. But the mate, of course, has double-crossed him, and the evil crew mutiny, forcing the ship to sail to Africa for one last slaving raid. How the captain outwits them, aided by a pugnacious cabin boy (Mickey Rooney), made a violent, brutal, not especially convincing film.

A few months later, *Souls at Sea* (1937) found Gary Cooper in a less ambiguous position as an officer who ships on slavers in the early 1840s but only to run them aground, steer them into British hands or otherwise make sure that their human cargo is freed. Working under cover for the British Government, he and his colorful sidekick (George Raft) sail as passengers aboard a packet bound from Liverpool to Philadelphia when it catches fire at sea.

Forced to play God by eliminating some of the more troublesome passengers to save the rest, Cooper finds himself charged with murder, the charge pressed by the girl he loves (Frances Dee), whose brother (Henry Wilcoxon), a secret slaver, was among the victims. The situation, based on an actual case of 1841, exactly anticipates *Abandon Ship* (1957), twenty years later, but the critical consensus was that the slave trade and the romance only confused what should have been a provocative moral issue about the hero's innocence or guilt.

A recurrent theme much easier to dramatize was the inevitable, often violent, conflict as each new means of transportation replaced, and in effect destroyed, its predecessor, with the railroads usually cast as the villain. In historical period the earliest of these, though made late in the decade, was *Stand Up and Fight* (1939), which the *Times* considered a brutal but "brisk and blood-tingling entertainment." At the Cumberland Gap in 1844 a bankrupt Maryland aristocrat (Robert Taylor) is working to extend the Baltimore and Ohio railroad across the Alleghenies—an aim which brings him into bloody collision with Wallace Beery, manager of an obsolescent stagecoach line, who also runs slaves on the side in the company's wagons. Despite countless beatings, the hero ultimately saves his attacker's life and job, and also, of course, gets the girl (Florence Rice).

Far more pastoral was *The Farmer Takes a Wife* (1935), Henry Fonda's film debut in the role he had created on Broadway, hailed by Andre Sennwald in the *Times* as "the most lovable of recent American folk plays." Based on Walter Edmonds' novel *Rome Haul*, it re-created in affectionate detail the 1850s, when the Erie "Canawl" had become such a permanent way of life to the boaters who plied it (at four miles an hour) that they still could not consider railroads a serious threat. Janet Gaynor, cook on the boat of Charles Bickford, naturally falls in love with quiet-spoken farm boy Fonda, but much of the folksy charm came from quaint background characters played by such as Slim Summerville, Andy Devine, Roger Imhof and Margaret Hamilton, and the fond recollection of an era even then beginning to pass away.

Besides *The Farmer Takes a Wife* and the musical *High, Wide and Handsome* (1937), two other films made vigorous use of historical local color of the 1850s, Goldwyn's *Barbary Coast* (1935) and Warners' *Frisco Kid* (1935), both, as is evident from the titles, set in San Francisco. Released hardly a month apart, the two films are curiously parallel, dealing with the violence of a newly rich, brawling frontier town that was also a seaport, its powerful gamblers and their light ladies, crusading newspapermen, fearless judges and the vigilante mobs respectable citizens felt compelled to organize in the name of law and order.

In *Barbary Coast*, written by Hecht and MacArthur, Edward G. Robinson played the owner of Frisco's leading gambling hell, Miriam Hopkins was his mistress, the lady known as Swan, and Joel McCrea the young prospector from the East who wins her heart in yet another variation on *Camille,* but Frank Craven as Colonel Cobb, proprietor of the town's first newspaper, got the best reviews.

In *Frisco Kid* the characters parallel to Robinson and Hopkins (Ricardo Cortez and Lily Damita) were secondary, and in the romance of the worldling redeemed by the love of a good person the sexes were reversed: Cagney was a violent Irishman who battles his way up from bouncer to king of the Barbary Coast, and Margaret Lindsay the high-minded newspaper owner who against all odds loves him and in the end saves him from vigilante justice.

Though considering the film "a blatant steal from Howard Hawks' *Barbary Coast*," Everson in program notes for a showing at the New School calls it "big, blustering and quite spectacular, yet it doesn't wallow in its own elegance (as perhaps *Barbary Coast* did) and gets on with its no-nonsense plot with no time wasted."

Except for these few, most films attempting to depict American life in the immediate pre-Civil War decades were musicals laid in the Old South—that totally idealized and romanticized South that was one of Hollywood's, and the nation's, favorite myths, replete with courtly, white-goateed colonels sipping mint juleps on their pillared porticoes, served by faithful Uncle Toms, while other docile darkies sang and strummed their banjos in the magnolia-scented moonlight.

Typical were two 1930 operettas, *Dixiana*, set in New Orleans in 1840, and *Cameo Kirby*, the same in 1850, the latter based on an old Booth Tarkington novel, as also was *Mississippi* (1935), a Bing Crosby vehicle which had been filmed in 1929 as *River of Romance*. Shirley Temple's *The Little Colonel* (1935), her first costume picture, in which she danced up and down stairs with trusty servitor Bill Robinson, was such a hit that it was virtually reprised later the same year in *The Littlest Rebel,* with Robinson again as a dancing slave, and Abraham Lincoln (Frank McGlynn) introduced as a benevolent *deus ex machina* to heal the wounds of a chivalrous, honorable Civil War in which neither side was wrong.

In a decade in which *Gone With the Wind,* the most expensive, spectacular and fantastically publicized picture the world had yet seen, was the climactic achievement, Hollywood could hardly be accused of ignoring the Civil War, yet otherwise it produced strangely few films that touched even indirectly on the most serious crisis in American history. This is all the more surprising since in the '30s

Henry Fonda and Janet Gaynor
in **The Farmer Takes a Wife**

any native-born American over seventy must have retained at least some childhood impressions of the great conflict, reinforced, especially in the South, by firsthand, often bitter, memories of parents and grandparents who had lived through the worst of it. Though the ranks of veterans in blue and gray turning out for G.A.R. and Confederate parades naturally thinned each year, spry octogenarians still survived who could recall their days as teen-aged buglers or drummer boys.

Except for the three spy melodramas already noted (*Only the Brave,* 1930, *Secret Service,* 1931, and *Operator 13,* 1934), almost as romantic as the musicals, the first '30s film with a Civil War background was *So Red the Rose* (1935), based on Stark Young's novel. Since its release preceded the publication of *GWTW* by more than a year, the numerous parallels can only be put down to coincidence or to the limited options open to any novelist writing about the effects of the war on the South.

As Valette Bedford, belle of Portobello plantation in Mississippi, Margaret Sullavan (with Walter Connolly and Janet Beecher as her parents) was conventionally coquettish, but with none of Scarlett O'Hara's fire, spirit and "gumption." Her crush on her reserved cousin Duncan (Randolph Scott) curiously anticipates Scarlett's relationship with Ashley, without Rhett and Melanie to complete the quadrangle.

The story simply traces the decline and fall of the Bedfords, climaxed by the burning of their beautiful home and ending on a note of "desolation, humbled pride and the remnants of a house in mourning for the men it sacrificed in a doomed cause." The frankly elegiac tone for the good old days way down South was too much for the *Times* reviewer:

It is difficult in this turbulent day to subscribe to the film's point of view or to share its rage against the uncouth legions of Mr. Lincoln as they dash about the lovely Southern landscape putting crazy notions in the heads of plantation slaves . . . The film has its moments of unconscious irony that shatter the mood it is trying to evoke, such as the enthusiastic cheering of the slaves when their master goes off to fight their liberators, and Margaret Sullavan's absurdly sentimental appeal to the slaves later on when they are primed for rebellion.

By October 1936, when Republic's *Hearts in Bondage* opened in New York, *GWTW* had already sold fifty thousand copies and was the most talked-about best seller of the year, causing Robert Garland to observe in the *New York American:* "And now thanks to Margaret Mitchell's *Gone With the Wind,* we are on the verge of a cycle of books, plays and motion pictures in which the American Civil War is utilized as a background. Among the forerunners is *Hearts in Bondage.*" His assumption, though understandable, was wrong, for although the film was late in reaching New York, *Film Daily* had reviewed it two months before the Mitchell novel was published.

Randolph Scott and Margaret Sullavan in **So Red the Rose**

Despite its misleading title, *Hearts in Bondage* dealt neither with slavery nor sadomasochism. Though panned by *Variety,* this ambitious production, Lew Ayres' directorial debut, won high praise from *Film Daily* for its professionalism. Don Miller in *B Movies* blames its relative failure on the miscasting of James Dunn and Mae Clarke as the leads.

Dunn is a Union naval officer dishonorably discharged when, during a Confederate attack on Norfolk, he sinks the *Merrimac* instead of burning it as ordered, thus enabling the rebels to raise and use it. However, he redeems himself by helping his uncle, John Ericsson (Fritz Leiber), perfect the *Monitor,* and volunteers to serve on it. In the climactic on-screen battle between the *Monitor* and the *Merrimac* (cited by Miller for the excellence of its special effects, done with miniatures), Dunn's fiancée's brother (David Manners), who had chosen the Southern side, is killed, but the lovers are eventually reconciled. Meeting at their old trysting place by the Potomac in Washington, they are surprised by President Lincoln (Frank McGlynn, as usual), who appears like a vision of a saint to speak a few mystic words of encouragement before marching on, to the strains of "The Battle Hymn of the Republic."

Two years later, Lincoln (now acted by John Carradine) played a somewhat more functional role in *Of Human Hearts* (1938), based on Honore Morrow's story *Benefits Forgot,* which told of a frontier couple (Walter Huston and Beulah Bondi) whose son (growing from Gene Reynolds into James Stewart) is driven from home by his father's stern, God-fearing ways, but later helped through medical school, at much sacrifice, by his widowed mother. He neglects her, however, until summoned from the front lines by Lincoln himself, admonished and sent home to mother. Except for this unconvincing *deus ex machina* ending, *Of Human Hearts* was praised for its simple, true picture of American rural life in the mid-nineteenth century.

Aside from these occasional guest appearances, Lincoln himself was the central character in three memorable films. He was, appropriately enough, the subject of the very first biographical talkie about an American, which was also D. W. Griffith's first sound film, *Abraham Lincoln* (1930). It was the only one of the three to attempt to cover his whole life, so the only one to include the Civil War.

With a script officially credited to Stephen Vincent Benét and set designs by William Cameron Menzies, it remains an impressive achievement, mainly, as *The New Yorker*'s brief notice suggests, because of Walter Huston's "towering" performance in the title role. The idealized romance with Ann Rutledge (Una Merkel) was deplored even in 1930 as too cloyingly reminiscent of silents at their worst, but the war scenes, including Sheridan's ride, were much admired. The assassination was fully dramatized, with Kay Hammond as a waspish Mary Lincoln and Ian Keith appropriately flamboyant as John Wilkes Booth. A frankly reverent tone was maintained through the end, in which a log cabin dissolves into the Lincoln Memorial.

Compared to this, the other two Lincoln films were far more modest in their aims, as indicated by their titles. In John Ford's splendid *Young Mr. Lincoln* (1939), the Ann Rutledge affair is lightly, if touchingly, sketched, and Mary Todd (Marjorie Weaver) appears as a minor character, but the script concentrates dramatically on the famous trial in which Lincoln as a young lawyer saved the two sons of the Widow Clay from a trumped-up charge of murder based on circumstantial evidence.

As the anguished mother, Alice Brady gave a marvelous performance, far more moving than the one in *In Old Chicago* (1937), for which she had won the Oscar the previous year. Of the star, the *Times* said:

Henry Fonda's . . . performance kindles the film, makes it a moving unity, at once gentle and quizzically comic . . . The result of it, happily, is not merely a natural and straightforward biography but a film which indisputably has the right to be called Americana.

Released in February 1940, but filmed in 1939, *Abe Lincoln in Illinois,* Robert Sherwood's adaptation of his own Pulitzer Prize play, was the most touching Lincoln study and the most psychologically penetrating in its presentation of the hero's prairie years.

Ruth Gordon was impressive as a frankly drawn, shrewish Mary Todd, as was Gene Lockhart as Stephen Douglas. As for Raymond Massey, "you will simply think of him as Lincoln." Certainly no later portrait of Lincoln on stage, screen or TV has ever surpassed this masterful, compassionate study of the Great Emancipator as a deeply troubled man.

Of those caught up in the aftermath of the assassination, the only one to receive screen attention was Dr. Samuel Mudd, the unfortunate physician who set Booth's broken leg, not knowing who he was, and in the hysteria of the day was sentenced to life in a pestilential Civil War prison that rivaled Devil's Island. Warner Baxter played the title role in *The Prisoner of Shark Island* (1936), an American Dreyfus who suffered for years until his heroism during a yellow fever epidemic finally won him a belated pardon. Thanks to Nunnally Johnson's script and John Ford's direction, the grim story moved briskly and convincingly, but one reviewer complained that, true or not, this kind of situation, in which injustice is finally righted and the innocent man vindicated, was already overfamiliar. (In an early scene, Lincoln was played once again by Frank McGlynn.)

The America that emerged from the Civil War into the gilded age of the Robber Barons, rejected in scorn by Henrys James and Adams and caustically satirized by Mark Twain, offered few heroic figures for dramatization by later generations. One must look long for even cameo glimpses of any Presidents after Lincoln (e.g., Grant and Arthur in *Silver Dollar,* 1932, McKinley and Teddy Roosevelt in *This Is My Affair,* 1937). Many Westerns were, of course, set in the decades immediately after the Civil War, but very few films dealt with life in the same period in the older

American cities (in fact, only *Romance,* 1930, upper-class New York in the 1860s, *The Age of Innocence,* 1934, the same in the 1870s, and *In Old Chicago,* 1937, 1870–71). Most films reflecting the 1870s and 1880s at all used them as background for one segment in through-the-years operettas or tycoon chronicles.

The only tycoon film set entirely in this period was *The Toast of New York* (1937), supposedly based on Bouck White's *The Book of Daniel Drew* and a story, *The Robber Barons,* by Matthew Josephson. The change of title, plus the addition of music and lyrics by Nathaniel Shilkret, were enough to telegraph that this was no muckraking exposé of American business piracy but a romantic melodrama, with emphasis on picturesque period detail. Said the *Times,* "[Edward] Arnold is getting to be to industry what George Arliss was to history: a general utility man."

This time he was "Jubilee Jim" Fisk, locked in deadly financial combat with "Uncle Dan'l" Drew (Donald Meek) and Commodore Vanderbilt (Clarence Kolb). The film forgives Fisk for causing "Black Friday" in 1869, ignores his connection with the Tweed Ring and lets him atone in a brave dying speech after being shot by his rival, Ned Stokes (Cary Grant), who for some reason is called "Nick Boyd." In the most startling change of all, Fisk's mistress, the notorious Josie Mansfield (Frances Farmer), is cleaned up to a dedicated, virginal young entertainer who was never more than a friend to Fisk and wanted only to entrust her pure love to his partner (Grant). It was just as well that no other biographical films about actual financiers were attempted, since *The Toast of New York* was even more sentimentalized than *Diamond Jim* (1935), and with less reason.

On the whole, the screen did better with heroic figures who needed no whitewashing: statesmen, pioneers, scientists, crusaders for justice. Oddly enough, considering how totally technology had transformed the world in the past century, no one thought of dramatizing the life of an inventor until *The Story of Alexander Graham Bell* (1939). Although to later generations the very mention of Don Ameche as Bell seemed such a laughable cliché that "ameche" for a time became a slang word for telephone, the film itself was praised by the *Times* as superior to *Suez* and *Jesse James,* if only because Tyrone Power was not in it.

Henry Fonda was Bell's assistant, Watson, and Loretta Young his deaf wife, backed (in a coup of type-casting that outdid even *Four Daughters*) by her three real sisters, Sally Blane and Polly Ann and Georgiana Young, as her screen sisters, all daughters of Charles Coburn and Spring Byington. In a not too convincing climax, Bell battles Western Union to protect his patent. Undoubtedly the success of *Bell* led MGM in 1940 to make both *Young Tom Edison* and *Edison the Man.*

20th Century-Fox's last biographical venture of the decade was *Stanley and Livingstone* (1939), highly commended for its authenticity. Among other qualities, it had the unique virtue of a truly international subject, emphasizing Anglo-U.S. solidarity, since, of course, one of its title characters was American, one British. "*Stanley and Livingstone,*" said the *Times,* "is the best break the Fourth Estate has had on the screen since the beginning of the Stereotype Era."

Spencer Tracy was Stanley, the New York newspaperman assigned to find the Scottish missionary Livingstone (Sir Cedric Hardwicke). A fictitious romance was added (Tracy lost Nancy Kelly to Richard Greene), but even this did not detract from the overall accuracy, which was marred only by a pseudo-pious ending in which Stanley, saddened and prematurely aged, returns to Africa to carry on Livingstone's unfinished missionary business.

Although the tycoon films and the other American parallels to *Cavalcade* necessarily touched on the Spanish-American War in their tour through modern history (with somewhat the same ambiguity with which the

British treated the Boer War), only one film took place entirely during the conflict, and not a very good film, at that: *A Message to Garcia* (1936), quite rightly dismissed by one critic as "ridiculous."

Historically, a Lieutenant Rowan in 1898 delivered an oral message from President Mc-Kinley to Cuban insurgent General Garcia to ask his help in the war against Spain. He made the trip safely without even seeing a Spaniard. Not the least of the many absurd departures from fact in the film was that Rowan (John Boles) is guided through the Spaniard-infested jungle by a strangely modern-looking, Brooklyn-accented Cuban señorita (Barbara Stanwyck).

Still in the same era, Stanwyck fared somewhat better in *This Is My Affair* (1937), as a cafe entertainer who manages to stay the execution of Robert Taylor, a veteran of Manila Bay, when a secret mission entrusted to him by McKinley (Frank Conroy) is ruined by the President's assassination. As in other films, Sidney Blackmer played Teddy Roosevelt.

If the Spanish-American War itself was virtually ignored, three films dealt with some of the problems inherited along with our new empire—especially the health problems. *The White Legion* (1936) concerned a yellow fever epidemic during the construction of the Panama Canal. An officious senator and his daughter are quarantined along with the doctors; the girl turns out to be an innocent carrier of the disease. But heroic doctor Ian Keith loves his medical colleague Tala Birell —one of the few women doctors to appear on screen in the '30s and in historical period the earliest.

This picture must have come as a surprise to those who had seen Sidney Howard's 1934 play *Yellow Jack*, which ended with the discovery of the true cause of yellow fever in Cuba in 1900. (The explanation was that despite all evidence the army brass refused to accept the mosquito "theory," and the same battle had to be fought all over again in Panama in 1905.) *Yellow Jack* itself, based

on Paul de Kruif's *Microbe Hunters,* reached the screen in 1938, its outlines fortunately intact, detailing the impressive triumph of Walter Reed (Lewis Stone) and his colleagues in isolating the carrier of the fever as a certain kind of mosquito—but the emphasis was shifted from the medical scientists to the privates who volunteered as human guinea pigs —especially one played by Robert Montgomery. A nurse (Virginia Bruce) was added as love interest.

Finally, *The Real Glory* (1939) dealt with the American army of occupation versus Moro "brigands" in the Philippines in 1906. As the plot would have it, the army abandoned Mindanao, leaving behind only five officers to train a native constabulary, an effort complicated by a cholera outbreak. Gary Cooper was the standard heroic army doctor in what the *Times* called "a whopping adventure film with more action, suspense and melodrama than even a *juramentado* could shake his bolo at."

Despite the sympathy noted for Californians of Spanish descent oppressed by American rule, despite even the good-neighbor policy, with the few exceptions just discussed Hollywood in the '30s remained almost totally indifferent to Latin America, past or present, merely touching on its picturesque possibilities in *Flying Down to Rio* (1933) and in various rumba, conga and bolero numbers in other musicals.[3]

Meanwhile, however, the '30s saw two notable attempts to deal with two crucial periods of Mexican history, fifty years apart. In 1934 MGM offered *Viva Villa!,* with a script by Ben Hecht and a much-praised starring performance by Wallace Beery as the bandit-patriot. Heavily publicized and shown at advanced prices, *Viva Villa!* included some grimly brutal footage of the life of the peons under the Díaz regime (Villa's father is hanged in an early sequence).

Leo Carrillo got second billing as Villa's

[3] Overcompensation came in the 1940s, with every kind of musical arbitrarily set in South America, especially in Rio and Buenos Aires.

chief henchman, but the cast also included Henry B. Walthall as President Madero (here sympathetically depicted) , Joseph Schildkraut as his treacherous aide and Stuart Erwin (replacing Lee Tracy) as an American newspaperman who becomes Villa's confidant and assures him, when he is finally gunned down, that he will at least receive good publicity in the "gringo" press.

All but lost in this predominantly male shuffle were Katherine De Mille as Villa's wife and Fay Wray as an aristocrat whom Villa humbles by horsewhipping. Although the film was based on a book by Edgcumb Pinchon, as also was *Viva Zapata* (1952) , it was by no means as serious, and although Villa appears as a character in *Zapata,* the latter is not listed in the cast of *Villa.*

Conceived, written and produced on an altogether grander scale was Warner Brothers' *Juarez* (1939—pronounced "War-ezz," warned the ads, causing one wag to suggest that the studio change its name to "Juarner Brothers") . Set some fifty years before *Villa,* this ambitious production was a monumental recreation of the ill-fated attempt by Napoleon III during the American Civil War to create a puppet empire in Mexico, with a Hapsburg archduke on the throne. The tragic story had been fictionized and dramatized before, notably in Bertita Harding's *The Phantom Crown,* credited as the main source for the script, but never before had it been given such a detailed, almost documentary treatment. A galaxy of major stars, backed by almost every available character actor in Hollywood, made a truly imposing cast of thirty-one recognizable names.

Though Bette Davis as the would-be Empress Carlotta (who went mad after her husband's death and lived for sixty years) was billed immediately below the star, now known as "Mr. Paul Muni," she was actually less important than Claude Rains, who in a mag-

nificent performance as the suavely scheming French Emperor became the only film actor to play both Napoleons I and III. His Empress Eugenie, who only the year before in *Suez* had been Loretta Young, had by now aged and darkened into Gale Sondergaard, then the screen's favorite dispenser of elegant female malevolence. Surprisingly cast, John Garfield was the youthful Porfirio Díaz. But it was Brian Aherne as the gentle, honorable Maximilian, sincerely convinced of his divine right to rule Mexico, who walked off with the acting honors.

In dark make-up, with features altered to make him look like the Zapotec Indian who was the elected President of Mexico, Muni in the title role fared least well of the stars, perhaps because much of the time he had only to look stoic and unyielding. As he does his best to convince Maximilian that the New World wants no part of even the most benevolent monarch, too often his speeches sound like position papers.

Then too, so thoroughly did the writers try to reflect every twist and turn of Mexican politics in the 1860s, without omitting a single plot or counterplot, advance or retreat, betrayal or reconciliation, that in spite of all the splendid performances, the more than two hours become something of a trial of endurance. Undoubtedly the emotional high point is the execution of the gallant, gracious Maximilian, as native musicians play, at his request, "La Paloma."

However ideologically unassailable and timely in 1939, the reaffirmation of the Monroe Doctrine and implied warning to European dictators to keep hands off the Americas now seem too heavily underlined. Nevertheless, in political maturity, authenticity and intelligence, *Juarez* remains a most impressive achievement, a ringing answer to the familiar charge that Hollywood in the '30s always simplified and distorted history.

15

CONTINENTAL STYLE
European Classics, Biography and Historical Fiction

The just rights, history, and feelings of any nation are entitled to most careful consideration and respectful treatment.
                    —The Motion Picture Production Code

If, as had happened to other classics, *The Scarlet Letter* had been "modernized," transposed, say to a contemporary, Sinclair Lewis kind of town, this tale of a young wife who in her elderly husband's absence has an affair with a hypocritical minister, bears his child, refuses to identify him and still comes off as morally superior to her accusers would have turned America's pure air blue with outraged shrieks of blasphemy, sacrilege and anti-clericalism, not to mention adultery condoned and sin glorified. The fact that nothing of the sort happened suggests an even stronger motive for Hollywood's enthusiastic rediscovery of the past in the mid-'30s, diametrically opposite to mere nostalgia for the sweet simplicities of an earlier day—the search for ways around the Production Code.

If mistresses, courtesans, marital infidelity and amorous intrigue were no longer permissible in a modern setting, on the other hand, as essential parts of a long-established classic, especially French or Russian, or as matters of historic fact (European history, that is), they could hardly be altered, even to suit the Legion of Decency. (Thus while taking one's own life was strictly forbidden by the Production Code, no one in the Breen

Office in 1936 was fool enough to object publicly to the suicides of Romeo and Juliet—although the following year the Legion did condemn *Mayerling*.)

In 1934, when this elaborate set of taboos was new, Samuel Goldwyn, understandably, if mistakenly, eager to stay on the safe side, allowed *Nana* to be bowdlerized into a romance too innocuous to offend even the most squeamish. Later the same year, however, he did much better with Anna Sten's second American film, *We Live Again,* based on Tolstoy's *Resurrection,* directed by Rouben Mamoulian in one of the truly fine classic adaptations of the '30s. The novel had already been filmed twice, well received as a silent in 1926 with Dolores Del Rio and Rod La Rocque, very poorly reviewed when done as a talkie in 1931 with Lupe Velez and John Boles.

Called by the *Times* "surely the most faithful of the three screen editions of Tolstoy's novel," one which "captures the theme of mystic socialism and Christ-like abasement," *We Live Again* was widely praised both for its superbly atmospheric re-creation of nineteenth-century Russia and the power of its unusual love story, with Sten and Fredric March sharing equally in the critical bouquets. Unlike *Nana*, this film left no doubt about what its peasant heroine became after she had been seduced and abandoned by the prince she loved.

March acted so well (and looked so right) as a Tolstoyan aristocrat and army officer that he was a natural choice to play Vronsky opposite Garbo in what remains the definitive version of *Anna Karenina* (1935)—marred neither by the modern dress and tacked-on happy ending of the silent version, *Love* (1928), nor the heavy-handedness of the 1948 remake with Vivien Leigh. Produced with all Selznick's scrupulous period authenticity and MGM's apparently unlimited budget, *Anna Karenina* is impressive not only in the poignance of its tragic story but its lavish depiction of elegant, frivolous Russian society in the 1870s: Garbo and March dancing a mazurka at the ball where they meet, playing croquet at a garden party, scenes at the opera, the race track, the officers' club.

The superb cast, including Basil Rathbone as Karenin, Freddie Bartholomew as little Sergei, Reginald Owen as Anna's brother

Basil Rathbone and Greta Garbo
***in* Anna Karenina**

Stiva and Maureen O'Sullivan as Kitty, the production values and Clarence Brown's masterful direction all contribute to the qualities that have led many to rank this film as perhaps second only to *Camille* in Garbo's career.

To be sure, Hollywood did not always do so handsomely by the great Russian novelists. One of the first filmed classics to be released in 1930, *Redemption,* based on Tolstoy's play *The Living Corpse,* drew such poor notices for all concerned that it undoubtedly hastened the end of John Gilbert's faltering career. A more conspicuous disaster was von Sternberg's ambitious version of Dostoyevsky's *Crime and Punishment* (1935), with Peter Lorre as Raskolnikoff, billed below Edward Arnold as Inspector Porfiry.

Four decades later, *The New Yorker,* listing a revival of the film, found "almost everything you can think of the matter with this Hollywood version . . . but it has got the greatest Raskolnikov of any of the screen versions: Peter Lorre." Also, "as the pawnbroker, Mrs. Patrick Campbell adds some distinction."

Literature's other most famous cat-and-mouse pair, hounding detective and hounded culprit, fared much better the same year: Javert and Jean Valjean in what is generally considered the best of the several film versions of Hugo's *Les Misérables.*

Between the two Tolstoy roles, Fredric March (who made no less than eleven costume pictures in the '30s and turned down several others—more than Ronald Colman, Leslie Howard or even Errol Flynn), pitted against Charles Laughton for the third time, gave one of his strongest, most universally admired performances as Valjean. The supporting cast included Sir Cedric Hardwicke as the Bishop, Florence Eldridge as Fantine and Rochelle Hudson and John Beal as the young lovers, Cosette and Marius. More than forty years later, the *Times* TV listing confirms its place of honor: "Splendid version of the Hugo classic. Fast, colorful, beautifully played. Even better now." Those last three rueful words tell a great deal.

Fredric March and Florence Eldridge
in **Les Miserables**

Four years later Laughton played an even more famous Hugo character, in a much showier role, as the grotesque Quasimodo in *The Hunchback of Notre Dame* (1939)—usually ranked in merit as it was in time between Lon Chaney's version of 1923 and Anthony Quinn's of 1957. Almost buried beneath horrendous make-up—a mountainous hump like a bison's, one eye peeking coyly from his cheek like a dimple—Laughton nevertheless achieved some moments of genuine pathos as the well-meaning monster who sacrifices his life for a gypsy girl.

Making her American debut in this elaborate production, Maureen O'Hara was a ravishing Esmeralda, even in black and white. The exceptionally strong cast included Walter Hampden as the Archbishop of Paris, Sir Cedric Hardwicke as his villainous brother, Alan Marshal as Esmeralda's beloved Phoebus, Edmond O'Brien as a Villon-like poet and Thomas Mitchell and Minna Gombell as the king and queen of the beggars. Despite all its

violent and spectacular scenes, this *Hunchback* did not go down in film history as Chaney's had done.

Set in exactly the same period and background, another familiar medieval tale had fared better the previous year: *If I Were King* (1938), Paramount's tasteful version of Justin Huntly McCarthy's romantic novel and play, which it had already filmed, and was to film again, in operetta form as *The Vagabond King.* Fresh from his triumph in *The Prisoner of Zenda,* Ronald Colman brought all his distinction to François Villon, hero of this thrice-told tale, Frances Dee was a lovely Lady Katherine, Ellen Drew an appealing Huguette (another of those good-bad girls who die saving the hero) and, most striking of all, Basil Rathbone, in one of his few non-villainous '30s roles, made a marvelously crotchety, doddering Louis XI (the same king routinely played by Harry Davenport in the 1939 *Hunchback*).

Frank Lloyd's direction and a witty screenplay by Preston Sturges kept the story moving briskly, although it had so clearly found its definitive form in operetta that it constantly ran the risk (especially in the scenes in which the rabble save Paris) of seeming like a version of *The Vagabond King* from which the music had been mysteriously cut.

In the same perennially appealing vein, decade after decade, no works have made more popular films than the swashbuckling romances of Alexandre Dumas *père,* and the '30s were no exception. In 1934, a year that produced more costume films than any other of the decade so far, one of the most lavish, well-received examples was the third version of that old favorite, *The Count of Monte Cristo.*

British star Robert Donat, who could easily have become an American matinee idol had he chosen, was highly praised for the "cool and even-tempered brilliance of his performance," in a role that so readily lends itself to hammy histrionics. Elissa Landi was a suitably lovely Mercedes, and in the long roster of well-cast character players, Louis Calhern, Sidney

Blackmer and Raymond Walburn as de Ville-
fort, Mondego and Danglars were villainy itself. Indeed, the 1934 *Monte Cristo* has never
been bettered, not even by the excellent TV
production starring Richard Chamberlain.

The following year RKO offered a rather
colorless version of *The Three Musketeers*,
with more emphasis on court intrigue than
swordplay. Walter Abel was oddly cast as
D'Artagnan, with Paul Lukas, Moroni Olsen
and Onslow Stevens as his three companions, Heather Angel as Constance, Margot
Grahame as Milady and Rosamond Pinchot
as the Queen. So quickly did this 1935 film
fade from public memory that less than four
years later 20th Century-Fox did not hesitate
to offer its own semiburlesqued interpretation
under the same title, featuring the Ritz Brothers as three lackeys and Don Ameche as
D'Artagnan. The *Times* deplored the whole
misguided venture, regretting that if a burlesque had to be made, it was not carried
further—"far enough, at least, to have escaped
the clutches of the Ritzes themselves."

On a somewhat higher level, *The Man in
the Iron Mask* (1939), produced by Edward
Small, who had made *Monte Cristo,* was rated
"a moderately entertaining costume piece."
Unlike the Fairbanks version, this one centered on Louis XIV and his twin, both played
by Louis Hayward, and his Spanish queen
(Joan Bennett), with D'Artagnan (Warren
William) getting third billing. Marion Martin, then of night club fame, was hopelessly
miscast as Louise de la Villiere. With proper
pacing, it could have been "a romance as
blithe as *The Prisoner of Zenda*," said Nugent
in the *Times,* but it suffers from "an over-
fondness for pageantry and stiff heroics."

Considering the possibilities for spectacle
and special effects, one would have guessed
that Jules Verne as a source of colorfully cinematic material would have been more popular than Hugo or Dumas (as indeed he became for a while in the 1950s), but, most
unaccountably, Hollywood in the '30s completely ignored his works, with one exception,
and this was not a science fiction fantasy but

his relatively realistic novel of Czarist Russia,
Michael Strogoff, released under what the
Times called "the deceptively tea shoppe alias
The Soldier and the Lady" (1937).

Despite the title, it was described as "a
forthright action film, adventurous, swiftly
paced and blood-thirstily satisfying . . . There
are almost perceptible welts on the Roxy's
screen from the lashings, knifings, spearings,
saberings and bullet wounds the picture gives
it. Siberia during Verne's Tatar revolt of 1870
was no place for the anemic." As the only concession to the squeamish, Strogoff (Anton
Walbrook in his first American film) is not
actually blinded, as in the book. Elizabeth
Allan was the not very important lady of the
title, Margot Grahame did her standard seductive adventuress bit and Akim Tamiroff was
ogreish Ogaroff, the terrible Tatar torturer.

As with the American material, not all pictures set in the European past were drawn
from the classics, though many were based on
once-familiar novels and plays. After the extremely lean years of 1930 and 1931, the first
really lavish historical spectacle of the talkie
era—also De Mille's first since his silent *King
of Kings* in 1927—was *The Sign of the Cross,*
released for the holidays in 1932.

The religious aspects, it may be unequivocally stated, were handled far more tastefully
and less heavy-handedly than in any of the
later Roman spectaculars of the '50s and '60s,
such as *Quo Vadis, The Robe, Salome, The
Big Fisherman* and too many others. Perhaps
one reason is that *The Sign of the Cross,* based
on an old play by Wilson Barrett, does not
attempt to deal with any biblical characters,
so there is no danger of either excessive reverence or the reverse. Except for Nero, Poppaea
and Tigellinus, all the characters are fictitious,
a cross section of ancient Rome, involved in
an extremely well-knit plot (scripted by
Waldemar Young and Sidney Buchman) that
covers a few days shortly after the great fire
of A.D. 64.

The picture opens with a kind of prologue,
with Rome in flames, while from the safety of
a lofty palace roof Nero (superbly played by

Charles Laughton), reveling in the destruction, plucks his lyre and chants of the burning of Troy. The story gets off to a brisk start in a street scene when Marcus Superbus, Prefect of Rome (Fredric March in the second of his many costume roles), in saving two elderly suspected Christians from a mob meets and is attracted to the innocent maiden Mercia (Elissa Landi).

From a nearby balcony, Dacia (Vivian Tobin), "a court butterfly with the sting of a wasp," notices his interest and cannot wait to report it to the Empress Poppaea (Claudette Colbert), whom she finds up to her armpits in asses' milk in her pool-sized bath (with a kitten lapping at the side to prove it's real).

Marcus' rival, Tigellinus (Ian Keith), has also observed the street incident and sees an opportunity to make trouble if the girl is a Christian.

After turning down Poppaea's latest brazen offer of herself, Marcus holds a lavish feast that turns into an orgy guaranteed to show Mercia all she has been missing. Ancaria, "the wickedest woman in Rome" (Joyzelle Joyner), starts to dance a number called "The Naked Moon," but is put off by the hymn-chanting of the Christians being herded through the streets to the arena dungeons.

Despite Tigellinus' efforts, Poppaea persuades Nero not to blame Marcus for harboring a Christian but, rather, the girl herself.

Charles Laughton, Claudette Colbert, Fredric March in **The Sign of the Cross**

The word "decadent" might have been invented for Laughton in this scene, lolling on a couch with chubby arms over his head, wriggling voluptuously as he recalls last night's "delicious debauchery." Ruled by Poppaea, he refuses Marcus' plea for Mercia's life.

The climactic Circus Maximus sequence, which takes up the last half hour of the film, could hardly be bettered even now, especially the little human touches not usually associated with De Mille: a married couple quarreling, as they climb upward, about the location of their seats, a pair of young lovers so absorbed in each other they are almost oblivious to the slaughter below, the wealthy eagerly placing bets, Nero gorging on sweetmeats—all avidly enjoying the bloody spectacle of a truly Roman holiday.

The entertainment is nothing if not varied: gladiators fighting to the death with trident and net, spearmen baiting bulls and bears, blond barbarian women from the North skewering African pygmies on their spears—all preludes to the main attraction of the hungry lions loosed on the Christians. These shots are constantly intercut with glimpses of the dungeon below, where Mercia tries to comfort others by reminding them of the words of Christ. A little girl whose mother was killed during the arrest laughs delightedly as her grandfather fashions a doll for her, then gently covers her head as all the Christians slowly mount the long stairs, still singing, to their death.

By Poppaea's order, Mercia is to enter the arena last, and alone. Marcus makes one last attempt to win her over, then, seeing that she is really willing to die for her faith, accepts it as his own in the hope of sharing eternity, and goes up the stairs with her into the arena. As the doors close behind them, the shadow forms the pattern of a cross—only the second time such a symbol has been used in the film.

Landi, so devout and dedicated as Mercia, was given a refreshing change of pace in Hollywood's next spectacle of the ancient world, based on Julian Thompson's satirical comedy *The Warrior's Husband* (1933), in which Katharine Hepburn had made her name on stage, a true original, unlike any other film before or since, and (except for the fantasy-farce *The Night Life of the Gods*) the only one in the whole decade to draw on the rich material of Greek mythology.[1]

Landi was Antiope, army officer and younger sister of Hippolyta (Marjorie Rambeau), Mae Westish ruler of Pontus, queendom of the Amazons in 800 B.C. (but full of intentional anachronisms), where women do the laboring, fighting and wooing while men, the weaker sex, sit at home curling their beards, embroidering pansy designs on samplers and complaining of neglect.

When invaded by the Greeks (whose press agent, Homer, speaks in rhymed couplets) in quest of Hippolyta's magic girdle, the first real men they have ever seen, the women warriors are only too glad to surrender, with Antiope ending in the arms of Theseus (David Manners). The closing subtitle adds: "In 1933 A.D. nothing has changed. Women are still fighters and think man's place is in the home."

As Stephen Harvey observed in his program notes for a showing of the film at the Museum of Modern Art in 1975:

This rowdy satire of female-ruled, Amazon society is fascinating both on its own terms and for what it reveals of Hollywood's free-wheeling screen mores during the early thirties . . . But the film is really more intriguing as a prime example of the kind of carefree ribaldry which the Legion of Decency and the Motion Picture Production Code sanitized out of the industry within just a few months after the premiere . . . Unquestionably, if Fox had waited just one year longer to adapt *The Warrior's Husband* for the screen, the result would have been radically different.

In Hollywood's next classically set film, also a comedy, Manners changed Greek armor for a Roman toga as the juvenile opposite Gloria Stuart as ingenue in *Roman Scandals* (1933), a typical Eddie Cantor vehicle, based on a

---

[1] This play was turned into a musical, *By Jupiter* (1942), the last collaboration of Rodgers and Hart.

story by Robert E. Sherwood and George S. Kaufman, but with wit replaced by slapstick and a plot formula unblushingly lifted from *A Connecticut Yankee.*

A modern native of West Rome, U.S.A., beset with various problems, after an accident awakes in ancient Rome, where he is given the highly hazardous job of food taster for the (fictitious) Emperor Valerius (Edward Arnold), a genial sadist in constant danger of being poisoned by his loving spouse, the Empress Agrippa (Verree Teasdale).

As Valerius' castoff favorite, Ruth Etting sang a torch song, "No More Love," and the rest of the Dubin-Warren-Gilbert score was equally forgettable. In the climactic Busby Berkeley production number, "Keep Young and Beautiful," all the Goldwyn Girls wore long blond wigs and apparently little else; one of them, at least, was considered promising enough to be given individual publicity shots in fan magazines and identified by name: Lucille Ball.

Unaffected by such comic variations, De Mille returned to the ancient Mediterranean scene with *Cleopatra* (1934), set a century before *The Sign of the Cross,* with no religious conflict involved. Said the *Times:* "It has substantial, decorative settings, a wealth of minor properties, an imposing array of histrionic talent and an army of extras. *Cleopatra* reveals Mr. De Mille in an emphatically lavish, but nevertheless a relatively restrained mood."

Fresh from her success in *It Happened One Night,* Claudette Colbert, even sexier than in *The Sign of the Cross,* made an intriguing, imperious Cleopatra, ably supported by Warren William, who had played so many ruthless executives, as a briskly authoritative Caesar, crew-cut rather than bald, and Henry Wilcoxon in his American debut as a splendidly heroic Antony. Ian Keith (already a De Mille regular, as Wilcoxon was to become) glowered sullenly as Octavian and C. Aubrey Smith was a rough-diamond Enobarbus, while Gertrude Michael and Claudia Dell bore like true Roman matrons their roles as the neglected wives, Calpurnia and Octavia.

The following year saw another spectacular set in the Roman Empire, which used the title but absolutely nothing else from Edward Bulwer-Lytton's once admired novel *The Last Days of Pompeii.* Preston Foster played Marcus, a sturdy blacksmith whose wife and baby, struck down by a hit-and-run chariot driver, die because he has no gold for proper medical care. Embittered, he turns professional gladiator, and, ruthless as any '30s tycoon, rises to the top of the trade, turning supplier of gladiators when he is too old to fight himself. Along the way he adopts the small son of one of his victims. While in Judea to do some unofficial border-raiding for Pontius Pilate (Basil Rathbone, who, unlike Anatole France's Procurator, never forgets the Crucifixion), he briefly glimpses Christ—who cures the boy of a serious injury—but Marcus refuses to become involved in trying to help the Master.

In consequence of the cure, the adopted son grows up so humane and idealistic that he secretly operates an underground service to help runaway slaves, thus undercutting his father as producer of spectacles for the arena in Pompeii, where hundreds die every week. On the climactic day, the boy is arrested along with the slaves he has helped, but just as they are about to be slaughtered, the eruption starts. Seeing the light at last, the father sacrifices his own life to help them escape.

The centuries between the fall of the Roman Empire and the emergence of medieval Europe, once known as the Dark Ages, perhaps because we are in the dark about them, have never been popular even in historical fiction, much less on the screen. Indeed (except for *A Connecticut Yankee,* 1931), the only '30s films reflecting any part of that long period were not set in Europe but in the world of the *Arabian Nights,* the legendary Baghdad of minarets and harems, caliphs and grand viziers. Neither of these films utilized this background with anything like the imaginative splendor of Fairbanks' *The Thief of Bagdad* (1924).

The first was that venerable theatrical warhorse *Kismet* (1930), a 1911 play which had already been filmed as a silent in 1920, with the distinguished Otis Skinner once more playing the role he had created both on stage and screen. The *Times* called his performance "firm and flawless"—as well it might have been by that time. Unlike his contemporary George Arliss, who replayed almost his whole stage career on screen, Skinner made only the two versions of *Kismet*.

The complicated tale, at times melodramatic, at times ironically witty, of how Hajji, a clever beggar, by bold intrigue outmaneuvers the wicked wazir (Sidney Blackmer) and succeeds in making his own daughter (Loretta Young) the bride of the caliph (David Manners) is enduring in its appeal.

In *Ali Baba Goes to Town* (1937), Eddie Cantor offered still another variation on the *Connecticut Yankee* formula, as Aloysius Babson who, while playing an extra in an Arabian movie scene, takes an overdose of painkiller and finds himself in the Bagdad of A.D. 937, where the sultan (Roland Young) is having trouble both with his 365 wives (led by Louise Hovick, known on stage as Gypsy Rose Lee) and with his nine elderly councilors. These last were, incidentally, a reference to FDR's problems with the Supreme Court. When the sultan runs for election, he carries only the outlying provinces of Maino and Vermontash—an obvious allusion to Alf Landon's 1936 defeat. Although favorably reviewed at the time, this *Ali Baba* would now be difficult to enjoy without a thorough grounding in the timely topics of 1937.

As for European history, it was simply passed over until the late twelfth century, as reflected fictionally in *The Adventures of Robin Hood* (1938, to be covered under British material) and scarcely less fancifully in De Mille's *The Crusades* (1935), a decidedly romantic treatment of Richard the Lion-Hearted, who, though nominally King of England, spent as little time there as possible.

Despite its sweeping title, *The Crusades* deals with only one Crusade, the third (though with Peter the Hermit, played by

C. Aubrey Smith, from the first unhistorically included). The action takes place almost entirely in the camps of the Crusaders and the Saracens in the Holy Land. Henry Wilcoxon made a swaggering, boisterous Richard, Loretta Young was decorative as Berengaria, Princess of Navarre, his reluctantly accepted bride whom (in this fictional treatment) he comes to love, and the rulers of France, Burgundy, Germany, Montferrat and Russia also appear, all more concerned with jealously spiting each other than in liberating the Holy Land.

The fact that C. Henry Gordon played Philip of France would have clued any '30s movie-goer that he would be a villain, as indeed he proves, trying to force his sullen sister Alice (Katherine De Mille) on the reluctant Richard. In a sympathetic role for a change, Ian Keith played by far the most likable character, Saladin, the gracious Moslem leader whose urbanity makes his European adversaries look even more boorish than they are. But the routine personal story was completely eclipsed by the military spectacle, especially the siege of Acre by night and a tremendous clash of armed horsemen on the plain before Jerusalem.

Said Sennwald in the *Times*:

> Mr. De Mille provides two hours of tempestuous extravaganza . . . *The Crusades* presents him at the top of his achievement, with the virtues of his method towering majestically above his faults. At its best *The Crusades* possesses the true qualities of a screen epic.

A century after the events depicted in *The Crusades,* medieval East and West met much more amiably in the extraordinary career of Marco Polo, but Polo's superior qualities did not extend to the film supposedly based on his exploits, *The Adventurers of Marco Polo* (1938). Despite a script attributed to Robert E. Sherwood, Gary Cooper was hopelessly miscast as the thirteenth-century Venetian traveler, and the rest of the cast represented an impossible mixture of accents, ranging from George Barbier's "nasal Philadelphian" as Kublai Khan through Sigrid

Gurie's "Garboesque Norwegian" to Ernest Truex's "burbanked Kansas-Broadway."

Another talented Italian, a rogue whose private escapades almost overshadowed his artistic achievements, had been given a lighter treatment in *The Affairs of Cellini* (1934), based on Edwin Justus Mayer's 1928 Broadway hit, *The Firebrand,* a witty boudoir romp inspired by Cellini's self-proclaimed reputation as lover and swordsman. Like *The Warrior's Husband* and *The Pursuit of Happiness,* this made no pretense of grappling with historic fact but was simply a comedy set in the picturesque past.

Fredric March, in the midst of his cycle of costume roles, made a fiery, dashing Cellini, whether fashioning immortal works of art, wooing a lady or engaging in Fairbanks-like feats of derring-do—but it was Frank Morgan, repeating his stage role, who walked off with acting honors as the perpetually bumbling, fumbling Duke of Florence, whose hot pur-

Louis Calhern and Constance Bennett in **The Affairs of Cellini**

suit of Cellini's lovely, stupid model (Fay Wray) enables his designing Duchess (Constance Bennett in one of her last good roles) to consummate her affair with the artist himself.

As will be detailed in the next chapter, the only film dramas set in the later 1500s were both laid in the British Isles, *Mary of Scotland* (1936) and *The Private Lives of Elizabeth and Essex* (1939). With the seventeenth century the spotlight shifts back to the rest of Europe, not only with the two versions of *The Three Musketeers* already noted, but with two more directly historical films.

Queen Christina (1933), the first screen vehicle created specifically for Garbo, had the advantages of Rouben Mamoulian's direction, a superb supporting cast, the usual sumptuous MGM production and literate dialogue by S. N. Behrman. ("This is the first time that any one has troubled to write a speech that really represents Garbo," observed C. A. Lejeune, a British critic. "It is sombre, thoughtful and withdrawn dialogue, created for sombre, thoughtful and withdrawn playing.")

Most of the characters were historical, like Chancellor Oxenstierna (Lewis Stone) and the war-minded Charles Gustavus (Reginald Owen), who is to succeed his cousin on the throne after her very moving abdication scene, but the plot centers on her doomed (fictitious) romance with a Spanish envoy (John Gilbert, reunited with Garbo after five years, at her request, in his last notable role). Even those who knew this was invention could hardly complain, since the affair occasioned some of the most beautiful emotional scenes Garbo ever played, especially the one in which, using only her face and eyes, she says farewell to the room at a country inn where she has spent her one night of love. As *The New Yorker* notes, "the film ends, historically, with a heartrending close-up of Garbo's face that runs for eighty-five feet."

Cardinal Richelieu turned up in several '30s films, usually as a villain, as in the first two talkie versions of *The Three Musketeers* (played by Nigel de Brulier in 1935 and

Miles Mander in 1939) and the British *Under the Red Robe* (1937, played by Raymond Massey). He received his most sympathetic interpretation in *Cardinal Richelieu* (1935), based on Bulwer-Lytton's blank-verse melodrama that had once been a standard item in the repertory of every nineteenth-century actor-manager (and was still played on stage by Walter Hampden as late as the 1930s).

This was the last American-made historical film of George Arliss, who, naturally, turned Richelieu into one more shrewd, witty old rogue, slyly outfoxing his adversaries by calling their bluff with an even greater hoax of his own. At one point he even pulls ecclesiastical rank by threatening his enemies with his priestly right to condemn them all to eternal damnation. Edward Arnold was Louis XIII, Maureen O'Sullivan and Cesar Romero the standard ingenue and juvenile. As in the play, the plot is a labyrinth of court intrigue, betrayals, confrontations and last-minute turns of the table worthy of Scribe.

Two years before, Arliss had played another wily Frenchman confronting a later Louis, in *Voltaire* (1933), based on an unproduced play, with Doris Kenyon as a surprisingly sympathetic Pompadour, Reginald Owen as an amiably stupid Louis XV and Margaret Lindsay and Theodore Newton as the young lovers without whom no Arliss vehicle was complete.

In a story line as fictional as *Richelieu,* but preserving the main outlines of Voltaire's extensively documented personality, the film was regarded as a worthy addition to Arliss' series of historical portraits, of which it was the third. Even here, however, an Arliss hero must cleverly expose the enemies of the state, who also happen to be his own. Little was made of Voltaire's writings except for a play in which he mocks the King without Louis's ever realizing it. Frederick the Great is barely mentioned.

When the following year Warners, flying in the face of a superstition that any actress who played Du Barry would be punished by the bad luck of the lady herself—an idea perhaps strengthened by Norma Talmadge's last film—decided to star Dolores Del Rio in *Madame Du Barry* (1934), Reginald Owen had merely to take up where he had left off in *Voltaire,* as Louis XV a few years older and more fatuous.[2]

The beautiful Del Rio gave her usual sprightly, superficial performance, perhaps inhibited by the new rigors of the Production Code, which made it difficult to hint that she had ever done more than hold hands with a married man. But as a boudoir comedy played by such polished performers as Verree Teasdale, Osgood Perkins and Victor Jory, the film at least did not freeze into the stately waxworks of some historical spectacles.

A number of famous episodes were incorporated: when Du Barry wants to go sleigh-riding in midsummer, Louis ransacks Paris for enough sugar to create the illusion of snow; when her enemies steal her gown for her presentation at Versailles, she appears in a nightgown. It would have been quite out of keeping with this lighthearted approach to follow her to the guillotine, so the film leaves her, after Louis's death, banished from court by the new queen, Marie Antoinette (Anita Louise), but with her head, still intact, held high.

The last Queen of France herself was given more than her due, four years later, in Norma Shearer's spectacular and long-awaited *Marie Antoinette* (1938), with Du Barry (Gladys George) now reduced to a coarse, spiteful secondary character. The most elaborate production MGM had yet undertaken, with a royal ballroom larger than the actual one at Versailles and Adrian-designed costumes for some 1,200 extras, the film remains a stunning spectacle, though regrettably made in black and white. Perhaps rightly regarding MGM's own *A Tale of Two Cities* (1935) as the definitive work on the more violent aspects of the French Revolution, those in charge made no attempt to rival the sweep and power of that

film's scenes but concentrated instead on the gathering storm as it was dimly perceived by the totally sheltered royal family and their courtiers.

All the facts were, of course, in public domain, but Stefan Zweig's popular 1935 biography of the Queen was given credit as the chief source, so it is perhaps thanks to his interpretation that her tentative, presumably unconsummated, relationship with Count Axel von Fersen, a gallant Swedish diplomat, is given more stress than it historically deserves, but certainly this was no fictitious "love interest" tossed in by cynical studio hacks. Tyrone Power, though undoubtedly chosen for his box-office value, actually looked remarkably like the surviving portraits of Fersen.

The film, which covers more than twenty years of Marie Antoinette's life, from her betrothal at fifteen until her execution at thirty-eight, was authentic and extremely well cast. Robert Morley could hardly have been better as the dull, well-meaning Louis XVI, John Barrymore was the epitome of weary debauchery as the aged Louis XV, Alma Kruger portrayed a brisk, matronly Maria Theresa, Marie Antoinette's mother, and Joseph Schildkraut as the treacherous, painted Orléans fairly reeked of decadence. Anita Louise, whose Dresden shepherdess daintiness was especially suited to eighteenth-century modes, this time was an appealing Princess de Lamballe, whose mutilated remains are dragged past the Queen's prison window.

The New Yorker's review-in-brief still dismisses the film as "a resplendent bore" and blames the studio's deference to Shearer as Thalberg's widow and a large MGM stockholder in making the Queen "lugubriously noble," but according to Morley, quoted in Shipman's *Great Movie Stars,* rumor had it that during production the front office, presumably L. B. Mayer, wanted to sabotage the film to force Shearer to sell her stock; thus her chosen director Sidney Franklin was replaced at the last minute by W. S. Van Dyke, known as a fast worker and supposedly receiv-

---

[2] Owen played Louis XV a third time in Bob Hope's *Monsieur Beaucaire* (1946).

Norma Shearer in **Marie Antoinette**

ing a large sum for every day he was ahead of schedule.

This off-screen struggle, if such it was, was apparently not suspected by most reviewers, who complained of the excessive star treatment given Shearer at the expense of the other players. Later viewers, indifferent to Shearer's 1938 unpopularity as First Lady of MGM or Power's as a matinee idol (automatically put down by male critics, just as Robert Taylor was), may be surprised to find *Marie Antoinette* an incredibly lavish, splendidly acted, historically accurate film biography.

Two of the very earliest biographical talkies had also used French Revolutionary backgrounds. *Du Barry, Woman of Passion* (1930)

was one in which the heroine survived, but the star, Norma Talmadge, did not. Adapted from a 1911 Belasco play, the film made no pretense to historical accuracy, being based, as the opening subtitle announced, "on a few romantic episodes in the life of Mme. Dubarry." Romantic they were indeed, to the point of having her rescued from the guillotine by her true love (Conrad Nagel).

Not even the presence of William Farnum as Louis XV could overcome the verbose screenplay nor the inadequacies of the star, a beautiful brunette here disguised in powdered wigs, at the end of a long career, with her delivery of the admittedly impossible lines in a flat, whiny monotone.

Captain of the Guard (1930), a semimusical called by the *Times* "ambitious but somewhat heavy-handed," purported to deal with the life of Rouget de Lisle (John Boles), composer of "La Marseillaise," but "with little French flavor." Laura La Plante was the heroine, "a prominent little person in the Revolution," imprisoned in the Bastille by an unpleasantly depicted Louis XVI and at one point threatened with hanging—presumably before the invention of the guillotine. The director had been changed in mid-production, and thus the direction in both senses had floundered. What was evidently meant as a "to the barricades" operetta in the vein of *Song of the Flame* or *The Vagabond King* turned out a mishmash.

Marie Antoinette's more fortunate contemporary, Catherine II of Russia, whose career paralleled hers in many ways (coming as a German-speaking princess to a foreign court, to be married to the unattractive heir to the throne, resented by an older woman still clinging to power), but who played her cards so much more wisely, was given two screen treatments in the '30s. Dietrich's *Scarlet Empress* (1934), her next to last film with von Sternberg, risked comparison not only with Garbo's successful *Queen Christina* but, more directly, with Elisabeth Bergner's British-made *Catherine the Great,* released earlier the same year, as Alexander Korda's immediate follow-up to *The Private Life of Henry VIII*. Critical opinion agreed that among these royal ladies Dietrich's Catherine ran a poor third. Though franker than the Bergner version in admitting that Catherine took lovers, von Sternberg's bizarre, exotic production, visualized in Hans Dreier's art direction, reduced the actors to puppets.

"For sheer idiotic affectation, Joseph von Sternberg's latest picture sets new and probably unassailable records," Richard Watts announced in the *Herald Tribune*. "The picture frequently seems a particularly cruel satire on the director's celebrated postures and innumerable weaknesses . . . Miss Dietrich's performance is astonishingly bad . . . That love scene in the haystack supplies the wildest farce of the season."

Several other reviews noted the off-putting resemblance of Sam Jaffe (as Catherine's half-mad husband, the Grand Duke Peter) to Harpo Marx, and most deplored the American diction and "frontier" manner of Louise Dresser as reducing the raffish Empress Elizabeth to the level of a fishwife.

Moving on to the turn of the nineteenth century, although naturally no American production remotely approached the scope of French director Abel Gance's extraordinary *Napoleon* (1927), that truly epic silent made to be projected on three screens, the Little Corporal was given excellent characterizations in two otherwise undistinguished Hollywood films.

A forgotten play, *Glorious Betsy,* which had once served as the basis for a Rodgers-Hart musical, was exhumed as a vehicle for Marion Davies and Dick Powell in *Hearts Divided* (1936). It dealt with the 1804 romance between Betsy Patterson, Baltimore belle, and Jérôme Bonaparte, younger brother of Napoleon. In real life they were married, but soon divorced to accommodate Napoleon's ambition to seat a Bonaparte on every throne in Europe.

In the film they are merely engaged, until, in yet another echo of *Camille,* not to mention *The Student Prince,* Claude Rains (who

had played Napoleon on stage in 1928 in *Napoleon's Barber* and was to play his nephew, Napoleon III, in 1939 in *Juarez*) as an extremely persuasive Emperor convinces Betsy that she must give Jérôme up for the sake of France. Without ever questioning why she as an American citizen should be concerned about the future of France or even pointing out that the Bonapartes were no more royal than the Pattersons, Betsy complies, for one of those tearful, "bittersweet" renunciations once so popular in operettas.

Napoleon was given even more detailed and authentically French characterization (aided by strong physical resemblance) by Charles Boyer in *Conquest* (1937), one of MGM's most ambitious productions, costing a then unheard-of $3,800,000. Despite a screenplay by Samuel Hoffenstein, Salka Viertel and S. N. Behrman, based on a Polish novel, this remains one of the least distinguished films of Garbo's career. Coming between the haunting *Camille* (1937) and the sparkling *Ninotchka* (1939), *Conquest* seems especially lackluster, for all its elaborate production and impressive cast. Critics complained of the languidness of Garbo's performance. Said John Mosher in *The New Yorker:* "I think that for the first time Madame Garbo has a leading man who contributes more to the interest and vitality of the film than she does."

Aside from the fact that few except Napoleonic scholars or students of Polish history had ever heard of Countess Marie Walewska, there seemed no way of making her essentially undramatic story interesting. In still another variation on *Boule de Suif,* she is urged by Poland's leaders to gain Napoleon's aid, by betraying her elderly husband (Henry Stephenson), to make their country independent. First from duty, then from love, she becomes his mistress and bears him a son, even though she is disillusioned by his insatiable lust for power. He divorces Josephine only to marry an Austrian princess, so when he goes into exile on St. Helena Marie is left in the same sinking boat as Betsy Patterson.

Perhaps some of what went wrong can be blamed on what *The New Yorker* describes as a two-year wrangle with the censors, who, among other restrictions, insisted on a final meeting of the parents and child that would represent "a forceful illustration of the tragedy of having been born out of wedlock." This is particularly ironic because historically the son, Count Alexandre Walewski, fared much better than his legitimate half-brother, the ill-fated "l'Aiglon," Napoleon's son by Marie Louise; after some success as a writer Walewski became an important diplomat and cabinet minister under his cousin Napoleon III in the Second Empire.

Perhaps even in fictional form Napoleon is still such a magnetic personality that he cannot play a secondary role in anyone else's story without completely overshadowing the intended protagonist. At least the stars seemed to survive better in those films in which Bonaparte barely figures or is mentioned only as an off-screen threat—e.g., *The Count of Monte Cristo* (1934), *Becky Sharp* (1935), *Lloyds of London* (1936), *Anthony Adverse* (1936) and *The Firefly* (1937).

Of all the '30s films set in Napoleonic Europe the most intelligent and original was *The House of Rothschild* (1934), which thirty-six years before the Broadway musical *The Rothschilds* used much of the same material with telling dramatic effect—especially Nathan's financial rescue of England by refusing to sell his stocks even when it was reported that Wellington had been defeated at Waterloo.

In two of his finest historical character portraits, "half Shylock, half Disraeli," as Watts put it in the *Herald Tribune,* George Arliss played both old Meyer Rothschild, with side curls and yarmulke, patriarch of the Frankfurt ghetto and founder of the famous clan, and his son, cosmopolitan, assimilated Nathan, head of the London branch of the family firm.

Aside from the perennial fascination of the story of how one gifted Jewish family overcame not merely prejudice but the formidable legal barriers of their day to become the financial masters of Europe, the theme of decent, hard-working Jews at the mercy of ruthless, ingrate, so-called Christians (here personified by Boris Karloff as a German baron) in 1934 held strong, timely overtones.

As Watts observed:

The House of Rothschild belongs very definitely to the type of historical narrative that is concerned, not with escape, but with a parallel to present-day conditions. With a shrewd eye on the current plight of the Jews in Hitler's Germany, the picture shows its Semitic family as the victims of race hatred and Nordic oppression.

This theme is driven forcefully home in old Meyer's dying words, proclaiming the right of Jews "to live with dignity, to work with dignity, to walk the world with dignity."

Another internationally set film of the Napoleonic era was *Anthony Adverse* (1936), Warners' 140-minute version of Hervey Allen's sprawling 1933 best seller (nearly two hundred pages longer than *Gone With the Wind*!).

Though set in the late eighteenth and early nineteenth centuries, the novel is not vitally involved with any major historic events or issues, unless one counts the slave trade, but confines itself to the more picturesque as well as picaresque possibilities of the period.

As all the publicity emphasized, translating this unwieldy epic to the screen involved some 2,500 players, 98 speaking parts and 36 principals, led by Frederic March, then at his height as Hollywood's favorite costume hero, in the title role; Louis Hayward and Anita Louise as his ill-fated parents; Claude Rains as the mother's husband, Don Luis, a vindictive Spanish grandee; Edmund Gwenn as John Bonnyfeather, a Scottish merchant living in Leghorn who is actually the boy's grandfather; Gale Sondergaard as Faith, his scheming housekeeper (her first screen role, for which she won the 1936 supporting Oscar); and Olivia De Havilland as Angela, Anthony's first love, who later becomes an opera singer and also Napoleon's mistress. Of all Anthony's loves and wives in the book, only An-

Noel Madison, Paul Harvey, Murray Kinnell, George Arliss,
Ivan Simpson (as the five Rothschild brothers), Helen Wesley, George Renavent,
Boris Karloff, Alan Mowbray in **The House of Rothschild**

gela and his African mistress Neleta (Steffi Duna) survived in the film.

While everyone was impressed with the grand scale of the production, this very grandeur had an "adverse" effect on reviewers, most of whom deplored it as typical Hollywood gigantism, a substitution of colossal quantity for any real quality in writing or acting. Unlike many of the best '30s films, which, even if seen only once at the time, lingered in viewers' memory forever, *Anthony Adverse* left no emotional impact, only an impression of a great many costumed actors and varied scenes.

Europe in the middle and later nineteenth century was also a favorite background for films other than classics, biographies and historical spectacles—especially the Vienna of Franz Josef as an attractive setting for operettas like *The Smiling Lieutenant* (1931), *The Night Is Young* (1935), *The King Steps Out* (1936), *The Great Waltz* (1938) and occasionally even for a drama such as Arthur Schnitzler's minor classic *Daybreak* (1931).

Directed by Jacques Feyder, and hailed by the *Times* as "an admirable screen contribution" full of "scenes set forth with considerable artistry," *Daybreak* depicts much the same caste-ridden Vienna as von Stroheim's *The Merry Go Round* (1924) and *The Wed-*

ding March (1928). A young officer (Ramon Novarro) in the Emperor's guards falls in love with a music teacher (Helen Chandler), though the tradition of the regiment, embodied by his uncle, a general (C. Aubrey Smith), dictates that he must marry for money. The same rigid code prescribes that any officer unable to pay a "debt of honor" must promptly kill himself. To help a friend in this plight, the hero gambles, at first successfully, but then loses so badly that he is almost driven to the same fate himself, until his uncle relents and provides the money.

Paris in the mid-nineteenth century served as background for a horror film, *Murders in the Rue Morgue,* two romantic dramas, *Nana* and *Camille,* as well as for most of an operetta, *Maytime.* Returning to straight biographical subjects, *Suez* (1938) was a highly romanticized account of the career of Ferdinand de Lesseps (Tyrone Power), whose chief motivation in building the Suez Canal, it seems, is his unrequited love for the Empress Eugenie (Loretta Young), though he is himself loved by a regimental sergeant's gamine granddaughter (Annabella), easily recognizable as a variation on Cigarette in *Under Two Flags.*

The *Times* found *Suez* "handsomely sepiatinted and ponderously implausible," especially Power's unchanging youthful appearance, as if "either the canal was built in a year or its builder had tapped the fountain of youth." An impressive cast that included J. Edward Bromberg, Joseph Schildkraut, Henry Stephenson, Sidney Blackmer, Miles Mander (as Disraeli) and Leon Ames (as Napoleon III) could not give the film its intended serious weight. "Mr. Power is such a young man in their presence, and he has so much to say!"

Another distinguished Frenchman of the same generation had been given far more significant treatment in Warners' *The Story of Louis Pasteur* (1936), Paul Muni's first step toward taking over the mantle of George Arliss, for which he received that year's Oscar, despite the fact that the picture telescopes

Pasteur's long career and delays his recognition until almost the end of his life.

If the medical establishment of the time (chiefly personified by Fritz Leiber as Dr. Charbonnet) is made to seem even more culpably ignorant and hostile than it was, and if Pasteur is virtually banished from Paris by a contemptuous Napoleon III (Walter Kingsford this time around), these seemed to reviewers harmless dramatizations of the essential truth. Quoting the *Times:* "It may not be the province—and probably it was not the primary motive—of a Hollywood studio to create a film which is, at the same time, a monument to the life of a man. But *The Story of Louis Pasteur* is truly that."

The following year, the same studio, director (William Dieterle) and star produced what was undoubtedly the most admired biographical film of the decade, *The Life of Emile Zola* (1937), an enduringly powerful example of what Hollywood at its most committed could achieve. "It is at once the finest historical film ever made and the greatest screen biography ever made," said the *Times* unequivocally. "It has followed not merely the spirit but, to a rare degree, the very letter of his life and of the historically significant lives around him."

Muni's magnificent, full-bodied performance, by far the best of his three historical portraits in the 1930s, was matched by Joseph Schildkraut's Oscar-winning characterization of Captain Dreyfus, Gale Sondergaard's (in a sympathetic role, for once) as Mme. Dreyfus and a long list of character actors as those who, directly or otherwise, helped either to frame or to clear Dreyfus. On the side of the angels, Vladimir Sokoloff portrayed the artist Cézanne, who acts as Zola's conscience, Donald Crisp was Maître Labori, Morris Carnovsky, Anatole France, Henry O'Neill, Colonel Picquart, and Grant Mitchell, Clemenceau.

Although most of the film concentrates on the Dreyfus case, Zola's earlier career as a controversial, naturalistic novelist is also sketched in, as well as his gradual acceptance by the public and his extreme reluctance, just as he is being considered for the Academy, to become involved in an affair that was already splitting French society from top to bottom. Much of the drama is his difficult decision to risk all for justice, the rest his brilliant stratagems to force the truth to light, climaxed by his thundering challenge to the government: *J'accuse!*

Captain Alfred Dreyfus, an officer in the French Army, was in 1894 accused on the flimsiest evidence (presumably because he was Jewish) of selling military secrets to the Germans and condemned to Devil's Island for life. Even when two years later a Colonel Picquart discovered proof that the incriminating letter had been written by a Major Esterhazy, who was indeed in the pay of the Germans, the general staff refused to reopen the case, disciplined Picquart and accepted forged evidence of Dreyfus' guilt.

Pressed by his brother, the general staff reluctantly court-martialed Esterhazy, but acquitted him. It was at this point that Zola published *J'accuse!* Brought back by inflamed public demand, Dreyfus was in 1899 retried and *again* found guilty, with extenuating circumstances, and sentenced to ten years. He was pardoned, but not until 1906 was he fully exonerated and restored to his rank—four years after Zola's death.

Unlike *The House of Rothschild, Zola* never mentioned the word "Jew," so to that extent the underlying anti-Semitic issue is obscured, yet the sense of outrageous wrong is never lost. True, some of the most villainous characters pulling strings behind the scenes are called only by their official titles, never by their family names: the Commander of Paris (Ralph Morgan), the Chief of Staff (Harry Davenport), the Minister of War (Gilbert Emery), but, after all, the events were scarcely a generation in the past, and these men no doubt had living descendants, who might well have sued Warners as successfully as Prince Youssopoff had MGM for using characters based on him and his wife in *Rasputin and the Empress.*

The actual culprits' names are used whenever their deeds are a matter of public record: Major Dort (Louis Calhern), Major Esterhazy (Robert Barrat). But this is quibbling. The ultimate vindication of Dreyfus, his public restoration to full rank and honors come through with overwhelming force as drama of the highest order. Yet Zola's accidental death and Anatole France's noble eulogy—"He was a moment in the conscience of man"—end the film on an even loftier note.

More than four decades have not weakened its impact. 1970s college students, totally ignorant of Dreyfus, much less Zola, have in discussion immediately drawn parallels with Watergate: the official cover-up on grounds of patriotism, the self-righteous denunciations from high places, the attempt to smear those exposing the truth, the ultimate collapse of an overconfident bureaucracy caught in its own endlessly proliferating lies.

New York critics named *Zola* as the best film of 1937 and Muni as the best actor. It also won the national critics' poll, the National Board of Review's award and Oscars for the best supporting performance (Schildkraut), the outstanding production and the best screenplay, making it deservedly the most honored film of its year.

16

"THERE'LL ALWAYS BE AN ENGLAND"
British Classics, Biography and Historical Fiction

If a steady diet of juvenile American sweetness and light might have grown too cloying (*Little Women,* after all, was the only really outstanding film of that cycle), and if the jaded worldlings of Tolstoy and Dumas *fils* might seem almost as remote from the average movie-goer as the royal rascals and dueling cavaliers of Dumas *père,* public domain offered still another treasure trove that combined the best of all worlds—the limitless riches of English literature, much of it at least vaguely familiar to anyone who had gone to high school. Here were works as excitingly plotted as any by Dumas or Hugo, full of varied, eccentric characters mingling in a complex, stratified society, yet all as delightfully cozy as an old-fashioned Christmas card, and —most important of all—unlikely to raise any awkward problems of censorship.

Indeed, Victorian novelists, unlike their French and Russian contemporaries, labored under much the same difficulties as Hollywood scenarists of the '30s, forbidden to tell as much of the truth about adult life as both they and their public knew. For them, the gentle reader, a.k.a. Mrs. Grundy, had been just as powerful an inhibiting force as the Production Code itself. Was it not Trollope who boasted that he had never written a line that would bring a blush to a maiden's cheek? Once this sexual taboo was accepted, however, the wonder was how otherwise free writers were to criticize every aspect of their society, often in the most scathing terms.

Even during the lean years, 1930–32, before the great costume revival, some producers tried for the best of both worlds (and only achieved the worst) by filming nineteenth-century classics in modern dress. Not only was *East Lynne* given this treatment as *Ex-Flame* (1931), but *Madame Bovary* became *Unholy Love* (1932). An updated *Vanity Fair* (1932), with Myrna Loy as a thoroughly modern Becky, Barbara Kent as Amelia and Conway Tearle as Rawdon Crawley, retained its title but necessarily omitted Waterloo.

These were all low-budget productions by independents, but even Paramount gave the same cavalier treatment to Dickens' *Dombey and Son* as *Rich Man's Folly* (1931), with George Bancroft as the father, David Durand as the son and Frances Dee as the daughter. The scene was transposed to contemporary New York and even the characters' names were changed, so not much was left but the essential situation of a tyrannical businessman who learns true values only after inadvertently causing the death of his idolized small son. And in 1933 Resolute Pictures announced a film of *The School for Scandal,* "brought up to date for present-day audiences"—a threat fortunately never carried out.

As with American novels, it is first necessary to distinguish between those that might now be regarded as classics and those acknowledged then. Chief among the former would be *Of Human Bondage* (1934), already twenty years old when first filmed. Though not done in proper period as were the two later versions and using only part of the novel, this first one is universally considered the best. Neither Eleanor Parker nor Kim Novak could approach the ferocity of Bette Davis' performance as Mildred, nor could Paul Henreid or Laurence Harvey match Leslie Howard's sensitivity. Of Maugham's other works, at least eight were filmed in the '30s, either in Hollywood or England, but it must be left to posterity to determine whether any of them will rank as classics.

In number of screen adaptations, no other Edwardian fared as well. Considering John Galsworthy's Nobel Prize and international fame as novelist and playwright, it seems strange that of his many novels Hollywood in the '30s filmed only his last, *One More River* (1934). *The Forsyte Saga,* at that time the best-known series of novels in English, would have seemed a natural during the through-the-years cycle, and indeed MGM was announced to have bought the rights to it, with plans to star Katharine Hepburn (who would have been all wrong) as Irene, but nothing ever came of this, unless it was the unfortunate *That Forsyte Woman* (1949).[1]

Of Galsworthy's plays, only *Old English* (1930) was made, the most vehicular of all George Arliss' early talkies and the most stage-bound, with divisions between the acts clearly evident on the rare occasions when the setting changes. A spry octogenarian shipowner in Edwardian Liverpool, "Old English," as Sylvanus Heythrope is nicknamed, constantly defies his prim spinster daughter (Ethel Griffies) to favor the teen-aged children of his late illegitimate son. To provide for their future, he pulls off a financial deal of questionable

[1] The only Forsyte to appear on the screen in the '30s was a barrister (Alan Mowbray) in *One More River,* identified as Very Young Roger in the novel, in which his client, the heroine, is a cousin of Fleur Forsyte's husband.

legality, then, before his enemies can expose him, orders a gourmet dinner with appropriate wines, which, warned by his doctor, he knows will kill him. As a theatrical tour de force, this once-famous scene works on screen just as well as it must have on stage.

Galsworthy's fellow Edwardians did not even do that well on screen. Conrad's *Victory* was released as *Dangerous Paradise* (1930). Arnold Bennett was represented only by the farcical *His Double Life* (1933, based on *Buried Alive* and later remade as *Holy Matrimony,* 1943). H. G. Wells did rather better, but only with his science fiction, not his novels of social criticism: *The Island of Lost Souls* (1933), *The Invisible Man* (1935), the British-made *Things to Come* (1936) and *The Man Who Could Work Miracles* (1937). Though undoubtedly the most publicized writer in the world and lionized by all the Hollywood hierarchy, George Bernard Shaw was represented on screen only by the British *Pygmalion* (1938).

It should be recalled that two writers generally considered Victorians were still living at the beginning of the 1930s, though the major part of their careers was over, and both were already looked upon as figures from the past: Sir James Barrie and Rudyard Kipling. Sir James had done extremely well on the silent screen, for which his delicate dream fantasies, *Peter Pan* and *A Kiss for Cinderella,* made perfect material (1924 and 1925). The first talkie version of any of his plays was *Seven Days' Leave* (1930), based on *The Old Lady Shows Her Medals,* a sentimental but touching war story.

Three other Barrie plays, all more down to earth, all vehicles for Maude Adams on stage and all filmed as silents, were remade in the '30s, their appeal heightened by dialogue. *What Every Woman Knows* (1934), first filmed in 1921 with Lois Wilson, was successfully made with Helen Hayes, who had also done it on Broadway. "A wise, crusty sentimental comedy, with a Scottish burr which crackles through the dialogue," said the *Times,* praising not only the star but Brian

Aherne as the pompous husband whose career she maneuvers, and Donald Crisp, Dudley Digges and David Torrence as the three bachelor brothers who make the match for her as a business deal.

Almost as warmly greeted was RKO's holiday gift to the nation in 1934, *The Little Minister* (made in the silents by both Betty Compson and Alice Calhoun), with Katharine Hepburn as Babbie, a laird's fey daughter, who, disguised as a saucy gypsy, likes to fraternize with and help the oppressed weavers in the village of Thrums. She wins the heart of a stiff young minister (John Beal), much against his better judgment and that of the elders of the kirk.

Most pleasing of the three Barrie films was *Quality Street* (1937), which had served Marion Davies well as a silent, again starring Hepburn, who seemed to have a special affinity for playwrights named Barrie or Barry, moving easily from Sir James to Philip. Unlike the other two plays, this is set not in Scotland but in Regency England, from 1805 to 1815, in a village whose demure costumes and manners are delightfully reminiscent of Jane Austen or Mrs. Gaskell's *Cranford*.

Acted with deft spinsterish delicacy by the star, Fay Bainter as her sister, Estelle Winwood and Florence Lake as equally unmarried neighbors, the story of Phoebe Throstle, who, fearing she has grown too old during the long absence of the dashing Captain Brown (Franchot Tone), pretends to be her own (nonexistent) giddy niece, is as fragile as a butterfly's wing, but here touched with just the right blend of gentle humor and rueful charm.

Kipling was not as consistently well done on screen. Two films supposedly based on his work were blown up out of all proportion, both marching to that determined drumbeat for the British Empire that was so much more common in American than in English films of the '30s: *Wee Willie Winkie* (1936), turned from a short story into a Shirley Temple vehicle, and *Gunga Din* (1939), a poem magnified into a military epic.

Two other Kipling novels, which had nothing to do with maintaining the thin red line in India, became much better films. In *Captains Courageous* (1937), the age of the leading character, Harvey Cheyne, was reduced from nineteen to twelve, but this only made his emotional growth all the more convincing. It also enabled Freddie Bartholomew to prove conclusively that he was more than just another pretty boyish face, by playing as obnoxious a brat as anyone ever longed to strangle.

Only when he falls overboard from an ocean liner and is picked up by a Portuguese fishing boat out of Gloucester does he begin to learn, unwillingly at first, what it means to be a human being. Spencer Tracy won his first Oscar as Manuel, the warmhearted fisherman who is the chief agent in the boy's transformation, and Lionel Barrymore was "flawless" as the captain.

Opening in New York on Christmas Eve, 1939, *The Light That Failed* was hailed by Nugent in the *Times*, chauvinistically enough, as a "man's picture, a relief from too many feminine films" as well as "a letter-perfect edition" of the novel. Unlike two previous film versions, this one hewed uncompromisingly to the original unhappy ending. The artist hero (Ronald Colman) not only goes blind but realizes that the vicious street girl (Ida Lupino) he used as a model—a sister under the skin of Mildred in *Of Human Bondage*—has destroyed his masterpiece. Refusing a pity-prompted offer of marriage from the girl he loves (Muriel Angelus), he goes back to the Sudan for a last charge against the Fuzzy-Wuzzies (a kind of fighting in which Colman had had plenty of experience in *Beau Geste* and *Under Two Flags*).

Though he died several decades earlier than Barrie or Kipling, Robert Louis Stevenson's career overlapped theirs in the Victorian sunset of the 1880s and 1890s (as also did Conan Doyle's). In the '30s five of Stevenson's works reached the American screen, two classic adventure tales and three of a more sinister, adult nature.

Treasure Island (1934) is surely the best of

the many film versions of this familiar story. Teamed for the third time, Jackie Cooper and Wallace Beery made an ideal Jim Hawkins and Long John Silver, strongly supported by Lionel Barrymore as the violent Billy Bones, Lewis Stone as Captain Smollett, Otto Kruger as Dr. Livesey, Nigel Bruce as Squire Trelawney and, surprisingly, Chic Sale as the pathetic castaway Ben Gunn. The film holds up extremely well in its eighteenth-century atmosphere, vigorous dialogue and action and especially the ambiguous love-hate attachment of Jim to Long John.

Trouble for Two (1936), based on Stevenson's Suicide Club stories, starred Robert Montgomery as Prince Florizel and Rosalind Russell as the mysterious Miss Vandeleur (who is actually the unseen princess he is scheduled to marry). They were supported by a splendid MGM cast including Frank Morgan, Reginald Owen and Louis Hayward, but the *Times* reserved its highest praise for the director. J. Walter Ruben "achieves results with a finesse which we have come to consider a trade mark of England's master melodramatist, Alfred Hitchcock."

On the other hand, the same reviewer could scarcely find words harsh enough to condemn *Kidnapped* (1938) as a complete desecration of Stevenson's novel, both in writing and casting. "Frail and wistful" Freddie Bartholomew was all wrong for "tall, determined" Davy Balfour, and "ruddy, boastful, swashbuckling Alan Breck is enveloped in the fatty tissues and quiet gentility of Warner Baxter." Not only that, but a love interest was added in the person of Arleen Whelan. The whole film, Nugent concluded, was "about as Scottish as a hot dog and about as much Stevenson as Darryl Zanuck permitted it to be."

Because of its tropical setting, Stevenson's *Ebb Tide*(1937) will be discussed in Chapter 18. Similarly, the most striking and memorable of all his filmed works, *Dr. Jekyll and Mr. Hyde* (1932), properly belongs in the great horror cycle of the early '30s, as does the very first British classic to appear in those years, *Svengali* (1931), based on du Maurier's

Trilby. Both of these had been made as silents and were to be made again as talkies. (For that matter, of course, the equally recurrent *Dracula* and *Frankenstein* also had respectable British literary antecedents.)

In sheer durability, indeed, the popular second-rate, especially if a hit play, is more likely than a masterpiece to be filmed over and over again. Thus du Maurier's *Peter Ibbetson,* long a favorite on stage, turned into a film in 1921 with Wallace Reid and Elsie Ferguson, was made again in 1935 with, surprisingly, Gary Cooper in the title role and Ann Harding as his beloved, Mary, Duchess of Towers.

This is the romance of two people who, after loving each other since childhood, are permanently parted when he is sentenced to life imprisonment for accidentally killing her husband. But they possess the mysterious power to meet every night in dreams, which become their real life. The film was praised on all scores, especially Henry Hathaway's direction, but perhaps the fragile, wish-fulfilling fantasy was too sentimental to survive World War II, as it has not been filmed again.

Not so with another perennial Edwardian favorite, Anthony Hope's *The Prisoner of Zenda,* made five times, first in 1915 and 1922 as silents, embellished with color in 1952, and finally turned into a Peter Sellers vehicle (1979). In between, in 1937, came what is generally regarded as the best version, one of the most richly enjoyable films of the decade, the Selznick-International production, directed by John Cromwell from a screenplay by John Balderston.

Ronald Colman played a dual role, as Englishman Rudolf Rassendyll and his royal cousin and double, the King of Ruritania, Madeleine Carroll was Princess Flavia, Raymond Massey the villainous Black Michael, Mary Astor his mistress, Antoinette de Mauban, and Douglas Fairbanks, Jr., the likable scoundrel Rupert of Hentzau. In lesser roles, C. Aubrey Smith was Colonel Sapt and the then unknown David Niven Fritz von Tarlenheim. Perhaps the predominantly Germanic names, perhaps the solid dignity of the Ruritanian court, gave this *Prisoner,* set in the 1880s, overtones not of just one more mythical kingdom but of the Hapsburgs' Austro-Hungarian Empire at its outwardly magnificent height.

As William K. Everson observed in program notes for a late 1960s showing of the film:

. . . the last of the great romanticist adventure films . . . The cast is hand-picked, and its equal just couldn't be found today . . . The staging is sumptuous, the sets and decor stunning, and one never has the feeling—as one does with so many spectacles—that the palaces and ball-rooms disappear into wooden flats immediately outside the range of the camera lens . . . What *style* it has, and how much in sheer zest, exuberance of acting and the sheer joy of solid craftsmanship in movie-making have we lost in the thirty years since it was made!

Moving back a generation, but still in the realm of the often revived work that now ranks less as a classic than as a subliterary curiosity, one cannot long avoid the exotic figure of the once famous, if not notorious, Ouida (Louise de la Ramée), who despite her name was English. In the '30s, three decades after her death, two of her novels were still considered worth filming.

A Dog of Flanders (1935), one of those once beloved childhood classics, like *Heidi* or *The Swiss Family Robinson,* the European equivalents of *Pollyanna* or *Rebecca of Sunnybrook Farm,* starred boy actor Frankie Thomas and an excellent cast of character players. A Flemish lad helps his grandfather (O. P. Heggie) deliver milk daily with the aid of his dog, but dreams of becoming an artist, as despite numerous setbacks he eventually does.

A Dog of Flanders was a modest "B" production, but Ouida's 1868 novel *Under Two Flags,* one of the first works of fiction to exploit the melodramatic possibilities of the Foreign Legion, already filmed twice in silents, in 1916 and 1922, was in 1936 given what the *Times* called "a spirited and colorful revival" with four stars. Cigarette (Claudette Colbert) is a saucy but golden-hearted *vivandière* beloved by rugged Major Doyle (Victor

McLaglen), though her heart belongs to the sensitive, mysterious Englishman, Sergeant Victor (Ronald Colman), who in turn loves the aristocratic Lady Venetia (Rosalind Russell).

When the jealous major sends the sergeant into hostile Arab territory with only a small patrol, who rides into the desert to warn him? Since the novel had first been dramatized in 1870, Cigarette must surely be the ultimate ancestress of all those near-heroines like Huguette in *If I Were King,* not quite good enough to marry the hero, just good enough to save his life at the cost of her own, then die contentedly in his arms.

With Ouida we are back among the mid-Victorians, who would seem to have been made to order for '30s film producers in providing colorful but blameless family fare, as indeed some did, but even more surprising is the number of illustrious English novelists whose works were ignored, while minor novels were filmed again and again, as were Wilkie Collins' *The Woman in White* (three times, none in the '30s) and his *The Moonstone* (once by Monogram in 1934). Yet nothing at all was made from Trollope, Eliot, Hardy, Austen or Scott.

The connection between the Production Code and the rediscovery of the more innocuous classics has already been suggested, but in fact the trend began even earlier, as one aspect of a general return to innocence in 1932 and 1933, when Marie Dressler, Will Rogers, Janet Gaynor and Wallace Beery (soon to be joined by Shirley Temple) replaced more sophisticated stars like Crawford and Garbo among the top ten. As evidence of this, the first major studio film of an English classic (other than *Svengali* and *Dr. Jekyll*) was Paramount's extremely elaborate production of *Alice in Wonderland,* presented, as if in answer to RKO's *Little Women,* as its big holiday attraction for Christmas 1933.

Although it is usually dismissed (as in *The New Yorker*'s brief listing) as a misguided monstrosity, this *Alice* was certainly closer to the original than Disney's prettied-up cartoon of 1951. If anything, it erred on the side of slavish fidelity not only to Lewis Carroll's text (episodes from *Through the Looking-Glass* were also used) but to the original Tenniel illustrations. Costumes were copied identically, and all the more bizarre characters wore grotesque masks over their heads, making facial expressions impossible.

The *Times* rated Charlotte Henry's performance as Alice inferior to Josephine Hutchinson's on stage, but some of the other casting seems inspired: Alison Skipworth as the Duchess, Edward Everett Horton as the Mad Hatter, Edna May Oliver and Louise Fazenda as the Red and White Queens, W. C. Fields as Humpty Dumpty, Charlie Ruggles as the March Hare, Ned Sparks as the Caterpillar. Other choices were merely inexplicable: Cary Grant as the Mock Turtle, Gary Cooper as the White Knight.

Almost a year before *Alice,* Monogram, the most enterprising of the independent studios, had produced an authentic, reasonably successful *Oliver Twist,* thus contributing the first film to what was to become a Charles Dickens cycle. No doubt its quality was in large part due to the supervision of Herbert Brenon, who had done so well as the director of the silent Barrie fantasies, *Peter Pan* and *A Kiss for Cinderella.* The *Times* found it "not especially successful from a dramatic viewpoint, but in some of the characters there is the suggestion of a Cruikshank drawing come to life."

Dickie Moore, a cherub-faced child who usually played the star's small son in mother-love dramas, made a most appealing Oliver, Irving Pichel was a suitably villainous Fagin, William Boyd (the former stage actor, not Hopalong Cassidy) was Bill Sikes and Doris Lloyd, Nancy. This *Oliver* has been so eclipsed by the 1951 British version starring Alec Guinness and Robert Newton (not to mention the splashy Lionel Bart musical, *Oliver!*) that Michael Pointer in *American Film,* December 1975, fails to list it among the screen versions of Dickens' novels.

Nor does he mention the far more ambitious, equally forgotten *Great Expectations,* which Universal presented at Christmas 1934 (still ahead of the MGM Dickens films). One would assume that it must have played in New York, yet the *Times* did not cover it, nor are any other metropolitan newspaper reviews in the collection at the New York Public Library at Lincoln Center. The only information available is in a few publicity stories and fan magazines (plus the fact that this writer has seen it twice).

This is all the more surprising in that it was a faithful version of the novel, expensively produced, with an unusually distinguished cast. Although Phillips Holmes, the rather wooden young actor who had helped deaden the impact of von Sternberg's *An American Tragedy* (1931), was no more than adequate as the grown-up Pip, his Estella was the lovely Jane Wyatt, in her second film. Stage veteran Florence Reed, in one of her rare talkie appearances, was a formidable Miss Havisham, Henry Hull was the convict Magwitch, Alan Hale and Rafaela Ottiano, Joe Gargery and his wife. In a curious link with David Lean's celebrated 1947 classic, Francis L. Sullivan was the lawyer, Jaggers, just as impressive as in 1947. Only a few minor characters, like Jaggers' clerk, Wemick, were omitted. The cast even lists some characters who do not appear, including Biddy, played, oddly enough, by Valerie Hobson, the 1947 Estella.

Meanwhile, in April 1934, Warners had announced a production of *Pickwick Papers* starring Guy Kibbee (not bad casting, at that), but nothing further was heard of this. Thus the next Dickens film was MGM's superb *David Copperfield* (1935), which has never been surpassed. Adapted by novelist Hugh Walpole, with a screenplay by Howard Estabrook, produced by David O. Selznick and directed by George Cukor, the film in every detail reflects the scrupulous artistic integrity implicit in those names. From the opening credits, which show the title page of the original edition of the book, while an off-screen choir sings "Noel," "I Saw Three Ships" and other Christmas carols, the atmosphere of cozy, traditional warmth is established.

Edna May Oliver might well have been born to play Aunt Betsey Trotwood, and even W. C. Fields, though unmistakably himself, stuck to the script and makes a fine, touching Micawber (perhaps even better than Charles Laughton, originally wanted for the role, would have been). Likewise, though Jackie Cooper, L. B. Mayer's choice for David, would undoubtedly have given a good performance, he could never have brought to it the peculiarly English grace and charm of ten-year-old Freddie Bartholomew, whom Cukor and Selznick chose out of more than ten thousand applicants. But indeed the whole large cast—an extraordinarily vivid and varied gallery, even for Dickens—was visually and histrionically perfect, from the sadistic Mr. Murdstone (Basil Rathbone in the first of his sneering villain roles) and warmhearted Peggotty (Jessie Ralph), down to such vignettes as Mrs. Gummidge (Una O'Connor) and Mr. Dick (Lennox Pawle).

While it is true that, as in the novel, the grown-up David (Frank Lawton) is less interesting than the child, perhaps because he suffers less, and his second wife Agnes (Madge Evans) is the least colorful character in the cast, still, the three main plot threads of his

Freddie Bartholomew, Edna May Oliver, Lennox Pawle in **David Copperfield**

adult life are all masterfully handled: his hopeless first marriage to the pathetically childlike Dora (beautifully played by Maureen O'Sullivan), the seduction of Little Emily (Florine McKinney) by Steerforth (Hugh Williams) and the exposure of Uriah Heep (Roland Young in his only villainous role) by Micawber.

"A screen masterpiece in its own right," said the *Times,* "the most profoundly satisfying screen manipulation of a great novel that the camera has ever given us." More than four decades later, it remains a savory Dickensian pudding, stuffed full with comic and dramatic plums.

A few months later, Universal continued the trend with *The Mystery of Edwin Drood* (1935), from the novel on which Dickens was working when he died. The solution devised by screenwriters John Balderston and Gladys Unger generally satisfied those familiar with the characters and situations Dickens had created. Claude Rains as John Jasper was revealed as the murderer of Edwin Drood (David Manners), Douglass Montgomery was Neville Landless, Valerie Hobson (in her almost forgotten American phase), Helena Landless, and Francis L. Sullivan, the aptly named Mr. Crisparkle. The *Times* was especially impressed with Rains' performance and the sinister atmosphere contrasted with the tranquillity of an English cathedral town.

But it remained for MGM to top off 1935 (this time making sure of a New York opening during the holidays) with its magnificent, still unrivaled *A Tale of Two Cities,* which, true to the novel, outdid even *David Copperfield* in spectacular scope and dramatic force.

Though Ronald Colman had done a dual role in *The Masquerader* (1931) and was to do another in *The Prisoner of Zenda* (1937), he played only Sydney Carton, not Charles Darnay, as other actors had done in silent versions. Thus he first saves Darnay (Donald Woods) at the treason trial not by trading on their identical appearance but by subtly blackmailing Barsad into withdrawing the charge. This use of his wits rather than a chance resemblance has the effect of making the climactic substitution less gimmicky.

In a running time of little more than two hours, the literate, intelligent script by W. P. Lipscomb and S. N. Behrman manages to include all Dickens' major characters, themes and subplots. The occasional use of informative subtitles, essentially a silent screen technique, was presumably necessary to fill in a a complex historical background. These interfere neither with the sharp, often subtle dialogue nor with the marvelous cinematic sweep of the big scenes, notably the breaking of the wine cask in the impoverished Faubourg St. Antoine, the storming of the Bastille and Darnay's trial before the Revolutionary tribunal.

In all these scenes, director Jack Conway's use of quickly glimpsed reacting faces is visual storytelling at its best. Also effective both in word and image are the reminders that the poor were treated literally worse than animals —the concern of the Marquis (Basil Rathbone) that one of his horses might have been

Walter Catlett, Donald Woods, Ronald Colman in A Tale of Two Cities

injured while running over a child, the grape-eating monkey perched on the shoulder of a bewigged, painted nobleman, the huge chunks of meat thrown to hunting dogs while the people starve.

Aside from the original musical theme composed by Herbert Stothart, the sound track makes haunting use of the "Marseillaise" and of "Adeste Fideles," which is reprised whenever Carton thinks of his hopeless love for Lucie Manette (Elizabeth Allan). In a tender Christmas Eve sequence (not found in the novel) she takes him to Midnight Mass (permissible by then at least to foreign Catholics because of George III's relative tolerance), where the hymn is sung in Latin; in the street outside carolers sing it in English as "O Come All Ye Faithful"—a touch typical of the director's attention to fine detail.

The final scenes, including those with the pathetic little seamstress (Isabel Jewell), who has nothing to do with the plot, yet adds so much, are utterly true to Dickens, even to the ending with Carton's famous words, "It is a far, far better thing . . ." Though one might question the addition, in subtitle, of the biblical quotation about the resurrection and the life, the very last moment, as the camera moves upward from the guillotine to the sky, sparing us the bloody details, while Carton's voice utters his own epitaph, still seems tasteful and moving.

Nothing in the acting is dated, certainly not Colman's beautifully shaded Carton. Almost every speaking part was filled by a distinguished stage player of long experience, not only Blanche Yurka as the implacable Madame Defarge (her first screen role and the best she was ever to have), but H. B. Warner as Gabelle, the tutor, Henry B. Walthall as Dr. Manette, Edna May Oliver as Miss Pross, Claude Gillingwater as Jarvis Lorry and Fritz Leiber as Jacques, father of the run-over child.

After the departure of Selznick to form his own studio, MGM made only one more Dickens film, *A Christmas Carol,* released for the holidays in 1938. Though much of the public regretted that Lionel Barrymore did not play

Scrooge, as he had often done on radio, Reginald Owen did his usual splendidly professional job, and the production was given just as much care as Selznick's. Leo G. Carroll was Marley's Ghost, Ann Rutherford the Ghost of Christmas Past, Gene, Kathleen and June Lockhart were Mr. and Mrs. Bob Cratchit and their oldest daughter, with bucktoothed little Terry Kilburn a lovably shy Tiny Tim. Scrupulously faithful to the original, this *Carol* still compares favorably with the later Alastair Sim and Albert Finney versions and is far superior to the many TV adaptations.

In the midst of all these Dickensian excursions, RKO, not to be outdone, opted for William Makepeace Thackeray, in what was not merely the only authentic, unmodernized talkie version of *Vanity Fair* but, more important historically, the first full-length film in the newly perfected three-component Technicolor. Hitherto audiences had seen only a few short subjects, notably *La Cucaracha,* and individual scenes that suddenly blazed into color in a few films like *The Cat and the Fiddle* and *The House of Rothschild* (both 1934), which had the side effect of making the rest of the picture look intolerably drab. But *Becky Sharp* (1935) was directed by veteran craftsman Rouben Mamoulian, with the color effects carefully orchestrated by Robert Edmond Jones, then at the height of his success as a stage designer.

1935 viewers and reviewers were so understandably dazzled by their first extended venture into what the *Times* called "a strange, beautiful and unexpected new world" that they could hardly see the forest for the brilliantly hued trees. Technical faults were dwelt on, such as long shots that turned faces into blurred masses, and the creators were said to be using "not the coloration of natural life but a vividly pigmented dream world of the artistic imagination."

Seen now, when color can be as tacitly taken for granted as sound in even the cheapest film, *Becky Sharp* can be judged more fairly on its own merits. Most highly praised was the dramatic use of color at the Duchess of Richmond's ball in Brussels on the eve of Waterloo, when the rumble of Napoleon's cannons summons the red-coated officers to immediate duty and throws all the Regency-gowned ladies into well-bred panic.

Dramatically, the *Times* found the film, based on Langdon Mitchell's 1900 dramatization, "static and land-locked" and "endlessly talkative," yet it is true to the novel in all essential respects except that at the end there is no hint that Becky will eventually dispose of Jos Sedley and end her days as a pious Lady Bountiful.

If Miriam Hopkins was not a particularly memorable Becky, the other characters were extremely well cast. Frances Dee's dignity and beauty indeed give Amelia more character than she ever shows in the novel, and the older players could hardly be improved upon: Sir Cedric Hardwicke as the Marquis of Steyne, Alan Mowbray as Rawdon Crawley, Nigel Bruce as Jos Sedley, Alison Skipworth as the worldly old Miss Crawley and Billie Burke as Lady Bareacres. Until a better *Vanity Fair* is made, *Becky Sharp* with its still beautiful color effects and many lively scenes must re-

G. P. Huntley, Jr. and Miriam Hopkins in **Becky Sharp**

main the best screen treatment ever given Thackeray until *Barry Lyndon,* forty years later.

With authentically produced classics crowning every major studio with new critical laurels, and corresponding rewards at the box office, Warner Brothers were not about to be written off as mere purveyors of assembly-line musicals and hard-boiled slices of contemporary life. They had produced elaborate costume dramas in *Voltaire* (1933) and *Madame Du Barry* (1934), but in 1935 they went all the way, hiring the world's most illustrious stage director, Max Reinhardt, to produce one of the most difficult plays, *A Midsummer Night's Dream,* by the world's greatest playwright. This was Hollywood's first attempt at Shakespeare since the disastrous Fairbanks-Pickford *Taming of the Shrew* (1929), which had achieved a kind of immortality by its credit: "Additional dialogue by Sam Taylor."

The marvel was that this *Dream* did not turn out, as was widely predicted, a total nightmare. Far from it, "a brave, beautiful and interesting effort," said the *Times.* "The sum of its faults is dwarfed against the sheer bulk of the enterprise." With Mendelssohn's music arranged by Erich Wolfgang Korngold, dances directed by "Nijinska" and William Dieterle's cinematic expertise to help translate Reinhardt's visions intact to the screen, the film was pleasing both to eye and ear. Its unique juxtaposition of ancient Athens, Elizabethan England and fairyland leaves the designer unlimited latitude, and Max Ree's costumes were an imaginative mélange reflecting all three worlds.

Almost every actor on the Warners contract list was drafted for the great enterprise, gangsters and low comedians cast as the rustics (James Cagney, Joe E. Brown, Hugh Herbert, Frank McHugh), upcoming ingenues and juveniles as the four young lovers (Olivia De Havilland and Jean Muir predictably outacting their swains, Dick Powell and Ross Alexander), dignified middle-aged players as Theseus and Hippolyta (Ian Hunter and Verree Teasdale) and as Oberon and Titania Victor Jory and Anita Louise (who was at least visually right).

Cagney was called by the *Times* too dynamic for Bottom, but Brown was rated highly as Flute, and fifteen-year-old Mickey Rooney as Puck was hailed as "one of the major delights."

Never outdone for long, MGM marshaled its mighty resources to produce what was intended to be, and in fact was, the most prestigious Shakespearean film the screen had yet seen: *Romeo and Juliet* (1936). George Cukor, who had succeeded so well with *Little Women* and *David Copperfield,* was entrusted with directing Talbot Jennings' reverent but thoroughly cinematic screenplay, a young choreographer named Agnes de Mille staged the period dances at the Capulet ball, and not even Adrian and Cedric Gibbons were considered quite up to designing the costumes and settings unaided.

Oliver Messel, an expert on the fifteenth century (the period chosen for maximum visual appeal), was imported from London, then dispatched to Verona, where his staff spent three months taking thousands of pictures, so that the Italian Renaissance could be reproduced on screen as never before. One can only regret that all this splendor was photographed in black and white; had it been done in color, its pictorial effect would surely have rivaled those of the British *Romeos* of 1954 and 1966, both made on location in Italy.

Viewing it now, especially in comparison with the two later versions, one is immediately struck by the fact that all the principals are years too old for their roles. But one should bear in mind that this had long been an accepted convention on stage, on the theory that by the time an actress was emotionally mature enough to play Juliet (or professionally big enough to form her own company and star herself), she could no longer look the part. Except for Maude Adams, the most acclaimed Juliets of the 1900s had been buxom, middle-aged women. Even in the 1930s Katharine Cornell was forty-two when she first played the role, the same year that Lynn Fontanne at forty-eight was playing Kate in *The Taming of the Shrew.*

In those years road companies were sent out only for hit musicals or commercial comedies; the greatest stars still took their acclaimed vehicles on national tours, so no doubt it was their public, the literate minority who subscribed to the Theatre Guild and read *Stage* magazine, at which MGM's *Romeo and Juliet* was aimed, rather than at the average Shirley Temple fan. For the same discriminating clientele, Random House, even before release of the film, brought out a handsome illustrated volume, which contained both the text of the play and the shot-by-shot screenplay—then a most unusual publishing venture—plus short articles by all the talented people involved, including the leading actors, explaining the reasons behind their artistic decisions.

Norma Shearer was actually only thirty-two (and could look much younger), and though she was the wife of Irving Thalberg, MGM's production chief, it must not be supposed that her Juliet was an expensive ego trip with a determined husband trying to force his untalented wife on an indifferent public. Shearer had already proved herself with an Oscar in 1930, and if she could hardly pass for fourteen (Juliet's stated age in the text), she was still a thoroughly convincing Juliet. Undoubtedly she was helped immeasurably by Cukor's direction, flattering photography and perfect lighting, but the performance (for which she received her third Oscar nomination) was still her own.

The other characters were cast accordingly. Leslie Howard at forty-three was an extremely sensitive, introverted Romeo, better at soliloquies and lyrical passages than scenes of action, and John Barrymore, though he looked his fifty-four years, carried off Mercutio, including the Queen Mab speech, by sheer professional bravura. Basil Rathbone at forty-four seemed a comparatively youthful Tybalt. Lady Capulet, twenty-eight by her own account, was stately, icy-faced Violet Kemble Cooper. C. Aubrey Smith, more often seen in grandfather roles, was an authorita-

tive, if decidedly elderly, Capulet, and the Nurse, in later years usually cast as a lusty wench, was another of Edna May Oliver's sharp-tongued old ladies.

But once this Victorian convention was accepted—that these apparently mature adults were totally subject to the whims of their aged parents—audiences could sit back and enjoy the most sumptuous Shakespearean production they had ever seen, while listening to the text, almost uncut, beautifully delivered by some extremely polished (mostly British) actors.

Frank Nugent, who had succeeded Andre Sennwald at the *Times,* wrote of *Romeo and Juliet* only in superlatives. "Never before, in all its centuries, has the play received so handsome a production . . . Logically, if not chronologically, it is the first Shakespearean photoplay . . . The screen is the perfect medium for Shakespeare."

Perhaps rightly concluding that from such resounding critical acclaim there was nowhere to go but down, neither MGM nor any other Hollywood studio took up the Shakespearean challenge again until nearly twenty years later, with the 1953 *Julius Caesar.*

Yet a decade so devoted to English classics could hardly ignore the Brontë sisters, Emily and Charlotte. In 1934 Monogram had done a faithful, well-mounted version of *Jane Eyre,* with Virginia Bruce in the title role, Colin Clive as Rochester and a number of excellent character players in the supporting parts. This forgotten film (not reviewed by the *Times*) has suffered the same fate as Universal's *Great Expectations;* it was so utterly overshadowed by later versions that even to the most omnivorous TV fan the title now suggests if not Joan Fontaine and Orson Welles, then Susannah York and George C. Scott.

But that *annus mirabilis* 1939, which produced such an extraordinary number of great films destined for permanent fame, contributed one that is perhaps the most vividly remembered and fervently admired filmed classic of them all, the one that comes closer than any to being a cult film: *Wuthering*

Heights. Produced by Samuel Goldwyn with all his usual care and taste, directed by William Wyler at the height of his powers, with a script by Hecht and MacArthur, it remains one of the cinematic monuments of the decade.

Omission of the second-generation plot left the interest totally concentrated on the blazing, almost demoniacal passion of Cathy and Heathcliff—and never has passion been more intensely and movingly conveyed on the screen than by Laurence Olivier in his first memorable screen role and Merle Oberon, giving the performance of her career.

With every nuance deepened by an unusually evocative Alfred Newman score, the tragic love-turned-hate relationship of "wild, sweet" Cathy Earnshaw and the mysterious, brooding Heathcliff, played out against the wind-swept moors of Yorkshire, achieved a piercing poignance perhaps even beyond the hopes of its creators. Scenes and lines remain in the mind forever: Cathy to Heathcliff on hearing he plans to marry Isabella: "Don't punish her, Heathcliff, punish *me!*" and his implacable reply: "I *am* punishing you." Or Isabella as his neglected wife pathetically pleading: "Look at *me*, Heathcliff! *I'm* young, *I'm* pretty!" To which he turns away in disdain, muttering, "Why doesn't *your* hair smell of heather?"

As Edgar and Isabella Linton, the innocent brother and sister whose lives are totally blasted by their unrequited love for the other two, David Niven and Geraldine Fitzgerald contributed considerably more charm and character than they are given in the book. As an odd historic footnote to the unique good fortune that seemed to bless this *Wuthering Heights,* not only the four stars but even the character players (Flora Robson, Donald Crisp, Leo G. Carroll, Cecil Kellaway) all remained alive and professionally active for at least twenty-five years after the film. (The next year Olivier played two other well-known heroes of English novels, Maxim de Winter in Daphne du Maurier's best-selling *Rebecca* and Mr. Darcy in the superb *Pride*

and Prejudice—two of the brightest sparks in the 1940 afterglow of fine films obviously written and planned in 1939.)

As with the American and European material, not all '30s films set in the British past were drawn from classic novels or plays. Some of the best-remembered were taken from history itself, from current best sellers, stage hits or even popular legend. At this many centuries' remove, Robin Hood and Little John, who never lived, seem at least as real as King Richard and Prince John, who did. Oddly enough, the rich Arthurian material was used only once during the decade, and then satirically.

Mark Twain's *A Connecticut Yankee* (1931), second of three screen incarnations, but, surprisingly, not based on the hit Rodgers and Hart musical of 1927, was an original adaptation, mechanically updated with such modern contraptions as cigarette lighters, radios, tiny Austin cars, "autogyros" (helicopters) and bombers. Will Rogers was well cast as the shrewd New Englander, Hank, who as "Sir Boss" brings twentieth-century Yankee know-how to Camelot, and unites the ingenue and juvenile (Maureen O'Sullivan and Frank Albertson), despite the evil machinations of Queen Morgan le Fay (Myrna Loy). His magic incantation, which apparently causes the eclipse of the sun, tells much about 1931 wishes: "Prosperity, farm relief, freedom for Ireland, light wines and beer!"

In the same vein, on a lower level, Wheeler and Woolsey, a team regarded by reviewers as the lowest of low comedians, made *Cock-eyed Cavaliers* (1934), in which, masquerading as a royal doctor and his assistant, they caused havoc in medieval England. They were, of course, following in the footsteps of Eddie Cantor (as in *Roman Scandals*, 1933) and Laurel and Hardy, who had already done *The Devil's Brother* (1933) and were to do two more period operettas. The fact that even such slapstick comedians turned to the picturesque past is added evidence of the extreme popularity of costume films in the mid-'30s.

In the same historical order as in the last two chapters, the most colorful film set in the medieval period as well as the most spectacular and best-loved Errol Flynn vehicle was surely *The Adventures of Robin Hood* (1938), the first outdoor costume picture in the new color, with a marvelous score by Korngold. A visual and aural delight still, it remains the best all-around version of the Sherwood Forest legend ever made.[2]

Robin Hood was Flynn's most attractive role, Olivia De Havilland made a winsome Maid Marian, Alan Hale (repeating the role he had played in the 1922 Fairbanks silent) was a properly bluff Little John and Eugene Pallette was just right as the food-guzzling Friar Tuck, but most of the superb cast were British: Patric Knowles as a graceful Will

[2] In 1933, before Flynn's discovery, Warners had announced plans to star Cagney as Robin Hood, with Guy Kibbee as Friar Tuck.

Basil Rathbone and Errol Flynn in
The Adventures of Robin Hood

Scarlet, Ian Hunter as King Richard and, most delectable of all, the three villains: Melville Cooper as the Sheriff of Nottingham, Claude Rains as Prince John and Basil Rathbone as Sir Guy of Gisborne. Teamed for the fourth time, Una O'Connor as Bess, Maid Marian's servant, and Herbert Mundin as Much the miller's son provided droll Cockney humor, but indeed the script (by Norman Reilly Raine and Seton I. Miller) was written and played with a lighthearted, tongue-in-cheek flair that gave the picture a blithe charm unmatched by any later Flynn swashbuckler.

Though supposedly dealing more directly with history, *Tower of London* (1939) was almost as completely fictitious, with Basil Rathbone even more malevolent as Richard III than as Guy of Gisborne. Without the slightest effort to do justice to the historical Richard, about whom the facts were by then well-known, the melodramatic script by Robert N. Lee was content to follow the Tudor party line in depicting Shakespeare's "poisonous, hunch-backed toad," based on Holinshed and Thomas More, the only sources available in Shakespeare's day.

But the venomous ex-queen Margaret, who adds so much to the play, is omitted, and a pallid romantic pair (Nan Grey and John Sutton) who try to save the little princes are added, along with a ghoulish torturer and executioner (Boris Karloff), billed immediately after Rathbone, the star. Otherwise the film was rather well cast: Ian Hunter as Edward IV, Barbara O'Neil as his Queen, Vincent Price as Clarence, Leo G. Carroll as Buckingham and Ralph Forbes as Henry Tudor, but the emphasis on macabre horror was so strong that the *Times* dismissed Richard's villainies as "almost too bad to be true" (as indeed they were).

Both *Robin Hood* and *Tower of London* were obviously fanciful departures from history, with Richard I as totally idealized in the one (as also in *The Crusades*) as Richard III was maligned in the other. In this same borderland of historical fiction, in which what is known of certain real personages is extended to involve them in imaginary incidents, belongs Mark Twain's *The Prince and the Pauper* (1937). An exciting adventure tale in which the son of Henry VIII (Montagu Love), the little Prince of Wales, soon to become Edward VI, playfully exchanges clothes with a beggar boy who is his double, only to find that they have exchanged identities as well, the film starred actual twins, Billy and Bobby Mauch, Errol Flynn as a soldier of fortune who saves the day for them and a magnificent cast of character actors headed by Claude Rains and Henry Stephenson. The film, which climaxes with the coronation of the boy king in Westminster Abbey, was shrewdly timed to open just before the actual coronation of King George VI and Queen Elizabeth on May 12, 1937.

In 1933 Helen Hayes had scored one of her greatest stage triumphs, on Broadway and on tour, in Maxwell Anderson's *Mary of Scotland*. Undoubtedly she could have repeated the role on screen, had she not firmly decided in 1935 to return to the stage. With the vogue for costume films mounting each year, such a choice dramatic property could hardly be left unfilmed, so RKO bought it for Hepburn.

With her red hair, her height and her ability to look every inch a queen, Hepburn was physically much better suited than Hayes to play the hapless Scottish Queen, yet despite John Ford's direction, a Dudley Nichols screenplay that turned the Anderson blank verse to prose and a distinguished cast headed by Fredric March (who else?) as her third husband, the fiery Bothwell, this was not one of Hepburn's major triumphs.

Both Bette Davis and Ginger Rogers (Ginger *Rogers?*) wanted to play Queen Elizabeth, but the role went to March's wife, Florence Eldridge, who played it as written, as a glittering spider spinning endless webs of Machiavellian intrigue to enmesh her trusting rival. Douglas Walton was outstanding as the weakling Darnley, Mary's second husband, and the other players included just about all those dependable veterans who lent their authority

to almost every costume film: Ian Keith, Donald Crisp, Ralph Forbes, John Carradine, Moroni Olsen, Alan Mowbray, Robert Barrat, Robert Warwick, Ivan Simpson and Lawrence Grant. As *The New Yorker*'s brief notice puts it, "The picture drips prestige."

Reviews were on the whole laudatory for the stars, if anything even better for March than for Hepburn, and though many pointed out that the real Mary and Elizabeth never met, it was understood that their climactic confrontation was as dramatically necessary for Anderson as it had been for Schiller. Only *Time* sounded a sour note by complaining that Ford overdid the somber atmosphere by shooting so many scenes in the dark.

Indeed, seen now, the black-and-white photography, the constant, murky overcast, the long, Scotch-burred speeches by dignified elders in dark robes, while occasionally dramatic, do at times suggest a Calvinist funeral service; one must respect the solemnity of the occasion, but will it never end?

Three years later, Bette Davis achieved her ambition to play Elizabeth in a handsome color version of an earlier Anderson play, *Elizabeth the Queen*, retitled (in an echo both of John Erskine's 1920s titles like *The Private Life of Helen of Troy* and of *The Private Life of Henry VIII*) *The Private Lives of Elizabeth and Essex*.[3] This change was reportedly made at Errol Flynn's insistence, to give equal billing to his character (for whom Davis had wanted Olivier), but after seeing the film Nugent of the *Times* thought the original title should have been retained. "It's Queen Bette's picture . . . [Flynn's] Essex lacked a head long before the headsman got around to him." Or, as another critic observed, Flynn was no diamond in the ruff.

The same year, 1939, also saw Davis in *Dark Victory, Juarez* and *The Old Maid*, but in none did she give a more remarkable performance. As Shipman notes in *The Great Movie Stars*, "with entirely the wrong-shaped

---

[3] When revived now, the original title is used.

face Davis managed an uncanny resemblance to the Queen, and she dominated the film as Elizabeth had her court." (Sixteen years later, nearer the right age, she was an even better Elizabeth in *The Virgin Queen.*)

She was supported by such stalwarts as Donald Crisp as Bacon, Vincent Price as Raleigh, Henry Stephenson as Burghley and Henry Daniell as Cecil, but it is undeniable that Flynn, faced for the first time with a role that demanded more than the ability to look good in costume, handle a sword well and toss off impudent quips with a devil-may-care smile, was a painfully inadequate Essex. "How much better it might have been with an Essex worthy of Miss Davis' Elizabeth, we can only surmise," said the *Times.* Perhaps Flynn was punishing Davis for having turned down *Gone With the Wind* rather than accept him as Rhett Butler. In 1940 when he made *The Sea Hawk,* about an Elizabethan adventurer, it was Flora Robson, repeating her characterization from *Fire over England* (1937), who played the Virgin Queen.

The only American film with a seventeenth-century British background was Sabatini's *Captain Blood* (1935), set in England and the West Indies in the 1680s—as rousing a pirate adventure film as Hollywood ever turned out, the one that not only launched Flynn on his starring career but created the new romantic team of Flynn and De Havilland. It also included a cameo glimpse of James II (the only Stuart monarch of England to appear in any American film), whose accession to the throne in 1685 restores Blood's fortunes. (No need to wonder what happened when James was deposed three years later.)

Here it might be noted that, although Hollywood had made free with the foibles of any number of royal Louis', from XI to XVI inclusive, it approached British royalty much more respectfully, with none of the saucy irreverence that sparked such made-in-England productions as Laughton's *Henry VIII* (1933) and Hardwicke's and Neagle's *Nell Gwyn* (1935), nor, for that matter, the poi-gnance of *Nine Days a Queen* (1936), about Lady Jane Grey. The nearer the present, the blander the attitude, as if in deference to the living royal family. Thus the Prince Regent (later George IV) was briefly but not unfavorably introduced in *The House of Rothschild* (1934) and *Becky Sharp* (1935). Queen Victoria was invariably seen as a benign grandmotherly figure in black satin and lace cap, whose function was to reward patient merit in films like *Disraeli* (1929), *Annie Oakley* (1935), *The White Angel* (1936) and *The Little Princess* (1939)—a role she continued to play in other films for decades thereafter, as certifiably above reproach as Lincoln.

Among films set in the eighteenth century, one of the most memorable is the magnificent *Mutiny on the Bounty* (1935), released with typical MGM prodigality scarcely a month before its other eighteenth-century spectacle, *A Tale of Two Cities.* Laughton added another portrait to his lengthening gallery of historical and literary psychopaths—which already included Nero, Henry VIII, Edward Moulton-Barrett and Javert—perhaps his most memorable of all, or at least the one most familiar to his impersonators: Captain Bligh.

For sheer, slavering sadism, Bligh surpassed any villain the screen had ever seen, all the more horrifying in that his atrocities were a matter of historic fact. As his chief antagonists, Fletcher Christian and Roger Byam, Clark Gable and Franchot Tone were manly and sympathetic, the supporting cast was full of fine character actors (notably Dudley Digges as the drunken doctor), the seascapes with the ship under full sail braving all kinds of weather were superb, there was even a scantily clad romantic interlude with the Tahitian girls—all these varied appeals woven into a powerful, still compelling drama.

No wonder the *Times* said: "Grim, brutal, sturdily romantic, made out of horror and deep courage, it is as savagely exciting and rousingly dramatic a photoplay as has come out of Hollywood in recent years." This verdict surely could not be applied to the strange 1962 remake, in which for some unknown

Dudley Digges, Franchot Tone, Clark Gable, unidentified actor, Charles Laughton, Ivan Simpson, Ian Wolfe in **Mutiny on the Bounty**

reason Marlon Brando played Christian as an eighteenth-century dandy more foppish than Sir Percy Blakeney (in *The Scarlet Pimpernel*) at his most effete.

The year after *Captain Blood* zoomed Flynn to stardom, another British-set costume drama from a rival studio created another new matinee idol: *Lloyds of London* (1936), in which Tyrone Power, after a few small roles, dropping the "Junior" from his name, came into a stardom that was to last until his death more than twenty years later. Possibly inspired by the 1934 success of *The House of Rothschild* (which Zanuck had made

for his 20th Century studio before combining with Fox), this somewhat parallel story dealt with the fictional Jonathan Blake, who, growing from Freddie Bartholomew into Power, becomes the head of a Lloyd's syndicate during the Napoleonic wars, and through his boyhood friendship with Lord Nelson changes the course of history (perhaps even falsifies it, since he announces the victory at Trafalgar before it has taken place).

Looking as beautiful as the Lawrence portrait for which she is posing in one scene, Madeleine Carroll was his titled beloved, the unhappy wife of George Sanders, then just beginning his career of elegantly sneering villainy. The supporting cast was rich with familiar character actors, led by Sir Guy Standing as John Julius Angerstein, an actual founding father of Lloyd's.

One of the best-remembered of all British-set costume dramas, if only because it was Katharine Cornell's greatest stage hit, was produced at least three times in the 1950s as a TV special (once with Cornell herself, once with Helen Hayes, once with Geraldine Fitzgerald), was filmed again in 1956 and also served as the basis for at least one musical, is that perennial war horse of genteel literary biography, *The Barretts of Wimpole Street* (set in 1845).

A household in which nine young adults (three sisters, six faceless, indistinguishable brothers) are all cowed into quivering submission by one tyrannical paterfamilias seemed just as outrageous when the play opened in 1930 as now, with perhaps then an added fillip of self-congratulation at having just outgrown such monstrous Victorian patriarchy—but once this situation is accepted, as it apparently was by the real Barretts and countless other nineteenth-century families, there is undeniable satisfaction in watching

Madeleine Carroll and Tyrone Power in **Lloyds of London**

the dashing young knight, Robert Browning, rescue the captive maiden, Elizabeth Barrett, from the cruel ogre who happens to be her father.

Uniting three Oscar winners, as all the ads emphasized, Norma Shearer as the invalid poetess, Fredric March back in costume again as Browning and Charles Laughton as the sinister Mr. Barrett ("They can't censor a gleam in my eye," Laughton is supposed to have said about the obviously Freudian undertones in Barrett's possessive love for his oldest daughter), the 1934 film, directed by Sidney Franklin, was given a typical MGM prestige production, perfectly cast and mounted.

The play, which is as completely confined to one room as the unhappy heroine herself, was gracefully opened up to include the rest of the house, the street and a park with a greenhouse where the lovers meet to plan their flight. A typical visual touch is the opening scene in which Flush, Elizabeth's beloved spaniel, is seen trotting briskly along Wimpole Street, then entering Number 50. In the front hall, as he passes the dining room where Papa Barrett is piously lecturing his brood, the dog flattens himself and creeps along the

Charles Laughton and Norma Shearer in **The Barretts of Wimpole Street**

floor until he is safe, then bounds up the stairs.

Maureen O'Sullivan, in the first of the several nineteenth-century ingenue roles she did so well (when not swinging from tree to tree as Tarzan's mate), was a delightfully spirited Henrietta, the rebellious youngest daughter, Katherine Alexander was the repressed Arabel and Una O'Connor as Wilson, Elizabeth's maid, provoked smiles every time she glided across the floor as if on wheels.

Presumably encouraged by the favorable reception of *The Story of Louis Pasteur* early in 1936, Warners later that year assigned the same director, William Dieterle, to a parallel story of a female counterpart of Pasteur, a pioneer in the health field battling against the entrenched army medical practices of her day during the Crimean War. This was, of course, Elizabeth Barrett's contemporary, Florence Nightingale, in a film rather too reverently titled *The White Angel* (1936).

Kay Francis, escaping for once from elegant clotheshorse roles, gave a "sincere and eloquent" performance, said the *Times,* but despite this and the usual impressive roster of character actors (Donald Crisp, Nigel Bruce and Montagu Love were among her antagonists), the film suffered from the bane of too many Hollywood biographies, an excessively worshipful approach.

As Nugent observed:

Miss Nightingale—as Kay Francis portrays her —talks, walks and thinks like a historical character . . . When she makes her nightly rounds you are sure she is trying to live up to Longfellow's "Lady With the Lamp." When she tells her opponents they cannot stop her work, you cannot escape the feeling that she is speaking less out of sublime faith than certain knowledge gleaned from a twentieth-century encyclopedia.

A 1928 silent, titled *Dawn,* starring Sybil Thorndike as England's second most celebrated nurse, Edith Cavell, had unleashed a fury of official protests from Germany and a flurry of apologies from high-ranking Britons, including Sir Austin Chamberlain, but by September 1939, when *Nurse Edith Cavell,* starring Anna Neagle, was released, World War II had begun, with Germany again the aggressor and Poland suffering even worse atrocities than Belgium had in the previous conflict.

Despite the tempting possibilities for recruiting poster propaganda à la *Confessions of a Nazi Spy, Cavell* was praised for its quiet restraint. "A dispassionate, uninflammatory and deeply affecting tale of individual heroism under the crushing influence of modern warfare," said the *Times.* Of course it quoted Edith Cavell's most famous words: "Patriotism is not enough."

Except for a few films like *A Woman Rebels* (1936), *Little Lord Fauntleroy* (1936) and *The Little Princess* (1939), the post-Crimean Victorian decades were almost overlooked, with one exception that was enough to make one wish they had been overlooked altogether. Between the Nightingale and Cavell films, in year of release as in historical period, came the most completely disappointing screen biography of them all, *Parnell* (1937).

Adapted from Elsie Schauffler's successful Broadway play, with a screenplay by John Van Druten and S. N. Behrman, and a cast of character players remarkable even in an MGM "A" production—and inspired, moreover, by a historic instance of the world well lost for love, a romance that might have seemed especially timely in June 1937, when the Duke and Duchess of Windsor were the world's most publicized newlyweds—*Parnell* apparently had everything possible going for it.

Yet it was ruined by the miscasting of two of Hollywood's most popular stars: beardless, Midwestern Clark Gable as Charles Stewart Parnell, the Anglo-Irish M.P. who almost won Home Rule for Ireland in the 1880s, and cool, quizzical Myrna Loy as Katie O'Shea, the tragic beauty whose divorce, with Parnell named as corespondent, caused his political downfall.

"We can look upon Parnell's life and death . . . and remain untouched by it," said Nugent in the *Times.* "His speeches ring with insincerity . . . Miss Loy is about as fiery as a Wellesley daisy chain." Nor could the supporting efforts of Edna May Oliver, Edmund Gwenn, Alan Marshal, Donald Crisp, Billie Burke and Montagu Love (as Gladstone) overcome the wrongness of the stars.

Yet a decade that had produced the definitive *Dr. Jekyll and Mr. Hyde, Of Human Bondage, Treasure Island, David Copperfield, A Tale of Two Cities* and *The Prisoner of Zenda,* a creditable *Vanity Fair,* an intriguing *Midsummer Night's Dream,* a still impressive *Romeo and Juliet* and an incomparable *Wuthering Heights* had no cause to feel ashamed at not having done justice to the English classics.

But not even all the films discussed in this chapter fully expressed the extent of Hollywood's fervent Anglophilia in the '30s, which sprang no doubt in part from the large colony of distinguished British players, who, according to Evelyn Waugh in *The Loved One,* banded together as in some remote outpost of the Empire.

Except for an occasional backward glance, as in *Forever and a Day,* World War II soon diverted Hollywood's attention to warmly sympathetic idealizations of England's beleaguered present in such films as *Mrs. Miniver, A Yank in the RAF, The White Cliffs of Dover, This Above All* and many others, but not even the most nostalgic traditionalist could say that the screen had not already done more than its share in re-creating England's literary and historical heritage—and this without even including the films to be discussed next, those directly concerned with glorifying the British Empire.

THE WHITE MAN'S BURDEN
Imperialism, Hollywood Style

17

"RULE, BRITANNIA!"
The Sun Never Sets

Though none of the real powers in Hollywood were British or even WASP, their loyalty to England was touching. Even outsiders to the Establishment came through in a pinch —e.g., the fictitious hero of *Lloyds of London* (1936), whose faith in Nelson is as gloriously justified at Trafalgar as is Nathan Rothschild's in Wellington at Waterloo (*The House of Rothschild*, 1934).

But by far the most spectacular and stirring expressions of Hollywood's fervent Anglophilia were those epics that stoutly beat the drum for the even then shaky British Empire. Crusty old actors like C. Aubrey Smith, Henry Stephenson and Sir Guy Standing spent half their screen lives as governors general or commandants of beleaguered outposts threatened by fanatic (though British-educated) khans or maharajas who were forever whipping the simple natives into frenzies of doomed rebellion against the benevolent rule of the crown.

In such far-flung garrisons of the Empire, in the name of King and country (or beauty, home and England), the thin red line would always hold at bay those filthy beggars kicking up a row in the hills, or alternately stop the hordes of mad Fuzzy-Wuzzies swarming across the desert.

Even after Gandhi's policy of passive resistance had made the front pages, American film-makers, more British than the British themselves (who except for *Drums* and *Four Feathers* made few Empire-building pictures in the '30s), continued to accept the old Kiplingesque imperial values as articles of unchallengeable faith. (This paved a smooth way for World War II propaganda films in which the same kind of stubbornly heroic British were holding the line for civilization against the Nazis.)

Although the English did indeed make *Rhodes* (1936), about the builder of their African empire, it was Hollywood that starred Ronald Colman in *Clive of India* (1935), described by the *Times* as "a dignified and impressive historical drama which misses genuine distinction by a comfortable margin," mainly because of its concentration on the domestic side of the hero's career, with some of his major battles reduced to subtitles. Typically, though the climax is his trial in the House of Commons, it stops short of his physical collapse and suicide, ending instead on a note of reconciliation with his wife (Loretta Young).

Having thus in effect seen the historical justification for the British conquest of India, audiences could now relax and cheer wholeheartedly for Clive's latter-day successors, still keeping the wicked natives firmly underfoot in their own country. As Russell Baker put it in his column a few years ago:

Many of us still have a large emotional investment in the empire we saw built in those Saturday matinees. They made us all imperialists in the same vague sense that the Westerns made us all racists. Who, after all, could possibly cheer for Eduardo Ciannelli's pit of cobras when Gunga Din—"you're a better man than I am, Sam Jaffe"—was willing to die to save India for the Queen, God save her?

The standard British Empire film, in fact, was little more than the Western in South Kensington accents. Even Gary Cooper at one point changed from chaps to jodhpurs long enough to head 'em off at Khyber Pass. Instead of turkey feathers, the bad guys usually wore turbans. The regiment marched to bagpipes instead of bugles, but this did not prevent it from arriving invariably in the nick of time.

If we pass over personal dramas, especially marital triangles which just happened to take place somewhere in the Empire, such as *The Road to Singapore, Friends and Lovers* and *Another Dawn,* the first major film set in modern India is still one of the best-remembered: *The Lives of a Bengal Lancer* (1935), which by coincidence opened in New York the same week as *Clive of India,* so that while Colman was conquering eighteenth-century India at the Rivoli, Sir Guy Standing, C. Aubrey Smith, Gary Cooper and Franchot Tone were guarding its modern border at the Paramount.

Using only the title of Francis Yeats-Brown's book, the entirely fictional film was hailed by the *Times* as "in the vigorously romantic tradition of Kipling . . . It is so sympathetic in its discussion of England's colonial management that it ought to prove a great blessing to Downing Street."

Skillfully blending studio-shot scenes with authentic backgrounds filmed in India several years before for another film, director Henry Hathaway made *Lives* one of the most outstanding and successful films of 1935. Cooper and Tone were stalwart officers who withstood the most diabolic Afghan tortures, but young Richard Cromwell, weakling son of cold martinet Sir Guy, actually betrays the corps, so must redeem himself heroically in the climax. Pitted against them were such wily native moguls as Douglas Dumbrille, Akim Tamiroff and J. Carroll Naish.

Later that year Paramount offered another, more modest, tribute to the Empire, *The Last Outpost* (1935). "No matter what the billboards say, it is not another *Bengal Lancers,*" warned Nugent in the *Times,* "but it is a well-made, if somewhat familiar, melodrama for all that." Rescued from death in the Kurdistan campaign in World War I by a member of the British Intelligence Corps (Claude Rains), Cary Grant, recuperating in Cairo, falls in love with his nurse (Gertrude Michael), never suspecting that she is the wife of his benefactor. It all comes to a climax in a beleaguered outpost in the Sudan when reinforcements arrive in time to rout the screaming tribesmen. Nugent deplored only the time spent on the romance: "It does seem, with all the drawing rooms available, that Paramount could have preserved the Sudan for the sterner things of life."

The days when India was still the crown jewel in the glittering imperial diadem, the heyday of the British raj, the pukka sahibs, the world of tiger hunts and pig-sticking, of regimental cricket and polo matches, of ceremonial dinners and balls at Government House, with turbaned native servants in deferential attendance, were never more glowingly portrayed than in Warners' *The Charge of the Light Brigade* (1936), set in mid-Victorian India, the very milieu so scathingly exposed by Barry England's 1969 play *Conduct Unbecoming.*

Hailed by the *Times* as "the 1936 model of *Lives of a Bengal Lancer* . . . a virile and picturesque saga of blood and empire in India, with the usual treacherous Amir lurking in one corner" (this time he was C. Henry Gordon), *Charge* on the personal level was another triangle, in which an older brother (Errol Flynn) sacrifices himself at Balaclava so that his younger brother (Patric Knowles) will get the girl (Olivia De Havilland).[1] As

---

[1] His heroism was repaid the following year in *Another Dawn,* when Ian Hunter as Kay Francis' unloved husband makes the same kind of sacrifice to clear the way for Flynn.

the *Times* put it, "The scene switches from India to Crimea only just in time to justify the title and offer as . . . glorious a spectacle as the screen has provided this year. That cavalry charge is its own excuse."

The stars were backed by a truly impressive cast that included Henry Stephenson, Nigel Bruce, Donald Crisp, David Niven and E. E. Clive. It need hardly be added that it was written and played absolutely straight, with no trace of the caustic irony that was the dominant tone of its 1968 British namesake.

Always quick to follow a safely established trend with a variation just wrong enough to cheapen it, 20th Century-Fox came up with

Wee Willie Winkie (1937), in which wee Shirley Temple saved India for the British simply by asking the rebellious Khoda Khan (Cesar Romero, called back from *Clive of India*) why he is so mad at her grandfather (C. Aubrey Smith as the gruff commanding colonel). Like a female Fauntleroy, Wee Willie has already won all other hearts, especially that of a rough-diamond Scotch sergeant (Victor McLaglen), whose death provides the little star with her obligatory choking-back-the-tears scene.

Shirley paid further obeisance to Queen and country in Technicolor in *The Little Princess* (1939), in which her father (Ian

Gary Cooper, Richard Cromwell, Franchot Tone, C. Aubrey Smith
in The Lives of a Bengal Lancer

Patric Knowles and Errol Flynn in **The Charge of the Light Brigade**

Hunter) is reported dead in the siege of Mafeking in the Boer War, but, of course, turns up alive in time to be rewarded by Queen Victoria herself (Beryl Mercer), who has already succumbed to the charm of the angelic moppet.

As if it were not humiliation enough for the British to have to depend on Shirley Temple to protect the Khyber Pass, in *I Cover the War* (1937), released a few days after *Wee Willie Winkie,* an Arab revolt in Mesopotamia is crushed by a couple of newsreel cameramen (John Wayne and Don Barclay), who not only unmask the rebel leader but save a whole company of Lancers from annihilation. As one reviewer put it, "When Hollywood goes to the border wars, almost anything can happen."

1938 brought the inevitable "B" variation Republic's *Storm over Bengal,* which re united several veterans of earlier Anglo Indian campaigns. Patric Knowles had move up to older brother hero, but Richard Crom well as his junior gave a replay of his *Live* performance, spoiled and petulant, failin miserably at first but in the end saving th regiment. Just to make him feel at home, th khan was his old tormentor, Douglas Dum brille.

In 1939, as war neared, Hollywood turne to Kipling again to step up the drumbea *Gunga Din* may have borne as little relatio to his poem of that name as *Wee Willi Winkie* had to his story, but it was unden ably a major production, based on an ide by Hecht and MacArthur, starring Car

Grant, Victor McLaglen and Douglas Fairbanks, Jr., as soldiers three, Sam Jaffe in the title role and Eduardo Ciannelli as the villainous khan, here a fanatical high priest. As the nominal love interest, Joan Fontaine scarcely stood a chance.

Said the *Times:* "jaunty as a Barrack Room Ballad, splendid as a Durbar, as exciting and at times as preposterous as a Pearl White serial . . . The charge of the Sepoy Lancers is the most spectacular bit of cinema since the Warner Brothers and Tennyson stormed the heights of Balaclava."

Kipling himself appears as a minor character, a young war correspondent who dashes off the famous poem in time for the commandant (Montagu Love) to read it over the water carrier's grave. "And for all 'is dirty hide, 'e was white, clear white, inside" would not now be considered a compliment, but in 1939 neither Hollywood nor anyone else had ever heard that any other color could be beautiful. Jaffe, however, brought such strength and dignity to the role that the *Times* considered him a serious contender for the Oscar.

Thirty-seven years later, *The New Yorker* called *Gunga Din* "an exhilarating, slapstick trouble-in-the-colonies adventure film that does for the genre almost what *Beat the Devil* later did to the international thriller . . . a rousing, superbly photographed production" on which "Joel Sayre and William Faulkner did some of the rewrite work."

If *Gunga Din* may be regarded as one of the high points of the "up the Empire!" cycle, then surely its nadir was reached a few months later in a film actually called *The Sun Never Sets* (1939). Though the cast included such familiar faces as Douglas Fairbanks, Jr., and C. Aubrey Smith, as well as Basil Rathbone (in a sympathetic role), the central family, colonial administrators who had been manning outposts of the Empire for generations, was too much for both reviewers and audiences.

As the crusty old patriarch, Smith literally kept a map of the world on his study wall with pins indicating the current locations of

Cary Grant and Sam Jaffe in Gunga Din

his far-flung descendants. The women (Virginia Field, Barbara O'Neil, Mary Forbes) behaved with the same stoic gallantry as the men. This time instead of India the scene is the gold coast of Africa, and instead of the conventional khan the villain (Lionel Atwill), who seems to have escaped from a *Flash Gordon* episode, is a would-be dictator who from his jungle hideaway spreads revolts, strikes, arson, bomb plots and war fever via his secret radio station. The whole charade was so full of "Chin up, stout fellow, carry on!" spirit that the *Times* suggested the family coat of arms must be "inscribed with a stiff upper lip rampant on a field of whiskey-sodas."

But Hollywood's final '30s word on British India came later in the year, opening in New

York just a few days after the outbreak of the war that was ultimately to lead to the dissolution of the Empire—20th Century-Fox's lavish version of Louis Bromfield's *The Rains Came*. Nugent of the *Times,* who evidently admired the novel, complained that the film was "the merest skeleton of the Bromfield work . . . which became a best seller." The earthquake and flood had in the book symbolized the awakening of a new spirit in India; in the film it was merely "a visually thrilling spectacle."

This may well be true, but the novel has not survived, and, taken on its own, *The Rains Came* is a richly enjoyable variation of the *Grand Hotel* formula, expanded to include a whole cross section of Europeans and natives in the teeming (fictitious) Indian state of Ranchipur—a worthy entry among the many fine films of 1939. Perhaps attention was too closely concentrated on the two romances, the doomed love of the hitherto promiscuous Lady Edwina Esketh (Myrna Loy), wife of a gross newspaper peer (Nigel Bruce), for a young Indian surgeon, Major Safti (Tyrone Power), and the more lightly treated affair between the British wastrel Tom Ransome (George Brent) and Fern Simon (Brenda Joyce), naïve daughter of American missionaries.

But among the secondary characters H. B. Warner and Maria Ouspenskaya could hardly have been better cast as the Maharajah and Maharanee, nor Joseph Schildkraut as the over-Anglicized Mr. Bannerjee. (As usual, all the Indian parts were played by Americans

Myrna Loy and Tyrone Power in The Rains Came

or Europeans, since the only Indian actor known to the rest of the world at that time was Sabu.) Mary Nash was the dour Scottish nurse, Miss MacDaid, and Jane Darwell, Marjorie Rambeau, Laura Hope Crews and Henry Travers were among the others in what was even for 1939 an outstanding cast.

If *The Rains Came* offered no startling new insights into Anglo-Indian relations on the turbulent subcontinent, neither did it indulge in the jingoistic flag-waving and military heroics of too many others. As with so many good '30s films, to appreciate its true worth, one has only to compare its miscast '50s remake starring Lana Turner and Richard Burton.

18

GOING NATIVE
Seldom the Twain Shall Meet

Miscegenation (sex relationship between the white and black races) is forbidden.
—The Motion Picture Production Code

Indirectly related to the films discussed in the last chapter were others set in more peaceful parts of the Empire, especially the South Seas, with the tropical setting used for idyllic effect, where every prospect pleased and only man—especially white man—was vile, lusting after priceless pearls, ivory or gold, of whose value the childlike natives had no inkling. Even so, when two young people of different races fell in love, it was a sin against ethnic purity for which the only proper wages was death for at least one, preferably the one with darker skin. (In practice the Production Code ban on miscegenation was extended to *all* races other than white.)

Thus, likable as were the characters played by Loy and Power in *The Rains Came,* it was impossible by film standards that their love could lead to marriage. So, while helping the surgeon try to prevent an epidemic as an aftermath of the flood, Lady Edwina drinks from an infected glass and dies, just like Leora, the first wife, in *Arrowsmith*. Since other heroines with dubious pasts had been redeemed by love, her death can only be taken as punishment for having crossed the color line. Perhaps the fact that the doctor survives to carry on for India might be inter-

preted as a tiny step forward, since in practically all previous doomed interracial romances the darker partner had died.

Although Kipling had written tenderly of such a relationship in his story *Without Benefit of Clergy* and by implication in *The Road to Mandalay* and other poems, the taboo remained all but unbreakable in major films of the '30s, and indeed for many years thereafter. The only possibility of happiness for such star-crossed lovers was if by some unlikely plot device it turned out that they were, after all, of the same race. Either the apparently darker one was actually white, orphaned and reared by kindly natives as their own, or, less commonly, the apparent white learned that one of his/her parents, usually the mother, was actually Indian, Malay or whatever. This dodge was used three times in 1930 alone,[1] twice involving Chinese, against whom (as will be detailed in the next chapter) prejudice was strongest.

In fact, the only 1930 film to tackle boldly the issue of what would happen if one of the lovers were *really* not white was an independent "B" called *The Love Trader*. What would happen, of course, could be nothing good. As the young wife of a ship's captain (Henry B. Walthall) hunting pearls in the South Seas, Leatrice Joy falls in love with a

---

[1] *Son of the Gods, East Is West* and *Whoopee.*

native (Roland Drew), and even though nothing comes of it, after they sail away, whether from shame, regret or frustration, she atones even more directly than Lady Edwina by drowning herself.

Even an upper-caste Hindu played by Ramon Novarro stood no chance, as proved by *Son of India* (1931), based on a story by F. Marion Crawford but considered by the *Times* a feeble variation on *The Sheik*. Madge Evans was a Boston Brahmin who forgot Back Bay in favor of Bombay, but in the end reverted to Beacon Hill.

MGM offered another such ill-fated affair in *The Cuban Love Song* (1931), essentially a variation on *Madame Butterfly* and *The Squaw Man*, among other sources. Like John Gilbert in *The Big Parade*, wealthy Lawrence Tibbett enlists during World War I (though in the Marines), and soon meets two comic sidekicks, Ernest Torrence and Jimmy Durante. In Havana he falls in love with a lively peanut vendor, Nenita (Lupe Velez, just then beginning to specialize in such spitfire native or half-caste heroines, in a style that anticipated Carmen Miranda). He leaves for the war, ten years pass, and, returning to Cuba, he finds a motherless nine-year-old boy singing the peanut vendor's special song. In the role corresponding to Lieutenant Pinkerton's wife, Kate, his wife (Karen Morley) agrees to accept the child as her own. Since Cubans are presumably of Spanish descent, the obstacle may have been class rather than race, but in any case the unfortunate Nenita joined the ranks of lovable gamines not good enough to marry the hero.

Another 1931 film, titled, frankly enough, *Never the Twain Shall Meet,* from a story by Peter B. Kyne, dealt with a San Francisco playboy (Leslie Howard) going to pieces on a Polynesian atoll until he is taken in hand by a lively half-caste girl (Conchita Montenegro). He makes the mistake of bringing her home to Frisco, to the pained embarrassment of his father (C. Aubrey Smith) and his ex-fiancée (Karen Morley again). But, of course, she just doesn't fit in at the best

homes and night clubs, so she must be shipped back to her own kind, and the supposed truth of the cliché title is once more underlined.

Even more pointedly, in a Tiffany production, *Aloha* (1931), Ben Lyon as a wealthy American actually marries a native girl (Raquel Torres) and brings her home, where, naturally, no one will accept her. On a return visit to the South Seas she tactfully leaps into a volcano, leaving her husband to his white ex-fiancée (Thelma Todd).

Perhaps she had seen the famous old play *The Bird of Paradise,* a 1912 hit for Laurette Taylor, filmed in 1932 and described by the *Times* as "a languid film with many beautifully photographed scenes." Still another American playboy (Joel McCrea) falls in love with a beautiful Polynesian (Dolores Del Rio) and even decides to remain with her on a remote island. Native hulas and luaus abound, climaxed by the quaint old custom that decrees the heroine must be tossed into a volcano—a fate she willingly accepts since she already knows that she could never fit into her beloved white man's world.

A few months later, Novarro was sheiking it again in *The Barbarian* (1933), a remake of his 1924 silent *The Arab,* in which he played a dragoman—actually a prince—in love with an English girl (Myrna Loy) visiting Cairo. More fortunate than in *The Rains Came,* Loy finds out just in time that her mother was Arabian, so "the call of the blood" is only natural. Even after he had descended to "B" films, Novarro gave one more, reverse, twist to this old cop-out, in *The Sheik Steps Out* (1937), in which he kidnaps and marries a spoiled American heiress (Lola Lane), who runs away—but then *he* is revealed as "an Italian count who has spent most of his life in Arabia."

Meanwhile, on a more realistic level, Francis Lederer made an auspicious Hollywood debut in *Man of Two Worlds* (1934) as a bright Eskimo guide to a British expedition in the Arctic. Falling in love with a picture of the leader's daughter (Elissa Landi), he asks to be taken to London, where, of

Joel McCrea and Dolores Del Rio in **The Bird of Paradise**

course, he is as hopelessly out of place as the Savage in *Brave New World,* so he returns to Greenland to his wife and family.

The first film to break the taboo against love between the races was *White Heat* (1934), actually filmed in Hawaii by Lois Weber, one of Hollywood's few women directors. In a plot like a tropical version of *The Animal Kingdom,* a young sugar planter (Hardie Albright) leaves his native mistress (Mona Maris) to marry an American girl (Virginia Cherrill) "of the San Francisco sugar aristocracy." Bored by the monotony of island life, the wife "narrowly escapes" an affair with a handsome native boy, then takes up with an old admirer from home, while the husband returns to his mistress.

As a parting shot, the far from sweet sugar heiress sets fire to the cane, to save her lover from a beating by her husband, who is, however, rescued by the loyal native woman. This startling reversal of roles moved Andre Sennwald of the *Times* to dismiss it as an "easy but unfair method of vilifying the white girl," when he should have been commending the director and the writer, James Bodrero, for letting love for once triumph over racial barriers and the native woman come off better than the white.

But *White Heat* is a forgotten "B" film.

The following year a major production, *Mutiny on the Bounty,* though best-remembered for other reasons, made an unheralded breakthrough in race relations in the Tahitian sequence: the joyous welcome of the English sailors, the spontaneous romances that spring up (with no frowning parents nor white fiancées to interfere) and the final choice of the majority of the mutineers, including the hero, Fletcher Christian (Gable), to stay happily on Pitcairn Island with their native wives.

Though neither of the actresses playing opposite Gable and Tone, Mamo Clark and Movita, had much of a subsequent screen career, both appeared in "B" pictures that continued the liberated tradition of *Mutiny.* In *Wallaby Jim of the Islands* (1937), Clark actually gets George Houston away from the white girl, who ends up with his partner. In *Paradise Isle* (1937) Movita defies the taboo by diving for pearls to raise money for an operation to restore the sight of the blind American artist she loves (Warren Hull). Back in New York he tries to forget her, but, when cured, returns to her. Thus except for *Mutiny* three obscure "B" films were the only ones in the entire decade in which interracial lovers were allowed to end happily together.

Meanwhile more important films had upheld the traditional code. As noted, 1936 had seen two noble redskins bite the dust: Uncas in *The Last of the Mohicans* took his white love with him, and Alessandro in *Ramona* left his half-white bride a widow. The decade's last two elaborate treatments of the situation reinforced the taboo more sharply than ever, each with a then unheard of unhappy ending, the death of the glamorous star herself. *The Rains Came* has already been discussed. Opening the day before (September 7, 1939), *Lady of the Tropics* found Hedy Lamarr and Robert Taylor in a sultry romance dreamed up by Ben Hecht, a conscious parallel to the opera *Manon,* even to the heroine's name.

While his yacht is anchored in the harbor of Saigon, wealthy American Taylor falls in love with a beautiful half-caste, who is also pursued by a politically powerful man of her own mixed background (Joseph Schildkraut in Chinese make-up). During the long time the story took to reach its necessarily unhappy ending, B. R. Crisler of the *Times* became convinced that Lamarr was a museum piece like the *Mona Lisa,* more beautiful in repose. "Under the Hays office," he observed, "there can be only one inevitable ending to these trans-Equatorial, trans-coloring romances."

To be sure, not all films set in the tropics dealt with unhappy, or even happy, interracial romances. Many offered simple escape from the humdrum realities of civilization. On this level, in the jungle dream world untrammeled by the restrictions of everyday probabilities, unquestionably the figure to capture the public imagination most completely and to appear in more forms and media than any other fictional character except Sherlock Holmes was Edgar Rice Burroughs' Tarzan of the Apes. Racial barriers were no problem for Tarzan, since, of course, he is really Lord Greystoke, not only white but a British lord of the bluest blood, so perfectly eligible to live with his Jane in jungle bliss, even without benefit of clergy.

Though by no means the first nor the last screen Tarzan, by far the longest-lasting and best-known was Johnny Weissmuller, already famous as a champion swimmer when MGM cast him in the title role of *Tarzan the Ape Man* (1932). Apparently the studio did not anticipate the great success of either picture or star, for in the original reviews "John" Weissmuller is listed seventh in the cast, below Neil Hamilton, Maureen O'Sullivan, C. Aubrey Smith and even Doris Lloyd, Forrester Harvey and Ivory Williams.

Indeed, who could have foreseen how utterly this Tarzan, with his weird, spine-tingling cry, his breath-taking tree-to-tree acrobatics, powerful swimming scenes, life-and-death struggles with lions and tigers and confidential chats with friendlier animals, would captivate the hearts and minds of adolescents of all ages, and especially of small boys who suffered many a bruise and fall in trying to ape the ape man? "Me Tarzan, you Jane" passed at once and forever into the language.

The *Times* rightly called it "a fantastic affair . . . filmed with a sense of humor." W. S. Van Dyke, who had directed *Trader Horn,* kept the jungle atmosphere reasonably convincing and certainly exciting, with one mortal hazard after another, climaxed when a thundering herd of elephants respond to Tarzan's call by trampling a village of evil pygmies.

Within a year Weissmuller was given stiff competition by Buster Crabbe, also a swim star, as Kaspa the Lion Man in Paramount's *King of the Jungle* (1933), an obvious derivative but in some ways superior. Crabbe was just as well muscled as Weissmuller, but with a handsomer, more expressive face, and his character, unlike Tarzan, was a quick study who soon learned to speak English as fluently as the language of the lions. Captured by a circus owner (Sidney Toler) for display along with his lions, Kaspa dives overboard near San Francisco, is befriended by a teacher (Frances Dee) and in civilization encounters adventures more complex and varied than Tarzan's, including a circus fire in which all the animals escape.

Apparently Paramount did not know how to follow up on this well-reviewed film, for Crabbe next appeared in *Tarzan the Fearless* (1933), a cheap independent production shown as a feature but actually the first four episodes of a serial. Burroughs would not sell exclusive rights even to MGM, so "B" Tarzans continued to proliferate concurrently with the Weissmuller series. Herman Brix (later known as Bruce Bennett) got into the act with *New Adventures of Tarzan* (1935), as did Glenn Morris in *Tarzan's Revenge* (1938), both badly reviewed.

Meanwhile in 1934 MGM had reassembled most of the 1932 *Tarzan* cast for *Tarzan and His Mate.* (Despite the mate, his vocabulary had not noticeably increased.) Presumably in the interim Tarzan and Jane (still listed

in the cast as "Parker") have been living together in what was then known as "sin"— and this was only one of their offenses. 1934, it will be recalled, was the year of the great moral purge, the organization of the Legion of Decency and the imposition of the Production Code. Even aside from the tempting turpitude of Mae West's films and the questionable life-styles of all the kept lady heroines, reformers were also incensed by the second MGM Tarzan film, not only by his unhallowed union with Jane but by the costumes or lack thereof.

Jane, who in the first film, like any English lady on safari, had dressed demurely in white, was now wearing a near-bikini, a bra and two

Johnny Weissmuller and Maureen O'Sullivan in **Tarzan and His Mate**

scant triangles of what looked like elephant hide, one in front, one in back—nothing at all at the sides. Tarzan himself wore just two barely minimal pieces of hide, as close to nudity as '30s films ever came. (Perhaps one reason for the popularity of jungle films was that under the Code they offered almost the only chance for stars to show off their bodies.) An underwater love scene between Tarzan and Jane (with O'Sullivan's double topless) was the last straw for the guardians of purity.

Both were more sedately covered when the series resumed with *Tarzan Escapes* (1936), but, as with all series, it was beginning to get a bit repetitive, even at two-year intervals, despite the comedy relief of Cheetah the chimp and the ingenious Rube Goldberg devices by which the arboreal love nest was supplied with running water and elevator service.

The title of *Tarzan Finds a Son* (1939) tells the story, for since under the Code it would have been impossible for Tarzan and Jane to have children of their own (in lieu of the prescribed twin beds, one assumes they slept in separate branches of the same tree), a son (Johnny Sheffield) is provided for them, an infant survivor of a plane crash. Five years later, predictably, come upper-class British relatives looking for the boy as heir to a title, but naturally he chooses the jungle.

No doubt many producers contemplated coming up with a female equivalent of Tarzan. The idea of a mysterious white goddess in the jungle had always been intriguing, as in the horrendous early talkie operetta *Golden Dawn* (1930) and *Trader Horn* (1931). *The Savage Girl* (1933) cast dainty Rochelle Hudson, of all actresses, in the title role of a Tarzan counterpart, even to the helpful ape, but that was the last ever heard of her. This long-felt want must have been filled at last with Sheena Queen of the Jungle, but Paramount meanwhile had found a far more salable variation.

By switching the locale from Africa to Malay or a South Sea isle where the natives were graceful and light-skinned rather than grotesque savages, cannibals or pygmies, and wore attractively brief sarongs, with hibiscus blossoms in their hair, the studio created a new star, one whose image was to remain forever wrapped in that sarong: Dorothy Lamour. *Jungle Princess* (1936), her first such film, was dismissed by one critic in half a column; worse, he described her sarong as "a calico shift." Despite a production in then rare color, *Her Jungle Love* (1938), in which Lamour played a Malay priestess of a crocodile cult in love with American aviator Ray Milland, was given equally short shrift, or shift. This one involved an obliging volcano that erupted on cue at crucial points in the plot.

Though the Lamour films were not considered musicals, she had, after all, started out as a singer, so, whatever jungle peril might threaten, she usually managed to warble a song or two—e.g., the sprightly "Moonlight and Shadows" in *Jungle Princess*.

Lamour's films were essentially variations on another, still lighter, genre, the South Sea, especially Hawaiian, musical, which simply exploited the lush, exotic atmosphere for its own sake: grass skirts, ukuleles, leis, torch-lit feasts with ritual native dances, pigs in palm leaves roasted in pits and all the other familiar clichés.

These would include *Let's Go Native* (1930), whose oddly assorted cast featured such stars as Jack Oakie, Jeanette MacDonald and Kay Francis; *We're Not Dressing* (1934), with Crosby and Lombard doing a variation on *The Admirable Crichton*; *Down to Their Last Yacht* (1934), another crew of shipwrecked socialites; *Waikiki Wedding* (1937), a pleasing Crosby vehicle; *Hawaii Calls* (1938), a less pleasing one for the unaccountably popular child star Bobby Breen; *Tropic Holiday* (1938), the same formula switched to Mexico, with Lamour still in a sarong on a moonlit beach; *Honolulu* (1939), Eleanor Powell's contribution to the South Sea bubble; and *Hawaiian Nights* (1939), a Universal "B" with Johnny Downs. Except for "Sweet Leilani" and "Blue Hawaii" from

Waikiki Wedding, none of these offered any memorable or even popular songs; the one factor all the Hawaiian ones had in common was some connection with the pineapple industry.

Clearly most of these films, even those that ended sadly, were a form of escape, the kind of exotic adventure that ever since Captain Cook's eighteenth-century explorations white men had been seeking, first in South Sea idylls (as in Melville's *Omoo* and *Typee*), later in African safaris. Many were variations on the romantic myth of the noble savage, in which the tropics were a pagan paradise, where Anglo-Saxon inhibitions were shed along with Western clothes—the kind of appeal epitomized by the silent *Moana, Aloma of the South Seas, White Shadows in the South Seas, The Pagan* and *Tabu.* At very least all made the Torrid Zone, even the jungle, seem an exciting place, attractive to white men (even if some of the natives were too fatally attractive).

At the opposite extreme, another very common genre of film was repeating its own, grimmer set of clichés, many inherited from prewar melodramas or cheap novelettes, the sort in which the tropics bring out the very worst in white people. As evidenced by the recurrence of the word "hell" in the titles (*Hell Harbor, Hell's Island, Passport to Hell, Safe in Hell*), in such films an equatorial climate was a metaphor for decadence, ruin and decay, the depth below which the characters could not possibly sink.

Among those who sought to bury themselves in tropic anonymity, members of the Foreign Legion would, like one-eyed men in the kingdom of the blind, rank as relative aristocrats—brothers-in-arms, almost, to the defenders of the British Empire, in the sense that they, too, were white men fighting to maintain the overseas conquests of a European power against dark-skinned natives, necessarily cast as villains. The difference was that the country was not their own.

In silents like *The Sheik, The Arab, Fazil* and others, an Arab chieftain might cut quite a dashing, romantic figure; the Riff uprising of 1925 even evoked a certain amount of sympathy, as reflected in *The Desert Song,* but in the vintage Foreign Legion epics the Arab leaders were, if anything, even more diabolically cruel than the rajas in the films set in India.

Presumably in life Legionnaires were, and are, no different from any other mercenaries, adventurers, bored between wars, unable to adjust to any other life, fleeing some guilty or unsavory past (as witness the number of ex-Nazis said to swell the Legion)—but in films the heroes were always gentlemen, usually British, who had enlisted for the most honorable, if quixotic, reasons, ready to sacrifice their lives as selflessly as if they had joined the Trappists.

Despite, or perhaps because of, the great success of the silent *Beau Geste* (1926) and its sequel, *Beau Sabreur* (1928), by the early '30s the Legion had become something of a cliché, mocked in jokes about the Legionnaire who couldn't remember what he had joined the Legion to forget, in a Laurel and Hardy short, *Beau Hunks,* and even in a popular comic strip, *Minute Movies,* which, as usual reflecting Hollywood's trends more or less tongue-in-cheek, did a Legion serial called *Sun and Sand.*

Of the only three "A" films of the '30s to use a Foreign Legion background, two, both romantic melodramas, have already been discussed: *Morocco* (1930) and *Under Two Flags* (1936). Not until the remake of *Beau Geste* in 1939 was there another Legion film with important stars. Meanwhile Legion buffs had to make do with such items as *Hell's Island* (1930), with Legionnaires Ralph Graves and Jack Holt battling (as they did in so many films) over a girl (Dorothy Sebastian), with the older one sacrificing himself for the younger. For once the plot had nothing to do with fighting Arabs.

Later the same year *Renegades,* based on a French novel, with Warner Baxter, Noah Beery (a veteran of *Beau Geste*), Gregory Gaye and *George* Cooper as a quartet of Legion privates, was dismissed by the *Times* as "a muddled and tedious offering." Myrna Loy, in her Mata Hari phase, was responsible for the disgrace which had made it necessary for Baxter, a French officer, to join the Legion, but in the end he and his three buddies save his former regiment.

Though written by the same author, Percival Wren, and directed by the same director, Herbert Brenon, *Beau Ideal* (1931) was hardly a worthy sequel to the two previous *Beaux*. A friend of the Geste brothers (Lester Vail) enlists to find the only surviving one (Ralph Forbes in his original role), and together they help defeat the treacherous emir and his Arabs, after which the friend returns to England to marry the Gestes' cousin Isabel (Loretta Young).

Two years later Loretta was again the beloved of a Legionnaire in *The Devil's in Love* (1933), opposite Victor Jory as a surgeon who flees when falsely accused of the murder of his commander. He returns to the beleaguered fort, however, to cure his stricken comrades, help drive off the attacking tribesmen and incidentally clear his name. "A slightly changed version of an old story," said the *Times*, "with spotty, unconvincing characterization and insufficient action to merit straight melodramatic rating."

Except for *Under Two Flags* (1936), the Legion was given a furlough from the screen until 1937, when it recurred twice. In *We're in the Legion Now* two American gangsters (Reginald Denny and Vince Barnett) on the lam hide out in the Legion, with emphasis on fights and slapstick humor. In *Legion of Missing Men* that veteran Legionnaire Ralph Forbes and his younger brother (Ben Alexander) are rivals for a cafe singer (Halla Linda); both prove brave when captured by Arabs, but for once it is the younger who gives up the girl and is killed in battle.

When *Adventure in Sahara* (1938) opened, the *Times*, which had not even covered the above two films, opened its review: "The French Foreign Legion can't possibly be as bad as some of the movies they make about

it." C. Henry Gordon, who had also sneered his way through *Renegades* and *The Devil's in Love*, was the standard sadistic officer, whose villainy causes the death of the hero's brother and almost that of the hero himself (Paul Kelly), abandoned in the desert until rescued by the heroine (Lorna Gray) in her private plane—surely a new high in *deae ex machinis*.

With the Legion such a tired joke among reviewers, Paramount's decision to remake such a dated item as *Beau Geste* in 1939 can only be attributed to the general resurgence of pro-military themes just before World War II. Gary Cooper, who had also starred in the silent *Beau Sabreur* (not about the Geste family), played the title role, once acted by Ronald Colman, with Ray Milland and Robert Preston as his brothers, and Brian Donlevy as the vicious sergeant formerly played by Noah Beery.

"The absurd nobility, brotherly devotion and self-sacrifice of the Geste tribe are still unflagging ingredients for action melodrama," said the *Times*. However, "the law of diminishing returns has got in its dirty work over the years," an impression furthered by the American accents of Cooper and Preston in roles calling for "eternal Britishness." For those who remembered the silent, this 1939 version did not measure up, but "what the present generation doesn't know, it will certainly never miss."

In other films, other Englishmen, the kind who, along with mad dogs, went out in the noonday sun, were still dressing for dinner in the jungle and drowning lives of quiet desperation in gin and bitters on remote rubber or tea plantations—a complaint that might well have been called "Maugham's syndrome"—while their bored wives were driven by the climate, the rain, the husbands' alcoholism, cruelty, indifference or absorption in their jobs to infidelity or violence or both (e.g., Leslie Crosby in *The Letter*, Kitty Vane in *The Painted Veil*).

Of this kind of wife, one example has already been noted, in *White Heat* (1934).

Others include Dorothy Revier in *Vengeance* (1930), Lillian Bond in *When Strangers Marry* (1933)—both, as it happens, married to Jack Holt—Eleanor Boardman in *Mamba* (1931), Ann Harding in *Prestige* (1932), Mary Astor in *Red Dust* (1932), Margaret Lindsay in *West of Singapore* (1933), Carole Lombard in *White Woman* (1933) and Fay Wray in *The Woman I Stole* (1933).

Maugham also created the best-known example of the only other kind of woman to be found in tropical melodramas: Sadie Thompson in *Rain,* who epitomizes a whole scarlet sisterhood, the camp followers of the Western imperial powers who start and often end in honky-tonk bars, anywhere from Panama to Shanghai.

As noted in Chapter 1, Harlow's character in *Red Dust* (1932) is perhaps the second-best example. In modified form, the type survived in the Maisie films, but in the early '30s such heroines were much more frankly depicted. Examples would include Sally O'Neil in *Girl of the Port* (1930), Dorothy Mackaill in *Safe in Hell* (1931) and *Picture Brides* (1934), Helen Twelvetrees in *Panama Flo* (1932), Peggy Shannon in *The Painted Woman* (1932), Dorothy Burgess in *What Price Decency?* and *Malay Nights* (both 1933), Betty Compson in *West of Singapore* (1933), Rosemary Ames in *Pursued* (1934), Arline Judge in *Sensation Hunters* (1934), Kay Linaker in *The Girl from Mandalay* (1936) and Judith Allen in *Port of Missing Girls* (1938).

Occasionally the two types of women clashed head on (Harlow and Astor in *Red Dust,* Lindsay and Compson in *West of Singapore*), but usually they moved in such different circles as to offer another variation of "never the twain." In such films, native women, if any, were usually evil—Myrna Loy in *Isle of Escape* (1930), Mona Maris in *The Man Called Back* (1933).

At the lowest ebb, the Sadie Thompson types were often mixed up with the kind of white men known as "renegades," dropouts from decent society, under the influence of the heat, drink or guilt, "going to pieces in the tropics."

Even if not literally fugitives from the law, such men were running away from some shameful secret in the past, without the youth or physical stamina to make the Legion. Whether in Africa, the South Pacific or the Caribbean, in Singapore, Hong Kong, Havana, Panama or some unnamed "banana republic" in Latin America, they had reached the last stop for disbarred lawyers, unfrocked clergymen, alcoholic doctors convicted of malpractice, captains who had deserted their ships, gentlemen who had cheated at cards, soldiers cashiered for cowardice—all those dropped through the trap door of respectable society, many of them "remittance men," paid by their families to stay as far away as possible.

Reduced to a common denominator now, haggard, unshaven, in rumpled, once-white linen suits, with Panama hats or solar topees, they sat brooding over their drinks or listlessly playing cards while overhead a four-bladed fan slowly stirred the dead air. Whatever the geographic locale, the setting remained much the same, some steamy dive (a.k.a. a hellhole, den of vice or sink of iniquity), full of cheap rattan and bamboo furniture, beaded portieres and hard-eyed, painted women of dubious origin (often "half-caste," that most scathing term of contempt) at the bar or tables awaiting customers. In the background lurked evil-faced, snaggle-toothed natives, ready to pull a knife at the flicker of an eyelid from the villain, who usually owned the hotel, cafe or trading post. The others were all so deeply in debt to him, they had lost their last chance of escape.

In a few films, tropical exile was not permanent, only the nadir from which the protagonists, having hit rock bottom, could begin the struggle back up. 1931 offered three of these, all mentioned in previous chapters: the Gaynor-Farrell *The Man Who Came Back,* the Garbo-Gable *Susan Lenox: Her Fall and Rise,* in which after prolonged decline the lovers recover each other just in time, and the

Bankhead-March *My Sin,* in which they start at zero in Panama and end rehabilitated in New York.

The degenerative effect of a hot climate on some whites was a subject that intrigued not only Maugham but Conrad and Stevenson as well. In fact, the first such tropical drama to appear in 1930 was *Dangerous Paradise,* according to the credits "based on incidents from a novel by Joseph Conrad." The novel was *Victory,* and the incidents used were fairly close to the book. Nancy Carroll was Alma (Lena in the novel), girl violinist who when stalked by East Indies hotel owner Schomberg (Warner Oland) seeks refuge with idealistic recluse Heyst (Richard Arlen). Their siege by three other criminal psychopaths follows the book, except that a well-armed Japanese servant turns the tables, and the lovers' victory is physical as well as moral. Alma just misses joining the ranks of heroines who die to save their lovers.

As one might gather from some of the titles mentioned above, most such films were lurid "B" melodramas, not reviewed by the *Times,* that hardly deserve detailed discussion. A few stood out by their sheer grimness. In *Safe in Hell* (1931) Dorothy Mackaill, a prostitute fleeing the New Orleans police, becomes "the only white woman on the island" in a West Indies hideout for criminals. To prove her virtue to the sailor she loves (Donald Cook), she kills her chief tormentor (Morgan Wallace), and at the end she is to be hanged rather than become the sex slave of the executioner.

Kongo (1932), remake of a Lon Chaney silent, starred Walter Huston in his original Broadway role as a crippled sadist obsessed with vengeance against the man who caused his injury and stole his wife. Instead of a native, his mistress (Lupe Velez) was Portuguese, and the standard derelict doctor was Conrad Nagel, as also in *The Man Called Back.* Laughton played a similar monster as Carole Lombard's husband in *White Woman* (1933), a Cockney turned king who rules his Malay empire from a houseboat, drives his wife into the arms of his superintendent (Kent Taylor) and himself ends as the prey of head-hunters.

A more notable self-styled monarch was Paul Robeson in *The Emperor Jones* (1933), Eugene O'Neill's celebrated variation on the theme of *The Man Who Would Be King.* Opening up the play, DuBose Heyward's script shows Brutus Jones' experience as a Pullman porter, his conviction for murder and his escape from a Georgia chain gang before settling down to the main narrative, in which he dominates the natives of a West Indian island by convincing them that he is a supernatural being who can be killed only by a silver bullet. Dudley Digges, who specialized in white men decaying in the tropics, was his Cockney confederate in this well-received film.

Also highly praised was *The Narrow Corner* (1933), from a Maugham story of regeneration in the East Indies, far superior to the remake, *Isle of Fury* (1936). Doug Fairbanks, Jr., was a young Englishman who, after killing a man in Australia, wanders about the Malaysian islands on a ship hired by his father. At a Dutch trading colony they pick up an outlawed doctor (Digges again), who likes his opium. Later on another island they meet a classical scholar (Reginald Owen) and his daughter (Patricia Ellis). When boy and girl fall in love, her devoted Danish fiancé (Ralph Bellamy) kills himself.

Other tropical dramas featuring major stars were mere romantic triangles in exotic settings, such as Maugham's *The Painted Veil* (1934), with Garbo, Herbert Marshall and George Brent as Britishers in Hong Kong, and *His Brother's Wife* (1936), with Barbara Stanwyck, John Eldredge and Robert Taylor in the parallel roles. In *Mandalay* (1934), Kay Francis is turned over by her smuggler lover (Ricardo Cortez) as a virtual white slave to his evil boss (Warner Oland); when she wins her freedom and falls for a clean-cut American doctor (Lyle Talbot), she poisons Cortez.

The only really offbeat South Sea adventure tale was *Ebb Tide* (1937), from a short novel by Robert Louis Stevenson and his stepson Lloyd Osborne. Barry Fitzgerald won warm praise from the *Times* as "the most engaging scamp the screen has captured." Three beachcombers, a ticketless skipper (Oscar Homolka), a well-bred weakling (Ray Milland) and a rascally Cockney (Fitzgerald), luckily coming into command of a plague ship, decide to steal it and its cargo—until they land on an uncharted island ruled by a fanatic (Lloyd Nolan) with a Bible and a Winchester.

Just the week before *Ebb Tide,* however, New York had seen the opening of the most memorable (indeed the only serious) South Sea film of the decade, John Ford's *The Hurricane* (1937). Even aside from one of the most breath-taking on-screen catastrophes, this was a revealing depiction of Polynesian life under even the best-intentioned colonial administration. This theme had been touched on before, but here no evil pearl traders provide melodramatic complications.[2] The near-tragedy unfolds in a grim chain of consequences as inevitable as the plot of an Ibsen play.

The framework, in which a narrator (here a doctor) recalls the past, with his words dissolving into a flashback that is the main story, was a favorite '30s device, used in *Romance* (1930), *Maytime* (1937) and other films, but the deeper-and-deeper plot, in which the hero, imprisoned for some minor offense, in his desperation to escape only enmeshes himself in an endless labyrinth of legalities, can be traced back at least as far as Hugo's *Les Miserables.*

The clash of two irreconcilable goods is always a more subtle conflict than the simple battle of good versus evil, so Manakoora's strict French Governor DeLaage (Raymond Massey) insists against his own better instincts

Dorothy Lamour and Jon Hall
in The Hurricane

on punishing the gentle Terangi according to the strict letter of the law.

As Terangi, as incapable of malice as of understanding the white man's law, Jon Hall, whose career went straight downhill from here, reaching its nadir in the absurd Maria Montez-Turhan Bey spectacles of the '40s, gives a fine, sensitive performance. His naïve pride in his first mate's cap, his eagerness to buy a little dancing doll for his bride Marama (Lamour, keeping her sarong in use between her first two *Jungle* epics), her desire to go with him to Tahiti, are not presented in any

2 MGM's *The Last of the Pagans* (1936) dramatized the exploitation of natives in a tin mine, but in true Horatio Alger style the hero rescues an overseer in a cave-in, the owner rewards him and the point is lost.

patronizing or demeaning way; these people may be childlike, but only in the most lovable sense, treated by Ford with the same compassion and tenderness he usually showed toward Indians in his Westerns.

Nordhoff and Hall, who also wrote the *Bounty* trilogy, provided four separate *raisonneurs* (all very well acted) to plead with the implacable governor, but he will not be moved by the ship's captain (Jerome Cowan), the doctor (Thomas Mitchell), the priest (C. Aubrey Smith) or even his own wife (Mary Astor). (As so often in '30s films, the humane, unsanctimonious priest is perhaps the most appealing character other than the young couple.)

As in *San Francisco*, the final cataclysm (devised by the same special effects man, James Basevi) is used for a moral purpose. Just as Gable's character is awakened to a truer sense of values by his apparent loss of his beloved (MacDonald), so is the governor momentarily made to see the light only when he thinks he has lost his wife (saved by Terangi) to the hurricane.

DeLaage is much more dangerous than a mere hedonist; he is the fanatic, the true believer who will sacrifice any human value whatever to his own self-righteous sense of duty. To the very last, he never admits in so many words that he was wrong; when at the end he puts down his binoculars and says, "It *was* a floating log" (actually the lovers escaping out to sea in a canoe), one half-suspects that he may really have seen it as such, for clearly the others, including his wife, believe he is still capable of hounding Terangi to the bitter end.

Though all the other major white characters are sympathetic, *The Hurricane* is by implication a telling indictment of colonialism. The casualness with which Terangi is condemned by the governor of Tahiti because the white bully he hit in a bar happens to have good connections and the inflexibility with which DeLaage upholds this outrageous injustice, because he cannot take a native's side against a fellow administrator, tell us more powerfully than any number of interracial romances or exposés of decadence precisely what was wrong with the whole imperial system.

19

THE HEATHEN CHINEE
Inscrutable Orientals

. . . the following words and phrases are obviously offensive to the patrons of motion pictures in the United States and more particularly to the patrons of motion pictures in foreign countries:

Chink, Dago, Frog, Greaser, Hunkie, Kike, Nigger, Spig, Wop, Yid.

—The Motion Picture Production Code

In all the films of interracial romance discussed in the last chapter, the darker partner, though implicitly inferior, hence doomed to be renounced, die or turn out to be white, was at least attractive, often pathetic, at times almost tragic. Even in the going-to-pieces melodramas, the worst villains, though they might use native henchmen, were themselves white. But racism on the screen in the '30s did not always take such relatively mild forms.

Discussion of the treatment of American Indians and blacks will be left until later. The other most grievously slandered group by far was the Chinese. Although after Pearl Harbor the Japanese suffered worse both on screen and in life, in the '30s the few Japanese characters to appear were usually sympathetic: Madame Butterfly, Mr. Moto, an occasional smiling houseboy.

This was, after all, an Oriental-fearing America, which had set severe limits on the numbers that could be admitted as immigrants. It still shuddered from nightmares of "the yellow peril," with innocent Caucasian maidens drugged and trapped into a fate far worse than death, white slavery. In the syndicated comic strip *Buck Rogers,* set in the twenty-fifth century, which ran from 1929 until several decades later, the super-villains even at that remote date were still identified as "Mongols," just as in Floyd Gibbons' futuristic novel *The Red Napoleon,* serialized with vivid illustrations in *Liberty* magazine in the early '30s, the conqueror of America was to be a Russian war lord of Genghis Khan-like appearance and background, whose battle cry to his victorious yellow hordes was "Conquer and breed!"

Many silents like Lon Chaney's *Mr. Wu* had made the most of the picturesque possibilities of pagodas and dragon gates, gongs and incense, Buddhist ceremonies, tong wars, joss houses, opium dens, doll-like, almond-eyed maidens flirting demurely over their fans with Western admirers, long-nailed mandarins in silken robes and, above all, unquestioning submission to inflexible codes of honor that usually involved ritual murder or suicide. The Chinese characters always talked in fortune-cookie sentiments: "Is it not written in the ancient books of wisdom, O Honored Father, that he who would enjoy the fragrance of the lotus blossom must first plant the seed?" But whether seen in their own land, Limehouse or San Francisco's China-

town (never New York's), they were usually depicted as quaint, exotic, "inscrutable," perhaps wise, but, more often than not, cruel, treacherous and murderously vindictive. *Any* taint of Chinese blood in the ancestry was a reproach; "half-caste" and "Eurasian" were always terms of contempt, often applied to the villain's henchman or his castoff mistress.

Though Maugham's *The Letter* was not filmed in the 1930s, the decade is bracketed by two excellent talkie versions, Jeanne Eagels' in 1929 and Bette Davis' in 1940, both of which reveal the same racial attitudes. All the British characters express shuddering, almost paranoid, horror that the murder victim has (secretly) kept a Chinese mistress, even though in both versions she is shown as a proud, elegant woman, quite conscious of her superiority to the lying, murdering heroine. (Would she have been more acceptable as a humble, brown-skinned maiden ready to toss herself into the nearest volcano?)

By such standards, of course, any Oriental man who dared to love a white woman (unless in the sexless worship-from-afar style of *Broken Blossoms*) was even more monstrously perverse. Thus white supremacy got off to a good start in January 1930, with *Son of the Gods,* from a story by Rex Beach, in which Richard Barthelmess as a presumed Chinese (socially and financially light-years above his lowly shopkeeper in *Broken Blossoms*) while on a world tour "to find himself" wins the love of a wealthy white girl (Constance Bennett) without telling her of his origins. (Apparently nothing in his appearance gives him away.)

When she learns the truth, she publicly lashes him across the face with her riding crop, screaming epithets, of which "yellow dog!" is one of the choicest. But (in the first of several such cop-outs) he later learns that the kindly Chinese who brought him up was not really his father. Still *feeling* Chinese and understandably embittered against whites, he nevertheless seeks out and gets the girl who had so brutally scorned him. The *Times* reviewer wondered, as no doubt did many in

Richard Barthelmess and Constance Bennett in Son of the Gods

the audience, how such a marriage could possibly succeed.

The following month saw another clash of East and West in *The Green Goddess,* from William Archer's old melodrama, in which George Arliss had already starred both on stage and in silents. "He had the manners of a Chesterfield—and the blood-lust of a Borgia," the ads proclaimed of the suave Rajah of Rukh, who though not Chinese is definitely Asiatic—symbolically seen in a turban and European clothes as impeccable as his Oxford-accented English.

When one of a party of British travelers, stranded in his isolated Himalayan realm by the breakdown of their plane, happens to sit on an altar sacred to the green goddess, all must die, especially since the Rajah moonlights as high priest of her bloodthirsty cult. He will make an exception only for an English lady (Alice Joyce) on whom he has designs. To give him credit, Arliss plays it tongue-in-cheek throughout—an impression confirmed at the end when, after his prisoners

have escaped, he shrugs off the Englishwoman with "Just as well. She'd probably have been a damned nuisance."

In the same antiquated tradition, four other melodramas, three by David Belasco, were filmed in the early '30s, all, like *The Bird of Paradise* (1932), the sort of prewar hokum that Broadway had long since outgrown. First came *East Is West* (1930), based on a 1918 play, with Lupe Velez as Ming Toy, the role that had made Fay Bainter a star, who is sold by her supposed father in China but rescued by a young American tourist (Lew Ayres) and a kindly Chinese patriarch, who takes her to San Francisco.

To save her from deportation, the old man sells her to the chop suey king of Chinatown (Edward G. Robinson in his first talkie), but the American kidnaps her and even announces his intention to marry her. All Nob Hill is petrified—until it comes out that she is really the child of murdered white missionaries. What more could any society ask? The *Times* called it "implausible" and the actors' task "a heavy and thankless one."

Another, more tragic victim of racism, male chauvinist piggery or perhaps Yankee imperialism was Cio Cio San in a forgotten version of *Madame Butterfly* (1932) starring Sylvia Sidney and Cary Grant. Like most plays turned into operas, the hoary Belasco production, based on a story by John Luther Long, was no longer considered dramatically viable even in the 1900s. Puccini's score was used as background music, but reviews complained of the excessively quaint pidgin English and humor of "whimsical antiquity." Yet Sidney's harakiri scene, viewed in 1973, was still touching, thanks to her poignantly wistful face and voice.

In *The Hatchet Man* (1932), also by Belasco, the title character (Robinson again) is the honorable executioner for a Chinatown tong who in the line of duty must kill an old friend (J. Carroll Naish), actually called Sun Yat Sen, though without apparent political implications. He later marries his victim's daughter (Loretta Young), who soon takes a

Sylvia Sidney and Cary Grant in **Madame Butterfly**

fancy to a gangster, also Chinese (Leslie Fenton). The code calls for her death, but even at the cost of expulsion from the tong the tenderhearted hatchet man kills only her lover.

An even more curious Belasco relic, surely the most bizarre of Helen Hayes' nine 1930s films, was *The Son-Daughter* (1933), from a 1919 play, with a distinguished all-white cast. Again set in San Francisco, this somber tale deals with the efforts of the local Chinese to send supplies and arms to the revolutionists then struggling to overthrow the Manchu dynasty. Though in love with a student (Ramon Novarro), the lovely daughter (Hayes) of a noble doctor (Lewis Stone), in order to help the cause, barters herself to the highest bidder (Warner Oland), who just happens to be a secret royalist, plotting to assemble all the rebels at his wedding feast and dispatch them to their honorable ancestors. After seeing her father and her lover butchered, the bride avenges them by strangling her evil husband with his own pigtail.

Opening the following week, as the first attraction at the new Radio City Music Hall, was a far better film, the first East-West romance in which the man—the Oriental, of course—rather than the woman, paid: Capra's

The Bitter Tea of General Yen (1933). Though the *Times* considered it still another variation on *The Sheik*, Barbara Stanwyck's biographer, Ella Smith, calls it the star's only "art" film. Nils Asther, a Swede exotically handsome enough to make a convincing Oriental (as he had in Garbo's 1929 *Wild Orchids*), was a Chinese war lord who captures a New England girl (Stanwyck) on her way to join her fiancé in missionary work.

Gradually she falls in love with him, and is even ready to stay with him on his terms, but a castoff mistress betrays him to his enemies so that he loses all his wealth and power. It is then that he sips the (poisoned) bitter

Nils Asther and Barbara Stanwyck in **The Bitter Tea of General Yen**

tea of the title and sends the white girl back to her own people. Both Capra and his cameraman, Joseph Walker, have spoken of this film as a labor of love, and indeed even now it holds up far better than most of its overworked genre.

Asian-American romance was given one more twist, in which the questionable lover was not a native prince nor a war lord but a suave financier, in *Shanghai* (1935). Charles Boyer was highly praised as a cultivated Eurasian, half Russian, half Chinese, who has risen to power and prestige only because no one knows his origins. When after falling in love with an American (Loretta Young) he publicly announces the truth, all Shanghai, including the girl, scorns him. Later she regrets it, but, even so, they must part, sacrificing love to prejudice. Why, one might ask, when the hero's own parents had presumably defied the ban? But such were the ways of the mysterious Occident in the 1930s.

All these films were, of course, meant to be taken seriously. On the level of simple, bloodthirsty melodrama, of a Limehouse full of trap doors and torture chambers, the most famous, or infamous, Chinese villain of them all was Sax Rohmer's Dr. Fu Manchu, for whom "insidious" was one of the kinder words, and whose lurid exploits were detailed in three early '30s films.

Perhaps inspiring, or inspired by, the two-edged Chesterfield-Borgia image of the Rajah in *The Green Goddess,* Fu was described as having "the brow of a Shakespeare, the face of Satan." Why Rohmer should have made his international archfiend Chinese may be as Freudian a question as why Conan Doyle gave his master criminal an Irish name. Was it because both China and Ireland were just then struggling to free themselves from foreign domination, stirring deep fears in the British who had been profiting by the exploitation, yet neither nation was yet strong enough to protest effectively against such monstrous caricatures?

The ultimate irony was that all this vogue for cinematic *chinoiserie* gave little or no employment to Oriental actors. Sessue Hayakawa, the only Japanese ever to gain Hollywood stardom, who was to make a comeback in the '50s, appeared in only one American film in the '30s, and Anna May Wong, the only Chinese actress who ever got more than bit roles, made scarcely half a dozen, usually as a scheming villainess. The best Oriental roles invariably went to Occidental actors.

Of these by far the most frequently seen was the Scandinavian Warner Oland. In silents he had played all kinds of character roles, from a Borgia in *Don Juan* to the Jewish father in *The Jazz Singer* (though he also played Chinese in *Old San Francisco* and *Chinatown Nights*), but his success as *The Mysterious Dr. Fu Manchu* in 1929 seemed to limit him from then on almost entirely to Oriental roles.

The New Adventures of Fu Manchu (1930) was regarded by the *Times* as less exciting than its predecessor. With an indestructibility worthy of Frankenstein's monster, he survived so many apparent deaths that even when he was tossed off a balcony with a lighted bomb in his hand the reviewer hesitated to pronounce him dead. O. P. Heggie was Inspector Nayland Smith, Neil Hamilton Dr. Petrie and Jean Arthur his fiancée, as they had also been in the 1929 film. Fu's original motivation had been to kill all members of the Petrie family in vengeance for the death of his wife in the Boxer Rebellion, but this was soon lost sight of as he hatched diabolically Machiavellian plots on a global scale seldom seen again until the James Bond films of the 1960s.

Sure enough, he survived that lighted bomb. In *Daughter of the Dragon* (1931) Wong in the title role got billing over Oland; third in the cast was Hayakawa as a Chinese detective. Nayland Smith had disappeared, and Neil Hamilton had given way to Bramwell Fletcher as Petrie, but otherwise Fu was still doing business at the same old illegal stand, this time bequeathing to his daughter the mission of exterminating the Petries.

As if to compensate, between his two '30s

Fu films Oland played a likable Chinese detective in two others, *Charlie Chan Carries On* and *The Black Camel* (both 1931), the first of a series that was to include eleven more by 1937 and give Oland his chief claim to posthumous fame.[1] However, he still found time to play Oriental villains in *Shanghai Express* (1932), *The Son-Daughter* (1933) and *Mandalay* (1934), a general in *The Painted Veil* (1934) and a Chinese ambassador in *Shanghai* (1935).

But even after Oland bowed out, Fu was not yet through. Moving over to MGM, he reappeared in the person of Boris Karloff in *The Mask of Fu Manchu* (1932), with the Petries forgotten, Lewis Stone as Nayland Smith and Myrna Loy in her last Oriental role as another daughter, musically named Fah So Lee. Jean Hersholt, Karen Morley and Charles Starrett were among those threatened with exquisitely torturous deaths. This time around Fu is seeking the mask and sword of Genghis Khan, intending to present himself as a reincarnation and lead the yellow race to world domination. In short, the yellow peril rode again.

But even though the final bamboo curtain may have fallen on Fu himself, his tradition lingered in such spiritual godsons as George Raft's "half-breed Chinaman," the scourge of Scotland Yard, in *Limehouse Blues* (1934). Shamelessly borrowing from *Broken Blossoms,* the "child-like scenario" traces the hero's hopeless love for the white Jean Parker. After bringing her together with the boy she loves (Kent Taylor), he is gunned down by the police, since his castoff mistress (Anna May Wong, who else?) has in the classic tradition of women scorned tipped them off.

Another Fu variation was Monogram's *The Mysterious Mr. Wong* (1935)—no connection with Karloff's later detective of the same name—in which Bela Lugosi, as if to prove that he could be just as sinister an Oriental as any Caucasian actor in Hollywood, played

a ruthless Chinese bent on collecting twelve gold coins distributed by Confucius which confer great power on the possessor but only when all together. Turning his hatchet men loose in Chinatown, he soon eliminates eleven other would-be collectors, but a brash newspaperman (Wallace Ford) intercepts his mad hunt for the twelfth coin.

Oddly enough, the first film to uphold Chinese values, even at the expense of American, was Harold Lloyd's *The Cat's Paw* (1934), from a Clarence Budington Kelland story that anticipated both *Mr. Deeds* and *Mr. Smith.* After spending his whole life in China, the earnest, naïve son of missionaries arrives in his American home town just in time to be run as a puppet mayor by the local political machine. Needless to say, he takes the job seriously and tries to throw the rascals out. When they frame him, he seeks the counsel of a wise Chinese, the only one in the film (played by Fred Warren), who shows him a way to terrify his opponents into submission by apparently beheading the ringleaders. Though *The Cat's Paw* is a melodramatic farce, the hero frequently quotes words of Oriental wisdom reflecting the honesty and integrity of his upbringing.

Perhaps out of growing sympathy for China's struggle against Japanese invasion, especially after the bombing of Shanghai, as the decade moved on, the screen began to present Chinese characters somewhat more favorably, even in "B" items like *Chinatown Squad* (1935), in which the villain is a man who misuses funds meant for Chinese Communists. *West of Shanghai* (1937) was actually an adaptation of the 1920 play *The Bad Man,* in which Karloff played, instead of a Mexican bandit, a "lovable, charming and ridiculous Chinese war lord who bumps off the villain and sets matters right for the nice people in the cast, then gracefully eliminates himself before a Nanking firing squad." The *Times* was impressed with the "atmospheric validity" and the use of Chinese extras. In *Daughter of Shanghai* (1937) Anna May Wong, for once a sympathetic heroine, tracks down her

---

[1] Lorre's Mr. Moto and Karloff's Mr. Wong were obvious spin-offs from Chan.

father's murderers by masquerading as a dancing girl in a Central American dive whence the villains illegally smuggle aliens to San Francisco.

It is probably no accident that most of the better films on Chinese themes were laid in China itself. A Limehouse or Chinatown setting almost invariably meant plots of criminal activities, smuggling drugs or aliens, tongs and hatchet men, while in the perpetually war-torn fatherland itself the conflict was usually military, the Chinese were the majority, not despised aliens, and even war lords, as we have seen, could be figures of warmth and dignity.

Two of the best such romantic melodramas have already been discussed, *Shanghai Express* and *The Bitter Tea of General Yen*. Not all were on that level. *Roar of the Dragon* (1932) sounds like an attempt to combine the appeals of the then current *Shanghai Express* and *Grand Hotel*. Richard Dix played a river boat captain trying to hold off Chinese bandits besieging a hotel where his passengers are staying while the boat is being repaired. Oddly enough, no Chinese characters at all are listed in the cast. As noted, *China Seas* (1935) was a maritime version of the same formula, with white characters attacked by Chinese pirates.

The last Chinese war lord of the decade was Akim Tamiroff in *The General Died at Dawn* (1936), billed just below the stars, Gary Cooper and Madeleine Carroll. Clifford Odets' first screenplay, based on an unpublished novel, was "active, preposterous, hairraising and entertaining in equal and generous proportions," said the *Times,* and in no way reflected the writer's well-known "social consciousness."

Anticipating his role in *For Whom the Bell Tolls,* as an idealistic American determined to interfere in another country's civil war, Cooper is entrusted with funds for a rebellion in the province ruled by the cruel General Yang, who sends a hireling (Porter Hall) and his daughter (Carroll) to trap him. The girl, of course, switches sides, and the money belt changes hands many times before the title comes true.

Like all its predecessors, *General* was at best a brisk melodrama. The only serious efforts to depict life in modern China as it might really be lived were two other films, both based on American novels. *Oil for the Lamps of China* (1935), which might have seemed a more natural subject for Odets, was blasted by Andre Sennwald in the *Times* for totally defeating the purpose of the novel on which it was based.

Where Alice Tisdale Hobart described the impersonal ruthlessness of a great oil corporation, the photoplay becomes a confused effort to applaud the company for its paternal and affectionate attitude toward the men who dedicate their lives to its service . . . It presents the Chinese Communist movement not as a struggle of a tragic people to find a path out of their degradation, but as a vulturous gangsterism preying on organizations like the Atlantis Oil Company, which stand for honor and decency.

Seen now, considering where and when it was made, the film seems an unusually strong indictment of corporate ethics or lack of them, as blind loyalty to the company turns the hero (Pat O'Brien) into a heartless automaton with no mind or will of his own. As a direct result of his fanatic devotion to the job, his baby dies, he alienates and fires his best friend (John Eldredge) and almost loses his wife (Josephine Hutchinson). Even after he has risked his life to save company funds from pillaging Communists, he is demoted—an irony on which the picture obviously should have ended. Instead, the company relents and rewards him handsomely for his service.

MGM's elaborate production of Pearl Buck's *The Good Earth* (1937), on the other hand, drew unqualified raves from the critics.[2] The cast actually included several Chi-

[2] *Lost Horizon,* released a month later, despite its Himalayan setting can hardly be considered pro-Oriental. The High Lama, after all, turns out to be an eighteenth-century French priest, and the Manchu princess whom the hero loved in the novel was replaced by two white girls.

nese actors, but no one thought it odd that the leads, farmer Wang and his long-suffering wife O-lan, should be played by Paul Muni and Luise Rainer, both of Austrian Jewish background. The more important fact was that they were the 1936 Oscar winners, he for *The Story of Louis Pasteur,* she for *The Great Ziegfeld*—a rare stroke of luck that MGM could hardly have foreseen, as the film was released a month before the Academy Awards were announced.

"The performances, direction and photography are of uniform excellence, and have been fused perfectly into a dignified, beautiful and soberly dramatic production," said Frank Nugent in the *Times.* This represented a real triumph over adversity, for in its four years of preparation and production the vast

Paul Muni and Luise Rainer in **The Good Earth**

project had suffered changes of both director and producer, the latter occasioned by Irving Thalberg's untimely death. More than two million feet of film were shot in China for use in process shots and atmosphere, then blended with several hundred thousand more made at the studio.

True to the novel, the picture stresses the theme of the peasant's love for the land and the tragedy that overwhelms him when he neglects it. The famine that drives Wang and O-lan from their farm, the looting of a mansion that enables them to return, Wang's prosperity and taking of a young second wife (Tilly Losch) who betrays him with his own son, all follow the novel, but the film adds a new climax, a terrifying plague of locusts that threatens to destroy the crop and brings Wang to belated appreciation of both O-lan and his land. Since all the characters are Chinese, no interracial complications or patronizing of quaint native customs mars this panorama of twentieth-century China seen from within.

Rainer's performance brought her a second Oscar, making her the first, and almost the last, actress to win two in succession, and this despite the competition of Stanwyck's *Stella Dallas* and Garbo's *Camille*. In retrospect *The Good Earth* seems a giant step forward; Holly-wood, which began the decade with the clap-trap melodramatics of *Son of the Gods, East Is West* and the Fu Manchu films, had at last stopped either maligning or patronizing the Chinese.

But anti-Orientalism was only latent, not dead; it was soon transferred, in even more venomous forms, from Chinese to Japanese. From Pearl Harbor until past the end of the war, the screen seethed with grinning little "Japs," caricatured even more grossly than the Nazis (who, after all, were white natives of a country with which many Americans felt strong ties)—all buck teeth and horn-rimmed glasses, torturing innocent GI prisoners while snarling, "Ah, so! You are su'plised I speak your ranguage!''

To the average American, never quite able to distinguish clearly between Chinese and Japanese, no doubt these seemed the natural heirs and successors to the sadistic war lords, tong leaders and hatchet men half remembered from earlier films. Worse still, the American Government in 1942 acted on the most lurid fears and fantasies of the unthinking (especially Californians) in the disgraceful "relocation" of thousands of innocent Japanese-Americans to concentration camps, even though none had ever been accused, much less convicted, of a single subversive act.

"NICE WORK IF YOU CAN GET IT"
Occupational Hazards

20

FOR THE GOOD OF THE SERVICE
It's a Grand Old Flag

The saber-rattling jingoism of the British Empire epics and the chauvinistic contempt for "lesser breeds without the law" evident in both the interracial romances and the anti-Chinese melodramas had their 100% American analogues in other films, both comedies and dramas, which under the guise of inspiring patriotism actually glorified militarism. The heroes were Yankee Doodle Dandies who as soldiers, sailors or Marines, while battling each other in barroom brawls from Singapore to Nicaragua, still managed aggressively to protect American "interests" from mere natives.

In a largely isolationist America, unthreatened by any nation on earth, bitterly disillusioned by the results of World War I and unable to accept the inevitability of a second, much less our involvement in it, a country in which a peacetime draft was literally unimaginable, any boy who could plan no better future for himself than to enlist in the service was presumed by most people to be extremely limited in his options or in his mentality, or both—an impression abundantly confirmed by the antics of the characters in most service films.

High school dropouts could not, of course, rush out and enlist at Annapolis or West Point, still less at expensive private military academies, so films set in those backgrounds had somewhat different, not necessarily

higher, aims. Even if not every boy could aspire to a congressional appointment, it was still reassuring to see what clean-cut young Americans our future officers were, how aglow with selfless patriotism and how admirably trained in the finest traditions of the Army and the Navy.

To any experienced movie-goer, such vehicles were only variations on the equally familiar college film, except that the students and faculty wore uniforms, school spirit was identified with patriotism, and winning the crucial football game meant upholding the honor of that branch of the service. In plot formula there was little difference between *The Spirit of Culver* (1939) and *The Spirit of Notre Dame* (1931), or, for that matter, *Boys Town* (1938). In each the brash newcomer, ignorant or scornful of sacred custom and ritual, has to be made to see the error of his ways—and in the end, of course, he becomes the most hidebound conservative of all.

The first '30s film set in a military prep school was *Tom Brown of Culver* (1932), which, with its obvious echo of *Tom Brown's School Days,* seemed deliberately to suggest a schoolboy rather than a soldierly atmosphere. Sticking closely to the standard pattern, the moody, rebellious hero, being sent through Culver by the American Legion because his father was supposedly killed in action, learns to grow misty-eyed over Culver and the Army, even after finding that his father (H. B. Warner) is living, a shell-shocked deserter.

Though considered an extended commercial for Culver, it was praised for its "restraint and intelligence" and natural acting by the boys. As Anne Shirley and Gig Young were later to do, the young actor in the title role took the character's name for his own. No women at all appeared in the cast, but among the youthful cadets were Richard Cromwell and Tyrone Power, Jr.

After a six-year lapse in which no uniformed prep school films appeared, *Lord Jeff* (1938) cast Freddie Bartholomew not only as a spoiled brat, as he had been in *Captains Courageous* (1937), but a thief as well. In one of the "Barnardo" orphan homes, where British boys are trained for maritime service, young Jeff learns all the usual ethical lessons, and at last ships out on the *Queen Mary.* "A compact little fairy tale," said the *Times,* "as predictable as one of our old Annapolis or West Point films and as easy to accept." With a nice sense of ethnic strains in the United Kingdom, Jeff's classmates include Irish Mickey Rooney, Scottish Terry Kilburn and Cockney Peter Lawford.

In terms of free public relations supplied by Hollywood, Culver still outdid all other prep schools, for early in 1939 Universal did an unacknowledged remake of *Tom Brown,* freshly rewritten by Whitney Bolton and Nathanael West, this time called *The Spirit of Culver.*

Though Tom (Jackie Cooper) is now surnamed Allen, other characters retain their original names, including his best friend, Freddie Bartholomew in the part once played by Richard Cromwell. Henry Hull was highly praised as the doctor-father, who wasn't a dead hero, after all. B. R. Crisler in the *Times* called it "the best picture in the *Spirit of Old* ——— tradition in years," but then went on to qualify his praise with a reflection that could apply to any of the films discussed in this chapter:

Now *The Spirit of Old* (Rutgers, Yale, West Point, Annapolis etc. etc.) . . . is one of the oldest and least worthy of cinema traditions—a gross and unwarranted presuming on the idea that any one who tries to go against the mob, armed with uniforms, flags, military bands, rifles and "tradition" . . . is bound to be ultimately either pilloried or persuaded. In a sense this is too true, alas, but it is likewise true that the future sometimes erects monuments to the memory of people who defied the mob, and were burned at the stake in the public square.

Warner Brothers, who had declared their own war on Germany with *Confessions of a Nazi Spy* (1939) and from then on rattled the jingoistic saber more belligerently than any other studio, contributed the most blatant example of all the boys-in-uniform series in *Dress Parade* (1939), in which they offered all six Dead End Kids to the cause.

Having attended crime school and played angels with both dirty and washed faces, the once delinquent half dozen were now given crisp WASPish names and packed off to "Washington Military Academy." Tough Leo Gorcey's father, an officer during the war, asks Colonel John Litel, head of the school, to take his incorrigible son in hand. Naturally, the boy resists every inch of the way, in spite of all the noble examples around him, but when a fire breaks out and hostile classmate Gabriel Dell is trapped, guess who rescues him? As Crisler observed: "It is a steadying thought, in these days of qualified national emergency, to know that Warner Brothers are in such a splendid state of preparedness."

Was this part of a gradual softening-up process by which traditionally antimilitary Americans were to be converted to worshiping the brass? At very least it seems more than coincidence that, even as newsreels showed Hitler and Mussolini reviewing endless parades of strutting, saluting, uniformed youngsters, three American films within a year should preach the value of military training for teen-agers. And these were only the high-school-level pictures, not half as elaborately produced and publicized as those made "with the full co-operation of" the service academies themselves.

That in return for this generous help the picture of academy life should be 100% flattering went without saying. Indeed, the services could never have bought such lavish publicity as Hollywood gave them, packaged with all its professional expertise and, at least on the "A" level, as at MGM, played by some of its most promising young actors. The first '30s example was typical enough: *Midshipman Jack* (1933—the same year as the antiwar *Cavalcade* and *Men Must Fight*), "Dedicated to Henry Latrobe Roosevelt, who as Assistant Secretary of the Navy keeps alive the navy traditions begun by Theodore Roosevelt in 1895 and so gallantly continued by Franklin D. Roosevelt." Who could criticize a picture with its heart so conspicuously in the right place?

This was a naïve tale of honor at Annapolis, in which a prankish upperclassman (Bruce Cabot) takes two lowly plebes (Frank Albertson and Arthur Lake) under his wing, then assumes the blame for an accident in which one of them is hurt, even though it almost costs him the love of the commandant's daughter (Betty Furness). Taking the Blame was a standard plot device in all service academy (and college and school) films, especially if the true culprit, usually a well-meaning, weak type, was not only the hero's room-mate but the brother of the girl he loved.

In *Annapolis Farewell* (1935), Tom Brown and Richard Cromwell, those old Culver classmates, were reunited as naval cadets, with Brown again as the smart aleck who must learn to respect tradition, especially as embodied by a doddering retired commander (Sir Guy Standing), a veteran of Manila Bay, who, after pleading vainly that his beloved former ship not be used as a target in naval maneuvers, dons his old uniform and goes down with her—a sacrifice that seems as pointless as Alec Guinness' as the rigid British admiral in *Kind Hearts and Coronets* (1950).

The same year saw *Shipmates Forever* (1935), second in Warners' series of flag-waving musicals. Filmed, as usual, at Annap-

olis itself, with unlimited technical help from the Navy, the story was still the same old formula. The brash hero (Dick Powell) would rather be a crooner than follow in the footsteps of his admiral father (Lewis Stone) —but before winning the girl (Ruby Keeler), he is converted to true Navy ideals by the heroic death during battle practice of a flunked-out classmate (John Arledge).

Annapolis Salute (1937) cast Van Heflin as the sneering antiacademy type, James Ellison as the boy with the Navy in his blood, Marsha Hunt as their dream girl and Harry Carey as the obligatory voice of tradition. In *Hold 'Em, Navy* (1937), however, Paramount took a welcome lighter approach to essentially the same formula. Noted one critic: "Lew Ayres, its hero, not only doesn't make the deciding touchdown in the game with Army but doesn't even make the game—a twist so ingenious that the creative strain is probably still being felt in the Paramount script department."

Predictably, MGM offered the glossiest version of all in *Navy Blue and Gold* (1937), in which Robert Young (the cynic this time) and James Stewart were the rivals, Florence Rice the girl and Lionel Barrymore the good old retired sea dog who by word and deed exemplifies the highest naval ideals. Tom Brown, as perennial an undergraduate in service academies as Eddie Nugent was in civilian colleges, was the girl's brother. Despite the familiarity of all the ingredients, the film was considered "one of the more agreeable entertainments the screen has provided this season."

The Army, of course, had to be given equal time, and West Point was used in just as many films as Annapolis, starting with *Flirtation Walk* (1934), first of Dick Powell's three patriotic musicals. As the *Times* rather bitterly pointed out, stirred by an American Legion band in front of the theater, "you went to your seat prepared to give until it hurt . . . A rousing recruiting poster, the new photoplay tells of the raptures, the sentimental joys, the minor difficulties and the

Robert Young, Florence Rice, James Stewart in **Navy Blue and Gold**

collegiate fun of life . . . at the Military Academy."

West Point of the Air (1936) departed from formula to the extent of centering on a sentimental sergeant (Wallace Beery), whose West Point graduate son (Robert Young) becomes so obnoxious that the old man knocks him down and so is cashiered out of the service. The son almost succumbs to the temptations of civilian life offered by a sleek actress (Rosalind Russell), but eventually chooses the daughter (Maureen O'Sullivan) of the commandant (Lewis Stone).

Using the same writers, director and some of the same players as in *Hold 'Em, Navy,* Paramount just a year later gave the same refreshingly irreverent treatment to sacred West Point rigmarole in *Touchdown Army* (1938), hailed by the *Times* as "the craziest and funniest football comedy in years." Even the climactic big game is kidded, when the backbone of the team must be flown in a pursuit plane from the guardhouse to the Army-Navy game to allow his rival to carry the ball over the goal line.

Pushing iconoclasm one serious step further, *The Duke of West Point* (1938) cast Louis Hayward as an Army officer's son educated at Cambridge who returns to become the fifth generation of his family to enter

Ruby Keeler and Dick Powell
in **Flirtation Walk**

West Point. Said the *Times:* "Fancy our chagrin and our secret delight when, as the film rolls on, we find our Cambridge-bred hero manfully having to civilize West Point. And judging by the ill manners, childishness and general Boy Scoutism of the academy, as set forth in the picture, West Point certainly needs it."

When he sneaks out of barracks at night to wire $1,000 to save the life of a friend's mother and can't explain his absence, he is ostracized by "the silence," that barbaric "tradition" that four decades later is still causing controversy. Whatever the intent of the film, the hero seemed more sensible and mature than his persecutors. Joan Fontaine, just beginning to emerge, was the girl, and among the other cadets were Richard Carlson, Alan Curtis and, yes, Tom Brown.

Turning from the problems of uniformed undergraduates in training to those of soldiers, sailors and Marines in actual service, one is immediately struck by the lower tone. If the films set in the service academies radiated youthful idealism, with pure romance culminating in a military wedding to the commandant's dewy-eyed daughter, Hollywood's depiction of the enlisted men and non-coms who would presumably serve under these dedicated young officers was much less reverent. In fact, it most commonly took the form of rowdy farce, mixed with crude melodrama.

Even while serious films were bitterly exposing the futility of all wars and the hypocrisy of those who profited from them, not only the academy films but these others, however ridiculed or ignored, were undercutting that message, at least among those who really thought a boy could see the world by joining the Navy, find fun and adventure in the Army or leave it to the Marines to "make a man" of him. (The Air Force did not yet exist as a separate branch.)

Free of all civilian restraints and responsibilities, the typical movie doughboys, gobs and leathernecks (who usually came in sets of two or three) proved their masculinity over and over in endless drinking sprees amid

"sez you, sez me" arguments that broke into barroom brawls, usually over the shopworn charms of some dubious blonde like Shanghai Mabel in *What Price Glory?* In the climax, of course, when duty really called, despite their running feud, one buddy invariably sacrificed himself to save the other's life, reputation or military rank.

Most of these assembly-line products were the bastard offspring of *What Price Glory?*, that much admired play by Maxwell Anderson and Laurence Stallings which in 1924 had seemed to Broadway the last word in hard-boiled cynicism about the war. Read now, or seen in the 1926 film version (with Edmund Lowe and Victor McLaglen as Captain Flagg and Sergeant Quirt, the definitive battling buddies, of whom they were to play variations in many another film), *What Price Glory?*, despite a few lip-service war-is-hell speeches, seems no more antimilitary than *The Front Page*, which it resembles, is antinewspaper.

The camaraderie created by front-line combat is seen as the ultimate male bonding, a harsh but deeply ennobling rite of passage that serves forever after as a sentimental mystique unsharable by anyone else, even noncombatant Army men, much less civilians or women (who appear only as whores).

Though far more men actually served in the Army than in any other service, Hollywood produced a disproportionate number of films about the Navy. Even with the omission of six about the Coast Guard, some thirty-seven pictures between 1930 and 1939 involved sailors, compared with fewer than twenty about the Marines and hardly a dozen about the Army (including such special branches as the cavalry and border patrols). Still more surprising is the fact that most of the naval films were either out-and-out farces or musicals.

Perhaps this pattern, which dates back at least as far as Gilbert and Sullivan's *HMS Pinafore* (1878), grew in part out of the non-military, almost comic look of the enlisted men's uniforms. Even in pacifist families little boys, and sometimes little girls, had always enjoyed dressing up in sailor suits. However absurdly anachronistic and unfunctional, the bell-bottom trousers and middy blouse, the Buster Brown collar and flowing black tie, topped by the jaunty little white cap, lend an undeniably "cute" look, at least to youthful figures, with none of the grim overtones of khaki and overseas caps. Then too, the decks of battleships offered irresistible opportunities for Busby Berkeley production numbers.

Besides the 1930 *Hit the Deck* and *Shipmates Forever,* two of the most tuneful film musicals of the '30s (both 1936) used naval backgrounds: the Astaire-Rogers *Follow the Fleet,* with a score by Irving Berlin, and the James Stewart-Eleanor Powell *Born to Dance,* which featured some of Cole Porter's brightest numbers.

Along with the uniforms went the moth-eaten humor about sailors, who, because of their months at sea, were presumed to be suffering, or rather enjoying, acute satyromania, which left them with not one but many girls in every port. Some of the titles alone suggest the tone: *Dames Ahoy, Navy Blues, True to the Navy, Way for a Sailor, Sea Legs* (all 1930), *Oh, Sailor Beware* (1931), *Sailors' Luck, Sailor Be Good, Her First Mate* (all 1933), *She Learned About Sailors* (1934), *Miss Pacific Fleet* (1935), *Sweetheart of the Navy* (1937), *Give Me A Sailor* (1938).

But these lighthearted diversions were more than balanced, if not entirely sunk, by the dead-serious melodramas. In the whole decade only two films attempted personal stories about Navy men. *Navy Born* (1936) despite its title was just another variation on the *Three Godfathers* theme, in which three naval officers try to hide the baby of a dead comrade so that it won't be given to his supposedly scheming sister-in-law. Need it be added that one of the men (William Gargan) falls in love with the young aunt (Claire Dodd), so they end by sharing the custody?

The woman's angle was exploited for the only time in *Wings over Honolulu* (1937), "gaily played and attractively mounted," with Wendy Barrie as a Navy wife bored with the stodgy social life among the brass at Pearl Harbor during the frequent absences of her husband (Ray Milland). She almost falls for a passing yachtsman (Kent Taylor) and eventually "stirs up a fine wasp's nest of crack-ups and court martials," said the *Times,* "but Uncle Sam forgives her and so does Mr. Milland, and the presumption is that she is content to stay knitting at the fireside thereafter."

The first '30s film "dedicated to the United States Navy" had the advantages of being both spectacular and timely: Capra's *Dirigible* (1931). Though on a personal level it was another of a series in which Jack Holt fought Ralph Graves against the background of some dangerous occupation (e.g., *Submarine, Flight*), what intrigued contemporary audiences were the convincing snowscapes of Antarctica (all photographed in California) and the dramatized conflict over the merits of planes versus lighter-than-air craft.

No doubt inspired, as was *The Lost Zeppelin* (1930), by the 1928 Arctic disaster of the dirigible *Italia, Dirigible* seemed to favor the subject of its title, since in the end it is such a craft that rescues the two half-frozen survivors of a plane crash. (This implied judgment was to be reversed forever six years later with the destruction of the *Hindenburg.*)

Much more typical was *Hell Divers* (1931), a combination of the academy and the battling buddy patterns, which dealt with "the curriculum of Uncle Sam's sailors of the air," but concentrated on two rival petty officers (Gable and Beery) attached to the battleship *Saratoga.* In the crisis Beery sacrifices his life to save Gable's, and the film ends with the sounding of taps.

Set in the same background, *Wings of the Navy* (1939), another Warners contribution to the prewar patriotic build-up, was a near-documentary of the Pensacola Naval Air Training station and its methods of turning raw recruits into seasoned pilots. "The United

States government, which always co-operates so beautifully with Warners in these affairs," noted the *Times,* "most obligingly trots out dozens of the navy's speedy two-seaters and flying dreadnaughts." The story was a variation of *The Charge of the Light Brigade* (1936), in which Olivia De Havilland again switches her affection from an older to a younger brother, here George Brent and John Payne.

Dramatically speaking, the submarine service fared somewhat better on screen than the naval air force, getting off to a good start with *Men Without Women* (1930), co-authored and directed by John Ford, a tense drama of a sub accidentally disabled by a steamer. The claustrophobic crisis, with the oxygen supply dwindling, brings out the true personalities of assorted crew members (none of them big names) Kenneth MacKenna, Frank Albertson, Warren Hymer and Stuart Erwin, who must be rescued one by one through a torpedo tube, with the last one necessarily left behind.

In reviewing *Hell Below* (1933) the *Times* deplored the jarring mixture of farce and melodrama. Here Walter Huston and Robert Montgomery were the rival officers, a rivalry complicated by the fact that Montgomery is in love with Huston's daughter (Madge Evans). During World War I submarine combat in the Adriatic the younger man disobeys orders by firing torpedoes at enemy warships and is dishonorably discharged, but later manages to get aboard the submarine and die a hero's death. Most critics thought Jimmy Durante stole the picture.

In *Submarine D-1* (1937) Warners used the same near-documentary technique as later in *Wings of the Navy* (1939), with the usual triangle thrown in. Pat O'Brien and Wayne Morris were another Flagg-Quirt team, rivals for Doris Weston, brawling in tropical dives in Panama. Said Crisler: "The submarine is the only thing in the film which gets beneath the surface."

Best received of the underwater dramas was John Ford's *Submarine Patrol* (1938), "the story of a cockleshell armada that sailed from Brooklyn in '17 with a cargo of TNT and a crew of green hands to chase the U-boats from the Mediterranean"—in particular one wooden ship commanded by George Bancroft. An exceptionally strong cast included some of Ford's regulars like John Carradine and Ward Bond, but also Preston Foster, Slim Summerville, Warren Hymer, Douglas Fowley and, as the young lovers, Richard Greene and Nancy Kelly. Said the *Times:* "We have no qualms about calling this the best of its type this year."

Thunder Afloat (1939), MGM's version of underseas warfare, might well have been titled "How Wallace Beery Avenged the Sinking of the Tugboat *Susan H.,*" though it was based on the German submarine raids on the Atlantic coast in 1918. Beery gets himself court-martialed, occasioning "synthetic tears" from daughter Virginia Grey.

Of the six films made about the Coast Guard between 1930 and 1939, all routine "B's," reviewers' opinions might well be summed up in Nugent's words in the *Times* on June 22, 1936:

We hope that [*Border Flight*] will be the last of the "service" films. It seems that, no matter which branch of the government Hollywood tackles, it always is stumbling on one patriot and one chap who thinks the uniform is so much spinach. They invariably are rivals for the same young woman and the scoffer inevitably repents his treasonable ways. Either Hollywood is all wrong about this thing, or we should have a Congressional investigation.

Second only to the Navy in the number of films made about it was the Marine Corps, but the quality was even lower. The over-familiar battling buddy formula was not even leavened by the youthful idealism of the films about Annapolis and West Point. Even in the '30s ex-Marines were not likely to feel misty-eyed nostalgia for their boot training at Parris Island (which through the 1970s continued to make the front pages with exposures and supposed reforms of sadistic, often fatal, brutality, almost as often as West Point and Annapolis did with academic cheating scandals). The gung-ho titles alone suggest the level of most

Marine films: *Leathernecking, Come On, Marines, The Marines Are Coming, The Leathernecks Have Landed, Join the Marines, Pride of the Marines, Come On, Leathernecks, The Marines Are Here, Calling All Marines.*

The only films involving Marines that did not follow the same rigid formulae were actually other kinds of film. Thus *Soldiers and Women* (1930) was a murder melodrama involving Marine officers and their wives stationed in Haiti (perhaps inspired by the Fortescue case, which had taken place among the military in Hawaii). A colonel's lady (Aileen Pringle) wants a captain out of the way because he knows of her affair with another officer, but the captain's young widow (Helen Johnson) brings the truth to light.

In *Sweethearts on Parade* (1930) an innocent country girl (Alice White) in the city is almost tricked into a false marriage aboard the yacht of an evil millionaire (Kenneth Thompson) until her Marine boy friend (Lloyd Hughes) and his buddies come to the rescue. In *The Stoker* (1932) the Marines perform the same last-minute function, like the convenient cavalry in a Western. In *Rain* (1932) Sadie Thompson (Joan Crawford) is in love with a Marine (William Gargan). In *Parachute Jumper* (1933), in which Bette Davis played one of her several Southern roles, Doug Fairbanks, Jr., and sidekick Frank McHugh start out as Marines in Nicaragua, but soon turn civilian and become involved with gangsters in New York.

In the main stream of Marine clichés, Flagg and Quirt, the original battling buddies from *What Price Glory?* proved so popular that they were revived, again played by Victor McLaglen and Edmund Lowe, in *The Cock-Eyed World* (1929) and once more in *Women of All Nations* (1931), which begins with flashes of the war, then swings to the Panama Canal, then to Sweden for a good-will mission (!), thence to Nicaragua and finally to Turkey, where they invade a harem.

A third reprise, *Hot Pepper* (1933), with Lupe Velez in the title role, continued the

misadventures of the two, whose personalities (quick-tongued Flagg, fumbling Quirt) must by now have been almost as familiar to audiences as those of Laurel and Hardy. Once again they leave the Marines for civilian life, with Flagg turning successful speakeasy owner. One reviewer thought the comedy "reprehensible" but admitted the audience loved it.

If these raucous comedies were among the most popular Marine films, what can be said of those on still lower levels? *Leathernecking* (1930), a farce which introduced Irene Dunne to the screen, depicted the Marines' life as "one continuous round of parties, yachting trips and pillow fights among the boys in the barracks." In the same vein, *Come On, Marines* (1934) featured Clara Lou (later known as Ann) Sheridan in a tale, by Philip Wylie, of all writers, about Marines sent from San Diego to the Philippines to rescue a group of "shipwrecked children," who turn out to be attractive schoolgirls. Among those involved were Richard Arlen and Ida Lupino.

A more familiar pattern recurred in *Devil Dogs of the Air* (1935). "Having glorified the Navy and the Military Academy, the patriotic Warner Brothers now atone for their neglect of the Marines," noted Andre Sennwald in the *Times.* Though as a peace-loving citizen he was no admirer of films publicizing the armed forces, in this case he made an exception, finding it "distinguished by the most remarkable stunt flying and aerial photography the screen has seen in years." As so often before and afterward, the rivals were James Cagney and Pat O'Brien, this time battling over Margaret Lindsay, Cagney as a cynical barnstorming pilot turned by flying school into "a loyal and gallant defender of the Constitution."

Still more routine was *The Marines Are Coming* (1935), yet another doomed attempt at a comeback by William Haines, a brash MGM juvenile in silents, here backed by other faded stars including Esther Ralston, Conrad Nagel and Armida. In *The Leathernecks Have Landed* (1935) it was Lew Ayres as a Marine in Shanghai, in a plot about avenging a buddy's death by infiltrating the smuggling gang responsible—a plot Republic liked so well that it was used four more times under different titles in the next seven years. Said John T. McManus in the *Times*:

> There seems to have been an honest doubt in the minds of those responsible for the picture over whether the forces of General Chang should be called bandits or rebels, but, under either label, the Leathernecks disposed of a lot of them in the process of protecting an oil company and a mining company in the interior of China.

Passing over such trivial recruiting propaganda as *Join the Marines* and *Pride of the Marines* (both 1936), both featuring heroes who despite all hardships end by re-enlisting, Warner Brothers with their usual sense of fair play for all the armed forces, having made a Dick Powell musical about the Navy (*Shipmates Forever*) and one about the Army (*Flirtation Walk*), could hardly do less than give the Marines equal time. The result was *The Singing Marine* (1937), the best received of the three, perhaps because it avoided the most familiar clichés to tell a story about a bashful young Marine who wins an amateur contest and becomes famous but almost loses the respect of the corps. Doris Weston, a real-life Major Bowes amateur hour winner, pinch-hit for Ruby Keeler, and even she shared in the general praise.

But this level was not long maintained. *Come On, Leathernecks* (1938) saw Richard Cromwell as another pouting juvenile, a reluctant Marine lieutenant forced into uniform by his father, though he would rather play pro football. A skirmish with gunrunners in the Philippines opens his eyes to the joys of military life. That overfamiliar pair, the battling buddies, also returned twice more in two other "B" films of 1938. In *The Marines Are Here* they were Gordon Oliver and Ray Walker in Manila, where the hero worship of a small boy inspires them to valiant deeds, convincing the child that he wants to be a Marine when he grows up. In *Air Devils* the two heroes when mustered out of the Marines join the native police on a South Sea isle. A

pack train attacked by natives is saved when a "bombing plane" (presumably American) arrives. They are decorated, and, naturally, re-enlist.

Fittingly, Marine films of the '30s ended on that note of spy hysteria discussed earlier, with *Calling All Marines* (1939), described by Crisler in the *Times* as "everything that a saboteur, a spy and a wrecker of our defense forces could wish it to be." A hoodlum (Donald Barry) enlists in the Marines to steal the plans of an aerial torpedo for an unnamed foreign power, but succumbs to the ideals of the service. The climax was that old stand-by, the nick-in-time arrival of the Marines.

Considering the fact that within a year after the end of the '30s millions of young Americans were to find themselves about to be drafted into khaki GI uniforms, it is surprising how small a role the prewar Army had played in the public imagination, compared to the two supposedly more glamorous services —perhaps because the uniform was as colorless as its "olive drab" name, sartorially no competition for Navy blues or whites, the Marine dress outfit or even West Point gray. Until the draft, few people had ever heard of any fort but Knox, nor had the screen done anything to inform them about peacetime Army life. Among the relatively few films made, the already obsolescent cavalry, no doubt for pictorial reasons, received a disproportionate amount of attention.[1]

The first of these utterly undistinguished items was *Troopers Three* (1930), the usual crude mixture of low comedy and melodrama, highlighted only by scenes of expert horsemanship. Rex Lease, another brash William Haines type, and his sidekicks Roscoe Karns and Slim Summerville are failed vaudevillians who join the cavalry only to keep from starving and are outraged to find they must stay three years. The standard feeble triangle involved a sergeant's daughter and climaxed in a fire in which the hero proves himself.

---

[1] In *This Sporting Age* (1930) Jack Holt played a devil-may-care, polo-playing Army officer.

In *Keep 'Em Rolling* (1934) a Fort Lee cavalryman (Walter Huston) is so devoted to his horse, Rodney, that when the animal is temporarily taken from him he goes on a binge that disgraces him. Even after redeeming himself in World War I, he is condemned as too old. After both man and horse go AWOL, Rodney is finally pensioned off, with Huston assigned to care for him.

An even more extreme case of hippophilia was *Sergeant Murphy* (1938), in which Ronald Reagan joins the artillery because his father has sold his pet horse, Sergeant Murphy, to the Army. When his hitch is up, he tries to buy the horse, but instead it's transferred to the cavalry, and so is he. Meanwhile he has fallen for Mary Maguire, daughter of officer Donald Crisp, but gets the horse to unseat him and thus be discharged. When both are out of the Army, he "shows" the horse successfully and trains him for the Aintree Grand National. Thus despite the title and background *Sergeant Murphy* used as many animal and horse-racing as Army clichés.

A less horsy view of the cavalry was seen in *Army Girl* (1939), Republic's "special" for the year, with an unusually good cast headed by Madge Evans, Preston Foster, James Gleason and H. B. Warner. The conflict is a technological one; a captain in the tank corps arrives at a cavalry post to demonstrate a new type of tank and eventually mechanize the regiment, despite die-hard resistance from the old guard. His tank wins a race against the cavalry, but he wins the old colonel's daughter even while breaking his heart. "Exciting bunk," said the *Times*.

The other branch of service to receive what seems undue attention was the border patrol, which bore the same peripheral relation to the Army as the Coast Guard to the Navy, both largely concerned with smugglers. In *Soldiers of the Storm* (1930) the hero (Regis Toomey) falls for the daughter (Anita Page) of a man with a financial interest in a ring smuggling narcotics and aliens across the Mexican border. He chases the fleeing culprits in a plane in this thoroughly routine item,

differing only in uniform from any other cops-and-robbers melodrama. Equally negligible borderline cases were *Happy Landing* (1934) and *Skybound* (1935).

Criminals of the Air (1937) was a variation, again dealing with alien-smuggling and notable, if at all, as one of Rita Hayworth's last "B" picture leads. Identical in setting and problem was *Forged Passport* (1939), which had the distinction of being the second of the five versions of Republic's favorite plot, first used as *The Leathernecks Have Landed* (1935), as noted above.

Self-evidently, most of these Army films were routine "B" productions, just as predictable as those about the Navy and the Marines, even if the hack-work took slightly different forms. What in retrospect seems almost sinister is the rediscovery, late in the decade, by the major studios of the romantic-melodramatic-comic possibilities of the First World War—not at all like the war so relentlessly exposed in earlier talkies, but a revisionist, almost nostalgic view of it as a jaunty, heroic crusade.

The first example of this was MGM's *The Shopworn Angel* (1938), the personal story of which was discussed earlier; the last and most blatant, closing the decade on a prophetically propagandistic note, was Warners' *The Fighting 69th* (released January 1940).

However ironically dismissed or ignored by conscientious critics and discriminating viewers, even the worst films discussed in this chapter were still being seen by millions of others, with their naïve, simplistic values no doubt being absorbed, if only subliminally, by many. Thus when the time came for Hollywood to make its all-out contribution to the war effort (starting long before Pearl Harbor), it had only to trot out the good old service clichés—with fancy, updated packaging—in all those '40s films that were among the major nuisances of life on the home front.

Indeed, one of the most deplorable effects of the war on film criticism as well as film-going was that, however spangled with big star names, polished to a high gloss by expert directors and introduced with dedications to our brave boys in the service, it was still the same old flag-waving hogwash as ever—but now it had to be taken seriously, at least in public, and judged only by its presumed value in keeping up morale and winning the war.

21

"EACH TIME YOU GO UP THERE..."
Dangerous Jobs

Military men, British, Foreign Legion and American, were not the only ones risking life and limb in the line of duty. Aside from spies, costumed swordsmen and equally brave cops and G-men, another whole army of relatively unsung civilian heroes struggled manfully—often against technological hazards undreamed of by earlier generations—to get the serum delivered, the plane landed, the bridge repaired, the dam built or the telephone line strung. Though the loyal, patient wife or sweetheart might try to adjust with a brave smile, there usually came the moment of truth when she begged her man to quit for her sake. "Don't you know, each time you go up (or down or out) there, I die a little?"

Indeed, if popularity is to be judged by sheer volume, then by far the most popular of all genres in the '30s (except Westerns), far outnumbering even gangster and mystery films, was the kind of adventure melodrama which pitted the hero not only against villains but against the forces of nature: forest fires, floods, blizzards, log jams, wild animals. The fact that the vast majority of these were "B" productions ground out by independent producers, featuring unknown or already faded names, is not hard to explain. Action, after all, is what movies have always done best, and given enough fast movement, suspenseful twists and a rousing fight or rescue for the climax, most audiences were willing to accept —perhaps even enjoyed—the familiar cardboard characters, wooden dialogue and mechanical plot.

Besides, the roles of rugged hero, pretty heroine and sneering villain were well within the range of the least talented players. Given such a cast, a limited budget and a week's shooting schedule, a shoestring producer would have been mad to attempt sophisticated comedy or probing psychological drama. The fact that many of the results turned out to be lively entertainment was a real triumph of directorial ingenuity over the material at hand.

Considering how much public attention was focused on Arctic and Antarctic expeditions in the early '30s (a full-length documentary about Admiral Byrd was given regular theater distribution), it is surprising that in addition to *Dirigible* (1931), only two other films exploited this decidedly hazardous pursuit. *The Lost Zeppelin* (1930) used a flight to the South Pole as background for an utterly routine marital triangle (Conway

Tearle, Virginia Valli, Ricardo Cortez). *SOS Iceberg* (1933) was much more highly rated, especially for its location photography shot in Greenland. It was an American version of a German original, with Leni Riefenstahl (famous later as director of the most spectacular Nazi films) repeating her role in English opposite Rod La Rocque and Gibson Gowland (who went mad, just as in *Greed*).

To go from one of the most publicized dangerous occupations to the least glamorous and most ignored, only three '30s pictures dealt with coal miners. Paul Muni's *Black Fury* (1935), which involved a prolonged and bitter strike, will be discussed among timely films. *Draegerman Courage* (1937), highly praised except for its strange title, saw Barton MacLane as an expert who rescues a mine owner, his foreman and a doctor trapped in a disaster. Like *Black Fury,* whose title it echoes, *Fury Below* (1938) also attempted, however ineptly, to dramatize the "mining situation of today, beset with labor troubles," so must also be classed among timely films. But none approached the level of *The Stars Look Down* or even of *How Green Was My Valley.*

Though doomed to working conditions just as dangerous and risking a death just as horrible, sandhogs were never taken as seriously as miners nor given even one "A" dramatic picture. 1935 was their big year—indeed their only year, until 1943, when Fred MacMurray played one in *No Time for Love.* First it was McLaglen and Lowe, again directed by Raoul Walsh, as Brooklyn sandhogs tunneling under the East River, in *Under Pressure,* which merely transferred their overfamiliar battle to a novel setting. Besides the usual rivalry between the heroes, they were also battling Charles Bickford as boss of the Manhattan sandhogs.

A few months later the *Times* called the second sandhog film, *Hard Rock Harrigan,* "the most aggressively mediocre entertainment of the season." This time the hero, George O'Brien, avoids a fight with a rival sandhog, Fred Kohler, only because he knows Kohler

has heart trouble; when Kohler finds out, they become friends. In *Too Tough to Kill* two tunnel construction gangs are such rivals that Victor Jory and his crew are saved from death only by a tip from a girl reporter (Sally O'Neil). In all three films the genuine dramatic possibilities of a sandhog's unique perils were missed.

Truckers fared no better, with only three "B" productions. *In Spite of Danger* (1935) anticipated the French *Wages of Fear* (1955), with a climax in which a dynamite-laden truck goes out of control in a "war" between a mob and honest truckers. In *California Straight Ahead* (1937) John Wayne was a trucker racing a railroad from Chicago to the Coast, along the way battling blizzards and steep mountain roads to deliver supplies to a Pacific liner. In *Born to Be Wild* (1938) truckers are offered $1,000 to drive what proves to be dynamite, which, after being hijacked and almost wrecked, they use to blow up a dam and save a town. (Truckers did not come into their own until *They Drive by Night,* 1940.)

Iron and steel workers, especially riveters poised on girders high above city streets, were given more attention, at least numerically. Of five films about them (two starring the inevitable McLaglen), one achieved some melodramatic excitement: *Two Seconds* (1932), a flashback from the electric chair as Edward G. Robinson recalls the chain of events that put him there. A naïve riveter, he married a dance hall tramp (Vivienne Osborne), and when his best friend (Preston Foster) tried to tell him about her, he caused him to lose his balance and fall to his death. Realizing the truth too late, he then killed the wife.

Firemen, who had six pictures to their credit, did not do so well; all were forgotten quickies, only two reviewed by the *Times.* (*The Third Alarm* and *The Fourth Alarm* were, aptly enough, released within a week of each other in 1930.) *Flames* (1932) anticipated *The Towering Inferno* with a burning office building. *She Loved a Fireman* (1937) starred Dick Foran and Ann Sheridan, but

Fireman Save My Child (1932) was a Joe E. Brown vehicle, not even about firemen.

Of the seven films dealing with telephone linemen or operators in dangerous situations (one coyly titled *I've Got Your Number*), the only one to win reviewers' praise was *Slim* (1937), which starred Pat O'Brien, Henry Fonda and Margaret Lindsay. Said the *Times:*

> The Freres Warner, who have done so much to immortalize the commissioned stalwarts of the army, the navy, the marine corps and the Department of Justice, have discovered—to their delight and ours—that there are peacetime heroes, too . . . It is, within certain readily explicable limits, an honest attempt to dignify and dramatize commonplace lives, to acknowledge the day-by-day heroism of ordinary men.

Of eight films dealing with the oil industry,[1] starting with the misleadingly titled *The Woman I Stole* (1933) and ending with *Blackmail* (1939)—with both *Flaming . . .* and *Burning . . . Gold* along the way—most might be summed up in the phrase the *Times* used to dismiss *Danger Patrol* (1937): "another of those high-powered adventure pictures which tell of the glories and hardships in the suicide occupations." Perhaps the most unusual was *Blackmail,* in which Edward G. Robinson, a fugitive from a Southern chain gang for a crime he did not commit, puts out fires in Oklahoma oil wells. The real culprit, Gene Lockhart, has him sent back, but is finally forced to confess on the brink of a burning well.

The strictly twentieth-century occupation of newsreel cameramen (to be supplanted within a generation by their TV successors) was used in nine films, none memorable, only one an "A" production. Though this was indeed a form of journalism, its physical risks made it so different from any other that its practitioners seem to belong here rather than with reporters. *Headline Shooters* (1933) was likened to *The Front Page,* with the hero (William Gargan) constantly leaving girls to rush off on new assignments, until he meets a newspaperwoman (Frances Dee) who can keep up with him.

Richard Cromwell starred in the next two, in *Above the Clouds* (1934) as the exploited assistant of alcoholic Robert Armstrong, saving the day in the wreck of a dirigible. In *Men of the Hour* (1935) Cromwell is again taken advantage of by a buddy (Wallace Ford), fumbles his big chance, but regains his job by filming the assassination of a visiting king. In *Ladies Crave Excitement* (1935) Norman Foster photographs for a story-behind-the-news series called *Events,* obviously suggested by *The March of Time.* In *Anything for a Thrill* (1937) Frankie Darro wants to be a newsreel cameraman like his brother and by chance gets shots of a bank robbery which expose a phony nobleman as a crook. In *Exiled to Shanghai* (1937) a newsreel cameraman (Wallace Ford) who covered the Spanish Civil War later finds himself fired for photographing the wrong person. But eventually he sells his pioneer idea for a "television newsreel," and it is his hostile editor (Dean Jagger) who is sent to China.

In *Sharpshooters* (1938), the first of a projected Camera Daredevils series, Brian Donlevy and Wally Vernon, covering the assassination of the king of a mythical country, save the young prince from the same fate. Second in the series, *Chasing Danger* (1939) involved an Arab revolt against the French, with a rescue by the Foreign Legion, but, as Don Miller puts it in *B Movies,* "there were more actual hotspots on the globe for newsreel cameramen than Ruritanian kingdoms and remote desert outposts. The inexorable world events of the late 1930's curtailed the series."

Meanwhile the only big picture to deal with this line of work was *Too Hot to Handle* (1938), MGM's obvious and immediate follow-up to the successful *Test Pilot* (1938), with Gable and Loy again co-starred, she as a round-the-world flyer who becomes his pilot on assignments that include a blazing munitions ship, a jungle rescue expedition and a gang siege in a tenement. Despite a cast that

---

[1] Though *Oil for the Lamps of China* (1935) also dealt with the oil industry, the executive hero's dangers were more moral than physical.

Henry Fonda and Pat O'Brien in Slim

included two Walters, Pidgeon and Connolly, nothing could redeem the basically synthetic script.

Grand Hotel formula films set on trains have been covered, but at least a dozen others were concerned with the problems of railroads and their workers. Many were titled from the names of the trains, like *The Silver Streak, The Midnight Special, The Lightning Flyer* and especially (like the *Grand Hotel* types) this or that *Express*, including *Phantom, Cannonball* and *Paradise.* Most were

routine triangles like *Other Men's Women* (1930), in which bachelor fireman Grant Withers falls in love with the wife (Mary Astor) of his engineer (Regis Toomey), differing from others only in that the climax was either a railroad wreck, a race or a rescue. Typical was *The Silver Streak* (1935), in which the young designer of a crack train proves its worth when only it can rush iron lungs to polio-stricken Boulder Dam.

The recurrent pattern, in which old and new forms of transportation were pitted against each other, turned up twice in 1937. In *California Straight Ahead* the hero was a trucker racing a railroad to the Coast—but in *Paradise Express* the receiver of a short-line railroad battles a crooked trucking company to regain the all-important contract for delivering the produce of a farmers' co-op. If ever paired on a double bill, the two films would have canceled each other out.

As with railroads, so with ships; many served as settings for *Grand Hotel* variants, as well as for the naval films discussed in the preceding chapter. The photogenic qualities of sailing vessels having always been obvious, they were frequently seen in costume dramas. But some thirty-four other films, with titles like *The Sin Ship* (1931), *Ships of Hate* (1931), *The Ship of Wanted Men* (1935), were lurid adventure melodramas ignored by many reviewers.

An exception was *The Sea Wolf* (1930), Milton Sills' last picture, a well-received version of the Jack London novel, remade ten years later with Edward G. Robinson—who also starred in *Tiger Shark* (1932) as an Ahab-like, one-armed Portuguese fisherman off the Pacific Coast, whose young wife (Zita Johann) loves another man (Richard Arlen). Trying to kill the lover, he is caught in a rope and flung overboard, but dies boasting that he's still the best fisherman—better even than St. Peter![2]

It should not be surprising that aviation, almost exactly contemporary with movies but growing and changing at an even swifter pace, should have received more attention than any other dangerous occupation. The dazzling possibilities of aerial photography, so well exploited in late silents like *Wings* and *Lilac Time* and early talkies like *Hell's Angels* and *The Dawn Patrol*, gave such films unique excitement.

Aside from the few films about women flyers and stewardesses, a few *Grand Hotel* types

set on planes, those about flying military men and air training academies and, of course, war films, the '30s saw at least forty others about commercial flying—more than triple the number made about any other professional milieu except the sea. Many would no doubt still be of documentary interest, if only because of the constant technical advances, so rapid that *Twenty Hours by Air,* to keep pace with reality, had to be retitled *Thirteen Hours by Air.*

This was, after all, the decade that saw the first scheduled coast-to-coast flights and by 1939 the first transatlantic clippers, so even to the vast majority of people who had never been up in a plane, flying was clearly the mode of the future, a fascinating new dimension which would one day affect everyone's life. This avid public interest was reflected in the number of serious aviation films which began to be made by major studios with top directors and stars.

One of the most prestigious was MGM's *Night Flight* (1933), with a cast to rival that of *Grand Hotel*: Helen Hayes, Clark Gable, both Barrymore brothers, Robert Montgomery, Myrna Loy and William Gargan. Set in South America (like so many '30s flying films), the story tells of the first night flights on that continent. (Before radar and other devices, any night flying was, of course, extra-hazardous.) John Barrymore was the martinet director of a company running air-mail service who orders the planes to take off regardless of the weather (especially one carrying serum). Hayes was the worried wife of pilot Gable, doomed when his plane is blown out to sea by an electric storm.

The *Times* was even more enthusiastic about Warners' *Ceiling Zero* (1936), directed by Howard Hawks, which, it said, "has taken what was essentially a brittle piece of good theatre and has converted it into a rugged and virile photoplay . . . in a very real sense, the record of a page torn from the swiftly moving history of aviation."

Pat O'Brien played the operations manager of an airport in Newark, out of which his war

[2] Lowe and McLaglen also starred, together and separately, in a number of ocean-going films, as salvage divers, stokers, merchant sailors and other able-bodied seamen.

buddies, Cagney and Stuart Erwin, work as pilots. Cagney's lighthearted attitude toward aviation indirectly causes Erwin's death. "The screen has presented no more effective episode of stark drama than that in which Erwin's plane . . . fights its way into the field, tears into high-tension wires and sears an agonizing path along the ground."

A few months later Warners followed this with *China Clipper* (1936), an unfaked, near-documentary account of Pan Am's first trans-pacific flight in November 1935 (from California to Macao, with five refueling stops). O'Brien was again the driving executive, with Bogart and Ross Alexander as his pilots. Nugent was especially delighted by the film's "refusal to describe the flying boat's journey in the stock terms of aerial melodrama . . ."

The new picture contains not a single crack-up . . . The giant plane makes its record hop without the menace of enemy sabotage, without even an attempt to filch the plans or bribe the pilot or designer into betraying its secrets. Still further, there is not the remotest hint that the flight had to be made to carry a precious serum to plague-ridden natives.

MGM returned to the skies with *Test Pilot* (1938), written by Frank Wead, who had also scripted *China Clipper,* and featuring three of its top stars, then at their height, Gable, Loy and Tracy. The *Times* termed it a "bang-up aviation drama," but overlong and repetitive and saved from tedium only by its exciting scenes in the air.

Loy played the classic case of the fear-ridden wife who, unable to adjust to her husband's constantly risking his life, can only drink with him and pretend she's not afraid. Tracy was his mechanic and best friend, with no hint of a triangle (unless one takes literally a line in which Gable asks Tracy, "Who do you love?" and Tracy answers, with only a faint smile, "You").

The only attempt at a cavalcade of aviation, from Kitty Hawk onward, was Paramount's *Men with Wings* (1938), directed by William Wellman, best remembered for his silent *Wings* (1927). "As a camera-wise director,

John Barrymore and Helen Hayes in **Night Flight**

with Technicolor at his disposal, he has created some stunning aerial shots," noted the *Times,* "but, as a dramatist, he has been unable to fuse these several excellencies into an effective unity." (Since Robert Carson, not Wellman, wrote the screenplay, surely he should have been the one blamed.)

As in *Ceiling Zero,* the conflict was between the stunt flyer (Fred MacMurray) and the scientific flyer (Ray Milland), the war-time flying ace versus the sober draftsman. Unfortunately, the director's sympathy seemed divided, Nugent thought. "It neither enkindles our grudging admiration for the reckless one, nor does it command our respect for the steady one . . . A dramatic history of aviation remains to be written for the screen."

The last big civilian air film of the decade, *Only Angels Have Wings* (1939), written

Clark Gable and Myrna Loy in **Test Pilot**

and directed by Hawks, boasted an attractive cast that included Cary Grant, Jean Arthur, Richard Barthelmess, Thomas Mitchell and Rita Hayworth (her first move into the big time after several years in "B's"). Like *Night Flight* (1933), *Storm over the Andes* (1935) and *Flight from Glory* (1937), it was set in South America, this time in the banana port of Barranca, in Ecuador, where Grant is the operating manager of a small air line which must maintain a regular schedule for six months to obtain the mail subsidy.

But romantic complications intrude. Arthur is a stranded show girl, Barthelmess an aging pilot with a serious blot on his record, Hayworth his discontented wife, once Grant's fiancée—approximately the same quadrangle as in *Red Dust* (1932), several Maisie films and numerous tropical dramas. Said the *Times*, "Mr. Hawks has staged his flying sequences brilliantly . . . But when you add it all up . . . it's a fairly good melodrama, nothing more."

Today, with international jet flights regularly scheduled by the thousands a week, patronized by millions a year and as casually taken for granted as railroad travel and ocean crossings once were, public curiosity about flight has gradually subsided. In recent years aviation has been largely confined to disaster films and nostalgic re-creations of the picturesque pioneer days, as in *Those Magnificent Young Men in Their Flying Machines* (1965), *The Blue Max* (1966), *The Gypsy Moths* (1969) and *The Great Waldo Pepper* (1975).

22

SPORTING BLOOD
Playing the Game

Wrong entertainment lowers the whole living conditions and moral ideals of a race. Note, for example, the healthy reactions to healthful sports, like baseball, golf; the unhealthy reactions to sports like cockfighting, bullfighting, bear baiting, etc. Note, too, the effect on ancient nations of gladiatorial combats, the obscene plays of Roman times, etc.
—The Motion Picture Production Code

Besides all the occupational heroes, another, smaller group of young men chose to defy danger and possible death less out of duty and dedication to their jobs than for the fun, thrills, glory and, of course, the big money that are at best the rewards of professional sports. Bearing out the evidence of the preceding chapter, the popularity of sports on screen was in precise ratio to their degree of danger.

The sole exception was bullfighting—to true *aficionados* like Hemingway a mystique, almost a religion, an honored way of life (or death), but to most other Americans of the '30s a sadistic blood sport—hence used only twice on screen. In *The Kid from Spain* (1932) the comedy climax was a Mexican *corrida* in which Eddie Cantor had to face a particularly vicious bull.

The only other American film that attempted to take the bull by the horns left everyone concerned badly gored. This was *The Trumpet Blows* (1934), in which Adolphe Menjou and George Raft were two Mexican brothers, the older a retired bandit. The younger upsets all plans by not only aspiring to the bull ring but inadvertently falling in love with his brother's fiancée (Frances Drake), but in the end both prove their courage and brotherly love. Thus the first talkie to do serious justice to a matador's career was Mamoulian's colorful *Blood and Sand* (1941).

On the other hand, certain sports, no matter how skillfully played, fast-moving and enjoyable to millions, are simply not hazardous enough for excitement on screen. Just as no one made perils-of-the-job films about mailmen or accountants, no one paid any cinematic attention to basketball, golf, tennis or even polo (except for atmosphere-establishing shots of millionaire playboys).[1] Football was seen only in college and service academy films. Surprisingly, though professional hockey was by no means as popular as in later decades, three routine films made use of it: *King of Hockey* (1936), *The Game That Kills* (1937) and *Idol of the Crowd* (1937), the last starring John Wayne.

Wrestling was scarcely more popular. *Sit Tight* (1931) was a foolish farce about a contender for the wrestling championship of the world, at the climax of which Joe E. Brown was forced to enter the ring against an enraged, masked opponent. In *Flesh* (1932), directed by John Ford, Wallace Beery played a German beer-garden waiter turned champion wrestler who murders his wife's lover, but this was really a marital triangle drama.

Released a week later, *The Sport Parade* (1932) saw Joel McCrea as a sports writer, a Dartmouth graduate who ends up winning a wrestling championship. This must have been the film the *Times* reviewer had in mind a few weeks later in praising *Deception* (1933) for "substituting Nat Pendleton for the glittering romantic juvenile whose talents as a wrestler are limited to the excellence of his profile." Pendleton, who not only starred in but wrote *Deception*, had himself been an Olympic champion wrestler, but this did not prevent his falling into the usual clichés of athletic sagas: a crooked manager, a designing blonde and lessons learned the hard way.

The only really original film about wrestling was *Swing Your Lady* (1938), a hillbilly comedy in which an itinerant wrestler (Pendleton again) must go to the mat with his beloved (Louise Fazenda), a powerful lady blacksmith.

Considering the hordes of fans packing Yankee Stadium, Ebbets Field and every other ball park in the country to shout themselves hoarse cheering "all-time greats" then at their peak, long since enshrined in the Cooperstown Hall of Fame, it is truly surprising that the national pastime served as background for a scant half-dozen films.[2] Whether this was the result, or the cause, of the popular belief that baseball films were box-office poison, none was in any way distinguished.

Joe E. Brown starred in two baseball comedies, both based on stories by Ring Lardner. In *Elmer the Great* (1933) he was a "mulish braggart, a swaggerer, a gloater and an ignoramus," who nevertheless won the big game and got the girl. In *Alibi Ike* (1935) Brown played another corn-fed rookie, famous for his fantastic excuses, who makes good in the nick of time to win Olivia De Havilland (in her film debut). In *Swell Head* (1935) Wallace Ford played a more serious variation on the same theme as a boastful home run king who goes blind when hit by a ball, disappears, is found by a hero-worshiping boy (Dickie Moore) and eventually recovers his sight.

When Hollywood turned to vehicular races, it was, statistically speaking, a case of four if by land to one if by sea. That is, only four films, with almost interchangeable titles and plots, dealt with motorboat-racing: *Speed Madness* (1933), *Speed Demon* (1933), *Motor Madness* (1937) and *Mile a Minute Love* (1937), also known as *Crime Afloat*. However, no less than seventeen films were made about car races, mostly "B's," with stock footage of the Indianapolis 500 providing built-in excitement as sure-fire as the Kentucky Derby in horse-racing films. But not even the strong-

---

[1] *Polo Joe* (1936) was a Joe E. Brown farce about a horse-fearing hero forced to play the game.

[2] Two mysteries also used baseball backgrounds, *Death on the Diamond* (1934) and *Girls Can Play* (1937).

est stars could raise the general level of mediocrity.

Triteness had set in as early as Cagney's *The Crowd Roars* (1932), written and directed by Howard Hawks, in which the speed-demon hero is at first torn between true-blue Joan Blondell and his "reprehensible brunette" mistress (Ann Dvorak). When the true-blue one marries his younger brother (Eric Linden), bitter sibling rivalry causes a fatal crash, but Cagney eventually redeems himself. It was considered his weakest film thus far.

In *Red Hot Tires* (1935), remade from a silent, it was Lyle Talbot who, convicted of murder after a fatal accident on the track, escapes to South America, where under an assumed name he becomes a racing sensation, but returns for love of Mary Astor to win the big race at Daytona and clear his name. In *Speed* (1936) Jimmy Stewart played a test driver for a huge auto plant, bent on making the perfect carburetor while wooing Wendy Barrie away from Weldon Heyburn. Said the *Times*: "Essentially a minor motor opera . . ."

In 1939 Warners did another of its unacknowledged remakes; scarcely seven years after the original, *The Crowd Roars* became *Indianapolis Speedway,* with most of the characters' names retained. Pat O'Brien, so often cast as Cagney's rival, buddy or boss, now played his former role, with Ann Sheridan (then being publicized as the "Oomph Girl"), Gale Page and John Payne as the others in the romantic quadrangle, and Frank McHugh repeating his original role of Spud.

"Another of those racing melodramas which roll around as regularly as the Indianapolis classic itself, and usually manage to whip up about the same excitement," said Nugent of the *Times,* but then devoted most of his review to O'Brien's cigar. "What the profile is to John Barrymore, an enigmatic smile to Marlene Dietrich, a broad New England 'a' to Katharine Hepburn, that's the beginning of a cigar to Mr. O'B."

The only car-racing picture of the whole decade to break the formula did it, like *Death on the Diamond* (1934), by turning to mystery. This was MGM's *Burn 'Em Up O'Connor* (1939), which was expertly packaged by an experienced director and writers to further Dennis O'Keefe's then budding career.

The drivers of one owner's cars seem jinxed by crash after fatal crash, with the hero slated to be next. In the climax he must drive the big race while temporarily blinded, guided by whistled signals as to when to turn for curves, etc. A crooked doctor (Charles Grapewin), who blames the cars' owner (Harry Carey) for having caused his son's death, drugged the drivers' drinks, making them go blind during the race.

But if there was one form of racing that outdid all others in popularity, it was, of course, the sport of kings (more than fifty examples from the '30s place it second only to boxing), which very early developed a whole repertory of plot formulae all its own. One was the discredited jockey who must clear his name, but the recurrent favorite was the one about the hopeless dark horse, the unpromising colt or the one injured by accident who is in danger of being shot, until nursed back to health by a kindly old trainer, a comic black stableboy and a determined child or adolescent light enough to ride as jockey in the climactic race (the ultimate example being *National Velvet,* 1944). In such films the real protagonist was the noble thoroughbred itself.

This was the inspiration for a mythical film outlined in Thomas Meehan's amusing satirical piece, *Add Hot Water, Serves Fourteen Million,* in which he suggests how entire old movies can be instantly reconstructed from a single quintessential snatch of dialogue, and then proceeds to invent several from typical genres of 1938, starting with one to be called *Kentucky Sunshine:*

"A freckle-faced eleven-year-old tomboy named Cindy (Marcia Mae Jones) is looking pleadingly up into the moist blue eyes of an old white-haired Southern gent (Walter Brennan)." She asks: "They won't have to shoot Firefly, will they, Gramps?"

The first notable racing film of the '30s was a kind of adult *Black Beauty, Sporting Blood* (1931), which gave Gable one of his few sympathetic roles in the eleven films he made that year. The principals were subordinated to the Blue Ribbon winner, Tommy Boy, whose rise and fall are traced through a series of owners, from millionaire sportsman to crooked gambler.

Racetrack (1933) offered a slightly different twist; gambler Leo Carrillo befriends a runaway boy (Junior Coughlin) and trains him as a jockey, but then at the request of his mother has him ruled off the turf—thus avoiding the obligatory climactic race.

The success of *Lady for a Day* (1933) and *Little Miss Marker* (1934), both of which involved small-time bookies and horse players, led to numerous other Damon Runyon adaptations including *The Lemon Drop Kid* (1934). Lee Tracy played a "horse medium" who knew what horses were going to do before they did, but the story veered toward *Liliom* when, trying to go straight for the sake of his small-town wife, he turns to robbery to get medical help for her.

Far better received was Capra's *Broadway Bill* (1934), adapted by Robert Riskin from a story by Mark Hellinger. A horse fancier (Warner Baxter), unhappily married to a chilly society beauty (Helen Vinson), risks all on the care and training of the horse of the title, encouraged by the sympathetic Myrna Loy. The *Times* found it "a sly and impertinent screen comedy, painlessly whimsical and completely engaging."

Two of Will Rogers' most popular vehicles also involved horse-racing: *David Harum* (1934), about a trotter that could perform only to the music of "Ta-ra-ra boom-der-e," and his last film, *In Old Kentucky* (1935), from an 1895 melodrama filmed twice before. Even more directly nostalgic was *The Gentleman from Louisiana* (1936), an elaborate Republic production based on the career of Tod Sloan, a real jockey of the 1900s whose temporary disgrace had also inspired George M. Cohan's 1905 musical *Little Johnny Jones*.

John L. Sullivan, Steve Brodie and other turn-of-the-century celebrities were introduced in cameo bits; in fact, it's Diamond Jim Brady himself (Charles Wilson) who buys a horse for Tod (Eddie Quillan) and gets him reinstated.

Strictly routine was *Saratoga* (1937), remembered, if at all, because Jean Harlow died while making it and some of her scenes had to be completed by her stand-in. She played the granddaughter of an old horse breeder (Lionel Barrymore), engaged to Walter Pidgeon, but quick to fall for a noble bookie (Gable), who makes sure the right horse wins in a photo finish.

A juvenile version of the same kind of story was *Thoroughbreds Don't Cry* (1937), in which Ronald Sinclair, in a role meant for Freddie Bartholomew, was a plucky English lad who comes to America with his grandfather (C. Aubrey Smith) to race their horse. When it's disqualified by a crooked jockey (Mickey Rooney), the old man dies of disappointment, but the boy, befriended by a girl his age (Judy Garland) and the repentant jockey, eventually rides his horse to victory.

Rooney stole the picture so completely that he was soon cast in *Stablemates* (1938), a race-track parallel to *The Champ* (1931), with Wallace Beery as a discredited veterinarian sunk far in drink until taken in hand and redeemed by a spunky orphan boy. Still another *Champ* variation was *King of the Turf* (1939), in which Adolphe Menjou played a drunken derelict at Saratoga befriended by a stableboy (Roger Daniel). Together they acquire a horse, and the boy turns out to be not only a prize jockey but Menjou's own son. However, ex-wife Dolores Costello, now married to Walter Abel, persuades Menjou to get drunk and urge the boy to throw the big race, thus disillusioning him in the track and driving him back to school. (This last twist may well have been borrowed from the climax of a hit of the previous year, *Angels with Dirty Faces*.)

The biggest horse-racing film of the late '30s, however, the only one in color, was 20th

Century-Fox's gift to the nation for Christmas 1938, *Kentucky*. With a prologue set during the Civil War, establishing one of those everlasting family feuds, this sounds like a remake of *In Old Kentucky* (1935), but it was only a reworking of the same familiar elements.

As the scion of one feuding family, Richard Greene, for love of Loretta Young, daughter of the other, conceals his identity to work as a trainer for her one-horse stable. Summed up one critic:

Its time-tested ingredients include the feud motive, the foreclosure of the old plantation, the two-year-old that promises to recoup the family fortunes, the climactic Derby in which he romps home by a length, and a happy ending pleasantly mixed with pathos for old Uncle Walter Brennan, the best judge of hoss-flesh in Kentucky, who just couldn't stand the excitement.

Still, by far the most popular spectator sport with film-goers, the one that was to all others as aviation was to other dangerous jobs, was prize-fighting, which provided the plot of more than sixty '30s films—ten more than horse-racing and more than three times as many as the next nearest rival, car-racing. Some blended with other genres such as comic vehicles, farces, service films and mysteries, but the classic formula was the rise, fall and comeback of a boxer who lets success go to his

Loretta Young and Richard Greene in **Kentucky**

head, a change symbolized by his temporary desertion of his faithful manager and especially of his true-blue wife or sweetheart for some shallow society girl or gold digger.

To be sure, of all physical contact sports then popular, professional fighting was by nature the most violent, the fastest-moving and the easiest to follow, but there may also have been a more Freudian reason for its constant use on screen. Aside from jungle and South Sea films, in what other kind could the hero spend so much of his time half naked? In a decade when scenes of near-undress were often "innocently" worked in—that is, without any direct sexual connection—just as backstage musicals included frequent "cheesecake" glimpses into the chorus girls' dressing room for the titillation of men in the audience, surely the "beefcake" scenes in gyms and locker rooms, with well-muscled athletes undressing, showering, or lounging about in strategically draped towels, must have added appeal for women who might otherwise have been bored by prize-fight films—a long-denied female taste that finally surfaced in the 1970s, with the *Cosmopolitan* centerfold boys, *Playgirl, Viva,* etc.

Oddly enough, the first boxing film to appear in 1930 was *Be Yourself,* Fannie Brice's first full-length talkie, in which the formula noted above was slightly varied by centering on the long-suffering girl friend of an ungrateful, alcoholic pug (Robert Armstrong). When he leaves her for the usual designing blonde, she avenges herself by urging his opponent to go for his recently altered nose, but, of course, all is forgiven.

Except for *The Champ,* which will be discussed with other films about father love, the only major-studio boxing film of 1931 was the relatively realistic *Iron Man,* directed by Tod Browning from a novel by W. R. Burnett. This time Armstrong was the trusty manager of Lew Ayres, a rising fighter saddled with a two-timing chorus girl wife (Jean Harlow) who manages to topple him from his championship. Oddly enough, no nice girl was waiting in the background to pick up the

pieces. Said the *Times:* "It is unfortunate that Jean Harlow, whose virtues as an actress are limited to her blonde beauty, has to carry a good share of the picture."[3]

1932 saw two examples of the standard formula released within a week of each other. In *Society Girl* it was James Dunn as a boxer who falls for the title character (Peggy Shannon) despite the opposition of his manager (Spencer Tracy). As a slight twist, he loses the big fight, but marries the rich girl and has hopes of a comeback. *Winner Take All* hewed even more closely to the stereotype. Cagney was an aggressive pug who loves a young widow (Marian Nixon) but falls under the spell of the usual blonde (Virginia Bruce), coming to his senses only just in time.

By 1934 the conventions had become so rigidly fixed that Andre Sennwald, reviewing *The Personality Kid* (in which Pat O'Brien, Glenda Farrell and Claire Dodd were the triangle), noted:

When the information gets out that a new film is a slugging drama of the ring you can be pretty sure that it deals with a good-natured leather-pusher who, coincident with his rise in the sporting world, abandons his faithful wife or sweetheart for a society girl, hits the skids and finally returns penitently to the little woman.

Meanwhile another Warners film, *The Life of Jimmy Dolan* (1933), had indeed broken this formula. A light heavyweight champion (Douglas Fairbanks, Jr.) accidentally kills a newspaperman at a party, then passes out, whereupon his crooked manager steals his girl, identification and money and is then burned to death in a car crash, giving the hero a chance to play dead and start a new life. Under the influence of a nice girl (Loretta Young) and a kindly woman (Aline MacMahon) devoting her life to orphans, he re-enters the prize ring under an assumed name to raise money for a health farm for the children. A persistent detective (Guy Kibbee) puts two and two together, but does he give

---

[3] *Iron Man* was remade in 1937 as *Some Blondes Are Dangerous.*

the truth away and take Jimmy back on a murder rap? No fan would have stood for it.

Much better received was *The Prizefighter and the Lady* (1933), in which Max Baer, then a contender for the world's heavyweight championship, made an extremely promising screen debut (which even included competent singing and dancing). The climactic bout, refereed by Jack Dempsey himself, was between Baer and champion Primo Carnera, playing himself. Myrna Loy, then MGM's all-purpose sophisticated leading lady, was a night club singer who gives up her wealthy protector (Otto Kruger) to marry Baer, leaves

Myrna Loy, Max Baer, and extras in **The Prizefighter and the Lady**

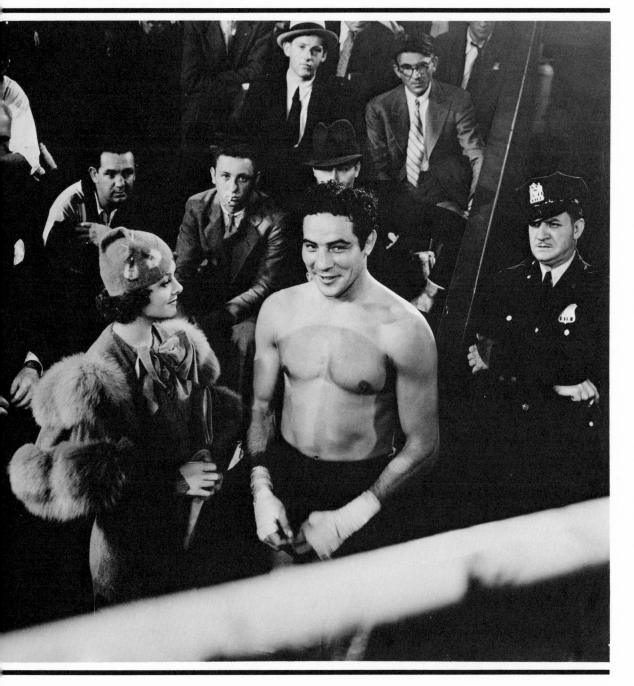

him when he strays, but comes through in the end. Walter Huston was the usual faithful manager.

A most bizarre melodrama was *Jealousy* (1934), in which a boxer (George Murphy) quarrels with his girl (Nancy Carroll) when she comes to his fight with another man (Donald Cook). He loses the fight, then in his dressing room knocks out and kills the other man. Sentenced to the chair, he asks to be "counted out" as in the ring, but wakes to find himself being counted out in the original fight and rises to KO the champ.

Passing over the numerous "B's" that came and went, as well as other films that involved boxing only incidentally (e.g., *The Irish in Us, Cain and Mabel*), the next one with an important star was *The Milky Way* (1936), adapted from a play into a hilarious vehicle for Harold Lloyd, supported by an excellent cast (Adolphe Menjou, Verree Teasdale, Helen Mack, Lionel Stander). Lloyd was a timid milkman who in a street brawl accidentally knocks out the middleweight champion (William Gargan), then is built up through a series of setups as a coming contender, for the sole purpose of letting the champ make mincemeat of him and regain his reputation.

A more credible variation on this idea was *Kid Galahad* (1937), in which the likable newcomer Wayne Morris in the title role was backed by a formidable Warners trio: Robinson, Davis and Bogart. This time the hero is a naïve bellboy who in self-defense knocks out an obnoxious champ and is built up by an unscrupulous manager (Robinson), whose girl friend (Davis) and sister (Jane Bryan) both fall for the clean-cut youngster. The only fault Nugent in the *Times* could find was that "the film ends with Miss Davis disappearing into the fog again just as she did in *Marked Woman*" (only a month before). In 1963 *Kid Galahad* was remade with Elvis Presley.

In *The Crowd Roars* (1938, no connection with Cagney's 1932 racing film of the same title), Robert Taylor continued to seek a more rugged image as the hard-boiled son of

a drunken ex-vaudevillian (Frank Morgan), who fights his way to the top, falling for a well-bred girl (Maureen O'Sullivan), who never suspects that *her* father (Edward Arnold) is a big, crooked gambler. "The story has a surprising amount of content and character for a picture involving Mr. Taylor," said the *Times*. (It was remade with Mickey Rooney as *Killer McCoy,* 1948.)

They Made Me a Criminal (1939) was a triumph of ingenious Warners packaging, "flatteringly assembled around Mr. John Garfield's ingratiating personality," as the *Times* put it. It was, in fact, a remake of *The Life of Jimmy Dolan,* with May Robson in the Aline MacMahon role, and the innocent orphans replaced by the Dead End Kids (who, the *Times* observed, were well on their way to becoming the Six Stooges), using their original *Dead End* names. Claude Rains was the almost relentless detective, Gloria Dickson the good girl and Ann Sheridan the bad one. Just as the combination of Sheridan and the Kids recalled one of 1938's biggest hits, *Angels with Dirty Faces,* so did the Garfield-Robson-Rains trio echo the equally successful *Four Daughters,* also 1938.

Even after Fred MacMurray had established himself as a light comedian, he was still called upon to enter the prize ring in *Invitation to Happiness* (1939), as a boxer who starts working toward the championship in 1928, so doggedly that he alienates his wife (Irene Dunne) and his son (Billy Cook). After an extraordinarily long build-up of ten years, he finally gets his crack at the title, and also, of course, wins back his family.

The most publicized fight film of 1939, however, was *Golden Boy,* directed by Rouben Mamoulian from Clifford Odets' much praised play, in which newcomer William Holden in the title role was backed by such stalwarts as Stanwyck, Menjou, Lee J. Cobb, Joseph Calleia and Sam Levene. The *Times* found it at its best when it cut loose from the play in "savagely eloquent" fight scenes possible only on screen.

The somewhat improbable dilemma of Joe

*Harry Carey, Humphrey Bogart, Bette Davis, Wayne Morris,
Edward G. Robinson in* Kid Galahad

Bonaparte, an Italian boy who must choose between becoming a concert violinist or a fighter, was faithfully retold, with the major exception of the denouement. Whereas Odets punished the unhappy hero and his manager's cynical mistress, whom he loves, with a fatal auto crash, the picture allows them a happy ending.

The unusual number of remakes suggests the limited number of variations possible in the boxing scene, yet the 1940s came up with a few originals. In *City for Conquest* (1940), made with typical Warners '30s vigor, the talents of Joe Bonaparte were somewhat more realistically divided between two brothers, Cagney, who boxes his way to fame but ends as a blind newsstand operator, and Arthur Kennedy, who, thanks to his brother's sacrifices, is educated to become a concert pianist and composer.

And who could forget *Body and Soul* (1947), *Champion* (1949) and *The Set-Up* (1949), all with downbeat endings, all exposing the seamier sides of the fight racket, as also did *The Harder They Fall* (1956)? Yet, though millions of fans continued to follow real prize fights, live or on TV, by the early 1970s the boxer as screen hero seemed as obsolete as the G-man or the Marine. Then came the extraordinary success of *Rocky* (1976) to

prove there was still a public for the underdog pug overcoming all odds. Despite the dead-on-target satire in *Movie Movie* (1978), 1979 brought not only *Rocky II* but two other expensive films with even bigger names: Barbra Streisand and Ryan O'Neal in *The Main Event,* Jon Voight and Faye Dunaway in a remake of *The Champ*—strong evidence that the fight film had not yet gone down for the final count.

23

STOP THE PRESS!
News Hawks and Sob Sisters

Among the most familiar secondary characters in the pictures about sports were the reporters who covered the events. Indeed, newspapermen figured in some way in almost every '30s genre set in modern times. But even aside from such incidental use, well over a hundred other films centered directly on newsmen's careers, making journalism by far the most popular occupation for '30s screen heroes, ahead even of medicine, which rated only seventy-odd films of its own. How to account for this extraordinary amount of attention? Pauline Kael offers one possible explanation: "In the silents, the heroes were often simpletons. In the talkies, the heroes were . . . smart and learned their way around. The new heroes of the screen were created in the image of their authors: they were fast-talking newspapermen."[1]

In *We're in the Money,* Andrew Bergman distinguishes two major character types in

newspaper films: "the slick scandal-crazed editor or publisher, and the cynical, puckish ace reporter or gossip columnist." (Reporters might be further subdivided into "cub," "ace," "star" and "demon," the latter three synonymous.) If they were indeed idealized images of the writers as they liked to remember themselves in their days as brash young news hawks back East, Kael suggests a more individual genesis for the hard-boiled editor: Walter Howey, city editor of the *Chicago Tribune* until lured away by Hearst to edit the *New York Mirror.*

At one time or another, just about all the Hollywood writers had worked for Walter Howey and/or spent their drinking hours with friends who had. He was the legend: the classic model of the amoral, irresponsible newsman who cares about nothing but scoops and circulation . . . A newspaper picture meant a contemporary picture in an American setting, usually a melodrama with crime and political corruption and suspense and comedy and romance. In 1931, a title like *Five Star Final* or *Scandal*

[1] *The Citizen Kane Book* (Bantam Books, 1974), pp. 26–27.

Sheet signalled the public that the movie would be a tough modern talkie, not a tearjerker with sound.[2]

Though Kael's observation is undoubtedly accurate, perhaps a further distinction should be made between cynical comedy-melodramas, all essentially variations on *The Front Page,* and another type, more seriously meant, attacking yellow journalism as a dire social evil, of which the prime example is *Five Star Final.*

If it seems incredible that a nation whose economy had collapsed could be so much concerned about such a relatively minor problem as an irresponsible press, it should be kept in mind that such films were actually reflecting the world of the '20s (*The Front Page* had opened on Broadway in 1928, *Five Star Final* in 1930), a decade that had seen tabloid sensationalism pushed to unparalleled depths of garish tastelessness. The well-named *New York Graphic,* with its "composographs," apparently showing photographs of real people in scandalous poses, outstripped even the *Mirror* and the *News.* Public suspicion grew that to boost circulation, unscrupulous publishers, editors and reporters did not hesitate to fabricate news and manufacture sensation where none existed. Just as the gold-digger comedies and backstage musicals revived an affluent Broadway already vanished, so did the newspaper films, however timely they seemed, actually recall the years when Americans could presumably imagine no more pressing problem than the excesses of a venal press.

That the newspaper film did indeed arrive with the complete acceptance of talkies by 1931 is confirmed by the fact that 1929, the year of transition, saw only two, *Gentlemen of the Press* and *Big News,* and 1930 only four, of which one (*Young Man of Manhattan*) was a variant or hybrid. Chronologically, the first such film of the decade was *Night Ride,* released in January 1930. Prophetically, it dealt—as also had *Big News*—with a reporter (Joseph Schildkraut) who exposes a powerful gangster (Edward G. Robinson in

his very first such role) and is consequently taken for a ride, but somehow manages to win out in the end. This might be taken as a foreshadowing of *The Front Page* type.

Night Ride was very soon overshadowed by *Roadhouse Nights,* scripted by the ever reliable Ben Hecht. "One cannot point to a single disappointing performance in this film nor to a scene that does not hold the attention," said the *Times,* with much praise for its grim realism. Charlie Ruggles played a Chicago reporter who in tracking down the murderer of a colleague finds that a suburban police chief (Fred Kohler) has been moonlighting as head of the bootlegging racket. In a situation borrowed from the play *Broadway,* Helen Morgan as a night club singer saves the reporter by killing the bootlegger.

On the other hand, the *Five Star Final* type, bent on a hanging indictment of corrupt journalism, was anticipated in *The Czar of Broadway,* released in June 1930. The *Times* critic complained about Hollywood's treatment of the press, quoting the heroine (Betty Compson), herself a night club hostess, who asks the reporter hero (John Harron): "Why did you have to pick such a rotten racket? . . . If you have to be a reporter, why can't you work on the society columns?"

His assignment is to get the goods on her gangster boss (John Wray), who, however, proves such a decent sort that he remains friendly with the hero even after learning the awful truth about his job. Before the exposé can be written, the gangster is mowed down by a rival and dies—after which the stricken reporter cannot possibly write the story. In fact, he tosses his "shield" on his managing editor's desk and announces that he is through, presumably about to seek some more honorable career (like his late friend's?).

In 1931 the number of newspaper films suddenly jumped to thirteen. Again anticipating *Five Star Final,* first to be released was *Scandal Sheet,* in which George Bancroft was the ruthless editor of a tabloid so compulsively determined to print all the news, no matter who's hurt, that when he discovers that his

[2] Ibid., p. 27.

wife (Kay Francis) loves a banker (Clive Brook), he murders the man—but then returns to the city room long enough to dictate the whole story before giving himself up. He is last seen in Sing Sing, busily editing a convict newspaper. According to Bergman, the story was roughly based on the case of Charles Chapin, onetime editor of the *New York Post,* who died in Sing Sing.

A month later came the first screen version of *The Front Page,* a faithful adaptation of Hecht and MacArthur's sardonic comedy, already recognized as the best of its kind—a judgment abundantly confirmed by time.

Breaking his long-established mold of suave sophistication, Adolphe Menjou made a superb Walter Burns (the character who is, according to Kael, the closest approximation of Walter Howey), Pat O'Brien as the reporter Hildy Johnson was fairly effective, and the long list of character roles was well cast, especially Edward Everett Horton as the hypochondriac Bensinger, George E. Stone as the pathetic condemned killer Earl Williams and Mae Clarke (what would early talkies have done without her?) as the tough-spoken streetwalker Molly Malloy, whose attempted suicide is a dramatic high point.

Six months later, *Five Star Final,* from Louis Weitzenhorn's play, made an equally

Clarence Wilson, Adolphe Menjou, unidentified player, Emma Dunn,
Pat O'Brien in The Front Page

strong impact in its own, very different way, as a serious, almost tragic, melodrama. As an editor constantly pressured by his publisher to boost circulation at all costs, Edward G. Robinson gave one of his strongest performances, his deepening revulsion revealed by his ever more compulsive hand-washing, as he drives a harmless middle-aged couple to suicide by raking up a twenty-year-old scandal in which the wife (Frances Starr) had been tried for murder.

In the climax, their daughter (Marian Marsh), whose engagement has been broken by the revelations, comes gunning for the editor, only to realize that nothing could punish him worse than his own conscience. Outstanding were Aline MacMahon as Robinson's secretary, quietly making her own moral judgments, and Boris Karloff (in one of his last pre-monster roles) as a slimy unfrocked minister paid by the paper to win the couple's confidence and obtain a damaging photo.[3]

Between these two films had come *Dance, Fools, Dance,* a mixed-genre melodrama in which a wealthy girl (Joan Crawford) in reduced circumstances goes to work for a newspaper where a friend, the star reporter (Cliff Edwards), is murdered by gangsters. Only when she is assigned to lure the gang leader (Gable) does she realize that her own weakling brother (William Bakewell) is mixed up in it. As the *Times* pointed out, "the story draws for its drama on two high spots in Chicago's recent crime history—the shooting of Jake Lingle and the celebrated St. Valentine's Day Massacre."

Released the same week, *The Finger Points* was also inspired by the career of Lingle, who, according to Frederick Lewis Allen in *Only Yesterday,* "led a double life as reporter for the Chicago *Tribune* and as associate of gangsters, and who was shot to death in a crowded subway." In this version Richard Barthelmess

Edward G. Robinson and Boris Karloff in Five Star Final

was a reporter earning $35 a week from his paper but charging as high as $100,000 to keep certain facts out of print. The *Times* found the newspaper background authentic and approved the ironic ending at the antihero's funeral, when another reporter says, "He was one fellow money couldn't touch," and headlines proclaim ENTIRE NATION MOURNS MARTYR. The review ends: "Clark Gable delivers another impressive characterization as a gangster."[4]

Other films in the same grimly accusing vein followed. In *Scandal for Sale* (1932) Charles Bickford was a ruthless editor who, in order to collect a money prize, sends his star reporter (Pat O'Brien) to his death in an attempted transatlantic flight, collects the money, but then leaves New York in disgust. *The Famous Ferguson Case* (1932) reminded

---

[3] Less than five years later, in 1936, it was remade, as *Two Against the World,* with Bogart in the Robinson role and a radio station substituted for the newspaper. Like most such remakes, it lacked the power of the original.

[4] *The Secret Six* (1931) also involved the gangland murder of a reporter on a subway.

the *Times* reviewer of the more sensational aspects of the Hall-Mills and Snyder-Gray cases, especially since the first name of the supposed lover of a murdered banker's widow is Judd (as in Gray). Unfounded but luridly headlined suspicions about Judd cause his wife a fatal heart attack.

The Crusader (1932), however, was vehemently denounced by the *Times*. "The inaccuracies that fill the new picture . . . make a disinterested spectator doubt that anybody connected with the production had ever seen the inside of a newspaper office." A reporter (Ned Sparks) feuding with a reforming D.A. (H. B. Warner) discovers that both the D.A.'s wife and his sister have apparently shady secrets, but right triumphs in the end.

Descending still further into "B" pictures, in *The Honor of the Press* (1932) the owner of a newspaper is also the head of a criminal gang until exposed by a cub reporter (Eddie Nugent). In *Behind Jury Doors* (1933) a reporter (William Collier, Jr.) helps a girl (Helen Chandler) clear her father, convicted by a crooked D.A., only to find that his own editor was in on the frame-up, so he takes the story to a rival paper.

In *The Return of Jimmy Valentine* (1936) a circulation booster (Roger Pryor) offers a reward for uncovering the once notorious crook. An innocent girl (Charlotte Henry) unwittingly gives clues that lead to her own father, now a banker, but his best friend, now his chauffeur, says *he's* Jimmy Valentine, so the booster, for the girl's sake, lets it go at that.

In *Missing Girls* (1936), called by the *Times* "a well presented re-statement of the thesis that the rackets and politics are bedfellows in Gotham," Pryor played a reporter who, like the author, Martin Mooney, serves a contempt sentence for refusing to tell a grand jury all he knows. His fiancé (Muriel Evans) is kidnaped, but thanks to the jail grapevine the reporter, when freed, is able to lead the G-men to the hideout.

In *Headline Crasher* (1937) another unethical paper frames a senator's son with a gangster's moll and almost wrecks the father's career, until an honest reporter (Kane Richmond) exposes the truth. A few months later, Warners' *Back in Circulation* dealt with a paper called by the *Times* "the yellowest rag of 1937." Those veteran news hawks Pat O'Brien and Joan Blondell were the hard-boiled editor and the sob sister who between them rescue from the death house a young widow (Margaret Lindsay) wrongly convicted of murder.

Exclusive (1937), however, written and produced by former newspapermen, seemed to John T. McManus of the *Times* "gratifyingly authentic," tracing the competition between a respectable newspaper run by Charlie Ruggles and its muckraking rival. Ruggles' cub reporter daughter (Frances Farmer) willfully takes a high-paying job with the other paper, but in the end must be rescued from a killer by her father, who dies in harness advising her to "write it simply and clearly and keep the paragraphs short."

Meanwhile a special journalistic type often filmed in the early '30s, when Walter Winchell's syndicated column and weekly broadcasts were making his name a household word, was the all-powerful Broadway gossip columnist. Winchell obviously inspired at least five films during 1931 and 1932, three of which were actually titled with phrases coined by him. They ran the gamut from lurid melodrama to wisecracking comedy, but generally remained closer to *The Front Page* than to *Five Star Final*.

In the first, *X Marks the Spot* (1931), a ruthless editor (Lew Cody) and an unscrupulous columnist (Wallace Ford) work hand in glove from a small-town paper to positions of power in New York in what the *Times* called a "spectacular melange of libelous journalism, omniscient newspapermen, cheap gunmen and publicity-mad showgirls," climaxing with a condemned murderer loose in a courtroom.

Is My Face Red? (1932)—a Winchellism to cover retractions—cast Ricardo Cortez as another such columnist, a "vain, unscrupulous fellow with a faculty for raking up petty scandal and a cold disregard for the ethics of his profession." The non-hero makes the mistake of announcing a gangland murder before the police have found the body and is himself almost killed in turn. Released in New York the same day, *Love Is a Racket* (1932) was "a hustling comedy of life among the Broadway chroniclers." This time Douglas Fairbanks, Jr., was the gossipmonger, in love with an actress (Frances Dee) for whom he risks his life, only to lose her to a producer.

Lee Tracy, who had played a secondary role in *Love Is a Racket,* came into his own with *Blessed Event* (1932) —Winchell's euphemism for an expected birth—which remains one of the definitive newspaper comedies. Mary Brian and Emma Dunn played much the same straight roles as in *The Front Page,* as innocent bystanders caught up in the journalistic frenzy, Ruth Donnelly was the standard wisecracking secretary, and Dick Powell, in his first noticeable role, played an obnoxious crooner given to singing "Too Many Tears." Tracy, with a machine-gun verbal pace that exceeded even Cagney's, launched himself successfully on a series of such roles—perhaps too successfully, for he was seldom afterward permitted to play anything but fast-talking newspapermen, press agents or ambulance-chasing lawyers.

Says William K. Everson, who has shown *Blessed Event* twice during the past ten years:

One of the best, yet least-known of all the high-pressure, irreverent comedies of the early '30's, it is basically a pungent satire on Walter Winchell. But in the best nothing-sacred traditions of the day, it also launches its lampoon ammunition against commercial radio, crooners and newscasters, mothers and racial, religious and sexual minority groups . . . Dick Powell . . . sings a marvelous parody of radio commercials, "Ten Little Fingers May Do As They Choose, But Ten Little Toes Need Shapiro Shoes."

A week later, *Okay America* (1932) —Winchell's weekly radio greeting—brought an end to this cycle, attempting a more serious tone in its tale of a columnist (Lew Ayres, miscast), who, after saving the kidnaped daughter

of a cabinet member, is murdered during his broadcast by the racketeer he has double-crossed (Edward Arnold). *Okay America* was remade in 1939 as *Risky Business.*

But the gossip columnist did not altogether vanish from the screen. Alice Brady in *Mind Your Own Business* (1936) and Richard Arlen in *Missing Daughters* (1939) were variants, and later years saw such malicious journalistic powers as Hedda Hopper in *The Women* (1939), Allyn Joslyn in *I Wake Up Screaming* (1941), Clifton Webb in *Laura* (1944), George Sanders in *All About Eve* (1950) and, most impressively, Burt Lancaster in Clifford Odets' powerful *Sweet Smell of Success* (1955), generally considered the most devastating portrait of Winchell.

Other specialized newspaper assignments were by no means as numerous or as prominent. Distinctly one-of-a-kind was *I Cover the Waterfront* (1933), based on Max Miller's grim book about the San Diego waterfront, but limited to the story of a sinister fisherman (Ernest Torrence), who smuggles Chinese into the country and does not hesitate to drop them overboard when the Coast Guard approaches. Claudette Colbert was his innocent daughter, cultivated by reporter Ben Lyon in his efforts to uncover the truth. Said *The New Yorker* about a 1970s revival: ". . . commonplace romantic melodrama . . . but the background is far from commonplace . . . There are several memorable . . . moments [such] as the heroine's passing the time of day with the madam of a brothel while waiting to take her boozed-up father home."

Despite the aura of international glamour surrounding such then famous foreign correspondents as Vincent Sheean, Walter Duranty, William Shirer and Quincy Howe, the only '30s film about their much-publicized branch of journalism was *Clear All Wires* (1933), adapted by the Spewacks from their stage farce, in which fast-talking Lee Tracy was the head of the foreign bureau of a Chicago paper, posted to Moscow, who constantly outscoops the *New York Times.* James Stewart in *Next Time We Love* (1936),

Gable and Franchot Tone in *Love on the Run* (1936) and Melvyn Douglas in *That Certain Age* (1938) were also foreign correspondents, but the plots did not concern their careers. The dramatic possibilities of such a role were not realized until Hitchcock's *Foreign Correspondent* (1940).

Advice to the Lovelorn (1933), "suggested by" Nathanael West's novel *Miss Lonelyhearts,* also starred Lee Tracy, and though the comedy phases succeeded, the picture fell apart when it attempted drama. A few weeks later, Paul Muni's *Hi Nellie* (1934), based on an identical idea—a newspaperman assigned as punishment to write an advice column under a female pseudonym—turned out much better. In this case a managing editor who apparently guessed wrong about a murder and caused a libel suit is demoted, and, of course, makes the heartthrob column a great success until he can prove his original hunch about the murder was right.

In addition to *Young Man of Manhattan* and *The Sport Parade,* sports writers appeared only in *The Pay Off* (1935), in which James Dunn is led by his worthless wife (Claire Dodd) to become the pawn for a crooked promoter, *Panic on the Air* (1936), in which Lew Ayres was a sports announcer investigating a gang fixing baseball games, and *Woman Wise* (1937), in which Michael Whalen collects a percentage from shady fight promoters, but only to expose them.

Small wonder, then, that in reviewing *Exclusive* in 1937, McManus of the *Times* voiced this overdue complaint:

The working newspaperman has been under considerable strain in the last few years trying to live up to, or live down, the Hollywood conception of the journeyman reporter. He has been represented by the Gables, the Powers et al. as a matinee idol with an heiress waiting outside while he bats out his invariable news beat for page one; by the McHughs and the Ruggleses as a diffuse individual with an overpowering failing for spirituous liquors and by the Lee Tracy school as a madly paced go-getter with no regard at all for the libel laws or for any other laws.

Yet later in that same year came the most original newspaper comedy of the second half of the decade, one whose astringent cynicism and frequent gallows humor remain fresh after more than four decades, the aptly titled *Nothing Sacred.* Unique if for no other reason than that it involved neither sob sister nor heiress, columnist nor gangster, this '30s classic centers, rather, on a small-town girl (Carole Lombard) supposedly doomed to die within a few weeks, but meanwhile promoted by a New York reporter (Frederic March)

***Carole Lombard and Fredric March** in* **Nothing Sacred**

into a national martyr-heroine, a kind of combined Amelia Earhart and Floyd Collins. When it turns out that she's not dying, after all, what can the vested interests do but go through with their elaborately orchestrated state funeral and a magnificent memorial, while she changes her name and drops out of sight?[5]

Once again Ben Hecht cast a jaundiced eye on his old editor, Walter Howey, this time under the fitting name of Stone, played by a dyspeptic Walter Connolly and described by March as "a cross between a Ferris wheel and a werewolf."

With so much attention devoted to newspaper*men*, it must not be supposed that women reporters—usually referred to as "sob sisters" —were overlooked. Though Carole Lombard in *Big News* (1929) seems to have played the first working newspaperwoman in talkies, Joan Crawford in *Dance, Fools, Dance* (1931) was the first whose job is an integral part of the plot. She was soon joined by Linda Watkins in a film actually called *Sob Sister* (1931), which was warmly praised for the authenticity of its newspaper scenes. Watkins and James Dunn were rival reporters—the first of many such couples, constantly scooping each other before admitting they're in love. 1931 also saw *Platinum Blonde*, in which Loretta Young was no more convincing as a reporter than Harlow was as a society girl.

Though girl reporters were never, to be sure, as popular as courtesans, Cinderellas or heiresses, among heroines who worked at all they ran second only to entertainers (including singers and dancers), figuring prominently in more than forty films of the '30s. Eight Torchy Blane films (1937–39) made Glenda Farrell the undisputed champion sob sister. (She was also a reporter in *The Mystery of the Wax Museum*, 1933, and a news magazine photographer in *Exposed*, 1938.)

Others who played similar roles more than once were Mae Clarke (*The First Edition,*

The Daring Young Man, Hats Off*), Joan Blondell (*The Famous Ferguson Case, Back in Circulation, Off the Record*), Claire Trevor (*Hold That Girl, Human Cargo, One Mile from Heaven*), Joan Bennett (*Big Brown Eyes, Wedding Present*) and especially Rosalind Russell (*Four's a Crowd* and *His Girl Friday*).

In *Four's a Crowd* (1938), the other three were Errol Flynn, Olivia De Havilland and Patric Knowles. In a typical '30s opening, the personable quartet are seen in full evening dress, gaily strolling along a New York street. This is a generally amusing farce made up of many familiar ingredients. As an ace reporter, daughter of a reporter, Russell with her quick speech and tailored suits clearly foreshadows her better-known role in *His Girl Friday* (1940). In fact, this is the first of those brisk career women who in the '40s became her trademark, and eventually her bane.

Aptly named Patterson Buckley, Knowles is the "ghost publisher" of a New York daily, engaged (just as in *It's Love I'm After*) to De Havilland as a bird-brained heiress, granddaughter of a crusty tycoon (Walter Connolly), who collects miniature trains and glories in being known as the most hated man in America. Fired as the editor of Knowles' paper, Flynn opens a public relations firm whose main project is to rehabilitate the image of the unpopular millionaire, whether he wants it or not. To accomplish this, Flynn must romance the granddaughter, with ensuing four-sided complications leading up to one of those weddings interrupted at the last minute so that the right couples can be paired off, Russell with Flynn, De Havilland with Knowles.

Surely Russell's deft handling of her role must have led to her casting as the screen's definitive newspaperwoman in the film that topped off the whole cycle, *His Girl Friday,* released in January 1940, obviously completed in 1939. What could be more fitting than that the '30s should begin and end with two different versions, both still admired, of the most enduring newspaper play of all, *The*

[5] *Nothing Sacred* became a Broadway musical, *Hazel Flagg,* in 1951 and a Jerry Lewis film, *Living It Up,* in 1954.

Cary Grant and Rosalind Russell in His Girl Friday

Front Page? This Charles Lederer adaptation is, of course, the one in which Hildy Johnson, name unchanged, is a top woman reporter, recently divorced from Walter Burns (Cary Grant), whose motivation is thus doubled—

not only to retain the valued employee but to regain the desired ex-wife.

In the preface to her *Citizen Kane Book*, Pauline Kael amiably discounts Howard Hawks' anecdote about how he accidentally discovered that Hildy's lines work even better for a girl.

After the surprise success of *It Happened One Night*—the new independent, wise-cracking girl was very popular, especially in a whole cycle of newspaper pictures with rival girl and boy reporters . . . Everybody had already been stealing from and unofficially adapting *The Front Page* in the "wacky" romantic newspaper comedies, and one of these re-writes, *Wedding Present* in 1936 (by Adela Rogers St. Johns' then son-in-law, Paul Gallico), had tough editor (Cary Grant) and smart girl reporter (Joan Bennett) with square fiance (Conrad Nagel). This was the mold that *The Front Page* was then squeezed into to become *His Girl Friday,* with Cary Grant, Rosalind Russell and Ralph Bellamy (already a favorite square from *The Awful Truth*) in the same roles, and Rosalind Russell was so obviously playing Adela Rogers St. Johns that she was dressed in an imitation of the St. John girl-reporter striped suit.[6]

Evidently Kael had never seen or had forgotten *Four's a Crowd.* Whoever first had the inspiration to change Hildebrand to Hildegarde, the result was a brilliant success, crackling with dialogue at the fastest pace ever

[6] Kael, op. cit., p. 61.

heard on the screen. Whenever the film is revived, *The New Yorker*'s recurrent comment is: "A hectic re-make . . . directed by Howard Hawks with a kind of terrific verbal slam-bang that has vanished from current film-making."

Though Molly Haskell in *From Reverence to Rape* points out that the title is ironic, since Hildy, far from a Girl Friday, is a star reporter whose services are clearly indispensable to the paper, she devotes two pages of enthusiastic analysis to the film, hailing Hildy as the truly fulfilled career woman, who yet had not sacrificed her femininity.

Later decades produced a number of newspaper films, even some good ones, but, as with most other genres, the '30s verve and exuberance had faded. Billy Wilder's 1974 remake of *The Front Page,* though done in proper '20s period, seemed heavy-handed, with Walter Matthau and Jack Lemmon looking years too old and jaded for Burns and Hildy. The best newspaper picture of the '70s was as far as possible removed from the breezy, wise-cracking melodramas of the '30s; it was Warner Brothers' sober, underplayed, quasi-documentary *All the President's Men.*

24

"SCALPEL! FORCEPS!"
Men—and Women—in White

The following subjects must be treated within the careful limits of good taste: . . . Surgical operations.
        —The Motion Picture Production Code

Except to perform necessary functions at

births, deaths and scenes of sickness or injury, doctors were not particularly popular as characters in nineteenth-century fiction—certainly not as heroic figures. The dull Charles Bovary might as well be a plumber, and Lydgate, though likable enough, is hardly the center of interest in *Middlemarch*. With the exception of Holmes' Dr. Watson, most medical men tend to be either mere ciphers (e.g., Allan Woodcourt in *Bleak House*), madly experimental scientists (Dr. Frankenstein, Dr. Jekyll, Dr. Moreau) or caricatures (all those in Shaw's *The Doctor's Dilemma*).

Perhaps it was Sinclair Lewis, the son and brother of doctors, who did most to humanize the profession, first in his sympathetic portrayal of Will Kennicott and his colleagues in *Main Street* (1920), but especially in his best-selling *Arrowsmith* (1925), with its medical details authenticated by Paul de Kruif. By the end of the '20s both novels about doctors (e.g., *Sorrell and Son*) and non-fiction books (de Kruif's *Microbe Hunters*) were selling well.

As in so many other areas, the screen lagged a decade behind. True, Monte Blue in Lubitsch's *The Marriage Circle* (1924) played a doctor, but the film deals with his marital misadventures, not his profession—a subject in which silent films showed little interest, except, as here, to lend the hero a touch of class. Early talkies followed suit, until *Doctors' Wives* (1931), based on a popular "problem" novel professing to probe the special difficulties of the ladies mentioned in the title.

A doctor's daughter (Joan Bennett), though warned by her embittered mother never to marry into the profession, nevertheless weds a busy surgeon (Warner Baxter), only to become so jealous of his designing female patients that she leaves him for a scientist (Victor Varconi). When the husband saves the lover's life by a successful operation, the wife returns, resigned to the demands of his practice.

Almost at the end of 1931 came the first serious picture centered on a doctor's career, *Arrowsmith* itself, a prestigious Goldwyn production, adapted by Sidney Howard, directed by John Ford, with Ronald Colman in the title role and Helen Hayes as his loyal wife, Leora. Said the *Times:* "It shines in its char-

acterizations and the sane fashion in which the story as a whole has been handled."

As faithful to the novel as was possible in a picture that ran less than two hours, it follows Martin Arrowsmith from a small-town practice to a research institute in New York to a West Indian island where he has the chance to test his serum against bubonic plague. Richard Bennett was the Swede Sondelius, DeWitt Jennings and Beulah Bondi were Leora's narrow-minded parents and Myrna Loy (listed fourteenth in the cast), just then emerging from Oriental servitude into Other Woman roles, played wealthy

Helen Hayes and Ronald Colman in Arrowsmith

Joyce Lanyon, who becomes Arrowsmith's second wife, after Leora's tragic death from a plague-infected cigarette.

Arrowsmith was the first film to raise what was soon to become the standard question in medical films: given the choice, should a young doctor take his Hippocratic oath literally and dedicate himself either to pure research or to an obscure slum clinic, or should he make hay while the sun shines with a lucrative practice (usually with a rich wife thrown in) ?

The next doctor film to pose this problem was Fannie Hurst's highly praised *Symphony of Six Million* (1932). One of the few early talkies to use a specific ethnic background, *Symphony* traces the climb of a gifted Jewish surgeon (Ricardo Cortez) from the Lower East Side to Park Avenue, always urged on by his ambitious parents (Gregory Ratoff and Anna Appel) and brother (Noel Madison). When in what the *Times* described as "one of the outstanding hospital episodes" all his skill fails to save his father's life, he renounces surgery to return to his old slum clinic. Only the plight of a crippled girl (Irene Dunne) who has all along served as his conscience compels him to operate and save her life.

In the totally misnamed *Once to Every Woman* (1934), the first of several A. J. Cronin (M.D.) novels to reach the screen, the conflict is purely professional, between an aging hospital head (Walter Connolly) and his brilliant young assistant (Ralph Bellamy) over the treatment of a patient in need of brain surgery—but too much time is wasted on the love of the head nurse (Fay Wray) for a medical ladies' man (Walter Byron).

A few months later, *Men in White* (1934) arrived, while the Sidney Kingsley play was still running at the Broadhurst—a play in every way superior to the film. Though the plight of a young doctor (Clark Gable) who seduces a nurse (Elizabeth Allan) while engaged to a wealthy girl (Myrna Loy, in much the same role as in *Arrowsmith,* only now billed second) is essentially unchanged, the role seemed too tailored to Gable as a matinee idol. Said *The New Yorker* more than forty years later: "Clark Gable seldom suggests the . . . brilliant young surgeon-hero . . . whose idealism over-rides any financial or romantic considerations."

Professional integrity versus quick money was by now as familiar a problem in young doctor films as in many other genres. *Society Doctor* (1935) dealt, none too convincingly, with an intern (Chester Morris) so disillusioned by the incompetence of his superiors that he is tempted to let a wealthy matron (Billie Burke) set him up in private practice. Disillusioned in her turn, his favorite nurse (Virginia Bruce) encourages another intern (Robert Taylor), but in the climax the hero, wounded by an escaping thug, directs his own operation by mirrors, and regains both his true ideals and the nurse.

Another MGM "B," *Between Two Women* (1937), from a story by Erich von Stroheim, found Virginia Bruce on the other side of the hospital charts as a wealthy appendectomy case who marries an idealistic young doctor (Franchot Tone), with by now predictable clashes of interest. Faithful nurse Maureen O'Sullivan suffers in silence, the more nobly because she is unhappily married to a ne'er-do-well.

When the socialite wife runs off with a less dedicated doctor (Leonard Penn), they are immediately punished by a train wreck, leaving them both injured, in the hands of the wronged husband. Does he do the right thing? Does the nurse's worthless husband get himself killed in time? As Everson observed in program notes for a showing of the film at the New School:

As a soap opera, it is clearly influenced by the '30s trend to make the idealistic doctor the stock Depression hero to take over from the now defunct and impractical aviator-explorer hero, who dominated the immediate post-Lindbergh era. From *Arrowsmith* in the early '30s, through the popular and much filmed works of Cronin and Lloyd Douglas, the dedicated (and fortunately medically non-explicit) doctor dominated the Hollywood scene of the '30s.

Noel Madison, Lita Chevret, Anna Appel, Ricardo Cortez, Irene Dunne,
Gregory Ratoff in **Symphony of Six Million**

A few months later, Virginia Bruce was back in uniform in still another medicated triangle, titled, frankly enough, *Wife, Doctor and Nurse* (1937), the other two sides being Warner Baxter as a harried doctor and Loretta Young as his frivolous wife. Done with a light touch, this film at least offered a novel solution: the wife and the nurse decide the doctor needs both of them—a decidedly unusual *ménage à trois* under the Production Code.

A young doctor's struggle and rise were given one more serious, perhaps definitive, treatment in the film chosen by the New York film critics as the best of 1938, A. J. Cronin's

The Citadel, one of MGM's first made-in-Britain productions, with a splendid cast: Robert Donat, Rosalind Russell (the only American), Ralph Richardson, Rex Harrison, Emlyn Williams. A kind of English analogue to *Arrowsmith,* it traces a young doctor from a selfless practice in a poor Welsh village to success as a fashionable specialist in Harley Street, then through the shock that brings him back to his earlier ideals. Said the *Times:* "A passionate affirmation of faith in the good physician, a passionate denunciation of the hypocritical, an appeal for broader medical service and a lesson in humility."

Though Everson's last-quoted statement

seems to link Cronin's novels with those of Lloyd Douglas, many critics and viewers who admired Cronin were totally repelled by Douglas' platitudinous, "uplifting" messages, starting with *Magnificent Obsession* (1935). This was the film that launched Robert Taylor's stardom, as a young wastrel whose recklessness costs the life of a distinguished brain specialist and the eyesight of his beautiful widow (Irene Dunne). Sobered and penitent, he decides to become a doctor, and within five years wins the Nobel Prize for his miracles of surgery!

The secret of his success (and the meaning of the title), as expounded by a mystical old stonecutter (Ralph Morgan), is to help others but keep your good deeds a secret (rewards as immediate and concrete as from inserting a coin in a vending machine!). With every step of the laborious plot leading toward the operation in which guess who restores the heroine's sight, this was a "woman's picture" in the worst sense. The anonymous *New Yorker* reviewer was never more precisely on target:

The woebegone trickeries of the material made the movie a four-handkerchief hit, and damned if Ross Hunter didn't produce another version in 1954 (with Jane Wyman and Rock Hudson), and the slop made money all over again. Irene Dunne spends a lot of time in the hospital and is at her most infuriatingly gallant and womanly.

Green Light (1937) dispensed more of Douglas' simplistic pseudo-philosophy, this time preached by Sir Cedric Hardwicke as a dean (Episcopalian?) whose optimism makes Dr. Pangloss look like a cynic. He advises all who are temporarily halted by life's red lights just to wait for the green. A young surgeon (Errol Flynn) takes the blame for an older colleague's fatal bungling, only to find himself discredited, outcast, scorned by the victim's daughter (Anita Louise)—until he decides to sacrifice his life by using himself as a guinea pig in testing a serum. Naturally, this turns on the green light, the serum succeeds, his name is cleared and he gets the girl.

Disputed Passage (1939), the last Douglas medical novel to reach the screen during the '30s, had still loftier aims—to "prove" the existence of the soul, or at least of Some Higher Power. Akim Tamiroff was the bearded medical cynic who in the end is forced to admit that science cannot solve everything. According to the *Times,* "the resolution of the drama," in which the cynic's mercy flight saves the life of a young idealist (John Howard), with the help of Dorothy Lamour, who supplies "the will to live," "strips it of its dignity, reduces it to the level of fortuitous melodrama."

Good, bad or indifferent, there was no denying the ever-increasing popularity of medical films. Whereas none at all had been made in 1930, only three in 1931 and five in 1932, the number rose to eight in 1934, and, including historical pictures like *The Story of Louis Pasteur* and *Yellow Jack,* stayed at that level for the rest of the decade. This, of course, does not even count those films in which the hero just happens to be a doctor (e.g., Leslie Howard in *Of Human Bondage,* Edward G. Robinson in *The Amazing Dr. Clitterhouse,* George Brent in *Dark Victory*), or those in which a doctor plays an important but secondary role (Dudley Digges in several tropical dramas, Thomas Mitchell in *The Hurricane* and *Stagecoach,* Donald Crisp in *Wuthering Heights* and *The Old Maid*). Significantly, though Sinclair Lewis' *Main Street* had been such a tremendous best seller that the title and its implications had since 1920 become part of the American language, in 1936 when it was filmed for the second time, even that obviously presold title was dropped in favor of what must have seemed one still more commercial: *I Married a Doctor.*

By the mid-'30s, series other than mysteries were beginning to appear, especially those involving likable characters with whom audiences could identify and whom they would enjoy seeing again. Considering the trend noted above, it was inevitable that sooner or later some film series would involve doctors.

Yet when *Internes Can't Take Money* (1937) was made, with Joel McCrea as young Dr. Jimmie Kildare, apparently no one at Paramount foresaw the future possibilities. In a self-contained story, Kildare with the aid of a grateful mobster (Lloyd Nolan) tracks down the long-missing child of a young widow (Stanwyck), and presumably ends up with her.

Not until MGM's *Young Dr. Kildare* (1938), with Lew Ayres in the title role, does crusty old Dr. Gillespie (Lionel Barrymore) first wheel his chair on the scene. Having by that time sat through so many of the doctor films mentioned above, Nugent in the *Times* found this one "happily free from the clichés of most of the men in white dramas." In fact, it defied one cliché: instead of joining his admirable father (Samuel S. Hinds) in a small-town practice, Kildare chooses to intern in a large city hospital, where he helps to cure a hysterical heiress.

By the second of the series, *Calling Dr. Kildare* (1939), along with Ayres and Barrymore, a number of others repeated their roles: Hinds and Emma Dunn as Kildare's parents, Lynne Carver as his small-town sweetheart, Nat Pendleton as the comic ambulance driver and Walter Kingsford as Dr. Carew. Three new faces were added to the continuing stock company: Laraine Day as nurse Mary Lamont, Alma Kruger as head nurse Molly Byrd and Marie Blake as the gabby switchboard operator. The *Times* called it "pleasingly entertaining" and dubbed it "the Hardy family of hospital pictures."

In *The Secret of Dr. Kildare* (1939), the young intern was still making only $20 a month, so could hardly propose to Mary, and Gillespie was still bullying everyone from his wheelchair, in a plot revolving around a girl's (Helen Gilbert) psychosomatic blindness. The *Times'* only quibble was that Gillespie seemed to be a specialist in everything, from research to pneumonia prevention to psychoanalysis.

Five more Kildare pictures were to follow

in the next two years, before Ayres, true to the pacifism of *All Quiet on the Western Front,* refused to fight in World War II (though he did perform medical service), thus temporarily derailing his career. But as all the world knows, young Dr. Kildare himself went marching on to TV immortality in the person of Richard Chamberlain.

Meanwhile, since the very beginning of the decade, all those sorely troubled young interns had not been alone in their battles for medical integrity. Almost as many films dealt with gray-haired, veteran practitioners who after a lifetime of humble service in country or city seem to have nothing to show for it.

The first of these was Ralph Morgan in *Humanity* (1933), laboring patiently in his Lower East Side office so that his motherless son (Alexander Kirkland) may complete his medical studies in Europe. But the son returns with a society girl (Irene Ware), who insists that he practice on Park Avenue. To get the money, he tends a fleeing rumrunner, the father takes the blame, loses his medical license and dies. Only then does the son repent and return to the East Side and the girl (Boots Mallory) who has been waiting all along. Evidently *Humanity* sought to combine the appeals of *Sorrell and Son* and *Symphony of Six Million*.

The same kind of selfless doctor, rural style, was paid further tribute in *One Man's Journey* (1933), from a short story called *Failure*. Like Morgan in *Humanity,* Lionel Barrymore played a widower with one son (Buster Phelps, growing up to be Joel McCrea), who follows in his medical footsteps. However, this father lives to be honored for his service, at a climactic dinner at which more eminent doctors pay tribute to his understanding of "the human heart."

This was followed within a month by *Dr. Bull* (1933), based on James Gould Cozzens' novel *The Last Adam,* directed by John Ford and starring Will Rogers as another small-town doctor. The victim of gossip about his visits to a widow (Vera Allen), he not only checks a typhoid epidemic but (more fortunate than Ibsen's Dr. Stockmann in *An Enemy of the People*) proves it was caused by pollution from the construction camp of the town's overbearing tycoon (Berton Churchill). (Oddly enough, Ralph Morgan appeared in this as an eminent specialist.)

The birth of the Dionne quintuplets in 1934, successfully tended by Dr. Allan Roy Dafoe, gave an immense public boost to the image of the country doctor. Inevitably, a story inspired by Dafoe, called, not surprisingly, *The Country Doctor* (1936), was filmed, with Jean Hersholt in the title role, typing him almost completely for the rest of his career. The *Times* found it "an irresistibly appealing brand of comedy and sentiment." John Qualen especially excelled as the flabbergasted father of the quints, who did not themselves appear until the final scene. As the plot would have it, their birth saves the doctor from being driven out of his practice and even ensures a new hospital.

The predictable follow-up, *Reunion* (later 1936), was based on the gimmick of a gathering of all the three thousand people brought into the world by Dr. John Luke (as the Dafoe character is called), who, said the *Times,* is "made out to be a combination of Paul Pry, Santa Claus and Mr. Fix-It" in solving all their assorted emotional problems. Though Qualen, Dorothy Peterson as the doctor's staunch nurse and Slim Summerville as a comic sheriff repeated their roles, the original ingenue and juvenile, still with the same fictional names, had unaccountably changed from June Lang and Michael Whalen to Rochelle Hudson and Robert Kent.

Almost as quick as Warners to retread used material, RKO in 1938, scarcely five years after *One Man's Journey,* offered a second version, *A Man to Remember*—one remake that was an improvement on the original. Directed by Garson Kanin from a script by Dalton Trumbo, it is called by Miller in *B Movies* "the B breakthrough"—that is, the first "B" to win spontaneous critical acclaim; indeed, it did so well across the country that in New York it opened at the Rivoli.

This version begins with the doctor's funeral, followed by the opening of his strongbox. Each memento, letter, unpaid bill or IOU leads to a flashback, until his whole unappreciated life is pieced together. No one seems to have noticed that this is the *only* '30s film other than *The Power and the Glory* (1933) to use this narrative structure, so much acclaimed a few years later in *Citizen Kane,* also from RKO. Edward Ellis' fine performance in the title role led to his casting in a less successful Barrymore remake, *Sweepings,* which became *Three Sons* but he failed to repeat his success.

In late 1939 the movie public was given three other venerable doctors to admire. When almost every variation on a genre had been worked, it was often given artificial respiration by crossbreeding with another equally popular type. Thus, in the tradition of Lincoln's doctor's dog, if old country doctors and convicts were both favorite screen heroes, why not send an old country doctor to prison? The result, Columbia's *Those High Gray Walls* (1939), was surprisingly good, full of "warmth, simplicity and freshness," said Nugent, as surprising as "a violet growing in the gravel of a jailyard." Walter Connolly played the small-town doctor sentenced for tending and shielding an outlaw whose family he knew. At first his humane philosophy is scorned by the cynical prison doctor (Onslow Stevens), but eventually his wisdom prevails.

Aptly enough, Jean Hersholt closed the "grand old man" phase of medical films of the '30s (and opened a new career for himself that would ultimately lead to TV) with *Meet Dr. Christian* (1939). "That all country doctors are sweet, heroic, self-sacrificing medical wizards who could have made a fortune in some metropolis if they had not chosen the Simpler Way is a part of the cinematic credo," observed Crisler in the *Times.* "He does his customary fine job of healing everybody and everything in sight except the plot."

But if the symbolically named Dr. Christian was the last of his kind to play the lead-ing role in a '30s film, there was a far more memorable, credible and admirable doctor. This was Dr. Meade (Harry Davenport), who figures prominently throughout *Gone With the Wind,* from the time he auctions off the ladies' dances at the bazaar until he warns Scarlett against any belated confessions at Melanie's deathbed. The unforgettable image of Dr. Meade struggling single-handedly to care for the thousands of Confederate wounded lying in the sun at the railroad sta-tion in Atlanta tells us more about medical heroism than all the patly contrived benefac-tions of Drs. Luke, Christian, Gillespie and company.

All these were main-stream doctors, of course, whose professional problems were relatively normal, even predictable. A num-ber of others faced more bizarre dilemmas. Some went to pieces in the tropics, as in *The Road to Singapore* (1931) and *The Man Called Back* (1932); one practiced hypnotism on his female patients for his own evil pur-poses (*The Love Captive,* 1934). Aside from the mad Dr. Moreau in *The Island of Lost Souls* (1933), at least one other practiced un-conventional plastic surgery. In *False Faces* (1932) Lowell Sherman played a medical charlatan much sought after by wealthy, ag-ing women for face lifts. Indicted for mal-practice, he is about to flee when killed by one of his victims.

Not even medicine was sacred to Warner Brothers. Just as they ruthlessly exposed crooked lawyers, politicians, columnists and tycoons, so in *Bedside* (1934), they offered Warren William as a veritable medical Elmer Gantry, a fake doctor with a publicity-in-flated reputation who realizes the seriousness of his offense only when he is unable to help his injured sweetheart (Jean Muir). It seems he was a medical student who gambled away his tuition but was given a diploma by a drug-crazed doctor (David Landau), who later threatens blackmail. As the *Times* said, "Its deviations from the formula are too wild-eyed to be classed as dramatic virtues." Sig-

nificantly, this was the only really bad doctor in the whole decade.

The subject of mercy killing, still a contro-versial issue in the 1980s, was gingerly ap-proached, if not explored, in *The Crime of Dr. Forbes* (1936), originally titled *The Mercy Killers.* A middle-aged scientist (J. Ed-ward Bromberg) whose young wife (Gloria Stuart) is in love with his protégé (Robert Kent), finding himself hopelessly injured in an accident, trapped in a cave, begs the younger man to end his suffering by an over-dose of opiate. This he apparently does and even confesses it to shield the widow from possible implication—but his lawyer proves that the victim actually committed suicide by saving and combining pellets from three dif-ferent doctors. "A straddle, of course," said the *Times,* "but a most entertaining one."

Ethical dilemmas of a different kind were faced by the characters in *The Man Who Lived Twice* (1936). A fugitive killer (Ralph Bellamy) ducks into a medical school auditorium, where he hears a doctor (Thurs-ton Hall) explain how brain surgery has re-formed the attitude of vicious dogs. He vol-unteers to serve as a human guinea pig in return for a new face, and emerges physically and mentally a new person, with no memory of his past. In ten years he is himself a noted medical scientist, until one of those Javert-like detectives tracks him down. Though con-victed of the offenses of his former self, he is pardoned, in what the *Times* termed "a di-verting, well photographed and nicely per-formed problem photo play."

Along with the hero of *Green Light,* those in *Grand Canary, Outcast, Dangerous In-trigue* and *Once a Doctor* were all wrongly discredited and had to practice under as-sumed names until they were cleared. And besides the son in *Humanity* and the surgeon in *The Man Who Lived Twice,* at least six other doctors, including those in *The Girl in 419, Emergency Call, Undercover Doctor, In-ternes Can't Take Money* and *Against the Law,* were involved, voluntarily or otherwise, with gangsters. Thus Paul Muni in *Dr. Soc-*

rates (1935) is kidnapped by thugs whom he finally outwits by injecting them with narcotics in the guise of scarlet fever shots.

Perhaps the most striking confrontation between the scientific and the criminal minds occurred in *Blind Alley* (1939), based on a stage melodrama, in which a vicious killer (Chester Morris) and his gang invade the summer home of an eminent psychoanalyst (Ralph Bellamy), who proceeds to root out the hidden cause of the gangster's recurrent nightmare—to the dismay of his moll (Ann Dvorak), an Oedipus complex. (This was remade in 1948 as *The Dark Past*, with William Holden and Lee J. Cobb.)

Considering the vogueishness of analysis among the well-to-do in the mid-'30s, as reflected, for instance, in the 1936 plays *End of Summer* and *The Women*, and a Rodgers and Hart lyric of that year, from *On Your Toes*, which lists psychoanalysts among the luxuries "too good for the average man," it is surprising that before *Blind Alley* only three '30s films had dealt with psychiatry at all, and of these one was the Astaire-Rogers musical *Carefree* (1938).

Amid all its scores of doctors, Hollywood paid even less attention to women in white than to lady lawyers—eight films in all, distributed among only five actresses. Surprisingly, three of them were played by the beautiful, mannequin-like Kay Francis, two by Ann Harding and one each by Claudette Colbert, Tala Birell and Frieda Inescort.

The first of these, *Mary Stevens MD* (1933), saw Francis as "a woman physician who has," said the *Times*, "a startling amount of trouble preserving a professional detachment toward the primitive emotions." Finding herself pregnant by a totally irresponsible fellow doctor (Lyle Talbot) who subsequently marries someone else, she flees to Paris, but the baby dies on the voyage home. Just as she is about to end it all by jumping out a window, her true love breaks in with the news that he has obtained a divorce, so can now make an honest woman of her. "One of the shabbiest of the Hollywood contemplations of

the medical profession," Sennwald observed.

Scarcely better was *Dr. Monica* (1934), adapted from a Polish play, with Francis as a famous obstetrician whose husband (Warren William) has a casual affair with her young friend (Jean Muir). Pregnant, the girl takes to drink, but even when she learns the truth the noble Dr. Monica remains friendly, presides at the birth and offers to give her husband up. The girl, however, returns him with thanks, and the selfish cad goes on as before. Self-evidently, neither of these plots had much to do with the heroine's professional life; Mary Stevens might just as easily have been a secretary and Monica a housewife.

Not counting *The White Angel* (1936), Francis' next venture into medicine was *King of the Underworld* (1939), an odd remake of *Dr. Socrates* with the sexes reversed, so that she played the Muni role, but received second billing to Bogart, replacing Ann Dvorak. This was so poor that one reviewer wondered whether Warners were deliberately sabotaging Francis' waning career.

Ann Harding, whose serene classical beauty made her especially convincing as a dignified professional woman, first played a doctor in *The Right to Romance* (1933), as Manhattan's most famous plastic surgeon. Though loved by a scientist (Nils Asther), she seeks escape in a California vacation, during which she re-encounters, and marries, a lively playboy (Robert Young), whose social butterfly habits soon clash with her quiet tastes. This was at least an honest switch on the dedicated husband-flighty wife situation of films like *Between Two Women*, and, as in those, the devoted professional colleague wins out in the end.

Harding set up practice again in *The Flame Within* (1935), as a psychiatrist who helps two troubled young people, a suicidal girl (Maureen O'Sullivan) and the charming, irresponsible alcoholic she loves (Louis Hayward in his screen debut). She straightens them out, only to find herself in love with the now reformed and married young man. As so often, Herbert Marshall was the patient suitor in the background. The implication, observed Nugent in the *Times,* was that "feminine psychiatrists may be terribly clever about resolving other people's riddles, but are pretty helpless when it comes to solving their own."

The Flame Within had the bad luck to follow by a few months a much more complex, absorbing drama of psychiatrists and their patients in a mental hospital, *Private Worlds* (1935), based on Phyllis Bottome's novel, about the clashes and reactions set off by the arrival of a new head doctor (Charles Boyer in his first important American role) and his predatory sister (Helen Vinson), whose brazen pursuit of a young doctor (Joel McCrea) drives his wife (Joan Bennett) insane. At the same time the head himself, who dislikes women doctors, at first resents and then falls in love with his able colleague (Claudette Colbert as the screen's first woman psychiatrist).

More than three decades later Everson paid it proper tribute:

One can recognize and applaud the original courage of a *Private Worlds* in 1935, when the Depression was calling for more and more escapism, and when the Production Code, at its height, was muzzling serious adult cinematic discussion . . . Despite occasional medical naïveté, *Private Worlds* holds up amazingly well; it is literate, well acted, unsensational. It makes far more sense, both emotionally and medically, than that curiously similar film of the '50s, *The Cobweb,* which, oddly enough, featured Charles Boyer in an almost identical role.

Except for Tala Birell in *The White Legion* (1936), a piece of period Americana, the only other woman doctor to appear on screen in the '30s was Frieda Inescort, in a forgotten "B" called, not very imaginatively, *Woman Doctor* (1939), which simply reversed the old cliché about the busy professional man and his neglected wife, sighing over the forgotten wedding anniversaries. Henry Wilcoxon was the fretful husband and Claire Dodd the other woman who almost gets him away before the doctor realizes that her marriage must come ahead of her career. (Forced

Charles Boyer and Claudette Colbert *in* **Private Worlds**

to make the same choice, male doctors, as in *Between Two Women,* invariably chose their careers.)

Nurses fared somewhat better. As humble handmaidens to doctors, they, after all, posed no threat to male supremacy; they were only performing the kind of ministering angel services that had always been expected even of untrained women. As noted above, they often figured sympathetically in doctor films, usually in wholesome contrast to the shallow society fiancée or wife, but they were also given several films of their own (not, of course, counting *Miss Pinkerton,* 1932, in which Joan Blondell was a sleuthing nurse, nor any of the films about Mignon G. Eberhart's Nurse Sarah Keating, all of which were mysteries).

Except for *War Nurse* (1930), covered under war films, the first professional nurse as heroine was Barbara Stanwyck in *Night Nurse* (1931), a rough-and-tumble, definitely pre-Code melodrama, in which a nurse on private duty finds the two children of a drunken divorcée (Charlotte Merriam) being systematically starved to death by a drug-addicted doctor (Ralf Harolde) who hopes to collect their trust fund—though the mother prefers her brutal chauffeur (Gable, billed eleventh, in one of his eleven 1931 roles). Only an honest bootlegger (Ben Lyon) helps the nurse save the children and has the chauffeur "taken care of." (The lip-curling scorn with which Stanwyck snarls, "All right, you *mother . . .*" probably gets a bigger laugh now than in 1931.)

More in the traditional pattern was *Registered Nurse* (1934), in which the heroine (Bebe Daniels) returns to her profession when her rich husband (Gordon Westcott) is knocked insane by a car crash. For a while she almost falls for lady-killer Lyle Talbot, playing much the same role as in *Mary Stevens MD,* but after the husband dies she ends up with the devoted chief surgeon (John Halliday—surely the only time he ever got the girl).

Dedicated "to the memory of the immortal Florence Nightingale," *The White Parade* (1934) was evidently meant to be the feminine equivalent of *Men in White,* tracing the probationary careers of a group of student nurses. Just as in the service academy films, some fall by the wayside, some must learn the hard way the true meaning of professional ideals, but the heroine (Loretta Young) proves the noblest of all. Even when offered marriage by rich Bostonian John Boles, she chooses nursing—the only film heroine on record to make such a choice. The *Times,* however, regarded the film as "altruistic . . . pious . . . flashy, glib and slightly opportunistic." Essentially, it was another variation on the multiple Cinderella pattern.

Except for Florence Nightingale herself in *The White Angel* (1936), and two added to *Yellow Jack* (1938), the nurse as heroine did not reappear until nearly four years later, and then only in routine "B" melodramas. In *Nurse from Brooklyn* (1938), Sally Eilers played the title character, whose kid brother (Maurice Murphy) is killed in a shoot-out

for which she blames a tough cop (Paul Kelly), until he proves the killer was really her boy friend (Larry Blake).

In *King of Alcatraz* (1938) Gail Patrick was a nurse who on shipboard must perform a critical operation guided only by wireless instructions from a surgeon on shore. Only a few weeks later the identical situation turned up again in *The Storm* (1938), with Nan Grey as the reluctant surgeon, but in neither film was the nurse the center of the plot. The luridly titled *Secrets of a Nurse* (1938) was actually more concerned with the troubles of a fighter (Dick Foran), temporarily blinded and later framed by the same crooks, ultimately exposed by big-time lawyer Edmund Lowe at the urging of the boxer's sweetheart (Helen Mack), who has known both men as patients.

Back in the multiple Cinderella pattern of *The White Parade, Four Girls in White* (1939) predictably traced the careers of four student nurses, Florence Rice, Una Merkel, Ann Rutherford and Mary Howard. Rice at first tries for surgeon Alan Marshal, ditches him for playboy Kent Taylor, but finally comes to her senses after heroic service in one of those catastrophic (and catalytic) train wrecks. By far the noblest nurse on screen in 1939 was Anna Neagle in *Nurse Edith Cavell.*

Thus the decade began and ended with films about nurses in World War I—but not until World War II did nurses as strong, heroic figures come fully into their own on screen, the true female equals of the GIs, Marines and sailors whose wounds they tended and whose dangers they shared, just as brave, dedicated and likely to get killed. In films like *Flare Path, So Proudly We Hail, Cry Havoc* and others, many top actresses did their bit for the war effort, either aiding, or, when necessary, taking the places of those selfless doctors whose image now became more sacrosanct than ever.

Throughout the next two decades, medical films of all kinds continued to flourish: biographies (*Dr. Ehrlich's Magic Bullet, The Story of Dr. Wassell*), the usual fiction (*Not* as a Stranger, the remade *Magnificent Obsession*), even the one about the dedicated old inner-city doctor (*The Last Angry Man*), but especially psychiatric dramas.

From the early '50s onward, however, they were overtaken and eventually overshadowed by TV doctors, in daytime soap operas and in prime-time series, of which *Dr. Kildare, Ben Casey, General Hospital, Medic, Doc* and *Marcus Welby, M.D.* (these last two direct

descendants of all the kindly old doctors in '30s films) are only a few of the best-known. But by the 1970s so much material had been used over and over (hysterical blindness, false pregnancy, amnesia, psychosomatic illness) that medical scripts had to try some new twist, either wild, sick humor or sardonic social comment, as in Paddy Chayefsky's *The Hospital* (1971) on theater screens and *M*A*S*H* on screen (1970) and TV.

25

IN HEAVEN'S NAME
Religion, True and False

The reason why ministers of religion may not be comic characters or villains is simply because the attitude taken toward them may easily become the attitude taken toward religion in general. Religion is lowered in the minds of the audience because of the lowering of the audience's respect for a minister.
— The Motion Picture Production Code

Among the traditional learned professions, clearly medicine ranked at the top, both in the number of films devoted to it and the reverential attitude toward its practitioners, who were, with the few exceptions noted, seen as dedicated benefactors of humanity. At the opposite extreme, lawyers were more often than not crooked, scheming shysters, as ruthless as any tycoon.

Far below either of these in numbers, teachers on screen were about as popular as swineherds. Discounting old-fogy professor stereotypes in college musicals and those few,

usually secondary characters, teaching in exclusive private schools (as in *Finishing School, These Three* and *Girls' Dormitory*), the only young teacher heroine was Ann Sheridan in *The Great O'Malley* (1935).

Otherwise, teachers were played exclusively by veteran character actresses in forgotten "B" films: May Robson in *Grand Old Girl* (1935), Alison Skipworth and Polly Moran in *Two Wise Maids* (1937) and *Ladies in Distress* (1938) and Edna May Oliver, later replaced by Helen Broderick and Zasu Pitts, in the Hildegarde Withers mysteries. Among men, schoolmaster heroes were equally rare: only John Barrymore as a science teacher in *Topaze* (1933), Norman Foster in the title role of *The Hoosier Schoolmaster* (1935), Lewis Stone as a high school principal in *Don't Turn 'Em Loose* (1936), professors James Stewart in *Vivacious Lady*, Henry Fonda in *I Met My Love Again* (both

1938), Richard Carlson in *Winter Carnival* (1939)—and, of course, Robert Donat in *Goodbye, Mr. Chips* (1939).

Thus one might infer that '30s film-makers (and their public?) not only respected but loved their doctors, distrusted their lawyers and had all but forgotten their teachers. As for their clergymen, only Catholic priests, and even among them only certain kinds, received any attention at all. The healthy briskness with which Hollywood in the '30s divorced preaching from entertainment, as firmly as the Constitution had separated church from state, can best be appreciated by comparison with the decades that preceded and followed.

As at least negative evidence of this total indifference to the mystical or spiritual aspects of religion, one might point out that in a decade that produced film biographies of almost every famous woman in history, from Cleopatra to Elizabeth Barrett Browning, no one made a picture about that truly unique heroine Joan of Arc, even though there were numerous screen Joans before and after the '30s and though Shaw himself hinted he would like to see Hepburn play his.

By later standards, one of the most deplorable aspects of that cloying sentimentality that pervaded too many silent movies, including Griffith's, was an overt, preachy religiosity, readily identifiable with middle-class respectability. Like parents and grandparents, clergymen, usually Protestant, were *ex officio* white-haired and saintly, played by patriarchal types like Theodore Roberts and Hobart Bosworth.[1] (Thus in *Sadie Thompson*, Gloria Swanson's 1928 silent version of *Rain*, the Reverend Davidson had to be carefully explained as not a *real* minister at all.)

The wages of sin—always equated with sex —was literal death, the more horrible the better (e.g., leprosy in the 1923 *Ten Commandments*), or, if some innocent character had to

die, like the baby in *Sparrows*, a misty Jesus bathed in radiant light would welcome His lamb into a flowery hereafter. And just in case the message was not already abundantly clear, some sanctimonious subtitle drove it home, quoting or echoing the Bible in high-flown phrases about the paths of righteousness, the pearl of purity or a better home above.

Thus in *The Birth of a Nation* (1915), when Mae Marsh jumps off a cliff to escape a black would-be rapist, the audience is admonished: "For her who had learned the stern lesson of honor we should not grieve that she found sweeter the *opal gates of death*." One has only to imagine how such words would sound spoken aloud on screen in 1930 to know why this kind of heavy-handed moralizing vanished with the talkies.

Even the Production Code had only negative effects. While it would certainly have prevented any antireligious or anticlerical film, had any producer been mad enough to attempt one in God-fearing, Bible-reading America, the Legion of Decency could not very well force Hollywood to make religious pictures for which there was no market. No '30s talkie even tried for the Christian fervor of the silent *King of Kings* or *Ben-Hur*.

The earliest talkie to touch on organized religion was *Laughing Sinners* (1931), from a play by Kenyon Nicholson called *The Torch Song*. As noted earlier, Joan Crawford was a night club singer seduced by salesman Neil Hamilton but consoled by street evangelist Clark Gable. But tastes had already changed so radically that the *Times* said: "By the time they start walking hand in hand through the park to the soft music of 'Brighten the Corner Where You Are' . . . it meant that the MGM cinema-smiths had blundered . . . [and] ended their story on a sentimental but undeniably false note."

Opening in New York two days later, *Salvation Nell*, based on Edward Sheldon's 1908 play, filmed as a silent in 1915 and 1921, fared even worse. Even in its own day, the play had been no *Major Barbara*, and by 1931

---

[1] *The American Film Institute Catalog . . . 1921–1930* lists ninety films about clergymen, only ten about priests.

its naïve sentimentality and maudlin melo-drama were hopelessly outdated. Helen Chandler was the saloon slavey who chooses the Salvation Army rather than a brothel, but continues to love a criminal (Ralph Graves), whom she finally reforms. According to the *Times,* the opening-day audience at the Beacon "chuckled . . . despite the fact that the picture has no pretensions to comedy."[2]

The Miracle Man (1932), a story that had been made into a play by George M. Cohan in 1914 and a popular silent in 1919, came close to suffering acutely from the same cultural lag. Sylvia Sidney and Chester Morris in the leads, John Wray as a grotesque fake cripple and Hobart Bosworth as "the Patriarch" were inevitably compared with Betty Compson, Thomas Meighan, Lon Chaney and Joseph Dowling in the original, not unfavorably, but with the implication that this "uplifting" tale of crooks reformed by an old man's miraculous cure of a lame boy belonged, after all, to an earlier and simpler theatrical era.

This was, of course, a variation on the once-revered pattern in which an enigmatic stranger with supernatural powers transforms a number of lives, redeeming even the most hardened sinners. Until *Strange Cargo* in 1940, the only pure American example of this genre was *Destination Unknown* (1933), which reminded one reviewer of both *The Rime of the Ancient Mariner* and *The Passing of the Third Floor Back* (filmed by the British in 1936).

A rum-running schooner swept out to sea by a storm is becalmed in the Pacific, with the ironic result that despite five thousand cases of whiskey aboard the crew is dying of thirst, especially since the bootlegger (Pat O'Brien) guards the water supply with his gun. But a stowaway (Ralph Bellamy) appears from behind a cross of light with the

news that there is enough water for all in the barrels supposedly containing wine. (A reversal of the miracle at Cana?) He also steers the ship by the stars, bringing it to shore safely, then disappears as mysteriously as he arrived. The *Times* wondered why such a celestial being should have bothered with this particular ship.

Unless one counts Ralph Morgan as the philosophic stonecutter in *Magnificent Obsession,* the only other semblance of a "mystic" character was Henry B. Walthall in *Dante's Inferno* (1935), as the operator of a modest boardwalk concession of that name who dispenses free moral advice along with the hellish entertainment. But the main story line is a twist on the tycoon cycle, in which ambitious Spencer Tracy marries the old man's ward (Claire Trevor) and makes the Inferno a howling success. Never satisfied, he then creates a floating pleasure palace, which at the height of the revelry catches fire and turns into a real inferno (recalling the *Morro Castle* tragedy of 1934).

Though by now Tracy has harmed many people and even driven two to suicide, he redeems himself by proving a hero during the fire and finally admits money isn't everything. As a morality play it left much to be desired, but undoubtedly the "What shall it profit a man?" theme and the satanic spectacle were meant to play on lingering Christian fears of hell-fire and damnation.

Except for the Lloyd Douglas films, the only other attempts at such direct preaching were both, predictably enough, based on once-popular novels, which, for whatever reason, had not been filmed in the period to which they properly belonged. Harold Bell Wright's *The Calling of Dan Matthews* was unfortunately "modernized," rendering its archaic plot all the more out-of-date in 1936.

Richard Arlen was the crusading minister (except for Gavin Gordon in *Romance* the *only* minister to appear as a leading character in any '30s film) who boldly exposes a lurid red-light district known as "Old Town," even though its unwitting absentee landlord (Fred-

---

[2] 1931 also saw *An American Tragedy,* in which the hero rejects the teachings of his street evangelist parents. Later, his mother's attempted comfort to him in the death cell rings particularly hollow.

erick Burton) is a pillar of respectability. Needless to add, the fighting parson not only beats the evil manager of Old Town (Douglas Dumbrille) man to man, but wins the landowner's sympathetic daughter (Charlotte Wynters).

In His Steps (1936), the first production of Grand National, "suggested" by Rev. Charles Sheldon's long-time best seller, first published in 1895, featured those familiar young lovers, Eric Linden and Cecilia Parker, but the *Times* reviewer regretted "the film's translation of the Golden Rule is to the effect that industry is its own reward."

Two wealthy young elopers by their heroic devotion to each other and to the life they have chosen tilling the soil finally overcome parental objections to their marriage. Says Miller in *B Movies: "In His Steps* may have dragged for sophisticates (the title was changed to *Sins of the Children* in some territories), but the plain folk appreciated it."

1936 seems to have been a banner year for pseudo- or would-be religious films.[3] Definitely not for the plain folk was *The Garden of Allah*. What could have led David O. Selznick to imagine a convincing film in Robert Hichens' bizarre 1904 novel, even in Technicolor (one of the first outdoor color films) and starring two smoldering European personalities, then at their height? An exotic Englishwoman (Dietrich), whose name alone, Domini Enfilden, should be clue to the tone, while staying at an inn in the Sahara meets and marries a mysterious stranger, Boris Androvsky (Charles Boyer), only to learn after a blissful interlude that he is a Trappist monk, tortured by guilt for having broken his vows.

The *Times*, though respectful, was chiefly impressed by the tastefully subdued color. In 1976 *The New Yorker* described the film, quite rightly, as "heavenly romantic kitsch, panting with eternal love . . . taken from Robert Hichens' old squash pie of a novel, it's

the juiciest tale of woe ever . . . Just about perfection of its insanely goopy type."

Another kind of religious film, much more popular in earlier and later decades, was the costume spectacle set in the ancient or medieval world, of which the '30s produced only four examples, none biblical, only three of which were commercially shown.

The Sign of the Cross (1932) is a fast-moving drama in which the Christians are seen as a gentle religious minority at the mercy of utterly decadent, sadistic Roman power—except by implication no more a tract for promoting Christianity than the anti-Nazi films were propaganda for Judaism. *The Last Days of Pompeii* (1935), though more akin to *Ben-Hur,* with the characters' lives influenced by one brief meeting with Christ, was more notable for the climactic eruption of Vesuvius than for the religious message. And *The Crusades* (1935), like the events on which it was loosely based, could scarcely be considered religious at all, primarily concerned as it was with military spectacle and the fictitious romance of Richard the Lion-Hearted and Berengaria.

The Great Commandment (1939), produced by a minister, Rev. James K. Friederich, at his own expense but listed in the *Film Daily Almanac* as a Fox film, was apparently never released commercially nor reviewed except by *Film Daily*, which liked it. Irving Pichel directed a respectable cast that included John Beal, Maurice Moscovich and Albert Dekker in a story of a rabbi's son who becomes a follower of Christ—but this well-meant venture had the misfortune to be made in the wrong decade. In the '50s it might have done at least as well as *The Big Fisherman*, if not *The Robe*.

Hollywood in the '30s showed so much more enthusiasm for exposing the hypocrisy of fake evangelists and supposed miracle workers, it is only surprising that in the years before the Code, when Sinclair Lewis' novels were at the peak of their popularity, no daring producer ever tried to make *Elmer Gantry*. The film that could have come closest, had

---

[3] *The Green Pastures* will be discussed with ethnic films.

not Capra in his own words "turned chicken," was *The Miracle Woman* (1931), released only a month after the *Times* had scorned *Laughing Sinners* and *Salvation Nell* and a year ahead of *The Miracle Man*.

Based on Robert Riskin's satirical play *Bless You Sister,* obviously inspired by the then flourishing Aimee Semple McPherson and bought by Columbia at Capra's insistence, *The Miracle Woman* starts with a strong scene. A smug rural congregation has replaced its old-fashioned pastor of thirty years with another more "modern"—but instead of hearing a benevolent farewell sermon, they are blasted from the pulpit in the most scathing terms by his daughter (Barbara Stanwyck), in whose arms the old man has just died. As Capra intended it:

From here this bitter, disillusioned young lady should have decided *on her own* to give the stupid "unwashed" the religion they "want": a potpourri of happy sermons, brotherhood, sisterhood and sex—all in the glittering trappings of "Xmas" paper and musical comedy. She wows them. She gets rich. *Variety* reports her weekly "take" in its show-biz columns. Then the Miracle—and her return to God. One woman's life in three acts: disillusion, venality, conversion.[4]

Instead, Capra continues, "the thought of a wicked evangelist deliberately milking poor, adoring suckers for money in the name of Christ was just too much for my orthodox stomach," so the guilt is transferred to her unscrupulous manager (Sam Hardy), raking in money on her flamboyant preaching (sincere or not? we are never sure), delivered in diaphanous robes in a cage of lions.

A blind ex-aviator (David Manners), by chance overhearing her on a neighbor's radio, is deterred from suicide, they meet and fall in love, but the villain, fearing exposure of his dirty tricks, sets fire to the tabernacle (a touch from *Elmer Gantry*) and is himself trapped in it, while the aviator saves the girl—who thereupon joins the Salvation Army.

As Capra puts it, "I dove into the pool of powerful ideas—and came up with a can of

[4] *The Name Above the Title* (Bantam Books, 1971), p. 148.

claptrap and corn." Considering the mocking, skeptical tone of so many early '30s films, his original concept might have been very well received, but even as it is, *The Miracle Woman* is still an impressive melodrama. Until *Elmer Gantry* nearly thirty years later, it remained by far the most powerful screen exposure of commercialized religion.

Half a Sinner (1934), based on a 1925 play, *The Deacon,* enabled Berton Churchill (a popular white-haired character actor whose pompous manner often cast him as a foil for Will Rogers) to re-create his stage role, "an Elmer Gantry of the box-cars," who works small towns for all they're worth. In one, a boy and girl (Joel McCrea and Sally Blane) whom he knew on the road are trying to go straight and fear his knowledge, but when the boy is wrongly accused of a robbery the self-ordained deacon straightens everything out. Although at times the satire on Midwestern small-town life "might have come straight out of Sinclair Lewis," the *Times* thought too much attention was wasted on the young couple and not enough given to the smooth-tongued deacon practicing his wily arts.

Klondike Annie (1936) was not one of Mae West's finer hours; it was, in fact, the beginning of her professional obliteration by the Production Code. As Nugent observed, she "does not function too well in a moral straitjacket." Fleeing a Barbary Coast murder charge, Frisco Doll boards a freighter for the Klondike, charms the skipper (Victor McLagen) and when a spinster missionary (Helen Jerome Eddy) dies, assumes her uniform and identity, so must live up to them. Though in Alaska she falls for a police officer (Phillip Reed), the virtuous mask becomes such a part of her that, renouncing her love, she returns to Frisco to face the law. The sight of America's bawdiest sex symbol in religious garb, preaching Christian virtue, was equally distasteful to those who revered religion and those who enjoyed Mae West.

A masculine parallel turned up in *Racketeers in Exile* (1937), in which George Bancroft, hiding out with his mob in his home town, discovers through a gift of eloquence that religion can be the most lucrative racket of all. Soon he runs his gospel tent operation into big business, with a charity front and a radio station featuring "The Voice of Your Conscience" to milk guilt-ridden businessmen —until (necessarily, under the Production Code) his own conscience stirs, and, like Klondike Annie, he hits the sawdust trail.

Still another variation on the crook-in-clerical-clothes formula was *Tarnished Angel* (1938), in which Sally Eilers, a jewel thief masquerading as a revivalist preacher, performs fake miracles, but after giving a real cripple courage to walk, converts herself. Finally, an obscure "B" actually called *Religious Racketeers* (1939), also known as *The Mystic Circle Murder,* featuring Betty Compson and Mme. Harry Houdini, exposed a phony spiritualist who dupes a bereaved heiress until shown up by her fiancé, a newspaperman.

Not all religious characters in '30s films were charlatans or criminals on the run. More than a dozen admirable professionally religious people played important roles in as many films—*all* of them Catholic priests, except for two nuns. With the noted exceptions of Gavin Gordon in *Romance,* Richard Arlen in *The Calling of Dan Matthews* and Sir Cedric Hardwicke in *Green Light,* ministers appeared only to perform necessary functions at weddings, baptisms and funerals, and since ethnic films were very rare, rabbis were virtually ignored.

Considering that Catholics were a relatively small minority in America, that practically all Hollywood producers were Jewish and that most of the stars were vaguely Protestant, if anything, one can only hazard a guess that such overwhelmingly favorable attention to the Church may have been meant to appease the ever-militant Legion of Decency or to placate Joseph Breen, administrator of the Production Code (which, it will be recalled, had been co-authored by Jesuit Daniel Lord). Whatever the explanation, in Hollywood of the '30s practical Christianity was identified

with Catholicism as exclusively as priests were with Irish names.[5]

On the screen, as in life, priests received at least five times as much attention as nuns. Indeed, discounting briefly glimpsed sisters serving as nurses or teachers in convent schools, or introduced as local color in period films or those set in Catholic countries, only two screen heroines took the veil, both in adaptations of established literary works written in prewar Europe, both treated with dignity and restraint. The '30s indulged in none of those relentlessly "human," coyly frolicsome, home-run-hitting, tennis-playing, bicycle-riding nuns that cluttered the screen from the '40s through the '60s.

In accord with MGM's policy of displaying its top stars in pre-tested vehicles of proven worth, *The White Sister* (1933), from F. Marion Crawford's 1909 novel, starred Helen Hayes and Clark Gable in the roles Lillian Gish and Ronald Colman had played in the successful 1923 silent. The story line was considered simplified, with a designing half-sister omitted, along with the climactic volcanic eruption and flood, but the essential crisis remained the same.

A high-born Italian girl, destined to wed a man of her father's choice, instead falls in love with a dashing young army lieutenant, who is subsequently reported dead. (Though Crawford himself had died in 1909, it was easy enough to update the period to World War I, with the hero, now a flyer, captured by Austrians rather than Arabs.)

Having lost her father as well, the girl decides to devote her life to God as a nun, with

---

[5] The few exceptions were either Italian (Edward Arnold in *The White Sister,* Jack LaRue in *A Farewell to Arms,* Henry O'Neill in *Anthony Adverse,* Joseph Calleia in *Full Confession,* Leo Carrillo in *Manhattan Melodrama*), French (Pedro De Cordoba in *Anthony Adverse,* Frank Sheridan in *The Man I Killed,* Jean Hersholt in *Seventh Heaven,* C. Aubrey Smith in *The Hurricane*) or Mexican (Robert Barrat in *Bordertown,* Victor Kilian in *Ramona*). Also, Walter Connolly played Chesterton's English priest in *Father Brown, Detective.*

May Robson and Helen Hayes
in **The White Sister**

the ceremony of her final vows pictured in authentic detail. Of course the lieutenant turns up alive and implores her to renounce the convent (as she could no doubt have obtained permission to do), but she firmly rejects him to continue her celibate life. Soon afterward he is injured in an air raid and dies with her at his side. The conflict between sacred and profane love was much the same as in *The Garden of Allah*, written in the same prewar decade, but the details were far more convincing.[6]

Of the three most publicized European actresses imported in 1933, Lilian Harvey, Anna Sten and Dorothea Wieck, the last-named was

---

[6] A lighter version of the same dilemma had appeared in the operetta-like *Call of the Flesh* (1930), in which Dorothy Jordan played a novice wooed back to the world by singing Ramon Novarro.

perhaps best-known to discriminating film-goers, for her performance in *Maedchen in Uniform. The Cradle Song*, G. M. Martinez Sierra's 1911 play of Spanish convent life, done on Broadway in 1927 by Eva Le Gallienne, seemed an ideal vehicle for Wieck's American debut, and indeed was hailed as such. The play itself is so pious, placid and lacking in conflict as to be almost soporific, but Marc Connelly's screenplay subtly heightened the dramatic possibilities without in any way falsifying the material.

When a foundling is left at a convent of cloistered Dominicans, the nuns after much debate decide to bring her up, though she will be nominally adopted by their doctor (Sir Guy Standing), a gently cynical agnostic, and live with the gardener's wife. But Sister Joanna of the Cross (Wieck), a young nun of strong maternal instincts, comes to love the child as her own and takes for granted that she will grow up to join the order.

When the girl (Evelyn Venable) decides instead to marry a young architect (Kent Taylor), who will take her to America, Joanna must painfully resign herself to the fact that her cradle song has ended. Louise Dresser was the firm but just Prioress, Georgia Caine her disagreeable assistant, the Vicaress, and Gertrude Michael a sympathetic sister who helps Joanna accept the truth. Indeed, such a gallery of recognizable, clearly distinguishable nuns was not to be seen again on the screen until *The Nun's Story* (1957).

No religious community of men has ever received comparable treatment. Rather, the typical '30s movie priest, whose commitment was at least as much sociological as theological, more concerned with enforcing common decency than preaching Catholic dogma, usually worked alone, but unlike his medical counterparts, he was always seen in an urban setting, running a settlement house, a slum mission or a poor parish (with never a curate to help). He was every inch a rugged he-man, who, confronting delinquents, juvenile or adult, never hesitated to lay it on the line (or, if necessary, on the jaw).

The first such pastor in a '30s film was Father Dan (Frank Sheridan) in *Donovan's Kid* (1931), whose faith helps straighten out the hitherto gangster hero (Richard Dix) and whose niece (Marion Shilling) marries him. Next came a priest in *Manhattan Melodrama* (1934), called "Father Pat" in the shooting script but listed as "Father Joe" in the cast of the finished picture, perhaps because he was played by the obviously non-Irish Leo Carrillo. (All such priests were always called by their Christian names, usually abbreviated.)

The film's original title, *Three Men*, suggests that the priest was meant to be as important as his two protégés (Clark Gable and William Powell), but as it turned out, he is brought in only at odd moments to voice benevolent comment and wise counsel. Indeed, his main function is as the chaplain of Sing Sing who in full church vestments walks with Blackie (Gable) on the last mile.

Prison films were extremely popular throughout the '30s, and those involving scenes in Death Row naturally included chaplains, usually Catholic. In *The Last Mile* (1932), for instance, Alec B. Francis was the would-be dispenser of spiritual consolation to the condemned, a service he also performed for Garbo in *Mata Hari* (1932)—but most of these were bit roles, as purely functional as ministers at weddings or doctors in hospital scenes.

After Father Pat/Joe, the next prison chaplain, and the first to play a prominent role, was Father Dolan (William Gargan), who in Fritz Lang's *You Only Live Once* (1937) pays with his life for trying to keep the hero (Henry Fonda) from escaping just when his pardon has come through. *Over the Wall* (1938), from a story by Warden Lewis E. Lawes, saw John Litel as Father John Connor, who drops the hero (Dick Foran) with a right hook at the beach one day, and subsequently reclaims him for society by proving he was framed. In *Mutiny in the Big House* (1939) Charles Bickford, usually on the wrong side of the law, was a heroic chaplain who helps quell a prison riot—a story based, surprisingly

enough, on an actual incident ten years before.

After Father Dan in *Donovan's Kid,* the next slum priest was played by William Harrigan in *Silk Hat Kid* (1935), a forgotten gangster film, in which Father Joe Campbell runs a settlement house where he puts hired killer Lew Ayres to work as a boxing instructor. He also forces Ayres and his rival in love (Paul Kelly) to throw away their guns and settle their argument by fists. All in all, he continued a vigorous tradition which many another movie priest was to follow.

The first major star to play a priest, however (and do it so well that he played two more within the next few years), was Spencer Tracy as Father Tim Mullin in *San Francisco*. Though the basic situation of boyhood friends who turn out opposites had been used before, most notably in *Manhattan Melodrama*, with Gable playing much the same character, also nicknamed Blackie, making the good man a priest, by definition sexless, eliminated all possibility of a triangle. Only thus could he serve as the stern voice of conscience without rousing suspicion that he really wanted the girl for himself.

The extraordinary zeal with which the Breen Office protected Catholic sensibilities is confirmed by Anita Loos' account in *Kiss Hollywood Goodby* of the off-screen struggles that preceded the filming of *San Francisco*. In one of the key scenes Father Tim tries to keep his rough-diamond friend Blackie Norton (Gable) from exploiting his fiancée (Jeanette MacDonald) by making her the Queen of the Barbary Coast. Says Blackie: "I'll have Mary pose in tights. I'll plaster pictures of her on trolley cars and ash cans all over Frisco." To which the priest replies: "You can't take a woman in marriage and then sell her immortal soul!" As he attempts to lead Mary out of Blackie's place, Blackie "hauls off and floors him with a sock to the jaw."

According to Loos, Breen was adamantly opposed to this scene. "Gable is such an idol that the public may take his side when he knocks out a priest and cheer for the triumph of evil . . . A priest has been humiliated in a way that will bring the whole Catholic church down on us."[7]

Loos and her collaborator Bob Hopkins consulted kindly, movie-wise Father Benedict, who ran a small Catholic chapel near the studio, and after a moment's thought he came up with the perfect solution. The priest is introduced in a new scene, in a gym, where he is shown as easily able to outbox, outslug and outsmart Blackie, so in the later scene when he deliberately *allows* Blackie to knock him out, he is "turning the other cheek," thus making him the hero of the encounter. Though probably not one viewer in a million saw the intended connection, not until Breen had been talked into this compromise was the film allowed to proceed.

Thus did the two-fisted Irish-American priest come into his own, and though his popularity never rivaled that of reporters or doctors, he remained a familiar figure for the rest of the decade and beyond. 1938 was a vintage year. In *The Devil's Party* a Hell's Kitchen gang first seen as children grow up to go their separate professional ways, one naturally becoming a shady gambler (Victor McLaglen), one a cop (William Gargan) and one a priest (Paul Kelly). In *City Streets* (essentially a children's picture) Frank Sheridan, who had played Father Dan in *Donovan's Kid* and Father Patrick in *The Great O'Malley,* played Father Ryan, another pastor in what is now called "the inner city."

But these were "B" films. The next important example of 1938, for which Tracy won his second Oscar, was *Boys Town,* in which he played the then living Father Edward Flanagan like an extension of his *San Francisco* role, only this time he redeemed Whitey (Mickey Rooney) instead of Blackie. Though the famous community for homeless boys was already twenty years old, and so presumably well established, the film depicts it as experimental, heavily mortgaged and dubi-

ously viewed, even by the Catholic hierarchy.

The plot was a variation on the formula so often used in service films: the cynical newcomer learns the hard way the true values of the institution he at first scorns—in this case a super-tough delinquent played by Mickey Rooney. As Nugent observed in the *Times,* "Mickey is the Dead End gang rolled into one . . . Mickey, as the French would understate it, is the original *enfant terrible.*"

Even the strong characterizations of Tracy and Rooney could not quite validate the melodramatic climax in which not only is Rooney's hero-worshiping little follower (Bobs Watson) struck by a car but his evil brother (Edward Norris) involves him in a bank robbery and kidnapping. Yet, Nugent concluded, "it manages, in spite of the embarrassing sentimentality of its closing scenes, to

Spencer Tracy and Mickey Rooney
in Boys Town

[7] *Kiss Hollywood Goodby* (Viking Press, 1974), pp. 131–32.

be a consistently interesting and frequently touching motion picture."

At very least it is one of the '30s films that has lingered longest in public memory. Thus nearly twenty years later in *A Hatful of Rain* (1957) when the heroine says to her sad-faced husband, "You look like Mickey Rooney leaving Boys Town forever," the line needed no explanation. By the 1970s the real Boys Town was called upon to cease its constant appeals for contributions and divest itself of some of its excessive wealth.

Within a few months of *Boys Town,* but much too soon to have been directly influ-

enced by it, came another of the best-remembered and most typical films of the '30s, *Angels with Dirty Faces* (1938), introducing Hollywood's other favorite priest, Pat O'Brien, as the sturdy Father Jerry Connolly, boyhood friend of the notorious Rocky Sullivan (Cagney) .[8]

With its usual skill in combining well-worn elements into pleasing new packages, War-

[8] *Angels Wash Their Faces* (1939) merely echoed the title. Except for the presence of Ann Sheridan and the Dead End Kids, there was no connection with the earlier film.

James Cagney and Pat O'Brien in Angels with Dirty Faces

ners added the Dead End Kids to the pattern of the two boys who take opposite paths. The relationship between the two men owes much to *San Francisco,* but even more to *Dead End* (Dave and Baby Face Martin), as does the mobster's influence on a gang of teen-aged admirers only too eager to learn the criminal ropes. Few who have seen the film have ever forgotten the climax, in which, in response to the priest's earnest plea to disillusion the boys, Rocky is dragged to the electric chair apparently a screaming, sobbing coward. Despite the familiarity of the material, the *Times* was deeply impressed by the realistic depiction of the gutter.

O'Brien's Irish face and authoritative manner seemed so right for a priest that he later played two more, putting him Roman-collared neck and neck with Tracy and one ahead of Bing Crosby, who played the same priest twice. Unfortunately, O'Brien's second clerical role, scarcely a year after *Angels with Dirty Faces,* was the famous military "padre" Father Duffy (whose statue stands at Broadway and Forty-seventh, in what is properly called Duffy Square) in *The Fighting 69th* (released in January 1940), one of the most blatant "revisionist" films, aimed at glorifying America's entry into World War I—an ominous hint of what was to come in the 1940s.

The supposed spiritual message was now barked out in "You better believe it!" tones, foreshadowing the wartime pseudo-epigram "There are no atheists in fox-holes." In short, church was now identified with state, and religion equated with patriotism. Blind faith in God and country was the order of the day, childlike and totally unquestioning.

With a few rare exceptions like *The Song of Bernadette* (1943) and *The Keys of the Kingdom* (1945), wartime religion on screen took on hysterical overtones of megalomania (*God Is My Co-Pilot*) or inspirational returns from the dead (*A Guy Named Joe*). On the civilian front, since whatever social problems America might still face had been swept under the rug for the duration, the hard-hitting slum priests gave way to crotchety old pastors and crooning curates in the cloying parochial sentimentality of *Going My Way* and *The Bells of St. Mary's,* pious pap that would have been hooted off the screen in the '30s.

Fighting Father Dunne (1948), O'Brien's third priest, seemed only an outdated, tearjerking variation on *Boys Town.* In the '50s, movie religion was expressed in a series of biblical and early Christian spectaculars from *Quo Vadis* (1951) to *Ben-Hur* (1959). Discounting Father O'Dowd (Frank McHugh), the bland pastor in Leo McCarey's hysterically anti-Communist *My Son John* (1952), among '50s film priests, only the fearless labor activist Father Barry (Karl Malden) in *On the Waterfront* (1954) showed any more serious concern than blessing the war effort (the Korean War in *My Son John*) or reassuring the faithful that all was indeed for the best in this best of all possible worlds.

CRIME AND PUNISHMENT
Cops and Robbers

26

"AW RIGHT, YOU GUYS!"
The Gang's All Here

There must be no display, at any time, of machine guns, sub-machine guns or other weapons generally classified as illegal weapons in the hands of gangsters, or other criminals, and there are to be no off-stage sounds of the repercussions of these guns . . . All discussions and dialogue on the part of gangsters regarding guns should be cut to a minimum.

—The Motion Picture Production Code

Of all the film heroes defined by their occupations, none cut a wider swath across '30s screens than the gangster, who could turn up in almost any kind of film set in modern times, not just those about newspapermen, doctors and priests. Curiosity about those living outside the law seems a perennial human trait by no means confined to the gallant Robin Hood tradition. Morbid fascination with more lurid crime has had an equally long history, as witness the bloodier Greek myths, folk ballads like "Edward, Edward," the gory Elizabethan and Jacobean revenge tragedies, the later Gothic tales of terror and their echoes in the criminal characters and violent scenes in many classic nineteenth-century novels.

Unlike the Lone Wolf, the Solitaire Man and other gentlemen jewel thieves, gangsters by definition operated in packs—hence such phrases as "the mob," "the syndicate" and "organized crime"—all expanded by Prohibition into a multimillion-dollar enterprise. Just as war has been defined as the continuation of foreign policy by other means, so the cold-blooded gang vendettas, ambushes and massacres, purely to eliminate rivals, seize power and increase profits, seemed in effect the extension of the methods of big business to their logical extreme—cutthroat capitalism without hypocritical pretense.

Thus some of the best gangster films at least subliminally invited the audience to identify with a hero who had, however outrageously, beaten the system and made it pay off in possessions that weaker men could only envy: beautiful women, fine clothes, big cars, lavish apartments. Who said crime didn't pay?

It is surely no coincidence that in 1931 and 1932, the years when the Depression hit rock bottom, Hollywood lashed out most bitterly against certain well-publicized figures who still seemed to have it made: yellow journalists, untouchable underworld czars, crooked lawyers and corrupt politicians, all apparently working hand in glove to fleece an already suffering public. No such cinematic attacks were ever launched against bankers, brokers, big-business men, economists or others whose activities might have seemed more directly connected with the financial crisis; all remained as invulnerable as doctors and clergymen. With the country paralyzed by total economic collapse, how simple and reassuring to find scapegoats in more easily identifiable and punishable wrongdoers!

In historic fact, the most flagrant excesses in all the areas exposed had been committed in the previous decade—e.g., the Teapot Dome scandal, the most luridly headlined gang slayings (Dion O'Bannion, Arnold Rothstein, the St. Valentine's Day massacre). William J. Fallon, "the great mouthpiece," had been dead since 1927. Jake Lingel was killed in 1930 and Legs Diamond in 1931, by which year Capone himself was behind federal bars.

With the election of Roosevelt in 1932, Prohibition and consequently bootlegging were doomed. Thus, as with the gold-digger and newspaper films, though screenwriters may have been drawing on their own earlier experience as reporters back East or in Chicago, their screenplays, however topical they may have seemed at the time, were really sensationalizing social evils already fading into the past.

Although von Sternberg's *Underworld* (1927), written by Ben Hecht, is often mentioned as the first gangster film, the protagonist is actually a lone jewel thief. *The Drag Net* (1928), an obvious attempt at a followup, in which von Sternberg used the same stars, George Bancroft and Evelyn Brent, more clearly involved gang warfare, but was dismissed by the *Times* as "a wholesale massacre."

By July 1928, when *The Racket* and *The Lights of New York* opened the same day, the reviewer was complaining of "a season somewhat overrun by melodramas and underworld mysteries." *The Racket,* from a 1927 play about two warring "bootleg kings" and an honest police captain, was hailed as relatively realistic, but *Lights,* the first full-length talkie, reviewed largely as a curiosity and condemned for poor acting, seems to have borrowed both the plot and the night club setting of *Broadway,* with none of the dramatic force of that long-running hit.

By November 1928, *Gang War* (prefaced by a title which "adjures the public to awaken to its duty to do what it can to put an end to murderous gangs") was greeted with "When earth's last gangster picture fades from the screen, it may, who can tell, be a relief to more than one person." Thus it would seem that, far from introducing the gangster film, talkies rather pumped sorely needed new blood into a genre well on the way to dying from overexposure.

Unquestionably, the sob of night club saxophones, the bark of an automatic, the chatter of a tommy gun, the roaring motor and squealing tires of a getaway car rounding a corner, the wail of police sirens and, above all, the harsh rasp of underworld slang snarled from menacing faces made all the difference—perhaps the most striking audible evidence that, just as silents had been uniquely able to invoke dreamlike fantasies, the first great triumph of talkies would be capturing the gritty realities of contemporary urban America.

Yet 1929 saw only eight examples: *Alibi* (acclaimed as "by far the best of the gangster films"), *Romance of the Underworld, Broadway* (turned into a musical), *Broadway Babies* (a variant, with Fred Kohler as a big-hearted mob leader), *Side Street, Skin Deep, Woman Trap* and *The Mighty,* in which Bancroft played a gangster turned by the war into a hero and subsequently an honest police chief—a causal connection to be reversed by many a later film.

Opening during the 1929 holidays, *The Mighty* was followed a week later by *The Racketeer,* which thus became the first gangster film to be released in New York in 1930. It also featured the first sympathetic gangster hero of the decade, a suave modern Robin Hood (Robert Armstrong) in love with a girl (Carole Lombard) who has left her husband for an alcoholic violinist (Roland Drew). Not only does our hero rehabilitate the musician, he arranges a concert, meanwhile winning a promise of marriage from the girl. But one of his henchmen kills a rival leader, and the chivalrous racketeer is shot down by the police, thus sparing Lombard the necessity of marrying him out of gratitude.

In even more improbably chivalrous form, the likable gangster turned up again in *Born*

Reckless (1930), based on Donald Henderson Clarke's novel *Louis Beretti.* Like Bancroft in *The Mighty,* Edmund Lowe redeems himself by going to fight in France—an idea almost as improbable as that of an Italian-American becoming such a powerful gang leader *before* the war. The plot involves his risking his life by double-crossing former associates to rescue the kidnaped child of a girl he admires.

This formula was apparently so successful that Lowe soon repeated it in *Good Intentions* (1930), as a gangster who sacrifices his life to save a polo player preferred by the girl he himself loves—again Marguerite Churchill. However, 1930's most extreme case of the noble gangster (who seems to have replaced the noble savage in the imagination of those who had never met a real one) was Lowell Sherman in *The Pay Off,* directed by himself, as a polished big shot who out of love for an innocent young wife (Marian Nixon) allows himself to be sent to the electric chair rather than let her and her husband (William Janney) be framed for a crime committed by his gang.

As a welcome antidote to all this underworld sweetness and light, late in 1930 came the grimly unsentimental *The Doorway to Hell,* called by the *Times* "intelligent and exciting . . . Racketeering as a ruthless industry . . . The police stand by powerless in the face of wholesale slaughter and gradually learn to adopt the weapons of the underworld they are fighting."

In an unusually cynical twist, a police captain (Robert Elliott) deliberately allows rival gangsters to arrange a jail break for Lew Ayres, knowing they will kill him, whereas the courts would only free him for lack of evidence. At the end, "the young man takes a look at the portrait of Napoleon, with whom he has always identified himself, and walks down the steps to his death."

When *Little Caesar,* filmed in 1930, opened in January 1931, the subject was not likely to bowl over any audience by its novelty. Robinson had already played three gangsters the previous year, in *Night Ride, Outside the Law* and *The Widow from Chicago.*

What made *Little Caesar* one of the three all-time best gangster films (along with *The Public Enemy* and *Scarface*) was not the over-familiar material but the extraordinarily sharp quality of the writing (W. R. Burnett), the direction (Mervyn LeRoy) and the acting (Robinson). Said the *Times:* "Little Caesar becomes at Mr. Robinson's hands a figure out of Greek epic tragedy [sic], a cold, ignorant, merciless killer, driven on and on by an insatiable lust for power, the plaything of a force that is greater than himself."

This hardly seems fair to Rico (who is called "Little Caesar" only by the newspapers, never by himself). He is driven by a desperate hunger not so much for power as such but for recognition. The power in itself means nothing without the symbols (especially diamond jewelry) and the rituals (the testimonial banquet).

Rico is by no means as bloodthirsty, treacherous and vindictive as, for instance, Macbeth, much less Richard III. Though working as a trigger man, he is shown killing only two known characters, once in self-defense, when the victim is the crime commissioner, once in the regretted execution (on church steps) of Tony Passa (William Collier, Jr.), a young weakling whose guilt-ridden babbling threatens the safety of the whole gang.

Moving up the ladder by superior cleverness, not mere brute force, Rico is even a generous victor to fallen rivals. When by winning the respect of the gang he takes over leadership from Sam Vettori (Stanley Fields), he still retains Sam as a trusted henchman, and even after his more nearly violent confrontation with Arnie Lorch (Maurice Black) he does no worse than banish Lorch and his hoods to Detroit. In fact, it is largely Robinson's gargoyle face and sneering voice that make Rico linger in the memory as malevolent; had he been played by a different kind of actor, he might have turned out a pathetic, if not sympathetic, hero.

Unlike Macbeth, he brings about his own

Edward G. Robinson in **Little Caesar**

downfall not by excessive ambition or cruelty but through his one human weakness, his love for his young protégé Joe (Douglas Fairbanks, Jr.). This relationship has definite homosexual undertones. Says Rico to Joe: "Who else have I got to give a hang about?" A moment later he is raging with jealousy of Joe's girl Olga (Glenda Farrell in her screen debut, miscast as a ballroom dancer.) "She and me can't both have you. One of us has gotta lose —and it ain't gonna be me! There's ways of stoppin' that dame . . ." It is this threat that drives Olga to call the police, enabling them to set a trap. Even then Rico cannot bring himself to kill Joe. Fleeing through the streets, he mutters, truthfully enough, "This is what I get for likin' a guy too much."

From here on it's all downhill for Rico— surely the most humiliating descent of any gangster hero. Even Ma Magdalena (Lucille La Verne), the old hag with whom he has occasionally hidden out and stashed most of his money, betrays him, turning him out with only a pittance. Soon he is reduced to drinking and sleeping in a flophouse, and becomes so changed in appearance and manner that when he tries to turn himself in, a police sergeant refuses to believe that this is the once-swaggering Little Caesar. His death, shot down by a detective as he reaches in his pocket for a comb, near a billboard advertising the stage success of Joe and Olga, is one of the classic closing scenes in '30s films, as his dying words are among the most memorable of movie curtain lines: "Mother of Mercy—is this the end of Rico?"[1]

Little Caesar was indeed a hard act to follow, yet 1931 proved to be the greatest of all years for gangster films, not only in the sheer volume produced (more than thirty clear-cut examples, plus many marginal items), but in the number that have remained of enduring interest. Not that the gangster with the heart of gold had altogether disappeared. In *The Last Parade* Jack Holt, about to go straight, stays outside the law just long enough to avenge the death of a young reporter (Weldon Heyburn), brother of the girl (Constance Cummings) Holt hopelessly loves.

Of *Hell Bound* the *Times* observed: "Romance has descended once more upon the bullet-riddled Broadway film sector and restored to the long-suffering gangster his old aura of gentleman adventurer." Leo Carrillo's Italian accent and genial personality made him a natural for a well-meaning mobster regenerated by his love for a singer (Lola Lane), even though she loves a doctor (Lloyd Hughes). When she unwittingly destroys an alibi, she feels obliged to marry the mobster so that she cannot be forced to testify against him, but noble Nick steps aside, into a hail of machine-gun fire.

In *Homicide Squad*, Carrillo did a virtual reprise of the same character. Finding his long-lost son (Russell Gleason) as a member of his own gang, he helps the boy go straight, but in consequence is framed and mowed down by police bullets. In *The Guilty Generation* Carrillo played a godfather type, eager for his daughter (Constance Cummings) to be accepted by Florida society. In a *Romeo and Juliet* variation, she falls in love with the son (Robert Young) of a rival gang lord (Boris Karloff). Both lovers deplore their disreputable fathers, but, unlike their Veronese counterparts, they survive.

But the most memorable gangster films of 1931 took a much less sentimental view of the underworld; some indeed set standards of brutal realism that may have been equaled but hardly surpassed. A borderline case was *Quick Millions,* in which Spencer Tracy as a truck driver risen to boss racketeer is mowed down after a long, treacherous career. While praising the film, the *Times* noted a tendency to glorify the forceful, magnetic hero.

City Streets—the very title evokes that whole sordid milieu of early talkie realism—directed by Rouben Mamoulian from a story by Dashiell Hammett, is now regarded as a minor classic. An underling (Guy Kibbee) assigned to rub out a rival lets his loyal daughter (Sylvia Sidney) take the rap. On her release, her lover, a budding beer-runner from the West known as the Kid (Gary Cooper), resents the big boss's interest in her. When the boss is shot by his discarded moll (Wynne Gibson), the girl is blamed and doomed to be rubbed out, but the Kid takes the three remaining hoods on a hair-raising auto ride that terrifies them into submission. The prevalent attitude toward the police is revealed in a remark of Cooper's. When invited to join the beer racket, he replies: "Beer? I'd as soon be a cop as that."

Less than a week later came *The Public Enemy,* an intended exposé, whose crusading purpose Warners strongly emphasized, branding gangsterism the most urgent national problem in an advertising campaign full of phrases like "It is real, real, DEVASTATINGLY real . . . a grim depiction of the modern menace! Come prepared to see the worst of women and the cruelest of men—as they really are." Oddly enough, in the printed cast the forgotten Edward Woods was given billing over Cagney, Harlow is listed fifth, and Mae Clarke, recipient of the most famous grapefruit in movie history, is twelfth and last.

---

[1] According to the press sheets, he was to have killed himself to avoid capture—a far less effective end.

Unlike most gangster films, in which characters are simply introduced as adults, with no attempt at psychological or sociological explanation, *The Public Enemy* went as far back as 1909 to establish childhood roots for later behavior; it was also the first film to link the war, Prohibition and the rise of the beer racket. Another novel feature was its use of Irish gangsters and even one Jew (Nails Nathan, played by Leslie Fenton)—an accurate reflection of such real-life mobsters as the O'Bannions and Hymie Weiss. The press sheet for the film, presumably prepared with the aid of the screenplay writers, Kubec Glasmon and John Bright, unequivocally states that the leading characters, Tom Powers (Cagney) and Matt Doyle (Woods), were inspired by pioneer bootleggers Frankie Lake and Terry Druggan.

What subverted the whole serious purpose of the film was, of course, Cagney's brilliant, vibrant performance. Just as Robinson made Rico, written more or less sympathetically, repellent, so did Cagney make Tommy, meant to be despicable, irresistible. As Andrew Bergman puts it: "With enough ingenuity, pluck and street-urchin wit to keep a dozen Alger heroes going, Cagney's Tommy Powers demonstrated again who the heroes really were and where the action lay."

However, Bergman dismisses the attempted environmental explanation by noting that Tommy's respectable brother (Donald Cook), product of the same background, is content to return from the war to his dull, safe job as a streetcar conductor. "Tommy accepts death more easily than he accepts the life of a drone. Even if his end is to be dumped lifeless into

Edward Woods, Joan Blondell, James Cagney, Mae Clarke in **The Public Enemy**

the family living room, swathed in bandages, Tommy's life had an agenda, has been restless and full of zest . . . In 1931, one didn't go to see trolley conductors working their way through night school."[2]

Less than two weeks later came MGM's most notable contribution to the gangster cycle, *The Secret Six,* whose title characters were not criminals but a vigilante group formed to fight them. The *Times* praised *The Secret Six* more wholeheartedly than it had *Little Caesar, City Streets* or *The Public Enemy.*

Set largely in "Centro," suburb and criminal center of an unnamed metropolis, the plot traces the rise and fall of another brutal Capone type (Wallace Beery), who kills his way to the top, guided by a corrupt alcoholic lawyer (Lewis Stone), whom he eventually murders. Gable, in one of his few non-gangster roles of 1931, was the inevitable reporter, working with the committee to avenge the death of a colleague (Johnny Mack Brown) — another echo of the Lingel case. Harlow played Beery's reluctant mistress, who turns state's witness at his trial.

What alarmed many concerned individuals and organizations at this time was that in this kind of film the police might just as well not have existed. Even though the gangsters usually killed only one another, they did so with a flagrant defiance of the law and with immunity from its penalties. As a result the contemporary American city, whether Chicago, New York or unspecified, seemed wider open than the wildest frontier town of the old West.

Compared to the last four films discussed, other gangster films of 1931 pale into mere routine variations on overfamiliar themes. For example, in *A Gentleman's Fate,* in a switch on *Great Expectations,* "socially resplendent" Jack Thomas (John Gilbert) learns to his shock that his still living father (Ernest Torrence) is a notorious "rum racketeer." After Jack is jilted by his fiancée, he

himself gets involved in the rackets and is finally killed.

In *The Ruling Voice* (originally titled *Upper Underworld*) Walter Huston was the chairman of a powerful underworld board of directors, rejected by his respectable daughter (Loretta Young) and betrayed by a henchman (Dudley Digges). As the publicity on *The Public Enemy* pointed out, few gangsters lived past thirty, but on screen it was remarkable how many were middle-aged men with grown children ignorant of the source of their fathers' ill-gotten gains.

No doubt partly in response to the mounting howls of protest from every type of civic and religious organization, 1932 saw a distinct falling off both in the number and the quality of gangster films. Thus, though involved with racketeers in *Taxi!,* Cagney himself was a hard-working cabbie bent on avenging his brother's murder.

However, the cycle ended not with a whimper but with a violent bang—in fact, went out in a blaze of gunfire, in the third of the classic trio (by far the most heavily publicized, even in advance), Howard Hughes' production of *Scarface* (1932), directed by Howard Hawks from a script by Ben Hecht.

Though it necessarily recapitulated certain elements of *Little Caesar* and *The Public Enemy, Scarface* differed from either in several significant respects. For one, it showed how easily innocent citizens could become victims—diners in a restaurant, pedestrians on a city street, a mother pushing a baby carriage, caught in the cross fire from speeding limousines. It also noted that Scarface was not only the shame of the nation but specifically of his own people; respectable Italian-Americans are shown protesting the disgrace he is bringing on all of them. Uniquely, the title character, both as written and acted, is a totally vicious psychopath, without a single redeeming quality—sadistic, treacherous, vindictive and, in the end, cowardly—and Paul Muni played him exactly that way.

As announced by the title, *Scarface* was based even more closely than *Little Caesar*

[2] *We're in the Money* (Harper, 1972), p. 13.

on the flagrant criminal career of Al Capone (who, from behind bars, actually asked to see the script in advance!). Even so the New York censor board in a fit of retroactive wishful thinking insisted that the movie Scarface be hanged instead of merely imprisoned or even rubbed out by his own kind. They also decreed the subtitle, *The Shame of a Nation,* which might have had more impact had Capone been still at large.

Unlike Rico taking over from Vettori (or, for that matter, Capone from Johnny Torrio, the real-life original), when this Scarface wrests power from his boss Johnny Lovo (Osgood Perkins), he immediately orders his henchman Rinaldo (George Raft in his first important role) to kill Lovo, while Scarface takes over his elegant moll, Poppy (Karen Morley), the only important character left alive at the end.

However, Tony's heart, if any, really belongs to his sister Cesca (Ann Dvorak), in a possessive passion barely short of incest. Thus when the faithful Rinaldo answers the door in Cesca's apartment wearing a dressing gown, Tony instantly shoots him, learning too late from the hysterical Cesca that they have been married. Nevertheless, she is killed at her brother's side in the final siege and shoot-out —the most prolonged and bloodiest climax in any major gangster film.

With the end of Prohibition, of course, went the bootleggers' chief source of income. Historically, it is true that most soon turned to bookmaking, drug-smuggling, labor racketeering, organizing chains of brothels and other sources of illegal loot, but these were less spectacularly visible to the public and so less viable for dramatization on the screen. As a few policemen began to emerge as heroes, most gangsters were reduced to villainous roles, played by coldly reptilian types like Eduardo Ciannelli, Joseph Calleia and Jack LaRue, or else turned into semicomic "retired" hoods in quest of overnight respectability.

By the time Bogart came along, the gangster was being viewed more and more as an ugly

Paul Muni, Ann Dvorak in Scarface: The Shame of a Nation

anachronism, however explicable as a product of the times, still evil, a threat to the public and a corrupter of youth. It is significant that Bogart's first important role, in *The Petrified Forest* (1935), was not the kind of hood he was later to play so often but a native Western outlaw who looked very much like Dillinger.

Public attention had by now been diverted from big-city Italian, Irish and Jewish gangsters to alienated sons (and daughters) of impoverished Yankee stock—that is, the rural bandits who in the mid-'30s roamed the Midwest in cars holding up small-town banks: Dillinger, Bonnie and Clyde, Ma Barker and her brood, Pretty Boy Floyd and their ilk. Except for Alvin Karpis, most had been killed by the FBI by the end of 1935.

Their take was penny-ante stuff compared to the riches reaped by the beer barons, and they lived on an accordingly modest scale, but what they did steal most effectively from the Capones and the Legs Diamonds was the front-page headlines. To prevent what might easily have become a cult glorifying them as homespun heirs to Billy the Kid and the

James boys, the Production Code in 1933 specifically banned any film based on Dillinger (and by implication the others), with the result that these incipient legends were nipped in the bud, not to bloom on screen until the 1950s and 1960s.

Even after public interest had waned, however, gangsters continued to appear in films, as minor, often comic, figures. Incredible as it may seem, they figured in well over twenty comedies or farces during the decade. Most typically, the gangster comedy centered on either some timid soul who through physical resemblance or some other accident finds himself embroiled with the underworld, or, after Repeal, a retired bootlegger striving for social polish.

Most of these (e.g., Eddie Quillan's *The Big Money*, 1930, and *The Tip Off*, 1931, Wheeler and Woolsey's *Hook, Line and Sinker*, 1930, and El Brendel's *Mr. Lemon of Orange*, 1931) were too negligible to merit comment here. Somewhat better reviewed was Jack Oakie's *The Gang Buster* (1931), in which the star survives endless farcical complications to outwit gang chief William ("Stage") Boyd.

The first case of a goodhearted ex-mobster yearning for social acceptance was Charles Bickford in *Men in Her Life* (1931). Bickford, who, like George Bancroft and Fred Kohler, often played rough diamonds of the underworld, hires as his mentor a financially embarrassed society girl (Lois Moran), stranded in France when a fortune-hunting nobleman made off with her jewelry and cash. Back in New York, when the evil Count threatens blackmail, the gangster accidentally kills him, but at the trial chivalrously refuses to mention the girl's name, so eventually wins her.

In *Night After Night* (1932) Raft played a speakeasy owner who for love of a Park Avenue girl (Constance Cummings) applies to *grande dame* Alison Skipworth for lessons in deportment and speech. The girl frequents his place only because it was once her home, before the crash, but despite a jealous discarded moll (Wynne Gibson) true love prevails. The film is most notable as the screen debut of Mae West, who in a secondary role walked away with it.

A third variation on this theme was *The Little Giant* (1933), Edward G. Robinson's first venture into comedy, as an ex-bootlegger so determined to crash Santa Barbara society that he even takes up polo. Though fleeced by the unscrupulous socialite family of Helen Vinson, who at first attracts him, he ends up with the charming lady (Mary Astor) whose house he rents.

The redoubtable Alison Skipworth, Paramount's answer to Marie Dressler, had meanwhile made *Madame Racketeer* (1932), as a lifelong con artist who, released from prison, returns to the town where she left her husband (Richard Bennett), but stays only long enough to straighten out the affairs of her two daughters before being taken off to prison again.

Sing and Like It (1934) was an amusing farce in which a sentimental gang czar (Nat Pendleton) is so taken with Zasu Pitts' rendition of a god-awful mother ballad that, like a low-comedy Citizen Kane, he tries to force her on the public, even if it means threatening the critics at gunpoint. Pert Kelton sparkled as his moll.

A further indication that the once-feared underworld leaders had now become figures of fun was *The Gay Bride* (1934), in which a script by the Spewacks turned an originally straight story called *Repeal* into a hilarious farce. Lombard played a dizzy chorus girl determined to nab a wealthy bootlegger, not realizing that the end of Prohibition had left them among the unemployed. Pendleton was again the softhearted mobster, the first in her series of victims before she falls for "poor but dishonest" ex-trigger man Chester Morris.

Passing over such forgettable items as El Brendel's *Olson's Big Moment*, Joe E. Brown's *A Very Honorable Guy* (both 1934) and Edward Everett Horton's *His Night Out* (1935), all of which dealt with milquetoast heroes besting gangsters, one might cite as typical Charles Butterworth's *Baby Face Har-rington* (1935, directed by Raoul Walsh), in which a henpecked clerk loses his job and also a roll of insurance money. He unwittingly steals the same amount from someone else, thinking it his, then after a brief career as a public enemy becomes a hero by his apparent capture of a mobster (Pendleton again). A female parallel, Zasu Pitts in *She Gets Her Man* (1935), becomes a national heroine by accidentally preventing a bank robbery. A gangster kidnaps her, but her influence leads even his gang to reform.

Better remembered than any of these is another Robinson comedy, *The Whole Town's Talking* (1935), in which the star played a dual role, a mousy bank clerk and his gangster double. This was recommended by the *Times* as "the best of the new year's screen comedies . . . With the topical excitement of the late Mr. Dillinger's exploits still warm in the memory, the city-wide search for Killer Mannion possesses the stuff of racy and biting melodrama." Given an identification pass to protect him from the police, the clerk is soon kidnaped by his lookalike, with predictable but entertaining consequences. Directed by John Ford, this bright film also gave Jean Arthur her first real opportunity to do comedy.

F-Man (1936) saw Jack Haley as a soda jerk with aspirations to the FBI. Given a mock appointment and induction, he outclasses the real G-men by capturing the most wanted criminal (Onslow Stevens)—a familiar pattern used earlier by Harold Lloyd and later by Danny Kaye. In *The Big Noise* (1936) Guy Kibbee was a retired textile manufacturer who buys half interest in a dry-cleaning business, which soon brings him into conflict with a protection racket and enables him singlehanded to rid his town of crime.

In a slight variation, *The Big Shot* (1937), Kibbee played a small-town veterinarian who inherits the money, estate and gang of a mysterious relative and uses them to eliminate the sources of his own income, thus exposing himself as Public Enemy Number One. In

Hideaway (1937) Fred Stone was a "Jeeter Lesterish" squatter in what turns out to be a hideaway of gangsters—"a modest little comedy . . . full of harmless rustic humors."

However, what is generally considered the funniest and most original gangster comedy of the decade was *A Slight Case of Murder* (1938), again starring the reliable Robinson. As a mobster about to go respectable, he is much embarrassed at finding in a back room of his rented house at Saratoga the bodies of four recently killed hoods, all still clutching their poker hands. Anticipating the black humor of *Arsenic and Old Lace,* this proved uproarious entertainment, with such added complications as a half-million-dollar note due before noon, a daughter (Jane Bryan) threatening to marry a state trooper and a tough, beer-guzzling juvenile delinquent (Bobby Jordan) named Douglas Fairbanks Rosenbloom.

To be sure, Robinson never altogether retired from serious crime. In the perhaps prematurely titled *The Last Gangster* (1937) he was seen as an unwelcome, threatening ghost from the past. Freed after ten years in Alcatraz on an income tax rap, he seeks out his ex-wife (Rose Stradner), to train his young son (Douglas Scott) in the ways of crime. But, like the movie public, she now prefers a cleancut newspaperman (James Stewart); it is clear where the audience's sympathies are meant to lie.

Fittingly enough, at the very end of the decade came the film that sounded a bittersweet taps for the whole gangster era. Although the end of the '20s, coinciding with the Wall Street debacle, marked them off forever as a decade unlike any other, as immediately recognized in Frederick Lewis Allen's *Only Yesterday* (1931), the feeling toward them at first was not nostalgia, only incredulity, dismay, even revulsion, like that of a hang-over victim confronted with his antics of the night before, perhaps because the '20s were still too close for fond recall or perhaps because values had in every respect so drastically changed.

All the more credit is due, then, to the one '30s film not merely set in the '20s but actually *about* them—*The Roaring Twenties* (1939), written by Mark Hellinger, with a script by Jerry Wald, Richard Macaulay and Robert Rossen, and directed by Raoul Walsh (all of whom had lived through the '20s)—Hollywood's first critical look back at the jazz decade, which perhaps could be faced with better perspective now that it was ten years in the past.

The film does indeed borrow from many an earlier gangster drama: the direct cause-and-effect connection between the war, Prohibition and the rackets from *The Public Enemy,* the year-by-year montage of '20s headlines, newsreels and song hits from *Three on a Match,* the hero's self-sacrifice to prevent the kidnaping of the child of the girl he loves from *Born Reckless* and a death on the steps of a church from *Little Caesar.*

Even aside from its quasi-documentary value as a vibrant recapture of the pulse and pace of New York's night life in that incredible decade, *The Roaring Twenties* features first-rate performances, especially by Cagney as a basically decent bootlegger who loses an innocent singer (Priscilla Lane) to an honest

James Cagney, Gladys George in **The Roaring Twenties**

lawyer (Jeffrey Lynn), while he himself is the object of a hopeless torch carried by a Texas Guinan-type night club hostess (Gladys George), later reduced by the Depression and Repeal to singing in a dingy bar. In the closing scene, it is she, cradling Cagney's bullet-riddled body, *Pietà*-like, on the snowy church steps, who utters the poignant epitaph that became the best-known curtain line of any gangster film since *Little Caesar,* and, in effect, marked the end of the era: "He used to be a big shot."

27

INNOCENT BYSTANDERS
Women and Children First

As is evident throughout this book, Hollywood in the '30s never overlooked the woman's angle, and this remained true even at the height of the cinematic crime wave. Thus a surprisingly large number of films centered not on the gangster as hero but on a nice girl, not necessarily a moll, in love with or married to a man whose underworld career she rejects in horror—but no matter how far she flees, he continues to blight her future with blackmail or threats to her life, as in *The Last Gangster* (1937).

The formula was already being used in the silents—e.g., *Romance of the Underworld* (1929), in which Mary Astor, happily married to wealthy John Boles, is blackmailed by former criminal associates. It turned up in several forgotten "B's" in 1930 and 1931—*Man Trouble, The Good Bad Girl,* Clara Bow's *No Limit* and Alice White's *Sweet Mama* and *Playing Around.*

Despite its provocative title, *The Single Sin* (1931) did not denote what Hollywood usually meant by "sin," but only a three-month sentence Kay Johnson served for bootlegging—a guilty secret to be kept at all costs from her husband (Holmes Herbert). When her former partner (Matthew Betz) turns up as her chauffeur, blackmail looms, but another old acquaintance (Bert Lytell) solves the problem.

A more youthful version of the same situation was *Hush Money* (1931), which sounds like a remake of *Romance of the Underworld.* This time it was Joan Bennett whom a friendly detective gets off the hook by turning the blackmailer over to another crook. In *Docks of San Francisco* (1932) Mary Nolan was a moll trying to go straight, forced by the gang to take bank loot to the cabin of the playboy she loves; she changes sides, and in the climactic gun battle is killed saving him. In *The Reckoning* (1932) it was Sally Blane struggling to escape the past, as Merna Kennedy did in *Red-Haired Alibi* (1932), which, incidentally, was Shirley Temple's first listing, ninth in the cast.

Similarly threatened in variations of the same situation were Claudia Dell in *Guilty or Not Guilty* (1932), Marian Marsh in *Notorious but Nice* (1933), Noel Francis in *The Important Witness* (1933) and Wynne Gibson in *Sleepers East* (1935). As the *Times* pointed out, *The People's Enemy* (1935) "entitled with a wink at Ibsen," illustrated the new Hollywood attitude toward crime—total condemnation. In this one "the millionaire scofflaw" (Preston Foster) is a rat who deserts his family, is jailed for income tax evasion and eventually loses his good wife (Lila Lee) to his mouthpiece (Melvyn Douglas).

In *Woman Wanted* (1935) Maureen O'Sullivan, wrongly convicted of murder, escapes in a car crash arranged by gang boss Louis Calhern, who wants information from her. A lawyer (Joel McCrea) shields her from both police and gangsters until he can pin the rap on Calhern. In *The Girl Who Came Back* (1935) a girl with a crooked past (Shirley Grey) goes West to reform and gets a job in a bank, but her former gang catches up, robs the bank and kidnaps the man she loves (Sidney Blackmer), so she confesses all to the police and brings about his rescue.

In *Public Enemy's Wife* (1936), though Pat O'Brien starred as a G-man, the title roles were played by Cesar Romero and Margaret Lindsay. After serving three years for a crime in which she took no part, the heroine divorces the man who got her into it and is about to marry a wealthy playboy (Dick Foran). But the vicious ex-husband escapes from a train to seek vengeance. After the usual shoot-out she ends with the G-man.

If Constance Bennett had been the perfect mistress and Rosalind Russell was to become the perfect career woman, then surely Sylvia Sidney, with her vulnerable face and wistful voice, was Hollywood's perfect victim. Not only was she betrayed by faithless lovers in *Confessions of a Co-Ed, An American Tragedy, Madame Butterfly* and *Jennie Gerhardt,* but, as noted earlier, she took the rap for her father in *City Streets* (1931).

Ill luck pursued her in *Ladies of the Big House* (1933), written by an actual convict named Ernest Booth, a fact for which the *Times* credited "the reality of its prison scenes . . . An atmosphere of shadow and desolation clings even to those scenes in which love is most plainly seen to be finding a way." As in other "shyster" exposés of the early '30s, the assistant D.A. takes his orders from the underworld, and the press is a ruthless monster eager to make a Roman holiday of other people's troubles. Through purely circumstantial evidence, an innocent young couple (Sidney and Gene Raymond) are arrested soon after their wedding for a murder committed by someone from her past. Prison and much suffering ensue before they are cleared.

In *Pick Up* (1933) her prison past continues to haunt her marriage to an honest cab driver (George Raft), especially when her vengeful first husband (William Harrigan) tries to kill her. Never had she come into such violent conflict with the law, however, as in *Mary Burns, Fugitive* (1935), which, as the *Times* put it, "studies the girl's nightmarish career as she sinks helplessly into the role of a gun-moll under the persecution of the police and the newspapers."

Alan Baxter was the "icy, tight-lipped" killer whom poor Mary, owner of a diner, believed was an oil salesman. Despite her innocence, she is sentenced as his accomplice, then allowed to escape with a female stool pigeon (Pert Kelton) to lead the police to Baxter. To free herself of the stigma now attached to her name, she is finally forced to kill him. Fortunately, as in *The People's Enemy,* Melvyn Douglas is waiting to console her.

In Fritz Lang's *You Only Live Once* (1937), generally recognized as one of the great films of the '30s, Sidney is once again living outside the law, but this time for the sake of the man she truly loves. Released from a third prison term with the warning that the next one will be for life, Eddie Taylor (Henry Fonda) wants only to go straight, aided by his bride, Joan (Sidney), and kindly Father Dolan (William Gargan) —but the world will not let him.

Convicted of a murder he did not commit, he is too embittered to believe it when a pardon arrives. Using a gun Joan smuggled to him in prison, he kills the priest trying to bar his escape. The young couple drive off on a hopeless cross-country flight to nowhere, like a much more appealing Bonnie and Clyde.

Sidney, who could wring the heart with a simple line, as when she speaks of her child, "We just call him . . . Baby," was at her poignant best. The shooting down of Eddie and Joan, viewed through the cross hairs of a sheriff's rifle, done with all Lang's somber power, was one of the unforgettable endings of the decade.

Despite Lang's unconventional directorial touches and an impressive musical score by Kurt Weill, *You and Me* (1938) could not be lifted above the level of mediocrity. An ex-con (Raft) is so disillusioned on learning that his wife (Sidney) has a similar past that he plans to rob a department store that has given him and others jobs despite their criminal records. The little woman, however, tips off the store owner and also convinces the gang that crime doesn't really pay, after all.

Meanwhile, despite this wealth of sad examples, throughout 1937 some of the greatest ladies of the screen had continued to marry into the underworld. Stanwyck, after all, would never have had all that trouble finding

Sylvia Sidney, Henry Fonda in You Only Live Once

her child in *Internes Can't Take Money* had she not married a crook in the first place. In *That Certain Woman,* a remake of Gloria Swanson's 1929 *The Trespasser,* what started Davis' endless chain of woes was her marriage at sixteen to a gangster; though she soon becomes a machine-gun widow, she is never permitted to live down her past. Even Crawford, having learned nothing from her experience with Gene Raymond in *Sadie McKee* (1934), made the same mistake all over again with the much nastier Alan Curtis in *Mannequin.* And where "A" pictures led, "B's" soon followed. Claire Trevor in *Big Town Girl* (1937), Evelyn Venable in *Female Fugitive* (1938) and Joan Woodbury in *Night Spot* (1938) all played variations on the same theme.

Even worse off than these harassed heroines were those who, like the frequently imprisoned Sidney, actually served time. On the whole, they were morally superior to the male convicts if only because, more often than not, their only mistake was loyalty to the wrong man.

As noted earlier, several female spies ended up before the firing squad, and even more long-suffering mothers, plodding in the footsteps of Madame X, ran afoul of the law for the noblest of reasons. Even heiresses were not exempt. In *Manslaughter* (1930) Colbert led off a list of nearly twenty '30s heroines who did a stretch in stir. The first working girl to suffer such a fate was Crawford in *Paid* (1931), the first talkie version of Bayard Veiller's 1912 melodrama *Within the Law,* on stage a vehicle for Jane Cowl and already filmed in silents both by Alice Joyce (1917) and Norma Talmadge (1923).

Mary Turner's three years behind bars were surely the traumatic experience that changed an innocent shopgirl into an embittered woman bent only on revenge against the store owner (Purnell B. Pratt) and the D.A. (Hale Hamilton) who sent her up. She and a tough prison friend (Marie Prevost) work a lucrative, technically legal "heart balm" racket against susceptible older men, until she marries for spite, then falls in love with, the son

(Kent Douglas) of her archenemy. After a melodramatic climax in which her crook friend (Robert Armstrong) saves her from a murder charge, she is finally cleared even of the original accusation of shoplifting.

Even the ladylike Elissa Landi landed in the clink in *Wicked* (1931), thanks to her bank-robber husband (Theodore Von Eltz), who is killed by police after handing her the stolen money. Trying to save him, she accidentally shoots a policeman, so is sentenced to from five to twenty years. A former admirer (Victor McLaglen) hires a lawyer to help, but meanwhile our heroine has borne a child, who is taken from her and given for adoption. On release she kidnaps the child, causing further legal complications before she is eventually freed.

In *Shopworn* (1932) Stanwyck was railroaded to prison on a morals charge, but survived to become a Broadway star. Her *Ladies They Talk About* (1933) was even more melodramatic, but livelier. According to Everson's program notes for a New School showing in 1971:

This slick prison and "confession" melodrama was ostensibly made to cash in on the notoriety surrounding the prison terms of Dorothy Mackaye and her actor husband Paul Kelly, after Kelly had killed her ex-husband in a brawl . . . Considering the realistic quality of most Warner melodramas of the period, it is all rather hokey and unconvincing, but it is enjoyable and briskly written nonsense . . .

Like a lower-class version of *Manslaughter,* the romance involves a crusading D.A. (Preston Foster), who puts a dashing lady bank bandit (Stanwyck) behind the bars of San Quentin, then falls in love with her. A major obstacle is her belief that he is responsible for frustrating a jail break in which two members of her gang were killed. Even after her release, she loses her temper and shoots her would-be lover, though she apologizes, "I didn't mean to do that." Gallantly, he replies, "Why, that's all right, Nan, it's nothing."

What little praise the film drew was for the gallery of inmates played by Lillian Roth,

Dorothy Burgess, Mme. Sul-Te-Wan and especially Maude Eburne as Aunt Maggie, an elderly con woman who acts as den mother to the others.

Bondage (1933), the *Times* noted, seemed to be influenced by *Maedchen in Uniform*. Dorothy Jordan, usually confined to ingenue roles, was an expectant unwed mother, having been seduced by a crooner (Edward Woods) and confined to an institution for "fallen women," at the mercy of a heartless matron (Rafaela Ottiano). When her baby dies, she flees, "completely disorganized by her brutalizing experiences and becomes a woman of the streets."

Unique among women's prison films was *Ann Vickers* (1933), based on Sinclair Lewis' novel, whose heroine is a crusading reformer rather than a victimized inmate. A social service worker (Irene Dunne) who remains cool to several suitors falls for a World War I officer (Bruce Cabot), but when he does not offer marriage she turns to a career of prison reform. Naturally, she is thwarted on all sides, but manages to bring out a book about one particularly disgraceful prison, so is appointed superintendent of an "industrial home." Not until later does she learn that a liberal judge (Walter Huston) has been quietly backing her career. When he is unjustly accused of grafting, she gets an opportunity to repay his confidence, but he is still convicted.

A modest "B," but well reviewed, was *School for Girls* (1934), which cast Sidney Fox as an innocent girl whose involvement with a jewel thief draws three years in prison, under the usual brutal matron (Lucille La Verne). Paul Kelly as the son of a wealthy campaign contributor appointed to the prison board takes an interest in her and eventually sets things right.

Jean Harlow (who had borne Gable a child while in prison in *Hold Your Man* in 1933) was back behind bars again in *Riff Raff* (1936), bearing Spencer Tracy's child after stealing for him, even though he had deserted her upon losing a strike he called on their wedding day. By this time Harlow had estab-

lished herself so firmly as a comedienne that Nugent in the *Times* lamented: "With so many Kay Francises around, Metro really should be able to stake off one small section of ground and post it with placards reading 'Miss Harlow's Plot: No Children Wanted.' "

In *Bridge of Sighs* (1936) an assistant D.A. (Onslow Stevens) suspects his girl (Dorothy Tree) loves a man he has doomed to the chair. She has herself committed to prison to gain the confidence of a moll who may have been the actual killer, not a mere accessory. They break out, the girl finds the crucial evidence, and, as it happens, the man she clears is really her brother.

As with films about men and boys in prison, a general amnesty seemed to prevail during the mid-'30s, followed by a sudden crackdown in 1938; the difference was that none of the later women's pictures featured any major actress.

Women in Prison (1938) used the slightly different twist of letting a vicious gang boss (Arthur Loft) confess, when shot, that he framed the daughter (Wyn Cahoon) of a dedicated warden (Sarah Padden), one of the few of her kind. *Prison Nurse* (1938), released a few days later, dealt with the plight of a doctor (Henry Wilcoxon) and his nurse (Marian Marsh) sent up for mercy killing, who "work out their joint sentence as best they can." *Condemned Women* (1938), with an excellent cast, was rated by the *Times* as "a first-rate production in the frankly third-rate, or pulpwood, class." Anne Shirley takes the rap for her boy friend, while Sally Eilers reforms, after knocking off a tough matron (Esther Dale) and a fellow con (Lee Patrick, as if warming up for *Caged*, which this film anticipated).

Better reviewed was *Prison Farm*, one of Paramount's crime series. Miller rates it second only to *Hunted Men* in the series. "It was all the prison stories ever seen on the screen rolled into one, and done in sixty-nine minutes."

To cover a far more serious crime, Lloyd Nolan takes a six-month rap on a prison farm, forcing his innocent sweetheart (Shirley Ross) to serve time as an accomplice. Says Miller:

Once inside the gates of the prison farm, we encounter all the standard types, including brutal guards J. Carroll Naish (male) and Marjorie Main (female) ; weaseling warden Porter Hall; cynically wise old-timer inmate May Boley; earnest young prison doctor John Howard; planned escapes, double-crosses, violent death, with all the precarious situations resolved for a happy ending. And it works beautifully, thanks to [director Louis] King, the cast, and some exceptionally realistic photography by Harry Fischbeck.[1]

With Columbia, Republic, RKO and Paramount each having contributed one of the above films, Warners could hardly let 1938 pass without getting into the act—hence *Girls on Probation,* which sounds a great deal like all the others about nice girls who keep bad company. Said the *Times:* "The heroine is nice but dumb; she blunders into jail. Her subsequent rehabilitation is therefore a matter more of plot contrivance than character building." Jane Bryan and Ronald Reagan were the stars, but among the inmates, listed twelfth in the cast, was Susan Hayward (her first billing under that name) —an ironic coincidence, considering that just twenty years later she would win an Oscar as a famous woman prisoner, Barbara Graham in *I Want to Live* (1958) .

After this quintet of female con films in one year, in 1939 all was quiet on the dames-behind-bars front—almost. As if to end the decade on a resolving chord, with a reprise from its beginning (as also happened in other genres) , MGM released the fourth film version of the venerable *Within the Law,* thereby making Mary Turner the equal of Madame X, whose tribulations had also been filmed four times.

Even the original title was retained, as were all the characters' names. Ruth Hussey was the wronged Mary, Rita Johnson her hard-boiled prison mate, Samuel Hinds the heartless store owner and Tom Neal his son. Except for the

interpolation of a few airplane sequences, the well-worn plot remained intact.

But if gangsters tended to be rough on their womenfolk, most of them were suckers for their (or even other people's) children. Not only did many, as noted earlier, take utmost pains to conceal the source of their ill-gotten gains from their grown offspring, they were even more susceptible to the clasp of tiny hands and the patter of little feet.

The earliest example was *Donovan's Kid* (1930) , in which the hoodlum hero (Richard Dix) is redeemed through love for his adopted son (Jackie Cooper) . *Tough Guy* (1936) offered another sure-fire combination: a runaway rich boy (Cooper again) and his dog (Rin Tin Tin, Jr.) fall into the hands of a gang leader (Joseph Calleia) who just happens to be a pushover for boys and their dogs, with G-man Harvey Stephens providing a satisfactory ending for all concerned. In *Gangster's Boy* (1938) a high school honor student (Cooper, who else?) is only temporarily embarrassed by the revelation that his prosperous father (Robert Warwick) is a retired gangster.

In *The Escape* (1939) Edward Norris, who had played Mickey Rooney's vicious brother in *Boys Town,* is the meanest hoodlum on the East Side—but when he finds that a little girl kidnapped by his gang is actually his own daughter, what can he do but sacrifice his life to ensure her freedom? The one exception among all these tenderhearted fathers was Bruce Cabot in *Mickey the Kid* (1939) . When the G-men put the heat on him, he sends his son (Tommy Ryan) to his grandmother's, where the boy prays for his safety— but then dear old dad tries to use Mickey and the school bus to cover his getaway. As the *Times* said, "No dice, Mickey has turned noble on him."

The far commoner connection between children or adolescents and crime, however, was as tough street urchins already in trouble with the police. Oddly enough, this note was first sounded in the '30s in a Buster Keaton comedy, *Sidewalks of New York* (1931) , in

---

[1] *B Movies* (Curtis Books, 1973) , p. 163.

which a playboy who falls for a Lower East Side girl (Anita Page) builds a gym to keep her kid brother's gang off the streets. A real gang thinks he's on to them and tries to bump him off, but the kids come to his rescue. The same problem—always soluble by a new athletic center or equipment—recurred more seriously in *The Silk Hat Kid* (1935).

As if determined to beat Goldwyn's long-heralded *Dead End* to the screen, *The Devil Is a Sissy* (1936) took another tentative step toward equating slum environment with juvenile crime. An English boy (Freddie Bartholomew) spending six months in New York with his divorced father (Ian Hunter) is fascinated by the new friends he makes in a public school: the leader of a youthful gang (Jackie Cooper again) and the proudly defiant son (Mickey Rooney) of a recently executed mobster.

To help his friend get money for a proper tombstone, the English lad leads a Raffles-like robbery of a Park Avenue home, an attempt that lands them all in juvenile court. From the vantage point of the '70s, Bergman rates it "halfhearted," judging Cooper and Rooney more like mischievous small-town pranksters than New York street toughs.

Thus it remained for *Dead End* itself (1937), adapted by Lillian Hellman from Sidney Kingsley's long-running play, to bring to the screen young hoodlums as close to the gutter in speech and manners as the Production Code would then permit. These, of course, were the original Dead End Kids, played by the same teen-aged actors as on stage: Billy Halop as Tommy, Leo Gorcey as Spit, Gabriel Dell as T.B., Bobby Jordan as Angel, Huntz Hall as Dippy and Bernard Punsley as Milty.

Their awed hero worship of Baby Face Martin (Bogart), the only local boy who ever made good—that is, achieved a life of at least temporary luxury—is obviously tempting them down the same criminal path, even though he is now on the lam and clearly doomed. *Dead End,* to be sure, involves many other social issues, but its sharp focus on en-

vironment as the breeding ground of criminals launched a whole cycle of films about young delinquents. It also launched the Kids themselves on careers of cinematic misbehavior that lasted them well into middle age.

The first follow-up, early in 1938, was *Boy of the Streets,* with Cooper, hailed by the *Times* as "the Walter Huston of juveniles," in his now familiar role of gang leader, and Marjorie Main again as the downtrodden slum mother, as in *Dead End.* Except for her, the *Times* said, the characters were "about as real as the virtuous folk in a comic strip." The young hero gets involved with real gangsters, doesn't like it and ends by joining the Navy, making this the first of many films in which a recruiting officer was the *deus ex machina* guaranteed to turn delinquents into heroes. In retrospect this seems almost prophetic, for in the end what cleared the jobless youngsters from the streets was the 1940 draft.

Oddly enough, in all Cooper's brushes with the law on screen he never actually served any time in a reformatory. Other movie j.d.'s were not so lucky. Throughout the decade, just as service films had their junior auxiliaries in those about the military academies and prep schools, and gangster pictures were paralleled in those about street gangs, the prison cycle also had its youthful counterpart in films, mostly "B's," about boys' reformatories.

The first was *Hell's House* (1932), which seemed to set the pattern in both title and tone—that of angry exposé. Though released by Capitol Film Exchange, it featured two future Warners stars, Pat O'Brien and Bette Davis, both billed beneath teen-aged Junior Durkin. Caught in a dry raid, the boy hero refuses to tell anything about his bootlegger friend (O'Brien), so is sentenced to three years in a particularly grim reformatory. When he finally escapes in a garbage container, the bootlegger's girl (Davis) persuades him to give himself up, and the boy is freed.

The following year the same kind of material was much more forcefully dramatized in *The Mayor of Hell* (1933), which the *Times* regarded as very nearly the equal of

I Am a Fugitive from a Chain Gang. A gang of young hoodlums led by Frankie Darro is sentenced to a reformatory that makes the one in *Hell's House* look positively idyllic, for it is run by a keeper (Dudley Digges) who for sanctimonious sadism would be hard to equal this side of Dickens.

An amiable ward heeler (Cagney) visiting the place learns the truth from a nurse (Madge Evans) and gets himself put in charge, but no sooner has he brought about long overdue reforms than he himself shoots a man and must go into hiding. His vicious predecessor returns, ready to wreak vengeance on all. Thus a consumptive boy who refuses to play stool pigeon is locked in a drafty guardhouse and allowed to die, whereupon the others take justice into their own hands and in effect lynch their tormentor.

Yet five years passed before another film was made about a boys' reformatory, predictably by Warners: *Crime School* (1938), the first vehicle to reunite the Dead End Kids after their original success, but not in the same league as *Angels with Dirty Faces,* which was to follow. Though the film was in part a remake of *The Mayor of Hell,* Bogart, their criminal mentor in *Dead End,* was now an enlightened deputy commissioner. Said the *Times:*

It presents its heroes as a tough and rough-spoken pack of rowdies whose ultimate regeneration we must accept with a hearty dredging of salt . . . If the script bears a family resemblance to *Dead End* and *San Quentin,* not to mention the old Cagney film, *The Mayor of Hell,* it is possibly as much the fault of environment as heredity.

The Mayor of Hell was, in fact, remade the following year, as *Hell's Kitchen* (1939), with

Madge Evans, James Cagney (standing) in The Mayor of Hell

Gale Page, Humphrey Bogart, the Dead End Kids—Leo Gorcey, Bobby Jordan, Bernard Punsley, Huntz Hall, Gabriel Dell (seated), Billy Halop—in Crime School

Crane Wilbur given sole screen credit, though it follows the original incident for incident, with the Dead End Kids the victims of sadistic Grant Mitchell, Ronald Reagan in the Cagney role and Margaret Lindsay replacing Madge Evans. This time the superintendent actually tortures a boy to death and is himself almost murdered, but the boys "end up in a burst of righteous glory and cake and ice-cream all around."

Meanwhile Columbia had produced the inevitable "B" version, *Reformatory* (1938), with Jack Holt as the benevolent new superintendent, Frankie Darro, still playing teenagers, and Bobby Jordan, borrowed from the Dead End crew. Darro also turned up in *Boys'*

Reformatory (1939), in which he takes the rap for a pal and is befriended by the prison doctor (Grant Withers). A gang leader springs the boys so they won't talk, but Darro finally traps him and his friend is cleared. In short, with the exception of the original *Mayor of Hell*, the boys-behind-bars cycle produced no film comparable to the best of the adult prison dramas or even of the others about juvenile delinquency.

Meanwhile, the third reunion of the Dead Enders, minus Leo Gorcey and Bobby Jordan, Universal's *Little Tough Guys* (1938), found the *Times* reviewer complaining that Hollywood would soon run out of novel nicknames for the youngsters, and also that "their stories are becoming increasingly redundant and therefore thin." *Little Tough Guys* was too directly reminiscent of both *Dead End* and *Crime School,* each time the originally powerful material diluted further, with less social consciousness and more comic cuteness.

Forced to the streets by the unjust conviction of his father, Billy Halop becomes a gang leader, with reform school looming at the end as "a hopeful regenerative haven"—the exact reverse of the message in all the other films on this theme. By now the Kids were beginning to remind B. R. Crisler of the Ritz Brothers—even more so in *Little Tough Guys in Society* (released late in 1938) .[2]

Code of the Streets (1939) featured the five "Little Tough Guys" in a typical melodrama about a police lieutenant (Harry Carey) broken because he believes in the innocence of a boy sentenced for murder. His son (Frank Thomas) joins a youthful gang who trap the real culprit.

Otherwise 1939 saw only the rapid erosion, perhaps from overexposure, of the Dead End

Kids' once vivid image, from *They Made Me a Criminal,* in which they were strictly subordinate to rising star John Garfield (and by now reminded Crisler of the Three Stooges) , through *Hell's Kitchen, Angels Wash Their Faces*—no connection with the film whose title it echoes—in which, Penrod-and-Sam style, they expose a politically backed arson ring while uniting Ann Sheridan with Ronald Reagan, and finally the deplorably militaristic *Dress Parade.*

The subsequent proliferation of such films throughout the 1940s and even into the 1950s in endless, overlapping series of lowbrow slapstick comedies (some with one of the original Dead End Kids, some with none) , featuring groups variously billed as the Little Tough Guys, the East Side Kids, the Gas House Gang, the Bowery Boys, was a degenerative process too complex (and dreary) to trace. What was most unfortunate was that the six talented young actors so soon reached dead ends in their careers. Leo Gorcey aged into a paunchy caricature of his youthful self, the sensitive Billy Halop died without ever having fulfilled his apparent promise. Of those living, only Gabriel Dell and Huntz Hall have retained any kind of names as actors.

---

[2] The fall of 1938, however, also saw two of the strongest juvenile delinquent dramas of the decade, *Boys Town* and *Angels with Dirty Faces,* covered earlier.

28

AROUND THE LAW IN EIGHTY WAYS
Shysters, Mouthpieces and Ambulance Chasers

The courts of the land should not be presented as unjust. This does not mean that a single court may not be represented as unjust, much less that a single court official must not be presented this way. But the court system of the country must not suffer as a result of this presentation.

—The Motion Picture Production Code

More vital to the survival of a successful gangster than his wife, molls, children, protégés or even henchmen was a good (i.e., unscrupulous) lawyer, whose fortunes usually rose and fell with his. Like doctors and clergymen, lawyers had always figured functionally in realistic fiction, though seldom as heroes. From Dodson and Fogg in *Pickwick Papers* through Jaggers in *Great Expectations,* Dickens alone contributed a whole rogues' gallery of generally unpleasant lawyers, at best pompous frauds (Stryver in *A Tale of Two Cities*), at worst sinister ghouls (Mr. Vholes in *Bleak House*). And surely Sydney Carton must be the literary ancestor of all the brilliant alcoholic lawyers.

One favorite kind of melodrama continued to hang on in the '30s, set almost entirely in a courtroom during a single trial (though perhaps with flashbacks dramatizing the witnesses' testimony), with suspense centered on the fate of the defendant.

Unusual in that it concentrated on the jurors rather than the defendant or the lawyers was *Ladies of the Jury* (1932), based on Frederick Ballard's play, in which Minnie Maddern Fiske had starred on Broadway in 1929. A determined society woman (Edna May Oliver), intuitively sure that a young actress (Jill Esmond) on trial did not murder her elderly husband, by hook or crook brings the other eleven jurors to her view. Remade in 1939 as *We're on the Jury,* with Helen Broderick and Victor Moore, it received equally good reviews as "a genial light comedy." In both versions Robert McWade played the harried judge.

A far more typical courtroom piece was *The Trial of Vivienne Ware* (1932), a variation on *The Trial of Mary Dugan* (1929), in which Joan Bennett was accused of murdering her unpleasant, older fiancé (Jameson Thomas) and defended by a lawyer (Donald Cook) who loves her. Said the *Times*: "It is nothing new for film producers to play fast and loose with court-room procedure . . . but in *The Trial of Vivienne Ware* . . . the tactics employed . . . make the liberties taken in other productions seem relatively restrained."

The next "pure" courtroom feature was *Midnight Madonna* (1937), of which the *Times* observed:

In contemplating courtroom procedure . . . it must have occurred to nearly every one what a fine . . . thing it would be to kidnap the judge and force the old gentleman to listen to the facts of the case, and that is precisely what Warren William does to that eminent jurist, Edward Ellis.

This one involved a child custody case, the child being Kitty Clancy, Paramount's attempted answer to Shirley Temple. Her dastardly father (Robert Baldwin) tries to prove his ex-wife (Mady Correll) is no lady, until her lawyer's seizure of the judge clears matters up.

To end the decade on an appropriately familiar note, Elmer Rice's old war horse, *On Trial,* that hit of 1914, already filmed twice in silents, in 1917 and 1928, was trotted out again in 1939, perhaps as a silver jubilee tribute. The *Times* noted certain enduring clichés of the genre: "Attorneys still gloat or glare when an objection is overruled, the defendant who insists he is guilty will be proved not, and the young attorney with his first big case will outsmart the criminal courts veteran." John Litel was the defendant, Margaret Lindsay his wife and James Stephenson the caddish victim, introduced in flashbacks. (*On Trial* had been the first stage play to use this cinematic device.)

In the early '30s, however, a new kind of lawyer had begun to emerge, in a whole cycle of what Andrew Bergman calls "shyster" films. Indeed, between 1930 and 1939 more than fifty films centered on lawyers (including twelve women and enough fictitious D.A.'s of Manhattan to pack a sizable courtroom). Many were true antiheroes, every bit as ruthlessly amoral as the criminals they so frequently, and successfully, defended. As Bergman puts it:

Their makers delighted in the rogues they were attempting to condemn. And this ambivalence was tied not only to the dismal position occupied by the law in 1931 and 1932 but to the fact that in depicting shysters during the nadir of the Depression they were administering relief, rather than addressing a central problem. In 1932, corruption must have seemed like an old and trusted friend.[1]

[1] *We're in the Money* (Harper Colophon Books, 1972), p. 18.

Not counting Fredric March, who played lawyers in *Manslaughter, Sarah and Son, My Sin* and *Night Angel,* as did Clive Brook in *The Laughing Lady* and *Anybody's Woman,* all discussed elsewhere, the first "mouthpiece" to appear on the screen in 1930 was William Powell (later to play many another lawyer) in *For the Defense.*

Photographed, like *Street of Chance* and other early Paramount talkies, on location in New York, a fact which now lends them unique documentary interest, *For the Defense* depicts the lawyer's downfall not through his admitted criminal associations but through his bribery of a juror in the case of a hit-and-run death involving his girl (Kay Francis). He pleads guilty and is sentenced to Sing Sing (where no doubt he will meet George Bancroft from *Scandal Sheet,* also put behind bars for love of Francis). Powell and Francis were becoming one of Paramount's most popular teams.

Legal dilemmas of a more conventional kind were faced by Clive Brook in *The Lawyer's Secret* (1931), when the brother (Charles Rogers) of his fiancée (Fay Wray) confides that he has been unwilling accessory to a murder, for which a sailor (Richard Arlen) has been convicted. Only when the execution is hours away do they track down a key witness and expose the murderer.

Released in New York the same week (the first week of June 1931), *A Free Soul* proved far more sensational, and won Lionel Barrymore the 1930–31 Oscar, as a brilliant, aging, alcoholic attorney, said to have been inspired by the father of the writer Adela Rogers St. Johns. As noted earlier, his daughter (Norma Shearer) becomes involved with one of his gangster clients (Gable, in another of his eleven 1931 roles). Alarmed, the father even promises to give up drinking if the girl will end the affair, but neither keeps the bargain. Pushed too far, her rejected, honorable suitor (Leslie Howard) kills the gangster, and is at the last moment defended by the father, who dramatically blames himself for having brought up his daughter too liberally, then drops dead. The *Times* was appalled by such lurid antics in a courtroom, but the worst was yet to come.

In 1932 so many mouthpiece films appeared in rapid succession, all apparently inspired by the much-publicized histrionics of the once notorious William J. Fallon (subject of Gene Fowler's biography, *The Great Mouthpiece*), that three major studio variations opened in New York within a month—preceded by a forgotten "B" from the Action studio, *Sin's Pay Day,* in which the wife (Dorothy Revier) of a mouthpiece (Forrest Stanley) leaves him in protest. He turns to drink, is redeemed by a kid (Mickey McGuire, later to be known as Mickey Rooney), and when the boy is accidentally killed by a gang bullet, exposes the leader.

Warners' *The Mouthpiece* starred Warren William as an assistant D.A. driven to drink when a man he has helped convict is proved innocent only after his execution. Thus he turns to criminal clients more out of disillusion than from simple greed. Sidney Fox was the naïve little typist he loved, and Aline MacMahon, as in *Five Star Final,* the wise secretary. Most unusually, this mouthpiece is mowed down by machine-gun bullets after sending a mobster to prison.

With *The Mouthpiece* only in its third

Warren William, John Wray, Aline MacMahon in **The Mouthpiece**

week at the Winter Garden, *State's Attorney* opened at the Mayfair, starring John Barrymore as another dazzling legal light. This time a boy who served a term in reform school becomes the confidant and lawyer of a racketeer he met there (William "Stage" Boyd), but when elected D.A. tries to go straight. Like Lionel in *A Free Soul,* John sustains his courtroom brilliance with heavy after-hours drinking. Though he marries a foolish heiress (Jill Esmond) for the sake of her father's political power, he loves a more vulnerable girl (Helen Twelvetrees) whom he saved from a prostitution charge, and eventually, after resigning his office, turns to her.

Three weeks later, *Attorney for the Defense* opened at both New York Paramounts, with Edmund Lowe as William J. Burton, still another D.A. who resigns his office to defend those accused of crime. To atone to the family of a man he wrongfully sent to the chair, he puts the victim's son (Donald Dillaway) through law school, and later hires him in his office. When his mistress (Evelyn Brent) for ulterior motives makes a play for the boy and is subsequently found dead, both the lawyer and his protégé are suspected on circumstantial evidence—but his crafty legal tactics soon flush out the real murderer.

Seven months later, almost at the end of 1932, William Powell returned to the bar in *Lawyer Man,* as a Lower East Side attorney of apparently Slavic origins, to judge by his name, Anton Adam, and that of his secretary, Olga (Joan Blondell). This one anticipates *Bordertown* (1935) in several respects, tracing the rise and fall of an ambitious ethnic-minority lawyer who, after discouraging setbacks, sells out for flashy success, is framed and almost destroyed by one woman (Claire Dodd), toyed with and dropped by a shallow socialite (Helen Vinson)—roles roughly parallel to those of Bette Davis and Margaret Lindsay in *Bordertown*—before returning in humility to work for his own people.

Lawyer Man was timely for 1932, with references to jigsaw puzzles, the Seabury investigation and even a political crook who keeps his money in "a little tin box" (a phrase associated with Jimmy Walker's cronies). In the style of the period, aptly chosen popular songs provide background music; thus the increasingly dismayed Blondell's signature tune is "Say It Isn't So," while Vinson's motif is "I Guess I'll Have to Change My Plan."

Even in the early '30s, a few screen D.A.'s did not resign their office in disgust or disgrace, but they were buried in "B" films, played by actors not half so magnetic as the high-powered stars. Thus in *Night Beat* (1931), praised for its realistic emphasis on the tradesmen victims of crime, an honest prosecutor (Jack Mulhall) calls in an out-of-town gangster friend to clean out the mob in his city. In *Behind Stone Walls* (1932) the wife (Priscilla Dean) of a D.A. (Robert Elliott) kills her lover, but her stepson (Eddie Nugent) takes the rap to spare his father, who, never suspecting the truth, prosecutes and convicts him. When he finally does catch on, he kills the wife, and the son, now pardoned, defends him in court.

In *The World Gone Mad* (1933), a new D.A. (Neil Hamilton) does not realize that his predecessor was murdered by the orders of an eminent financier (Richard Tucker) to prevent an investigation of his chicanery; it takes one of those ace reporters (Pat O'Brien) to expose the truth. In *Shadows of Sing Sing* (1934) an assistant D.A. (Bruce Cabot) falls in love with the sister (Mary Brian) of a powerful gangster (Harry Woods). The police bureau of identification provides "a surprise ending to the tale of love and woe."

Though pictures about lawyers continued to be made, the mouthpiece cycle was drawing to a close with 1932. 1934 saw only *The Defense Rests* and 1935 *Behind the Green Lights,* plus *Special Investigator,* in which Richard Dix was the "big shot" lawyer—but with a new post-Production Code twist. When his kid brother, a G-man (Owen Davis, Jr.), is gunned down, the hero switches his ruthless skill to the side of the law as an undercover man for the Justice Department.

Still praised as timely and based on recognizable incidents, *Criminal Lawyer* (1937), starring Lee Tracy, was an unacknowledged remake of *State's Attorney,* as *Midnight Court* (1937) seems to have been of *The Mouthpiece,* with a happy ending.

Despite its title, *Counsel for Crime* (1937) was primarily concerned with father love, as the hero (Otto Kruger) goes to prison to live up to the ideals of his unacknowledged illegitimate lawyer son (Douglass Montgomery). Youngest mouthpiece of the decade, fresh out of law school, was Robert Cummings in *I Stand Accused* (1939). Though Thomas Beck as his partner never lowers his high standards, Cummings repents in time to get the girl (Helen Mack).[2]

All screen lawyers, of course, were not wealthy mouthpieces, even in the '30s. Some were mere ambulance chasers, like Lee Tracy in *The Nuisance* (1933), which at various stages was to have been called *The Chaser, Accidents Wanted, Ambulance Chaser* and *Never Give a Sucker a Break.* Emphasis was on satirical comedy in this film, called by the *Times* "a hilarious diversion." Adapted by Samuel and Bella Spewack in apparently their first screenwriting assignment, it reveals the title character as an irresistible rogue who works hand in glove with a drunken doctor (Frank Morgan) and a professional accident victim (Charles Butterworth).

A transit company, fleeced once too often, hires a pretty private detective (Madge Evans) to trap the nuisance, but, needless to say, she falls for him, and by barely legal means he outwits everyone in the end. Like so many lawyer pictures, *The Nuisance* was remade within the decade, as *The Chaser* (1938), still using some of the Spewacks' script, the characters' names unchanged, with Dennis O'Keefe in the title role, Lewis Stone as the doctor and Dorothy Morris as the girl.

As is already evident, certain actors (Pow-

ell, Clive Brook, March) seemed naturals to play lawyers. Thus in 1937 Lee Tracy was practicing again in *Criminal Lawyer,* and in 1939 played *The Spellbinder,* still another mouthpiece, the last one of the decade. But perhaps the busiest lawyer of all was Otto Kruger, who plied his skill in *The Women in His Life* (1934), *They Won't Forget* (1937), *Counsel for Crime* (1937), *Disbarred* and *A Woman Is the Judge* (both 1939).

Occasionally the screen even touched on honest lawyers: Warner Baxter (though unjustly ostracized for serving as mouthpiece to Nat Pendleton) in *Penthouse* (1932), remade by Walter Pidgeon as *Society Lawyer* (1939); William Powell in *Evelyn Prentice* (1934), remade by Pidgeon as *Stronger Than Desire* (1939).

However, by far the most convincing of the good attorneys appeared in what was undoubtedly the best lawyer picture of all, completely outside the mouthpiece cycle: Elmer Rice's adaptation of his own 1931 play, *Counsellor-At-Law* (1933), starring John Barrymore in the role created on stage by Paul Muni. The structure is a variation on the *Grand Hotel* pattern Rice had used so effectively in *Street Scene,* with a large, variegated cast connected only by the fact that all are associates, clients, employees, friends or relatives of George Simon, who has climbed from a Lower East Side ghetto to a palatial suite of offices in the Empire State Building, where all the action takes place.

If any fault could be found, it might be that Simon's law practice is almost *too* varied; he does corporation work but also handles murder cases, breach of promise suits and divorces—yet this slight improbability makes possible a series of strong, vividly realized scenes (one with an amorous murderess whose acquittal he has won, one with a blackmailing chorus girl, one with a passionately bitter young radical).

Within a few hectic days Simon finds his professional life threatened by disbarment over an alibi faked years before and now dug up by a rival; at the same time his personal

---

[2] Still further outside the law, a few lawyers even turned murderers—e.g., Claude Rains in *Crime Without Passion* (1934) and Charles Bickford in *A Notorious Gentleman* (1935).

Thelma Todd, Bebe Daniels, John Barrymore in **Counsellor-At-Law**

life is cracking up with the dawning realization that his idolized socialite wife (Doris Kenyon) would really rather not have him go with her to Europe as long as she can enjoy the company of a gentleman of her own background (Melvyn Douglas). Only his loyal secretary (Bebe Daniels) fully appreciates him. As always in Rice's work, New York's then dominant ethnic strains, especially Jewish, Irish and WASP, and their attitudes toward each other, are sharply and accurately portrayed.

The following year Powell played another lawyer in *Manhattan Melodrama* (1934), the film which achieved accidental historical fame as the one that Dillinger saw the night he was killed. It is one of the earliest, and perhaps most obviously contrived, examples of the Cain and Abel pattern noted in *San Francisco* and *Angels with Dirty Faces,* the diametrically opposed friends (in earlier melodramas they would have been brothers, preferably twins), one of whom upholds or practices the law, while the other defies it. "One went up the ladder to the throne," said the ads. "One went up the river to the chair."

Orphaned by the *General Slocum* disaster of 1904, when an excursion steamer burned in the East River, the two boys grow up on the Lower East Side, with Gable (called Blackie, as later in *San Francisco*) becoming a big-time gambler, Powell a lawyer, then D.A., then governor, along the way marrying Blackie's ex-mistress (Myrna Loy). Loyal to the end, Blackie kills a disgruntled political hack to spare his friend a mudslinging campaign, refuses to explain in court, is convicted by Powell as D.A. and finally rejects a commutation of his death sentence by Powell as governor—which seems an excess of nobility even for a '30s film. But, as Everson notes, "It is also an incredibly fast-paced and well-made film, full of solid craftsmanship."

Not until the later '30s, however, after the successful and highly publicized conviction of Lucky Luciano and other racketeers by New York's special prosecutor Thomas E. Dewey, did the boldly crusading (as distinguished from merely ambitious) D.A. come into his own as a film hero—neither as glamorous nor as frequently portrayed as the G-man, but, on the other hand, smoother and more articulate than a cop.

In *Exclusive Story* (1936), based on an exposé by journalist Martin Mooney, Franchot Tone was a special prosecutor appointed to wipe out the policy racket, Madge Evans was his fiancée, kidnaped to force him to drop the investigation, and Joseph Calleia played another of his menacing hoods as Ace Acello, lieutenant of the numbers king, caught at last by the FBI.

By far the strongest of such films was *Marked Woman* (1937), in which Bogart, for once on the right side of the law, played an assistant prosecutor who nails the malignant Eduardo Ciannelli when five clip joint hostesses, led by Bette Davis (already scarred on the face as a warning), finally turn state's witnesses after the murder of Davis' innocent sister (Jane Bryan). The parallel to Luciano, then in Dannemora, was obvious, though as Nugent in the *Times* noted, "In the interests of the Hays Office and the Legion of Decency, the sphere of influence of Johnny Vanning, the picture's Luciano, has been transferred

from the bagnio to the bistro." He considered Davis' performance her best since *Of Human Bondage*.

The other D.A. films, three released the same month (August 1938), were more routine. *Smashing the Rackets,* based on a *Saturday Evening Post* series about Dewey, starred Chester Morris, who rather easily (said the *Times*) "assumes the investigation of a big city's crime, traces its involutions right down to one big shot, sends the felon to the jug and picks up a wife in the bargain."

Opening a few days later, *Racket Busters*, by the same writer (Robert Riskin) and director (Lloyd Bacon) as *Marked Woman*, saw Bogart revert to type as king of the food and trucking rackets. Called by the *Times* "hard-grained and generally exciting," the story, based on court records, centered on a trucker (George Brent) who at first holds out against a crooked union, later capitulates, but finally exposes it—a pattern parallel to Bogart's in *Black Legion*.

A few weeks later, in *I Am the Law*, Robinson, cast against type, was playing a mild-mannered law professor drafted by a citizens' committee to clean up the city, in which Mr. Big turns out to be Otto Kruger, father of Robinson's honorable young assistant (John Beal). In a scene that Crisler considered "a climax in silliness," the hero takes on single-handedly three tough hoodlums in a rousing fist fight.

Next variation in 1938 was *Crime Takes a Holiday*, in which Jack Holt was the racket-busting D.A. who by fair means or foul exposes the big shot as, of all people, a publisher of popular songs. Finally, in December 1938, in *Gang Bullets*, the last of this cycle, a clever gangster eludes the D.A. (Charles Trowbridge) so consistently that a newspaper blames the D.A. in a series of accusing letters. He is actually tried and convicted, but it was all a scheme with the assistant D.A. (Robert Kent) to get evidence.

The only remaining good lawyer of the decade was Edward Ellis in *Main Street Lawyer* (1939), an attempted follow-up on the very well-received *A Man to Remember* (1938), but described by Crisler as "a rickety little horse-and-buggy opera," in which, to conceal the fact that his presumed daughter (Anita Louise) is really the child of a woman convict, a hitherto respected attorney allows himself to be blackmailed into throwing an important prosecution and suffers temporary disgrace.

It is typical of the esteem in which the two professions were held that, although there were at least seven '30 films about kindly old small-town or country doctors (not counting their urban counterparts), Ellis' character in this film is the only such lawyer—unless one might include Will Rogers in *Judge Priest.*

Speaking of neglected minorities, one must now turn to women lawyers, who, as noted earlier, numbered twelve, four more than women doctors, but played by a greater variety of actresses. Only Frieda Inescort played more than one. It seems significant that three of these films (one a remake of another) involved self-sacrificial mother love.

The first was *Scarlet Pages* (1930), in which Elsie Ferguson, re-creating her 1929 stage role, played a lawyer defending a night club entertainer (Marian Nixon) accused of murdering her adopted father when he tried to attack her. Need it be added that the girl turns out to be the lawyer's own illegitimate daughter? In another forgotten "B," *Drifting Souls* (1932), a playboy (Theodore Von Eltz) framed for manslaughter marries a girl (Lois Wilson) for an alibi, but she falls in love with him and wins his case, as she's a lawyer.

Like Strindberg's *Comrades, Ann Carver's Profession* (1933) openly preached that woman's place was in the home. When a lawyer wife (Fay Wray) begins to earn more than her architect husband (Gene Raymond), he is just as resentful as if she were an heiress. Rather oddly, he then becomes a night club crooner and gets involved in a sensational murder case, in which his wife successfully defends him—after which she gives up her career to save her marriage (just as Frieda

Inescort was to do six years later in *Woman Doctor*).

Next lady of the law was Jean Arthur in *The Defense Rests* (1934), which was a late example of the mouthpiece cycle, with Jack Holt as still another undefeatable legal wizard, until thwarted by idealistic young law school graduate Arthur, determined to expose him as a perjurer. Her role, however, was distinctly secondary to his.

Altogether unique was *Two Heads on a Pillow* (1934), in which Neil Hamilton and Miriam Jordan played a young married couple, both lawyers, separated by her mother's interference. Seven years later (anticipating *Adam's Rib* by fifteen years), they meet as opponents in court in an alienation suit, he representing a rich girl, she a poor boy. She wins the case, but they get back together. Even more surprisingly, no triangle was involved, nor does she give up her career.

Behind the Green Lights (1935) was more seriously intended. A veteran police lieutenant's daughter (Judith Allen) never questions the tactics of the mouthpiece (Sidney Blackmer) in whose firm she works, until a criminal she helped free shoots her father during a robbery, whereupon she changes sides and helps a young detective (Norman Foster) capture the criminal and expose the lawyer.

Equally routine was *The Law in Her Hands* (1936), whose sole distinction was that the co-heroines, Margaret Lindsay and Glenda Farrell, are the only women law partners in any '30s film. Also, Lindsay, from the usual motives of curdled idealism, becomes the only female mouthpiece of the decade. In the end she not only succumbs to the pleas of an idealistic assistant D.A. (Warren Hull), but institutes proceedings for her own disbarment. As in *Ann Carver's Profession*, the message seemed to be that the more successful a woman became as a lawyer, the more quickly she had to be hustled out of competition.

Though not reviewed by the *Times, Career Woman* (1936) was by all odds the most realistic, least melodramatic, of any of the films about women lawyers. A high-minded law school graduate (Claire Trevor) and her colleague (Michael Whalen) differ sharply about legal ethics. The girl takes the case of Isabel Jewell, who seems doomed to execution for having killed her brutal father. Trying to help, Whalen gives the jury a biting lecture on its prejudices, but this backfires. Trevor apologizes, offers a simple plea and wins. Most remarkably, she does not then abandon her career.

With *Portia on Trial* (1937) we return to the more familiar ground of mother-love melodrama. Frieda Inescort in the first of her several professional women roles played a lawyer defending a girl (Heather Angel) accused of shooting the son (Neil Hamilton) of a ruthless publisher (Clarence Kolb) —as the lawyer herself had come near doing years back, when she was involved with him. She not only gets the girl off but exposes the old man and reclaims the son he took from her in infancy—meanwhile conducting a mature romance with the prosecuting attorney (Walter Abel).

The Lady Objects (1938) was an unacknowledged remake of *Ann Carver's Profession* (1933), with Gloria Stuart as the lady lawyer and Lanny Ross as the disgruntled husband turned night club singer. Just as before, when he is wrongly accused of murder, she makes an impassioned plea to the jury, blaming herself for her selfish ambition and promising to give up her career, only in this version she is not even serving as his lawyer.

In *Disbarred* (1939) Gail Patrick was a lawyer whom a disbarred mouthpiece (Otto Kruger) tries to use as a stooge to prolong his own unsavory career—but she is won over by the usual young assistant D.A. (Robert Preston).

Finally, as if to end a decade of lady lawyers on the same maternal note on which it began, Frieda Inescort, now elevated to the bench, appeared in *A Woman Is the Judge* (1939), apparently based on *Scarlet Pages* (1930). Her first assignment is the case of her own long-lost daughter (Rochelle Hudson), charged with murder. She disqualifies herself, resigns her judgeship, becomes defense attorney in a new trial and proves justifiable homicide by bitterly confessing her own negligence as a mother. Just as in *Portia on Trial,* she ends with the prosecuting attorney (Otto Kruger this time), thus becoming the fourth woman lawyer to marry the D.A. or assistant who opposed her—a variant on the usual fate of career women in '30s films.

29

LAW AND ORDER
The Enforcers

Considering the extraordinary popularity in the 1970s of policemen (and policewomen) both on theater screens (*The French Connection, The New Centurions, Serpico,* etc.) and in TV series (*Baretta, Columbo, Kojak, Starsky and Hutch, Police Story, Police Woman*) —perhaps an attempt to atone for or altogether erase the hated "pig" image of the 1960s—it may come as a surprise how few policemen appeared as the central characters in early talkies. At the height of the gangster cycle, the law was either entirely absent or powerless to interfere in the bloody vendettas. In most other films, cops, by definition Irish, usually played by heavy-set actors like Robert Emmett O'Connor and Tom Kennedy, tended to be low-comedy flatfeet, no match for either criminals or clever amateur sleuths.

One exception was *Officer O'Brien* (1930), in which the hero (William "Screen" Boyd) is embarrassed by his lawless father (Ernest Torrence), who redeems himself only at the end by killing the chief gangster. O'Brien vows he will quit the force, but at the sound of a siren he's off again.

In *Framed* (1930), which borrowed both from *Broadway* and *The Racket,* a night club hostess (Evelyn Brent) is seeking vengeance against the police chief she blames for her father's death, but she falls for his son (Regis Toomey), also a cop, and double-crosses her gang for his sake. In *Those Who Dance*

(1930), which featured several silent favorites, a cop (Monte Blue) disguises himself as a gunman from Detroit to find the murderer of his brother, also a cop, a crime for which the young brother (William Janney) of the heroine (Lila Lee) has been framed. William ("Stage") Boyd and Betty Compson were the villain and his moll. In *The Costello Case* (1930) Tom Moore was the usual Irish cop, who uses psychological trickery to trap the killer of a speakeasy owner and at the same time clear a suspected young couple. That makes only four policemen heroes in 1930 (five if John Holland in *Defenders of the Law* was indeed a cop), compared with at least a dozen gangsters.

In 1931, while gangsters proliferated, the policeman hero had altogether disappeared. The only protagonist working for the law was female; Mary Nolan in *Enemies of the Law* was a police spy who falls for a gang leader (Johnny Walker), but, unlike the heroines of most spy pictures, she turns him in.

In 1932, as the gangster began to decline, the cop made a comeback, to the extent of six films, none major, and certainly none with the impact of *Scarface.* MGM's contribution was *The Beast of the City,* written by W. R. Burnett, starring Walter Huston as Fighting Fitzpatrick, a zealous police captain eager to jail an underworld leader named Sam Belmonte (played, in an odd piece of casting, by Jean Hersholt), who is always sprung by his elderly mouthpiece (Tully Marshall).

Exiled to the sticks for his efforts, Fitzpatrick is nevertheless appointed by an honest mayor as chief of police. His weakling younger brother (Wallace Ford) falls for Belmonte's moll (Jean Harlow) and even aids in a bank theft, but later repents and testifies for the state. Harlow got her first good review, pronounced by the *Times* "a distinct asset."

In *Disorderly Conduct* Spencer Tracy played an honest motorcycle cop punished for arresting the daughter (Sally Eilers) of a powerful politician and bootlegger (Ralph Morgan) and for refusing bribes. Embittered by this treatment, he apparently turns crooked, constantly defying his honest captain (Ralph Bellamy), but in the end proves his courage. *Radio Patrol* introduced the first cops in the then new patrol cars, Robert Armstrong and Russell Hopton. Here they are concerned with protecting the payroll of a packing company. Noted the *Times:* "Of the five chief male characters, four are killed, three in the performance of duty."

In *Midnight Morals* a crusty detective (De-Witt Jennings) opposes the romance of his cop son (Charles Delaney) with a taxi dancer (Alberta Vaughn) framed in a gang murder, but the boy sticks with her, and she unmasks the real killer. In *Me and My Gal,* Spencer Tracy was again an Irish cop, this time in love with a pert luncheonette waitress (Joan Bennett), whose sister (Marion Burns) is involved with a gangster. A paralyzed man (Henry B. Walthall) gives the crucial clue by blinking his eyes in Morse code.

As 1932 ended, Jack Holt joined the forces of righteousness in *Man Against Woman,* as a tough detective in love with a torch singer (Lillian Miles), who in turn loves a crook (Gavin Gordon) and even helps him escape from a train to Sing Sing. Catching the fleeing pair en route to Bermuda, Holt has the girl paroled in his custody. The *Times* thought everyone miscast.

January 1933 brought *The Big Pay Off,* in which a cop (Victor Jory) loses his nerve, is dropped from the force, tries suicide, but later redeems himself by saving an innocent man from the chair. Said the *Times:* "As a 1932 urban version of the old Westerns, *The Big Pay Off* has a lot to be said for it. The action is plentiful, the crooks are wicked, the policemen are brave, the hero is good-looking and the heroine is wistful."

The only other 1933 film with a policeman hero was even less distinguished: *State Trooper,* with Regis Toomey as an incorruptible motorcycle cop who arrests an oil tycoon (Edwin Maxwell) but is subsequently hired by him to protect his plant against gangsters working for a rival; he also, of course, gets the tycoon's daughter.

1934 continued in the same minor key. *Woman Unafraid* starred Lucille Gleason as the only police*woman* of the decade, one who supervises dance halls and befriends girls on parole. One, an ex-moll, gives information that enables the lady cop to trap a powerful gangster. In *Hold That Girl* James Dunn was a good-natured Irish detective in love with Claire Trevor, a worldly sob sister whose professional zeal leads to her being kidnaped. In *Hell Bent for Love* a cop (Tim McCoy) is framed by a racketeer and fired from the force, but gathers a gang of ex-cons who after much hijacking put the villain out of business. In *The Fighting Rookie* the title character (Jack LaRue) must alienate everyone and get himself dropped from the force to gain the confidence of a gang leader—only, of course, to obtain evidence.

As is obvious from the stories and the casts, all these films, however competently made, were strictly run-of-the-mill "B's." Even after gangster heroes went out of fashion, policemen could not hope to rival the appeal of reporters, doctors and lawyers in the eyes of screenwriters, and hence the public.

1935 at first seemed to herald a reversal of this trend. February brought the first well-mounted, well-cast picture really attempting to reflect the problems of a modern police force, *Car 99,* starring Fred MacMurray, a fast-moving adaptation of a *Saturday Evening*

Post factual series about the radio cars of the Michigan State Police. Most unusually, the mastermind behind a series of bank robberies is an urbane professor (Sir Guy Standing), who realizes that his only chance to pull his biggest job is to paralyze the police radio communications system. But it happens that the Massachusetts police radio operates on the same wave length, so relays the necessary information by phone. Nugent thought *Car 99* "one of the best melodramas to come from Hollywood in many a moon."

But this did not, after all, start a cycle, still less signify the dawn of a new cinematic appreciation for your friendly neighborhood cop. Within a few months he was totally eclipsed by the highly publicized national glamour of the then hero-worshiped G-men. For the rest of the '30s only eight films, none notable, centered on city or state police, compared with nearly thirty about FBI agents, and even these eight were on much the same modest level as their pre-1935 predecessors.

The only even slightly different cop film was *The Great O'Malley* (1937), a remake of a Milton Sills silent, which cast Pat O'Brien (who had also played a cop in *The Irish in Us,* a minor ethnic comedy of 1935) as a compulsively zealous patrolman who makes his neighborhood miserable by scrupulously enforcing every last meaningless city ordinance, to the dismay of his mother (Mary Gordon) and his pastor (Frank Sheridan), as well as the intense displeasure of his superior (Donald Crisp).

When his nit-picking about a car muffler keeps a desperate man (Bogart) from getting his first job in years and drives him to crime and prison, only growing affection for the man's little lame daughter (Sybil Jason) and the influence of her warmhearted teacher (Ann Sheridan) gradually humanize O'Malley. Thus even when the father, released from prison and misunderstanding O'Malley's interest in his family, shoots him, the once strict enforcer refuses to press charges.

Contrived as it sounds, the film had Warners' usual solidly detailed atmosphere of the Lower East Side (where O'Brien and Ann Sheridan were to meet again the next year in *Angels with Dirty Faces*), including an authentically run-down old grammar school.

Meanwhile in the more routine pattern *We're Only Human* (1936) starred Preston Foster as a tough cop in love with a reporter (Jane Wyatt), and involved with the usual gangsters. In *The Man in Blue* (1937) a gangster's son (Robert Wilcox) brought up by the cop (Edward Ellis) who killed his father is lured by his con man uncle (Richard Carle) into a life of crime, but after a prison term is reformed by love and understanding, especially from Nan Grey.

In a juvenile variation of the same situation, *Tenth Avenue Kid* (1938), Bruce Cabot was a cop who kills a gangster, then tries to win over his tough son (Tommy Ryan), who's sent to reform school for not talking, but later comes round and ends in a military academy. In *State Police* (1938) the head of that force compels his playboy son (William Lundigan) to become a trooper in a mining town, where bootleg coal racketeers try to use him to get his father to call off troops he is sending, but the son refuses and proves himself.

1939 saw only four cop films, three typical "B's" and one relative "A" with a major star. *Inside Information,* like one of those cavalry versus tank epics, pitted the new police methods of the hero (Dick Foran) against the old ones of his future father-in-law (Harry Carey). The new win out. Presumably by coincidence, the other three films had almost identical plots: the good cop father forced to hunt down his worthless son.

In *My Son Is a Criminal* Alan Baxter was the black sheep son of retired police chief Willard Robertson who uses his father's connections to alert a hijacking mob whose stolen trucks he camouflages in the garage he runs as a front. In the climax the father shoots the son as he flees a robbery.

Released two days later was MGM's *Sergeant Madden,* starring Wallace Beery and directed by Josef von Sternberg, of all people. Ever the indulgent father, Beery was even

Pat O'Brien, Humphrey Bogart in **The Great O'Malley**

more bitterly disappointed in his son than in *West Point of the Air* or *Port of Seven Seas.*

This time the no-good son whom the father must track down was Alan Curtis, beyond redemption even by his sweet young bride (Laraine Day in her screen debut) —but, of course, there was always the good son (Tom Brown) around for consolation. The *Times* gave *Sergeant Madden* credit for "pace, at least an attempt at characterization, and more running interest than the theme deserves."

Since *Heroes in Blue* was released eight months after the other two, it is impossible not to suspect direct influence. Those old favorites, the contrasting brothers, turned up again, one a cop (Dick Purcell), one a crook (Charles Quigley). The latter gets in trouble with his gangland boss and flees a murder rap, which forces his father (Frank Sheridan), also a cop, to let crime flourish in his precinct so the bad son won't be killed. The good son cleans up the gang, and the bad one is saved, after all.

In concluding this brief survey of cop films of the '30s, it must be noted that never was any occupation more ethnically exclusive. In every single example for which the names of the characters are available, the hero is always specifically Irish, and so usually is the girl he loves—no doubt a reflection of a social reality in many American cities at that time.

The faded slang phrase "to come on like Gangbusters" referred to the current radio program of that name, but it might well have been applied to the speed and thoroughness with which G-men took over and all but monopolized legal violence on the screen—eight films each in 1935 and 1936 and four each for the remaining years of the decade, not to mention others in which they played a minor role. This was a quite deliberate turn to the right, brought about partly by the antigangster pressures of the Production Code and the Legion of Decency, partly by genuine public revulsion at the Lindbergh kidnapping and at various bloody Midwestern shooting sprees.

On a deeper level, the changed attitude was a reflection of the vigorous confidence of the New Deal. After Herbert Hoover had plumbed depths of alienation from the public not to be paralleled by any later President until Nixon, Roosevelt, especially in his first term, moved quickly to restore faith in the system. Of all the members of his team, none was more visible or more highly respected than J. Edgar Hoover. Not the least reassuring aspect of Washington's benevolent paternalism was declaring kidnapping a federal offense and arming the FBI to handle it.

Predictably, Warners was the first studio to capitalize on this new spirit by casting Cagney himself in *G-Men* (1935), making the most of his established on-screen criminal record. "Hollywood's Most Famous Bad Man Joins the G-Men and Halts the March of Crime," the ads proclaimed.

The transition was rendered credible by giving Cagney's character approximately the same tough background as in *The Public Enemy* (1931)—only this time a benevolent bootlegger (William Harrigan), the last of his breed on screen, has put him through law school to keep him *out* of the rackets. Unwilling to become a mouthpiece, but unable to build up a practice otherwise, he is urged by a college friend (Regis Toomey) to join him in the FBI, but does so only when the unarmed friend is gunned down by a hood Cagney knows.

From there on, "the blazing melodrama" tears along at breakneck pace, in fusillades of gunfire as frequent as in any gangster film ever made. Though Hollywood had been forbidden to use any character based on Dillinger, some episodes of his career were incorporated by the arbitrary device of an urban gang transferring their activities to the small-town Midwest. Indeed, the most spectacular massacre was a reproduction of the government's raid on Dillinger's hideout in a Wisconsin hunting lodge, in which Cagney's old benefactor, forgiving to the end, is among those mowed down.

The two women characters were as minimal as in a service film, Margaret Lindsay as the extremely nominal love interest, and Ann Dvorak in her standard good-bad girl role, for love of Cagney revealing the whereabouts of a kidnap victim, as in *Three on a Match*, and being shot down, as in *Scarface,* this time in a phone booth by her loving husband (Barton MacLane). The *Times* summed up: "The headiest dose of gunplay that Hollywood has unloosed in recent months."

Other studios were quick to jump on the federal band wagon. Four weeks after *G-Men*, Reliance Pictures' *Let 'Em Have It* opened, the second in the cycle (unless one counts *What Price Crime?*, a forgotten Beacon quickie). As the *Times* put it: "Hollywood has stripped the underworld assassins of their glamour and exposed them as furtive rats who squeal and scurry for their submachine guns when Richard Arlen and his Department of Justice men close in on them."

An heiress (Virginia Bruce) in danger of

James Cagney, William Harrigan in **G-Men**

being kidnapped refuses to believe that her chauffeur (Bruce Cabot) is one of the conspirators. She even wins a parole for him, a favor he repays by springing the rest of his mob and terrorizing the Midwest. Only when her young brother (Eric Linden) joins the G-men and is killed does she change her mind. The *Times* reviewer noted "the familiar Dillinger motif in the government's assault on the lodge where the outlaws are hiding."

That the urban mobsters of the earlier '30s had completely vanished from the screen was proved again a week later by MGM's *Public Hero Number One*. In an attempt to run the notorious Purple Gang to earth, the govern-

ment plants agent Chester Morris as the cell-mate of the leader (Joseph Calleia) and even arranges an escape. Again paralleling Dillinger, the antihero after his few frantic days of freedom is mowed down by the Feds in a theater, here a vaudeville house. In this film, too, Jean Arthur furthered her reputation as a comedienne, begun in *The Whole Town's Talking,* and Lionel Barrymore played that familiar figure, the alcoholic doctor.

The same month (June 1935) brought Paramount's *Men Without Names,* marred for the *Times* only by the monotonously unbroken triumphs of the G-men. "Hot" money turning up in a small Kansas town leads the

Justice Department to suspect that a gang led by Leslie Fenton is hiding out near there, so agent Fred MacMurray assumes a false identity to track them down.

Warners' *Special Agent* (1935) provided a slight variation: T-men instead of G-men. As Nugent observed in the *Times:*

Already having elevated the G-men into a position of lofty grandeur comparable to that once held by William S. Hart, Tom Mix, Tarzan the wonder horse and Rin-Tin-Tin, the Warners have set about the job of glorifying the special agents of the Internal Revenue Bureau with commendable thoroughness and a neat sense of gun play.

Special Agent, from a story by Martin Mooney, then a well-known crime reporter, concerned a gang lord (Ricardo Cortez) sentenced to thirty years in Alcatraz for income tax evasion, thanks to his patriotic book-keeper (Bette Davis, still not quite free of this kind of role) and a zealous Treasury agent (George Brent). As in all the other films of this cycle, the climax was a raid and shoot-out at the racketeers' hideaway. A "B" version promptly turned up, *Confidential,* in which Donald Cook infiltrated the mob and Evelyn Knapp was the helpful bookkeeper.

Then T-men were at it again in *Counterfeit* (1936), in which Chester Morris went to great lengths to ingratiate himself with Lloyd Nolan, leader of a gang which kidnapped a master engraver right out of the bureau in Washington and forced him to make counterfeit bills. In *Wanted: Jane Turner* (1936) it was the postal service authorities led by Lee Tracy who round up a gang that robbed a mail truck and killed the driver. This plot was based on an actual case of 1926. In *Midnight Taxi* (1937) still another federal agent (Brian Donlevy) works as a cab driver and even becomes a mobster's henchman to catch a counterfeit gang.

Meanwhile, back in the FBI, among pure G-men, 1935 ended in a blaze of gunfire in *Show Them No Mercy,* inspired by the Weyerhauser kidnapping case, in which Kubec Glasmon, who was co-author of *The Public En-*emy, "resumes his mood of realistic ferocity."

An innocent young couple (Edward Norris and Rochelle Hudson) with a sick baby seek shelter in an apparently deserted house, only to find it the hideout of a gang who have just collected the ransom on a successful kidnapping. Edward Brophy and Warren Hymer were, as always, the dumb henchmen, so the conflict is between the sleek, relatively civilized leader (Cesar Romero) and a chillingly sadistic psychopath (Bruce Cabot), eager to kill all possible witnesses.

Through ransom money passed in a nearby town, the G-men begin to close in on the house, their efforts complicated by the presence of the hostages. In program notes for a New School showing, Everson describes *Show Them No Mercy* as

. . . far more of a suspense piece than a standard gangster epic. The mood is carefully created and sustained by excellent sets and lighting, and it is quite a raw little picture, even though much is left unsaid . . . There is no individualized police hero this time, à la Cagney in *G-Men.*

As with most cycles, the G-men had just about run their course within a year. By January 1936, only eight months after *G-Men* itself, B. R. Crisler was likening *Man Hunt* to a hash made of leftovers—"edible, if not exactly appetizing." Ingredients included G-men, a country editor and the usual Dillinger parallel (Ricardo Cortez). But again as with most cycles, where "A's" no longer deigned to tread, "B's" rushed in.

In June 1936 Grand National launched a G-man series starring Conrad Nagel and Eleanor Hunt. In *Yellow Cargo* Nagel, alerted by girl reporter Hunt, poses as an actor to uncover an unusual alien-smuggling racket: a phony movie-producing unit each day sends costumed extras to a nearby island (Catalina?), then Chinese wearing the same costumes are brought back to the mainland unnoticed.

By *Navy Spy* (1937) Hunt has become Nagel's assistant, helping him catch the mysterious group who have kidnapped a scientist to get his poison gas formula. In *The Gold Racket* (1937) the team catch a mob that has been shortchanging the Mexican Government by smuggling gold across the border to a California mine, then selling it to the United States "at the attractive New Deal figure of $35 an ounce." The fourth and last in the series, *Bank Alarm* (1938), also struck a timely note. The gang steals WPA funds as well as kidnaps Nagel's sister. Hunt becomes a press agent for a night club owner who's the real brains of the mob.

Meanwhile in *36 Hours To Live* (1936) a public enemy (Douglas Fowley) wins a sweepstakes, but en route by train to collect his money he encounters a girl reporter (Gloria Stuart) and a G-man (Donlevy). Need more be said?

In a still more obscure film, unaccountably reviewed twice by *Film Daily*, in May 1936 as *Rio Grande Romance*, in October as *Put on the Spot*, even that veteran collegian Eddie Nugent turned up as a G-man, one who while vacationing in the West finds his sister's husband jailed for murder. Only by having himself jailed as cell-mate to a tough suspect does he prove that the killer is his brother-in-law's supposed best friend.

As is evident, G-men had become by now as familiar rescuers as the cavalry in old Westerns, in almost any kind of film. That their novelty had worn off was indicated by the sharp drop in 1937 of films involving federal agents of any kind.

In *River of Missing Men* G-man Jack Holt pretends to be a bank robber for the usual reasons, escapes from prison, shoots rapids in a canoe to find the forest hide-out and even "proves" himself by sending the dumbest member of the gang to get his partner (Wynne Gibson). As expected, the dumb one falls for her and reveals the location of the hideaway.

Federal Bullets, the only one of these 1937 films to be reviewed by the *Times,* was considered too routine even for a plot summary, distinguished only by the "superb underworld characterization" of Zeffie Tilbury as

a little old lady, aptly named Mrs. Crippen, a supposed humanitarian, actually the queen of the mob broken up by undercover G-man Milburn Stone.

When G-Men Step In (1938) virtually gave away its whole plot in the title; the gimmick was that old standby, the good and bad brothers. G-man Don Terry must arrest racketeer Robert Paige. By this point the *Times* was dismissing G-men films in a scant two paragraphs. This was true even of such relatively good examples as *Tip-Off Girls* (1938), in which G-man Lloyd Nolan cleans up the hijacking racket, which has been using female decoys to prey on innocent truckers.

Held for Ransom (1938) featured the decade's only G-*woman* (Blanche Mehaffey) operating on her own rather than assisting a male agent, to clear up a case involving stolen ransom money. Perhaps the nadir of G-men films was *Paroled from the Big House* (1938), a fifty-seven-and-a-half-minute quickie from Syndicate Exchange with a cast of total unknowns, about a G-man posing as a criminal to get evidence on parolees seeking vengeance against those who jailed them.

Federal Manhunt (1939) rated the usual dismissive two paragraphs from the *Times,* just long enough to scorn its overfamiliar story of a criminal trying to flee the country, thwarted by G-men.

Despite the early 1938 fade-out of Grand National's G-man series, Warners launched another in 1939, with Ronald Reagan as Brick Bancroft, an undercover FBI agent, and Eddie Foy, Jr., as his supposedly comic sidekick. *Secret Service of the Air* was the first, about smuggling aliens across the border.

Miller says of this series: "They had a kind of wild, devil-may-care sort of headlong movement about them . . . if no great reflection on the G-men." In *Code of the Secret Service* (1939), Brick is sent to Mexico to catch counterfeiters operating out of an abandoned monastery. (One would have thought counterfeiting the province of the Treasury rather than the Justice Department, but perhaps the T-men were shorthanded and given Brick on loan.) This film, says Miller, "unwinds like twelve chapters of a serial rolled into one. Of the four productions in the series, it's undoubtedly the best."

In the third one, *Smashing the Money Ring* (1939), to catch another counterfeiting ring, Brick gets himself imprisoned, makes friends with the mob, even takes part in a break before discovering that the bogus money is coming from the prison print shop. The fourth and last of the series, *Murder in the Air,* was not released until the summer of 1940.

Meanwhile Paramount without any special fanfare had begun its own anticrime series, using not the same characters but the same actors in various combinations: Anthony Quinn, Lloyd Nolan, Lynne Overman, J. Carroll Naish, Buster Crabbe, Akim Tamiroff and, as juveniles, Robert Preston and Richard Denning. These films, which included *King of Gamblers* (1937) and *Tip-Off Girls,* (1938), Miller considers exceptionally well written, directed and acted, as well as four based on J. Edgar Hoover's non-fiction best seller, *Persons in Hiding.*

The first one, which used his very title, released in March 1939, starred Patricia Morison (a Broadway singing star, who, like Gladys Swarthout in *Ambush,* 1939, in this one never sang a note), Overman, Naish and a strong supporting cast, but the *Times* gave it only a patronizing, tongue-in-cheek review. Morison as a cold-blooded, greedy beauty teams up with a small-time hoodlum (Naish) to become half of the nation's most wanted criminal pair. The parallel to Bonnie and Clyde was noted even by Crisler.

It is easy to see how the idealized G-men, with their quasi-military training and discipline, their unquestioning obedience to their superiors, their instant black-and-white judgments of good (us) and evil (them), not to mention their way of shooting first and asking questions afterward, paved the way, along with the service and academy films, for the simplistic, jingoistic flag-waving of so many World War II pictures.

But the end was not yet. Surely no veteran watcher of TV need be reminded that no sooner had the FBI men faded from the big screen than they turned up, more numerous and more authoritarian than ever, in many a popular series of the '50s, of which *The Untouchables* was only the most famous—continual free propaganda designed to maintain and polish the sacrosanct legend of J. Edgar, an image that in the late 1970s was still being chipped away.

30

"I'M BUSTIN' OUT!"
Our Fettered Friends

. . . the important objective must be to avoid the hardening of the audience, especially of those who are young and impressionable, to the thought and fact of crime. People can become accustomed even to murder, cruelty, brutality, and repellent crimes, if these are too frequently repeated.
—The Motion Picture Production Code

As is evident, many leading characters in the films discussed in the last four chapters, whether crook, moll, mouthpiece or undercover federal agent, served time in prison, but the '30s also produced another distinct genre, still vividly remembered, set mainly or wholly behind bars.

Except for those occasional star vehicles like *Within the Law* and *Manslaughter,* silent films had paid little heed to convicts. By the later '20s, however, the growing national concern about "the crime wave," as heralded by the success of a doleful 1924 ballad, "The Prisoner's Song," and the long Broadway runs of *The Last Mile* and *The Criminal Code,* was intensified not only by the gangland slayings already mentioned but by an unusual number of prison riots and jail breaks. In the summer of 1930 newsreels and front pages were less concerned with the deepening depression, not yet recognized as such, than with rioting convicts.

Yet despite this built-in timely interest the whole decade produced fewer than seventy

pure prison films, compared with nearly three hundred about gangsters. Perhaps one reason why these relative few have lingered in the collective memory is that the plot variations were so limited that the stereotyped characters and clichés of both language and situation recurred more often and thus were more readily recognized and mocked.

June 1930 saw three prison films released within a few weeks. Perhaps not quite a pure example, *The Shadow of the Law,* from a novel called *The Quarry,* seems a variation on *Les Miserables,* in which the hero (the ever-busy William Powell) in a scuffle accidentally causes another man to fall out a window to his death, whereupon the alluring blonde (Natalie Moorhead) over whom they were fighting, the only one whose testimony could clear him, disappears, and he is sentenced to life for manslaughter.

With the aid of another convict, he escapes, changes his identity and two years later is supervising a mill in the South. To clear his name, he offers the blonde a bribe to tell the truth, instead of which she tries to blackmail him. As fingerprints are the only evidence to link him to his former identity, he resorts to the drastic extreme of allowing his fingertips to be destroyed in a factory machine so that he will be free to wed the owner's daughter.

Numbered Men, from a play called *Jail Break,* was ridiculed for its improbabilities, especially the free-and-easy, country club atmosphere of the prison, spoiled only when a particularly hard case (Ralph Ince) insists on trying to escape. The young hero (Raymond Hackett) is ultimately cleared of a false counterfeiting charge by a real counterfeiter (Conrad Nagel) and gets the girl (Bernice Claire), at whose home the road gang convicts were always welcome to drop in for a snack.

After these two films, *The Big House,* the first prison talkie written especially for the screen, an Oscar-winning script by Frances Marion, looked and sounded like grim realism itself. A playboy (Robert Montgomery) sentenced to ten years for manslaughter while driving drunk is put in the same cell with a basically decent forger (Chester Morris) and "Butch" (Wallace Beery), a superficially genial murderer, the ringleader of the cons. The boy is persuaded to turn stool pigeon, and, of course, pays with his life. After discouraging a violent jail break, the forger succeeds in saving the warden and the keepers, and eventually wins the playboy's sister (Leila Hyams).

What most impressed critics and viewers was the brute force of the dialogue and action and the apparent firsthand authenticity of such details as a cockroach race on which the prisoners bet cigarettes.

The title phrase "the big house," along with other prison slang ("stir," "spring," "chow," etc.), immediately passed into the language of movie-goers, especially the young, augmenting a vocabulary already enriched by other underworld films. The popularity of the film also ensured that many of the then fresh touches would, in less skillful hands, soon harden into the stereotypes and clichés noted above. *The Big House* included most, if not all, the stock characters: the innocent man being railroaded to the chair (until the last-minute reprieve from the governor), the hard-bitten old lifer, the squealer or stool pigeon, the sadistic guards (male or female), the weak-kneed (or humane) warden, the kindly chaplain, the comic relief (usually black).

Likewise, among the obligatory scenes were the dimming of the lights and outbursts of hysteria as someone gets the electric chair, the poker-faced exploratory conversations in the recreation yard, the banging of tin cups on plates to protest the food ("I'm bustin' out! I can't take no more of this slop!"), the elaborately planned climactic break, with sirens moaning from the watchtowers, bloodhounds baying and searchlights playing over the grounds until the inevitable showdown resulting in the deaths of several characters.

The Squealer (September 1930), according to the *Times,* not only echoed *Street of Chance* and *Broadway* but "recall[s] the recent prison break pictures and present[s] nothing new."

Jack Holt was a racketeer fronting as a real estate operator, whose troubled wife (Dorothy Revier) summons the police to his hideaway only to save him from being killed by a rival gang. During his seven years in prison he becomes convinced that she really wanted him out of the way so that she could marry his best friend (Matt Moore), but when he overhears the truth, he walks out into the machine-gun fire, like Robert Armstrong, Edmund Lowe, Leo Carrillo and other noble gangsters.

October, surprisingly, brought one of the few prison comedies of the decade, *Up the River,* written by Maurine Watkins, author of *Chicago* (1927), and directed by John Ford, with Spencer Tracy and Humphrey Bogart (his second film). Most of the plot concerned the standing of the prison baseball team and an amateur theatrical in which some of the inmates play women's roles.

Tracy and moronic yegg Warren Hymer escape in drag—but only to ensure smooth sailing for the young lovers (Bogart and Claire Luce); they report back inside in time for the big game. This was remade in 1938 under the same title, with Preston Foster and Arthur Treacher, and football substituted for baseball.[1]

[1] The only other prison comedies of the decade were Laurel and Hardy's *Pardon Us* (1931), Wheeler and Woolsey's *Hold 'Em, Jail* (1932) and *The Daring Young Man* (1935).

Chester Morris, Wallace Beery in **The Big House**

1931, the gangsters' year of screen glory, was just the opposite for those inside; perhaps one fact explains the other. It is impossible to imagine Rico or Tommy Powers submitting to the ignominy of imprisonment, and only the censors dictated the incarceration of Scarface. Of all actors typed as gangsters, George Raft, less dynamic than the others, was most often seen as a prisoner or ex-con.

Except for those involving women, the only prison film of 1931 was the first screen version of Martin Flavin's 1929 stage hit, *The Criminal Code,* in which a crusading D.A. (Walter Huston) is appointed warden of a state prison full of convicts he helped send there. Among them is a sensitive young man (Phillips

Holmes) doing ten years for manslaughter, whom the warden chooses to work in his office and with whom the warden's daughter (Constance Cummings) falls in love. In the climax a squealer is killed and only the boy knows what happened, but, true to the code of the title, he will not talk. Only when the murderer himself is killed by a guard does the truth come out.

"Grim and gruesome," said the *Times,* were the events of *The Last Mile* (1932), adapted from John Wexley's 1930 play, in which Howard Phillips repeated his stage role as a businessman wrongly convicted of murder. Preston Foster, however, played the much stronger role of Killer Mears (done by Spencer Tracy on Broadway and by Gable on the road), who grabs the keys of a guard and frees all the inmates of Death Row, putting guards in their places as hostages. The warden refuses their demands for a car and a four-hour start, and more killings ensue. In spite of all this, the film was introduced by a lengthy foreword in which the then well-known Warden Lewis Lawes of Sing Sing expressed his opposition to capital punishment.

These indeed seemed to be the years for "grim and gruesome" depictions of prison life, sympathizing with the inmates against the system, as evidenced by the recurrence of the word "hell" in the titles: *Hell's House* (1932), *The Mayor of Hell* (1933), *Hell's Highway* (1932) and *Laughter in Hell* (1933), the latter two about the horrors of chain gangs in the South. More important than either of these, *I Am a Fugitive from a Chain Gang* (1932) offered the most startling revelation yet of brutal injustice, but this was so much more than a prison picture that it will be discussed among films of social consciousness.

With the success of *I Am a Fugitive,* Warners seemed encouraged to establish a virtual monopoly on this kind of material. Early 1933 brought *20,000 Years in Sing Sing* (the grand total of all the sentences being served there), inspired by Warden Lawes' book. Though necessarily fictionized for the screen, the film

retained a quasi-documentary realism that impressed reviewers. "Truth is more interesting than fiction here," said the *Times.*

Spencer Tracy played a gangster who expects his political connections to work just as well in prison and learns the hard way they do not. Allowed to leave just long enough to visit his girl (Bette Davis), injured in an auto accident, he is prevented from returning on time, but reports later, even though it means being executed for a murder he did not commit.

The only other prison films of 1933 were those about women or boys' reformatories. Except for incidental scenes, as in *Manhattan Melodrama,* 1934 was equally negligible, producing only four of any kind. In these years when, partly in response to the Production Code, backstage musicals, through-the-years cavalcades and costume classics were favored, convicts received even less attention than gangsters.

Unless one counts *The Daring Young Man,* which included "satire on prison life," and *Escape from Devil's Island,* 1935 saw no prison films at all, and 1936 produced only a few obscure "B's" (*One Way Ticket, Road Gang, Parole, Bridge of Sighs, Jailbreak*), a historical variant, *The Prisoner of Shark Island,* and Harlow's prison term in *Riff Raff.* Despite its title, which echoes such G-men epics as *Let 'Em Have It* and *Show Them No Mercy, Don't Turn 'Em Loose* was less concerned with prison conditions than with the iniquities of the parole system. Bruce Cabot was the criminal son of a small-town high school principal (Lewis Stone) who serves on a parole board. By threatening to reveal his identity and disgrace the family, the son gains his freedom, but ultimately dies at the hands of his father, thus anticipating the plots of *Sergeant Madden, My Son Is a Criminal* and *My Son Is Guilty* (all of 1939).

In 1937, for no apparent reason unless because both the gangster and the G-men cycles had been exhausted and public taste for criminal violence had to be satisfied by other means, prison pictures began to stage a strong comeback, not only in numbers but in the level of casts and directors. From four in 1937, they rose to twelve in 1938 and eleven in 1939—far more than had been made in any earlier year of the decade.

Though based on a book by a man who had indeed been saved when his conviction for murder was reversed, *We Who Are About to Die,* starring Preston Foster, Ann Dvorak and John Beal, the first such film to be released in 1937, only moved the *Times* reviewer to list all the clichés it embodied:

> the innocent man framed for a payroll robbery and murder, the loyal sweetheart and the conscientious detective working against time to establish his innocence, prison riots, another murder or two and the last-minute reprieve as the doomed man is being led to the gallows.

With *San Quentin* (1937), its first "A" film on an adult prison theme since *20,000 Years in Sing Sing* (1933), Warners reasserted its vigorous mastery over such material. A number of the old familiar faces were on hand: Pat O'Brien as the captain of the guards, Bogart as a "misanthropic mug," Ann Sheridan as his sister, a night club singer whom the captain loves. Resisting all attempts at rehabilitation, Bogart joins a jail break, then, realizing his mistake too late, returns, wounded, to die remorsefully at the prison gates.

A few months later, California's other most famous prison was given the Warners treatment in *Alcatraz Island,* with Sheridan in top billing and John Litel rather oddly cast as a "practical" racketeer caught on income tax evasion. In prison he finds himself side by side with the would-be kidnaper of his daughter, a juxtaposition which leads to a murder and almost sends the repentant mobster to the gallows.

The fourth 1937 film, reviewed by the *Times* as *The Outer Gate,* the title which appeared on screen, but billed on the marquee as *Behind Prison Bars,* was a Monogram production, disappointing to true *aficionados* of life among our fettered friends. "Heck, there isn't even a jailbreak!" Crisler com-

plained. "Some of the customers are going to get awfully mad!"

In a rather unusual story, its theme of implacable revenge reminiscent of the previous year's *Fury,* an innocent youth (Ben Alexander) is convicted of embezzlement, framed by a guilty cashier. His employer (Ralph Morgan) despite the boy's engagement to his daughter (Kay Linaker) lifts not a finger to clear him. Five years later the cashier confesses and kills himself, and the embittered victim accepts a job from his former boss only to even old scores. He tips off a bond robbery for which Morgan is convicted. Not until he is awaiting sentence does the young man relent, retrieve the bonds and exonerate him. Obviously, this was not a pure prison picture, but the change of title indicates how popular they had become.

The 1938 crop included several already noted in other connections: five films about women's prisons, two about boys' reformatories, remakes of *The Criminal Code* (as *Penitentiary*) and *Up the River,* and *Over the Wall,* discussed elsewhere because of the role of the chaplain. In fact, the only one not covered elsewhere was *Prison Break,* which the *Times* praised for avoiding at least some clichés.

Instead, the message, surely not new, even then, was that it was wrong to confine an honest, essentially decent sort like tuna fisherman Barton MacLane with hardened offenders like Ward Bond. The condition of parole by which a parolee is forbidden to marry was also called into question. Whether intended as just another prison drama or an indictment of the system, Crisler thought it "not a bad show at all."

1939 was a big year for prison pictures from all studios, but Warners clearly maintained its lead with six. Besides *Smashing the Money Ring,* Reagan also appeared in *Hell's Kitchen,* Bogart starred in *You Can't Get Away with Murder,* Cagney in *Each Dawn I Die* and Garfield in both *Blackwell's Island* and *Dust Be My Destiny.*

Chronologically first came *Blackwell's Is-*

land, based on the New York Welfare Island scandal of 1934, in which Garfield played an investigative reporter who exposes conditions: the island prison is completely run by a cheap gangster (Stanley Fields). Said the *Times:* "It's sound melodrama . . . and amusing, too, in a cynical way . . . convicts making book on the races, playing poker, lolling about in striped silk pajamas, ordering the keepers about like lackeys. The Warners find it laughable and so, reluctantly, must we."

Warners balanced off this lightness a few weeks later with the dead-serious *You Can't Get Away with Murder*, from a play coauthored by Warden Lawes, "where the big punch-line in the final sequence is when the warden says 'Get the Governor on the wire' "— a line from which the whole plot can be reconstructed.

A few days later came a far more effective version of the same situation, Columbia's *Let Us Live*, praised by the *Times*. Based on *Murder in Massachusetts*, the story of an actual incident in Lynn in 1934, it told of a near-tragic miscarriage of justice that might have turned into another Sacco-Vanzetti case.

Henry Fonda, wrongly identified by several witnesses (just as he had been in *You Only Live Once* and was to be again nearly twenty years later in Hitchcock's *The Wrong Man*), comes all too close to execution.

Fonda, Maureen O'Sullivan as his frantic sweetheart, Ralph Bellamy and Alan Baxter all came in for praise, but especially the writers, Allen Rivkin and Anthony Veiller, and John Brahm, whose "forceful and eloquent direction . . . has underscored his physical drama with the psychological . . . the quality that raises it above the death-house thriller class and gives it dignity and maturity."

But by June 1939, MGM's *6000 Enemies* had Crisler protesting, "We've been sentenced to so many prison pictures by now we begin yammering at the sight of a stone wall." This is the one "about the tough prosecutor who finally gets sent up the river himself." He (Walter Pidgeon) was framed on a bribery charge, just as his girl (Rita Johnson) was on embezzlement, both arranged by the villain (Harold Huber). The climax was the standard jail break.

By July, when *Each Dawn I Die* opened, Crisler was so stir-crazy that he failed to appreciate its generally recognized merits. But others thought more highly of this offbeat melodrama, in which Cagney was a newspaperman framed on a manslaughter charge by the powerful enemies made by his by-lined exposés of crime and corruption. Raft was a big-shot gangster who becomes his friend and subsequent liberator, even at the cost of his own life.

It was, alas, followed only by such run-of-the-jute-mill items as *Behind Prison Gates* and *Smashing the Money Ring*, in both of which G-men had themselves imprisoned. Somewhat better were *Those High Gray Walls*, covered among doctor pictures, and *Mutiny in the Big House*, discussed with religious films.

Unless one counts *The Roaring Twenties*, the last, though by no means the best, of Warners' sociologically oriented crime films of the '30s was *Dust Be My Destiny*, but even John Garfield's image as "official gall-and-wormwood taster for the Warners" was beginning to wear thin. Said the thoroughly jaded Crisler:

It's not even fun, any more, outguessing the script. The moment we meet Joe Bell riding a freight car, looking for work, we knew he was going to be sent to a prison camp. The moment we saw the prison gang foreman (whose stepdaughter is Priscilla Lane) and heard about his whiskey heart, we knew Joe was going to be blamed for his death.

The film attempted to wring all hearts with the tear-choked plea of the defense attorney (Moroni Olsen): "If you convict this boy" (quaver) "you are convicting thousands like him, not criminals, not murderers, just nobodies trying to find a place to hang their hats." Crisler sympathized with Lane, having to redeem Garfield all over again in every picture.

With all their built-in limitations, prison

James Cagney, George Bancroft in **Each Dawn I Die**

dramas have never ceased to fascinate the public in the decades since 1940—e.g., *Brute Force, Bird Man of Alcatraz, Cool Hand Luke, Fortune and Men's Eyes* and, on the distaff side, *Caged* and *I Want to Live*. We have even seen a successful prison comedy in *The Longest Yard*.

In conclusion one must acknowledge that in spite of occasional misfires, in making crime pay, Warner Brothers surpassed all other studios, producing two of the three classic gangster films (*Little Caesar* and *The Public Enemy*), one of the best lawyer films (*The Mouthpiece*), the best G-man film (*G-Men* itself), one of the best juvenile delinquent dramas (*Angels with Dirty Faces*) and practically all the best prison films, from *I Am a Fugitive* to *Each Dawn I Die*.

BLOOD WILL TELL
The Nonprofessionals

31

THIS WILL KILL YOU
Murders Without Mystery

The techniques of murder must be presented in a way that will not inspire imitation.
—The Motion Picture Production Code

Although gangster films may well have accounted for more bloodshed than any other film genre except possibly Westerns, professional criminals have never held a monopoly on violence. Crimes of passion among friends, or, even more often, among relatives, have, after all, been a staple of the world's literature ever since Cain and Abel and the fratricidal, parricidal families of Greek mythology. The vogue of the eighteenth and early nineteenth century (roughly from 1760 to 1820) for luridly melodramatic "Gothic romances," though it produced few enough masterpieces of its own, did spawn a goodly number of murderous descendants, some of which are still with us today.[1]

One such genre, in which British writers have particularly excelled, is the drama of skulduggery in genteel, middle-class surroundings (often Victorian), with motivations carefully traced through all the events leading up to the crime and then its consequences, especially to the perpetrator. The modern theater has produced many examples, usually termed "suspense dramas" or "psychological thrillers," some involving ironic twists of fate, some plots of adultery, blackmail and revenge, some the unpredictable patterns of a psychopathic killer.

Though at no time anywhere nearly as popular as straight mysteries (scarcely fifty during the '30s compared with nearly two hundred), the kind of melodrama in which the identity of the murderer is known from the start enjoyed certain advantages. At best it could use more realistic, less mechanical plotting, with more subtle characterization and psychological probing, especially of the torments of guilt, as in *Her Private Affair* (1930), based on a Viennese story, with the original setting and the characters' names retained. Ann Harding as the wife of a judge kills a threatening blackmailer, then must see an innocent man accused. Even after he is acquitted, she suffers until she has confessed the truth to him in the presence of her husband (Harry Bannister), who forgives her.

At worst this kind of picture was mere gimmicky melodrama, like *The Locked Door* (1930), from Channing Pollock's 1919 play, *The Sign on the Door*, filmed in 1922 by Norma Talmadge and remade as Barbara Stanwyck's first talkie and first starring film.

---

[1] This does not include what are now called Gothic novels, descendants of *Jane Eyre,* mostly written by women, in which a beleaguered heroine is brought to a sinister old manor house, where she falls in love with its Byronic, diabolically fascinating master—e.g., *Rebecca, Dragonwyck.*

Like many early talkies based on plays, it is extremely stage-bound, with the act divisions easily discernible, though Everson (in program notes for a 1969 showing) calls it "rather above average for its period . . . The camera keeps on the move to offset the limitations of the locale, many sequences are played silent, and dialogue exchanges are at least broken down via cutting."

Yet, however cinematic director George Fitzmaurice may have tried to make it, nothing could be done with the plot. Another vulnerable wife (Stanwyck), trying to protect her young sister-in-law (Betty Bronson) from a blackmailing cad (Rod La Rocque) out of her own innocent but compromised past, is accused of his murder. Her husband (William "Stage" Boyd) confesses to save her, but then the villain revives just long enough to clear them both; he was shot by accident. As Stanwyck herself put it in 1958, speaking of *The Locked Door* to the *Los Angeles Times:* "They never should have unlocked the damned thing."

Far more original was *Guilty Hands* (1931), of which the *Times* said: "a fresh and arresting story . . . The camera for a change sees all and knows all." Lionel Barrymore was a lawyer who, to save his daughter (Madge Evans) from marriage to another of those notorious roués (Alan Mowbray), murders the man and places the gun in his hand to make it look like suicide.

To establish his alibi, he uses the novel device of a small cardboard silhouette of himself attached to the turntable of a phonograph in his room, so that with each revolution the enlarged shadow cast on a drawn window shade looks from outside like Barrymore himself pacing back and forth. Even when the victim's mistress (Kay Francis) confronts him at the scene of the crime, he threatens to pin the murder on her—until the lawyer is shot dead by the corpse as its stiffening fingers pull the trigger.

Still another cad who must be dispatched to protect an innocent girl turned up in *Neighbors' Wives* (1933), but in a plot closer to *The Locked Door* than to *Guilty Hands.* Dorothy Mackaill as the wife of a cop turned lawyer (Tom Moore) is covering for his kid sister (Mary Kornman), involved with a shady type; in fact, she kills him to save the girl's "honor"—but her husband thinks she was unfaithful, until a kindly judge provides an alibi.

The loyal wife, innocently involved in a murder through blackmail or some other reason that makes it impossible for her to tell the truth, recurred several more times during the '30s. In *Without Regret* (1934), based on *Interference,* an international stage hit of the '20s (and in 1928 Paramount's very successful first full-length talkie), Elissa Landi, to save herself in China, marries drifter Kent Taylor.

Back in England, believing him dead, she later marries Paul Cavanagh, whose embittered castoff mistress (Frances Drake), learning the facts, blackmails the heroine as a bigamist. The ne'er-do-well first husband, having only a short time to live, does one good deed by poisoning the blackmailer and confessing it, so that the second husband never knows the truth.

In *The Woman in Red* (1935) Barbara Stanwyck played a professional horsewoman married into the snobbish society of Chicago's North Shore. To save a friend (John Eldredge), wrongly accused of murder, she must risk her marriage to Gene Raymond by providing an alibi that apparently compromises her reputation.

Even more genteel was *The Unguarded Hour* (1936), set in England, with Loretta Young paying off to save her husband (Franchot Tone) from the threats of a blackmailer (Henry Daniell), using letters written to another of those troublesome ex-mistresses (Aileen Pringle). Not at all incidentally, Tone is prosecuting an innocent man (Dudley Digges) for having allegedly pushed his wife off a cliff; only a missing woman witness can save him (guess who), but *she* cannot explain her presence at the scene without revealing the letters, etc., etc. Despite obvious holes in the plot, reviewers found it an entertaining melodrama.[2]

To be sure, not all protagonists in this kind of film were as innocent as these hard-pressed heroines One of the most theatrically effective examples was *The Kiss Before the Mirror* (1933), directed by James Whale and strikingly photographed by Karl Freund, from a play by Ladislas Fodor. When a distinguished Viennese doctor (Paul Lukas) kills his faithless wife (Gloria Stuart), he is defended by a lawyer friend (Frank Morgan), who has good reason to suspect his own wife (Nancy Carroll).

As did the defendant, he uses as a test the embrace mentioned in the title; a woman who shrugs off her husband's attentions at such a moment must be making herself beautiful for someone else. For a while it looks as if a parallel murder will take place, but instead the lawyer insists his wife be present in court for his summation to the jury.

So powerfully does he re-enact the crime and re-create the betrayed husband's feelings that his own wife screams and faints; later she comes to her senses in more ways than one. Morgan, not yet typed in dithering comic roles, gives an extraordinarily strong performance, as does Lukas.

A supposed remake of this story, *Wives Under Suspicion* (1938), not only transferred the locale to America but completely changed the somber, near-tragic tone. The lawyer (Warren William) is a ruthless D.A. bent on convicting a professor (Ralph Morgan) of the murder of his actress wife (never seen). Only when he wrongly suspects his own neglected wife (Gail Patrick) of an affair with a young friend (William Lundigan) does he learn compassion and ask that the charge against Morgan be reduced to manslaughter.

1934 was particularly productive of murder melodramas based on marital triangles. In *Journal of a Crime,* from a French play, Ruth Chatterton, an actress, kills the mistress (Claire Dodd) of her husband (Adolphe Menjou) and gets away with it. An innocent man is accused; she is about to confess, when a car accident brings on amnesia, whereupon her husband forgives her. On the other hand, in *The Crime Doctor* a criminologist (Otto Kruger) pins a murder on the lover (Nils Asther) of his wife (Karen Morley) so neatly that the charge sticks, but then, realizing that she still loves the other man, he confesses and kills himself. (In *Night Club Scandal,* 1937, John Barrymore went him one better, as a doctor who murders his wife and pins it on her lover [Harvey Stephens] so cleverly that only the framee's sister [Louise Campbell] and a reporter [Lynne Overman] can expose the truth.)

A superior example was Ben Hecht's *Upperworld* (1934), titled no doubt to suggest a companion piece to his famous silent *Underworld* (1927). A railroad tycoon (Warren William), ignored by his busy socialite wife (Mary Astor), becomes "innocently" (this being post-Production Code) involved with a likable show girl (Ginger Rogers), who in shielding him is killed by her blackmailing ex-lover (J. Carroll Naish), who is in turn shot by the tycoon in self-defense. Fearing the scandal, he flees—but a vindictive cop (Sidney Toler), whom the hero had exiled to the Bronx for giving him a speeding ticket, finds an incriminating fingerprint and pursues it relentlessly until he can make the arrest as his quarry is host at an elegant dinner party. Unexpectedly, the wife stands by him and he is acquitted. On the whole the film holds up very well indeed. Everson in his notes calls *Upperworld* "quite an honest and touching movie, up until its somewhat hard to accept finale."

The other best murder melodrama of 1934 also involved Hecht. *Crime Without Passion,* the first of four films written, produced and directed by Hecht and MacArthur at Paramount's New York studio, dealt with a coldly unscrupulous lawyer (Claude Rains) who decides to end his affair with a fiery Spanish dancer (Margo) by killing her, so that he can

---

[2] Other murder plots involving blackmail include *Silence* (1931) and *Champagne Charlie* (1936).

marry a desirable socialite (Whitney Bourne). The girl doesn't die, after all, but before he learns this, he has killed someone else in trying to establish an alibi.

The *Times* reviewer was much impressed by the clever dialogue and striking photography, which *The New Yorker* now dismisses as "a lot of symbolism and dated avant garde novelties." Yet the opening shot, in which the three Furies, mythical avengers of hidden crime, are unleashed on New York, with rolling eyes, bloody fangs and shrieks of demoniacal laughter, floating among the skyscrapers with Greek draperies streaming in the wind,

however arty it may seem now, is at least unforgettable.

Still another homicidal lawyer cropped up in *A Notorious Gentleman* (1935), in which Charles Bickford played one of those ruthless mouthpieces who plots the death of a rival (Sidney Blackmer) and even gets away with it through a jury's disagreement. But a determined D.A. (Onslow Stevens) sees that justice is served even at the price of a frame-up.

The strongest murder melodrama of 1935, however, and one of the best of the decade, was *Bordertown,* which gave Bette Davis her first worthy role after *Of Human Bondage.*

Paul Muni, Bette Davis in Bordertown

Though it starts out, like *Lawyer Man* (1932), with an ethnic minority lawyer (Paul Muni as a Chicano from Los Angeles' "Mexican quarter," graduate of a bilingual law school), it soon turns into a grim study of retribution in the style of James M. Cain.

Losing his first case against a reckless driver, another decadent debutante (Margaret Lindsay), he also loses his temper and his right to practice law when he attacks his sneering Anglo opponent (Gavin Gordon). Bitterly determined to make money any way he can, within two years he is manager of a sleazy gambling casino in a flashy border town like Tijuana, working for vulgar, good-natured Eugene Pallette, whose oversexed wife (Davis), smoldering with boredom, takes a violent fancy to the Mexican. Despite all rebuffs from him, she murders her husband by leaving him sleeping drunk in his car in the garage with the motor running.

Financially backed by her, the erstwhile manager converts the casino into a superglamorous night spot, which naturally attracts jaded L.A. socialites like Lindsay. In no time they are enjoying an affair, while the frustrated, haunted widow rages in vain—until she is driven to confess to the police, adding that Muni forced her to commit the murder. In court, however, she breaks down, babbling so incoherently that her insanity is obvious.

But the notoriety has been too much for the rich girl, who now tells Muni that he is, after all, "a different tribe"—whereupon she is run down by a passing car. (Not even the Legion of Decency could complain that any sin went unpunished.) Our hero sells the club, uses the money to endow a law school for Chicanos and returns to the ghetto, welcomed by his mother (Soledad Jiminez) and his pastor (Robert Barrat), who knew all along that he should never have left his own people.

In notes for a 1976 showing Everson said: "As melodrama, it owes most of its strength to Bette Davis, who arrives on the scene quite late, but then proceeds to take over totally, playing some scenes for bravura, others with effective restraint."

Not all murder melodramas, of course, involved sexual triangles. Some were "different" to the point of being bizarre. *The Witching Hour* (1934), from Augustus Thomas' venerable warhorse of 1907, filmed in 1916, dealt with murder committed under telepathic suggestion. In *The Case Against Mrs. Ames* (1936), a widow (Madeleine Carroll), acquitted of her husband's murder but still suspected by the assistant D.A. (George Brent), offers a reward if he can prove her guilty, hoping to clear her name so that she can regain custody of her child.

In *The Man Who Cried Wolf* (1937) an actor (Lewis Stone) repeatedly confesses to murders he did not commit so that when he does kill the man who took his wife and child, his confession won't be believed. However, when his own son is convicted, he must convince the police that this time he's guilty, and, of course, pays the penalty.

Even further off the beaten path was *Full Confession* (1939), the only film until Hitchcock's 1950 *I Confess* to dramatize the dilemma of a Catholic priest who has heard a murderer's confession, yet is bound by his vows not to break the seal of silence even to save the life of an innocent man. Unfortunately, the treatment, said the *Times,* was "only spottily effective at its best and bordering on the banal at its worst."

Victor McLaglen was the culprit who confesses when he thinks he's dying, then later recants. Though all the other leading characters are Irish, the troubled priest is unaccountably Italian, perhaps because played by Joseph Calleia, in one of his rare sympathetic roles. No doubt hoping to wring another Oscar-winning performance from the star, director John Farrow tried too hard to suggest parallels with *The Informer* (1935).

Of all non-mysterious murder films, however, the rarest and generally the most haunting were those sinister, macabre thrillers in which the motive was nothing so hot-blooded as sexual passion but, rather, implacable hatred, greed, revenge or the pure evil, the "motiveless malignity" of a psychopath capable of killing without scruple or regret. In such films the emotional horror was all the more chilling for being set in the everyday world, growing out of the sheer depravity of human nature.

An early example, bizarre enough to resist any other classification, was Lon Chaney's only talkie, *The Unholy Three* (1930), a remake of his 1925 silent hit, also directed by Tod Browning. Unlike most of Chaney's more famous vehicles, this cannot be considered a horror film, since during most of it he is disguised as a sweet old lady. The other two of the title are a carnival strong man (Ivan Linow) and a malicious midget (Harry Earles), palmed off as the old lady's infant grandson.

Along with an accomplice (Lila Lee), they open a pet shop as a front, specializing in parrots who talk only because Chaney is an expert ventriloquist. When customers complain, the old lady and the supposed baby visit their homes, to case them for valuables. But thieves fall out when the strong man and the midget pin a needless murder on an innocent clerk (Elliott Nugent), for whom the girl has fallen. The ventriloquist finally comes through for the defense, and the other two are killed off.

In the decidedly offbeat *Thirteen Women* (1932), from Tiffany Thayer's novel, a homicidal anticipation of Mary McCarthy's *The Group,* Myrna Loy, just emerging from her Oriental phase, was a half-caste (half Hindu, half Javanese) bent on avenging slights suffered long ago while attending an exclusive girls' school. Aided by an evil swami (C. Henry Gordon), she writes letters to twelve former sorority sisters predicting dire tragedies, which in some cases come true. Among the intended victims were Jill Esmond, Florence Eldridge, Kay Johnson and Julie Haydon, but strong-minded Irene Dunne, whose little son is threatened, with the aid of detective Ricardo Cortez ends the chain of deaths.

But by far the best murder melodrama of 1932, the first American-made British psycho-

logical thriller of the decade, was *Payment Deferred,* in which Charles Laughton re-created the role in which he had scored in London and New York in Jeffrey Dell's play. The plot is a grim variation on the "postman always rings twice" theme: even if you get away with one murder, fate will trip you up in some other way.

A mousy bank clerk, deeply in debt, poisons his rich Australian nephew (Ray Milland), buries the body in his garden and runs the money up to a fortune. He takes to drink, neglects his devoted wife (Dorothy Peterson) for a flashy French adventuress (Verree Teasdale) and generally makes a fool of himself, but can keep neither his gaze nor his thoughts from the grisly secret in the garden. When his grieving wife suspects him first of embezzlement, then of murder, she takes her own life by putting an overdose of drugs in a cup of tea he innocently served her—so on circumstantial evidence he is convicted and hanged for her murder. Though Laughton naturally overshadows everyone else, all the performances hold up extremely well.

Double Door (1934), from Elizabeth McFadden's 1933 play (said to have been inspired by the last, reclusive members of the Wendel family of Fifth Avenue), was a most absorbing thriller, meticulously set in the New York of 1910. Mary Morris and Anne Revere admirably repeated their stage roles as the spinster Van Brett sisters, Victoria and Caroline, one the domineering embodiment of fanatic family pride, the other her cowed victim, kept in line by threats of an asylum.

When their young half-brother (Kent Taylor) brings home an unwelcome bride (Evelyn Venable) to live in the gloomy mansion, Victoria, who is given to playing mad organ solos in the style of the Phantom of the Opera and leading the way up dark stairways by the light of a flickering candelabra, first tries to accuse the girl of an affair with her doctor (Colin Tapley), then, when all else has failed, to lure her, on the pretext of giving her the famous Van Brett pearls, into a secret vault, guarded by the double door of the title, of

***Dorothy Peterson, Charles Laughton, Maureen O'Sullivan** in* **Payment Deferred**

which only Victoria knows the combination. Though experienced movie-goers might guess who will end fatally trapped in the vault, the mounting suspense and the sense of ruthless evil are powerful indeed.

An even more disturbing mood of claustrophobic menace pervades *Kind Lady* (1935), based on *The Silver Mask,* a short story by Hugh Walpole, in which Aline MacMahon starred in a role created on stage earlier that year by Grace George.

Coming home from the opera one snowy Christmas Eve, a wealthy London spinster is maneuvered into befriending an untalented but aggressive painter (Basil Rathbone), especially when his supposed wife apparently faints from hunger near her door. In no time they have not only moved in but introduced a whole knavish crew; with a criminal doctor's aid, they keep the woman on drugs, murder her faithful maid, intercept notes she tries to smuggle out, convince chance visitors she is mad and at last imprison her in an attic room, where she will obviously be killed as soon as

Mary Morris in **Double Door**

they have finished selling all her valuable paintings. In the story this is her fate, but in all the dramatic versions she is rescued in the nick of time.

Another cold-blooded killer, whose obsession is academic ambition rather than family pride or avarice, figured in *Under Cover of*

Night (1937), in which a professor of science (Henry Daniell), the very opposite of Pierre Curie, has been passing off the important discoveries of his wife (Sara Haden) as his own. When she threatens to leave him, what can he do but kill her? But she has had the foresight to entrust her precious research notes, outlining future work, to an unnamed colleague. Determined to recover them, the professor virtually decimates his department, killing off several others before detective Edmund Lowe catches up with him.

However, by far the most notable American film about a murderous psychopath ("homicidal maniac" seems too violent a term) was *Night Must Fall* (1937), based on Emlyn Williams' international hit play. As on stage, the film version opened almost simultaneously with that of Frank Vosper's *Love from a Stranger* (British-made), which also dealt with a smooth-tongued murderer of women, but far from killing each other off, both films attracted all who wanted to compare them, both were admired and both hold up well today.

As the laughing, blarneying Irish bellboy Danny, Robert Montgomery in his first opportunity in a genuinely dramatic role astounded critics with a performance that in effect made the rest of his career. Whether he is charming the foolish, selfish old Mrs. Bramson (Dame May Whitty in her American debut), alternately attracting and terrifying her repressed niece (Rosalind Russell) or impudently defying a suspicious police inspector (Matthew Boulton), Danny is a frighteningly credible character, as genuinely likable at one moment as he is subtly menacing at the next. His mysterious hatbox, whose contents are never shown, conveys a more effective suggestion of horror than many a more gruesome sight in later films.

Most variations on the murder theme have continued to flourish in more recent decades, particularly in the 1940s, which saw not only several notable examples from Hitchcock such as *Suspicion* (1941), *Shadow of a Doubt* (1943) and *Rope* (1948) but a number of

Basil Rathbone, Aline MacMahon in Kind Lady

Robert Montgomery, Rosalind Russell in Night Must Fall

those hard-boiled melodramas sometimes called *films noirs: Scarlet Street* (1946), *Double Indemnity* (1944), *Mildred Pierce* (1945), *The Postman Always Rings Twice* (1946), the latter three based on novels by James M. Cain. The genteel British thriller likewise persisted in such familiar films as *Ladies in Retirement* (1941), *Gaslight* (1944), Mrs. Belloc Lowndes' *The Lodger* (1944) and *Ivy* (1947), and Joseph Shearing's *Moss Rose* (1947) and *So Evil My Love* (1948).

32

"AH, BUT YOU MADE ONE SLIP!" The Butler Never Did It

Another descendant of the Gothic romance, by way of Poe, Gaboriau, Wilkie Collins and Conan Doyle, the pure puzzle plot, commonly called the detective story or murder mystery, was never more popular than in the '30s, the heyday of novelists like Agatha Christie, Dorothy Sayers, Ellery Queen and S. S. Van Dine. "Whodunits," as they soon came to be known, provided talkies with some of their earliest— and tritest—series. Most remained rigidly locked in the stage convention by which all the characters are brought together in a sinister old mansion for some occasion and then picked off one by one—until the great success of *The Thin Man* (1934) launched a whole new cycle, in which bright young couples wisecracked their way to the surprise solution. Thus the gambits open to a mystery writer were quite limited. Megalomaniacs ambitious to take over the world, like Fu Manchu and Professor Moriarty, were rare; most murderers were driven by simple greed, jealousy, revenge or fear of blackmail. The nuances of abnormal psychology, repressed guilt, love-hate relationships and other perverse quirks of human nature, so brilliantly explored by later suspense novelists like Ross Macdonald and

Patricia Highsmith and in many of Hitchcock's films, might occasionally turn up in those murder dramas discussed in the last chapter, or in horror films, but almost never in pure mysteries.

Indeed, it would almost seem that the more intelligent and subtle the mystery writer, the less likely his/her works were to be filmed in the '30s. (Dashiell Hammett is an exception.) Thus none of Dorothy L. Sayers' novels were done, and of Agatha Christie's only *Love from a Stranger,* by way of a British-made adaptation of Frank Vosper's play. Only four Sherlock Holmes films were made (none between 1933 and 1939), only two Nero Wolfe mysteries and two Ellery Queens (both poorly done), as contrasted with six Perry Masons, eight Philo Vances, nine Bulldog Drummonds and twenty Charlie Chans, most ground out as mechanically as any TV series and certainly not worth extended analysis. Yet the genre was undeniably popular, especially in the later '30s, when from twenty to thirty mysteries were made each year.

By far the most popular formula was that of the "old dark house," mostly based on hit plays of the '20s, with their origins often showing all too clearly. Aside from the economy of limiting the action to a few interiors, this enforced unity of place also gave all the characters equal opportunity to commit the crimes. Another perhaps inevitable convention was that the first victim should be so generally disliked as to spread suspicion evenly among all the survivors. Later victims, of course, might be killed merely for knowing too much about the first murder.

Characters likewise tended to be drawn strictly from the stockpile. They frequently included an eccentric millionaire whose will is full of outrageous codicils and contingencies, a crotchety spinster aunt, a family lawyer, a doctor, a wastrel nephew or cousin, a blond adventuress, one or more creepy or comic servants and, of course, the ingenue and the juvenile (who was often an amateur sleuth, only too ready to show up the bumbling police).

All are brought together in the sinister mansion for some ostensible purpose: the reading of the will, a séance, someone's twenty-first birthday or the anniversary of some earlier crime. Often they are marooned by a washed-out bridge, bad weather or some other natural force. Lights mysteriously fail, then go on to reveal another murder, corpses fall out of closets and chimneys, valuable papers or jewels disappear and turn up, clutching hands (or claws or paws) reach out from secret panels, women scream and faint, until in the final roundup the know-it-all hero reconstructs the whole plot, unmasks the killer (always the least likely suspect) and assures the heroine of her inheritance.

Two typical examples, remarkably parallel in several respects, were *The Bat*, a 1920 play by Mary Roberts Rinehart and Avery Hopwood, based on Rinehart's novel *The Circular Staircase*, and an obvious derivative, *The Cat and the Canary*, a 1922 play by John Willard. Most of the clichés just noted appeared in both, with the additional bizarre note that in both the killer calls himself by an animal name and even assumes animal disguise.

Though mysteries were not especially popular in silents, perhaps because the necessary exposition, interrogation and recapitulation placed too much of a burden on subtitles, both these plays had been successfully filmed, *The Bat* in 1926, *The Cat and the Canary* in 1927, the latter highly praised for its unusual photography. Still parallel, both were remade as early talkies, with the titles changed by the addition of a verb: *The Cat Creeps* (1930) and *The Bat Whispers* (1931).

The Cat Creeps, in which Helen Twelvetrees played the role Laura La Plante had done in the silent, suffered by comparison with its highly stylized predecessor, was routinely dismissed by the *Times* and has seldom, if ever, been revived anywhere. It was, however, remade in 1939 under the original title as a vehicle for Bob Hope. Said the *Times:* "Paramount has had the wit and wisdom to produce a nonsense edition of John Willard's old shocker . . . Streamlined, screamlined and played to the hilt for comedy, the new version is more hare-brained than hair-raising."

The Bat Whispers, on the other hand, directed by Roland West, when shown at the Huff Society in 1965, found Everson "bowled over by the marvelous stuff it contains."

Other films of this type, however, without the benefit of West's direction, were strictly formula. *The Gorilla* (1931) played it for laughs as two low-comedy Irish detectives disguised themselves as the beast of the title and were alternately mistaken for and attacked by the real thing. In 1939 the two were increased to three, and the Ritz Brothers did for *The Gorilla* what Bob Hope had done for *The Cat and the Canary*, only not as well. *The Menace* (1932), from an Edgar Wallace novel, featured a hero (Walter Byron) disguised by plastic surgery seeking the murderers of his father. (Though listed second in the cast, Bette Davis was not mentioned in the *Times* review.)

Of *Miss Pinkerton* (1932), based on a magazine serial by the prolific Mrs. Rinehart and starring Joan Blondell as a nurse, the *Times* noted:

The producers have dragged in the eccentric butler, the spiritistic housekeeper, the evil-looking doctor, the cloaked man with the clutching fingers and the frightened juvenile. Mix well with shadows, creak a few doors, let the midnight wind howl, and what have you? An old story.

A more typical example, according to Don Miller "one of the few independent productions to receive overwhelmingly good notices from the critics," was Monogram's *The Thirteenth Guest* (1933), which, surprisingly, starred Ginger Rogers and Lyle Talbot. The plot involved the midnight reading of a will in a sinister old mansion on the thirteenth anniversary of a fatal family reunion, a deadly electrified telephone, a heroine in peril, a jaunty private investigator—all the standard ingredients, but blended well enough to please everyone.

A less original variation was *Strange People* (1933), in which twelve jury members who sentenced an innocent man to death are summoned to the home of the victim, where the defense attorney stages a fake murder that turns out to be real. The *Times* reviewer could only list the clichés (a device that almost became a cliché in itself):

Rain, shadows and half-human sounds the wind makes when it whistles around the gables of a house at night; stairs that creak and floors that groan; the stifled screams of women who imagine they can see the silhouette of a man hanging dead on the balcony; and the look on the face of a corpse when it tumbles out from behind a screen.

In *The Secret of the Blue Room* (1933) the setting was a Continental castle containing a locked room, supposedly haunted, where twenty years before three people were murdered. As one of the three suitors of Gloria Stuart, William Janney, to prove his courage, offers to spend a night in the room, from which he disappears. A strong cast including Lionel Atwill, Paul Lukas, Edward Arnold and Onslow Stevens helped make this one of the better examples of the genre.

In *The Ninth Guest* (1934), from a play by Owen Davis, eight people (including Edward Ellis, Hardie Albright and Helen Flint), all apparently successful, all connected politically, financially, emotionally or otherwise, most on bad terms with one another, are invited by telegrams signed "Your Host" to dinner at a penthouse, where they are greeted only by a radio voice that seems to know everything about them. The ninth guest is, of course, death. With poisoned wine, electrically charged gates and other devices, they are picked off one by one—except for a pair of disillusioned ex-lovers (Donald Cook and Genevieve Tobin).

The format was indeed far from dead. MGM, with its passion for making and remaking prewar melodramas (e.g., *Madame X, Within the Law*), in 1937 exhumed Bayard Veiller's 1916 hit, *The Thirteenth Chair,* which had already been filmed twice, in 1919 and 1929. This time Dame May Whitty played the old Irish medium at whose séance an attempt to solve one murder leads to another. An excellent cast (Lewis Stone, Edmund Lowe, Henry Daniell, Madge Evans, Janet Beecher) impressed the *Times* reviewer: "Assured direction and competent performances by an established troupe of featured players are the film's chief attributes, for little ingenuity has gone into the revising of the script."

Though necessarily more varied in background, the numerous detective series that flourished throughout the '30s were in most other respects just as limited as the old-dark-house films. To deal first with the most famous fictional detective of all time, Clive Brook, who in 1929 had starred in *The Return of Sherlock Holmes,* in 1932 made, for Fox, just plain *Sherlock Holmes,* updated to the then present, but still featuring Moriarty (Ernest Torrence) as chief villain. In this version, which owes little to either Doyle or Gillette, Holmes is about to marry one Alice Faulkner (Miriam Jordan). Watson was Reginald Owen, perfectly cast.

The following year, in an astonishing piece of casting *against* type, this same Reginald Owen played Holmes himself in World

Wide's *A Study in Scarlet,* with Warburton Gamble as Watson. Despite modernization, the script, adapted by Robert Florey, with dialogue by Owen himself, was reasonably faithful to the original and acted by an almost entirely British cast.

Not until nearly six years later, at the end of the decade, did the next American Holmes film appear, the memorable *The Hound of the Baskervilles* (1939), done in proper Victorian period, with Basil Rathbone and Nigel Bruce at last assuming the roles for which they seemed to have been born.

Six months later, as a follow-up, came *The Adventures of Sherlock Holmes* (1939), which Everson in program notes for a 1976 showing calls "arguably the screen's best." Though said to be based on Gillette's play, it bears no more resemblance to it than did the 1932 film, but "the admirably complicated screenplay is excellent pseudo-Doyle," centering on Moriarty's announced plan to steal the crown jewels from the Tower.

Until the Holmes revivals of the '60s and '70s (mostly British), this was the last Holmes film done in period. All twelve of the Rathbone-Bruce series made by Universal (1942–46), though eight were loosely based on Doyle stories, were anachronistically set in the present of World War II, usually in America.

As noted, in the number of '30s films based on his exploits, Holmes was easily surpassed by Vance, Mason, Drummond and especially by the longest-lived screen sleuth of them all, Charlie Chan, who smiled his first inscrutable smile and uttered (in subtitles) his first "Confucius say" aphorisms in a Pathé serial, *The House Without a Key* (1926), played by a Japanese actor, George Kuwa. In 1928 Universal made *The Chinese Parrot* with another Japanese Chan, Kamiyama Sojin, and in 1929, talking for the first time, he appeared as a minor character in *Behind That Curtain,* played by an English actor, E. L. Park.

Not until Warner Oland assumed the role in *Charlie Chan Carries On* (1931) did the bland Oriental detective come into his own. So successful did he carry on that within four months he was back, in a film that, uniquely for this original series, did not include his name in the title, *The Black Camel* (1931).

Others soon followed, at first only one a year (*Charlie Chan's Chance,* 1932, *Charlie Chan's Greatest Case,* 1933), then two a year (*Charlie Chan's Courage* and *Charlie Chan in London,* the first one not written by Chan's creator, Earl Derr Biggers, both 1934), then three a year (*Charlie Chan in Paris,* . . . *in Egypt* and . . . *in Shanghai,* all 1935). According to Don Miller in *B Movies,* in the last two, "the mystery and suspense elements, so valuable to the success of the Chans, were all but absent, with the emphasis placed on action and hairbreadth escapes."

It was at this point that Fox merged with 20th Century, to the great benefit of the Chan series. *Charlie Chan's Secret* was given a quality production, as were his visits to *the Circus, the Race Track* and especially *the Opera* (all 1936). Yet of *Secret* the *Times* reviewer observed:

With the passing of the years the Charlie Chan mystery film has grown to be as much standardized and about as uniform in quality as any other consistently selling product of the industrial age. Any one sufficiently antiquated to have seen the earliest Chan will know what to expect of the latest.

Opera, however, was regarded by the *Times* as the best so far, and is considered a classic by the continuing Chan cult. Among other assets, it included Boris Karloff as a crazed singer and original operatic music composed by Oscar Levant.

1937 took Chan to the 1936 Berlin *Olympics* via the *Hindenburg* (which unfortunately had crashed before the release of the film), to *Broadway* and *Monte Carlo,* at which point the series was temporarily curtailed by the death of Oland. But not for long. Charlie survived not only his author but his most popular interpreter. He was soon back in the person of Missouri-born Sidney Toler in *Charlie Chan in Honolulu* (1938), . . . *in Reno* and . . . *at Treasure Island* (both 1939), the last-named regarded by *aficionados* as the best of all. *Charlie Chan in the City in Darkness* (which meant Munich during the 1938 crisis) was the last entry for the '30s, but five more followed at Fox, 1940–42, before Monogram took over the series, making eleven low-budget productions with Toler (1943–47) and six more with equally Occidental Roland Winters (1947–49).

In the midst of this series, 20th Century-Fox, presumably on the principle that one can never have too much of a good thing, launched the Mr. Moto series, starring Hungarian-born Peter Lorre as J. P. Marquand's Japanese detective in eight films within two years (1937–39). But despite Lorre's subtle, underplayed characterization of the inconspicuous Mr. Moto, he could not rise above the familiar material: murders, jewel thefts, smuggling, carried out against international backgrounds, especially the Orient. Presumably Mr. Moto was cut off in his cinematic prime by the growing tension between the United States and Japan.[1]

Though in 1929 William Powell had played Philo Vance for Paramount in both the *Canary* and *Greene Murder Cases* (S. S. Van Dine's titles always involved a six-letter word), the first Vance to appear in 1930 was none other than Basil Rathbone (the only actor ever to play both Holmes and Vance) in MGM's *The Bishop Murder Case,* which the *Times* praised chiefly for its sound recording.

This is the one in which the killer, who styles himself "the Bishop" after the chess piece of the same name, announces each crime by sending the police a nursery rhyme, then arranging a murder to fit it (e.g., a hunchback is toppled off a wall to re-enact Humpty Dumpty). This twist afforded Vance an unusually good chance to display that random erudition (chess, etymology, folklore) that made him at times the most irritating and supercilious of amateur sleuths.

[1] Not to be outdone, Monogram came up with its own Oriental detective, Mr. Wong, played by the ever-busy Karloff in five films between 1938 and 1940.

A few months later Powell resumed the Vance role, with Eugene Pallette again as Sergeant Heath, in *The Benson Murder Case* (1930). One of the first films to make use of the previous year's market crash, it dealt with the murder in a hunting lodge of a broker (Richard Tucker) who had sold out several of his clients.

After a three-year lapse and a switch from Paramount to Warner Brothers, Powell and Pallette were back in the same roles in *The Kennel Murder Case* (1933), with a large cast and a plot so absurdly complicated as to seem almost a parody of the genre.[2] So many people want to kill Archer Coe (Robert Barrat) that he is in effect murdered more than once; at least two people think they have done it. Says *The New Yorker:* "The plot involves some lively Scotties and a handsome Doberman, as well as that sinister figure, the connoisseur of Oriental objects of art; in the thirties, Ming and murder always seemed to go together."

Perhaps because Powell now moved to MGM, where he presently began playing that much more likable sleuth, Nick Charles, Vance for the rest of the decade was portrayed by a whole gallery of different actors. First it was Warren William in *The Dragon Murder Case* (1934), while Pallette continued as Heath, as did Robert McWade as D.A. Markham and Etienne Girardot as medical examiner Doremus. By MGM's *The Casino Murder Case* (1935)—the ingenue role Rosalind Russell regarded as the low point of her screen career—Vance had become Paul Lukas, with Ted Healy as Heath. In *The Garden Murder Case* (1936), still at MGM, Edmund Lowe was Vance, Nat Pendleton Heath.

To add to the confusion, Paramount now

[2] In 1940 Warners remade it as *Calling Philo Vance,* with James Stephenson in the title role and Edward Brophy as Ryan, substitute for Heath. The plot now involved "priceless plans for a new air bomber and assorted foreign agents." This was the last of Vance on screen until three Producers' Releasing Corporation quickies in 1947, one with Will Wright, two with Alan Curtis.

did a poor remake of *The Greene Murder Case* under the title of *A Night of Mystery* (1937), with Grant Richards as Vance, Roscoe Karns as Heath. To crown it all, Paramount then brought back Warren William as Vance in *The Gracie Allen Murder Case* (1939), but with William Demarest as Heath.

It should be noted that all these unrelated films, made by different studios, with seven different Vances (one British with Wilfrid Hyde-White) in less than ten years totally destroyed any sense of the continuity of the Chan series. Successive Vance films also drew increasingly cool reviews, competing as they were now with fresher, more original mysteries. Though Powell never again played Vance after *The Kennel Murder Case,* he was the one that lingered in the memory and continued to be invoked as the definitive embodiment of the character.

An even sharper decline in quality was evident in the Bulldog Drummond films. The original 1929 *Bulldog Drummond,* United Artists, Ronald Colman's first talkie, was hailed as an artistic and technical triumph.[3] *Bulldog Drummond Strikes Back* (1934), Fox, again starring Colman, was regarded by the *Times* as "excellent entertainment." Warner Oland, never too busy with Charlie Chan to play Oriental villains in between, was trying to unload a fortune in furs from a cholera-plagued ship.

These two Colman films stand apart from the series which Paramount began with *Bulldog Drummond Escapes* (1937) with Ray Milland in the title role, Sir Guy Standing as Nielson, his Scotland Yard superior, and Heather Angel as his fiancée. Yet five months later, in *Bulldog Drummond Comes Back* (1937), he came back as John Howard, with John Barrymore (who got top billing) as Nielson and Louise Campbell as the put-upon fiancée, Phyllis.

The following month found Republic getting into the act, releasing *Bulldog Drummond at Bay,* very poorly reviewed, one of several British versions, most not shown in the United States. Still in 1937, the Howard-Barrymore-Campbell team were back in *Bulldog Drummond's Revenge,* which, as the *Times* pointed out, involved no revenge at all, only interminable delays to Drummond's intended marriage.

Bulldog Drummond's Peril and *Bulldog Drummond in Africa* followed in 1938, to increasingly scornful reviews. In the second one Heather Angel returned as the perpetual fiancée, and H. B. Warner succeeded Barrymore. By *Arrest Bulldog Drummond* (1939) the constantly delayed wedding had become such a joke that the *Times* reviewer bet it would not take place by 1940. In this he was wrong, for after one more postponement, in *Bulldog Drummond's Secret Police* (1939, apparently a disastrous remake of the 1930 *Temple Tower*), Hugh and Phyllis finally made it to the altar in *Bulldog Drummond's Bride* (1939), which mercifully put an end to this thoroughly uninspired series.

"With S. S. Van Dine's Philo Vance temporarily on the shelf," the *Times* noted, perhaps too optimistically, in its review of *The Case of the Howling Dog* (1934), "the cinema has sought out a new detective. He is Perry Mason." The reviewer was much impressed by the relative realism of the film and its avoidance of clichés. Warren William was praised as "infinitely better suited to the part than he was to that of Philo Vance where he was stumbling over William Powell's footsteps." Yet this did not save Mason from going through almost as many different screen embodiments as Vance.

By *The Case of the Curious Bride* (1935), Della Street, originally played by one Helen Trenholme, never heard of again, had become Claire Dodd. This was a fast-moving tale of a disappearing bridegroom, a small part, played by the as yet undiscovered Errol Flynn. "The pace is swift," the *Times* noted, "the solution well hidden, the comedy good, and—but isn't that enough?"

---

[3] *Temple Tower* (1930), with Kenneth MacKenna as Drummond, was so poorly reviewed it hardly deserves mention as one of the series.

In *The Case of the Lucky Legs* (1935) William was still Mason, but Genevieve Tobin was Della, in a film the *Times* hailed as "a gay, swift and impudent excursion into the sombre matter of murder . . . Nonsensical? Of course, but that seems to be the style in murders ever since *The Thin Man* came along."

Despite their apparent success, after these first three, the Perry Mason films were reduced to lower budgets—in fact, became "B's." William and Dodd were in one more, with Perry and Della as newlyweds, *The Case of the Velvet Claws* (1936), but the *Times* was less than enthusiastic. In *The Case of the Black Cat* (1936) Ricardo Cortez and June Travis had taken over; the *Times* gave it a fair but very brief, perfunctory notice. Finally, the ultimate ignominy: *The Case of the Stuttering Bishop* (1937), with Donald Woods, considered the best Mason so far, and Ann Dvorak as Della, was not even reviewed by the *Times*. But who does not know that Perry and Della reached their true apotheosis on TV in the 1950s and still enjoy world-wide rerun immortality in the persons of Raymond Burr and Barbara Hale?

Female detectives—amateurs, of course—were naturally much rarer than men, but few though they were, they suffered from the same kind of confused identities. Thus Stuart Palmer's spinster schoolteacher, Hildegarde Withers, appeared in only six films, but was played by three different actresses. Mignon G. Eberhart's Nurse Sarah (or Sally) Keate (or Keats or Keating) fared still worse, in six films portrayed by five wildly varied actresses. Only Nancy Drew was consistent.

Miss Withers started out well enough in *The Penguin Pool Murder* (1932), as the crisply authoritative Edna May Oliver, with James Gleason as her slow-witted foil, Inspector Oscar Piper of the NYPD. The setting was so novel (the New York Aquarium) and the comedy so amusing that the *Times* reviewer was not inclined to pick apart the plot. *Murder on the Blackboard* (1934) was good enough for the critic to speak of Hildegarde's

"rivalry of Sherlock Holmes, Father Brown, Philo Vance and Charlie Chan." The plot was termed "quite ingenious," with the crucial clue a musical notation on a blackboard, which, properly interpreted, identified the killer.

Even more successful was *Murder on a Honeymoon* (1935), co-authored by Robert Benchley. The *Times* reviewer ended with this plea: "Note to RKO-Radio. One Gleason-Oliver picture a year seems awfully stingy. Couldn't we have two or three?" (No one had ever asked for more Charlie Chans or Philo Vances.)

Yet, for whatever misguided reason, RKO now broke up this winning team, not only substituting Helen Broderick for Oliver but also changing the director and writers. The result: *Murder on a Bridle Path* (1936) was described by Crisler as "boring dialogue between James Gleason and Helen Broderick." It even included an old dark house with a creepy butler.

The series was finally done in by an even worse piece of miscasting. In *The Plot Thickens* (1936), while Gleason continued as Piper, Hildegarde was now taken over by Zasu Pitts. Gifted comedienne though she was, Pitts' helpless, wispy personality was the very opposite of the firm, tart-tongued Miss Withers. Predictably, the *Times* scarcely mentioned *Forty Naughty Girls* (1937), again with Pitts and Gleason, the unmourned end of a series that had started off unusually well.

No such falling off can be traced in the fortunes of Mignon G. Eberhart's sleuthing nurse, who started out at a low level in *While the Patient Slept* (1935) and never rose above it. At first known as Sarah Keate (middle-aged as in the novels), she was played by Aline MacMahon. Between murders she found time for a coy little romance with Guy Kibbee, who bore the unlikely name of Lance O'Leary.

In *The Murder of Dr. Harrigan* (1936) as Sally Keating she had become an elegant young brunette (Kay Linaker), but got even worse reviews. Next played by Marguerite

Churchill in *Murder by an Aristocrat* (1936), she fared no better, perhaps because the plot came far too close to the old-dark-house formula.

Undaunted by these three Warners failures, 20th Century-Fox, with more courage than discretion, bought another Eberhart novel, which emerged as *The Great Hospital Mystery* (1937), with stout, grandmotherly Jane Darwell as "Miss Keats." It drew the same dismal notices. With persistence worthy of a lemming, Warners returned twice more to the losing battle. *The Patient in Room 18* (1938) starred youthful Patric Knowles as Lance O'Leary and Ann Sheridan (soon to be proclaimed "the Oomph Girl") as Sarah Keate. Two months later she found herself opposite a new O'Leary, Dick Purcell, in *Mystery House* (1938), to which the *Times* gave even shorter shrift.[4]

Thus the only sleuthing heroine in a mystery series who stayed on the same level, modest but entertaining, was Nancy Drew, the enterprising high school girl already nationally known through a series of juvenile novels by Carolyn Keene. Nancy had the good fortune to be played by only one actress, an extraordinarily talented teen-ager, Bonita Granville, in all four films: *Nancy Drew Detective* (1938), *Nancy Drew Reporter*, *Nancy Drew Trouble Shooter* and *Nancy Drew and the Hidden Staircase* (all 1939).

Says Miller:

The ensuing films satisfied adolescents and entertained their elders as well, possibly because of the unanimity of the staff. In each of four films, John Litel played Nancy's exasperated father, and Frankie Thomas her dubious accomplice in crime-solving . . . This teamwork accounted for a smoothness not often found in series films.

One late-starting series successful enough to continue beyond the '30s was the one begun in *The Saint in New York* (1938). As Leslie

[4] The availability of surgical masks, scalpels, hypodermic needles and deadly drugs made hospitals a favorite background for murder mysteries, such as *The Mystery of the White Room* (1939).

Charteris' adventurous hero, Simon Templar, Louis Hayward was well received, but when the next one appeared a year later, *The Saint Strikes Back* (1939), George Sanders had taken over. He continued in *The Saint in London* (1939), praised by Crisler as "the handsomest and most urbane of all the currently practicing gentlemen detectives." But after four more films, through 1941, RKO lost the rights to the character and switched Sanders to the practically indistinguishable Falcon series, in which he was presently replaced by his real-life brother, Tom Conway.

Some series never got further than two entries. Such was the case with Anthony Abbot (pseudonym of Fulton Oursler, editor of *Liberty* magazine), whose mystery titles followed the pattern of *About the Murder of . . .* and whose sleuth was no amateur but, rather, the New York police commissioner himself, Thatcher Colt, played by Adolphe Menjou in both films. With the title shortened, *The Night Club Lady* (1932) dealt with a Guinan-like cabaret hostess (Mayo Methot), who is warned that she will not live a minute past midnight New Year's Eve, and despite all protection does not. She was operating an international blackmail business on the side, so there's no lack of suspects. Skeets Gallagher was the standard comic sidekick and Ruth-elma Stevens the loyal, wisecracking secretary (so soon to become a cliché, as in the Mason films).

She survived, but the sidekick disappeared in the second film, *The Circus Queen Murder* (1933), about the murder of a trapeze artist (Greta Nissen) in full view of the horrified audience—perhaps inspired by the real-life tragedy of aerialist Lillian Leitzel. Both films were so well received for the novelty of their settings and motivations that it is hard to guess why Columbia, which had no other detective series going, never made a scheduled third about Thatcher Colt.

Even more inexplicable was the cinematic fate of Nero Wolfe. *Meet Nero Wolfe* (1936), well cast, with Edward Arnold as Rex Stout's sedentary sleuth and Lionel Stander as his assistant Archie, was hailed as most promising. Wolfe, said John T. McManus, somewhat ungrammatically, in the *Times,* "presages brisk competition for such current screen masterminds as Philo Vance and Perry Mason, both in matters of deduction as well as aesthetically." His immobility, of course, made the final roundup of suspects unavoidable.

In *The League of Frightened Men* (1937) Nero had become Walter Connolly, with hot chocolate substituted for his beloved beer. The plot, parallel to that of *Thirteen Women,* dealt with ten Harvard alumni who as undergraduates had in a hazing prank crippled another student for life. When three have died under mysterious circumstances and the rest have received threats, they engage Wolfe. The *Times* considered it "a well-knit mystery and well played out," but nevertheless Columbia chose to spurn the Wolfe series from its door.

At that, Nero made out better than Ellery Queen, whose ingenious, literate adventures, supposedly written by himself (actually by Frederic Dannay and Manfred B. Lee) and at first always using a national adjective followed by a noun in the title (e.g., *The Greek Coffin Mystery, The Egyptian Cross Mystery*), enjoyed a very wide following in the '30s and later. The intellectual son of a likable police inspector, though well informed in many fields, Queen never became as obnoxious as Vance.

Yet his only '30s screen incarnations were both "B's," one worse than the other. In *The Spanish Cape Mystery* (1935), Donald Cook was not badly cast as Queen, but the original clever plot was reduced to a shambles. In *The Mandarin Mystery* (1937), supposedly based on *The Chinese Orange Mystery,* the ruin of the script was completed by the casting of Eddie Quillan, a breezy juvenile more suitable for college musicals, who had nothing in common with Ellery Queen but the initials.

In a sense, all these independent investigators (except Charlie Chan, who worked for the Honolulu Police Department), even Holmes, were "private eyes"—though certainly not in the hard-boiled, grim, seedy pattern created by Dashiell Hammett, Raymond Chandler and other writers for *Black Mask* magazine, later debased by Mickey Spillane and countless imitators and ultimately redeemed by Ross Macdonald, among others.

The archetypal private eye, Hammett's Sam Spade, made his first screen appearance in 1931, in the first of the three versions of *The Maltese Falcon,* played by Ricardo Cortez, with Bebe Daniels as the *femme fatale,* whose name was changed for some reason from Brigid O'Shaughnessy to Ruth Wonderly. Except for this and a slightly softened ending, in which Sam visits her in prison and instructs the matron to take good care of her, this film, crisply written, directed and acted, is completely faithful to the novel. Perfectly cast were Dudley Digges as Gutman, Dwight Frye as Wilmer, Una Merkel as Effie and Thelma Todd as the amorous widow, Iva Archer.

No more striking example in film history can be found of the difference a director and script writers can make, given the same story. *The Maltese Falcon* was filmed three times within ten years; Roy Del Ruth's 1931 version is a superior piece of work, John Huston's 1941 *Falcon* became an all-time classic.

But in between, a 1936 variation, retitled *Satan Met a Lady,* directed by William Dieterle from a script attributed to Brown Holmes, who had also co-authored the earlier version, with all the characters' names changed, including Spade's to Ted Shayne, was so bad that it drove Bette Davis into open rebellion against Warners—a move with which anyone seeing the film can warmly sympathize. Among other pointless changes, Gutman, the Fat Man, had become Mme. Barabbas (Alison Skipworth). Cut to sixty-six minutes and speeded up to the point of incoherence, what is left of the plot is buried in a blizzard of feeble wisecracks. Crisler in the *Times* minced no words:

So disconnected and lunatic are the picture's incidents, so irrelevant and monstrous its people, that one lives through it in constant expectation of seeing a group of uniformed individuals appearing suddenly from behind the furniture to take the entire cast into protective custody.

Meanwhile, however, other private eyes—three of them Hammett's—had maintained higher standards. In *Mr. Dynamite* (1935), based on Hammett's story *On the Make*, Edmund Lowe played one T. N. Thompson (hence his nickname), the scourge of the San Francisco detective squad. Said Nugent in the *Times:* "Mr. Hammett's distinction among mystery tale spinners is that he never takes his corpse as seriously as his detective, and he never lets his detective take himself seriously at all . . ."

This was followed within a month by Hammett's *The Glass Key* (1935), which won even higher praise. George Raft was Ed (not Ned) Beaumont in this complex tale of a ward heeler (Edward Arnold) who in trying to go in for clean politics finds himself framed for the murder of a colleague's son (Ray Milland).[5] Praising the somber tone, Nugent wrote: "Now, just when we were beginning to fear that the imitators of *The Thin Man* were becoming overly jocose on the subject of assassination, Mr. Hammett comes along with proof that murder isn't necessarily funny."

Clearly, Hammett could do no wrong. Thus when *Muss 'Em Up* (1936), from a novel called *The Green Shadow,* opened, Harry T. Smith in the *Times* observed:

It is a compliment to James Edward Grant, who wrote the novel on which the film is based, to say that his Tip O'Neil might have been invented by Dashiell Hammett himself. Tough, witty, eminently practical, Tip (short for Tippecanoe) is a perfect illustration of the modern detective hero.[6]

What had every studio bidding for Hammett's work or a reasonably exact facsimile thereof was not this kind of hard-boiled private-eye tale at all, but the film that truly

revolutionized the genre by combining it with genuinely witty comedy: *The Thin Man* (1934), after more than four decades and countless imitations still the most sparkling example of its kind.

David Shipman in writing about Loy in *The Great Movie Stars* comes close to suggesting the film's charm:

It was something quite new: Nick and Nora Charles, affluent private eye and wife, bantering and affectionately bitching each other; their chief interest seemed to be alcohol, and neither could be said not to have a philandering nature . . . There was a spontaneous gaiety (it looks fresh today) which had much to do with the understated incisiveness of the stars' playing. Their styles matched perfectly and it is obvious (as Loy has confirmed) that they loved acting together. The team became one of the keystones of MGM in the '30's.[7]

It should not be forgotten that, even aside from its bubbling wit, *The Thin Man* has a strong, unhackneyed plot, well acted by a first-rate cast that included Maureen O'Sullivan, Nat Pendleton, Minna Gombell and Cesar Romero (not to mention Asta, the wise wire-haired terrier).

While such a success clearly called for a series, this, unlike too many others, was not to be a three-or-four-a-year series doomed to early death from overexposure, but one that kept the fans waiting from two to three years, until they were clamoring for the next—and always, to the very end, with the two original stars. The studio must have been hard pressed to come up with variations on the title, since, of course, "the thin man" was not Nick (William Powell) but Clyde Wynant (Edward Ellis), the first murder victim.

But *After the Thin Man* (late 1936, more than two and a half years after the first) fitted well enough, since one of the key characters was also a thin man. Again directed by W. S. Van Dyke, and scripted by Frances Goodrich and Albert Hackett, it proved that extreme rarity, a sequel almost worthy of the original.

The plot involved Nora's stuffy Nob Hill

---

[5] A better-known version of *The Glass Key* was made in 1942 with Alan Ladd and Brian Donlevy.

[6] The hero whose nickname anticipated that of the future Speaker of the House was played by Preston Foster.

[7] *The Great Movie Stars* (Bonanza Books, 1970), p. 350.

William Powell, Myrna Loy, Henry Wadsworth in **The Thin Man**

relatives, ruled by a matriarch (Jessie Ralph), who insists on calling Nick "Nickel-ahss." Loy's cousin Elissa Landi, ardently loved by young James Stewart, is unhappily married to caddish Alan Marshal, the first victim, who was carrying on with night club entertainer Dorothy McNulty (later to be known as Penny Singleton). Considering the type-casting then prevalent, the identity of the killer must indeed have surprised 1936 audiences, but what mattered most was that Nick, Nora and Asta were back in fine form.

Nearly three years later came *Another Thin Man* (1939), again with the same director and writers. "The third of the trade-marked *Thin*

Man takes its murders as jauntily as ever," wrote Crisler. However, he felt that the law of diminishing returns was about to set in.

But in the end even MGM pressed its luck too far. *The Shadow of the Thin Man* (1941), *The Thin Man Goes Home* (1945) and *Song of the Thin Man* (1947), none with the original director or writers, gradually ran downhill. Still, for sheer longevity the Thin Man series was in its own time outrun only by Charlie Chan. Ten years after the last film, Nick and Nora turned up on TV as Peter Lawford and Phyllis Kirk in a series that lasted seventy-two episodes. And in *Murder by Death* (1976) among the five famous fictional sleuths and their sidekicks affectionately parodied, no pair was more instantly recognizable, and certainly none more debonair, than Dick and Dora Charleston, gracefully played by David Niven and Maggie Smith.

Meanwhile, back in the 1930s, *The Thin Man* had spawned a whole new cycle of tongue-in-cheek mysteries from almost every major studio, two with Powell himself, several with other bright young couples. Earliest was RKO's *Star of Midnight* (1935), with Powell opposite Ginger Rogers in "a sleek, witty and engaging entertainment" about the murder of a gossip columnist. *The Ex-Mrs. Bradford* (1936) starred Powell and Jean Arthur. "Of all the attempted copies of the justly celebrated William Powell-Myrna Loy comedy, *The Ex-Mrs. Bradford* comes closest to approximating the gaiety, impudence and ability to entertain," said McManus in the *Times.* Arthur played the title role, an apparently bird-brained mystery writer who in solving murders at a race track recaptures her ex-husband.

Between these two came Universal's *Remember Last Night?* (1935). "Betraying the influence of *The Thin Man* in its merry attitude toward homicide, the film . . . is an active bit of slaughter and can be enjoyed in moderation." But Nugent on the whole was not much amused by the alcoholic antics of the Long Island smart set. (It was based on a novel called *The Hangover Murders.*) The main difficulty for the police is that everyone was so drunk no one can remember just *what* happened last night. Edward Arnold and Edward Brophy were the cops, Constance Cummings and Robert Young the standard bright young couple.

Perhaps unwilling to risk direct competition with *After the Thin Man,* in 1937 no studio produced any such mystery-comedies at all. The next one came from Columbia, *There's Always a Woman* (1938), with Joan Blondell and Melvyn Douglas as Sally and Bill Reardon, another amiably sparring couple. He was an unsuccessful private eye, about to give up when offered a $300 fee by Mary

Astor. "An excellent job of all-around spoofing—a *Thin Man* of the lower income brackets," said Crisler.

But when the Reardons returned in *There's That Woman Again* (1939), with Virginia Bruce replacing Blondell, Nugent complained:

> This sequel business is driving us crazy. *Topper* was succeeded by *Topper Takes a Trip. Four Daughters* was to be followed by *Four Daughters Meet Four Sons,* but its producers decided to take a short-cut and call it *Four Wives* . . . Any pessimist can forecast the next in the series: *There's Always a Woman Again, That Woman Takes a Trip* and *That Woman Is Here Again.*

Concurrently, MGM had begun in effect competing with itself, by starting still another bright-young-couple mystery series, with *Fast Company* (1938), "made," according to John Douglas Eames in *The MGM Story,* "to mollify exhibitors who complained of the long wait between *Thin Man* movies." Melvyn Douglas, likewise competing with himself, starred with Florence Rice, as Joel and Garda Sloan, owners of a rare-book shop. "A brash and amusing story, of the light weight or *Thin Man* school," said Crisler.

But when Joel and Garda reappeared in *Fast and Loose* (1939), they had been upgraded to Robert Montgomery and Rosalind Russell. In this one the theft of a priceless Shakespearean manuscript causes two murders, with the usual range of suspects including Reginald Owen and Ralph Morgan. Reviews were still favorable. Yet in the third film of the series, *Fast and Furious* (1939), Joel and Garda had unaccountably turned into Franchot Tone and Ann Sothern, as Crisler noted with annoyance, adding, "Metro seems to be stretching an original idea to infinity . . . Mr. Tone and Miss Sothern banter through it in the manner of third-string substitutes who know that the game is hopelessly lost." After that, there was nowhere for the fast-moving Sloans to go except off the screen for good.

Like every other formula, this one soon

wore thin. Yet between the last two *Fast* films MGM gave it still another try, with what sounded like a sure-fire combination of talent: a script by Ben Hecht from a story by him and Herman Mankiewicz, directed by W. S. Van Dyke and co-starring (for the only time) Claudette Colbert and James Stewart, supported by several veterans from the MGM roster—but Nugent in the *Times* found *It's a Wonderful World* (1939) "almost too strenuous for relaxation . . . a killing farce about a private detective, an unwanted feminine assistant (who finally, of course, effects the murderer's capture) and a couple of comedians from the Homicide Bureau."

Clearly even the best series and the most popular genres sooner or later ran into difficulties in devising suitable material without recycling. Some praise, then, must be reserved for the very small number of '30s mystery films which avoided both the banalities of the old-dark-house school and the built-in pitfalls of the series—those few which by novelty of plot, setting, motivation or means of murder stood out as relatively original in a field where true originality was virtually impossible.

Truly unique in setting was *Subway Express* (1931), based on a 1930 play. Aboard a Seventh Avenue train, bound north from Fourteenth to Seventy-second Street, after a brawl in which a shot is fired, a stockbroker is discovered dead in his seat. Instead of the usual amateur sleuth, a police inspector (Jack Holt) sifts the suspects, several of whom had peculiar reasons for riding in that particular car.

70,000 Witnesses (1932), by sports writer Cortland Fitzsimmons, was indeed as novel as its title. A college football star is killed on the gridiron just as he is about to make the crucial touchdown. A gangster (Lew Cody) had tried to get his varsity team kid brother (Phillips Holmes) to drug a team-mate (Johnny Mack Brown), and though the boy refuses, the halfback still collapses at the right moment.

Somewhat similarly, in *Death on the Diamond* (1934), a killer stalks the St. Louis Cardinals, shooting one from the stands, strangling another in the locker room and so on, with suspicion well distributed among several people who want the Cardinals to lose the pennant.[8]

The Crime of the Century (1933), from a play by Walter Espe, was despite its hyperbolic title rated unusual not only in its plot but in pausing after an hour for one minute to give the audience a chance to decide who was the killer. A scientist (Jean Hersholt) asks the police to lock him up, as he feels an irresistible urge to kill a banker—who is then killed, anyway. A reporter (Stuart Erwin) solves the case.

Menace (1934), based on a story by Philip MacDonald and ranked by Nugent "several notches higher than the average murder film," used a pattern seldom seen again until *The List of Adrian Messenger* (1963). In British East Africa three people (Gertrude Michael, Paul Cavanagh, Berton Churchill) persuade a young engineer (Ray Milland) to leave the dam on which he is working, to make a fourth at bridge. In his absence a violent storm destroys the dam and also his sister's house; he kills himself. An insane brother, unknown to the three, threatens them, but is confined to an asylum. Two years later, when all three are living in California, the threats are renewed, but which of several new acquaintances is the mad brother?

Shadow of Doubt (1935, not to be confused with Hitchcock's *Shadow of a Doubt,* 1943), released the same week as *Murder on a Honeymoon* and *While the Patient Slept,* caused Nugent to anticipate a new cycle of "female crime detectors." In *Shadow of Doubt,* not intended as one of a series, Constance Collier, in her talkie debut, played a formidable dowager who emerges from twenty years of seclusion to solve the murder of a playboy and his butler.

In 1939, with the various series virtually monopolizing the mystery scene, two other

---

[8] A minor variation, *Girls Can Play* (1937), dealt with a girls' softball team, with Rita Hayworth, the catcher, among the murder victims.

suspense films made more of an impression. Using colorful background footage he had filmed on a tour of the Orient, Tay Garnett directed *Trade Winds,* from a story by himself, written for the screen by Dorothy Parker and Alan Campbell, with Fredric March, Joan Bennett, Ralph Bellamy and Ann Sothern in the leads.

"It is light, agreeable and extremely interesting technically," said Crisler, "including the technical switch from blond to brunette of Miss Bennett." Beginning her Hedy Lamarr lookalike phase, she was fleeing halfway around the world to beat a Frisco murder rap, pursued by March and Bellamy as detectives. Sothern was "surprisingly successful as the leech on the bloodhound." At the very opposite extreme from the stagebound old-dark-house melodramas, *Trade Winds* is as much travelogue and romantic comedy as mystery (though it does have a surprise ending).

Finally, *Tell No Tales* almost foreshadowed the complexities of Ross Macdonald and later suspense novelists in exploring a startling variety of vividly realized milieux within a single city, connected only by the guilty secrets at the heart of the plot. Melvyn Douglas was an editor tracing a ransom bill from a kidnapping, a trail that leads him to a wedding, a night club, backstage at a police benefit, the home of a fashionable, elderly doctor with a young wife and a Negro death wake "almost alarming in its unexpected authenticity."

By the 1970s, though mystery novels continued to be published by the hundreds each year and routine whodunits abounded on TV, very few were ever seen on stage or on theater screens. Except for an occasional oddity like *Klute* (1971) or an adaptation of a rare Broadway thriller like *Night Watch* (1974), the only film mysteries of the '70s (as distinguished from suspense or horror dramas) were those that deliberately recalled the '30s (*Chinatown* and *Murder on the Orient Express,* both 1974) or the '40s (*The Long Goodbye,* 1973, *The Late Show,* 1976) or spoofed the whole genre (*Sleuth,* 1974, *Murder by Death,* 1976)—still another echo of Hollywood's golden age.

33

"IT'S ALIVE!" (AND WELL AND LIVING IN TRANSYLVANIA)
Sheer Horror

A third descendant of the Gothic school is the tale of pure horror that, like Dickens' Fat Boy, "aims to make your flesh creep." This may be further subdivided into at least two categories, one as old as superstition and folklore, the other strictly a nineteenth-century development. The first, of which *Dracula* is the prime example, ultimately traces to Old World folk tales involving supernatural beings, always malevolent: ghosts, vampires, werewolves, witches, zombies, demons, perhaps the devil himself, whose powers admit of no rational explanation. The other is a precursor of science fiction, in which a fanatically determined doctor or scientist (usually called "mad") in tampering with the laws of nature unleashes forces beyond human control, with monstrous results. The ancestor of these is, of course, *Frankenstein*.

One of the several unique facts about the unsurpassed cycle of horror films of 1931–35 is that, though certainly not all were of equal merit, "B's" among them were almost as rare as "B" costume films, perhaps for the same reason: they could not be mass-produced. Whereas romantic comedies, conventional mysteries or almost any other contemporary genre could be turned out by the score in standing modern sets with any reasonably competent cast, a horror film, to come off at all, had to have convincingly sinister settings (castles, cemeteries, laboratories), careful, mood-setting photography, evocative music and sound effects, elaborate, specialized make-up and, above all, first-rate character actors who could make the impossible seem at least momentarily real—not only such horror specialists as Boris Karloff, Bela Lugosi and Lionel Atwill but such versatile veterans as Lionel Barrymore, Ralph Morgan and Otto Kruger.

Thus while the *Times* ignored some 1,500 films of other genres, it took horror seriously enough to review all but two of the entire output (thirty-four). Likewise, of those American examples made in the '30s, William K. Everson includes twenty-two in his *Classics of the Horror Film* (1974), with favorable mention of several more—well over half his entire collection. For that matter, what other genre has had at least three serious books devoted to it? Everson's and Alan G. Frank's *Horror Movies* (1974) are both excellent, but surely Carlos Clarens' *An Illustrated History of the Horror Film* (1967), though now a bit dated, is the definitive work.

Horror, to be sure, has always been an element in literature and art, as witness the frightful punishments meted out in Greek myths for equally frightful crimes—but it must be kept in mind that such myths were only written and read or recited aloud, not dramatized. When Athenian playwrights used violent legends like those of the royal houses of Thebes and Mycenae, not even synthetic blood was shed on stage.

It was the Romans who, sated with their orgies of mass sadism in the arena, found mere reported violence too tame and demanded that the carnage be shown, as in the tragedies of Seneca. And it was Seneca who was the strongest classical influence on Elizabethan playwrights of the late sixteenth century, and an even stronger influence on the Jacobeans of the early seventeenth.

While deploring ancient pagan excesses, one must not overlook the nauseating horrors taken casually for granted during the nominally Christian centuries. Beggars, hideously pock-marked, diseased, deformed or mutilated, monstrosities such as would later be exhibited in freak shows, swarmed the streets, especially around churches, flaunting their stumps and sores. As if that were not enough, the same public as late as the seventeenth century delighted in going over to Bedlam for a good laugh at the lunatics, and watching bears and bulls torn to pieces by dogs. Chopping off the right hand, cropping the ears and/or nose, branding on the forehead or cheek were considered mild deterrents. The favorite spectator sport was public executions. Burning at the stake, the punishment for heresy and witchcraft, was regarded as relatively humane, since it seldom lasted longer than ten or fifteen minutes. True execution buffs preferred to watch criminals at Tyburn not merely hanged but taken down alive and conscious to be "drawn and quartered"—first castrated, then slowly disemboweled, organ by organ. On the Continent, impalement, as practiced by Vlad the Impaler, the supposed inspiration for Dracula, could last for days as the stake slowly worked its way up through the body.

Thus the excessive violence so constantly deplored in films and TV programs of the 1970s had a long, if not honorable, tradition behind it. The eighteenth century, after all, gave the world the Marquis de Sade and the Reign of

Terror. Then in the Romantic era the morbid vein of love identified with death, of suicidal mania, rape, incest, castration, necrophilia, demon lovers, implied homosexuality, curses potent from beyond the grave and other Gothic paraphernalia turn up in some of the greatest writers—e.g., Coleridge's *Geraldine*, Shelley's *The Cenci*, Keats' *Isabella* and several of Byron's long narrative poems.

The results of Gothic childhood influences on the Victorians are evident in such characters as Heathcliff, Mr. Rochester and many of Dickens' sinister grotesques like Fagin and Quilp. In fiction, the purely Gothic vein, totally detached from the realities of everyday life, reached its culmination in the macabre tales of Poe, with their obsessively recurrent themes of madness, premature burial, returns from the dead, diabolic revenge, physical and emotional torture.

Even as the façade of Victorian gentility screened the eyes of the respectable ever more discreetly from what they did not wish to see, this very repression exacted its own dark price, as we now know from such belated revelations as *My Secret Life* and the dichotomy of superego and id most strikingly symbolized in *Dr. Jekyll and Mr. Hyde*.

It was only a year after Queen Victoria's Golden Jubilee in 1887 that Jack the Ripper, never caught, stalked Whitechapel and terrorized London with his gruesomely sadistic murders of prostitutes. And if Paris had its Grand Guignol Theater (now closed), whose repertoire consisted exclusively of plays of inhuman tortures, one of London's prime tourist attractions was the Chamber of Horrors in Mme. Tussaud's Wax Museum.

Thus it seems no coincidence that the '30s' first four horror talkies (all 1931) were all based on nineteenth-century British novels: *Dracula* (1897) by Bram Stoker, who had been Sir Henry Irving's business manager; *Svengali* (from *Trilby*, 1894, by George du Maurier); *Frankenstein*, written in 1818 by Mary Godwin Shelley; and *Dr. Jekyll and Mr. Hyde*, written by Robert Louis Stevenson in 1886. (The fifth in the cycle, *Murders*

in the Rue Morgue, 1932, was at least inspired by Poe's 1840s story.)

Horror, then, had proved to be a most profitable business long before films undertook their first ventures into it. Obviously the silents' unique power to evoke dreamlike fantasies, as in costume romances, could be turned inside out to produce nightmares to haunt the imagination forever.

No viewer of *The Phantom of the Opera* (1925) will ever forget Lon Chaney as the mad Eric with his skeleton's face, plumed hat and operatic cape poling his boat through the subterranean canals under the Paris Opéra. Though some of Chaney's monsters, like Quasimodo in *The Hunchback of Notre Dame*, were touched with pathos, all were physically horrible to an unparalleled degree.

As to why the marked Gothic revival in early talkies should coincide with the worst years of the Depression, no one has yet offered a convincing explanation. Perhaps, considering the overwhelmingly drab, nitty-gritty atmosphere of most serious films during those years when almost no musicals or costume films were made and even mysteries were prosaically housebound, the great horror films, set in nineteenth-century Paris or London or Transylvania, provided a kind of escape into exotic, if sinister, worlds, not otherwise available on screen. Or perhaps their ghoulish thrills made the worries outside—breadlines, bank failures, unemployment, mortgage foreclosures—seem relatively manageable, man-made evils that could and would be overcome.

Of all horror figures, those hardy perennials, Dracula and Frankenstein's monster, have had the longest careers (still going strong in the 1980s), in many ways remarkably parallel. Each typed the star in his role forever, in Bela Lugosi's case perhaps no great loss, but Boris Karloff had a far greater range than horror parts. The 1931 *Dracula* and *Frankenstein* films were each followed after several years by one good sequel (considered by many superior to the original), then later degraded into ludicrous travesty as the title characters spawned more descendants, met each other, the Wolf Man and even Abbott and Costello. Yet, as if their creators had endowed them with true immortality, both survived these indignities, to be resurrected in the late '50s in gory color by Britain's Hammer Studios, thereby launching the careers of Peter Cushing and Christopher Lee, only to be done in again in the 1970s by Andy Warhol (and in Frankenstein's case by Mel Brooks).[1]

Dracula (early 1931), the first of the horror cycle, directed by Tod Browning, had originally been scheduled for Chaney, but after his death in 1930 was taken over for practically all time by Bela Lugosi, the Hungarian actor who had played it on Broadway in 1927. The *Times* greeted it rather casually, concluding, ". . . the best of the many mystery films"—an extremely mysterious comment, since, of course, from the moment Dracula is first seen as a muffled coachman driving the dapper young lawyer Renfield (Dwight Frye) over fog-shrouded mountain roads at midnight, it is perfectly clear who he is, especially when he turns into a bat as they near his castle.

When he next appears as the suave Count in evening clothes, dispensing hospitality Transylvanian style, then leading the way up a spiral stone staircase, passing through thick spiderwebs without breaking them, while Renfield must entangle himself in them to follow, the spider-fly analogy is obvious—an image later recalled by Renfield's mad craving for "nice, juicy" flies and spiders.

The sight of Dracula's three silent brides in their gauzy draperies rising at sunset from their coffins is surely weird enough, as is the set of the moldering castle, but once the scene has shifted to England, where the action is largely confined to Dr. Seward's house and sanatorium, the stage origins become all too apparent. This, of course, is where the play

[1] The most original spin-off was the film *Love at First Bite* (1979), in which Dracula, evicted from Transylvania, turns up in present-day New York, with hilarious results.

Bela Lugosi, Helen Chandler in Dracula

begins; all that went before was an effective picturization of Dracula's background, inspired, it would seem, by *Nosferatu* (1929).

Even Dracula's ability to turn himself at will into a bat or a wolf, the mirror in which he is not reflected and other vampire trademarks, easily managed on screen, can hardly seem as startling now as in 1931. Certainly sensationalism was kept at a minimum. The music over the credits is *Swan Lake,* no blood is shown, not even teeth marks, nor the final driving of the stake through Dracula's heart. What horror is generated is more psychological than physical: the apparent eagerness of Mina Seward (Helen Chandler) to reject and even prey upon her mortal suitor, John Harker (David Manners), to follow Dracula. The lingering mood is quietly eerie rather than terrifying.

Dracula's Daughter (1936), though made five years later by another director, Lambert Hillyer, takes up the story as the previous film ends. Renfield is dead, thrown downstairs by Dracula, Mina and Harker have left, not to be heard from again, but Professor Van Helsing (Edward Van Sloan), the vampire expert who drove the stake, is arrested for the apparent murder of Dracula, whose body is temporarily stored at a police station. When a mysterious black-caped woman (Gloria Holden), aided by her hunchbacked assistant (Irving Pichel), hypnotizes and kills the policeman in charge, steals the vampire's body and burns it in a remote graveyard, the meaning of the title is clear enough, but we next meet her as a Hungarian countess, a portrait painter, at a fashionable London party. ("My guests are just *dying* to meet you," twitters the hostess, Hedda Hopper.)

Holden's beauty, dignity and intelligently restrained performance add immeasurably to the effect, for it is plain that the Countess would go to any length to escape her vampire nature. Desperately she appeals to a psychoanalyst (Otto Kruger) for help, then falls in love with him, and when he realizes that she is murdering innocent people for their blood, especially a pathetic street waif (Nan Grey), he calls in the police. Dracula's daughter in turn kidnaps the doctor's assistant and would-be fiancée (Marguerite Churchill) and flees back to Transylvania, thus reversing the geographic movement of the earlier film.

The last scenes of the Dracula saga are played out in the same half-ruined castle. The Countess will spare the English girl's life only if the doctor agrees to stay with her as one of the undead—but before this can happen her jealous henchman shoots her through the heart with a wooden arrow. He is about to do the same for the doctor when Scotland Yard men, alerted by Van Helsing, arrive. Seen now, *Dracula's Daughter* is distinctly superior to *Dracula*. Unlike Lugosi, Holden provokes *no* unintended laughs, and the sense of a surrounding normal world she longs in vain to share intensifies the somber mood.

The only other '30s film involving a true vampire was *Condemned to Live* (1935), one of the few "B" horror films, in which Ralph Morgan played a gentle professor by day who at night turns into a batlike monster terrorizing an English village. The natives seeking his help are inclined to blame his hunchbacked servant (Pedro De Cordoba) until another doctor (Russell Gleason) finally routs the vampire.

The only two other American vampire films of the '30s (both between the Dracula pictures) ended by explaining away the apparently supernatural. In *The Vampire Bat* (1933) Lionel Atwill, who soon ran a close third to Lugosi and Karloff in playing villains in horror films, took up where he had left off in *Dr. X*. Set, typically, in "Kleinschloss, somewhere in Central Europe," it pitted Melvyn Douglas as Karl Breetschneider against some mysterious "thing" preying on the population. Naturally, the peasants blame werewolves or vampires. Dwight Frye, who met horrendous fates not only in *Dracula* but in the first two Frankenstein films, was a peasant who domesticates bats for his amusement and is ultimately chased with torches through the night. But, as the *Times* said, "It seemed rather a comedown, after the terror of the good folks of Kleinschloss had been described in such eerie detail, to discover that all the pother in *The Vampire Bat* was the work of just one more mad scientist."

Mark of the Vampire (1935), which Browning made for MGM, was partly a remake of a Chaney silent, *London After Midnight* (1927), but it also showed the influence of *Dracula*. Lugosi was the same kind of sinister count, this time the terror of the Czech peasantry. This film may even have inspired *Dracula's Daughter*, since "Count Mora" has just such a daughter (Carol Borland). Lionels Atwill and Barrymore were both on hand, A. as a police inspector, B. as a delver into the occult. In a decidedly anti-climactic ending the supposed vampires turn out to be vaudeville performers hired to terrify the real murderer into showing his hand.

Though akin as fellow creatures of the undead, zombies, as indigenous to the West Indies, especially Haiti, as vampires are to Transylvania, are much less autonomous, usually animated only to perform menial labor at someone else's bidding. The *Times* greeted *White Zombie* (1932) with open derision, merely noting that Lugosi played a "necromancer" with the power "to turn corpses into automatons" and quoting some of the worst lines of dialogue. Another reviewer suggested that the sequel would probably be called *Zombie and Son*.

The title character, an American girl (Madge Bellamy), arriving in Haiti to join her fiancé (John Harron), attracts the attention of a wealthy planter (Robert Frazer), who conspires with "Murder" Legendre (Lugosi), the island's notorious zombie master, to gain control over the girl. During the wedding banquet she collapses, apparently dead, and is placed in a mausoleum, but she has actually become the "white zombie." When the groom discovers her body missing, with the aid of a missionary and a native witch doctor he locates Legendre's mysterious castle. The planter, belatedly repentant, summons up enough will power to drag the sorcerer, along with himself, over the castle ramparts to death on the rocks below, thus releasing the heroine from the evil power.

Historians of horror rank the film very high indeed, mainly echoing Carlos Clarens' three pages of unreserved praise. "Whatever period feeling *White Zombie* possessed at the time of its release has been erased by the intervening third of a century, making the images more faded, the period more remote and the picture itself more completely mysterious."

Not even a zombie could put up forever with such "inhuman" working conditions,

and 1936 brought *Revolt of the Zombies,* with Dorothy Stone, Dean Jagger and an otherwise obscure cast. "Even a zombie has his rights, and we loyal necrophiles will fight to the last mandrake root to protect them," wrote Thomas M. Pryor in the *Times.* The most unusual sequence was a war scene in which a high priest of Angkor brings to the Franco-Austrian front a company of Indonesian zombie soldiers who walk serenely through enemy bullets—but even this proves to be a trick of hypnosis.

Not directly concerned with zombies, *Black Moon* (1934) dealt with another aspect of West Indian folklore: voodoo. Little does Jack Holt realize when he marries West Indian Dorothy Burgess that as a child she had been inducted by her Negro nurse into the rites of blood sacrifice. After several apparently normal years as wife and mother in New York, she finds herself drawn back to her native island, where she is installed as high priestess of a voodoo cult. While noting the resemblance of a native ritual dance to a Busby Berkeley routine, the *Times* concluded, "But it is difficult to think of details like that when Mrs. Lane picks up the knife to slaughter her own child."

Still another case of the not quite dead was *The Mummy* (1933), directed by the celebrated cameraman Karl Freund, in which Karloff returns to life after some 3,700 years to terrorize a field expedition of the British Museum. He also falls in love with a modern girl (Zita Johann), whom he identifies with a priestess from his own time—but he had been embalmed alive for having even then tried to restore her to life—strictly taboo. The most striking feature was Karloff's all too convincing make-up, created, like that of Frankenstein's monster, by an artist in that field, Jack Pierce. Says Alan G. Frank in *Horror Movies:*

The full-length mummy is seldom seen, horror being conveyed with close-up shots of head, shoulders and hands, covered with rotting bandages and ancient, flaking clay. The combination of Karloff—billed by surname only as

"Karloff the Uncanny" (an honor previously accorded only to Garbo!) —Freund, Pierce and magnificent photography credited to Charles Stumar, *The Mummy* was to remain the key film of its genre.[2]

Supernatural (1933) played still another variation on the theme of the restless dead. Alan Dinehart was a fake spiritualist attempting to extort money from a rich girl (Carole Lombard) by pretending to be in touch with her dead brother. But, unknown to him, the spirit of his former mistress (Vivienne Osborne), who had been executed for strangling three of her lovers, invades the girl's body, turning her into a murderess who gives the charlatan his comeuppance.

Among supernatural creatures, second only to the vampire in terrorizing the peasantry was the werewolf, usually associated with Central European or Balkan superstition but found in the mythology of many countries.

The apparently harmless citizen who turns into a bloodthirsty beast when the moon is full made his talkie debut in *The Werewolf of London* (1935). Opening the same week as *Mark of the Vampire* and *The Bride of Frankenstein,* it was considered by Nugent in the *Times* another variation on *Dr. Jekyll and Mr. Hyde,* but the werewolf, often an involuntary victim, infected by another of its kind, seems more like a vampire. "Designed solely to amaze and horrify, the film goes about its task with commendable thoroughness, sparing no grisly detail," Nugent noted.

Henry Hull played an English botanist bitten by a werewolf (Warner Oland) in Tibet while searching for a rare flower that blooms only in the moonlight. Of course he himself becomes a werewolf at the next full moon, bites someone and soon there are two of them ravaging London. Because such a creature instinctively seeks to kill the thing it loves best, Hull eventually attacks his wife (Valerie Hobson), but is shot by the police, at death (like Jekyll) turning back into his human self.

Films requiring the audience to suspend

disbelief and accept supernatural creatures and events as real were far rarer in the '30s than in later decades. In fact, they number only seven: *Dracula, White Zombie, The Mummy, Supernatural, Condemned to Live, The Werewolf of London* and *Dracula's Daughter.*

All other '30s horror films, however visually or emotionally shocking, were variations on the theme of the mad scientist (or surgeon or hypnotist or artist), who might indeed "tamper with" or violate the laws of nature, but without resorting to demonic powers (though he was often suspected of doing just that). By the 1970s this pattern was completely reversed.

Certain memorable horror films, especially 1931–33, do not fit into any category. Very early—between *Dracula* and *Frankenstein*—came Warners' first entry in the cycle, based on another bizarre British classic, George du Maurier's novel *Trilby* (1894), turned into *Svengali* (1931)—perhaps not a true horror film in the strictest sense, but considered such by Clarens, who notes that "the Victorian flavor of the original was spiced with a good dose of the macabre."

Next to pictures of John Barrymore, with long, matted black hair and beard, glaring malevolently from beneath craggy eyebrows, ran the text:

HE is genius—madman—lover! His hypnotic spell reaches out of darkness controlling love—hate—life itself. SHE is the beauty who has all Paris at her famous feet—who wins men with a smile—who hates Svengali, the sinister love maker—until his magic spell forces even *her* heart to his *manufactured love.*

As indicated by the title (also by the billing in the ads, with Marian Marsh's name and photo running a poor second to Barrymore's), the emphasis had shifted from the beautiful model to the sly, sinister hypnotist whose powers make her a great singer. (Yet Marsh is very good; her faltering rendition of "Don't You Remember Sweet Alice, Ben Bolt?" is almost as haunting as Angela Lansbury's "Goodbye, Little Yellow Bird" in *The*

---

[2] *Horror Movies* (Derbibooks, 1974), p. 77.

Picture of Dorian Gray.) Except for the scenes of hypnosis, Barrymore, using what sounds like a Jewish accent, plays Svengali less frightening than oily and pseudohumble, fawning like a combination of Fagin and Uriah Heep.

Whenever the film is revived, *The New Yorker* states:

In one startling sequence, Svengali, his eyes a blank white, stands at a window and casts his spell over the rooftops to the room where Trilby lives, and there are affecting moments, too, like the failure of Trilby's voice when Svengali's influence wanes . . . The scene designs and Archie Mayo's direction occasionally suggest the German Expressionist films of the preceding decade.

A few months later, still before *Frankenstein,* came Paramount's first entry, *Murder by the Clock* (1931). Though technically a macabre mystery, it is not really much of one, since it is fairly obvious from the start that designing Lilyan Tashman, slinking about in clinging satin gowns, is up to no good. Seen now, the film seems slow-paced, but it does have its chilling moments, especially those involving a mausoleum that can be opened from the inside, with "an eerie horn that can be turned on to proclaim that the occupant is not dead" (Everson).

Blanche Frederici was the eccentric matriarch of a wealthy clan of neurotics, including lecherous psychopath Irving Pichel. The old lady's apparent return from the dead to confront her murderer is a high point. Actually, of course, it's the disguised Tashman, who at various times turns her synthetic charm on fellow villain Lester Vail, the psychopath and even the detective (William "Stage" Boyd) —but, as in *The Maltese Falcon* a few months earlier, he turns her in, anyway.

One other '30s horror film defies classification. It had no antecedents and fortunately no sequels or follow-ups, yet it remains one of the most unforgettably horrifying pictures ever made. This was *Freaks* (1932), directed by Tod Browning (between *Dracula* and *Mark of the Vampire*), which the *Times*

thought should have opened at the Medical Center rather than at a theater.

A heartless trapeze performer (Olga Baclanova) marries a midget (Harry Earles), intending to poison him and take his money for herself and her real love, a professional "strong man" (Henry Victor). At the wedding feast she cannot conceal her revulsion from her misshapen guests and even humiliates her little husband by prancing around the room carrying him like a baby. When the freaks realize her murderous plans, in the horrendous climax, one rainy night they trap the guilty pair, kill the man (the original intent was to emasculate him) and mutilate the woman into "one of us," a hideous, legless "hen-woman," last seen squatting, cackling in a bran pit.

Alan G. Frank calls it "perhaps the most disturbing and terrifying" film ever made. It was at least disturbing enough to be banned for thirty years by the British censor. Says *The New Yorker:*

It uses images of physical deformity for their enormous potential of horror, and at the end, when the pinheads and the armless and legless creatures scurry about to revenge themselves on a normal woman . . . the film becomes a true nightmare.

Yet Clarens finds them to be "sensitive, vulnerable and intensely human characters. Freaks among themselves cease to be freaks."

A few months later came a more genial horror classic, James Whale's *The Old Dark House* (1932), adapted by Benn Levy and R. C. Sherriff from *Benighted,* a novel by J. B. Priestley. This time an ill-assorted group is thrown together by a violent storm which forces some of them to seek refuge in a weird mansion in the wilds of the Welsh mountains. The relatively normal travelers are Raymond Massey and Gloria Stuart as a married couple, Melvyn Douglas as their friend, Charles Laughton as a rough-diamond Yorkshire tycoon and Lillian Bond as his heart-of-gold show-girl mistress.

As *The New Yorker,* which regards the picture as "tremendous fun" thanks to Whale's "witty, perverse and creepy" direction, puts it:

They seek shelter in a gloomy mansion, which is inhabited by a prize collection of monsters and decadent aristocrats: a mute, scarred brute of a butler (Boris Karloff) attends a prissy madman (Ernest Thesiger), his religious-fanatic hag of a sister (Eva Moore), his pyromaniac-dwarf brother (Brember Wells), and their father—a hundred-and-two-year-old baronet.

Released by the drunken butler (who's right out of Charles Addams), the mad dwarf soon gets hold of a carving knife, and the ensuing action is nothing if not fast and furious.

1932 ended with another unique horror film, which despite two later remakes remains a favorite in its own right: *The Most Dangerous Game.* For those not familiar with Richard Connell's short story, "game" here means the kind to be hunted for sport—in this case two-legged game.

The concept is simple but bold: a mad Russian count (brilliantly played by Leslie Banks in his film debut), bored with hunting animals, takes to hunting down any men unfortunate enough to be shipwrecked (with his help) on the reefs near his Malayan island. Using either a bow and arrow or a rifle, he allows them only a knife and time enough to hide. If the quarry manages to elude him and his bloodhounds till morning, he (never she) is set free; if not, his head may well join the other trophies mounted on the walls of the madman's game room.

Despite a rather bland performance by Joel McCrea as the one who finally gets the best of him and the presence of a girl (Fay Wray) not found in the story, it is a taut thriller. Produced by Ernest Schoedsack and Merian C. Cooper at the same time they were making *King Kong,* it benefited from the use of the same jungle sets and also a Max Steiner score—"quite probably the best score written for any movie to that date."[3]

[3] The 1946 remake, *A Game of Death,* was reasonably faithful to the original, but *Run for the Sun* (1956) was twice as long without being half as effective.

Two other unforgettable horror films seem to straddle the line between the unique ones and the more familiar "mad doctor/scientist" genre: *The Mystery of the Wax Museum* (1933) and *The Devil Doll* (1936). Both involve extraordinary experiments in "tampering with nature," but neither protagonist is a scientist; one is a sculptor of wax figures, the other an escapee from Devil's Island who accidentally acquires the secret of reducing humans to doll size.

The Mystery of the Wax Museum was not the first horror film in Technicolor (still two-toned); *Dr. X.* had that distinction, but the color prints (according to Everson) were used only for key opening dates in major cities, so that most of the public saw *Dr. X.* only in black and white. *Wax Museum,* however, was the first in which the color design was so essential to the horror effects that it could not have been released any other way.

The horror was all the more intensified by the film's setting, not in Transylvania or in some remote tropical jungle but in contemporary New York—the first time (unless one counts *King Kong* as a horror film) it had ever been used for such a tale of terror.

Aside from the grisliness of the plot—a mad genius, apparently a benevolent museum owner confined to a wheelchair, kidnaps people who happen to resemble historical characters, dips them in boiling wax, then displays them like the figures in Mme. Tussaud's—the film abounds in incidental macabre touches. When a girl reporter notes the resemblance of "Voltaire" to the missing Judge Ramsay (which in 1933 suggested the vanished Judge Crater), scratches the waxen hand and feels the dead flesh beneath, the whole audience shared her shudder.

Glenda Farrell in the first of many breezy reporter roles and Frank McHugh as her editor provided a welcome note of sanity in a picture the *Times* called "too ghastly for comfort . . . too intent on its extravagantly blood-curdling ideas . . . as much horror as is well-nigh possible." The scene in which Fay Wray, scheduled to become the waxen

Marie Antoinette, slaps the smooth face of Ivan Igor (Lionel Atwill) only to have it crack to pieces and reveal the hideously gnarled, burned flesh inside, is still justly regarded as the second greatest unmasking in horror film history, topped only by the parallel confrontation between Mary Philbin and Lon Chaney in the silent *Phantom of the Opera* (1925).

The Devil Doll (1936), Tod Browning's second-last film, is far less physically horrifying. Trick photography that could make people look like giants or reduce them to miniature had been toyed with ever since the earliest experiments of Méliès, but most often for whimsical effect (*Peter Pan* and *Alice in Wonderland*).

Both *The Lost World* and *King Kong,* to be sure, had done the opposite—i.e., made small models look like prehistoric monsters—but *The Devil Doll* was the first to exploit the macabre possibilities of tiny people, in this case hypnotically compelled by their master to commit crimes that are literally undetectable, since the rest of the time they are immobilized, passing as cleverly detailed dolls. Like Chaney in *The Unholy Three,* Lionel Barrymore spends most of the film disguised as a kindly old lady shopkeeper, using instead of a midget his remarkably lifelike "dolls," selling them to his enemies as Christmas gifts for their children.

An innocent man wrongly imprisoned for twenty years, he has escaped and returned to Paris to avenge himself on the three men who framed him. Escaping with him is a scientist (Henry B. Walthall), who for the usual high-minded reasons has perfected a formula for reducing humans and animals to one sixth their normal size. Walthall dies, leaving his laboratory to his widow (Rafaela Ottiano), who at first accepts Barrymore as a partner, but later turns against him when he does not share her ambition to "make the whole world small!"

Granted this premise, the treatment is remarkably restrained, with even the young love interest well acted by Frank Lawton and

Lionel Barrymore in The Devil Doll

Maureen O'Sullivan (who had played Dora to his David Copperfield) as Barrymore's daughter, who knows him only as the old lady. But what has intrigued all audiences is the ingenious perfection of the special effects, as the reduced Arthur Hohl and Grace Ford go about their criminal business. Nearly four decades later, Everson pronounced these scenes "infinitely superior to the cheaper, simpler work in the similar *Dr. Cyclops* and *The Incredible Shrinking Man.*"

Meanwhile, back in 1931, to follow up on Lugosi's success in *Dracula,* Universal soon embarked on a production of *Frankenstein,* almost equally familiar and bizarre, and in public domain. Lugosi turned it down, so director James Whale chose for the monster a hitherto busy but not particularly successful British character actor whose professional name was Boris Karloff.

The result was the picture that *The New Yorker* calls "probably the most famous of all horror films and one of the best."

As the protagonist of Mary Shelley's novel, Dr. Frankenstein was, of course, the first notable "mad scientist" in fiction as well as talkies. Despite a chorus of Mittel-European peasantry reminiscent of a Viennese operetta —women in dirndls and flowered headdresses, men in lederhosen and Tyrolean hats dancing the Schützplattl, all celebrating Dr. Frankenstein's wedding—tension mounts as the monster, scheduled for painless mercy killing, hangs his tormenting dwarf guard (Dwight Frye) and lurches toward the village.

In the famous scene with a little girl, the first person who has not run shrieking in horror from him, it is plain from the monster's smile (his first) that he means her no harm as he joins in her childish game of tossing wreaths of flowers into a lake to watch them float. In the version shown in the United States the actual drowning of the child is not seen; the follow-up is the heartbroken father

Boris Karloff, Marilyn Harris in **Frankenstein**

carrying her body along the village street, silencing one group of merrymakers after another.

Meanwhile the monster has been menacing Frankenstein's bride (Mae Clarke). In the climax the enraged villagers pursue him with torches and dogs until, seizing Frankenstein himself, he takes refuge in an old windmill, which the mob sets afire. Clearly it was intended that Frankenstein should perish along with his monster, as in the novel (with his bride presumably turning to his friend Victor, played by John Boles, an otherwise useless character)—but instead the monster flings him from the top of the blazing mill and his fall is broken by one of the arms.

Though the monster apparently dies in the flames, the ending of the film is discordantly cozy, as testy old Baron Frankenstein (Frederick Kerr) stands outside his son's bridal chamber drinking toasts with three pretty servant girls.

As with *Dracula*, the sequel, *The Bride of Frankenstein* (1935), is considered superior to the original. In a well-done prologue, Elsa Lanchester as Mary Shelley does far more acting than in her brief closing scenes as the man-made "bride" (not of Frankenstein, of course, but of his monster; the bride of Frankenstein, once Mae Clarke, had now become Valerie Hobson). While a thunderstorm rages outside, Mary explains to the intrigued Shelley and Byron (visually well cast, Douglas Walton and Gavin Gordon) what *really* happened after the end of *Frankenstein*.

The monster's survival is easily enough explained, by his having fallen through to the flooded cellar of the mill. A few inconsistencies remain: not only Frankenstein's bride but the burgomaster and the parents of the drowned child are played by different actors; also the boring Victor has disappeared without explanation, and old Baron Frankenstein has apparently died quite suddenly, as the doctor has inherited the title. But these small discrepancies are soon forgotten as the story gets under way.

Unwittingly spreading terror wherever he goes, the monster at one point frightens a shepherdess so that she tumbles into a pond, from which he rescues her, but even this does not still her screams. Shot in the arm by the villagers and chained in a dungeon, he escapes again, wandering through the forest until he is drawn by the music of a violin to the hut of a blind hermit (O. P. Heggie).

Sensing only that the stranger is in need of help, the old man embraces him as a friend, dresses his wound, gives him food and wine and even teaches him to enjoy smoking cigars. That night as the hermit kneels by the monster's bed weeping in gratitude to God for sending him a friend, and the monster, tears oozing between his misshapen eyelids, awkwardly pats his shoulder, the pathos is genuinely touching. Within a few days the still nameless monster (whose brain is that of a criminal, not a moron) has learned to speak in simple but intelligible phrases (in fact, his vocabulary is soon larger than Tarzan's after several years with Jane).

But this idyll is shattered when a traveler (John Carradine) recognizes him and gives the alarm, which results in the burning of the old man's hut. Fleeing once more, the monster stumbles through a graveyard into a catacomb occupied by Dr. Pretorius (Ernest Thesiger), a gleeful lunatic who dines on a coffin and delights in creating miniature human beings whom he keeps sealed in separate bottles. Without batting an eyelash, Pretorius enlists the monster as an ally in blackmailing Frankenstein into creating another humanoid creature—an idea Frankenstein had earlier indignantly rejected. "Make . . . woman!" the monster commands, and when Frankenstein still balks, kidnaps the Baroness as a hostage.

Only the latter part of the film is concerned with this creation, managed as before with parts of corpses, stolen this time by Pretorius' two criminal henchmen. In the climax, as impressively staged as in the first film, amid the roar of thunder and flash of lightning the synthetic woman comes to life (Elsa

Lanchester in one of the weirdest make-ups ever devised). When the monster gently approaches her, asking "Friend?" her piercing shrieks and writhing revulsion tell him that he is doomed to loneliness forever. Rather inexplicably pushing Frankenstein and his wife to safety ("Go! You . . . live!"), the monster pulls enough switches to ensure an explosion that will destroy him, his intended bride and Pretorius along with the laboratory.

But even now he does not stay dead. In *The Son of Frankenstein* (1939) he is brought back without explanation, lying on a marble slab in the Frankenstein crypt, guarded by Ygor, a once-hanged shepherd (Lugosi), all ready to be reanimated when Wolf (Basil Rathbone), son of the late Dr. Frankenstein, returns to claim his inheritance. Since the first two films were set in modern times, one wonders how the Frankensteins could within a few years have produced a son apparently in his forties, but this is only one of the difficulties in what was considered to be the weakest Frankenstein film.

This time the monster ends in a pit of boiling sulphur, after kidnaping Wolf's small son (with whom, however, he played amiably in an earlier scene). *The New Yorker* comments: "Karloff gets a few inventive scenes (the Monster's revulsion when he sees himself in a mirror, his agonized scream when he discovers that Ygor is dead) but Rowland V. Lee's stodgy direction crosses over from the creepy to the distasteful."

Less than a month after the first Frankenstein film, *Dr. Jekyll and Mr. Hyde* (1931) opened in New York. The *Times* flatly proclaimed it "far more tense and shuddering" than John Barrymore's 1922 silent. Certainly all agree that Fredric March's portrayal of the dual role (for which he won his first Oscar—the only time a horror character was even in the running) was far superior to Spencer Tracy's pallid version in MGM's misguided 1941 remake.

Since few people alive today have ever had the opportunity to see Barrymore's Jekyll-Hyde, the Mamoulian-March version remains unquestionably the one most buffs remember best. Full credit goes to its marvelously cinematic qualities, especially the transformation scenes, in which the handsome March turns into a horrendous simian creature worthy of Chaney, managed not by trick photography but by changing filters, revealing successive layers of already applied make-up.

The noble Dr. Jekyll, it will be recalled, wanted only to free the good side of human nature from the evil by isolating it; the disastrous results are too well-known to need recapitulation here. Though the Stevenson story contains no female characters, all dramatized versions have introduced two women, to symbolize what appeals to the two sides of the hero's split personality: a pure, devoted fiancée for Jekyll and a tempting, tartish type for Hyde.

Thus in this version Jekyll chivalrously gives first aid to Ivy Parsons (superbly played by Miriam Hopkins), a Cockney pub entertainer whose provocative theme song is "Champagne Ivy is me nime—good for any gime at night, me boys." Says Everson: "Mamoulian's caressing close-ups and long, lingering dissolves give the scenes between March and sexually provocative Miriam Hopkins a sensual and erotic intensity rare on the American screen, even in those pre-Production Code years."

With her shapely leg, dangling out of bed, still swinging in his mind's eye, when Jekyll next turns (involuntarily) into Hyde, he heads straight for Ivy, eventually driving the girl half-mad with terror. Meanwhile she confides her fears to Jekyll, and when Hyde quotes, in his snarling, sneering rasp, her very words, she is convinced he must be the devil. Her murder, just off camera, is one of the screen's genuine highlights of horror.

The next horror film (also the next mad doctor) in order of release was *Murders in the Rue Morgue* (1932). Only the third in Universal's horror series, it was the first to receive poor reviews, and ominously pro-

Miriam Hopkins, Fredric March in **Dr. Jekyll and Mr. Hyde**

phetic of things to come—i.e., a respected Poe title tagged on a story that would have set the master revolving in his premature grave.

On the assumption that most people would think "Rue Morgue" was the name of a morgue rather than a street, the scenarists naturally provided such a morgue. C. Auguste Dupin, fiction's first detective, becomes Pierre Dupin, romantic medical student (played by Leon Waycoff, later known as Leon Ames), and Camille L'Espenaye, one of the victims in the original, becomes just one more threatened ingenue (Sidney Fox), though her

mother, as in the story, is murdered and stuffed feet first up a chimney.

Lugosi, who had presumably rejected *Frankenstein* in favor of Dr. Mirakle (accent on the second syllable), lures girls off the street for his unholy experiments in mixing human and gorilla blood. Arlene Francis as a streetwalker is bled to death, then dropped through a trap door into the Seine. About the only survivor from Poe was the murderous gorilla.

Six months later came the next mad scientist film, *Dr. X.* (1932), which marked Lionel

Atwill's debut in horror films. As clubfooted Dr. X. (short for Xavier), he certainly seemed sinister enough, but he turns out to be only an effective red herring for the maniacal, one-armed "moon murderer" (Preston Foster), whose kick is tearing out the left deltoid muscle from his victim's back and devouring it. He makes up for a missing arm by creating a spare one from the "artificial flesh" he has devised. In an especially grim climax, he ends as a human torch. Fay Wray, also making her horror debut, was for once Atwill's daughter, not his victim, and Lee Tracy was the standard wisecracking reporter.

"A grand chiller of the old school," said Everson, "replete with clutching hands, a weird laboratory, a hooded killer, gas jets, secret panels, a wonderful group of suspects."

Atwill's triumph in *Mystery of the Wax Museum* has already been noted. A few months later in 1933 he returned to the horror field for the third time, in *Murders in the Zoo*. Perhaps more akin to the Count in *The Most Dangerous Game* than to your run-of-the-lab mad scientist, this big-game hunter is also a zoologist who collects wild animals for zoos, but still manages to keep a sharp eye on his young wife (Kathleen Burke).

After leaving one suspected lover tied in the jungle with his lips sewn together, he exposes another to a mamba's poisonous fangs, and finally topples the faithless lady herself into a pool of waiting crocodiles. Randolph Scott and Gail Patrick were the nominal love interest and Charlie Ruggles as a bibulous press agent provided comedy, but the *Times* found Atwill "almost too convincing for comfort . . . Judged by its ability to chill and terrify, this film is a successful melodrama."

Both actresses just mentioned had been among the finalists in Paramount's well-publicized search for a "panther woman" to appear in *Island of Lost Souls* (1933), based on H. G. Wells' *The Island of Dr. Moreau*, with Burke the winner but Patrick destined for a more successful career. Running concurrently

with *The Sign of the Cross* (and coming immediately after *Payment Deferred* and *Devil and the Deep*), *Island* helped establish Charles Laughton as the screen's favorite psychopathic villain—much less the gentleman than Atwill and even more decadent.

A ghoulish doctor has succeeded in turning various animals into creatures almost, though not quite, human. His fatal mistake is trying to mate his masterpiece, the panther woman, with a man, Richard Arlen. Led by an ape-man (Lugosi), the beast-men chant their creed as their creator cracks his whip: "What is the Law? Not to spill blood, not to chase other men, not to go on all fours, not to eat flesh: that is the Law. Are we not men?" But when Dr. Moreau breaks his own law by drawing blood, the dog-men, pig-men and other monstrosities take him to his own dreaded "House of Pain" and (as in *Freaks*) there vivisect him.

Authorities on the horror film quote the term "tasteless" applied at the time, and indeed it was (again like *Freaks*) kept off British screens for some thirty years. Wells himself denounced Philip Wylie's adaptation as a parody of his work. (Under its original title the story was remade in 1977 with Burt Lancaster and Michael York, to generally disastrous reviews.)

1934 brought one of the most sinister of mad scientists, in *The Black Cat,* whose connection with Poe was even more tenuous than that of *Murders in the Rue Morgue*. But it did bring together for the first of several times the two reigning kings of horror, Karloff and Lugosi, in what is generally considered the best of their co-starring vehicles. An extremely macabre tale (said by Everson to have been inspired by the career of Aleister Crowley, once the notorious high priest of devil worship), it cast Karloff in one of his most effective characterizations, the very embodiment of evil for its own sake.

The slow, gliding camera work, the use of classical music in the background and the coldly modernistic sets all contributed to the dark mood. Despite eccentricities such as his morbid dread of cats, Lugosi is for once the relatively innocent victim, who loses first his wife, then his daughter to Karloff (who keeps the wife's preserved body on display for old times' sake). But all scores are evened at last when Lugosi first skins Karloff alive on an embalming rack, then blows up his castle-fortress.

Not much can be said for *The Raven* (1935), another highhanded appropriation of a familiar Poe title, with no relationship to the original. The scenarist professed to have been "inspired" not only by the poem whose title he used but by *The Pit and the Pendulum*.

Nugent in the *Times* regarded this claim as "amazing effrontery," to describe "the season's worst horror film." This time Lugosi was a mad surgeon with a torture chamber full of devices drawn from Poe's stories which he delights in trying out on guests. One of his jolliest pranks is to perform a facial operation on Karloff which leaves him horribly disfigured.

A few months later Karloff redeemed his reputation with *The Black Room* (1935), one of Columbia's few entries in this field, and, oddly enough, one of the only two '30s horror films not reviewed by the *Times*. (The other was *Condemned to Live*.) In the familiar pattern of *The Man in the Iron Mask*, Karloff played twins, one good, one bad. Set in Middle Europe of the nineteenth century, complete with a prologue, a family curse, the hidden black room of the title and other Gothic accoutrements, the story (an original by Arthur Strawn) might well have been written in the period it depicts. Stylistically, the brooding sets of castle, church and cemetery recall Whale's Frankenstein films. The evil brother murders the good one and assumes his title and identity with almost complete success—exposed at last only by the good one's loyal dog, a device also used in Bette Davis's *Dead Ringer*.

Before reaching the point at which *Times* reviewers hastily dismissed such films without even bothering to tell what they were about,

the horror cycle offered one more striking example, novel in that it starred neither Karloff, Lugosi nor Atwill. If the mad surgeon did not resurrect a whole criminal, he did make functional use of parts of one, for *Mad Love* (1935), the properly horrifying American debut of Peter Lorre, already famous for Fritz Lang's *M*, was based on *The Hands of Orlac*, a French novel made into a German film in 1925.

The maniacal surgeon (whose total baldness makes him literally an egghead) loves an actress (Frances Drake) in a "théâtre des horreurs" like the Grand Guignol, where night after night he watches avidly while on stage she is tortured and branded as a faithless wife. When she repeatedly rejects his overtures, he consoles himself with a life-size wax image of her—but his real chance comes when her husband, Stephen Orlac (Colin Clive), a concert pianist, has his hands mangled in a train wreck, and in all Paris only Dr. Gogol (Lorre) can help.

What he does is graft the hands of a recently guillotined murderer (Edward Brophy) onto Orlac's arms, with the result that while he finds it difficult to play the piano, it is alarmingly easy for him to hurl knives with deadly accuracy. Playing on Orlac's uneasy sense of guilt, Gogol almost convinces him that he has killed his own stepfather. In another terrifying sequence Lorre pretends to be the criminal returned from the dead to reclaim his hands. Gone completely mad at last, he is about to strangle Mme. Orlac with her own braids when her husband's unwanted dexterity with a knife dispatches him just in time. Most observers agree that *Mad Love* is by any standards one of the best, as it was one of the last, Hollywood chillers of the '30s.

By the end of 1935 it was apparent that the great wave of cinematic horror was rapidly receding. What could have brought about such a rapid decline in a genre that in the previous five years had produced at least a dozen acknowledged masterpieces? Had the gradually improving economic conditions made this particular form of escape less necessary? Or had the great popularity of light-hearted, whimsical, "screwball" comedy, which affected all genres, made it more difficult to approach even horror with a straight face?

Early 1936 saw a minor Republic effort, *The Crime of Dr. Crespi,* supposedly "suggested" by Poe's *The Premature Burial*—a film about which the *Times* observed: "The Rialto audience was unable to restrain a kind of uncalled-for mirth." Even Erich von Stroheim, who as well as a great director had been one of the silents' favorite villains ("the man you love to hate"), failed to register as a murderous doctor who, years after losing the girl he loved to his assistant, perfects a drug by which he can totally suspend the animation of his rival for exactly twelve hours—intending, of course, that he shall be buried alive and awake in the grave, but he's dug up in time and the evil doctor kills himself.

The only other horror films of 1936 were two Karloff vehicles, in one of which he played a mad scientist, and in the other a dead man revived by one. In *The Invisible Ray* he was Dr. Janos Rukh, who in discovering a new element, "Radium X," acquires the deadly power to kill whatever he touches. Naturally, he sets out to rid the world of his wife (Frances Drake), her lover (Frank Lawton), the woman he suspects brought them together (Beulah Bondi) and a few professional rivals, including Lugosi. In the end, about to be consumed by his own radioactivity, he fumbles with a lifesaving antidote, but his own mother (Violet Kemble Cooper) smashes the syringe, reproaching him for having broken "the first rule of science."

In an effort to lend the story scientific weight, producer Carl Laemmle in a printed foreword warned that what the audience was about to see might soon turn into fact. To which Nugent in his review retorted, "Boo right back at you, Mr. Laemmle."

The Walking Dead, released two months later, was more favorably received. An ex-convict, Karloff is adroitly framed by a gang for the murder of the judge who sentenced

him, but after electrocution is restored to life by another of those scientists (Edmund Gwenn). In a variation on *The Count of Monte Cristo* and *The Devil Doll,* he proceeds to avenge himself on the five men who framed him. His mere reappearance among them starts a chain of events that leads each one to bring about his own death. He himself at last dies for good, just as he is about to reveal what it was like the first time. As Gwenn murmurs, "It will never be known."

Whatever the explanation, the years 1937 and 1938 produced not a single horror film. Karloff and Atwill turned to other kinds of roles, but Lugosi was in effect technologically unemployed between *The Invisible Ray* (1936) and *The Son of Frankenstein* (1939).

1939 saw only two more variations on the already overworked theme of the executed criminal revived. In *The Man They Could Not Hang,* Karloff was both scientist and victim. As the former he discovers how to revive the dead, but is charged with *causing* the death of a student with whom he was experimenting. Hanged, he is brought back to life, and then, in a plot remarkably parallel to *The Walking Dead,* avenges himself on the D.A., the judge and the jury who condemned him to the gallows. After killing six jurors, he gathers the rest at his house, but is finally himself killed, inevitably destroying his lab and taking his secret with him.

With the last horror film of the decade, *The Return of Dr. X.* (neither a sequel to nor a remake of the 1932 *Dr. X.*), the '30s cycle ended not with a bang but with a feeble whimper. John Litel was the usual doctor experimenting with blood to revive the dead. His first success is the recently executed Humphrey Bogart, who requires a particular type of blood to keep alive—hence everyone with that type disappears from a hospital. Litel himself is murdered, but not before he reveals the truth about Bogart. Said Crisler in the *Times:*

The resuscitation of the dead is a cinematic commonplace these days; the real problem is to get the boys to do something constructive after you have got them out of the trenches. Once they return from that bourne from which the traffic grows more congested daily, they usually tend to lead a life of crime, and to look like something which has literally been dug up.

Though horror films of later decades, thanks to the end of censorship, the use of color and other technical devices, may produce more violently jolting shocks, achieved by effects more bloodcurdling, revolting or downright nauseating than were permissible under the Production Code, to the true horror buff nothing will ever equal, much less surpass, those classic chillers of the '30s.

THE LIGHT FANTASTIC
Flights of Fancy, Musical and Otherwise

34

FANCY FREE
Fantasies, from <u>Just Imagine</u> to <u>The Wizard of Oz</u>

As is evident, the many "mad doctor" films, however tricked out in pseudoscientific apparatus and jargon, were scarcely less fantastic than the avowed tales of the supernatural. Yet, considering the limitless possibilities of the camera, it is surprising how very few pure fantasies were filmed in the '30s, and how few even among these exploited the trick photography so imaginatively used in such silents as *The Thief of Bagdad* and *Peter Pan*. Perhaps the '30s' ultimate flights of fancy appeared in the altogether new genre of the animated sound cartoon in color, especially Disney's delightful Silly Symphonies (which won Oscars every year from 1931–32 through 1939) and their logical culmination in the first feature-length cartoon, *Snow White and the Seven Dwarfs* (1938).

Excluding the horror films already noted and a few others covered under other genres, Hollywood in the '30s produced scarcely twenty films that could be considered true fantasies, more than half of them adapted from other media. Unless one counts *Just Imagine* (1930), it never attempted the kind of provocative, futuristic science fiction the British did so well, as in *Transatlantic Tunnel* (1933) and *Things to Come* (1936), still less the '70s' spectacular exploration of outer space, as in *2001* and *Star Wars*.

Of the eight film fantasies created directly for the screen, several made notable use of special effects, but only one captured the public imagination strongly enough to become a classic in its own right: the truly unique adventure-thriller *King Kong* (1933). Of the six fantasies based on novels (three British), five did indeed use special effects, two for dramatic purposes, three for comic, but in the sixth and most famous, *Lost Horizon* (1937), only the *idea* was fantastic.

Of the seven based on well-made stage plays (that is, with only one or two sets), five were British or European, all involved either the personification or the transcendence of death and none required much imaginative cinematography. Only one joyous fantasy, the first in color (based on material that had been successively a series of novels popular since the 1900s, a stage musical comedy and a silent film), escaped all conventions and became an enduring favorite for all subsequent generations: *The Wizard of Oz* (1939).

Among fantasies written especially for the screen, the earliest was the bizarre creation of Buddy G. De Sylva, Lew Brown and Ray Henderson, *Just Imagine* (1930), which after fifty years remains unique as the only science fiction musical comedy ever made. At times it suggests a comic *Brave New World,* though it appeared two years before the publication of the Huxley novel.

The New Yorker now scoffs at it as "an oddly tacky concoction: papier-mache skyscrapers soar into painted heavens," but in fact the futuristic sets (obviously influenced, as Clarens notes, by Lang's *Metropolis, 1927*), with multileveled streets of Art Deco buildings and the air dense with the traffic of small open planes, still look impressive in surviving ads and stills, as they certainly do on screen.

As Miles Kreuger noted for a showing of the film at the Museum of Modern Art in 1971:

Picture telephones, exploration of Mars, a rocket ship called Pegasus, pants suits and reversible dresses for women, sleek cardigan jackets for men, pills for nourishment, automatic doors, heated hand-driers, air traffic controls, test-tube babies, and personal flying devices are just a few of the dreams of the screen-writers that have come to pass . . .[1]

Reversing the usual time-traveler's direction, El Brendel, a comedian with a broad Scandinavian accent, was a Rip Van Winkle from 1930, whose putdown comments on the superefficient world of 1980 no longer sound funny. The music is negligible, and the story goes downhill after the landing on Mars (where all the natives are born twins, one good, one bad), but otherwise *Just Imagine* has much to recommend it. Maureen O'Sullivan and John Garrick are appealing young lovers, their comic sidekicks, Marjorie White and Frank Albertson, are breezily amusing, and the blast-off to Mars, with the earth receding until the whole spinning globe can be seen, with the continents clearly outlined, was in 1930 a breathtaking glimpse into a future that has now almost come true.

Fox, which produced more fantasies than any other studio, came up with another in *Six Hours to Live* (1932), a most unusual film which combined the familiar back-from-the-dead motif with the kind of let-us-save-humanity-from-itself message so often heard in high-minded early talkies.

At an international trade conference in Geneva, the representative (Warner Baxter) of a mythical country is assassinated because of his opposition to a destructive policy. But a scientist (George Marion), who has been experimenting with animals, restores him to life —for six hours. Though his political views remain unchanged and he carries his point at the conference, he has acquired a mellow understanding of life and death that enables him to comfort others whom he had earlier spurned, especially a widow (Beryl Mercer), mourning the loss of her only son, and a prostitute (Irene Ware) to whom he gives money to get out of the life.

1933 brought the most famous original film fantasy of all time: *King Kong,* after nearly five decades still a marvel not only of trick photography but of breathlessly exciting filmmaking. Says Clarens: "Nor (wisely) does the film aspire to be a horror tale. It is instead a most successful adventure romance."

Surely audiences who had in the previous two years shuddered through the extraordinary cycle of genuine horror films did not flock to *King Kong* (which opened simultaneously at the Roxy and Radio City Music Hall, with a combined seating capacity of ten thousand) in the same mood of terrified fascination. It offered no mad scientist, no supernatural menace, not even a real villain.

Rather, it combined the appeal of jungle films like *Trader Horn* and the Tarzan series, the startling special effects of *The Lost World* and a new, quite conscious element of the beauty-and-the-beast legend, confirmed by Robert Armstrong's famous closing line: " 'Twas beauty killed the beast." It also introduced the then entirely novel element of mass urban disaster.

Other commentators have been content to marvel at the superb pacing, the effective use of music and especially the technical expertise of all the special effects, which indeed have never been surpassed. Clarens calls it "the most accomplished thriller of the decade . . .

[1] In one respect the writers were overpessimistic; in their 1980, Prohibition, described as "a noble experiment," is still in effect.

New York in 1980 as envisioned in **Just Imagine**

the best apology for Hollywood's technical proficiency, the perfect admixture of a multitude of talents."

Although the 1976 *King Kong* was not as disastrous as most remakes, the critical and popular consensus was that despite the addition of color, the World Trade Center and would-be topical references, it could never match the speed, power and pathos of the original; indeed, its chief effect seems to have been a revival of interest in the earlier version. As an indication of changing standards, a number of touches long excised from the 1933 film as too "brutal" have now been re-

stored: Kong gobbling down a sailor, trampling a native village, reaching in through an apartment window to grab a woman, then, finding she is not Fay Wray, dropping her many stories to her death.[2]

The sequel, *Son of Kong* (1933), hurried out within a year, though directed by Ernest

[2] In an interview printed in the *London Times* in 1978, Miss Wray expressed pride in having become part of a legend. She had been sent the script of the 1976 version in the hope she might play a part in it, but she was so appalled at the attempted modernizing that she did not even go to see the completed film.

King Kong, Fay Wray in King Kong

Schoedsack, who had produced the first, with Robert Armstrong playing the same character, was even at the time dismissed as a too obvious attempt to cash in on a box-office bonanza. For one reason, Kong Jr. measured a mere thirty feet tall, and was much more benevolent than his sire. Indeed, in the climactic earthquake and flood he actually saves Armstrong. Clarens terms him "little more than an emasculated version of the great Kong —funny and endearing as a big teddy bear."

Original screen fantasy had fallen on hard times that were to last the rest of the decade. What can be said for *It's Great to Be Alive* (1933), a feeble Fox musical about a world in which only one man (Raul Roulien), isolated by chance on a tropical isle, survives an epidemic called "masculitis"? The idea was not new even then, and was, of course, to be repeated in later years with pseudoscientific variations about atomic radiation. Predictably, the hero is fought over by female racketeers, the government and a world congress of scientists headed by Edna May Oliver, but Roulien was so lacking in appeal that the *Times* reviewer sympathized with a character played by Emma Dunn who complained: "Of all the men in the world, he *would* be the only one left."

Perhaps an indirect descendant of *King Kong* and certainly the first film of the decade based on a mass disaster, *Deluge* (1933) ranks as a fantasy only because its premise is the destruction of New York by flood rather than some historic catastrophe. Unlike other such films, it is mainly concerned with the adjustment of the survivors *after* the tidal wave has receded. The hero (Sidney Blackmer), believing he has lost his family, falls in love with a girl (Peggy Shannon), only to learn that his wife (Lois Wilson) and children have survived, after all. What can the poor girl do but swim out to sea? Reviewers were not impressed, even with the deluge itself.

Far more delicate and original was the idea behind the exquisitely photographed and tinted *I Am Suzanne*, which (except for *Death Takes a Holiday*, adapted from a play, and the operetta *Babes in Toyland*) was the *only* film of 1934 to use any element of fantasy. It was the third of four forgotten American pictures made by Lilian Harvey, a dainty British star who had enjoyed her greatest success in German films, notably *Congress Dances* (1932).

She played a temporarily crippled acrobatic dancer in love with a puppeteer (Gene Raymond), who, anticipating Mel Ferrer in *Lili* (1953) by nearly twenty years, talks to his creations like real people. Indeed, the heroine becomes so jealous of her puppet lookalike that she shoots it (but does not destroy it). In a dream sequence, the most imaginative segment of the film, Suzanne is tried, à la Alice in Wonderland, before the King and Queen of Puppet Land and their minions, who in real life were the then famous Podrecca's Piccoli Marionettes. (In one of his two American film appearances, Leslie Banks shone as Suzanne's Svengali-like manager.)

The only original fantasy of 1935, generally considered the best of the four films written, produced and directed by Hecht and MacArthur, was *The Scoundrel* (originally titled *Miracle in 49th St.*), which gave Noel Coward his first starring role on screen. With his inimitable, icy aplomb, he played a ruthless publisher (supposedly inspired by Horace Liveright), who drives fading novelists to suicide just as casually as he breaks the heart of a naïve young poetess (Julie Haydon).

So embittered is she that she calls down a curse on him, praying that his plane may crash and he die knowing no one will mourn him. This happens, but, as in other fantasies of survival beyond death, he is given a chance: a month's return to life to find someone who will shed a tear for him. In the nick of time he manages to bring about the resuscitation of the poetess' true love (Stanley Ridges), and is presumably saved by her grateful tears.

It was not this conventional plot, however, still less the sentimental ending, that led Nugent in the *Times* to hail *The Scoundrel* as "the most dazzling writing this column has ever heard on screen . . . a distinctly exhilarating event of the cinema."

This was a film that could only have been made in Manhattan, because the social scenes glitter with such genuine New Yorkers as Alexander Woollcott (as "Vandermeer Veyden"), Hope Williams and others who were not lured to Hollywood. The elegant, jaded bitchery of the dialogue probably comes as close as anything could to capturing the malicious wit long associated (at least in legend) with the Algonquin Round Table.

Though Coward himself expressed dissatisfaction with his work and explained that he had accepted the role only because Helen Hayes was to have played the poetess, no one else has ever agreed with his regrets. Said Nugent: "Mr. Coward is so perfectly attuned to the part that we cannot help suspecting that he contributed to the dialogue."

Among the six '30s film fantasies adapted from novels, it is surely no coincidence that the three British entries (all by well-known writers, all remembered, revived and remade) were serious, while the three American ones (all by Thorne Smith) were comic.

The Invisible Man, with its frequent visual and verbal humor, struck 1935 critics and audiences as intriguingly novel—indeed unique —science fiction, of a kind that could be done *only* on screen. Claude Rains had never before made a film, but one can hardly call this his first "appearance," since until the last minute he is heard but not seen. He played a scientist, one driven mad by the same mysterious chemical, "monocane," that has rendered him invisible. In the presence of others he keeps his face wrapped in bandages and wears dark glasses and gloves. When the usual prying villagers (British this time) get too curious, he simply unwinds the bandages and discards his clothes, revealing nothing whatever inside.

He does not realize, however, that the drug induces megalomania. Presently he is derailing a train, robbing a bank, committing needless murders, all with perfect impunity, since no one can see him. Finally a snowstorm forces him to take refuge in a barn, where the

sound of his breathing gives him away. As footprints appear in the snow, the police open fire. Like Dr. Jekyll and the Werewolf of London, as he dies he resumes his normal look, visible at last.

Aside from the startling and amusing special effects (e.g., a pair of trousers dancing down a country road), critics were impressed with the literate dialogue in which R. C. Sherriff and Philip Wylie had brought the H. G. Wells novel to the screen. Five later variations, starting with *The Invisible Man Returns* (1940) and ending inevitably with *Abbott and Costello Meet the Invisible Man* (1951), proved of as little interest as most of their kind.

When *She,* H. Rider Haggard's 1887 novel, reached the screen for the third time in 1935, the *Times* found that getting there was more than half the fun; the adventures of scientist Randolph Scott in search of the mysterious walled city of Kor were more exciting than what happened inside it. "She" (Helen Gahagan, Melvyn Douglas' wife, later a congresswoman, in her only screen role) is the ruthless priestess-ruler, who long ago stood in "the Flame of Life," to gain not only immortality but eternal youthful beauty.

It seems "She" was in love with an ancestor of the scientist some five hundred years ago, but is perfectly willing to settle for his twentieth-century descendant, and indeed is ready to sacrifice his mortal sweetheart (Helen Mack) to that end. But a second trip through the Flame of Life suddenly withers "Her" to her proper age of five centuries.[3]

With four decades' hindsight, *The New Yorker* comments:

The stagey decor of Kor is in the Art Deco style of Radio City Music Hall, and you keep expecting the Rockettes to turn up. The dialogue, however, belongs to an earlier age . . . The picture is deadly slow, and those lovebirds could try anybody's patience, but camp like this is a rarity.

She, however, had one element in common with the most admired, even beloved, non-

---

[3] A 1965 remake drew very poor reviews.

musical fantasy of the decade, Frank Capra's version of James Hilton's *Lost Horizon* (1937) : the instantaneous old age that overtakes Margo in the climactic scene. It is impossible to doubt Capra's sincerity or the zeal with which he and his favorite scenarist, Robert Riskin, worked to bring this idyll to the screen on the grandest possible scale. Ronald Colman was a particularly apt choice to play Conway, the sensitive British diplomat kidnaped at the order of the High Lama of Shangri-La,[4] to become his successor. Though it was released in March, the *Times* confidently hailed it as sure to be on everybody's ten best list.

To some extent it follows the *Grand Hotel* pattern, with a plane full of assorted passengers fleeing a revolution in Baskul "shanghaied" (the later term would be "skyjacked") to Shangri-La, a secret Utopia hidden in a protected valley high in the Himalayas, where an eighteenth-century Belgian priest, still living as the High Lama (Sam Jaffe), has sought to preserve all that is best in our culture against the approaching day when Western civilization will destroy itself.

Capra gives no hint to explain some rather strange departures from the novel. On the one hand, a woman missionary was turned into a consumptive prostitute (Isabel Jewell); on the other hand, the Manchu princess beloved by Conway in the book was split into two characters, neither Oriental: Jane Wyatt as his love interest and Margo (who might be Eurasian) opposite his rebellious young brother (John Howard), who, ignoring all warning signs, leads her out of Shangri-La, with the disastrous results noted above.

Perhaps the appeal of this particular fantasy is now as specifically dated to the '30s as it was rooted in them. To those struggling between the Depression and the ever-darkening clouds of World War II, a tranquil never-never land where time stood still would obviously have the strongest possible charm. To later generations, it smacks of an elitist cop-out, as *The New Yorker* puts it: "Part popular adventure and part prissy, high-flown cracker-barrel sentimentality." Both an attempted Broadway musical and Ross Hunter's ludicrous musical remake (1937) were unmitigated disasters, ridiculed by both press and public.

American writers have generally been less interested than the British in serious fantasies, either as plays or as novels. In fact, in the '30s American novels of fantasy (always comic) seemed the exclusive province of a now forgotten humorist named Thorne Smith, who at the time enjoyed a reputation as a kind of sexier Wodehouse. Smith turned out novels with titles like *The Bishop's Jaegers,* with jackets like *Esquire* cartoons in which leering old men chased scantily clad blondes. Despite the Production Code, five of these, three in the '30s, made it to the screen—all, unfortunately, after Smith's death.

The Night Life of the Gods (1935), the only film of the decade other than *The Warrior's Husband* (1933) and the opening of *Crime Without Passion* (1934) to make use of the abundant material of Greco-Roman mythology, is basically a parody of the mad-scientist formula. Alan Mowbray played the inventor of a ray that could not only turn humans into statues but vice versa. Seven members of the cast portrayed well-known denizens of Olympus, while an eighth was Perseus, demigod slayer of the Gorgon Medusa. All were discreetly garbed within the Code, rather than as they usually appear in classical art.

Lowell Sherman, in his last directorial effort before his death, had "performed," Sennwald in the *Times* found, "an amusing and occasionally hilarious screen transformation of the novel," as the inventor first petrifies his obnoxious family, then proceeds, à la Pygmalion, to bring the statues in a museum to life.

The next Smith novel filmed remains one of the relatively small number of '30s films al-

---

[4] The name soon passed into the language as a synonym for Utopia. The name of FDR's plane in World War II, it was also the name of the presidential enclave now known as Camp David.

most universally familiar, if only because it inspired a long-running TV series. This, of course, was *Topper* (1937), in which George and Marion Kerby (Cary Grant and Constance Bennett) immediately took their place beside Nick and Nora Charles among the screen's most sophisticated young couples.

Perhaps understandably, the *Times* reviewer, who by that time had had more than his fill of whimsy and screwball comedy, noted, "Whimsy is a delicate and perishable commodity and nobody need be blamed for slight spoilage in the transit." In an opening that would have been the tragic climax in another kind of film (indeed Bennett herself had suffered just such a fate in *Outcast Lady,* 1934), the Kerbys smash their roadster into a tree and emerge from the wreckage as elegant, frivolous ghosts.

In a comic variation on the plot of *The Scoundrel,* they must do at least one good deed before their eternal destiny is decided. The beneficiary is that favorite antihero of '30s comedies, the worm long overdue to turn, the henpecked, downtrodden millionaire, neglected by his selfish wife and family (as in *A Successful Calamity, Fifth Avenue Girl,* several Will Rogers vehicles or, for that matter, *Dodsworth*—in this case Cosmo Topper (Roland Young), a suburban banker at the mercy of his wife (Billie Burke at her flightiest) and their sardonic butler (Alan Mowbray), whose acid delivery of the line "Bless our happy home" closes the film. The Kerbys liberate Cosmo, innocently enough, by introducing him to champagne and his wife to lacy lingerie.

Much of the hilarity is purely cinematic, the kind of thing that Noel Coward exploited even more wittily in the film of *Blithe Spirit* (1945), with characters materializing and vanishing at will, objects whisked about by unseen hands—all the trickery of *The Invisible Man* turned around for comic effect.

The first sequel, *Topper Takes a Trip* (1938), with most of the same principals, moved the *Times,* predictably, to observe: "The spirits are willing, but the freshness is

weak." Cary Grant was no longer on hand, having done his good deed and moved on to higher planes.

But since the *Times* had not liked the first film, it could hardly be expected to like the second, which takes place largely in Paris (where Mrs. Topper has gone for a divorce) and Monte Carlo. Verree Teasdale shone in one of her elegantly bitchy roles as a supposed friend of Mrs. Topper. Those who had enjoyed *Topper* (or still enjoy it) loved (or would love) the sequel. Only in *Topper Returns* (1941, not based on a Smith original) did the series begin to show its age, with a different director and writers and Joan Blondell as a ghost who was no substitute for the irrepressible Kerbys.

Of film fantasies adapted from plays, *Outward Bound* (1930), British Sutton Vane's 1924 hit, was the first to reach the talking screen. Directed by Robert Milton, who had also staged the Broadway production, and featuring several of the original cast, *Outward Bound* was a good example of one type of early talkie, the faithfully photographed play. This was the gentle tale of souls after death (in the familiar vein of *The Passing of the Third Floor Back, Servant in the House,* etc.).

Almost the whole familiar stock company was present and accounted for aboard the mysterious ship: the young lovers (Douglas Fairbanks, Jr., and Helen Chandler), the haughtily hyphenated Mrs. Cliveden-Banks (Alison Skipworth), the humble charwoman (Beryl Mercer), the likable alcoholic (Leslie Howard in his film debut), the ruthless tycoon (Montagu Love) and the Cockney steward (Alec B. Francis).

As on stage, Dudley Digges played the Examiner, who calls these recently dead people to account and metes out justice to all except the lovers, who in despair had turned on the gas, but are recalled to life when their dog jumps through a window and lets in fresh air.

A few weeks later a more distinguished fantasy opened: Fox's version of *Liliom,* Molnár's only serious play, written in 1909 but not successful until after the war, a work for which the word "bittersweet" might have been coined. First presented in New York by the Theatre Guild in 1921, it made stars of Eva Le Gallienne and Joseph Schildkraut.

Though less sentimental, the background (lower-class urban European) and the story (a conceited but essentially decent young man is transformed and redeemed by the love of a humble "slavey") are so parallel to Austin Strong's 1922 play *Seventh Heaven,* which in 1927 had made Janet Gaynor and Charles Farrell the most romantic young lovers of the silent screen, the only wonder is that Fox did not make *Liliom* sooner.

With Frank Borzage again directing, it might well have been the Budapest equivalent of *Seventh Heaven,* had not Gaynor been off salary, waiting in vain for the studio to meet her terms. As a result, the role of Julie went to the competent but colorless Rose Hobart, and the film has been forgotten—never revived, never seen on TV and not important enough to be mentioned in any standard film history.

Though it probably did not rank with Fritz Lang's French version (1933), starring Charles Boyer, the *Times* reviewer found it "a most compelling talking picture," not the least surprise being Farrell's effective performance as the devil-may-care carousel barker. The film was well cast, with Estelle Taylor as Mme. Muscat, the amorous carousel owner, Lee Tracy as "the Buzzard," a petty criminal who tempts Liliom into a bungled payroll robbery, and H. B. Warner as his supernatural guide.

Surprisingly for the time, even Liliom's suicide was retained, and his experience after death only slightly cinematized by the use of a train which whisks his astral self from his deathbed to the court of judgment and another, fiery one that carries him off to purgatory. The epilogue, in which he is allowed to return ten years later to see his child (and ends by slapping her as he had slapped her mother) was faithfully dramatized. *Liliom* is now, of course, better-known to the world

in musical form, transposed to nineteenth-century New England as Rodgers and Hammerstein's *Carousel.*

A minor British play, *The Monkey's Paw,* which hung on in high school anthologies long after it was forgotten everywhere else, was filmed by Fox in 1933 with a respectable, almost all-English cast. Like other antique melodramas, it conveys well-bred British shudders at the sinister powers of the Orient. It is also a variation on the familiar folk motif of the three wishes, the first of which does so much harm that the other two must be used to undo it.

The monkey's paw with such supernatural powers comes into the hands of a couple (C. Aubrey Smith and Louise Carter) whose first wish is for great wealth. This leads to the death of their only son (Bramwell Fletcher) in a factory accident. The mother wishes him back to life, but when he appears at the door looking just as he did immediately after the tragedy, horribly mangled and maimed, they can only wish him dead again. Whatever effect this denouement might have had was undercut in the film by letting the whole episode turn out to be a dream.

Three months later, Fox released one of the most poignant and haunting of film fantasies: *Berkeley Square* (1933), adapted by John L. Balderston from his own 1929 play (suggested by Henry James' story *The Sense of the Past*), and directed by Frank Lloyd, fresh from his triumph with *Cavalcade.*

This was the decade's one serious treatment of the traveler-in-time motif, otherwise used only for humorously anachronistic effects by comedians like Will Rogers, Eddie Cantor and even Wheeler and Woolsey. A few years before, Fox might have made *Berkeley Square* with Gaynor and Farrell; the hero, Peter Standish, is, after all, a forthright young American, and the heroine, Helen Pettigrew, gentle and wistful, would have been just Gaynor's cup of tea. As it was, Leslie Howard recreated his stage role, with the lovely, then new, Heather Angel as Helen.

A modern American taking over an inherited London house, Standish is fascinated by a theory that time is a river, of which we can see only the part that bears us along, while to God it all appears simultaneous. He becomes so obsessed with the charm of eighteenth-century England that presently he finds himself transported back there, changing places with an ancestor whose name and appearance he shares, at the exact moment in 1784 when the earlier Peter first set foot in the house.

Though a thunderstorm rages outside, Peter, to the astonishment of his cousins, the Pettigrews, is perfectly dry. Worse, having read his ancestor's diary, he blunders by referring to events that have not yet taken place, and indeed terrifies his intended fiancée, Kate Pettigrew (Valerie Taylor) into fleeing the house. When Sir Joshua Reynolds (Olaf Hytten), painting his portrait, is about to give it up because he cannot capture the expression of the eyes, Peter assures him that he will indeed complete the picture and even tells him where it will hang. At a ball he frightens

Leslie Howard, Olaf Hytten, Valerie Taylor, Heather Angel in **Berkeley Square**

the Duchess of Devonshire (Juliette Compton) by rattling off a tribute as if she were already dead. Meanwhile he is disillusioned by the callousness and coarseness behind all the elegant façades. In the climax, revealing his true identity, he shouts, "Eighteenth-century London *stinks!*"

Only Helen, Kate's sister, has understood that he is not a charlatan or a devil but a man from another time. But even she, looking deeply into his eyes for a glimpse of the future, sees an apocalyptic vision of racing cars, battleships, traffic jams, gang wars, soldiers in gas masks.

Though he loves her, Peter knows from history that his ancestor will marry Kate. Helen can only hope they will meet again, "Not in my time, nor in your time, but in God's time!" Returning to the present, more alienated than ever from his puzzled fiancée (Betty Lawford), he finds an Egyptian amulet Helen left for him, and seeking out her grave, learns that she died shortly after he left her.

The personification of death is certainly not a new form of fantasy. It can be traced back to the most ancient religions, and was extraordinarily popular in the Middle Ages, both in the morality plays and in church sculpture and paintings. Seldom, however, has Death appeared as a suave, handsome young man in an otherwise realistic modern setting. *Death Takes a Holiday* (1934), from Alberto Cassella's 1929 play, as it follows a party of Italian aristocrats from a street carnival to a suburban villa, seems at first like a sophisticated comedy of manners. Adapted by Maxwell Anderson and directed by Mitchell Leisen, who had done so well with another European drama, *Cradle Song*, the film won high praise from most reviewers, from *Variety* to *Time*.

Bored with his eternally lonely mission, Death (Fredric March) assumes the body of a Russian prince to spend three days as the house guest of a nobleman (Sir Guy Standing), to find out why people fear him so. Though two titled ladies (Katherine Alexander and Gail Patrick) are temporarily at-

tracted to him, the only one not terrified of him even when he tells her the truth is the strangely mystical Grazia (Evelyn Venable). Despite the grief of family and fiancé, she walks into eternity with Death.

One cinematic touch impossible on stage was showing what happens in the rest of the world while Death takes his holiday. As Mordaunt Hall put it in the *Times,* "Wilted flowers regain life, a man leaps from the Eiffel Tower and gets up and walks away, no one is even injured in a school fire and no casualties are reported in fighting between rival nations."

What must have been the least distinguished film fantasy based on a play was *The Return of Peter Grimm* (1935), one last go-round for Belasco's hoary 1911 melodrama (revived in 1921 and filmed as a silent in 1926). Its not very startling premise, actually a variation on *A Christmas Carol,* is the second chance given a selfish old businessman (Lionel Barrymore), allowed to return from the grave just long enough to undo the wrong he had done in committing his adopted daughter to a loveless marriage with his nephew. The *Times* review was completely derisive.

Barrymore encountered Death more directly and successfully in *On Borrowed Time* (1939), based on Paul Osborn's 1939 Broadway hit, which had been adapted from a novel by Lawrence Watkin. This is the one about the stubborn old codger who corners Death, embodied as a Mr. Brink (Sir Cedric Hardwicke), in a magical apple tree because he is determined not to die until he can secure the future of his small grandson (Bobs Watson).

The *Times* liked its "warmth and sentiment and just enough ornery human acidity to keep it off the alkaline, or mawkish, side"—but found it not nearly so effective on screen as on stage, mainly because Barrymore was no Dudley Digges.

The enormous success of Disney's *Snow White* (1938), which set the whole country whistling and humming "Someday My Prince Will Come," "Wishing," "Heigh-Ho" and "Whistle While You Work," quickly awak-

Fredric March, Evelyn Venable, Kent Taylor, Kathleen Howard,
Sir Guy Standing in Death Takes a Holiday

ened other producers to a hitherto untapped vein of public fancy—the pleasure of musical return to the half-forgotten fairy-tale kingdoms of childhood. Thus 1939 brought from MGM not only *On Borrowed Time* but an infinitely more memorable fantasy, one that has become a part of our popular cultural heritage to a degree attained by very few films, even '30s films—the ever-fresh, ever-enchanting *The Wizard of Oz.*

Thanks to MGM's shrewd policy of well-timed theatrical reissues in the '40s and, from the '50s on, of carefully limited showings on TV, *The Wizard of Oz* has become as much a seasonal treat for generations of American children as Lionel Barrymore's annual broadcast of *A Christmas Carol* was to radio listeners in the '30s.

L. Frank Baum's first Oz book was published in 1900 and turned into a stage musical as early as 1903, the first starring vehicle of Montgomery and Stone. There were also two silent *Wizards* in 1910 and 1925, both forgotten. This was not, of course, the first musical in color—that was *Dancing Pirate* (1936) — nor MGM's first such project—that was *Sweethearts* (1938) —nor even MGM's first venture into musical fantasy—that was *Babes in Toyland* (1934) —but this *was* the first film which used color not merely to imitate or reproduce reality but to defy and transcend it just as gaily as cartoons had been doing for years.

No doubt the songs would sound just as tuneful and the characters seem just as lovable even in black and white, but how much would be lost! Not only the Yellow Brick Road itself, the Ruby Slippers and the Emerald City, but the exuberantly fanciful landscape, the delicate pink bubble in which Glinda, the Good Witch (Billie Burke), appears and disappears, the ever-changing Horse of Another Color and, above all, the green-faced, red-eyed Wicked Witch of the West (Margaret Hamilton), with her hourglass full of blood-red sand to measure Dorothy's remaining minutes. As if she were determined to outdo Snow White's stepmother, Miss Hamilton's fiendishly cackling performance remains the ultimate in wicked witchcraft, just as some

scenes, such as those of her squadrons of flying apes dropping on the Haunted Forest to seize Dorothy and Toto, are still eerie enough to terrify the more susceptible young.

This brilliantly imaginative visual production, directed by Victor Fleming, with special effects by Arnold Gillespie, was given the final magic touch by one of the most appealing scores ever composed for a film: one rippling,

Ray Bolger, Jack Haley, Judy Garland, Bert Lahr in **The Wizard of Oz**

bubbling number after another, with E. Y. Harburg's always neat and frequently witty lyrics perfectly matched to Harold Arlen's melodies, most by now so familiar that they seem like traditional nursery songs: "Ding-Dong! the Witch Is Dead" (sung in the piping voices of the Munchkins), "Follow the Yellow Brick Road," "We're Off to See the Wizard" and the three variations of "If I Only Had . . ." Who could forget the Scarecrow's (Ray Bolger) longing for a brain, the Tin Woodman's (Jack Haley) yearning for a heart and especially the Cowardly Lion's (Bert Lahr) hilarious account of all he would do if he only had "the nerve." (Among the finest performances was Frank Morgan's, as a cranky doorman, then the Cockney cab driver of the chameleon horse and then a softhearted palace guard before being exposed as the somewhat fraudulent Wizard himself.)

Ironically, the poignantly wistful "Over the Rainbow," identified with Judy Garland for the remaining three decades of her life, is virtually thrown away in the film: sung only once, in the black-and-white opening sequence in Kansas, and never even reprised, except for a few faint echoes on the sound track.

Surely it was her unforgettable rendition of this song, with the same warm sincerity that had made "Dear Mr. Gable" the standout number in *Broadway Melody of 1938* (1937), as much as anything else in her performance as Dorothy that made the seventeen-year-old Garland an immediate and beloved star of the first magnitude.

Yet history records that MGM had wanted Shirley Temple for the role, but Fox was not willing to lend her. Had it done so, *The Wizard,* even with everything else going for it, might now be resting in oblivion as deep as most of Temple's vehicles, including *The Bluebird* (1940), Fox's own blunder into fantasy, which proved almost as heavy-handed a disaster as the Russian-American version in 1977.

Thus it seems most probable that long after *The Wiz* (the 1978 black reinterpretation) has come and gone, future generations will still be humming the Arlen-Harburg score and romping with Garland, Bolger, Haley and Lahr down the 1939 Yellow Brick Road.

35

ANYTHING FOR A LAUGH
Farce and Low Comedy

In addition to fantasies labeled as such, one must note that the slapstick farces that gradually gave way to, or paved the way for, the screwball comedies were for all practical purposes stylized fantasies, with only the faintest resemblance to reality. If farce may be defined as the ultimate extension of comedy, in which probability and logic are tossed overboard for the sake of immediate laughter, or a genre in which endless coils of complication are spun out of some initial misconception or misunderstanding or some preposterous condition to which the hero must submit, then it is obvious that many of the comedies already discussed, especially those classed as "screwball," were, in fact, farces.

Then too, many musicals were adapted from farces or built on farcical premises, and all the vehicles of the great comedians, which often included wildly surrealistic scenes and effects, were by their very nature farcical—but there was also another, more venerable tradition of "pure" farce, of which one of the oldest playable examples, Brandon Thomas' hit of 1892, *Charley's Aunt,* was successfully filmed in 1930, with Charlie Ruggles as the disguised Lord Fancourt Babberley.[1]

Likewise, *The Man From Blankley's,* another British antique, from 1903, was resurrected as John Barrymore's third talkie (1930). This is the one about a drunken British peer who wanders into the wrong party and is mistaken by the hostess for a paid guest she hired to make a fourteenth at dinner. As Barrymore's first comic effort in years, it was hailed with delight.

Most of the popular screen farces of the early '30s, however, came from Broadway of a season or two before. Thus in *Bachelor Father* (1931) C. Aubrey Smith repeated his 1928 stage hit as a rakish British nobleman who rounds up three illegitimate children by different mothers, then finds the one he prefers (Marion Davies) is not his, after all. *It's a Wise Child,* on the stage in 1929, also made it to the screen in 1931, with Davies as the lively heroine who visits a midwife and is suspected of being pregnant when she's only covering up for a servant girl (thus anticipating the plot of *Kiss and Tell*).

Still in 1931 came *The Man in Possession* (on Broadway, 1930), with added dialogue by P. G. Wodehouse, and Robert Montgomery as an impecunious younger son who becomes a sheriff's man guarding a house under writ, but for love of its mistress (Irene Purcell) serves as her butler. This was filmed again in 1937 as *Personal Property,* with Rob-

ert Taylor and Jean Harlow; in both versions Reginald Owen played the hero's stuffy brother.

Preston Sturges' *Strictly Dishonorable,* a sensation on Broadway in 1929, was likewise filmed in 1931, surprisingly intact in its risqué implications, with Sidney Fox as the Southern belle of determined virginity and Paul Lukas as the suave Italian singer whose "dishonorable" intentions she deflects. In purified form, this was remade in 1951 with Ezio Pinza and Janet Leigh.

One Rainy Afternoon (1936), based on a French story and set in a Paris as amorous as only Hollywood could imagine it, had an actor (Francis Lederer) keeping a rendezvous with a married woman in a movie theater. Given the wrong seat, he kisses the wrong girl (Ida Lupino), who screams, thereby rousing a band of moral vigilantes determined to protect French womanhood. Hauled into court, the actor, to shield his mistress from scandal, pleads the gallantry and romantic ardor of the French nature and thus becomes something of a national hero before ending up with Lupino.

That same year, Hollywood raided Broadway again by adapting Mark Reed's 1935 hit, *Petticoat Fever,* as a vehicle for Robert Montgomery, cast as a wireless operator isolated in Labrador so long that he goes berserk at the sight of a white woman (Myrna Loy) when a plane with her and her fiancée (Reginald Owen) is forced down. Nugent, who disliked Montgomery, was not pleased with the film, but others thought it among the funniest farces of the year.

A 20th Century-Fox "B" production, *Thank You, Jeeves* (1936, a Wodehouse adaptation), despite the perfect casting of Arthur Treacher and David Niven as Jeeves and Bertie Wooster, became too involved with less interesting characters. *Step Lively, Jeeves* (1937), not from a Wodehouse story, with Treacher but not Niven, was even milder and ended the projected series.

Perhaps the last more or less original farce of the decade was Hal Roach's *The House-*

---

[1] Jack Benny made another version in 1941, and Ray Bolger starred in the musical version, *Where's Charley?,* in 1952.

keeper's Daughter (1939), based on a novel by Donald Henderson Clarke—"the funniest specimen in years and years," said the *Times*. Chronologically between *A Slight Case of Murder* (1938) and *Arsenic and Old Lace* (1940), this, too, drew "black" humor from mass murder, here done with randomly distributed cups of poisoned coffee. In the title role, Joan Bennett was an ex-moll who goes home to mother (Peggy Wood), who works for wealthy would-be newspaperman John Hubbard—but Adolphe Menjou, William Gargan and George E. Stone took comic honors. This was, incidentally, Victor Mature's first film.

But it was not any of these more or less genteel adaptations that roused the loudest belly-laughs of the '30s; it was the farce-comedies of the greatest array of clowns the screen has ever seen. The one genre in which the silents are usually considered to have excelled the talkies is their kind of slapstick comedy, often called "low."

Yet, admitting that for certain styles more may have been lost than gained with the advent of sound, the '30s were still extraordinarily rich in varied comic talent, much of it drawn from the stage, where laughs depended at least as much on the well-timed delivery of wisecracks as on pantomime and sight gags. A decade that saw practically all the best work of the Marx Brothers, Laurel and Hardy, W. C. Fields, Eddie Cantor and Joe E. Brown, as well as the rise of Mae West, Jimmy Durante, Burns and Allen, Jack Benny and Bob Hope as screen favorites can hardly be considered a comedown from the '20s.

While the three greatest names among silent comedians, Chaplin, Keaton and Lloyd, did, technically, survive the talkies, their careers were, of course, affected: Chaplin's by his own prolonged refusal to talk on screen, Keaton's by a studio system that took artistic control of his work out of his hands and Lloyd's by increasing difficulty in finding vehicles to suit his established image of the bespectacled timid soul.

Since Chaplin had withdrawn to a solitary eminence beyond competition or even commercial considerations, he made only two films—both silent—during the whole decade, as compared with a dozen in the '20s.

Many moments in *City Lights* (1931) have become part of the permanent Chaplin heritage. From the opening scene, in which our hero is found asleep in the arms of a statue of Peace and Prosperity as it is unveiled, until the close, in which the blind girl (Virginia Cherrill), now in her own flower shop, her sight restored, thanks to his efforts, recognizes by his touch that this grotesque little ragamuffin is her benefactor (followed by the final shot of his face, full of apology, humiliation and anguish), *City Lights* abounds in typical Chaplin touches.

Five years later (in a decade when even major comedians made at least one film a year and minor ones three or four) came *Modern Times* (1936), still mostly silent, except for a few lines of dialogue and a hilarious gibberish song by Chaplin himself.

As Lewis Jacobs observes in *The Rise of the American Film*: "*Modern Times* presented the shifting background of modern life: the factory, the streets, the jail, the waterfront, the hospital, Hooverville, department stores and cabarets . . . The world has become a place of speed-ups, unemployment, starvation, riots, oppression." The foreword by Chaplin announcing that "*Modern Times* is a story of industry, of individual enterprise—humanity crusading in the pursuit of happiness" sounds grim enough, but fortunately Chaplin was too fine an artist to sacrifice his comic genius to a heavy social message.

Despite reminders of the troubled '30s world, the assembly line on which he must endlessly tighten nuts with the same monotonous gesture, the automatic feeding machine gone berserk that holds him down while pelting him with food, to cite but two, are among the funniest scenes in the Chaplin canon. This was his last appearance as the little tramp, for in his long-awaited talkie, *The Great Dictator* (1940), Chaplin rose to the political challenge of the times by satirizing Hitler.

Since during most of the '30s silents were considered of no historic interest, much less of commercial value, revivals were rare. Thus movie-goers then growing up, judging Buster Keaton only by the pictures they saw, had no way of knowing what a great comedian he had been. To them he seemed far less funny than the Marx Brothers, Joe E. Brown and other new favorites. Now considered on the same artistic level as Chaplin, superior to Lloyd, he was not so shrewd a businessman as either, and in effect lost control of his career when he signed with MGM.

His last few silents for the studio were great hits, and his first talkie, *Free and Easy* (1930), was hailed by the *Times*. As the setting is Hollywood, this will be discussed later. Likewise, his second talkie, *Dough Boys* (1930), less favorably received, is covered among films about World War I.

Parlor, Bedroom and Bath (1931) was a remake of a typical *Up in Mable's Room*-type farce, previously filmed in 1920. Despite the support of Charlotte Greenwood and a good cast, this was hardly worthy of the comedian who had created *The Navigator* and *The General. Sidewalks of New York* (1931), touched on earlier because of its juvenile-delinquent motif, was rated by Keaton as one of his worst films; the *Times* did not even review it.

As his box-office value faded, MGM made Keaton split star billing with Jimmy Durante, then new to the screen, in *The Passionate Plumber* (1932), a burlesque version of *Her Cardboard Lover* (1929); *Speak Easily* (1932), a feeble farce with a show-biz setting; and *What! No Beer?* (1933), which will be dealt with among films reflecting aspects of Prohibition.

As a team, Keaton and Durante were no rivals for Laurel and Hardy. Reviews indicate that Durante's aggressive, verbal style of comedy virtually wiped Keaton's understated, deadpan humor off the screen. His popularity gone, Keaton left Hollywood, returning only to make a series of short subjects for Educational, 1935–37. His only other feature films

in the '30s, all in subordinate roles and all for Fox in 1939, were *Hollywood Cavalcade, The Jones Family in Hollywood* and *Quick Millions.*

Harold Lloyd, third of the great silent trio, was the least comic in appearance. Indeed, much of his effect came from his air of flustered normality, frantically trying to cope with the bizarre predicaments thrust upon him, a bashful bumpkin in the famous straw hat and the shell-rimmed, lens-less glasses that became his trademarks.

At his silent height, in such hits as *Safety Last* (1922), *The Freshman* (1925) and *Speedy* (1928), he had outdone even Chaplin and Keaton at the box office, even though his comic effects usually sprang more from plot and situation than from his own invention. One of his favorite specialties was teetering perilously on the roof or window ledge of a skyscraper—dizzying sequences that thrilled, even as they swept audiences into gales of near-hysterical laughter.

Lloyd's adjustment to talkies was not as reluctant as Chaplin's, nor was his descent as precipitous as Keaton's, for he did remain a star, in control of his own pictures, but a decline was noticeable in *Welcome Danger* (1929), which had been converted to a talkie, and was by no means as funny as his last silent. From then until the end of the '30s, he made only one picture every two years, releasing them, as Ibsen did with his plays, in the even years.

Feet First (1930) revived the vertiginous antics of *Safety Last* (1922), with the hero dangling on a scaffold being hoisted on a skyscraper by workmen unaware of his plight. Starting as an inept shoe clerk in Honolulu, he ends up in Los Angeles in one of his typical, hilarious, worm-turning plots. The results at the box office were so disappointing, however, that Paramount considered canceling its agreement to distribute Lloyd's films.

Movie Crazy (1932), a variation on the *Merton of the Movies* theme, fared much better, and will be discussed among films about Hollywood. "After the gangster films and those concerned with the more or less serious activities of gossip mongers and crooners," the *Times* noted, "this offering came to those in the packed audience as a relief."

Lloyd's next film, *The Cat's Paw* (1934), based on a story by Clarence Budington Kelland, in the familiar pattern of the naïve yokel who outsmarts the city slickers, set in Chinatown, with an unusually positive view of Oriental values, was discussed among films about Orientals. Similarly, *The Milky Way* (1936) is among boxing films. The fact that both were adapted from other media rather than created as vehicles for Lloyd perhaps strikes at the root of his problem, for they could just as easily have been made with any hayseed hero type.

By now Gary Cooper, Henry Fonda and James Stewart, all younger than Lloyd and all with greater range, were, or soon would be, playing exactly his type of nice, homespun young man who bumbles his way to success: Cooper in *Mr. Deeds Goes to Town* (1936) and *Meet John Doe* (1941), Fonda in *The Farmer Takes a Wife* and *Way Down East* (both 1935), Stewart in *The Shopworn Angel* (1938) and *Mr. Smith Goes to Washington* (1939).

Professor Beware (1938), Lloyd's last film of the '30s and almost his last film ever, followed the same pattern, but the gags provoked Crisler in the *Times* with their antiquity and familiarity. As Lloyd himself observed in 1940: "I had come to the conclusion that no one had any particular use for me as a comedian any more."

One comic star of the silents who not only survived but soared, in one of the most remarkable comebacks in theatrical history, was the beloved Marie Dressler. A success in vaudeville, revues and musical comedy, this self-styled ugly duckling ("too homely for a prima donna, too big for a soubrette") also made silent films, but by the mid-'20s she had faded into total obscurity, until MGM scenarist Frances Marion persuaded Thalberg, in a brilliant piece of casting, to team Dressler with Polly Moran in *The Callahans and the*

Murphys (1927), based on a novel by Kathleen Norris.

Though the film was bitterly boycotted by the American Irish, it launched Dressler and Moran as the only successful female comedy team full-length pictures have ever known, to be reunited over the next six years in seven more.

Her low-comedy vehicles invariably cast her and Moran, both conspicuously plain older women of the type usually described as "battle-axes" (Dressler's visage suggested a tired but determined bulldog, Moran's a beady-eyed ferret), as rival neighbors, landladies, boardinghouse keepers or even competitive sisters; often the son of one fell in love with the daughter of the other.

Caught Short (1930), supposedly "suggested" by Eddie Cantor's (non-fiction) book about the stock market crash, was typically full of gags such as a refractory folding bed and even a laxative joke that gave double meaning to the title—just the sort of thing deplored by some critics but loved by the public. *Reducing* (1931) referred to the then novel craze for losing weight. Moran was the prosperous owner of a beauty parlor, Dressler her dowdy country sister; their daughters were also rivals in love. "There are several really moving moments," the *Times* complained, "but they are meaningless because of the predominating hilarious mood of the film."

In *Politics* (1931) Dressler played an outspoken widow who unexpectedly finds herself running for mayor of her town, backed by all its women, who, taking a leaf from Lysistrata's book, go on strike, forcing their husbands to keep house. The *Times* continued to deplore what it considered the waste of Dressler's talents.

Even after winning the 1930–31 Oscar for *Min and Bill* and almost getting another for *Emma* (1932), Dressler made one more comedy with Moran: *Prosperity*, an attractive title in 1932, and the Capitol Theatre opened at 9:30 A.M. to admit the long waiting line. Again a widow, Dressler was the president of a small-town bank, whose son marries Moran's

Marie Dressler and Polly Moran costumed for **The Hollywood Revue of 1929**

daughter. Unwittingly, Moran causes a run on the bank, but all ends well. It seems significant of how closely these films adhered to formula that in three out of the four the ingenue was Anita Page, and in two the juvenile was William Bakewell, menaced by villain John Miljan.

Few viewers can have missed seeing two other survivors from the silents, the very popular Laurel and Hardy. Not only are they continually on TV, but their work has been compiled in at least three theatrical films. Who could forget Stan's helpless cry-baby routine when his well-meant efforts produce chaos, or Ollie's elaborately mounting exasperation, slower than Edgar Kennedy's slowest burn?

Yet, they never aspired to be anything but simple funny men; their fun is more primitive than that of the greatest screen clowns, and never pretended to be otherwise. First teamed in 1927 by Hal Roach, they turned out short comedies for the next three years almost at the rate of one a month before doing one skit in *The Hollywood Revue of 1929* and providing comedy relief in Lawrence Tibbett's operetta *The Rogue Song* (1930).

Their first full-length feature, *Pardon Us* (1931), reflected the then current vogue for prison films. Sent up for brewing beer, the two escape, blacken their faces and work on a cotton plantation until an overaffectionate bloodhound licks the burnt cork off Hardy's face. Prison seemed a subject no comedian of this period could resist, any more than the First World War, which Laurel and Hardy turned to in *Pack Up Your Troubles* (1932).

In 1933 they starred in *The Devil's Brother,* based on Auber's comic opera *Fra Diavolo*—a musical diversion so successful that MGM followed it up with Laurel and Hardy versions of *Babes in Toyland* (1934) and *The Bohemian Girl* (1936).

Despite the title, *Sons of the Desert* (1934) was not a burlesque of sheik or Foreign Legion films but a good-natured spoof, written by Frank Craven, of a then sacred American tribal ritual, the annual convention of one of those fraternal lodges, still popular in the '30s, at which henpecked husbands traditionally sought escape from hawk-eyed wives.

Along with several other comedians, Laurel and Hardy were trapped in the generally disastrous *Hollywood Party,* released the same month as *Sons of the Desert.* *Bonnie Scotland* (1935), which, though not reviewed by the *Times,* proved their biggest money-maker, saw Laurel as heir in a Scottish will which turns out to leave him only bagpipes and a snuffbox. He and Hardy then get involved with troops bound for India, an episode which leads to a Bengal Lancers travesty and, inevitably, a harem sequence.

Our Relations (1936), in a variation on *A Comedy of Errors*, cast Laurel and Hardy in dual roles, one respectable, one black sheep, with all the possibilities for confusion. "Custard pies can be funny . . .," said the *Times*. "Laurel and Hardy are a funny pair, but they should know when to stop—and that is after the third reel."

Indeed, even some of their warmest admirers still feel that their most inspired gags went into their short subjects, which they no longer made, rather than the more elaborate full-length features. *Way Out West* (1937), which involved standard frontier ingredients including the deed to a gold mine, was greeted by the *Times'* pointing out how much of their effect depended on Hardy's girth and cherubic dimples and Laurel's skinniness and vacant face. *Pick a Star* (1937), like *Hollywood Party*, saw the two as themselves, in what would later be called cameo roles.

Reviewing *Swiss Miss* (1938), B. R. Crisler confessed himself a recent Laurel and Hardy convert, and praised its "almost Disney-ish disregard for reality . . . in the best two-reeler tradition of screen humor."

This time the two were mousetrap salesmen in Switzerland, paid in counterfeit francs. Among the highlights were their attempt to move a piano along the edge of a precipice and a scene in which Laurel outwits a St. Bernard to get its keg of brandy. Technically, *Swiss Miss* was supposed to be an operetta, with singers Della Lind and Walter Woolf King as the lovers, but the three songs by Arthur Quenzer and Philip Charig were never heard again.

Block Heads (1938), the last film Laurel and Hardy made for Hal Roach at MGM, seemed to Crisler only slightly less funny. "Masters of the delayed and double takes, the slow burn, the dead pan, the withering (or vacuous) looks, the tailspin and asthmatic

wheeze, Laurel and Hardy seem equally at ease with or without plot material." In this case the material was minimal.

Flying Deuces (1939), produced by RKO and based on a French farce once filmed by Fernandel and Noel-Noel, was described by Crisler as "a situation and little more." They join the Foreign Legion, desert and finally escape in a runaway plane, in the film's funniest sequence.

A Chump at Oxford and *Saps at Sea* (1940), both made for Roach and United Artists, were so indifferently received that it became clear that the greatest days of Laurel and Hardy were over. Thus their joint career as top-flight comedians in full-length features, from *Pardon Us* to *Flying Deuces*, fell entirely within the '30s.

Among other comedians who made the transition to sound successfully were three "legendary" Ziegfeld stars, who during the '20s had managed to keep a foot in both the stage and screen worlds: Will Rogers, Eddie Cantor and W. C. Fields. Rogers' films were, of course, neither slapstick nor farcical, but, rather, gentle domestic comedies.

Like Dressler and Moran and Laurel and Hardy, most of the other stars discussed in this chapter were in some way involved with music, if only as comic relief in someone else's musical—but none was so consistently a singing, dancing comedian as Eddie Cantor, in the '30s at his zenith, both on radio's *Chase and Sanborn Hour* and on screen as Samuel Goldwyn's biggest star.

In the Depression years, his cheerful song "Now's the Time to Fall in Love" was heard on the air and played in movie theaters far oftener than "Brother, Can You Spare a Dime?" Though he certainly did not rival Will Rogers as a political wit, he kidded the 1932 campaign in a number, "When I'm the President," reprised weekly, in which each chorus added some absurd promise.

Through most of the decade, a Cantor picture, always lavishly produced, usually with a top comedienne opposite him and a secondary romance between an ingenue and a juvenile,

Laurel and Hardy in Swiss Miss

good songs and elaborate production numbers featuring the Goldwyn Girls (who became the screen's equivalent of Ziegfeld Girls or Rockettes), seldom disappointed expectations. If his well-known style of prancing and bouncing back and forth, often in blackface, with white-rimmed spectacles, clapping his hands and rolling his famous "banjo" eyes, was not the subtlest way of putting over a number, it expressed his exuberant personality, which, unlike Jolson's, never came across as obnoxiously overconfident.

Except for a brief appearance, billed as himself, in a skit in the *Ziegfeld Follies* sequence of *Glorifying the American Girl* (1930),

Cantor's first talkie was *Whoopee* (1930), a perfect example of a Broadway musical transferred to the screen intact. His six other '30s films were all screen originals, some co-authored by himself, starting with *Palmy Days* (1931), in which, with Charlotte Greenwood opposite him, he played a crystal-gazer turned efficiency expert in a large bakery.

Though to the credit of Cantor and his writers, he never resorted to the wartime army, prison, a mythical kingdom or other locales overused by other comedians, even he could not avoid at least one campus. *The Kid from Spain* (1932) begins with his expulsion from college after being caught in a girls' dormitory. The usual mad train of events leads him to Mexico, where in the climax, mistaken for a famous matador, he must fight an enraged bull.

Roman Scandals (1933) and *Ali Baba Goes to Town* (1937), both variations on the *Connecticut Yankee* theme, in which the modern hero is transported back to earlier times, were both well received. Between these two came two other films, both opposite Ethel Merman.

"Sam Goldwyn, the Ziegfeld of the Pacific, has mounted the million-dollar orbs of his favorite comedian in a rich and merry setting for the annual Eddie Cantor show," said Sennwald of *Kid Millions* (1934).

As a Brooklyn boy who inherits a fortune in Egyptian treasures from his unknown father, he must first outwit a bloodthirsty Arab sheik who thinks he has a prior claim. A sequence in an ice-cream factory, done in the new Technicolor, was hailed as "the most successful example of fantasy in color that Broadway has seen outside of the Disney cartoons."

Strike Me Pink (1936), which had no connection with the 1933 Broadway revue of that title, provoked "considerably less hilarity than we have come to expect of the annual Goldwyn-Cantor shows," the *Times* observed. Based on a Clarence Budington Kelland story originally intended for Lloyd, the script evidently suffered in adaptation. The plot had something to do with saving an amusement park from a gang of slot-machine racketeers, so the climax, naturally, took place on a careening roller coaster. This was Cantor's last film for Goldwyn.

Ali Baba Goes to Town, made for 20th Century-Fox, was well reviewed, especially its touches of political satire, but nevertheless Cantor moved to MGM, where *Forty Little Mothers* (1940), a straight sentimental comedy, cast him opposite Judith Anderson, as a professor at a girls' college who must care for an abandoned baby.

Like Chaplin, Keaton and, to a lesser extent, Lloyd, Laurel and Hardy (though not Cantor) have become cult figures—but no cult is more aggressive in proclaiming the supremacy of its idol than those worshiping at the battered shrine of W. C. Fields, the only comedian of them all who made absolutely no pretense of being likable. If the others appealed to the public by being, however inept, basically vulnerable and even fleetingly wistful, Fields' comedy was that of pure misanthropy, a style that often pleased critics more than audiences, until the rise of "black" or "sick" humor in the 1950s, at which time Fields came posthumously into new glory. Not that he had been neglected in his lifetime, but he had never achieved (nor has he still) the universal appeal of the greatest clowns.

Starting with *Sally of the Sawdust* (1925), a film version of his 1922 stage hit, *Poppy,* Fields starred in nine silent films, with apparently indifferent success; none except the first has ever been revived. His first talkie was a two-reel short, followed by a supporting role as Marilyn Miller's disreputable father in *Her Majesty Love* (1931).

After four more shorts for Mack Sennett, he signed with Paramount, but at first appeared only with other comedians in such films as *Million Dollar Legs* (1932), in which he was billed second to Jack Oakie and supported by Lyda Roberti (as a spy named Mata Machree), Andy Clyde, Ben Turpin and Hugh Herbert. The film was aptly characterized by Bergman as "a plotless pastiche of ancient slapstick and sight gags that utilized nationhood and the Olympic games for manic purposes."

In Klopstockia, a land where all the men are named George and all the women Angela, Fields as President stays in office only by winning at Indian wrestling each morning. "The sight humor and verbal gags seem to run independent of each other," says Bergman, "creating an effect both unsettling and very funny." The fact that it works at all is due no doubt to the lunatic inspiration of a script by Joseph Mankiewicz.

In one of the funniest episodes in *If I Had a Million* (1932), Fields was teamed for the first time with Alison Skipworth, presumably as Paramount's answer to MGM's Dressler and Beery, but for comedy an even more effective pairing, without a trace of sentimentality. As a couple whose precious new car is wrecked by a road hog, Fields and Skipworth use some of their million to buy a fleet of old tin lizzies, with which they spend a day gleefully wrecking the cars of other road hogs.

International House (1933), another multistarred effort, taking off from the *Grand Hotel* pattern saw Fields as Professor Quail, who lands in a helicopter. "With his regal and somewhat beery manner, his precious silk hat, his frozen face and his unlit cigar," said the *Times,* "he keeps his audiences in perpetual roars."

Fields and Skipworth were reunited in *Tillie and Gus* (1933), this time as stars, with no competition from anyone but Baby LeRoy, an infant phenomenon for whom Fields' loathing has become part of his legend. The title characters were artful card sharps who must win a race between two decrepit ferryboats to regain the rightful inheritance of Tillie's niece.

For a comedian of such pronounced individuality, Fields played a surprising number of "literary" roles, the first in *Alice in Wonderland* (1933), well cast, even if unrecognizable, as the cantankerous Humpty Dumpty. In *Mrs. Wiggs of the Cabbage Patch* (1934) he appears toward the end as Mr. Stubbins, fortune-hunting suitor of Miss Hazy (Zasu Pitts), and in *David Copperfield* (1935), even without an English accent, he made, under George Cukor's direction, a perfectly acceptable Micawber—the only role he ever attempted so far outside his chosen persona as embittered victim of a malevolent world. What a Falstaff he would have made!

But it is not for such roles that he is remembered, nor are those films often revived. Even in the hilarious *Six of a Kind* (1934), Fields and Skipworth had to take second billing to Charlie Ruggles and Mary Boland and share the limelight with Burns and Allen. The plot involved a cross-country auto trip by the other two couples, with Fields as a Western sheriff

introduced rather late in the film, in which he revived his famous billiard routine.

You're Telling Me (1934), a remake of his 1927 silent *So's Your Old Man,* was the first talkie in which Fields was the sole center of comic attention, as a small-town inventor of puncture-proof tires. His golf sketch, used on Broadway and also in silents, was exhumed and drew as many laughs as ever.

The Old-Fashioned Way (1934), a reflection of the extreme popularity of prewar period atmosphere, cast Fields as the Great McGonigle, leading a broken-down acting troupe on tour in *The Drunkard.* The *Times* still considered Fields "the drollest of the current screen comics."

It's a Gift (1935), partly written by the star himself, is regarded as vintage Fields. A small-town storekeeper, henpecked husband and again the victim of Baby LeRoy, he drives his family across the country to a California orange grove he has bought—but this was no more than a framework on which to hang the usual gags and routines.

Mississippi (1935) was a Bing Crosby musical, presumably meant as Paramount's answer to *Show Boat,* in which Fields was given second billing but managed to get most of the attention in the *Times'* review. Captain of a Mississippi show boat, he is described as "the beery aristocrat of the river, the bogus Indian fighter, the prodigious quaffer of rum, the greatest liar afloat." A highlight was a poker game in which, surrounded by gamblers with primed pistols, he deals himself five aces.

To Fields *aficionados, The Man on the Flying Trapeze* (1935) remains one of the finest examples of his art. In a story partly written by himself, he was once more the victim of a relentlessly nagging wife (again Kathleen Howard, as in *It's a Gift*)—but, Sennwald noted with glee:

He finally asserts his battered ego in one of the most satisfying scenes in recent motion picture history. He runs amuck for a few magnificent seconds, slugging his brother-in-law into insensibility and aiming a brilliantly erratic haymaker at his terrified mother-in-law.

Poppy (1936) , a remake of his 1922 stage hit with its original title restored, found Nugent in the *Times* just as captivated as Sennwald. "Gettysburg, Waterloo, Actium, Jutland: great battles these, but have you ever seen Mr. Fields in a fight to the finish with a shirt front, a croquet mallet, a suspender strap or a cigar-box fiddle?" A carnival medicine man and shell-game expert, he tries to pass off his adopted daughter Poppy (Rochelle Hudson) as a missing heiress and is exposed, but, who would have thought it, she *is* the heiress!

In *The Big Broadcast of 1938* (1938) , one of the least inspired of the Paramount series begun in 1932, Fields was given top billing, but a year's absence from the screen due to a serious illness seemed to have flawed his effects, as Nugent noted with concern:

The rasping voice has lost its fine nasal resonance, as though some one had scraped the rust from the old trombone . . . The shadow of his radio debacle with Charlie McCarthy has fallen upon the script, and W.C., who never had to stoop so low before, makes a Durante-like play upon his nose and jokes morosely about strong drink and the d.t.'s. We prefer to forget it.

At this point Fields moved from Paramount to Universal, at an even bigger salary, plus percentage, but his next film, *You Can't Cheat an Honest Man* (1939), was deplored by Nugent as "a drab, labored and generally misguided comedy. Considering that he wrote it himself, . . . Mr. Fields seems singularly ignorant of the qualities that have endeared him to his millions." His character was so viciously unsympathetic (perhaps reflecting too directly his well-known off-screen personality) that, as on radio, he came off a poor second to Charlie McCarthy, Edgar Bergen's wisecracking dummy.[2]

My Little Chickadee (early 1940) , with Mae West, was less a co-starring vehicle than a head-on collision of superegos, each deter-

mined to write his/her own dialogue and not be overshadowed by the other. *The Bank Dick* (1940) is indeed regarded as one of the good Fields vehicles, but *Never Give a Sucker an Even Break* (1942) is definitely not. By this time the screen popularity of W. C. Fields had for all practical purposes passed. As with so many stars, the limited number of films recognized as his best fall almost entirely within the 1930s.

Other than those already discussed (and Will Rogers) , the only popular film comedian of the '30s to have appeared in silents was Joe E. Brown, whose trademark was an enormous mouth, in a funny face almost as rubbery as Bert Lahr's. He has, however, not become a figure of cult or legend. Thus he truly belongs in the tidal wave of talent from the stage (Broadway, vaudeville or stock company) that inundated Hollywood in those once-in-a-lifetime years 1928–30.

Brown's first film of 1930, *Song of the West,* in which he played John Boles' faithful sidekick, exemplified still another trend of the day, the filmed operetta. He was starred in his next two, *Hold Everything* and *Top Speed* (both 1930) , but both were based on Broadway musicals. *Maybe It's Love* (1930) was a college football comedy, but in *The Lottery Bride* (1930) Brown was once more providing comic relief in an operetta.

Not until *Going Wild* (1931) was he starred in a non-musical comedy, a typical mistaken-identity farce of the kind that was to provide his vehicles for the rest of the decade. *Sit Tight* (1931) forced him into the wrestling ring with a ferocious masked opponent. Both *Broad Minded* and *Local Boy Makes Good* (both 1931) seemed to the *Times* reviewer like musical comedies without music to make them bearable. The last-named, which took Brown back to a campus setting, said Sennwald, "spreads a half hour's worth of amusement through an hour and a quarter."

Yet by now Brown was clearly established as a popular comedian with a dependable following, so Warners continued to star him in

---

[2] Bergen made four films in 1938 and 1939, in all four playing himself as straight man to Charlie, so cannot be regarded as a leading screen comedian.

two or three films a year, most based on the same formula (also used by Lloyd, Cantor and others) of the timid soul compelled to perform some impossible feat of daring or athletic prowess. Several have been, or will be, mentioned in other chapters: e.g., *Fireman Save My Child* (1932), among hazardous occupations, and *The Tenderfoot* (1932), Kaufman's *The Butter and Egg Man* transposed to a Western setting.

The *Times* reviewers were generally as cool to Brown's comedies as they were lavishly enthusiastic about Fields and Laurel and Hardy—and, indeed, his vehicles do seem too closely cut to a standard pattern. Among the exceptions, *Elmer the Great* (1933) and *Alibi Ike* (1935) were both baseball comedies. *Son of a Sailor* (1933) clearly belongs among Navy comedies, while *Bright Lights* (1935) was a typical, though well-received, backstage musical.

Good reviews always stressed Brown's genuine acting talent; as Flute in Max Reinhardt's all-star production of *A Midsummer Night's Dream* (1935), he was singled out by the *Times* as "giving the best performance in the show"—yet for the rest of the '30s he was handed thoroughly routine assignments.

Crisler rather liked *Earthworm Tractors* (1936), but *Polo Joe* (1936), Brown's last film for Warners, was one of his worst. *When's Your Birthday?* (1937) for RKO was so little better that Crisler wrote in distress: "We shall never cease to regret him, for at heart he is a fellow of infinite possibilities, a unique clown who must always be in dead earnest to be funny."

Of his six remaining '30s films, only *The Gladiator* (1938), from a novel by Philip Wylie, was well received. "Not since Chaplin have we beheld so unbrokenly successful a pattern of pure cinematic clownery," wrote Crisler. As a retread college student, Brown is given a serum devised by a benevolently mad scientist that turns him into an incredible superathlete.

Next in order of seniority on screen, the first major comedy team to emerge with talkies, were a trio who soon became a legend around the world as they already were on Broadway: the Marx Brothers. Zeppo, a dull juvenile, dropped out after their first five films, but the other three offered riotous comedy on every possible level.

Harpo achieved the unique feat of remaining a silent star in talking pictures, communicating by honking an auto horn, with a battered top hat on his curly mop and a capacious overcoat from which he could instantly produce anything from a lighted candle to a cup of coffee. Clearly Harpo followed the pantomime tradition of Chaplin and Keaton. Chico always looked like a vaudeville Italian, whose losing battle with the English language, producing many an outrageous pun, recalled the dialect comedy once so popular on stage, records and radio.

Though Groucho's painted mustache and active eyebrows, his perpetual cigar and loping stride were certainly part of his act, he was essentially a verbal comedian, best remembered for his lightning retorts, *double-entendres* and sardonic asides to the audience. Some of his wittiest lines, to be sure, were written by George S. Kaufman and S. J. Perelman, but in later years on TV Groucho's devastating ad libs and put-downs on *You Bet Your Life* more than proved that he needed no writers. Besides these particular qualities, all three brothers also shared innumerable daring and original slapstick routines.

During the still affluent summer of 1929, when the dazzling novelty of full-length talkies had not yet worn off, delighted fans went back to see over and over *The Cocoanuts*, based on the Marxes' 1925 Broadway hit (with one forgotten song by Irving Berlin, "When My Dreams Come True") and filmed at Paramount's Astoria studios.

Animal Crackers (1930), based on their 1928 stage hit, had something to do with a priceless painting stolen from the home of Mrs. Rittenhouse (that imperturbably dignified stooge, Margaret Dumont). Lillian Roth was the singing ingenue. In *Monkey Business* (1931), their first film made in Hollywood, they used their own first names. The script, co-authored by Perelman, had them stowing away aboard an ocean liner, with Thelma Todd as their foil. *Horse Feathers* (1932), in which Perelman also had a hand, in an inspired bit of lunacy cast Groucho as a college president, with the other two passing themselves off as students. The highlight was the funniest football game since Lloyd's *The Freshman* (1925).

Duck Soup (1933), their last film for Paramount, was not well received at the time by either critics or public. Hall complained in the *Times* that "this production is, for the most part, extremely noisy without being nearly as mirthful as their other films." But it is now regarded as one of their best.

Seven years before Chaplin's *The Great Dictator, Duck Soup* was a wild burlesque of dictatorship and even of government in general, sharp enough so that Mussolini banned it in Italy. In the mythical country of Freedonia, Groucho as Rufus T. Firefly is handpicked by his predecessor's widow (Dumont) to take over as dictator. By way of respect for his office, he slides down a fire pole into his inaugural ceremony and plays jacks while presiding over the Chamber of Deputies.

In retaliation for a fancied slight to his honor, he blunders into war with the rival country of Sylvania. What follows is a grotesque parody of all the hypocrisies and idiocies of blind wartime superpatriotism. Andrew Bergman attributes its failure to the timing of its release. After a year of the popular, activist New Deal, government was no longer an acceptable subject for satire.

The Marxes were then brought, on very favorable terms, by Thalberg to MGM, where they soon proved they had not lost their lunatic touch. *A Night at the Opera* (1935), with a screenplay by Kaufman and Morrie Ryskind, authors of *Of Thee I Sing,* was their most successful picture to date, and remains their best-known and most frequently revived. The young lovers, Kitty Carlisle and Allan Jones (replacing Zeppo), had good voices and even a good song, "Alone," but the famous scenes are the one in which an incredible number of people are jammed into a tiny stateroom, and the climax in which a performance of *Il Trovatore,* presumably at the Met, is reduced to an utter shambles.

They virtually duplicated this success in *A Day at the Races* (1937). As with the previous film, the brothers had polished every gag by testing it before live audiences. Groucho was a horse doctor who on the side also treated rich hypochondriacs like the durable Dumont, and the plot, such as it was, hinged on winning the big race.

Next the Marxes moved to RKO for *Room Service* (1938), their first film not written especially for them. As directed by George Abbott, it had been a great hit on Broadway and the road, full of fast lines and frantic, farcical complications. Instead of one of his usual weirdly named con artists, Groucho played Gordon Miller, a shoestring producer holed up with his partners and cast (including Lucille Ball and Ann Miller) in a Times Square hotel while trying to get a backer so that their play can open. The plot was preserved intact, so inevitably there was less scope for the usual freewheeling antics, but it was still well received.

Meanwhile back at MGM Thalberg had died, and this affected the Marx Brothers' careers as adversely as it did those of many other stars. *At the Circus* (1939) was a distinct comedown. "A rather dispirited imitation of former Marx successes," Crisler called it, and it marked the beginning of a decline. With the exception of *The Cocoanuts* (1929), the Marxes' whole unbroken string of comic masterpieces, from *Animal Crackers* to *Room Service,* were all made in the '30s.

Next of the comic immortals to make his screen debut was Jack Benny, who retained his hold on public affection continuously from the early '30s until his death in 1974. This long reign was admittedly not so much thanks to his films as to his very successful radio and TV careers. Nevertheless, he did make nine films in the '30s, one of the very few radio stars (Cantor and Crosby were the only others) to achieve a simultaneous screen career.

One comedian who would never have succeeded in silents, his effects depended on his perfect timing and his pained tone of voice. Thus, like Brown and the Marxes, he was signed in the first onset of Hollywood's mad craze for musicals, but used in only a few routine skits in *The Hollywood Revue of 1929*. In *Chasing Rainbows* (1930), a backstage musical, as the stage manager he received third billing and made the deadpan most of an occasional line like "Sorry, folks, but the leading lady just broke her leg and we had to shoot her."

From MGM he descended briefly to Tiffany, for *The Medicine Man* (1930), another backstage yarn, but his career really picked up in the early '30s with the success of his weekly radio program, sponsored by Jell-O, at seven-thirty Sunday evenings, which soon became as much a ritual in most American homes as Eddie Cantor's *Chase and Sanborn Hour*, immediately following. Essentially, he acted as straight man, maintaining an image of being vain (about his age, looks, musical talent), self-pitying and, above all, stingy. Even his valet, "Rochester" Anderson, put him down.

Voted radio's favorite comic in 1934, Benny was next featured in *Transatlantic Merry-Go-Round* (1934), one of the seagoing variations on *Grand Hotel*. In MGM's *Broadway Melody of 1936* (1935) he received top billing as an obnoxious gossip columnist harassing producer Robert Taylor, but this was another backstage musical. *It's in the Air* (1935) successfully teamed him with Ted Healy as a pair of con men who flee the Internal Revenue by way of a balloon into the stratosphere.

In spite of this, MGM let him go, but Paramount then starred him in *The Big Broadcast of 1937* (1936) as program director of a radio studio, and in the very lightweight *College Holiday* (1936), in which he first attempted to play "Love in Bloom" on the violin. In the well-reviewed *Artists and Models* (1937), which cast him as the head of a failing advertising agency, he was hailed by the *Times* as "the drollest comic on the screen."

In *Artists and Models Abroad* (1938)—no connection with the other except title—he was head of a theatrical troupe stranded in Paris, but by now Nugent was growing tired of the bland Benny manner. "His Buck Boswell has a score of amusing lines . . . but he airs them as though he were rehearsing a radio script. We resent being treated as 'the vast unseen radio audience.' "

This must be one of the few poor reviews Benny ever got. If he seemed bored, perhaps he had a right to be, after so many inconsequential musicals. A new Paramount contract for two pictures a year started auspiciously with *Man About Town* (1939), from a story by Morrie Ryskind and Allen Boretz, in which Rochester, said the *Times*, "has restored Mr. Benny to the comic map and cleared a sizable place there for himself."

Though it included songs, this was a lighthearted farce, the kind usually thought of as French, in which Benny, notably lacking in sex appeal but determined to impress Dorothy Lamour, pretends affairs with two wealthy married women, one English (Binnie Barnes), one French (Isabel Jeans), only to find their jealous husbands (Edward Arnold and Monty Woolley) gunning for him.

Unlike most of the other stars discussed in this chapter, Benny was *not* at his height as a screen comedian in the '30s. His career in straight, non-musical comedy began with *Buck Benny Rides Again* and *Love Thy Neighbor* (both 1940). *Charley's Aunt* (1941), *To Be or Not to Be* (1942)—the one most often revived—*George Washington Slept Here* (1942) and others from the '40s are surely the films Benny fans recall most fondly —but even these were overshadowed by his great and lasting success on TV.

In the same early talkie rush from Broadway to Hollywood that launched so many stage comedians on screen careers came two others, a team, who, far from becoming cult idols, are now all but forgotten, not even mentioned in any of the standard histories, yet between 1930 and 1937 they made twenty features—more than Fields, more than twice as many as the Marx Brothers.

They were (Bert) Wheeler and (Robert) Woolsey—not at all the poor studio's Laurel and Hardy, but, if anything, more in the zany vaudeville vein of the Marxes, with Woolsey a kind of road-company Groucho and Wheeler like a combination of Zeppo and Harpo. In the *only* recent critical comment on them, at the time of a rare revival in 1977, the anonymous *New Yorker* reviewer noted: "Round-faced Wheeler was the teary, innocent, eternal juvenile; skinny, bespectacled Woolsey was the con-man, nibbling on a long cigar and spitting out quips."

Like so many of their colleagues and rivals, they came to the screen as comic relief in an operetta, in their case *Rio Rita,* one of the biggest hits of 1929. They performed the same function in *Dixiana* (1930), but in between began starring on their own, in *The Cuckoos* (1930), this, too, from a stage musical comedy, *The Ramblers,* which on Broadway had starred Clark and McCullough. The *Times* said, "Wheeler and Woolsey are almost as mad as all the Marx brothers together."

If the title *Cracked Nuts* (1931) sounds too close an echo of *The Cocoanuts,* on the other hand, the film itself used a mythical kingdom to burlesque political and military pretensions over a year before *Million Dollar Legs* and two years before *Duck Soup*—rather effectively, according to the *New Yorker* reviewer, who was particularly taken by cross-eyed Ben Turpin as a precision bomber.

Even if they created no immortal scenes or familiar routines, Wheeler and Woolsey reflected every current fad in screen comedy—not only the mythical kingdom but the World War (*Half Shot at Sunrise,* 1930), gangsters (*Hook, Line and Sinker,* 1930), prison (*Hold 'Em Jail,* 1932), the costume vogue (*Cockeyed Cavaliers,* 1934), the Old West (*Silly Billies,* 1936) and many more, often with feebly punning titles.

Occasionally they rose above this level, as in *Girl Crazy* (1932), which the *Times* re-viewed favorably without even mentioning the Gershwin score. Occasionally, too, Betty Grable or some other promising starlet would replace Dorothy Lee, their usual ingenue, but otherwise most of their vehicles were cut from the same overfamiliar pattern. The *Times* critics grew increasingly weary of the moth-eaten vaudeville routines, slapstick gags and painful puns, but apparently Wheeler and Woolsey had their public, or RKO would not have continued to star them two or three times a year. Their last five films, however, made from 1935 to 1937, were done on severely reduced budgets that relegated them to the bottom of double bills. As Woolsey died in 1938, there is no telling how much longer the team might have lasted.

The next major comedian to make the transition from stage to early talkies was Jimmy Durante, the beloved "Schnozzola" himself, whose career was determined by the shape of his nose just as surely as Brown's was by the size of his mouth. Though of Italian descent, unlike Chico Marx, he never used that dialect, but instead hoarsely parodied a Brooklyn accent, liberally sprinkled with malapropisms, in which every "th" became "d" and "turmoil" was turned (or "toined") into "toimurl."

Biographical references state that he entered films in 1929, but his first picture, *Roadhouse Nights,* was released early in 1930, and he is listed immediately after the three principals. From the fact that his vaudeville partners, Lou Clayton and Eddie Jackson, were also in the cast, plus the knowledge that much of the action takes place in a roadhouse featuring entertainment, one may hazard a guess that Clayton, Jackson and Durante merely provided comic relief from the melodramatic plot, perhaps doing some of their vaudeville routines.

Indeed, unlike most of the comedians discussed so far, Durante was for several years limited to secondary roles in films starring someone else. Of his second film, the first of many for MGM, *The New Adventures of Get-Rich-Quick Wallingford* (1931), supporting William Haines, the *Times* noted: "A good deal of the twisted comedy is supplied by Jimmy Durante, who is known in the film as Schnozzle."

In *The Cuban Love Song* (1931) he was again the hero's comic sidekick. As noted in the discussion of Keaton's career, the two comedians were teamed in *The Passionate Plumber* (1932), *Speak Easily* (1932) and *What! No Beer?* (1933), none noticeably successful, but with Durante gradually overshadowing Keaton as principal laugh-getter. Meanwhile he had also appeared (billed eleventh in the cast) in *The Wet Parade* (1932), as Robert Young's not so comic sidekick, a fellow dry agent killed by a bootlegger.

By *Blondie of the Follies* (1932) the *Times* reviewer had become a convert: "Jimmy Durante pops in . . . long enough for him to break up the show. He sings one of his 'disa and data' songs, heaps vigorous and haughty scorn on his imaginary enemies and does a mad impersonation of John Barrymore in an episode in which Marion Davies figures as Garbo." Shortly afterward, in *The Phantom President* (1932) he even managed to hold his own with the star, George M. Cohan.

In *Hell Below* (1933) Durante, along with Eugene Pallette, provided comic relief in a routine service film; one of the highlights was his boxing match with a kangaroo. In *Meet the Baron* (1934) Durante was called upon to help launch the (unsuccessful) career of another comedian, Jack Pearl, then very popular on radio as Baron Munchausen, whose repeated "Vas you dere, Charlie?" became a comic byword.

If MGM (perhaps because it already had Laurel and Hardy under contract and would soon have the Marxes) confined Durante to such thankless roles, United Artists gave him a better break in *Palooka* (1934), based on a then popular comic strip about a naïve young boxer (Stuart Erwin), a precursor of Kid Galahad, pushed by his streetwise manager, Knobby Walsh (Durante), but the picture itself was a mediocrity. Moving to Fox for *George White's Scandals* (1934), Durante

was given billing second only to Rudy Vallee and praised for his enlivening of an otherwise routine backstage musical.

Back at MGM, in the hopeless *Hollywood Party* (1934) he played what was really the starring role, but had to take second billing to Laurel and Hardy. In *Strictly Dynamite* (1934), he played, "appropriately enough," said the *Times,* "a radio comedian who is having gag trouble."

Though Sennwald's review included an appreciative inventory of Durante's assets ("his comic exuberance, his pride in his profile . . . his delight in multi-syllable words"), it concluded that "in his valiant struggle with the boys who write the jokes the master comes out second." *Student Tour* (1934) was an even lower point in the careers of all concerned, including Durante. In *Carnival* (1935), a sentimental comedy made by Columbia, he was back to sidekicking again, this time for Lee Tracy.

After a three-year absence, during which he was starring on Broadway, Durante returned to the screen in *Sally, Irene and Mary* (1938), for 20th Century-Fox, billed seventh in the cast, below Fred Allen and Gregory Ratoff. He was starred, however, in *Start Cheering* (1938), another college musical, described by Nugent as "one of the funniest of the year's admittedly minor productions," but whatever ground he gained was soon lost in *Little Miss Broadway* (1938), a typical Shirley Temple vehicle in which all attention centered on her. Durante's last film of the decade was *Forbidden Music* (1938), a British production of a "mildly sedative" Oscar Straus operetta, in which (said the *Times*) "Mr. Durante's nose is in everything but a good script."

After a decade of alternating between leading parts in inferior "B's" and throwaway roles in other stars' vehicles, how did Durante survive at all, much less achieve his permanent niche in the cinematic hall of fame? The fact is that during those very years of negligible screen assignments, he was heard regularly on radio, made records, appeared in night clubs, and, most surprisingly, he outdid even Walter Huston and Leslie Howard in shuttling between coasts, starring in *four* successful Broadway musicals: *Strike Me Pink* (1933), *Jumbo* (1935), *Red, Hot and Blue* (1936) and *Stars in Your Eyes* (1939).

As with Benny, his screen career began to pick up after 1940, with a number of big MGM musicals, and by the end of the decade, of course, TV welcomed him.

When Jack Benny died just as he was about to film *The Sunshine Boys*, the only possible choice to replace him (and in 1980 the only comedian of their generation still active) was his lifelong friend George Burns, the survivor of the most successful husband-and-wife team in the history of screen comedy—indeed the only one since Mr. and Mrs. Sidney Drew.

When Burns and Allen appeared in *The Big Broadcast* (1932), they were hardly new faces; besides their years in vaudeville and on radio, they had also filmed a number of two-reel comedies. Their success was immediate; for conveying sheer, bird-brained imbecility, Gracie had no equal, and George's dry, controlled exasperation made him the ideal straight man.

In most of their films, however, they were part of a whole cast of comedians, as in the original *Big Broadcast* and those of 1936 and 1937. *International House* (1933) and *Six of a Kind* (1934) have been mentioned in connection with Fields. *We're Not Dressing* (1934) was a Bing Crosby musical, as *Damsel in Distress* (1937) was a Fred Astaire vehicle, with Burns and Allen supplying only incidental laughs. In *Honolulu* (1939) they supported Robert Young and Eleanor Powell.

Thus only three—not necessarily the best—of their fourteen films together (all in the '30s) can be considered pure Burns and Allen comedies. In *Many Happy Returns* (1934), Gracie was a daffy heiress who plans to have her father's department store demolished to make way for a bird sanctuary. A psychoanalyst prescribes that she marry Burns, who agrees only when offered ten dollars for every mile he travels as her husband. "They seem

to have run out of really funny lines," said Hall in the *Times*.

Love in Bloom (1935) did not fare much better, with Burns and Allen given top billing but with interest centered on a struggling songwriter (Joe Morrison) and his girl (Dixie Lee). If nothing else, the score by Mack Gordon and Harry Revel introduced to a waiting world that immortal ballad "Lookie, Lookie, Lookie, Here Comes Cookie"—so naturally the next Burns and Allen film was *Here Comes Cookie* (1935), which, said Nugent, "clips Miss Allen from the lunatic fringe and sews her on to the border of absolute idiocy." To discourage a fortune-hunting suitor for his other daughter, Gracie's father (George Barbier again, as in *Many Happy Returns*) deeds his fortune to her for sixty days—a decision that makes one wonder who was the biggest idiot in the family.

From then on Burns and Allen were cast in secondary roles, with the peculiar exception of *The Gracie Allen Murder Case* (1939), which pitted Gracie, without George, against Philo Vance. Like so many of their contemporaries, they found a whole new career on TV in the '50s, in a typical sitcom series which set a new generation laughing at Gracie's inimitably vacuous giggle and air of sweet reasonableness while uttering the wildest absurdities.

Surely no survey of film comedy in the '30s could fail to note that the same month that introduced Burns and Allen in *The Big Broadcast* (October 1932) also saw the screen debut of a lady whom many regard as the wittiest, most provocative of all screen comediennes, the unique Mae West. (The film was *Night After Night*.) Her four vehicles set in the '90s have been discussed with nostalgia films; those set in modern times were classed among gold-digger comedies.

A comedienne of a completely opposite type, a funny lady whose laughs depended on her exaggerated unattractiveness, joined Paramount's ever-growing roster of comic talent in 1936: Martha Raye. Even in the Bing

Crosby musical that introduced her, *Rhythm on the Range,* her impression was overwhelming—"a stridently funny comedienne with a Mammoth Cave or early Joe Brown mouth," Nugent said.

She was cast opposite Bob Burns, a rustic comedian from radio, whose drawling delivery and homespun humor Paramount presumably hoped would remind people of Will Rogers, but who after ten films faded out in the early '40s. Like Burns and Allen and almost everyone else at Paramount, Raye appeared in two of the obligatory college musicals, two *Big Broadcasts* and an *Artists* and *Models,* but vehicles were soon being tailored to her special talents.

Mountain Music (1937), again with Burns, was reviewed as an entertaining hillbilly romp; in *Double or Nothing* (1937), a farcical variation on *If I Had a Million* (1932), in which four strangers must compete in doubling a sum of money given them, Raye was billed immediately after Bing Crosby, though they did not play opposite each other. She and Burns, together again, stole *Tropic Holiday* (1938), a Mexican-set musical, from the nominal leads, Dorothy Lamour and Ray Milland.

In *Give Me a Sailor* (1938), Raye and newcomer Bob Hope furiously try to break up a romance between the objects of their affections, Jack Whiting and Betty Grable, but, of course, end up with each other. They played opposite each other again in *Never Say Die* (1939), with Bob as a millionaire hypochondriac at a European spa and Martha as a Texas heiress unhappily engaged to a Prince (Alan Mowbray). To save her, Hope, thinking he is about to die, marries her himself, only to find he will live. After a duel with the Prince, among other complications, all ends well, as the *Times* put it, "with the eternal Raye of Hope."

Inevitably, perhaps by way of administering "mouth to mouth" resuscitation to Joe E. Brown's expiring film career, he and Raye were brought together in *$1000 a Touchdown* (1939), but this was "a painfully witless foot-

ball farce of almost fantastic unoriginality" (the *Times*), which did nothing for either star.

As is already evident, Bob Hope had by now arrived on the Hollywood scene—the last important comedian to do so in the '30s and surely one of the most durable. To those who know him only in his later phases, it may be impossible to imagine how fresh he seemed, in every sense of the word, to the public of 1938.

By then many of the greatest earlier clowns were fading; the funny hat, the bulbous nose, the painted mustache no longer seemed quite so hilarious. Though already in his mid-thirties (ten years Benny's junior), Hope still looked then, and for years thereafter, young, slim and, despite the ski-nose, personable enough to play opposite and win, on screen, some of the most beautiful stars in Hollywood. A stand-up comedian who could toss off, or throw away, wisecracks as deftly as any and still serve as juvenile singing lead was a rare and welcome find.

"Thanks for the Memory," his bittersweet, wryly self-mocking duet with Shirley Ross, which was to become his lifelong signature tune, was not only the high point of the otherwise negligible *Big Broadcast of 1938* but one of the unforgettable movie songs of the decade.

This was followed by two films opposite Raye, *College Swing* and *Give Me a Sailor* (both 1938). But naturally he and Ross had to be reunited in a picture called *Thanks for the Memory* (still 1938), a remake, with even the characters' names unchanged, of *Up Pops the Devil,* which in 1932 had starred Carole Lombard and Norman Foster. The *Times* greeted it with unmixed joy: ". . . in *Thanks for the Memory* with a feather-brained story, an arsenal of effective gags at his disposal and no *Big Broadcast* trappings to stumble over, Bob assumes his rightful stature as the most debonair and delightful of the screen's romantic comedians."

In this simple marital tale, he keeps house and tries to write while his wife works; they break up and are brought together again by friends.

After *Never Say Die* (1939), he and Ross did another remake, titled *Some Like It Hot* (1939)—no connection with the famous Billy Wilder comedy of 1959. This one, based on a flop play by Ben Hecht about seedy show-biz characters, had been poorly received when Jack Oakie made it in 1934 as *Shoot the Works,* and it fared no better now.

Hope's next film (still another remake), opposite Paulette Goddard, a hilariously far-cical version of an old mystery, *The Cat and the Canary* (1939), proved a solid hit. Just around the corner in 1940 was *Road to Singapore,* the first of his seven immensely success-ful co-starring vehicles with Bing Crosby and Dorothy Lamour.

In an overall view of the '30s, even aside from this extraordinary array of top-flight comics, most then at the peak of their powers, one must not forget the younger, more glam-orous stars who sparkled so merrily in the more sophisticated comedies covered in other chapters. Then too, working with both kinds of comedians, on all levels, were a host of character actors, many of whom were quite capable of playing dramatic roles but who found their lighter talents more in demand. Some were occasionally starred in "B's" of their own or in the two-reel short subjects that continued to flourish throughout the decade, but most were continually employed adding solid support in many of the films already discussed.

Truly unique was the double screen life of Edward Everett Horton, who, when he was not doing double takes and biting his nails as the flustered fuss-budget, the nervous con-fidant, cuckolded husband or unwelcome suitor in some of the most elegant high come-dies of the decade (e.g., *Holiday,* 1930 and 1938, *Trouble in Paradise,* 1932, *Top Hat,* 1935), "moonlighted" as the star of any num-ber of forgotten farces (at least fifteen) for independent studios.

Since this study is meant as a complete survey rather than mere reaffirmation of the greatness of the great, some mention should be made of those comedians who amused the '30s movie public briefly, if at all, then faded from the screen.

If even the greatest of the silent clowns, Chaplin, Keaton and Lloyd, had difficulty adjusting to talkies, others of lesser stature simply disappeared. Harry Langdon, a fey, Kewpie-doll type once considered in their league, after a promising silent career (ruined by himself, according to all accounts) was in talkies relegated to short subjects or to sup-porting roles in long-forgotten films: with Slim Summerville in *See America Thirst* (1930), with Ben Lyon in *A Soldier's Play-thing* (1931), with Al Jolson in *Hallelujah, I'm a Bum* (1933). In *My Weakness* (1933), he played Cupid in the most literal sense of those words, then did comic bits and shorts for the rest of his life.

Ben Turpin, whose crossed eyes made his face one of the most unmistakable in silent comedy, did brief scenes in *Show of Shows* (1929), *Swing High* (1930), *Cracked Nuts* and *Ambassador Bill* (both 1931), had slightly better roles in *Make Me a Star* and *Million Dollar Legs* (both 1932), then did nothing recorded until resurrected, along with other old-timers, for the Keystone Kops sequence in *Hollywood Cavalcade* (1939).

Even comedians who were brilliantly suc-cessful in other media, before and afterward, did not always come across in early talkies, usually through no fault of their own. Pre-dictably, those who had gained fame chiefly in radio sometimes failed to register on screen. The immensely popular Amos and Andy (Freeman Gosden and Charles Correll), two white men who did Negro dialect, in a fifteen-minute, five-nights-a-week program that was a seven o'clock ritual in most American homes throughout the '30s, made one film, *Check and Double Check* (1930), but despite fair reviews never made another. Only slightly more successful was the best-known blackface team before them, Moran and Mack, once famous in vaudeville and on records as "the Two Black Crows," who made three films,

Why Bring That Up? (1929), *Anybody's War* (1930) and *Hypnotized* (1933), all fairly well received, but then were heard of no more on screen.

It took only two films to finish the screen career of Jack Pearl, radio's Baron Munchhausen (whose repeated retort "Vas you dere, Sharlie?" seemed hilarious at the time): the aforementioned *Meet the Baron* (1933) and *Hollywood Party* (1934). Even the brilliantly caustic Fred Allen, so highly rated on radio and later on TV, whose screen debut in *Thanks a Million* (1935) was hailed by the *Times* as "a happy success," made only one other film in the '30s, *Sally, Irene and Mary* (1938). Other casualties from radio, who made only a film or two without lasting success, include Seth Parker (Phillips Lord), Myrt and Marge, and singers Kate Smith, Lanny Ross and Rudy Vallee (who came into his own as a character comedian only in the 1940s).

The radio comic who tried hardest was Joe Penner, whose catch phrases "Wanna buy a duck?" and "You . . . *nasty* . . . MAN!" (the basis for a song sung by Alice Faye in *George White's Scandals*) were once familiar to every school child. Between 1934 and 1939 Penner made eight films, plus two more in 1940, without any lasting impression on the movie public, still less the critics.

Though in *College Rhythm* (1934) he was welcomed by the *Times* as "an amiable and likable comedian," by *Collegiate* (1936) he was dismissed as "a pantaloon and a buffoon, not a humorist." Only in *Go Chase Yourself* (1938) and *The Day the Bookies Wept* (1939) did he ever get a kind word from the *Times*, but by then it was too late, and he made no films after the poorly received *The Boys from Syracuse* (1940).

At that, he fared better than the Ritz Brothers, whose popeyed, frenetic antics, however they affected audiences, in their nine films between 1937 and 1939 (in all but one of which they played themselves), drew nothing but groans and sneers from the *Times*. When their night club routines were simply tossed into a picture, as in *On the Avenue* (1937), they were bearable, but starring them was something else again. In *The Three Musketeers* (1939) they did *not* play the title roles, but "three lackeys," with Don Ameche as D'Artagnan and the rest of the cast playing it straight—a combination everyone agreed should not have happened to Dumas.

Even more surprising were the failures, at least the first time around, of some of Broadway's biggest comic names. The last of the Red Hot Mamas, Sophie Tucker, made her debut in *Honky Tonk* (1929), which mixed night club numbers and maudlin mother love so ineptly that she was not seen again until *Broadway Melody of 1938* and *Thoroughbreds Don't Cry* (both 1937), both with Judy Garland. The first two talkies starring Fannie Brice, the original funny girl-funny lady, *My Man* (1928) and *Be Yourself* (1930), both cast her in long-suffering roles, carrying the torch for heartless heels, but in those pre-Streisand days the public was not yet ready for homely heroines. Not until she played herself, most amusingly, in *The Great Ziegfeld* (1936) did she make any real impression, but even that led to only one other, negligible film, *Everybody Sing* (1938), which the *Times* deplored for its waste of her talent, as a Russian maid in a theatrical household, billed below Judy Garland and Allan Jones. By this time, of course, she was known to millions of radio listeners as Baby Snooks.

Another famous singing comedienne, Ethel Merman, was a little more fortunate in that she made eight films in the '30s, most on a fairly high level and none sentimental—but in every one of them she was supporting someone else: Ed Wynn in *Follow the Leader* (1930), Bing Crosby in *We're Not Dressing* (1934) and *Anything Goes* (1936), Eddie Cantor in *Kid Millions* (1934) and *Strike Me Pink* (1936), Sonja Henie and Don Ameche in *Happy Landing* (1938), Ameche, Tyrone Power and Alice Faye in *Alexander's Ragtime Band* (1938); and as the ultimate indignity, in *Straight, Place and Show* (1938) Merman was billed below the Ritz Brothers.

Only in *Anything Goes,* repeating her original role of Reno Sweeney, belting out Cole Porter's "You're the Top" and "I Get a Kick out of You," was she given any scope; obviously, even this was not enough for her to achieve on screen anything like her long reign as musical comedy queen of Broadway.

Strangest of all was the Hollywood fate of Beatrice Lillie, whose second talkie (she had done a few numbers in *Show of Shows,* 1929), *Are You There?* (1930), had originally been designed to showcase her unique personality, with seven songs composed especially for her. But before its scheduled release in the summer of 1930 Fox decided that the market for musicals had dried up and deleted four numbers. Even so, the first reviews from the trade publications were so negative that the studio never released the film at all—a circumstance that naturally gave rise to the myth that Lillie's comedy style could not be transferred to the screen.

Yet when the film was shown at the Museum of Modern Art in 1971, one of its few public showings anywhere, the audience loved it. As a lady detective of many disguises, Lillie certainly had more scope than in *Dr. Rhythm* (1938), her only other '30s talkie. Miles Kreuger calls *Are You There* "a near masterpiece of lunatic comedy by any standards . . . Beatrice Lillie's position at the helm of screen comedy is reassured with the rediscovery of this lost gem."

Joe Cook, called by Percy Hammond "the funniest man in America," made but one film, *Rain or Shine* (1930), based on his stage hit of the same name, but without the music! Well reviewed, this circus story, according to Frank Capra, who directed it, also did well at the box office, but Cook's career was presently cut short by ill health.

Olsen and Johnson, along with William Gaxton, suffered a parallel experience, appearing in their Broadway hit *Fifty Million Frenchmen* (1931) without the Cole Porter score that had been its main attraction. What was left was not even enough to amuse fifty Frenchmen. In *Gold Dust Gertie* (1931),

Olsen and Johnson were bathing suit salesmen, billed below Winnie Lightner. Two Republic films, *Country Gentlemen* (1936) and *All Over Town* (1937), did nothing for them, yet from there they bounced back to Broadway for their greatest hit, *Hellzapoppin,* which ran more than three years.

Ed Wynn made one silent, *Rubber Heels* (1927), which he hated so much that he wanted to buy it up and destroy it; the critics wished he had. Nevertheless, he returned to films in *Follow the Leader* (1930), based on his stage hit *Manhattan Mary,* benefited by sound, yet despite the presence of Ethel Merman and Ginger Rogers the picture failed to click.

The Chief (1933), made to capitalize on Wynn's popularity on radio as the Texaco Fire Chief, was so bad that MGM never released it in England. Not until 1958 did Wynn come into his own as a fine character actor in such films as *Marjorie Morningstar* and *The Diary of Anne Frank.*

Even Bert Lahr was not immediately appreciated. *Flying High* (1931), which he had made Broadway's biggest musical hit of 1930, was fairly well received, but six years passed before he made another film. *Merry Go Round of 1938* (1937), a musical mélange, was dismissed by the *Times* as "indigestible" except for the contributions of Lahr and Jimmy Savo (another once-famous Broadway clown, who made only one other film in the '30s, the unsuccessful Hecht-MacArthur *Once in a Blue Moon,* 1936).

In *Love and Hisses* (1938) Lahr played fourth fiddle to Walter Winchell, Ben Bernie and Simone Simon; in *Josette* (1938) he provided incidental comic relief in a romantic triangle; in *Just Around the Corner* (1938) he was interred in that graveyard of so many comedians, a Shirley Temple vehicle; in *Zaza* (1939), though billed third, he was not even mentioned in the *Times* review. Not until *The Wizard of Oz* (1939) was he given material at all worthy of his unique comic gifts.

The last well-known comedian to fall on his face in '30s films was Milton Berle, who in *New Faces of 1937* (1937), starring Joe Penner, was termed by Nugent "variably effective except for his usual tendency to overdo things . . . his material always has the advantage of being tested by other comedians first." In *Radio City Revels* (1938)—a title RKO had been planning to use since 1929—Berle starred as one of a team of dried-up songwriters, but the film, said the *Times,* was "an unfortunate botching of comic talents." Berle did indeed make a few more successful films in the 1940s, but even then who could have imagined that he would be TV's first superstar?

For, of course, from the late '40s onward, it was TV that would make a comedian's name overnight (and, all too often, unmake

it almost as quickly, as he used up in one season material that would have lasted a vaudevillian a lifetime). Unless one counts such undistinguished teams as Abbott and Costello and Martin and Lewis, the last important comedians (until Woody Allen) to gain fame primarily on screen were Red Skelton, who began in 1941, and Danny Kaye, whose first picture was released in 1944. A new generation of clowns was waiting, all unheralded, in the wings; Jackie Gleason made a film in 1941 and Sid Caesar in 1946, without attracting the slightest notice, and by 1939 Lucille Ball, a Goldwyn Girl in 1933, was no more than a promising starlet at RKO, the studio whose property she would one day buy for Desilu Productions.

36

DIRECT FROM BROADWAY
Musical Comedies from the Stage

Clearly, the connections between comedy and music were constant and strong. As has been seen, almost all the comics discussed in the last chapter made their talkie debuts in the musicals to be covered in this and subsequent chapters. Chaplin composed scores for his films, Laurel and Hardy starred in MGM operettas, as Benny, Hope, Burns and Allen did in Paramount's *Big Broadcasts.* Even the Marx Brothers' vehicles usually included a song or two.

In the strict sense, *any* film in which the actors (even non-singers) burst into song, accompanied by an unseen orchestra and presently joined by large numbers of strang-

ers, all knowing the lyrics and dancing in unison, must be regarded as a form of fantasy. Surely the most striking evidence of the pathetic hunger of '20s movie audiences for just such entertainment was the extraordinary number of Broadway musicals and operettas filmed as *silents,* presumably with the actors pantomiming the songs to appropriate accompaniment. Thus Fields, as noted, made a silent version of *Poppy* as *Sally of the Sawdust* (1925), as Cantor did of *Kid Boots* (1926). Others in this bizarre cycle of "silent musicals" included *Sally, Irene and Mary* (1925), *Sally* (1925), *Irene* (1926), *Tip Toes* (1927), *Oh, Kay* (1928) and *Lady Be Good* (1928).

As a matter of fact, there had never been any such thing as a literally silent film. Long before sound tracks, as far back indeed as *The Birth of a Nation* (1915), in the largest picture palaces full orchestras played special scores supplied by the studios, the second-run chain theaters echoed to the throb of the mighty Wurlitzer and in even in the smallest neighborhood houses a pianist sat grinding out "ride, rape and rescue" music—or, from the mid-'20s on, the theme song.

Thus the public appetite for sound movie musicals, when the first ones appeared, early in 1929, was well-nigh insatiable. Since in this field 1929 and 1930 form one continuous period, it has seemed better to cover both years rather than to start arbitrarily with January 1930. Fortunately for those New Yorkers interested in the complete history, during the summer of 1971 at the Museum of Modern Art Miles Kreuger, foremost authority on musical films, arranged and introduced an extraordinary series, under the title of *The Roots of the American Musical Film (1927–32)*, which showed an unbelievable number of musicals from those truly pioneer, relatively forgotten years. Many of the observations in this and the following chapters owe much to Mr. Kreuger's excellent program notes, as well as to his book *The Movie Musical from Vitaphone to 42nd Street,* which he compiled and edited from reviews, ads, articles, interviews and photographs that appeared in *Photoplay* magazine 1926–33.

Long before the end of 1929 Hollywood had found its own musical voice, but, even so, almost every successful musical comedy and operetta of the '20s was filmed (most during 1930), many in Technicolor, some with their original stage stars. A few silent stars, notably Bebe Daniels and Ramon Novarro, surprised everyone with their good singing voices, but far more musical performers were imported from Broadway (or vaudeville, night clubs, radio or even the Met). Few of these achieved lasting success on the screen. John Boles and Walter Pid-

geon, who had acted in silents, survived by returning to straight dramatic roles. Likewise Jeanette MacDonald, Ginger Rogers and Irene Dunne were versatile enough to hold their own in non-musicals whenever necessary.

Self-evidently, then, one of Hollywood's top priorities in those years was to give the fans what (unless they lived in New York or some other large city) they had been missing: the latest hits of the Broadway musical stage, of which radio had made them more aware than ever before.

As distinguished from operettas, the typical musical comedies of the '20s, the kind of thing perfectly parodied in *The Boy Friend,* were usually strung on story lines flimsy to the point of absurdity—some, incredibly, based on long-forgotten farces, others regularly turned out by such expert practitioners as Guy Bolton, William Anthony McGuire and P. G. Wodehouse. Since many were built around female stars, the titles often included girls' names (*Irene, Sally, Sunny, No, No, Nanette, Oh, Kay*); the alternative was snappy two-word phrases (*Sit Tight, Hold Everything, Follow Through, Good News, Great Day, Top Speed, Queen High*).

Who cared about the plot, if any, as long as it left plenty of openings and provided cues for the musical numbers? The score customarily included, for the stars, several love duets and solos (interchangeable not only from one scene to another but from one show to another, since they never grew out of character or situation), a few lively patter numbers for the comedians or sidekick couple, full of topical references to rumble seats and bathtub gin and New York "in" jokes about Hoboken and Yonkers and, of course, high-stepping, kick-in-a-row dance routines for the chorus.

Although the heroine of Ziegfeld's *Sally* becomes a star in his *Follies,* backstage plots were not especially popular. More typically, the standard ingredients were tossed together in some attractive modern setting familiar to well-to-do Americans, such as a country club, a Long Island estate, a yacht or a luxury liner, a college campus, a resort hotel, a dude ranch or anywhere else where sheiks and flappers could enjoy their flaming youth making whoopee. Unfortunately, almost all the theater music composed in the '20s by Berlin, Kern, Porter, Rodgers, Youmans and even Gershwin had to be fitted to these conventions.

The ads for *Paris* (1929), the first musical comedy to make the transition to talkies, sounded what was to become the dominant note in publicizing such films:

You'll see a famous stage star in *Paris*—Irene Bordoni . . . with all the color, songs and comedy that captivated critical Manhattan. See for yourself why thousands paid $4.40 per seat . . .

This was a bit disingenuous, considering that none of Cole Porter's score was used. Yet it is clear that even before the Wall Street crash, the chance *at last* to see and hear at neighborhood movie prices the very shows and stars for which "critical Manhattan" had shelled out the then astronomical prices of $4.40 or $6.60 was undoubtedly a strong selling point—but even more so as affluent 1929 darkened into troubled 1930.

In a 1930 interview in *Photoplay* John Murray Anderson flatly predicted: "The legitimate stage, except in New York, will die. For who in the world will pay five or six dollars to see a revue done on the stage with shoddy scenery, second-rate actors and second-rate musicians, when for less than a dollar they can see a show like *The Rogue Song* . . ."

Still, although *Paris* was enthusiastically hailed by reviewers, Bordoni's only other early talkie appearance was a single number in *Show of Shows*, released the same month. However durable her "naughty" Gallic charm, invariably compared to Anna Held's, how many musicals could be built around a heavily accented, decidedly mature lady who had made her American debut in 1912?

Marilyn Miller's screen debut in *Sally* (late 1929) was given an even more hyperbolical build-up. "Now the Screen has Robbed the Stage of its Most Prized Possession!" exulted the Warners ads.

Though *Sally* had enjoyed its stage success

in 1920, the *Times* found much still to praise in it: ". . . the most beautiful picture that has come to the screen and so far as Miss Miller is concerned one never wearies of her nimble dancing." Though five new songs by others were added to the Kern score, no attempt was made to update the simple Cinderella tale of a foundling who, while flipping pancakes in a restaurant window, attracts a wealthy young man (Alexander Gray) and, after becoming a *Follies* star, eventually gets him, in a standard bridal finale, with everyone singing "Look for the Silver Lining."

Miller made two more films, spaced a year apart, each timed for the holiday trade: *Sunny* (1930), opposite Lawrence Gray, based on her 1925 stage hit, in which she played a circus bareback rider and sang Kern's "Who?", and *Her Majesty Love* (1931), in which her lowly position as a barmaid in a Berlin cabaret stands in the way of her marriage to wealthy Ben Lyon. Both were well reviewed, but did not click at the box office.

Nevertheless, 1930 brought fourteen more musicals (not even counting operettas) adapted from the stage, and still more announced, notably MGM's superelaborate *The March of Time,* then quietly shelved before the end of the year, as were *Rosalie* and *The Five O'Clock Girl,* both scheduled for Marion Davies.

The year (1930) had started off with the release of two Youmans stage hits. *No, No, Nanette* marked the apparently auspicious screen debut of Bernice Claire (who lasted through only six films) opposite Alexander Gray (ditto), but did *not* include the Youmans music, now considered standard.

A middle-aged Bible publisher (Lucien Littlefield), who takes a purely philanthropic interest in young women with names like Betty from Bridgeport and Flossie from Frisco, is trailed by his suspicious wife (Louise Fazenda) to Atlantic City, where their niece, Nanette (Claire) is trying to produce a musical. The only two numbers in the film were both parts of the show within the show.

The other Youmans musical, *Hit the Deck,*

Bernice Claire in No, No, Nanette

though made by the director of *Rio Rita,* was blasted by both newspapers and magazines. "The fun is labored," said the *Times,* "and the romance is more painful than sympathetic." The big hit, "Hallelujah!," a rousing choral number sung by blacks, was worked into a story largely set on a battleship. Jack Oakie played an amorous gob and Polly Walters the waitress he was pursuing.

The New York premiere of *Hold Everything* in April 1930 marked the opening of the elaborate new Hollywood Theatre, at Broadway and Fifty-first, an event that quite overshadowed the film, a routine vehicle for Joe E. Brown and Winnie Lightner, with a prize-fight background. Unseasonably released in July, and largely ignored, *Spring Is Here,*

the first Rodgers-Hart musical on screen, again teamed Bernice Claire and Alexander Gray and included the original song hits, "Yours Sincerely" and "With a Song in My Heart," but others had been added by other writers, "Have a Little Faith in Me" and "Cryin' for the Carolines."

August brought a trio of recent Broadway hits, Joe Cook's *Rain or Shine* (made without the music), *Top Speed,* another Joe E. Brown vehicle, involving motorboat racing, and *Queen High,* which received by far the best reviews. Frank Morgan and Charlie Ruggles were partners in a garter business, one of whom loses a bet that requires him to work for a year as the other's butler. Meanwhile Morgan's nephew (Stanley Smith) and

Ruggles' niece (Ginger Rogers) fall in love.

In September came *Follow Through,* with Jack Haley repeating his stage role as a woman-hating millionaire and Nancy Carroll and Buddy Rogers as the lovers whose romance is played out against a background of professional golf. The big production number featured chorus girls dressed as angels who turn into devils, but the hit song was "Button Up Your Overcoat!" A few weeks later *Heads Up,* again with Buddy Rogers as juvenile, allowed Victor Moore to re-create *his* stage role in a mishmash involving bootleggers and the Coast Guard.

But undoubtedly the best of the Broadway-to-Hollywood musicals, the one that topped off this 1930 cycle, was the Goldwyn-Ziegfeld production (the only film Ziegfeld ever supervised) of his 1928 hit *Whoopee,* which not only retained its score and its original star, Eddie Cantor at his height, but also much of the original New York talent, especially the irrepressible Ethel Shutta and her husband, George Olsen, whose fifty-man dance band had played for the show during its run at the New Amsterdam.

One departure from the stage production was Busby Berkeley's flexible use of the camera in the dance routines, including some of his first overhead shots. This was the film that introduced the Goldwyn Girls, including recognizably, Claire Dodd, Virginia Bruce and, as chorus leader, Betty Grable. Unlike Berkeley's later spectacles for Warners musicals, the "Cowboy," "Mission" and "Indian" numbers are integrally related to the locale and to the story line, such as it is.

In this funny, lighthearted version of Owen Davis' play *The Nervous Wreck,* Cantor plays a comic hypochondriac, with Shutta as his energetic nurse. The secondary romance is resolved by a typical racist cop-out, in which juvenile Paul Gregory is proved to be not an Indian, after all, but white, so worthy to marry ingenue Eleanor Hunt.

From the score, the only survival is "Makin' Whoopee," which, typically, has nothing to do with either couple. Cantor sings it di-

rectly to the audience, as a lightly cynical comment on marriage à la mode, from the wedding to the divorce.

Cantor's exuberant performance makes one understand why, out of all the musical stars and comedians who made early talkies of their stage hits, he was the only one to enjoy instant and lasting success. Said *Photoplay* (October 1930) : "There is no attempt at realism. It's simply a rollicking, roistering, beautiful production that will make you forget Hoover's advice to sit tight because better times are coming. Heck! They are *here!*"

Even so, by the end of 1930 the public was sated with such a surfeit of Technicolor bonbons. Now when reviewers found themselves liking a musical, they began to sound apologetic or defensive. Thus it was no coincidence that 1931 saw only *three* musical comedies taken from the stage: *Fifty Million Frenchmen,* shorn of its Cole Porter score (later used in a short subject, *Paree, Paree*), Bert Lahr in *Flying High* and Eddie Dowling in a poorly reviewed version of his forgotten 1925 vehicle, *Honeymoon Lane,* something about the visit of a king of another of those mythical kingdoms to an American health resort.

1932 brought only a single filmed stage musical, Gershwin's *Girl Crazy,* which the *Times* reviewed without mentioning the music, "but with Bert Wheeler and Robert Woolsey at their best, it offers a brand of humor that few could resist." In fact, though the Western setting was retained, it had been turned into a Wheeler-Woolsey vehicle.

The Gershwin songs were virtually thrown away: "Bidin' My Time" as background to a comic scene in the cemetery where the town's short-lived sheriffs are buried, the wistful "But Not for Me" likewise played for laughs by Eddie Quillan and Arline Judge and reprised by Mitzi Green impersonating Bing Crosby, George Arliss and Edna May Oliver. "I Got Rhythm" is indeed given a production number, with even the cactus plants swaying in time to the music, but Kitty Kelly, who sings it, was no Merman.

Nat Pendleton, Bert Wheeler, Robert Woolsey, Kitty Kelly in **Girl Crazy**

For the rest of the decade, only one or two stage musicals a year were filmed. The only pure examples of the farcical type (both 1936) were *Sons O'Guns,* a Broadway hit of 1929, with Joe E. Brown turned loose in wartime France (and no mention of the music in the *Times* review), and *Anything Goes,* with Charlie Ruggles replacing Victor Moore as Moonface Martin, Public Enemy Number Thirteen, in itself a bright and amusing film. For once, Ethel Merman was allowed to belt

out the Cole Porter numbers she had done on stage, especially "I Get a Kick out of You" and "You're the Top."

One main reason why so few stage musicals were filmed in the later '30s is that, pending the great rebirth that was to begin with *Oklahoma!* (1943), not that many great musicals were being written for Broadway itself. In fact, many of the very best musicals of the day were being created, by the most talented composers, directly for the screen.

37

"LET'S FACE THE MUSIC AND DANCE"
From Imitations to Originals

As suggested by the number of original scores dropped from the screen versions of Broadway musicals, a common fear among producers, despite all evidence to the contrary, was that even the biggest hits of a season or two before might meanwhile have been overplayed to the point of saturation. Why take that risk when one could just as easily (and perhaps less expensively) assign studio songwriters or, for that matter, hire the best New York talent to dream up something new, created expressly for the screen? Thus even while transplanting so many stage musicals, Hollywood very quickly learned how to produce not only reasonably exact facsimiles thereof but its own original musicals.

One of the first cycles to blaze across early talkie screens like skyrockets, though at the time the most novel, yet, like all such pioneer musical genres, played out before the end of 1930, was the all-star revue, each designed to showcase the talents of a studio's whole roster of contract players, as if to prove that every last one of them could not only talk, but, if called upon, sing and dance.

On Broadway, of course, the '20s were the golden age of the annual revues, not only the familiar *Follies, Vanities* and *Scandals* but the *Music Box Revues,* the *Passing Shows,* the *Garrick Gaieties,* the *Blackbirds,* the *Greenwich Village Follies, Artists and Models* and several more. Thus the format of MGM's

The Hollywood Revue of 1929 (originally to have been called *Revue of Revues*) could hardly be considered a daring experiment, yet for *movies* it was indeed a departure, and, while it lasted, a most successful one.

Proof of the pudding was the rapidity with which four other major studios followed the leader: Warners' *Show of Shows,* late in 1929, and in 1930 Fox's *Happy Days, Paramount on Parade* and, last of the cycle, Universal's *King of Jazz.* RKO several times announced *Radio City Revels,* even updating the title to *Radio City Revels of 1930,* but it was never made. At this point Columbia was too small, hardly a level above the independents, with no galaxy of stars to mount such a venture, and United Artists, of course, was a releasing organization for individual producers.

Despite their titles, *Fox Movietone Follies* (1929) and *New Movietone Follies of 1930* were not revues but backstage musicals, as also was *Happy Days.* The other four films mentioned were indeed Broadway-type revues, with tuxedoed masters of ceremonies introducing black-out skits, stand-up comedians, star solos and duets and huge production numbers; in some, a curtain was lowered between scenes, to create the illusion that the viewer was watching a live performance from an orchestra seat.

The inclusion of the date in the title *The Hollywood Revue of 1929* seemed to promise an annual edition, but before a year had passed, not only had the Depression set in, but the screen's first musical wave had subsided. Among those present in *Hollywood Revue* were Jack Benny, Buster Keaton, Laurel and Hardy, Dressler and Moran, but it also used almost everyone at MGM except Ramon Novarro, William Haines and the two stars the public would probably have given most to see, Garbo and Lon Chaney.

Though it may now look like filmed vaudeville, choppy and poorly paced, *Hollywood Revue* pointed the way other such productions were to take. It included color sequences with elaborate sets, it paid lip service to culture with Norma Shearer and John Gilbert doing the balcony scene from *Romeo and Juliet,* it used trick photography to miniaturize stars (Bessie Love and Marion Davies), its tongue-in-cheek version of "While Strolling Through the Park One Day" was one of the talkies' first examples of the Gay '90s nostalgia that was soon to become so prevalent, and it ended with a grand finale in which the whole cast sang chorus after chorus of the big number—"Singin' in the Rain," which was to serve MGM so well in many a later musical.

Warners' *Show of Shows* picked up these cues and tried to go MGM one better. The entire film was in Technicolor, with *only* stars and featured players, more than seventy, in every role, right down to the chorus. Again the Gay '90s vogue was reflected in three numbers, the comic Florodora Sextette, "Singin' in the Bathtub," done in '90s bathing suits, and "A Bicycle Built for Two." Culture was served in an elaborately staged scene from *Henry VI, Part 3,* in which John Barrymore as Gloucester, the future Richard III, gloats fiendishly over the deaths of his enemies.

Fairly original (for movies) was a variation on the girls-of-all-nations motif then popular in stage revues, in which eight pairs of real off-screen sisters, in costumes of the lands of their ancestors, did brief song and dance routines before combining in an inter-national finale. They included Dolores and Helene Costello (American), Loretta Young and Sally Blane (French) and Sally O'Neil and Molly O'Day (Irish).

One amusing skit featured Beatrice Lillie, Louise Fazenda, Frank Fay and Lloyd Hamilton reciting alternately lines of four different ballads, which combine to tell an altogether different story. Fay, however, with his vain, patronizing manner, was an unfortunate choice for M.C., and the finale, "Lady Luck," in which the entire cast finally pops their heads through a giant curtain, is danced to exhaustion and sung to stupefaction.

By any standards, the weakest of these all-star specials was *Happy Days* (1930), which Fox opened at the Roxy with much fanfare as the first picture filmed in "Grandeur," a new wide-screen process. As if, despite the success of *Hollywood Revue* and *Show of Shows,* the producers feared to release a film without some shred of a story, the star turns were presented in a feeble framework, as all part of a benefit to save an old show boat. Janet Gaynor and Charles Farrell, Victor McLaglen and Edmund Lowe, and even Will Rogers were all worked into the act, all playing themselves in forgettable numbers.

Paramount on Parade (1930) was considered the best of its kind so far, if only because of its use of eleven directors, supervised by Elsie Janis, whose varied styles made it more cinematic than the others. It also depended less on spectacular production numbers than on the sly, mocking wit so often found in Paramount's early talkies. Jack Oakie, Skeets Gallagher and Leon Errol were the comic M.C.'s.

Chevalier got top billing, but he shared the plaudits with, among others, that remarkably talented child Mitzi Green, who did deadly impersonations of George Arliss, Helen Kane (the original "Boop-boop-a-doop" Girl, who also appeared in this film) and even of Chevalier himself. The obligatory cultural note was sounded by Nino Martini as a gondolier singing "Torna a Sorrento," but far more effective were such highlights as *Murder Will Out,* a satire on mysteries, in which Warner Oland as Fu Manchu kills both Sherlock Holmes (Clive Brook) and Philo Vance (William Powell). In another sketch, *Impulses,* George Bancroft and Kay Francis are among the guests at a formal dinner party at which everyone exchanges polite banalities; then the same people are shown speaking and acting out what they *really* feel. Bancroft ends by tossing his hostess' obnoxious brat out a window.

Surprisingly, the most impressive and the last of the all-star extravaganzas came from Universal: *King of Jazz* (1930), directed by John Murray Anderson, then at the height of his fame as the creative genius behind some of the most lavish Broadway musicals, including several editions of Ziegfeld's *Follies.* Among the major assets of *King of Jazz* are truly imaginative settings and photography. As the only one of these revues shown in New York in recent years in the original Technicolor, it holds up beautifully; except for the absence of real blue, the color is by no means as garish or distorted as might be feared; flesh tones come through very well.

After a cartoon opening depicting Paul Whiteman's coronation as King of Jazz, Whiteman himself introduces his orchestra by opening a suitcase, from which forty tiny musicians emerge, then grow to normal size. Some of the comedy black-outs may now seem deplorable, but all else works beautifully, including John Boles' solo of "It Happened in Monterey," which became one of the hits of the year. The Whiteman orchestra's rendition of *Rhapsody in Blue* (the only Gershwin music used) must be approximately what the audience heard on that historic night when it was first played in Aeolian Hall.

It is, however, the visual spectacle that is most striking. One number, "The Bridal Veil," depicts exquisitely costumed brides of several different epochs, starting with the seventeenth century—a favorite pattern in stage revues of the time—all leading up to the modern bride, with sixteen bridesmaids car-

rying the biggest veil ever made. The "Tapping Feet" number has chorus girls descending onto a carefully constructed large-scale miniature of New York, anticipating by three years Busby Berkeley's climactic number in *42nd Street.*

Best of all, both in concept and execution, is the finale, "The Melting Pot," in which, to appropriate imagery, the folk songs of various nations all blend into an American jazz symphony. To quote Everson, *King of Jazz* is "not only an accurate reconstruction of a typical Anderson Broadway revue, but an accurate mirror of the tastes in comedy, music, fashion *et al.* of the period. This is the kind of thing that just cannot be reproduced."

Indeed it never has been. Five films made within one year hardly constitute a genre, but this was surely a significant and, on the whole, creative cycle. Though the format and much of the talent came from the stage, instead of statically photographing a Broadway revue, then attaching a backstage story, as was done, for instance, in *Glorifying the American Girl* (1930), the specific aim was to display all that film, and *only* film, could do with sound and color and dazzling camera magic. An original screen revue was not even attempted again until MGM's *Ziegfeld Follies* (1946). Both *Star-Spangled Rhythm* and *Thank Your Lucky Stars* had stories.

If half the appeal of such spectacular revues was that their effects could be achieved *only* on screen, there was still money to be made from more conventional fare. During 1929 indeed it seemed that almost *any* kind of musical made a hit. Thus began the westward trek that, before the decade was half over, brought every major (and many a minor) composer for the theater to Hollywood.

Among the first, Irving Berlin began by writing theme songs: "Marie" for Vilma Banky's last silent, *The Awakening* (1928), and the title song for *Coquette* (1929), Mary Pickford's first talkie, then the title song and two others for *Puttin' On the Ritz* (1930), though not the biggest hit, "There's Danger in Your Eyes, Cherie!"

Rodgers and Hart started with a screen original, *The Hot Heiress* (1931), Gershwin with *Delicious* (1931), Harold Arlen with *Let's Fall in Love* (1934), Kern with *I Dream Too Much* (1935) and Porter (perhaps disappointed by the fate of the scores of *Paris, Fifty Million Frenchmen* and *The Gay Divorcee,* but pleased by the fidelity of *Anything Goes*) with *Born to Dance* (1936).

Unique was the team of De Sylva, Brown and Henderson, who, from 1929 onward concentrated almost exclusively on writing and producing musicals for Fox. Others, perhaps less famous but equally adept at turning out popular hits, included such composers and teams as Victor Schertzinger, first at Paramount, then at Columbia, Herbert Stothart, Arthur Freed and Nacio Herb Brown at MGM, at Paramount Richard Whiting, Robin and Rainger, and Gordon and Revel, who later moved to Warners, where Sammy Fain and Warren and Dubin also worked. Jimmy McHugh and Kalmar and Ruby wrote for various studios. This does not include, of course, those composers, generally considered to be more "serious," who wrote not popular songs but background music for non-musical films. Among these the most important names in the '30s were Alfred Newman, Max Steiner, Erich Wolfgang Korngold and Franz Waxman.

The first truly *original* screen musical, both in the sense of being written for the screen and in the much rarer sense of avoiding the prevailing 1929 clichés: backstage (starting with *Broadway Melody*), country club (*Tanned Legs* was the first), collegiate (as in *The Time, the Place and the Girl*) and American Cinderella (of which *Sunny Side Up* was the prime example), was MGM's *Marianne,* released in October 1929, in which Marion Davies, who surely could have chosen the most glamorous possible vehicle for her talkie debut, courageously appeared as a simply dressed French peasant girl and even spoke with a convincing accent—at a time when foreign stars were frantically taking English diction lessons or else heading back to Europe.

Though not an operetta either in musical ambitions or style, its lightly romantic tone and rural setting in wartime France make it a kind of tuneful adieu to those lovers so popular in late silents, the French ma'amselle and her soldier boy (as in *The Big Parade, What Price Glory?, Seventh Heaven* and *Lilac Time*)—in this case a Yank. As Kreuger notes, "*Marianne* is a modest bauble that deserves to be better known."

In a more familiar vein, perhaps the film that did most to diminish the impact of Warners' *Sally* on 1929 holiday audiences was Fox's very popular *Sunny Side Up,* released the same month as *Marianne.* Written by De Sylva, Brown and Henderson, it starred the screen's favorite young lovers, Janet Gaynor and Charles Farrell, in their joint all-talkie debut, in a story remarkably parallel to *Sally,* about a poor East Side girl, a wealthy boy, his haughty mother and his catty debutante fiancée, all happily resolved at a big charity benefit show at a Long Island estate. The all-*new* score included at least four immediate hits: the title number, "I'm a Dreamer, Aren't We All?", "Turn on the Heat" and the timely "If I Had a Talking Picture of You."

The successful *Sunny Side Up* was soon followed by *High Society Blues* (1930), in which Gaynor and Farrell reversed social positions. Her parents (William Collier, Sr., and Hedda Hopper) are Scarsdale blue bloods, while his (Lucien Littlefield and Louise Fazenda) are parvenus from Iowa. The forgotten score (by McCarthy and Hanley) included at least one timely number, "I'm in the Market for You."

In the same amiably romantic vein was Paramount's hit *Honey*[1] (1930), based on a 1921 play, *Come Out of the Kitchen.* Nancy

---

[1] The title, evidently meant to recall the 1929 football musical, *Sweetie,* also starring Carroll and Smith, is meaningless. The score does *not* include the popular song of the day "Honey."

Carroll and Skeets Gallagher, sister and brother, impoverished Virginia aristocrats, rent their mansion to a pushy Yankee matron (Jobyna Howland) and her daughter (Lillian Roth), but stay on, serving as cook and butler. Of course the daughter and the brother pair off, as do her fiancé (Stanley Smith) and the sister.

Though the credits announce it as "a musical farce," it is another gentle, harmless little Cinderella romance, with some good comedy supplied by Zasu Pitts as a perpetually tearful upstairs maid and Mitzi Green as her bratty daughter. One wistful number, "In My Little Hope Chest," reprised three times, sounds exactly like the kind of thing spoofed in "A Room in Bloomsbury" from *The Boy Friend* —but the only hit, as irrelevant as "Hallelujah!" was in *Hit the Deck,* was the lively "Sing You Sinners," energetically sung by Roth at a Negro revivial meeting.

Before the end of 1930 the whole iridescent bubble had burst for this kind of musical comedy, as well as for most others. To cite but one example, after contributing three songs to Harry Richman's *Puttin' on the Ritz* (1930, a backstage story), Irving Berlin next applied his talents to Douglas Fairbanks, Sr.'s first modern-dress film in several years, *Reaching for the Moon,* which opened in December 1930, a few days after *Sunny.* Written and directed by Edmund Goulding, from an idea supplied by Berlin himself, this at least tried to be different, and to some extent succeeded. Said the *Times:* "Buffoonery de luxe, a soupcon of musical comedy plot, a hybrid conception of French farce, streaks of sentiment, acrobatics and clever modernistic settings . . ."

Set mainly aboard an ultraluxurious French liner, it cast Fairbanks as a tycoon so involved in his wheeling-dealing that he is strangely bashful with women—until all his inhibitions are dissolved by a wildly potent cocktail called "Angel's Breath." Bebe Daniels, turned blond, was the object of his affections. But, though surely the title song must have been written for this film, the *Times* review reports "There is only one song, which is called 'High Up and Low Down.'" Even more oddly, *Photoplay* says "Written by Irving Berlin, but no songs." To make the confusion complete, Miss Daniels' own explanation, quoted by John Kobal in *Gotta Sing, Gotta Dance,* is: "When it came out, the public had gone off musicals, and all except one or two numbers were cut. I had a song, 'Lower Than Lowdown,' which I sang while standing by the ship's bar." The upshot was that Berlin did not write for the screen again until *Top Hat* (1935), the first of three musicals he composed for Astaire and Rogers.

Presumably produced before the change of taste was apparent, *The Hot Heiress,* the first venture of Rodgers and Hart in writing for the screen, with a script by Herbert Fields, was released early in 1931. By coincidence, Ben Lyon, who was to be Bebe Daniels' husband, co-starred, playing a riveter. In an interview for the Kobal book, he recalled his work on the film:

It was an original story, which for the time was rare for musicals. Most of them were copies of stage hits, musical all-star revues or copies of *Broadway Melody* . . . It was all about an heiress (Barbara Hutton type, played by Ona Munson) who lives in a plush apartment house alongside of which a new building was being put up. When the new building reached her level, we saw each other and fell in love . . . As the buildings progressed in height, she kept moving to the flat above so we could keep meeting.[2]

In an interview with *Cinema* in 1930, Rodgers expressed his pleasant surprise at the congenial working conditions he found in Hollywood. He also articulated the difference between writing music for the stage and for the screen:

Most important in songs for the screen is their relevance. We are not making them numerous. They are seldom reprised. And they are all definitely connected with the story, pertinent to the actors and the action. We ease into them in the dialogue, so that before you know it, you realize

[2] *Gotta Sing, Gotta Dance, A Pictorial History of Film Musicals* (Hamlyn, 1970), p. 47.

that the characters are speaking lyrics and their gradual entry into the song appears very logical.[3]

Nevertheless, *The Hot Heiress,* from which no songs survive, was rather coolly received. Said the *Times,* "The story is too fragile and stale even for the films . . . but the comedy is bright and the tunes are in the gay Rodgers and Hart manner."

1931 was most definitely not a good year for musicals, original or otherwise. In fact, except for Cantor's *Palmy Days,* Chevalier's *The Smiling Lieutenant,* Lawrence Tibbett's *The Prodigal* and *The Cuban Love Song* (all black and white) and a few leftovers made late in 1930, 1931 produced practically no musicals at all.

Thus the timing of *Delicious,* the third Gaynor-Farrell musical, with Gershwin's first score written for a film, released for the 1931 holidays, could not have been worse. The best *Photoplay* could find to say about it was, "Encourage this clean picture by attending it." While conceding that it "found favor with the audience, among whom were many children," the *Times* rated it "a conventional piece of sentimentality."

Though admittedly a Cinderella romance, the story by Guy Bolton is fresher and livelier than those of *Sunny Side Up* and *High Society Blues,* which had been well received. As a wee, bonnie Scots lassie with a convincing burr in her speech, poor young Gaynor meets rich young Farrell (again) aboard the liner on which she is immigrating to America, when he comes down to steerage to check on his favorite polo pony.

Refused entrance to the country because a relative withdraws his promise to support her, the girl jumps ship and is from then on pursued by a relentless immigration officer. Aided by comic butler El Brendel, she first hides out in Farrell's palatial Long Island home, then with a warmhearted Russian family she met on the boat (including composer Raul Roulien, whom she almost marries, thinking she has lost Farrell). In the end she

is deported but aboard finds Farrell, who has learned that it was his fortune-hunting fiancée (Virginia Cherrill) who betrayed Gaynor to the authorities.

The title song, pronounced in four syllables, "de-li-ci-ous," rhymed with "ca-pri-ci-ous" and "am-bi-ti-ous," is a big too coy, but the two production numbers were both highly original. The first is a dream sequence, the night before landing, in which the girl is welcomed to the city by Mr. Ellis (of Ellis Island), a jazzy Statue of Liberty, eight Uncle Sams and other symbolic figures. This is counterpointed by a nightmarish scene near the end, in which she flees through menacing Manhattan streets to themes from the "Second Rhapsody," here called "The New York Rhapsody." As Kreuger notes, the "montage keeps pace with the eccentric rhythms of the music . . . A brilliant sequence contains the most fluid use of a camera in any musical until Rouben Mamoulian's *Love Me Tonight* the following year."

For the next year or more, the only kind of musical to survive, chiefly at Paramount, was the lightly whimsical variety, in which characters burst into song without pretext, often leading up to it by rhymed dialogue—just what Rodgers and Hart had tried to achieve in *The Hot Heiress* and did, in fact, achieve in the above-mentioned *Love Me Tonight.* Then when the tide turned back with *42nd Street* (1933), these and almost all other musical genres were overwhelmed by endless variations on the backstage formula.

Other than Cantor's annual extravaganzas, among the few films to carry on the tradition of lighthearted musical comedy were the very relaxed and relaxing vehicles built around Bing Crosby, who was already well-known on radio and through short subjects when he appeared in *The Big Broadcast* (1932), which made him a movie star overnight. To be sure, he did his share of backstage epics (*Too Much Harmony,* 1933, *The Star Maker,* 1939), campus capers (*College Humor,* 1933, *She Loves Me Not,* 1934), one good Broadway adaptation (*Anything Goes,* 1936), a

---

[3] As quoted in Kobal, p. 47.

Western spoof (*Rhythm on the Range,* 1936), even one South Sea musical (*Waikiki Wedding,* 1937), but his best were usually a little further off the beaten path, even if based on plays or novels that clearly could not have held their own without music.

One of the better ones was *We're Not Dressing* (1934), which *The New Yorker* accurately describes as "a light, easy-going Paramount musical comedy about the wreck of a yacht on a desert island, taken (very loosely) from J. M. Barrie's *The Admirable Crichton.*" Crosby was a sailor, Carole Lombard the spoiled heiress, and among the other passengers were Ethel Merman and Leon Errol. The island is far from deserted, for Burns and Allen turn up as naturalists living there. (In his series of polite song titles, Crosby in this film sang "May I?", as he had earlier introduced "Please" and "Thanks.")

Here Is My Heart (1934) was based on a 1925 stage hit, *The Grand Duchess and the Waiter* (filmed by Adolphe Menjou in 1926), one of the first of many plays to spoof royalty exiled by the revolutions growing out of World War I. With Kitty Carlisle well cast as a bored, haughty Russian ex-Princess and Alison Skipworth (repeating her stage role), Roland Young and Reginald Owen as her dotty relatives, *Here Is My Heart,* said the *Times,* "in its satirical study of these pompous and indigent aristocrats, jabs with urbane skill at the arrogant and useless members of an outmoded royalty."

As a millionaire entertainer icily spurned by the Princess, Crosby masquerades as a waiter to insinuate himself into her favor, but eventually must buy the hotel to keep his future in-laws from being tossed into the street. Such sophisticated whimsey, set in Monte Carlo, so typical of Paramount, might well have made a Lubitsch operetta for Chevalier and MacDonald, but these three, alas, had moved to MGM to make *The Merry Widow.* The three songs by Rainger, Gensler and Robin, perfectly tailored to Crosby's style, were decidedly swinging hits: "Love Is Just Around the Corner," "I Think of You

with Every Breath I Take" and "It's June in January."

Mississippi (1935), from Booth Tarkington's novel *Magnolia,* which had been filmed in 1930 as *River of Romance,* was described by the *Times* as "a good-natured burlesque of the Mississippi duelling code." W. C. Fields co-starred, but Crosby was also given an excellent Rodgers-Hart score that included "Soon," "Easy to Remember" and "Down by the River."

Of his sixteen other '30s films, perhaps the best was *Sing You Sinners* (1938), in which he played the black sheep of a country family, the son of Elizabeth Patterson and brother of Fred MacMurray and Donald O'Connor (then a child), who finds fortune in Los Angeles by buying a horse that eventually wins. The hit songs were "I've Got a Pocketful of Dreams" and "Small Fry." Every Crosby musical included at least one big hit.

Yet the most elegant, visually entrancing film musicals created for specific talents in the '30s were the nine in which Fred Astaire and Ginger Rogers danced their way into a truly immortal niche in screen history, a team as ideally mated as William Powell and Myrna Loy or Katharine Hepburn and Cary Grant. Thus perhaps the most significant event of the musical screen in 1933 was not, after all, the backstage counterrevolution started by *42nd Street,* but the teaming of Astaire and Rogers later that year as decidedly secondary characters, not even a couple, in RKO's *Flying Down to Rio,* in which non-singing, non-dancing Dolores Del Rio and Gene Raymond were the romantic leads.

This was for its time a decidedly innovative musical, one of the first to exploit the possibilities of Latin-American rhythms and settings, later to become so popular. The truly spectacular finale (satirized in Ken Russell's film of *The Boy Friend,* 1971) is the one in which chorus girls dance to the title number apparently on the wings of planes flying high over Rio. The Youmans score also included the sensuous tango "Orchids in the Moonlight" and the beautifully staged "Carioca," the first number ever danced on screen by Fred and Ginger.

Of their remaining eight films, only the first two were based on stage musicals, *The Gay Divorcee* and *Roberta.* The rest were written for them by some of Broadway's best composers. Despite their flimsy, boudoir farce plots, they still glitter with high polish, far above the prevailing movie musical clichés of their day. They are simply among the best American screen musicals of the decade, and therefore of all time.

In a work of the scope of the present one, it is impossible to do more than take note of these delightful films, chiefly distinguishable by which songs and dances they featured. Although in 1932 Astaire had starred successfully (248 performances) on Broadway in Porter's *The Gay Divorce,* the film (1934) not only added an "e" to the title but dropped the Porter score, except for the unforgettable "Night and Day." Four new songs were added, notably "Don't Let It Bother You" by Gordon and Revel and the big dance number, "The Continental," by Conrad and Magidin.

The book by Dwight Taylor was no more than a standard mistaken identity farce, in which, because he happens to utter a certain remark at a certain time ("Chance is the fool's name for fate"), Rogers thinks Astaire is a professional correspondent (Erik Rhodes) hired to help her get a divorce. Edward Everett Horton and Alice Brady were the comic older couple who became standard in the Astaire-Rogers vehicles, but the interest, of course, is in the dance numbers, especially "Night and Day," which Arlene Croce in her *The Fred Astaire and Ginger Rogers Book* calls "this incomparable dance of seduction."

Despite the great success of *The Gay Divorcee,* Astaire and Rogers were back playing the secondary couple again in *Roberta* (1935), based on the Kern-Harbach Broadway hit of 1933–34, with Irene Dunne (billed first) and the non-singing Randolph Scott (billed fourth) in the nominal leads. The book, from Alice Duer Miller's novel *Gowns*

by Roberta, about an American football hero who inherits a Parisian dress salon from his aunt (Helen Westley), a famous *couturier,* and falls in love with her assistant, an exiled Russian princess, was not much more than an excuse for a lovely Kern score and a lavish fashion show, but the songs include the classic "Smoke Gets in Your Eyes," as well as well as "Yesterdays," "I Won't Dance" (adapted for Astaire and Rogers from a number in the unsuccessful Kern-Hammerstein operetta *Three Sisters,* seen only in London, 1934) and "Lovely to Look At," written for the film.

What makes *Roberta* still enjoyable is the contribution of Astaire and Rogers as the wisecracking secondary couple played on stage by Bob Hope and Lyda Roberti. As Croce puts it: "The vitalizing presence of Astaire and Rogers converted *Roberta* from Continental operetta to American musical comedy, and the film paved the way for *Swing Time.*"

Meanwhile came their second film of 1935 —one of their most admired—*Top Hat,* the first written specially for them, with a brilliant score by Berlin (his first movie music since *Reaching for the Moon* in 1930), around which Dwight Taylor built a script that was essentially a variation on *The Gay Divorcee,* which he had also written in its stage form. That fall, all America, if not dancing to "The Piccolino," was whistling or humming "Cheek to Cheek," "Isn't This a Lovely Day?" and "Top Hat, White Tie and Tails."

Edward Everett Horton was back, as were Erik Rhodes and Eric Blore, with sardonic Helen Broderick replacing Alice Brady as the older woman. Again the entire plot hinged on a mistaken identity that could have been cleared up at any point by one minute of simple explanation; Rogers goes through the whole film convinced that Astaire is the husband of Broderick, her best friend.

The total artificiality of *Top Hat* is underlined by the highly stylized, all-white set supposed to be Venice (without a single back projection), which bears no resemblance whatever to the real city, where, as any tourist knows, all gondolas are painted black. Yet in fairness it must be noted that all the musical numbers, unlike Busby Berkeley's, could conceivably be done on an actual stage.

Croce sums it up best:

In the class-conscious Thirties, it was possible to imagine characters who spent their lives in evening dress—to imagine them as faintly preposterous holdovers from the Twenties, slipping from their satin beds at twilight, dancing the night away and then stumbling, top-hatted and ermine-tangled, out of speakeasies at dawn.[4]

Follow the Fleet (1936) brought them back to America and down to earth in San Francisco, with Astaire and Randolph Scott as sailors, Rogers as an entertainer (not a hostess) in a dime-a-dance palace and Harriet Hilliard as her mousy sister, a music teacher. Though supposedly based on *Shore Leave,* the same 1922 comedy that had inspired *Hit the Deck,* the plot bears little resemblance. What is clearest in the rather tedious story is that, though Astaire and Rogers get star billing (as well they might at this point!), they spend most of their time when not dancing trying to get the other two back together.

Despite the dead weight of the plot, Astaire and Rogers were, as *The New Yorker* notes, "at their most buoyant," and the Berlin numbers include "We Saw the Sea" (a march tune with comic lyrics), "Let Yourself Go," with which the stars win a ballroom dance contest, "I'm Putting All My Eggs in One Basket," one of the few of their dances ever played for laughs, and the highly dramatic "Let's Face the Music and Dance," a veritable mini-ballet, acting out a playlet that has nothing to do with the plot, even symbolically, with the stars as a pair of ruined gamblers at Monte Carlo who save each other from suicide.

All the Continental chic of their previous films was concentrated in that one number; otherwise, *Follow the Fleet* bounced Astaire

[4] *The Fred Astaire and Ginger Rogers Book* (Galahad Books, 1972), p. 56.

and Rogers into mid-'30s America, the home of swing and big bands, where they were to remain for their next three films. *Swing Time* (1936), for which Jerome Kern wrote an exceptionally fine score (with lyrics by Dorothy Fields), is in the opinion of many the very peak of the series. As Croce puts it: "It is a world of night-time frolics . . . but it is also a middle-class, workaday, American world. It is top hats and empty pockets: Fred as a Depression dandy hopping a freight car, Ginger being sung to with soap in her hair." Yet on its opening the *Times* pronounced it "neither good Kern nor good swing."

The film is full of amusing reversals; in "Pick Yourself Up" Astaire pretends to learn to dance so that Rogers won't lose her job as instructor, "A Fine Romance" (surely the best of their sarcastic duets) is first sung by Rogers to Astaire, in a snowy landscape, and even the tender "The Way You Look Tonight" (which won the Oscar for best movie song of the year) was deliberately de-romanticized. Ginger is washing her hair as Astaire sings it. "Waltz in Swingtime," however, as well as "Bojangles of Harlem" and the climactic "Never Gonna Dance" are done straight.

As usual, the plot is negligible, but it does have a certain symmetry. It begins with Astaire missing his elaborately planned wedding to Betty Furness, and ends with Ginger walking out on her equally elaborate wedding to Georges Metaxa. A dancer with a talent for gambling, Astaire will be permitted a second chance to wed Furness, if he can make $25,000, so, once in love with Ginger, he tries to keep his winnings below that amount. Victor Moore and Helen Broderick as the comic sidekicks were certainly more fun than Scott and Hilliard in *Follow the Fleet.*

Shall We Dance (1937), for which Gershwin composed his first film score since *Delicious* (1931), was hailed by the *Times* as "one of the best things the screen's premiere dance team has done . . . Of course the pictures are formularized. But the amazing thing about them is their knack . . . of

Ginger Rogers, Fred Astaire in **Swing Time**

seeming fresh and individual and sparkling.''

By the mid-'30s ballet was becoming familiar to more Americans than ever before. Balanchine's *On Your Toes* was a hit on Broadway, and both Warners' *A Midsummer* *Night's Dream* and MGM's *Romeo and Juliet* had featured extended ballet sequences. Thus in *Shall We Dance* Astaire played an American ballet star who dances under a Russian name, then falls in love not only with Rogers, a successful ballroom dancer, but with that style of dancing.

The usual farcical complications ensue when, after meeting aboard a luxury liner bound for New York, the two stars, pursued by reporters, are wrongly publicized as secretly married and even expecting a child—a serviceable enough plot, but, as always, the main interest is in the numbers: "They All Laughed," "Let's Call the Whole Thing Off" (the by now standard quarreling duet), danced on roller skates in Central Park, and the wistful "They Can't Take That Away from Me," sung on a ferry from New Jersey, where they go to be married just so that they can be divorced.

For the first time in three years, the fall (1937) brought no new Astaire-Rogers film. The reason for their parting was, as Croce explains, not personal enmity but professional pride. Neither wanted to be known exclusively as half of a team. Thus Ginger appeared successfully in *Stage Door* (1937) and only slightly less successfully in *Vivacious Lady* (1938) and *Having Wonderful Time* (1938), while Fred made only *Damsel in Distress* (1937), opposite non-dancing Joan Fontaine.

It had a story (set in England) and screenplay by P. G. Wodehouse, music by Gershwin (his last completed film score), Burns and Allen in good form and, as the older couple, in this case the girl's father and aunt, impressively British Montagu Love and Constance Collier. The *Times* reviewer was well pleased with the results, but demure, twenty-year-old Fontaine was no substitute for Ginger, and though the plot was no more foolish than any of the others and "A Foggy Day" and "Nice Work If You Can Get It" became standards, the film was Astaire's first flop.

Thus the reunion of Astaire and Rogers in *Carefree* (1938), with Berlin providing his third score for them, was greeted with rapture by press and public. Written by Dudley Nichols and Hagar Wilde, the creators of *Bringing Up Baby* (1938), it is consistently amusing. The writers seemed to be deliber-

ately avoiding the formulae and clichés of the previous Astaire-Rogers films. No one mistakes anyone's identity, and there's not even another couple, unless one can count Luella Gear as Ginger's aunt and Clarence Kolb as her occasional escort.

Worried because Ginger, a radio singing star, keeps putting off their wedding, Ralph Bellamy, already typed as the perennial stuffy fiancé, sends her to his good friend Astaire, a psychoanalyst, who, to get her to dream, prescribes a horrendous assortment of indigestible food. But her dream (danced in slow motion to "I Used to Be Color Blind") reveals that she is in love with the doctor. To hold his interest, she invents a wildly complicated dream that convinces him she is indeed seriously maladjusted.

Under the influence of a drug meant to relax her inhibitions, she wanders out of his office, and, in a truly screwball sequence, acts out her every (mostly destructive) impulse, from smashing a plate-glass window to kicking a cop. Conscientiously, the doctor hypnotizes her into believing that she hates him and loves her fiancé. Realizing too late that he loves her, Astaire must spend the rest of the film undoing what he has done. A new dance step, "The Yam," never caught on, but the big number, "Change Partners," danced while Ginger is under hypnosis, responding to Fred's every move like a puppet, includes some of the most striking effects of the whole series.

The last Astaire-Rogers film of the '30s, *The Story of Vernon and Irene Castle* (1939), was a complete departure from all the others, set as it was from 1911 to 1918, based on the lives of a real dance team, using period music and close adaptations of the dances the Castles had done (supervised by Irene herself). As already mentioned, the film is one of the most charming expressions of the '30s' incurable nostalgia for the prewar years.

Judging by *The Whirl of Life* (1915), a film in which the Castles at their height played themselves, the 1939 picture sticks far closer to the truth than most show-biz "biopics," then or now. The sequence of their debut at the Café de Paris and its effect, for instance, is almost identical in both films. The one noticeable departure, to which Irene rightly objected, was that Walter Ash, the faithful servant who accompanied the Castles to Paris, was in life a Negro; in the 1939 film he is played by Walter Brennan.

In the very year (1937) that Astaire and Rogers first broke their established two-a-year pattern, thus foreshadowing the approaching end of the legendary series, a new musical cycle dawned, at times, like theirs, somewhat akin to operetta, yet distinctly different enough to be considered simply original screen musicals: the Deanna Durbin films.

MGM's one-reeler *Every Sunday* (1936), co-starring and, in effect, audience-testing the then unknown teen-agers Deanna and Judy Garland, is now a historic document. Not only did it foreshadow the disparate futures of the two, Judy as a singer of "pop" or "hot" songs, Deanna of "sweet" or "long-haired" music, but MGM's surprising retention of Judy, leaving Deanna free to be picked up by Universal, also determined their careers as stars, Judy as one of the mainstays of MGM, Deanna as quite literally the singlehanded savior of Universal—even more so than Mae West had been of Paramount or Shirley Temple of 20th Century-Fox.

Universal had fallen on evil days, with the Laemmle regime eased out and all the major directors gone, but fifteen-year-old Miss Durbin changed all that. As Everson notes, "Quite apart from the fresh and enchanting quality of both her personality and her movies, the money they made (and the best theaters clamored for them) not only helped keep Universal solvent but began to pile up assets in the bank."

Aside from her own beauty, voice, assured personality and keen comedy sense, credit for creating and maintaining Durbin's delightful screen image must also be given to the producer-director team of Joe Pasternak and Henry Koster, who had also worked together in Europe. In fact, *Three Smart Girls* (1937), their choice for her first vehicle, was a remake of a film they had done there.

Deanna, Nan Grey and Barbara Read, living in Switzerland with their mother (Nella Walker), on hearing that their estranged father (Charles Winninger) is about to remarry, rush to New York, where they stop at nothing to save him from a particularly rapacious gold digger (Binnie Barnes) and her scheming mother (Alice Brady), along the way arranging romances for the two older girls.

Perhaps the most remarkable fact about Durbin's quick and lasting success is that (like Garland) she achieved it at precisely that "awkward" age that was to end the career of Shirley Temple, as it had those of many another child star. Though her voice was mature enough to encompass the most demanding classical selections with ease, she always played a girl her own age, a bright, even mischievous, Miss Fixit, whose well-meant meddling in the affairs of others, especially adults, often got her into hot water. But though she might have cause to shed a few tears of regret or embarrassment, she was never threatened with the dire calamities that regularly overtook Temple.

Her second film, released later in 1937, was *One Hundred Men and a Girl*—a provocative title that meant nothing worse than that Deanna was trying to help that many unemployed musicians, including her father (Adolphe Menjou), to form their own symphony orchestra. This she manages by enlisting the aid of a wealthy couple (Alice Brady and Eugene Pallette, virtually replaying their *My Man Godfrey* roles) but, more important, by getting Stokowski (played by himself) to conduct them. The *Times* reviewer was completely enchanted:

The climactic scene . . . is as thrilling . . . as State's last-second touchdown, the hero's arrival at the Bloody Gulch saloon or the way the Bengal Lancers stormed the heights at Balaklava. Mr. Stokowski, having resisted all the importunities of Miss Durbin and her musical proteges, has retreated to his home. There the unemployed 101 follow him and, ranging themselves on the stairway, break appealingly into Liszt's Second Hungarian Rhapsody. The Maestro hears them, begins a gesture for silence; then, swept away by the defiant chords, by the entreaty and faith of the players, bethinks himself of his musicianship and enthusiastically becomes their conductor.

Mad About Music (1938) found Deanna back in Switzerland, this time in one of those exclusive schools, the daughter of a movie star (Gail Patrick), who loves her, but must keep her out of sight to protect her own glamour-girl image. To quiet inquisitive classmates (especially hostile Helen Parrish), the girl invents an explorer father, writes herself letters and, when challenged to produce him, drafts total stranger Herbert Marshall for the role.

Eventually, in Paris she brings him and her mother together. This was a pleasant change of pace for both Patrick, who usually played menaces, and Marshall. Says Everson: "The sight of Deanna and her school-mates bicycling through a California substitute for Switzerland, while Deanna sings 'I Love to Whistle,' is one of the most enjoyable images of pleasure from the late '30s."

A touch of youthful romance with Jackie Moran, barely hinted at in *Mad About Music,* was further developed with another Jackie, Cooper, in *That Certain Age* (1938), an intentionally "different" Durbin vehicle. Directed by Edward Ludwig instead of Koster, this is the one film in which the hitherto foolproof formula momentarily faltered. Based on a rather sophisticated story by F. Hugh Herbert, it cast Deanna as the daughter of a publisher (John Halliday) and his wife (Irene Rich).

When famed foreign correspondent Vincent Bullitt (Melvyn Douglas)—whose name combines those of real correspondent Vincent Sheean and Ambassador William Bullitt, then both very much in the public eye—becomes their house guest, Deanna develops such a deep crush on him that it takes all his efforts and those of his fiancée (Nancy Carroll) to disillusion the girl and send her back to her own contemporaries "Rather less sprightly, less infectiously musical and less finished a piece of cinema than *Mad About Music,*" said the *Times.*

Three Smart Girls Grow Up (1939) reunited Deanna with Koster and also with most of her screen family from *Three Smart Girls,* the same parents and butler and sister Nan Grey, but with Helen Parrish substituting for Barbara Read. In this one she rearranges the romances of her two sisters with Robert Cummings and William Lundigan. "Still her delightful self," reported the *Times.*

As noted earlier, *First Love* (1939) was a charming updating of the Cinderella story, in which Deanna was allowed to grow up, at least to the extent of receiving her first on-screen kiss, from Robert Stack. Two films later, she crossed the border into Viennese-style operetta, in *Spring Parade* (1940), with Henry Stephenson again playing Franz Josef, as he had also done in *The Night Is Young* (1935). Deanna's career continued until 1948, but it is still her earlier films, set in the then modern world of the '30s, that retain the greatest appeal.

Thus, quite apart from the many well-known films still to be discussed as operettas or backstage musicals, Hollywood had in a few short years gone from the crudity of stage-bound reproductions of Broadway hits to slavish imitations thereof to true screen originals, polished by the finest talents available to a level of grace, skill and charm that was, to be sure, sometimes equalled in the '40s and '50s when enhanced by color (especially at MGM), but has still never been surpassed.

38

SO THIS IS COLLEGE?
Campus Capers

Of all musicals with neither aspirations to operetta nor backstage frameworks to justify their songs, one of the most persistent throughout the decade was the college football musical, in itself an almost redundant term, since to movie-goers "college" and "football" were synonymous. Why else would anyone go to college except to play on or root for the varsity team?

Before skimming through the history of this peculiarly American phenomenon and its much rarer variant the non-musical (or even non-football) college film, note should be taken of the unique role of college in the popular imagination. This, to be sure, had been building up since the rollicking prewar years of Frank Merriwell, Dink Stover, Brown of Harvard and George Ade's *The College Widow*, and, of course, it meant not college as actually known to the small minority attending (only 1.1 million by 1930) but as fondly dreamed of by millions of others, a way of life at once caricatured and idealized not only in films but on radio, in popular songs, magazines and cartoons, as remote from most people's experience as a penthouse or a mythical kingdom, almost as exclusive a privilege of gilded youth as playing polo or wintering in Palm Beach.

The basis of all this fascination with college was the convergence of two national passions: for youth and for sports, never more frenzied than in the '20s. College football as played by the Ivy League was followed by millions of fans every Saturday on radio, then a few days later watched in newsreels.

Thanks to the leading jazz orchestras of the day (many of which looked and sounded collegiate), like Rudy Vallee and his Connecticut Yankees and Fred Waring and his Pennsylvanians, as well as theater organ recitals, vaudeville, band concerts and radio programs, college medleys, especially during the football season, were almost as popular as those from the Gay '90s. Children learned all the "fight" songs: "On, Wisconsin," "Cheer, Cheer for Old Notre Dame," "Anchors Aweigh," "On, Good Old Army Team," while their elders, most of whom had never gone to college, listened appreciatively to wistful glee club numbers like "The Whiffenpoof Song" and "The Sweetheart of Sigma Chi" or more rousing ones like "The Maine Stein Song," which Vallee in 1930 popularized into a best seller.

Not only college songs but songs *about* college life flourished. Two were variations on the "campus flirt" or "college coquette" theme: "Betty Co-ed" and "The All-American Girl."

Visually as well as aurally, the public was constantly reminded of the college generation. John Held, Jr.'s cartoons were only the best-known; the daily papers, *The Saturday*

Evening Post, Collier's, Judge, Life and, of course, *College Humor* itself were full of more or less good-natured caricatures of Joe College, with slicked-back hair parted in the middle, in a raccoon coat and pork-pie hat with the brim turned up in front, holding a football pennant, or, alternately, in a striped blazer and bell-bottomed flannels, or a letter sweater and plus fours, or any combination thereof, often playing a saxophone or a ukulele.

Naturally, Hollywood could not ignore this national fad. One of Harold Lloyd's biggest silent hits was *The Freshman* (1925), even Keaton made *College* (1927), and Clara Bow's first talkie was *The Wild Party* (1929), set in a girls' college. Indeed, *The American Film Institute Catalog . . . 1921–1930*, which classifies films by subject matter, lists seventy others about college during those ten years. Forty-five specifically concerned football, as indicated by such titles as *Drop Kick, Kick Off, The Forward Pass, Making the Varsity* and just plain *Varsity*. By 1929 reviewers were complaining of such films as a seasonal hazard.

As with gold-digger comedies and other genres, in this kind of film the '20s never ended. While real colleges, like most other institutions, were struggling with Depression problems: budget cuts, declining enrollments, radical student protests and strikes such as were not to be seen again until the late 1960s, on screen the campus remained untouched by the times, not so much a grove of academe as a youthful country club, in which the only important issues were sorority dances, fraternity pins, prom queens, freshman hazing and football rallies.

Just as if Wall Street had never laid an egg, Big Men on Campus, with only their fads and slang updated, went right on speeding in snappy, rumble-seated convertibles from frat house to roadhouse (where, alas, the star halfback was all too often tricked into getting drunk the night before the Big Game). Faculty members, if glimpsed at all, were invariably absent-minded professors, frumpish, eccentric oddballs quite capable of flunking important athletes merely because they couldn't pass the course.

The archetypal college musical was *Good News,* by De Sylva, Brown and Henderson, deservedly one of Broadway's biggest hits in 1927–28 (322 performances), but this did not reach the screen until 1930, by which time half a dozen other films had stolen the ball, so to speak. Warners kicked off in July 1929 with *The Time, the Place and the Girl,* which followed Grant Withers from gridiron stardom to success in Wall Street. This was followed a month later by Universal's *College Love,* a full-length spin-off from a popular silent series of short subjects collectively known as *The Collegians.* An ad in *Photoplay* for October 1929 says it all:

Red-hot youth aflame on the campus! A football game that will thrill you to the core! Moaning melodies put over by the University of California Glee Club! College chatter that will surprise you! Sorority parties, fraternity dances, roadhouse affairs that will amaze you.

The same month brought Pathé's *The Sophomore,* with Eddie Quillan and Sally O'Neil as the singing lovers, followed in October by Paramount's *Sweetie,* which introduced both Jack Oakie and Helen ("Boop-boop-a-doop") Kane to a waiting world, along with the song "My Sweeter Than Sweet." November saw MGM's *So This Is College,* with Elliott Nugent and Robert Montgomery among the undergraduates, and First National's *The Forward Pass,* which featured Douglas Fairbanks, Jr., and Loretta Young and four songs. It was set, said the *Times,* in "an institution that excels in football, saxophonists and romance." Even Tiffany, an independent studio, got into the act with the inept *Sunny Skies* (1930), whose title echoes those of both *Blue Skies* and *Sunny Side Up.*

Thus by the time *Good News* reached the public in September 1930, football musicals were hardly a novelty. Even so, the score was one of the best the composers had ever written: the title song, "Just Imagine," "Lucky in Love," "The Best Things in Life Are

Free" and, as the dancing grand finale, "The Varsity Drag."

As noted, De Sylva, Brown and Henderson created several successful musicals for Fox, notably *Sunny Side Up* (1929) and *Just Imagine* (1930), but they also sold their stage hits to other studios. What they themselves might have made of a screen version of *Good News* will never be known, but it would surely have been preferable to what MGM did with it, which was to make it not better but cheaper. "Just Imagine" and "Lucky in Love" were cut altogether, while the other hits were minimized or thrown away, except for the title number and "The Varsity Drag," both energetically put over by Dorothy Mc-Nulty (later known as Penny Singleton), though Bessie Love was the star. New songs added by Nacio Herb Brown, Arthur Freed and others in no way compensated for those dropped.

Said the *Times*: "*Good News,* as a film, combines all the faults of the poor musical comedy. This picture . . . is patterned and dull as it is raucous and unfunny."

This is one of the rare instances when a remake was far better than the original. The 1947 Technicolor version with June Allyson and Peter Lawford was done in proper '20s atmosphere, with the full score restored, as a good-humored spoof of flapper-age musicals.

Despite the poor reception of *Good News,* two more college football musicals of no distinction whatever, *Maybe It's Love* and *College Lovers,* rounded out 1930, after which they fell victim to the general moratorium on musicals during 1931 and 1932. Eight football films were made, including the bizarre mystery *70,000 Witnesses,* but not until 1933 did another campus musical appear: *College Humor,* which was well enough received to encourage Paramount to make five more variations during the decade.

In this one Bing Crosby was a professor at Mid-West U., Burns and Allen were on hand as caterers and Jack Oakie and Richard Arlen (veteran of several straight football films) were somewhat overaged students. Bing's best number was "The Old Ox Road," and the whole thing was done with such a light hand that the *Times* reviewer observed, "There are delightful moments when it seems to be on the verge of satirizing all the dreary collegiate films of the last decade."

1933 also saw Monogram's pleasant, "quasi-musical" *The Sweetheart of Sigma Chi,* which stood out if only because the sport on which the story hinged was not football but varsity rowing. Mary Carlisle is an insatiable collector of fraternity pins until she succumbs to love in the form of Buster Crabbe in time for him to stroke the crew to victory. Even more unusual was Fox's *Bachelor of Arts* (1934), which included many glee club numbers but involved no sport at all. A lazy student (Tom Brown), taken in hand by a co-ed (Anita Louise), buckles down and gets a job when he thinks her father has lost all his money.

MGM again proved its ineptitude at this kind of thing with *Meet the Baron* (1933), mentioned in connection with Durante and Jack Pearl. Though it did not involve football, the setting was Cuddle College, where Edna May Oliver was Dean Primrose. Even more disastrous was *Student Tour* (1934), which wasted the talents of both Durante and Charles Butterworth in a labored account of a world cruise of the co-eds and athletes of a college, in which the wallflower gets her man at a masquerade dance by the even then antiquated device of taking off her glasses.

Paramount reasserted its collegiate pre-eminence with a musical version of Howard Lindsay's hit farce *She Loves Me Not* (1934), in which a fiery cabaret dancer (Miriam Hopkins) who witnessed a gangland slaying hides out in a Princeton dormitory, with complications like *Charley's Aunt* in reverse, since she must be passed off as a boy. The romantic leads were Crosby and Kitty Carlisle, to whom he warbled the film's biggest hit, "Love in Bloom."

Collegiate (1936), also from Paramount, based on Alice Duer Miller's 1920 play *The Charm School,* brought Jack Oakie back sup-

Eddie Nugent, Bing Crosby, Miriam Hopkins in She Loves Me Not

porting Joe Penner, whom the *Times* dismissed, as noted, as a buffoon, not a humorist. In a variation on *Roberta,* also by Miller, Oakie was a playboy whose aunt's will makes him dean of a girls' school.

Relentlessly, Paramount continued the series with *College Holiday* (1936), with Benny, Burns and Allen and Martha Raye. As Benny observes in a curtain speech, they never permitted the story to interfere with art, but tossed both out the window. Mary Boland played a nutty millionaire who takes over a bankrupt hotel to use it as the laboratory for a eugenic experiment, with Benny

hired to comb the nation for perfect mating specimens.

With *College Swing* (1938), Paramount rounded out the decade, with the *Times* reviewer suggesting: "It might be a good thing all around if some enterprising company—why not Paramount?—would just stop trying to keep up plot appearances in musicals of this type, and advertise them frankly as variety shows . . ." Burns and Allen, Bob Hope and Edward Everett Horton were among those trapped in the wreckage. In all fairness, it must be admitted that none of these last four Paramount entries involved football.

The gridiron musical had meanwhile been taken over by 20th Century-Fox, with *Pigskin Parade* (1936), which gave all the old clichés some new satirical twists, to the delight of the *Times* reviewer: "*Pigskin Parade . . .* moves down the entertainment field with gusto and eclat, emerging as a genuinely funny burlesque of football and its musical comedy concomitants . . ."

Jack Haley played a new coach at an obscure Texas college that by a fluke finds itself scheduled to play Yale. When his aggressive wife (Patsy Kelly) causes the star halfback to break his leg, she scouts a hillbilly tosser of muskmelons (Stuart Erwin), who, using the credentials of a jailed campus radical (Elisha Cook, Jr.), beats Yale even though it means playing barefoot in the snow. As his kid sister Judy Garland in her first full-length film role put over three numbers, especially "It's Love I'm After," quite outshining such veteran co-eds as Arline Judge, Betty Grable and Dixie Dunbar.

Unfortunately, 20th Century-Fox went on to star the Ritz Brothers in *Life Begins in College* (1937), working their way through as proprietors of Klassy Kampus Klothes and bench warmers for the football team, until the inevitable climactic game.

Warners' only contribution to the campus musical was *Varsity Show* (1937), in which the students of Winfield College hire an alumnus (Dick Powell), a producer-director of musicals currently between jobs, to stage their annual show, against the bitter opposition of their faculty adviser (Walter Catlett), who wants them to do something more classical. Rather than let his supporters be expelled, Powell withdraws, but in their spring vacation the students, led by the co-ed (Rosemary Lane) who loves him, follow him to New York, take over an empty theater and, of course, produce a hit show, climaxed by a Busby Berkeley finale that includes just about every familiar college song.

The hit number was "Have You Got Any Castles?"; amusing also was "We're Working Our Way Through College" ("to get a lot of knowledge that we'll probably never, ever use again"). Though the *Times* welcomed the return of Ted Healy to the screen, its review was patronizing. In the *Herald Tribune*, the usually supercilious Lucius Beebe liked it much better. "Gay stuff, tuneful, fast and glittering . . . It belongs in the brighter category of Hollywood's travesties on the American scene with music."

Start Cheering (1938) offered Jimmy Durante one of his best opportunities, in a farce about a Hollywood star of the collegiate type (Charles Starrett) who, pursued by his frantic agent (Walter Connolly), enrolls in a real college, only to find himself, as the *Times* put it, "entangled in the average plot he left behind him, except that this time he doesn't make the winning touchdown."

Hold That Co-Ed (1938), the *Times* decided, was "altogether too wishy-washy a title for impious satire of two great American institutions—football and politics." John Barrymore was Governor Gabby Harrigan, running for the Senate. As a grandstand play, he develops a sudden interest in the run-down State U., for which he builds a 100,000-seat stadium, in which the greatest star is Lizzie Olsen (Joan Davis), the only female drop-kicker in the history of college football.

The last college musical of the decade, *Freshman Year* (1938), was praised by *Film Daily* for its "authentic" campus atmosphere. At least it did not involve football. William Lundigan rejects a fraternity that will not accept his two room-mates. One of them writes a scathing editorial on an antiquated political science course, whereupon the professor (Ernest Truex) changes his methods, most of the class flunks and our heroes' "flunk insurance" scheme goes in the red. To raise money, their girl friends put on a show (what else?), which the emancipated professor steals by dancing the shag.

Thus only twenty-five college musicals were made 1929–39, even counting hybrids like *College Lovers*, and of these only fourteen directly concerned football. If they seemed like an endless stream to reviewers, perhaps it was because so many other college films, especially those about football, used clichés so similar that they seemed like musicals from which the songs (and often the humor) had been removed.

Closest to the lighthearted spirit of the best musicals were the occasional satires. The first out-and-out spoof of the whole football business (and very big business it had become by this time) was Joel Sayre's *Rackety Rax* (1933), in which a big-shot mobster (Victor McLaglen) decides to muscle in on the lucrative action by founding Canarsie College and hiring professional pugs and wrestlers, who are soon winning every game with scores like 148 to 0. A rival gets the same idea, leading to an all-out armed battle between the two phony colleges.

In *Hold 'Em Yale* (1935), Damon Runyon's hilarious variation on O. Henry's *The Ransom of Red Chief,* a spoiled, shrewish heiress (Patricia Ellis) is lured to New York by a fortune-hunting gigolo (Cesar Romero), then left with four smalltime hoods (William Frawley, Andy Devine, Warren Hymer, George Stone), whose apartment and lives she is soon running like a perverse Snow White with a whim of iron. When they realize that even her father (George Barbier) will not take her back at any price, the only solution is to marry her off to her sweetheart (Buster Crabbe) by making him the hero of the Yale-Harvard game, no matter how that has to be fixed.

The only film to satirize, or even deal with, that perennial collegiate ritual the alumni homecoming reunion, was *We Went to College* (1936), which the delighted *Times* reviewer thought worthy of a *cum laude* honorary degree for all concerned. Hugh Herbert was a professor of economics and perpetual alumni secretary, and Charles Butterworth, Walter Abel and Walter Catlett were among the recognizable old grads.

To all these musicals and comedies must be added the collegiate vehicles of the star comedians: Cantor's *The Kid from Spain* and *Forty Little Mothers,* the Marx Brothers'

Horse Feathers, Keaton's *Speak Easily,* Joe E. Brown's *Local Boy Makes Good* and *The Gladiator* (in addition to *Maybe It's Love*) and Laurel and Hardy's *A Chump at Oxford,* which brings the total of light treatments to thirty-five.

Among the twenty-odd non-musical football films of the '30s (including those set in the service academies) meant to be taken more or less seriously, it would be futile to seek fine distinctions except perhaps to divide them into those which totally idealized alma mater loyalty, team spirit and the character-building effect of the sport and those that seemed to question such values.

The Spirit of Notre Dame (1931) was very much in the idealistic vein. Whatever the reason, a popular saying of the '20s held that every man had two alma maters, his own and Notre Dame. Hollywood evidently subscribed to this wholeheartedly, for the film, "dedicated to the memory of Knute Rockne" (who had been killed in a plane crash earlier that year), gave Notre Dame the most priceless world-wide publicity ever bestowed on any American university.

J. Farrell MacDonald played Rockne, looking more like him than Pat O'Brien did and coaching several real Notre Dame grid stars, including the famed Four Horsemen as themselves. Lew Ayres was the hot-shot hero who must learn his lesson before being allowed to make the winning touchdown in the last minute of the big game, William Bakewell was his buddy (as in *All Quiet on the Western Front,* 1930) and Andy Devine was a super-loyalist who insists on playing even with a broken rib.

The same season, *Touchdown!* was highly praised for realism, if only because the ruthless coach (Richard Arlen) does not, after all, let an injured player return to the field and so sacrifices the big game. A month later, however, in *Maker of Men*—presumably the title referred to football—Richard Cromwell, a juvenile who specialized in young weakling roles, rebelled against his father (Jack Holt), a fanatical coach, but after being disowned by his girl and the college as well as his father, the misguided youth is forced to realize that nothing, after all, is as important as winning the game.

Huddle, unseasonally released in June 1932, cast Ramon Novarro as an Italian-American worker in a steel mill who wins a scholarship at Yale, where some of the scenes were photographed. His ethnic background and difficulties in a WASP milieu were depicted honestly enough, but he does win the big game against Harvard.

The All American (1932), first football picture of the fall season, assembled several real "pigskin manipulators," supporting Richard Arlen in a rather grim drama about what happens to college heroes who let fleeting fame go to their heads. Like Red Grange, this hero quits after his last game to go commercial by endorsing products. In no time he has learned to drink, pass phony checks and even peddle choice seats for his alma mater's games to scalpers. However, he saves his younger brother (John Darrow) from following in his footsteps.

In *That's My Boy* (1932), Richard Cromwell, backsliding from all he had learned in *Maker of Men,* went Arlen one better by turning commercial while still playing, demanding his share of the university's gate receipts. An alumnus forms a holding company based on the boy's reputation, but when small hometown investors are wiped out, of course he does the right thing. Three years later poor Richard had to be taught the same lesson all over again in *The Most Precious Thing in Life* (1935), this time by his unknown mother (Jean Arthur), a scrubwoman at the college.

Meanwhile *Saturday's Millions* (1933) offered the most cynical view yet, with Robert Young as "a callous and world-weary young artist who is fooled neither by the sentimental back-slapping of the old grads nor the excited yippings of the sports reporters," said the *Times,* but the writers compromised by bringing him back to the fold in time for the big game—which he loses. *College Coach* (1933) also played both sides of the street, satirizing

the shrewd public relations campaign by which a Napoleonic coach (Pat O'Brien) puts himself and his college on the map, but then backing away from the implications.

Young was back in a numbered jersey again in *The Band Plays On* (1934), which followed four lifelong friends known as the Four Bombers (like Notre Dame's Four Horsemen) from childhood to college football stardom. When one is injured in a car accident, the other three quit the team, but, of course, are reunited in time to play in the big game.

The Big Game itself (1936), though scripted by Irwin Shaw, was no more original than its title; the same goes for *Rose Bowl* (1936), *Over the Goal* (1937), *Campus Confessions, Swing That Cheer* (both 1938) and *$1000 a Touchdown* (1939). Football also figured prominently in several service films including *Hold 'Em, Navy, Navy Blue and Gold* (both 1937) and *Touchdown Army* (1938), as well as in such prison comedies as *Hold 'Em, Jail* (1932) and the second version of *Up the River* (1938).[1]

Saturday's Heroes (1937) led the *Times* reviewer to observe: "College football pictures hardly ever vary by so much as one esthetic milligram in either plot or intellectual weight from year to year, and . . . all of them are tinged with a rather melancholy note of cynicism and disillusionment concerning college football." In this one Van Heflin, expelled for ticket scalping, sells a rival college on the idea of openly subsidizing athletes, and eventually wins against his former alma mater.

The last football film of the decade was one of the most unusual, in that the title character (Charles Grapewin) in *Hero For a Day* (1939) is not a young grid star but one of thirty years before. Though once named "most likely to succeed," he now works as a night watchman—but as the only man in New York who graduated from McKinley, an obscure college in Texas, he is drafted by a pub-

---

[1] *Cowboy Quarterback* (1939), a Bert Wheeler comedy, was the *only* film of the decade about pro, rather than college, football.

licity man to welcome his alma mater's team, arriving to play against "Gale." Uneasily, he lets himself be passed off as a successful contractor, but does some real good by using his own sad example to straighten out an overconfident halfback (Dick Foran), who gets drunk the night before the big game. Though he loses his job, the older man is made assistant coach at McKinley, while his niece (Anita Louise) presumably gets Foran.

More than twenty college films did *not* involve football, including eight that concerned other sports: one about basketball, *Girls Demand Excitement* (1931), two about track, *Local Boy Makes Good* (1932) and *Girl of My Dreams* (1934) and, in addition to the musical *Sweetheart of Sigma Chi*, four others about rowing: *Freshman Love* (1936), *All-American Sweetheart, A Yank at Oxford* (both 1938) and *Million Dollar Legs* (1939) —no connection with the 1932 W. C. Fields film) and one based on winter sports, *Winter Carnival* (1939). Most of these simply applied the familiar collegiate formula, substituting the big track meet or boat race for the big game, but neither *A Yank at Oxford* nor *Winter Carnival* was a mere sports story; indeed, both retain a certain historic interest.

The first of MGM's British-made productions, *Yank* was essentially an elegant variation on the brash-newcomer-learns-traditions formula, but an intelligent script (written by *seven* well-known scenarists), the beauty of Oxford itself and a variety of impeccable British accents gave the film a pleasing sense of authenticity. Clashes between American pep and drive and centuries-old English customs were handled so as to amuse audiences

Maureen O'Sullivan, Robert Taylor, Vivien Leigh in **A Yank at Oxford**

on both sides of the Atlantic, and, of course, in the end the Yank helps stroke the winning crew against Cambridge.

Robert Taylor as a brash Midwestern athlete and Lionel Barrymore as his father were almost the only Americans in the cast. Especially notable were Edmund Gwenn as a quizzical dean, C. V. France as a vague tutor and Edward Rigby as a Dickensian "scout" (porter-valet for students). The hero is almost "sent down" when a local bookseller's tartish wife (Vivien Leigh in her first American film) is found in his rooms—but, of course, he was only shielding the haughty brother (Griffith Jones) of the girl he loves (Maureen O'Sullivan). Louis B. Mayer had rejected Leigh for the O'Sullivan role because he did not consider her important enough for such a prestige production.

Not only is *Winter Carnival* the only '30s film other than Sonja Henie's to deal with winter sports, it enjoys the accidental distinction of being the picture on which Budd Schulberg was assigned to work with F. Scott Fitzgerald (who got no writing credit). Their disastrous experience at Dartmouth was clearly the inspiration for the climax of Schulberg's fine novel *The Disenchanted*.

Aside from that, both the setting and the story itself are decidedly off the beaten movie campus path. Ann Sheridan (who had just been named "the Oomph Girl") played an American heiress divorcing the latest of several titled husbands. To dodge reporters, she joins her kid sister (Helen Parrish) aboard a special train bound for the Dartmouth carnival, where whom should she meet but old flame Richard Carlson (at this point succeeding Franchot Tone as the screen's favorite young intellectual), now a faculty member. When the sister, elected Snow Queen, as Sheridan had once been, shows signs of falling for a hand-kissing count (Morton Lowry), Sheridan really turns on the "oomph" and takes him away, just to make her point. Needless to add, both sisters end up with clean-cut Americans.

One other unusual college film deserves mention: *Soak the Rich* (1936), one of the four films written, produced and directed by Hecht and MacArthur, and one of the only three in the '30s that took any cognizance of the controversial issue of campus radicalism. Though praised for witty dialogue, *Soak the Rich* was as uneven in tone as if (the *Times* reviewer speculated) Hecht had wanted a satire while MacArthur held out for a farce—or vice versa. One piece of dialogue quoted seems astonishingly prophetic of the 1960s:

Theirs is not radicalism, sir. They will grow up to be quite conventional gentlemen. While they are young, they sing, struggle and dream of something else. A few years ago it was the fashion to be Don Juans. Today ideas have taken the place of drink, and revolt is the latest form of necking.

Walter Connolly played a choleric tycoon whose daughter (Mary Taylor) enrolls in his private university, but falls in love with the leading radical (John Howard). Soon they are leading a protest against the dismissal of a professor who endorsed a soak-the-rich program.

The other two films to deal with this problem took it very seriously indeed. The appallingly reactionary *Red Salute* (1935) dramatized the issues in simplistic terms. Said the outraged *Times* reviewer: "With the subtlety of a steamroller and the satirical finesse of a lynch mob, the film goes in for some of the most embarrassing chauvinism of the decade."

Barbara Stanwyck, the co-ed daughter of a general (Purnell Pratt), disgraces the family name by falling in love with a speechmaking radical (Hardie Albright), so her horrified father hustles her off to Mexico, where she meets a red-blooded, true-blue American soldier (Robert Young). Circumstances force them to flee in a stolen car.

When they are caught, Stanwyck defiantly returns to her first love, while the soldier faces a long prison term. But the general—no fool he—releases the two-fisted lad so that he can disrupt a student rally, beat up the agitator and win the girl. Albright and all his cohorts in the "Liberal League of International Students" were made as villainous as possible, so that the film turned out (said the *Times*) "a burlesque of the Americanism for which it is presumably battling."

A companion piece was *Fighting Youth* (1935), which touched incidentally on football, but was primarily a crusade against subversive organizations in our universities, led by Left Wing agents cleverly disguised as students, calling themselves the "Student League for Freedom" (another echo of the real-life League Against War and Fascism). The leader, Ann Sheridan, another misguided heiress, is only a pawn of Alton Chase as a bushy-haired Red with shell-rimmed glasses. They succeed in disrupting the football team, but that, one is warned, is only the beginning; today the campus, tomorrow the world. Among those involved were Charles Farrell and that perennial aging undergraduate Andy Devine. These last three films, one farcical, the other two naïvely propagandistic, were Hollywood's sole reflections of what was on many campuses a serious political issue.

Merely amused by such student social consciousness was the charming *Spring Madness* (1938), which some critics thought better than its source, Philip Barry's play *Spring Dance*. Lew Ayres and his eccentric roommate, "the Lippincott" (Burgess Meredith), campus liberals, are planning a trip to see at first hand life in the U.S.S.R.—but they reckon without the loyal sorority sisters of Maureen O'Sullivan, who scheme to keep Lew in town long enough to squire her to the spring dance and, with any luck, to the altar.

Other non-athletic college comedies that year included *Vivacious Lady* and *Brother Rat*, one of the many hit farces staged by George Abbott in the '30s, whose cast included practically the whole roster of Warners' young players: Priscilla Lane, Wayne Morris, Jane Bryan, Eddie Albert, Ronald Reagan and Jane Wyman. Set entirely in the Virginia Military Institute, where "Brother Rat" is a friendly greeting among cadets, the complicated plot centers on the pregnant wife of one, who, against regulations, has secretly married, but all three boys are, as the *Times* put it, in "girl trouble, class trouble, faculty trouble, biology trouble and, well, just plain trouble."

MGM's *These Glamour Girls* (1939) took a considerably less amiable view of college girls than had *Spring Madness*. When a group of undergraduates on a lark in the city stop in a ten-cents-a-dance palace, the wealthiest, Philip Griswold (Lew Ayres), jokingly invites a young dance hostess (Lana Turner) to a house party at his college, forgetting that he already has a date with an impoverished socialite (Jane Bryan) who plans to marry him for his money.

But Lana takes him at his word, and, as one reviewer observed, "shows up the debs in their own way and on their own ground." Among those present were Anita Louise and Tom Brown, both cast against type in unsympathetic roles, and Marsha Hunt as a tragic "always a bridesmaid" prom-haunter. When all the cards have been put on the table, Bryan, after all, chooses (good old) Richard Carlson, the only one working his way through college, leaving Lew to Lana. Writing before the release of *The Women*, the *Times* critic hailed *These Glamour Girls* as "not only the best college comedy of the year but the best social comedy of the year," and called the satire "more brutally acidulous than Clare Boothe ever dreamed of being."[2]

Poised midway between comedy and drama were four mysteries with a college setting (in addition to the murder melodrama *Under Cover of Night,* 1937): *A Shot in the Dark* (1935), *College Scandal* (1935), *Murder Goes to College* (1937) and *Extortion* (1938).

Of these, *College Scandal* (remade in 1942 as *Sweater Girl*) was the most original; it even had music. A few years after the death

___

[2] Two months later, MGM attempted a follow-up with *Dancing Co-Ed* (1939), with Turner and Carlson in the leads; the plot, about a starlet planted by a studio at a college as part of a fake search for a dancing co-ed, will be discussed among films about films.

of a student during a freshman hazing, a number of other student deaths occur, this time murders. Arline Judge played a co-ed who saves her boy friend (Eddie Nugent) from being next. The ultimate clue is a particular typewriter finally found in the house of a respected professor, whose wife (Mary Nash in her screen debut), it turns out, was the mother of the hazing victim.

Were there *no* college films that an audience could take seriously? Their number was surprisingly small, and their quality uneven. The two recurrent campus problems were (of course) sex and social snobbery, especially feminine snobbery. Thus in *Confessions of a Co-Ed* (1931), the *Times* noted, "the students devote their whole time to discussing affairs of the heart, never for an instant revealing any inclination for work."

Just as in *An American Tragedy,* later that year, Sylvia Sidney is seduced by Phillips Holmes, but he also dallies with another co-ed (Claudia Dell). While fleeing in a borrowed car from an out-of-bounds roadhouse, they cause the death of a pursuing motorcycle cop (as in *Manslaughter,* 1930). Both are eventually expelled, leaving the pregnant heroine to turn to a stauncher type (Norman Foster). But three years later, returned from South America a new man, the erstwhile weakling arrives to claim his child and his true love.

Though the *Times* reviewer found the young people in *The Age of Consent* (1932) more like high school students, the film, directed by Gregory La Cava, when shown at the New School in the summer of 1978, seemed "both sympathetically handled and intelligently written."

In hardly more than an hour, it dramatizes the dilemma of a young couple (Dorothy Wilson and Richard Cromwell), ardently in love but unable either to marry, because that would mean leaving college, or to have an affair, because that would be against her principles. Frustrated, the boy goes home with a pert coffee shop waitress (Arline Judge), they drink too much and fall asleep. Innocent or not, in the morning they are confronted by

her furious father (Reginald Barlow), who demands that they marry at once.

Disillusioned, the good girl accepts a ride from the campus playboy (Eric Linden), which leads to a crash, leaving him fatally and her seriously injured. Accompanying the boy to the hospital, the waitress, seeing where his heart is, defiantly tells her father that she will not steal what never belonged to her. When the girl recovers, the couple leave college to be married, with the blessings of an older couple, a sympathetic professor (John Halliday) and a house mother (Aileen Pringle), who had once loved each other but put off marriage until too late. There is not a single reference to football, fraternities, proms or any of the other preoccupations of most college films, a fact which makes *The Age of Consent* unique.

Six years were to pass before another film set on an American college campus appeared that could be taken seriously even by the characters on the screen.[3] Meanwhile there was *Girls' Dormitory* (1936), which, after one of the biggest publicity build-ups in history, introduced Simone Simon ("pronounced See-MOAN See-MOAN") to the American public.

An exclusive boarding school in Switzerland could hardly be further removed from the average American college; on the other hand, it is even further removed from the average American high school. The professors all hold doctorates and are recognized scholars in their fields, so the institution, perhaps a *lycée,* must count as the European equivalent of a junior college, at the very least.

Girls' Dormitory, from a play by Ladislas Fodor, was evidently meant to be a poignant, bittersweet love story, a heterosexual *Maedchen in Uniform.* It came just close enough to make its ultimate failure the more disappointing.

A schoolgirl (Simon) secretly worships the

---

[3] One can hardly count *Finishing School* (1934), in which the girls are satirically shown as being taught absolutely nothing but etiquette and social graces.

headmaster of the school (Herbert Marshall), who is also silently loved by an esteemed colleague (Ruth Chatterton). When the girl writes some passionate letters about a purely imaginary affair with an unnamed lover, they are pounced upon by two prying faculty members (Constance Collier and J. Edward Bromberg), who insist on her immediate expulsion. Though spared this, she runs away through a thunderstorm and seeks refuge in an isolated cottage, where her idol finds her and impulsively makes love to her. As fictionalized in *Screen Romances* magazine for September 1936, the intended ending was that the girl, who also hero-worships the woman, bravely denies her love for the man, leaving him free to turn to his contemporary while she presumably settles for a boy her own age (Tyrone Power)—but, as released, she quite unrealistically gets the older man.

Somewhat of an American analogue, in that it involved an innocent schoolgirl in a scandal, was *Girls' School* (1938), which the *Times* praised for avoiding the romantic clichés of other school pictures. "Is it possible that nice girls actually go to boarding schools and miss having affairs with the biology instructor, or fail to smolder beneath all manner of repressions . . . and be content with poetry?" Nan Grey and Kenneth Howell were the leads, Anne Shirley was a monitor, and the faculty included Gloria Holden, Marjorie Main and Cecil Cunningham.

In *I Met My Love Again* (1938), a routine romantic drama whose structure anticipated *Winter Carnival* (1939), Henry Fonda played a professor of science at a small New England college, still embittered after ten years at having been jilted by Joan Bennett, who eloped to a bohemian life in Paris. When she returns as a widow with a small daughter and enrolls at the college, she is generally resented, especially by the professor's family. Meanwhile another student (Louise Platt) threatens suicide unless he marries her.

Here I Am a Stranger (1939), the last pure (non-musical non-football) college film of the '30s, set in a college "without a co-ed and

where the faculty holds classes instead of bets on the big game," starred Richard Greene as the son of divorced parents, brought up by his mother (Gladys George), who remarried well, and estranged from his father (Richard Dix), a boozy, broken-down newspaperman, whose whole life has been a comedown from his days of college football glory.

As the boy gets to know his father better and also comes under the influence of a whimsical, Mr. Chipsish English professor (Roland Young), he realizes that the future laid out for him by his mother and his stuffy fiancée (Katharine Aldridge) is not for him, so he turns to the professor's charming daughter (Brenda Joyce). Though criticized by the *Herald Tribune* as both "static" and "meandering," it was praised for "a certain honesty in its reconstruction of undergraduate life."

Was there any life after college for the graduates of all these fabulous institutions? Hollywood's interest was indeed minimal, but besides the two already noted about old grads, *We Went to College* and *Hero for a Day*, two other films dealt with young alumni, starting on graduation day itself.

Change of Heart (1934), based on Kathleen Norris' novel *Manhattan Love Song*, traced the fortunes and misfortunes of four ambitious young graduates of a California college (first seen in their caps and gowns receiving their diplomas) when, after an exciting *fifteen*-hour flight coast to coast, they face the career challenges of New York.

Janet Gaynor and Charles Farrell (in their eighth year as a team) were obviously meant for each other, but their final union is delayed by James Dunn and Ginger Rogers in a four-sided *La Ronde:* Gaynor wants Farrell, who thinks he wants Rogers, who wants Dunn, who thinks he wants Gaynor. The background glimpses of Manhattan avenues still shadowed by the elevated lines and the dialogue (not ironic) about the thrills and opportunities of the big city lent the film, when shown in 1977, a quite unintended nostalgic charm.

Parallel but typically more serious and timely was Warners' *Gentlemen Are Born*

(1934), which, Everson pointed out at a showing in 1978, is a perfect male counterpart of *The Group* (1966), but less than half as long. This, too, begins on commencement day, with the academic procession, a solemn alma mater hymn and much idealistic talk about the bright future ahead.

But the four young friends are faced with the somber realities of Depression-stricken New York. Athlete Dick Foran, who wanted only to be a coach, after slugging it out as a small-time preliminary fighter, winds up dead, shot by a cop after a ten-dollar theft from a pawnbroker. Robert Light collapses when his idolized father (Henry O'Neill) jumps out a window to escape an embezzling scandal. Ross Alexander settles for a low-level job in a brokerage, marriage to Jean Muir and early

Dick Foran, Jean Muir, Robert Light (top row), Ann Dvorak, Franchot Tone, Margaret Lindsay in Gentlemen Are Born

fatherhood. Franchot Tone, the central character and *raisonneur,* who works as a reporter for a ridiculous salary, is reasonably content when Margaret Lindsay, Light's sister, finally decides not to marry wealthy Charles Starrett even for her family's sake. Everson notes that the film was very popular in Russia as an apparent exposé of the evils of capitalism.

Like a number of other genres, the college film, including the football musical, died with the '30s, extinguished by World War II, which virtually shut down men's colleges throughout the country.

After the war came the GI Bill, which overnight democratized college by making it every soldier's right instead of a privilege of the rich or the exceptionally gifted. On an altogether new kind of campus, married veterans and their wives lived in Quonset huts or other improvised housing, as young parents too tied down to think about prom-trotting or fraternity hazing. Sorority snobbery and football no longer seemed important. Perhaps the only real, if misbegotten, heir to the '30s college comedies, appropriately vulgarized for contemporary tastes, is *Animal House* (1978) .

39

GAÎTÉ PARISIENNE AND CAPRICE VIENNOIS
Light Operettas

The operetta, as it came to be enjoyed all over Europe and America in the late nineteenth century, originated not in Vienna, as might be supposed, but in Paris during the Second Empire, largely the creation of one man, Jacques Offenbach, who between the 1850s and his death in 1880 wrote more than a hundred operettas. (The word itself means "little opera," and is often used interchangeably with "light opera" or "comic opera.") By the 1870s, Johann Strauss, Jr., in Vienna and Gilbert and Sullivan in London were making their own unique contributions, of which most of theirs and three of his are still playable.

The approach of these earliest practitioners was strictly tongue-in-cheek, witty and satirical. Behind the classical draperies of *Orpheus in the Underworld* and *La Belle Hélène,* Offenbach was burlesquing the pomposities of

the court of Napoleon III, as Gilbert and Sullivan were to do for the stuffy conventions of Victorian England.

Thus it is possible to distinguish two main streams in the history of the operetta, on screen as on stage, one in the *Fledermaus-Merry Widow* style, akin to French farce, an airy blend of nonsense and satire, in which flirtatious wives, straying husbands, amorous bachelors and saucy soubrettes gaily pursue each other in quest of naughty extramarital rendezvous. The milieux were those the original audiences knew, or would have liked to know, the favorite playgrounds of the European aristocracy: Paris or Vienna, Monte Carlo or Baden, or, if a mythical kingdom, one that spoofed the pretensions of real monarchies.

The other main-stream, romantic operettas,

unfortunately more familiar to most Americans, thanks to popular scores by the later Lehár and Straus, Herbert, Friml, Novello and especially Romberg, are what has given the very word "operetta" such heavily sentimental connotations.

The first operetta composed exclusively for the screen (by Victor Schertzinger), Chevalier's second talkie (and Lubitsch's first), *The Love Parade,* released in November 1929, was precisely in the sparkling, sophisticated vein noted above.

It was indeed a mythical kingdom romance, based on a European play, *The Prince Consort,* but, as the *Times* observed, "Mr. Lubitsch has seized every opportunity to lift it out of any suggestion of sentimentality by bright satirical shafts." Jeanette MacDonald in a most promising screen debut played the Queen of Sylvania, and Maurice Chevalier was Count Alfred, a diplomat whom her country recalls from Paris because of his formidable reputation as a Don Juan. As the Queen's husband, he can at first take no part in affairs of state, but manages most adroitly to assert himself in the end. Lillian Roth as the Queen's maid and Lupino Lane as the Prince's valet provided comic counterpoint.

But, of course, the story was less important than the brilliant proof that talkies had in no way impaired the famous "Lubitsch touch." Though none of Schertzinger's songs became standards, the title number is at least vaguely familiar, as is "Dream Lover."

Chevalier's two 1930 films were among his weakest, conventional musicals, with new songs added to old comedies, although in *The Big Pond* he introduced the very popular "You Brought a New Kind of Love to Me," and in *The Playboy of Paris,* "My Ideal."

Lubitsch did indeed direct one of the two sophisticated operettas of 1930, but with Mac-Donald and British star Jack Buchanan, in a role that would have been perfect for Chevalier. *Monte Carlo,* based on a play, *The Blue Coast,* is an amusing variation on *Monsieur Beaucaire,* in which an impoverished Countess, about to marry for money, instead flees to the Riviera to seek her fortune at the gambling tables, singing as she goes the opening number, "Beyond the Blue Horizon," with the chugging of the locomotive, the whistle, the click of the train wheels along the track all forming part of the accelerating rhythmic pattern.

A count (Buchanan) falls in love with her, and, after trying every other way to get to know her, disguises himself as a hairdresser. The truth comes out as she watches a musical version of *Monsieur Beaucaire.* As the *Times* noted, "The humor is a combination of satire and sparkling fun."

The producers might well have buried most of the dreary Warners-First National operettas of 1930—with one charming exception. However it happened, of the two original operettas that studio produced that year, the apparently more promising one, *Viennese Nights,* sank without trace, but *Sweet Kitty Bellairs,* written by the then totally unknown team of Robert Emmett Dolan and Walter O'Keeffe, based on a 1903 comedy by Belasco (one of his few, and the only Belasco work to succeed on screen in the 1930s), was a witty ballad opera that captured the flavor of eighteenth-century Bath with surprising authenticity.

The plot hinges on an appropriately antique device, the situation in which a married lady's reputation is saved when an innocent woman steps forward to claim the compromising letter, slipper or fan (as in *Lady Windermere's Fan* and *The Merry Widow*). Likewise, the characters might have stepped out of a comedy of the period: a gouty old cuckold (Ernest Torrence), his dallying young wife (June Collyer), a dandy (Perry Askam), a gallant highwayman (Walter Pidgeon) and the wife's sister, Sweet Kitty herself (Claudia Dell).

All the songs are so closely linked to the characters and the period that they stood little chance of becoming popular, but when seen in 1971, *Sweet Kitty Bellairs* seemed a true original, pleasing proof that Paramount did not have a monopoly on the only kind of musical that was to survive 1931 and 1932.

Jeanette MacDonald, Jack Buchanan
in Monte Carlo

Having directed MacDonald without Chevalier in *Monte Carlo,* Lubitsch went on to score an even greater hit, directing Chevalier without MacDonald, but with two other charming leading ladies, Claudette Colbert and Miriam Hopkins, in *The Smiling Lieutenant,* the *only* musical of 1931 other than Cantor's *Palmy Days* to be successful. Filmed, like *The Big Pond* (1930), at Paramount's Astoria studios, adapted from Oscar Straus' 1907 operetta *A Waltz Dream,* with most of the original score dropped but with new songs added by Straus himself, *The Smiling Lieutenant* more than restored Chevalier's *Love Parade* image.

Once again he was a reluctant prince consort in a mythical kingdom, but this time in even more complex and amusing circumstances. As Nikki, a dashing lieutenant in Franz Josef's Vienna, he is enjoying a blissful affair with Franzi (Colbert), a pretty young violinist in an all-girls' orchestra. While on duty at a royal parade, he winks at her, but the wink is intercepted and misinterpreted by the dowdy Princess Anna (Hopkins), just then passing in a state coach with her pompous father (George Barbier), the King of Flausenthurm. The Emperor makes it clear that for diplomatic reasons Nikki must marry

the insulted Princess—but their wedding night finds him playing checkers with his father-in-law.

When Franzi comes to Flausenthurm to resume their affair, she is summoned to the palace by the Princess, but after a comic face-slapping confrontation, the two girls realize their common interest: both love Nikki. Generously, Franzi tells Anna all she should know about how to hold a man, and leaves with the rueful observation, "A girl who stays for breakfast seldom gets invited to dinner." Nikki returns to find his hitherto prim wife properly made up, in a sexy negligee, smoking a cigarette while playing jazz, with a cocktail set on the piano; he quickly adjusts to the possibilities.

Oddly but typically of the time, as in *Daybreak, Dishonored, The Registered Woman* (all 1931) and even Max Ophuls' *Liebelei* (1932), all specifically set in Hapsburg Vienna before or during World War I, the girls wear modern clothes (a matter of economy?) —but this is a trifling flaw in an otherwise delightful operetta. According to *Chevalier* by Gene Ringgold and DeWitt Bodeen, its reception from coast to coast was rapturous.

Even without Lubitsch, Paramount, called by Kreuger "easily the most creative studio during this period," revealed a unique flair for airy farce, sophisticated in the best Continental sense (and invariably set in Europe). *This Is the Night,* directed by Frank Tuttle, from Avery Hopwood's 1925 play *Naughty Cinderella,* once a vehicle for Irene Bordoni, was one of the few delights of early 1932.

Moving from Paris to Venice, it traced the complications created by Roland Young's affair with the blond wife (Thelma Todd) of an Olympic javelin-thrower (Cary Grant). To divert the husband's suspicions, Young must produce a wife of his own (Lily Damita). Of the three musical numbers, by far the best was "Madame Has Lost Her Dress" (after Todd's skirt has been ripped off by a closing car door), which sets all Paris, including the Eiffel Tower, singing out the vital news.

When Lubitsch decided to make a musical of his celebrated 1924 hit *The Marriage Circle,* with Chevalier in the Monte Blue role, as a philandering doctor wavering between his wife and her supposed best friend, the two women were to have been played by Carole Lombard and Kay Francis, but when they had other commitments, Lubitsch brought Mac-Donald back from Fox, where she had made three non-musical farces, and cast Genevieve Tobin as the other woman.

By the production date of *One Hour With You* (1932), Lubitsch was still involved with his one serious American film, *Broken Lullaby (The Man I Killed)*, so George Cukor directed several scenes. Then Lubitsch became available and took over, and Cukor was relegated to the side lines, but still insisted on credit, so the ads read "Under the supervision of Ernst Lubitsch . . . Directed by George Cukor."

Delightful as *The Marriage Circle* still is, it is much heavier than its musical version. Samson Raphaelson's screenplay, which shifts the setting from Vienna to Paris, perfectly integrated with six sparkling songs by Oscar Straus and Richard Whiting, avoided any discordantly serious note.

The film departs at will from the earthbound limitations of realism. The hero when in doubt turns to confide directly in the audience. At any moment characters may not only burst into song but lead up to it by conversing in couplets, which soon sound pleasantly natural.

This device is used from the very opening, as the police commissioner of Paris (George Barbier) metrically exhorts his men to clear the parks of lovers. When a gendarme finds a particularly amorous couple on a bench, he cannot believe that they are the respectably married Dr. and Mme. André Bertier (Chevalier and MacDonald) —but their marital bliss is confirmed in their bedroom as they sing "What a Little Thing Like a Wedding Ring Can Do."

Next morning André involuntarily shares a taxi with a most provocative lady, and later is startled to find her lunching with his wife, Collette; she is her friend, the formidable Mitzi (Genevieve Tobin), bored wife of a professor (Roland Young). Meanwhile the two women have exchanged confidences in verse:

C: And how's the composer you went with so much?

M: He's gone—but he had such a wonderful touch!

C: And the artist who painted you all draped in gauze?

M: One night I found out what an artist he was!

From this Collette leads gracefully into the charming waltz "We Will Always Be Sweethearts."

She cannot understand André's reluctance when summoned to Mitzi's bedside ostensibly to treat a strange feeling she gets "Three Times a Day." Most of the action, however, takes place on the evening of a formal dinner-dance for about twenty couples in the Bertiers' elegant Art Deco home, where Mitzi, without her husband, under the guise of helping Collette divert André's attention from another woman, by skillful maneuvering of place cards and dance partners does all she can to lure him into a rendezvous, even as Collette playfully fends off the ardor of a bachelor friend, Adolphe (Charlie Ruggles).

As they dance, both couples sing special lyrics to "One Hour with You" (a song which later served not only as the gibberish Klopstockian anthem in *Million Dollar Legs*, 1932, but for years as Eddie Cantor's sign-off song on radio). After putting his dilemma to the audience in "Oh, that Mitzi!", André succumbs to her wiles and accompanies her home, while Collette turns tearfully to Adolphe, sobbing, "Oh, I was wrong!"—to which he replies, "And why not? You had a perfect right to be wrong. I *like* my women wrong!"

Next morning, after musically asking the audience "What Would *You* Do?" ("That's

Jeanette MacDonald, Maurice Chevalier
in One Hour With You

what I did, too!"), André is confronted by the professor, who on a private detective's evidence threatens to name him as co-respondent. Not to be outdone, Collette pretends she let Adolphe make love to her; thus, having apparently evened the score, the Bertiers are ready to start over.

If *One Hour with You* is a near-perfect screen operetta, *Love Me Tonight* (also 1932) is perfection itself—a judgment on which most leading film historians and commentators have long agreed. As Rouben Mamoulian freely explained, he was not at all pleased at being asked to direct the next Chevalier-MacDonald musical, after their several successes with Lubitsch, but once he had accepted the assignment, instead of trying to out-Lubitsch Lubitsch, he set about it in his own original way.

With no more than an idea for a story supplied by Leopold Marchand, he inspired Rodgers and Hart (despite their flop with *The Hot Heiress*) to write their first successful score for a film. Of the eight numbers, three have become standards: "Isn't It Romantic?", "Lover" and "Mimi." The title number is not so well-known, and the others (with the exception of "The Poor Apache," sung by Chevalier as a specialty number at a costume ball) are so tightly integrated into the specifics of the film that the lyrics would scarcely mean anything apart from it. The whole score was finished before Samuel Hoffenstein, Waldemar Young and George Marion, Jr., under Mamoulian's firm guidance, began working on the script, in which rhythmic dialogue and verses flow in and out of song numbers with never an awkward shift of gears.

Love Me Tonight is essentially a satirical fairy tale of an emotionally sleeping beauty awakened not by a prince but by a humble tailor—a unique blend of stylized fantasy and everyday reality. The opening sequence (even if it does owe something to René Clair) is one of the most effective in musical film history, as a number of ordinary morning sounds in a poor quarter of Paris gradually merge into a triumphant symphony, ended with a shot of Chevalier's straw hat hanging on his bedroom wall.

Once his personality has been established, as well as his friendship with an impecunious Vicomte (Charlie Ruggles), who owes him for twenty suits, as he works he absently begins to sing "Isn't It Romantic?" The tune is picked up by a taxi driver, overheard by a composer, who sings it on a train full of soldiers; they march to its strains through the countryside, whence, played by a gypsy violinist, it floats through a forest and brings a Princess (Jeanette MacDonald) out on her balcony to sing the final chorus, thus linking the future lovers before they have even met.

Trying to collect, Maurice appears at the family château of the Vicomte, who, to avoid telling the truth, introduces him as his house guest, a baron, to his aristocratic relatives—all those under sixty wasting away from boredom, especially the widowed Princess (whose husband died of old age) and her man-hungry cousin, Countess Valentine (Myrna Loy), who, when asked if she could go for a doctor, instantly brightens. "Certainly! Bring him right in!"

Lord of the château is a crusty old Duke (C. Aubrey Smith), whose idea of lively diversion is endless games of bridge. Most amusing are three elderly aunts (Elizabeth Patterson, Blanche Frederici, Ethel Griffies), usually seen sitting around a table in their tower room, like benevolent witches brooding over the future of their niece.

Almost all of the numbers are introduced in unexpected, always functional, ways. One sequence is a balletic hunt, in which the horses and even the stag bound to the meter of the music, and surely the most hilarious is the denouement, "The Son of a Gun Is Nothing but a Tailor," in which not only the nobility but all the servants rhythmically denounce the impostor.

Totally cinematic to the end, the climax finds the Princess racing her horse against the train that is taking Maurice back to Paris, passing it, then dismounting to plant herself

Myrna Loy, Maurice Chevalier, Jeanette MacDonald in **Love Me Tonight**

on the tracks, defying the engineer not to stop. But the last shot is of the three aunts, gently beaming as they sum up the tale of her rescue by a man who "wasn't a prince—but he *was* charming!"

According to Kobal's book, Arthur Freed, Vincente Minnelli and Charles Walters, creators of some of MGM's best musicals, all agree that *Love Me Tonight* had the greatest influence on their work. (Even Stephen Sondheim, who composes in a far different mode, when asked his opinion in 1976, agreed that *Love Me Tonight* is "perfect of its whipped-cream kind.")

No doubt encouraged by the reception of *Love Me Tonight,* Rodgers and Hart stayed on at Paramount to contribute to two other films. In *The Phantom President* (1932), a political satire, one of George M. Cohan's few

pictures, only one of their songs was used.

More unusual was *Hallelujah, I'm a Bum* (1933), adapted by S. N. Behrman from a story by Ben Hecht. Al Jolson, for once giving a relatively restrained performance, played Bumper, "mayor" of the hobos in Central Park, who enjoys a friendly relationship with the "real" mayor (Frank Morgan), a very kind version of Jimmy Walker, who hates public ceremonies and lunches daily at the Park Casino.

When Bumper's quaint constituents gather (including Egghead, a vaguely radical "white wings" played by Harry Langdon), they try Bumper for the offense of having gone to work. What drove him to this drastic measure was love of a mysterious girl (Madge Evans) whom he rescued from drowning herself in the park lake, an experience that left her with amnesia. Little does he suspect that she is the mayor's missing fiancée, who disappeared after a lovers' quarrel. Like the blind girl in *City Lights* (1931), when she regains her memory, she sees her benefactor only as a pathetic tramp.

Though Kobal asserts that this was "one of the few musicals to deal with the Depression," Bumper and his friends have simply *chosen* not to work, acting out the escapist '30s pseudo philosophy expressed in one of the five undistinguished songs, "What Do You Want with Money?"—an attitude practical only for those who have plenty of it. Undeniably, the film has a certain wistful charm, but it is basically a sentimental fable, and too many couplets strained even Hart's ingenuity.

Rhymed dialogue was also used in RKO's *Melody Cruise* (1933), called by the *Times* "an adroit mixture of nonsense and music." Aboard a ship bound from New York to California, a wealthy bachelor (Phil Harris) is trying to avoid marriage, while his married friend (Charlie Ruggles) is trying to elude his wife (Marjorie Gateson), but they become involved with a pair of involuntary stowaways (Helen Mack and Greta Nissen), left over from a *bon voyage* party. The songs by Val Burton and Will Jason at least do not sound sentimental: "I Met Her at a Party," "He's Not the Marrying Kind," "This Is the Hour" (combining *This Is the Night* and *One Hour with You,* both films in which Ruggles had appeared) and "Isn't This a Night for Love?"

By 1933 operetta was barely hanging on. Yet it was at this point that Fox, which up until now had taken no part in all the rhymed dialogue, chose to make *Adorable* (1933), co-authored by Billy Wilder (his first Hollywood credit). Though it was based on a German film, *Ihre Hoheit Befiehlt* (1931), it seems safe to say that it would never have been made but for the success of *Love Me Tonight;* it even used two of the same character players in parallel roles, C. Aubrey Smith and Blanche Frederici.

The tone was set by the opening subtitle:

"On the map of Europe, somewhere between Munich and Vienna, there is no such kingdom as Hipsburg-Legstadt. In this secluded little kingdom we begin our story." Dancing incognito at a servants' ball, a Princess (Janet Gaynor) passes herself off as a manicurist so as not to overawe a young man (Henri Garat) who says he keeps a delicatessen. When she learns that he is really a lieutenant, she arranges for a series of quick promotions which make him a general in no time.

Whimsical touches abound: the Princess' slippers continue to dance after she has gone to bed, and even the bed sways in time to the music. The mysterious King (never seen till the end), of whom everyone seems in awe, is the Princess' small brother. Of its kind *Adorable* was not at all bad, but it could hardly be counted a success, since Gaynor made no more musicals and it was Garat's only American film.

The year before, he had starred in the extremely popular German film operetta *Congress Dances,* set during the 1815 Congress of Vienna, in which as Czar Alexander I in disguise he falls in love with a milliner (Lilian Harvey). In what must have seemed a coup, Fox, which seemed to favor petite, elfin actresses (Gaynor, Heather Angel, later Simone Simon, Sonja Henie, Annabella), imported not only Garat but Harvey as well. Perhaps one reason was that the senior resident elf, Gaynor, who had, after all, won the first Oscar in 1929 for her strongly dramatic performances in *Sunrise, Seventh Heaven* and *Street Angel,* had begun to rebel against being cast in cream-puff musicals.

Thus one may suppose that Harvey's three Fox films, made in rapid succession, might originally have been meant for Gaynor. *My Weakness* (1933), a De Sylva-Robin-Whiting musical, was a personal triumph for the star, but the *Times* deplored "so many silly and antiquated jokes and painful puns." It was one more Cinderella-Ugly Duckling-Pygmalion tale, in which a playboy (Lew Ayres) bets his uncle (Henry Travers) that he can transform a slavey into a lady of fashion.

Harry Langdon literally played Cupid, a rather middle-aged Cupid, who comments on the action and intervenes now and then. China cats, dogs, monkeys and a statuette of Rodin's *Thinker* join in the singing, especially the hit song "Gather Lip Rouge While You May," and, needless to add, people often talk in rhyme.

A few months later, *My Lips Betray* (1933) offered Lilian Harvey a vehicle more suitably Continental in origin and setting. The plot is the one about the innocent girl who, from being seen riding in the King's car, is assumed to be his mistress. John Boles was King Rupert of mythical Ruthenia, but despite dialogue by S. N. Behrman and four forgotten songs, the *Times* termed it "a club-footed duckling of the Graustark family," which forced the star to be "aggressively coy."

The only traditional operetta of 1933 was *The Devil's Brother*—traditional in the sense that it was based on Auber's 1830 comic opera *Fra Diavolo* (libretto by Eugène Scribe), a kind of Italian parallel to *Sweet Kitty Bellairs* —but it was turned into a vehicle for Laurel and Hardy. In Dutch bobs and eighteenth-century costumes, they played unwilling henchmen of the title character (Dennis King in one of his rare screen appearances), a daring highwayman who poses as a marquis to woo a married lady (Thelma Todd). The *Times* reviewer would have preferred more of King and less of Laurel and Hardy, but audiences loved it, and MGM subsequently gave the same revivifying shock treatment to two other old operettas.

Even as backstage musicals continued to flood the screen throughout 1934, operettas, too, staged a comeback of sorts. Though seldom as heavily sentimental as Romberg's and set in less exotic backgrounds, Jerome Kern's works were surely light-years beyond the average Broadway musical. Though the two to be discussed here involve backstage situations, both have the light operetta touch.

As the anonymous writer of *Musicals of the 1930s* says of *The Cat and the Fiddle* (book and lyrics by Otto Harbach), which ran

nearly four hundred performances in Depression-stricken 1931–32, it "had no chorus-girl routines, no synthetic comedy, no set spectacular numbers. The story moved easily, and the characters were believable human beings."

Thus it made a perfect vehicle for Jeanette MacDonald (her first film since *Love Me Tonight*) and Ramon Novarro (his first musical since *Call of the Flesh* in 1930), who played, for a change, composers (though they also sang), she American, he Romanian, who meet in Brussels. Even *The New Yorker* concedes that, although Novarro is "a disaster," MacDonald has "some nice light comedy scenes" and the film "has pace and flavor."

While her song "The Night Was Made for Love" becomes the toast of Paris and then of Europe, he has great difficulty getting his first operetta staged, especially when the entire cast walks out. Though she was about to marry wealthy Frank Morgan, Jeanette replaces the resigned prima donna (Vivienne Segal) and saves the show. *The Cat and the Fiddle* was certainly a critical success, yet despite a score that included "Try to Forget" and "She Didn't Say Yes" and a closing sequence in the newly perfected Technicolor, it was not the resounding hit MGM had expected, and did nothing to revive Novarro's waning career.

As if still determined to become the cinema capital of Mittel-European *gemütlichkeit,* as Paramount had once been, Fox, despite *Adorable* (1933), *Caravan* (1934) and the Harvey films, redeemed itself with *Music in the Air* (1934), the charming Kern-Hammerstein operetta which had been Broadway's biggest musical hit of 1932–33. "A romantic story without recourse to formula—a fable flowing naturally out of a full-brimming score," says *Musicals of the 1930s*. The film was faithfully produced by Erich Pommer, directed by Joe May and co-written by Billy Wilder, all Europeans, though the stars and, of course, Kern and Hammerstein themselves were Americans.

Set in Bavaria, it tells of a kindly old music

master (Al Shean), who goes to Munich to visit an old friend, now a music publisher (Reginald Owen). With him are his daughter (June Lang) and her fiancé, a schoolmaster (Douglass Montgomery), who soon find themselves caught up in a temperamental battle between the prima donna (Gloria Swanson) and the lyric writer (John Boles) of a forthcoming operetta. To spite each other, the older couple pair off with the young sweethearts, whose heads are temporarily turned. The delightful score included "I've Told Every Little Star" and "The Song Is You."

Opening in New York the same week as *Music in the Air* was Laurel and Hardy's inimitable version of Victor Herbert's 1903 classic *Babes in Toyland,* by far the best of their three operettas, which reflected not only the renewed interest in musicals but the post-Code trend toward innocuous childhood fancies.

The original libretto was scrapped (no loss!) in favor of a new one about Oliver Dee and Stanley Dum, apprentice toymakers and boarders with the Widow Peep (Florence Roberts), who also happens to be the Old Woman Who Lived in a Shoe. Since this is Mother Goose Land, the widow's daughter, Bo, the well-known shepherdess (Charlotte Henry, who a year before had been Paramount's Alice in Wonderland), is loved by Tom, Tom the Piper's Son (Felix Knight), but coveted by the villainous Barnaby (Henry Kleinbach), who holds the mortgage on the shoe.

This was MGM's most imaginative fantasy until *The Wizard of Oz* in 1939. Given an order for six hundred one-foot wooden soldiers, Stanley instead makes one hundred six-footers, and it is they who, to the crashing strains of "March of the Toys," save the Mother Goose people from Barnaby's bogeymen. "Toyland," "Never Mind, Bo Peep" and indeed most of Herbert's score survived in this truly comic operetta, still frequently shown on TV.

Meanwhile, back at Paramount, Chevalier's two brilliant 1932 hits had proved impossible to match. *A Bedtime Story* (1933) was a mildly amusing variation on the *Bachelor Mother* situation, in which an unmarried person is left with a foundling, who is immediately assumed to be his/her illegitimate child. Chevalier thus became the first of several stars to fall victim to the scene-stealing charm of Baby LeRoy, a remarkably appealing infant, who after eight films retired, presumably rich, before he turned four. The film, in which despite the competition of more sophisticated ladies the baby's governess (Helen Twelvetrees) wins Chevalier, contained but one fairly good number, "In a Park, in Paree." As for *The Way to Love* (also 1933), this was so poor that Sylvia Sidney asked to be removed from it (replaced by Ann Dvorak), and Chevalier left Paramount for MGM.

When after the disasters of *The Merry Widow* (1934) and *The Night Is Young* (1935) (to be discussed later) MGM announced *Naughty Marietta* with Jeanette MacDonald and (instead of Allan Jones, who could not get out of a Broadway commitment) Nelson Eddy, a concert baritone, who had sung one number in each of three films but had never acted, lovers of operetta anticipated the worst.

Yet, whoever made the basic decisions, whether producer Hunt Stromberg or director W. S. Van Dyke, the scenarists, John Lee Mahin, Frances Goodrich and Albert Hackett, started by reversing the treatment given *The Merry Widow,* which had come close to turning champagne into flat beer. They simply junked Rida Johnson Young's heavy-handed 1910 book, retaining only the two leading characters and the eighteenth-century New Orleans setting, but with the emphasis very much on bubbling wit and humor. For the first time since *Love Me Tonight,* the public was reminded that an operetta, even an MGM operetta without Laurel and Hardy, could be fun—not, to be sure, Lubitsch's sly, risqué, pre-Code fun of 1929–32, but still light and amusing.

Gone was the tedious subplot about the governor's wicked son Etienne, who's really

Bras Pique, the notorious pirate, and his quadroon mistress, Adah. As in *Love Me Tonight,* MacDonald was a spirited French princess (also a dedicated music student) , who, to escape an arranged marriage to an elderly Spanish grandee (Walter Kingsford) , takes the place of her maid, Marietta, as one of the "casket girls," sent to New France with a dowry from King Louis XV to become the wives of colonists. Captured by pirates, the girls are rescued by Captain Dick Warrington (Eddy) and his fighting mercenaries, who sing as they march "Tramp, Tramp, Tramp Along the Highway."

To avoid having to marry the first farmer who asks her, "Marietta" uses a typical post-Code stratagem. "Surely," she says, with a knowing smile, to Louisiana's royal governor (Frank Morgan) , "there's a place in New Orleans for a girl who doesn't necessarily wish to become a housewife, but who likes to be . . . charming?" The flustered governor is overwhelmed, as are all the young gallants about town, who beat a path to her door, until routed by Warrington, who has refused all along to believe that she is "just a little indiscreet girl from Marseilles."

Almost all Herbert's score was retained, each number functionally introduced, flowing directly out of the action, from the sparkling "Chansonette," sung by Parisian students in the highly cinematic opening sequence, to the triumphant duet of "Ah, Sweet Mystery of Life" (a song the heroine has been

Elsa Lanchester, Jeanette MacDonald, Frank Morgan in **Naughty Marietta**

trying to compose throughout) as the lovers ride off to a new life in the wilderness. Comedy on one level is supplied by Morgan and Elsa Lanchester as his termagant wife, while broader humor comes from Edward Brophy and Harold Huber as two of the hero's backwoods followers.

The reception was all that MGM could have hoped. It at once established MacDonald and Eddy as the most successful singing team the screen would ever see, and, according to Kreuger's liner notes for the RCA-Victor recording *Jeanette MacDonald and Nelson Eddy,* it remains easily the most popular operetta ever to reach the screen. The same public that had stayed away in droves or squirmed once through *The Merry Widow* went back to see *Naughty Marietta* again and again in sheer delight. It won *Photoplay*'s coveted Movie of the Year Award—in a year that included many strong dramatic films now considered classics.

Yet this is the picture *The New Yorker* routinely dismisses as "an atrocity, of course, and one of the most spoofed of all the Jeanette MacDonald–Nelson Eddy operettas, and yet it has vitality and a mad sort of appeal . . . It's beyond camp, it's in a realm of its own." Even further off the mark is John Baxter's astonishing comment in discussing Van Dyke's career in his book *Hollywood in the Thirties:* "His Nelson Eddy–Jeanette MacDonald vehicles *Naughty Marietta* (1935), *Rose Marie* (1936) and *Sweethearts* (1938) did little to counteract the reaction against the duo in sophisticated circles while it led to their being christened 'The Singing Capon' and 'The Iron Butterfly.' "

Nothing could be further from the truth. Aside from the fact that these snide sobriquets were not applied to the stars until years later, the first three Van Dyke films, plus Robert Z. Leonard's *Maytime* (1937), were the *best* films MacDonald and Eddy ever made; it was their other four (the last three released in the early '40s) that left that lingering, apparently ineradicable misconception that *all* their pictures were dreadful beyond endurance, the

kind of thing that gave operetta a bad name.

As a matter of fact, to "sophisticated circles" in the '30s, the first MacDonald-Eddy vehicles were a delightful change from the drearily repetitive musicals being ground out by other studios: backstage sagas with Busby Berkeley spectacles at Warners, collegiate capers and *Big Broadcasts* at Paramount, mechanical Shirley Temple fairy tales at Fox. Van Dyke, after all, had just directed *The Thin Man* (1934), and the same public that had enjoyed that made *Naughty Marietta* one of the box-office smashes of 1935.

After such a great success, whatever MacDonald and Eddy made next seemed doomed to suffer by comparison—but such was not the case. The choice of *Rose Marie* (1936), the highly successful operetta of 1924 composed by Friml and Stothart, with book and lyrics by Hammerstein and Harbach (which Joan Crawford had made as a silent), was a logical one, and, even more logically, it was given the same drastic treatment as *Naughty Marietta* by two of the same writers, Frances Goodrich and Albert Hackett, along with Alice Duer Miller, plus the same kind of brisk direction by Van Dyke.

Though the original, starring Mary Ellis and Dennis King, had run 557 performances on Broadway, the plot was a crudely melodramatic affair about a singer in a Saskatchewan hotel who, to save the man she loves from a false charge of killing an Indian, promises herself to the man who framed him. The real murderer is Wanda, an Indian girl in love with the villain. The scenarists wisely scrapped all this, retaining nothing but the Canadian setting and the music.

With MacDonald and Eddy under contract, MGM had no need to import singers from the Met. In graceful recognition of the current operatic cycle, however, the heroine is now a soprano—for once not a struggling one but at the height of her fame, "Canada's Own Marie de Flor," first seen singing in Gounod's *Romeo and Juliet* in Montreal (MacDonald's first operatic singing on screen). And a most imperious, temperamental prima donna she is, quite capable of firing her faithful manager (Reginald Owen) in public when he opens a window too near her. ("Dear Mr. Myerson! Always thinking of my comfort! . . . How I shall miss him when he leaves me *at the end of next week!*")

The plot gets under way very quickly when an Indian guide (George Rigas) brings word that Marie's wild younger brother (James Stewart), serving a prison sentence for a shooting, has escaped and is hiding out, wounded, in a cabin in the north woods, in urgent need of her help. Reaching a remote but lively trading post, she soon encounters a Mountie sergeant (Eddy), who, neatly sidestepping a cliché, instantly recognizes her by name. To account for the "R" on her suitcase (borrowed from her maid), she tells him her name is *Rose* Marie and hints that she is on her way to a secret rendezvous with a tenor, far from prying eyes.

In a number of tartly comic scenes she scorns both him and his proffered help, but when the treacherous guide robs and deserts her, she has no choice but to let the sergeant escort her as close as she dares to where her brother waits. Despite their growing love (expressed in "Indian Love Call"), the Mountie has known all along that she would lead him to his man, whom he now arrests and takes away, presumably to be hanged.

Back in Montreal, during a performance of *Tosca* (with Allan Jones singing a few brief notes as Mario), she reaches a doubly dramatic climax as Tosca realizes that Scarpia has tricked her and Marie realizes she is not hearing her cues but the sergeant's voice echoing "Indian Love Call." With a scream she collapses, the curtain is rung down and we next see her in a snowy mountain retreat, apparently recovering from a breakdown, wan and listless, until Myerson brings in the Mountie. As in *Naughty Marietta,* all the songs are adroitly introduced, the script is witty wherever possible and totally avoids operetta clichés.

Rose Marie was an even bigger hit than *Naughty Marietta.* Four months later, Mac-

Donald followed it with another box-office bonanza, that unique dramatic musical *San Francisco,* in which, following the operatic trend (her only role as an aspiring singer), she did a scene from *La Traviata* and in a montage sequence several excerpts from *Faust.*

For the rest of the decade the only operetta satirical or sophisticated enough to merit comparison with the best of those discussed so far in this chapter, the only one with an American setting, was also a MacDonald-Eddy vehicle (their last good one), *Sweethearts* (1938), which despite its Victor Herbert origins was, if not exactly antiromantic, quite tartly unsentimental; even the title is ironic.

In this very handsome production (MGM's first in the new Technicolor) the two stars, for the first time both well dressed in modern clothes throughout, had never looked or sounded better. As with their first three filmed operettas, all that survived of the original was the title and some of the music. In place of the 1913 libretto, apparently set in Holland, something about a widowed laundress and her seven marriageable daughters, Dorothy Parker and Alan Campbell produced a witty, amusing backstage comedy that, if anything, recalls at times both *The Guardsman* and *The Royal Family.*

An opening shot of Broadway theater marquees proclaims (not at all accurately) that *I'd Rather Be Right* has been running for two years, *Idiot's Delight* for three, *Victoria Regina* for four, *Tobacco Road* for five and the musical hit *Sweethearts* for six years! Stars of the last-named are a married couple (MacDonald and Eddy), who have never missed a performance, yet are still enough in love for the husband to write daily notes like "Six years with you are like six minutes; six minutes away from you are like six years"—which the wife saves.

The first half hour of the film, supposedly during a performance of *Sweethearts,* offers one lilting Herbert number after another, in what looks like a typically Graustarkian operetta, full of colorfully clad peasant maidens and dashingly uniformed hussars. Though the weary stars would prefer to unwind by them-selves, their producer (Frank Morgan) insists on their appearance at a lavish night club party to celebrate the sixth anniversary of the show, and since it is to be broadcast, they must go right on singing. Home at last, they are immediately beset by a swarm of devoted but parasitic relatives on both sides, all living off them and long-past theatrical triumphs, and all committing them to unwelcome en-gagements in every free hour for weeks ahead.

Thus they are more than ready to listen to the blandishments of a suave Hollywood stu-dio representative (Reginald Gardiner), de-spite the alarm of all who depend on them as meal tickets. Planning her wardrobe, Mac-Donald is treated to a lusciously tinted Adrian fashion show. Egged on by the frantic pro-ducer, the librettist of their show (Mischa Auer) steals the husband's love notes and in-corporates them in a play, telling the wife he got them from another woman. Instantly jealous, she suspects their faithful secretary (Florence Rice).

Abandoning all thoughts of joint stardom in Hollywood, the couple splits up, starring in separate road companies of the inescapable *Sweethearts,* though both hate leaving New York. Then both read in *Variety* a bad review of the librettist's new play, based on the same trick he played on them, so they rush back to New York to reopen in (what else?) *Sweet-hearts.* (Besides those mentioned, the players include Ray Bolger, Herman Bing, George Barbier, Lucile Watson and half a dozen other recognizable names.)

The subtle, "Lubitsch touch" sophistica-tion of the first three Chevalier-MacDonald musicals had vanished from the screen by 1940—yet two later films, ten years apart, came close to capturing that vintage sparkle. Though not at all nostalgic, both were set at the turn of the century, one aptly enough in imperial Vienna and environs, the other in Paris and Trouville.

In *The Emperor Waltz* (1948) Billy Wil-der turned a Bing Crosby vehicle into a sly, though affectionate, spoof of the Hapsburg Austria of his youth, especially of the protocol at the court of Franz Josef. In *Gigi* (1958), Lerner and Loewe, with the inspired help of Cecil Beaton and Vincente Minnelli, evoked Colette's Paris of La Belle Époque, its jaded *boulevardiers* and past, present and future courtesans, with wit, warmth and elegance. Thus the account of this kind of operetta on screen must end where it began on stage, in Paris and Vienna.

40

"IF LOVE WERE ALL"
Romantic Operettas

The other kind of operetta, briefly mentioned in the last chapter, is that in which, despite comic relief, the story is meant to be taken seriously, misunderstandings lead to bitter quarrels and sacrificial partings (to the reprised strains of the main love song) —all set as glamorously far away as possible from the audience in space or time or both. The main function of the plot is to provide as many opportunities as possible for lyrical solos, tender love duets and stirring male choral numbers (especially marching and drinking songs). Almost always, the score far transcends the book, or, to put it another way, the composer was at the mercy of his librettist.

Just as with musical comedies, a distinct cultural lag was evident on Broadway in the '20s. In a strange double standard of taste, the same public that welcomed so many sophisticated, innovative, ground-breaking dramas and comedies continued to enjoy operettas like Romberg's *Blossom Time* and *My Maryland* that might well have been written in the 1900s. Again as with musical comedies, their popularity was reflected even on the silent screen, in voiceless versions of *Maytime* (1924), *The Merry Widow* (1925—the famous von Stroheim–Mae Murray–John Gilbert version), *The Student Prince* (1927—Ramon Novarro and Norma Shearer, directed by Lubitsch), *The Red Mill, The Lady in*

Ermine (both 1927) and *Rose Marie* (1928).

In Hollywood's grand passion for music during 1929 and 1930, operettas swept the screen, divided, like less ambitious genres, between recent Broadway hits and new works commissioned by the studios. Of the former, the first to appear was Romberg's *The Desert Song* (1929), starring John Boles and Carlotta King. As an ad in *Photoplay* for July 1929 put it: "Love's heart beat . . . set to the golden notes of the most famous music-play of our generation . . . Love's immortal melodies—in the enchanting atmosphere of moonlit desert nights . . ."

On Broadway in 1926, *The Desert Song* had seemed a timely reflection of the current Riff rebellion against the French in Morocco. Given the '20s passion for sheik and Foreign Legion films, plus a lush Romberg score, who cared that the story was an uninspired reworking of the Scarlet Pimpernel–Zorro formula, in which an apparently effete weakling is leading a double life, by day the governor's son, by night the Red Shadow, daring leader of the Riffs?

According to Miles Kreuger's program notes from the Museum of Modern Art early sound musicals series, "the picture was so well received that Warners engaged Sigmund Romberg and Oscar Hammerstein II to compose one original screen operetta every year thereafter."[1] (They actually wrote only two.) Cinematically, it was something else.

With ponderous, declamatory acting that would have seemed inadequate in a high school production, cinematography that consists largely of some one having flipped a switch to turn on the cameras, and pacing that verges on the funereal, one wonders just what Roy Del Ruth was doing all that time behind his megaphone.

The next stage operetta to reach the screen was RKO's *Rio Rita* (released October 1929), the smash hit with which the Ziegfeld Theatre had opened in 1927. The longest talkie to date, over two hours, with the last forty minutes in the best Technicolor yet seen, this was an overwhelming success, artistically and commercially, named as one of the ten best pictures of the year. A south-of-the-border romance involving Texas Rangers, a Mexican señorita and a mysterious bandit called "the Kinkajou," *Rio Rita* had everything going for it, including its stars, John Boles and Bebe Daniels.

Though Harry Tierney's songs did not become standards, as have so many of Romberg's, the title number, "The Rangers' Song," "You're Always in My Arms" and "If You're in Love, You'll Waltz" were all extremely popular at the time.

Though in many ways a filmed stage show, with singers performing directly to the camera, in other ways, as Kreuger points out: "*Rio Rita* is tremendously innovative, for it is the first lavish screen musical in which the scope and type of musical numbers are directly relevant to the dramatic situation."

December 1929 brought Ramon Novarro's successful talkie debut in *Devil May Care*, a fast-moving tale of Napoleonic intrigue, based on *The Battle of the Ladies* (1851), by Eugène Scribe and Gabriel Legouve, with an all-new score by Herbert Stothart. As distinguished in type from *The Love Parade*, which

had opened a month before, *Devil May Care* is the first romantic costume operetta composed expressly for the screen. Though *The New Yorker* dismisses it as "one of those tumultuous romantic costume dramas with musical numbers added," as if the songs had been tossed in as an afterthought, Kreuger's comment seems more to the point: "Instead of a series of solos or duets for the stars (a common formula in early screen musicals), there is a fully developed score with ballads, comedy numbers, and a marching song for a large male chorus."

Though Novarro continued to appear in dramas, he made four more operettas, usually cast as a lighthearted but gentle playboy, two in 1930, *In Gay Madrid* (originally titled *The House of Troy*), in which he played a student, and *Call of the Flesh* (*The Singer of Seville*), as an entertainer, both set in Spain, both opposite Dorothy Jordan and neither as well received as *Devil May Care*.

As with other musical genres, 1930 was a boom-to-bust year for operettas: seven more from the stage, eight romantic originals, including Novarro's two, and two of the sophisticated variety, *Monte Carlo* and *Sweet Kitty Bellairs*, the only originals that were not complete disasters. *Cameo Kirby*, musical version of a 1909 play by Booth Tarkington and Harry Leon Wilson, filmed as a silent in 1923, reuniting the stars of *Married in Hollywood*, Norma Terris and J. Harold Murray, set in New Orleans and on a riverboat in 1850, with the hero one of those Mississippi gamblers (just close enough in time and place to recall *Show Boat*), must have looked like a sure hit—but the music was undistinguished, and Terris, who did not even sing in it, made no more films.

Equally promising, set in exactly the same locale and period, *Dixiana*, starring Bebe Daniels and Everett Marshall, composed and directed by the same men who had created *Rio Rita*, was a distinct letdown for all concerned, despite lavishly costumed scenes of the Mardi Gras in color. The *Times* reviewer was growing weary of old New Orleans

---

[1] *Married in Hollywood* (1929) was advertised and is still sometimes mentioned as the first operetta written for the screen, but this is not quite true, as the two Oscar Straus songs used were from his 1907 operetta *A Waltz Dream*.

plucky girl entertainers spurned by their lovers' haughty mothers, and even of Wheeler and Woolsey.

One of the strangest cases of 1930 was an aborted operetta called *The Three Sisters*—no connection with Chekhov—which, to judge by the press sheets, some of which are aimed at theaters not yet equipped for sound, started out as a late silent mother-love melodrama (probably 1929), set in war-torn Italy, starring Louise Dresser, with L. Wolfe Gilbert and Abel Baer credited as writers of two songs. Yet both *The American Film Institute Catalog . . . 1921–1930* and the *Blue Book of Hollywood Musicals* list *The Three Sisters* as having seven songs by Kern and Hammerstein, titles given, though in standard reference books it is not among their credits.

Far more bizarre was Cecil B. De Mille's highly publicized *Madam Satan* (October 1930), aptly termed by John Douglas Eames in *The MGM Story* as "the apex of cuckoo supercolossalness." Starting from the familiar *Fledermaus-Guardsman* premise, in which a suspicious wife (Kay Johnson) tests the fidelity of her husband (Reginald Denny) by masquerading as someone far more glamorous, it ends as a spectacular disaster thriller as hundreds of guests at a lavish costume ball, dressed as everything from a golden pheasant to Henry VIII, are forced to parachute over New York from a collapsing dirigible, broken away from its mooring mast. The contrasting behavior of the wife and the girl friend (Lillian Roth) brings the straying husband back into line.

Everson comments:

Once aboard the Zeppelin, the whole pace and mood change, and it becomes the kind of wild, vulgar, spectacular, no-holds-barred frolic that all De Mille films are supposed to be and almost never are . . . Culturally, this may be one of the worst films—but it's certainly also one of the most entertaining and unique.

1930 ended with the first screen operettas by two composers so illustrious that the results were all the more disappointing. In *Viennese Nights,* in Technicolor, the first of the series

Warners had signed Romberg and Hammerstein to write, the creators certainly played it safe. The book is a veritable pastiche of operetta clichés, one of those hopeless-love-through-the-years chronicles that reminded the *Times* reviewer of *Bitter Sweet.*

In Vienna in 1880 a young composer (Alexander Gray) loses the girl he loves (Vivienne Segal) to a nobleman (Walter Pidgeon), and on the rebound marries another (Alice Day) who does not appreciate his talent. In New York in 1890 as a second violinist in an opera house he meets his true love again, but she decides to return to Europe with her husband. Finally, forty years later, in 1930, the woman, now old, hears a familiar theme in a new composer's symphony and realizes her lover's son succeeded where he failed.

Friml's first and last screen operetta, *The Lottery Bride,* which opened in New York the day after *Viennese Nights,* made it and even *Madam Satan* look like almost documentary slices of life. "It is a pictorial composition that causes one to wish that the performers would sing more and talk considerably less," said the *Times* with commendable restraint. Based on Herbert Stothart's "tale" *Bride 66,* it was a fantastic mishmash.

Set in Norway, it told of a girl (Jeanette MacDonald) who forces her boy friend (John Garrick) into a three-day marathon dance, after which they drop from exhaustion. She then enters herself in a "wife lottery," and he wins her but doesn't realize it. So he boards a dirigible bound for the Arctic Circle, it crashes, but the lovers are reunited. If MacDonald's career could survive this, obviously it could survive anything.

The seven operettas from the stage fared somewhat better, starting with *The Rogue Song,* which introduced the magnificent voice and commanding personality of Lawrence Tibbett, leading Metropolitan Opera baritone, the first opera star to make a full-length film since Geraldine Farrar's curious silent career (1915–22). Supposedly based on Lehár's *Gypsy Love,* it used only one Lehár number, "Sweet White Dove"; Stothart wrote

Judith Vosselli, Catherine Dale Owen, Lawrence Tibbett in **The Rogue Song**

the other songs, including the most popular, "When I'm Looking at You."

The story, set in pre-Revolutionary Russia (with comic relief by Laurel and Hardy), was at least coherent, if melodramatic. Tibbett was a bandit leader disguised as a Cossack, in love with a princess (Catherine Dale Owen), whose brother he kills for having wronged his (the bandit's) sister. But to critics and audiences all that mattered was Tibbett's glorious voice and the lavish all-color production.

Also about a romance between a thief and a princess and also in color was Paramount's *The Vagabond King,* in which Dennis King

repeated the role of François Villon which he had successfully created on Broadway in 1925. Based on Justin Huntly McCarthy's *If I Were King,* long popular as a novel and a play (and again popular, even without the music, in Ronald Colman's 1938 film), with one of Friml's best scores, Jeanette MacDonald (her second film) as the patrician Lady Katherine, Lillian Roth as the pathetic gamine Huguette and O. P. Heggie as the wily Louis XI, *The Vagabond King* was praised on all counts.

In Kreuger's 1971 series at the Museum of Modern Art, only excerpts could be shown, but of these he says: "The romantic and illusory atmosphere of *The Vagabond King* is bewitchingly brought to life in this 1930 screen adaptation through the use of the sharpest, most subtly toned two-color Technicolor ever seen."

The film, though poorly remade in 1956, has never been revived, but, judging by stills, the production was elaborately authentic, the performers had all proved their talent, the score included "Only a Rose," "Some Day," the haunting "Huguette Waltz" and the rousing "Song of the Vagabonds," so one would suppose it represented romantic operetta at its very best.

Warners' next entry, *Song of the West*, based on the Youmans-Hammerstein *Rainbow* (1928), teamed John Boles and Vivienne Segal (her film debut) in the first outdoor musical in color. The *Times* complained of "the temperamental microphone or acoustics . . . If the songs came forth effectively, it might be another matter, but as they do not, the idea of Captain Stanton (Mr. Boles) and Virginia (Miss Segal) suddenly bursting into melody in the midst of romantic discussion seems strange."

Attempting the American epic vein, with caravans of covered wagons trekking westward against picturesque mountain scenery, it also included a quota of clichés: a cashiered Army officer who masquerades as a minister, then turns gambler, scenes in San Francisco, etc. As *Photoplay* said, "The *Song* is faint, in spite of excellent singing by John Boles and a vigorous tragi-comic performance by Joe E. Brown . . . Ambitious but dull."

Presumably inspired by the success of *The Rogue Song*, Warners next dusted off *Song of the Flame*, a 1925 Gershwin-Hammerstein operetta about a Russian peasant Joan of Arc known as "the Flame" (Bernice Claire), who, naturally, falls in love with a prince (Alexander Gray). As the ads would have it:

Russia of the Czars . . . splendor . . . magnificence. Pampered princes and their perfumed gallantries—squandering a nation's wealth in riotous revelry! And then from the lips of a glorious girl pours a soul-stirring song to light the fierce flame of revolt and free her people from the yoke of fate. What irony that the fire she kindled should sear the man she loves! What drama when the freedom she won for others makes her the slave of the man she hates!

As the hated one, Noah Beery was a bass-voiced villain, a traitor to the people's cause, who sings even when facing a firing squad, which politely waits until he has finished. Oddly, the *Bluebook* lists this film as having *no* Gershwin numbers, only several by Clark and Akst.

But the worst were yet to come. A few weeks after *Flame*, Warners were at it again, with *Bride of the Regiment*, based on a 1922 operetta, *The Lady in Ermine*, a heavily whimsical period piece set in nineteenth-century Italy, starring Vivienne Segal, Allan Prior and Walter Pidgeon, with Lupino Lane, Myrna Loy, Louise Fazenda and Ford Sterling trying hard for laughs. *Photoplay* said it all: "This is another of First National's gorgeously dressed, sumptuously mounted and very slow-paced operettas taken from the theatre. It positively glitters, and some of the Technicolor is grand, but it is a ponderous piece of business . . ."

Screen operetta surely plumbed one of its all-time nadirs with *Golden Dawn*, which was to stage adaptations what *Lottery Bride* was to screen originals: the dregs. On Broadway in 1928 as the first American work of the famed Hungarian composer Emmerich Kálmán, with a book by Harbach and Hammerstein, it had run 184 performances, presumably on the prestige of those names. As Vivienne Segal's third clinker in a row, the film almost finished her screen career (only *Viennese Nights* lay ahead), and certainly did no good for Walter Woolf King or Noah Beery, as another singing villain.

Set in German-occupied British East Africa during World War I, it sounds like a musical variation on *Trader Horn*, with a golden-haired white girl about to be dedicated by natives (who talk like Amos and Andy) for life as a virgin priestess. Lucius Beebe summed it up in the *Herald Tribune*: "Reason totters at the thought that any one could have conceived in seriousness such a definitive catalogue of vulgarity, witlessness, and utterly pathetic and preposterous nonsense."

The operetta form almost redeemed itself at the end of 1930 with MGM's *The New Moon,* with Met stars Tibbett and Grace Moore doing full justice to the melodious score of the 1928 Romberg-Hammerstein hit, which was originally set, like *Naughty Marietta,* in eighteenth-century New Orleans, but, presumably in homage to *The Rogue Song,* was now served *à la russe,* transposed to pre-Revolutionary Russia.

Tibbett was a dashing lieutenant, Moore a princess destined to wed another, but no one cared about the story when the two superb voices blended in "Lover, Come Back to Me," "One Kiss" and "Wanting You" or when Tibbett led the male chorus in "Stout-hearted Men." The *Times* was lavish in its praise, but in another illustration of Gresham's law, too many bad operettas had killed the public for good ones, and Moore's contract was not renewed.

No doubt this shift in taste accounts for the delay in the release of Warners' version of *Mlle. Modiste,* which was favorably reviewed in *Photoplay* for August 1930, under the title of *The Toast of the Legion,* but did not open in New York until January 1931, as *Kiss Me Again.*

The plot is a simple combination of *Camille* and *Cinderella,* in which the humble shopgirl Fifi (Bernice Claire), scorned by the haughty family of the young lieutenant she loves (Walter Pidgeon), sends him away (to Algiers), while she becomes a famous opera singer, the toast of Paris, acceptable even to his gouty old father (Claude Gillingwater). Like so many other musicals, it ends with a charity fete at an aristocratic estate.

As Everson noted for a Huff Society showing on June 8, 1965:

Kiss Me Again, however, does hold up fairly well considering that its basic values—the songs —have been so severely rationed . . . Fortunately the background score makes *constant* use of the lilting melodies, and this also helps quite

a little to overcome the lethargy of the creaking plot mechanics.

This was the last romantic stage operetta to be filmed for several years—until, in fact, another Herbert favorite, *Naughty Marietta,* in 1935. Meanwhile 1931 produced four screen originals, two of them Tibbett vehicles, artistically pleasing but financially unsuccessful. In *The Prodigal* (also known as *The Southerner*), he played his first contemporary role, a black sheep of a Southern family who prefers to wander as a hobo with his two sidekicks (Roland Young and Cliff Edwards). When he returns home after several years, he falls in love with the beautiful wife (Esther Ralston) of his despicable brother (Purnell B. Pratt), but gives her up to return to the road. Though no original score was written, Tibbett sang "Without a Song" (left over from the abandoned *Great Day*), Oscar Straus' "Life Is a Dream" and "Home, Sweet Home."

As noted earlier, in *The Cuban Love Song* Tibbett was back in uniform, as a World War I Marine, again with two comic buddies, Jimmy Durante and Ernest Torrence. However trite the story, the film when shown in 1971 was termed by Miles Kreuger "a work of astonishing beauty," which "adheres strictly to the story line, and neither music nor comedy is allowed to intrude." Besides the title song, Tibbett sang "The Peanut Vendor," "The Marine Hymn" and other military songs. (Never in any of his four MGM films did he sing a note of opera.) But, whatever its merits, *The Cuban Love Song* came too late, and Tibbett returned to the Metropolitan.

Samuel Goldwyn's only venture into operetta, *One Heavenly Night* (also known as *Lilli* and *The Queen of Scandal*), released in January 1931, was obviously a holdover, or hang-over, from 1930. The script by Sidney Howard, from a story by Louis Bromfield, surely put no strain on the talent of either Pulitzer Prize winner, for it was scarcely weighty enough for a ballet.

An innocent flower girl (Evelyn Laye in her American film debut) is persuaded to masquerade as a notorious music hall performer (Lilyan Tashman) when the latter is exiled by police from Budapest to Zuppa. There a dashing count (John Boles), taking her at face value, treats her accordingly, until at the end he realizes her true worth. The *Bluebook* lists only two songs, both forgotten, one by Nacio Herb Brown, the other by Bruno Granichstaedten.

Romberg and Hammerstein, still working out their contract to write an operetta a year for Warners, ended it once and for all, though perhaps not intentionally, with *Children of Dreams*, "a musical romance" about migrant workers in Western apple orchards. "The story is a simple one," said the *Times*, "and there is little or no effort at characterization or motivation." Except for Charles Winninger, even the cast was obscure.

To save her father from prison, the heroine (Margaret Schilling) "agrees to enter an opera career," is wooed by the son of her benefactor, but returns to the orchards and her true, apple-picking love (Paul Gregory). Said *Photoplay:*

Another reason why the box-office turned thumbs down on musicals. Sigmund Romberg and Oscar Hammerstein II are responsible for the tale, which has . . . a hero tenor warbling to the girl friend, "And Every Morning at Seven A.M. We'll Go Climb a Tree."

It was clear long before the end of 1931 that the romantic, sentimental operetta was, if not dead, at least dormant in Hollywood. Oddly enough, the only 1932 film to resemble the form at all was Pola Negri's American swan song, *A Woman Commands,* which, though supposedly based on the life of a real queen of Serbia, sounds exactly like a Graustarkian operetta—but its only song was the haunting "Paradise."

But despite all these portents the traditional operetta, old-fashioned in the worst sense, was not dead yet. Fox, which had scuttled Lilian Harvey's career in three films, fortunately was unable to do the same for the more durable stars of *Caravan* (1934), Charles Boyer and Loretta Young.

In spite of a tuneful score by Werner Heymann and direction by distinguished Erik Charell, both Europeans, *Caravan* seemed like a parody of all Hungarian gypsy operettas, from *The Gypsy Baron* to *Countess Maritza.* "If lyric loveliness and photographic charm were all a picture needed to keep an audience enthralled," said the *Times,* "Mr. Charell could be toasted in good Tokay."

Unfortunately, there was the story, about a Countess (Young) who must marry by midnight or else forfeit her lands. Naturally, she picks the least likely man, a proud gypsy (Boyer), who (as quoted by the *Times*) strikes a pose and recites: "A hundred pengoes is not enough, my lady. I may be a gypsy, but I'm not for sale." Nevertheless, he marries her, but she falls in love with a young lieutenant of her own class (Phillips Holmes) and "keeps the audience waiting around for an hour and fifty minutes while she flits coyly from one to the other."

Considering that Jean Parker gets third billing in the cast, one assumes that the lieutenant settles for her, while the Countess somehow manages to keep the gypsy. Though Boyer had played a few small parts in Hollywood in 1931–32, this was his first American lead, and surely only his unique magnetism could have survived such an inauspicious debut. As the *Times* perceptively noted, "M. Boyer, who has a reputation on the Gallic screen, plays the gypsy lover with liquid-eyed ardor, and his voice has the vibrant tenderness of accent which makes ladies suspire."

But undoubtedly the longest-heralded, most eagerly awaited, most lavishly produced operetta of the year, when it opened in October 1934, was MGM's *The Merry Widow,* for which Thalberg had finally reunited the winning Paramount team of Lubitsch, Chevalier and MacDonald. Louis B. Mayer and Chevalier himself had wanted Grace Moore, who was indeed eager to play Sonia, but Lubitsch, backed by Thalberg, insisted on MacDonald.

The opening at the Astor was celebrated with a glittering, star-studded premiere, and the *Times* raved, "The Winter season has been royally crowned." Apparently many reviewers (though not the public, which did not turn out for it), dazzled by the prestigious names, suffered from an "emperor's new clothes" syndrome, guiltily reminding themselves, "This is MGM's big production of the year. A Chevalier-MacDonald-Lubitsch musical! It's *got* to be great!"

Though Lubitsch is listed as associate producer as well as director, it is impossible to believe that he had final artistic control, so leaden is the tone of this *Merry Widow,* so completely the opposite from his four earlier musicals. In fact, the tiresome screenplay by Ernest Vajda and Samson Raphaelson turns the perennially popular *Merry Widow* from the elegant, amusing jewel that has held the stage the world over for over seventy-five years into something much closer to a drearily sentimental operetta.

Though *The Merry Widow* opened in Vienna in 1905 and swept London and New York two years later, the film is for no apparent artistic reason backdated twenty years to 1885—which means that the women must wear stiffly basqued and heavily bustled costumes so effective in gaslit Victorian thrillers and so wrong for a musical, instead of the graceful princess gowns in which the first Merry Widows waltzed.

The original operetta is set entirely in Paris, within the course of a day or two, the first act in the Marsovian Embassy, the second in the garden of Sonia's villa, the third at Maxim's, or, in some versions, a salon in Sonia's house redecorated to look like Maxim's. The whole plot, airy as it is, springs from the fact that Sonia, once a poor girl in mythical Marsovia, though in love with and loved by Count Danilo, was scorned as a commoner by his aristocratic family. On the rebound she married a rich old man, who soon left her with enough money to control the Marsovian economy. Enjoying her wealth in Paris, she is wooed by many titled Frenchmen, but Danilo, now a diplomat, is ordered to win her to keep her money in the country.

An interlocking subplot involves the wife (Natalie) of the Marsovian ambassador to France, Baron Mirko Zeta, and a young French vicomte, Camille, with whom she has been carrying on an indiscreet flirtation. When he writes of his love for her on her fan, she loses it, causing no end of complications. When in a last rendezvous in Sonia's summer pavilion they are almost caught by her husband, Sonia takes Natalie's place, letting Danilo believe the worst.

Only when she has teased him through the third act at Maxim's by pretending that she will forfeit all her money if she remarries does she get him to propose, after which she explains that the money will go to her second husband. To be sure, it is the music, not the book (by Victor Léon and Leo Stein), that keeps *The Merry Widow* alive wherever light opera is enjoyed, but the plot is at least coherent, less nonsensical than that of *Fledermaus* and, above all, it never takes itself seriously.

As if playing it safe at all costs, the MGM adapters took care that every scene looked familiar, recalling some previous Chevalier or MacDonald hit; Lubitsch seems not only to be repeating himself but even copying Mamoulian! The first several scenes, pointlessly set in Marshovia, introduce the King (George Barbier, just as in *The Smiling Lieutenant,* 1931) and the Queen (Una Merkel, with no funny lines) and re-establish Chevalier as a ladies' man, with the same personality and uniform as in *The Love Parade* and *The Smiling Lieutenant.*

Sonia is a wealthy, extremely reclusive widow in deep mourning, with no explanation of her marriage except the hint that it was happy. Regarding her as a challenge, Danilo, a total stranger, climbs the wall of her estate, preceded by a note describing himself as a "terrific" lover, but is coldly rejected by the lady, whose face he does not see, as she wears a black lace mask. Left alone, for no reason she sings "Vilia" from her balcony, to gypsy violin accompaniment (just as the Princess had sung "Isn't It Romantic?" in *Love Me Tonight,* where it made sense).

With no explanation she suddenly leaves for Paris, where she blossoms out in a new, non-mourning wardrobe. Danilo, caught in a compromising situation with the Queen, is hastily dispatched to Paris to woo Sonia, reversing the opening of *The Love Parade,* in which the hero for similar reasons was summoned home from Paris to marry the Queen.

From her hotel window Sonia sees and overhears Danilo order a hansom cab to take him to Maxim's (which, incidentally, did not open until 1893). She follows him there, but instead of an elegant, Art Nouveau setting for discreet rendezvous or for socializing among already paired couples of the demi-monde (as accurately shown in *Moulin Rouge,* 1953, and *Gigi,* 1958), it looks like a brightly lit, wide-open bordello of the Barbary Coast—several times its actual size.

Despite her elaborate gown, jewels and haughty manner, Sonia is at once mistaken for a cocotte, and goes along with it, accompanying Danilo to a *chambre séparée* for a long, serious scene; then, when he tries to make love to her, she leaves in high dudgeon. Not until *Girl of the Golden West,* more than three years later, was MacDonald called upon to do so much lip-biting and winking away of angry tears. "Merry" is the last adjective one would apply to this difficult, humorless widow.

At the embassy, hundreds of endlessly waltzing couples in identical uniforms and gowns, mechanically alternating black and white (choreographed by Albertina Rasch), look more like one of Busby Berkeley's massive spectacles than like people enjoying themselves at a ball. When the fuss-budget ambassador (Edward Everett Horton), apparently a bachelor, prematurely announces Sonia's engagement to Danilo, more bitter misunderstanding ensues. Danilo is arrested and sent back to Marshovia to be court-martialed.

At his quite unfunny trial, Sonia testifies that he did indeed try to woo her, but he is sentenced to prison. She is locked in the cell with him until she agrees to marry him, whereupon champagne, wedding rings and

even a clergyman are instantly produced.

No wonder Lubitsch went back to Paramount, where the following year he became production head. As for Chevalier, though offered several promising vehicles by MGM, evidently fearing that he would soon be playing second fiddle to MacDonald, he asked to be released from his contract, and after one more film, *Folies Bergère* (1935), an elaborate backstage musical for 20th Century, he returned to France, not to be seen in an American picture again for more than twenty years.

1935 began with Warners' uninspired version of *Sweet Adeline,* the 1929 Kern-Hammerstein musical that on stage had been one of the first evidences of the growing nostalgia for the '90s. Then, in a last vain effort to salvage Ramon Novarro's career, MGM produced *The Night Is Young,* from a story by Vicki Baum, into which Romberg and Hammerstein, as if they had learned nothing from *Viennese Nights* (1930), stuffed every possible *alt Wien* cliché, from Franz Josef to Wiener schnitzel. MacDonald was luckily otherwise engaged, so Novarro's co-star was the genuinely beautiful and talented Evelyn Laye, again, as in *One Heavenly Night* (1931), the victim of her material.

Set in Vienna in the 1880s (and thus perhaps utilizing some of the extras' costumes from *The Merry Widow*), *The Night Is Young* is essentially a simple variation on *The Student Prince* (one of Novarro's silent hits). Instead of the heir to a mythical kingdom, Paul Gustave is a Hapsburg archduke, nephew of Emperor Franz Josef (Henry Stephenson, who was also to play him in Durbin's *Spring Parade,* 1940). To camouflage his affair with a married countess (Rosalind Russell), Paul feigns a passion for an innocent ballet girl (Laye), only to find that he really loves her.

Of course he also enjoys her comic friends, fellow dancer Una Merkel and her beau, Charles Butterworth, who drives a horsecar. But when the Emperor gets wind of the romance, he solemnly reminds the young man of his sacred duty to go through with an arranged marriage of state. What can the lovers do but sit in a Prater beer garden and sadly sing "When I Grow Too Old to Dream"? This is a truly charming song, by the way, as also is the title number.

In a similarly trite vein Paramount offered *All the King's Horses* (also 1935) , which had run only a few months on Broadway in 1934. Possibly the studio had hopes of building the dimpled Danish star, Carl Brisson, into another Chevalier, but he made only three films, of which this was the last. Though it gave him "A Little White Gardenia," his signature tune in his later successful career as a supper club performer, it also saddled him with a dual role too much like Chevalier's in *Folies Bergere,* which had opened a few weeks before.

Again an entertainer is the double of a man of importance—in this case the King of another of those mythical countries—and again he is called upon to take his place not only in official duties but in the boudoir as well—to the consternation of the Queen (Mary Ellis) . "The photoplay is a rattletrap confection," said the *Times,* "which progresses so slowly that, unless you watch closely, you become convinced it is being unreeled backwards."

Whatever the artistic limitations of Columbia's Grace Moore vehicles, their financial (and even critical) success was too marked for other studios to ignore. Most were content to showcase their Metropolitan Opera songbirds in variations on the struggling-singer-makes-good formula, but Paramount, where Lubitsch was now in charge, in introducing mezzo-soprano Gladys Swarthout early in 1936 attempted to avoid that cliché, only to fall into a worse one. The decision (surely not Lubitsch's?) to turn Belasco's 1906 melodrama *The Rose of the Rancho* (first filmed in 1914) into an operetta, despite the repeatedly proved unsuitability of Belasco to the '30s screen, was, to say the least, ill-advised.

Once more we are back in the Ramona-Zorro country of Mexican California so popular in '30s films, with a preposterous plot in which the daughter of a *ranchero,* a demure señorita by day, is by night the mysterious

Don Carlos, leader of the vigilantes against the land-grabbing Yankees. John Boles was the government agent set to trap "him." The score by Robin and Rainger was undistinguished, and the time and place, of course, prevented Swarthout from singing a single operatic note. Said the *Times:* "It is the misfortune of the film that, instead of combining the most fascinating qualities of operetta and the six-shooter drama, it merely accents the weaknesses of both forms in one handsome blur."

This was surely an inauspicious start both for Swarthout and for 1936, yet in addition to *Rose Marie* the year was to produce two other first-rate operettas and two pleasant ones as well. To touch on the minor ones first, in *The Bohemian Girl* Laurel and Hardy did for Balfe what they had already done for Auber and Herbert: turn an otherwise unfilmable operetta into a slapstick romp, while retaining some of the story and the best of the music. The libretto, about a little princess kidnapped by gypsies, must have seemed fairly threadbare even in 1843, but the two stars as a pair of bumbling gypsies kept it from bogging down. The score includes the familiar "I Dreamt I Dwelt in Marble Halls," "Then You'll Remember Me" and "The Heart Bowed Down."

Dancing Pirate, produced by Pioneer Pictures and released by RKO, was the first musical—and only the third full-length film of any kind—in the new Technicolor (preceded only by *Becky Sharp,* 1935, and *The Trail of the Lonesome Pine,* 1936) . Designed by Robert Edmond Jones with a painterly palette that won rapturous praise from the *Times,* it was also graced by a Rodgers and Hart score (two forgotten songs) and a story that was at least unhackneyed.

An umbrella-toting dancing master (Charles Collins, warmly acclaimed as a most promising musical juvenile and never heard of again) is shanghaied by pirates from early nineteenth-century Boston to a sleepy Mexican village, where Frank Morgan is the alcalde and Steffi Duna his nubile daughter. Need it be added that the hero with his trusty umbrella gets the best of the pirates and wins the girl? It sounds like a precursor of the much-admired Judy Garland-Gene Kelly *The Pirate* (with faint overtones of *Mary Poppins*), yet it is utterly forgotten, never revived anywhere, not even mentioned in Kobal's book or in Daniel Blum's *Pictorial History of the Talkies.*

Perhaps tiring of the backstage framework of her last two films, however profitable, Grace Moore now appeared in the second of the only two pure operettas she ever made (the first was the 1930 *New Moon*): *The King Steps Out,* based on Fritz Kreisler's *Cissy,* with new lyrics by Dorothy Fields. Though it involved that favorite operetta device, royalty incognito, for once both lovers were of equal rank, thus eliminating the standard renunciation scene.

More unusually still, the kingdoms were not mythical but the real Bavaria and Austria of the 1850s, and the protagonists were the youthful monarch Franz Josef (Franchot Tone) and his cousin Elisabeth (Moore), whose nickname was "Cissy." Even the basic facts of the story, however fancifully embroidered, were more or less authentic. He *had* been slated by their mothers (sisters) to marry Cissy's sister Helene, who loved another, until Cissy does everyone a favor by capturing Franz Josef for herself, though in the film it means disguising herself as a dressmaker. (The fact that they were first cousins, brought up in neighboring countries by mothers on the best of terms, makes one wonder how *any* disguise could have fooled anyone in the family.) The film was well cast, with coolly regal Frieda Inescort as the sister, Nana Bryant as their mother and Elizabeth Risdon as the Dowager Archduchess Sophie, mother of the young Emperor.

In effect disowned by its director, von Sternberg, who asked that it not be included in any retrospective of his films, *The King Steps Out,* seldom revived or seen on TV, acquired an unmerited reputation as an impossible piece of schmaltz—but when shown in a revival

series in the '60s Everson wrote: "It holds up well, both as a piece of cinematic froth, *and* as a von Sternberg film."

"No fledgling prima donna this time but a gamine princess of Bavaria," the *Times* noted with relief, "Miss Moore is spared the necessity of impressing an impresario to gain an audition, but breaks into song with or without provocation all during the picture." Besides some songs from the stage version of *Cissy* (produced in Vienna but apparently not in New York), other Kreisler melodies were borrowed from *Apple Blossoms.* "The Old Refrain" and "Caprice Viennois" were also adapted.

Contemporary reviews praise Walter Connolly as the father of the girls, the beer-guzzling Duke Max of Bavaria, described by his wife as "a grease spot on the pages of history," and Herman Bing in a role so juicy that Everson considers this the definitive Bing film. He also judges it easily Moore's best vehicle, the one that dates least of all. She sings no opera, only the lovely Kreisler music.

But undoubtedly the American operetta of the year, perhaps of the decade, was Universal's definitive film of *Show Boat.* From the first, the 1927 Ziegfeld production had been an enormous hit (surely no other '20s musical has ever been revived as often, both here and abroad), so much so that Billy Rose was able to convince Universal that the public was tired of its songs by 1928, and all but "Ol' Man River" were dropped from the misguided 1929 film in favor of several, long forgotten, by Rose himself.

But with the perspective of more than half a century, *Show Boat* seems, if anything, an even more monumental achievement than was realized at the time. Though it had no immediate influence, surely *Show Boat,* not *Oklahoma!* (1943), was the first fully integrated American musical play—"integrated" in every sense, for it touched honestly on Southern racism, a topic generally taboo even in straight plays of its period.

Perhaps the main reason for its perennial appeal is that Hammerstein's libretto sticks faithfully to Edna Ferber's novel, which dealt, however romantically, with a genuine, hitherto unrecorded phase of Americana, the theatrical troupes who plied the Mississippi in the nineteenth century, bringing to thousands of small-town, rural and even backwoods people their only taste of professional entertainment. Written with no thought of adaptation to the musical stage, the novel was not tacked together out of prefabricated, interchangeable parts, like the librettos of, for instance, *Rose Marie* and *The Desert Song* (also by Hammerstein). Each song grows directly out of Ferber's characters and situations and could not possibly be transferred to any other musical.

The 1936 film, directed by James Whale, not only restored all the glorious Kern music but added two new numbers, "Ah Still Suits Me," a comic number for Paul Robeson, and "Gallivantin' Around," also comic, which Irene Dunne sings in blackface.

Aside from its fidelity to the spirit and letter of the original, the film is totally cinematic. Even the credits are given on antique-lettered posters and banners, as in a show boat parade through town. Irene Dunne made a perfect Magnolia, from youth to maturity, using her fine dramatic and comic talents as well as her excellent voice, and Allan Jones was ideally cast as Gaylord Ravenal.

Even more valuably from a historical point of view, Helen Morgan as the tragic mulatto Julie, the role she had created on stage, gives a marvelously affecting performance both in the dramatic scene in which she and her white husband (Donald Cook) are forced to leave the *Cotton Blossom* and in her two unforgettable numbers, "Can't Help Lovin' Dat Man" and "Bill."

Though Paul Robeson was not the original Joe, he had played it in the first London production in 1928 and in the first New York revival in 1932; certainly he never appeared to better advantage on screen. "Ah Still Suits Me," with scornful comments by Hattie McDaniel, is irresistibly droll. Unlike the laundered MGM version of 1951 (in which Lena

Helen Morgan, Irene Dunne in Show Boat

Horne was not allowed to play Julie for fear of offending the South), this one retains the strong original lyrics of "Ol' Man River," with its blunt opening about "darkies" working while the white folks play and its fervent plea to be taken away from the white man boss. As Joe sings, we *see* him and other "darkies" toting barges, lifting bales, getting a little drunk and landing in jail, all with immensely moving effect.

To make way for the two new numbers and several added scenes, "Why Do I Love You?" and "Life upon the Wicked Stage" were reduced to background music, but otherwise this was the *Show Boat* for all seasons. The scene of Magnolia's eventually triumphant debut at Chicago's Trocadero after Ravenal's desertion reflects the '30s fondness for the '90s, for she sings "Goodbye, My Lady Love" and finally wins the crowd over with repeated choruses of "After the Ball."

A montage of programs, theater marquees and newspaper clippings (which turn into a scrapbook kept by Ravenal) quickly conveys Magnolia's rise as an international musical comedy star and her retirement after her daughter Kim makes her debut. As in the stage version (not the novel), both Captain Andy (Charles Winninger, as in the original production) and Parthy (Helen Westley in a wonderfully tart performance) remain alive to the end, when Ravenal turns up as stage doorman at Kim's theater and Magnolia invites him to join her in a box to applaud their daughter—a sentimental ending not in the novel, but in the context most satisfactory.

No doubt encouraged by the enthusiastic reception of *Show Boat,* Hammerstein and Kern made another ambitious attempt at creating a genuinely indigenous American musical, using purely native idiom in basic material, lyrics and music. This was *High, Wide and Handsome* (1937), directed by Rouben Mamoulian, a truly original concept that cannot be compared with any earlier musical, but, rather, with those examples of rugged Americana in which two rival forms of transportation battle it out.

The *Times* was wholly enthusiastic, finding the film "a colorful chapter of American history"—an unfamiliar one, too, since it dealt with the discovery of oil near Titusville, Pennsylvania, in 1859. Randolph Scott was one of the lucky discoverers, but with no means of getting the oil to the refineries except by the railroads, which were out to ruin him. The only solution was to build a direct pipe line, as laborious an undertaking as the famous irrigation ditch in *Our Daily Bread,* and saved from destruction (by Charles Bickford and his railroad gang) only by Irene Dunne, daughter of a circus owner, and her professional friends, including elephants.

The *Times* continued:

Like *Show Boat* and *San Francisco,* it defies ready classification. "Musical romance" is closer to it than "operetta," yet has too tinkling a sound to be applied to a rugged and virile historical saga. "Symphonic drama" is the phrase

fastened to it by Hollywood's Idwal Jones . . . Against it, *Show Boat* was an effeminate piece, nostalgic and sentimental.

Whereas *Show Boat* and at least five of the Rodgers-Hammerstein musicals (*Oklahoma!, Carousel, South Pacific, The King and I* and *The Sound of Music*) had scores from which every leading number became a standard, the music from *High, Wide and Handsome* has not survived. One recalls but dimly that the big romantic ballad, popular at the time, was "Can I Forget You?"

Meanwhile, earlier in 1937 MacDonald and Eddy had, quite incredibly, topped their two previous triumphs with *Maytime,* hailed by the *Times* unequivocally as "the most entrancing operetta the screen has given us." (As noted above, the *Times* considered the Kern-Hammerstein musicals something other than operettas.)

Even more than in *Naughty Marietta* (1935) or *Rose Marie* (1936), the stage original was completely abandoned, not only the story and the characters' names but almost the whole score. All that survived of Romberg's 1917 *Maytime* was the title and the most popular song, already a standard, "Will You Remember?"

To judge by an unfavorable review of a 1922 silent based on it, the 1917 book was about a girl named Ottilie van Zandt who falls in love with her family's gardener, but both are forced to marry others. Years later, their grandchildren fall in love, with happier results. According to MacDonald's biographer, Thalberg had actually started a production of this *Maytime,* which was to have been MGM's first film in the new color, with a cast that included, besides the two stars, Paul Lukas, Frank Morgan and Julie Haydon.

Although Thalberg's death in 1936 had an adverse effect on the careers of many stars such as the Marx Brothers, this is one case when one can only be grateful for Mayer's decision to scrap the unfinished film and assign Noel Langley to come up with a completely new script, to be made with a different supporting cast.

As is evident from the opening credits, in which, to the strains of "Will You Remember?", the names are spelled out in letters formed of blossoms floating on a pond, *Maytime* was meant to be a romantic operetta, a form which films had seldom done so well. The triumph of Langley's script, Robert Z. Leonard's direction and the performances of the stars is that the love story comes through as gently poignant, tastefully touching rather than maudlin or oversentimental.

With its framework of an old lady telling the story of her own tragically lost love to a troubled girl torn between romance and career, this *Maytime* owes a good deal to Coward's *Bitter Sweet*—but the climactic murder is much better motivated, the outcome of seven years' smoldering jealousy, and the musical background is greatly enriched by the heroine's position as a world-famous opera star. True, this reflects the still popular operatic cycle, but again, as in *Rose Marie,* Mac-Donald is spared the struggling soprano routine; until her retirement the heroine remains internationally acclaimed—ironically counterpointing the emptiness of her personal life.

The "May Day" theme is evoked from the very first shot, of school children dancing around a Maypole on the green of an American town of 1905. As old Miss Morrison, Mac-Donald never overplays, but moves with sprightly dignity and speaks without excessive doddering. As she sits beneath a' blossoming tree in her garden, a young friend (Lynne Carver) comes weeping to confide her dilemma; she has been offered the chance of an operatic career in New York, but her beau (Tom Brown) is totally against it. She longs to be a great singer like Adelina Patti or Nellie Melba—or Marcia Mornay . . .

This, of course, is the old lady's cue, and we flash back to 1868, when *she* was Marcia Mornay, an American soprano who after a brilliant debut at the Paris Opéra has been invited to sing before Napoleon III and Empress Eugenie at a gala soiree in the Tuileries. During the banquet Nikolai Nazarov (John

Barrymore), her coach, manager and impresario, adroitly maneuvers an important composer, Trentini (Paul Porcasi), into promising to write an opera especially for her.

Though alcoholism had cost Barrymore the role of Baron de Varville in Garbo's *Camille* (1937), he made up for it in his strongly etched characterization of Nazarov, whose total domination of his protégé, on stage and off, recalls his 1931 triumphs in *Svengali* and *The Mad Genius.*

MacDonald's spirited rendition of "Les Filles de Cádiz," with "Les Deux Grenadiers" for encore, is short and tuneful enough to please any ear, further enlivened by constantly changing camera angles and reaction shots (Eugenie suspicious of Napoleon's rapt attention, Nazarov amused at Trentini's inability to contain his enthusiasm).

Later, Nazarov most humbly proposes marriage, urging Marcia not to feel in any way obligated—but, of course, she does, since he has made her triumph possible. Unable to sleep, she daringly goes for an open carriage ride around Paris, but the horse breaks away, leaving her stranded near a students' cafe on the Left Bank.

An atmosphere of lighthearted gaiety reminiscent of the opening scenes of *La Bohème* is quickly established as an American voice student, Paul Allison (Nelson Eddy), improvises an amusing song about ham and eggs, a pastiche made up of snatches from many familiar operatic numbers: "Caro Nome," "Largo al Factotum," "O Evening Star," "La Donna è Mobile," "The Soldiers' Chorus" and the *"William Tell* Overture."

Captivated by the charming young diva, Paul playfully refuses to let her leave until she has promised to come to lunch next day in his top-floor apartment. Chaperoned by his overzealous teacher (Herman Bing), the two Americans sing a duet of "Carry Me Back to Old Virginny" and realize a rapport that leads to further plans. Against her better judgment, Marcia agrees to spend May Day with Paul. Meanwhile she must sing that evening in *Les Huguenots,* during which Paul is ejected from an orchestra seat when the rightful ticket holder appears.

Cedric Gibbons' settings and Adrian's costumes re-create nineteenth-century Paris as vividly as they had a few months before in *Camille,* but they outdid themselves in the lively sequence of the May Day celebration at St. Cloud, with every detail exactly right for the time and place: the headdresses of the peasant women, the flower-decked swings, the blossom-wreathed arches carried by the dancers.

The love scene (their only one), in which Marcia explains to Paul all the reasons why she must marry Nazarov, is quite brief and restrained, leading naturally into their duet of "Will You Remember?"

The subsequent montage, conveying seven years of her operatic career: ocean liners, trains, programs, posters, theater curtains, is extremely well done, suggesting constant travel, triumph after triumph, but with Marcia's face gradually maturing and Nazarov implacably in the background, with the metronome ticking away. Among the operas she is seen and heard singing are *Tannhäuser, Lohengrin, La Traviata, Norma, The Bohemian Girl* and *Lucia di Lammermoor.*

When we pick up the story again in 1875 in New York, where she has been engaged to sing, the girlish ringlets and ruffled hoop skirts of the Second Empire have given way to a matronly chignon and the elaborately bustled silhouette of the '70s. Her face and manner have also subtly aged. When her maid remarks on the pleasant hotel suite, her weary murmur, "Yes, they all are," conveys a world of lonely boredom.

The climactic opera, *Czaritza,* supposedly the one Trentini composed for her, is actually a pastiche, adroitly adapted by Herbert Stothart from Tchaikovsky's Fifth Symphony, with French lyrics especially written for it. (The libretto seems to be about Catherine the Great.) Paul is cast as the leading man, and though they give no sign of recognition, Nazarov suspects the truth from watching the way they sing together. After the opening,

Marcia asks for her freedom and he deceptively agrees, but instead goes to Paul's apartment and shoots him; Marcia arrives just in time for him to die in her arms. (He was the first operetta hero to die since Carl in *Bitter Sweet,* and the last until Billy Bigelow in *Carousel.*)

When we dissolve back to the 1900s framework, all that remains, of course, is for the girl to profit by Marcia's sad example, and for Marcia, still seated beneath her favorite tree, to die peacefully on this anniversary of the one happy day of her life. A youthful "spirit" arising from the dead body was a favorite device for softening a protagonist's death, used in Barrymore's silent *Beau Brummel* (1924), Shearer's *Smilin' Through* (1932) and *The Story of Vernon and Irene Castle* (1939).

Restored to their 1868 selves, Paul and Marcia, like the ghostly lovers in *The Enchanted Cottage* (1924), smile indulgently as the reunited ingenue and juvenile walk away. Their final duet of "Will You Remember?" as they fade arm in arm down a path into a curtain of blossoms closes *Maytime* on the same tender note on which it began.

Maytime was not merely the best, it was the *only* good film operetta of 1937. Otherwise, it was a year of disasters, starting with *Champagne Waltz.* Still trying to give Swarthout the kind of success MacDonald enjoyed at MGM and Moore at Columbia, Paramount dusted off the battle, trite even then, of "long-hair" music versus swing, the former written by Johann Strauss, Jr., the latter by no less than seven studio composers. The result was somewhere between musical comedy and operetta, combining the worst of both worlds.

A popular waltz palace in Vienna, run by maestro Fritz Leiber, is deserted when an American jazz band, led by Fred MacMurray, moves in next door. Predictably, the band leader incognito woos the maestro's daughter (Swarthout), even teaching her to chew gum (an echo of *It Happened One Night*), all leading up to a monstrous finale which, said the *Times,* "appears to be staffed by the combined orchestras of the Metropolitan, the Phil-

Nelson Eddy, Jeanette MacDonald in **Maytime**

harmonic, Paul Whiteman and Fred Waring . . . completely absurd."

Like Astaire and Rogers, MacDonald and Eddy, after one successful picture in 1937, temporarily parted company, but with much less fortunate results. MacDonald made an extremely elaborate, sepia-toned version of Friml's 1911 operetta *The Firefly,* but despite an adaptation by Ogden Nash, a screenplay by Frances Goodrich and Albert Hackett, new lyrics by Gus Kahn, Bob Wright and Chet Forrest, musical direction by Stothart, over-all direction by Robert Z. Leonard and, of course, sets and costumes by Cedric Gibbons and Adrian—all people of proven talents—*The Firefly,* though financially successful, failed to light up the screen.

The *Times* noted that "a toy-soldier tale of

Bonaparte's invasion of Spain is glibly substituted for the New World background against which the Friml tunes were first introduced twenty-five years ago," but how far it departed from the original is now impossible to judge. The title character, a singer and dancer, actually a Spanish spy, wins the heart of an important French officer (Warren William), but loses her own to Don Diego (Allan Jones), a counterspy for France. Much too plotty for an operetta, it drags on for well over two hours before Wellington's victory finally reunites the lovers. Many of the original songs were retained, notably "Giannina Mia," "Sympathy" and "Love Is Like a Firefly," but the outstanding hit, sung by Jones, was a Friml piano work adapted by Forrest and Wright as "The Donkey Serenade."

Eddy's solo venture was even more disastrous; *Rosalie,* a Ziegfeld extravaganza of 1928 written for Marilyn Miller, with music by Gershwin and Romberg, was resurrected, but given a new score by Cole Porter. "In the Still of the Night" became a standard, but according to Porter's own account, he composed the title song "in hate," after L. B. Mayer had rejected six previous versions. The deliberately inane lyrics sound like a parody of the kind of love song based on a girl's name, especially "Rose Marie."

The equally brainless book mixed West Point cadets with a mythical kingdom, actually called Romanza, of which Eleanor Powell is the princess (attending Vassar), daughter of battle-ax queen Edna May Oliver and dithering king Frank Morgan (a role he had played on stage), whose hobby is ventriloquism. Of all the overproduced numbers, the worst was a stupefying bridal finale—a cliché of Broadway musicals of the '20s. The *Times* described *Rosalie* as "one of the most pretentious demonstrations in sheer mass and weight since the last Navy games . . ."

Reunited by executive decision responding to popular demand, MacDonald and Eddy were next cast, or miscast, in a totally misguided musical version of Belasco's creaking 1905 melodrama *The Girl of the Golden West* (1938), which had inspired Puccini's 1910 opera and had already been filmed twice, in 1923 and 1930. Undaunted by the all but unbroken record of Belasco fiascoes in '30s films, most recently Paramount's *Rose of the Rancho* (1936), MGM gave the doomed venture the full treatment, including sepia photography and a score by Romberg, as well as some old standbys like "Liebestraum" and "Ave Maria" for MacDonald.

Nothing, however, could lighten the dead weight of that dreadfully hokumish plot, lumbering toward the stagy climax in which Mary, the virtuous saloon-owner, plays poker with the sheriff (Walter Pidgeon), with the stakes her hand and the life of her wounded lover, a federal agent masquerading as a Mexican outlaw.

Such a hero was as ludicrously unsuited to Eddy as a gun-totin', homespun frontier gal was to MacDonald's crisply urban, sophisticated personality. Both artistically and financially, this was the least successful MacDonald-Eddy film so far, and indeed marked the beginning of their decline.

After three such clinkers in a row, MGM at last came up with an operetta that can be ranked as at least a qualified success, *The Great Waltz* (1938), which was nothing if not Continental in its talent: French director Julien Duvivier, German scenarist Gottfried Reinhardt, Russian musical arranger Dmitri Tiomkin (working with the music of Austrian Johann Strauss, Jr.) and the three stars, French Fernand Gravet, in one of his rare American appearances, as Strauss, Austrian Luise Rainer as his wife, the former Poldi Vogelhaber (entirely fictitious), and Hungarian Miliza Korjus (publicized as "the gorgeous Korjus") as Karla Donner, an equally imaginary prima donna who almost comes between them.

On stage, where *The Great Waltz* had been a hit in 1934 largely thanks to a superspectacular production at the long-vanished Center Theatre in Radio City, the story concentrated on the bitter rivalry between Johanns Jr. and Sr. for the title of Waltz King of Vienna, with a romance only incidental to the triumph of the son. In the film, however, the exhilarating music is all but bogged down in a dull marital quadrangle, of which Lionel Atwill was the fourth side, as the singer's titled protector. Rainer was once again the neglected wife, smiling bravely through her tears, and the dialogue was full of lines like "Something difficult and honest had to be said. It was just like you to say it."

Although in his comments on *Love Me Tonight*, Kobal notes its "delicious parody of that film operetta staple 'the drive through the country,'" he finds its use in *The Great Waltz* "unforgettable," in the sequence in which Strauss and the singer "drive through the woods at dawn in an open carriage; the rhythm of the trotting horse, the birds' trill, the shepherd's call, a postilion's horn, the snug improvisations of the soprano and carriage driver, all weave together to re-emerge from Strauss' head as the famous Waltz of the Vienna Woods."

Oddly enough, Henry Hull, who only the year before had played Crown Prince Rudolf to Dudley Digges' Franz Josef in Maxwell Anderson's Broadway play *The Masque of Kings,* had, so to speak, grown into his own father. In *The Great Waltz* he appears as Franz Josef in two scenes, one at the time of the revolution of 1848, and again more than forty-three years later, when he honors Strauss at Schönbrunn.

The Great Waltz was released for Thanksgiving 1938, but MGM still had its main holiday treat in store, the delightful version of *Sweethearts.* Since most of the country saw this in 1939, this continued the MacDonald-Eddy patterns of an operetta each spring. But during the same year she made *Broadway Serenade,* an execrable backstage musical, while he fared somewhat better in *Let Freedom Ring,* written by Ben Hecht presumably as MGM's answer to *High, Wide and Handsome* in the field of rugged, two-fisted Americana.

Said the *Times:* "Ben Hecht, henceforth to be known as the George M. Cohan of the movies, is waving the flag like mad in *Let Freedom Ring,* the burstingly patriotic lesson in Americanism . . ." But it was still "sound dramatic stuff," with "fortunately, Mr. Eddy's singing."

Set in Colorado in the 1880s in a town on the right of way of a land-grabbing railroad headed by ruthless tycoon Edward Arnold, it was still another variation on the Pimpernel-Zorro pattern, in which a local boy returned from college in the East apparently sells out the home folks to work for the enemy. But secretly he's "the Wasp," the mysterious anti-railroad leader who publishes a literally underground newspaper edited in a cave, converts the railroad workers to democracy, including even the tycoon's chief henchman (Victor McLaglen), and incidentally wins Virginia Bruce.

Just as the first filmed stage operetta of the decade, *The Rogue Song,* had been set in Russia, so was the last, *Balalaika,* MGM's holiday offering for 1939. Based on Eric Maschwitz's London hit, never done in New York, it cast Eddy as a Cossack prince who in Czarist days masquerades as a student to woo a beautiful girl (Ilona Massey) working for the revolution.

Critical opinion was mixed; the *Times* on the whole liked it, especially a scene in which on Christmas Eve at the front Eddy sings "Silent Night" and is faintly answered by Austrian soldiers in their trenches, just before a signal to attack. The film ends with a happier Christmas celebration, after the revolution, in that milieu so popular in '30s films (e.g., *Here Is My Heart, Roberta, Café Metropole, Tovarich, Ninotchka*), the world of Russian *émigrés* in France, in this case Paris, where some of them now run a cabaret called the Balalaika.

The *Herald Tribune* critic pronounced it a "dull diversion . . . Screen operetta has rarely seemed more synthetic, Slavic or sluggish." He was, however, charmed by Ilona Massey, who after being wasted as a lady in waiting in *Rosalie* here came into her own.

The provenance of the score of *Balalaika* remains confused. The *Blue Book* lists five songs, including "At the Balalaika," as by Stothart, Forrest and Wright, three by Kahn and Romberg, and one, "The Magic of Your Love," by Kahn and Lehár. Since it seems unlikely that either Romberg or Lehár would have been hired to contribute so little, no doubt, as with "The Donkey Serenade," new words by Kahn were put to music already owned by MGM.[2] Yet Eames in his *MGM Story* calls both "At the Balalaika" and "The Magic of Your Love" adaptations by Stothart of music by George Posford and Bernard Gruen from the original London stage show.

But the romantic operetta did not die with the '30s, either on stage or screen. Thus Eddy was successfully teamed with Risë Stevens in *The Chocolate Soldier* (1941), which, as in *Sweethearts,* ignored the original Straus operetta and rather neatly adapted *The Guardsman,* making the jealous actor and his wife stars in a Viennese production of *The Chocolate Soldier.*

As noted at the end of the last chapter, such films were generally overshadowed by the newer, more innovative works for which no satisfactory term was ever found (musical play? dramatic musical?), the classics of the '40s, '50s and '60s pioneered by Rodgers and Hammerstein, soon joined by Lerner and Loewe, later by Harnick and Bock, Kander and Ebb, occasionally even by Leonard Bernstein, and, of course, by Stephen Sondheim—those brilliant productions in which the stories made sense, every song and dance expressed time, place and situation, and even sympathetic characters could die. Almost all these were filmed.

Also as noted, at first most were in the homespun American style of *Oklahoma!,* but even in those years both *The Merry Widow* and *Fledermaus* (under the title of *Rosalinda*) enjoyed Broadway runs, as did Herbert's *Sweethearts* and *The Red Mill* a few years later. Even some of the practitioners mentioned above sometimes chose the colorful or exotic milieux associated with earlier operettas, though used with different effect (as in *Brigadoon, Camelot, Fiddler on the Roof* and *Cabaret*). Nor should it be forgotten that Rodgers and Hammerstein's last work, *The Sound of Music,* the biggest film musical hit of the '60s, was as coyly sentimental as *Blossom Time* or *The Song of Norway,* and that Stephen Sondheim, whose boldly original "concept" musicals are as far as possible from the traditional operetta, enjoyed his greatest commercial success so far, on stage if not on screen, with the prettily romantic *A Little Night Music* (1973).

[2] "The Magic of Your Love" is the same Lehár waltz called "Sweet White Dove" in *The Rogue Song.*

THE SHOW MUST GO ON
Behind the Scenes

41

"AH...GIVE THE KID A BREAK!"
Backstage Musicals

Although backstage plots had never been particularly popular on Broadway except for a few late '20s hits, *The American Film Institute Catalog . . . 1921–1930* lists seventy-six films about the theater, many more on agents and backers, and literally hundreds on actors. To this already marked trend, talkies gave new urgency.

Even though characters spontaneously bursting into song, with unseen accompaniment, was a convention taken for granted in the theater for centuries, from the Greek chorus to grand opera, not to mention all those musical comedies and operettas, yet in the early talkie years many producers, fearing despite all evidence to the contrary that such imaginative musical flights might prove too much for literal-minded fans, unaccustomed to hearing their favorites talk, much less sing, hedged their bets with those backstage musicals that became the most overworked cliché of 1929 and 1930.

A backstage story could play both sides of the street, providing an apparently "realistic" framework (however trite, maudlin or fantastic on an absolute scale), in which no character ever sang or danced unless rehearsing for or performing in a show. Unlike those covered in the previous chapters, these were some of the least "integrated" musicals ever made. The songs, at least the love songs, in the show-within-a-show might vaguely parallel the backstage romance, but more often they were simply presented for their own sake, while the story stood dead still, waiting in the wings.

After all, the great breakthrough film itself, *The Jazz Singer* (1927), had been a backstage musical based on a Broadway hit, in which at first only the songs were meant to be heard, until Jolson's ad lib, "You ain't heard nothin' yet!" opened up the possibilities of dialogue and revolutionized the industry.

The first full-length talkie, *The Lights of New York* (1928), however inept, was set mainly in a night club, with the musical sequences the only ones the *Times* praised. Other backstage films with sound sequences included *Show Girl* (1928) and *Lucky Boy* (1929), which, as *Photoplay* put it, was "patched and vulcanized with sound and talk." Thus MGM's *The Broadway Melody*, released in February 1929, could hardly be said to be breaking new ground—but it was the first *all-talkie musical*, and that was enough to make it the runaway hit of the year. It even won the Oscar for best picture.

"So far as its entertainment value is concerned," the *Times* reviewer complained, "it is a matter whether one likes to see and hear so much of the upsets of chorus girls and their ilk." But he was in a minority of one. When Charles King, in white tie and topper, against a stylized Art Deco Times Square setting, urged his audience not to bring a frown to old Broadway, it was just what the 1929 public had been longing to hear. "All Talking! All Singing! All Dancing!" shouted the theater marquees, and people everywhere flocked to it.

Edmund Goulding's story, enlivened by James Gleason's slangy, wisecracking dialogue, was indeed obvious and sentimental enough (though not then as hackneyed as countless follow-ups would make it seem) — but, as with gangster films, sound made all the difference. Soon almost everyone was singing and dancing to not only the title song but "You Were Meant for Me"; even "The Wedding of the Painted Doll," done as a production number in Technicolor, is at least still recognizable.

The standard Manhattan milieu of predatory millionaire "angels" ever on the prowl for pretty new faces in the chorus (played for laughs in the gold-digger comedies) was here used seriously, as naïve young Queenie (Anita Page), the prettier half of a small-time sister team, in her determination not to come between the devoted Hank (Bessie

Bessie Love, Charles King, Anita Page in **The Broadway Melody**

Love) and her fiancé, songwriter Eddie Kerns (King), almost succumbs to a suave playboy (Kenneth Thompson, in the kind of role Franchot Tone would play a few years later). As the plain, plucky, losing side of the triangle, Love gave an Oscar-nominated performance that still rings true after more than fifty years.

No wonder that the very word "Broadway" in a title was thought to guarantee success. *Broadway* itself was soon followed by *Broadway Babies, Broadway Scandals, The Gold Diggers of Broadway*, and in 1930 *Broadway Hoofer, Broadway Vagabond* (changed to *Puttin' on the Ritz*), *Lord Byron of Broadway* and *The Royal Family of Broadway* (not a musical, but obviously, like *The Gold Diggers*, changed to suit the trend).

It would be pointless to trace all the variations on the same few, soon threadbare themes, but one backstage musical, released in April 1929, before most of the others, was unique in its setting, its story line and, above all, in its star: Maurice Chevalier's triumphant talkie debut in *Innocents of Paris*, in which he introduced "Louise," as a singing junk dealer who rises to stardom in a revue like the *Folies Bergère*.

As Miles Kreuger observed in notes for a showing of the film in 1971, "It reveals almost none of the technical limitations that fettered so many early talkies . . . There is no attempt in the settings or costumes to glamorize Paris artificially."

For historic purposes, too, one should note the first talkie appearance of that most notorious of all backstage musical clichés, the unknown going on at the last moment in place of the star. However often it may have been used in silents, this chestnut made its talking debut in *Fox Movietone Follies of 1929*, in which Lola Lane replaced the temperamental leading lady (Sharon Lynn). This opened in New York two days before the much-better-remembered *On with the Show*, the first talkie all in color. Indeed, the "prismatic tones" were all that the *Times* found to praise.

Whenever *On with the Show* is revived in New York, *The New Yorker*'s anonymous reviewer-in-brief states: "The same story was later used for *42nd Street*." As will be proved below, this simply is not true. *On with the Show* was based on an extremely plotty story by Humphrey Pearson, involving a robbery of the box office during a producer's (Sam Hardy) frantic efforts to stave off his creditors—but it does preserve the classic unities of time and place. All the action occurs during the first out-of-town performance of a Broadway-bound musical (of which it is even possible to follow the plot). Betty Compson as the bitchy star refuses to go on after the first act unless she is paid immediately in cash, so a talented hat-check girl (Sally O'Neil) takes her place. This substitution is the *only* point of resemblance to *42nd Street*. Of seven songs, only "Am I Blue?", sung by Ethel Waters, has survived.

Both *Broadway* (1926) and *Burlesque* (1927) had been hits on stage as straight plays, but since both were backstage stories, naturally in 1929 they reached the screen as musicals. The former, set in a midtown night club, opened in the few days between *Fox Movietone Follies* and *On with the Show* and drew a better review than either from the *Times*, which, however, complained that the numbers merely got in the way of the melodramatic gangster plot.

Because of the embarrassing possibilities of the word "burlesque" on the marquees of respectable movie houses, the play of that name was retitled, lamely enough, *The Dance of Life*. Though Nancy Carroll played Bonnie, the loyal, long-suffering wife, the role that had made Barbara Stanwyck a Broadway star, Hal Skelly effectively re-created his original characterization of Skid Johnson, the dancing (and drinking) comedian whose head is turned by Broadway success. This pattern soon became the second most popular cliché of backstage musicals.

The Gold Diggers of Broadway fared better than most of its kind, perhaps because it was basically a romantic comedy, not concerned with some trouper's breaking heart. On the other hand, *Glorifying the American Girl* (1930), despite the novelty of a climactic *Follies* opening filmed in New York, introducing such contemporary celebrities as Jimmy Walker, Texas Guinan, Jack Dempsey and Otto Kahn, and the presence of Ziegfeld stars Mary Eaton, Helen Morgan, Rudy Vallee and Eddie Cantor performing just as on stage, was rightly dismissed as trite, even if the glorified girl did lose her man in the end.

When *Chasing Rainbows,* MGM's intended follow-up to *The Broadway Melody,* opened in February 1930, the *Times* critic headed his totally adverse review "More Backstage Bickering." And indeed the film did combine the two most overworked backstage clichés of the day: another of those conceited heels, this time a hoofer (Charles King), ignores his loyal partner (Bessie Love) to marry a designing leading lady (Nita Martan), who eventually walks out on him and the show, leaving guess whom to go on in her place?

And yet, to anyone not forced to sit through a year of such musicals, as 1930 reviewers had been, *Chasing Rainbows* has much to offer. As Kreuger put it in his notes for a 1971 Museum of Modern Art showing:

Chasing Rainbows . . . presents quite an intriguingly original situation: all the performers are members of a touring road show, and, like the characters in *Grand Hotel* . . . they cannot escape the environment that links and imprisons them . . . *Road Show* was, in fact, the pre-release title . . . and a far more appropriate one than *Chasing Rainbows.*

Love and King were given strong support by Marie Dressler, Polly Moran and Jack Benny (in his first dramatic role). To judge by the uniforms and stage settings, the musical in which they are touring is set in wartime France. The finale, which seems to be celebrating the Armistice, was "Happy Days Are Here Again," which two years later became FDR's campaign song, and so gained a wholly unexpected place in popular history.

Only the week before *Chasing Rainbows,* an even more egotistic protagonist (Harry Richman) had figured in *Puttin' on the Ritz,* but had received a much warmer welcome from the *Times.* A performer and songwriter, taken up by a society woman (Aileen Pringle), anticipating *Pal Joey,* high-hats all his old friends and true-blue girl friend (Joan Bennett), until temporary blindness from wood alcohol brings him to his senses. Berlin supplied the title song and "With You," but the big hit was "There's Danger in Your Eyes, Cherie."

A few weeks later, in the oddly titled *Lord Byron of Broadway,* came the worst of all such despicable show-biz antiheroes, another songwriter-singer (Charles Kaley), who turns even his best friend's (Cliff Edwards) death into salable Tin Pan Alley sentiment. The Brown-Freed score included the standard "Should I?" Only in *Children of Pleasure* (1930) was the formula varied, if not reversed. A composer-performer (Lawrence Gray), engaged to an heiress (Wynne Gibson), finds she plans to continue an affair with his understudy (Kenneth Thompson), so turns to his understanding co-worker (Helen Johnson). None of the songs survived.

At the opposite extreme from all these cads and bounders was the kindly hero of *Song O' My Heart,* in which the beloved Irish tenor John McCormack, then forty-five, made his first screen appearance. Released in time for St. Patrick's Day 1930, directed by Frank Borzage, filmed partly in Ireland and featuring a dozen of the singer's concert favorites, the picture was warmly praised for its exceptionally fine photography and perfect sound recording, especially the star's rendition of "Little Boy Blue," during which the camera cuts away from him to depict the story of Eugene Field's touching little poem.

To provide some semblance of plot, McCormack as a singer must look out for the orphaned children of his late beloved (Alice Joyce). Using an exceptionally clouded crystal ball, *Photoplay* said, "Maureen O'Sullivan was brought to this country from Dublin to carry the heart interest. She doesn't make the grade, but Tommy Clifford, the eleven-year-old kid playing her brother, is a sensation. Maureen will undoubtedly go back to the old fireside."

Like the stock market a year earlier, long before the end of 1930 the wave of backstage musicals had crested, then crashed so heavily that none at all were released in 1931 or 1932. But Darryl Zanuck, then studio manager at Warners, took a shrewd gamble and produced *42nd Street,* from a gutsy 1932 novel by Bradford Ropes. Apparently confident of its success even before release, the studio in January 1933 announced a follow-up, whose title was changed from *High Life* to *The Gold Diggers of 1933.* In a heavily covered publicity stunt, a "42nd Street Special" train was sent across the country to Washington for FDR's inauguration, bearing a flock of Warners contract players, including Bette Davis. Perhaps the most unusual feature was that none of them had any connection with the film.

Later generations who know Forty-second Street between Seventh and Eighth avenues as the most blatantly sleazy block in New York may well wonder why any novel or film was ever named for any part of such a street —but until the early '30s those very theaters now showing pornography housed so many hit musical comedies that "Forty-second Street," even more than "Broadway" itself, came to symbolize the musical stage.

Like the film, the novel traces the birth pangs of a Broadway-bound musical, *Pretty Lady,* from casting call to out-of-town opening, but it involves several relationships taboo on screen even before the Production Code. Julian Marsh, the great director himself, is having an affair with an ambitious chorus boy, Billy Lawlor. A naïve chorus girl, Peggy Sawyer, is the only one in the company to ignore this and treat Billy pleasantly, so when the demanding, promiscuous star, Dorothy Brock, is injured in a drunken fall downstairs, Billy persuades Marsh to let

Peggy take her place. Brock is the jealous mistress of Pat Denning, a smalltime gigolo who divides his strictly commercial favors between her and dance director Andy Lee's oversexed wife, whom at the end Pat plans to marry. The wife was not used in the film.

Those familiar with the film may recognize the characters' names, but surely not much else. In the film, after the accident the show's sugar daddy-backer (Guy Kibbee), who does not appear in the book, wants to give Dorothy's role to another chorus girl, "Any Time Annie" (Ginger Rogers), who, most improbably, declines it and urges Marsh (Warner Baxter) to choose Peggy (Ruby Keeler) ("She can dance rings around Brock"). The end pairs off Peggy and Billy (Dick Powell), while Dorothy (Bebe Daniels) happily settles for basically decent Pat (George Brent). Yet the last shot is of Marsh, who has no love life, sitting on a fire escape in the theater alley, looking profoundly depressed. In any case, it is clear that *42nd Street* is not, as *The New Yorker* insists, "an unofficial re-make of the 1929 *On with the Show.*"

Even cleaned up, the story, told largely in swift wisecracks, is, unlike *The Broadway Melody,* as lively and unsentimental as the music, epitomized by the jaunty, pounding rhythm of the title song ("Hear the *beat* of dancing *feet?* It's the song I love, the melody of Forty-second Street!"). Of the four songs, "You're Getting to Be a Habit with Me," Daniels' one number, is seen only in rehearsal.

In what came to be the standard Busby Berkeley pattern, the other three increasingly elaborate production numbers are presented back to back at the end, supposedly during the first performance of the show. "Young and Healthy," sung by Powell to Toby Wing, is fairly routine, but "Shuffle Off to Buffalo" (which established a honeymoon number as another cliché of this kind of musical), neatly staged aboard a Pullman car, remains a pleasure, especially the cynical added chorus sung by Rogers and Una Merkel as cold-

Ginger Rogers, George E. Stone, Una Merkel in **42nd Street**

creamed chorus girls commenting on the happy couple's prospects.

Only the climactic "42nd Street" number takes off into the surreal, when Keeler is suddenly revealed to be dancing atop a taxi in the middle of traffic. The quick, balletic impressions of midtown types and situations (including a momentary vignette of a girl in a hotel room who is stabbed, then falls out a window and through a marquee), the sense of the pulsing, frantic tempo of New York, though attempted in many another film, was seldom so vividly captured. As Powell musically sums it up, "Naughty, bawdy, sporty, gaudy Forty-second Street!" This film set a new pattern for all subsequent backstage musicals, especially at Warners, which may be why so many of the others seem like ever-paler carbon copies.

Its instant success evidently took the other studios so completely by surprise that there was not even a follow-up until Warners' own shrewdly timed *Gold Diggers of 1933* was released in June 1933. This was indeed a remake of the 1929 *Gold Diggers of Broadway*, based on the Hopwood play, but with a new score and the added motivation that the girls are trying to raise money for a show called off just as they were about to open.

Considering the cheerful intent of the film, reflecting the surge of optimism generated by the New Deal, it is surprising that the opening and closing numbers were not transposed. It is the decidedly upbeat "We're in the Money," full of topical references, with the chorus girls decked out in giant coins—who could forget Ginger Rogers singing one chorus in pig Latin?—that is interrupted by the sheriff taking over the theater.

Later, after all the difficulties have been

ironed out and "Pettin' in the Park" and "The Shadow Waltz" have been staged, the film's closing number is the somber, socially conscious "Remember My Forgotten Man," sung principally by Joan Blondell, Hollywood's equivalent of Broadway's "Brother, Can You Spare a Dime?" and no less poignant. Indeed, this powerfully conceived and staged mini-drama conveys images of the Depression more haunting than any non-musical had thus far attempted. The contrast with the frivolity of the offstage story, whether or not intentional, is effectively ironic.

The first spin-off in the new backstage cycle came, surprisingly, from Universal: *Moonlight and Pretzels* (August 1933), a low-budget production shot in a small New York studio, enough, as Everson noted for a 1976 showing, to make one "gasp at the devil-may-care attitude which prompted Universal to release the film in direct competition with so many bigger and better musicals."

Leo Carrillo contributed another of his genial gangster roles as a gambler who backs Roger Pryor's musical, then loses control to a rival (Herbert Rawlinson), who offers the starring role to inexperienced ingenue Mary Brian—but, in a switch, she refuses, insisting that the real star (Lillian Miles) go on.

The score, by E. Y. Harburg and Sammy Fain, among others, was nothing if not timely. The title number, set in a beer garden, joyously anticipated Repeal, due in December. "Are You Makin' Any Money?" was a question any early '30s girl might have asked her boy friend. "I've Got to Get Up and Go to Work" celebrated that experience as a welcome novelty. "Dusty Shoes," sung by Alexander Gray, is a long, stylized montage of conditions 1929–33, ending with a tribute to FDR.

In October 1933 Warners released a third blockbuster, *Footlight Parade,* the first to be adversely reviewed by the *Times.* Keeler and Powell were again the young lovers, Kibbee the hayseed backer, Blondell was promoted—or demoted—from gold digger to faithful secretary, but a dynamic new element was

added: James Cagney in his first screen musical. Sennwald appreciated Cagney, but spoke of the "dull and turgid" film that "rumbles along with the elephantine splendor of its kind."

Cagney played another hard-pressed producer, who gets the idea of packaging live musical prologues to accompany feature films; they can be syndicated and staged simultaneously. He must grind out three of these extravaganzas in as many days. Thus "Honeymoon Hotel," "By a Waterfall" and "Shanghai Lil" take up nearly the whole second half of the picture.

By now Berkeley had abandoned all pretense of reality. The spectacles are dreams bounded only by his imagination, not so much choreographed as photographed: girls, girls, girls, forming every kind of geometric pattern, shot from every conceivable angle, especially from overhead, while the chorus of the song is endlessly repeated. In *Footlight Parade,* as still another twist on the oldest cliché, the juvenile, a no-talent protégé of the backer's wife (Ruth Donnelly), gets drunk, so Cagney must go on for him, joining Keeler in the "Shanghai Lil" finale, which concludes with a tribute to the stars and stripes, FDR and the blue eagle of the NRA.

Considering its major role in the first musical cycle, MGM was slow to respond to the second. Its first attempt was *Broadway to Hollywood,* released in September 1933, a backstage soap opera which reflected the popular through-the-years pattern, but was certainly no competition for the fast, up-to-the-minute Warners musicals. Despite fine performances by Frank Morgan and Alice Brady as the Hacketts, a married vaudeville team, the film remains flat, obvious and predictable throughout.

From Tony Pastor's in 1886, the Hacketts are followed through the heyday of vaudeville as their son, who grows from Jackie Cooper into Russell Hardie, becomes successful enough to star in a Weber and Fields show, in which they are given only bit parts. At this point MGM quite anachronistically tossed in an absurdly overblown production number salvaged from the abandoned 1930 *March of Time.*

While the parents are reduced to playing in obscure movie houses, the son and his wife (Madge Evans) become headliners, but he drinks and philanders, and after a quarrel she is killed in a fall downstairs. The Hacketts take their grandson (Mickey Rooney, who was then thirteen but looked about six, dancing up a storm) while his father continues to drink and eventually dies in World War I.

In no time it's 1929 and the grandson (Eddie Quillan) is a big movie star, the kind who walks off the set while studio heads rage. Of course his grandfather tracks him down, convinces him he must be a true Hackett, the show must go on, etc., then quietly expires while the boy is shooting a scene. *Broadway to Hollywood* is totally without laughs, convincing drama, good music or even nostalgic appeal.[1]

Thus by the fall of 1933 MGM had not yet come out with a hit musical. In the 1960s, Joseph Mankiewicz told how hard he tried to persuade Louis B. Mayer to buy an exquisite operetta he had seen in Paris. All Mayer said, logically enough, was, "Give me *43rd Street!"*

What he got instead, produced by his then son-in-law, David O. Selznick, directed by Robert Z. Leonard, from a novel by James Warner Bellah, was *Dancing Lady*, released in December 1933, almost a year after *42nd Street*, but not too late to be a resounding hit on its own. Joan Crawford was well cast as a brash, ambitious dancer, first seen being hauled off by the police from a raided burlesque house.

In the first of his many charming playboy roles, Franchot Tone falls hard for her, but she has eyes only for a tough dance director (Clark Gable). In his eagerness for her to give up her career, Tone withdraws his financial backing from her show, but this only drives her into Gable's arms. The closing superproduction number featured both Fred Astaire (film debut) and Nelson Eddy in non-speaking roles. Among the songs written by three different teams was "Let's Go Bavarian," another echo of "I Luff Louisa," which Astaire had introduced on Broadway, but the biggest hit was "Everything I Have Is Yours."

Obviously the backstage musical had staged a comeback—but fortunately 1934 did not repeat 1930's mistakes. There were fewer made, and even these tried studiously to avoid the hoariest clichés. Three were melodramas, all involving death; one was a mystery. In *Bolero,* five years before *The Story of Vernon and Irene Castle,* George Raft played an ambitious dancer, Raoul, whose career spanned those same dance-mad years (c. 1912–20), costumed with Travis Banton's usual precise sense of period. Helped by his loyal brother (William Frawley) and any number of women, Raoul rises from humble origins to expensive gigolo in Parisian cabarets to top ballroom dancer, firing any partner who falls for him, until one (Carole Lombard) turns the tables and leaves him.

Just as he is about to realize his long-cherished dream of opening his own club, where he will dance his definitive interpretation of Ravel's *Bolero,* comes the war, from which he returns with a weakened heart and warnings that he must not dance again.[2] On opening night when his current partner (Sally Rand) turns up drunk, his true love, though now married to a British peer (Ray Milland), takes her place for a most impressive and haunting *Bolero.* In his dressing room Raoul dies with the applause still ringing in his ears—surely an unusual ending for a film about dancing.

Wonder Bar (a pun on the German word

---

[1] As a follow-up Brady was also starred in *Stage Mother* (1933), an unpalatable mixture of *Mother Knows Best, Applause* and *Stella Dallas,* in which daughter Maureen O'Sullivan is driven into breaking away from her.

[2] This was an anachronism; Ravel composed his *Bolero* in 1928.

Joan Crawford, Clark Gable in **Dancing Lady**

wunderbar, "wonderful") is a spectacular night club in Montmartre, where in a single night half a dozen stories interweave in true *Grand Hotel* fashion. A Latin dance team (Dolores Del Rio and Ricardo Cortez) quarrel when she finds that he is also the lover of a banker's bored wife (Kay Francis). In a jealous rage, Del Rio stabs Cortez during a passionate tango, but good old Al Jolson, owner and star of the Wonder Bar, who also loves her, not only convinces her that Cortez is not dead but disposes of the body in the car of a suicidally bent German officer (Robert Barrat)—only to lose Del Rio to Dick Powell.

The plot is so strong that the Berkeley numbers come as tedious interruptions, especially the relentlessly reprised "Don't Say Goodnight" and Jolson's blackface "Goin' to Heaven on a Mule," done in Uncle Remus terms that would later be considered outrageously patronizing.

Murder at the Vanities, also from the stage, mixed music, comedy and mystery with fair success, thanks to a strong cast and good numbers, one of which became a standard, the timely, post-Repeal "Cocktails for Two" ("Oh, what delight to be given the right to be carefree and gay once again, no longer slinking, respectably drinking, like civilized ladies and men"), introduced by Carl Brisson in his talkie debut, and another of which three years later would have been banned as illegal, celebrating the joys of marijuana!

Jack Oakie was the show's press agent and Victor McLaglen a detective investigating the strange occurrences on opening night, when first the body of a private eye (Gail Patrick) is found on a catwalk far above the stage, then an unpopular star (Gertrude Michael) is killed by a falling sandbag, and the heroine (Kitty Carlisle) is in constant danger. The identity of the murderer is as much a surprise as in most mysteries.

Another of 1934's better backstage musicals was *Moulin Rouge* (based on Constance Talmadge's 1925 silent *Her Sister from Paris*), in which another Constance (Bennett) not only sang but successfully played a dual role, one a brunette with a French accent.

It was the familiar *Fledermaus-Guardsman-Madam Satan* plot, in which a neglected spouse masquerades as someone more glamorous to test the partner's fidelity. Here she impersonates her sister, a French musical comedy star, so well that her husband (Franchot Tone) is completely captivated. The Warren-Dubin score includes "Coffee in the Morning" and the wistful "Boulevard of Broken Dreams."

The following year Chevalier did something similar in *Folies Bergere* (1935), in which he played two roles, one an important financier, the other his double, a Parisian revue star. When the banker must be in two places at once, the performer is hired to take his place for certain public appearances, which leads to no end of complications with the banker's wife (Merle Oberon) and the impersonator's girl friend (Ann Sothern). Both the story and the spectacularly staged numbers, especially "Rhythm of the Rain" and "I Was Lucky," were highly praised, as was Chevalier's dual performance, but it was his last American film for over twenty years.

Among backstage musicals, the least original were those in series, of which by the mid-

'30s each major studio had its own: Paramount's *Big Broadcasts,* Fox's *George White's Scandals,* MGM's *Broadway Melodies* and Warners' *Gold Diggers,* most distinguished, if at all, only by their songs. Warners indeed ground out more standardized products than anyone else; the *Gold Diggers* label might just as easily have been attached to *Dames* (1934, in which the hit song was "I Only Have Eyes for You"), *Go into Your Dance* (1935, in which Jolson sang "A Latin from Manhattan" and "About a Quarter to Nine"), *Colleen* (1936, no distinguishing feature), *Stage Struck* (1936, in which ingenue Jeanne Madden went on in place of rich, untalented backer Blondell) and *Ready, Willing and Able* (1937, in which Keeler and Lee Dixon danced on giant typewriter keys).

Gold Diggers of 1935 was but a trivial background for "Lullaby of Broadway," Berkeley's most elaborate and dramatic spectacle, the closest to a ballet, in which Wini Shaw suffers death by defenestration. Likewise, *The Broadway Melody of 1936* (1935) is the one that introduced tap dancer Eleanor Powell, as well as three standard songs, "I've Got a Feelin' You're Foolin'," "You Are My Lucky Star" and "Broadway Rhythm." *The Broadway Melody of 1938* teamed Powell and Robert Taylor again, but is remembered, if at all, as the one in which sixteen-year-old Judy Garland sang (to Clark Gable's photo) the unforgettably touching "Dear Mr. Gable," Roger Edens' specially written extension of "You Made Me Love You."

By mid-decade the backstage musical film, especially the series, had become such a standing national joke that in the 1936–37 edition of the *Ziegfeld Follies* the Act One finale was an extravaganza titled "The Big Broadway Love Melody Cast of 1937," in which the big dance number was "The Gazooka" and Bobby Clark and Fannie Brice played characters named Bing Powell and Ruby Blondell.

But some of the most distinctive backstage musicals, even from the same studios, were not part of any series. No doubt because of his success as the director in *42nd Street,* Warner Baxter apparently had his choice of similar roles. In the brightly satirical *Stand Up and Cheer* (1934), which the *Times* hailed as "close to a conception of what a modern Gilbert and Sullivan opus might be," Baxter was a producer appointed by the President to the new cabinet post of Secretary of Amusement, charged with "bringing smiles to the face of the nation." The score, now forgotten, was full of upbeat numbers like the title song, "I'm Laughin'" and "We're Out of the Red." The large cast included "a delightful child named Shirley Temple"—her first notice by the *Times.*

In *King of Burlesque* (1936), which the *Times* rated "one of the screen's more entertaining ventures in the musical comedy line," Baxter played the title role. Even after he has risen to be a producer of successful Broadway revues, his Park Avenue bride (Mona Barrie) finds them too vulgar for her taste, but when his experiments with art ruin him, she deserts him, leaving him to fight his way back with the help of a burlesque alumna, Alice Faye.

In *Vogues of 1938* (1937), the first modern musical in the new color, lavishly produced by Walter Wanger, Baxter, in a slight switch, was the head of a fashion house, unhappily married (as twice before) to Helen Vinson, whose avant-garde theatrical ventures are driving him to ruin, until he hits on the idea of using the sets from her latest flop play to stage the big fashion show that puts him on top again, ready to face the future with Joan Bennett, who as a society girl turned supper club chanteuse introduced one of the song hits of the season, "That Old Feeling."

20th Century-Fox's *On the Avenue* (1937), a veritable compendium of '30s movie conventions, now seems all the more charming on that account. The plot is a variant of *Love Is News* (released by the same studio a month later), in which "America's Richest Girl" (Madeleine Carroll) is feuding not with a reporter but with a stage star (Dick Powell) because his current revue features a lam-

poon of her, her yachtsman father (George Barbier) and her wildly eccentric aunt (Cora Witherspoon). The star is also loved by a singer (Alice Faye), who gives him up but is last seen flirting with the old millionaire. The whole film moves along lightly, to one of Berlin's very best scores: "This Year's Kisses," "You're Laughing at Me," "I've Got My Love to Keep Me Warm," "Slumming on Park Avenue" and, the inevitable Gay '90s number, "The Girl on the Police Gazette."

Although Berlin has wisely never permitted his private life to be subjected to the indignity of a "bio-pic," *Alexander's Ragtime Band* (1938) was a cavalcade of his professional career thus far: twenty-six songs, from ragtime to swing. The plot follows Tyrone Power, Alice Faye and Don Ameche (the same trio as in *In Old Chicago*), backed by Ethel Merman, from 1911 to 1938 during which time no one ages a day. Despite the nonsensical story, the *Times* called it "the best musical show of the year."

No one ever said that about *Rose of Washington Square* (1939), which reunited Faye and Power as a loyal Ziegfeld star and her crooked husband, so obviously based on Fannie Brice and Nicky Arnstein that it is surprising the studio was not sued. Faye sings, not very convincingly, several songs associated with Brice, especially the title number and "My Man," but the characters were deracinated, with WASP names, and though much was made of the period, Faye's strictly 1939 dresses, hats and hairdos make the film one long, painful anachronism. The only bright spot was Al Jolson, reprising some of his most celebrated hits.

Though 1939 is rightly considered the outstanding year in Hollywood history, producing classic films in almost every genre, the backstage musical was definitely not one of them. MGM perpetrated two of the worst on two of its top female stars. Joan Crawford's *Ice Follies of 1939,* with James Stewart and Lew Ayres, and Jeanette MacDonald's *Broadway Serenade,* also with Ayres, were dreary (and unsuccessful) soap operas in which conflicting careers cause marital problems, like inept parodies of *A Star Is Born.*

Two filmed Rodgers and Hart musicals opened in New York on two successive days in October 1939, one successful, the other not. *Babes in Arms,* on Broadway in 1937, had one of the composers' finest scores, yet other songs were added, by Brown and Freed, Arlen and Harburg. The title number, "Where or When" and "The Lady Is a Tramp" survived, but, inexplicably, not the equally familiar "My Funny Valentine," "I Wish I Were in Love Again" and "Johnny One Note." Brown and Freed added "I Cried for You" and "Good Morning." As Eames notes in *The MGM Story,* it started a cycle of "Come on, kids, let's put on a show!" films. Even Judy Garland was overshadowed by the exuberant Mickey Rooney, who did everything, including deadly impersonations of Lionel and John Barrymore.

On Your Toes, in 1936 the first Broadway musical to incorporate a ballet (choreographed by George Balanchine), somehow didn't come across on screen, though it stuck to the story of a third-generation vaudeville hoofer (Eddie Albert) who writes a ballet, *Slaughter on Tenth Avenue,* and gets involved with a mad Russian troupe, especially the prima ballerina (Vera Zorina). As on stage, the big hit was "There's a Small Hotel."

Almost as old as the backstage musical itself was the kind supposedly based on the career of a real singer, composer or producer —too scattered to constitute a cycle, yet just numerous enough to rank as a special subgenre of the biographical film.

In the first such talkie, *A Lady's Morals* (1930), Grace Moore, in the earliest anticipation of the operatic cycle, played Jenny Lind. The film was a musical smorgasbord, with two classical arias, four songs by Oscar Straus, two by Stothart and one by Carrie Jacobs Bond, but the story, said the *Times,* was "one of half-truths and fiction," something about her true love (Reginald Denny) going blind and giving her up.

Wallace Beery played P. T. Barnum, who brought the Swedish Nightingale to America. Thus when 20th Century made *The Mighty Barnum* in 1934, Beery repeated the role, this time with Virginia Bruce as Lind, her singing remarkably well dubbed. As for authenticity, the *Times* noted: "With gleeful whoops Gene Fowler thumbs his nose at the grave processes of history and biography . . . an entertaining fable."

Stephen Foster was the victim of two pseudobiographical films in the '30s, about which the only relevant question is which was worse. Republic's *Harmony Lane* (1934), with Douglass Montgomery and Evelyn Venable, attempting to dramatize how Foster drank himself to death, "lapses into the lachrymose and beery piety of an ex-drunkard preaching prohibition on a street corner" (said the *Times*).

20th Century-Fox's *Swanee River* (1939), starring Don Ameche, was dismissed as "a rather badly Technicolored song-slide for a half-dozen of the more famous Foster tunes . . . in which Al Jolson is forever appearing at the head of a minstrel troupe to sing the Foster melodies as though they were all called 'Mammy.' "

Although, surprisingly, Hollywood never filmed Romberg's popular *Blossom Time,* Fox offered its own equally fanciful version of Schubert's unhappy life in *Love Time* (1934). Nils Asther played a Schubert so poor that he gives up the girl he loves (Pat Paterson), never suspecting she's of noble blood. She runs off with traveling musicians, nurses him back to health and arranges for him to play at court for a synthetic happy ending.

Though not a musical, the next biographical film about a show-biz figure was the lively *Annie Oakley* (1935), which was to have been called *Shooting Star.* Barbara Stanwyck was warmly praised as the backwoods Ohio girl whose marksmanship made her world-famous, with Preston Foster as her true love and Moroni Olsen as Buffalo Bill Cody—but to later generations the film is bound to seem like a de-musicalized version of *Annie Get Your Gun*.

Pictures titled *The Great* (Someone) usually court disaster, but one major exception was MGM's *The Great Ziegfeld* (1936), the most lavish and successful backstage biography made thus far. In the title role William Powell was suavity itself, and Luise Rainier, both in her dramatic scenes and in her two musical numbers, made such a delightfully piquant Anna Held that no one questioned her winning the Oscar.

Miriam Hopkins would have been Billie Burke's first choice to play her youthful self, but Myrna Loy, so often cast as Powell's wife, fitted in smoothly, as did Nat Pendleton as Sandow and Virginia Bruce as Audrey Dane, a hard-drinking, gold-digging Ziegfeld girl said to have been inspired by Lillian Lorraine. Fannie Brice and Ray Bolger sparkled as themselves. The incredible scale of some of the numbers, especially "A Pretty Girl Is Like a Melody," outdid anything possible on stage even for Ziegfeld, but this was by now an accepted screen convention, and the musical interludes never get in the way of a leisurely but well-knit narrative.

The chronology, major events and most names are correct, but in 1936 Lillian Lorraine and Marilyn Miller were both living and would not allow their names or any suggestion of their relations with Ziegfeld to be used.

The Great Waltz has already been discussed, as has *The Story of Vernon and Irene Castle.*[3] The only remaining backstage biographies were two inferior 1939 offerings from Paramount. *The Star Maker* cast Bing Crosby as Gus Edwards, once famous producer of kiddie revues called *School Days*, which show-

[3] Other operettas with backstage stories include *Music in the Air, The Cat and the Fiddle, Rose Marie, Show Boat, Maytime, Sweethearts* and *Balalaika*. Other such nostalgic films were *The Florodora Girl*, all Mae West's '90s vehicles, *The Bowery, The Old Fashioned Way, Sweet Adeline, San Francisco, We're Going to Be Rich* and *Zaza*.

William Powell, Virginia Bruce
in The Great Ziegfeld

cased such future celebrities as Eddie Cantor, George Jessel and Walter Winchell. None of the youngsters in the film were ever heard of again.

Still worse was *The Great Victor Herbert*. Portly Walter Connolly was well cast in the title role, but the film strayed so far from the truth that it added an apologetic afterword. Too much of it concerned the tiresome marital troubles of a couple of fictitious singers (Mary Martin and Allan Jones), but the worst problem was that Paramount had acquired rights to the music but *not* to the operettas for which it had been written, so

Herbert fans were subjected to such horrors as a number from *Naughty Marietta* done in a snowy Arctic landscape.

Among forms of live entertainment other than the stage, the circus provided the background for only four musicals, three from the stage, all covered earlier: *Rain or Shine, Sunny, Poppy* and *High, Wide and Handsome*. A surprising number were set in radio stations, often featuring radio stars as themselves and usually satirical of crass sponsors and idiotic commercial jingles, but seldom of the medium itself.

Throughout the '30s the two dominant media were less rivals than collaborators. Premieres of important films were broadcast live; comedians often spoofed them, providing further free publicity; Hollywood gossip columnists soon took to the air; fading stars (e.g., Pickford, Chatterton) found temporary refuge in weekly series, and still flourishing ones guested on variety programs.

Within a few weeks in 1932 Warners released two comedies about radio-made celebrities. *Crooner* amusingly kidded the whole phenomenon, tracing the meteoric rise and even faster fall of a conceited band leader (David Manners), who by singing through a megaphone affects women like catnip. The best lines were Ken Murray's as an utterly cynical agent, who, while frankly despising the crooner, manipulates him into a national craze. It also included two hit songs, "Sweethearts Forever" and "Three's a Crowd." In *Blessed Event* Lee Tracy played a Winchell-like columnist whose archenemy is another crooner (Dick Powell); both work on radio programs whose commercials are lampooned.

Equally mocking of crooners was Paramount's first *Big Broadcast* (1932), in which Crosby, in his full-length film debut, played "Bing Hornsby," idol of the air waves, fired by a sponsor but restored to success by a Texas millionaire (Stuart Erwin); the film also had a number of radio stars who in "the big broadcast" sing the songs they made famous. In addition to Burns and Allen's comedy, the film was livened by many wild

sight gags—e.g., a "hot" clarinet melts, a clock-face comes to life, a cat liquefies long enough to slide under a closed door and other phenomena hitherto seen only in cartoons. Besides the familiar radio theme songs, the score included two new Crosby hits, "Please" and "Here Lies Love."

RKO next took up the good-natured spoofing of radio in the very funny *Professional Sweetheart* (1933), with Ginger Rogers as a sexy singer trapped as "The Purity Girl" of the *Ipsie Wipsie Radio Hour,* sponsored by Ipswich Wash Cloths, forbidden even to smoke or drink, much less do anything else. A hillbilly (Norman Foster) is selected from among her fans for a publicity-plotted romance and wedding; when dragged off to his old Kentucky home, she finds she prefers the simple life, after all, until brought back to the air by her sponsor's rival.

Rogers appeared in another satire on radio, *Twenty Million Sweethearts* (1934), opposite Powell as another crooner, discovered as a singing waiter and pushed to fame by Pat O'Brien, but forbidden to marry so as not to lose his fans. Other musicals involving radio singers include *The Loud Speaker* (1934—Ray Walker), *Broadway Gondolier* (1935—Powell again), *Stars over Broadway* (1935—James Melton), *Every Night at Eight* (1935—a girl trio, Alice Faye, Frances Langford and Patsy Kelly), *Millions in the Air* (1935—John Howard, Wendy Barrie and others), *Wake Up and Live* (1937—Jack Haley) and *Mr. Dodd Takes the Air* (1937—Kenny Baker).

Among variations of the backstage musical, the last to arrive (and the shortest-lived) was the operatic cycle (1934–37), which consisted not of filmed operas but of stories of the professional struggles of classically trained singers. Sparked by the unexpected success of Columbia's *One Night of Love* (1934), which launched Grace Moore on a second screen career that lasted only slightly longer than her first, every major studio soon signed its own Metropolitan Opera stars, to play unknowns striving for the big break.

At the time *One Night of Love,* directed by Victor Schertzinger, who also composed the title song, was hailed with delight. "After reels and reels of torch singers and crooners," said the *Times,* "it is indeed a joyous relief." The heroine, after singing all over Europe, finally makes her debut at the Met, where her exacting voice teacher (Tullio Carminati) appears in the prompter's box, proving he loves her.

The sentimental nature of Moore's films is indicated by their distractingly similar titles. *One Night of Love* was followed by *Love Me Forever* (1935), opposite Michael Bartlett, which the *Times* considered "the most distinguished musical photoplay of the season." But *When You're in Love* (1937) despite Cary Grant as leading man, a score by Kern and Moore's much-publicized rendition of "Minnie the Moocher" was dismissed as "a glib re-working of an ancient operatic formula." *I'll Take Romance* (1937), with Melvyn Douglas, was accused of having no story at all. The only one of Moore's pictures that holds up today is the pure operetta *The King Steps Out* (1936).

First to leap aboard the operatic band wagon, however briefly, were Warners, but their *Stars over Broadway* (1935) retained a sense of humor. Said the *Times,* "It merits praise chiefly for its failure to fawn completely upon the Diamond Horseshoe." Pat O'Brien played another cynical manager who persuades James Melton to give up opera for a lucrative radio career—but art triumphs in the end. In *Sing Me a Love Song* (1936) and *Melody for Two* (1937) Melton sang no opera at all.

A month after Melton's screen debut Nino Martini, who had sung one number in *Paramount on Parade* (1930), appeared in Fox's *Here's to Romance* (1935), which the *Times* found "a sedate bore," in which wealthy art patrons Genevieve Tobin and Reginald Denny almost come between singers Martini and Anita Louise. In *The Gay Desperado* (1936), directed with a light touch by Rouben Mamoulian, Martini, surrounded by good comedians, fared much better, but *Music for Madame* (1937), opposite Joan Fontaine, even with music by Friml, finished his brief screen career.

In the same month as *Here's to Romance,* Moore's former co-star, Lawrence Tibbett, returned with considerable triumph in *Metropolitan* (1935), one of the first productions of the newly formed 20th Century-Fox, highly praised by the *Times* as "a gay and spirited satire on the social exclusiveness of opera management," as well as "the best musical film of the season."

Yet in *Under Your Spell* (1936) Tibbett was given no operatic music, only a Dietz and Schwartz score on which to exercise "the most beautifully controlled vocal instrument on the contemporary screen." The story of his ultimate capture by another of those heiresses (Wendy Barrie) was so unworthy of his talents that Tibbett made no more films.

A month after Martini's and Tibbett's return to the screen, Lily Pons made a promising debut in *I Dream Too Much* (1935), with Henry Fonda as her composer-husband and a score by Kern to sing, as well as the obligatory arias. *That Girl from Paris* (1937) was praised by the *Times* as the culmination of that

revolution begun in Grace Moore's *The King Steps Out* and continued in Nino Martini's *The Gay Desperado.* No longer are the Metropolitan songbirds sacrosanct, requiring reverential handling and the protracted adulation of script and camera . . . the operatic film has climbed off its high horse and started to frolic on the floor.

But Pons' *Hitting a New High* (1937) was generally thought to have hit a new low. She played a night club singer who allows a press agent (Jack Oakie) to plant her in a jungle, there to be discovered as a twittering "bird girl," like Rima in *Green Mansions.*

Next singer to be lured from the Met was mezzo-soprano Gladys Swarthout, two of whose films, *Rose of the Rancho* and *Champagne Waltz,* were among the more dismal operettas. In *Give Us This Night* (1936), she was, the *Times* thought, sacrificed to Jan

Kiepura, who did most of the singing in a slight tale about a new operatic version of *Romeo and Juliet* (with music by Erich Wolfgang Korngold).

Romance in the Dark (1938) was even worse. A simple country girl in Budapest, she is transformed by a tenor (John Boles) into "the Persian nightingale," to lure his rival (John Barrymore) for the love of a countess (Claire Dodd). Paramount finally gave up on Swarthout; her last film was *Ambush* (1939), a crook melodrama in which she sang not a note. At that, she lasted longer than

Marion Talley, who made but one film, *Follow Your Heart* (1936).

Except for *One Night of Love*, none of these films are ever revived, yet at its height the cycle was undoubtedly responsible for such interesting spin-offs as *Charlie Chan at the Opera* and even the Marxes' *A Night at the Opera* (both 1936). While soon wearing out their welcome with the general public, the operatic films irked true music-lovers with their repeated snippets from the same overfamiliar arias, sung with a perfection, it was suspected, achieved by electronic means.

12

"FIVE MINUTES TILL CURTAIN!"
Straight Films About the Theater

As noted earlier, plays about the theater had never been especially popular on stage, except for a few minor pieces like Eugène Scribe and Ernest Legouvé's *Adrienne Lecouvreur* (1849), Pinero's *Trelawney of the Wells* (1899), Belasco's old French-born war horses *Zaza* (1899) and *Kiki* (1922)—both unsuccessfully filmed in the '30s—and those three late '20s hits, *Broadway, Burlesque* and *The Royal Family,* two of which reached the screen as musicals.

Amid the flood of backstage films in 1929, some, despite interpolated vaudeville, night club or burlesque routines, remained more melodramas than musicals, especially those about mothers whose involvement in the bedraggled fringes of show business shocked their gently reared daughters—e.g., Sophie Tucker's one-shot *Honky Tonk* and Louise

Dresser's maudlin *Not Quite Decent.* (Edna May Oliver's *Fanny Foley Herself,* 1931, also followed this pattern.)

Akin to these, but only in basic premise, was Rouben Mamoulian's first talkie, the remarkable *Applause.* Helen Morgan, then at the height of her Broadway fame, between *Show Boat* and *Sweet Adeline,* showed rare courage in taking—and playing honestly—the role of Kitty Darling, a blowsy, aging burlesque queen, a kind of backstage Stella Dallas, whose seventeen-year-old daughter (Joan Peers), brought up in a convent school, is horrified to be thrust into the seedy lives of a burlesque troupe, especially by the unwelcome attentions of her mother's lover (Fuller Mellish, Jr.). Faced with this and the fading of her career, Kitty takes poison, only to regret it, too late.

Applause would be historically significant if only because of Mamoulian's then highly innovative use of actual New York street scenes and noises, but it is also a powerfully grim drama, unsparing in its exposure of the sordid milieu. Close-ups of the crudely made-up, overweight "chorines," intercut with the leering, loose-lipped faces of their patrons, look as decadent as anything ever caught by von Stroheim, with the added shock impact that Mamoulian's grotesques are not of Hapsburg Vienna but of contemporary New York.

As for those other, often tawdry forms of entertainment, the circus, the carnival and the amusement park (or pier), so extraordinarily popular in silents (*The American Film Institute Catalog . . . 1921–1930* lists sixty-six such films!), the '30s saw fewer than twenty, even including some already covered, such as *Freaks* and *Charlie Chan at the Circus.*

Sinners' Holiday (1930), pointlessly retitled from *Penny Arcade,* would be notable if only for introducing both Cagney and Blondell to the screen, repeating roles they had played on stage. The nominal stars were Grant Withers as a barker and Evalyn Knapp as the daughter of a penny arcade owner (Lucille La Verne), but Cagney stole the film as Knapp's weakling brother, who commits a murder and with his doting mother's help tries to pin it on Withers.

Among the all too many backstage films of 1930, the one that holds up best had no musical connection whatever: Kaufman and Ferber's charming 1927 comedy *The Royal Family,* neatly adapted by Herman Mankiewicz and Gertrude Purcell and directed by George Cukor. Even aside from the supposed box-office lure, the addition of the words *"of Broadway"* to the title was wise; otherwise the average movie-goer would surely have assumed this was another Graustarkian romance.

As was obvious from the moment the play opened, the Cavendishes, distinguished three-generation theatrical dynasty, were inspired by the Barrymores. Ethel was said to be mortally offended, though it is hard to under-

stand why; her counterpart, Julie (Ina Claire in one of her few good film roles), a chic, glamorous star at the peak of her career, is most likable. Her brother Tony, an outrageously flamboyant matinee idol who has "sold out" to Hollywood, as played by Fredric March, is a hilarious but not malicious caricature.

But the most memorable character is their mother, the feisty matriarch, Fanny Cavendish, perhaps suggested by the Barrymores' grandmother, Mrs. John Drew, beautifully played by Henrietta Crosman, herself a star of the 1900s, who embodies all that was finest in troupers of the old school. While Tony flees to Europe to escape lawsuits, amorous women and angry husbands, Julie is tempted to leave the stage for a wealthy marriage (to Frank Conroy, as one of the talkies' earliest stuffy suitors), as her daughter Gwen has already done—but when the old lady, determined to make one last tour, collapses and dies in her dressing room just as she is about to go on, Julie, realizing where she truly belongs, dons her costume and takes her place. This, perhaps the most moving version of that familiar situation, was not in the play.

If *The Guardsman* was the most sophisticated backstage comedy of 1931, then surely the most bizarre backstage melodrama was *The Mad Genius,* another triumph for the real John Barrymore. Though evidently intended as a follow-up on *Svengali* (1931), it was different enough to be judged on its own. In the milieu of international ballet in Berlin and Paris, even more exotic to most Americans then than now, Barrymore played a famed ballerina's castoff son, a clubfooted puppeteer, burning with impotent talent until he discovers a gifted boy (Frankie Darro) whom he molds and drives into becoming one of the world's great dancers (Donald Cook).

The parallel with Diaghilev and Nijinsky is obvious, but homosexual undertones are not even hinted, as in *Little Caesar.* The older man is shown as a womanizer, with Carmel Myers (who had played a similar role in *Svengali*) as his castoff mistress. When the protégé marries against his orders, his fury is not from jealousy but professional outrage that the boy can put anything ahead of his art. After he has kept every other ballet company from hiring him and finds him reduced to dancing in a Montmartre cabaret, it is not difficult to persuade the girl (Marian Marsh) to leave him for his own good.

But in the climax, during the first performance of a *ballet mécanique,* of which we catch only glimpses, Barrymore's half-mad assistant (Luis Alberni), whose drugs he has cut off, goes berserk and murders him; the horrified audience sees his impaled body dangling grotesquely upside down from a descending piece of scenery.

Katharine Hepburn, who made her screen debut as Barrymore's daughter in *A Bill of Divorcement* (1932), won her first Oscar in her third film, *Morning Glory* (1933), aptly cast as an intense young actress from New England, who calls herself Eva Lovelace, fiercely determined to be a star at all costs. In the opening scene she is standing in a theater lobby, gazing reverently at portraits of Ethel Barrymore, Maude Adams, Sarah Bernhardt and other immortals, and throughout the film

Douglas Fairbanks, Jr., Katharine Hepburn in **Morning Glory**

there is much dropping of names like Cornell, Molnár, Shaw and even Gilbert Miller, lending a superficial air of authenticity, but the Zoe Akins play, adapted by Howard Green, is far from convincing.

After too much champagne at a theatrical party, Eva recites both a soliloquy from *Hamlet* and the balcony scene from *Romeo and Juliet,* so sensitively that she attracts the attention of a producer (Adolphe Menjou) long enough for a brief affair, but her true love is a young playwright (Douglas Fairbanks, Jr.). When the temperamental star (Mary Duncan) walks out on the opening night of his play, Eva, though never shown rehearsing the part, goes on and is an instant sensation.

Despite warnings that she may be no more than a "morning glory," she is last seen taking curtain calls, defiantly proclaiming over and over, "I'm not afraid!" The critics quite rightly acclaimed Hepburn's glowing performance, but surely this case of the unknown becoming a star overnight is even farther-fetched than those in *On with the Show* and *42nd Street.*

Though *Dinner at Eight* (1933) is not primarily about the theater, among its gallery of characters Kaufman and Ferber created a quite different theatrical *grande dame* from their Fanny Cavendish—Carlotta Vance (Marie Dressler in the film), who lives in luxurious retirement on the Riviera, as an international hostess entertaining the likes of "Wales" and Noel and Winston, after a turn-of-the-century career that, as vividly recalled by herself, Oliver Jordan (Lionel Barrymore) and Dan Packard (Wallace Beery), makes her sound like a glittering combination of Lillie Langtry, Lillian Russell and Maxine Elliott.

What Hecht and MacArthur had done for (or to) the newspaper business in *The Front Page,* they did even more hilariously for the theater in *Twentieth Century* (1934), with the same expert blend of fast pace, hard-boiled satire and sheer slapstick. The film attacks theatrical egos with a sharp, cynical bite not usually found in the average screwball farce.

Happiest inspiration was the casting of John Barrymore as Oscar Jaffe, "the Napoleon of Broadway," maker of stars and megalomaniac par excellence. In *Svengali* and *The Mad Genius* he had seriously played two obsessed impresarios whose domination, on and off stage, had a sinister, even fatal, influence on an idolized protégé, and he was later to do another such tyrant in *Maytime.* In *Twentieth Century* he simply turned that character inside out, parodying every hammy mannerism to the exact point where it becomes uproarious—from the rolling eyes and ear-splitting yell of rage at each new "betrayal" by an underling, to the backward stagger and hushed, heartbroken whisper of a nobly martyred fake death scene.

If Walter Hovey is generally believed to be the original of Walter Burns in *The Front Page,* then surely the inspiration for Jaffe was Jed Harris, that *enfant terrible* of Broadway in the '20s (with perhaps a few touches of Belasco). Thus Jaffe is first seen staging a play about a Southern girl whose lover, Michael, is killed by her father—the exact situation in the 1928 play *Coquette,* which starred MacArthur's wife, Helen Hayes. Since Harris produced both *Coquette* and *The Front Page,* the authors had ample opportunity to observe him in action.

Unlike the play, set entirely aboard the famous train, the film traces Jaffe and protégé Lily Garland's tempestuous love-hate relationship, from the time he discovers her as Mildred Plotka, a lingerie model, and in rehearsal gets her to produce a convincing scream by jabbing her with a hatpin, until her furious departure for Hollywood after discovering he has had a private eye shadowing her. His total domination and her attempts to escape are, of course, comic variations on the Svengali-Trilby situation, which is indeed mentioned twice in the dialogue.

Aside from affording Barrymore the finest comic role of his screen career, *Twentieth Century* is even more significant for giving Carole Lombard her first real chance as a zany

Carole Lombard, John Barrymore in **Twentieth Century**

comedienne—many would say the best of her generation—and led to her other classic comedies. As *The New Yorker* puts it, "Lombard's talents here are not of the highest, but her spirits are, and in her skin-tight satins she incarnates the giddied glamour of Thirties comedy."

1935 was the year when, cinematically speaking, Jean Harlow turned *Reckless* and Bette Davis was pronounced *Dangerous* (a few years before, both adjectives would have been followed by the word *Lady*), both opposite Franchot Tone.

Harlow, a musical comedy star, unwisely marries a persistent playboy (Tone in a neurotic variation on his roles in *Dancing Lady*, *Sadie McKee* and *The Girl from Missouri*), then later overhears him confide to his jilted fiancée (Rosalind Russell) that he was hooked while drunk. In remorse he kills himself in suspicious circumstances, and though his widow wants none of the family money, the scandal temporarily ruins her career. Eventually she makes a comeback and marries her agent (William Powell), who has loved her all along.

No one could miss the parallel to Libby Holman, the "Moanin' Low" torch singer, whose husband, tobacco heir Zachary Reynolds, had committed suicide in 1932, the same year as Harlow's own husband, Paul Bern. The result was a glossy but sentimental semi-musical melodrama. As Curtis Brown put it in his Harlow book, "Time hasn't been kind to *Reckless;* it seems today less a dramatic experience than a topical, exploitative weeper."

An even more lurid *roman à clef* was *Dangerous,* in which Davis played Joyce Heath, a "jinxed" actress whose drive toward alcoholic self-destruction most vividly recalled the tragic career of Jeanne Eagels. When a slumming architect (Tone), who remembers her great days, finds her as a sodden habitué of a cheap gin mill, he tries to rehabilitate her, even backs her in a new play, and they fall in love.

Her weakling husband (John Eldredge) refuses a divorce, so she tries to get rid of him by crashing her car into a tree, but both survive, he crippled for life. When her play opens triumphantly, in belated guilt she sends Tone back to his ex-fiancée (Margaret Lindsay), while she sacrifices her future to her husband—an ending that convinced no one, even in 1935. As *The New Yorker* says, "This is the mawkish, trashy movie in which she won her first Academy Award." Dazzling as Davis was in the role, it was generally believed that the Oscar was overdue recognition for *Of Human Bondage* (1934).

By far the best film of the decade to deal with theater people, on an all-time basis second only to *All About Eve* (1950), was *Stage Door* (1937), which owes absolutely nothing to the 1936 play by Kaufman and Ferber except the title, the setting (a theatrical boardinghouse for girls) and the names of a few of the characters.

Unlike *Once in a Lifetime, Boy Meets Girl* and other broad satires on Hollywood, this insufferably self-righteous play is less a good-natured spoof than a hanging indictment. The heroine is Terry Randall, a small-town doctor's daughter, whose dominant trait is her determination to stick to the stage at all costs. Personally, she is torn between Keith Burgess, a young radical playwright who sells out to Hollywood at the first opportunity ("Odets," everyone thought), and David Kingsley, a supposedly sensitive film producer who despises the industry so much that he even urges Terry to reject the contract he has been authorized to offer her.

At the end, when her friend Jean Maitland, returning as a triumphant movie star, proves inadequate during rehearsal for a play the studio has bought for her, Kingsley suggests Terry, but when Adolph Gretzl, the grossly thick-skinned studio head, rejects her, Kingsley buys the play and will star Terry in it. Thus the authors had it both ways—endorsing stubborn integrity, yet providing a Cinderella ending. Unconnected with this main plot, a minor character named Linda Shaw becomes someone's mistress and another, Kaye Hamilton, takes poison rather than return to a rich, psychotic husband.

Anyone familiar with the film will realize that it bears no more resemblance to the play than the screen versions of *Naughty Marietta* and *Rose Marie* did to the original operettas. In the brilliant screenplay by Morrie Ryskind and Anthony Veiller, Terry is a spoiled rich girl who wants to take a fling at acting (a role even more perfectly suited to Hepburn than Eva in *Morning Glory*). Her manners and assumptions unwittingly alienate the other girls at the Footlights Club, especially Jean Maitland (Ginger Rogers), a wisecracking hoofer who must share a room with her.

Both they and Linda Shaw (Gail Patrick) are involved with Anthony Powell, a middle-aged producer (Adolphe Menjou), for whom the term "casting couch" might have been invented. Linda, whose chauffeured limousine, expensive clothes and furs are smilingly attributed to her "Aunt Susan"—a euphemism that fools no one—is obviously Powell's mistress. Terry by apparently compromising herself with Powell (actually to disillusion and protect Jean) and then getting the lead in his play (secretly engineered by her father, who hopes she will flop and give up the stage) is naturally suspected by the others, especially Jean, of having taken the easiest way.

What Terry does not realize is that the role she won so easily is the very one on which sensitive Kaye Hamilton (Andrea Leeds), a Powell protégée of last season, has fixed her last professional hope. An Olivia De Havilland lookalike, the long-forgotten Leeds was nominated for a supporting Oscar, one of the four nominations the film received. On opening night Kaye tries to be a good sport and even gives Terry a ring for good luck, but after Terry leaves for the theater Kaye walks slowly upstairs, to the sound of imaginary cheers and thunderous applause, and jumps out a window.

Jean cannot wait to break the tragic news, hoping Terry will be too unnerved to go on —but Constance Collier as a has-been actress turned coach, in one of the most eloquent "the show must go on" speeches ever filmed, convinces Terry that she must not only go on but play the role as Kaye would want it played. Though she was seen in rehearsals as wooden and obtuse, her shock and grief for Kaye enable her for the first time to convey real emotion in her lines, beginning with the famous speech from Hepburn's own 1933 flop play *The Lake:* "The calla lilies are in bloom again."

Four months later, now an established star, Terry is still living at the Footlights Club, Linda is back with Powell, the other girls continue to bicker as a newcomer moves in, the last scene echoing the first. In minor roles, Lucille Ball, Eve Arden and Ann Miller clearly reveal the talents that were to make them stars, while the real stars, Hepburn and Rogers, trading some of the brightest bitchy lines every heard on screen before *The Women,* were perfect foils.

Even after four decades, *Stage Door* remains unique in that it involved *no* love interest at all, only the emotional (non-Lesbian) bonding of a number of young women drawn together by their dedication to the theater. Thus while the play is hopelessly dated, the film, concerned with more subtle problems of theater tradition, integrity and what makes an actress a star, remains timelessly fresh, funny and touching.

A few weeks later came *The Great Garrick,* a surprising novelty in that it made no pretense of being a serious biography of the eighteenth-century actor but was frankly a period farce, with Brian Aherne well cast in the title role. "We felt his kinship with the man he played," said the *Times.*

As scenarist Ernest Vajda imagined it, members of the Comédie Française, insulted by Garrick's slighting reference to their invitation to act with them, take over an inn where he must stay and stage an apparently real drama meant to frighten him back to London, after which they will reveal the hoax and make him a laughingstock. But their plans are upset by a runaway countess (Olivia De Havilland). "It is boldly, richly, unabashedly an excuse for Mr. Aherne's gallant play-acting."

Less than a month later, Olivia was back again, in *It's Love I'm After* (1937), as another of those heiresses, this one with a crush on a famous actor. In a delightful change of pace, Bette Davis and Leslie Howard, who had played so well together in the serious *Of Human Bondage* (1934) and *The Petrified Forest* (1936), proved themselves equally adept at sophisticated farce, as America's leading (and most furiously battling) theatrical couple, almost—but never quite—married.

Perhaps in sly allusion to the Lunts, the film opens, as did *The Guardsman,* with the two stars performing on stage, here in the tomb scene of *Romeo and Juliet,* muttering insults and threats under their breath, unsuspected by their entralled audience. Patric Knowles as the smitten Olivia De Havilland's frantic fiancé begs the actor to disillusion her once and for all. As the house guest of her

Ann Miller (seated), Eve Arden, Lucille Ball, Ginger Rogers in Stage Door

family in Pasadena, Howard is impossibly rude and boorish, but nothing, not even sneaking into her room at night, can cure the silly girl—until Davis turns up as the wronged but excruciatingly noble wife, complete with pictures of her children.

"As a variant, almost a sequel, to *Stage Door*, it is a surprisingly fresh, uncommonly diverting, remarkably well done film," said the *Times* of *Letter of Introduction* (1938), though the chief resemblance was the presence of Andrea Leeds and Adolphe Menjou, the latter as a fading matinee idol, as also in *The Great Flirtation* (1934) and *Sing, Baby, Sing* (1936).

Leeds was a daughter he had all but forgot-

ten in the twenty years between his first wife and his fourth. Since he is reluctant to admit publicly to a grown daughter, his interest in the girl is naturally misunderstood by everyone, especially her hotheaded suitor (George Murphy).

"Unlike *Stage Door* and *Letter of Introduction,* which plowed the same field," said B. R. Crisler of the *Times* about *Dramatic School* (1938), "Mr. Le Roy's film is steadfastly sober-sided . . ." It was, in fact, Luise Rainer's last MGM picture, and much better than several of her previous ones. Adapted from a Hungarian play but transposed to Paris, it was mainly set in a very professional national school of drama like the Comédie

Française, where the older actors train the next generation.

Rainer played a fervently dedicated student who must work in a factory at night and who, by winning the coveted role of Joan of Arc, breaks the heart of the great star (Gale Sondergaard) whose career first inspired her. In an unusually strong cast, the other aspirants included Paulette Goddard, Virginia Grey and Ann Rutherford, Genevieve Tobin was a glittering boulevard star, the kind the girls are trained to despise but can't help envying, and Henry Stephenson was the dignified director of the school, whose son (Rand Brooks) has inherited no talent at all. Its careful avoidance of clichés, many fine performances and sense of authenticity (both European and theatrical) should have earned *Dramatic School* greater success than it attained.

Despite all its other glories, 1939, as noted, was not a good year for backstage films, musical or otherwise. In fact, the only one to receive a favorable review from the *Times* came at the very end of the year, a kind of somber variation on *Letter of Introduction* titled *The Night of Nights,* written by Donald Ogden Stewart, directed by Lewis Milestone and starring Pat O'Brien as a playwright-actor-producer whose life stopped when his wife left him.

Eighteen years later his daughter (Olympe Bradna) appears and urges him to return to the theater. Encouraged by his old friends Roland Young and Reginald Gardiner, he hesitantly undertakes to revive one of his plays—and, of course, succeeds. Said the *Times,* "The Night of Nights is an uncom-

Gale Sondergaard, Luise Rainer
in Dramatic School

monly interesting study of a man's mind, subtly written and directed, presented with honesty and commendable sincerity . . ."

Thus it will be seen that, far from returning in kind the constant, often bitter, attacks of Broadway, Hollywood in the '30s for the most part treated its legitimate parent with affection and respect.

43

WHAT PRICE HOLLYWOOD?
Films About Filmland

From the beginning, the screen had always been more narcissistic than the stage in dramatizing itself. In the 1910s the sheer novelty of the new medium fascinated the whole world, and the '20s, according to *The American Film Institute Catalog . . . 1921–1930*, saw thirty-three films about Hollywood and ninety-three about "motion pictures," with only a few overlapping. Thus talkies about talkies were inevitable. The '30s produced more than seventy such films, if one counts those that used stars as characters in romantic comedies, including some twenty musicals, more than twenty comedies, nine mysteries and even a few serious dramas. Indeed, in a number of hard, searching looks into the mirror, Hollywood peeled away its own glamorous mask far more ruthlessly than even Broadway could do.

Chronologically, except for the operetta *Married in Hollywood* (1929), the first musical about the new talkies was *Let's Go Places* (1930), but the first *good* one was *Show Girl in Hollywood* (1930). Pert, blond Alice White, who had made the part-talkie *Show Girl* in 1928, repeated the role of J. P. McEvoy's Dixie Dugan in what Everson calls "one of the best and most convincing yarns *about* Hollywood."

Brought to the Coast to make a movie musical, *The Rainbow Girl*, Dixie, egged on by a vain, pretentious director (John Mil-

jan) soon "goes Hollywood," to the disgust of her songwriting boy friend (Jack Mulhall). In fact, her temperamental clashes with the producer (Ford Sterling) cause the production to be shut down, thus dashing the last comeback hope of her friend Donna Harris (Blanche Sweet), a faded star, ruined not by talkies but by her age (thirty-two).

Her poignant song "There's a Tear for Every Smile in Hollywood" is less like the upbeat "Broadway Melody" than like the melancholy, prewar "There's a Broken Heart for Every Light on Broadway." The scene in which she attempts suicide, entirely in silence, is most unusual for such an early talkie. This barely averted tragedy jolts Dixie back to her senses in time to finish the picture. The last scene, originally shown in Technicolor, is the triumphant premiere, which (as so often in films about Hollywood) introduces several real stars as themselves, including Jolson and Keeler, Loretta Young and Walter Pidgeon.

The general 1931–32 moratorium on musicals lasted even longer for those with a movie background. Not until nearly four years after *Show Girl in Hollywood* did they begin to reappear—four, from as many studios, within a few months of the winter of 1933–34. First was Paramount's *Sitting Pretty* (1933), in which Jack Oakie and Jack Haley were a songwriting team who in hitchhiking across the country to Hollywood pick up a pert waitress (Ginger Rogers) who wants to be a hoofer. Thanks to a drunken director (Lew Cody), they are given a chance to air their talent for the heavily accented producer (Gregory Ratoff). Of ten Gordon and Revel songs, "Did You Ever See a Dream Walking?" was the biggest hit.

Though by no means as amusing as Marion Davies' satirical silent, *Show People* (1928), MGM's *Going Hollywood* (1933) was a pleasant little Cinderella romance in which Davies quits her job teaching in a stuffy boarding school to follow her idol, a radio crooner (Bing Crosby), aboard a train to Hollywood, to the annoyance of his fiery co-star and fiancée (Fifi D'Orsay). Needless to say, Davies eventually gets both Crosby and D'Orsay's co-starring role opposite him.

Except for glimpses of Shearer, Dressler, Montgomery and a few other MGM stars, no Hollywood atmosphere was attempted, but the score by Arthur Freed and Nacio Herb Brown was unusually good: "We'll Make Hay While the Sun Shines," "Cinderella's Fella," "After Sundown" and the sensuous tango "Temptation." Oddly, it also reprised "Beautiful Girl," introduced earlier that year in *Stage Mother*.

Ratoff returned as another producer in Columbia's *Let's Fall in Love* (1934), which the *Times* praised as "a nimble-witted romantic comedy," despite the familiarity of the material. Edmund Lowe was a famous director searching for a Swedish girl to replace his Garbo-like star (Tala Birell), who has returned to Europe. In desperation he pulls a Pygmalion and in six weeks passes off a Brooklyn girl (Ann Sothern) as the latest Scandinavian find. When she falls in love with him, his jealous fiancée (Miriam Jordan) gives the hoax away, but their picture is a hit. Surprisingly, the Harold Arlen score included only one good song, the continually reprised title number.

Fox's *Bottoms Up* (1934) starred Spencer Tracy as one of a trio of con men (along with Herbert Mundin and Sid Silvers) who palm

off a Canadian beauty prize winner (Pat Paterson in her American debut) as the daughter of a British peer and themselves as members of her entourage. She falls in love with a star (John Boles), to whom in the end Tracy gives her up. For a change, the illiterate producer was not Ratoff but Harry Green. The lively score by Burton Lane, Richard Whiting and Gus Kahn included "Turn On the Moon" and "Waitin' at the Gate for Katy."

Passing over such forgettable items as *Hollywood Party* (1934), which was livened only by the interpolation of a Disney cartoon, *Hot Chocolate Soldiers,* and Mascot's *Young and Beautiful* (1934), which purported to tell the story of the Wampas Baby Stars while introducing that year's crop (with William Haines as the studio publicity man and Joseph Cawthorn as the inevitably Jewish producer), one might note Fox's *365 Nights in Hollywood* (1935), which the *Times* dismissed in short order as "a lightweight musical comedy romance dealing with the less than epic theme of a studio-struck blonde from Peoria who enrolls in a fly-by-night movie school and, through the efforts of its one-man faculty (formerly a boy wonder among directors), becomes a picture star." Alice Faye was the blonde and James Dunn her Pygmalion.

The *Times* ignored two other Hollywood musicals from Fox, despite respectable casts. In *Redheads on Parade* (1935), John Boles and Dixie Lee were starring in a musical film backed by an angel (Raymond Walburn), who falls for Lee. Press agent Jack Haley persuades her to string him along, causing predictable misunderstandings not cleared up till the premiere of the film.

Marginally more original was *Music Is Magic* (1935), which *Film Daily* described as a "satire on picture-making." A vaudeville troupe hits Hollywood after touring with a washed-up star (Bebe Daniels in her last American film) still trying to play ingenues. An accident leads her to admit that her supposed sister is really her daughter, and Alice Faye takes over the starring role—one of the last examples, at least in the '30s, of this venerable cliché.

Surely this could have been no more trivial than Paramount's *Three Cheers for Love* (1936), which the *Times* described as "Hollywood's equivalent of the employees' annual picnic." Despite a good cast of character players, the only notable touch was the first use of the familiar gag about Miracle Studios, whose slogan is "If It's a Good Picture, It's a Miracle."

Fox (now 20th Century-Fox) redeemed itself with *Sing, Baby, Sing* (1936), one of the most hilarious satires of the decade. John Barrymore had indeed laid himself wide open to such attack by his much-publicized cross-country flight from youthful Elaine Barrie, who became his fourth wife. Instead of Caliban and Ariel, to whom these two were likened, broken-down, alcoholic matinee idol Bruce Farraday (Adolphe Menjou at his best) and his night club singer (Alice Faye) are headlined as Romeo and Juliet. The *Times* was so amused that it even praised the Ritz Brothers and Tony Martin's rendition of "When Did You Leave Heaven?"

Like most Warners stars, sooner or later, Cagney rebelled, in 1936, and, while waiting to get his terms, made two films for the independent Grand National, the second of which was *Something to Sing About* (1937), his first musical since *Footlight Parade,* conceived, composed and directed by Victor Schertzinger.

Cagney played a band leader lured to Hollywood "to be developed into a composite of Dick Powell and Fred Astaire (heaven help us!)," said the *Times,* which liked the film's satire on Hollywood's star-building methods, as the hero is worked over by a make-up expert, a stylist, a press agent, a diction coach and finally by the studio's leading siren (Mona Barrie). Much of the fun was at the expense of a pompous producer, Bennett O. Regan (Gene Lockhart), unpopularly known as "B.O.," initials that in the '30s meant that social handicap from which only Lifebuoy soap could save you.

Hollywood Hotel (1938) was hailed by the *Times* as "the best Warner musical in recent history . . ." Benny Goodman's swing orchestra, then at its height, was a major asset. Though the writers borrowed "If It's a Good Picture, It's a Miracle," most of the quips were original, and the tone was refreshingly irreverent, as reflected in the best number, the exuberant "Hooray for Hollywood!" ("where any bar maid can be a star made . . . where any young mechanic can be a panic with just a good-looking pan").

Dick Powell played a saxophonist brought to the Coast but released from his contract when instead of dating a bitchy star (Lola Lane), as ordered, he prefers her twin sister and stand-in (Rosemary Lane). Powell is soon hired back on his own terms, to voice-double for the non-singing Alan Mowbray. In the climax Mowbray, determined to keep Powell indefinitely as his unbilled voice, is forcibly detained just long enough so that Powell must go on in his place on Louella Parsons' *Hollywood Hotel* radio program, thus establishing his own identity.

Released the month after *Hollywood Hotel, The Goldwyn Follies* (1938) was not only the producer's first film in the new color but the realization of his long-time dream of producing the cinematic equivalent of Ziegfeld's *Follies.* Despite a dazzling array of first-rate talent in every field: the Gershwins, Vernon Duke, Kurt Weill, Ben Hecht, George Balanchine, Vera Zorina, Helen Jepson and, in the comic line, both Bergen and McCarthy and the Ritz Brothers, the consensus was that Goldwin would have done better to follow Ziegfeld all the way and produce an out-and-out revue, like those of 1929 and 1930, without the pretext of a story line.

Instead, Hecht provided a bland situation about a girl (Andrea Leeds) whose tastes are so average that producer Oliver Merlin (Adolphe Menjou) hires her as "Miss Humanity" to test her reactions to his films in production.

The nineteen numbers, freed from this lame invention, might have done as well as

MGM's *Ziegfeld Follies* did eight years later. Even so, the effects are often impressive. George Gershwin had completed only four songs at the time of his death in 1937, but they include the standard "Love Walked In" (reprised four times by Kenny Baker), "I Was Doing All Right" (sung by Ella Logan) and "Love Is Here to Stay." Zorina appeared in a striking water-nymph ballet choreographed by her then husband, Balanchine, and Helen Jepson and Charles Kullmann of the Met sang "Libiamo" and "Sempre Libera" from *La Traviata*.

The next Hollywood-set musical, 20th Century-Fox's *Second Fiddle* (1939), was still another spin-off from *Gone With the Wind*, specifically from Selznick's endlessly publicized search for the perfect Scarlett O'Hara. Here the quest is for "Violet Janson" in Consolidated Productions' long-delayed *Girl of the North,* and the winner is an unknown Minnesota schoolteacher (Sonja Henie). A studio press agent (Tyrone Power) creates a publicity romance between her and a star (Rudy Vallee), even to writing the love notes, so successfully that he finds himself in the position of Cyrano, with his words winning the girl he loves for someone else. The score by Berlin was not one of his best, though it included the amusing "Sorry for Myself."

Even more minor was MGM's *Dancing Co-Ed* (1939), an attempt to follow up on the success of *These Glamour Girls* (1939). In another of those publicity-inspired talent searches, a studio is supposedly seeking the perfect dancing co-ed, but, leaving nothing to chance, they plant a dancer (Lana Turner) at Midwestern U., there to be discovered at the right time. She falls for the student newspaper editor (Richard Carlson), and when he catches on to the dastardly plot, we have the perfect setup for one of those "why didn't you tell me?" misunderstandings. Artie Shaw and his orchestra were also on hand, so perhaps the one result of the film, though hardly lasting, was the Turner-Shaw marriage.

This was obviously an era when a name band was thought to ensure box-office appeal for any film, so in *That's Right, You're Wrong* (1939), the last movie-inspired musical of the decade, it was Kay Kyser, whose *Kollege of Musical Knowledge* was a popular radio program of the day. The *Times* gave it "a cautious and conservative passing grade." In an almost Pirandellian confusion of reality and illusion, the non-plot dealt with the difficulties of a screen-writing team, Village and Cook (Edward Everett Horton and Hobart Cavanaugh), in devising a suitable film vehicle for Kay Kyser and his band. Adolphe Menjou was once again the producer, but it was Lucille Ball, as a movie star, who solves the problem by falling for Kyser's manager (Dennis O'Keefe) and insisting the studio retain Kay and his boys—who, of course, prove to be a hit.

Although *Free and Easy* (1930) is listed in *The American Film Institute Catalog . . . 1921–1930* as "a musical farce," with five forgotten songs specified, tossed-in musical numbers were so much a part of almost any 1930 talkie that no commentator at the time or since has ever mentioned them, or written about the film as anything but a slapstick farce, and a triumphant talkie debut for Buster Keaton, whose voice exactly matched his deadpan face. In fact, one of the funniest scenes depends on his constant inability (as a bit player in a costume epic) to deliver the tongue-twisting line "Alas, woe is me, the queen has swooned!" Time after time it comes out "the sween has quooned" or "the coon was sweened" or something similar.

As the manager of a Kansas beauty contest winner (Anita Page), Keaton drives her and her formidable mother (Trixie Friganza) to Hollywood, where, as was common in such films, they glimpse a number of MGM stars at a premiere. Later, in a comic chase through several sound stages, Keaton disrupts scenes apparently being directed by Fred Niblo, Lionel Barrymore and De Mille, in which Gwen Lee, John Miljan, William Haines, Karl Dane and Dorothy Sebastian all play themselves.

Predictably, though the beauty gets her man (Robert Montgomery), she fails to click on camera; it is her mother and Keaton who are signed as comedy stars. This was the first talkie instance of this pattern, in which someone through sheer ineptitude stumbles into Hollywood success.[1]

The only film about Hollywood released by any major studio in 1931 was Paramount's *Newly Rich*, from a most uncharacteristic story by Sinclair Lewis, *Let's Play King*. Edna May Oliver and Louise Fazenda, who two years later would play the Red and White queens in *Alice in Wonderland*, were rival mamas of two child stars, Mitzi Green as her usual likable self and Jackie Searl (who had already established himself as a juvenile menace, starting with *Tom Sawyer*, 1930) as an obnoxious movie brat known as Tiny Tim Tiffany.

In London they meet a boy king (Bruce Line) and his unassuming mother (Virginia Hammond). After running away together, the three youngsters are kidnaped, but rescued by a gang of children. Said the *Times*, which on the whole liked the film: "The burlesque of child actors, and of their mothers, is all there, and even the magnates of the industry come in for part of it."[2]

Surprisingly, 1932 brought eight films about Hollywood, four comedies, four dramas. To start with the worst, *The Cohens and the Kellys in Hollywood* was the second-last of a series of crude farces Universal had begun in 1926, part of the cycle of Irish-Jewish ethnic comedies that sprang up in the wake of *Abie's Irish Rose*. Though the rest of the cast changed, George Sidney and Charlie Murray, like male counterparts of Dressler and Moran, were always the rival fathers. In

this one the Kelly daughter (June Clyde) becomes a silent star, but is ruined by talkies, whereupon the Cohen son (Norman Foster) makes a hit writing songs for early talkies, but is finished when the first musical cycle ends, so both families end up as poor as they began.

Much better was Paramount's *Make Me a Star*, based on Harry Leon Wilson's *Merton of the Movies*, which, having already been a novel (1922), a play (1922) and a silent film (1924), may be regarded as the ultimate source of the stumbling-to-success pattern noted in connection with *Free and Easy*. This time Stuart Erwin played the naïve, small-town grocery clerk who takes a correspondence course in acting and dreams of becoming a great cowboy star.

In Hollywood Merton glimpses the usual assortment of stars (almost every Paramount luminary, from Bankhead to Chevalier), but finds the going rough until taken under the wing of Joan Blondell, a worldly-wise girl who falls for the innocent she started out to exploit.

Merton is given a chance to star in a Western, but no one tells him that it is a take-off on the films he reveres. He is photographed powdering his face in his dressing room, his voice is mechanically raised to a piping falsetto and his soulful talks with his horse come out addressed to other characters, all with hilarious effect. At the premiere he is, of course, crushed and humiliated, until Blondell convinces him that she did it all for him, knowing the only way he could ever become a star was as a comedian.

"After the gangster films and those concerned with the more or less serious activities of gossip mongers and crooners, this offering came to those in the packed theatre as a relief," said the *Times* of *Movie Crazy* (1932), Harold Lloyd's second talkie, which opened scarcely two months after *Make Me a Star*, with an almost identical story.

Lloyd was the bumbling would-be actor and Constance Cummings the helpful girl. The slapstick climax was a formal dinner at

---

[1] *Free and Easy* was remade as *Pick a Star* (1937) with Jack Haley, Patsy Kelly and Rosina Lawrence.

[2] The only other '30s films to deal with child stars were *Million Dollar Baby* (1935), in which a midget played a child, Jane Withers' *Keep Smiling* and Edith Fellows' *Little Miss Roughneck* (both 1938).

a producer's house, at which Lloyd by mistake dons a magician's tail coat, with a boutonniere that squirts water and a hidden menagerie of rabbits and mice. Later, when he accidentally breaks into a scene being filmed, the producer (Robert McWade) is so amused that he signs him for a series of comedies. *Movie Crazy* was the best-liked and most successful of Lloyd's five '30s talkies, but original it surely was not.

The following month (October 1932) brought a film that no one believed ever could or would be made, Universal's screen version of Kaufman and Hart's satirical farce *Once in a Lifetime* (1930), one of Broadway's first and broadest blasts at Hollywood. Carl Laemmle introduced the film with a self-congratulatory foreword, pointing out his own courage and defying anyone to say he had pulled any punches. As James Parish and Michael R. Pitts note in *Hollywood on Hollywood,* "What resulted was one of the most brilliant satires ever devised about the movie world. Universal filmed the story line intact, deleting none of the punch of the theatre original."

Possibly on the grounds that directly ridiculing a rival studio would be neither good taste nor good business, references to the Schlepkin brothers, who grew rich on Vitaphone, were omitted, as was the name of the gossip columnist's house, "Parwarmet," the gift of Paramount, Warners and MGM. Otherwise the satire is undiluted—not so much evidence of masochism on Hollywood's part as a gesture of supreme self-confidence, a recognition that all the wild lampooning was only Broadway's desperate whistling in the dark, to cover its mortal fear of what talkies would do to it.

The film begins with the opening of *The Jazz Singer,* then shows crowds lined up outside movie theaters while vaudevillians play to almost empty houses. Soon we zero in on a particular trio: acid-tongued May (superbly played by Aline MacMahon), debonair Jerry (Russell Hopton), whom she loves, and dim-witted George (Jack Oakie), whose monu-

mental stupidity is the source of most of the laughs. As a last resort, May suggests that they take their "once in a lifetime" chance to make big money by heading for Hollywood, where anyone with stage experience can palm himself off as a voice-training expert. On the train she meets an old friend, Helen Hobart (Louise Fazenda), now a powerful movie columnist, who eventually gets them in to see studio head Herman Glogauer (Gregory Ratoff in the most amusing of all his accented tycoon roles).

When George boldly talks back to Glogauer, telling him truths his yes men keep from him, he is made studio supervisor. He promptly stars his totally untalented girl friend (Sidney Fox) in a picture he produces by mistake from a 1910 script, shoots scenes in near-darkness while cracking Indian nuts (a noise the mike picks up) and, of course, is fired when Glogauer sees the results. But critics read all kinds of subtle artistry into George's every blunder, and once again he's on top—surely the funniest of all the stumbling-into-success variations.

Most of the fun now seems rather genial; the one bitter note is sounded by Lawrence Vail, played by Kaufman himself on stage and by Onslow Stevens in the film, a desperate writer literally driven frantic by his inability ever to see Glogauer.

Yet the best Hollywood satire of the decade was an inside job: MGM's hilarious *Bombshell* (1933, sometimes billed as *The Blonde Bombshell,* so as not to be mistaken for a war picture), wittily scripted by Jules Furthman and John Lee Mahin, centering on a few typical days in the hectic life of Lola Burns (Harlow), a glamorous sexpot movie star with a wistful desire to settle down and be just like any other girl.

As Curtis Brown suggests in his Harlow book, some details may have been drawn from Harlow herself, but at the time most fans immediately thought of Clara Bow: the rhythm of the name, the alliterative sobriquet (Bow had been publicized as "the Brooklyn Bonfire"), trouble with a scheming secretary

Jack Oakie, Aline MacMahon, Russell Hopton in **Once in a Lifetime**

(Una Merkel), romantic involvement with a director (Pat O'Brien). Her pursuit by a European nobleman (Ivan Lebedeff), of course, recalled Gloria Swanson, Constance Bennett, Pola Negri and other stars who married titles.

But the film need not be taken as a *roman à clef*. It is an uproarious farce in which Lola epitomizes all harried stars, torn in a dozen directions by people living off their fame—but in her case never failing to give as good as she gets, especially in her verbal bouts with Space Hanlon (Lee Tracy), the fast-talking studio publicity man, who ends her romance

with the nobleman by having him arrested and prevents her adopting a child by staging a noisy brawl in her home in front of the inspectors from the adoption agency.

Fleeing to Palm Springs to get away from it all, Lola meets a sensitive, cultured Bostonian (Franchot Tone) and his distinguished parents (C. Aubrey Smith and Mary Forbes), but Hanlon turns up with Lola's disreputable father (Frank Morgan) and brother (Ted Healy). Back at the studio, she finds that even the proper Bostonians were bit players hired by Hanlon, who, of course, wants her for himself and eventually gets her,

Lee Tracy, Jean Harlow in **The Blonde Bombshell**

though they are battling to the very end. One of the high points of Harlow's career, *Bombshell* remains as fresh as when made.

Indeed, no other movie-based comedy for the rest of the decade came even close—perhaps because several were essentially romantic comedies, in which the heroines were movie stars, but which did not deal with their careers as such. For example, in *In Person* (1935) Ginger Rogers, between Astaire films, played a star so tired of being mauled by her fans that she wears a disguise, then flees to a rural retreat, where she meets George Brent, who is not the least impressed on learning who she is—another variation on the spoiled

heiress getting her comeuppance. Similar were Gertrude Michael's character in *It Happened in New York* (1935) and Carole Lombard's in *Fools for Scandal* (1938).

As a "comedy romance," *The Moon's Our Home* (1936), from a novel by Faith Baldwin, with "added dialogue" by Dorothy Parker and Alan Campbell, was very well received. Margaret Sullavan and Henry Fonda played a movie star and a best-selling travel writer who, without having met, despise each other's reputations. When they do meet incognito, they marry in haste, part when he proves allergic to her perfume, then have the greatest difficulty finding each other.

A fine supporting cast that included Charles Butterworth, Beulah Bondi, Henrietta Crosman, Walter Brennan and Margaret Hamilton helped make this one of the year's most enjoyable comedies.

On stage, Lawrence Riley's *Personal Appearance,* starring Gladys George, had been a hilarious send-up of a Hollywood glamour girl, not too bright or literate, who while on a promotional tour falls for a small-town gas station attendant, until her press agent convinces her that the boy "has to" marry his local girl, thus giving the star a chance to replay the big renunciation scene right out of her current film, *Drifting Lady.*

Since no one could imagine Mae West as naïve or sentimental, her rewrite of the play as a vehicle for herself, retitled *Go West, Young Man* (1936), though it retained some of the malapropisms ("Leave me, I must commute with myself") lost much of the satirical bite. In the play she is married to her producer, Benjamin Z. Feinberg, and her last line to the press agent (still considered shocking in the '30s) is "You son of a bitch!" In the film she apparently plans to marry him.

Stand-In (1937), from a Clarence Budington Kelland novel, followed his favorite formula: the shrewd hick outwits the city slickers (as in *The Cat's Paw, Strike Me Pink, Mr. Deeds Goes to Town* and *Mr. Dodd Takes the Air*). This time another Mr. Dodd (Leslie Howard), a precise, cautious New York banker, is sent to Hollywood to protect the investment in Colossal Studios of the millionaire Pettypacker family.

When a former child star, now a stand-in (Joan Blondell), takes him under her wing, he becomes friendly with a hard-drinking producer (Humphrey Bogart). In the climax, after the bank has sold the studio and fired all the employees, Howard persuades the workers (in a variation on a sit-down strike—very timely in 1937) to occupy the property for forty-eight hours while Bogart re-edits the crucial film, which was being sabotaged by the star (Maria Shelton) and

director (Alan Mowbray), and the studio is saved.

Boy Meets Girl, by Samuel and Bella Spewack, produced and directed by George Abbott (on stage even funnier than *Personal Appearance* because it satirized the follies of the system itself, not merely the indiscretions of a star), had been bought by Warners in 1935, originally for Marion Davies and Olsen and Johnson, but Davies did not like the script.

One of the few plays or films to satirize screenwriters as well as stars and producers, it centers on a team supposedly inspired by Hecht and MacArthur, whose Katzenjammer Kid antics and practical jokes drive the studio head to near-apoplexy. By 1938, when the play was at last filmed, adapted by the Spewacks and produced by Abbott himself, the original stars, Jerome Cowan and Allyn Joslyn, both urbane, polished farceurs, were already in pictures, but in secondary roles, and, of course, their names meant nothing at the box office.

Thus their roles went to James Cagney and Pat O'Brien, who were simply not right for this, more like fugitives from Hell's Kitchen than from the Algonquin. In the play they are bent on making a star of the unborn illegitimate child of a waitress who faints in their office, mainly to spite a pompous cowboy star (Dick Foran in the film) by co-starring the baby with him. Much of the humor was broadened and much lost—e.g., the Production Code required that the waitress be the victim of a bigamous marriage. Though she was well played by Marie Wilson and Ralph Bellamy was fine as the studio head, the results were generally disappointing.

A few months later, however, Nugent of the *Times* welcomed *The Affairs of Annabel,* first of a projected series. The debt to *Bombshell* is obvious, but Lucille Ball in her first starring role held her own with Jack Oakie. To revive a career troubled by clashes with the studio, Oakie arranges, when Ball is cast in a prison film, for her to spend a month in jail. When she is to play a servant, he gets her a job in a wealthy household, little suspecting that the teen-age son will develop a crush on her, etc., etc.

It was followed, perhaps too soon, by *Annabel Takes a Tour* (1938), which the *Times* still liked, but which Miller in *B Movies* says "met the fate of most sequels, an overstaying of the original welcome." According to Parish and Pitts' *Hollywood on Hollywood*, it was Oakie's excessive salary demands that put an end to the series. In any case, that was the last of Annabel (though the following year Ball played another movie star in *That's Right, You're Wrong*).

Last intentional comedy of the decade to be set in Hollywood was *The Jones Family in Hollywood* (1939), thirteenth out of seventeen in an inexplicably long-lived series that all too clearly foreshadowed TV sitcoms of the '50s. Taking up approximately where *The Cohens and the Kellys in Hollywood* had left off, when Pa Jones (Jed Prouty) is a delegate to an American Legion convention in Los Angeles, the whole family trails along, and daughter Lucy is given a screen test, thanks to an obnoxiously overconfident teenaged star, Danny Regan (William Tracy), whose original could not have been more obvious had he been called Rickey Mooney.

Even among the dozen seriously intended films about Hollywood, most must be regarded as melodramas. The first of these was *The Lost Squadron* (1932), unique at the time, in that it dealt with those World War I aces who, ten years later, made their living as stunt pilots, performing the spectacular aerial feats in films like *Wings, Lilac Time, The Dawn Patrol* and *Hell's Angels*. Written by one of them, Dick Grace, it was, said the *Times*, "a story about aviators which can boast of a rich vein of originality and clever dialogue . . . excellent melodrama, ably directed" (by George Archainbaud).

As the villain of the piece, director Erich von Furst, ruthless stickler for realism at all costs, von Stroheim played the popular image of himself. Three disillusioned vets (Richard Dix, Joel McCrea and Robert Armstrong) daily risk their lives for fifty dollars a stunt, until the director, whose wife was once Dix's sweetheart, tampers with his plane, in which Armstrong is killed.

To utilize some of the unused footage, a spin-off film was made, *Lucky Devils* (1933), in which stunt men William Gargan and William ("Screen") Boyd both love Dorothy Wilson; when Gargan is killed in the line of duty, Wilson marries Boyd, but after he's badly hurt forces him to quit his hazardous job. *Hollywood on Hollywood* comments: "It was not populated by glamorous Hollywood types nor by tyrannical directors. Instead it concerned real people in real stunting situations—it focused on the lack of security, both financial and healthwise, that was part of every stunt man's existence."

An extremely bizarre little item was James Cagney's *Lady Killer* (1933), justly described by Everson as giving "the impression of either having been constructed as it went along, or hurriedly scripted on the back of a studio menu. It never decides whether it wants to be a thriller, a regeneration drama or an outright comedy."

Cagney starts out as a pugnacious moviehouse usher, then, when lured into a crooked card game by Mae Clarke, joins her gang, led by Douglas Dumbrille, in burglarizing the mansions of the rich. When caught in Los Angeles, however, they let Cagney take the rap. Upon his release, he gets work as a bit player in a prison film, then (like George Raft) becomes a favorite in gangster and tough guy roles. In the most unusual scene he forces a film critic literally to eat his words—chew and swallow a copy of the offensive review.

Naturally, the gang returns to blackmail him into fingering the homes of other stars, but, after dragging Clarke across a room by her hair, he manages to trap them all, though with a plea of leniency for the moll, so that he is free to marry fellow star Margaret Lindsay.

In *Hitch Hike to Heaven* (1936) Henrietta Crosman played a variation on her role in *The Royal Family of Broadway*, as a veteran stage actress, head of her own troupe, who hates movies, even though (or perhaps because) her son (Herbert Rawlinson) is a screen star. Polly Ann Young, ingenue in the company, loves Crosman's grandson (Russell Gleason), but becomes innocently involved in Rawlinson's divorce. When all is cleared up, the whole company goes over to the movies.

1936 also brought *Hollywood Boulevard,* a mixture of routine murder melodrama and sympathetic depiction of the desperate ploys of a fallen matinee idol, played by the impeccably suave John Halliday. An unscrupulous pulp magazine publisher (C. Henry Gordon) offers him $25,000—in 1936 a fortune—for serialization of his memoirs, but, as sensationalized without his knowledge, the first installment proves painfully embarrassing to his ex-wife and especially to his beloved daughter (Marsha Hunt).

He begs for release from his contract, in vain, until it comes out that the next victim of the scandal will be the publisher's own wife (Frieda Inescort). In a furious quarrel, the publisher shoots the ex-star, then tries to pin the murder on the victim's daughter—but her fiancé (Robert Cummings) outwits him by playing back a dictaphone recording of the conversation leading to the crime.

What was unique about *Hollywood Boulevard,* however, was its extraordinary cast of forgotten silent stars. Esther Ralston and Betty Compson played speaking roles, but the rest, extras, bit players and background, included more than twenty once famous names such as Francis X. Bushman, Maurice Costello, Mae Marsh, Jack Mulhall, Roy D'Arcy and Creighton Hale. The *Herald Tribune,* which generally disliked the picture as "often lurid, dull at times and painfully average throughout," concluded by saying, "It is nice to encounter old friends again."

A more cheerful variation on the theme was *It Happened in Hollywood* (1937), based on Myles Connolly's story *Once a Hero.* A cowboy star (Richard Dix) fades out with talkies because he looks ill at ease in evening clothes

and for the sake of his youthful following will not play gangster roles. When his leading lady (Fay Wray), whom he loves, becomes a bigger star than ever, they drift apart. Several years later, alone and forgotten, he is heartened by the loyalty of a boy fan (Billy Burrud) who seeks him out. Coincidentally, he shoots a trio of bank robbers, makes the front pages and finds himself in demand again, even co-starring with Wray.[3]

Also accentuating the positive was 20th Century-Fox's ambitious Technicolor *Hollywood Cavalcade* (1939), which was to have been called *Falling Stars.* It was, as the *Times* said, "the motion picture's first large-scale attempt to dramatize its own history. It has been, by and large, a successful attempt, although the history is more effective than the drama." After the very amusing opening sequence with Buster Keaton, Ben Turpin and the Keystone Kops as themselves, the rest was mainly downhill, plodding along with that basically synthetic, hokumish air that marred so many 20th Century-Fox efforts—as an Alice Faye film certainly better than *Rose of Washington Square,* but not as good as *Alexander's Ragtime Band.*

Don Ameche played an early director named Michael Linnett Connors, who seemed to be a composite of D. W. Griffith and Mack Sennett, with perhaps some touches of De Mille (all three were living at the time), who, with his producer (J. Edward Bromberg), in 1913 signs a stage star, Molly Adair (Alice Faye), a combination of Mabel Normand and Mary Pickford, to do a slapstick comedy opposite Keaton.

It's a hit, but Connors is too busy developing every screen innovation, from close-ups to custard pies, to notice that Molly loves him,

---

[3] Other '30s films in which cowboy movie stars off screen lived up to their heroic images include Tom Keene in *Scarlet River* (1933), Buck Jones in *The Thrill Hunter* (1933), Charles Starrett in *The Cowboy Star* (1936), Gene Autry in *The Big Show* (1936), Jones again in *Hollywood Round Up* (1937) and George O'Brien in *Hollywood Cowboy* (1937).

so eventually she marries a matinee idol (Alan Curtis), who reminded the *Times* reviewer of Valentino, Fairbanks Sr. and Wallace Reid. They become leading stars of the '20s, which are glossed over with no period atmosphere at all—e.g., at a banquet circa 1928, even as the orchestra plays "Ramona," Faye and the other women are wearing floor-length '30s evening gowns.

The two stars are making a silent version of *Common Clay* when an auto crash kills Curtis and injures Faye. The studio plans to shelve the film, but Ameche, whose career meanwhile has slumped, is so thrilled at seeing and *hearing* Jolson in *The Jazz Singer* (a re-enactment, not the original film) that he steals the negative of *Common Clay* and re-shoots some scenes with sound. Released as a part-talkie, it is, of course, a smash, and puts both Faye and him back on top, together at last.

The writers of *Hollywood on Hollywood* are among the film's warmest admirers: "While *Hollywood Cavalcade* did not adhere strictly to history, the feature contained a relatively accurate and—more importantly—loving account of the rise of the movie industry from its fledgling flicker days to the debut of the talkies." Loving it may be, but interesting or convincing it's not, once past the Keystone Kop era.

This leaves only the very small number of films that attempted to deal with the darker, more tragic side of Hollywood. As noted, the first faded star to appear in a talkie was Blanche Sweet's character in *Show Girl in Hollywood* (1930). The next, aptly enough, was her erstwhile Griffith co-star, Henry B. Walthall, in his first important talkie, a Monogram picture that the *Times* reviewed adversely as *Fame Street* (1932), but which *Film Daily* praised, under the title of *Police Court*.

Walthall played a once great star ruined by drink, trying to make a comeback for the sake of his son (Leon Janney). The cast included Aileen Pringle, King Baggott, Al St. John, Edmund Breese and Lionel Belmore, all prominent in silents. *Film Daily* thought Walthall gave "a very believable and touching performance as the great actor gone to the dogs with drink . . . The Hollywood studio atmosphere is well done."

Another modest attempt to evaluate the price of fame was *Hollywood Speaks* (1932), in which a despondent actress (Genevieve Tobin), envying the famous at Grauman's Chinese Theater, is about to take poison, until stopped by a reporter (Pat O'Brien). Through his influence she is given a test by a vain, saturnine director (Lucien Prival, who looked like von Stroheim), notorious for his affairs with actresses. Though she resists his advances, his wife (Leni Stengel) kills herself, leaving a note that incriminates the girl, and the scandal ends her budding career. But she happily abandons it for marriage to the reporter.

Less than a month before the utterly forgotten *Hollywood Speaks,* another film opened with a similar theme and denouement, RKO's *What Price Hollywood?* (1932), produced by Selznick and directed by Cukor, from a story by Adela Rogers St. Johns, which has become, if not exactly a cult film, almost a minor classic of its kind, still revived in New York. Everson ranks it with *Bombshell* (1933) and *Sunset Boulevard* (1950) as "one of the best and most honest movies about Hollywood."

Originally titled *The Truth About Hollywood,* it was intended to be a comeback vehicle for Clara Bow, whose career had been ruined by several scandals, but it was Constance Bennett who played Mary Evans, a movie-mad Brown Derby waitress befriended by Max Carey, a brilliant, alcoholic director (Lowell Sherman, in a superb performance, some details of which he may have drawn from his then brother-in-law, John Barrymore). Though he presumably finds Mary attractive, his attitude is avuncular, and hers is only one of gratitude.

In a very well-done studio sequence, he coaches her from awkward amateurism to a degree of polish that impresses the studio head (Gregory Ratoff). She is given the full treatment, and in a montage in which her cut-out figure looms ever larger against a starry background we see her rise to major stardom, popularly known as "America's Pal."

At her height, Mary (like Bennett herself) marries a polo-playing millionaire (Neil Hamilton), whose superwhimsical courtship may well make theirs the first screwball romance. The studio stage-manages their elaborate wedding, and even the honeymoon must be postponed because of retakes. The husband is soon fed up with Mary's demanding hours, the prying interviews, the incessant shoptalk, and especially Max's increasingly irresponsible antics. In fact, he leaves her and gets a divorce shortly before their son is born.

Fired by the studio, Max goes from bad to worse. After one drunken escapade, Mary bails him out and takes him to her house, promising to send him to a sanatorium. Instead, during the night (in a marvelously

Constance Bennett, Lowell Sherman, Gregory Ratoff in What Price Hollywood?

acted scene), after looking at a picture of himself as he once was and then into a mirror, Max shoots himself. The scandal ruins Mary's career overnight as tabloid headlines imply the worst, and screaming fans turn against "America's Pal" with abuse and boycotts. A montage shows her cut-out figure dwindling to insignificance.

She retires with her child to the South of France, where her ex-husband seeks her out for a happy reconciliation, after which she firmly declines an offer from the producer of a comeback film. As implied by the title, for her the price was too high. Why should she sacrifice her marriage and personal happiness to a fickle public that could not wait to tear her down even faster than it had built her up?

What Price Hollywood? may to some extent be, as Everson states, "a fore-runner of *A Star Is Born*," but only to the limited degree that *On with the Show* can be called a forerunner of *42nd Street*.

As anyone familiar with *A Star Is Born* (1937) will recall, what gives the story all its poignance, tension and irony is precisely that the rising star, Vicki Lester (Janet Gaynor), and the falling star, Norman Maine (Fredric March), are married and in love. Whereas in *What Price Hollywood?* the success of the director's protégée could only reflect favorably on his judgment in having discovered her, Vicki's growing fame as Norman's fades out can only be a constant humiliation to him—in fact, it drives him back to drink.

Even more crucially, the motivation for the suicide and its consequences in the two films are precisely the opposite. Max Carey apparently gives no thought of what it will do to the recently divorced Mary's career for him to kill himself in her house. Norman, on the other hand, overhearing Vicki's anguished decision to quit the screen to devote herself to him, walks into the Pacific to free her, to give her back the career he made possible.

Since his death is considered accidental, it causes no scandal for Vicki, and though she is mobbed by fans at his funeral, they are trying to express misguided sympathy ("Don't you

care, Vicki, he wasn't so much!"). The famous closing scene, in which, instead of leaving Hollywood forever as she intended, Vicki (given new courage by her indomitable grandmother, played by May Robson) makes her first public appearance at the premiere of her new film and announces herself proudly as "Mrs. Norman Maine," makes it clear that his sacrifice was not in vain. Unlike Mary Evans, Vicki Lester, having paid the price of losing the man she loved, will go on being a star.

In addition to a witty, literate screenplay by Dorothy Parker and Alan Campbell, among other distinctions, this was the first full-length film to use the new Technicolor in a modern urban setting. Despite the disenchanted tone of the story, Hollywood had never looked more glamorous: Grauman's Chinese Theater, the Hollywood Bowl, Santa Anita, Malibu, the Oscar ceremonies at the Biltmore, the glittering panoramic view from the Trocadero over the city at night—all seen as never before by the movie public.

Though it was one of Janet Gaynor's last films, she was never finer than as farm girl Esther Blodgett, rechristened Vicki Lester. Fredric March, who in 1937 surely looked more like a matinee idol than did James Mason in 1954, received a well-deserved Oscar nomination for his moving portrayal of the likable, self-destructive Norman Maine. Adolphe Menjou, cast, as so often, as a producer, was the very antithesis of the accented Ratoff stereotype.

The manner of Norman's suicide is said to have been suggested by that of John Bowers, husband of Marguerite de la Motte, but neither of them was ever a star on anywhere near the Norman Maine-Vicki Lester level. A more likely inspiration (as Lawrence J. Quirk points out in *The Films of Fredric March*) was the tragic decline of silent idol John Gilbert, who did not directly kill himself but drank himself to death by 1936, after his third wife, Virginia Bruce, had risen to stardom.

All in all, the film impressed critics and public alike. The *Times* called it ". . . the

Fredric March, Janet Gaynor in **A Star Is Born**

most accurate mirror ever held before the glittering, tinseled, trivial, generous, cruel and ecstatic world of Hollywood . . .''

From any point of view, there can be no doubt that *A Star Is Born* was the decade's finest film drama about Hollywood; even on an all-time basis, most critics would rank it with *Sunset Boulevard*.

PEOPLE LIKE US
Everyday Folks—More or Less

44

DOWN TO EARTH
Domestic Comedies

Self-evidently, Hollywood in the '30s offered escapist entertainment of unparalleled abundance and variety—escapes into the lives of millionaires, spies, jewel thieves, escapes into the past, into exotic climes and adventurous occupations including crime, into sheer fantasies, frightening or pleasing, into every level of musical life as well as the supposed glamour of life behind the scenes of stage or screen. But was no attempt ever made to reflect the lives most Americans were leading in those years? Yes—a number of films, most modestly budgeted, and seldom revived, did deal with at least the surface of middle-class family life.

Many were what were once known as "domestic comedies," direct ancestors of TV's ubiquitous sitcoms. The plots usually centered on some minor contretemps in a supposedly typical American family. The cast was often made up of convenient stereotypes—e.g., the henpecked father, the social-climbing mother, the daughter whose choice of the right young man determines the happy ending, perhaps a bratty younger brother (that was how Andy Hardy started) and usually a peppery older relative, a grandparent or spinster aunt, to comment tartly on the others. A comic maid was also standard.

The climax often involved the worm turning: the browbeaten or neglected spouse or overshadowed sibling or taken-for-granted breadwinner at last rebels and comes into his/ her own. Just as often, some handy *deus ex machina* solved everything: the supposedly phony stock Father bought proves to be a gold mine, the crazy invention with which Junior was always tinkering brings a fortune or at the very least someone gets a long overdue raise, promotion or inheritance.

Such domestic comedies were the staple middle-brow fare on Broadway in the 1920s, passing from successful runs and tours into the catalogue of Samuel French, thence to be continually resurrected by the then flourishing stock companies, little theater groups and school productions, because they were so safe, sure-fire and easy to put on (one living-room set, seven or eight characters, contemporary clothes and furniture) .

The only such plays by playwrights whose names are still remembered are Booth Tarkington's *Clarence* (1919), filmed 1922 and 1937, *Dulcy* (1921) by Marc Connelly and George S. Kaufman, filmed 1923, 1930 as *Not So Dumb* and 1940, George Kelly's *The Show Off* (1924), filmed 1926, 1934 and 1946. Others like *Your Uncle Dudley* (1929), filmed 1936, *Apron Strings* (1930), filmed 1932 as *The Virtuous Husband,* and *Broken Dishes* (1930), filmed 1931 as *Too Young to Marry* and 1936 as *Love Begins at Twenty,* were once as familiar to '20s theater-goers as their plots were to '30s film-goers.

From the dates this was obviously another

of those cultural lags apparent in so many genres. Throughout the '30s Hollywood continued to depict middle-class life as cheerfully as in the '20s, with never an economic cloud on the horizon, or at least none that could not be cleared away in time for the happy ending.

Since the youthful characters were generally secondary, many of these plays made ideal film vehicles for the middle-aged to elderly stars so extraordinarily popular in early talkies, notably George Arliss, Will Rogers, Marie Dressler and May Robson. Of these, the Arliss films, all but one for Warners, were by far the most elaborately produced and highly polished. Although Arliss is perhaps best-remembered for his gallery of historical portraits, from Disraeli to Richelieu, during his American career he also made several films laid in the modern world, in all of which he was always the spruce, spry, wealthy old gentleman who outfoxes not only his enemies but, if necessary, his own disagreeable family.

In *The Millionaire* (1931), from a story by Earl Derr Biggers, dialogue by Booth Tarkington, Arliss played an auto tycoon who on doctors' advice retires, but grows so bored that he buys half interest in a gas station and secretly works there, furthering the career of his young partner (David Manners), who ends up with Arliss' daughter (Evalyn Knapp). In a single scene James Cagney as a dynamic salesman made one of his first strong impressions on screen.

The Man Who Played God (1932), remade from an Arliss silent, based on a play, was more serious, with the star cast as a famous concert pianist permanently deafened by an explosion. Driven almost to suicide, he acquires a new lease on life by learning to read lips. From his apartment overlooking Central Park, through strong binoculars he can literally see what people are saying, and anonymously intervenes in their lives to help them, mostly with money. But eventually he eavesdrops once too often and learns that his youthful fiancée (Bette Davis in her first Warners role) really loves a boy her own age (Donald Cook); he breaks their engagement and turns to the faithful friend (Violet Heming) who has loved him all along.

In a lighter vein, in *A Successful Calamity* (1932), from a 1917 play by Clare Kummer, Arliss played still another millionaire, who, to test the character of his apparently selfish family, a social butterfly second wife (Mary Astor), a polo-playing son (William Janney) and a bridge-playing daughter (Evalyn Knapp), pretends he has gone broke. To no one's surprise but his, the daughter drops her fortune-hunting suitor (Hardie Albright) in favor of a worthier young man (Randolph Scott), the son not only goes to work but scores a coup meant to save the father, and, though it looks until the last minute as if the wife were going to run off with a gigolo, she was really only arranging for him to sell her jewels.

In *The King's Vacation* (1933), the second film to play Radio City Music Hall, Arliss naturally was a king, but bored with the formalities of his position and yearning for the commoner wife (Marjorie Gateson) and child he had been forced to give up for the throne. So he abdicates, leaves his Queen (Florence Arliss) and seeks out his true love in France, only to find that she has become a snobbish title-worshiper, eager to become queen but not the wife of a private citizen. After seeing that their daughter (Patricia Ellis) gets the right boy (Dick Powell), the King returns to his unassuming Queen and presumably his throne.

The Working Man (1933) resembled a plottier version of *The Millionaire,* with Arliss as a shoe tycoon who, with no children of his own, promotes his conceited nephew (Hardie Albright) to head the firm. Vacationing in Maine, he meets the two spoiled orphaned children (Bette Davis and Theodore Newton) of a late rival, whose wife Arliss had loved in their youth. To spite his nephew, without revealing his identity he builds up *their* company at the expense of his own and generally straightens everyone out so that the girl ends up with the chastened nephew. (Surprisingly, less than three years later, 20th Century-Fox in its attempt to launch Irvin S. Cobb as a successor to Will Rogers remade *The Working Man* as *Everybody's Old Man*.)

Arliss' last modern-dress vehicle in Hollywood was *The Last Gentleman* (1934), an excellent production of Zanuck's 20th Century before its merger with Fox, and indeed one of the most delightful films of the decade, with an array of character players that now seems incredible. A crusty octogenarian New England millionaire, Cabot Barr (Arliss), who looks like John D. Rockefeller, summons the scattered members of his family to their first reunion in years, at a house party on his estate. They include his spinster sister (Edna May Oliver), her adopted son (Frank Albertson), his widowed daughter-in-law (Janet Beecher), long estranged, his hitherto unrecognized granddaughter (Charlotte Henry), his scheming son (Donald Meek) and *his* bitter wife (Rafaela Ottiano).

Aided by his faithful secretary (Ralph Morgan) and ex-convict valet (Edward Ellis), Barr proceeds to manipulate everyone into doing what he knows is best for them. The boy and girl, strictly forbidden by him to have anything to do with each other, naturally fall in love, as he planned. The detestable son, trying to have his father declared insane because he collects clocks and stuffed peacocks, is hilariously hoist with his own petard.

Not unexpectedly, Barr dies—but instead of a written will he has made a talking film in which he announces the bequests from the screen, exactly anticipating how each heir will react. In 1934 such a denouement was a startling novelty, carefully kept secret in the reviews. But the whole film glows with such mellow autumnal charm that the ending is genuinely touching, as the old man's image walks off the screen to the strains of his favorite song, "Put On Your Old Gray Bonnet."

But if Arliss was always the supremely confident man of the world, in full command of every situation, Will Rogers was the perennial homespun hayseed who'd be gol-derned if he'd take any hifalutin nonsense from any city slickers—an American folk figure that goes at

least as far back as *The Contrast* (1787), the first play by an American about Americans. Though he, too, sometimes played millionaires, they were *nouveau riche* tycoons, meat packers or razor blade kings, ill at ease in high society, yet his common horse sense invariably cured the misguided ambitions of his flighty wife.

Several Rogers vehicles dealt with American-European cultural contrasts, not in the Jamesian sense, but very much in the tradition of Twain, as the not-so-innocent abroad exposes the phony nobleman and wins the respect of the real one. It would be pointless to discuss all his films, since most were cut from much the same pattern, tailored expertly to his nationally familiar personality and allowing him every opportunity to ad-lib timely witticisms, as he did in his widely syndicated column.

As with Arliss, some vehicles were adapted from plays or novels, others were written specially for him, as were *They Had to See Paris* (1929) and *So This Is London* (1930), both with Irene Rich as his wife. *Lightnin'* (1930), based on a long-running 1918 play, cast him as the slow-talking owner of a hotel half in California, half in Nevada, enabling a young fugitive (Joel McCrea) to escape the law.

In *Young as You Feel* (1931), which the *Times* compared to Arliss' *The Millionaire*, from George Ade's *Father and the Boys*, Rogers was a tycoon who despite his two stuffy sons discovers fun as embodied by Fifi D'Orsay. In *Ambassador Bill* (1931), one of his least original films, he helped save the throne of the boy king of the mythical Sylvania.

In *Business and Pleasure* (1932), from Booth Tarkington's *The Plutocrat*, amid the usual complications he explored Algiers and Damascus. *Down to Earth* (1932) revived his character from *They Had to See Paris*, with the spoiled family properly chastened and, on the whole, improved by the Depression. *Too Busy to Work* (1932), his most serious film, was a remake of his silent *Jubilo* (1919), in which he played a tramp who long ago lost his wife (now dead) and daughter to a judge; he straightens out the girl's romance without ever revealing his identity.

Mr. Skitch (1933), with Zasu Pitts as his wife, was an extremely slender story about a cross-country trip in an open car. In *Handy Andy* (1934), based on a play, *Merry Andrew,* Rogers was a small-town druggist who regrets selling his store to a chain, but at least curbs the singing ambitions of his wife (Peggy Wood). *Life Begins at Forty* (1935), using the title of a non-fiction best seller, saw Rogers as a small-town editor who clears a wrongly accused boy (Richard Cromwell). His last modern-dress vehicle, *Doubting Thomas* (1935), though based on George Kelly's successful 1922 comedy *The Torch Bearers,* a satire on the amateur little theater groups so popular in the '20s, was harshly dismissed by the *Times* as "old hat for 1935"—but, fortunately for the sake of Rogers' well-loved image, his last two films, released after his death, *Steamboat Round the Bend* (1935) and *In Old Kentucky* (1935), were solid, nostalgic hits.[1]

Most of the equally beloved Marie Dressler's films have been discussed elsewhere. Those with Polly Moran indeed come close to domestic comedy except for their broadly farcical tone. But Dressler made four other comedy-dramas that seem to belong here. *Min and Bill* (1931), deplored by the *Times* as "far from pleasant," was nevertheless the biggest box-office hit of the year and won Dressler the 1930–31 Oscar. Teamed for the first time with Wallace Beery, she played the owner of a broken-down waterfront hotel, who, to protect the future of a waif she brought up (Dorothy Jordan), kills the girl's disreputable mother (Marjorie Rambeau).

Even more emotional was *Emma* (1932), in which Dressler was a motherly housekeeper who rears the children of a widower (Jean

Hersholt). When all are grown, he proposes, but soon after their marriage he dies of a heart attack, leaving her his money, whereupon the ingrate children not only take her to court but accuse her of causing his death. Cleared, she turns the money over to them, as she had always intended, and is last seen in a new job, ready to offer the same selfless love to another family of children.

Tugboat Annie (1933), based on a series of *Saturday Evening Post* stories by Norman Reilly Raine, was an obvious—and successful —attempt to follow up on *Min and Bill,* with Dressler and Beery again a battling lower-class couple, she running their tug while he drinks. Their son (Robert Young) becomes the youngest captain in the merchant marine; when his ship is almost driven on rocks by a storm, guess who redeems himself by saving it? Nevertheless, both stars were praised.

In *Christopher Bean* (1933), Dressler's last film, based on Sidney Howard's 1932 play, she again played a faithful housekeeper, this time for country doctor Lionel Barrymore, his wife (Beulah Bondi) and their daughters. In a variation on the plot of Henry James' *The Aspern Papers,* she had long ago befriended Bean, an alcoholic artist whose work, scorned locally, is now priceless. Despite all the family's efforts to cheat her, she refuses to part with a portrait of herself, and in the end she triumphs over all—a pleasant comedy but hardly a memorable one for Dressler's final curtain.

Unlike Arliss, Rogers and Dressler, who never played any less than starring roles, May Robson (who had been Miss Prism in the first American production of *The Importance of Being Earnest* in 1895), though starred several times, continued throughout the '30s and until her death in 1942 to accept supporting roles, as the vigorous, tart-tongued mother, mother-in-law, aunt or grandmother of some of the decade's top stars (Crawford, Shearer, Hayes, Harlow, Loy, Gaynor, Flynn).

In fact, after eight silents (1915–28), Robson starred in her first talkie, reviewed by the *Times* as *She-Wolf* (1931), based on a 1923

---

[1] In attempts to replace Rogers, vehicles were built around Victor Moore, Charles Winninger, Charles Grapewin, Fred Stone, Irving Cobb and Harry Davenport, but none ever caught on with the public.

play, *Mother's Millions.* Her name, Hattie Brean, recalls that of Hetty Green, the notorious millionaire miser who dressed and lived like a pauper and let family members die rather than spend money for medicine—but this was a decidedly softened Hetty Green. After alienating both her son (Lawrence Gray) and her daughter (Frances Dade) by interfering in their romances, she relents when the son refuses a bribe of millions to betray her secrets and her secretary (James Hall), the daughter's young man, proves equally loyal.

After fourteen non-starring roles, and the extremely successful *Lady for a Day* (1933), in which she was unquestionably the star and as such nominated for an Oscar, Robson played another Hetty Green type, this time called Hannah Bell, in MGM's *You Can't Buy Everything* (1934), set between the financial panic of 1893 and that of 1907, during which her loved but stingily reared son (William Bakewell) falls in love with the daughter (Jean Parker) of her most hated rival (Lewis Stone).

In what must have seemed a doubly surefire combination of two tested box-office appeals—a mother who was also a tycoon!—*The Mills of the Gods* (1935), Robson played an indomitable widow who, after running a plow factory for forty years, comes out of retirement to summon her idle children home from the fleshpots of Europe to ask their financial help in keeping the Depression-stricken business open. Naturally, they refuse. One reactionary son (Raymond Walburn) even calls the police so that the family can get away without facing the protesting workers, thus provoking a riot in which a grandson is killed by a stray police bullet. The old lady restores order with a stirring speech and a promise to reopen the plant at her own expense. Meanwhile a granddaughter (Fay Wray) has fallen in love with the union leader (Victor Jory), perhaps symbolizing the dawning peace between capital and labor? Even for Hollywood in 1935, this was social thinking based on the wishful premise that

the world's weightiest problems can be solved by a heroic mother figure (preferably rich).

In the pseudo-Runyonesque *Three Kids and a Queen* (1935) Robson starred as still another crusty millionairess who, when thrown from her carriage in Central Park, is picked up by three orphans and taken to the home of their guardian, an Italian barber (Henry Armetta). At first she is thought to be kidnaped, then a real kidnaping plot develops, until the old lady is finally softened in a story the *Times* said ran "relentlessly from burlesque to bathos."

After several more secondary roles, mostly in MGM "A's," Robson starred in another RKO "B," *Strangers All* (1935), as the widowed mother of four grown children, all dependent on the oldest son (Preston Foster). Of the other two, one son (James Bush) is a radical, one a would-be actor (William Bakewell), while the only daughter (Florine McKinney) goes to college. The mother has a suitor (Samuel S. Hinds), but emphasis is on the selfish children's misuse of money the oldest needs for a store. The radical is arrested and bailed out by the mother, the actor ends as a Hollywood extra. Dreary as it sounds, the ads emphasized "all fun."

They also compared *Strangers All* with *Three-Cornered Moon* (1933), which is usually credited (or blamed) for starting the cycle about daffy screwball families. Mary Boland played a widow who bought worthless mining stock, thus wiping out the family fortune and leaving the Rimplegars with nothing but their large, unsalable Brooklyn house. Claudette Colbert was the standard sensible daughter, engaged to a vain, unpublished writer (Hardie Albright), but her brothers seem less eccentric than merely inept: William Bakewell was a would-be actor, Wallace Ford a law student and Tom Brown a college boy (again!) forced to drop out. Eventually the writer finds a richer girl and the heroine turns to a dependable doctor (Richard Arlen) who boards with them. Realistic it may be, but funny it certainly is not.

Though seldom starred by herself, Boland,

an unusually gifted comedienne (e.g., *The Women, Pride and Prejudice*), was teamed with Charlie Ruggles in twelve films, in all but one as his wife. Six of these have already been noted; the others include some of the decade's most amusing domestic comedies. Typically, they played a middle-class, middle-aged couple with a marriageable daughter, she the genteel but dominant wife, he the flustered, timid husband. With polished teamwork they starred in *Mama Loves Papa* (1933), *Melody in Spring* (1934), a musical meant to launch radio singer Lanny Ross on a screen career, *People Will Talk* (1935), of which the *Times* said, "Miss Boland and Mr. Ruggles are unmatched on the screen as exponents of domestic comedy and their work has the remarkable faculty for touching life"; *Early to Bed* (1936), *Wives Never Know* (1936) and *Night Work* (1939), a.k.a. *Boy Trouble*. The last-named was meant to be the first of a series about the Fitch family, but got no further.

Continually paired acting teams (including James Dunn and Sally Eilers, Slim Summerville and Zasu Pitts, Kent Taylor and Evelyn Venable) were so popular in '30s films that the next step was using whole casts in more than one picture—in other words, series. The Tarzans, Dr. Kildare films and the many mystery and horror series have already been discussed, but others revived the family pattern of the silent and early talkie Cohens and Kellys.

First to appear was the Jones family in *Every Saturday Night* (1936), with Jed Prouty and Spring Byington as the parents, Florence Roberts as Granny, three sons, a teen-aged daughter and a grown one played at various times by June Lang, Shirley Deane and Joan Valerie. The closest precursors of routine TV sitcoms, the Joneses made an incredible fifteen films 1936–39, whose titles indicate their level—e.g., *Educating Father* (1936), *Off to the Races* (1937), *A Trip to Paris* (1938) and *Down on the Farm* (1939). Along with the plots, even some of the titles were borrowed from earlier films: *Hot Water*

(1937), *Safety in Numbers* (1938), *Quick Millions* and *Too Busy to Work* (both 1939) —surely enough to merit Don Miller's dismissal of the series as "regional disasters."

It was a Hollywood truism that MGM's "B's" were more than equivalent to most other studios' "A's." Thus its entry in the family series cycle is the only one still remembered, the Hardy family of fictitious Carvel, Idaho. *A Family Affair* (1937), based on Aurania Rouverol's forgotten 1928 play *Skidding*, seemed like a follow-up on *Ah, Wilderness!*, since it cast Lionel Barrymore and Spring Byington as the parents, Eric Linden and Cecilia Parker as the young lovers, and especially Mickey Rooney as Andy, the girl-crazy teen-aged son. An older, married daughter (Julie Haydon) was soon dropped from the series, but spinster Aunt Milly (Sara Haden) hung on throughout. The modestly budgeted film was so full of wholesome American values that Mayer decreed a sequel, then the series. The plot of the first was another variation on Ibsen's *An Enemy of the People*, in which Judge Hardy alienates the town and even his family by restraining the construction of an aqueduct, but everyone agreed Rooney stole the film.

In *You're Only Young Once* (1938) Lewis Stone and Fay Holden took over for good as Judge and Mrs. Hardy, and the older daughter was dropped. Said the *Times,* "Here at least is a 'series' family . . . in which the individual members react like human beings instead of third-rate vaudevillians." On a family vacation at Catalina the daughter is temporarily smitten with a lifeguard and Andy falls in puppy love "with a modern model of the baby-talk girl," almost forgetting home-town sweetheart Polly Benedict (Ann Rutherford).

Judge Hardy's Children (1938) took the family to Washington, where the Judge is serving on a federal commission investigating the power industry; the daughter becomes involved with blackmailing lobbyists, and an idea of Andy's saves the day. Man-to-boy talks between the Judge and Andy were now becoming a regular feature of the series.

Love Finds Andy Hardy (1938) centered squarely on the title character, who, said the *Times,* "ranks second to Walt Disney's Dopey as our favorite movie hero of the year. Watching Mickey's Andy on screen is practically as good as reading Mark Twain or Booth Tarkington; he's the perfect composite of everybody's kid brother." Besides Polly, he was now involved with two other promising newcomers, Judy Garland (billed third) and Lana Turner (eighth). In *Out West with the Hardys* (the fourth Hardy film of 1938), the daughter, still unmarried, falls for a widowed ranch foreman—temporarily, of course—but the *Times* said of Rooney, "As Andy Hardy, he is still the dominating member of the family."

Reviewing *The Hardys Ride High* (1939), the *Times* spoke of Rooney as "that gnomish prodigy . . . who is as old in cinema ways as Wallace Beery and twice as cute." In a variation on *Juno and the Paycock,* the Hardys are led to believe that they are about to inherit a Detroit auto fortune, but are on the whole relieved to find it's not true. In *Andy Hardy Gets Spring Fever* (1939) he becomes involved with a teacher of dramatics, while the Judge is almost ruined in a confidence game.

Judy Garland, Mickey Rooney, Ann Rutherford, Lana Turner in Love Finds Andy Hardy

Clearly, ideas were running thin and situations were beginning to repeat themselves, but the Hardys lasted through nine more films, until 1958, when Rooney was thirty-eight. With the years they have become a byword for the cleaned-up, prettified, all-American niceness later associated with such TV series as *Father Knows Best* and *My Little Margie*.

Other studios were quick to jump on the family band wagon. In a true triumph of type-casting, Republic offered James Gleason, his wife Lucille and their son Russell (who had also been involved with the Jones family) as *The Higgins Family* (1938), but, according to Miller, the tone was "unadulterated, hectic situation comedy," in which the senior Gleason was always the dupe. Not even Harry Davenport as Grandpa could save the series, which ran its course with *My Wife's Relatives, Should Husbands Work?*, *The Covered Trailer* (all 1939) and *Money to Burn* (1940). An attempt to revive it with a different cast fared even worse.

Other projected family series such as Standard's *The Headleys at Home* (1938) and Warners' *Everybody's Hobby* (1939), like the Fitches, never got beyond Square One. The only other such series to enjoy lasting success —clearly an immediate ancestor of *I Love Lucy*—was the incredibly long-lived Blondie films, twenty-eight in all, from *Blondie* (1938) to *Beware of Blondie* (1950), all starring Penny Singleton in the title role, Arthur Lake as Dagwood Bumstead and Larry Simms as Baby Dumpling.

The *Times*, which incorrectly called *Blondie* the first picture "admittedly based on a comic strip," dismissed it briefly as belonging "somewhere between the Katzenjammer Kids and Boob McNutt"[2]—but there was evidently a large public for such antics, later repeated

on radio and TV. Titles of the three 1939 entries explain themselves: *Blondie Meets the Boss*, *Blondie Takes a Vacation* and *Blondie Brings Up Baby*.

However farfetched their predicaments, all the series families were considered in the main stream, reflecting more or less normal American folks at home, as distinguished from that peculiar '30s phenomenon, the screwball family. As noted elsewhere, this kind of madcap humor affected many genres, especially films about heiresses and bright amateur detectives, but the cycle also produced a number about families as such, a few rich, some newly poor, most middle-class.

Discounting *Three-Cornered Moon*, the first such clan appeared in Chesterfield's *In the Money* (1934), described in *Film Daily* as a "nutty family," the motherless children of a "screwy" scientist, all dependent on the oldest daughter (Lois Wilson). One sister with a parasite husband is mad about art, another is involved with a boxer whose manager (Skeets Gallagher) eggs him into a championship match, saving the family from ruin.

Next was Warners' *The Merry Frinks* (1934), panned by *Film Daily* but still remembered by those who saw it as one of the funniest of its kind. "Absolutely the daffiest collection of bottled-in-bond crackpots that ever gave the world the jitters," proclaimed the ads.

In a New York tenement setting, downtrodden Aline MacMahon is even on Mother's Day completely ignored by her husband (Hugh Herbert), a reporter always getting fired for drunkenness, her two sons, a foolish radical lawyer (Allen Jenkins), a teen-ager known as Stinky (Frankie Darro) and a needling mother-in-law (Helen Lowell). When she cooks the wildly indigestible favorite dish of rich, eccentric Uncle Newt (Guy Kibbee), he dies, leaving her his fortune on condition that she leave her family. But the life of a Park Avenue matron, complete with gigolo (Ivan Lebedeff) is not for her, and she ends as she began, only minimally more appreciated.

---

[2] There had been silent versions of *Ella Cinders* (1926), *Tillie the Toiler* (1927), *Bringing Up Father* and *Harold Teen* (both 1928). Talkies included *Skippy* (1931), *Little Orphan Annie* (1932 and 1938), *Palooka* and another *Harold Teen* (both 1934).

Between the last two films had come the first of another subgenre, about once wealthy families who do not let sudden poverty interfere with their madcap ways—titled, aptly enough, *The Poor Rich* (1934), in which a clan that includes Edward Everett Horton, Edna May Oliver, Andy Devine and Leila Hyams tries to recoup its fortunes by marriage to foreign nobility, only to find the titled family equally poor—so they go into business together selling fried chicken.

Next such entry was *We're Rich Again* (1934), based on a play called *And Let Who Will Be Clever,* in which the *nouveau* poor couple (Billie Burke and Grant Mitchell) try to marry off their daughter (Joan Marsh) to a wealthy broker (Reginald Denny) while dodging bill collectors. The grandmother (Edna May Oliver) keeps up her morale by playing polo, but a garrulous country cousin (Marian Nixon) solves all their problems and gets the broker for herself.

Even "wackier" was *Down to Their Last Yacht* (1934), in which Mary Boland was the daffy queen of a South Sea island where the yacht of hard-up socialites, chartered by a *nouveau riche* family, with the owners serving as crew, is beached. Said the *Times:* "The film is a sorry melange of Hollywood native dancing, theme song singing and preposterous comedy." Last of this limited cycle was *Society Fever* (1935), in which another broke but nutty family puts up a front to impress rich visitors, everything goes wrong, but the visitors are won over. Lois Wilson was again the only sane one and Lloyd Hughes the scion of wealth.

To be sure, one of the best-known screwball families of the decade, the Bullocks in *My Man Godfrey* (1936), were still rich, as were their counterparts in *Merrily We Live* (1938), but middle-class examples continued to abound—e.g., 20th Century-Fox's *Danger, Love at Work* (1937), which the *Times* praised. Besides the parents (Mary Boland and Etienne Girardot) the clan included an artist (John Carradine) who does surrealistic paintings on windowpanes, Aunts Pitty and

Patty (played by the famous pixilated sisters from *Mr. Deeds Goes to Town* [1936], Margaret Seddon and Margaret McWade) and a ferocious ten-year-old prodigy (Bennie Bartlett) more than ready for college. Even the daughter (Ann Sothern) brings home a new fiancé every second day, until she falls for the lawyer (Jack Haley) who is trying vainly to get them all together long enough to sign an important legal document.

A few weeks later, too soon to have been influenced, by apparent coincidence Boland and Sothern were playing approximately the same roles in RKO's *There Goes the Groom* (1937), about another scatterbrained, ne'er-do-well family whose only hope is to marry a daughter to a former suitor (Burgess Meredith) returned rich from Alaska. He must feign amnesia to avoid being married off to his true love's younger sister.

Although the title *Rich Man, Poor Girl* (1938), a remake with Robert Young and Ruth Hussey of *The Idle Rich* (1929), clearly announced its Cinderella theme, the girl now had "an amiable, slightly nuts" family.

In Frank Capra's *You Can't Take It with You* (1938), Jean Arthur and James Stewart, excellent as they are as Alice Sycamore (the only sane one) and Toby Kirby, Jr., her upper-class beau, are overshadowed by the character players: Lionel Barrymore as philosophical Grandpa Vanderhof, who quit the business world thirty-five years ago to enjoy life; Spring Byington as his delightfully vague daughter, Penny Sycamore, Alice's mother, writing a novel because someone left a typewriter at the house; Ann Miller as Alice's sister, Essie, would-be ballerina forever pirouetting about on point, though her teacher, Boris (Mischa Auer), loudly proclaims to one and all, "Confidantially she *steenks!*" Essie makes candy, which her xylophone-playing husband, Ed, sells, enclosing in each box messages like "Dynamite the White House!" Of course the FBI men arrive the very evening of the visit of Tony's haughty parents (Edward Arnold and Mary Forbes), who are hauled off to jail with the rest.

James Stewart, Jean Arthur, Dub Taylor, Lionel Barrymore (seated), Spring Byington,
Ann Miller, Edward Arnold (seated), Mary Forbes, Mischa Auer (on floor), Lillian Yarbo,
Eddie Anderson, Donald Meek, Samuel Hinds, Halliwell Hobbes in You Can't Take It with You

From the play, only Gay Wellington, the alcoholic actress, and the Grand Duchess Olga, the Childs waitress ambitious to work at Schrafft's, are missing, along with the hilarious word-association game with which Penny embarrasses the Kirbys. In their place, Robert Riskin devised an elaborate populist fable in which ruthless tycoon Kirby as head of a cartel plans to destroy the Sycamores' neigh-borhood to make way for a munitions plant—until, like Scrooge, he is made to see the error of his ways by getting to know his lovable victims. His ultimate humanization, symbolized by joining Grandpa in a harmonica duet, is surely a touch more Capra than Kaufman and Hart. *You Can't Take It with You* was so clearly the culmination of the whole screwball cycle that it virtually ended it.

45

NO PLACE LIKE HOME
Domestic Dramas

Except for some star vehicles, most of the films discussed in the previous chapter were comedies, but Hollywood also produced just as many serious family films, most involving misunderstandings between parents and grown children—e.g., *The Bargain* (1931), based on Philip Barry's 1923 play *You and I,* with Lewis Stone as a frustrated soapmaker who wanted to be an artist and is so disappointed when his son (John Darrow) makes the same mistaken choice that he himself retires and tries to paint, too late—but then the son goes off to study art, after all.

Oddly enough, in *New Morals for Old* (1932), based on John Van Druten's play *After All,* Stone played just the opposite sort of father, as a wallpaper manufacturer who *discourages* the artistic ambitions of his son (Robert Young). A daughter (Margaret Perry) is in love with a married man, but after several years pass the two young people come around to thinking exactly as their parents did.

The title of *Looking Forward* (1933) was borrowed from a non-fiction book by President Franklin D. Roosevelt, but the film itself was based on a British play, *Service,* by C. L. Anthony (Dodie Smith). This time Stone was the husband of faithless Benita Hume and the father of Elizabeth Allan and Phillips Holmes. Their centuries-old London department store is saved from ruin only by a venerable bookkeeper (Lionel Barrymore).

In *This Side of Heaven* (1934), Barrymore was still adding up figures, as an accountant, with Fay Bainter in her screen debut as his wife, who has just sold a book to Hollywood. Their children were Mae Clarke, a schoolteacher, Tom Brown, a college boy, and Mary Carlisle, about to start college. All five are involved in crises, from a car crash to suspicions of embezzlement, but all are neatly resolved within twenty-four hours. The *Times* thought it as refreshing as *Little Women,* "blessed with the proper restraint . . . each character is developed in a believable fashion."

An American family drama of far more universal appeal was *Alice Adams* (1935), illumined by one of Katharine Hepburn's finest performances. The pecking order in a small Indiana town among various levels of WASP families may seem even more trivial a subject now than in 1935, yet it is just such trivia—snubs, exciting dates, embarrassing moments, ruined evenings—that make up most young people's lives.

Less sentimental than most of Booth Tarkington's novels, *Alice Adams* had been filmed as a silent in 1923 with Florence Vidor, an actress so strikingly beautiful as to seem miscast as a small-town social climber. One of Hepburn's peculiar gifts was that while she could when necessary look radiant, she could also seem convincingly gawky and awkward.

The New Yorker describes Alice as "one of the few authentic American movie heroines." From the moment we first meet her furtively hurrying out of a five-and-ten, then striking a leisurely debutante pose in front of a fashionable shop, Alice is always "on," pretending to be what she's not—yet her efforts always come across as pathetic rather than irritating. As her needle-tongued mother (Ann Shoemaker) never ceases driving home to her underdog father (Fred Stone), all Alice lacks is money, and in this town "money *is* family."

For most of its length the film is remarkably honest, constantly hovering between hilarity and heartbreak, especially in two classic sequences. One is the formal dance to which Alice is unwillingly escorted by her loutish brother Walter (Frank Albertson), who promptly leaves her stranded in the foyer in her two-year-old organdie gown, with her homemade corsage (plucked from the city park), a desperately smiling wallflower with no one to ask her to dance but fat Frank Dowling (Grady Sutton).

The other sequence is the disastrous dinner at which the Adams family puts its best foot forward to entertain wealthy Arthur Russell (Fred MacMurray), serving course after course of steaming food on the hottest night of summer, while the drunken maid (Hattie McDaniel) hired for the occasion, her cap askew, lurches about spilling and dropping things and Mr. Adams' starched shirt front keeps coming between him and his plate. Except for the lame Cinderella ending, in which Arthur assures Alice that he loves her for herself, *Alice Adams* remains a minor masterpiece of quiet realism.

A few weeks later a far more flamboyant family, one of the most popular in fiction, reached the screen in *Jalna* (1935), based on the prize-winning first novel (1927) of Mazo de la Roche's best-selling series. In what seems perfect casting, Jessie Ralph was the redoubtable hundred-year-old Gran, C. Aubrey Smith and Halliwell Hobbes were her septuagenarian sons, crusty Uncle Nicholas and fussy Uncle Ernest, Ian Hunter and Peggy Wood

were the middle-aged children of the late Philip Whiteoak, Renny, the master of Jalna, and spinster Meg, and David Manners and Theodore Newton were Eden and Piers, two of their young half brothers.

As in the novel, Eden is a writer, who on a visit to his New York publisher marries reserved Alayne Archer (Kay Johnson) and brings her back to Jalna, the Whiteoak estate in southern Ontario, where she is fairly overwhelmed by his tumultuous family. Piers meanwhile has married Pheasant (Molly Lamont), illegitimate daughter of neighbor Maurice Vaughan (Nigel Bruce), who had been about to marry Meg when Pheasant was left on his doorstep. Soon the philandering Eden tries to seduce Pheasant, but before any real harm can be done he dies in a fall (not from tuberculosis, as in the book). About to leave Jalna, the widowed Alayne instead stays on to marry Renny. Said the *Times:* "The Whiteoaks are an interesting family . . . and this first photoplay about them manages to do them justice."

The next non-series, non-screwball family of any distinction was in *Call It a Day* (1937), from Dodie Smith's pleasant comedy-drama of a London family on the first day of spring, during which the four leading members all have brief encounters with temptation. The daughter (Olivia De Havilland) throws herself at a married artist (Walter Woolf King) but is deflected by his wife (Peggy Wood); the son (Peter Willes) is ready to run off to the Continent until he meets the new girl next door (Anita Louise). Even the parents, happily married twenty years, flirt with indiscretion; Father (Ian Hunter) is being stalked by an amorous actress (Marcia Ralston), and Mother (Frieda Inescort) receives a "shameless" proposition from a pixyish bachelor (Roland Young). But by the end of the day, as the *Times* put it, "nothing has been altered really and practically nothing of importance has happened." The charm was all in the dialogue and the performances.

Another charming British family, of an altogether different sort, were the protagonists

Ann Shoemaker, Fred MacMurray, Hattie McDaniel, Katharine Hepburn, Fred Stone in Alice Adams

of *The Young in Heart* (1938), adapted from I. A. R. Wylie's novel, *The Gay Banditti*. The Carletons (Roland Young and Billie Burke) and their children (Janet Gaynor and Douglas Fairbanks, Jr.) are supremely skilled con artists, operating on the principle that "the family that preys together stays together." The father, known as "Sahib," was supposedly a colonel in the Bengal Lancers, though in truth he came no closer than touring Canada in a musical comedy about the Lancers.

Given one-way tickets to London when expelled from a Riviera resort, on the train they meet dear, wealthy old Miss Fortune (Minnie Dupree), at first hoping to get her to make a will in their favor, but soon genuinely fond of her. Meanwhile the daughter falls in love with a strait-laced young Scot (Richard Carlson) and the son with a girl (Paulette Goddard) who makes the unthinkable demand that he go to *work*. (In one amusing scene father and son stand looking down on a con-

struction site, talking about the workers like scientists discussing the habits of ants.) Aided by a witty script, all the principals gave sparkling performances, but critics agreed that the film was stolen by the veteran Miss Dupree.

The last heart-warming family saga of the decade, and one of the best-loved, began with *Four Daughters* (1938), taken from a story by Fannie Hurst, about the musically gifted Lemp family, which Jack Warner considered the climax of his producing career. The *Times* agreed that it was indeed one of the best pictures of *any*one's career, if only for the introduction of a fascinating new actor, John Garfield, at twenty-five a stage veteran, as a bitter, brooding loser whom one of the daughters marries. In an era when dimpled Adonises like Robert Taylor, Tyrone Power and Richard Greene were the reigning matinee idols, Garfield's sardonic image was indeed stunningly different.

Even aside from his unique impact, the

film was a strong one, full of fresh characterization and unhackneyed situations. Claude Rains was the widowed father of four girls, played, in a triumph of type-casting, by the three Lane sisters, Priscilla, Rosemary and Lola, with Gale Page as the fourth sister. May Robson was the doughty aunt who keeps house for them. All is harmonious in this household of classically trained musicians until the arrival of a modern composer (Jeffrey Lynn) and his orchestrater (Garfield), the eternal outsider, who, in a twist surprising in this kind of film, ends as a suicide, freeing Priscilla presumably to turn to Lynn, whom she had mistakenly given up to one of her sisters. Said one critic, "It may be sentimental, but it's grand cinema."

Like any other studio, Warners lost no time in reassembling such a winning combination, but since Garfield's character was dead, a sequel was out of the question. Instead, *Daughters Courageous* (1939), with the same cast, was a kind of parallel, about another family of four daughters. The *Times* found that the two films had much in common: "warmth, humor, poignance." In a completely different story line that recalls both *Mary Jane's Pa* and *A Bill of Divorcement,* not to mention *Enoch Arden,* a father (Rains) who had deserted his wife (Fay Bainter) and children twenty years before returns just as she is about to remarry, to a worthier man (Donald Crisp). The daughters naturally give him a chilly reception, until eventually won over. Garfield was Gabriel Lopez, a fisherman's impertinent son with whom one of the girls falls in love.

But a true sequel was inevitable, and it arrived, three days after the opening of *Gone With the Wind,* as *Four Wives.* Except for Garfield (who appeared in a flashback), the original cast took up where they had left off. Gale Page is still married to Dick Foran, as Lola Lane is to Frank McHugh, so only Rosemary and the widowed, pregnant Priscilla figure in the plot. As hinted in the earlier film, she ends up with composer Lynn, while Rosemary weds a new character, a doctor played by Eddie Albert. The secret of the success of

these films, said the *Times,* was that "they seemed a natural enough family when first we met them, not the usual caricature family Hollywood enjoys inventing."

There were many other films in which the family served as the mere background or foils for one leading character, whether a child, a mother (not the self-sacrificing kind!), a father or, most rarely, even an aged grandparent. Child stars had, of course, been popular in silent films, as they had been on stage for centuries. Besides such forgotten favorites as Baby Peggy and Wesley Barry, silent fans doted on Our Gang, Mary Pickford even in her thirties was still *perceived* as a spunky little girl, and in the mid-'20s Jackie Coogan was surely the most famous little boy in the world.

But the '30s were the true heyday, with hundreds of films written for and about (and at times it seemed *by*) children. Though occasional forays were made into the more familiar childhood classics, American (*Peck's Bad Boy, Mother Carey's Chickens, Mrs. Wiggs of the Cabbage Patch, Little Lord Fauntleroy*) or European (*A Dog of Flanders, Heidi*), most such vehicles stuck to contemporary America and necessarily domestic situations with the emphasis shifted to the supposedly talented tots.

Except for *Tom Sawyer* and *Huckleberry Finn,* the first "kids'" picture of the decade was the highly successful *Skippy* (1931), based on a popular comic strip, which launched the first child star of the decade, Jackie Cooper, a nine-year-old veteran of Our Gang. *Skippy* not only placed high on most "ten best" lists but won an Oscar for director Norman Taurog.

It holds up remarkably well, especially in the performances of Cooper in the title role and of Jackie Coogan's five-year-old brother Robert as the wistful ragamuffin Sooky, from Shanty Town, where Skippy is forbidden to go, but does. With many touches true to small-town American boyhood, the rather leisurely story climaxes with the two friends' efforts to save Sooky's mongrel pet from a particularly mean dogcatcher. When even Skippy's savings bank, which he deliberately lets be run over by a truck, does not yield enough to pay the fine, the dog is shot. The two little boys' grief, especially Sooky's, is genuinely heartbreaking. Only this childhood tragedy finally softens Skippy's strict father (Willard Robertson).

Inevitably, such a critical and financial success led to a sequel, *Sooky* (1931), which met the fate of most sequels. Despite the same cast and writers, *Sooky* seemed to work too hard at tear-jerking, for it dealt with the death of the little hero's mother (Helen Jerome Eddy), after which he comes to live at Skippy's house. Between these two films, Cooper had made *Donovan's Kid,* the first of his many screen encounters with gangsters, and the unforgettable *The Champ,* in which King Vidor turned Frances Marion's sentimental story into the most touching film of its kind since Chaplin's *The Kid* (1921).

Wallace Beery's performance as a broken-down pug hopelessly addicted to drink and gambling, yet still idolized by his loyal little son, won him half the 1931–32 Oscar, which he shared with Fredric March, but Cooper's all-out emotional performance was no less affecting. *The Champ* was indeed the ancestor of all those heart-tugging comedy-dramas in which a sensible child rejects conventional upbringing to look out for a lovable, irresponsible father.

The Cooper-Beery combination proved so effective that they were teamed again in *The Bowery* (1933), *Treasure Island* (1934) and also *O'Shaughnessy's Boy* (1935), a circus-set variation on *The Champ,* in which the now adolescent Jackie had to have a still younger boy play him as a small child. The *Times* dismissed it as a "tear festival . . . as relentless as a dentist's drill."

From then on Cooper played almost nothing but street boys and potential juvenile delinquents. He often shared top billing with his near-contemporaries Mickey Rooney and Freddie Bartholomew, notably in *The Devil Is a Sissy* (1936). Bartholomew's career, starting with *David Copperfield* (1935) and con-

tinuing mainly in classic and/or costume films, has been covered elsewhere, except for a graceful, lavish and surprisingly de-sentimentalized *Little Lord Fauntleroy* (1936), with the still beautiful Dolores Costello as his mother and C. Aubrey Smith as his grandfather, the crusty old Earl of Dorincourt. Rooney's career has also been covered elsewhere, but, unlike the other two, in dozens of films before the Hardy series he played roles too small to mention.

But, of course, *the* unique juvenile phenomenon of the decade—or any decade—was Little Miss Millions herself, Shirley Temple, who at her height in 1938 was earning $100,000 per film, far more than any adult star, in fact, more than anyone else in Hollywood except L. B. Mayer—with '30s buying power, no big income tax and protected by a law passed after Jackie Coogan lost all he had earned in silents to his mother and stepfather. Besides this unique salary, Shirley was making even more than the Dionne Quintuplets from royalties on various wholesome products that she smilingly endorsed. Unquestionably she was the most successful child performer of all time. Yet with the occasional exception of *Little Miss Marker* (1934) and *Now and Forever* (1934), her films are seldom revived, at least not in theaters in New York.

An ambitious mother had Shirley at three or four playing both in short subjects and bit roles in "B" films. She first attracted attention in Fox's "timely" musical *Stand Up and Cheer* (1934), singing the climactic number, "Baby, Take a Bow."

Meanwhile on a two-picture deal with Paramount she made a tremendous impression in *Little Miss Marker* (1934), a typically sentimental Damon Runyon yarn about soft-hearted hoods, touts and race-track hangers-on (Adolphe Menjou, Dorothy Dell, Lynne Overman), all suckers for a lovable four-year-old left as security by her washout father, who kills himself after losing all on the wrong horse. Beguiled by the King Arthur legend, the little girl casts all these roughnecks as characters in *Camelot,* so naturally they arrange a costume party at which they appear as such. Though Shirley was billed fourth, the *Times* called her "the stellar performer . . . no more engaging child has been beheld on the screen." Even the bad guy (Charles Bickford) comes through with a blood transfusion needed to save her life. In an appealing secondary role she was in a good position to steal the picture, and did.

Scarcely a month later Fox released *Baby Take a Bow,* in which Shirley for the first time got top billing. Still charmed, the *Times* reviewer observed, "She takes the picture under her little arm and toddles off with it." Two goodhearted ex-cons (James Dunn and Ray Walker) lose their jobs as chauffeurs when their employer's pearls disappear, but Shirley (as the daughter of Dunn and Claire Trevor) finds them and gets the reward.

Four months later she was involved in another jewel robbery, in her other Paramount film, *Now and Forever,* in which she was billed below Gary Cooper and Carole Lombard as an international thief and his girl. Shirley is his daughter by a late wife, whose family despise him; her insistence on the whole truth at all costs causes him endless embarrassment, but eventually leads him to surrender her to a wealthy benefactress (Charlotte Granville) while he goes off to prison. As in *Little Miss Marker,* Shirley made an impression all the more appealing because she was not allowed to dominate the story or do anything a child her age might not have done.

With *Bright Eyes* (still 1934) began the financial bonanza and the artistic decline; from now on all Shirley Temple films—and there were four a year—were the most vehicular of vehicles, built entirely around her and designed only to display her soon familiar bag of tricks to maximum advantage. The question very soon rose among reviewers as to just how extensive *were* Shirley's talents.

As Everson noted in *Films in Review* for November 1976, "Children were not uniform and automatic fans of Shirley Temple. If they were in the same age group, Shirley represented a challenge and a threat; she was always

being held up as an example, an impossible model to emulate . . . The *real* fans of Shirley were probably the aunts and mothers, who used their own children as an excuse to attend Temple vehicles."

The titles of her films, always descriptive of her, tell a good deal: *Bright Eyes, Curly Top, Dimples,* and all those *Little* creatures: *The Little Colonel, The Littlest Rebel, Our Little Girl, Poor Little Rich Girl, Little Miss Broadway, The Little Princess,* etc, etc., in which Shirley pranced and strutted and showed off her relentless cuteness. Most included an obligatory scene in which she literally or figuratively climbed onto the lap of some stern authoritarian figure and melted all resistance: Abraham Lincoln in *The Littlest Rebel* (1935), a hostile khan in *Wee Willie Winkie* (1937), a bearded miser whom she mistakes for Uncle Sam in *Just Around the Corner* (1938) and in *The Little Princess* (1939) Queen Victoria herself.

As Everson also points out, Shirley often suffered vicissitudes worthy of the most lurid Victorian melodrama: "Shirley had an incredibly traumatic history of mothers who were run over by buses or done in by pneumonia, of fathers who were away at the war or awaiting execution, with long periods in stern orphan asylums in between. Her problems ranged from the Victorian era and the Civil War to being chased by a sex maniac in New York."

Invariably Shirley was the good fairy who reunited her parents or straightened out the romance of the juvenile and ingenue—but whereas this latter situation seemed perfectly natural for a wise old Arliss or Rogers, it was less acceptable for a precocious child to manipulate the lives of adults. As an impersonator Temple could not hold a candle to Mitzi Green, as a child actress she was never in the league with Bonita Granville or Margaret O'Brien, and as an all-around singer-performer she never made the adult grade as Garland and Durbin so triumphantly did (not to mention Elizabeth Taylor and Natalie Wood).

On the other hand, the lively Jane Withers made her debut in Shirley's own *Bright Eyes* (1934), as a youthful monster who delights in practicing surgery on her dolls by hacking off their limbs. This "talented little imp" proved such a welcome relief from Shirley's angel-child image that the *Times* hailed her as the female equivalent of Jackie Searl, who had been playing sniveling brats ever since *Tom Sawyer* (1930). But while Jackie never went beyond secondary roles, Jane very soon became a star in her own right, and at Shirley's own studio, with *Ginger* (1935). Her films were never as elaborately produced or publicized as Shirley's—in fact, they were meant to fill out double bills, but they caught on and continued to be made, three or four a year, for the rest of the decade, with titles like *Little Miss Nobody, Pepper, The Holy Terror, Wild and Woolly, Rascals* and *Always in Trouble*.

Other studios' attempts to cash in on the Temple craze led to the brief, forgotten careers of such once well-known youngsters as Sybil Jason, Edith Fellows, Gloria Jean and that most obnoxious of all child stars, Bobby Breen, one of Eddie Cantor's least fortunate discoveries. When plump little Master Breen put one chubby hand on his full bosom, operatic tenor style, and turned his face heavenward, men fainted and strong women wept.

Least offensive were the child actors who were seldom starred but worked steadily in adult films, playing either the stars' children or the stars *as* children, without ever being compelled to carry the burden of the picture. Among those who appeared in many of the best films of the decade were Dickie Moore, Cora Sue Collins, Scotty Beckett and Virginia Weidler.

One bizarre variation on films about supposedly average families was a surprising flurry of films about *selfish* mothers! If some of May Robson's millionairesses were at least outwardly ruthless and domineering, they were nothing compared to these others in manipulating their families (though their number was, of course, insignificant compared to the martyred madonnas covered earlier).

Even silents had seen *The Goose Woman* (1926) and *Mother Knows Best* (1928), in both of which Louise Dresser played decidedly unmotherly mothers. The first talkie example was Irene Rich in *On Your Back* (1930), as a self-made couturier who stops at nothing to keep her son (Raymond Hackett) from marrying a chorus girl (Marion Shilling).

By what can only be coincidence, all the other notably selfish mothers (all of sons) appeared in a single year, 1933, starting with *Out All Night,* a comedy in which Slim Summerville was the overprotected son of Laura Hope Crews, who tries to prevent, then break up, his marriage to Zasu Pitts.

Crews' character sounds like a caricature of the better-known one she had created on stage and repeated on screen, the formidable Mrs. Phelps, in that *locus classicus* of clinging motherhood, *The Silver Cord* (1933), an admirably faithful adaptation of Sidney Howard's sharp, Ibsen-like problem play, the first American work to drop the bomb on Mom. Joel McCrea was her stronger, older son, who barely escapes with his wife (Irene Dunne), while his weaker brother (Eric Linden) jilts his fiancée (Frances Dee), whom the mother had almost let drown. Opened up just enough, the film drove home its points most powerfully, especially in the climactic confrontation between Mrs. Phelps and her scientist daughter-in-law.

A few days before *The Silver Cord* opened, Eric Linden had appeared as a son victimized in another way in *The Past of Mary Holmes,* talking version of *The Goose Woman,* a bizarre story by Rex Beach, obviously inspired by "the Pig Woman," the key witness in the sensational Hall-Mills murder trial of 1926. Helen MacKellar played an eccentric alcoholic recluse dreaming of her past operatic glory and hating her son, whose birth she blames for the loss of her voice. When she accidentally witnesses a murder, she unwittingly gives testimony that convicts her innocent boy, and then barely succeeds in saving him from the chair.

In *Another Language* (1933), based on Rose Franken's hit play, the son-devouring Mom Hallam (Louise Closser Hale) is another Mrs. Phelps, even to the fake heart condition, only her insignificant husband (Henry Travers) is still living, and she has *four* sons and their wives to dominate on her famous Tuesday evenings, which no one dares miss. The son (John Beal) of the oldest brother (Willard Robertson) falls in love with the bride (Helen Hayes) of his youngest uncle (Robert Montgomery); it is these two who speak "another language"—a situation that leads to the crisis and resolution. In itself *Another Language* is an excellent comedy-drama of middle-class American life; it suffers only by comparison with the more concentrated and forceful *The Silver Cord*.

But by far the strongest of 1933's dramas of warped mother love was John Ford's extraordinary *Pilgrimage,* from a story by I. A. R. Wylie titled *Gold Star Mother*. Like Selina Peake in *So Big,* Hannah Jessup (Henrietta Crosman) is a hard-working Midwestern farm woman before World War I with an only son (Norman Foster)—but there the parallel ends. Determined to break up his romance with a neighbor's daughter (Marian Nixon), she deliberately asks the local draft board to take him, and he is killed in battle, leaving the girl to bear his child.

With no signs of remorse this hard, bitter woman continues to ignore her grandchild and his mother, until fourteen years after the war she is persuaded to join a pilgrimage of Gold Star mothers to their sons' graves in France. When in Paris she meets a young couple (Heather Angel and Maurice Murphy) about to be broken up by his hostile mother (Hedda Hopper), Hannah at last gains new insight into her own self-destructive pattern and returns home to make peace with her only remaining kin.

This small number of selfish mothers was balanced by a scarcely larger minority, the selfless fathers of grown children—those who sacrificed far above and beyond the Lewis Stone-Lionel Barrymore call of duty. Most, in fact, were closer to Madame X than to King Lear. Indeed, the shadow of Emil Jannings loomed heavily over several father-love talkies, starting with the first, *Sins of the Children* (1930), starring Louis Mann as a humble German-American barber, who gives his all for his thankless children, sending one out West for his health, putting up collateral when another (Elliott Nugent) is accused of embezzling, even mortgaging his shop to set one son (Robert Montgomery) up in business. Then the ne'er-do-well turns inventor, saves the day and reunites the family.

Oddly enough, *Man to Man* (1931) also involved a put-upon barber (Grant Mitchell) with a son (Phillips Holmes) accused of embezzlement. The father has served time for a (justifiable) homicide, a disgrace that years later forces the son to leave college and embitters him. Yet when the money is missing, each confesses, thinking the other guilty, until the true culprit is caught.

Although Richard Bennett in Fannie Hurst's *Five and Ten* (1931) as a Woolworth-type tycoon certainly suffers, what with a wife (Irene Rich) who takes up with a gigolo and a suicidally neurotic son (Kent Douglas), his troubles are solved by his daughter (Marion Davies), one of the first sympathetic heiresses in a '30s film. Bennett faced even worse problems in *This Reckless Age* (1932) as a mining expert falsely accused of fraud whose apparently spoiled wife and children (Frances Starr, Charles Rogers and Frances Dee) rally round to save him. In *Skyline* (1931) Thomas Meighan accepts his illegitimate son (Hardie Albright) as an admiring protégé and makes his career before disclosing their relationship.

This Sporting Age (1932) cast Jack Holt as a polo-playing Army captain whose idolized motherless daughter (Evalyn Knapp) is engaged to a young polo star (Albright again) but compromises herself with another player (Walter Byron) so seriously that she attempts suicide, leading her father at the next polo match to cause a fatal accident to the cad and suffer the consequences.

But by far the finest father-daughter drama of the decade was *A Bill of Divorcement* (1932), closely adapted from Clemence Dane's play, which had starred Katharine Cornell on stage. After years in an insane asylum, Hilary Fairfield (John Barrymore) suddenly returns, apparently cured, ready to take up life exactly where he left off. But his wife (Billie Burke) has divorced him and is about to marry another man (Paul Cavanagh). When their daughter, Sydney (Katharine Hepburn in a sensational screen debut), learns that insanity is hereditary in her family, she urges her mother to go ahead with her plans and gives up her own fiancé (David Manners) to devote herself to her father. Despite a certain staginess in the dialogue, *A Bill of Divorcement* remains a most moving film, thanks to the riveting performances of Hepburn and Barrymore.

Equally serious was *Whom the Gods Destroy* (1934), which the *Times* compared to "the thunderous dramas of the Emil Jannings school." The tormented hero, a theatrical producer caught in a shipwreck comparable to that of the *Titanic,* first behaves with great courage, then in a moment of panic saves himself by donning a woman's coat. After a stay incognito in a fishing village, he returns to New York to find that he is venerated as a dead hero, so can hardly reveal himself as a live coward. Concealing his identity, he follows the fortunes of his beloved wife (Doris Kenyon) and their son (who grows into Robert Young), and in the guise of a friend of the father's steers the boy to theatrical success. Even when the wife recognizes him and begs him to stay with her, he goes out of their lives again.

In *Sins of Man* (1936) both the star and much of the setting were European. While finding it "uncompromisingly tearful," the *Times* noted that "it happens also to have been splendidly performed, honestly directed and handsomely produced." The long-suffering life of an Austrian bell ringer (Jean Hersholt) is traced from the late nineteenth century, when his wife dies bearing their sec-

ond son, born deaf. The other son, interested in aviation, emigrates to America, where the father later follows him to seek help for Gabriel, the deaf son. But the aviator is killed testing a plane, World War I breaks out, the Tyrolean village is bombed and Gabriel is reported missing.

Years later the father, reduced to a Bowery derelict, hears a recording by a famous Italian maestro that includes a bell arrangement that he recognizes as native to his village. Seeking the maestro out, he finds that Gabriel's deafness was cured by the bombardment, that he was sheltered and musically trained by an Italian family whose name he took. Hersholt was highly praised and radio star Don Ameche, playing both sons, was considered to have made a promising film debut.

Rarest of all family variants were four that centered on old people not as sly old foxes, ultimately triumphant, as in the vehicles for elderly stars, nor yet as pathetic martyrs, but as they normally appear in life, trying to adjust to failing powers and reduced income while fitting into the busy lives of indifferent grown children. Of the four, one centered on an old lady, two (actually two versions of the same story) on an old man and only one on an old couple.

Over the Hill (1931) was based on Will Carleton's famous nineteenth-century poem in which an aged mother tells how her large family has sent her "over the hill to the poorhouse." This had been made twice in silents, notably in 1920, and was even then described as "deliberately sentimental." The talkie version was praised as "infinitely more restrained" than its predecessors. Mae Marsh was the mother and James Dunn the good son who rescues her from the poorhouse where the skulduggery of a hypocritical son (Olin Howland) has put her.

Edna Ferber's story *Old Man Minick,* which had also been a play, was first filmed as *The Expert* (1931), starring comedian Chic Sale, whose "intimate acting" was praised, though the film was not. The story concerns his misadventures in the Chicago home of his son

(Earle Foxe) and daughter-in-law (Lois Wilson). Eventually he feels so much in the way that he decides to live in an old men's home. Remade in 1939 as *No Place to Go,* with Fred Stone, Dennis Morgan and Gloria Dickson, the story was changed only slightly. Given a job in his son's office, he suspects it's token; he ends up in "a club for gentlemen," convincing his son it's better that way.

The only serious, realistic American film about old age during the whole decade was Leo McCarey's classic *Make Way for Tomorrow* (1937), adapted by Viña Delmar from Josephine Lawrence's novel *The Years Are So Long* (1934). At the time of Miss Lawrence's death in 1978 the *Times* noted that "Although *Make Way for Tomorrow* had its premiere forty-one years ago, in 1937, it is still regarded as the best motion picture presentation of the problems faced by aged parents who must depend on the largesse of their children." Yet this uniquely touching film was not even nominated for a single Oscar.

When Barkley and Lucy Cooper (Victor Moore and Beulah Bondi) break the news to

Beulah Bondi, Victor Moore in **Make Way for Tomorrow**

four of their five middle-aged children (a fifth is never seen) that they are about to lose the family home and hope the children will buy them a smaller house, all four are dismayed at this financial impossibility. They decide instead that, temporarily at least, Mother will live with the eldest son, George (Thomas Mitchell), and his wife Anita (Fay Bainter) in their New York apartment, while Father will stay with Cora (Elizabeth Risdon) and her family in a remote town. Then, after three months, the childless, apparently well-to-do Nellie (Minna Gombell) and her husband (Porter Hall) will provide a home for both parents.

But, of course, nothing works out as planned. One of the distinctions of the film is its scrupulous fairness to both sides. The children are not heartless monsters, simply busy people caught up in their own lives, and the old couple, unwillingly separated and uprooted from their lifelong surroundings, are admittedly not easy to live with. Their poignant plight reflects a Depression-stricken America, where millions of people had seen their life's savings wiped out, and where Social Security, Medicare and unemployment insurance were still hotly debated issues.

The film gains immeasurably by the very triviality of the issues that cause friction—old Mrs. Cooper's kibitzing Anita's bridge lessons, her creaking rocker, Mr. Cooper's biting the finger of the young doctor examining him, his stubborn defiance of Cora.

Realizing after several awkward incidents how much she is in the way, Mrs. Cooper pretends she *wants* to go to an old ladies' home; her husband will be sent to the daughter in California, supposedly for his health. But they deliberately skip the farewell family dinner the children planned to spend their last hours alone together. A kindly car salesman drives them to an old-time luxury hotel where they spent their honeymoon and where they are now given a cordial welcome by the new manager. They even dance, to "Let Me Call You Sweetheart." In these closing scenes, criticized as a false touch of Hollywood glamour, what comes through most hauntingly is that Bark and Lucy, though old in years, are still capable of enjoying all the pleasures of life, if only they could afford them. As it is, no thanks to their children, they cannot even afford to spend their last years together.

At Grand Central they keep up cheerful talk about how he will soon get a job and send for her, but both know that they will never see each other again. As the train pulls out, Lucy stands watching, then trudges slowly off, into her own bleak future—one of the most poignant endings in any '30s film. As the *Times* put it, *Make Way for Tomorrow* had "three qualities rarely encountered in the cinema: humanity, honesty and warmth."

BOY MEETS GIRL
The Path of True Love

With the exception of *Stage Door* and a few all-male war pictures, almost every one of the thousands of films discussed so far involves a romance, however subordinated to other plot elements. Indeed, the love story was often primary—but with special obstacles: her guilty past, her wealth, his dangerous job. There were other films, however, which were purely and simply love stories, tenderly tracing, without melodramatic or comic distortions, the fortunes of a young couple, either single or married, through a series of crises to some resolution—in a few cases even to death.

The most famous youthful love story of the late silents (as distinguished from the more sophisticated affairs of the Garbo-Gilbert films) was Frank Borzage's *Seventh Heaven* (1927), set in Paris during World War I, which made stars of Janet Gaynor and Charles Farrell, and even after more than fifty years remains a beautiful, touching film. It was fitting, therefore, that Borzage also directed the first widely acclaimed talkie about young married love.

Bad Girl (1931), based on a Viña Delmar novel, was, in keeping with the times, much less starry-eyed than *Seventh Heaven*, set in contemporary, working-class New York. The title was unfortunate, for the heroine, Dot Haley (Sally Eilers), was not a bad girl in any sense. The story traces her perfectly respectable romance with Eddie Collins (James

Dunn in a promising screen debut), who works in a radio store, from their first meeting, through marriage on a shoestring, to the birth of their first child a year later.

Along the way Eddie rents and furnishes an apartment as a surprise to Dot, only to find her more concerned about her pregnancy, as yet unknown to him. Once he learns, he stints himself on every small comfort and even enters amateur boxing bouts to raise enough money to pay an expensive obstetrician, who is so touched that he makes no charge. With no hint of a triangle or other standard devices, *Bad Girl* made enough of a hit to launch Dunn and Eilers as a romantic team[1] as well as to spawn a cycle of films about struggling young couples, most ending with the expectation or birth of a child.

The first one was *Consolation Marriage* (1931), released two months after *Bad Girl*, in which Irene Dunne, jilted by Lester Vail, and Pat O'Brien, rejected by Myrna Loy, marry each other, with the understanding that either is free to leave should the former love return. But they have a child and, of course, realize they love each other.

Even more in the vein of *Bad Girl*, with an equally misleading title, was *Play Girl* (1932),

[1] Their other films were *Over the Hill* (1931), *Dance Team* (1932), *Sailors' Luck* (1933), *Don't Get Personal* (1936) and *We Have Our Moments* (1937).

which cast Loretta Young as an ambitious working girl named Buster and Norman Foster as a boy she meets at a dance hall and marries before she discovers how much he likes to gamble. They quarrel, he leaves, she stakes her last money on a horse race, etc. A few months later Young and Foster were teamed again in *Week-End Marriage,* based on Faith Baldwin's novel *Part-Time Marriage.* When he loses his job and with it his self-respect, while she succeeds at hers, the result is a "weakened" marriage—solved only when she gives up her job to devote herself to him—in 1932 the only possible solution.

Between these two films had come still another variation, reviewed in the *Times* as *Love Starved* (1932), in which Helen Twelvetrees as a lonely librarian marries "a scatterbrained dance palace sheik" (Eric Linden), who loafs while she works. Learning she is pregnant, he goes on a binge, finally promises to reform—as if a baby would solve all their problems instead of creating new ones.

A similar ending, treated more lightly, was used in *The First Year* (1932), from Frank Craven's popular 1920 play, which had been filmed as a 1926 silent. Janet Gaynor and Charles Farrell, thought the *Times,* had not appeared to such advantage since their silent films, as a young couple whose courtship, alternately abetted and frustrated by her family, is amusingly traced, then their post-honeymoon life in another town, climaxed by a crucial dinner at which they must entertain an important business contact and his wife while everything conceivable goes wrong. Humiliated, the young wife returns to her parents, but her kindly uncle (Dudley Digges), a doctor, solves it all by telling the husband about the little stranger on the way.

Perhaps the archetypal example of domestic comedies about squabbling newlyweds was Maxwell Anderson's Pulitzer Prize play *Saturday's Children* (1927), filmed three times within eleven years: first as a part-talkie (1929) with Corinne Griffith and Grant Withers, again in 1940 with Anne Shirley and John Garfield, both times with the original

title, and in between as *Maybe It's Love* (1935), the only version poorly reviewed, with Gloria Stuart and Ross Alexander as white-collar workers Bobby Halevy and Rims O'Neill. Egged on by her married sister (Ruth Donnelly), Bobby keeps Rims from taking a foreign job by inventing an imaginary suitor, thus spurring him into an unintended proposal. Her interfering family and an amorous boss lead to the inevitable split and equally inevitable reunion.

The Depression, blithely ignored by the films discussed so far, was the main obstacle in *I'll Love You Always* (1935), in which Nancy Carroll and George Murphy were a young couple in jobless New York, whose marriage cracks up under "the endless futility of trying to get somewhere." Said the *Times,* "Even the reconciliation over the baby's crib, the brat cooing and the customers getting their money's worth in stifled sobs, is bearable after what has gone before."

What went before was the husband's futile search for the right opening in engineering, a profession in which he graduated with highest honors. His wife, who used to be on the stage, becomes a dance hall hostess without telling him. When he finds out, they quarrel and agree to separate. He pretends he has the prospect of a job in Russia, but instead goes to prison for stealing money to buy her gifts. His letters are relayed by way of Russia, she has a baby but is too proud to tell him.

Meanwhile in 1934 Borzage had re-established his pre-eminence in directing moving love stories with the justly acclaimed *Little Man, What Now?,* faithfully adapted from Hans Fallada's novel, set in pre-Hitler Germany and acted by an unusually large, able cast. Douglass Montgomery played Hans Pinneberg, a young bookkeeper in a small German town who tries to conceal his charming bride Lammchen (Margaret Sullavan) from his employer (DeWitt Jennings), whose plain daughter (Muriel Kirkland) wanted to marry Hans.

When the truth comes out, the young couple move to Berlin, to live in the large house of his worldly stepmother (Catharine Doucet), whose lover (Alan Hale), a good-hearted crook, befriends them, gets Hans a job in a department store and otherwise helps out before being taken off to prison. The step-mother seems to be having parties every night for tired businessmen, but not until someone points out an ambiguous ad in a newspaper does Hans realize that she is running a high-class bordello.

He and Lammchen next find refuge in a loft over a secondhand furniture store owned by a kindly old wagon driver (Christian Rub), and there she bears their son, to whom his father tenderly addresses the words of the title. Though he has lost his job, a former colleague offers him a better one in Holland, so the picture ends on a hopeful note. As in so many Hollywood films of the '30s, casting and art direction were so perfect that even lo-cation photography in Germany itself could hardly have looked more authentic.

Passing over Borzage's next attempt to deal with married love, *The Big City* (1937), a hopeless mishmash in which Spencer Tracy and Luise Rainer were wasted as a taxi driver and his immigrant bride, the closest American parallel to *Little Man, What Now?* was *Made for Each Other* (1939), produced by Selznick and directed by John Cromwell, but the con-trasts are more significant than the similari-ties. The young husband (James Stewart) is a lawyer in a good New York firm, his wife (Carole Lombard) studied journalism, and their plans for a European honeymoon are frustrated only by an important case he must handle. Though there is much talk of scrimp-ing and saving, they live in a large apartment with a series of maids. In short, to genuinely struggling European couples like the one in *Little Man, What Now?* they would seem to be wallowing in luxury, a point no one no-ticed, so completely was such a standard of living taken for granted for '30s film char-acters. *Made for Each Other* has much to recommend it, especially the appealing per-formances by the stars, supported by Lucile Watson as Stewart's clinging widowed mother

Carole Lombard, James Stewart
in Made for Each Other

and Charles Coburn as the crusty head of his firm.

Most of the incidents are human enough: Stewart asking for a promotion and taking a cut instead, his feeling of failure at the tenth reunion of the Harvard class of 1928, the bickering between wife and mother, a diffi-cult dinner party. Only in the last part does the film lapse into melodrama, suspenseful but irrelevant. The baby, dying of pneu-monia, can be saved only by a serum that must be flown from California for $5,000. Does the crusty boss come through with the money? Does the pilot, forced to bail out of his open plane in a blizzard, reach New York in the nick of time? Is Stewart made a partner, after all? Despite these *dei ex machinia,* on the whole *Made for Each Other* was rightly hailed as one of Hollywood's more honest efforts to depict the troubles of a young couple.

Of the relatively few unmarried couples whose romances provided the main plot, some faced serious problems indeed; in six cases one lover or both died. A minor example was Bor-zage's *After Tomorrow* (1932), from John

Golden's 1931 play, in which Charles Farrell and Marian Nixon are sorely put upon by their selfish mothers, Josephine Hull and Minna Gombell. When *her* two-timing mother runs off with a boarder, the bereft father (William Collier, Sr.) suffers a breakdown for which the young couple must pay with their savings. Only "an unexpected stroke of good fortune" finally enables them to marry.

A more prestigious Borzage film was *A Man's Castle* (1933), still fondly remembered by some as what *The New Yorker* calls "a depression idyll." It is an obvious attempt at another *Seventh Heaven,* but the script by Jo Swerling, from a story by Lawrence Hazard, is even closer to *Liliom.* In Central Park a swaggering drifter (Spencer Tracy), who sometimes works as a sandwich man, picks up a starving, humbly adoring waif (Loretta Young), whom he constantly ridicules and threatens to leave. They live in "Hoover Flats," an improvised shantytown of the unemployed along the East River, among other dispossessed "little people," including a self-styled preacher (Walter Connolly), a heart-of-gold alcoholic (Marjorie Rambeau) and a lecherous crook (Arthur Hohl).

When the girl becomes pregnant, Tracy, egged on by Hohl, attempts and bungles a robbery, whereupon Rambeau shoots Hohl. Tracy and Young are last seen riding in a freight car. Surely the most heavily sentimental of all Borzage's films, *A Man's Castle* fails to live up to its legend.

As if in training for *Little Man, What Now?,* earlier in 1934 Douglass Montgomery had played another young German in *Eight Girls in a Boat,* whose setting in an austere school for girls reminded the *Times* reviewer of *Maedchen in Uniform.* Dorothy Wilson played a sensitive schoolgirl who, finding herself pregnant by a medical student (Montgomery), contemplates suicide, but, unable to go through with it, confides in an understanding teacher (Kay Johnson), who arranges a marriage, despite the opposition of the girl's father (Walter Connolly). The setting in a European school anticipated *Girls' Dormitory,* but the story was closer to such studies of troubled American heiresses as *Coming Out Party* and *Finishing School.*

Also set in a girls' school, but in America, was *These Three* (1936), Lillian Hellman's surprisingly powerful adaptation of her 1934 play *The Children's Hour.* So "notorious" had the play become because of its sympathetic treatment of a latent Lesbian that even its innocuous title could not be used on screen. Since the plot obviously could not be used either, what, then, had Samuel Goldwyn bought? As it turned out, all the values of the play were preserved intact by an adroit switch of sexes, a job of literary carpentry that the *Times* called "little short of brilliant." After all, the play was not *about* Lesbianism, any more than *The Winslow Boy* was about theft, but about the malevolent power of a wanton lie that destroys three lives.

In the play two young women, Karen Wright and Martha Dobie, run a very successful private school. Martha's exasperating old Aunt Lily, tolerated as an acting teacher, in a moment of pique hints that Martha resents Karen's forthcoming marriage to Dr. Joe Cardin and is, in fact, jealous. Their conversation is overheard by Mary Tilford, a viciously psychopathic teen-ager who hates all her teachers. Forcing another girl to back her up, Mary whispers the suspicion as fact to her doting grandmother, and in no time the school has no students. Even a libel suit fails to clear the victims' names. In the end, Martha, after confessing to Karen that she has indeed always loved her "that way," kills herself, and Karen and Joe, unable to trust each other ever again, part.

In the film this basic triangle remains, but instead of Karen and Martha (Merle Oberon and Miriam Hopkins) being branded, Martha is accused of carrying on a secret affair with Joe (Joel McCrea). (Bonita Granville gave an unforgettable performance as the malicious brat.) The dialogue is the same almost word for word, only now Martha feels guilty for loving Joe, and Karen is left wondering how much of the scandal was true. To be sure, Martha goes out of their lives, but does not kill herself, and Karen and Joe eventually get back together, yet this does not weaken the impact of a "strong, turbulent and caustic" drama.

So many of the most popular silents were re-made in the '30s that a talkie of *Seventh Heaven* (1937) was inevitable. What could be more logical than to star 20th Century-Fox's heavily publicized French *gamine* Simone Simon as Diane? But her Chico was James Stewart, who was, of course, as Parisian as Mom's apple pie. Despite a good cast that included Gale Sondergaard as Diane's wicked sister, the remake, directed by Henry King, bore no trace of the haunting charm of the original.

A more successful remake, also set in France, was *Port of Seven Seas* (1938), MGM's forgotten version of Marcel Pagnol's *Fanny*. Though the heroine's name was changed to Madelon, the atmosphere of the Marseilles waterfront was retained, as was the lifelong relationship of the two old friends, Cesar (Wallace Beery), a bar owner, and Panisse (Frank Morgan), a prosperous ship chandler. When Cesar's son Marius (John Beal) seduces Madelon (Maureen O'Sullivan), daughter of seafood vendor Honorine (Jessie Ralph), then goes to sea, leaving her pregnant, the kindly, childless Panisse marries her—with predictable complications when the boy returns. As Eames notes in *The MGM Story*, *Port of Seven Seas* was "no disgrace to the original."

In 1937 Leo McCarey had proved that he could direct both deeply touching drama (*Make Way for Tomorrow*) and sophisticated comedy (*The Awful Truth*) with equal skill. Two years later he combined the two genres in a film outstanding even in that year of extraordinary films, 1939: *Love Affair*, which teamed Irene Dunne and Charles Boyer for the first time, as Terry Mackay and Michel Marnay, two experienced worldlings who have decided to marry for money. When they meet aboard a luxury liner bound for New York, at first they keep each other at arm's length with witty repartee, but when at the last European port of call they stop to visit Michel's delightful grandmother (beautifully played by Maria Ouspenskaya), Terry sees a hidden, tender side of the international playboy, and they admit they are in love.

Promising to break their respective commitments to others, they agree to meet atop the Empire State Building after six months of probation (during which she works as a night club singer and he as a sign painter). Hurrying to keep their rendezvous, Terry is run down by a car and apparently crippled for life. Naturally, she doesn't want to be a burden, naturally he thinks she stood him up. Even when they meet by chance at a theater, he with his wealthy fiancée (Astrid Allwyn), she with her suitor (Lee Bowman), she remains in her seat, so that Michel will not see that she can't walk. When eventually he does find her and realizes the truth, their reunion movingly climaxes what many feel was the best film romance of the decade.

Aside from the doomed romances in such classics as *Anna Karenina, Romeo and Juliet, Camille* and *Wuthering Heights,* and most interracial romances, only six major Hollywood films of the '30s ended with the death of one or both lovers. Surely Theodore Dreiser meant *An American Tragedy* to be far more than a tragic triangle drama, but in Paramount's plodding version (1931), adapted by Samuel Hoffenstein and directed by von Sternberg, that is all that is left. In fact, Dreiser was so furious that he tried unsuccessfully to keep the picture from being shown. The unhappy childhood of Clyde Griffiths as the son of street evangelists, so important in the novel in warping his values, is passed over, but perhaps the most serious flaw in the film was the performance of Phillips Holmes, a handsome but extremely limited young actor. As the *Times* noted, he "gives a peculiarly flabby conception of his role."

While working as a foreman in his uncle's shirt factory, Clyde seduces one of the girls, the pathetically vulnerable Roberta (Sylvia

Irene Dunne, Maria Ouspenskaya, Charles Boyer in Love Affair

Sidney), but by the time she finds herself pregnant, he has fallen in love with wealthy Sandra Finchley (Frances Dee). As *The New Yorker* puts it, "Sylvia Sidney is so appealing that the pathos of Roberta's situation is intensified." Desperate to get rid of her, Clyde takes her out in a rowboat, planning to drown her, but changes his mind, only to let her drown accidentally; the circumstantial evidence leads to his being charged with murder. Undoubtedly the best segment of the film is the pro-

longed courtroom sequence, enlivened by Irving Pichel's performance as the relentless D.A. who brings about Clyde's conviction.

As in the book, Clyde's mother (Lucille La Verne) reappears and tries to help, in the end offering him meaningless religious consolation as he awaits execution. This is definitely one of those rare cases when a later version, *A Place in the Sun* (1951), was better than the original.

A far more effective tale of doomed love

was *One Way Passage* (1932), one of the best-remembered romantic films of the '30s. When they meet about to board a liner from Hong Kong to San Francisco, Dan Hardesty (William Powell) does not know that beautiful Joan Ames (Kay Francis) is dying of an incurable heart ailment, nor does she suspect that he is a convicted murder being taken back (by detective Warren Hymer) to be executed at San Quentin.

When they stop at Honolulu, Dan sacrifices his only chance to escape in order to carry Joan back to the ship after a heart attack. A shock would kill her, he is warned,

so to the accompaniment of a haunting musical theme he continues his tenderly gallant deception. Even when they disembark, he manages to conceal his handcuffs. By this time Joan has learned the truth, but she gaily agrees to meet him New Year's Eve in Agua Caliente—a date both know they can never keep. In the last scene, at the appointed time and place, two empty cocktail glasses on a bar suddenly meet as if in a toast and shatter.

Opening in New York the day after *One Way Passage, Smilin' Through* (1932) was a bittersweet romance in an altogether more conventional theatrical vein. Based on a 1919

William Powell, Kay Francis in One Way Passage

play by Jane Cowl and Jane Murfin, which Norma Talmadge had filmed as a silent in 1922, it must have originally been set in Ireland, judging by the girls' names and a reference to County Wicklow, but in this version it seems to be England, close enough to the Channel to hear the guns booming during World War I.

At the turn of the century John Carteret (Leslie Howard), reclusive bachelor, is reluctantly persuaded to bring up little Kathleen (Cora Sue Collins), orphaned niece of his long-dead fiancée, Moonyeen Clare. When by 1915, now grown into Norma Shearer, Kathleen announces her love for Kenneth Wayne (Fredric March), a dashing young American, old Carteret tells her for the first time the bitter story that makes Wayne unthinkable for her.

In a long flashback to the 1860s we meet Wayne's father (also played by March), a rejected suitor of Carteret's bride, Moonyeen (Shearer in a blond wig) —so madly jealous that during the wedding he tries to shoot the groom, but instead kills the bride, who stepped between them. This is the loss from which Carteret has never recovered. Convinced, Kathleen agrees to give Kenneth up, but when he comes back from the war wounded, Carteret finally relents and is free to join Moonyeen's loving ghost, who has often visited him through the years. Though the plot is pure hokum, the three stars acquit themselves well. But with MGM's usual high-handed disdain for authentic period atmosphere, throughout World War I Shearer wears 1932 clothes and drives a 1932 car.

An equally jarring anachronism marred *Three Comrades* (1938), which takes place between 1918 and 1922, but in which Margaret Sullavan, again playing a German girl, looks throughout like Adrian's ideal Miss 1938. But in every other respect the film is a triumph: sensitive direction (Borzage at his best), good writing (the only screenplay for which F. Scott Fitzgerald got even partial credit), fine acting and convincing German background.

Based on Erich Maria Remarque's poignant novel, it traces the struggles of three disillusioned veterans (Robert Taylor, Robert Young, Franchot Tone) in the early days of the Weimar Republic to make a living from their auto repair shop. All three are attracted to charming Pat Hollman (Sullavan), who is also desired by wealthier men, but she loves Erich (Taylor). They marry and the other two remain on the same terms with them, but nothing can prevent the casual killing of Gottfried (Young) in a meaningless street riot, nor the more lingering death of Pat from tuberculosis in an Alpine sanatorium. Of Sullavan, the *Times* said, quite justly, "Hers is a shimmering, almost unendurably lovely performance."

Undoubtedly the most exotic, at least in locale, of these sadly ended romances was *Algiers* (1938), John Cromwell's close remake of Julien Duvivier's French film *Pepe Le Moko* (1937). This is the film in which Charles Boyer does *not* say "Come with me to the Casbah," for the simple reason that he spends most of the picture *in* the Casbah, and, in fact, leaves it only at the cost of his life. The Casbah is, of course, the squalid but picturesque native quarter of Algiers, a sanctuary for fugitives, whom the police cannot touch. Such is the situation of Pepe le Moko (Boyer), who chats daily with patient Inspector Slimane (Joseph Calleia), playing an endless cat-and-mouse game, yet never gets over his keen nostalgia for Paris.

Meanwhile he lives like a lord, surrounded by "a wonderful gallery of underworld types who behave like Fritz Lang characters as they might have been rewritten by Damon Runyon" (Everson) and comforted by a lovely half-caste (Sigrid Gurie). Gene Lockhart plays a slimy informer whose treachery causes the death of Pepe's young protégé, Pierrot (Johnny Downs). But what brings about Pepe's own downfall is his passionate love for a beautiful visitor—from Paris, where else?— (Hedy Lamarr in her American film debut), traveling with her elderly "fiancé" (Robert Greig), one of the few post-Production Code kept heroines. While rushing to join her on a ship to France, Pepe, betrayed by the other girl, is shot, in the denouement of what Emerson calls "a kind of lush Greek tragedy which one can appreciate and enjoy at a distance, without really believing in it . . ."

One of the most unforgettable of all '30s doomed heroines, perhaps second only to Marguerite Gautier in *Camille,* and like her in her feverish pursuit of pleasure, was chain-smoking, hard-drinking Judith Traherne in *Dark Victory* (1939), the willful heiress to end them all, one of Bette Davis' greatest roles. Nugent of the *Times,* in fact, thought her 1938 Oscar should have been deferred for *Dark Victory.*

Based on a 1934 play in which Tallulah Bankhead had flopped on Broadway, *Dark Victory* is at once a character study, a case history and a love story, as Judith, madcap darling of the Long Island horsy set, thinking an operation has cured her, learns by accident that she has less than a year to live. Her first

reaction against her surgeon (George Brent), whom she loves, and her secretary and closest friend (Geraldine Fitzgerald) is violently bitter; she will not be pitied. But after a few more months of living it up, she is convinced by her horse trainer (Humphrey Bogart) that she should make the most of what time she has left. So she marries the doctor and they retreat to his Connecticut farm to live a simple life until the inevitable hour strikes.

However deep and valid its emotional appeal, on one subliminal level *Dark Victory* was saying to audiences still struggling out of the Depression: "What good was all her money? It couldn't save her life." Though *The New Yorker* dismisses the film as a "kitsch classic," more than four decades later viewers are still moved by the beautifully restrained death scene, in which Judith is by her own choice left alone. As Gene Ringgold says in *The Films of Bette Davis,* "Judith . . . smiles, knowing that she has won a small victory over death."

47

"WE CAN'T GO <u>ON</u> THIS WAY!"
The Honeymoon Is Over

Literature has always dealt with marital triangles, but since until modern times the wife was considered first her father's property, then her husband's, it was always the woman who paid, from Bathsheba and Jezebel, to Clytemnestra and Helen, to Guinevere and Isolde, to Madame Bovary and Anna Karenina, not to mention Hester Prynne. Literally hundreds of films incidentally involved

marital problems, but hundreds of others concentrated specifically on the unhappily married and those they loved. Many were "women's pictures," often adapted from novels by such feminine favorites as Faith Baldwin, Fannie Hurst, Kathleen Norris and Ursula Parrott. As Everson says in notes on *One More River* (1934), "It was a kind of story especially prevalent on the screen in the

Thirties, a natural for the afternoon trade, for housewives and spinsters to see together after some shopping and tea. They'd all avidly consume the book, argue over the casting choices, see the film and argue some more."

Even before the Production Code, there seemed to be an unwritten law that, however much forgiveness was required on either side, the husband and wife always ended together. One exception to this rule was *The Office Wife* (1930), based on a Baldwin novel, in which a secretary (Dorothy Mackaill) spurns her slangy young suitor to set her cap for her married boss (Lewis Stone), whose neglected wife (Natalie Moorhead) amuses herself with younger men, then divorces him, leaving him to the secretary. *Wife Versus Secretary* (1936), though also by Baldwin, was *not* the same story; in that one, noble secretary Harlow, though in love with boss Gable, hands him back untouched to unjustly suspicious wife Loy.

As with mistresses and mothers, so many of the same actresses were cast again and again as wronged, tempted or straying wives (only occasionally as the other woman) that it seems best to discuss this phase in the careers of several leading practitioners. Numerically, undoubtedly the queen of the triangular scene, almost always as the wife, was the actress whom David Shipman, in reference to her inability to pronounce "r's," calls "wavishing Kay Fwancis."

As early as *A Notorious Affair* (1930) Francis almost took violinist Basil Rathbone away from his devoted wife (Billie Dove), but she really came into her own with *The Virtuous Sin* (1930), co-directed by Cukor from a European play set in Russia in 1914. When her husband (Kenneth MacKenna), a scientist unsuited to army life, gets himself condemned to death for disobeying an order, what can a loyal wife do but offer herself to the haughty general (Walter Huston), the only one who can spare his life, even though it means making assignations in an elaborate bordello? But she falls in love with the general, and the husband, released, after

threatening to kill him, gives her up. The one remarkable feature of the film is that Francis wears beautifully accurate 1914 gowns, hats and hairdos.

A few months later she was at it again in *Passion Flower* (1930), from a Kathleen Norris novel, in which she is married to invalid Lewis Stone but almost steals the husband (Charles Bickford) of her cousin (Kay Johnson)—in fact, loses him only because of his love for his children.

In *Scandal Sheet* (1931) Francis was the faithless wife of editor George Bancroft, who kills her lover (Clive Brook), while in *Transgression* (1931) she was married to Paul Cavanagh but in love, at least temporarily, with Ricardo Cortez, who, however, is killed by a dead girl's father, leaving Kay free to return to her husband. In *Twenty-Four Hours* (1931) she was the bored wife of alcoholic Clive Brook, who is charged with the murder of his mistress (Miriam Hopkins).

In *Man Wanted* (1932), a successful career woman married to Kenneth Thompson, she falls in love with her secretary (David Manners). In *Jewel Robbery* (1932) she played for the first of three times the straying wife of elderly Henry Kolker—in this case attracted to the thief (William Powell) who stole her jewels.

Cynara (1932), however, directed by King Vidor from a 1930 British play, was one of the finest marital dramas of the decade. It was courageous of Samuel Goldwyn even to retain the title; how many people would catch the allusion to Ernest Dowson's line "I have been faithful to thee, Cynara, in my fashion"? Francis played the trusting wife, aptly named Clemency, of a London barrister (Ronald Colman), who, while she is away, has a casual affair with a pathetic shopgirl (Phyllis Barry) that ends with the girl's suicide and his public disgrace. Unlike the play, the film is told in flashback, starting as the unhappy couple are apparently about to part forever, then detailing what led up to this. In the end the bachelor friend (Henry Stephenson) who encouraged the affair persuades the wife to for-

Kay Francis, Ronald Colman in **Cynara**

give, if not forget, in this truly romantic film.

In *The Keyhole* (1933) Francis again played Henry Kolker's faithless wife, who falls for the private eye (George Brent) hired to spy on her in Cuba, and in *Wonder Bar* (1934) she cuckolded Kolker for a third time with heartless night club dancer Ricardo Cortez. Between these two she made *Storm at Daybreak* (1933), set in Serbia during World War I with an early sequence recreating the assassination at Sarajevo. Though Walter Huston had been her lover in *The Virtuous Sin,* here he is her husband, a wealthy peasant, who, finally realizing that she is in love with a dashing Hungarian officer (Nils Asther), obligingly eliminates himself by driving his carriage over a gorge.

In *Dr. Monica* (1934) Francis was on the deceived side, almost losing her husband

(Warren William) to Jean Muir. In *Give Me Your Heart* (1936), though married to George Brent, she is tormented by thoughts of the child she bore titled Patric Knowles and gave up to him, but finally realizes her son is better off with Knowles and his wife (Frieda Inescort). In *Another Dawn* (1937), set in a tropical outpost of empire, married to Ian Hunter, she falls for Errol Flynn as the reincarnation of her dead lover; ever self-effacing, Hunter gets himself killed in a native uprising.

After all these routine triangles, interspersed with heavy mother-love dramas, Francis appeared in what may be the best marital drama of 1939, *In Name Only,* as a perfectly cold-blooded schemer who, while loving someone else, marries Cary Grant for his money and social position. In fact, she writes to the other man to explain, driving him to suicide, whereupon his mother sends the incriminating letter to Grant as a wedding present.

To him, of course, the marriage is a hollow sham, yet Francis passes as a model wife so successfully that when at last he falls in love with a widowed artist (Carole Lombard), mother of a small girl, it is the wife who gets all the sympathy, even from Grant's parents (Charles Coburn and Nella Walker). She agrees to a Paris divorce, but returns to say she has no such intention. If the husband tries to divorce *her,* she will sue the artist for alienation of affection and even drag her child into court. In despair Grant gets drunk, falls asleep near an open window on a freezing night and catches pneumonia. Only at his near deathbed does the wife inadvertently reveal her true nature to her parents-in-law, and for once the other woman deservedly wins.

Though Ruth Chatterton was thirteen years older than Kay Francis, by no means as beautiful but an incomparably better actress, their careers were curiously parallel. Both played an inordinate number of suffering mothers, both moved from Paramount to Warners with eventually unhappy results and

Cary Grant, Carole Lombard, Kay Francis in **In Name Only**

both made temporary comebacks playing supremely bitchy wives.

In *Charming Sinners* (1930), from Maugham's *The Constant Wife,* Chatterton was an ideally understanding wife, who tolerates her husband's infidelities without committing any of her own. *Unfaithful* (1931), adapted by John Van Druten from his own play, is also reminiscent of Maugham. The basic plot twist in which the heroine shields her brother's wife recalls *Lady Frederick,* while the upper-crust London milieu is precisely that of *Our Betters.* Like Constance Bennett in that film, American Chatterton soon finds out that her titled husband (Paul Cavanagh) married her strictly for money. He has a mistress (Juliette Compton), but as she is the wife of Chatterton's highly neurotic brother (Donald Cook) divorce is out of the question. Instead, she flings herself into the hectic whirl of the Bright Young People, despite the disapproval of a worthy admirer (Paul Lukas). In the climax, Cavanagh and Compton, driving to an illicit rendezvous, crash; he is killed and she flees, forgetting her purse in the car and unable to explain. Cook grows wildly suspicious, until resourceful Chatterton convinces him that the guilty pair were hurrying on their way to keep *her* from spending the night with Lukas. Repeating this at the inquest ruins her reputation, but she is now free to marry Lukas.

Tomorrow and Tomorrow (1932), from Philip Barry's 1931 play, had a plot remarkably like *Strange Interlude,* with Tad Alexander playing an exactly parallel role, but it beat the O'Neill play to the screen by several months. Here the problem is a superhorsy husband (Robert Ames), who has no interest in fathering a child. His unfulfilled wife (Chatterton) has an affair with a visiting Viennese brain surgeon (Lukas again) and bears him a son, without letting either man know the truth. When the boy at eight is seriously injured in a fall from horseback, the surgeon, still not suspecting, saves his life. The woman then tells him, but decides to stay with her husband.

A few months later Chatterton returned to high society in *The Rich Are Always with Us* (1932), a complex but not very interesting drama in which she is again married to a cad (John Miljan), who is carrying on with Adrienne Dore. Even after divorcing him, she feels responsible when all her friends withdraw their accounts from his brokerage, and still more when he is injured in a crash which kills his second wife. Though she has been in love all along with a foreign correspondent (George Brent), their union is interminably delayed by one misunderstanding after another. Perhaps the most notable fact about this film is that it gave Bette Davis one of her first attractive roles as a flashy society girl in shameless pursuit of Brent. Chatterton was secure enough in her own stardom to allow Davis several juicy scenes.

The Crash (1932) was even worse. Again married to a stockbroker (Brent), who loses all his money, Chatterton wants to divorce him for an Australian (Cavanagh), but eventually after much to-do about a necklace stolen by her maid, whom she refuses to prosecute, she returns to Brent.

Four years later, her career at low ebb, Chatterton gave what most critics considered her most brilliant performance, in one of the most admired films of the decade, *Dodsworth* (1936), which won eight Oscar nominations—surprisingly, none for her. Given a lavish Goldwyn production, directed by William Wyler, adapted by Sidney Howard from his hit play, based on Sinclair Lewis' 1929 novel, *Dodsworth* was, of course, much more than just another triangle (or hexagon); it was Lewis' variation on that favorite theme in American literature, the shrewd but trusting Yankee corrupted by the charming, decadent Europeans. Though never pretty, Chatterton in every glance and nuance conveys the manners and airs of a spoiled beauty who has always fed on masculine admiration.

Walter Huston—not at all hurt by the fact that he looked and sounded like the first Henry Ford—gave a legendary performance as Sam Dodsworth, an auto tycoon, who, retiring rich in his fifties in Lewis' fictitious city of Zenith, agrees to take his adored wife on an indefinitely extended holiday in Europe.

While he eagerly absorbs all the history and culture, shallow, spoiled Fran, fighting middle age, becomes involved in a series of increasingly deeper relationships with other men—first a shipboard flirtation with a British officer (David Niven), then an indiscreet summer at a villa with a suave international banker (Lukas again) and then, when Sam has forgiven that, a proposal of marriage from an Austrian baron (Gregory Gaye).

Reluctantly agreeing to a divorce, Sam wanders forlornly around Europe, until in Naples he runs across Edith Cortright (Mary Astor), an attractive expatriate whom he first met coming over on the *Queen Mary.* Meanwhile the baron's mother (Maria Ouspen-skaya, in a superb, Oscar-nominated portrayal), an icy Viennese aristocrat, sternly forbids the marriage and shatters Fran by asking, "Have you ever thought what it would be *like* to be the *old* wife of a *young* husband?"

Though Sam has been starting a whole new life with Edith at her villa, he feels he must stand by Fran. They are actually aboard the *Rex,* about to sail, when he realizes that Fran will never change; far from feeling any remorse, she is still blaming him. In a worm-turning scene that still brings applause from audiences nearly five decades later, Sam leaves, telling Fran, "Love has to stop somewhere short of suicide!" The ship's whistle drowns out her outraged shrieks. In a memorable wrap-up, Edith, looking sadly down on the Bay of Naples, suddenly sees Sam in a motor-boat approaching her dock. Among the best

Paul Lukas, Ruth Chatterton, Mary Astor, Walter Huston in Dodsworth

features of this splendidly civilized film, the art direction, which won an Oscar, perfectly reproduces Paris, Vienna and Naples.

Next in number of unhappy screen marriages was Irene Dunne, who played the other woman as often as the wife. In fact, she starred in the first version of the most famous of all films about the plight of the kept woman, *Back Street* (1932). Poor Ray Schmidt, Fannie Hurst's drably suffering heroine, does not even have a child to comfort her in her twenty-five long years as the discreetly hidden mistress of banker Walter Saxel (John Boles), who does not even keep her in style. After his death, even his son (William Bakewell) is surprised to learn that his father gave her only two hundred dollars a month. Nor did he remember her in his will. Yet, true to the last, she is apparently about to join him in death when the picture ends—none too soon for the *Times* critic, who noted, "Saxel seems to live much too long and Ray is exasperatingly silly."

In *No Other Woman* (1932), based on Eugene Walter's play *Just a Woman,* Dunne was the loyal wife of a Pittsburgh steel worker (Charles Bickford), who, when he becomes rich on a dye formula, falls for a blonde (Gwili Andre) and, to get a divorce, frames the wife by bribing witnesses, before he comes to his senses. *If I Were Free* (1934), from Van Druten's British play *Behold We Live,* was another triangle, in more genteel surroundings, in Paris and London. Though Dunne's husband (Nils Asther) leaves her, the wife of the man she loves (Clive Brook) refuses to divorce him, at least until the end of the picture. In *This Man Is Mine* (1934) Dunne was married to Ralph Bellamy—happily, until an old flame (Constance Cummings) turns up after a recent divorce, to make the usual kind of trouble until the wife outwits her. The *Times* called it "a mediocre, verbose picture."

These last three films were based on long-forgotten plays, but 1934 brought *The Age of Innocence,* based on Edith Wharton's 1920 Pulitzer Prize novel, a hit on Broadway with Katharine Cornell. Dunne and Boles were reunited as the unhappy lovers, American-born Countess Ellen Olenska and Newland Archer, trapped by the conventions of New York society in the 1870s. The film was well cast: Julie Haydon as Ellen's cousin May, Archer's bland, naïve bride, Lionel Atwill as Julius Beaufort, unscrupulous banker, said to be based on August Belmont, and Helen Westley as the indomitable old Mrs. Manson Mingott, grandmother of the two girls.

Said the *Times,* "To experienced film-goers the drama has a rather dreadfully familiar look," and went on to compare it with *Back Street* (1932) and *The Life of Vergie Winters* (1934), in both of which Boles had played the same kind of thankless role. As in the book, the film ends unhappily; Ellen unselfishly returns to Europe and Newland sticks with his unloved wife.

Dunne did only one more triangle, *When Tomorrow Comes* (1939), a feeble attempt to follow up on *Love Affair,* in which she played a waitress and Boyer a violinist tied to an insane wife (Barbara O'Neil), just as he was to be again the following year in *All This and Heaven Too* (1940).

Next in line among nobly suffering screen wives was Ann Harding. Besides several films already covered among other categories, she made *Westward Passage* (1932), in which, as in a more serious version of *Private Lives,* she divorces her temperamental writer husband (Laurence Olivier) to marry a solid businessman (Irving Pichel), but on a voyage back from Europe re-encounters the first one, now successful, and ends up with him. In *Double Harness* (1933) she traps playboy William Powell into marriage, which he resents, but before the divorce he realizes he prefers her to his mistress (Lillian Bond). In *The Fountain* (1934), faithfully adapted from Charles Morgan's much-admired novel, set in Holland during World War I, Harding was an Englishwoman married to a disabled German officer (Paul Lukas) but in love with a British officer (Brian Aherne) interned there; the husband dies. In *The Lady Consents*

(1936) she agrees to divorce her doctor husband (Herbert Marshall) so that he can marry athletic Margaret Lindsay—a mistake he soon regrets.

In all six of her 1931–32 films Tallulah Bankhead played unhappy wives—three of them no better than they should be, but in the other three she was the injured party. In *The Cheat* (1931), a lurid old melodrama that had already been filmed twice in silents, in 1915 with Fannie Ward, in 1923 with Pola Negri, she played a woman who loses twenty thousand dollars gambling, and, to pay it without her husband's knowledge, "compromises" herself with a sadist (Irving Pichel), who collects Oriental art objects, and who, to enforce his claim, pretends to brand her shoulder (actually using ice, accompanied by the smell of burning flesh). Understandably, she shoots him, but her husband (Harvey Stephens) takes the blame, and the villain lives to back up his false confession. Perhaps it should be regarded as some kind of progress that in both previous versions he *was* Oriental (Sessue Hayakawa the first time), and he really did brand her, as she revealed in court.

In *Thunder Below* (1932), set in Central America, Bankhead was married to Charles Bickford, an oil rigger, who never suspects that she is in love with his best friend (Richard Arlen). The husband goes blind, she goes off with a third man (Ralph Forbes), then ends all her problems by throwing herself over a cliff. Even more melodramatic was *Devil and the Deep* (1932), in which Bankhead was married to a psychotic submarine commander (Charles Laughton), apparently German, insanely jealous, who wrongly accuses her of loving Cary Grant, then with better reason suspects Gary Cooper. Determined to destroy the lovers, in the climax Laughton deliberately crashes his sub into a ship, but Cooper manages to rescue everyone except Laughton.

In addition to playing deceived wives in *Let Us Be Gay* (1930) and *The Women* (1939), as well as a rebellious one in *Private*

Lives (1931) (all comedies of manners), Norma Shearer also played three other wives in dramas of marital infidelity. One of the most provocative films of 1930 was *The Divorcee,* based on Ursula Parrott's best-selling novel *Ex-Wife,* which boldly advocated the single standard. Finding her husband (Chester Morris) involved with another woman, the heroine (Shearer) repays him in kind; she frankly tells him that from now on her door will be open to any man but him. They are divorced, she encourages the attention of a former suitor (Conrad Nagel), now unhappily married, and toys with a wisecracking playboy (Robert Montgomery), but, running across her ex-husband in Paris, she rather unconvincingly takes him back.

When produced on stage in 1928, Eugene O'Neill's *Strange Interlude* was a sensational success, not only because of its then "daring" subject matter, but also because of the famous "asides," in which each character, supposedly unheard by the others, speaks his secret thoughts, and the novelty of its extreme length—nine acts, necessitating a dinner break for the audience.

Although the screenplay by C. Gardner Sullivan and Bess Meredyth compressed the five-hour play to less than two hours, it is an extremely faithful adaptation, briskly directed by Robert Z. Leonard and well acted by a strong MGM cast (1932). The actors do not speak the asides on screen but merely register the thoughts their voices are expressing on the sound track.

Shearer was excellent as the neurotic Nina Leeds, forever tortured by the loss in World War I of Gordon Shaw (never seen), whom her father (Henry B. Walthall) kept her from marrying. After a fling at promiscuity, she decides on the advice of brusque Dr. Ned Darrell (Clark Gable), with the approval of Charlie Marsden (marvelously played by Ralph Morgan), a prissy bachelor who loves her in a wistful, sexless way, to marry apparently healthy, normal Sam Evans (Alexander Kirkland).

But her mother-in-law (May Robson) soon

tells her that, unknown to Sam, insanity runs in his family. In the play Nina is already pregnant, so has an abortion; in the film—the only change—she is not, but her dilemma remains the same. If she does not give Sam a child, he may suffer a mental breakdown from frustration; if she does, the child will inherit the mad streak. The only solution is to have a child by another man; who more logical than family friend Darrell? The plan works; Sam is so happy with "his" son, inevitably named Gordon, that Nina and Ned, though now in love, cannot destroy him by running off together, still less by telling him the truth.

As a boy of eleven young Gordon (Tad Alexander) worships Sam but hates his real father, almost as if suspecting the connection. When as a young man (Robert Young) Gordon wants to marry Madeline Arnold (Maureen O'Sullivan), Nina, repeating her father's pattern, is about to interfere, but is prevented by Ned. Still never suspecting the truth, Sam dies of a heart attack, leaving Ned and Nina free, but they no longer want each other. Instead, she turns at last to good old "Uncle Charlie" Marsden, in what will presumably be a sexless marriage. The characters, however, age as if they had just been taken out of Shangri-La. At the end Nina and Ned, in their mid-forties, with snow-white hair, haggard faces, quavering voices and doddering steps, look at least ninety.

After an absence from the screen of a year and a half, Shearer returned in *Riptide* (1934), written and directed by Edmund Goulding, set in the world of American heiresses married to British titles. After five happy years of such a marriage, the lordly husband (Herbert Marshall) goes to New York on business, and his wife (Shearer) is persuaded by his worldly aunt (Mrs. Patrick Campbell, making her screen debut at sixtynine) to take a holiday on the Riviera, where she encounters an old American flame (Robert Montgomery), who after too much to drink falls from a balcony outside her room, causing a much-publicized scandal. Naturally suspicious, the jealous husband contemplates

divorce, but after endless discussion decides against it.

Also set in titled British society was *Christopher Strong* (1933), Katharine Hepburn's second film and her only venture into a marital triangle. As Lady Cynthia Darrington, prize-winning "aviatrix," she defends the right of a friend (Helen Chandler) to love a married man (Ralph Forbes), but when *she* falls in love with the friend's father, Sir Christopher Strong (Colin Clive), an important M.P., and gives up flying to become his mistress, the other girl, now respectably married to her lover, is shocked. Finding herself pregnant, a circumstance that would compel Strong to divorce his wife (Billie Burke) and ruin his career, Cynthia deliberately cuts off her oxygen while seeking an altitude record. Says *The New Yorker,* "The film was a flop, but it's not one that independent-minded women can easily forget."

Still another triangle set among Britain's best families was *One More River* (1934), the only American film made from any of Galsworthy's works during the '30s. This was his last novel, only tangentially linked to *The Forsyte Saga* in that the Charwell family are cousins of Michael Mont, Fleur Forsyte's husband. In the book the heroine is Dinny Charwell; in the film Dinny (Jane Wyatt) is subordinated to her sister Clare (Diana Wynyard in her last American picture), Lady Korven, who has left her brutal husband, Sir Gerald (Colin Clive), in Ceylon and returned to England. On the ship she met the charming young Tony Croom (Frank Lawton), they fall in love and spend much time together in London, quite innocently, but Korven has them shadowed, then sues for divorce, naming Tony as co-respondent. Clare hires as her barrister "Very Young" Roger Forsyte (Alan Mowbray), while Korven retains the sneering Mr. Brough (Lionel Atwill). The *Times* called the trial "one of the finest courtroom episodes ever projected on a screen."

What gives the film great charm and distinction is the absolute sense of authenticity, an illusion helped by a splendid array of character actors. C. Aubrey Smith and Kathleen Howard played General and Lady Charwell, the girl's parents, Henry Stephenson and Mrs. Patrick Campbell were Sir Lawrence and Lady Em Mont, their aunt and uncle, Reginald Denny was David Dornford, Dinny's fiancé, Gilbert Emery was the judge, and even the private detective was played by E. E. Clive.

Even Garbo herself could not escape the eternal triangle. Besides her costumed adulteresses in *Anna Karenina* and *Conquest*, she played a modern one in *The Painted Veil* (1934), based on Somerset Maugham's novel. Instead of Kitty, the heroine is called Katrin, and her lover is Jack, rather than Charlie, Townsend, but otherwise the film was reasonably faithful to the book. The wife of a bacteriologist (Herbert Marshall), bored with Hong Kong's British colony, Katrin falls in love with a lively diplomatic attaché (George Brent), also married, but he will not endanger his career by a divorce, so she returns to her embittered husband.

About to go inland to fight a cholera epidemic, he takes her with him, expecting them both to die. When he relents and urges her to return to Hong Kong, she decides to stay with him. In the book he died, but here he survives, and they find they love each other, after all. The *Times* noted that Garbo was "the most miraculous blend of personality and sheer dramatic talent that the screen has ever known."

One of the few triangles set in middle-class suburban America, *There's Always Tomorrow* (1934), from a novel by Ursula Parrott, for a change sympathized with the husband. Frank Morgan gave one of his finest characterizations as a gentle, patient family man whose wife (Lois Wilson) and five children (including Robert Taylor) have gradually tuned him out of their lives. Even on their wedding anniversary, when he has theater tickets, his wife suggests he go alone. No wonder he is grateful to find that a former sweetheart (Binnie Barnes in her American de-

but) still cares for him. When his children discover the relationship, they try to break it up without letting their mother know, but the other woman, far from being a homewrecker, helps bring the family back together, then goes out of their lives forever. The *Times* called the film an "album of natural, human and living portraits."

Much further off the beaten path was Goldwyn's *The Wedding Night* (1935), directed by King Vidor, from a story by Edwin Knopf, written in hopes of saving Anna Sten's floundering career. The film was rich in the local color of a rural Polish-American community in the Connecticut tobacco country, with Sten well cast as Manya, daughter of one such traditional farmer (Sig Rumann). A hard-drinking New York novelist (Gary Cooper), writing a book about the Polish, finds it turning into a love story, with Manya as heroine and himself as hero as despite the difference in their backgrounds, they fall deeply in love. Even his wife (Helen Vinson, for once not a bitch) understands when she reads the manuscript, but refuses to consider a divorce. Besides, Manya has been betrothed by her family to a local lout (Ralph Bellamy). When on their wedding night the drunken bridegroom, enraged by her coldness, sets out to murder the novelist, it is instead the girl who dies, in a fall downstairs. Newspaper reviews praised Sten, but it was too late to retrieve her career.

Among lighter variations on the eternal triangle (actually a quadrangle), one of the most charming was *To Mary—With Love* (1936), based on Richard Sherman's novel, which used as background a mini-cavalcade of the years 1925–35. After ten years of marriage to architect Jock Wallace (Warner Baxter), Mary (Myrna Loy) is sadly seeking the legal advice of their close friend Bill (Ian Hunter), who has offices in the Empire State Building. Nostalgically they recall her wedding reception in the old Waldorf-Astoria, the night of Jimmy Walker's election.

To the hit songs of the day, starting with "Valencia," the ups and downs of the marriage are traced, as Jock and Mary attend the Dempsey-Tunney fight, watch the Lindbergh parade and suffer in the Wall Street crash. Meanwhile there has been a stillborn child, Jock's off-and-on affair with speakeasy girl Kitty Brant (Claire Trevor), an auto accident and a drinking problem (his). Bill has always loved Mary, but now when he has the chance to get her on the rebound, instead (being Ian Hunter) he brings the couple back together. What was most remarkable in this delightfully authentic film, directed by John Cromwell, was that Loy and Trevor had the courage to don the cloches and flapper styles of the previous decade—fashions some other '30s actresses were apparently unwilling to wear on screen.

One of the most unusual marital dramas of the decade involved only two people; a triangle among Wife, Husband and House. Though George Kelly's *Craig's Wife* won the Pulitzer Prize in 1926, it now reads as an extremely clumsy, contrived play. Many of the speeches are intolerably stagy, and the climax arbitrarily hinges on the offstage murder and suicide of two people the audience has never seen. Moreover, though Harriet Craig has generally been accepted as the archetype of the fanatically house-proud woman, surely by 1925 any woman with her ruthless drive, executive ability and passion for organization would have sought independence and security in a career rather than marriage.

Be that as it may, the 1936 film, written by Mary McCall, Jr., and directed by Dorothy Arzner, is in every respect a vast improvement on the play. In the title role, Rosalind Russell made the most of her first dramatic opportunity on screen to create a completely convincing heartless domestic tyrant to whom the perfect order of her house is far more important than anyone's feelings, including her husband's. John Boles, for once a victim rather than the victimizer, played Walter Craig, who seems not to realize what has been done to him until it is forcefully pointed out by his aunt (Alma Kruger). In

a sex reversal it is he who must escape to become his own person—but somehow his symbolic gestures of breaking a prized vase and dropping ashes on the carpet seem feeble rather than defiant.

Having driven away Walter, his aunt, her own niece (Dorothy Wilson), a kindly neighbor (Billie Burke), the housekeeper (Jane Darwell) and even the maid (Nydia Westman), Harriet is left to pace through her immaculate, empty house and reflect on what she has done to herself. The ideal title would have been the one announced for Joan Crawford's 1948 version (released as *Harriet Craig*) —*The Lady of the House.*

Colin Clive played another sadistic husband in the extremely bizarre, almost unclassifiable *History Is Made at Night* (1937). As *The New Yorker* puts it, "The plot is so preposterously arbitrary it's as if several scripts were chopped up and stuck together." Directed, surprisingly, by Borzage, from a script by Gene Towne and Graham Baker, the film was widely criticized for its indigestible hodgepodge of farce, melodrama, comedy and tragedy. Clive was a shipbuilder, insanely jealous of his wife (Jean Arthur), who falls in love with an urbane Parisian headwaiter (Charles Boyer). The husband tries to frame Boyer for a murder he himself committed, then, when all else fails, determined to destroy the lovers, he arranges for his superliner to crash into an iceberg, thus providing a spectacular *Titanic*-style climax, which resolves the triangle once and for all.

As with so many other genres, 1939 was a banner year for marital triangles. Besides the admirable *In Name Only, The Women* (whose plot was made up of intersecting triangles) and such minor items as *Beauty for the Asking* (Lucille Ball, Patric Knowles, Frieda Inescort) and *Wife, Husband and Friend* (Loretta Young, Warner Baxter, Binnie Barnes), at least three other vehicles for major stars offered variations on the familiar theme.

The Shining Hour, a British play transposed to Wisconsin, was given a glossy MGM production and a high-powered cast which could not quite disguise the soap opera material. A famous New York night club dancer (Joan Crawford) of questionable past on impulse marries a Midwestern gentleman farmer (Melvyn Douglas), to the extreme disapproval of his stuffy brother (Robert Young), happily married (to Margaret Sullavan). The neurotic spinster sister (Fay Bainter) of the two men resents the new bride even more. Since all live under the same luxurious roof, as in *Jalna,* trouble soon brews.

Crawford and Young find themselves drawn into an incipient affair, which everyone pretends not to notice. A new house is built on the estate for Crawford and Douglas, but before they can move into it the spinster, in the great tradition of Mrs. Rochester and Mrs. Danvers, sets fire to it. In the confusion, Sullavan, convinced that she has lost her husband's love, rushes into the flames to immolate herself, but Crawford, not to be outdone in self-sacrifice, rushes in after her and saves her life. She decides to leave, but Douglas goes with her. "It's an unconvincing, overly classy film," says *The New Yorker,* "with the selfish characters being ennobled by love in a way that nobody gets ennobled in movies any more."

On an infinitely higher level was *Intermezzo: A Love Story,* Ingrid Bergman's triumphant American debut, a close remake of a Swedish film she had done in 1936. Taking no chances on having her turned into another Hollywood glamour girl, David O. Selznick insisted that even her make-up and lighting be the same as in Europe. Astonished to see a star with a simple hairdo, unplucked eyebrows, even a slight shine on her nose, critics raved about her freshness, simplicity and natural dignity.

A world-famous Swedish violinist (Leslie Howard), contentedly married (to Edna Best) and father of two children, finds himself falling in love with his daughter's dedicated young piano teacher (Bergman) and asks her to be his accompanist. On a tour of the concert halls of Europe they enjoy, to the recurrent strains of "Intermezzo," a tender affair which gives him the illusion of renewed youth. But this being post-Production Code 1939, divorce of an innocent wife is out of the question. Prodded by her conscience and the admonition of his former accompanist (John Halliday), who serves as *raisonneur,* the girl sends her lover back to his family in Stockholm. His daughter, rushing to meet him, is hit by a car, and the ensuing crisis cements the reconciliation with his wife and son. This last seems an unnecessary touch of melodrama in an otherwise "mature, eloquent and sensitive" film that immediately established Bergman as a star of the first rank.

The last marital triangle of the decade was a tragic one indeed, *We Are Not Alone,* adapted by James Hilton from his novel and called by the *Times* "a film of rare tenderness and beauty, compassionate and grave." In Edwardian England, just before World War I, a kindly village doctor (Paul Muni) and his sternly pious wife (Flora Robson) hire a plain German girl (Jane Bryan) as governess for their little son (Raymond Severn). Inevitably the gentle doctor and the warmhearted Fräulein are drawn together, in an entirely innocent relationship, and inevitably the wife suspects the worst.

When she is found dead of poison, the two are tried for her murder, and in the rising anti-German hysteria of 1914 there is no doubt about the outcome. Though protesting their innocence to the end, they are convicted and hanged. Only the audience knows that it was the little boy who, innocently switching the places of two bottles on a cupboard shelf, had accidentally caused his mother's death.

All the performances were highly praised, but especially Jane Bryan's, in the best role she was ever to get. Since Bette Davis (to whom Bryan had played sister, daughter and rival in other films) was the undisputed queen of the Warners lot, it seems probable that *We Are Not Alone* had been bought with her in mind, but perhaps she could not fit it into an already crowded 1939 schedule.

Ingrid Bergman, Leslie Howard in **Intermezzo**

It seems likely that Hilton must have been at least partly inspired by the once notorious case of the Duc de Praslin and Henriette Desportes (an ancestress of Rachel Field), which was the direct basis of Field's best seller *All This and Heaven Too* (which Davis was to film in 1940) with the real names used. In the misery of a quiet Edwardian doctor who is married to a relentless shrew and who turns to an idealistic young woman for comfort, Hilton may also have had in mind the 1909

execution of Dr. Crippen (who, however, actually killed his wife). The result transcended both of these possible sources in a touching story of two innocents destroyed by circumstantial evidence and jingoistically inflamed public opinion.

Thus in exploring almost every conceivable kind of marital problem, from adultery to divorce to murder, Hollywood in the '30s produced a number of memorable films and at least one superb one, *Dodsworth*.

48

FROM SEA TO SHINING SEA
Ethnic and Regional Films

Although the films discussed in the last three chapters generally dealt with middle-class Americans as families, lovers or unhappily married couples, in one respect—so completely taken for granted at the time that no one ever mentioned it—they were *not* typical Americans. They were all WASPs, with nice WASPish names like Adams, Archer, Cooper, Craig and Hardy. This is all the more surprising considering the extreme popularity in late silents of ethnic comedy-dramas, especially about assimilating Jews (e.g., *His People, The Jazz Singer*) and endless variations on *Abie's Irish Rose*.

True, the moribund Cohens and Kellys series, starring George Sidney and Charlie Murray, gave a few last gasps before expiring in 1933, and there were other feeble, sentimental comedies such as *Around the Corner* (1930), in which Sidney and Murray played not Cohen and Kelly but a pawnbroker and a cop, guardians of a girl who loves a rich boy despite their opposition. Exclusively Jewish was *The Heart of New York* (1932), from a play called *Mendel Inc.*, which sounds as if it might have originated in the Yiddish theater, in which Sidney, supported by the vaudeville team Smith and Dale, played an inventor whose sudden wealth causes the usual troubles.

The first serious depiction of New York's ethnic mix was, of course, Elmer Rice's *Street Scene* (1931), discussed earlier, which included accurately observed characters of Jewish, Irish, Italian, German and Scandinavian backgrounds, all living in the same tenement. Though the stereotypes for Jews on screen were tailors, pawnbrokers, delicatessen owners and occasional movie producers, Abraham Kaplan in *Street Scene* is a writer for radical publications, his daughter Shirley a spinster schoolteacher and his son Sam an intellectual college student, who falls in love with Rose Maurrant, daughter of an Irish stage electrician.

In *Bought* (1931) Constance Bennett played the illegitimate daughter of her real-life father, Richard Bennett, who, though never specified as Jewish, is named Dave Mayer and owns a garment firm. When he realizes who she is, he takes her to lunch at the Ritz, introduces her to opera, gives her new books and gets her a desirable job—an altogether sympathetic character. But undoubtedly the warmest depiction of middle-class Jewish life was *Symphony of Six Million* (1932), which while primarily a doctor film, abounds in ethnic details. In *Uptown New York* (1932) another kind of Jewish doctor (Leon Waycoff, later Leon Ames) is forced by his ambitious family to marry for money, jilting the girl he loves (Shirley Grey), who on the rebound marries Irish Eddie Doyle (Jack Oakie). When he realizes the truth, he offers her a divorce, but, though not loving him, she stays with him.

No Greater Love (1932) reverted to maudlin clichés as a kindly old Jewish delicatessen owner (Alexander Carr) sells his store to raise money to cure a little crippled girl and ends nearly dying himself. In the same sentimental vein was *Hearts of Humanity* (1933), involving the usual Lower East Side melting pot, in which a kindly old Jewish pawnbroker (Jean Hersholt) adopts an Irish orphan (Jackie Searl); his daughter (Claudia Dell) loves an Irish cop. The only other drama to use a specifically Jewish background was *Straight Is the Way* (1934), based on the play *Four Walls,* a gangster melodrama in which Franchot Tone was wildly miscast as an ex-con named Benny Horowitz trying to go straight.[1]

The Irish turned up more often in the background as landladies, cops, detectives, bartenders and priests than in leading roles, though several of the heroines already covered had Irish names (e.g., in *Blondie of the Follies, Personal Maid, The Shining Hour. McFadden's Flats* (1935), a once-famous old comedy, starring Walter C. Kelly, well-known in vaudeville as the Virginia Judge, struck the *Times* reviewer as hopelessly dated. The heyday of ethnic humor and dialect comedians had long since passed.

Warners' comedy *The Irish in Us* (1935), though well cast, was a real Irish stew of clichés. Mary Gordon played the widowed mother of three sons, a fight promoter (James Cagney), a policeman (Pat O'Brien) and a fireman (Frank McHugh). The first two are rivals for a girl (Olivia De Havilland) in this totally predictable film, which was in no way redeemed by authentic ethnic details. Again Mary Gordon's son, O'Brien played another cop in *The Great O'Malley* (1937). *In Old*

Chicago (1937) also involved an Irish widow with three sons, but though Alice Brady won an Oscar as Mrs. O'Leary, owner of the famous cow, the whole film now seems as forced and synthetic as the brogues.

Full Confession (1939) involved several Irish families, especially that of Barry Fitzgerald and Elizabeth Risdon, whose son (Malcolm McTaggart) is wrongfully convicted of murder, but oddly enough, their priest (Joseph Calleia), who heard the real murderer's confession but, of course, can't reveal it, is Italian. In *The Escape* (1939) almost all the characters are specifically Irish or Italian.

Numerically, by far the commonest occupation among Italians on screen was crime, but kindlier, older men (Leo Carrillo, Paul Porcasi, Henry Armetta) were often seen as comically hot-tempered waiters, barbers, musicians or keepers of fruit stands. The first to escape these stereotypes was Edward G. Robinson in *A Lady to Love* (1930), based on Sidney Howard's 1925 Pulitzer Prize play, *They Knew What They Wanted,* which had been filmed only two years before as a silent, *The Secret Hour,* with Jean Hersholt and Pola Negri. In the play Tony, the naïve, effusive California Italian, who wins a mail-order bride by sending a photo of his handsome hired man, was a bootlegger; in this version he's a grape grower. Vilma Banky was the bride and Robert Ames the other man, who fathers a child that Tony eventually accepts. Still further from the common Italian stereotypes was George Bancroft in *Ladies Love Brutes* (1930), who as a newly rich contractor in love with a divorced socialite (Mary Astor) tangles with the kidnapers (also Italian) of her son and his.

Throughout the '30s Leo Carrillo was practically a one-man ethnic unit in himself. When he was not playing lovable gangsters, he was playing equally lovable Italians in other occupations—a barber in *Obey the Law* (1933), a laborer in *Men Are Such Fools* (1933), a barber again in *The Winning Ticket* (1935), with an Irish wife (Louise

---

[1] *Having Wonderful Time,* Arthur Kober's delightfully authentic comedy about young Jewish New Yorkers at a summer camp in the Catskills, filmed in 1938, though adapted by the author himself, was completely de-racinated, with the names Anglicized.

Fazenda), a ditchdigger, along with George Raft, in *It Had to Happen* (1936), and in *Fisherman's Wharf* (1939), starring Bobby Breen, Carrillo was, needless to say, a fisherman. Meanwhile MGM's bizarre *Song of the City* (1937), a mélange of musical and melodrama, had used the same San Francisco locale, with J. Carroll Naish and Nat Pendleton supplying the Italian interference to a romance between native Margaret Lindsay and playboy Dean Jagger (then known as Jeffrey Dean).[2]

The decline of ethnic subject matter was nowhere more marked than in the virtual disappearance of German-Americans from the screen. Though in both *The Way of All Flesh* (1927) and *Sins of the Fathers* (1928) Emil Jannings had played patriarchs of that hyphenated background, the talkies saw only *Sins of the Fathers* (1930), *Song of the Eagle* (1933) and the slight comedy *Best of Enemies* (1933), about two feuding German-American fathers (Frank Morgan and Joseph Cawthorn) reconciled, à la the families of Romeo and Juliet, by the union of a son and a daughter (Buddy Rogers and Marian Nixon).

This decline was surely not due to any lingering anti-German prejudice; the '30s produced several films set in Germany itself, two even depicting the war and its consequences from the German point of view (*All Quiet on the Western Front*, 1930, and *The Man I Killed*, 1932). Also the early '30s, perhaps as a result of Repeal, saw a resurgence of enthusiasm for the kind of *Gemütlichkeit* associated with German beer. Thus in an early scene of *Back Street* (1932), set in Cincinnati, Irene Dunne is seen demurely waltzing in a beer garden. There was even a vogue (1931–33) for pseudo-German songs, unthinkable a decade before: "I Luff Louisa," from *The Band Wagon*, hit Broadway revue of 1931; the title number, set in a beer garden, from *Moonlight and Pretzels* (1933);

"Listen to the German Band" and "Was Willst Du Haben?", both popular 1932–33, and the "Let's Go Bavarian" number in Joan Crawford's *Dancing Lady* (1933).

Minorities with roots in other European countries got even shorter shrift. Only *The Man Who Dared* (1933) used Bohemians, while Poles appeared only in *As the Earth Turns* (1934), *Black Fury* (1935) and *The Wedding Night* (1935), all discussed elsewhere. As for Scandinavians, unless one counts Swedish dialect comedian El Brendel's films, the janitor in *Street Scene* (1931) and a few in *I Married a Doctor* (1936), the only such characters appeared in *Come and Get It* (1937).

If even white minorities were subjected to benign neglect, other races suffered far worse indignities. Treatment of Orientals, whether in their own lands or in America's Chinatowns, ranged from patronizing to bitterly hostile. In a country that had recently supported the Ku Klux Klan in the North as well as the South, a country which practiced Jim Crowism both officially and unofficially, which still tacitly accepted the idea that the only good Indian was a dead Indian, in which WASPs looked down on all other whites and even those ethnic minorities despised one another according to religion or country of ancestry, it is not surprising that many American films reflected prejudices that now seem outrageous. In a white America that doted on Amos and Andy and read Octavus Roy Cohen's stories in *The Saturday Evening Post* about ludicrously caricatured blacks, Hollywood was hardly likely to lead a crusade for racial justice.

The Uncle Tom-Aunt Jemima stereotypes have been so thoroughly exposed in so many books and articles as to need no further underlining of the obvious here. Black actors like Stepin Fetchit, Willie Best, Louise Beavers and Leila Bennett were often criticized by their own people for continuing to play demeaning roles, but as Hattie McDaniel (quoted by Gary Null in *Black Hollywood*) put it, she had a choice of working as a maid

---

[2] *Tiger Shark* (1932), *He Was Her Man* (1934) and *Captains Courageous* (1937) all involved fishermen of Portuguese descent.

for seven dollars a week or playing maids for seven hundred.

To be sure, all-black films were made by black producers for black audiences, but these were never seen outside of Harlem and other ghettos. The only all-black picture to receive general distribution was *The Green Pastures* (1936), adapted by Marc Connelly from his own play, based on Roark Bradford's stories *Ol' Man Adam an' His Chillun*, a retelling in heavy dialect of the major incidents in the Old Testament as they would be visualized by a Sunday-school class of Deep South black children. De Lawd (Rex Ingram) is pictured as a dignified, gray-haired minister, and the angels wear straw hats as well as wings and enjoy fish fries and cigars. It won high praise from the *Times* for its fidelity to the play (a Broadway hit). Null includes two stills from it but makes no comment, so presumably he had no objections to it but did not consider it worth praising.

In the whole decade only two films other than *Gone With the Wind* (1939) took their black characters seriously—both, as it happened, Universal and both involving legally black women passing as white. Most memorable was the subplot of *Imitation of Life* (1934), in which rebellious Fredi Washington, determined to be accepted in the white man's world, breaks off relations with her adoring mother (Louise Beavers), then regrets it too late. White audiences certainly sympathized with the mother, but Null notes that even in 1934 many critics, white as well as black, felt that the mother was entirely too self-effacing and that the daughter was essentially right in demanding her share of the good things of life, even if it meant denying her race.

The other film was *Show Boat* (1936), in which the very sympathetic leading lady, Julie Lenoir (Helen Morgan), idolized by Magnolia, the heroine, is exposed as "black" by a vengeful stagehand. Her loyal white husband (Donald Cook) cuts her finger and sucks a little blood from it so that he can truthfully swear that he has "Negro blood"

in him, and they will not be arrested for violating the laws against miscegenation.

As for those now known as "native Americans," though they were the bad guys in countless Westerns, they did come in for at least occasional sympathetic treatment, as in the silents *The Vanishing American* (1925) and *Redskin* (1929), both starring Richard Dix as noble red men. He also starred in *Cimarron* (1931), in which the hero may have Indian blood and encourages his son to marry an Indian princess. Very few '30s films dealt with leading Indian characters, none very well.

First came *The Squaw Man* (1931), Cecil B. De Mille's third film version of a 1905 play, which, critics agreed, was beginning to show its age. This time Warner Baxter played the title role, an Englishman who loves his cousin's wife (Eleanor Boardman) so much that he takes the blame for her husband's theft of charity funds and must leave England. In Arizona his life is saved by a humble Indian maiden (Lupe Velez), who then camps on his doorstep until he takes her in.

A few years later we find them parents of a small boy (Dickie Moore). As a birthday surprise the mother laboriously carves and paints a little wooden horse, only to watch sadly as the child ignores it in favor of a miniature train given to him by the white ranch hands. When an English friend (Roland Young) arrives with the cousin's widow, now free, the Indian wife quite rightly fears the worst: her son will be taken from her to be brought up as an English gentleman. Though her dialogue is minimal, Lupe Velez gives a remarkably restrained and moving performance. Using the same gun with which she once saved her husband's life, the squaw kills herself.

In the misnamed *Massacre* (1934) Richard Barthelmess played an educated Indian, who makes good money as a crack shot and rider in a Wild West show. When called back to the reservation by his dying father, he is appalled to find that the white administrators, led by Dudley Digges, are all crooks, whom he ultimately routs, with the aid of Washington, and as reward is made federal representative at the reservation. Though he had plenty of white girls after him, he chooses one of his own tribe (Ann Dvorak).

Laughing Boy (1934), from Oliver La Farge's 1929 Pulitzer Prize novel, produced by MGM and directed by W. S. Van Dyke, proved a disappointing dud. Lupe Velez played a different kind of Indian, Slim Girl, corrupted by white men into prostitution. Not only does she persuade her husband (Ramon Novarro) to leave his people, but when she goes to town supposedly to sell silver jewelry he makes, it is actually to live with a white man. Aiming an arrow at the lover, the ironically named Laughing Boy accidentally kills his wife instead. Oddly enough, the film had censorship problems on grounds of being derogatory to government officials.

The squaw man theme was given one more go-round in *Behold My Wife* (1935), with Sylvia Sidney as the red-skinned bride of playboy Gene Raymond, who married her only to spite his family, since they had made him give up a secretary he loved, driving her to suicide. Does the Indian girl take New York as Pocahontas took London? Does her husband come to appreciate her true worth? Based on a novel, *Translation of a Savage*, this was called by the *Times* "the most wild-eyed scenario of the year." It was arguably Sidney's worst film.

Warners, who had made *Massacre*, two years later again took up the tomahawk, in *Treachery Rides the Range* (1936), this time on behalf of the Cheyennes, who were promised by treaty that there would be no more buffalo hunting in their territory. But the buffalo traders stir up trouble between the Indians and the Army, and despite the efforts of sympathetic cavalry captain Dick Foran the Cheyennes end up worse off than ever.

1936 also brought *Ramona* and *The Last of the Mohicans,* both featuring doomed Indian heroes. Like all the other films about Spanish California, *Ramona* was both ethnic and regional, but many others set in the con-temporary United States depicted regions apparently inhabited only by WASPs.[3]

New York was probably the setting for more films than any other city in the world. Self-evidently, anything about the theater, including backstage musicals, had to take place there, as did most gangster films (unless specifically located in Chicago), most romantic comedies, whether about heiresses or working girls, for no functional reason except that New York was the paradigm for all big cities. Wherever movies were shown throughout the world, its skyline was instantly familiar, nor did anyone anywhere need to be told the symbolic significance of Broadway, Park Avenue, Wall Street or the Lower East Side. In fact, the words "New York," "Manhattan" or specific street names were used in nearly thirty film titles during the decade. The second most popular city was the other glamour capital, Hollywood itself, followed by San Francisco and Chicago. Other American cities were almost totally ignored. Far more Hollywood films were set in Paris, Budapest and Vienna than in, say, Boston, Philadelphia or Detroit.

Considering its historical and cultural importance, and the number of famous writers it produced, New England was the background of very few films, except for *The Last Gentleman* (1934) all rural. First was *Way Back Home* (1932), an attempt to launch a film career for Phillips Lord, a popular radio actor better known to his fans as a Maine preacher named Seth Parker. "All the real and mellow phases of Yankee village life" appealed to the *Times* reviewer, as did Seth's personality, but they were panned elsewhere. The cast was largely unknown except for the young lovers, Bette Davis and Frank Albertson.

As the Earth Turns (1934), based on Gladys Hasty Carroll's popular novel of Maine farm life, traced four seasons in the difficult lives of the Shaw family and their

[3] The only Mexican-American film hero of the '30s was Paul Muni in *Bordertown,* set in California.

new neighbors, the Janowskis, Poles distrusted as "foreigners." Daughter of David Landau and stepdaughter of Clara Blandick, levelheaded Jen Shaw (Jean Muir) despite the designs of a troublesome stepsister (Dorothy Appleby) ends up with Stan Janowski (Donald Woods), both dedicated to farming, though his parents return to Boston.

Unlike New England, the South received more screen attention, not necessarily favorable, than any other section of the country except the West, but the tendency was either to romanticize its pre-Civil War past or its Kentucky thoroughbreds or to indict its current social backwardness. One of the few films simply to depict the contemporary South without any axe to grind was *Cabin in the Cotton* (1932). The *Times* gave it a totally negative review, but anyone seeing it now would be inclined to agree with Everson's estimate: "Quite one of the best of the early Warner talkies that mixed social comment with all-out melodrama."

Richard Barthelmess, the son of sharecroppers, a clerk in the village store where all must trade, is the protégé of a paternalistic plantation owner (Berton Churchill), who has educated him above his station and in return expects unquestioning loyalty. The boy's dilemma, torn between his own impoverished people and the man to whom he owes so much, is aptly symbolized by two girls, his naïve little childhood sweetheart (Dorothy Jordan) and the planter's brazenly seductive daughter (Bette Davis, brilliant in the first of her several Southern roles). Leaning across the counter, she murmurs, "Ah would let yuh kiss me, but Ah just washed muh hayah."

Promoted to bookkeeper, the hero soon learns that the planter has been cheating his tenants, who are plotting a rebellion. When a neighboring planter is killed by a cotton thief, the latter is hunted down and lynched. In retaliation, the share-croppers burn down the store, destroying the records of their overdue accounts. Forced to take sides at last, the clerk produces a duplicate set of books, with which he compels the planter to agree to a new

contract guaranteeing fairer conditions. Of course he returns to his sweetheart in calico, but to the end Davis looks as if she hasn't given up.

An even more melodramatic view of the South, but taken seriously by the critics, was *The Story of Temple Drake* (1933). Paramount in buying Faulkner's sensational novel *Sanctuary*, which he freely admitted was a potboiler, acquired a property so hot that even the title could not be used. Even in cleaned-up form, the film was one of the last straws that brought about the imposition of the Code.

Though some of the characters' names were changed—Horace Benbow (William Gargan) became Stephen and the sadistic villain Popeye (Jack LaRue) was rechristened Trigger—about as much of the story was left as was allowable even before the Production Code. Miriam Hopkins, herself a Southerner, was well cast as the thrill-seeking, decadent Temple, who scorns beaux of her own class and ends up Trigger's prisoner in a Memphis brothel, where she rubs elbows with such sisters under the skin as Ruby Lemar (Florence Eldridge) and Miss Reba, the madam (Jobyna Howland). As in the book, Trigger casually kills one henchman and pins it on another (Irving Pichel), but is eventually himself killed by Temple.

Says Everson: "The obvious depravities were removed, the stress on horror and melodrama somewhat expanded · . . The overall effect is decidedly downbeat and intrinsically faithful to Faulkner."

A third negative view of decaying Southern aristocracy was *Carolina* (1934), based on Paul Green's 1931 play *The House of Connelly*, the first production of the Group Theatre. Lionel Barrymore was the unbalanced patriarch of an impoverished but fiercely proud old family; as his sister-in-law Henrietta Crosman breathed icy scorn for anyone born north of the Mason-Dixon line. As Joanna, the unwelcome Yankee (in the play Patsy, a poor white share-cropper) loved by the Connelly heir (Robert Young), considerably less of a weakling than in the play, Janet Gaynor has the greatest difficulty in persuading his stiff-necked family that they can save themselves only by switching from cotton to tobacco—in North Carolina in the 1930s surely a message long overdue. Stepin Fetchit contributed another of his many caricatures of moronic sloth to this generally well-received film.

Besides *Show Boat* (1936), other films utilizing the local color of the Mississippi Valley include *River of Romance* (1930), remade as *Mississippi* (1935), the two versions of *Tom Sawyer* (1930 and 1938) and *Huckleberry Finn* (1931 and 1939), *The Flood, Heaven on Earth* (both 1931), *Lazy River* (1934), *Steamboat Round the Bend* (1935), *Banjo on My Knee* (1936), *On Such a Night* (1937) and *St. Louis Blues* (1939).

Moving up from the Deep South, a few films were also set in border states, especially in the Appalachians or Ozarks, where the inbred natives, rifle-toting moonshiners clinging to primitive superstitions and speaking in heavy dialect, were already being caricatured both in *Esquire*'s hillbilly cartoons and in the comic strip *Li'l Abner*.

First of these was *Tol'able David* (1930), set in West Virginia, remake of a famous 1922 silent, with Richard Cromwell replacing Richard Barthelmess in the title role. David is the youngest of a family, constantly being told he is not yet man enough to do this or that. He gets his chance when he must drive the U.S. mail wagon from his town to the railroad station through the territory of the thieving, murderous Hatburn brothers. He has to kill all three to make sure the mail gets through. The *Times* found this version even better than the first.

In the most grotesque miscasting of her career, Katharine Hepburn in *Spitfire* (1934) played a simple Ozarks faith healer (oddly named Trigger), who kidnaps a baby for its own good and is almost stoned to death as a witch by her outraged neighbors. Meanwhile she has fallen in love with an engineer (Robert Young), not knowing he's married, but at the end when she accepts exile from the community there's a hint she may get Young's boss (Ralph Bellamy).

The Trail of the Lonesome Pine (1936), the third film version of John Fox, Jr.'s 1905 novel, had the distinction of being the first outdoor film made in the new Technicolor, its colors chosen to represent nature. "Paradoxically," said the *Times*, "it improves the case for color by lessening its importance."

The story involved another of those everlasting feuds of two backwoods families "in the Blue Ridge Mountains of Virginia." The daughter of one clan (Sylvia Sidney) shocks everyone by falling in love with a "furriner" (Fred MacMurray), another of those engineers, who has come into the mountains to build a railroad despite native opposition. Henry Fonda was his local rival, Fred Stone and Beulah Bondi were Sidney's parents, and little Spanky McFarland was an innocent victim caught in the cross fire.

Opening a week later, *The Voice of Bugle Ann* (1936), based on MacKinlay Kantor's novel, was set in the Missouri fox-hunting country. The ubiquitous Lionel Barrymore and his crony, Charles Grapewin, along with their sons (Eric Linden and Henry Wadsworth) take great pride in their hunting hounds. When an unpleasant new neighbor (Dudley Digges) builds a wire fence around his property, they politely ask him to take it down so as not to injure their dogs, but he rudely refuses. Later, when he is suspected of killing the beloved Bugle Ann, the finest hound of them all, Barrymore shoots him down and at seventy-one faces a twenty-year term for murder. Ruined, too, is his son's romance with the victim's daughter (Maureen O'Sullivan). The film was especially praised for its simplicity and rich local color.

The upper Midwest may be discussed in terms of the novelists who depicted it. Except in his historical novels, Booth Tarkington's works were usually set in a typical Indiana town, as were *Bad Sister* and *Alice Adams*. Sinclair Lewis' favorite settings were his native Minnesota and the composite Midwestern state he created, Winnemac, whose metropolis is Zenith. In addition to *Arrowsmith* and *Dodsworth,* both *Babbitt* and *Main Street* were also filmed in the '30s.

Though *Babbitt* (1934) was suitably cast, with Guy Kibbee in the title role and Aline MacMahon as his patient wife, it is considerably plottier than the novel, with the designing Tanis Judique (Claire Dodd) attempting to blackmail Babbitt into going along with a crooked real estate deal. The film is pleasant enough entertainment, but much of the bite of the satire is lost.

Main Street, rechristened with the confessional-sounding and entirely misleading title of *I Married a Doctor* (1936), was also well cast with character players, but, among other changes, it was updated from 1915–18 to the then present, necessarily omitting all the satire on wartime superpatriotism and also not taking into account how twenty years of movies and radio had affected the real Main Streets. The town's name was changed from the aptly depressing Gopher Prairie to Williamsburg, whether in tribute to a section of Brooklyn or the restored Virginia city equally inept.

Pat O'Brien was Dr. Will Kennicott, with Josephine Hutchinson as Carol, his city-bred wife, determined to impose culture on a town that loathes and fears it. Unlike the novel, in which her misunderstood interest in the sensitive young Eric Valborg (Ross Alexander) was only one of many strands used to expose the viciousness of small-town gossip, the film centered almost entirely on this triangle. As in the book, Carol leaves her husband and the town temporarily, but this makes Main Street admit its errors and welcome her back. As the *Times* said, "That . . . may be good box office, but it is bad drama. It is the difference between *Main Street* and *I Married a Doctor.*"

Even more disappointing to admirers of the book was a version of that supremely regional novelist Willa Cather's *A Lost Lady* (1934), with Barbara Stanwyck as Marian Forrester, Frank Morgan as her elderly hus-

band, Ricardo Cortez as her lover and Lyle Talbot as Neil, the young man through whose eyes the story is told. First off, it was taken out of the nineteenth-century context so important to its meaning, then everything that had been hinted at was spelled out, and even the ending was changed; Marian settles down to "a life of gentle resignation with her husband." On the basis of her experience with *A Lost Lady,* Cather in her will expressly forbade any further theatrical or cinematic adaptations of her fiction.

Perhaps the most authentic depictions of the rural Midwest, specifically Iowa, were the films based on the novels of Phil Stong. *State Fair* (1933), the first of three film versions, made a perfect vehicle for Will Rogers, as Abel Frake, a shrewd, easygoing farmer, though he shared the honors with Janet Gaynor (given top billing) as his daughter Margy, Louise Dresser as his wife Melissa and Norman Foster as his son Wayne. Each of the four Frakes has some objective to accomplish during their week at the annual fair: Abel to show his prize hog, Blue Boy, Melissa to enter her mincemeat in a food competition, Wayne to even the score with a con artist who took him the year before and Margy just to have a good time.

Margy falls in love with a reporter (Lew Ayres), her brother has a one-night fling with a trapeze artist (Sally Eilers), the parents win their prizes (the mother because more than one family member added brandy to her mincemeat), not without suspense when Blue Boy takes sick. The material is the simplest, yet the film, directed by Henry King, is so full of little human touches and so well captures the carnival atmosphere of such annual fairs that it became almost a legend.

Much less familiar than *State Fair* but much stronger dramatically was the film based on Stong's *The Stranger's Return* (1933), directed by King Vidor. Miriam Hopkins played a sophisticated New Yorker, separated from her husband, who comes to stay at the prosperous Iowa farm still run by her patriarchal grandfather, an eighty-five-

Sally Eilers, Norman Foster, Lew Ayres, Janet Gaynor, Will Rogers (inset) in State Fair

year-old Civil War veteran (Lionel Barrymore in one of his finest performances), with the aid of an alcoholic but faithful hired man (Stuart Erwin). A bitter stepdaughter (Beulah Bondi) and her supine husband (Grant Mitchell) treat the girl as an unwelcome interloper, especially when she becomes involved with a neighbor (Franchot Tone), an educated farmer, whose wife (Irene Hervey) everyone likes.

In the climax, Barrymore is triumphant at a sanity hearing instigated by the scheming relatives trying to get his property. Then he dies, after changing his will to leave the farm to his granddaughter, who will run it with the aid of the loyal lush, minus the step-daughter and her entourage. There can be no happy ending for the romance. Much as he loves farming, Tone accepts a teaching post at Cornell, previously rejected, to take himself and his family out of Hopkins' life for good. As with other Vidor films, the rustic details were exceptionally well conveyed: "the great house, the shade trees, the white silos and the hay barns, the shimmering fields of alfalfa."

After these two almost idyllic pictures of rural Americana, Stong joined rather belatedly in the "revolt from the village." *Village Tale* (1935) exposes a town in which practically everyone is unpleasant. Though Kay Johnson is making the best of her marriage to dull Arthur Hohl, his vicious brother (Robert Barrat), envious of the town's leading citizen (Randolph Scott), spreads rumors that inflame the loutish husband into trying to kill Scott. The wife leaves, taking refuge at a neighbor's house, where they are subjected to a menacing "shivaree."

When an old servant defending Scott is beaten, the town finally turns against the villain and almost lynches him until Scott intervenes. The husband is frightened into getting out of town, presumably leaving Johnson free eventually to marry Scott. The ugly picture of the malice of small-town minds anticipates the lynch mob scenes in *Fury* (1936) and *They Won't Forget* (1937). On the other hand, *Career* (1939), from another Stong novel, was an obvious attempt to follow up on the success of *A Man to Remember,* (1938), with Edward Ellis as a small-town storekeeper who solves everyone's problems. This was still regarded as an honest, worthwhile film.

In the same bitter vein as *Village Tale* was *Party Wire* (1935), in which the return of a creamery heir (Victor Jory) to his native town greatly impresses everyone but Jean Arthur and her father (Charles Grapewin). But the heir and the girl fall in love, her former beau grows jealous and plans to go to New York. When on a party line someone overhears her complain about "the mess" he's leaving her in, meaning some unbalanced church books, the whole town is at once convinced she's pregnant. In disgust the hero fires all the local workers, who gather to run him out of town. But his aunt (Helen Lowell), who knows all their secrets, denounces the townspeople and silences them, at least for the present—hardly a flattering picture of American small-town life.

Most regional novelists stick to the region they know best, but the versatile Edna Ferber offered lively, colorful depictions of almost every section of the United States. In *Cimarron* (1931), it was Oklahoma, starting with the great land rush of 1889, in *So Big* (1932), a Dutch farming community near Chicago, in *Show Boat* (1936), the Mississippi and Chicago, and in *Come and Get It* (1937), her native Wisconsin.

Considerably simplified from the novel, this vigorous drama offered Edward Arnold one of his more sympathetic roles as ambitious Barney Glasgow, the lumber camp chore boy who becomes a timber tycoon. Though in 1884 he loves Lotta (Frances Farmer), a beautiful singer, he prudently marries the boss's daughter (Mary Nash), leaving Lotta to marry his Swedish friend, Swan Bostrom (Walter Brennan in his first Oscar-winning performance).

Twenty-three years later, in 1907, Barney at fifty, rich and powerful, father of two grown children (Joel McCrea and Andrea Leeds), on a visit to the town where he first knew Lotta, finds that though she is dead, she left a daughter who looks exactly like her (also Frances Farmer, in her best role). Of course he falls in love with her, but when he establishes her, chaperoned by an aunt (Mady Christians), in his own city, his son is also smitten, and the girl naturally prefers him.

In a showdown during an employees' garden party at his estate, he and his son almost come to blows, and only when Lotta restrains the boy by reminding him "He's your *old man*" does Barney face what a foolish figure he has cut. Though suspecting the truth, his wife says nothing. The details of logging in the opening scenes (directed by Howard Hawks), the splendid period atmosphere and the strong emotional conflicts make *Come and Get It* a superb piece of Americana.

Self-evidently, the West has received more film attention than all other sections of the country combined; it is to regions what New York is to cities. The Western has been a popular genre as far back as *The Great Train Robbery* (1902). Indeed, except for a few popular melodramas (*The Girl of the Golden West, The Great Divide, The Bad Man, The Dove*), all set mainly in saloons, the Western arrived with movies, since its most picturesque elements of rugged scenery, chases on horseback, bone-crunching barroom brawls and climactic shoot-outs on a town's ominously deserted main street could never have been done so well on stage. The appeal has been world-wide, for no other country has ever had anything like the nineteenth-century American West. Yet few silent Westerns have endured or would be of even historic interest now. *The Covered Wagon* (1923) and *The Iron Horse* (1924) are less conventional Westerns than pioneer epics, depicting in heroic terms white American expansion across the continent.

This theme was echoed in *The Big Trail* (1930), directed by Raoul Walsh and starring John Wayne in his only major role before disappearing into nearly ten years of "B" films. The *Times* described it as a monumental work. The story was secondary, but the spectacular highlights included a buffalo stampede, an Indian attack on encamped covered wagons, the fording of a river, the lowering of cattle and wagons over a cliff, a blizzard and a trek across the desert. Wayne played a scout who eventually wins Marguerite Churchill. The villain was Tyrone Power, Sr., father of the later '30s star.

MGM's only contribution to the short-lived cycle of early talkie Westerns was *Billy the Kid* (1930), directed by King Vidor, but dismissed by the *Times*. Everson deplores the use of silent-type subtitles and the absence of a musical score, but praises it as "easily the best *Billy the Kid* ever." William S. Hart worked with Vidor, tutoring Johnny Mack Brown in the use of the real Billy's own guns. Unfortunately a happy ending was tacked on for the American public; Europe saw the true ending, Billy's death.

In Old Arizona (1929), from a story by O. Henry, was the first talkie filmed outdoors, and Warner Baxter won one of the earliest Oscars playing the Cisco Kid, so *The Arizona Kid* (1930) and *The Cisco Kid* (1931), in which he played the same character, were no doubt inevitable, but certainly not distinguished. Although *Cimarron* (1931) cannot be classed as a true Western, covering as it does forty years during which the Oklahoma frontier town of Osage grows into an oil metropolis, it does include an early scene in which Yancey Cravat (Richard Dix) shoots it out on the main street with an outlaw known only as "The Kid" (William Collier, Jr.).

The last and grimmest of the cycle was *Law and Order* (1932), from the novel *Saint Johnson* by W. R. Burnett, with an all-male cast headed by Walter Huston and Harry Carey. As Johnson, Huston imposes law and order on Tombstone, Arizona, even though it means decimating the population. "One of the goriest exhibitions of shoot-'em-down gunplay since the gangster and machine-gun era," said the *Times*, rather curiously implying that era was over.

But the public was still more interested in contemporary gangsters than in nineteenth-century outlaws. Consequently after 1932 the few Westerns made by major studios were given to stars of the second rank like Richard Dix, Richard Arlen, the upcoming Randolph Scott and especially George O'Brien, who made several a year. While it is true that Gary Cooper first attracted attention in the silent Western *The Winning of Barbara Worth* (1928) and scored a big hit in his first talkie, *The Virginian* (1929), followed by *The Texan* (1930), which wasn't a Western at all, and *Fighting Caravans* (1932), he did not settle into a Western rut.

The apparently insatiable appetite for this extremely stylized genre among rural and small-town audiences was satisfied by routine horse operas, many based on Zane Grey's novels, ground out by independent producers, seldom given first-run theater showings in New York, starring such exclusively cowboy actors as Buck Jones, Ken Maynard, Hoot Gibson, Tim McCoy, Bob Steele, Tom Tyler and William ("Screen") Boyd, who as early as 1935 was making the Hopalong Cassidy films that later became a staple of TV.

The first critically praised Western in several years was RKO's *The Arizonian* (1935), written by Dudley Nichols and directed by Charles Vidor. A two-fisted stranger (Richard Dix) rides into Silver City, rescues an imperiled maiden (Margot Grahame) from a crooked sheriff (Louis Calhern) and is asked to take over as marshal. As the *Times* said, "This one has all the advantages of a rich production, a sense of humor and a splendid cast."

Apparently other studios took the hint. MGM came up with the third of four film versions of *The Three Godfathers* (1936), Peter B. Kyne's dramatic tale of three outlaws (Chester Morris, Lewis Stone and Walter Brennan) who find a baby beside his dying mother in the desert and, rather than abandon him, sacrifice their own lives by returning to the town they just robbed.

Hailed as delightfully different was *The Last Outlaw* (1936), in which Harry Carey played a once-famous bandit released from prison after twenty-five years, who at first cannot adjust to the new, modern West, in which phony cowboys croon from movie screens, but eventually, aiding the sheriff who caught him (Henry B. Walthall), rounds up a modern mob of the Dillinger sort.

Paramount led the way toward a Western revival, at first ineptly, with *The Texas Rangers* (1936), made in honor of the state's centennial, in which two bandits (Fred MacMurray and Jack Oakie) become rangers and eventually dispatch an unregenerate third (Lloyd Nolan). Far more successful was Cecil B. De Mille's *The Plainsman* (1937), which was not only Gary Cooper's first Western in five years but the first since *Billy the Kid* to deal with historical figures. Its authenticity was seriously questioned by the *Times,* but the public flocked to see Cooper as Wild Bill Hickok, James Ellison as Buffalo Bill Cody and Jean Arthur as a decidedly cleaned-up Calamity Jane. The last stand (1876) of General Custer (John Miljan) was also worked into the act, and even President Lincoln (Frank McGlynn, as usual), indicating a considerable compression of time or confusion of chronology.

Wells Fargo (1937), also Paramount, directed by Frank Lloyd, was thought to have bitten into more themes than any one film

could chew—the opening of the West, the gold rush, Indian raids, the Pony Express, the Civil War. Joel McCrea played an advance man for Wells Fargo as the mail service is gradually extended from Buffalo to St. Louis and eventually to San Francisco, "always a horse's head in front of the railroad or the telegraph." McCrea's off-screen wife, Frances Dee, played his Southern bride, whose sympathies force them apart during the Civil War (when Frank McGlynn was Lincoln once again). The supporting cast was thick with familiar names, but the *Times* reviewer felt that the human story was lost in the rush of great events hurried over too quickly.

1938 was not a notable year for Westerns. Paramount did little better with *The Texans,* set in Reconstruction years, than with *The Texas Rangers,* and MGM's *The Badman of Brimstone* was called by the *Times* "the Madame X of the horse operas." In one more of his frequent paternal dilemmas, Wallace Beery as a grizzled old desperado discovers that an annoying new tenderfoot in town (Dennis O'Keefe) is his own son, unknown to the boy, whom the father secretly educates and whose life he eventually saves.

1939, a notable year in so many other ways, saw the dawn of a new golden age of Westerns; among the thirteen released by major studios, six were "grade A" productions, featuring top stars. Earliest in the year came *Jesse James,* the first pure Western in color, greatly enhanced by being photographed in the actual locale of Pineville, Missouri. Tyrone Power played the title role, with Nancy Kelly as his wife, Henry Fonda as Frank and John Carradine as Bob Ford, "the dirty little coward that shot 'Mr. Howard' and laid poor Jesse in his grave," but Henry Hull as Major Rufus Cobb, small-town editor and friend of the James boys, walked off with the critical laurels. "Handsomely produced," said the *Times,* "it becomes an authentic American panorama, enriched by dialogue, characterization and incidents imported directly from the Missouri hills."

The Oklahoma Kid was perhaps most significant as a straw in the wind, indicating that Warners thought it expedient to put cowboy outfits on even Cagney and Bogart. Cagney was a Robin Hood type of bandit of the Cherokee Strip, out to get Bogart's gang, who had lynched Cagney's law-abiding father. The *Times* found it on the border line of cheerful satire: "Mr. Cagney [is] just enjoying himself and if you want to trail along, so much the better for you."

Much more lavish but also more conventional was *Dodge City,* in color, with Errol Flynn as a frontier marshal, Olivia De Havilland as a girl who temporarily despises him for having shot her brother, Ann Sheridan as a lively dance-hall girl, Bruce Cabot as the villain and the whole Warners stock company to back them up. The *Times* found Flynn too invulnerable and the film too violent.

De Mille returned to the Old West with a truly spectacular epic, surprisingly not in color, *Union Pacific,* the biggest of all the films about transportation. In all the others the railroads had been the villains, but here was the talkie successor to *The Iron Horse* (1924), dramatizing in backbreaking detail all that went into the building of the first transcontinental railroad. Even the *Times* reviewer was awed by the tremendous energy and sweep of the film. Joel McCrea was a U.P. trouble shooter assigned to see that the track reaches Ogden before the C.P.'s tracks get there, even though Brian Donlevy has been hired to lure the laborers with gambling, liquor and women.

Worse, McCrea's Civil War buddy, a likable gambler (Robert Preston), is also in the pay of the enemy, and they are rivals for the heart of Irish spitfire Mollie Monahan (Barbara Stanwyck), daughter of the U.P.'s first engineer (J. M. Kerrigan) and postmistress of "End of Track," the town that moves with the railroad's progress. Akim Tamiroff and Lynne Overman supplied the comic relief. Stanwyck was especially praised in this "big, old-fashioned De Mille show . . . easily the best he has made in years."

All these films were released in the first half of the year, but one of the outstanding Westerns of 1939 did not open until late fall. Universal's *Destry Rides Again,* loosely based on a novel by Max Brand, would be memorable if only for Marlene Dietrich's startling break from her exotic von Sternberg image. It was equally a change of pace for James Stewart as Destry, the hard-hitting son of a sagebrush sheriff, who brings law and order to the town of Bottleneck.

Delighted critics noted that as Frenchy, the rough-and-ready saloon entertainer, Dietrich was just as hard-boiled as in *The Blue Angel* (1930), belting out cynical ballads like "The Boys in the Back Room." One high point was a knockdown, drag-out fight between Dietrich and Una Merkel. But though she loves Destry, according to an unwritten law, Frenchy could not get him; that reward goes to good girl Irene Hervey, while Frenchy, in the tradition of Cigarette in *Under Two Flags* and Huguette in *If I Were King,* dies saving her hero's life. Despite this semisad ending, the impression left by *Destry* was of hilarious, rowdy comedy.

The finest Western not only of the year but of the decade had been released the previous March, but on all scores deserves the climactic place in this chapter. John Ford's *Stagecoach,* one of the unquestioned classics of the screen, is considered, if not exactly the archetypal Western, the best cinematic use ever made of Western material. While staying well within the conventions and even using such stereotypes as a basically decent outlaw (John Wayne as the Ringo Kid, the role that launched him as a major star), a "bad" girl with a heart of gold (Claire Trevor as Dallas, one of the few such to get her man), an alcoholic doctor (Thomas Mitchell), a chivalrous Southern gambler (John Carradine) and an absconding banker (Berton Churchill), *Stagecoach* manages to transcend most of the tiresome clichés of the genre.

With its pounding, relentless pace and its constant, marvelously sustained sense of a literal flight for life, against magnificently photographed scenery, *Stagecoach* is less a con-

Claire Trevor, John Wayne in Stagecoach

ventional Western than a variation on the *Grand Hotel* in transit pattern, in which a number of strangers are thrown into temporary intimacy by traveling in the same stagecoach.

Said the *Times:* "Here, in a sentence, is a movie of the grand old school, a genuine ribthumper and a beautiful sight to see . . . This is one stagecoach that's powered by a Ford."

In a career article on Wayne in *Films in Review* (May 1977) Jim Beaver calls it "a film that singlehandedly rescued the Western from the doldrums in which it had sunk for the previous decade." Undoubtedly the resounding success of *Stagecoach* did much to revive the waning genre and inspire the long parade of big-budget Technicolor Westerns (many directed by Ford himself) throughout the '40s and later.

12 SECTION 12

IN TIMES LIKE THESE
Films of Ideas

49

THEY GAVE HIM A GUN
From Antiwar to Prowar

Most films provided escapist entertainment, a legitimate social function in itself, but in addition to reflecting normal American life and dramatizing our colorful past, Hollywood made a number of attempts to speak out on timely issues, especially one controversial in the early '30s, patriotism versus pacifism, on which the best movies were uncompromisingly antiwar. One may compare this attitude with that of 1965–73, when, freed of all censorship restraints and playing to far more sophisticated audiences, all the time the Vietnam War was polarizing the country and provoking the most violent protests and demonstrations in our history, Hollywood fiddled while Rome burned.

As the watershed event of the twentieth century thus far, the 1914–18 war was reflected in countless films, sometimes directly, as in all the through-the-years chronicles, sometimes indirectly, as in the nostalgic films; it was precisely the postwar disenchantment that made the 1900s look better all the time to the 1930s.

But aside from these incidental uses, many other films concentrated on the war itself, including some of the biggest late silents (e.g., *The Big Parade, What Price Glory?, Wings, Lilac Time*), which, when seen now, with their emphasis on heroism and romance, do not seem at all as antiwar as they were thought to be at the time.

1930 was a particularly big year for war films, not all necessarily antiwar. The most spectacular (and least distinguished), *Hell's Angels,* is perhaps best-remembered for giving Jean Harlow her first leading role. At the time it was more notable for having cost "young Howard Hughes" four million dollars, including a silent version that had to be shelved and reshot. The story was trivial, a routine triangle in which two brothers (Ben Lyon and James Hall) are rivals for the love of Harlow, but reviewers were dazzled by the unprecedented power of the air scenes, especially an elaborately staged Zeppelin raid on London, in which the German crew is ordered to jump out, without parachutes, and the dirigible itself is finally destroyed. Several critics complained of the three principals' ludicrous attempts at British accents, which Harlow accomplished by pronouncing "either" as "eye-ther."

English characters fared much better in *The Dawn Patrol,* an all-male drama of the Royal Flying Squadron, in which Richard Barthelmess and Douglas Fairbanks, Jr., close friends, fly under the command of Neil Hamilton. Barthelmess is promoted to Hamilton's post, which means sending new men to their deaths every day, including Fairbanks' younger brother (William Janney), a tragedy which ends their friendship. But when an ammunition dump must be raided, a suicide mission, Barthelmess sacrifices himself, Fairbanks succeeds him as commander and the slaughter goes on. Reviewers again marveled at the scenes of aerial combat and bombings.[1]

Also made without women, but written on a much higher level, was *Journey's End,* a faithful adaptation of R. C. Sherriff's quietly sensitive drama of life in the British trenches, directed by James Whale, who had also done the London and New York stage productions. Colin Clive played the strong, decent Captain Stanhope, the role he had created on stage. Most of the action is confined to a dugout, except for the ill-fated raid that takes Osborne (Ian MacLaren) and Stanhope's protégé, young Raleigh (David Manners), into no man's land. Critics praised the stiff-upper-lip British restraint, which deepened the sense of despair, symbolized by the end, when a last flickering candle dies out.

The most powerful and moving of all these antiwar films, however, dealt with *German* soldiers—surely conclusive proof that the anti-Hun hysteria of 1914–18 had totally died out. This was Universal's magnificent version of Erich Maria Remarque's novel *All Quiet on the Western Front,* adapted by Maxwell Anderson and George Abbott and directed by Lewis Milestone. Cheered on by their teacher and their fathers, in 1914 a group of school-boys, barely sixteen, joyously enlist to fight for the Fatherland, and, of course, find nothing but degradation, suffering and early death—a true slaughter of the innocents.

As the young hero, Paul Baumer (Lew Ayres in a classic performance), sees his friends picked off one by one (they include William Bakewell, Russell Gleason, Ben Alexander and Owen Davis, Jr.), then on leave finds the older generation still preaching the glories of war, his disillusion is complete. He feels more at home with his comrades at the front than with civilians, who understand nothing. A particularly touching detail is the prized pair of boots that passes from one boy to the next as one after another is killed.

[1] *The Dawn Patrol* was remade in 1938 with Errol Flynn, David Niven and Basil Rathbone in the roles played by Barthelmess, Fairbanks and Hamilton.

In a gallery of convincing characterizations, outstanding was Louis Wolheim as Katczinsky, the tough, middle-aged veteran who becomes a father to each successive wave of new recruits. The scene in which Paul continues to carry him on his shoulders, not realizing he has died, is unforgettable, as is the one in which Paul kills a Frenchman in a shell hole, then, finding a picture of his wife and family, weeps and begs his forgiveness—and so, of course, is the famous ending in which Paul reaches out to catch a butterfly and is killed, on a day when the official dispatches announce "All quiet on the Western front."

Indeed, so insistent had the "war is hell" message become in serious films that in November 1930, reviewing *Suspense,* a British drama, the *Times* critic complained that a "scathing indictment of war" had become a cliché. Possibly he was thinking of inferior examples like *The Case of Sergeant Grischa* and *War Nurse* (both 1930), with their hearts in the right pacifist place but ineptly done. *Beyond Victory* (1931) brought more of the same. The *Times* reviewer observed that "if all the men who thought up some of these war pictures had to sit through them, there wouldn't be any more war pictures."

Diana Wynyard, who had suffered so poignantly through two wars in *Cavalcade,* was recalled to duty in *Men Must Fight* (1933), the most original of the antiwar films, for it dealt not with the last war but with the *next* one, the United States versus "the Eurasian States," projected for 1940—off by only one year. A Red Cross nurse in the First World War, in love with a flyer (Robert Young), who is killed, the heroine finds herself in trouble, until an older suitor (Lewis Stone) offers to marry her to give her child a name. By 1940 the foster father has become Secretary of State, but his wife, a militant pacifist, has brought up her son (Phillips Holmes) to be the same. As war looms, she vehemently urges a giant congress of mothers not to let their sons go, in fact, to stop bearing sons who only end up as cannon fodder sacrificed to old men's political ends.

Almost as happened in real life, during the isolationist-interventionist struggle of 1939–41, her crusade is bitterly denounced, the Secretary's home is stoned, his wife and son scorned as "yellow-bellies," especially by the boy's fiancée's superpatriotic family. But, just as happened after Pearl Harbor, when the enemy bombs New York, destroying the Empire State Building, and the mother is injured, the boy finally enlists and is last seen flying an Army plane. Once war hysteria has taken over, pacifism is futile—a downbeat but undeniably honest conclusion, at least up until Vietnam.

Paramount's *The Eagle and the Hawk* (1933), with Fredric March and Cary Grant, depicts the emotional disintegration of an officer in the Royal Flying Squadron who must daily send his juniors to death. His understanding superior (Sir Guy Standing) gives March ten days' leave in London, where he enjoys a brief romance with Carole Lombard, but he is appalled by all the lighthearted civilian chatter about war as a great adventure.

On his return, the last straw is the death of his very young observer (Kenneth Howell). In a radical departure from other war films, the acclaimed hero can no longer bear the strain, so kills himself. But his former gunner (Grant), the "hawk" of the title, who can take all the deaths in his stride, smuggles March's body aboard a combat plane, riddles it with bullets and crashes it, so that March will still be remembered as a hero.[2]

Gabriel over the White House (1933) and *The President Vanishes* (1934) also scored antiwar points, but they are political films. The same message was conveyed more obliquely in *No Greater Glory* (1934), directed by Borzage, based on Molnár's novel *The Paul Street Boys*, a touching parable about two "armies" of boys in Budapest, who, aping their elders, become so obsessed with rank, uniforms, discipline and "honor" that the little hero (George Breakston) dies of pneumonia, but with an officer's cap on his head.

The last effective antiwar drama of the decade (unless one counts *Idiot's Delight*, 1939) was *The Man Who Reclaimed His Head* (1935)—"head" meaning professional integrity—from a French play. Like *The Man Who Would Be King*, it begins with a half-crazed man (Claude Rains) about to tell his story; he opens a handbag to reveal something unspeakably horrible. We flash back to the time when as a brilliant writer, to please his ambitious wife (Joan Bennett), he sold his talents to an unscrupulous newspaper publisher (Lionel Atwill) by ghosting pacifist editorials. But on the eve of the world war the publisher betrayed him and sold out to the "merchants of death," the munitions makers who will profit by the war. In the trenches the writer broods over this until he goes quite mad, obsessed with the idea of reclaiming his head, which he does by removing the publisher's.

If that was the last antiwar film, then the first major production to romanticize, if not glorify, militarism was *The Road to Glory* (1936). Despite the title, there is no irony whatever in this 1936 film, co-authored by Joel Sayre and William Faulkner and directed by Howard Hawks. "Glory" is apparently meant in the French sense, *la gloire,* to be taken at face value.

It is an extended, even fulsome, tribute to French patriotism, heroism and gallantry under fire, in which the rightness of the Allied cause is never even momentarily questioned. Warner Baxter plays a war-weary captain, Fredric March his lighthearted lieutenant and rival for a quite unnecessary nurse (June Lang). Baxter's father (Lionel Barrymore), a Franco-Prussian veteran, despite his age insists on re-enlisting for combat service. In momentary panic he tosses a grenade among his own men, but later redeems himself by guiding his blinded son to an advanced position where they'll both be killed.

---

[2] In *Suzy* (1936), MGM's muddled spy romance, also set in World War I, Franchot Tone performed exactly the same service for Grant.

March takes over as captain, and at the end greets the newest recruits, absolutely straight-faced, with the same proud, patriotic appeal that Baxter had given twice earlier. Though grim enough in its physical details and sense of suffering, *The Road to Glory* basically honored the whole military mystique.

Just what brought about this total reversal of attitude remains unclear. In 1936 Hitler and Mussolini were not yet perceived as threatening American interests. In fact, in that very year, Congress passed the Neutrality Act, intended to keep us out of any future European conflict. Yet Hollywood, whether spontaneously or with official encouragement, had already begun to rattle the saber. As spy plots turned domestic, climaxing with *Confessions of a Nazi Spy* (1939), more and more films were made glorifying the Army, the Navy, the service academies and even military prep schools. Said an ad for *The Spirit of Culver* (1939): "It's better to die on your feet than live on your knees."

According to Lewis Jacobs in *The Rise of the American Film,* Paramount's *Men with Wings* (1938) "had its pacifistic ending changed on the advice of the War Department so that America's air-preparedness was emphasized and the men who build bombers, glorified." This is the only recorded incident of direct government intervention before World War II, but presumably the studios were allowed to use Army and Navy bases on the strict understanding that the films would serve as animated recruiting posters.

There were, of course, other war films which took no sides but were simply adventure stories, some already covered under other headings. They included *The Doomed Battalion* (1932), much admired, about Alpine warfare between Austrians and Italians, and *Hell in the Heavens* (1933), about the Lafayette Escadrille. John Ford contributed three such films, all well received: *Men Without Women* (1930), the grimly harrowing *The Lost Patrol* (1933), about British cavalrymen lost in the desert being picked off by Arabs, and *Submarine Patrol* (1938).

Besides all the dramas concentrating on the plight of those in combat, in which women played little or no role, a number of other films used the war as a mere backdrop or convenient plot catalyst for triangular romances, usually about two officers, rivals for the same girl or one in love with the other's wife, occasionally with an *Enoch Arden* twist—e.g., *Smilin' Through* (1932), *The Dark Angel* (1935), *The Shopworn Angel* (1938)—all remade from silents—*Chances, Surrender* and *Waterloo Bridge* (all 1931), *Captured, The Fountain* and *Today We Live* (all 1933), *All Men Are Enemies* (1934), *Suzy* (1936) and *The Woman I Love* (1937), most long forgotten. In all of these films the uniforms and the military equipment may be authentic to the last degree, but following that perverse movie law of the 1930s that fashion accuracy stopped about 1910, the women are always dressed in the styles of the year the film was made.[3]

Perhaps the outstanding wartime love story of the decade, the only such film drawn from a respected literary source, was *A Farewell to Arms* (1932), directed by Frank Borzage, with Gary Cooper as Frederic Henry and Helen Hayes as Catherine Barkley. Though it was criticized as too sentimental, the film's reputation has grown with the years, especially in comparison with Selznick's overblown 1957 version. It was generally agreed that Cooper, so marvelously right for any Hemingway hero, quite overshadowed Hayes, competent though she was. In an excellent cast standouts were Adolphe Menjou as Lieutenant Rinaldi and Jack LaRue, cast against type, as the priest.

As in the book, the tender romance between the wounded Frederic, a young American lieutenant attached to an Italian ambulance unit, and Catherine, a British nurse, follows its doomed course. Caught up in the calamitous retreat from Caporetto, he almost loses

---

[3] The worst offenders in this respect were MGM, Universal and Samuel Goldwyn; the most faithful were Paramount and Warners.

touch with her; finding her, he deserts and they row across a lake to Switzerland to await the birth of their child. The baby is stillborn and Catherine dies, with Frederic at her side. It is not true that a happy ending was tacked on for American consumption; rather, it was left ambiguous. Although the dialogue makes it clear that Catherine has no chance, she seems to rally as the Armistice bells ring out. The tone of the film, like that of the novel, is disillusioned enough to rank it among anti-war films—the only one with a strong love story.

Another subgenre that contributed some of the best pacifist films was the type that offered only brief glimpses of combat but explored the emotional after-effects on the survivors. An early example was *The Last Flight* (1931), adapted from his own novel by John Monk Saunders, who also wrote *Wings* (1927) and *The Eagle and the Hawk* (1933). A fine, sensitive film, *The Last Flight* is nevertheless so incredibly parallel to *The Sun Also Rises* that it is surprising Hemingway did not sue. Although the heroine, Nikki (Helen Chandler), is not as promiscuous as Lady Brett Ashley, she is just as eccentric and enjoys the same kind of comradeship with four burnt-out aces, expatriates in Paris, too shattered by the war to adjust to any life but endless drinking and wry, self-mocking wit.

Like Jake Barnes, the hero, Cary Lockwood (Richard Barthelmess), is impotent; there is even an obnoxious fifth wheel (Walter Byron), like Robert Cohn, who keeps horning in and making unwelcome passes at the heroine. Instead of Pamplona, they all impulsively take off for the bullfights in Lisbon, where the most extroverted, an ex-football star (Johnny Mack Brown), gets himself killed by foolishly jumping into the arena, the obnoxious one fatally wounds the most likable (David Manners in his finest performance) and is in turn mowed down by an apparently catatonic one (Elliott Nugent), leaving Cary and Nikki to return to Paris alone, with no more hope than Jake Barnes and Lady Brett.

But the most powerful of these postwar studies, almost like a sequel to *All Quiet on the Western Front* (1930) (and likewise about Germans), was *The Man I Killed* (1932), Ernst Lubitsch's one serious American picture, based on a play by Maurice Rostand. Robert E. Sherwood called it the best talking picture yet made, but it is now dismissed by *The New Yorker* as "drab, sentimental hokum." Sherwood was closer to the truth, for the film fully merits an honored place in the Lubitsch canon.

While the credits appear in the kind of Gothic printing used in Germany, a bell tolls, solemn organ music plays, and the somber mood is set. But it opens in Paris, on November 11, 1919, during a celebration of the first anniversary of the Armistice, amid much visual irony, as the camera cuts from a triumphal military parade to hospital wards of permanently disabled veterans, and from a peace sermon preached in a vast church to the sunlight glinting on officers' spurs, sabers and military decorations.

One young man (Phillips Holmes in his best performance) remains alone in the church, anxious to ease his tortured conscience in confession. Paul has had a traumatic experience. As we see in flashback, he shot at close range a young German as he was writing a letter to his fiancée, which Paul read, learning to his horror that the other boy, too, was a musician, who had studied two years in Paris. The priest (Frank Sheridan) gives Paul the standard rationalization, that it was all in the line of patriotic duty, but when Paul bitterly rejects this, finally advises him to seek out the family of his victim, Walter Holderlin, the only child of a doctor (Lionel Barrymore).

In a German town, authentically pictured to the last detail, Walter's heartbroken parents keep his room intact, including his violin. His fiancée, Elsa (Nancy Carroll), lives with them like a daughter. In a touching scene in a cemetery, we see the mother's hands tenderly arranging flowers on Walter's grave before we see her face. Then she (Louise Carter) and another grieving mother (Emma

*Nancy Carroll, Phillips Holmes
in* **The Man I Killed**

Dunn), whose son "would be twenty today," talk quietly of their boys.

Paul, too, seeks out Walter's grave and is seen putting flowers on it by the puzzled Elsa. When he comes to visit the father, who at first angrily denounces him merely for being French, Elsa mentions the flowers, whereupon both parents wishfully assume that Paul must have been a friend of Walter's in Paris, so welcome him warmly to their home. The other townspeople, with all the bitterness of the defeated, hate all Frenchmen and are extremely critical of the doctor's attitude, but at the cafe where the older men lunch every day he eloquently denounces them for being, as he says, too old to fight but not too old to hate, and for having cheered their sons on to their deaths, as he himself did.

More guilt-racked than ever, Paul finally convinces Elsa of who he is by quoting Walter's last letter. Momentarily stunned, she quickly rises to the occasion and instead of telling the parents assures them that Paul will stay with them forever, meanwhile warning him that to leave now would be for them like losing another son. In the last scene the father brings out Walter's violin and Paul hesitantly begins to play, while Elsa accompanies him on the piano and the old couple happily embrace. Except for *Cavalcade* (1933), *The Man I Killed* was the only film to dramatize the anguish of parents who lost their sons in the war.

Also set in postwar Germany were *Little Man, What Now?* (1934), *Three Comrades* (1938) and *The Road Back* (1937), which, though based on a novel by Remarque, with a script by R. C. Sherriff, directed by James Whale, with a huge cast of familiar names, went seriously awry. Nugent of the *Times* took the trouble to reread the novel and then the script, which could not be faulted, nor did he blame Whale. The problem was in the casting and editing, he concluded, which placed undue emphasis on the comic elements in what he describes as "a savage and bitter sifting of the ashes of war." Slim Summerville and Andy Devine were billed third and fourth, preceded only by John King and Richard Cromwell. "Universal has narrowed it and cheapened it and made it pointless . . . as though it were dealing with a routine comedy of the trenches."

A few weeks earlier MGM had released its own treatment of postwar trauma in the accusingly titled *They Gave Him a Gun,* which Eames in *The MGM Story* describes as "one of 1937's strongest pictures, dramatically if not box-officially." Franchot Tone was a meek clerk transformed by his Army experiences into a killer, and Spencer Tracy was his Army buddy, a circus barker. Gladys George, the Army nurse loved by both, loves Tracy but is nobly sacrificed by him. Only when Tone is killed by a cop, his gunnery instructor in the Army (ah, irony!), do the other two find happiness. The *Times,* which hated the film, described Tone as "the singularly unconvincing head of the vaguest racket and the most completely movie gang that has operated hereabouts in months." The connection between the war, Prohibition and the rackets had, of course, been shown much more forcefully in *The Public Enemy* (1931) and MGM's own *The Wet Parade* (1932), and was to be again in *The Roaring Twenties* (1939).

War was a subject for comedy as far back as Aristophanes. During World War I Chaplin presented *Shoulder Arms* (1918) so it is not surprising that, in addition to all the Flagg-and-Quirt, battling-service-buddy films, several leading comedians also poked fun at military life. First were Moran and Mack, "the Two Black Crows," in *Anybody's War* (1930), followed by *Dough Boys* (1930), Keaton's second talkie, *Half Shot at Sunrise* (1930), with Wheeler and Woolsey, *A Soldier's Plaything* (1931), with Harry Langdon, *Suicide Fleet* (1931), with William ("Screen") Boyd, Robert Armstrong and James Gleason all in love with Ginger Rogers, *Sky Devils* (1932), with Spencer Tracy and William ("Stage") Boyd pursuing Ann Dvorak, *Pack Up Your Troubles* (1932), with Laurel and Hardy as Army buddies, and *Sons O' Guns* (1936), with Joe E. Brown. The title *Pack Up Your Troubles* was used again in 1938 for another wartime comedy with Jane Withers and the Ritz Brothers. The one that got the best reviews, however, was *Private Jones* (1933), described as a satire on the Army, in which Lee Tracy rebelled against the system, personified by his lieutenant, Donald Cook.

Besides all thees films about the war itself and its consequences, several others were made about two historical developments that grew directly out of the war, the Russian Revolution and the Irish "troubles." Russian themes had been popular in late silents, and the '30s saw several musicals and comedies involving Russian émigrés in Paris, but the first talkie drama about the Revolution was *The World and the Flesh* (1932), in which a group of disguised aristocrats attempt to flee the country in a boxcar, among them a dancer (Miriam Hopkins), mistress of a grand duke (Alan Mowbray). They are about to embark for France when the town is taken over by a sea captain (George Bancroft) and his crew. In the end only the dancer escapes execution. In *Scarlet Dawn* (1932), in pre-Revolutionary Russia Douglas Fairbanks, Jr., was an Army officer and Nancy Carroll a servant girl who saves his life. Using some family jewels for bribery, they escape to Constantinople. The *Times* found the film unsatisfactory.

But by far the most ambitious and impressive treatment of the Russian Revolution was *Rasputin and the Empress* (1932), which would be historically significant if only because of the unique appearance together of the three Barrymores, John, billed first as Prince Chegodieff (a composite of the young noblemen who killed Rasputin), Ethel as the Czarina and Lionel as Rasputin. Written by Charles MacArthur and directed by Richard Boleslawski, the film was not only superbly acted but lavishly produced. Ralph Morgan could hardly have been better as the gentle, naïve Czar and Diana Wynyard shone as Natasha, a lady in waiting (fictitious), the fiancée of Chegodieff.

The picture opens in 1913, with the celebration of the three hundredth anniversary of the Romanoff dynasty. Following the facts of history, when the Czarevitch (Tad Alexander), the adored little brother of four older sisters, seems near death from hemophilia, the Czarina, willing to try anything, calls in the bizarre monk Rasputin, who apparently heals the boy by hypnosis, and in no time has the imperial family in his power. He is not only politically ambitious but lecherous as well; at one point he rapes Natasha—a fictional touch that cost MGM a fortune when the real Prince and Princess Youssopoff successfully sued on the grounds that Chegodieff and Natasha were based on them.

The anonymous *New Yorker* reviewer, now identified as Pauline Kael, asserts that all three Barrymores were at their worst. The

Ralph Morgan, Ethel Barrymore, Gustavf von Seyffertitz, Lionel Barrymore,
John Barrymore, Tad Alexander in **Rasputin and the Empress**

fact is that Lionel gives an extremely flamboyant performance, but how else could any actor play the monster Rasputin? The prolonged scene in which Chegodieff apparently cannot kill him, neither with poison, bullets nor a crowbar, and finally holds his head under the icy water of a river is harrowing indeed. According to legend, the real Czarina on a visit to London about 1912 asked to meet the beautiful American actress who was said to resemble her, so who could have been better cast than Ethel?

Irish subjects were very popular in silents, but less so in talkies. Four were made about Ireland's final, bitter battle to free itself from English rule, a struggle that erupted with the doomed Easter Week rising of 1916.

The Key (1934) took no sides politically, but used the Black and Tan occupation of Dublin in 1920 as the setting for an adult, extremely well-acted triangle drama. A philandering British Army officer (William Powell) finds a former love (Edna Best) now married to a British Intelligence officer (Colin Clive), who at first suspects nothing. But when he finds the two together, he goes on a tour of pubs which leads to his capture by the Irish freedom fighters as a hostage, to be traded only for the life of their leader (Donald Crisp), about to be hanged. How Powell redeems himself by getting the husband freed makes a most impressive film, in which the atmosphere of the time and place are very well captured.

Of the other three films on the troubles, two were obviously made as attempted follow-ups on a much-admired third. Among the lesser, *Beloved Enemy* (1936), which was to have been called *Love Under Fire,* was a rather incredible tale of an Irish rebel leader (Brian Aherne) who falls in love with the titled daughter (Merle Oberon) of a British diplomat (Henry Stephenson)—a romance termed by one New York critic *"The Informer* in evening clothes." It was evidently inspired by the fate of Michael Collins, an Irish leader who negotiated the agreement with England that created the Free State but left the four northern counties still under British rule—an arrangement that after six decades is still causing endless bloodshed.

In this version the Collins character is Dennis Riordan, and his innocent but indiscreet romance with Lady Helen Drummond is what causes his men to suspect that he has sold out to the enemy. Chief among them are his best friend and bodyguard O'Rourke (Jerome Cowan in his film debut) and die-hard Burke (Donald Crisp). O'Rourke is given the job of assassinating Riordan; he does it, then turns the gun on himself, while Riordan dies in Lady Helen's arms in a Dublin drugstore.

1937 brought not only the dreadful *Parnell,* but a disappointing version of *The Plough and the Stars,* based on Sean O'Casey's tragic drama of the Easter Week rising, written by Dudley Nichols and directed by John Ford, the same team who in 1935 had dazzled the critics with *The Informer.* Barbara Stanwyck and Preston Foster played Nora and Jack Clitheroe, a young married couple caught up in the strife when he is appointed an officer in the rebel army. The cast included half a

dozen present or former Abbey players, notably Barry Fitzgerald as Fluther Good, Arthur Shields and Una O'Connor.

According to Ella Smith's *Starring Miss Barbara Stanwyck,* after the picture was finished, a new executive producer decided a married couple was not exciting enough, so the two stars should be lovers. An assistant director shot some scenes with this change, "ruining Ford's film, O'Casey's story and Stanwyck's performance." The original version was shown in England and Ireland, but not unfortunately in the United States. What admirers of the play resented most was not only softening O'Casey's ending, in which Jack is killed and Nora goes mad, but sacrificing the rich variety of background characters to their love story.

It is unlikely that either *Beloved Enemy* or *The Plough and the Stars* (both totally lacking in period atmosphere) would ever have been made were it not for the universal acclaim that had greeted *The Informer* (1935), John Ford's classic version of Liam O'Flaherty's novel. Ford and his favorite scenarist, Dudley Nichols, had been hoping to make this film ever since 1930, but only when Ford had repeatedly proved himself with hits like *The Lost Patrol* (1934) were they given the green light. So well had they planned every detail that the production was completed in an incredible three weeks, and since it was not regarded as important, executive interference was minimal. Most film historians pay detailed tribute to Ford's masterful use of the camera, lighting and the sound track to establish mood, atmosphere and smooth transitions, as well as to suggest symbolism.

From the opening shot of hulking, stupid Gypo Nolan (Victor McLaglen in a performance well worth its Oscar) lumbering along a shadowy street while a boy in a ragged cap and sweater leans against a lamppost singing "The Rose of Tralee," the feel of strife-torn Dublin in 1922 is overwhelming. A poster offering a British reward of twenty pounds for fugitive Frankie McPhillip (Wallace Ford) reminds Gypo, in a brief flashback, of their good days together; he tears the poster off the wall.

Then he sees his girl, Katie Madden (Margot Grahame), who has obviously taken to the streets, picking up a man, whom Gypo furiously tosses into the gutter. Taunting him with his lack of money, Katie points out a window display advertising passage to America for ten pounds, then rushes off. The poster Gypo threw away is picked up by Frankie, who presently finds Gypo eating in a cheap hash-house. On the run for six months, Frankie has come home to see his mother. We also learn that Gypo was thrown out of the rebel organization, presumably the IRA, because he could not kill as ordered. All the while Gypo is picturing the poster and the steamship ad, so he is next seen in British headquarters betraying Frankie's whereabouts.

While Frankie is visiting with his mother (Una O'Connor) and his sister Mary (Heather Angel), a British truck pulls up, he tries to escape and is shot down in his own house. Gypo gets his reward from the contemptuous British, but, as he leaves, outside stands a blind beggar, who from now on follows him everywhere, like the voice of conscience. To divert suspicion, Gypo goes to Frankie's wake. Outside the house the street singer is sadly crooning "The Minstrel Boy"; inside, the mourners are reciting the Rosary. Gypo behaves so loudly and clumsily that he gives himself away, especially when some of his coins drop on the floor. As a trap, Gallagher (Preston Foster), Mary McPhillip's fiancé, asks Gypo's help in tracking down the informer. At random he names one Rat Mulligan, but no one believes him, and two men are assigned to follow him as he wanders from pub to pub, squandering his blood money on strangers, especially a fawning toady (J. M. Kerrigan), who hails him as "King Gypo."

At Madame Betty's after-hours "shibeen," he treats everyone, leads boozy choruses of Irish songs and ends up giving an unhappy English girl (Grizelda Hervey) five pounds

Margot Grahame, Victor McLaglen in The Informer

for passage home, whereupon the madam (May Boley) demands four pounds more for the girl's board. The IRA men, who have been keeping track of every penny Gypo spent, now close in and take him to a kangaroo court, but by this time he has forgotten he even accused Mulligan (Donald Meek), a timid little tailor, who, in the only humorous scene, readily clears himself.

Gypo finally breaks down, but still manages to escape and flees to Katie's room, where by her fireside he enjoys a few moments' solace. As he sleeps, she leaves him to plead with Mary and Gallagher for his life, but his executioner has already been chosen. By now it is morning, and as Frankie's mother attends early Mass, Gypo, shot down on the street, staggers into the church and falls at her feet, begging her forgiveness, which she grants: "Sure you didn't know what you were doin'." Looking up toward heaven, Gypo cries, "See, Frankie? Your own mother forgives me!" and dies—a highly theatrical, yet totally convincing, end to this remarkable film.

To everyone's surprise, *The Informer* was the most honored film of its year, winning four Oscars (best actor, director, screenplay and musical score) and the New York Film Critics' prize for best picture. Even *The New Yorker* still finds "the work all of a piece—naive, yet powerful."

50

"RIPPED FROM TOMORROW'S HEADLINES" Timely Films

The futility of war was by no means the only serious issue dealt with on screen in the '30s. The phrase "socially conscious," usually associated with plays and novels, could be applied with equal justice to a surprising number of films. Considering the Production Code, the power of the New York offices, the general fear of offending anyone and the public's overwhelming preference for escapist fare, the wonder is not that more outspoken films were not made but that any were made at all.

Even the gangster cycle and films exposing yellow journalism and ruthless mouthpieces, though couched in melodramatic terms, were timely in reflecting trends of the day. Many of these revealed the general contempt for the Eighteenth Amendment, unpopularly known as Prohibition. *That* national problem at least was solved once and for all with Repeal, in December 1933. Meanwhile, in addition to incidental references in scores of films, four were made specifically about Prohibition, two comic, two serious.

What! No Beer? (1933) teamed Keaton and Durante as partners in a brewery whose beer proves to have no alcoholic content. "Mr. Durante's peculiar form of humor rather puts Mr. Keaton in the shade," the *Times* noted, but the film contained "many hilarious incidents," including a car chase in which the pursuing gangsters are stopped by beer barrels rolling downhill. More sophisticated was *A Lady's Profession* (1933), in which Alison Skipworth and Roland Young were a titled British brother and sister operating a New York speakeasy where they serve only nonalcoholic beverages and so run afoul of the booze-pushing mob.

MGM's *The Wet Parade* (1932), based on an Upton Sinclair novel, was an ambitious film over two hours long, which so thoroughly explored both the dangers of drink and the evils of Prohibition that it ended up taking no side. The cast was listed in two parts, "The Parade in the South" and "The Parade in the North." In the South in 1915 we meet the Chilcote family, Roger (Lewis Stone), a courtly aristocrat but a hopeless drunk, who after a two-day binge kills himself in a pigpen, to the shock of his wife (Emma Dunn), his son Roger Jr. (Neil Hamilton), who goes to New York to become a writer, and his daughter Maggie May (Dorothy Jordan).

In New York young Roger stays at a small residential hotel run by hard-working Mrs.

Tarleton (Clara Blandick) and her son Kip (Robert Young), while Mr. Tarleton (Walter Huston) spends his time talking big in saloons. The 1916 Wilson-Hughes election, the declaration of war and the advent of Prohibition are all accurately depicted. Tarleton must now pay exorbitant prices even for phony whiskey. When his wife breaks a bottle, in a drunken rage he kills her and is sentenced to life.

Meanwhile Maggie May has come North and married Kip, who becomes a dry agent, working with his comical friend Abe (Jimmy Durante). Roger Chilcote, Jr., a successful playwright, is involved with Eileen (Myrna Loy), an entertainer, who deserts him when he goes blind from rotgut liquor. In the climax Kip is kidnaped by bootleggers and saved from death by Abe at the cost of his own life. Even the dry agents themselves speak of the hopeless futility of their task and note how Prohibition has actually increased drinking.

Dedicated to President Roosevelt, Paramount's *Song of the Eagle* (1933), which was to have been called *The Beer Baron*, took a firmer stand, showing how a decent German-American brewer (Jean Hersholt), who lost a son in the war, is forced out of business by Prohibition, but refuses to violate the law. As his fortunes decline, one of his former drivers (Charles Bickford) becomes a leading bootlegger, who ultimately kills the old man. His surviving son (Richard Arlen) gathers his American Expeditionary Force buddies for a showdown with the gangsters and restores law and order. At the end the film boldly prophesies that the end of Prohibition will mean the end of racketeers.

Prohibition and organized crime were not the only current problems dramatized on screen. In *Breach of Promise* (1932) a senatorial candidate (Chester Morris) is almost ruined when a girl (Mae Clarke) falsely brings such a suit against him. *Alimony Madness* (1933), very badly reviewed, told of an architect (Leon Waycoff) who loses all his money in the crash and is sent to alimony jail.

Later he marries a nice girl (Helen Chandler), but their life is made so miserable by his ex-wife (Charlotte Merriam) that the second wife finally kills her—and is acquitted. Other films took a lighter approach. Several already covered satirized radio, especially sponsors and commercials: *Crooner* (1932), *Blessed Event* (1932), *Professional Sweetheart* (1933), *Romance in the Rain* (1934). *Grand Slam* (1933) kidded the public's passion for bridge tournaments.

Another kind of timely film dealt with real people, thinly disguised, still living or only recently dead. *Silver Dollar* (1932) did this for H. A. W. Tabor as *I Loved a Woman* (1933) did for Samuel Insull, a trend that culminated in *Citizen Kane* (1946). There were also the numerous variations on the careers of Walter Winchell and mouthpiece William Fallon. These were not the heavy-breathing *romans à clef* of later decades like *Valley of the Dolls, The Carpetbaggers,* and *The Greek Tycoon,* but with a few exceptions were tastefully done.

Based on a story, *The Goldfish Bowl, It's Tough to Be Famous* (1932) was clearly inspired by the public idolatry of Lindbergh, but the object of the satire was not the modest hero himself but the people exploiting him for their own profit. A young naval officer (Douglas Fairbanks, Jr.) who risks his life to save a submarine crew finds himself overwhelmed with national adulation that destroys his privacy and almost wrecks his romance.

Considering the possibilities, even *The Night Mayor* (1932) was relatively mild in its treatment of a dapper playboy mayor named Bobby Kingston (Lee Tracy) who loves sports, the theater and especially one actress (Evalyn Knapp) even while his administration is being investigated. To avoid scandal he marries his girl off to a writer (Donald Dillaway). He is last seen leading a "Bring Back Beer" parade. In 1932 Jimmy Walker and Betty Compton were hardly in a position to sue, but in any case films have always been kind to Walker, as in *Hallelujah, I'm a Bum* (1937) and *Beau James* (1957).

In *The Half-Naked Truth* (1932) Tracy, having meanwhile done the best Winchell take-off in *Blessed Event,* offered another satirical cartoon as a press agent based, according to the *Times,* on the once well-known Harry Reichenbach. Because of its then daring title, this film acquired a notorious reputation unjustified by its content. To publicize the career of a singer (Lupe Velez), masquerading as Princess Exotica, an escaped harem beauty, the press agent uses such devices as introducing a lion into her hotel suite as her supposed pet. Tracy played much the same kind of role in *Bombshell* (1933), which might be considered part of this trend, since it was thought to be a spoof of Clara Bow.

Other films took their real-life subjects more seriously. *The Match King* (1932), though adapted from a novel, was clearly based on the rise and fall of Ivar Kreuger, who was said to have invented the "three on a match" superstition to increase his sales by one third. The film covers only 1929–32, during which the antihero (Warren William in his most ruthless tycoon role) returns from Chicago to Sweden, where he takes over a failing match factory and raises a loan on his supposed American assets. As he goes from swindling to forgery to blackmail and murder, he uses women all over Europe until he falls for a glamorous film star, Marta Molnar (Lily Damita), who leaves him for Hollywood and then a gypsy violinist. When his empire collapses, the match king kills himself.

The only one of these films deplored as tasteless was *Sing, Sinner, Sing* (1933), in which Leila Hyams was oddly cast as a torch singer tried for the murder of her playboy husband (Donald Dillaway), who presumably killed himself—an obvious attempt to cash in on the Libby Holman-Smith Reynolds scandal, which was also the inspiration for *Reckless* (1935).

On the other hand, *The Man Who Dared* (1933) was an altogether sympathetic biography of an admirable politician, Anton Cermak, the mayor of Chicago who early in 1933 was killed by a man trying to assassinate the newly elected President Roosevelt. The hero (Preston Foster) is called Jan Novak, but otherwise the film sticks close to the facts. In spanning more than six decades, it followed the through-the-years pattern so extraordinarily popular in 1933, with impeccable period atmosphere all the way. The hero's Bohemian background is also solidly detailed, making this one of the few ethnic films of its time.

An opening subtitle pays tribute to the immigrants who have contributed so much to America. Beginning the year of the Chicago fire, 1871, we follow Jan from boyhood. Fired from a mine, he goes to Chicago, where he meets a waitress (Zita Johann), whom he later most happily marries. Encouraged by an Irish politician (Frank Sheridan), he becomes a state senator and makes his name vigorously defending a miners' strike. After quick glimpses of the war and Prohibition, a montage shows Chicago becoming the crime capital of the country. As mayor Jan hopes to rehabilitate the city's good name with the Century of Progress exposition, but before it opens he is shot. Even then he says he's glad it was he, not FDR.

Stolen Holiday (1937), like *The Match King,* dealt with financial skulduggery in high European circles. Despite a vehement disclaimer, no one doubted that this lavishly produced film was based directly on the Stavisky affair, which had rocked France a few years before, when it was revealed that a multimillion-franc swindler had been protected by police officials, legislators and even cabinet ministers, whom he presumably paid off. As the Stavisky character, called Stefan Orloff, Claude Rains gave an unusually brilliant performance, but as his wife (Kay Francis), a mannequin who becomes a modiste, was the star, perhaps too much time was given to her troubled love for Ian Hunter. At the end Orloff is rather unconvincingly murdered, because, the *Times* suggested, the Legion of Decency would not permit him to commit suicide, as the real Stavisky had apparently done.

Walker, Cermak and Stavisky were real political figures, but most screen politicians were fictitious, running for mayor of imaginary cities or representing unnamed states in Congress. Compared to doctors, lawyers and reporters, they were a tiny minority, scarcely thirty in all, including even border-line cases.

Marie Dressler's *Politics* (1931), covered elsewhere, was a farce with no particular point of view, but some of the best '30s films on political themes were sharply satirical, starting with *The Dark Horse* (1932), which sparkled with that delightful irreverence that was a Warners specialty. By a fluke the Progressive party finds itself saddled with a candidate for governor (Guy Kibbee) "so dumb that every time he opens his mouth he subtracts from the sum total of human knowledge." Obviously he can't be left to his own devices, so at the suggestion of a loyal party worker (Bette Davis) the leaders hire as campaign manager a smooth operator (Warren William) whom she loves, even though he is in jail for delinquent alimony payments to his ex-wife (Vivienne Osborne).

He adapts a Lincoln speech for the candidate's first public utterance, but the opposition candidate, who speaks first, uses the same speech, whereupon the manager denounces him for plagiarism. But the dark horse by answering every question with "Yes . . . and, again, no" forges so close to victory that the opposition frames him with the manager's ex-wife. To avoid scandal, he must remarry her, but after the election he proves the second marriage isn't valid. The plot was routine, but the pace was fast and the lines funny, especially in an election year.

1932 was a big year for political films, both serious and light—even musical, though, surprisingly, *Of Thee I Sing*, the first musical to win a Pulitzer Prize, was never filmed. George M. Cohan made his talkie debut in *The Phantom President*, a fairly amusing blend of satire and mistaken identity farce. He played a candidate totally lacking in charisma and his double, a charming medicine show man,

who is hired to appear for him in public, with all the expected complications. Though Cohan at fifty-four looked old enough to run for President, he also looked too old to woo Claudette Colbert, who falls for the medicine man. In fact, the candidate grows so jealous of his double that he plots to have him shanghaied out of the country—only he himself is taken instead. The Rodgers and Hart songs have not survived, but the film is full of sly touches characteristic of Paramount comedy: presidential portraits come to life, characters speak in rhyme and in one memorable shot the image of a senator's pompous face dissolves into that of a horse's rear end.

The Fox musical *Stand Up and Cheer* (1934), dealt with elsewhere, also had elements of satire, with Warner Baxter appointed Secretary of Amusement, but far sharper was another musical, *Thanks a Million* (1935), in which Dick Powell, steered by cynical Fred Allen (in an apparently promising film debut), runs for governor of Pennsylvania on sheer charm and singing ability, replacing lush Raymond Walburn. In the climax Powell, who has lost his girl (Ann Dvorak) along the campaign trail, confesses to the voters that he is a fraud, without qualifications, but they are so charmed by his candor that they sweep him into office. The Yacht Club Boys contributed an amusing number that satirized the proliferating alphabetical agencies of the New Deal.

But undoubtedly the wittiest political satire of the decade was *First Lady* (1937), from a play by George S. Kaufman and Katharine Dayton, a Broadway hit with Jane Cowl. As an opening subtitle noted, in Washington the hand that rocks the cradle frequently rocks the capital, for this was a comedy of archrivalry among official wives. Lucy Chase Wayne (Kay Francis), supposedly the granddaughter of a turn-of-the-century President, vaguely suggestive of Alice Roosevelt Longworth, is now the wife of the Secretary of State (Preston Foster), whom she hopes to make the next President. She suspects, however, that her dearest enemy, Irene Hibbard

(Verree Teasdale in a deliciously catty performance), the bored heiress wife of an elderly Supreme Court justice (Walter Connolly), is about to divorce the old gentleman and marry a young congressman (Victor Jory), whom she will maneuver into the presidency. How Lucy and her cohorts try to prevent this by starting a small boom for the judge, which then gets out of hand, makes a hilarious film, which along with Washington officialdom nails to the wall such familiar types as a superclubwoman (Louise Fazenda), head of the Women's League for Peace, Patriotism and Purity, and a smug newspaper tycoon (Grant Mitchell).

The last comedy of the decade to involve politics was *The Great Man Votes* (1939), starring John Barrymore as an erudite lush, widowed father of two children, now reduced to a lowly night watchman, who happens to be the last registered voter in a factory district. When the local party machine pins its hopes on the way this district goes, his vote becomes important and so does he. To please his children, he allows himself to be exploited, but gradually pulls himself together, with the aid of their teacher (Katherine Alexander). At the end he is about to start life anew as the commissioner of education. For a comedy, this leaned too heavily toward sentimentality, but avoided the melodrama of many political films.

This surely could not be said of *Washington Masquerade* (1932), in which John's brother Lionel starred as a widowed Midwestern senator trapped into marriage by a designing blonde (Karen Morley), who persuades him to take a bribe from the Water Power lobby. During an investigation he admits the truth, and at the end of his testimony collapses and dies.

Equally sensational was *The Washington Merry Go Round* (1932), released just before the election, which applied the title of a best-selling book and widely syndicated political column to an original story by Maxwell Anderson, about a crusading young congressman (Lee Tracy) whose battle against corruption leads to his being unseated by a phony recount. With difficulty he convinces an elderly senator (Walter Connolly) that, though above bribery, he continually wins large sums at poker only because an ambitious lobbyist (Alan Dinehart) lets him. About to attack the lobbyist, the senator is poisoned, but his granddaughter (Constance Cummings) and the young man finally expose the truth and the lobbyist kills himself.

Unique in the decade was *Gabriel over the White House* (1933), based on a British novel about a party-hack President of the United States (Walter Huston) who, while recovering from an auto accident, has a mysterious vision—pictured only as a fluttering of the curtain on his window—which transforms him into a different, much better, man. He fires his corrupt cabinet, starting with the Secretary of State (Arthur Byron), and, just as he is about to be impeached, dismisses Congress, establishing himself as a benevolent dictator, who communicates directly with the people via radio (anticipating FDR's fireside chats).

An army of a million unemployed is marching on Washington (as indeed had almost happened a year before). He meets them in Baltimore, but unfortunately their leader (David Landau) is gunned down by a powerful gangster (C. Henry Gordon), who is later executed by presidential order. Having solved unemployment and the crime wave, he turns to foreign policy. Inviting representatives of important countries aboard his yacht, he insists that instead of squandering billions arming for the next war they pay the debts owed the United States from the last one.

Just as success crowns all his efforts, he dies of a heart attack, mourned by his faithful secretary (Franchot Tone) and his assistant (Karen Morley). The most amazing fact about this powerful film, which attacked head on so many burning national issues, is that it was ever made at all, much less by MGM.

In the exciting topical melodrama *The President Vanishes* (1934), with the country on the brink of war, whipped on to hysteria with the slogan "Save America's honor!", the President (Arthur Byron) suddenly disappears. Said the *Times:* "The enemies of the republic . . . are the anonymous czars who dominate the munitions and banking fields, the publisher of a large newspaper chain, the lobbyists and propagandists who inflame the legislators and the populace at the bidding of their masters." In the midst of them all was Rosalind Russell (billed fifth) as a Washington hostess, wife of Sidney Blackmer, at whose dinner table the war plans are hatched by the likes of Walter Kingsford, Edward Arnold, Jason Robards and Osgood Perkins.

As the war fever cools, all the President's enemies are blamed for kidnaping him, including the Gray Shirts, a violent Fascist group led by a fanatic (Edward Ellis), but it was actually the President himself who engineered the plan, with the aid of a secret service man (Paul Kelly), and succeeded in turning the mood of the country around.

There were any number of films about crusading D.A.'s and reform mayors or governors routing the forces of corruption (e.g., *Manhattan Melodrama, The Cat's Paw, The Glass Key, Judge Hardy's Children*), most covered elsewhere, but one of the most successful po-

Peggy Conklin, Paul Kelly, Andy Devine, Arthur Byron, Janet Beecher in The President Vanishes

litical films of the decade and certainly the best-remembered was Frank Capra's *Mr. Smith Goes to Washington* (1939). When the junior senator of a Western state dies in office, the governor (Guy Kibbee), ordered by the state boss, media tycoon Jim Taylor (Edward Arnold in his nastiest tycoon role) and senior Senator Joe Payne (Claude Rains) to appoint someone harmless, who will not question their profitable plans to build an unnecessary dam, at the suggestion of his young sons names Jefferson Smith (James Stewart), a leader of the Boy Rangers with no political experience. The son of a murdered liberal editor, he idolizes his father's dear friend, the distinguished Senator Payne, known as "the White Knight of the Senate."

To everyone's consternation he disappears from Union Station and takes a sight-seeing bus to view all the national shrines, especially the Lincoln Memorial, where he overhears a small boy reading the Gettysburg Address to his grandfather. When he finally turns up at his office, his awe is not at all shared by Saunders (Jean Arthur), the cynical Washington secretary assigned to him, still less by Diz (Thomas Mitchell), the alcoholic reporter who loves her.

When the press corps traps him into foolish statements and embarrassing candid shots, he is the laughingstock of Washington. Senator Payne (whose office is lined with autographed photos of real celebrities of the '20s and '30s) kindly counsels more discretion. In the Senate Chamber (*exactly* reproduced in Hollywood, since the real one could not be used), to his great pride Smith is given Daniel Webster's desk. Hostile senators comment on his adverse publicity. Further baited by reporters in the press bar, he goes around town knocking several out.

Hesitantly he introduces his cherished bill to establish a boys' camp, with kindly encouragement from the Vice-President (Harry Carey). Pennies pour in from the eager boys. Shortly after, when the conflicting bill for the dam on the same site is introduced, Payne arranges for his attractive daughter (Astrid

Jean Arthur, James Stewart in
Mr. Smith Goes to Washington

Allwyn) to lure Smith away for the day. Knowing what's ahead, Saunders gets drunk with Diz, tells Smith of plans for the dam and warns him to go home. He questions Payne, who alerts all the other crooks, especially Taylor, who reminds Payne that he wants a national nomination. Confronted again by Smith, Payne tries to justify thirty years of compromise; to accomplish any good, he had to become part of the system.

Unconvinced, Smith speaks out in the Senate, where Payne charges that Smith owns the land in question and wants to profit on it. False testimony and forged documents seem to confirm this. Shattered by this stab in the back, Smith wanders to the Lincoln Memorial, where Saunders finds him weeping and heartens him: "You can't quit now!" He returns to face expulsion from the Senate, but the Vice-President recognizes him and he seizes the floor for a filibuster—one of the most intensely emotional sequences in any '30s film (yet lightened by well-timed touches of humor).

Furious, Taylor uses all his resources of newspapers and radio stations to smear Smith as a megalomaniacal crook. Saunders contacts Smith's mother and the staff of the Boy Rangers' newspaper to print the real facts, but Taylor's goons drive them off the streets. As Smith begins to wear out from sheer exhaustion, Payne brings in huge loads of anti-Smith mail. Discouraged, he nearly breaks down, but directly pleads with Payne. When he finally collapses on the floor, Payne rushes into an anteroom and tries to shoot himself, but, when prevented, shouts that every word Smith has said is true.

Far from recognizing this as a triumph of democracy in action, a warning against incipient home-grown fascism of the Jim Taylor brand, in 1939 senators who should have known better outdid each other in hysterical denunciations, despite critical raves. Punitive legislation against the movie industry was even threatened.

Joseph P. Kennedy, then American ambassador to England, urged Columbia not to release the picture in Europe. Columbia head Harry Cohn replied with a sheaf of laudatory American and Canadian reviews, but Kennedy was still dubious. Eventually, freedom prevailed, and in 1942 when the Nazis banned American films in France, *Mr. Smith* was deliberately the last one shown, and roundly cheered—surely a picture that has earned the often misused word "classic."

None of these films about American politics was in any way propagandistic or ideological, still less favoring one political party over another; fond references to President Roosevelt and the New Deal were regarded as mere healthy patriotism. The few attempts at anti-Red indoctrination were uniformly

disastrous. *Red Salute* and *Fighting Youth* (both 1935) were discussed among campus films, but *Forgotten Commandments* (1932) attacked Russia on its home ground in a lurid exposé of the horrors of life among the Communists. Scenes from De Mille's silent *Ten Commandments* were incorporated as a priest (Harry Beresford) risks his life to tell some young people about Moses and the commandments.

Irving Pichel was a villainous scientist who orders the priest shot, sneers at religion and formulates his own mock commandments. When his mistress (Sari Maritza) falls for a young husband (Gene Raymond), who divorces his wife (Marguerite Churchill) for her, the scientist kills her and wounds her lover. "An emphatic attack against the Soviet pagan ideas," the *Times* noted with approval, but apparently not a successful one, because nothing of the sort was tried again.[1]

The only other '30s film touching on Communism took quite the opposite approach, gaily satirizing the grimness of a party-line life. The unique, delightful *Ninotchka* (1939) was the one in which, MGM proclaimed to the world, "Garbo laughs," as if she had never done so before. In fact, as a commissar she revealed hitherto untapped resources as a comedienne, at first playing her character as glumly deadpan as Buster Keaton, later holding her own in a duel of wits with stage veteran Ina Claire as a haughty Grand Duchess.

From a script by Charles Brackett, Billy Wilder and Walter Reisch, based on a story by Melchior Lengyel, *Ninotchka* was basically an ugly duckling tale, but the particular milieu, the contrast of French and Russian values and the constant sly Lubitsch touches make one wish that MGM had given Garbo

---

[1] Of the three films using the Spanish Civil War as background, one, *Love Under Fire* (1937), was a comedy, *Last Train from Madrid* (1937) was a routine *Grand Hotel* melodrama and *Blockade* (1938) had a spy plot. In none of the three were the opposing sides ever named or identified.

more such opportunities instead of scuttling her career with the totally unworthy *Two-Faced Woman* (1941).

Sent to Paris to raise money for farm machinery by selling jewels once belonging to a Grand Duchess, three minor Soviet functionaries (Sig Rumann, Felix Bressart and Alexander Granach), the most lovable grotesques since Disney's dwarfs, are stymied when the Duchess files an injunction to stop the sale. Meanwhile they are introduced to the joys of *la vie Parisienne* by the Duchess' suave lover, Leon (Melvyn Douglas).

Sent to investigate, their superior, Ninotchka (Garbo) is at first a rigid, humorless bureaucrat, but when Leon goes to work on her she soon thaws, won over especially by luxurious Parisian clothes. While she and Leon are enjoying their love affair—her first —a waiter hired by the Duchess steals the jewels. In a crucial scene the Duchess agrees to return them if Ninotchka will give up Leon and return to Russia. Unable to follow her, he meets her in Constantinople, where her three friends have decided to stay and open a restaurant.

To most Americans the threat of a Communist take-over was totally unreal compared to the pressing internal problems of the troubled decade: the continued crime wave, rebellious youth, miscarriages of justice (especially in the South), mob violence and, always in the background, creeping into everyone's life like a poisonous gray fog, the pervasive, inescapable effects of the Depression. All these issues were dealt with in films—not frequently but forcefully.

In the '20s "youth" had always meant the flaming variety, those dancing daughters, jazz babies and campus sheiks who cavorted through so many silents. They lingered for a while in a few films like *Wild Company* (1930), *The Naughty Flirt* (1931) and *Young Sinners* (1931), but writers had begun to discover another kind of youth, the middle- or lower-class youngsters, especially boys, whose wild ways brought not merely parental worry but trouble with the law—

those who would later be called juvenile delinquents. Some such films had hopeful endings, such as Borzage's *Young America* (1932), in which a druggist (Spencer Tracy) is determined to prosecute two runaway boys who broke into his store, but instead his wife (Doris Kenyon), influenced by a kindly judge (Ralph Bellamy), persuades him to let one of the boys (Tommy Conlon) live with them.

Of much sterner stuff was *Are These Our Children?* (1931), a timely problem drama about a smart-aleck high school dropout (Eric Linden), who defies his kindly grandmother (Beryl Mercer), spurns a nice girl (Rochelle Hudson) for a faster one (Arline Judge) and while burglarizing a Queens delicatessen owned by a family friend (William Orlamond) inadvertently kills the old man. For a while he gets away with it, and even when arrested basks in the publicity and insists on conducting his own defense, which depends on a phony alibi, but when one of his friends (Ben Alexander) breaks down and blurts out the truth, the other two boys get life and our hero gets the chair. The prison scene in which he says his last goodbye in turn to his grandmother, the nice girl and his weeping little brother (Billy Butts) is a powerful one. Said the *Times*: "It is a lithograph of one section of the feverish New York scene that will not be lost on New Yorkers."

One of the first films to deal specifically with a familiar Depression disaster, a run on a bank by depositors terrified of losing their savings, was Capra's neatly plotted, if melodramatic, *American Madness* (1932). As president of a big New York bank, Walter Huston believes that character is the greatest asset a client can have and makes loans on that basis—but so busy does this keep him that he neglects his wife (Kay Johnson), who turns for consolation to a crooked cashier (Gavin Gordon).

The honest assistant cashier (Pat O'Brien), in love with the president's secretary (Constance Cummings), catches on to the guilty pair and goes to the man's home to confront them. At exactly this time the bank vault, left conveniently open, is robbed of one hundred thousand dollars. The cashier planned it this way, to pay off gambling debts to gangsters, and, of course, he has the perfect alibi. Innocent O'Brien is suspected of complicity because he cannot explain his whereabouts without giving the president's wife away. The amount of the robbery is so quickly exaggerated that people believe it was five million, and the run begins. O'Brien calls on the small-business men to whom Huston has made easy loans, and in true Capra populist style "the little people" rally round and start making deposits, thus turning the tide. The truth comes out, the guilty cashier is caught and the president forgives his erring wife. *American Madness* caught very well the panicky mood of 1932.

Almost all other topical dramas came from Warners, which, starting with the classic gangster films *Little Caesar* and *The Public Enemy* (both 1931), boldly tackled current social problems with almost documentary realism. The first and in many ways the best was *I Am a Fugitive from a Chain Gang* (1932), which on one level reflected the popularity of prison pictures in the early '30s but went far beyond any other in indicting the system, especially Southern justice.

Based on a pseudonymous autobiography, this powerful film traces the misfortunes of an ex-sergeant in the AEF (Paul Muni) who while looking for work cannot even pawn his Army medals. Trapped by a chance acquaintance (Preston Foster) into robbing a lunch wagon, he is sentenced to five years on a chain gang, the inhumanity of which is pictured in brutal detail. In desperation he escapes and starts a new life in Chicago, in five years rising to a good position in a bridge-building firm. But his spiteful blond landlady (Glenda Farrell) first blackmails him into marrying her, then later turns him in. He returns to the prison camp to serve a nominal ninety days, but at the end of that time the redneck prison commissioner refuses to release him.

Once again he escapes, only now into Depression America, with no chance even of a job. In the unforgettable last scene he sneaks home to say goodbye to his loyal second wife (Helen Vinson, sympathetic for once), and when she asks how he lives, he says simply, "I steal." Thus through no fault of his own he has again been forced outside the law in this uncompromisingly grim tragedy.

Parallel in some ways but not quite as harrowing (reflecting, faintly, the spark of hope kindled by the New Deal) was *Heroes for Sale* (1933), which also dealt with the problems of a returning veteran (Richard Barthelmess), in this case rather specialized. Cheated of a medal which was given to a banker's cowardly son, he was also led by his war injuries into morphine addiction. To support his habit, he embezzles from a bank, is fired and sent to a "narcotics farm" for a year and is apparently cured.

Now the plot moves off in a completely different direction. In Chicago he finds work in a laundry, where his ideas quickly bring promotion. But a Communist inventor (Robert Barrat) perfects an automatic laundry device and quickly turns capitalist. The hero invests in it and persuades other workers to do so, with the understanding that it will not cost them their jobs. Then a new owner fires them all, and in true Luddite style they attack the machines, not the boss. Though Barthelmess tries to stop the ensuing riot, in which his wife (Loretta Young) is killed, he is blamed for inciting it and sent to prison. Even when released he is chased from Chicago by "Red Squads" as a dangerous agitator.

Meanwhile he has contributed all his profits to a soup kitchen for the unemployed, run by Aline MacMahon, while he himself becomes a hobo and to those who remember him a kind of folk hero. This was an occasionally powerful but extremely confused film, yet it still remains "a major filmic reflection of the Depression."

Warners' next timely venture, released in September 1933, was *Wild Boys of the Road*, about high school youngsters forced to leave

Paul Muni and David Landau (at right) in **I Am a Fugitive from a Chain Gang**

home to lessen the burden on their unemployed parents, one of the most pathetic of Depression phenomena. The heroes (Frankie Darro and Edwin Phillips) ride in freight cars hoping to find work but find instead an ever-growing army of young hobos. When a railroad official forces them off a train, they beat him, but only because he raped one of their number (Rochelle Hudson).

In Cleveland they establish a "sewer city" to live in, and when police come to eject them, they fight back with stones, only to be routed by fire hoses. In New York they settle in a garbage dump. Darro is used by some thieves and arrested, but, unlike the victimized heroes of *I Am a Fugitive* and *Heroes for Sale,* he comes before a kindly judge (Robert Barrat)

with a Blue Eagle on his wall. With rimless glasses he even looks a bit like FDR. "I know your father will be going back to work soon," he tells the boy, and we feel the worst is now over. Despite this overoptimistic ending, *Wild Boys* remains one of the most vivid pictures of one phase of its time.

The last three films all involved violence, the last two between police and embattled minorities. But a more sinister form of violence also reared its ugly head, a form not confined to the '30s but as American as black slavery, the Salem witchcraft trials and the Ku Klux Klan: lynching—the public murder of a helpless victim (in life, though not in films, most often a black man) by a mob of hysterical, sadistically gloating, supposedly respectable citizens. A federal anti-lynching bill drafted by NAACP lawyers in 1935 was defeated by a Southern filibuster.

As film historians have observed, the early '30s saw a number of films with fascist undertones, in which the villains, usually gangsters, are punished outside the law, either by a strong leader, as in *Gabriel over the White House,* or by outraged citizens who take the law into their own hands, as in *Song of the Eagle* and De Mille's *This Day and Age* (1933), in which a group of clean-cut high school boys, led by Richard Cromwell, Eddie Nugent and Ben Alexander, avenge the murder of a beloved old man (Harry Green) by kidnapping a notorious, hitherto untouchable gangster (Charles Bickford). In a night scene ominously suggestive of a Hitler youth rally, with hundreds of youngsters carrying torches and chanting in unison, in a deserted brickyard the leaders tie a rope under the man's arms, hoist him in the air and then proceed to lower him, inch by inch, into a pit of rats! Of course, he confesses, so Q.E.D., the end justified the means.

This Day and Age was the last film to advocate mob rule. In *The Frisco Kid* (1935) the 1850 vigilantes, however justified in their own minds, are shown as wrong in lynching Ricardo Cortez, and only Margaret Lindsay saves Cagney from the same fate. Then in 1936 came *Fury,* Fritz Lang's first American film and the best he was ever to make in Hollywood. Based on a story by Norman Krasna, it centers on an innocent man (Spencer Tracy) jailed in a strange Midwestern town as a suspect in a kidnaping of which he knows nothing. "People don't land in jail unless they're guilty," the townspeople tell each other as rumors spread and hysteria rises. In no time at all a mob is storming the jail. Unable to reach the prisoner, they set fire to the building and cut the firemen's hose, hoping to see him burned alive, before the very eyes of his hysterical fiancée (Sylvia Sidney). For political reasons the governor declines to send in the national guard, but a newsreel camera records everything.

Now comes the twist. The prisoner has secretly escaped, traumatized into a man with one aim in life: revenge. Twenty-two mob leaders are arrested and prosecuted by a conscientious D.A. (Walter Abel). After they have all perjured themselves and produced phony alibis, the newsreel is shown, and they are convicted. From a secret hide-out, unknown even to his fiancée, the intended victim gloats. Morally the twenty-two are as guilty as if they *had* killed him. When his girl tries to convince him that he has already had his revenge, he refuses to relent, until the very last minute. Even this compromise ending does not really weaken this powerful film. "A mature, sober and penetrating investigation of a national blight," said the *Times*.

Mountain Justice (1937), a strong topical melodrama, also involved an attempted lynching. Robert Barrat played a grim backwoods patriarch who horsewhips his grown daughter (Josephine Hutchinson) to teach her respect. Encouraged by her downtrodden mother (Elizabeth Risdon), a kindly doctor (Guy Kibbee) and his perennial fiancée (Margaret Hamilton), the girl goes to New York to study nursing and falls in love with a lawyer

Sylvia Sidney, Spencer Tracy in **Fury**

(George Brent) who had earlier helped convict her father of a shooting. Returning to work with the doctor in a chain of free clinics, she is spurned from the house by her father. When her little sister (Marcia Mae Jones) flees to her rather than become a child bride, the father again tries to horsewhip his older daughter, but this time she fights back and accidentally causes his death. Though defended by Brent, she is convicted of murder and sentenced to twenty-five years, but even this does not satisfy her redneck neighbors, who don their Klan-like hoods to lynch her. Disguised in the same outfits, Brent and Kibbee manage to whisk her to a waiting plane and another state, from which she cannot be extradited.

After *Cabin in the Cotton, I Am a Fugitive from a Chain Gang* and *Mountain Justice,* one might think that Warners had declared its own private Civil War against the unreconstructed South. Though the title of Ward Greene's novel *Death in the Deep South,* based on the 1913 lynching of Northerner Leo Frank in Atlanta, was changed to *They Won't Forget* (1937), presumably meaning the South would never forget having lost the Civil War, the indictment was no less scathing. "A trenchant film editorial against intolerance and hatred," said the *Times.*

Produced and directed by Mervyn LeRoy, from a script by Aben Handel and Robert Rossen and superbly acted, the film reminded some viewers of the Scottsboro trial, a then recent case of Southern injustice. In a middle-sized Southern city an ambitious D.A. (Claude Rains) is waiting for the big case that will send him to the Senate. He gets it when sexy teen-ager Mary Clay (Lana Turner in her film debut) is murdered in Buxton Business College. The audience is led to believe the killer was courtly old Colonel Buxton himself, but he comes from too fine a family to be suspected. There would be no political profit in convicting the terrified black janitor (Clinton Rosemond); he is merely browbeaten into saying what the D.A. wants to hear. But Robert Hale (Edward

Norris), a young teacher, was in the building that day. Though he is happily married (to Gloria Dickson), it is known that the late Mary had a crush on him. Best of all, he's a damned Yankee.

On the flimsiest of circumstantial evidence, Hale is indicted and the case soon becomes a national *cause célèbre.* The North charges prejudice, the South interference. A New York detective is beaten, Hale's New York attorney (Otto Kruger) is stoned. The town has already made up its collective mind. Both lawyers try every flashy trick in the book, but the conclusion is foregone. When the governor signs a pardon, the enraged mob drags Hale from a train and lynches him. No one is arrested. In the last scene a reporter (Allyn Joslyn), who helped whip up the frenzy with his slanted stories, says to the D.A., "Now that it's over, Andy, I wonder if Hale really did it," and the prosecutor replies, almost absently, "I wonder."[2]

Clearly Hale was the victim of inflamed sectional prejudice, but in all fairness it must be remembered that not only did the Ku Klux Klan then flourish in many states outside the South, but so did other native fascist organizations like the Silver Shirts, all dedicated to 100% Americanism, white supremacy and hatred of Negroes, Jews and Catholics, in that order. Three films, two "B's" and an "A," dramatized the institutionalized terrorism of such secret brotherhoods.

First to reach the screen was Columbia's *Legion of Terror* (1936), a routine but fast-moving melodrama in which Bruce Cabot as a Post Office investigator breaks up the "Hooded Legion," though not before it has framed and murdered Ward Bond, brother of Cabot's girl, Marguerite Churchill. In this case the governor does send the national guard in time.

A Nation Aflame (1937), produced by the Halperin brothers for their Treasure Pictures,

[2] *Transient Lady* (1936) and *White Bondage* (1937) also involved attempted lynchings in the Deep South.

Otto Kruger and Claude Rains (both standing) in **They Won't Forget**

was supposedly taken from a story by Thomas Dixon, author of the novel on which *The Birth of a Nation* was based. If so, he must have undergone a radical change of politics, for here the "Avenging Angels," as the bigoted organization is known, are the villains, run by racketeers even as they disseminate antiforeign and "pure womanhood" propaganda.

In a complex plot, the heroine (Norma Trelvar) is the daughter of a governor, who is the puppet of the chief mobster (Noel Madison) but is eventually assassinated by his orders. The girl then goes to her former fiancé, a crusading D.A. (Roger Williams), and offers to set the evil leader up for a scandal that will discredit him. She arranges for some of his trusting followers to break in on him after an apparent all-night orgy with her. He is ruined, but so is she, as she cannot

tell the truth. Her ex-fiancé runs successfully for governor. The highly ironic last scene is at his inaugural parade, in which he is riding with the President of the United States, who pauses for a smile and a salute to the girl standing in the onlooking crowd. She smiles bravely back, but for her there is no happy ending.

Between these two films had come Warners' *Black Legion* (1937), which used the actual name of an organization that had in 1935–36 terrorized the Midwest, especially Michigan. Humphrey Bogart played a factory worker, married to Erin O'Brien Moore and content with his lot until a promotion he expected goes to a Polish-American. Embittered, he falls prey to a nativist group secretly organizing in his town.

Though they preach the standard line about protecting true-blue Americans from the foreign menace, the leaders' motives are as mercenary as ideological, since they profit on the guns and robes members must buy. They run the Pole out of town and Bogart gets his job, but soon loses it by spending too much time proselytizing for the Legion. He takes to drink, beats his wife and in the climax is forced to kill his best friend (Dick Foran), who opposed the Legion.

However, the Legion does not let him down. It provides a defense that rests on the perjured testimony of tartish Helen Flint, who swears that the murder was the outcome of a jealous quarrel. As Bogart sees the horrified looks on his wife and Foran's fiancée (Ann Sheridan), he breaks down and turns state's evidence. The Legion members get life imprisonment. "Editorial cinema at its best," said the *Times,* noting that it was based on the case of a member who had blown the whistle on the real Legion.

Outbreaks of mob violence and lynchings were recognized as antisocial aberrations and condemned by all decent citizens, nor were they exclusive to the '30s. But what of the petty adjustments and frustrations of the Depression, so much less easy to dramatize? Did no films attempt to deal with them? Very few, and even most of these had to climax in melodramatic violence to attract an audience.

One of the few to attack a Depression theme honestly was not made by a major studio, though it was by a major director. This was *Our Daily Bread* (1934), not only written and directed by King Vidor but produced with his own money, a true labor of love. According to his autobiography, he had difficulty raising the money; banks were not interested, until he gained the support of financially sound friends like Chaplin.

Charles Silver's notes for a 1972 showing of the film put it *"Our Daily Bread . . .* is naive, simplistic and awkward. It is also an extremely lovely and lovingly-made film." What Vidor meant to do was a sequel to his justly admired silent, *The Crowd* (1928), by showing what might have happened to the same average young couple, had they been faced

not with the anonymity of a mechanized metropolis but with the much more pressing difficulties of the Depression.

One problem of the film was that Vidor had the very limited cowboy star Tom Keene and Karen Morley, usually competent but not at her best here. They get the rights to an abandoned farm, but, ignorant of agriculture, open up the property to dispossessed passersby, starting with a Swedish family (led by John Qualen).

One by one, with a too perfect symmetry, farmers, carpenters, plumbers, bricklayers, a tailor, even a concert violinist, all of different ethnic backgrounds, contribute their skills to form a perfect co-operative. The very idea of a "commune" frightened off some exhibitors, critics and audiences, especially when the Hearst press denounced it as "pinko." Silver considers the film the kind of thing D. W. Griffith would have done had he been allowed to remain active in the '30s. Its optimism likewise parallels Capra's faith in the goodness of the simple and humble.

But the determining factor that makes *Our Daily Bread* now a historical curiosity rather than a really good film is that Vidor was not that great a writer. He failed to take into account the drive for individual success that motivates most people's lives, even in a Depression. As Andrew Bergman says, "Most of the competitive tensions dissolve when the inhabitants reach the farm, as if it were a kind of Oz."

The only threats to this idyll come not from human inability to co-operate but from two completely extraneous elements: a platinum blond vamp (Barbara Pepper), who almost lures Keene, the chosen leader, away from his people, and then a drought, which leads to the laborious construction of an irrigation ditch, the completion of which makes the last twenty minutes one of the most joyously cinematic finales in any '30s film.

The *New York Times* was ecstatic, hailing it as "a social document of amazing vitality and emotional impact." The *Los Angeles Times,* on the other hand, refused even to advertise it. The leftist press was divided between those who appreciated what Vidor had tried to do and those who put him down as another guilt-ridden liberal. In either case, *Our Daily Bread* has the tone of an earnest editorial or a nobly motivated cartoon.

Another, more sentimental "idyll" about a random assortment of people banding together to weather the Depression was *One More Spring* (1935), a "fantastic and rollicking fable," based on Robert Nathan's 1933 novel. In this case they number only three: a former antique dealer (Warner Baxter), a temperamental concert violinist (Walter King) and an out-of-work actress (Janet Gaynor), who in the novel was a prostitute. In Central Park a kindly street cleaner (Roger Imhof) lets the three of them live in a tool shed in return for violin lessons. They are presently joined by a banker (Grant Mitchell), saved from suicide. In a typical post-Production Code device, when Gaynor turns up with money at the right moment, both Baxter and the audience are allowed to assume the worst, but, of course, she only borrowed it from the street cleaner's wife.

How they get through the winter makes a gently charming comedy-drama. The ending is hopeful, but as Everson puts it, "clearly only a stop-gap, stepping-stone kind of solution awaiting the prosperity that is still elusively just around the corner."

The next film to attack a serious social problem was *Black Fury* (1935), a hotly disputed melodrama about labor strife in the coal mines of Pennsylvania. It became itself a cause of raging controversy between those who thought Warners should be commended for tackling such a subject and those who felt that it completely avoided the very questions it purported to raise. The trouble was blamed not on an unjust economic system or on the owners but on a racketeering strike-breaking agency. Though aware of its limitations, the *Times* called *Black Fury* "by all odds the most notable experiment in social drama since *Our Daily Bread*."

As Joe Radek, a simple, good-natured Polish miner, Paul Muni gave a remarkable performance, perfectly conveying not only the man's accent and mannerisms but the appalling naïveté that lets him be manipulated by a shyster detective agency into leading a wildcat strike, deplored by the responsible union leaders almost as heartily as by the management. Taking refuge in drink when his girl (Karen Morley) runs off with a company cop, he is easily led into walking out of a union meeting to protest the terms the leaders have accepted. The benevolent owners reluctantly call in scabs while striking workers' families starve. But, of course, this is all the fault of the scheming strike-breaking agency, which must foment conflict in order to prosper.

When one of their goons kills a close friend (John Qualen), Joe sneaks into the mine and sets off explosives, threatening total destruction unless the company meets his terms, but the crisis is resolved when the federal government sets everything right and the men go back to work on the terms they should have accepted in the first place. John L. Lewis praised the film, but the liberal weeklies denounced it as completely dishonest.

The next three socially conscious dramas were all based on hit Broadway plays. First came Warners' faithful version of Robert E. Sherwood's 1935 philosophical melodrama *The Petrified Forest* (1936), in which Leslie Howard not only re-created his stage role—a chance few stars were given in the '30s—as Alan Squier, failed writer and rueful, doom-haunted drifter, but also insisted that Humphrey Bogart be granted the same opportunity as his foil, Duke Mantee, a Dillinger-like desperado, a role Warners wanted Cagney or Robinson to play. This was the real beginning of Bogart's screen career.

Though, like the play, the film takes place largely in a roadside lunchroom in the Arizona desert, when Mantee and his henchmen hold the others as hostages, the fact that they cannot leave this room adds to the claustrophobic menace that breaks down inhibitions and crumbles social façades. Bette Davis plays Gabrielle Maple, a spirited girl. half-French, who longs for Paris, where her mother lives, but instead must stay with her sour, super-patriotic father (Porter Hall) and her lively old grandfather (Charles Grapewin), who remembers Billy the Kid and is delighted to meet Mantee.

Gabrielle is loved by Boze Herzinger (Dick Foran), a college football hero now reduced to manning the gas pumps, but from the moment Alan wanders in on his walking tour to nowhere, she is taken with his cosmopolitan air. He goes on his way, only to be brought back along with the wealthy Chisholms (Genevieve Tobin and Paul Harvey) as prisoners of Mantee. Since his life means nothing to him, Alan begs Mantee to kill him, but Mantee is reluctant to kill in cold blood a man he rather likes. In the end, he does and is himself killed by the police. Not until Alan is dead does Gabrielle learn that he left her an insurance policy that will free her to fulfill her dreams. From the plot, it is impossible to convey how perfectly the film captures the atmosphere of the Depression, above all the despair, the conviction that all the frontiers have been closed, that once venerated American institutions have become as fossilized as the ancient trees in the petrified forest.

In 1935 the New York critics were so annoyed when the Pulitzer Prize went to *The Old Maid* that they formed the Drama Critics Circle and started their own annual awards. The first was given to Maxwell Anderson's verse tragedy *Winterset,* filmed in 1936, with several members of the original cast—an act of courage by RKO, since none were screen names. Anderson's poetic dramas have been derided as pretentious, hollow and florid, but they did not sound that way at the time. On both stage and screen, the actors seemed to believe passionately in what they were saying, and consequently so did the audiences.

Winterset returns to a theme Anderson had used before, the notorious Sacco-Vanzetti case. On very scanty evidence, two Italian laborers, known to hold radical views, were convicted of murder in a payroll robbery, and in spite of appeals that dragged on for years and pro-

tests from all over the world, the governor of Massachusetts refused to pardon them, and in 1927 they were executed.

Winterset supposes that one of them left a small son, who at seventeen, stirred by renewed public interest in the case, seeks to avenge his father's death by finding a witness never called, whose testimony could have saved him. The boy, Mio Romagna (Burgess Meredith), when he has tracked the witness, Garth Esdras (Paul Guilfoyle), to the family home in the shadow of the Brooklyn Bridge, falls in love with his sister, Miriamne (Margo). But Mio is not the only one looking for Esdras. Trock Estrella (Eduardo Ciannelli, in a menacing performance), the ruthless gangster who committed the murder, is determined to keep Esdras silent, and Judge Gaunt (Edward Ellis), who sentenced Romagna, driven out of his mind by his conscience, wants reassurance that he acted rightly.

The film adds an effective opening sequence, establishing Romagna (John Carradine) as a kindly, idealistic man and showing the crime being carried out. In the play the young lovers are killed by Estrella, but their deaths are really even more gratuitous than Romeo's and Juliet's. No one faulted the film for allowing them a happy ending. Trapped in a short block with Estrella and his henchmen waiting at both ends, they start playing a hand organ, a violation of the law that brings a policeman running—a perfectly plausible *deus ex machina.*

Of the few dramas of social consciousness filmed, by far the most sensational was *Dead End* (1937), adapted by Lillian Hellman from Sidney Kingsley's 1935 play, and directed by William Wyler. True to its symbolic title *Dead End* conveyed an overwhelming sense of futility, clearly meaning to indict all of society and by implication the capitalistic system. Almost too schematically, Kingsley shows the various effects of slums: juvenile delinquents (the six Dead End Kids) will grow up into either gangsters like Baby Face Martin (Humphrey Bogart) or jobless dreamers like Dave (Joel McCrea). Girls either toil in a sweatshop like Drina (Sylvia Sidney) or become prostitutes like Francey (Claire Trevor), a broken-down streetwalker, or like Kay (Wendy Barrie), an elegant kept woman.

The film, like the play, resembles a Greek tragedy, preserving unity of place (a single gigantic set, part of a street that ends in the East River, where the service entrance of a luxury apartment confronts slum tenements) and of time (a single day) —but definitely not of action. Instead, we see a series of juxtaposed scenes often unrelated to each other except thematically. Even when well acted, most of the characters remain one-dimensional illustrations of social types. Both Francey and Baby Face's mother (Marjorie Main), though marvelously played, are seen only in one short scene each with Baby Face; we are told nothing else whatever about them.

On stage the hero, known as Gimpy, was a cripple, the victim of improperly treated childhood disease. In the film he becomes clean-cut Dave, an architect whose main problem is unemployment. In the climax he personally kills his erstwhile friend Baby Face instead of merely turning him in to the police. Except for these changes and the cleaning up of the language, the film is utterly faithful to the play—perhaps too faithful. Although the mobile camera tries to keep it from looking stagebound, all the characters seem to be spending too much time hanging around the street waiting to encounter each other, even when it would be more natural to move inside.

But what makes *Dead End* an interesting piece of '30s social protest rather than a timeless human drama is that the whole structure depends on the coincidence of two contrivances: the street repair that makes it necessary for the wealthy apartment dwellers to use the service entrance and Baby Face's one-day visit to his old home. Neither of these situations is necessary or rooted in either character or the milieu, yet without them the play would not exist, since there would be no possibility of the constant class confrontations. *Street Scene* gives an infinitely richer sense of people living their everyday lives, yet *Dead End* will always

retain a certain historic interest as a compendium of '30s social problems.

Sylvia Sidney was again a slum girl in *One Third of a Nation* (1939), also with a kid brother (Sidney Lumet, the future director). Freely adapted from Arthur Arent's play written for the Federal Theatre project, the film was described in the *Times* as "an interestingly presented editorial for slum clearance." A wretched old-law tenement dominates the picture, "the very symbol of reaction, of greed, oppression and human misery." It even speaks, in the croaking voice of a miserly old man. Thus its destruction by fire comes as a happy ending of sorts.

1939 had started off with a film that was timely in a unique way, concerned not with economic inequities but with the most seriously looming international crisis, the approach of the next European war. With Robert E. Sherwood's adaptation of his 1936 play *Idiot's Delight* (1939) we seem to have come full circle, or cycle, back to *Grand Hotel* itself; the setting is a luxury hotel in central Europe, with a largely Continental clientele. As the long-dreaded outbreak of World War II overwhelms all personal stories, the cosmopolitan European society, so fascinating in earlier films, is exposed as decadent, jingoistic, ready once more to destroy itself and the rest of the world.

The prospect sent chills through 1939 audiences, with its forecast of a war that broke out seven months to the day after the New York opening of the film. "As timely as tomorrow's front page," said the *Times* with unconscious accuracy, hailing the film as "profound because its bitterness wears the mask of comedy." By exposing the suicidal greed, the essential lunacy that hurls the world toward destruction, *Idiot's Delight* was the last antiwar film for years.

Interest centers on the two leading characters, played on stage by the Lunts, Harry Van (Clark Gable), a smalltime hoofer traveling with six chorus girls known as "Les Blondes," and a supposed Russian countess (Norma Shearer), with a blond pageboy wig, a long cigarette holder and a heavy Slavic accent. Unlike the play, the film definitely shows that Harry, a wounded World War I vet making his way in vaudeville in the '20s, had a brief fling in Omaha with a brash dancer named Irene—now the mysterious countess, mistress of munitions magnate Achille Weber (Edward Arnold).

Perhaps because it was being written in 1938 after the Austrian *Anschluss* and Munich, the antiwar message is not quite as vehement as in the play, nor are any actual countries named. We can only assume from the surnames that Quillery (Burgess Meredith), a pacifist, in the play a Communist, is French and Dr. Waldersee (Charles Coburn), a scientist, is German. The young honeymooners (Pat Paterson and Peter Willes) are English.

Irene still gives her scathing denunciation of Weber as a profiteer of death, to which he coolly replies that he does not start wars, he merely sells what governments crave. When hostilities break out, he deserts her without a passport. Even the pacifist and the scientist revert to rabid nationalists. The hotel must be evacuated because of its closeness to an airfield, but Harry chooses to stay with Irene during an air raid, and at last she admits knowing him in Omaha. The bombers recede, and they will apparently survive, not as in the play. Still, all the main sardonic points have been made.

In January 1940, but obviously made in 1939, came the film that marks the climax of Hollywood social consciousness in the '30s, a cinematic masterpiece, John Ford's *The Grapes of Wrath*, adapted by Nunnally Johnson from John Steinbeck's best-selling 1939 novel. (Within the previous year Ford had directed *Young Mr. Lincoln*, *Stagecoach* and *Drums Along the Mohawk*—an unparalleled record!)

The Joads are a poor, hard-working farm family in Oklahoma, the heart of the Dust Bowl, "Okies," driven off their farm by drought and dust storms. Their land, presumably acquired in the land rush of 1889, is literally "gone with the wind."

To the haunting strains of "Red River Valley," we first meet laconic Tom Joad (Henry Fonda) coming out of prison, and encountering Casey (John Carradine), an itinerant preacher who has "lost the call" from too much fooling around with women. They find the Joad house empty except for a desperate neighbor, Muley (John Qualen), who has been driven almost out of his mind by being forced off his land and seeing his house bulldozed. Tom's family, his parents (Russell Simpson and Jane Darwell), his grandparents (Charles Grapewin and Zeffie Tilbury) and several younger brothers and sisters including Rosasharn (Dorris Bowdon) and her husband Connie (Eddie Quillan), are staying with an uncle before setting out for California, where they expect to make a new start.

In one unforgettable scene, fat, indomitable Ma Joad burns her most precious mementos: a postcard from New York, a china dog, earrings from her youth. At the last minute rebellious Grandpa balks at being uprooted and must be sedated with soothing syrup. Though the battered old truck is already overcrowded, Casey decides to go along. A montage of Highway 66 shows countless similar trucks full of the same kind of refugees, all streaming westward toward the promised land of California.

Soon Grandpa dies of a stroke and must be buried by the roadside. Everywhere the Joads meet others like themselves—to their dismay, some on their way *back,* after bitter experiences. When they reach California, Grandma dies.

One disaster follows another. At a transient camp full of Okies, Tom hits a crooked sheriff and the family must flee. Pregnant Rosasharn's petulant husband, Connie, leaves her. An angry mob tries to stop all Okies. In a confused strike of underpaid farm laborers, a deputy kills Casey and wounds Tom, who is now a fugitive, hidden by the family.

Even at a Department of Agriculture camp, where conditions are relatively comfortable, the local citizens are hostile. Tom must flee the police again. In a farewell scene with his mother he gives a rather mystic speech about

Dorris Bowdon, Jane Darwell, Henry Fonda in **The Grapes of Wrath**

being "everywhere." Perhaps as an outlaw he can find out what went wrong with the country to reduce so many people to such a plight. At the end the Joads are pushing off to somewhere else where a few days' work is promised. Comforting Rosasharn, about to give birth, Ma assures her, *"We're* the people!" as they join another endless stream of battered jalopies.

Clearly *The Grapes of Wrath* was unique in presenting so unflattering a picture of some of the seamiest sides of American life: poverty, injustice, prejudice, violence. Yet when it was shown in Russia, publicized as an exposé of the horrors of life under the failed capitalistic system, it had to be withdrawn. Presumably

used to hardships of their own, the one thing Russian audiences noticed was that, no matter how poor the Joads were, they still had their own car.

What most impressed American critics and viewers was the totally unglamorized authenticity. Though these were familiar Hollywood actors, they made absolutely convincing Okies, not only Jane Darwell (who won an Oscar for best supporting actress, as did Ford for best director) but Fonda (nominated for an Oscar) and the entire cast. That Hollwood could produce such a socially critical film at all, much less do it with such truth, integrity and force, was surely proof that by 1939 the screen had come of age.

"OVER THE RAINBOW"
1939: The Best of Everything—Almost

Just as the European capitals are said to have glittered more splendidly than ever in 1914, on the eve of the war that was to change them forever, so Hollywood in the equally fateful year of 1939 reached a fabulous zenith it was never again to attain. Who can now imagine a year in which Garbo in *Ninotchka*, Bette Davis in *Dark Victory*, Irene Dunne in *Love Affair* and Greer Garson in *Goodbye Mr. Chips* were the Oscar nominees who lost to Vivien Leigh in *Gone With the Wind?* Or when Laurence Olivier in *Wuthering Heights*, James Stewart in *Mr. Smith Goes to Washington*, Mickey Rooney in *Babes in Arms* and even Clark Gable in *Gone With the Wind* lost to Robert Donat in *Goodbye Mr. Chips?*

In *American Film* for December 1975, Larry Swindell calls 1939 "the apogee—the midpoint as well as the high point in what is now romanticized as the movies' Golden Age." 1938 had been so prosperous that the bankers who underwrote the studios were more tolerant of artistic freedom, and the producers in turn more willing to indulge their most creative directors. By coincidence exactly 365 feature films were released, among them an amazing number now considered classics or the best of their kind.

In the order in which they opened in New York, some of the outstanding examples include *Gunga Din, Idiot's Delight, Made for Each Other, Stagecoach, Love Affair, The Hound of the Baskervilles, The Story of Vernon and Irene Castle, Wuthering Heights, Dark Victory, Juarez, Only Angels Have Wings, Goodbye Mr. Chips, Young Mr. Lincoln, Bachelor Mother, On Borrowed Time, In Name Only, The Old Maid, The Wizard of Oz, Golden Boy, The Rains Came, The Women, Intermezzo, Babes in Arms, Mr. Smith Goes to Washington, Drums Along the Mohawk, Ninotchka, The Roaring Twenties, Destry Rides Again, The Private Lives of Elizabeth and Essex* and, in December 1939, as the culminating cinematic event of the decade, *Gone With the Wind*.

Like *The Wizard of Oz*, with which it has much in common (both released by MGM, both directed by Victor Fleming, both among the mere eight feature films in color in 1939, both full of universally familiar characters), *Gone With the Wind* seems never to have lost its grip on the public imagination since the novel was published. From 1936 through 1939 the amount of publicity it received, some promoted by Selznick, much spontaneous, was unparalleled in this century. Who cared if Chamberlain appeased Hitler at Munich? The only important question was who would play Scarlett O'Hara. Of course everyone *knew* who would play Rhett Butler.

References to *Gone With the Wind* turned up constantly in every other medium. A popular song of 1937 used the title, with the cover of the sheet music a replica of the jacket of the book. In one verse of Rodgers and Hart's "The Lady Is a Tramp," the singer announces that she *won't* play Scarlett in *Gone With the Wind,* and when a line from "Our Love Affair" proclaimed that the world would soon forget all other lovers, from Adam and Eve to Scarlett and Rhett, no one needed an explanation.

The comic strip *Li'l Abner* attempted a crude parody, using names like Ashcan Wilkes, Wreck Butler and Melancholy Hamilton, until Margaret Mitchell legally stopped it. In a cartoon Bugs Bunny disguised himself as a character named Crimson O'Hare-Oil. At least three other fictional works were spin-offs from the endless search for Scarlett. Clare Boothe Luce's comedy *Kiss the Boys Goodbye* was all about a quest for an actress to play Velvet O'Toole. Richard Sherman's novel *Premiere* dealt with the fierce rivalry of four actresses for the lead in the historical film epic of the decade. As noted, the film *Second Fiddle* (1939) also involved a hunt for the right girl to star in a much-publicized film.

Greater love hath no studio than to mention a film about to be made by another, yet in Columbia's *The Awful Truth* (1937) Joyce Compton sings a song, later parodied by Irene Dunne, about how her dreams are all gone with the wind. In Paramount's *King of Gamblers* (1937) Claire Trevor, thinking she'll never see Lloyd Nolan again, shrugs and sighs, "Gone with the wind!" In Warners' *Hollywood Hotel* (1938), Lola Lane as a movie star is making a Civil War epic in which she and Alan Mowbray play characters named Lucy O'Mara and Captain Cutler.[1] At one time or another just about every female American star in Hollywood was announced on the front pages as being considered, rejecting or out of the running for the role of Scarlett.

While almost any successful film spawns a litter of inferior follow-ups, *GWTW,* like some mighty meteor blazing across the late '30s skies, attracted into its orbit satellites that heralded it almost like "coming attractions," and, far from diminishing its impact, only whetted public hunger for the real thing. Thus MGM (though it was to release the film) tried to jump its own gun with *The Toy Wife* (1938), based on *Frou-Frou* (1869), a forgotten French play by Henri Meilhac and Ludovic Halévy, with the setting transposed from Paris to New Orleans.

"Frou-Frou" is the nickname of a shallow coquette (Luise Rainer), who marries the man (Melvyn Douglas) loved by her older sister (Barbara O'Neil), then neglects her home and child for a gay social life, asks the sister to take over her household, becomes jealous of her, runs off with an adventurer (Robert Young), whom the husband kills in a duel, whereupon Frou-Frou goes into a decline and dies. The plot of this tiresome film surely does not resemble *GWTW,* but the atmosphere of the *ante bellum* South and the parallel of the four leading characters to Scarlett, Ashley, Melanie and Rhett was unmistakable.

Warners' infinitely superior entry in the Scarlett O'Hara sweepstakes, also set in pre-Civil War New Orleans, based on a 1933 play in which Miriam Hopkins had flopped on Broadway, was *Jezebel* (1938), for which Bette Davis deservedly won her second Oscar. Again the same quartet: a spoiled Southern belle (Davis), a chivalrous gentleman (Henry Fonda), the self-effacing girl he marries (Margaret Lindsay) and a dashing rascal (George Brent). Though determined to marry Pres Dillard (Fonda), perverse Julie Marsden is equally determined to have her own way by wearing a red gown to the Olympus Ball, where tradition decrees white for unmarried girls. Painfully embarrassed, Pres evens the score by forcing her to continue dancing until they are the only couple on the floor.

Realizing she has gone too far when Pres leaves the city, on his return Julie is ready, all

---

[1] In Paramount's *Louisiana Purchase* (1941) Bob Hope carries on a filibuster by supposedly reading *GWTW* in its entirety.

in white, to apologize, but it is too late; he is married—to a Yankee (Margaret Lindsay)! Livid with rage, Julie goads another suitor, crack shot Buck Cantrell (George Brent), into challenging Pres to a duel, but in his absence his inexperienced younger brother (Richard Cromwell) fights in his place—and, much to everyone's astonishment, kills Buck. Sternly denounced by her aunt (Fay Bainter, in an Oscar-winning performance), Julie is at her wit's end, until she hears that Pres is among the yellow fever victims to be shipped to a leper isle. She begs his wife to let her go along to nurse him, to atone for all she has done, and the wife agrees. Despite this ending, *The New Yorker* rightly terms *Jezebel* "a dazzling romantic melodrama," in which Davis displays her full powers. The parallel to Scarlett was so obvious that Davis' picture on the cover of *Time* was simply captioned "Gone before the wind."

Both *The Toy Wife* and *Jezebel* were re-

Vivien Leigh, Evelyn Keyes, Alicia Rhett, Howard Hickman (in back), Ann Rutherford, Thomas Mitchell in **Gone With the Wind**

leased in the first half of 1938, so had come and gone long before the opening in Atlanta on December 15, 1939, of *Gone With the Wind*—surely the most eagerly awaited premiere in film history. A few days later it opened in New York simultaneously at the Capitol and the Astor, and in January 1940 in other major cities, on a reserved seat basis. If it had been given the greatest advance build-up of any film ever, the finished product disappointed no one. Selznick's passion for getting every detail right had paid off.

The longest, most expensive picture made thus far, the first major spectacle in color, with a cast of glamorous stars, *Gone With the Wind* epitomized to a remarkable degree almost every favorite trend and taste of the 1930s. Applying the genres used in this book, Scarlett was as hard-boiled as any gold digger; at one point she offers to become Rhett's mistress and would always have done as much for Ashley, eventually creating two interlocking marital triangles. Her story has elements of both the working-girl Cinderella and the spoiled heiress themes, as she falls from riches to rags and fights her way back again. Rhett as the dashing blockade runner and rakish social outcast has the same devil-may-care charm as the jewel thieves, gamblers and gangsters of other films. *Gone With the Wind* was deeply nostalgic, and not only for Southerners; it had the through-the-years structure of a family chronicle, it was a costume picture on the most elaborate scale, based on what to the public had already become a fictional classic, dealing with the greatest crisis in American history—the ideal combination of realism and escape.

It even involved hospital scenes and a heroic doctor. Though it is, of course, primarily a romantic drama, the most popular love story in American fiction, it also contains a great deal of humor, especially Rhett's ironic quips at Scarlett's expense. The musical score by Max Steiner was among the first such sound tracks from a non-musical film to become generally recognizable and popular. It was perhaps the most deeply regional American film

ever made, as well as one of the most specifically ethnic, with its emphasis on the O'Haras' Irish background and the number of carefully drawn black characters.

Though not really a film of ideas, it was at least implicitly antiwar. The scenes of boys dashing blithely off to enlist, sacrifices on the home front, anguished partings, bereaved parents and casualty lists all took on a poignant timeliness for Americans 1941–45. *Gone With the Wind* truly gave movie-goers the best of everything they had ever dreamed of getting from a film.

Obviously anyone interested in movies does not need the plot recapitulated, so this discussion will be limited to a few incidental observations. In recent years comments in *Cue, The New Yorker et al.* have indicated that the black characters are dated stereotypes. This is totally untrue. Mammy (for which Hattie McDaniel won an Oscar, the first black actress to do so) is one of the strongest, most dignified people in the film, more than once serving as Scarlett's conscience as well as the final authority on what's "fittin'." The relationship of mutual respect that grows between her and Rhett is beautifully delineated.

Granted that Prissy (Butterfly McQueen) is, as Rhett terms her, "a simple-minded darky," and an irritating one, on the other hand, Aunt Pittypat (Laura Hope Crews), the flower of Southern aristocracy, who has enjoyed all the advantages Prissy never had, is an even worse idiot, constantly exposing her folly.

Likewise, the unidentified vigilante group which Rhett, Ashley and Frank Kennedy join to avenge the attack on Scarlett at Shantytown, leading to Frank's death and Ashley's injury, may well be the Ku Klux Klan, but it is not specified as such. How can critics complain about this while accepting the blatant, hysterical racism of *The Birth of a Nation* (1915), in which *both* white heroines (Lillian Gish and Mae Marsh) are threatened with rape by monstrous blacks and the climax is the triumphant ride of the Klan in full regalia

***Hattie McDaniel, Clark Gable in* Gone With the Wind**

to enforce white supremacy? (After all, it was based on a novel called *The Klansman.*) It is a curious bit of symmetry that almost exactly twenty-five years passed between these two historic films, both about the Civil War and Reconstruction from the Southern point of view, one introducing an era, the other marking its high point.

GWTW was an enormous hit in London, where it ran four years, right through the Blitz, and by 1945 a whole new European public in the liberated countries was eager to identify with Scarlett in her postwar battle back to affluence. When all-time box-office grosses are compared, it should be kept in mind that during its original run and first revivals movie tickets cost a dollar or less, even at first-run theaters, compared to the four or five dollars charged for recent blockbusters. If the number of paid admissions were counted rather than the total amount of money, *Gone With the Wind* would probably still emerge the winner.

The 1970s brought three large books about it: Gavin Lambert's *The Making of Gone With the Wind*, Roland Flamini's *Scarlett*,

Olivia De Havilland, Ward Bond, Clark Gable, Leslie Howard in **Gone With the Wind**

Rhett and a Cast of Thousands and William Pratt's and Herbert Bridges' *Scarlett Fever*. Evelyn Keyes, who played Suellen O'Hara, could think of no more surefire title for her autobiography than *Scarlett O'Hara's Younger Sister*. Ann Rutherford, who played Carreen

O'Hara, has said, "If nothing else, it assured me of an epitaph. It was a passport to the world. It was something for the ages. There is something evidently quite timeless about the appeal of *Gone With the Wind*."[2] In 1980 not

[2] *New York Times,* December 31, 1979.

one, but two, TV specials concerned the prolonged quest for Scarlett: *The Selznick Years,* a documentary which included the actual tests made by Jean Arthur, Paulette Goddard, Susan Hayward and others, and a segment of Garson Kanin's *Moviola* series. Frankly, a lot of people still give a damn.

After the triumphant reception of *Gone With the Wind,* the climax of this unique decade, what could have gone wrong? As with the reason why 1939 was the greatest year, the answer is both economic and political. In the fall of that year Congress passed a bill prohibiting "block booking," the system by which the seven major studios, plus United Artists, had profitably filled movie houses from coast to coast with double features contracted for in advance "blindly"—i.e., not chosen by the theater owners.

More seriously still, in September 1939 World War II broke out, within months cutting off what remained of Hollywood's most lucrative foreign market, Western Europe. Once more production supervisors had to capitulate to the fears of New York home offices, and though a certain afterglow lingered through much of 1940, with the release of films started or planned in 1939, not yet affected by the war (e.g., *Rebecca, Pride and Prejudice, The Philadelphia Story*), the handwriting, even if invisible, was on the studio walls.

An additional factor (whether it was voluntary or "suggested" by the government) was harnessing every possible feature film for propaganda, to prepare the American people for entry into the war. The 1940s, though financially the most profitable decade in American film history, were from the beginning poisoned by this self-consciously patriotic slant, which infected even films not directly about the war. When the only permissible question was "Will this picture help the war effort?" artistic integrity was the first casualty.

Profits soared because Americans working in war plants had more money to spend than since before the Depression, prices were frozen, travel was restricted, most consumer goods were unavailable, TV was only a deferred postwar dream—so what was there to do but join the crowds lining up around the block to see a movie? The only genres in which the '40s excelled (and which the '50s inherited) were the period musical in color (e.g., *Meet Me in St. Louis,* 1944), an outgrowth of that '30s nostalgia noted elsewhere, and the so-called *films noirs* (e.g., *Double Indemnity,* 1944), downbeat murder and mystery melodramas, an offshoot of '30s private eye films.

With but a few exceptions (Garbo, Shearer, Rainer, Kay Francis), most '30s stars continued to reign throughout the 1940s, though generally in vehicles less fresh and original than those of the previous decade. It is surely no coincidence that from Ginger Rogers and James Stewart in 1940 through Olivia De Havilland and Broderick Crawford in 1949, *all* the '40s Oscar winners for best actor and actress had been active in the '30s. (Yes, even Jennifer Jones had been appearing in "B" films under her own name, Phyllis Isley.) Even in the 1950s, Bogart, Cooper, Holden and Niven all won Oscars, as did Leigh, Bergman (a second for each) and Susan Hayward. On other levels, America's favorite singing screen star of the '40s, Judy Garland, and even the most pinned-up sex symbols of World War II, Betty Grable, Rita Hayworth, Lana Turner and Dorothy Lamour, had all been well established by the late '30s.

Not to minimize the talent and charm of the many pleasant young players who emerged in the 1940s, but compared with the hundreds of '30s immortals, who really remembers them? Only a few ever reached anything like the old superstar status: Brando, Clift, Kirk Douglas, Heston, Gene Kelly, Lancaster, Peck, Sinatra, Ava Gardner, Liz Taylor, Bacall and, among British imports, Deborah Kerr, James Mason, perhaps one or two others.

As surest evidence of what had been lost, in the panicky '50s almost every well-loved masterpiece of the '30s was remade in splashy color, often under a new title. Even if the same script was used (as seldom happened) the results could only make the viewer long for the original. Remakes had always been part of the Hollywood system; countless silents were redone as early talkies, and by the end of the '30s most studios were turning hits of less than ten years before into inconspicuous "B's"—but these were concessions to the then insatiable market for second features, not publicized to cash in on the success of the earlier version.

As further proof of the inimitable touch of the '30s, of the scores of remakes, the overwhelming majority have been unmitigated disasters, ruined by blundering attempts at updating and players simply not in the same league with their predecessors. Among romantic comedy-dramas the sole exception was *An Affair to Remember* (1957), written and directed by Leo McCarey, as was the original 1939 *Love Affair*. Deborah Kerr and Cary Grant surely did not suffer by comparison with Irene Dunne and Charles Boyer.

Some '50s actresses seemed especially prone to stumble in their betters' footsteps. June Allyson risked comparison with Hepburn in *Little Women* (1949), with Colbert in *You Can't Run Away from It* (a 1956 remake of *It Happened One Night* so poor that it was not even reviewed by the *Times*), with Shearer in *The Opposite Sex* (1956, a hopeless mishmash supposedly based on *The Women*) and even with Lombard in *My Man Godfrey* (1957). Lana Turner almost equaled this record, playing Myrna Loy's role in *The Rains of Ranchipur* (1955), taken from *The Rains Came,* Colbert's in *Imitation of Life* (1959), and in *Madame X* (1966) a part played in earlier talkies by both Ruth Chatterton and Gladys George.

But if Allyson was the queen of inept remakes, surely the king was producer Ross Hunter, who must assume full blame for the falsely glamorized remakes not only of *My Man Godfrey, Imitation of Life* and *Madame X,* but also of *The Magnificent Obsession* (1954) and *Back Street* (1961). He threatened to give the same lethal treatment to *Stella Dallas* (presumably with Turner), but

nothing came of this, perhaps in consequence of his ghastly *Lost Horizon* (1973), which instantly replaced *Goodbye Mr. Chips* as the worst film musical of the 1970s.

Otherwise, '30s films turned into musicals —that is, transmuted into an altogether different art form, given an added dimension by a good composer—fared rather well, especially those made in the 1950s, which despite the war seemed to have retained much of the '30s' innocent optimism. *Daddy Long Legs* (1955), a frail little Cinderella tale filmed in 1931, actually worked better as a musical with Fred Astaire and Leslie Caron. *State Fair* was enhanced by a Rodgers-Hammerstein score in 1945, though done less well again in 1962. *Four Daughters* (1938) became the agreeable *Young at Heart* (1955), as *Ninotchka* (1939), thanks to a tuneful Cole Porter score, turned into the reasonably pleasant *Silk Stockings* (1957).

The finest musical remake was, of course, *A Star Is Born* (1954), enriched by Harold Arlen's excellent score and performances by Judy Garland and James Mason as charismatic as those of the 1937 originals, Janet Gaynor and Fredric March. The 1977 version, with the principals changed to rock stars, though fairly faithful in story line, was generally dismissed as a monstrous ego trip for Streisand, with Kris Kristofferson all but wiped off the screen.

By the 1960s, of course, TV had completed its conquest, the damage was irreversible and it was only a matter of time until the shambles of the '70s and no doubt the '80s, often blamed on the fact that the real decisions are being made not by creative movie-makers but cost-conscious executives from the conglomerates that have taken over most of the studios.

It seems not unfair to note that American TV is now more than twice as old as full-length films were in 1930, yet during more than three decades how many programs has it produced that anyone would want to see revived? Aside from its unique power to cover live news events, especially sports, and certain other useful functions, its level of dramatic entertainment has actually declined since the 1950s, when programs like *Studio One* and *Playhouse 90* were telecast live. In recent years the only TV programs to compare in quality with good '30s movies (which never had anything to sell but themselves) have been those on the public channels, the best ones usually of British origin, especially *Masterpiece Theatre,* which has kept Edwardian England alive forever.

The one positive contribution of commercial TV to cinema history has been accidental; in its desperate need to fill twenty-four hours a day, it has bought and shown thousands of old films that would otherwise be forgotten, and thus created generations of new fans for stars long dead or retired. Seeing films that way (often heavily "edited" and with the mood shattered every few minutes by hard-sell spot commercials) is better than not seeing them at all, but once the taste is acquired, buffs, even the youngest, soon learn to seek out museums, revival theaters and university series, where the old films can still be enjoyed as intended.

Who could have imagined that all these pictures, taken for granted at the time as mere popular entertainment, would not only long outlive their makers but would one day be cherished and studied as among the finest examples of an all but lost art? Dazzled by the sparkling stream of 1939 hits into assuming it would flow on forever, the crowds waiting in line to see *Gone With the Wind* could not have believed that Hollywood's greatest decade was even then passing into history, leaving later generations to echo one of its best movie songs: "Thanks for the memory . . ."

BIBLIOGRAPHY

Allen, Frederick Lewis, *Since Yesterday*. New York: Harper & Row, 1940.

The American Film Institute Catalog of Motion Pictures. Feature Films 1921–1930. New York and London: R. R. Bowker Company, 1971.

Baxter, John, *Hollywood in the Thirties*. London: Tantivy Press; Cranbury, New Jersey: A. S. Barnes & Company, 1968.

Bergman, Andrew, *We're in the Money, Depression America and Its Films*. New York: Harper Colophon Books, 1972.

Brown, Curtis F., *Jean Harlow*. New York: Pyramid Books, 1977.

Burton, Jack, *Blue Book of Hollywood Musicals*. Watkins Glen, New York: Century House, 1953.

Capra, Frank, *The Name Above the Title*. New York: Bantam Books, 1972.

Chierichetti, David, *Hollywood Costume Design*. New York: Harmony Books, 1976.

Clarens, Carlos, *An Illustrated History of the Horror Film*. New York: Capricorn Books, 1967.

Conway, Michael, McGregor, Dion, and Ricci, Marc, *The Films of Greta Garbo*. New York: Bonanza Books, n.d.

Croce, Arlene, *The Fred Astaire and Ginger Rogers Book*. New York: Galahad Books, 1972.

Dickens, Homer, *The Films of Katharine Hepburn*. Secaucus, New Jersey: Citadel Press, 1971.

Eames, John Douglas, *The MGM Story, the Complete History of Over Fifty Roaring Years*. New York: Crown, 1975.

Everson, William K., *Classics of the Horror Film*. Secaucus, New Jersey: Citadel Press, 1974.

———, Program notes for film series given at the New School for Social Research, 1960s through 1980.

Film Daily, Film reviews January 1, 1930, through December 31, 1939.

Frank, Alan G., *Horror Movies*. Secaucus, New Jersey: Derbibooks, 1975.

Gabree, John, *Gangsters from Little Caesar to the Godfather*. New York: Galahad Books, 1973.

Gill, Brendan, "Philip Barry," *The New Yorker*, September 15, 1975.

Griffith, Richard, editor, *The Talkies: Articles and Illustrations from Photoplay Magazine 1928–1940*. New York: Dover Publications, 1971.

Halliwell, Leslie, *Mountain of Dreams, The Golden Years of Paramount Pictures*. New York: Stonehill Publishing Company, 1976.

Haskell, Molly, *From Reverence to Rape, The Treatment of Women in the Movies*. New York: Holt, Rinehart & Winston, 1974.

Jacobs, Lewis, *The Rise of the American Film*. New York: Harcourt, Brace & Company, 1939.

Kael, Pauline, "Cary Grant" (profile), *The New Yorker*, July 14, 1975.

———, *The Citizen Kane Book*. New York: Bantam Books, 1974.

Kobal, John, *Gotta Sing, Gotta Dance, A Pictorial History of Film Musicals*. London, New York, Sydney, Toronto: Hamlyn, 1970.

Kreuger, Miles, editor, *The Movie Musical from Vitaphone to 42nd Street, as Reported in a Great Fan Magazine*. New York: Dover Publications, 1975.

———, Program notes for *The Roots of the American Musical Film (1927–32)*, series given at the Museum of Modern Art, Summer 1971.

Loos, Anita, *Kiss Hollywood Good-by*. New York: Viking Press, 1974.

Marill, Alvin H., *Samuel Goldwyn Presents*. Cranbury, New Jersey: A. S. Barnes & Company, 1976.

Miller, Don, *B Movies*. New York: Curtis Books, 1973.

Musicals of the 1930s. New York: Museum of the City of New York, n.d.

The New York Times Film Reviews, 1913–1968. New York: The New York Times and Arno Press, 1970.

Null, Gary, *Black Hollywood*. Secaucus, New Jersey: Citadel Press, 1975.

Parish, James Robert, *The Jeanette MacDonald Story*. New York: Mason/Charter, 1976.

——— and Pitts, Michael R., with Gregory W. Mank, *Hollywood on Hollywood*. Metuchen, New Jersey, and London: The Scarecrow Press, Inc., 1978.

Quirk, Lawrence J., *The Films of Fredric March*. New York: Citadel Press, 1971.

———, *The Films of Joan Crawford*. New York: Citadel Press, 1971.

Ringgold, Gene, *The Films of Bette Davis*. New York: Citadel Press, 1966.

———, and Bodeen, DeWitt, *Chevalier, The Films and Career of Maurice Chevalier*. Secaucus, New Jersey: Citadel Press, 1973.

Rosen, Marjorie, *Popcorn Venus*. New York: Avon Books, 1973.

Selznick, David O., *Memo from David O. Selznick* (edited by Rudy Behlmer). New York: Viking Press, 1972.

Sennett, Ted, *Lunatics and Lovers*. New York: Arlington House, 1973.

Shipman, David, *The Great Movie Stars*. New York: Bonanza Books, 1970.

Smith, Ella, *Starring Miss Barbara Stanwyck*. New York: Crown Publishers, 1974.

Trent, Paul, *Those Fabulous Movie Years: The '30's*. Barre, Massachusetts: Barre Publishing, 1975.

Vizzard, Jack, *See No Evil: Life Inside a Hollywood Censor*. New York: Simon & Schuster, 1970.

INDEX OF NAMES
OF PERSONS

(See also Index of titles
and of names other than of persons.
Italic numbers indicate photographs.)